Margaret Thatcher
The Authorized Biography

ALSO BY CHARLES MOORE

Margaret Thatcher:
From Grantham to the Falklands

MARGARET THATCHER

The Authorized Biography

AT HER ZENITH:
IN LONDON, WASHINGTON AND MOSCOW

Charles Moore

ALFRED A. KNOPF · NEW YORK · 2016

THIS IS A BORZOI BOOK
PUBLISHED BY ALFRED A. KNOPF

Library of Congress Control Number: 2015954069

ISBN 978-0-307-95896-9 (hardcover)
ISBN 978-0-307-95897-6 (eBook)

Grateful acknowledgment is made to Penguin Books Ltd.
for permission to reprint the poem "Mrs Thatcher" from
The Growing Pains of Adrian Mole by Sue Townsend,
copyright © 1984 by Sue Townsend. Reprinted by
permission of Penguin Books Ltd., London.

Jacket photograph: Margaret Thatcher at Isle of Wight, 1983
© PA Images
Jacket design by Stephanie Ross
Manufactured in the United States of America
First Edition

To Kate, Will and Hannah,
who are too young to have seen what happened

and in memory of
W. F. Deedes, who saw it all

Contents

No coward soul is mine,
No trembler in the world's storm-troubled sphere

—*Emily Brontë*

Preface

The life of Margaret Thatcher constantly confounds the philosophers. I noted at the beginning of the first volume of this biography how she had wrong-footed Socrates. His dictum that the unexamined life is not worth living cannot be applied to hers. She also disproved Francis Bacon, who famously said that 'All rising to great place is by a winding stair.' Her climb began lower – and therefore reached further – than those of her predecessors, but she moved upwards as straight as she could. And although she could certainly be more cunning in tight situations than she would ever admit, her method was rarely circuitous. The man rising up the winding stair cannot see where he is going. The woman fighting to reach the summit and stay there had the end always in view. She was impelled upwards by a combination of intense personal ambition and her fervent belief in the capacities of a free country, particularly the capacities of her own country. She had enough time at the top to try to unlock those capacities and realize much of that vision.

Mrs Thatcher served as prime minister of the United Kingdom for eleven and a half continuous years – a record unique in the era of universal suffrage. This book covers the zenith of her power, from the aftermath of the Falklands War in 1982 – and her subsequent (and consequent) victory in the general election of 1983 – to her third election victory in 1987. It therefore contrasts strongly with the first volume of this authorized biography (*Margaret Thatcher: From Grantham to the Falklands*), which was published shortly after her death in 2013. That told the story of the lonely rise of the Midlands grocer's daughter to become the first woman leader of the Conservative Party and then, four years later, Britain's first woman prime minister. It showed her always battling against the odds, wrestling with the huge difficulties that were thrown in the way by many of the male sex (and by some of her own), by political opponents and by the economic problems that beset her country. This book shows her on top – more dominant, perhaps, than any peacetime predecessor, and more famous on the world stage than any British prime minister except for Sir Winston Churchill.

So one might have thought that the second part of the story would be less dramatic than the first – a triumphal progress along the red carpet of global renown instead of the earlier, terrifying precariousness. But to think this is to impose upon past events an order which they did not, to their participants, possess. No one knew at the time that Mrs Thatcher would win all three general elections which she would contest as leader. Very few in the West, in 1983, had heard of Mikhail Gorbachev, or imagined that the Iron Lady, of all people, would be the first to try to bring the Soviet Union in from the cold. No one, in March 1984, knew that the miners' strike, which began in that month, would last for a year and would end in the absolute defeat of organized trade union power in British politics. And no one, at the beginning of December 1984, would have dreamed that the affairs of a small Somerset helicopter company would, within a few weeks, taint her reputation and force her to think that she might have to resign. It was not in the character of Mrs Thatcher herself, or in the nature of her times, that things would jog along peacefully. Indeed, in this period – at Brighton in 1984 – she nearly lost her life to a terrorist attack by the IRA.

Only by writing this book did I come to understand just how insecure Mrs Thatcher's position often felt in these years – not least to her. Within months of her landslide win in 1983, she became aware that many of her senior colleagues did not want her to fight the next general election as leader. At several moments in the miners' strike, it seemed quite possible that she would lose. On issues like the sale of British Leyland, South African sanctions or Britain's membership of the Exchange Rate Mechanism (ERM) of the European Monetary System, she found herself dangerously isolated from Cabinet colleagues. Despite overwhelming polling evidence to the contrary, she was intermittently convinced that she would lose the 1987 election. Even her close friendship with President Ronald Reagan – one of the most important themes of this book – was troubled by bad moments. After the US invasion of Grenada, she felt her trust in him had been betrayed. After Reagan's attempt at the Reykjavik summit with Gorbachev in 1986 to bargain away all nuclear weapons, she briefly believed that the cause of the free world might be lost.

This was the era when Mrs Thatcher scored some of her greatest successes – her visit to Moscow in 1987, large-scale privatization, the settlement of the five-year row about Britain's rebate from the European Community, the reduction of inflation and the return of prosperity, and the defeat of the miners' extremist leader, Arthur Scargill, not to mention two overwhelming election victories. But it was also the period in which she presided over the invention of the poll tax, incurred the anxiety of the

Queen about South Africa and the Commonwealth and developed what would later become fatally bad relations with her most senior colleagues. In these years, she revealed her full qualities as a leader – both her astonishing abilities and her sometimes equally astonishing flaws. The week in December 1984 which began with her meeting Gorbachev for the first time, continued with her signature of the Anglo-Hong Kong Agreement in Peking and ended with President Reagan at Camp David is one of the most remarkable in modern political history. The day in June 1987 when she lost all sense of proportion about the election campaign she was fighting is one of the most embarrassing. Mrs Thatcher's appetite for achievement and change and the degree to which she was the commanding personality of the era is beyond question; but, hard as she fought for everything she wanted, this was not always what she got. In the process, many of her loyal but exhausted staff often asked themselves, in the words of a pop song at the time, 'Somebody tell me, won't you tell me / Why I work so hard for you?' Their answer was that she made everything seem to matter: their boss made a difference, and passionately wished to do so. Whatever her critics said, she always cared.

This book was conceived in 1997, when Lady Thatcher decided to choose an authorized biographer and offered the role to me. This allowed me full access to all her private papers, most of which she gave on permanent loan to the archives centre at Churchill College, Cambridge. (She chose Cambridge because her own university, Oxford, had refused her an honorary degree, a decision which – see Chapter 19 – hurt her more deeply than any other insult offered to her during her time in office, apart from the vote that forced her out in 1990.) By extension, and at her request, the Cabinet Secretary at the time, Sir Richard Wilson (now Lord Wilson of Dinton), granted me full access to the prime ministerial papers for the whole of her time in government, regardless of the restrictions of the 'thirty-year rule' (now a twenty-year one), but under the established conventions which require quotations from such papers to be vetted for national security.* This permission continues under his successors. Lady Thatcher also gave me interviews for the book, and encouraged all those close to her – many of whom had been discouraged from speaking before – to do the same. To my great benefit, she also insisted that she should not read the book's manuscript and that it should not be published in her lifetime. This meant

---

* Nothing important for the book has been lost in this process. Sensitive matters struck out tend to be operational details of intelligence or military matters which are not central to the Thatcher story.

that she could not be accused of trying to control it – something which, to my surprise, she never seemed tempted to do.* As well as sources reached by these means, there are numerous others, from many countries, most notably the United States, where the rich material from the presidential libraries and other archives has been trawled and more than sixty witnesses have been consulted. The consequences of all of the above have been that hundreds of people have been interviewed, thousands of papers have been studied and millions of words have been read in the making of this book. By the time it is finished, it will have taken twenty years.

This leads me to an apology for inadvertently misleading readers of Volume I. In its preface, I promised that there would be two volumes. In fact, as it turns out, there will be three. I was originally contracted for three in the 1990s, then decided that two would do it, and then realized, when I worked on the second volume and saw how good and extensive the material was, that three would be better after all. It means that faithful readers will have to wait a little longer to reach the end of the story, but at least it does also mean that the second volume will not be too heavy to read in bed. The third volume will cover Mrs Thatcher's last three years in office, her fall, her life out of office and her death and funeral.

The material for Volume II is rather different from that for Volume I. There, in the early years, the problem was of too few sources, although this was largely overcome by the revelations contained in the young Margaret's letters to her sister Muriel. Here, the problem is of too many. There, Mrs Thatcher had more of a private life. Here, there is very little distinction between her life and her work. She and Denis lived over the shop in Downing Street. She brought work home at the weekends (to Chequers), took minimal holidays and, notoriously, worked all the hours that God sent. When she did buy a house of her own, in Dulwich in 1985, it was a mistake (see Chapter 19). Even her love of clothes became much more an expression of her use of power than of her private identity, reaching its apotheosis in her 1987 trip to Moscow (see Chapter 18). Except for Denis's constant, reassuring presence, family life was largely sacrificed. Carol lived in Australia for part of the period, and never in Downing Street. Mark was driven by criticism of his business dealings to base himself in Dallas, Texas, from 1984, which caused anxiety for his mother about his security (see Chapter 9).

So, as one would expect of a workaholic, most of the evidence about

---

* Lady Thatcher did not pay me for my work. The book was contracted by my publishers, Penguin.

her life derives from studying her at work. Luckily for the biographer, Mrs Thatcher was in the habit of writing her views most expressively all over government papers, often adding exclamation marks, underlining what she liked and putting a wiggly line under what she thought 'feeble' or bureaucratic or excessively European. She was also of the last generation – being pre-email – who expressed their views in a systematic way on paper (usually by means of private secretaries, above all Charles Powell) without the terror of being hacked or going viral. Although she was by nature secretive about information and extremely conscious of the dangers of leaks, she was also almost incapable of concealing what she really thought. It is possible to see from official sources alone the extraordinary way in which she governed. It is sad to think that technology and Freedom of Information have made such frankness on paper very rare in government today. Life for the biographers of twenty-first-century prime ministers who succeeded her will, in this sense, be much harder than it has been for me. Private sources are also, of course, immensely important – take, for example, Sir David Goodall's private account of the Anglo-Irish negotiations (see Chapter 10), Lord Burns's contemporary notes on the disastrous 1985 meeting about the ERM (see Chapter 13) or Lord Young of Graffham's amazing diary of the 1987 election campaign (see Chapter 20), all here quoted extensively for the first time. So are the memories of those who saw her in action. In the period covered, she became a global and a mythological figure: this book draws on the witnesses to this phenomenon.

Because there is so much material in these five years, there is a problem of narrative structure. Wherever possible, the author should convey the fact that a prime minister must deal with completely disparate things, frequently without notice, all at once. In this volume, for example, on the same day in 1986 as US aircraft, taking off from British bases, bombed Libya, Mrs Thatcher also had to face the defeat of her Shops Bill (to permit Sunday trading) – the only time any of her governments lost a second reading vote in the House of Commons. The easiest way to convey this mêlée of events is to stick to a single, blended, chronological narrative of everything. Quite often, however, this is not possible, because of the need to give a clear, detailed and coherent account of one important issue at a time. In this book, most of Mrs Thatcher's dealings with Reagan and with Gorbachev in Cold War matters are presented in this way. So are the miners' strike, the Anglo-Irish Agreement and the story of South African sanctions. Every effort, however, is made to remind the reader, as the story unfolds, that other things are happening off-stage. One apparently unrelated incident frequently affects another, and almost always affects the main player in the drama, her attitudes, her political fortunes and her decisions. It should be borne in mind that this is the biography of Margaret Thatcher, rather than the complete history of her governments. There were important areas on which even her active gaze seldom fell – for example, rather surprisingly, most Home Office matters. These can therefore – usually at least – be omitted. She is the one constant presence – which is what, due to the force of her personality, it felt like to colleagues at the time. This book is Act Two of a three-act play in which the central character almost never leaves the stage.

For similar thematic reasons, although the broad chronological framework is maintained, there are some issues better grouped with related matters, rather than presented at the exact time they occurred. This applies to her dealings with intelligence and with privatization, both of which featured relatively little in the first volume but appear extensively here. By the same token, most of Mrs Thatcher's reforms of the social security system and of the National Health Service will appear in the final volume, although they were quite important in the period covered by this one. The same applies to her attitude to AIDS and public health, the row about the publication of the book *Spycatcher* and most of her somewhat uneasy relationship with Scotland. In some subjects, such as the discussion in Chapter 19 of Mrs Thatcher's mythological status in the culture of the time, matters covered sometimes run beyond the 1982–7 dates. In two instances – the US invasion of Grenada and the leaking of the Solicitor-General's letter in the Westland affair – I have departed from the chronological sequence to imitate the fact that, in both cases, it was only later that the main participants discovered what had really happened. To assist the reader, a chronology, collating different subject areas against the dates, is provided at the front of the book.

There is another difference between Volume I and Volume II. The first was written when Lady Thatcher was alive, most of the second when she was dead. This probably affects the way I have written: it certainly affects the way people read. On 17 April 2013, as the Queen stood in St Paul's Cathedral, beside the coffin of the longest-serving of her twelve prime ministers and the only one who shared her sex, Margaret Thatcher passed into history. This meant that interest in her became even stronger, but also that the mythology, both favourable and unfavourable, grew stronger too. The biographer must not succumb to this. He must never answer the many 'What would Mrs Thatcher do today about x?' questions which he is asked, for the simple reason that he does not know. Rather than becoming marmoreal, or speculative, his work must continue to be detective. He is still trying to discover the truth about this extraordinary woman who was too driven ever to examine herself.

I have given well over 100 talks about Mrs Thatcher since she died. At first, I was surprised by how rarely audiences asked me about politics. She was a political obsessive, and her political legacy – in terms of economic policy, national sovereignty, international alliances, attitudes to liberty, military affairs, totalitarianism and society itself, the '-ism' which bears her name – is of immense interest. Yet these subjects are rarely raised directly, whereas ones about her as a worker, a colleague, a wife and mother, a public performer, a leader and a Christian very frequently are. I have concluded that people are not bored by Margaret Thatcher's politics, but what they want to get at is *her*. It is her character in relation to great ideas and great events which fascinates them. This is closely connected to the most obvious fact about her – that she was the first woman, in the whole of Western democratic history, who truly came to dominate her country in her time. The pronoun 'she' is where it all starts, and perhaps where it will finish.

Acknowledgements

As in Volume I, I must first thank the late Lady Thatcher for inviting me to write this book. She fulfilled her promise of complete access – including interviews, support in seeking interviews from others and the sight of all her papers. From her offer flowed the help of her family. I interviewed her late husband, Sir Denis Thatcher, at the end of the twentieth century. Her children, Sir Mark Thatcher and Carol Thatcher, have also been interviewed, more often and more recently, and have been most kind throughout.

After Lady Thatcher died in 2013, most of her personal staff dispersed, but I have still been greatly helped in the preparation of this volume, and in the whole enterprise, by the former director of her private office, Sir Julian Seymour. He was the first person to tell me, back in 1997, of Lady Thatcher's idea for the book, and he has been the book's constant supporter – and occasional trenchant critic – ever since. I am also grateful to Sir Mark Worthington, Lady Thatcher's long-standing private secretary after she left office, and Mrs Cynthia Crawford ('Crawfie'), who served her both in and out of office.

Once I had accepted Lady Thatcher's invitation all those years ago, I had to find a publisher for the book. With the help of Gillon Aitken, my great literary agent, the proposal was accepted by Penguin. For most of the work's long career, its editor there has been Stuart Proffitt, the most talented, helpful and conscientious editor in British publishing. He may, with good reason, have regretted the delay, but his kindness and his enthusiasm for the book itself have never failed. I am also grateful to Clare Alexander, Gillon Aitken's partner in the agency, for her involvement in this current volume.

The two main sources of Thatcher documentation are her own papers and those held by the government. The former are deposited in the Churchill College Archives Centre, Cambridge, which is Britain's pre-eminent modern political archive. There they are beautifully kept, under the overall supervision of Dr Allen Packwood, by Andrew Riley, the Thatcher archivist, ably assisted by Sophie Bridges. Andrew is the constant wise counsellor to this project and often makes suggestions which open up new lines of inquiry, or produces papers which I should otherwise have missed.

It is a question which I cannot solve whether Andrew Riley or Christopher Collins knows more about this book's subject. Certainly, both know more than I do. Dr Collins is the founder and editor of www.margaretthatcher.org, the Margaret Thatcher Foundation website. This is the best online documentary archive of any public individual in the world, and is constantly expanding. By collecting all Margaret Thatcher's public remarks – and much else – in one place, it has saved me literally years of searching. Dr Collins is the most inveterate discoverer of new material, and there are times in this book when his reading of a particular document has been decisive for me.

The Churchill Archives Centre needed a whole new wing built to house the papers. The government papers are even more voluminous. Many of those covered in this volume have now been released to the National Archives at Kew, but I studied them chiefly, before they were released, in Whitehall. Every effort has been made to update the relevant endnote citations to include the PREM or CAB references used at the National Archives (supplemented by a web link to the Margaret Thatcher Foundation website when the document is available online). For documents that remain closed or retained by the department, it was necessary to keep the older file references provided when I consulted them in the Cabinet Office. I must thank Tessa Sterling, the head of the Cabinet Office Official Histories Team, and her deputy Sally Falk, for their constant helpfulness in obtaining the documents for me and in pushing the project forward if ever bureaucratic obstacles loomed. Roger Smethurst, the head of the Archives Team, was most helpful in this cause; and I must thank Sue Gray, also of the Cabinet Office, for helping to cut the Gordian knot when a last-minute delay threatened the book's timetable. David Richardson, Ron Lawrence and Deborah Neal, stalwarts of the Archives Team, so often found the files in the bowels of the Treasury and brought them to me. I have frequently shared a room with official historians, and have been particularly grateful for conversations with them, especially Sir Stephen Wall, Ian Beesley and Gill Bennett. I have also been helped by Professor Patrick Salmon, the Chief Historian of the Foreign Office.

Although an authorized rather than an 'official' historian, I was granted, in 1998, the official status required for clearance to see the necessary documents by the then Cabinet Secretary Sir Richard Wilson. This privilege has continued under his successors, Lord Turnbull, Lord O'Donnell and Sir Jeremy Heywood. The book's progress has been followed with kindly interest by successive prime ministers since it began – Tony Blair, Gordon Brown and David Cameron. I must also thank Mr Blair and Mr Cameron for agreeing to be interviewed for it. (The latter will appear in Volume III.)

I should like to express my gratitude to Sir Christopher Geidt, the private secretary to HM the Queen, and other members of the Royal Household and Royal Archives, for their courteous assistance.

The American material in this volume is even richer than in the last. This is due both to the importance of the relationship between Margaret Thatcher and Ronald Reagan in the period covered and also to the huge amount of scholarly research performed by Daniel Collings. Although, overall, I have done the bulk of the research for this book myself, in the case of the United States I soon realized that I would not be able to be there often enough to cover the necessary ground. I therefore made Dan my US Director of Research. His assiduity, good organization and interpretive intelligence, proved to me over ten years and more, are beyond praise. Indeed, his formal title does not do justice to the breadth and importance of his role as my trusted adviser on all aspects of the book. In self-aggrandizing moments, I think of Dan as my Charles Powell. With this task accomplished, he will also have proved himself a fully fledged historian in his own right. I want also to thank, and apologize to, Dan's wife Sonja and their daughter Clara, who let me take up far too much of what should be their time.

After Daniel Collings, Dr David Shiels, my research associate, has been the most important part of the team. He has continued the Irish research which he contributed to the last volume, but his work has now extended over a much wider field of primary research at Kew, the Churchill Archives and elsewhere. He has also been deeply involved in the preparation and consolidation of the whole volume. His care and diligence are outstanding.

For Volume II, it fell to Daniel Collings to conduct most of our interviews in the United States (which for this volume number around sixty), as well as taking relevant testimony from former occupants of Whitehall and King Charles Street. More time-consuming was US documentary research. Here we owe a debt to the Presidential Libraries of Ronald Reagan and George H. W. Bush. At the Reagan Library we would like to thank Mike

Duggan, Steve Branch and, above all, the indefatigable Shelly Williams, our cheerful and extraordinarily wise sherpa for over ten years. At the Bush Library our sincere thanks to Robert Holzweiss, who runs a very tight ship, and Zach Roberts, who dealt with our numerous requests with military precision.

This book has benefited from FOIA and Mandatory Review requests for documents spanning many thousands of pages. In part we have been guided by the knowledgeable staff at the Presidential Libraries, but we have also submitted numerous requests directly. We would thus like to thank the FOIA staff at the State Department, Department of Defense, CIA, NSA and Exim Bank. Those helping us at Foggy Bottom deserve special mention, especially Lorraine Hartmann, the Appeals Officer, who has so often gone above and beyond the call of duty in search of obscure documents.

Our research has also relied upon the expertise and documentary collections of a number of US institutions. These include the National Security Archive at George Washington University in Washington, DC, where we would like to thank Mary Curry and, particularly, Svetlana Savranskaya, who generously shared the fruits of her research at the Gorbachev Foundation in Moscow. We also acknowledge with gratitude assistance from the Library of Congress, the National Archives and Records Administration, the Lauinger Library at Georgetown University, the Mudd Library at Princeton University, the Hoover Institution at Stanford University, the archives of the United Nations and the public libraries of the District of Columbia.

In our efforts to understand Mrs Thatcher's interlocutors we have benefited greatly from the support of Mrs Nancy Reagan and those who continue to look after the interests of President Reagan, above all Joanne Drake and Fred Ryan. Our debt to them is huge. We are similarly appreciative of the support received from President George H. W. Bush and his office. President Bush receives only a walk-on part in this volume, but will, of course, take centre stage in Volume III. George Shultz has also been a stalwart supporter of this book throughout – generous with his time and unfailingly shrewd in his insights. So has Peter Robinson. Others from whom we have learnt much for this volume include Bud McFarlane, Jack Matlock, Richard Perle, John Poindexter, Roz Ridgway and Colin Powell. Our gratitude to them, and to all our interviewees, is immense.

I also thank my US publishers, Alfred A. Knopf, and my editor there, Dan Frank. The speakers' bureau, Leading Authorities, has helped me spread the word about the book in the United States.

*

Other institutions whose records have been consulted include the National Archives of Ireland in Dublin, the Public Record Office of Northern Ireland and the Archives Nationales in Paris. I am, as always, much in the debt of the London Library. Numerous individuals have made documents available to me. I should like to thank Sir David Butler for arranging access to his archive of contemporary election interviews at Nuffield College, Oxford (where Sir David, now over ninety, continues to provide the most active and generous help); the late Lord Deedes, my first editor (to whose memory this book is co-dedicated), for glimpses of his own records; Harry Hart for the use of the papers of his late father, David; Professor Sir Brian Harrison for material relating to Mrs Thatcher's honorary-degree controversy at Oxford and to her relationships with intellectuals; Graham Turner for the unpublished transcripts from his published interview on the latter subject; Henry Hardy for permission to quote a letter from the late Sir Isaiah Berlin; John Whittingdale for sight of his unpublished diaries of the period; Dame Patricia Hodgson for personal papers; Lady Walters for permission to quote from the notes and diaries of her late husband, Sir Alan; Gerald Bowden for his private article about the Thatchers in Dulwich; Archie Brown for his contemporary notes about Soviet matters; Martin Nicholson for unpublished extracts from his memoirs and assistance rendering obscure Russian phrases into wonderfully approachable English; Azriel Bermant for his thesis on Margaret Thatcher and the Middle East (which is expected to be published by Cambridge University Press in 2016); Lord Burns for his private notes of meetings; Alice Coleman for her contemporary graphological analysis of Mrs Thatcher's hand; Sir David Goodall for his private memoirs of the Anglo-Irish Agreement and of the character of Mrs Thatcher; Sir John Coles for several private papers; Sir Peter Marshall for the use of his private diaries; the estate of the late Lord Wyatt of Weeford for permission to quote from previously unpublished passages from his journals; Lord Young of Graffham for the use of his private Election Diary of 1987.

The following have kindly given interviews for this volume. Many of them have never spoken before on this subject. In a few cases, their interviews are not quoted or referred to directly, but the background information provided has been of great use: General Jim Abrahamson; Sir Antony Acland; Kenneth Adelman; Raymond Albright; Rosie Alison; the late Martin Anderson; Lord Armstrong of Ilminster; Jacques Attali; Lord Baker of Dorking; James Baker; HRH Prince Bandar Bin Sultan; Dr Wendy Barron; Lord Bell; the late Lord Biffen; Lord Birt; the late Tony Bishop; Eivind Bjerke; Tony Blair; Sir Kenneth Bloomfield; Lord Blyth of

Rowington; Roger Bone; Sir Gerald Bowden; Dame Colette Bowe; Sir
Rodric Braithwaite; the late Lord Brittan of Spennithorne; Keith Britto;
Lord Brooke of Sutton Mandeville; Sir Nigel Broomfield; Professor Archie
Brown; William Brown; Sir Colin Budd; Vladimir Bukovsky; Lord Burns;
Conor Burns; Richard Burt; Lady Butler of Brockwell; Lord Butler of
Brockwell; Sir David Butler; the late Sir Michael Butler; Frank Carlucci;
Lord Carrington; Sir Brian Cartledge; Bishop Richard Chartres; Charles
Clarke; Duane Clarridge; Tyrus Cobb; Professor Alice Coleman; Sir John
Coles; Tony Comer; the late Robert Conquest; David Cornwell (John
le Carré); the late Sir Percy Cradock; Sir James Craig; Cynthia Crawford;
Chester Crocker; Peter Cropper; the late Sir Brian Cubbon; the late Lord
Cuckney; Ian Curteis; the late Sir Christopher Curwen; Kenneth Dam;
Timothy Deal; Sir Richard Dearlove; the late Michael Deaver; Lord Deben
(John Gummer); the late Lord Deedes; Ken deGraffenreid; F. W. de Klerk;
Jacques Delors; Carol Dinkins; Lord Dobbs; Noel Dorr; Ken Duberstein;
Lady Dunn; the late Lawrence Eagleburger; Lord Egremont; Richard
Ehrman; Sir Brian Fall; Sebastian Faulks; Lord Fellowes; Fred Fielding;
the late Garret FitzGerald; Marlin Fitzwater; Tim Flesher; Lord
Fowler; Charles Freeman; Tessa Gaisman; Nicholas Garland; Sir Victor
Garland; Dr Robert Gates; John Gerson; Sir David Goodall; Sir Nicholas
Goodison; Oleg Gordievsky; Lord Gowrie; Sir Peter Gregson; Lord Grif-
fiths of Fforestfach; Sir Gerry Grimstone; Lord Hamilton of Epsom;
Sir Claude Hankes; Lord Hannay of Chiswick; Sir David Hare; Robin
Harris; Professor Sir Brian Harrison; the late Arthur Hartman; Sir Max
Hastings; Sir Terry Heiser; Philip Hensher; Lord Heseltine; Sir William
Heseltine; Charles Hill; Dame Patricia Hodgson; Sir Michael Howard;
Sir Gerald Howarth; Lord Howe of Aberavon; Jonathan Howe; Lord
Hurd of Westwell; Angela Huth; Sir Bernard Ingham; Sir Martin Jacomb;
Lord Jenkin of Roding; Lord Jopling; John Kelly; Dr Geoffrey Kemp; Lord
Kerr of Kinlochard; Robert Kimmitt; Lord King of Bridgwater; the late
Lord Kingsdown; the late Bob Kingston; Lord Kinnock; Dr Henry Kiss-
inger; Andrew Knight; Lord Lamont of Lerwick; Sir Tim Lankester;
Andrew Lansley; Lord Lawson of Blaby; the late Nelson Ledsky; Dr John
Lehman; Dr Ronald Lehman; Sir Mark Lennox-Boyd; Oliver Letwin;
Burton Levin; Michael Lillis; Ken Livingstone; Sir Michael Llewellyn
Smith; Rachel Lomax; the Marquess of Lothian (Michael Ancram); Jose-
phine Louis; Lord Luce; Romilly, Lady McAlpine; the late Lord McAlpine
of West Green; Sir Colin McColl; Robert 'Bud' McFarlane; Lord Maginnis
of Drumglass; Gerald Malone; Lord Mandelson; Martin Mansergh; the
late Lord Marshall of Knightsbridge; Sir Peter Marshall; Jack Matlock;
Lord Maude of Horsham; Lord Mayhew of Twysden; Roger Maynard;

Ed Meese; Sir Peter Middleton; Oliver Miles; Frank Miller; Lord Mogg; Chris Moncrieff; David Montgomery; Lord Moore of Lower Marsh; Pierre Morell; the late Lord Moser; Tony Motley; Sir Richard Mottram; Ferdinand Mount; Brian Mulroney; Jane Mulvagh; Rupert Murdoch; Richard Murphy; the late Dermot Nally; Andrew Neil; Martin Nicholson; Thomas Niles; David Norgrove; Oliver North; Sir John Nott; Dr Stanley Orman; John O'Sullivan; Lord Owen; Claire Pakenham; Sir Michael Pakenham; Lord Parkinson; David Pascall; Lord Patten of Barnes; Richard Perle; John Poindexter; Amanda Ponsonby; Lady Powell of Bayswater; Lord Powell of Bayswater; Colin Powell; the late Charles Price; Jonathan Pym; the late Sir Michael Quinlan; Sir Shridath 'Sonny' Ramphal; Katharine Ramsay; Mrs Nancy Reagan; John Redwood; the late Lord Rees; Lord Renwick of Clifton; William Rickett; Roz Ridgway; Sir Malcolm Rifkind; Peter Robinson; Jill Rutter; Richard Ryan; Lady Ryder of Wensum; Lord Ryder of Wensum; Lord Saatchi; Wafic Said; Sir John Scarlett; Dr Michael Schluter; Sir Michael Scholar; Raymond Seitz; Lord Sharkey; Sir Nigel Sheinwald; Lord Sherbourne of Didsbury; George Shultz; Jeremy Sinclair; Geoffrey Smith; Sir John Sparrow; Dick Spring; Lord Sterling of Plaistow; Edward Streator; Barry Strevens; William Taft IV; Lord Tebbit; Howard Teicher; Horst Teltschik; Carol Thatcher; the late Sir Denis Thatcher; Sir Mark Thatcher; Lord Thomas of Swynnerton; Sir Derek Thomas; Harvey Thomas; Lord Turnbull; Graham Turner; Sir Brian Unwin; Sir John Ure; Hubert Vedrine; Lady Wakeham; Lord Wakeham; Lord Waldegrave of North Hill; George Walden; the late Lord Walker of Worcester; Sir David Walker; Sir Stephen Wall; Sir Dennis Walters; Peter Warry; the late Lord Weatherill; Sir John Weston; Ron White; the late John Whitehead; Sir Clive Whitmore; John Whittingdale; Sir Nigel Wicks; Philip Wilcox; David Willetts; the late Lord Williamson of Horton; the late Richard Wirthlin; Revd John Witheridge; Paul Wolfowitz; Lord Wolfson of Sunningdale; the late Sir Oliver Wright; Lord Wright of Richmond; Bob Young; Lord Young of Graffham.

In the last volume, several people were interviewed on the condition that they remained anonymous. For this volume, only one interviewee made this stipulation (though many spoke off the record on some subjects). I am grateful to her/him for her/his contribution too.

Many others have helped in a variety of ways:

- at Allen Lane, Richard Duguid and Rebecca Lee have (as last time) been the book's efficient editorial managers; Peter James has again been my meticulous and brilliant copy-editor; Taryn Jones and

Sandra Fuller have been the production controllers, Chris Shaw and Stephen Ryan the proofreaders, Lisa Jackson the design manager, Antonio Colaco the jacket designer, Christine Shuttleworth the indexer, Cecilia Mackay the picture researcher, Donald Futers and Ben Sinyor successive assistants to Stuart Proffitt. All of them have worked hard to ensure that the book met its publication date in good order. Chantal Noel has ably organized serialization. I should like retrospectively to thank Liz Sich and Sarah Watson for their cheerful and effective publicity work for Volume I. As the book goes to press, Pen Vogler is doing a similar job for this volume.

- All those who have helped with research. My dear friend Miriam Gross did research to help me understand Mrs Thatcher and the arts. To aid the final, immensely complicated process of getting 3,000 endnotes right, Dan Collings advised me to recruit Foley Pfalzgraf, in Washington, DC. Demonstrating extraordinary precision and determination throughout, she has done a splendid job.

- I am particularly grateful to the owners of the Telegraph Media Group, Sir David and Sir Frederick Barclay, and Sir David's son, Aidan, for their warm support for this book. The chief executive, Murdoch MacLennan, and the editor, Chris Evans, have been equally enthusiastic and, in the case of both volumes, have serialized the book. Chris Evans kindly permitted me a sabbatical to get Volume II finished. Other members of the paper's staff – Ian Macgregor, Richard Preston, Philip Johnston, Harry de Quetteville, Robert Colvile (who has now left the paper) and Sally Chatterton – should also be thanked for their co-operation and patience. In my work at the *Daily Telegraph*, Pat Ventre is my assistant. The Thatcher book is not part of her duties, but her presence has greatly helped me organize my life. I am much in the debt of Fraser Nelson, the editor of the *Spectator*, who has tolerated too frequent absences from my column on Thatcher business.

In the previous volume, I mentioned friends whose conversations over many years about my subject and the age in which she flourished have been particularly valuable. I shall not rename most of them here, but what I said then applies still. One or two should be singled out for special relevance to this volume. They include the late Nicholas Budgen, Richard Ehrman, Christopher Fildes, Nicholas Garland, Dean Godson, Nigel Lawson, Oliver Letwin, Ferdy Mount, Owen and Rose Paterson, Alan Petty, Katharine Ramsay, Norman Tebbit and William Waldegrave.

On Irish matters, Lord Bew has been essential; Professor Eugenio Biagini has also been most helpful. Jane Mulvagh, Carla Powell, Cynthia

Crawford, Amanda Ponsonby and Romilly McAlpine have, in very different ways, explained to me about clothes.

Among those particularly close to Mrs Thatcher, I am so grateful to Amanda Ponsonby for hospitably bringing together the important but little-known people behind the scenes who often knew her the best; also to Richard and Caroline Ryder, who have helped me at every turn. The person, among the leading cast of Thatcher characters, who has assisted my inquiries most often is Charles Powell (Lord Powell of Bayswater), whose memory is prodigious and range of subjects unique. He must have spent more time with Margaret Thatcher, and certainly knew more of her political mind, than anyone else in the period covered. His co-operation has been unstinting.

Charles Powell was a distinguished civil servant, if of an unusual kind. Several others from his profession have been vital for this book, contributing the sort of accuracy which politicians, whatever their other virtues, rarely possess. I thank, in particular, Robert Armstrong (Lord Armstrong of Ilminster), Robin Butler (Lord Butler of Brockwell), who served Mrs Thatcher both as principal private secretary and, later, as Cabinet Secretary, and Andrew Turnbull (Lord Turnbull).

Friends, expertly and kindly, read the manuscript to try to improve it. They were Mervyn King (Lord King of Lothbury), particularly for the bits about money; Richard Ehrman; James Sherr (for everything concerned with the Cold War); Andrew Riley; David Willetts; Sir Noel Malcolm. My father, Richard Moore, also read it most carefully. At home in Sussex, Jackie Ashdown has cleaned round it with the greatest possible tact.

As with Volume I, Virginia (Ginda) Utley, towards the end of the process assisted by her sister, Catherine, and Kate Ehrman both helped anchor the book. Ginda is in charge of the manuscript, a very arduous task when working with an author who does not get the best out of computers. Kate translated from the French and checked the 2,000 or so quotations from those interviewed. Both, having worked with me on and off for many years, have developed exceptional gifts of patience and humour.

As in the previous volume, I want to thank Diana Grissell, MFH, and my horse Tommy, for whom she cares. As in hunting, so in writing a book, a good rule is that of Lucy Glitters, 'Throw your heart over it, and then follow it as quickly as you can,' though I concede that it may not look to the outside world as if I am being quick at all.

Finally, I must thank all my family, especially our twins, Will and Kate, who were seven when all this started and are now, as I write, twenty-five.

Truly, they have borne a great deal, and have made plenty of jokes (and, in Will's case, drawn cartoons) to remind me of this. Now my daughter-in-law, Hannah, is an additional victim. To her and them, this book is dedicated.

My wife Caroline has borne the most. I just do not know how to thank her enough: I hope, by the time I have finished Volume III, I shall have found the answer.

Charles Moore
Etchingham
August 2015

List of Illustrations

Every effort has been made to contact all copyright holders. The publishers will be happy to make good in future editions any errors or omissions brought to their attention.

TEXT ILLUSTRATIONS

LIST OF PLATES

Chronology

	Politics	Economics
1982		
Jul		19 – Plans to privatize British Telecom announced
Aug		
Sept	18 – Leak of CPRS paper for radical welfare reform	9 – Unemployment reaches 3 million
Oct	4–8 – Conservative Party conference in Brighton 19 – MT appoints Anthony Parsons as her special adviser on foreign affairs	
Nov	Early – Keith Joseph presents modified education voucher scheme	
Dec		
1983		
Jan	6 – Cabinet reshuffle: Michael Heseltine replaces John Nott at MOD 16 – MT declares support for 'Victorian values'	
Feb	24 – Bermondsey by-election (Lab loss to Lib)	

East/West	Other Foreign	Northern Ireland
	17–29 – MT begins Far East visit (agrees to open Hong Kong talks with China)	
10 – Soviet leader Leonid Brezhnev dies	1 – Helmut Kohl becomes West German chancellor	
	28 – MT visits Kohl in Bonn and (29) Berlin (attempt to build up ties)	
		24 – General election in Republic of Ireland
	24 – Draft of Franks report on Falklands War exonerating MT reaches No. 10	14 – Garret FitzGerald elected taoiseach after forming a coalition with the Irish Labour Party
	7 – MT visits the Falklands	
	4 – Kohl visits MT at Chequers (mutual support for INF deployment)	
	8 – British troops join MNF in Beirut	

	Politics	Economics
Mar	8 – MT rejects Joseph's latest plan for education vouchers	15 – Budget (tax allowances raised 8.5 per cent above inflation)
	24 – Darlington by-election (Lab hold)	
Apr		
May	9 – General election campaign begins	
Jun	9 – Election day: MT returns as PM with majority of 144	
	10 – Cabinet reshuffle as MT forms new government: Nigel Lawson becomes Chancellor; Geoffrey Howe to Foreign Office; Willie Whitelaw to Leader of the House of Lords; Leon Brittan becomes Home Secretary	
Jul	15 – Bernard Weatherill becomes new Commons Speaker	7 – £500 million in spending cuts announced
	13 – Commons rejects restoration of capital punishment	
	28 – Penrith by-election (Cons hold)	
	29 – CPRS formally abolished	
Aug	3 – MT hospitalized for eye-operation	

East/West	Other Foreign	Northern Ireland
8 – MT meets József Marjai (Hungarian deputy PM) at No. 10 23 – President Reagan announces plan for SDI		21 – MT meets FitzGerald on fringes of Brussels EEC summit (first meeting after FitzGerald's return to office)
1 – Reagan authorizes MT to confirm her de facto veto over use of US missiles on British soil 28 – MT attends G7 summit in Williamsburg (endorses INF deployment)		30 – First meeting of New Ireland Forum in Dublin
	17–19 – Stuttgart European Council (MT wins one-year temporary budget rebate)	

	Politics	Economics
Sept	1 – Ian MacGregor becomes NCB chairman	
Oct	2 – Neil Kinnock becomes Labour Party leader 7 – White Paper on GLC abolition published 11–14 – Conservative Party conference at Blackpool 14 – Cecil Parkinson resigns (Norman Tebbit to DTI)	
Nov		
Dec	21 – Rate-capping Bill introduced	

East/West	Other Foreign	Northern Ireland
1 – Korean Airlines Flight 007 shot down	22 – New Constitution comes into effect in South Africa	
9 – MT holds East–West seminar at Chequers (decides to engage with the Soviet Union)		
28–30 – MT visits Reagan in Washington, DC (shares thinking on engagement)		
19 – Maurice Bishop, Grenadian PM, killed in *coup d'état*	23 – Bombing of US Marine barracks in Beirut	
22 – Reagan agrees to OECS request to intervene in Grenada		
25 – Howe declares that he knows of no US intention to invade Grenada		
25 – US invades Grenada		
2–11 – NATO conducts ABLE ARCHER exercise	22–29 – CHOGM in New Delhi (MT faces early disagreements over South Africa)	7 – FitzGerald visits MT at Chequers (MT closes down Goodall–Lillis channel but discussions continue elsewhere)
23 – Deployment of US INF missiles in Europe begins		
		7 – Unionist politician Edgar Graham shot dead by IRA
		17 – IRA bombing of Harrods
		24 – MT visits Northern Ireland

	Politics	Economics
1984		
Jan	25 – GCHQ union ban announced	
Feb		
Mar	8 – Miners' strike begins: pits close in Yorkshire and Scotland 14 – MT meets with Ian MacGregor (subsequently stiffens police resolve)	13 – Budget (tackles inflation and reforms business tax)
Apr	19 – Arthur Scargill reduces national ballot threshold to approve strike to 50 per cent	
May	3 – Local elections (Cons lose seats)	
Jun	14 – European elections (Cons lose seats) 16 – Portsmouth by-election (Cons loss to SDP) 18 – 'Battle of Orgreave' (violent clashes between police and striking miners)	

East/West	Other Foreign	Northern Ireland
16 – Reagan calls for dialogue with Soviets		
2–4 – MT visits Hungary	8 – UK troops withdrawn from MNF	
9 – Soviet leader Yuri Andropov dies		
14 – MT visits Moscow for Andropov's funeral		
14 – Kinnock meets Reagan in Washington		
	16 – Nkomati Accord (non-aggression pact) signed between South Africa and Mozambique	
	29 – Brussels European Council (no agreement over UK budget rebate)	
	17 – WPC Fletcher killed by gunfire from within Libyan Embassy	
	2 – Kohl visits MT at Chequers (MT hints that Britain may give a little to reach budget deal)	2 – New Ireland Forum report published
	2 – P. W. Botha visits MT at Chequers (clashes over apartheid but dialogue established; MT 'raises question' of Mandela)	1–4 – Reagan visits Ireland
	25–26 – Fontainebleau European Council (MT secures permanent UK budget rebate)	

	Politics	Economics
Jul	9 – National dock strike begins	
	18 – NUM–NCB talks on the future of uneconomic pits break down	
	19 – National dock strike ends	
Aug		
Sept	2 – MT authorizes Patrick Jenkin's review of local government finance	
	10 – Cabinet reshuffle: Douglas Hurd replaces Jim Prior in Northern Ireland	
	15 – Birth of Prince Henry of Wales (Prince Harry)	
	28 – NACODS vote to strike	
Oct	9–12 – Conservative Party conference at Brighton	
	24 – NACODS call off planned strike	
	25 – NUM assets sequestered	
	28 – MT attends Chequers 'teach-in' on local government finance	
Nov	30 – David Wilkie killed by concrete post dropped on his taxi while driving a miner to work	20 – British Telecom share flotation

East/West	Other Foreign	Northern Ireland
	28 – Howe begins visit to China to complete Hong Kong negotiations	
26 – Reagan receives Andrei Gromyko at the White House for the first time	5 – P. W. Botha sworn in as executive state president of South Africa 13 – Shimon Peres becomes Israeli PM	3 – FitzGerald visits MT at No. 10 28 – Irish security forces intercept the *Marita Ann*, importing arms for the IRA
	16 – Desmond Tutu awarded Nobel Peace Prize 23–25 – François Mitterrand makes state visit to UK (discusses Channel Tunnel) 31 – Indira Gandhi assassinated	12 – IRA bombs the Grand Hotel in Brighton: MT narrowly escapes injury, but five people killed
6 – Reagan re-elected president of the US 16 – Reagan calls off Grand Jury investigation into BA	3–4 – MT attends Mrs Gandhi's funeral in Delhi 29 – MT visits Mitterrand in Paris (becomes enthusiastic about Channel Tunnel)	18–19 – Anglo-Irish summit at Chequers (MT rejects New Ireland Forum Report ('out . . . out . . . out'))

	Politics	Economics
Dec	10 – 'Everything She Wants' released by Wham!	

1985		
Jan	1 – Vodafone launches first UK mobile phone network	14 – Run on sterling (interest rates raised to 14 per cent)
	29 – Oxford University declines to grant MT honorary degree	
Feb	13 – MT discusses possible ERM membership with ministers	
	13 – Results of Scottish rates revaluation announced	
Mar	3 – Miners' strike ends: NUM conference votes to return to work	19 – Budget (rise in personal tax allowances)
	27 – Peacock Committee (investigating BBC financing) established	
	31 – At Chequers meeting, MT approves community charge in principle	
Apr		
May	2 – Local elections (Cons lose seats)	
Jun		

East/West	Other Foreign	Northern Ireland
16 – Mikhail Gorbachev visits MT at Chequers (MT calls him 'a man to do business with')	17 – MT meets Prince Bandar for the first time (begins talks leading to Al-Yamamah deal)	3–4 – MT attends European Council meeting at Dublin Castle (makes amends with FitzGerald)
22 – MT visits Reagan at Camp David (agrees 'four points' on SDI/ arms control)	19 – MT signs Hong Kong Agreement in Peking	
7 – Gromyko and Shultz meet in Geneva to agree new arms control negotiations	31 – P. W. Botha makes a conditional offer of release to Nelson Mandela	
19–21 – MT visits Washington (attends Reagan's 'arms control seminar'; addresses Congress)	11 – King Hussein and Yasser Arafat agree on joint approach to Arab–Israeli dispute	
11 – Soviet leader Konstantin Chernenko dies		
13 – MT attends Chernenko's funeral in Moscow (meets with Gorbachev)		
15 – Howe attacks SDI as a 'Maginot Line in space'		
	18 – Kohl visits MT at Chequers (reacts positively to MT's suggested agenda for Europe)	15 – District council elections in Northern Ireland: Sinn Fein win fifty-nine seats
	28–29 – European Council in Milan (MT's proposed European agenda hijacked and turned into plan for new treaty)	

	Politics	Economics
Jul	4 – Brecon and Rador by-election (Cons loss)	
	24 – Commons rebellion over TSRB proposals (majority cut to 17)	
Aug		
Sept	2 – Cabinet reshuffle: Tebbit becomes party chairman; Brittan demoted to Trade and Industry; Hurd becomes home secretary; Lord Young to Employment; Kenneth Clarke joins Cabinet as paymaster-general.	22 – Plaza Accord (effort to tackle overvalued dollar and restore exchange rate stability)
	9–10 – Handsworth riots	
	28 – Brixton riot	
	30 – MT holds seminar on possible ERM membership	
Oct	1 – Kinnock attacks Militant in his speech at Labour Party conference	17 – Lawson delivers Mansion House speech dropping £M3 target
	6–7 – Broadwater Farm riot (murder of PC Blakelock)	
	7–11 – Conservative Party conference in Blackpool	

East/West	Other Foreign	Northern Ireland
22 – Oleg Gordievsky arrives in UK after exfiltration from Soviet Union 25–27 – MT visits Washington (meets with Vice-President George Bush and addresses IDU)		25 – Cabinet approves draft of Anglo-Irish Agreement 30 – BBC governors prevent transmission of *Real Lives* documentary
	15 – South African President P. W. Botha delivers 'Rubicon' speech in Durban (fails to promise reform)	30 – Unionist leaders James Molyneaux and Ian Paisley meet MT in Downing Street
12 – Gordievsky's defection announced; twenty-five Soviet officials expelled from the UK	17–20 – MT visits Egypt and Jordan: agrees to meet Jordanian-Palestinian delegation 26 – Heseltine signs formal Al-Yamamah agreement	2 – Tom King appointed Northern Ireland secretary
	13 – MT cancels planned meeting with joint Jordanian-Palestinian delegation 16–20 – CHOGM in Nassau (acrimonious exchanges as MT resists imposition of sanctions on South Africa)	30 – Unionist leaders Molyneaux and Paisley meet MT in Downing Street

	Politics	Economics
Nov	13 – MT isolated at full ministerial discussion of ERM membership 29 – Heseltine engineers NAD agreement to block Sikorsky bid for Westland	
Dec	3 – *Faith in the City* report released 9 – Press stories emerge about row over Westland 12 – Heseltine attempts to raise Westland at Cabinet but ruled out of order 13 – Westland board votes to recommend Sikorsky takeover bid 19 – Cabinet reaffirms that shareholders alone should decide Westland's future	

1986

	Politics	Economics
Jan	6 – Patrick Mayhew's letter warning Heseltine of 'material inaccuracies' leaked 9 – Heseltine resigns during Cabinet meeting (replaced at Defence by George Younger) 9 – Cabinet approves community charge 13 – Brittan ambushed by Heseltine during statement to the House 15 – MT gives lacklustre performance in debate on Westland 23 – MT reports the results of Robert Armstrong's Westland inquiry to the House	31 – Unemployment reported at a peak of 3.4 million

East/West	Other Foreign	Northern Ireland
19–21 – Reagan and Gorbachev hold first summit in Geneva	27 – Kohl visits MT in London (preparation for Luxembourg summit)	15 – MT signs Anglo-Irish Agreement in Belfast 23 – Unionists rally against Anglo-Irish Agreement
6 – UK signs SDI participation agreement	2–3 – Intergovernmental conference in Luxembourg (MT secures agreement for European Single Market, but concedes mention of EMU)	2–3 – MT meets FitzGerald on margins of Luxembourg summit ('You've got the glory') 11 – First meeting of the Intergovernmental Conference established by the Anglo-Irish Agreement 17 – Ulster Unionist MPs resign in protest at Anglo-Irish Agreement
16 – Gorbachev launches surprise proposal for the elimination of nuclear weapons by 2000 28 – Space Shuttle *Challenger* disintegrates after launch, killing seven crew	7 – Delors becomes president of European Commission 20 – MT visits Mitterrand in Lille (announces plans for Channel Tunnel) 31 – P. W. Botha outlines limited reforms including restoration of citizenship rights to black South Africans	23 – All Ulster Unionists but one re-elected in by-elections

	Politics	Economics
Jan – *cont.*	24 – Brittan resigns (replaced at DTI by Paul Channon)	
	24 – Wapping printworkers' dispute begins	
	27 – MT survives emergency Commons debate on Westland	
	28 – Green Paper on community charge published	
Feb	4 – Sale of Austin Rover to Ford dropped	
	12 – Westland shareholders vote to accept Sikorsky bid	
Mar	17 – Wedding of Prince Andrew and Sarah Ferguson	18 – Budget (basic rate cut 1 per cent to 29 per cent)
	25 – Sale of Land Rover dropped	
	31 – GLC abolished	
Apr	10 – Fulham by-election (Cons loss to Lab)	
	13 – Chequers meeting on election strategy (exposes MT rift with Tebbit)	
	14 – Government defeated on the Shops Bill	
May	8 – Ryedale by-election (Cons loss to Libs); also local elections (major Cons losses)	
	12 – John Biffen branded 'semi-detached' by Ingham	
	21 – Cabinet reshuffle: Nicholas Ridley to Environment; Kenneth Baker to Education; Keith Joseph leaves Cabinet	
	29 – Peacock report on BBC	

East/West	Other Foreign	Northern Ireland
	12 – MT signs Channel Tunnel Treaty 17 – MT signs Single European Act	25 – Unionist leaders Molyneaux and Paisley meet MT at No. 10
	12 – EPG meets Nelson Mandela, who asks for message to be passed to MT	3 – Unionist 'Day of Action' in protest at Anglo-Irish Agreement
5 – Bombing of La Belle discothèque in Germany 15 – US bombing of Libya (involving assets based in the UK) 26 – Chernobyl disaster	18 – Bodies of two murdered British hostages recovered in Beirut	
4–6 – Tokyo G7 (MT reports to Reagan that Gorbachev claims to be eager for a new summit) 23 – Reagan warns MT that US will no longer adhere to SALT II limits	19 – South African Defence Forces launch raids on ANC offices in Botswana, Zambia and Zimbabwe; condemned by MT 24–27 – MT visits Israel	

	Politics	Economics
Jun	23 – Election Strategy Group ('The A-Team') first meets	
Jul	20 – *Sunday Times* reports that the Queen is at odds with MT 30 – Tebbit confronts MT about hostile press stories he believes came from No. 10	
Aug	5 – MT hospitalized for operation on right hand 8 – MT and Tebbit reach truce: hostility diminishes 29 – BBC chairman Stuart Young dies	
Sept	10 – Mini-reshuffle: John Major becomes minister of state for social security	

East/West	Other Foreign	Northern Ireland
	12 – Eminent Persons Group reports (South Africa not making progress towards eliminating apartheid)	23 – Northern Ireland Assembly dissolved
	24 – FCO Minister of State Lynda Chalker meets head of the ANC, Oliver Tambo, in London	
	26 – MT attends European Council in The Hague (some sanctions against South Africa agreed)	
17 – UK–US Extradition Treaty ratified 25 – Reagan first proposes abolition of ballistic missiles	9 – Howe begins EC mission to the Frontline States 15 – Howe writes to MT, worried that Britain is seen as 'sole defender' of apartheid 24 – Edinburgh Commonwealth Games	
	1 – Howe writes to MT, expressing 'extreme concern' at Ingham's presentation of Cabinet decision on South Africa 3–5 – Commonwealth review meeting in London (MT agrees to 'further measures' if agreed by EC)	
	16 – EC sanctions imposed on South Africa	

	Politics	Economics
Oct	6–10 – Conservative Party conference in Bournemouth 26 – Jeffrey Archer resigns as deputy party chairman	27 – Big Bang transforms City of London
Nov	26 – Bill to abolish domestic rates in Scotland introduced	14 – Sharp drop in unemployment to around 3.2 million
Dec	29 – Death of former Prime Minister Harold Macmillan, Earl of Stockton	3 – British Gas flotation

1987

	Politics	Economics
Jan	29 – Alasdair Milne resigns as BBC director-general; replaced by Michael Checkland	
Feb	6 – Wapping print dispute ends 26 – Greenwich by-election (Lab loss to SDP)	11 – British Airways flotation
Mar	27 – Kinnock humiliated during visit to Washington, DC	17 – Budget (basic rate cut to 27 per cent)
Apr		
May	7 – Local elections (Cons gains) 11 – General election campaign begins	
Jun	4 – 'Wobbly Thursday' 11 – Election day: MT returned to office with a majority of 102	19 – Unemployment reported to have fallen below 3 million

East/West	Other Foreign	Northern Ireland
11–12 – Reagan and Gorbachev meet in Reykjavik (come close to agreeing the abolition of all nuclear weapons)		
3 – Iran-Contra scandal first becomes public		
15–16 – MT visits Reagan at Camp David (agree to pull back from Reykjavik proposals in favour of a more modest agenda)		
		20 January – FitzGerald's coalition ends after the Labour Party withdraws its support
28 – Gorbachev agrees to INF talks separate from SDI negotiations		
28–1 Apr – MT's visit to the Soviet Union	23 – MT sees Mitterrand in Normandy and Kohl in Bonn (consultations ahead of her Moscow visit)	10 – Charles Haughey forms a minority government and returns as taoiseach
8–9 – G7 summit in Venice (MT leaves early due to election campaign)		

PART ONE

Foundations

I

Liberal imperialist

'I'm leader of this great nation,
and I haven't made up my mind'

In October 1982, Margaret Thatcher became the senior elected leader in the Western world. Her three years and five months as prime minister meant that she had led her country continuously for longer than any of her counterparts among the major Western powers. It was a position she was to retain for more than eight years, until her fall in November 1990. Since her arrival in office in May 1979, Ronald Reagan had replaced Jimmy Carter as president of the United States, and François Mitterrand had defeated Valéry Giscard d'Estaing in France. On 1 October 1982, Helmut Schmidt, who had been chancellor of West Germany since 1974, lost a vote of confidence in the Bundestag and resigned, to be replaced – initially without an election – by the Christian Democrat Helmut Kohl.* In little more than three years, therefore, Mrs Thatcher had moved from being the ingénue of international politics to being the doyenne. And because of the huge change in her international standing brought about by victory in the Falklands, the transformation was swift and dramatic. Although she was not a great one for noticing dates and ticking off anniversaries, she was undoubtedly conscious of her new status, and pleased with it. She felt that her beliefs were being vindicated, and that she was more than ever entitled to expound and export them to the whole world.

Within ten days of her Falklands victory on 14 June 1982, Mrs Thatcher was addressing the General Assembly of the United Nations in New York, expounding her doctrine of 'peace with freedom and justice', rather than 'peace at any price'.[1] She boldly described the nuclear deterrent as a 'priceless achievement', because it made such peace possible globally.[2] In her speech to her party's conference on 8 October, she made it clear that freedom and justice were not just the guarantors of the carve-up between West and East,

---

* Helmut Kohl (1930–), educated Heidelberg University; Minister-President, Rhineland Palatinate, 1969–76; Leader, CDU/CSU, 1976–98; Chancellor of Federal Republic of Germany, 1982–90; of reunified Germany, 1990–98.

but dynamic forces opposed by 'political systems *evil* enough to seek to
enslave the whole world'. She declared that the Communists had attempted
to crush Solidarity in Poland because the Soviets 'knew that the beginning
of freedom spelt the beginning of the end for Communism'.[3] Her message
was that freedom everywhere was on the march. Back at home, 370,000 families had now bought their council houses since the Conservatives came into
office ('There is no prouder word in our history than "freeholder"'). Citing
her government's privatizations, Mrs Thatcher claimed that 'already we
have done more to roll back the frontiers of socialism than any previous
Conservative Government.'[4] In short, her battles, both at home and abroad,
had the same purpose, and she was winning them.

Mrs Thatcher's dealings with her ministers reflected her new dominance.
One official witnessed this first-hand during the summer of 1982:

> In Cabinet, Mrs Thatcher's authority seemed absolute, and her manner that
> of a headmistress dealing with recalcitrant staff. Willie Whitelaw,* massive,
> bushy eyebrows raised, was allowed something of a moderating role. But
> Peter Carrington had by that time resigned, and her other male colleagues . . .
> seemed uncertain how to disagree with her without provoking rebuke: as
> someone said, she came across as though she were 'everyone's mother in a
> bad temper'. 'WHO authorised this memorandum?' she demanded at one
> of my first Cabinet meetings, waving a paper indignantly before her. Silence.
> 'WHO authorised it?' Eventually, the Secretary of State for Wales, who sat
> at an awkward angle from her, poked his head cautiously round the Cabinet
> Secretary (Robert Armstrong†) and said, 'I did, Prime Minister.' Pause. 'But
> I cleared it with the Chancellor of the Exchequer.' Geoffrey Howe‡ simply
> studied his papers. 'And with the Foreign Secretary.' Francis Pym§ remained
> similarly silent. 'Well, it should NEVER have been issued.'[5]

---

* William Whitelaw (1918–99), educated Winchester and Trinity College, Cambridge; Conservative MP for Penrith and the Border, 1955–83; Secretary of State for Northern Ireland,
1972–3; for Employment, 1973–4; Home Secretary 1979–83; created Viscount Whitelaw,
1983; Leader of the House of Lords and Deputy Prime Minister, 1983–8.
† Robert Armstrong (1927–), educated Eton and Christ Church, Oxford; principal private
secretary to the Prime Minister, 1970–75; Permanent Under-Secretary, Home Office, 1977–9;
Cabinet Secretary, 1979–87; Knighted, 1978; created Lord Armstrong of Ilminster, 1988.
‡ Geoffrey Howe (1926–), educated Winchester and Trinity Hall, Cambridge; Conservative
MP for Bebington, 1964–6; for Reigate then Surrey East, 1970–92; Chancellor of the Excheq-
uer, 1979–83; Foreign Secretary, 1983–9; Deputy Prime Minister, 1989–90; knighted, 1970;
created Lord Howe of Aberavon, 1992; retired from House of Lords, 2015.
§ Francis Pym (1922–2008), educated Eton and Magdalene College, Cambridge; Conserva-
tive MP for Cambridgeshire, 1961–83; for Cambridgeshire South East, 1983–7; Government
Chief Whip, 1970–73; Secretary of State for Northern Ireland, 1973–4; for Defence,

It had always been Mrs Thatcher's way to hector her colleagues, but in the past this tendency had been somewhat restrained by her inexperience and the weakness of her own political position. Now these restraints were lessened. An official himself, Goodall noted how the situation was less irksome for his breed than for her fellow politicians: 'Often outspokenly rude to Ministers (especially, as time went on, to Geoffrey Howe) and invariably acerbic in argument, she was never, in my experience, actually rude to officials.'[6] He described her thus:

> Although equally assertive both at the meeting table and in informal conversation away from it, Mrs Thatcher's personality is in other respects dramatically different; at a meeting there is something actually repellent about the poisoned smile and didactic way in which she reiterates her points. In informal conversation, she sheds her scaly covering, her smile becomes normal, her femininity apparent and one can argue with her in a friendly, even bantering way. But it is still extraordinarily difficult to find a point of entry to put a case counter to the one she is making.[7]

Mrs Thatcher's refusal to provide that easy 'point of entry' was essential to her way of working. Given that she was radical, always kicking against the pricks of bureaucracy and inertia, she would not have been able to maintain momentum if she had made life easy for nay-sayers. But it is also true that her way of working – though usually invoking huge loyalty and admiration from her own staff – stored up resentment from Cabinet colleagues, even those who were her political allies. In the latter part of 1982, however, this did not seem to matter much. She took advantage of her new situation to preach and to prevail.

One of the more common complaints against Mrs Thatcher from Tory critics was that she was not really a conservative at all. The Wets* and their allies in the press tended to describe her as a 'nineteenth-century liberal', a doctrinaire free-marketeer who wished to reduce the subtleties of human society to the dry facts of a balance sheet. This was never the case. Although it is true that, for a Conservative politician, Mrs Thatcher was exceptionally and tenaciously devoted to certain economic beliefs – for example, that inflation is 'a disease of money' – it is not true that economic doctrines were the source of her beliefs. She was much more historically minded than

---

1979–81; Chancellor of the Duchy of Lancaster and Leader of the House of Commons, 1981–2; Foreign Secretary, 1982–3; created Lord Pym, 1987.
* The 'Wets' was the name given to Mrs Thatcher's centrist critics at the top of the party in her first administration, such as Jim Prior, Ian Gilmour and Pym.

that, although her sense of history was more romantic than accurate. She was also much more specifically British and less austerely theoretical than her critics alleged. Thatcherism was more like a vision than a doctrine. She carried in her head a picture of her country derived from its past greatness and energetically projected on to its future. It was more restorationist than revolutionary, though the restoration would sometimes require revolutionary methods. From her earliest political declarations as a young candidate in Dartford, this vision had been present, but, after victory in the Falklands, she made it more explicit.

In a lecture on 'Women in a Changing World', delivered in July 1982, Mrs Thatcher said she took inspiration from a Latin motto on her inkstand at Chequers. Translated, it read:

> To stand on the ancient ways,
> To see which is the right and good way,
> And in that way to walk.[8]

To her party conference in October, she said that the Falklands had not brought about the recovery of British patriotism, but had proved that such patriotism 'was never really lost'.[9] Speaking of the young men who had just fought, she said: 'If this is tomorrow's generation, then Britain has little to fear in the years to come.'[10] At the end of 1982, for a television programme broadcast in March 1983, Mrs Thatcher showed the South African writer Sir Laurens van der Post* round 10 Downing Street. Disarmed by van der Post's flattery, she revealed how much her choice of pictures and decorations for the house was influenced by her self-identification with the high points of Britain's greatness. She pointed out the Chinese Chippendale table which had belonged to Clive of India, Pitt the Younger's desk and the portraits of Nelson and Wellington ('I . . . thought of him very much because I was very upset at the people who lost their lives in the Falklands . . . he walked around the battlefield [of Waterloo] totally and utterly sickened and grief-stricken by it').[11] She showed off the silver from Belton House near her home town of Grantham, lent by 'a great friend of mine, Lord Brownlow', which had belonged to one of his ancestors who was Speaker of the House of Commons. In acknowledgment of her own scientific background, she was building up 'a little scientific gallery' in the small dining room, with pictures or busts of Humphry Davy, Joseph Priestley and Grantham's most famous son, Isaac Newton. A bust of Michael Faraday, who pioneered the generation of electricity, was too heavy for the

---

* Laurens van der Post (1906–96), Afrikaner; writer, farmer, soldier, explorer, conservationist; friend of Prince Charles; knighted, 1981.

room, and stood downstairs. In the Cabinet Room, she pointed out, she sat in 'Winston's chair'.

With the Downing Street setting providing these props for the Thatcher psychodrama, van der Post drew her out. 'Would you have been a Roundhead or a Cavalier?' he inquired. 'Oh, no slightest shadow,' replied the woman often accused of being a puritan, '. . . I'd have been a Cavalier, a Royalist.'[12]* Reminiscence about the wartime 'dam-busters' being received in Grantham when her father was mayor caused her to reflect that 'the battles of peace are even more difficult to solve than the battles of war'. In peace, she said, 'it's a question of creating your own inner challenge.' 'The values of a free society' derived from religion, not from the state, she went on. She invoked her favourite hymn 'I Vow to Thee, My Country', with its phrase about 'soul by soul', to show that individuals must take up the challenge, because 'you believe in something which is greater than yourself'.

In material transcribed but not broadcast, Mrs Thatcher gave even fuller rein to her beliefs about English-speaking freedom and law. She reverted to her childhood fascination with India, in whose civil service she had aspired to work. She said that the British record there had been blemished by the colour bar, but all the same 'we taught what was right and we upheld what was right,' and it was the Lord Chief Justice Lord Mansfield who had, as she put it, 'let the black go' in a famous eighteenth-century court case (*Somerset* vs *Stewart*, 1772), thereby signalling the end of slavery. The Empire had stood for 'incorruptible law – the incorruptible military – the incorruptible civil servants'. And the common law, as pointed out by Blackstone and Coke, was 'greater than the King' – 'fantastically courageous men . . . who said to the king: "No. These things do not come from a king . . . these rights come from God, and you are not entitled to set them aside." ' The American Constitution ('that wonderful document') arose from the same spirit. Much of civilization, she slightly grudgingly admitted, came from Continental Europe, 'And yet the law came from us. Perhaps because we are an island off Europe and therefore just a little bit different, we've developed a little bit differently.'

'If one were to go into a pub at a time of national crisis,' Mrs Thatcher averred to van der Post, speaking of something which, because of her traditional attitudes to the role of her sex, she had never done unaccompanied, 'possibly the phrase you'd hear on everyone's lips as they discuss things would be: "We're a free country." ' This freedom, she asserted, was

* When Woodrow Wyatt raised the Cavalier or Roundhead question with Mrs Thatcher in private, however, at lunch at Chequers in 1986, she said she 'must be a bit of a Puritan, particularly as she doesn't draw her full salary as Prime Minister but now they've bought [their house in] Dulwich she rather wishes she had . . . "I'm a Cavalier," says Denis.' (Woodrow Wyatt, *The Journals of Woodrow Wyatt*, vol. i, Macmillan, 1998, 19 January 1986, p. 62.)

a beacon to those under Soviet tyranny. She had watched Alexander Solz-
henitsyn being interviewed on the BBC and found it 'one of the most
moving experiences I have ever seen on television . . . his eyes flashed his
sincerity and conviction.' She believed that the Soviet dissidents were saying to her: 'Keep them [your values] alive. Defend them, and one day we
shall hope to have the same things which you take for granted.' Soviet
Communism, she said, 'will end . . . There are many religious currents at
work in the Soviet Union, and those will not for ever be denied.'[13]

A critic of Mrs Thatcher's historical assertions, reading the full transcript, could easily have mocked her odd mixture of Liberal imperialism
and the Tory bloody-mindedness of Lord Salisbury ('I often look back at
his work,' she claimed). Such a critic could have caricatured her as a member
of the Conservative Primrose League – which, before the First World War,
was the largest political organization in British history – marching under
its slogan of 'Imperium et Libertas' ('Empire and Liberty'). He could have
poked holes in her factual accuracy and laughed at her romantic schoolgirl's
idea of a national past teeming with great men and great ideas. But she had
her answer for such people. They were, she told the Lord Mayor's Banquet
in November 1982, part of the 'army of professional belittlers' who had held
sway in the 1970s. 'They denigrated our past, undermined our present and
had no faith in our future.'[14] She had been criticized for preaching 'the parables of the parlour. But I do not repent: those parables would have saved
many a financier from failure and many a country from crisis.'[15] She maintained her grand simplicities. They may have been historically shaky; they
may have sounded, to some, faintly embarrassing; but, whatever they were,
they were not arid and utilitarian. They were passionate declarations of
belief, made now more clearly than ever.

In January 1983, Brian Walden,* who, of all Mrs Thatcher's regular
television interviewers, was closest to her way of thinking, gave her, on air,
a phrase to sum up her creed. Having ascertained from her that she wanted
the next general election to be held the following year, but would contemplate calling it as early as June 1983, Walden asked her what vision she
would campaign for. Listening to her answer, he said that what she was
really putting forward was 'an approval of what I would call Victorian
values'.[16] Mrs Thatcher grabbed the phrase: 'Oh exactly. Very much so.
Those were the values when our country became great, but not only did
our country become great internationally, also so much advance was made

---

* Brian Walden (1932–), educated West Bromwich Grammar School, the Queen's College
and Nuffield College, Oxford; Labour MP for Birmingham, All Saints, 1964–74; for Birmingham, Ladywood, 1974–7; television and radio presenter and journalist.

in this country.' Her interpretation of the period was that 'As our people prospered, so they used their independence and initiative to prosper others, not compulsion by the State.'[17] She cited voluntary schools, hospitals endowed by benefactions, improved prisons and new town halls.[18]* The phrase 'Victorian values' stuck, and was quickly used against Mrs Thatcher. For many, it seemed to stand for inequality and to remind people of poverty, workhouses, children being sent up chimneys and other horrors. But Mrs Thatcher did not retreat. She pointed out that the privations of the period were fewer than those of earlier times. What she liked was the Victorian spirit of improvement and what, a generation later, the Conservative Prime Minister David Cameron would call the 'Big Society'. In her view, even the social reforms proposed in the wartime years, usually claimed by the left, had at first tried to uphold the obligations enjoined by Victorian values. The Beveridge Report of 1942, credited with the invention of the welfare state and the National Health Service, had maintained that 'The State in organising social security should not stifle incentive, opportunity, responsibility'.[19] 'In a caring society,' she glossed Beveridge, 'we all care.' When she attacked trade unions for organized selfishness, she did not condemn unions as such, but reminded them of their Victorian roots as friendly and provident societies. She accused them of straying from their benevolent origins.

The world's heightened expectations of Mrs Thatcher, and her own post-Falklands rhetoric about the British commitment to freedom, were soon put to the test by the issue of Hong Kong. This prosperous, capitalist port was a British colony which had flourished despite the hostility of neighbouring Communist China. The island of Hong Kong itself had belonged to Britain absolutely since 1842, but the surrounding New Territories, on which Hong Kong island depended for, among other things, water, were rented from China on a 99-year lease which would expire in 1997. In any case, China rejected Britain's rights over both freehold and leasehold, claiming that they had been extorted by 'unequal treaties'. Since Britain could not sustain its claim to the New Territories after 1997, it was obvious that some new arrangement for Hong Kong would have to be agreed. China wanted the whole place back. Although the Chinese leader, Deng Xiaoping,† had told Hong Kong businessmen in 1979 to 'set their hearts at ease' about

---

* In a letter to John Evans, MP, dated 5 May 1983, Mrs Thatcher explained that when she spoke of Victorian values 'I mean respect for the individual, thrift, initiative, a sense of personal responsibility, respect for others and their property, and all the other values that characterised the best of the Victorian era.'

† Deng Xiaoping (1904–97), leader of People's Republic of China, 1978–92. He never held formal offices that reflected his power, but was in complete control.

the preservation of the capitalist system there, huge doubts remained. The markets and citizens of Hong Kong were becoming increasingly nervous. It seemed to most that Hong Kong's future needed to be settled soon. The British feared that, if they did not move to obtain an agreement, the Chinese would simply sit still as the deadline approached and 'wait for the lease to fall in'.[20] Then China would occupy the place – if resisted, by force.

In approaching the subject, Mrs Thatcher had no clear model to follow. Hong Kong was not a typical British colony whose people could be given independence, because independence was not on offer. What loomed was the absorption of a free entity – and, worse, a free people – into the dictatorship of the Communist mainland. Emotionally, though not physically, ethnically or economically, Hong Kong more closely resembled the Falklands: most of its people were pro-British and dreaded the rule of the country which laid claim to it. But, unlike in the Falklands, there was a lease which was running out, a land border with the hostile power, and the overwhelming might, in the last resort, of the People's Liberation Army.

Because of her visit to China as leader of the Opposition in 1977,[21] and her general opinion of Communism, Mrs Thatcher strongly disliked the place and feared Chinese power, but she had not until now given the region a great deal of thought. Her first anxiety, after becoming prime minister, had been about immigration. When the 'Boat People' had started to flee the Vietnamese Communist regime in 1979, she had been notably reluctant to offer them places in Britain. In a private conversation with her then Foreign Secretary, Lord Carrington, in June 1979, in which he had raised the Boat People's plight, she had tastelessly remarked, 'Well, people go on cruises, don't they?',[22] words for which she subsequently apologized. Hong Kong presented a greater risk of an influx to Britain if things went wrong, because its citizens held British passports, albeit of an inferior sort which did not guarantee them right of abode.

In March 1982, shortly before his resignation over the Falklands, Carrington wrote to her about the future of Hong Kong. His argument did not focus on the freedom of the more than 5 million people for whom Britain was responsible, but on the danger of them trying to get into Britain if things went wrong. 'The option of unilateral withdrawal is not really open to us,'[23] he wrote, because Hong Kong people* would demand right of admission. Mrs Thatcher underlined his words, and did not, at this point,

---

* 'Hong Kong people' was the phrase for the colony's inhabitants preferred both officially and unofficially to 'Hong Kong citizens' because it avoided the question of whether their status was British, Chinese or something in between. Since the British Nationality Act of 1981, they had lacked right of abode in the UK.

take up those people's cause. Nor had she previously been visibly attracted to the idea of bolstering Hong Kong against Chinese threats by giving its people more democratic rights, despite (or because of?) the advocacy of the idea by the young left-leaning MP and former head of the Conservative Research Department Chris Patten* in 1979.[24] The colony was run by a combination of business power and the colonial Governor and administration. In January 1982, Sir Percy Cradock,† the British Ambassador in Peking‡ and the most important of the Foreign Office's 'China hands', reported to London that 'a willingness to <u>cede sovereignty</u> . . . will be <u>essential</u> to an [sic] satisfactory settlement.'[25] On her copy of the telegram Mrs Thatcher's underlining indicated her approval. No mention was made of the people of Hong Kong. It suited both Communist China and the Foreign Office that the people's wishes should not be the decisive factor in any equation for the territory's future. Mrs Thatcher disliked both these entities, but until the second half of 1982 she did not get in their way.

Immediately after the Falklands victory, however, she focused, belatedly, on the issue. The suggestions for her visit to China, planned for late September, were set out by Sir Antony Acland,§ the Permanent Under-Secretary at the Foreign Office. Once of the 'Main Objectives' was 'To contain public expectations of progress . . . so that confidence in Hong Kong is not undermined'.[26] Mrs Thatcher jibbed at this. Her foreign affairs private secretary, John Coles,¶ offered a stronger alternative: 'To confirm that in discussions

---

* Christopher Patten (1944–), educated St Benedict's School, Ealing and Balliol College, Oxford; director, Conservative Research Department, 1974–9; Conservative MP for Bath, 1979–92; Secretary of State for the Environment, 1989–90; Chairman, Conservative Party, 1990–92; Governor, Hong Kong, 1992–7; European Commissioner, 1999–2004; Chancellor of Oxford University, 2003–; chairman, BBC Trust, 2011–14; created Lord Patten of Barnes, 2005.
† Percy Cradock (1923–2010), educated Alderman Wraith Grammar School, Spennymoor and St John's College, Cambridge; Ambassador to People's Republic of China, 1978–83; leader of UK team in negotiations over Hong Kong, 1982–3; Deputy Under-Secretary of State, FCO, supervising Hong Kong negotiations, 1984; Prime Minister's foreign policy adviser, 1984–92; knighted, 1980.
‡ At this time, the Chinese capital was always referred to in government in its Europeanized 'Wade–Giles' version – Peking. Gradually, from the 1980s, people in the West started to use the 'Pinyin' rendering – Beijing.
§ Antony Acland (1930–), educated Eton and Christ Church, Oxford; head of Arabian Department, FCO, 1970–72; Ambassador to Spain, 1977–9; Permanent Under-Secretary and head of Diplomatic Service, 1982–6; Ambassador to the United States, 1986–91; Provost of Eton, 1991–2000; Knight of the Garter, 2001.
¶ John Coles (1937–), educated Magdalen College School, Brackley and Magdalen College, Oxford; private secretary to the Prime Minister, 1981–4; Ambassador to Jordan, 1984–8; High Commissioner to Australia, 1988–91; Deputy Under-Secretary, FCO, 1991–4; Permanent Under-Secretary and head of Diplomatic Service, 1994–7; knighted, 1989.

with the Chinese on Hong Kong's future our aim will be to secure a prosperous and secure future for the people of Hong Kong'.[27] 'I much prefer
your version,' Mrs Thatcher scribbled to Coles. With her elevation of the
rule of law over the assumptions of diplomacy, she began to pay attention
to the treaties with China themselves, questioning the Foreign Office's idea
that these should be discarded just because the Chinese wished them to be.

At a meeting on 28 July with Cradock, Acland, Edward Youde,* the
new Governor of Hong Kong, and Francis Pym, the Foreign Secretary, the
whole approach was debated. Mrs Thatcher was concerned that China
had 'a fundamental lack of comprehension' of what was needed to maintain confidence in Hong Kong: 'The only real guarantee of our position
was the international treaties on which it was based.'[28] Cradock argued
back that the Chinese were determined to assert the sovereignty they
believed they had never truly surrendered. Unless Britain surrendered
sovereignty in 1997, there would be confrontation. He tried to reassure
the Prime Minister that Deng Xiaoping would stick to any agreement he
made. Mrs Thatcher did not maintain, head-on, that sovereignty must be
preserved at all costs, but she wanted to park the matter and discuss
administrative arrangements to perpetuate the current free-market system
after 1997. Could Britain not obtain some sort of 'management contract'
for the territory? She continued to worry about the dangers of immigration. She was not sure what she should do, but she was sure that 'What
she could not do, particularly in the light of the recent Falkland Islands
problem, was simply to announce that we had conceded sovereignty over
Hong Kong.'[29] The meeting agreed that the minimum objective of her visit
to China should be that talks about the future of Hong Kong could get
going without prejudicial statements being made.

There was a tension between her and the Foreign Office. As John Coles
put it, she had 'a very strong feeling in her mind that it was inconsistent
to hand over British territory'. The Foreign Office worked on 'the long,
slow process of overcoming this'.[30] Or, as Robin Butler,† her principal
private secretary at the time, judged, 'The Foreign Office was nervous.
Her reaction was: "Let them be nervous."'[31] Percy Cradock, for whom
Mrs Thatcher felt respect, even though she tended to disagree with him,
recalled what he called the 'fog' of her style: 'She would dot about . . .

---

* Edward Youde (1924–86), educated School of Oriental and African Studies, University of
London; private secretary to the Prime Minister, 1969–70; Ambassador to People's Republic
of China, 1974–8; Governor of Hong Kong, 1982–6; knighted, 1977.
† Robin Butler (1938–), educated Harrow and University College, Oxford; principal private
secretary to the Prime Minister, 1982–5; Second Permanent Secretary, Public Expenditure,
Treasury, 1985–7; Cabinet Secretary, 1988–98; created Lord Butler of Brockwell, 1998.

sometimes total rubbish and sometimes pretty sharp.' He would spend his time 'trying to persuade her of what needed to be done: she'd slide down the cliff face.'[32] As the visit to China approached, Mrs Thatcher tried to climb back up the cliff. At a private lunch with Youde and leading Hong Kong people at Downing Street in early September, she challenged the orthodoxy that the Chinese were pragmatic: 'They were Marxist and their system was centralist. Having been born and bred under a Marxist/Leninist system, they did not understand what was necessary to maintain confidence. Our duty was to the people of Hong Kong, who wished to live under our administration. Her instinct was to concede nothing until it was clear we could obtain precisely what we wanted.'[33] Cradock expressed 'some serious reservations' about the emerging negotiating stance. It was important to 'make a bow to the Chinese position on sovereignty', he warned Pym, to avoid an 'unhelpful salvo'.[34] Putting sovereignty on one side risked the 'complete failure' of the visit. Robin Butler recalled that the 'overwhelming preoccupation was to avoid a collapse of confidence in Hong Kong',[35] where the markets had fallen badly in August. The situation was precarious.

Mrs Thatcher arrived in Peking, after a short visit to Tokyo, on 22 September. The journeys were particularly arduous because she had recently been in hospital for an operation on her varicose veins. The next day she met the Chinese premier Zhao Ziyang.* Just before heading into their meeting, Zhao told reporters that 'China will certainly take back its sovereignty over Hong Kong.'[36] This effort to pre-empt the issue publicly infuriated the British. 'I realise that some of these points may be unwelcome. But I must be candid,' Mrs Thatcher told Zhao. 'Confidence in Hong Kong, and thus its continued prosperity, depend on British administration.' Sovereignty was a difficult issue for her, she warned, because it was for Parliament, not her, to abrogate treaties. Abrogation alone would be 'unthinkable': 'It would produce immediate panic in Hong Kong.' What she wanted was an agreement with China which would define the new arrangements. If she were 'satisfied that they . . . were acceptable to the people of Hong Kong . . . there would then be a new situation in which I could consider the question of sovereignty'.[37] In reply, Zhao was polite, but firm. The capitalist system in Hong Kong would remain, but the return of sovereignty to China could not be delayed after 1997. If it came to a choice, sovereignty would take precedence over prosperity.

The following morning, Mrs Thatcher met Deng Xiaoping. Those

* Zhao Ziyang (1919–2005), Premier of China, 1980–87; General Secretary of the Chinese Communist Party, 1987–9.

present at the meeting were conscious of an air of unease and of two formidable individuals confronting one another. 'They were mirror images,' recalled Percy Cradock.[38] Robin Butler remembered a 'great diatribe' by Deng, with Mrs Thatcher being 'pretty equally aggressive'. While she spoke, Deng started hawking, and expectorating into the spittoon which was uncomfortably near to her: 'She moved her legs. It threw her.'[39] Once Deng had heard Mrs Thatcher repeat her points about sovereignty and confidence, he declared that if sovereignty over Hong Kong were not recovered 'it would mean that the new China was like the China of the Ching Dynasty and the present leaders were like Li Hongzhang.'[40] (In Chinese political myth, the Ching Dynasty was proverbial for its weakness in the face of foreigners, and its late nineteenth-century minister, Li Hongzhang, was considered the archetypal traitor.) Without recovered sovereignty, Deng said, his government 'ought to retire voluntarily from the political arena'. Why should Britain not want to abandon its claim? Britain should be pleased to end its colonial era.

Mrs Thatcher hit back. This was not a normal colonial situation, she explained. 'Her duty, which she felt deeply, was to reach a result acceptable to the people of Hong Kong.'[41] She was not contesting the termination of the lease, but the treaties for Hong Kong and neighbouring Kowloon were 'valid in international law' and so must be changed only by agreement. She wanted talk 'based on a certain formula' which would reassure people – British administration after 1997. Deng flatly refused: 'Mr Deng Xiaoping said that he was very sorry,' but sovereignty would return to China in 1997. 'That was certain.' It was a precondition of any agreement. He made dark remarks about the danger of 'disturbances' in Hong Kong. Mrs Thatcher snapped back that if there were disturbances they would not be caused by Britain: the outside world would draw its own conclusions.

'After two and a half hours,' according to Robin Butler, 'it all seemed disastrous,'[42] but then, when the question of a communiqué about the meeting was raised, a form of words provided by Cradock, which said nothing about sovereignty, made quick progress. At first, the Chinese wanted the statement to mention 'differences' between the two countries, but this was replaced by the more emollient 'Both leaders made clear their respective positions on this subject.' The statement also said that both sides wish to secure 'the stability and prosperity of Hong Kong' and agreed to start talks. To British surprise, the thing 'went through as easy as anything'.[43] 'Deng snapped his fingers in approval.'[44]* As she left the meeting,

---

* It showed how the Chinese government wished to make life uncomfortable for Mrs Thatcher that, as she gave the 'return' banquet to her hosts in the Great Hall of the People that evening,

A less than auspicious departure from the Great Hall of the People, Peking, in September 1982.

Mrs Thatcher stumbled on the steps of the Great Hall of the People, which, according to Chinese superstition, was an ill omen.

She flew on to Hong Kong – the first visit there by a British prime minister when in office. Intimations that the tension between the two countries had not been resolved caused the Hang Seng index of the Hong Kong stock market to fall 7.5 per cent in one day. Mrs Thatcher herself welcomed the communiqué to Hong Kong audiences ('So far, so good,' she said at the

most of the leadership did not attend, but caroused with the North Korean dictator, Kim Il Sung, in another part of the building (see Percy Cradock, *Experiences of China*, John Murray, 1994, p. 181). The British team were also ill treated by being given inferior accommodation. Only Denis Thatcher overcame this indignity by complaining so loudly (in the apparent privacy of his own room) that he did not have a gin and tonic that the eavesdroppers arranged for some to be supplied. (Interview with Lord Butler of Brockwell.)

press conference) but was combative: 'I shall speak not only for Britain but for Britain's moral responsibility and duty to the people of Hong Kong,'[45] she told a lunch of Hong Kong businessmen. Hong Kong people were pleased that she had come in person to tell them what was going on, but were extremely nervous all the same. China's public comments on the situation were tough. Within ten days of Mrs Thatcher leaving China, the Hong Kong stock market had fallen 25 per cent. Some in Washington were not impressed by her visit. 'Bah!' wrote one National Security Council (NSC) staffer against a report from the American Embassy in Peking which suggested that the British had 'got what they hoped for'.[46] As Cradock himself acknowledged, however, Mrs Thatcher's visit to China did 'secure our main objective'[47] – the agreement to begin talks.

A war of nerves ensued. The Chinese put out belligerent propaganda, and prevaricated about sitting down for talks. Hong Kong people demanded a clearer British response. The British worried inconclusively about what public line to take, until Mrs Thatcher, who did not share Cradock's anxiety about what he called 'widening the circle of knowledge', authorized Youde to brief the press as he saw fit. Mrs Thatcher, who had been studying the memoirs of Henry Kissinger,* was struck by his point that the Chinese often found a subtle way of giving a signal of their intentions without stating them. Subtle signals were not usually her best thing; but, on a report from Cradock about how the ceding of sovereignty might be turned into a 'working hypothesis' in order to get talks started, she wrote: 'Can't we use their technique and indicate that we gave them a signal in our opening statement about sovereignty, bearing in mind that I have to put it through Parliament and with as little trouble as possible for all our sakes.'[48] What she was saying, in a roundabout way, was that sovereignty was not, for her, a sticking point at all. For political and negotiating reasons, however, she needed to appear robust.

Next month, Mrs Thatcher, in particularly robust form, gave Kissinger dinner at No. 10. 'That whole evening was her fighting the idea of giving Hong Kong up at all,' he recalled. 'And then seeing various levels of retreat.'[49] Having visited the Chinese leadership in October, Kissinger reported that they 'were not angry with the Prime Minister. They respected her and did not regard her as hostile.'[50] The problem was that their style of negotiating was not, like the Russians, to state maximal positions from

---

* Henry Kissinger (1923–), born in Germany; educated George Washington High School, New York City and Harvard University; US Secretary of State, 1973–7 (National Security Advisor, 1969–75); member, President's Foreign Intelligence Advisory Board, 1984–90; Hon. KCMG, 1995.

which they then retreated, 'because everything then becomes a question of pride'. The best tactic was not to make any demands about sovereignty, but just to discuss administration. A month later, Kissinger wrote to her stressing that the Chinese thought everything was fine in relation to Britain and Hong Kong so long as sovereignty was conceded. They would welcome informal talks.[51] But Mrs Thatcher remained unhappy. The Chinese ideas, she replied, 'still fall a long way short of a really satisfactory package'.[52] They wanted an 'autonomous, capitalist-style Hong Kong under <u>China's</u> control'. They did not offer 'any genuine guarantees whatsoever' for preserving freedom, prosperity and stability.

On Christmas Eve 1982, Mrs Thatcher called in Sir Frank Cooper, the Permanent Secretary of the Ministry of Defence. The two agreed that 'there was no realistic prospect of defending Hong Kong from the Chinese if they were determined to take it over.'[53] Cooper recommended that, as 'a defence for the Prime Minister', she should discreetly get an assessment from the Chiefs of Staff about reinforcing and defending Hong Kong. This was set in hand. The unsurprising official verdict was that Hong Kong could not be militarily defended for any length of time.

China's refusal to engage in talks until the question of sovereignty was settled divided the British side. Mrs Thatcher characteristically sought ways of spreading public support for her approach: 'Perhaps we should now develop the democratic structure [in Hong Kong] as though it were our aim to achieve independence or self-government within a short period.'[54] Equally in character, the Foreign Office was anxious to prevent Hong Kong people having a say in the matter, and feared that what it saw as Mrs Thatcher's impossibilist position would provoke China. In January, reports suggested that China intended to announce its plans for Hong Kong unilaterally by the middle of the year. Francis Pym sent Mrs Thatcher a paper on the future of Hong Kong. In his covering letter, he wrote: 'We must . . . think very carefully and realistically about the possibility that . . . we may have no alternative but to accept Chinese recovery both of sovereignty and administrative control after 1997 . . . It follows, therefore, that . . . we should say nothing publicly which would rule out an eventual accommodation.'[55] 'By extension,' he continued, 'we must not allow our consideration for the "wishes of the people" to develop into acceptance of the paramountcy of the will of the population.' The paper itself advocated 'the avoidance of unhelpful or unrealistic commitments for the future, in particular, the acceptance of responsibility with no power to fulfil it'. It recommended recognizing Chinese sovereignty over the whole of Hong Kong and accepting that British administration should cease 'when the time is ripe'. The phrase was badly judged: it was already being used, to Mrs Thatcher's irritation, to express British policy about entry into the Exchange Rate Mechanism of the European Monetary System.

Ill disposed to Pym at the best of times, Mrs Thatcher put cross wiggly lines under or alongside much of what he wrote. When she got to the paper itself and its caution about accepting responsibility, she exploded: 'It is <u>not</u> a question of <u>new</u> acceptance of responsibility WE HAVE IT ALREADY BY VIRTUE OF THE TREATIES.'[56] At the top of the letter she wrote: 'This paper is <u>pathetic</u> – it is a recipe for a sell-out. There <u>are</u> other possibilities.' Her response advocated dual sovereignty after 1997, by which China got back the New Territories, Britain kept Hong Kong proper and the two countries ran the place together.

As was often the case when she argued most strenuously, Mrs Thatcher was well aware that she was in a tight spot. Her tenderness towards British honour and Hong Kong rights did not blind her to the perils. She agreed to a new tactic. On 10 March 1983, she wrote a secret letter to Zhao Ziyang, which Percy Cradock, who devised it, called 'the first finesse'. The key passage read:

> Provided that agreement could be reached between the British and Chinese Governments on administrative arrangements for Hong Kong which would guarantee the future prosperity and stability of Hong Kong, and would be acceptable to the British Parliament and to the people of Hong Kong as well as to the Chinese Government, I would be prepared to recommend to Parliament that sovereignty over the whole of Hong Kong should revert to China.[57]

The letter was carefully worded. It correctly deferred both to Parliament and to Hong Kong people and did not, strictly speaking, concede anything. On the other hand, it effectively acknowledged China's rights and that Chinese sovereignty would be recognized if all went well. It said that Mrs Thatcher would 'recommend', rather than merely 'consider', the transfer of sovereignty if the right conditions were in place. The Chinese duly leaked the fact that the letter had been sent, and Zhao, in his reply, deliberately misinterpreted it to be saying that the recovery of sovereignty by China was 'the premise and basis for further talks'.[58] But he also declared the way now open to prepare for negotiations. Mrs Thatcher wrote: 'We are still treading on eggshells but it looks as if we can start talks.'[59] She felt able to tell this to the Cabinet on 12 May. Then came the general election.

According to the Foreign Office view, the process described above was a year's work in getting Mrs Thatcher to see reason. The 'China hands' knew all along that sovereignty would have to be ceded: they simply had to convince Mrs Thatcher of the inevitable. There is something in this. As time passed, Mrs Thatcher, who always had a 'genuine regard and affection'[60] for Percy Cradock, did end up tacitly accepting many of his arguments. The path towards eventual agreement with China was one strewn with concessions which she did not want and had to make despite herself.

But there is a counter-case to be made. According to John Gerson,* who at the time was one of the government's greatest China experts, and who first won Mrs Thatcher's confidence when he accompanied her on her visit to China as leader of the Opposition in 1977, she understood something which the Foreign Office sinologists did not. She had a very clear sense of the evil of the regime – the fact that, as late as 1978, peasants in Guandong province were so hungry that they were eating children, the vicious persecution of dissidents, the telling statistic that there were often as many as 1,000 people a day trying to escape from China to Hong Kong. People like Cradock, in Gerson's view, tended to see the nastiness of the Communists as a reason for concessions: 'It became a mantra that "This is a question of sovereignty for the Chinese," at which point the Foreign Office always wanted to give in to them.'[61] Mrs Thatcher's opposite reaction – to harden up – gave the Chinese pause. 'She went without knowing what her final objective would be and brilliantly left them not knowing what theirs was.' Her treatment of Deng as an equal when they met was 'completely baffling for the Chinese. It made them say: "Hang on! They've just squashed the Argies. They have got Polaris. Perhaps they *won't* give Hong Kong back." ' In this view, if Mrs Thatcher had behaved according to diplomatic norms, the Chinese would have won hands down. By being bolder, she achieved 'seismic uncertainty'. Where Cradock and colleagues saw the handover as a classic piece of necessary diplomacy, she saw it as surrendering people for whom Britain was responsible to a totalitarian regime: 'She felt, "I'm leader of this great nation, and I haven't made up my mind." '[62] Because of her stubbornness, both parties had time to adjust and discuss. Luckily, China *was* changing. By a paradox, Mrs Thatcher's 'unreasonableness' made real negotiation possible in a way that conventional diplomatic behaviour would not have done.

---

* John Gerson (1945–), educated Bradfield and King's College, Cambridge; diplomat; First Secretary and Consul, Peking, 1974–7; First Secretary, later Counsellor, FCO, 1979–87; Counsellor, Hong Kong, 1987–92; Counsellor, FCO, 1992–9.

2

A radical disposition

'when people are free to choose,
they choose freedom'

The arrival of Helmut Kohl as chancellor of West Germany seemed at the time to be good news for Mrs Thatcher. Although his predecessor, Helmut Schmidt, had been personally tough-minded about the nuclear deterrent, Schmidt's Social Democrat Party (SPD) was split on the deployment of American cruise and Pershing missiles (known collectively as Intermediate-range Nuclear Forces (INF)) in Western Europe. Kohl's conservative Christian Democrats, on the other hand, were considered more reliable allies. Mrs Thatcher had met Kohl in January 1982, when he was leader of the German opposition, and she had been pleased by his resistance to neutralism. Kohl, who, though already Chancellor, had yet to win an election, believed Mrs Thatcher's prestige could assist him politically.

From his early days as chancellor, Kohl planned to hold federal elections the following March. A few days after he took power in October 1982, a visit to Britain was proposed. The British Ambassador in Bonn, Sir Jock Taylor,* reported that the new Chancellor wanted to visit Mrs Thatcher and 'lay the basis for an effective personal dialogue with the Prime Minister'.[1] Flatteringly, Kohl sought 'some advice on how to handle his discussions with President Reagan'.[2] Mrs Thatcher was happy to help. The visit was quickly arranged for 19 October. In preparation, John Coles wrote to her: 'I suggest that the main aim, without ever letting it appear obvious, is to begin a process of establishing a special relationship with Germany within the European Community (EC) (in order to balance – we certainly cannot replace – the special Franco-German relationship).'[3] Kohl was keen on a public presentation of friendship: Coles suggested a photo-call outside 10 Downing Street, 'emphasising a meeting of minds'.[4]

---

* John ('Jock') Taylor (1924–2002), educated schools in Prague and Vienna and Imperial Services College, Windsor, Cornell University and Trinity College, Cambridge; Ambassador to Venezuela, 1975–9; to the Netherlands, 1979–81; to Federal Republic of Germany, 1981–4; knighted, 1979.

Mrs Thatcher was keen that minds should indeed meet. But even before Kohl had arrived, there was already one area where both parties had their doubts. Taylor reported, after conversation with Kohl before his visit, that 'The only subject where he thought differences might arise between us was the Community.'[5] Mrs Thatcher underlined this message with her pen. She had already been studying Kohl's address to the Bundestag earlier in the month in which he discussed his government's vision of Europe. Kohl wanted 'progress towards the unification of Europe', driven by Franco-German friendship. European institutions should be reformed. The Council of Ministers should have more power and 'it must reach its decisions by majority vote ... The European Parliament should be strengthened. Its powers should be enlarged and its work on a European constitution developed.'[6] This passage was noted down the side by Mrs Thatcher's hostile wiggly line. It was the sort of stuff to which, six years later, she would say 'No. No. No,' with politically fatal results. Francis Pym told her that such ideas were 'innocuous in substance'.[7] She was not, at this point, looking for trouble, but, from the first, she did not agree.

When the two leaders met in Downing Street, they were mostly in accord. Once satisfied that Kohl was, in his own word, 'resolved' to install US missiles on West German soil if disarmament negotiations failed, and determined to be 'full friends and partners of the United States', she was inclined to agree with some of Kohl's criticisms of President Reagan's aggressive approach. 'She had the clear impression', she told Kohl, 'that the Americans now recognised that the action which they had taken over the [Siberian gas] pipeline [see Volume I, Chapter 20] was a mistake and were looking for a way out.'[8] Kohl complained that Reagan did not understand the problems of Europe in relation to the Cold War: 'The recent action of the Pope [John Paul II] in initiating the canonisation of a Polish priest [Fr Maximilian Kolbe, martyred at Auschwitz] had done more to affect opinion in Poland than the whole of the Reagan policy on sanctions.'[9] Mrs Thatcher defended Reagan as 'a [sic] honest politician with certain strong views', but she added that 'in her view the approach proposed by Chancellor Kohl was better.' The two speculated on the future of the Soviet Union. Kohl said that he was 'not a fan of Brezhnev but thought that the next generation would be no better'. Mrs Thatcher responded that 'time was on the side of the West, provided that the West played their cards shrewdly.'[10]

There was no set-to about the European Community, although Mrs Thatcher reiterated her long-running demand for a permanent settlement of the dispute about Britain's excessively high contribution to the European budget. In this the Germans, being the only other net contributors, were natural allies; but at root the attitudes of the two countries were entirely different. West Germany saw ever closer European integration as the guarantee of its post-war legitimacy. Britain was constantly worried about any further sacrifice of national independence. Speaking jointly to the press afterwards, Mrs Thatcher used the approved phrase about 'a true meeting of minds'. Kohl agreed, but also said: 'I am the first Federal Chancellor who is a child of the post-war generation . . . and I will do what is in my power to make sure that we will move forward to the unification of Europe in the course of this decade.'[11] Mrs Thatcher could not say later that she had not been warned. Their difference of approach was fundamental and unalterable.

Now it was her turn to visit West Germany. Ten days later, she appeared with Kohl in Bonn. The apparently happy couple announced that they were off to Berlin together to see what Kohl called 'the division of our fatherland'. 'That wall', Mrs Thatcher said, 'is an ever-present reminder that, when people are free to choose, they choose freedom.'[12] In Berlin, on 29 October 1982, Mrs Thatcher was greeted by enthusiastic crowds, who 'told her that they were heartened by her actions in the Falklands'.[13] From the viewing platform in the Potsdamer Platz, she contemplated the Berlin Wall for the first time in her life. Tears came into her eyes. 'I think it's even worse than I imagined,' she told waiting reporters. 'I laid flowers. There was one young girl [shot trying to escape to the West], she was only 18 . . . they do these terrible things and they flaunt it publicly, it just shows you the atrocities and barbarism of that system.'[14] Speaking at a ceremony to sign the city's Golden Book, she quoted the moral that 'It is weakness that tempts the aggressor. It is strength that leads to discussion and negotiation.' The 'lesson of Poland' under Soviet-backed martial law was that 'pitiless ideology only survives because it is maintained by force': it would be overcome in the end by popular anger. 'One day,' she concluded, 'liberty will dawn on the other side of the wall.'[15]

Even at this early stage, personal relations between Mrs Thatcher and Kohl were not particularly cordial. John Coles remembered them as 'always very poor'.[16] Mrs Thatcher found Kohl boring and long-winded. She considered him intellectually inferior to her and to his predecessor, Helmut Schmidt.[17] With his great girth, ponderous manner and unglamorous looks, Kohl was not her type of man. Besides, being very much a child of the home front in the Second World War, she had a prejudice against his nationality which something in his demeanour brought out. Once she took the present author aside, as if to share a confidence. 'You know the trouble with Helmut Kohl?' she asked, and did not pause for an answer before revealing, '– He's a *German*.'[18] But nothing in the official records at this time suggests any problem serious enough to inhibit friendly exchanges between allies. Notes scribbled by Mrs Thatcher for an informal speech of thanks for her late October visit say things like 'Touched us most deeply', 'Spirit of humanity', 'Pulse of freedom', 'full of goodwill' and 'Thank you' with the parenthesis – as if she needed to remind herself – '(warm and friendly)'.[19] 'It might sound unfashionable nowadays,' Kohl later wrote, 'but it is a fact: the Federal Government was deeply grateful to Mrs Thatcher for her visit to Berlin. It was a gesture of friendship and solidarity with the Germans.'[20]

By early 1983, the West's struggle with the Soviet Union over the deployment of American INF missiles was coming to a head. With no breakthrough in arms control talks visible, NATO had agreed to deploy these weapons on European soil to counter the SS-20 missiles that the Soviets had already put into the European theatre (see Volume I, Chapter 20). Despite considerable resistance from the left and the 'peace movement' across Europe, the American missiles were due to arrive later that year. Successful deployment promised to hand the West a significant victory in the Cold War. Mrs Thatcher was determined to keep the plan on course. The strength of neutralism in Germany alarmed her. The Campaign for Nuclear Disarmament (CND), with covert Soviet backing, stirred up such feelings across Europe and generated extreme nervousness in Western capitals. Even in Britain, there had been a growth of anti-nuclear feeling which she found worrying. Refusal to accept the missiles on German soil, a policy by now actively advocated by the opposition SPD, would probably be fatal to the whole enterprise. She duly arranged for Kohl to pay a visit to Chequers on 4 February 1983.[21] There she told him of the 'unimaginably damaging consequences' if the SPD were to succeed, and assured him that she 'wished to do all we could presentationally to help Chancellor Kohl at the present time'.[22] She and Kohl agreed that it was unlikely that the Soviets would accept President Reagan's 'zero option', which would have removed all INF missiles from Europe. Therefore the planned deployment would have to go ahead. Mrs Thatcher expressed her perennial anxiety that Russia would try to throw the British and French independent nuclear deterrents into the negotiations (she also feared an American tendency to do the same), and Kohl supported her, loyally saying that, by guarding their own security, France and Britain were guarding Germany's. The two discussed a date for deployment, looking at it purely politically. At this stage, Mrs Thatcher was doing everything possible to keep her election-date options open (her last possible poll date was not until May 1984), but she confided in Kohl that she proposed to tell Vice-President Bush, whom she was shortly to see, that she favoured November 1983, implying an election in or before October. INF deployment was not her only electoral concern. 'It would be impossible for her to go into the British Election with the European Budget problem unsolved,'* she told Kohl.[23] He agreed, but, reflecting his own European approach, told her that he wanted the British government to be able 'to go into its Election with its European colours flying high'.[24]

At a press conference, Kohl and Mrs Thatcher spoke of their commitment to INF deployment. It was an opportunity for Mrs Thatcher to explain the nature of her commitment to peace: 'We really are a true peace movement ourselves and we are the true disarmers, in that we stand for all-sided disarmament, but on a basis of balance.' The two presented complete harmony. 'You can rely on the Germans,'[25] Kohl declared. Whatever their inner thoughts, the two leaders had become close allies.

As she prepared for the next election, Mrs Thatcher sought help from another close ally, her friend Ronald Reagan. Although the US administration tried to avoid public comment, the prospect of the Labour Party taking power horrified them. When Denis Healey, Shadow Foreign Secretary, visited Washington in March 1983, the US Embassy in London urged that he be given 'a clear warning on where and how Labor's prospective policies harm American and Western interests'.[26] As Richard Perle, then US Assistant Secretary for Defense, recalled, 'Michael Foot's† election would have been a very serious blow to us.'[27]

In early 1983, an opportunity for the administration to help Mrs Thatcher – and thus hinder Foot – arose. In Britain, as in other INF-deployment countries, there was growing public concern that, in the event of conflict, there was nothing to stop the Americans deciding unilaterally to launch their missiles from British soil. Pressure grew for the weapons to be fitted with a 'dual key' requiring physical activation from both Britain and the US. With the Americans, who still owned the missiles, vociferously opposed, Mrs Thatcher saw no need for a key. She knew that, since 1952, the Truman–Churchill agreement had provided the British Prime Minister with a veto over the use of the US nuclear weapons on British soil.‡ But,

---

* Although this is, in fact, what happened.

† Michael Foot (1913–2010), educated Leighton Park School, Reading and Wadham College, Oxford; Labour MP for Plymouth Devonport, 1945–55; for Ebbw Vale, 1960–83; for Blaenau Gwent, 1983–92; Secretary of State for Employment, 1974–6; Leader of the House of Commons, 1976–9; Leader of the Opposition, 1980–83.

‡ It was noted, in Cabinet committee, that in the highly unlikely event that the President failed to make good on this commitment, British personnel could 'take action which would make it virtually impossible for the Americans to launch their weapons' (MISC 7(83) 1st

because this agreement remained shrouded in secrecy, in public she could offer only the limp assertion that the use of such weapons 'would be a matter for joint decision' by the American and British governments.[28]

The Americans believed that the less said about these matters the better. Even repetition of the 'joint decision' formula set their teeth on edge. Theoretically, the existence of any veto weakened the deterrent effect of deployed missiles because it made it less likely that they would ever be launched. More important, most other European countries to which missiles were to be deployed would not have such a veto. If Britain's position became public knowledge, Washington feared similar demands from far less reliable allies. To Mrs Thatcher, engaged in a battle for public opinion over deployment, these arguments were unpersuasive. In mid-April, she despatched the British Ambassador in Washington, Sir Oliver Wright, to seek Reagan's help. 'Mrs Thatcher will be asking for your approval in saying more openly that she has a veto over the use of those weapons,' Judge Clark, the National Security Advisor, warned Reagan.[29] Expert opinion in Washington was deeply opposed. 'So far we have resisted British requests to acknowledge the secret agreement and have insisted they not go public,' Clark told the President. 'When Sir Oliver delivers this latest request, you will want to say that we feel the agreement should be kept secret, but will review Mrs Thatcher's request and respond to it.'[30]

Advocates for the status quo swiftly realized the game was up. 'We were all worried that anything Margaret Thatcher asked for, Ronald Reagan would want us to give her,' recalled Ron Lehman of the NSC staff.[31] Sure enough, Clark recorded that the President wished to 'support the Prime Minister as much as he possibly can'.[32]* Reagan authorized Mrs Thatcher to tell Parliament that 'no nuclear weapon would be fired or launched from British territory without the agreement of the British Prime Minister'.[33] Trying to close the stable door after the mare had all but disappeared from view, the Americans insisted that the President would not personally confirm this arrangement, although other US government spokesmen would be authorized to do so.† Reagan thus 'gave Mrs Thatcher

Meeting Minutes, 27 Jan. 1983, CAB 130/1224 (http://www.margaretthatcher.org/document/128288)).
* Robin Renwick, at the British Embassy, was told by his NSC contacts that 'Reagan had responded that he would mortgage the Washington Monument, if necessary, to help get Margaret Thatcher re-elected' (Robin Renwick, *A Journey with Margaret Thatcher*, Biteback, 2013, p. 140).
† President Reagan seemed blissfully unaware of this nuance. On 26 May, in the heat of the 1983 British general election campaign, he was asked whether he or Mrs Thatcher would be in charge of launching the INF missiles. 'I don't think either one of us will do anything independent of the other,' he replied. 'This constitutes a sort of veto power, doesn't it?'

the assurance that she needed'.[34] In her memoirs, Mrs Thatcher merely notes that she made sure the existing position concerning missile launches was satisfactory and she 'cleared personally with President Reagan the precise formula we should use to describe it'.[35] This significantly downplays her achievement. She had persuaded the President to overrule official caution and overturn forty years of precedent at a particularly sensitive moment. Not only had she asserted a principle central to Britain's national interest, but she had gained valuable ammunition for the election campaign to come.

In domestic politics, following victory in the Falklands, the question of the election date quickly came to colour all decisions. Mrs Thatcher's natural inclination was always to press on with reform, but its timing carried electoral risks. Despite the gradual improvement in Britain's economic and financial situation in 1982, the problems of public spending remained almost as severe as ever. In January 1982, total unemployment had risen above 3 million for the first time.[36] At the beginning of July, the *Financial Times* reported sluggish economic growth: the consensus forecast was for growth of just over 1 per cent for the year (down from an expected 1.5 per cent) and 2 per cent for 1983.[37] On 15 July, armed with the latest growth figures, Geoffrey Howe warned the Cabinet that the progress of recovery was 'hesitant and patchy'.[38] Leon Brittan, the Chief Secretary to the Treasury,* said that, 'contrary to all we stand for', public expenditure had risen from 41 per cent of GDP in 1979 to 44.5 per cent: borrowing and spending must come down. Mrs Thatcher wanted tight control of spending, not least because 'The next Budget is the last in which tax reduction can be made and take effect before the next election.' This could not be done by increasing the deficit: 'We can't go the US way.† We must make room for personal taxation cuts; I know of no better way.'[39] Against the prime ministerial and Treasury view, the critics

(Reagan, Interview with Foreign Television Journalists, 26 May 1983 (http://www.reagan.utexas.edu/archives/speeches/1983/52683b.htm).)

* Leon Brittan (1939–2015), educated Haberdashers' Aske's School, Trinity College, Cambridge and Yale University; Conservative MP for Cleveland and Whitby, February 1974–83; for Richmond, Yorkshire, 1983–8; Chief Secretary to the Treasury, 1981–3; Home Secretary, 1983–5; Secretary of State for Trade and Industry, 1985–6; knighted, 1989; created Lord Brittan of Spennithorne, 2000.

† For all their common purpose in East–West relations, Mrs Thatcher and President Reagan did not share the same economic outlook. He was the sunny Californian optimist who cut taxes first and hoped that higher growth would address the resulting deficit, while she was the stern Methodist who insisted on balancing the books before contemplating tax cuts.

counter-attacked. Jim Prior* said that 'The Chancellor does not pay enough attention to unemployment.' Michael Heseltine† spoke fiercely: unemployment would be the 'crucial issue' at the next election – 'We are stretching the credibility of the party in many parts of the UK.'[40] He wanted more help for selected industries and faster privatization. Unlike the previous summer, the Cabinet did not fail outright to agree a strategy, but scepticism was strong.

Over the spring and summer of 1982, the 'Think Tank' (the Central Policy Review Staff) had set to work on the problem of high spending on a projection of very low growth. It scrutinized the main areas of public spending – education, social security, health and defence – and proposed radically different ways of running them that would permit major cuts. By now under the directorship of John Sparrow,‡ a merchant banker who had advised Mrs Thatcher on City and economic matters, the CPRS was considered to have shed its Heathite origins and embraced a more Thatcherite ethos. Its report was commissioned by Geoffrey Howe to take forward the Treasury's concerns. It proposed such dramatic changes as an end to the state funding of higher education (to be replaced by student loans), the possibility of education vouchers for schools, the de-indexing of all social security payments, so that in future they would rise less than inflation, and the replacement of the National Health Service with a system of private health insurance. It was, Sparrow recalled, 'only a brief for an argument',[41] but naturally, given its contents, that argument soon exploded.

After Mrs Thatcher had received the Think Tank paper, her principal private secretary, Robin Butler, asked her permission to circulate it to Cabinet colleagues. 'She didn't give a clear answer,' he recalled,[42] but he circulated it anyway. It appeared, along with the normal Cabinet papers, in ministers' boxes on 7 September, for discussion at Cabinet two days later. When the Cabinet met, its first gathering since the summer break, there was a storm of protest. Even Cecil Parkinson, who supported the thrust of reform, warned that 'If we are going to think the unthinkable,

---

* James Prior (1927–), educated Charterhouse and Pembroke College, Cambridge; Conservative MP for Lowestoft, 1959–83; for Waveney, 1983–7; Minister of Agriculture, 1970–72; Lord President of the Council and Leader of the Commons, 1972–4; Shadow Employment Secretary, 1974–9; Secretary of State for Employment, 1979–81; for Northern Ireland, 1981–4; created Lord Prior, 1987.
† Michael Heseltine (1933–), educated Shrewsbury School and Pembroke College, Oxford; Conservative MP for Tavistock, 1966–74; for Henley, February 1974–2001; Secretary of State for the Environment, 1979–83 and 1990–92; for Defence, 1983–6; President, Board of Trade, 1992–5; First Secretary of State and Deputy Prime Minister, 1995–7; created Lord Heseltine, 2001.
‡ John Sparrow (1933–), educated Stationers' Company's School and LSE; head of Central Policy Review Staff, 1982–3; chairman, Horserace Betting Levy Board, 1991–8; knighted, 1984.

do so privately and outside Gov't machines.'[43] Ministers insisted that the discussion of the CPRS report should not be minuted. Peter Walker* said that it was 'ludicrous to discuss at 24 hours' notice', and that such things were 'for party matters, not Whitehall'. Mrs Thatcher hit back (as abbreviated by Armstrong): 'Are you saying not in Cab.? That is astonishing.' She did not seek any decisions, she said, other than that the ideas in the report should be 'pursued': 'We must not duck them.'[44] Walker said: 'I regret that the CPRS paper was circulated. I have no doubt that it will leak.' Just to make sure that his prediction came true, he leaked it.[45] The main contents of the CPRS paper appeared in the *Economist* on 18 September 1982.

There was outrage. The government, it was claimed, was trying to abolish the welfare state. Mrs Thatcher was belatedly furious at the decision to circulate, though she had effectively acquiesced in it, and had defended in Cabinet the need for a cross-Whitehall debate about the report's contents. She was terrified by the possible electoral consequences. 'I was horrified by this paper,' she wrote in her memoirs.[46] This was not so. Although the report's suggestions were certainly not her own private thoughts, still less a secret plan, they did reflect her direction of travel. Nothing about them upset her, except for the political embarrassment they caused.

The fiasco had two consequences. The first was the end of the Think Tank. Its constant problem was that, as John Redwood,† who later ran the No. 10 Policy Unit, put it, it did 'good work to no good effect'.[47] The CPRS was attached by the rules and by Whitehall geography to the Cabinet Office, rather than to the Prime Minister. It was on the wrong side of her green-baize door. It was structurally incapable of working fast to a political agenda.

Mrs Thatcher herself resented the idea that the CPRS did not work for her. She felt outgunned by the firepower of the big government departments. In June, well before the leak, Mrs Thatcher had told a 'flabbergasted' John Sparrow, whom she had appointed as director as recently as April, that she wanted to wind it up.[48] Sparrow talked her out of it, but then she began to argue that the CPRS should become part of her office instead. Sparrow objected to this, and Robert Armstrong wrote to her in support of his view that the CPRS 'could be diminished if it became visibly part

---

* Peter Walker (1932–2010), educated Latymer Upper School; Conservative MP for Worcester, 1961–92; Secretary of State for the Environment, 1970–72; for Trade and Industry, 1972–4; Minister of Agriculture, Fisheries and Food, 1979–83; Secretary of State for Energy, 1983–7; for Wales, 1987–90; created Lord Walker of Worcester, 1992.
† John Redwood (1951–), educated Kent College, Canterbury and Magdalen College and St Antony's College, Oxford; Fellow of All Souls College, Oxford, 1972–87, 2003–5, 2007–; head of No. 10 Policy Unit, 1983–5; Conservative MP for Wokingham, 1987–; Minister of State, DTI, 1990–92; Environment, 1992–3; Secretary of State for Wales, 1993–5.

of the Prime Minister's office'. 'Perhaps I could add', he went on smoothly, 'that the Cabinet Office, including the CPRS, is very much your Department.'[49] Mrs Thatcher was not falling for that: 'and yet its influence is diminished if it is my department!', she scrawled, throwing back Armstrong's own argument in his face.

By now she had overcome some of her early resistance to employing political advisers in government, and so the role of the Policy Unit, working exclusively for her, grew. Under Ferdinand Mount,* who replaced John Hoskyns as director of the Policy Unit during the Falklands War, the unit became more capable of giving form to her often rather inchoate ideas and projecting them across Whitehall. In Mount's view, the CPRS report was a 'total disaster politically' because it attempted to present a complete plan, 'an absurd list of unthought-out though dramatic ideas'.[50] The unit could act with a cunning, flexibility and speed which were denied to the Think Tank. Instead of Hoskyns's strategic approach with which Mrs Thatcher had always felt uneasy, Mount saw Mrs Thatcher as needing a 'peg' for a suggestion: 'If we could catch her enthusiasm she would immediately run with it and haul in the relevant minister and carpet him. He would glare at us.' It was a matter of enlisting Mrs Thatcher's 'angry will'.[51] On each issue – local government reform, education, family policy and so on – the unit would get into the detail of policy, developing it along Thatcherite lines. It would send her crisp, clear memos designed to push the issues forward. These generally went to her alone, rather than floating round Whitehall, and they usually avoided the grand ideological sweep which, if leaked, could cause such mayhem. According to Tim Flesher,† one of her private secretaries at the time, the Policy Unit was successful because 'they were the only ones working flat out for her.'[52] So the disaster of the Think Tank leak ultimately improved Mrs Thatcher's ability to prevail. She reprieved the Think Tank for the time being, but abolished it after the 1983 election.

Another aspect of the debate about advice to the Prime Minister was Mrs Thatcher's desire, in order to avoid another disaster like the Argentine invasion of the Falklands, for independent policy work on foreign affairs

* Ferdinand Mount (1939–), educated Eton and Christ Church, Oxford; journalist and author; political columnist, *Spectator*, 1977–82, 1985–7; head of No. 10 Policy Unit, 1982–3; editor, *Times Literary Supplement*, 1991–2002.
† Timothy Flesher (1949–), educated Hertford College, Oxford; private secretary to the Prime Minister, 1982–6; Home Office: head of After Entry and Refugee Division, 1986–9; Personnel Division, 1989–91; Probation Service Division, 1991–2; Director of Administration, OFSTED, 1992–4; Deputy Director General (Ops), Immigration and Nationality Directorate, Home Office and Chief Inspector, Immigration Service, 1994–8; Deputy Chief of Defence Logistics, MOD, 2003–7; Chief of Corporate Services, Defence, Equipment and Support Organisation, MOD, 2007–10.

and security – areas which were outside the Policy Unit's remit. In August
1982, she canvassed the idea of a full, separate foreign affairs and security
policy unit. She wanted Sir Anthony Parsons,* the hero of British
diplomacy at the United Nations during the Falklands War, to head it.
This caused the sucking of bureaucratic teeth. Robert Armstrong warned
her that the presence of so senior a man as Parsons would 'bring us into
the problems of appearing to set up a separate centre of activity in foreign
affairs . . . competing with the FCO'.[53] Francis Pym, the Foreign Secretary,
was beside himself at the idea. He feared, Armstrong reported, that it
would be 'very damaging to the morale of the diplomatic service (already
bruised)' and that it 'would be seen as a "slap in the face" for himself'.[54]
There would be consequences for policy too: 'We should thus (it is feared)
drift inexorably . . . to a situation like that which prevailed (and was so
damaging) in the United States when Kissinger and Brzezinski were at the
White House.'[55] Mrs Thatcher maintained her position – 'I have made a
firm decision and every day I realise how necessary it is to have a unit
here,'[56] but she agreed to see Pym about it. Robin Butler prepared the
ground by explaining to Pym's office how a similar arrangement with her
economic adviser, Alan Walters,† often worked as a force for harmony
rather than conflict: 'On submissions from the Treasury and the Bank, he
[Walters] is often able to reassure the PM about their merits as a result of
his earlier involvement [at meetings with them] . . . he has contributed
significantly to increasing the PM's confidence in what the Treasury and
the Bank are doing.'[57]

When Pym and Mrs Thatcher met on 18 October, the conversation was
sufficiently unpleasant for Butler to write John Coles a covering note on
his record of the meeting saying: 'I propose to keep it in my cupboard for
the time being and not show it to anyone.'[58] Pym 'said that he found it
difficult to understand' why Mrs Thatcher had not consulted him earlier.
Of course she should have advice, 'but not in a form which would create
divisions between her and himself. He was already disturbed by reports
of such divisions.' Mrs Thatcher replied tartly that 'she was surprised that
anyone should contest her wish to have more support on these matters
within her own office.'[59] With an ill grace, Pym accepted Parsons's appointment a day later, but when the story leaked on the same day, he had what

---

* Anthony Parsons (1922–96), educated King's School, Canterbury and Balliol College,
Oxford; Ambassador to Iran, 1974–9; UK Permanent Representative to UN, 1979–82;
special adviser to the Prime Minister on foreign affairs, 1982–3; knighted, 1975.
† Alan Walters (1926–2009), educated Alderman Newton's School, Leicester, University
College, Leicester and Nuffield College, Oxford; Professor of Economics, LSE, 1967–76;
chief economic adviser to the Prime Minister, 1981–4 and 1989–90; knighted, 1983.

Ferdinand Mount remembered as 'a complete hissy fit'.[60] He saw Mrs Thatcher in the Commons and accused her staff of leaking against him. 'It was clear to him that such an article would not have been written without guidance from 10 Downing Street.'[61]

Pym had some reason for his complaint: Mrs Thatcher admitted that she had seen Anthony Shrimsley, the author of the article, though she denied saying anything slighting about her Foreign Secretary. The fact was that Mrs Thatcher did indeed have a low opinion of Pym, and made little effort to conceal it. Parsons was appointed as her foreign affairs adviser, and Roger Jackling, a less senior official from the Ministry of Defence, became her adviser on defence and intelligence. The latter post turned out to make little difference to things. Even the appointment of Parsons did not fulfil Pym's fears. He was, in most of his views, a 'Foreign Office man', and did not antagonize his old department. His genial, well-informed presence in fact helped to make Mrs Thatcher less jumpy about what the Foreign Office might be up to. It would nowadays be considered strange indeed if the Prime Minister had no adviser on foreign affairs.

The second consequence of the CPRS leak, however, was bad for Mrs Thatcher. The impetus for reform of the great spending programmes of government was gravely slowed. When the Cabinet met on 30 September 1982, it gloomily reviewed the aftermath of the leak. Norman Fowler, the Health and Social Services Secretary, was in the middle of an NHS pay battle. He told colleagues that the CPRS story 'added a new dimension to the dispute. We are under attack for wanting to abolish the NHS.'[62] The annual party conference was imminent. Willie Whitelaw intoned (again as abbreviated by Armstrong): 'Grave political danger abt NHS, following CPRS paper. The PM alone can kill it.' George Younger, the Scottish Secretary, warned, 'There will be a lot of pretty nurses at Brighton [where the conference was being held]. Be careful with the media.'[63] When Mrs Thatcher addressed the conference, therefore, she had to box herself in more than she would have liked:

> let me make one thing absolutely clear. The National Health Service is safe with us. As I said in the House of Commons on December 1 last [this example was chosen to show that the policy was in place before the CPRS leak rather than cooked up as a desperate response to it], 'The principle that adequate health care should be provided for all, regardless of ability to pay, must be the foundation of any arrangements for financing the Health Service.' We stand by that.[64]

Between then and the general election the following June, Mrs Thatcher made no speeches about any of the social policy areas covered in the CPRS report. She was frequently criticized for trying 'to dismantle the welfare state', but in truth she was more open to the very different charge that she shied away from serious reform. The effects of this hesitation would be visible throughout her time in office.

Not that policy work on all these subjects abruptly ceased. In education, where the Conservatives felt slightly less nervous than in health, Keith Joseph* – ever restless for improvement, though ever susceptible to official obfuscation – was active. At the beginning of November 1982, he fulfilled Mrs Thatcher's request for a report on education vouchers. This long-standing idea, put forward by market-minded people, was that parents should be offered state-funded vouchers for the value of a school education which they could then redeem at the school of their choice. After a year's cogitation, Joseph had concluded that a full voucher scheme was not possible all at once, because of the transitional difficulties. Instead, he offered vouchers for those wishing to send their children to independent schools, and what he called more 'open enrolment' in state schools for education authorities which wanted to take part in pilot projects. The experiment would begin in Tory-run Kent. Learning from the mistake of the CPRS leak, the bureaucracy did not circulate Joseph's ideas to colleagues. Geoffrey Howe was the only other Cabinet minister informed. The obvious problem with this proposal was that it would only be quickly and widely effective within the independent sector, and was therefore, in effect, little more than a larger version of the existing Assisted Places Scheme. Ferdinand Mount sent his own commentary to Mrs Thatcher: 'It has been a tremendous struggle for Keith to advance the cause of vouchers as far as this. At every step, the opposition of the bureaucracy has been fierce and unremitting. We are facing nearly 40 years of fossilised prejudice.'[65] Joseph's scheme, he went on, 'bears too many scars inflicted by a hostile DES [Department of Education and Science]'. It must be made clear that *every* parent would receive a voucher. Joseph should be encouraged to produce 'a shorter, simpler and more positive version'. Beside this, Mrs Thatcher drew an arrow and underscored her support. 'If we just go on saying that "vouchers are under consideration",' Mount wrote, 'the whole idea will dribble away into the sand.'[66]

Due to Mount's pushing, Joseph's ideas were put before the relevant Cabinet sub-committee, MISC 91, early in February 1983. It asked Joseph

* Keith Joseph (1918–94), 2nd baronet; educated Harrow and Magdalen College, Oxford; Conservative MP for Leeds North East, 1956–87; Secretary of State for Social Services, 1970–74; for Industry, 1979–81; for Education and Science, 1981–6; created Lord Joseph, 1987.

to come back quickly with a full scheme of education vouchers. But when Joseph returned with his adjustments, which included the idea that most parents who availed themselves of the voucher would have to pay something towards their children's education, Mount commented that 'In many ways, the latest draft is worse than the first. It is obviously politically dangerous. I also think it is both unjust and unnecessary.'[67] Mount proposed amendments to help the idea along, but the MISC 91 meeting on 24 February 1983 to discuss it all was cancelled because of political sensitivity. Instead, Mrs Thatcher met Joseph on 8 March: 'the Prime Minister said that it was clear that the scheme as set out in the paper before the meeting was neither politically nor educationally acceptable,' but 'vouchers remained at the heart of Conservative education policy.'[68] Searching for 'a more modest scheme', the ever complicated Joseph then came up with two new alternatives, but it became clear to all involved that nothing would be ready in time for the election. Discussion now, fulfilling Mount's fear, deteriorated into anxiety about referring to vouchers at all, and whether 'a system of credits' would be better.[69] According to Oliver Letwin,* Joseph's special adviser, there was 'nothing Keith liked more than being asked to think again . . . he was devoted to reason as opposed to dogma.'[70] The trouble was that if what Mount called 'the architect of the whole enterprise' was so prone to doubt, it was hard for Mrs Thatcher to push on with the scheme. Joseph was the intellectual driving force of Thatcherism, but he was also, by character, a Hamlet. So education reform was 'sicklied o'er with the pale cast of thought'. A key moment was missed.

The choice of election date also affected the progress of privatization. Privatization policy had taken shape only gradually and was still, even by 1982, far from settled. Until 1979, the Conservatives had usually opposed the Labour nationalizations of the post-war years, but had been cautious about reversing them. As leader of the Opposition, Mrs Thatcher certainly favoured denationalization, and had commissioned Nicholas Ridley to study the possibilities. But when he reported in 1977, she decided that the subject was too dangerous to pursue at the time. As Nigel Lawson†

---

* Oliver Letwin (1956–), educated Eton and Trinity College, Cambridge; member, No. 10 Policy Unit, 1983–6; Conservative MP for West Dorset, 1997–; Minister for Government Policy, Cabinet Office, 2010–15; Chancellor of the Duchy of Lancaster, 2014–; Cabinet minister in overall charge of government policy, 2015–.
† Nigel Lawson (1932–), educated Westminster and Christ Church, Oxford; Editor of the *Spectator*, 1966–70; Conservative MP for Blaby, February 1974–92; Financial Secretary to the Treasury, 1979–81; Secretary of State for Energy, 1981–3; Chancellor of the Exchequer, 1983–9; created Lord Lawson of Blaby, 1992.

34 FOUNDATIONS

recalled, 'In the 1970s, Mrs Thatcher was far more nervous of the trade unions than she ever made out.'[71] A seventh of the British workforce was employed by nationalized industries. She feared the claim that privatization would produce mass unemployment: it could provoke an unstoppable wave of strikes if those industries were brought to market. In addition, it was believed that the state of most of the nationalized industries was simply too parlous for them to be able to find a buyer.

This was a widespread view, even among those attracted to privatization. In 1976, John Redwood, who, as head of the Prime Minister's Policy Unit, was later to become a leading figure in pushing privatization forward, wrote that 'It is neither possible nor desirable to return to a free market economy. There would be too much upheaval involved in dismantling the large State and private monopolies currently operating in the economy.'[72] This way of thinking was unsurprising given the wide range of industry in the state sector before May 1979. Coal, rail, ports, steel, shipbuilding, aerospace, electricity, water, telecoms, gas, large parts of the motor, airline and oil industries, and many more, were either nationalized or controlled by a state majority shareholding. A mass change in their status seemed too daunting to contemplate. The word 'privatization' was not used in the party's manifesto for the 1979 general election. The only sell-offs mentioned there were those of the recently nationalized shipbuilding and aircraft industries, and the sale of shares in the National Freight Corporation.

After the Conservative victory in May 1979, it was the Treasury, more than Mrs Thatcher, who had pushed the subject forward. In his first Budget speech, Geoffrey Howe spoke about the 'substantial' scope for the sale of public assets: 'such sales are not justified simply by the help they give to the short-term reduction of the PSBR [the Public Sector Borrowing Requirement: what is now known as the budget deficit]. They are an essential part of our long-term programme for promoting the widest possible participation by the people in the ownership of British industry.'[73] The word 'privatization' was first officially used in a Cabinet sub-committee meeting on 20 June 1979,[74] but Mrs Thatcher herself did not use it in public until July 1981, and she still avoided it in her party conference speech that autumn. She preferred the word 'denationalization'. Ministers tended to speak of 'disposals' and 'special asset sales'. The inability of government to settle on a single agreed term more than two years into office is evidence that the policy was somewhat improvised.

Although Howe set out from the start some of the wider aims of privatization, the most immediate reason for sell-offs was the need for money. Any sale by which the government gave up control of the industry in question counted as a reduction in the PSBR. In November 1979,

£290 million was raised from the sale of part of the government's remaining 51 per cent stake in BP (a precedent for such a sale had been set by the Labour government, desperate for money in 1977). A sub-committee of the powerful economic E Committee of the Cabinet was established, with three Treasury ministers sitting on it.* It was known as E(DL). 'DL' stood for 'disposals'. In the early days, by far the most important privatization – though it was not usually, then or later, so described – was the sale of council houses permitted by the 1980 Housing Act. Its form was quite unlike that of the privatization of nationalized industries. It had none of the particular problems associated with the placing and pricing of shares. But its success in spreading popular ownership and getting the state out of a large area of life showed that such an approach could reap political rewards. Council house sales helped create a political climate in which privatization began to make sense.

Gradually, progress was made. At this early stage, the focus was on asset sales (usually shares in private companies that, through historical accident, had ended up on the government's books). In February 1981, the first of two tranches of shares in British Aerospace (BAe) were offered for sale. In October, the sale of Cable and Wireless was oversubscribed 5.6 times. In February 1982, Amersham International, a specialist producer of radioactive isotopes for use in medicine, was floated. The offer was oversubscribed 24 times. 'I was acutely embarrassed,'[75] recalled Nigel Lawson who, as energy secretary at the time, had refused the idea of a 'tender' for the shares in favour of a fixed-price offer to encourage small investors. But the underpricing did send out a clear message to the markets that there was money to be made in privatizations. In the same month, agreement was reached for a management buy-out of the National Freight Corporation. And in October 1981, Lawson announced the privatization of the entire oil-producing business of the British National Oil Corporation (BNOC) and the British Gas Corporation's offshore oil assets. Arguing his case, Lawson enunciated the general doctrine: 'No industry should remain under State ownership unless there is a positive and overwhelming case for it so doing.'[76]

When it finally came to market just over a year later, Britoil – as the company hived off from BNOC was named – found its sale by tender severely undersubscribed because of the vagaries of the oil market. Nevertheless, the sale's gross receipts for the government of £549 million were the largest yet. By the end of 1981, privatization had become a major aim

---

* They were the Chancellor (Howe), Chief Secretary (Biffen) and Financial Secretary (Lawson). The committee also included the secretaries of state for Industry, Agriculture, Environment, Trade and Energy.

of the Thatcher government, rather than a chapter of accidents or a mere
scramble for cash. Increasingly, the ministers concerned tried to establish
the general intentions of privatization, weighing the desire to maximize
proceeds against other claims – wider share ownership, employee share
ownership, greater management efficiency and the creation of competition. In July 1982, Howe wrote to Mrs Thatcher complaining that most
departments were still not paying enough attention to the opportunities
for privatization: 'We need a major push now if we are to achieve maximum progress before the election and to put ourselves in the best position
to make further progress on major candidates after it.'[77] At his request,
Mrs Thatcher sent him a 'personal minute', to be copied to all Cabinet
ministers, to urge them on. 'Suitable candidates (institutions and functions) need to be identified,' she wrote. 'And subsequent preparations for
privatisation need to be pursued as vigorously as possible.'[78]

Given that privatization eventually became Mrs Thatcher's best-known
global export, it is notable that she was not yet its cheerleader. Lawson
regarded her, in the first term, as 'distinctly unenthusiastic about privatisation'. She 'went along with it initially entirely because of the money it could
raise'.[79] Some colleagues, officials and advisers – Cecil Parkinson,* David
Norgrove† – analysed her quite differently. They considered that her main
interest in the subject derived from her desire for wider share ownership.
But more believed that privatization was for her, at first at least, more of
a solution to a problem than a grand ideological principle in itself. The
problem – 'much the top of her priorities', according to Oliver Letwin – was
'getting the industries concerned to run properly and getting rid of their
subsidy'.[80] In the case of natural monopolies, such as water, she started
from the proposition that they would be better regulated by government,
and 'had no strong feeling that these citadels should be stormed'.[81] She
nourished certain superstitions, maintaining, for example, that the Post
Office should not be privatized because, as the name Royal Mail implied,
'It's Her Majesty's.'[82] She worried that the sale of Britoil might threaten
'our oil'. Partly to solve these anxieties, Lawson introduced the concept of
the 'golden share', which retained government control *in extremis*.

* Cecil Parkinson (1931–), educated Royal Lancaster Grammar School, Emmanuel College,
Cambridge; Conservative MP for Enfield West, then Hertfordshire South, then Hertsmere,
1970–92; Secretary of State for Trade and Industry, June–October 1983; for Energy, 1987–9;
for Transport, 1989–90; Chairman, Conservative Party, 1981–3 and 1997–8; created Lord
Parkinson, 1992.
† David Norgrove (1948–), educated Christ's Hospital, Exeter College, Oxford, Emmanuel
College, Cambridge and LSE; Treasury, 1972–8 and 1980–85; private secretary to the Prime
Minister, 1985–8.

Although she supported the general principle, Mrs Thatcher was always ready to make exceptions if the time was not ripe. In February 1983, for example, when Mount wrote to tell her that the Scottish Secretary, George Younger, should not be allowed to exempt the Scottish Transport Group from privatization, she did not disagree, but she was nervous. 'Do not circulate,' she wrote on the document. 'These things are best said. Orally!'[83] Perhaps the simple fact that she disliked the word 'privatization' ('a dreadful bit of jargon to inflict on the language of Shakespeare', she later complained),[84] yet could not find a substitute, slowed her down a bit. She did come to believe that, as she wrote in her memoirs, 'privatization is at the centre of any programme of reclaiming territory for freedom',[85] but she also was immensely cautious (on this her memoirs are less explicit) about when and how that territory should be reclaimed. According to Peter Gregson, who was working at the Department of Trade and then at the Cabinet Office in Mrs Thatcher's first term, there was 'not a lot of "We must forge ahead with this" from Mrs Thatcher; more, "I hope they know what they're doing" '.[86]

Mrs Thatcher did not make the common ministerial mistake of getting so excited by improvements in nationalized industries that she allowed them to expand their monopoly power. At the heavily loss-making British Leyland, she was reluctant to give the dynamic chairman, Michael Edwardes, the extra backing he constantly demanded. After her chosen candidate, Ian MacGregor,* had become the chairman of British Steel, he wanted to grow the company by buying an American firm, Kaiser Steel.[87] She forbade him. 'You do not sell off the public sector by expanding it,' she told David Young.[88]† In the view of Michael Scholar, her Treasury private secretary, she was assisted in the Kaiser case by Denis, who, with his superior knowledge of business, often gave her advice on particular companies. 'I'd sometimes see Denis's writing on a submission. She would have rubbed it out inadequately.'[89]

By far the most important first-term test of privatization and of Mrs Thatcher's attitude to it came with the case of British Telecom. This gigantic monopoly, spun out of the Post Office on 1 October 1981, controlled almost all the telephones in Britain. The entire company, employing nearly

* Ian MacGregor (1912–98), educated George Watson's College, Edinburgh, Hillhead High School, Glasgow and Glasgow University; chairman and chief executive, British Steel Corporation, 1980–83; chairman, National Coal Board, 1983–6; knighted, 1986.
† David Young (1932–), educated Christ's College, Finchley and University College London; director, Centre for Policy Studies, 1979–82; Secretary of State for Employment, 1985–7; for Trade and Industry, 1987–9; Deputy Chairman, Conservative Party, 1989–90; created Lord Young of Graffham, 1984.

250,000 people, was unionized. It had no serious internal accounting and did not really know from which parts of the business its profits derived. George Jefferson,* who became the new company's chairman and chief executive, recalled that, in that year, there was a waiting list of a quarter of a million people for a new phone line, and no promise from BT of a date by which each line could be installed. Towards the end of his first year, he went to tea with Gordon Richardson, the Governor of the Bank of England: 'He told me that, unless I could rapidly improve telecom services in the City, it was almost certain that the City would lose its position as major financial centre.'[90]† There was a desperate need for modernization, but no prospect of increasing the External Financing Limit – the system by which the Treasury controlled the spending of nationalized industries – which would have an unpleasant impact on the PSBR. So the search for new money was on.

The need for investment in the nationalized industries was a broader problem at this time, with the Treasury trying to develop ingenious models whereby they could borrow to invest without it counting towards the PSBR. In the case of BT, initially Keith Joseph, the Industry Secretary, favoured allowing the company to raise money directly through a 'revenue bond' (known as the 'Buzby bond' after the cartoon bird used in the BT advertisements), but the Treasury warned that even this funding would need to be included in the PSBR. In July 1981, Kenneth Baker,‡ Joseph's Minister of State, and David Young, who was Joseph's special adviser in the department, gave dinner at Young's house to their boss to persuade him to privatize.[91] In Baker's view, privatization was not a great issue of principle, but 'we were at the end of our tether about how it [BT] could be better run.'[92] The two men knew that, of all the Cabinet, Joseph was best placed to persuade Mrs Thatcher of the rightness of the cause. Shortly afterwards, Joseph saw her, and won her support. At the same time, Baker and Young were working to issue a licence to Mercury, a consortium put together by Cable and Wireless, to set up its own telephone networks,

---

* George Jefferson (1921–2012), educated Dartford Grammar School, Kent; chairman, British Telecommunications plc, 1981–7, and chief executive, 1981–6; knighted, 1981.

† Around this time Jefferson visited Mrs Thatcher in Downing Street and she showed him the new BT phones in her flat: 'To my horror, when she picked up the telephone, the base also lifted off the table and dangled on the end of it. I have to admit that, after profuse apologies, I left.' He told his area managers to go and put weights in the new phones. (Remarks at BT privatization seminar, Churchill Archive Centre, 6 December 2006.)

‡ Kenneth Baker (1934–), educated St Paul's and Magdalen College, Oxford; Conservative MP for Acton, then St Marylebone, then Mole Valley, 1968–97; Secretary of State for the Environment, 1985–6; for Education and Science, 1986–9; Chairman, Conservative Party, 1989–90; Home Secretary, 1990–92; created Lord Baker of Dorking, 1997.

which Mrs Thatcher warmly welcomed. The beginning of competition was provided for. On 28 July, the objective of privatizing was endorsed by Treasury ministers, but without any public announcement until the huge logistical problems involved had been more fully addressed.[93]

In September 1981, Mrs Thatcher moved Joseph to Education and replaced him at Industry with Patrick Jenkin,* a slightly odd choice for this important post in view of the fact that 'as it later transpired, she didn't trust his judgement.'[94] Jenkin was keen to push ahead with privatization, believing that it was, among other things, the only way for BT to raise all the money it needed; but her initial line was 'It's a monopoly. At least if it's in the public sector, we have control of it.'[95] She told Jenkin: 'You can't have a monopoly [once the industry was privatized]. Why not break it up into its sixty-one separate areas?'[96] Jenkin's counter-argument was that the company had always been run from the top and it would take much too long to break it up before any sale. David Young was more supportive of Mrs Thatcher's view, urging that BT be divided into an international company and six or seven regional companies, but it was 'a battle I lost'.[97] The Treasury, ever keen on maximum proceeds, wanted the company sold whole.

Despite her misgivings about monopoly, Mrs Thatcher did not seek to delay the BT privatization. Progress was made politically easier by victory in the Falklands. Jenkin announced the plans for BT to the House of Commons on 19 July 1982, and from then on Mrs Thatcher was anxious to push ahead. An attempt by the Department of Trade to include BT in its annual referrals of state industries to the Monopolies and Mergers Commission was firmly blocked by the Prime Minister: 'I take the view that denationalisation must <u>not</u> be jeopardised.'[98] At the party conference in October, Mrs Thatcher highlighted the privatization of BT and, for the first time when speaking to her most important annual audience, used the word itself. Adapting Dr Johnson's famous remark about the effect on a man of knowing that he will be hanged, she said: 'Depend on it, when you know you are going to be privatised in a fortnight it concentrates the mind wonderfully.'[99] She was noting one of the most striking effects of privatization – that the mere prospect of it changed the behaviour of everyone involved.

She herself was no exception to the rule. Peter Benson, a City auditor who helped handle the BT privatization, summed her role up thus: 'I do not believe that Mrs Thatcher had a clear idea at all until the last moment

---

* Patrick Jenkin (1926–), educated Dragon School, Oxford, Clifton College and Jesus College, Cambridge; Conservative MP for Wanstead and Woodford, 1964–87; Chief Secretary to the Treasury, 1972–4; Minister for Energy, 1974; Secretary of State for Social Services, 1979–81; for Industry, 1981–3; for the Environment, 1983–5; created Lord Jenkin of Roding, 1987; retired from House of Lords, 2015.

what she really wanted to do. The great thing was she wanted to do something, and she was certainly going to do it.'[100] It was not, of course, in a fortnight, or anything like it, that BT privatization took place. Mrs Thatcher's decision to call the general election for 9 June 1983 caused the Bill to fall before it had completed its passage through Parliament. But, should the Conservatives be returned for a second term, it was certain to be reintroduced. None of the biggest and most controversial privatizations had yet taken place, but the way towards them now lay open.

Few subjects were more fraught for Mrs Thatcher's first government than local government spending and the increase in the domestic rates which raised the revenue. She had been pitched into this area in the general election of October 1974 when, as Ted Heath's Environment spokesman, she had made the public promise that a Conservative government would abolish the rates. As she wrote in her memoirs, she 'had considerable doubts' at the time, 'for we had not properly thought what to put in their place'.[101] Eight years on, this remained the problem, though Mrs Thatcher's personal antipathy to rates was not in doubt. Domestic rates were extremely unpopular, particularly with likely Conservative voters. Because they were a tax on property, they were payable only by householders. This meant that fewer than half of the 35 million local electors in England were liable for them, or, because of various rebates, paid them in full. They therefore bore disproportionately on those who did pay them. Militant Labour councils, using their rate-raising power to spend up and protest at national Tory policies, were only too happy to make that disproportion even greater. Since central government contributed more than 60 per cent of the money consumed by local government, Mrs Thatcher's ministers devoted a great deal of time and trouble trying to control the excesses of local spending and to devise ways of making councils more accountable to all their voters. But in the 1979 manifesto the party had said that it would defer the abolition of domestic rates for the time being. The implication was that it would come up with something for the election after that. Now that election approached, and still no solution readily offered itself.

In 1982, the Cabinet sub-committee MISC 79, chaired by Willie Whitelaw, tried to bring some sort of coherence to the problem. The Environment Secretary Michael Heseltine's memo to the sub-committee rehearsed the options. A local income tax was ruled out by the government's overall taxation policy and a local sales tax was considered too complex and unaccountable. A poll tax (so described) – a tax on every voter – could be working by 1985–6. It would have advantages – getting rid of an unfair tax, getting more people contributing, more accountability. But Heseltine set out the biggest problem: 'The main complaint about rates is that the means of taxpayers are not fairly judged in assessing rates.'[102] A poll tax would do nothing to address this. The government wanted to help the victims of this unfairness but 'At this point the politics become crucial. We can offer a financial benefit [to some] . . . but part of our intention is that there shall be losers. It is a fact of politics that it is no less hard to persuade those who will benefit from any change to feel gratitude in support of the policy than it is to convince the losers of the virtue of the policy.'[103] A few days earlier, Heseltine had also supplied a preliminary study, for which Mrs Thatcher had asked, about reorganizing local government in the metropolitan areas, which suffered – or, according to taste, benefited – from an extra layer of local government. The idea was growing that the 'mets' and the Greater London Council (the GLC), which harboured the greatest groupings of Labour councillors keen to make difficulty for the government, could be abolished. In a separate memorandum to Mrs Thatcher the following day, Heseltine urged caution. The Conservatives must not, he said, 'forget our fundamental beliefs about the constitutional role of local government'.[104] The controls already in force had achieved 'the first serious check on the expectations and aspirations of local government for some 30 years'. Heseltine fought hard and, for the year 1982–3, successfully, against an attempt by Leon Brittan, then Chief Secretary to the Treasury, to impose a 'holdback' of government grant to recalcitrant councils.

Shortly after this, MISC 79, unable to see its way through, ruled out the abolition of domestic rates for the time being. Since there was no agreement, this was the only thing to be done, but the indecision made the government more desperate for other ways of alleviating the problem of local overspending. In the Policy Unit, Ferdinand Mount could see the dangers. In a paper entitled 'The Local Government Impasse', written immediately after MISC 79 had decided not to decide, Mount warned Mrs Thatcher of 'the dangers of ill-advised action'. The abolition of the mets and the GLC was 'superficially attractive', but 'we should not saddle ourselves for the duration of the next Parliament with a commitment whose virtues and defects are not fully explored, as in the case of the promise to abolish the rates'.[105] 'Can it be right', he continued, 'to dispense with some kind of directly-elected council for Greater London which speaks for all citizens who regard themselves as Londoners?' He pointed out the 'unhappy results' of previous Conservative structural reforms, such as the Heath–Walker abolition of many old counties in the early 1970s. Mrs Thatcher underlined the phrase. Might it not, wondered Mount, be better to arrange for more frequent elections to hold councils to account, rather than abolishing elected bodies?

But time was running short for such careful thinking. If the Conservatives could not offer the abolition of the rates at the next election, they had to come up with something eye-catching. For the remainder of the year, inconclusive argument continued, with Mrs Thatcher siding with Leon Brittan about imposing selective controls on extravagant councils ('very worrying', she wrote against one of Heseltine's objections to direct control),[106] and MISC 79 tending to side with the Environment Secretary. At the turn of the year, Whitelaw reported that his committee lukewarmly recommended abolishing the mets and the GLC, and had failed to agree on the direct control of rates and spending. As Whitelaw put it with characteristic ruefulness, his committee 'were aware that their recommendations on rates might disappoint the Cabinet. They had perhaps identified problems rather than solved them. Nevertheless, he had to warn the Cabinet that the problems were intractable.'[107] The Cabinet meeting proved his point. George Younger, the Scottish Secretary, complained about the rating system: 'If we don't do something, we have a disaster on our hands.'[108] Mrs Thatcher lamented that MISC 79 had done nothing to address the unfairness of rates to old people and families. Heseltine, on the other hand, who by now had been moved from Environment to Defence, said that the House of Commons had 'a general understanding that there isn't an alternative to rates'. More work was set in hand on abolishing the mets and the GLC and to look at rates yet again, under Tom King,* who succeeded Heseltine at Environment, but nothing was actually decided.

By this time, Mrs Thatcher's dominant and immediate concern was electoral. 'There would be a great political prize', she told King at a meeting a fortnight later, 'in a decision that there would be no further increases in rates.'[109] She toyed with paying for this by a local VAT, increasing the central grant which funded the police, or taking the salaries of teachers away from local government and funding them from the centre. None of this transpired. As she told *The Times* with surprising frankness, when asked about the rates on 3 May 1983: 'The first thing you always have to look at in politics is – "I know what I want to get away from, but what am I going to put in its place?" '[110] Government indecision was almost final, waiting until the moment when the election was called.

---

* Tom King (1933–), educated Rugby and Emmanuel College, Cambridge; Conservative MP for Bridgwater, March 1970–2001. Secretary of State for the Environment, January–June 1983; for Transport, June–October 1983; for Employment, 1983–5; for Northern Ireland, 1985–9; for Defence, 1989–92; created Lord King of Bridgwater, 2001.

3

Landslide

'I live in a big house called 10 Downing Street.
I'm going to live there for a long time'

The Conservatives were almost bound to win the general election of 1983. The Falklands effect was too strong and the Labour Party, under the leadership of Michael Foot, too weak for any other result to be at all likely. Even without the Falklands, there had been some Tory recovery. From the week before the Falklands crisis broke, the Conservatives were continuously ahead of Labour in the opinion polls until polling day. But, to the woman who had ultimately to decide when the election should be called, matters were not so obvious.

Under the British unwritten constitution,* the sitting prime minister had the right to ask the sovereign for the dissolution of Parliament at any point up to the moment when the Parliament's statutory five years were complete. The sovereign could, in theory, have refused, but, in modern times, this became extremely unlikely. The freedom to choose the date gave great power to the prime minister, but also caused her (or him) enormous anxiety.

Few prime ministers can have been more anxious than Mrs Thatcher. On top of her natural caution, and her obsession with collecting all possible relevant data before arriving at a decision, was an overpowering sense that a mistake would be fatal for her purposes and for her career. She had always said that the restoration of Britain would take two or even three terms of Conservative government. 'If we lose, we lose it all,' she told Ferdinand Mount.[1] 'She knew that this was a massive decision, and that she alone was responsible,' remembered Cecil Parkinson who, as chairman, ran the party's campaign.[2] As a result, she was extremely tetchy until the decision was finally made.

Mrs Thatcher knew, and stated publicly, that she should not try for a

---

* This was altered when the Conservative–Liberal Democrat Coalition passed the Fixed-Term Parliaments Act in 2011. It fixed each Parliament for five years, preventing an early dissolution in all normal circumstances.

snap election after the Falklands. The Tories had been in government for
little more than three years and, with a good working majority, had no
need to refresh their mandate. Any early rush to the polls would have been
seen as opportunist, and punished accordingly by the electorate. The decision not to go to the country in 1982 was easily made. Everything else was
more complicated. Mrs Thatcher's own original preference was for running the full five years. As this looked less and less sensible, she favoured
waiting until October 1983. In her urging that US missile deployment in
Europe should take place in November 1983, and that the Germans should
settle the EEC budget question during their presidency which was to begin
in July 1983, one can detect that, until well into 1983, October was her
target date.*

   One factor which affected her calculations more than most realized
was the inquiry, which she had commissioned from Lord Franks, into the
failures which had led to the Argentine invasion of the Falklands. Although
the public appetite for questioning a clear British victory was low, Mrs
Thatcher genuinely feared that Franks might find against her and so force
her out of office. 'If he had concluded that government inefficiencies had
caused war,' recalled Robin Butler, 'she thought she'd be done for.'[3] On
Christmas Eve 1982, when she knew that the draft of the report had
arrived at Downing Street, she came into the private secretaries' room,
where Butler and John Coles were sitting. 'Read me the conclusion,' she
said.[4] Franks, whose commission included privy councillors from all parties, concluded that 'The invasion of the Falkland Islands . . . could not
have been foreseen' and that the government could not be blamed for the
decision of Argentina to invade. She was in the clear. In the new year, Mrs
Thatcher therefore felt free to celebrate (although Franks's conclusions
were not yet made public) by visiting the Falklands, which she had never
before seen, in conditions of great secrecy.† She was, needless to say,

---

* Mrs Thatcher always wanted to keep open the option to go early, however. In September
1982, she wrote to President Reagan, who was at that time proposing to hold the G7 economic summit in Williamsburg on 11 June 1983. She told him that the date was difficult for
her, without explaining why. The first draft, not sent, even pretended that she could not come
to the United States because of the Sovereign's Parade ('Trooping the Colour') ceremony in
London. (Perhaps Mrs Thatcher rejected that draft because its stated reason was bogus.) The
President, always anxious to help her electorally, took the hint, and replied that, because of
her anxiety, 'we left the timing vague.' (Draft message from Thatcher to Reagan, 30 September 1982, TNA: PREM 19/1007; Reagan to Thatcher, 1 October 1982, CAC: THCR
3/1/25 (http://www.margaretthatcher.org/document/123491).)
† One reason for this secrecy was that Mrs Thatcher feared that Argentina might try to
intercept her aircraft. The Cabinet Secretary, Robert Armstrong, was authorized to turn her
plane round should news of her visit break. She was recognized during her stopover on

warmly received, although Butler recalled that she 'was disillusioned with the locals, whose lethargy shocked her, and fell asleep in their company'. On the other hand, she 'was very happy with the military and behaved like a young filly'.[5]* Once she had returned to Britain, election speculation grew and she unintentionally added to it when she said publicly that it was contributing to the fall in the value of sterling. It was becoming harder to get on with the business of government.

Although Labour's weakness was well known, Conservative electoral calculations also had to include a factor which, as a deliberate tactic, Mrs Thatcher hardly ever mentioned in public – the centrist SDP–Liberal Alliance. The Alliance had fallen from its pre-Falklands poll ratings to third place, but it remained a threat. The conventional ideological response to the Alliance was to argue that the Conservatives should tack to the centre. Moderate Tories fretted that Mrs Thatcher was too extreme, and that this would give an opening to the new force. For a background interview in November 1982, Chris Patten, the rising young hope of the Tory Wets, 'denied that there had been any change in national attitudes in favour of privatisation and the like. He thought the Tory party was completely off the rails under Margaret,' and he wanted 'people of principle to put out public markers that they dissented'.[6]†

In fact the Conservatives found themselves challenged by the emergence of the SDP, not only in the centre, but on the right. Previously, they had felt confident that they could hoover up the votes of those who resented trade union power, but in the course of 1982, the SDP – which was, after all, a party formed in revolt against the unions' dominance of Labour – began to attack the Tories for not going far enough. In October 1982, Norman Tebbit,‡ the hardline Employment Secretary, pointed out to E Committee that the SDP was now making the 'political levy' – the system by which union members automatically paid money to the Labour Party – 'a matter of public debate'. The Tories, he went on, were too hesitant about reforming the levy because, for their own reasons, they did

---

Ascension Island, and Armstrong endured a sleepless night waiting for the dreaded leak, but the news held until she arrived. (Interview with Lord Armstrong of Ilminster.)
* Years later, her time with the Scots Guards stuck in her mind: 'One or two of the very ordinary guys I went round to said "Keep on against Europe, Maggie, we don't want to fight for them, we fight for Britain"' (Thatcher Memoirs Materials, CAC: THCR 4/3).
† This was one of many unpublished background interviews conducted by David Butler and Denis Kavanagh for their series of British general election studies.
‡ Norman Tebbit (1931–), educated Edmonton County Grammar School; Conservative MP for Epping, 1970–74; for Chingford, February 1974–92; Minister of State, Department of Industry, 1981; Secretary of State for Employment, 1981–3; for Trade and Industry, 1983–5; Chairman, Conservative Party, 1985–7; created Lord Tebbit, 1992.

not want the argument straying into the broader issue of the funding of political parties.[7] They feared too much scrutiny of their business donors. Yet even Tebbit himself was suspected of not pushing trade union reform hard enough. Ferdinand Mount, though generally more politically moderate than the man Michael Foot called 'the semi-house-trained polecat', wrote a fierce memorandum to Mrs Thatcher that same month: 'I think there is a danger of complacency and timidity creeping into our approach to the reform of trade union law. Both the paper from Norman and the discussion last week were extremely defensive and limited.'[8] 'I agree,' wrote Mrs Thatcher. Mount was particularly exercised about the need to include strike ballots in Tebbit's forthcoming Green Paper, a subject on which he sensed that 'the Department of Employment is determined to do nothing.'[9] In the end, strike ballots made it into the Green Paper and so did changes to the political levy, but in the conciliatory form that unions should try to find their own ways of sorting these questions out. Politics was becoming more multi-dimensional at a time when most Conservatives, including Mrs Thatcher, were happy with straightforwardly bashing the left.

The Conservatives watched with interest the Bermondsey by-election of February 1983. Michael Foot had originally declared that he would prevent the candidacy of the radically left-wing Peter Tatchell* but eventually failed to do so. Supporters of the outgoing right-wing Labour MP Bob Mellish made crude jokes against Tatchell's homosexuality (which, though he later became the nation's best-known gay campaigner, he did not acknowledge at the time). These slurs were echoed by Liberal campaigners and a weird atmosphere of farce and bitterness prevailed. The by-election was a test case of Labour's difficulties with its left, but the result, an overwhelming victory for the Liberal candidate, Simon Hughes,† with the largest swing (over 44 per cent) in by-election history, was not good news for the Tories. They feared that Labour might go into such national decline that the SDP–Liberal Alliance would overtake it, with frighteningly unpredictable electoral results.

---

* Peter Tatchell (1952–), educated Mount Waverley High School, Melbourne and Polytechnic of North London; activist/organizer on gay rights and environmental issues; Labour candidate in Bermondsey by-election, 1983; resigned Labour Party, 2000; Independent Green candidate for Greater London Assembly, 2000; joined Green Party, 2004.

† Simon Hughes (1951–), educated Llandaff Cathedral School, Cardiff, Christ College, Brecon, Selwyn College, Cambridge and College of Europe, Bruges; MP for Southwark and Bermondsey, February 1983–97 (Liberal, 1983–8; Liberal Democrat, 1988–97); Liberal Democrat MP for North Southwark and Bermondsey, 1997–2010; for Bermondsey and Old Southwark, 2010–15; shadow to Attorney-General, 2005–7; to Leader of House of Commons, 2007–9; Deputy Leader, Liberal Democrats, 2010–13; Minister of State at the Ministry of Justice, 2013–15.

There followed, on 15 March, the last Budget before the election. Neither showy nor particularly memorable, Howe's plan reduced taxes on businesses, while seeking to cement Conservative support with a rise in personal tax allowances of 8.5 per cent more than inflation. A little over a week later came the Darlington by-election, considered the key barometer of Tory fortunes. If Labour lost the seat, there was a real possibility that the party would ditch Michael Foot as leader and veer suddenly towards electability. The Alliance went all out to win. In the event, Labour narrowly held the seat from the Conservatives. The SDP candidate got a good vote but did not break through. This result was satisfactory for the Tories.

Even now, Mrs Thatcher hung back. Sensing the pressure on her to go to the country, and trying to make it difficult for her to do so, Denis Healey heckled her in the House of Commons for wanting to 'cut and run'. She became so heated at this suggestion of cowardice that she let slip a bit of the Lincolnshire dialect which her education had ironed out of her:

> The right hon. Gentleman is afraid of an election, is he? Afraid? Frightened? Frit? Could not take it? Cannot stand it? If I were going to cut and run, I should have gone after the Falklands. Frightened! Right now inflation is lower than it has been for 13 years – a record which the right hon. Gentleman could not begin to touch.[10]

Without quite meaning to, she was campaigning already. Good results in the local elections on 5 May removed the last obvious remaining objection to going to the polls, although Mrs Thatcher still harboured doubts ('I wasn't quite certain whether the results were good enough').[11]*

The manifesto was ready, and so were the troops. The press was also gearing up for an election. In his summary of the weekend's news coverage, Bernard Ingham† advised Mrs Thatcher that 'there is only one topic: the election . . . and <u>when</u> (and whether) an announcement will be made.' On this note she scribbled the words '<u>Calm Down</u>.'[12] That Sunday, 8 May, Mrs Thatcher held a meeting of those most involved in the campaign, at Chequers. To it came Whitelaw, Parkinson and his Vice-Chairman,

---

* Another factor which accelerated the decision was the need for a by-election in Cardiff North West, following the death of the Conservative MP Michael Roberts in February. Mrs Thatcher saw the merit in calling a general election early enough to make the Cardiff North West contest unnecessary: 'The last thing you want is a by-election just before the Election,' she later recalled (Thatcher Memoirs Materials, CAC: THCR 4/3.)

† * Bernard Ingham (1932–), educated Hebden Bridge Grammar School; reporter, *Yorkshire Post*, 1952–61; *Guardian*, 1961–5; director of information for Department of Employment, 1973; Energy, 1973–7; chief press secretary to the Prime Minister, 1979–90; knighted, 1990.

Michael Spicer,* Howe (who was in charge of the manifesto), Tebbit, the Chief Whip, Michael Jopling,† her parliamentary private secretary (PPS), Ian Gow‡ and various advisers. The politicians liked to refer to themselves ironically as 'the Magnificent Seven'. Denis Healey mocked them as 'Snow White and the Seven Dwarfs'.[13] The idea of the meeting, which was Cecil Parkinson's, was to take her through everything – 'the main thing was to reassure her that you *had* thought it through.'[14]

It was absolutely obvious to all concerned that an election should be called – to all, that is, except Mrs Thatcher herself. She was, perhaps, 'frit'. She was given an exhaustive presentation of the local election results, which suggested a large Tory majority in a general election, and she also had in her hand an ORC poll privately conducted for the Conservative Party. It gave the Tories a lead of 10 per cent over Labour (44 per cent to 34 per cent), and put the Alliance, by now a formal electoral pact between Liberals and SDP, on 20 per cent.[15] Even this did not seem good enough to her. Neither did any of the other omens. She did not want to call the poll for 16 June because that was the week of the royal race meeting at Ascot and she 'was not going to have people in grey suits and toppers heading the news pages at a time when three million were unemployed'.[16] She complained that if she called the poll earlier she would not be able to attend President Reagan's G7 summit at the end of May. She still fretted about the unseemliness of 'going early'.

The main meeting finished without any decision. Parkinson, Jopling and Gow stayed to supper. Mrs Thatcher tried one last, futile way of avoiding the issue. The Queen, she objected, would not be available at such short notice to grant a dissolution. Ian Gow slipped out of the room and returned to say that he had spoken to the Palace, and the Queen would be happy to see the Prime Minister at noon the following day. 'If looks

---

* Michael Spicer (1943–), educated Wellington College and Emmanuel College, Cambridge; Conservative MP for South Worcestershire, February 1974–97; for West Worcestershire, 1997–2010; Parliamentary Under-Secretary, 1984–7, and Minister for Aviation, 1985–7, Department of Transport; Parliamentary Under-Secretary, Department of Energy, 1987–90; Minister of State, Department of the Environment, 1990; chairman, 1922 Committee, 2001–10; knighted, 1996; created Lord Spicer, 2010.

† Michael Jopling (1930–), educated Cheltenham College and King's College, Newcastle-upon-Tyne; Conservative MP for Westmorland, 1964–83; for Westmorland and Lonsdale, 1983–97; Parliamentary Secretary to HM Treasury, and Chief Whip, 1979–83; Minister of Agriculture, Fisheries and Food, 1983–7; created Lord Jopling, 1997.

‡ Ian Gow (1937–90), educated Winchester; Conservative MP for Eastbourne, 1974–90; PPS to the Prime Minister, 1979–83; Minister for Housing and Construction, 1983–5; Minister of State, Treasury, 1985; resigned from the government over the completion of the Anglo-Irish Agreement; murdered by the Provisional IRA, who exploded a bomb under his car at his home in Sussex, July 1990.

could kill, she'd have killed him.'[17] As Parkinson explained: 'Her resistance to an idea is a technique meaning "Persuade me." '[18] It was also, as Jopling observed, a way of shifting responsibility: 'She was saying, "If this is what you want to do, do it, but don't blame me if it all goes wrong." '[19] After the supper guests had left, Mount heard Mrs Thatcher say to Denis: 'I'm not sure it's the right thing to do at all. I shall sleep on it. It's always best to sleep on these things.' As Mount wrote: 'For the only time when I was around (though there must often have been such occasions in the privacy of their boudoir), Denis lost patience. "You can't do that, Margaret. They've all gone back to town saying it's going to be the 9th. You can't go back on that now. The horses have bolted." '[20] So 9 June it was.

Parkinson was in no rush to start campaigning. As soon as the election was called, there was a surge in favour of the Conservatives. One poll, on 12 May 1983, even gave them a 21-point lead over Labour. On 13 May, honouring a long-standing commitment, Mrs Thatcher visited the Scottish Conservative Party conference in Perth. She sensed 'tremendous enthusiasm' and a 'really great feeling of togetherness'.[21]* It was not until 18 May that the party's manifesto was launched. Its process of composition had been more concentrated than in 1979. All departments had been asked for manifesto ideas, of course, but most of the work, under Howe's chairmanship, was done by Mount and Adam Ridley, Howe's special adviser ('Ferdy was excellent,' Mrs Thatcher later judged).[22] As is generally the case in government, the manifesto came under closer central control than in opposition, and the process of party policy formulation was winding down,[23] with results which would be deleterious in the longer term. Mrs Thatcher herself, however, had less to do with it than in 1979. She was very busy and, now that she had an actual record on which to fight, the manifesto had become less important in her mind. In her memoirs, she recorded that she was 'somewhat disappointed'[24] by the document that emerged, which she believed reflected Howe's over-cautious nature, but colleagues did not remember her complaining at the time.

The tone of the Conservative manifesto mostly reflected the more 'small c' conservative and less radical side of her party's nature. In her foreword,

---

* In her Perth speech Mrs Thatcher said that the election provided a 'chance to banish from our land the dark divisive clouds of Marxist socialism' (Speech to the Scottish Conservative Party conference, 13 May 1983 (http://www.margaretthatcher.org/document/105314)). The comments were picked up by Christopher Monckton in the Policy Unit, who was concerned about the tone of the speech and urged Mrs Thatcher not to 'stoop to personal abuse' of her opponents. She underlined this comment with her squiggly line and added, 'Where was the personal abuse in that speech? Please give me one example.' (Thatcher's annotations on Monckton to Gow, 16 May 1983, THCR 2/7/3/36 (http://www.margaretthatcher.org/document/131412).)

Mrs Thatcher spoke not of revolution, but of recovery. Britain had renewed its 'confidence and self-respect'. The task was 'to defend Britain's traditional liberties and distinctive way of life'. 'Abroad,' the manifesto concluded, 'Britain is regarded for the first time in years as a country with a great future as well as a great past.' Emphasis was laid on the importance of Britain's independent nuclear deterrent and of the deployment of US missiles in Europe if disarmament negotiations failed. Labour's anti-nuclear policy would 'shatter the NATO Alliance, and put our safety in the greatest jeopardy'. Oddly though, and, as Mrs Thatcher later publicly admitted, by mistake the new submarine-borne Trident nuclear missiles were not mentioned by name.

The document was quite short, and its specific promises were few. Trade union members would be given the right to ballot for election to their governing bodies, and the legal immunity of unions would be withdrawn if a strike were called without a secret ballot. Members must decide every ten years whether their union should have party political funds and should be guaranteed a right of choice (perhaps only by 'contracting out') about whether they paid the political levy. On unemployment, the manifesto promoted the enormous Youth Training Scheme devised the previous year by David Young and Norman Tebbit to ensure that every school-leaver not in further education would be in work or training: 350,000 young people would be in the scheme by the autumn. Health was presented in terms of extra money spent and higher numbers of people employed: questions of structural reform were avoided. The Conservative claim was that only £7.75 billion had been spent on the National Health Service in 1979, compared with £15.5 billion in 1983. Voucher schemes having run into the sand, serious education reforms were not mentioned. Promises on tax were studiously vague, and modest, in no way presaging the huge tax reform programme of which radicals like Nigel Lawson dreamed. The only eye-catching announcements fell in two areas. BT, Rolls-Royce, British Airways and parts of several other named nationalized industries, including British Steel and British Leyland, would be sold off. Replacement of the rates was not promised, though local authority high spending would be curbed. The GLC and the metropolitan counties would be abolished.

The Conservative manifesto was, in fact, a well-constructed document, creating the space for widespread reform without alarming people with strident language or dangerous detail. But the Tories had much more relish for Labour's manifesto – famously described by the Labour MP Gerald Kaufman* as 'the longest suicide note in history' – than for their own.

---

* Gerald (Bernard) Kaufman (1930–), educated Leeds Grammar School and the Queen's College, Oxford; Labour MP for Manchester, Ardwick, 1970–83; for Manchester, Gorton,

With its pledges to renationalize industries, end the sale of council houses, get out of the European Community and disarm unilaterally, it was an electoral gift to the Conservatives. Mrs Thatcher carried it round with her at all times in the campaign, and quoted from it gleefully in almost all her main speeches. She counted 'at least forty seven new ways' in which it would put Britain in 'a Socialist straitjacket'.[25]*

The press conference which launched the Conservative manifesto set the tone of the campaign. Mrs Thatcher was fizzing with energy, and in no mood to play things down. The choice at the election was 'absolutely stark in philosophical terms',[26] she said: did Britain want greater liberty and a smaller public sector, or a return to state socialism? Although Geoffrey Howe also spoke, and she invited questions to other members of her Cabinet sitting on the platform, she dominated the show, and tended, to the amusement of the press, to butt in. One questioner† noted that the manifesto seemed to leave the way open for talks with Argentina about the Falkland Islands, and asked Francis Pym if this was the case. Pym starting talking about 'further sensible conversations' with Argentina. Mrs Thatcher could bear it no longer, and cut across him: 'No I'm sorry, I thought you [the press] were going to misunderstand that. The Foreign Secretary said quite clearly on commercial links . . . but not on sovereignty.'[27] In fact, the Foreign Secretary had said no such thing, and his discomfiture at the general laughter was visible. The next day, Pym rashly declared that a landslide victory for the Conservatives would not be healthy. Mrs Thatcher responded, when challenged on this, that Pym had exhibited 'a natural . . . Ex-Chief Whip's caution. You know there's a club of Chief Whips. They're very unusual people.'[28]‡ It was apparent that Pym's political career was drawing peacefully to its close.

The preparation for each day's press conference was excellent. Mrs Thatcher began listening to the radio at 6.30, before appearing at Central Office at 8.15 for an exhaustive briefing. She loved this chance to suck in

1983–; Minister of State, Department of Industry, 1975–9; Shadow Environment Secretary, 1980–83; Shadow Home Secretary, 1983–7; Shadow Foreign Secretary, 1987–92; knighted, 2004.

* Much as she loved attacking Labour, Mrs Thatcher drew the line at anything personal against Michael Foot. A proposed advertisement by Saatchi and Saatchi showed a picture of the sixty-nine-year-old Foot, with his familiar walking stick, over the line 'As a pensioner, he'd be better off with the Conservatives.' Mrs Thatcher was 'appalled'. Tim Bell, presenting the advertisement for Saatchis, recalled that she 'threw me out of the office'. (Tim Bell, *Right or Wrong: The Memoirs of Lord Bell*, Bloomsbury, 2014, p. 80.)

† The present author.

‡ The most prominent ex-Chief Whip was, of course, Ted Heath, a fact which, in making this comment, Mrs Thatcher probably had in mind.

yet more information, and the exercise stopped her from having time to fret. Cecil Parkinson and Stephen Sherbourne,* who, despite a former association with Edward Heath, had become her chief political minder for the campaign, were 'accomplished diplomats, who were brilliant at keeping her on course, her tangential monologues to a minimum and generally jollying everyone along'.[29] Her absolute mastery of the material – what Sherbourne called her 'mania for facts' – contrasted very favourably in public with Michael Foot's windy vagueness. The most dangerous issue, obviously, was unemployment, but Parkinson and Tebbit had developed a theme of what they called 'shared responsibility', in which the unions and the Labour Party, rather than just the government, were blamed for the problem of joblessness. One of the party's posters reminded voters that no Labour government had ever brought down the level of unemployment. By frequent references to the subject and the detailed policy remedies being applied, Parkinson and Tebbit somehow managed to bore the press into the ground, and prevent Mrs Thatcher herself from being too closely identified with it. The media enjoyed the confidence and theatricality of Mrs Thatcher's daily press conferences. The political scientist David Butler,† who attended them, noted privately, halfway through the campaign: 'Mrs Thatcher at her press-conferences was extraordinarily self-confident and outgoing. She did sound as though she was completely on top of her situation and on top of all her colleagues. People laughed at her, but admiringly.'[30] The pleasure the press took in these occasions emanated in their favourable coverage.

Parkinson was somewhat worried, however, that she 'mustn't allow herself to exhaust herself'.[31] He wanted to ensure that she could have her interviews 'in the can' by the early evening, and to plan her travel 'so that she could come back to No. 10 and think about the next day'.[32] The best thing, once the press conferences had set the day's agenda, was to get Mrs Thatcher away from London, charging up and down the country campaigning. This suited her temperament. As Stephen Sherbourne saw it: 'It's a

* Stephen Sherbourne (1945–), educated Burnage Grammar School, Manchester and St Edmund Hall, Oxford; Conservative Research Department, 1970–75; head of the office of Edward Heath MP, 1975–6; special adviser to Patrick Jenkin (then Secretary of State for Industry), 1982–3; political secretary to the Prime Minister, 1983–8; chief of staff to Leader of the Opposition, 2003–5; knighted, 2006; created Baron Sherbourne of Didsbury, 2013.
† David Butler (1924–), educated St Paul's and New College, Oxford (MA, DPhil); Fellow of Nuffield College, Oxford, 1954–; served as personal assistant to HM Ambassador in Washington, 1955–6; author/editor of many publications, including, since 1951, the Nuffield Election Studies, a reference series for each UK election since 1945. Co-authors/editors have included Professor Richard Rose, Professor Anthony King and, since 1974, Professor Dennis Kavanagh. Knighted, 2011.

shooting war, and she's a footsoldier. She's not the general back at HQ. She's in the front line.'[33] Except for a few setpiece speeches, the purpose of these journeys was not to make political arguments, but to be seen in a good light.

This succeeded. According to Frank Johnson, in his daily sketches of her campaign in *The Times*, Margaret and Denis had managed to become part of the national furniture. In Cornwall, Denis was 'instantly recognised and acclaimed. Perhaps he is the quintessential Englishman of our time. "You look after her, won't you?" they often cried.'[34] As for Margaret, wrote Johnson, 'having her as Prime Minister seems to be part of the natural order of things.'[35] It was also true that Mrs Thatcher was highly unpopular in some areas, and was followed all round the country by a tiny mob of protesters from the Socialist Workers' Party trying to disrupt her every word; but, in enough people's eyes, this probably enhanced and certainly did not diminish her standing. Mrs Thatcher enjoyed the 'old-fashioned style of campaigning which we used to do'. She relished the chance to respond to hecklers and 'was thrilled to bits' when they showed up.[36] For the most part, she was photographed from favourable angles in pleasant places. In the Isle of Wight (which the Conservatives nevertheless failed to win), she swept up the beach at the prow of a hovercraft, as if she were the figurehead of Britannia on a man o' war. At a Finchley supermarket, she went on one of her manic pretend shopping trips, spending £11.94 on goods which included part-baked rolls, cling-film and the unpleasant new English cheese Lymeswold. 'I went to the supermarket and said "Please have you got any English bacon?" And they said they only had Danish bacon.'[37] She forgot to take any money, and so Carol, accompanying her to write a diary of the campaign, had to pay. While Mrs Thatcher was photographed making fast, orderly and usually friendly progress round the country, Michael Foot had a hard time. There was no discernible pattern to his outings, and he himself, with his poor sight, lack of a sense of direction and inadequate staff, was seen to wander confusedly about. Accompanied by his walking stick and his dog Dizzie (sportingly named after the Tory Prime Minister Disraeli, about whom he had written), Foot was an endearing figure to most of the voters who saw him, but not remotely a prime ministerial one.*

In these circumstances, attacks on Mrs Thatcher which, in more normal

---

* As in 1979, though much more readily, Mrs Thatcher refused to take part in a television debate. 'You simply cannot make up your mind as a result of a couple of programmes between the Prime Minister and the Leader of the Opposition.' Equally she saw no reason to give the Alliance a platform: 'We can't have a debate between three, certainly. The elections are too important to be considered as a matter of entertainment, or as a matter of successive soundbites, or as a matter of who is better at repartee.' (Thatcher Memoirs Materials, CAC: THCR 4/3.)

times, might well have struck home, failed. The Conservatives' private polling did pick up some anxiety about the NHS and that Mrs Thatcher was considered too 'uncaring'. In the view of some party officials, she was 'excessively arrogant'[38] in the early stages of the campaign. But, to a surprising degree, political assaults on her backfired. This was particularly true of anything in relation to the Falklands, a subject on which she wisely said little. Denis Healey accused her of 'glorying in slaughter'* over the recapture of South Georgia, and was forced to retract this, saying that he had meant to say 'glorying in conflict'. Labour's rising star, Neil Kinnock,† hitting back at a heckler who shouted that Mrs Thatcher had 'guts', said it was 'a pity that people had to leave theirs on the ground at Goose Green in order to prove it'.[39]‡ These remarks damaged only Labour. The party's activists reported that voters 'really admired' Mrs Thatcher over the Falklands and that, as a result, 'Labour was now seen as the unpatriotic party.'[40]

The Conservatives could not push this line directly in relation to the Falklands, but they could and did in relation to nuclear weapons. Especially among working-class voters, the idea that Labour would leave Britain undefended rendered it automatically unfit for government. This point was brought out most effectively by the Labour former Prime Minister James Callaghan. On 25 May, halfway through the campaign, he launched a fierce attack on his party's anti-nuclear policy, pointing out the Russians' game: 'The Soviet Union's propaganda clearly wishes to use public opinion in this country to get the West to reduce its own arms while doing nothing themselves. In this way they would gain nuclear superiority. This is simply not on.'[41] Most voters agreed. As defence secretary, Michael Heseltine took on CND directly, charging them and, by implication the Labour Party, with advancing the Soviet cause. This impressed Mrs

---

* Apart from anything else, no one was killed in the recapture of South Georgia.

† Neil Kinnock (1942–), educated Lewis School, Pengam and University College, Cardiff; Labour MP for Bedwellty, 1970–83; for Islwyn, 1983–95; chief Opposition spokesman on education, 1979–83; Leader of the Labour Party, and Leader of the Opposition, 1983–92; member, 1995–2004, and a vice-president, 1999–2004, European Commission; chairman, British Council, 2004–9; created Lord Kinnock of Bedwellty, 2005.

‡ It was over the Falklands, however, that Mrs Thatcher suffered one of her rare embarrassments of the campaign. In a BBC television phone-in, she was asked by Mrs Diana Gould, a member of the public, about the sinking of the *Belgrano*. Mrs Gould appeared to catch her out about the direction which the ship had been taking when she was torpedoed. Mrs Thatcher was flustered. (See BBC1 *Nationwide*, 24 May 1983 (http://www.margaretthatcher. org/document/105147).) The interview 'really made me jolly cross . . .' she later recalled; 'they had no idea what it was like to be in charge' (Thatcher Memoirs Materials, CAC: THCR 4/3). Even on the *Belgrano*, however, it was the view of her advisers that the subject was 'a total plus' for Mrs Thatcher with the electorate (David Butler interview with Ferdinand Mount, 1 July 1983, David Butler Archive, Nuffield College, Oxford).

Thatcher, who recalled with pleasure Heseltine's success in inflicting a 'series of defeats on CND and the Labour Left'.[42] Once the word 'unilateral' was delatinized and rendered as 'one-sided' – a conscious decision of the Tory campaigners – it spelt electoral death to Labour. 'Patriotism' had been 'restored to our vocabulary',[43] Mrs Thatcher told party supporters in Cardiff. Even more importantly, it had become linked, for the first time in modern British politics, with only one party.

In the middle of the campaign came the G7 economic summit at Williamsburg. Mrs Thatcher had agonized constantly about whether or not she dared be out of the country at such a time.* Once she had decided to call the election, she informed Reagan that she would not be able to make their planned pre-summit meetings in Washington, but hoped to attend the summit itself: 'I have to weigh this against the requirements of the Election campaign and possible criticism here if I attend.'[44] Reagan wrote asking her to attend the tail end of the meeting in Williamsburg, arriving on the Sunday and leaving on the Monday, the last in May. 'I wish you every success in the election,' he wrote, 'and in gaining another mandate to carry out the courageous and principled policies which you have begun.'[45] Reagan's aide Michael Deaver† rang the British Embassy in Washington to relay the President's private thought which was 'Hell, the main thing is to get her re-elected,'[46] so there should be no pressure on her to attend if it was considered politically dangerous. On the other hand, Deaver added, if she did come, there would be excellent photo-opportunities. She decided to go. Events at home seemed to confirm the rightness of her decision. On 27 May 1983, the day before Mrs Thatcher set out, the Labour Party put out a strange press release stating that 'the unanimous view of the campaign committee is that Michael Foot is the Leader of the Labour Party,' which suggested, naturally, that he very nearly was not. She could fly across the Atlantic without due anxiety.‡

Despite the fact that her friend President Reagan was the host and was

---

* In one discussion with officials, in which she protested that she could not go, she declared: 'I'll send somebody else.' 'Mr Pym?' presumed an official. Mrs Thatcher looked horrified. 'No, no, not him,' she said. 'I'll send Mike [Michael Scholar, her Treasury private secretary].' (Interview with Sir Michael Scholar.)

† Michael Deaver (1938–2007), educated San José State College; aide to Ronald Reagan, 1967–85 (known for arranging memorable photographic backdrops for his public appearances); founder Michael K. Deaver & Associates (lobbying firm); convicted in 1987 on three counts of perjury for lying to a House sub-committee and a federal grand jury about efforts to use the White House to support his lobbying.

‡ Mrs Thatcher had earlier been asked by Robert Armstrong if she intended to fly to the United States, like President Mitterrand, by Concorde. 'No,' she wrote, mindful of the

doing everything he could to be helpful politically, Mrs Thatcher harboured serious worries about the content of the summit, as well as its timing. On top of her normal dislike of international platitudes was a fear that the world's economic powers might take a turn in the wrong direction, undermining her own economic policies and therefore making her more vulnerable electorally. Ever since the breakdown of the Bretton Woods system (the world monetary order worked out, under American leadership, in 1944) in 1970–71, and the inflation that ensued, many political leaders had hankered after a new way of fixing the international system through the management of exchange rates, a dream which Mrs Thatcher did not share. As in Europe, so globally, Mrs Thatcher did not believe that problems could be solved by fixing exchange rates. After preparatory meetings in March, Robert Armstrong reported that the 'sherpas' for the summit, of whom he was one, were working on collective action to get 'a measure of growth', 'promoting greater stability in exchange rates' and strengthening the machinery for international financial co-operation. She put a wiggly line under the point about exchange rates, and wrote, 'This is quite different from the basis on which Alan [Walters] and I are working.' She concluded: 'I do not like the way this is developing. We are not seeking new institutional arrangements or links. We are in danger of becoming committed to something fundamentally unsound just for the sake of saying something in a communiqué.'[47]

Alan Walters himself warned her, from American sources, that 'there is a danger that the President may be induced to agree in general terms to some programme involving some degree of fixity in exchange rates. This he might do in an unthinking way.'[48] The problem was the size of the US deficit, and only Mrs Thatcher, said Walters, had the standing to put this to the President. Geoffrey Howe backed this up: 'The key way may be to point out to the President the gains – economic and political – which have accrued to us from our demonstration, in the 1981 Budget, of our commitment to reduced borrowing.'[49] Shortly before she called the election, Mrs Thatcher met Edwin Meese, Reagan's emissary, to discuss the summit. She pushed hard against making statements at Williamsburg about co-ordinating exchange rates. 'All that we could usefully do', she insisted, 'was try to pursue stable economic policies. That was the way to achieve stable exchange rates.'[50] The two agreed to try to lower expectations of what the summit would say. They also discussed East–West relations. The Americans were now looking for a statement at Williamsburg on INF deployment in the autumn. Mrs Thatcher was cautious. Naturally she wanted a

---

election image, '– much too expensive.' (Armstrong to Thatcher, 20 April 1983, TNA: PREM 19/1007.)

statement, but only 'provided this can be agreed without difficulty with our other summit partners'.[51] If the Europeans fell out on this subject, at this moment, one of her best electoral advantages would collapse.

As the summit grew close, Reagan and Mrs Thatcher became ever more complicit. She continued to worry about leaving Britain in the midst of the election campaign but suggested she might come to Williamsburg on the Saturday. He begged her to stay on into the Monday, instead of leaving on the Sunday night as she now wished, because 'it would be a great help to me'. The President wanted her to outmanoeuvre her own sherpa, Armstrong, who was trying to mediate between the Americans and the French. Reagan sought not mediation, but alliance against the French, who were proposing exchange rate control of the sort devised after the war. He wanted 'a tone of realistic optimism . . . we must resist a call for a new Bretton Woods.'[52] In reply, Mrs Thatcher repeated, with regret, that she must get back to Britain on the Sunday night, but supported Reagan on exchange rates. In her memoirs, she recorded approvingly that, unlike at previous summits, the Americans had insisted that the communiqué, rather than being precooked, should be drawn up in the light of the discussions that actually took place. This was 'far more sensible', she wrote. 'But I took along a British draft just in case it was needed.'[53] This was somewhat disingenuously expressed. The draft *was* precooked, but according to her recipe.

Behind the scenes, the summit was not easy. At dinner on the Saturday night, a few hours after Mrs Thatcher arrived, the leaders debated arms control. Disagreements emerged. These continued in a heated discussion of the draft communiqué among the leaders the following morning. Mrs Thatcher naturally pronounced the draft 'an excellent document',[54] but François Mitterrand, because of France's special position outside the NATO command structure, objected to the declaration's endorsement of NATO policy, though not to that policy's content. Helmut Kohl, on the other hand, argued that the need to issue the statement was 'urgent' in order to counter Soviet claims that 'the deployment of Pershing missiles in Germany would destroy all German hopes of national unity'. The Canadian Prime Minister, Pierre Trudeau,* objected that the statement was sending 'the wrong message, utterly and tragically wrong'. It should not call for deployment by the end of the year, but should offer 'something about mutual trust'.

Mrs Thatcher pointed out that she was fighting, and Kohl had recently fought, a general election on this issue: Trudeau's words were 'utterly devastating and could only give comfort to the Soviet Union'. This would come 'at

---

* Pierre Trudeau (1919–2000), Prime Minister of Canada, 1968–79 and 1980–84; Leader of the Liberal Party of Canada, 1968–84.

a time when it would be particularly embarrassing for those of them who were fighting elections'. With some conciliatory words about how 'very moving' it was to be sitting round the table with former enemies from the Second World War, Reagan urged his fellow leaders to accept the proposed declaration: 'What was wrong with taking the moral high ground against the use of these weapons [Soviet SS-20s]?' There would be 'a barrage of headlines' if they failed to agree, and besides, the strategy would work: 'The Soviet Union were at full economic stretch, and could not afford to increase the resources devoted to defence. The United States and the West could do so, and the Soviet Union knew that they could do so, because they had seen us do it. So, faced with the possibility of an arms race, the Soviet Union would pull back.'[55]

After permitting a few drafting changes to please Mitterrand, which, according to Mrs Thatcher, actually strengthened the statement,[56] Reagan won the day. Mrs Thatcher returned to London well pleased. On economics, the summit had resisted co-ordination mechanisms for economic policy and pushed for lower interest rates. On defence, it had endorsed INF deployment. 'It is practically the policy on one's own manifesto,' she told a press conference in London the day after her return.[57] She was delighted not only by the substance, but by the skill and charm which Reagan had deployed at Williamsburg. 'The President was wonderful,' she told Parkinson. 'He had done his homework.'[58] Reagan was equally pleased. In his letter of thanks to Mrs Thatcher, he wrote: 'Thanks to your contribution during Saturday's dinner discussion of INF, we were able, in our statement, to send the Soviets a clear signal of allied determination and unity.' And he described the Declaration on Economic Recovery as 'a victory for the future. Your government's economic policies have proved the wisdom of the key principles laid out in the declaration.'[59]

On 2 June, a Harris poll put the Conservatives on 46 per cent, Labour on 28 per cent and the Alliance on 24 per cent. When asked why they supported the Tories, 46 per cent of those who did so replied that it was because of Mrs Thatcher's leadership, with only 31 per cent attributing their support to the party's policies.

As the election campaign progressed, Mrs Thatcher was vindicated in her then unfashionable view that the SDP–Liberal Alliance would not prove the political force which her party had feared. The Alliance campaign, with its dual leadership of Roy Jenkins, comically entitled 'Prime Minister-designate', and David Steel* as the Alliance leader, was unhappy.

---

* David Steel (1938–), educated Prince of Wales School, Nairobi, Kenya, George Watson's College, Edinburgh and Edinburgh University; Liberal MP for Roxburgh, Selkirk and

Jenkins, who, according to his colleague and rival David Owen,* made the mistake of seeing Mrs Thatcher as 'an aberration',[60] rather than a radical and transformative political phenomenon, was diffuse in his speeches and slow in his electoral reactions. There was plenty of public goodwill for the Jenkins and Steel combination, but the Alliance showed little sense of direction. Jenkins had declared that they would not 'play a fuddled fiddle somewhere in the muddled middle', but this phrase seemed an accurate enough reflection of the style of the Alliance campaign for Cecil Parkinson to throw it gleefully back at him at every opportunity. While Mrs Thatcher was in Williamsburg, the Alliance leadership called a summit at Steel's home at Ettrick Bridge in the Scottish Borders, and agreed to sideline Jenkins for the last ten days of the campaign. It was an admission of weakness.

This, combined with Williamsburg and the travails of Labour, caused Mrs Thatcher to put aside some of her habitual caution.† Arriving at Manchester airport on 1 June, she approached a small boy riding in a 10-pence-a-ride miniature aeroplane. According to the *Manchester Evening News*, she announced: ' "My name's Margaret Thatcher and I live in a big house called 10 Downing Street. I'm going to live there for a long time." The bemused tot hid in the tiny cockpit.'[61] She could see her rivals floundering. On television two days later, she broke her normal rule of not referring to the Alliance at all, and enunciated her theory about British political parties. Dismissing the SDP as people 'who . . . hadn't the guts to stay within the Labour Party',[62] she explained that 'the Labour Party will never die.' Its problem was that it had become 'state socialist' instead of being, as she said it once had been, the party of 'fraternity' and the 'voluntary spirit'. The Liberals were just a 'miscellaneous mishmash in the middle'. She predicted – a prophecy which served her electoral turn, of course – that Labour would hold on in its strongholds and the Alliance

---

Peebles, 1965–83; for Tweeddale, Ettrick and Lauderdale, 1983–97 (Liberal, 1983–8; Liberal Democrat, 1988–97); Liberal Chief Whip, 1970–75; Leader of Liberal Party, 1976–88; co-founder Social and Liberal Democrats, 1988; knighted, 1990 (KT, 2004); created Lord Steel of Aikwood, 1997.

* David Owen (1938–), educated Bradfield and Sidney Sussex College, Cambridge; Labour MP for Plymouth Sutton, 1966–74; for Plymouth Devonport, 1974–81; SDP MP for Plymouth Devonport, 1981–92; Foreign Secretary, 1977–9; Leader, SDP, 1983–7; created Lord Owen, 1992.

† Even so, Mrs Thatcher was reluctant to finalize plans for her likely return to Downing Street for a second term. 'Let's not count chickens,' she scribbled on a note from Bernard Ingham and Robin Butler outlining media planning for 10 June. 'We can always make arrangements quickly.' (Thatcher annotations on Ingham to Thatcher, 2 June 1983, CAC: THCR 5/1/1E/42.)

would come third. 'If you want a good Opposition,' she went on, 'you've got to reform the Labour Party, as Gaitskell [the Labour Leader until his death in 1963] was trying [to do].'[63] At the time, most commentators thought that Labour was all but finished. But Mrs Thatcher took a longer view, one which was eventually adopted by a young man who was first elected to Parliament in the 1983 general election, Tony Blair.*

There were now no serious dangers for the Conservative campaign. Mrs Thatcher felt sufficiently confident to spare the party's coffers by ordering Cecil Parkinson to cancel the three-page newspaper advertisements designed by Saatchi and Saatchi to run on the last Sunday of the campaign. These would have devoted a page to Conservative policies, a page to Labour ones (sticking to their belief that they had only to repeat Labour policies to gain votes for the Tories), and an almost blank page for the policies of the Alliance. She felt that it was unnecessary to give the Alliance extra publicity by attacking it and that the £1.5 million cost of the advertisements was too great, but it is clear from the diaries of the party's Vice-Chairman Michael Spicer that Mrs Thatcher made Spicer pass on her command to Parkinson, who was reluctant to quarrel with Saatchis and Tim Bell on the point.[64]† The only embarrassment of the last days of the campaign occurred at the Conservative Youth Rally at Wembley on Sunday 5 June. Mrs Thatcher's speech, a surprisingly high-falutin' oration for such a gathering, quoting Pericles and Kipling, and praising Elizabethan merchant adventurers, passed off without incident, but the comedian Kenny Everett treated the crowds to jokes like 'Let's bomb Russia' and 'Let's kick Michael Foot's stick away.' There was widespread disapproval. In her memoirs – as at the time – Mrs Thatcher sought to downplay this: 'Some of the sourer critics chose to take offence,' she wrote,[65] but she did not repeat any of the tasteless jokes.

It has become a historical orthodoxy that Mrs Thatcher dominated the election campaign of 1983. This is true, in the sense that her personality, energy and record were the focus of attention, but it is not correct to say that 'The Tory campaign was frankly concentrated on Mrs Thatcher.'[66]

* Anthony ('Tony') Blair (1953–), educated Durham Chorister School, Fettes College, Edinburgh and St John's College, Oxford; Labour MP for Sedgefield, 1983–June 2007; Leader of the Opposition, 1994–7; Prime Minister, 1997–2007; Leader of the Labour Party, 1994–2007.
† In his memoirs, Parkinson said that it was his initiative to cancel the Sunday advertisements (Cecil Parkinson, *Right at the Centre*, Weidenfeld & Nicolson, 1992, p. 232). In any event, Tim Bell was upset. Parkinson was, in turn, concerned for Bell because he believed Bell was suffering from a drug problem: 'On one occasion, we were at a meeting of donors in Central Office and Tim suddenly rushed from the corner into the middle of the room. He thought the walls were closing in on him' (Interview with Lord Parkinson).

Most of the party posters did not feature her, and there was always anxiety that she might put off as many floating voters as she might attract. It was only in the last party political broadcast of the campaign, two days before polling, that she was put at the centre of her own party's propaganda. By this stage, consistently strong polls had stilled the earlier fears about the negative electoral effects of too much Thatcher. The broadcast spoke of the things achieved 'because of one woman' and contained interviews with people praising her. Then the woman herself appeared in a grey-blue suit against a background of roses, offering 'the certainty of liberty' and 'the chance of property ownership'. Everything that mattered, she went on, depended on the nation being properly defended. Voters should ask themselves 'who would best defend our freedom, our way of life, and the much loved land in which we live'.[67]

Amid the steady success of the Conservative campaign, a few people noticed something which the public did not. Interviewing Cecil Parkinson on 27 May 1983, David Butler noted, the day after seeing him, 'I thought he was in a slightly hysterical state . . . and showed extraordinary anxiety for someone who was 15 per cent ahead in the polls . . . I think I was seeing a man under great strain, though why he should have been under such strain I can't imagine.'[68] At Saatchi and Saatchi, where election posters were being devised, 'we were puzzled that what seemed to us a perfectly good piece of work kept being rejected by Central Office,' recalled Jeremy Sinclair, then Saatchis' chairman.[69] It showed a newborn baby held by a midwife, and boasted of the government's increase in the number of nurses and midwives under the slogan: 'Even labour's better under the Conservatives'.

The explanation was tragi-comic. On the day before polling day, after the last press conference of the campaign, Mrs Thatcher, now confident of victory, turned gratefully to Parkinson and said, 'Come to tea tomorrow at No. 10 and tell me what you want.'[70] By this she meant that he could name the Cabinet job he would like. He went as commanded. 'I'd thought of Foreign Secretary,'[71] she told him. 'Foreign Secretary for two or three years, then Chancellor; then it's up to you.' Plucking up the courage to tell her something which he had withheld during the campaign, Parkinson said, 'I'm afraid I've got a very big personal problem.' He had made his former secretary, Sara Keays, pregnant (she had left his employment in 1979).* Mrs Thatcher reacted in a way which surprised him: 'What's that

---

* In her memoirs, Mrs Thatcher records this meeting with Parkinson, but notes that she learnt of the pregnancy in a letter from Sara Keays's father, Colonel Hastings Keays, which she saw only on the day after polling day (*The Downing Street Years*, HarperCollins, 1993,

Mrs Thatcher scribbles out her early thoughts on the post-election reshuffle. She soon learnt that her desire to make Cecil Parkinson foreign secretary was a political impossibility.

got to do with anything?' she asked. 'They tell me Anthony Eden [Prime Minister at the time of the Suez disaster of 1956] leapt into bed with any good-looking woman. You can sort this out.' 'Not with two Special Branch men next to me all the time,' said Parkinson, referring to the protection he would receive if he became Foreign Secretary. Mrs Thatcher continued to look at the matter realistically. 'If the successful party Chairman isn't in government,' she said, 'everyone will be asking why.'[72] The solution, they decided, was that Parkinson should become head of a new department which would combine the existing ministries of Trade and of

---

p. 310). This cannot be the case. Parkinson, who had better reason to recall the course of events than Mrs Thatcher, insisted that he told Mrs Thatcher about the pregnancy on polling day (Interview with Lord Parkinson): if he had not done so, why would he have mentioned his affair to her at all? In his letter, Colonel Keays complained of Parkinson's behaviour and said that the matter would very likely become public. This obviously raised the sense of political danger in Mrs Thatcher's mind. A draft response from Mrs Thatcher suggests that it was arranged that Colonel Keays should speak 'to the person concerned' (that is, Parkinson), presumably to calm things down, and that she returned his letter to him (Thatcher to Colonel Hastings Keays, 12 June 1983, CAC: THCR 2/5/1 (http://www.margaretthatcher. org/document/132255)).

Industry. The job was important, but did not have such a high profile. They did not discuss what would happen about Miss Keays's pregnancy.

As usual, Mrs Thatcher spent election night at the count in her Finchley constituency. Although the earliest returns suggested a good result for the Alliance and made the Tories nervous – they lost Yeovil* to the future Liberal leader, Paddy Ashdown – it soon became clear, once the Conservatives had gained Nuneaton from Labour, that the night was theirs. Her own result, in which her majority increased to 9,314, was:

Mrs M. Thatcher (Conservative)	19,616
L. Spigel (Labour)	10,302
M. Joachim (SDP–Liberal Alliance)	7,763
(Eight minor party candidates)	736

The Conservative national vote had, in fact, fallen by nearly 700,000 to 13,012,316, but the Labour vote had collapsed from 11.5 million in 1979 to 8,456,934. Voters had deserted Labour in droves in favour of the Alliance. In 1979, the Liberal Party had received 4,313,811 votes. In 1983, the Alliance received 7,780,949 votes. It had 25.4 per cent of the total vote. Labour had only 27.6 per cent. The Conservatives had 42.4 per cent, compared with 43.9 per cent in 1979. They won 397 seats, Labour 209 and the Alliance 23. The Tories had an overall majority of 144, the largest for either party since the Labour landslide of 1945.

There were scenes of jubilation in Central Office and Mrs Thatcher, arriving there shortly before four in the morning, got Cecil Parkinson to join her at the window to acknowledge the cheers in Smith Square. She said little publicly during the evening, beyond declaring her 'very great sense of responsibility and humility'.[73] One witness to that night was the long-serving Peter Cropper, the head of the Research Department. For him at least, the moment of victory was ambiguous: 'She really did start walking on water. It was wonderful in a way. But the triumphalism horrified me.'[74]

* The Conservatives did not recover this seat until the general election of 2015.

4
Jobs for her boys

*'To write the concerns and views of your
Government into the grammar book of politics'*

After her landslide victory on 9 June 1983, Mrs Thatcher received a note setting out the statistical and historical scale of her triumph. Her private office informed her that, in the twentieth century, she was the first leader of any party to serve a full term and then increase her majority, and the first Conservative Prime Minister to win two elections in a row.[1]* The increase in the government's majority was the greatest in parliamentary history and the Labour share of the vote was the smallest since the party had begun to contest every seat. The margin of votes by which she had won (over 4.5 million) was the greatest since 1931.

Only two years earlier, until victory in the Falklands, most people, including most at the top of her party, had believed that she could not win another election. Now her enemies – outside her party and within it – lay prostrate before her. The leaders of the Labour Party and of the SDP, Michael Foot and Roy Jenkins, announced their resignations and the Liberal leader, David Steel, retreated to Ettrick Bridge for several weeks in a state of near-collapse. Robin Butler, who remained her principal private secretary, recalled that, faced with this vacuum, 'It was not so clear what she was supposed to do.'[2] Mrs Thatcher herself – safely back in, rather than starting the job for the first time – did not pause to reflect on the overall situation which she now enjoyed. 'She had no list of three main things to do.'[3] She was simply relieved, and, as always, eager to get on with her work. She does not seem to have analysed the political consequences of her own triumph. The scale of her success was a problem in itself, as Bernard Ingham, writing to her before the result, warned it would

---

* The last time the Conservatives had increased their majority was in 1959, when Mrs Thatcher was first elected to Parliament. 'I imagine that you must have felt much as I do after your great triumph in 1959,' she wrote to Harold Macmillan. 'There is so much to do.' (Thatcher to Macmillan, 17 June 1983, CAC: THCR 2/4/1/19 (http://www.margaretthatcher.org/document/131137).)

<u>Post Election Psychology</u>

   After this rather dirty election the public will be looking for a
rest from it all. The bigger your majority the more they will expect
magnanimity from you. You will be able to afford to be generous, subject
to certain provisos.

   The honeymoon will be shorter this time. At most it will run to
Christmas.

   Longer term, what you will have to cope with is the boredom factor.
It will be necessary to generate your own excitement as a Prime Minister
and an Administration.

   Nor should you under-estimate the British capacity to reject success.
The more successful you are - ie. the bigger your majority - the more
the media will seek to bring you down to earth and humble you.

<u>Stance</u>

   In the light of all this, it is important you underplay your success,
make no rash promises, send everyone on holiday on a note of re-assurance,
play down expectations and prepare people for a quiet life.

   That is what the Speaking note at Annex I seeks to do.

B. INGHAM
7 June 1983

Mrs Thatcher carefully annotated Ingham's advice warning her not to overplay her electoral success.

be: she should not 'under-estimate the British capacity to reject success' but rather 'play down expectations and prepare people for a quiet life'.[4]

Stephen Sherbourne, appointed at Cecil Parkinson's request to revive Mrs Thatcher's political office in Downing Street, recalled the atmosphere as he entered No. 10 to take up his new post: 'It was as if I was in a very well-run country house and the couple had gone away for a three-week cruise, and everything was working just as before. The whole machine was ticking over and the whole machine was expecting them back.'[5] The usually restless chatelaine was 'very comfortable with everybody and everything'. 'There was no discussion about what we were going to do,' Sherbourne added. 'It was just straight down to business.' Unlike in 1979, Mrs Thatcher had no new surroundings with which to familiarize herself; she was happy with her able and mostly, by this time, quite long-serving private secretaries and personal staff. She treated them all as 'part of the family',[6] fussing over them in what her diary secretary Caroline Ryder called 'her Jewish-mother style'.[7]

One of the first jobs for Mrs Thatcher was to reshuffle her Cabinet, a job she disliked. 'I'm not a good butcher,' she told the BBC's Robin Day, 'but have had to learn to carve the joint,' implying that this traditionally male role was not to her taste.[8] At last, however, Mrs Thatcher was able to forge a Cabinet more or less as she wanted it, rather than as she reluctantly acknowledged it had to be. The most important change was to make Nigel Lawson, the greatest exponent of her free-market philosophy, Chancellor of the Exchequer. This was a bold move which she might not have risked with a small majority: the 'establishment' candidate was Patrick Jenkin, then Industry Secretary. Jenkin had been a 'very good lawyer', and was sound on economics ('not real right but centre-right'), but this was not what she was looking for at the Treasury.[9] Lawson, by contrast, 'had a creative mind, he was imaginative', she thought.[10] And after years of struggle, it did feel as if the economic doctrines of Thatcherism – tax cuts, privatization, deregulation and tax reform, as well as strong monetary controls – having been tested in adversity, could now be boldly applied in what was beginning to look like prosperity. Alan Walters went so far, in private, as to suggest that the pound might now start to replace the dollar and the Swiss franc as a world currency.[11] This was comically hubristic, but it showed how much confidence, and with it the sense of possibility, had grown.

It was, noted her Treasury private secretary Michael Scholar, as he liaised between Mrs Thatcher and her new Chancellor, 'a very sweet time for both of them'.[12] Early in this glad, confident morning, Scholar was summoned to Chequers. Mrs Thatcher needed to discuss public spending cuts with Lawson and had decided the issue would be best tackled in the relaxed setting of her country retreat. Scholar was supposed to be with her in advance of Lawson's arrival, but his car would not start and then he got lost in Slough en route. He arrived forty minutes after Lawson, cursing himself and fearing the wrath of his boss: 'I felt desperate, but they were sitting there wreathed in smiles.'[13] 'Don't worry, Michael,' Mrs Thatcher told him, 'Nigel and I have fixed the whole thing – it's all done.' It was evident that they felt 'very pleased with one another'.

Mrs Thatcher was able to build most of the rest of her Cabinet as she – though not always they – wanted it. When John Wakeham,* whom she saw

* John Wakeham (1932–), educated Charterhouse; Conservative MP for Maldon, February 1974–83; for Colchester South and Maldon, 1983–92; Government Chief Whip, 1983–7; Lord Privy Seal, 1987–8; Leader of the House of Commons, 1987–9; Lord President of the

as 'another of my boys',[14] became her new chief whip, he was summoned to discuss the reshuffle. His arrival coincided with the Sovereign's Birthday Parade, so it was only after bands had tootled and regiments had marched below the windows, a display followed by the traditional lunch for Commonwealth high commissioners, that he sat down with her. Instead of discussing the matter, she simply handed him a complete list of her proposed Cabinet which she had already worked out with Willie Whitelaw, Cecil Parkinson and her outgoing Chief Whip, Michael Jopling, whom she now made minister of agriculture. Reluctantly she had accepted that Cecil Parkinson could not become Foreign Secretary owing to the expected birth of his extramarital baby (see Chapter 3). Instead, she followed his suggestion of amalgamating two government departments, and put him in the post he had invented, making him secretary of state for trade and industry. This left Lord Cockfield* and Patrick Jenkin without jobs. Jenkin she sent to Environment, which Mrs Thatcher considered to be 'a really big job' because of plans to press ahead with the abolition of the Greater London Council;[15] Cockfield she kept in the Cabinet as Chancellor of the Duchy of Lancaster and a supernumerary adviser on tax and trade. Parkinson's elevation upset Norman Tebbit, who had been wanting to move on from Employment and hoping for a version of this job.[16] Mrs Thatcher intended it as no insult to Tebbit, however. She agreed with the reshuffle advice from David Wolfson, the unpaid chief of staff to her political office, that 'The crucial battle over the next 5 years will be with the Unions,'[17] and that Tebbit was the best person to fight it. But Tebbit was irritated that his old friend Parkinson was ahead of him.† His lack of promotion marked the beginning of increasingly fractious relations between Mrs Thatcher and her toughest public defender.

Francis Pym, originally appointed Foreign Secretary for the sake of party unity in the wake of the Falklands invasion, was the major casualty of the reshuffle. He had sealed his fate during the election campaign with his gloomy warning of the dangers of a landslide majority. It was a mark

---

Council, 1988–9; Secretary of State for Energy, 1989–92; Minister responsible for co-ordinating development of presentation of government policies, 1990–92; Lord Privy Seal and Leader of the House of Lords, 1992–4; chairman, Royal Commission on Reform of House of Lords, 1999; of Press Complaints Commission, 1995–2002; created Lord Wakeham, 1992.

* Arthur Cockfield (1916–2007), educated Dover Grammar School and LSE; Minister of State, Treasury, 1979–82; Secretary of State for Trade, 1982–3; Chancellor of the Duchy of Lancaster, 1983–4; Vice-President, European Commission, 1985–8; knighted, 1973; created Lord Cockfield, 1978.

† The Tebbit–Parkinson relationship went back to their days together as young Conservative activists in Hemel Hempstead in the early 1960s. As upwardly mobile, ambitious young men, they felt rivalry as well as friendship.

of how power had shifted that his dismissal did not present Mrs Thatcher
with a serious political problem. She removed him altogether from the
government, without regret ('He was soft'), but with a slight sense of
guilt.[18] By way of compensation, she hoped to engineer the Speakership
of the Commons for him: 'with a history like his in the family' (his ances-
tor, John Pym, had been one of the 'Five Members' who had resisted the
power of King Charles I), she believed he would welcome the chance.[19]
Without disclosing her intentions about Pym, she had already asked
Jopling to tell Jack Weatherill,* the most likely candidate to succeed
George Thomas as Speaker, that she would prefer it if he did not stand.
Jopling had pleaded with her that this was an impossible request since the
choice rested with MPs, not with her. She had insisted that he make it
regardless. Weatherill, as predicted, had said 'Go jump in the lake.'[20] She
was attempting something which she had in the past wisely left to others –
the management of the House of Commons.

Pym was naturally angry about being sacked as Foreign Secretary and
'absolutely refused'[21] her offer of the Speakership, on the correct grounds
that it was not hers to offer.[22] He said he preferred the freedom of the back
benches, which was exactly what she did not want him to have. He quickly
became a focus for discontented Tory MPs. In his stead, Mrs Thatcher
appointed Geoffrey Howe, whom, before she learnt of Parkinson's affair,
she had pencilled in for the Home Office. The Foreign Office was what
Howe wanted. With what she saw as his preference for negotiation and
discussion (the Foreign Office's 'two stars in the firmament')[23] over making
decisions, he was well suited to it. At the time, however, she seems not to
have foreseen any differences with Howe in their European outlook. He
was greatly respected by colleagues because of how, as Chancellor, he had
borne and overcome the economic difficulties of the early years.

In relation to Willie Whitelaw, Mrs Thatcher faced a delicate situation.
She wanted to remove him from the Home Office, where she felt he had
'not been the most overwhelming success'.[24] He and she had differed over
crime and punishment, especially capital punishment, which he opposed
and she always supported. On the other hand, she regarded him as 'quite
simply, indispensable to me in Cabinet'[25] because 'When it really mattered
I knew he would be by my side and because of his background, personality
and position in the party he could sometimes sway colleagues when I could

* Bernard ('Jack') Weatherill (1920–2007), educated Malvern; tailor; Conservative MP for
Croydon North East, 1964–92; Deputy Government Chief Whip, 1973–4; Deputy Oppos-
ition Chief Whip, 1974–9; Speaker of the House of Commons, 1983–92; created Lord
Weatherill, 1992.

not.'[26] She wanted to retain him as her Cabinet fixer and elder statesman, by 'kicking him upstairs' to be Leader of the House of Lords. Perhaps aware that Whitelaw would not be pleased, she took a cowardly way out and got Jopling to ring him. Contrary to what he later told colleagues, Whitelaw had not expected this turn of events and was indeed 'very, very disgruntled'.[27] He said to Jopling that he feared a bad result in the by-election in his constituency that his elevation would cause. Besides, he wanted to stay in the House of Commons.

Using the well-tried technique of piling honours and flattery upon those whom she was dropping, Mrs Thatcher consoled Whitelaw by reviving the dormant right to create hereditary peers. She made him a viscount.* This readiness to put the clock back was evidence of the romantic, high Tory streak in her nature. She also emphasized more strongly than in the past that Whitelaw was deputy prime minister, an office 'unknown to the constitution' but useful in establishing hierarchy.† He accepted, without further complaint. The consequence of Whitelaw's move was that he had more time to assist Mrs Thatcher in the management of the Cabinet, but much less knowledge of what was going on in the Commons. To effect the change she desired, Mrs Thatcher had to jettison the existing Leader of the Lords, Lady Young, whom she liked but regarded as far too cautious. She persuaded her ('By God she was difficult')[28] to become minister of state at the Foreign Office. Characteristically, Mrs Thatcher seems to have been unworried that she was removing the only woman in the Cabinet apart from herself. There would never be another, so long as she was prime minister.

The new Home Secretary was Leon Brittan, promoted from the relatively junior Cabinet post of chief secretary to the Treasury, where Mrs Thatcher had considered him a great success. His proved the most controversial of her appointments. Being one of the three 'great offices of state', the Home Office was traditionally filled by a senior politician of independent standing. Brittan was not such a man, but an extremely able barrister who had risen, it was widely considered, as a creature of Mrs Thatcher. This was an unfair view, not least because, with his strongly pro-European opinions and liberal social views, Brittan was a Thatcherite only in strictly economic matters. He was a member of the so-called

* The hereditary honour had no practical consequences, since all Whitelaw's children were girls and therefore could not inherit his title.
† In the UK, unless there is a coalition government, the title of 'Deputy Prime Minister' is given to a Cabinet minister as recognition of seniority in the governing party. It is not unusual for the position to be vacant. There are no required official duties, and no automatic rights of succession associated with the role.

'Cambridge mafia' who had been at the university together in the late
1950s and early 1960s. Other mafiosi included Norman Fowler,* Kenneth
Clarke,† John Selwyn Gummer‡ and Norman Lamont,§ most of them on
the left of the party. These men owed their political careers to Mrs
Thatcher, although they were not necessarily Thatcherites. Contained in
the adverse reaction to Brittan's appointment was a submerged element of
anti-Semitism: the belief that it was all very well for Jews to take 'clever'
ministries to do with money, but in matters of law and order the Tory
Party tended to prefer someone 'more English'. Peter Rees, who replaced
Brittan as chief secretary, and subsequently fell out with Mrs Thatcher,
alleged to the present author that she had a 'freemasonry' of Jews in her
Cabinet – Brittan, Keith Joseph (who stayed on at Education) and Lawson.[29] Harold Macmillan made the same point more obliquely when, in
1986,[30] he privately joked that there were now 'more Estonians than Eton-
ians' in the Cabinet. Mrs Thatcher certainly had no thought of creating
a defined Jewish group among her ministers, and anyway Brittan and
Lawson were not close; but her sympathy with Jews was part of her
anti-establishment instincts and her belief that conservatism was a creed
of opportunity. She did, however, later come to accept the view that she
had promoted Brittan too fast. 'If I had my time again,' she recalled, 'I
would know that people who are excellent lawyers, excellent at taking a

---

* Norman Fowler (1938–), educated King Edward VI School, Chelmsford and Trinity Hall,
Cambridge; Conservative MP for Nottingham South, 1970–74; for Sutton Coldfield, February 1974–2001; Minister of Transport, 1979–81; Secretary of State for Social Services,
1981–7; for Employment, 1987–90; Chairman, Conservative Party, 1992–4; created Lord
Fowler, 2001.
† Kenneth Clarke (1940–), educated Nottingham High School and Gonville and Caius Col-
lege, Cambridge; Conservative MP for Rushcliffe, 1970–; Minister of State, Department of
Health and Social Security, 1982–5; Paymaster-General and Minister for Employment,
1985–7; Chancellor of the Duchy of Lancaster and Minister for Trade and Industry, 1987–8;
Secretary of State for Health, 1988–90; for Education and Science, 1990–92; for Home
Department, 1992–3; Chancellor of the Exchequer, 1993–7; Lord Chancellor and Secretary
of State for Justice, 2010–12; Minister of State (Minister without Portfolio), 2012–14. Holding his first government job (a junior whip) in 1972, and leaving his last in 2014, Clarke was
the longest-serving elected government minister of modern times.
‡ John Selwyn Gummer (1939–), educated King's School, Rochester and Selwyn College,
Cambridge; Conservative MP for Lewisham West, 1970–February 1974; for Eye, Suffolk,
1979–83; for Suffolk Coastal, 1983–2010; Chairman, Conservative Party, 1983–5; Secretary
of State for the Environment, 1993–7; created Lord Deben, 2010.
§ Norman Lamont (1942–), educated Loretto School and Fitzwilliam College, Cambridge;
Conservative MP for Kingston-upon-Thames, 1972–97; Financial Secretary to the Treasury,
1986–9; Chief Secretary to the Treasury, 1989–90; Chancellor of the Exchequer, 1990–93;
created Lord Lamont of Lerwick, 1998.

brief, aren't much good at ... deciding a line to take.'[31] She did not acknowledge, for these purposes, that she was a lawyer herself.

Among the Cabinet ministers who fairly fundamentally disagreed with Mrs Thatcher's whole approach and had dominated her first Cabinet in 1979, only three survived – Michael Heseltine, who remained at Defence after fighting unilateral disarmament successfully during the election campaign, Jim Prior, now clearly in the autumn of his career, who stayed on in Northern Ireland, and Peter Walker, whom she promoted from Agriculture to Energy, in the expectation that he would have to deal with coming confrontations in the coal industry. She respected Walker's talents. Besides, 'I didn't frankly want to take Peter Walker out of the Cabinet because he would have been a deadly enemy on the backbenches.'[32]

As usual, finalizing changes in the junior ranks took a bit longer. Alan Clark,* longing for his first government job, became impatient. On Monday 13 June, he wrote in his diary, 'I had been getting more and more irritable all day as the "junior" appointments were leaking out on to the TV screens.'[33] At last, his wife Jane came across the lawn at Saltwood Castle, which he was mowing, to tell him that Ian Gow was on the telephone. Clark, Gow revealed, was to become parliamentary under-secretary of state at the Department of Employment, a position of great unimportance. Unknown to Clark, his appointment had come about in a strange way. He had written and photocopied a letter to Mrs Thatcher saying that he was running what (in his diary though not in his letter to her) he called a 'Shadow Cabinet' to keep her government up to the mark with right-wing policies. He seems not to have sent the letter, but he had carelessly left a copy in a Commons copier; someone found it and brought it to John Wakeham.

Wakeham showed it to Mrs Thatcher. 'Oh dear,' she said, 'I'll speak to him.' 'No!' exclaimed Wakeham. 'That would be dangerous. Make him a minister.' Mrs Thatcher, who had a soft spot for Clark, agreed. Wakeham encountered a uniform resistance to Clark among Cabinet ministers, however, and it took a long time to find a taker. This was Norman Tebbit, who accepted on the grounds that 'I don't really mind who my junior ministers are, so long as they keep out of my hair.'[34] Thus did the era's

---

* Alan Clark (1928–99), educated Eton and Christ Church, Oxford; Conservative MP for Plymouth, Sutton, February 1974–92; for Kensington and Chelsea, 1997–9; Parliamentary Under-Secretary of State, Department of Employment, 1983–6; Minister for Trade, 1986–9; Minister of State, MOD, 1989–92. Three volumes of his diaries have been published. The first, originally called *Diaries*, but subsequently subtitled *In Power 1983–1992*, came out during his lifetime (1993); the second and third were published posthumously, subtitled *Into Politics*, covering the period 1972–82 (2000) and *The Last Diaries*, covering the period 1993–9 (2002).

most celebrated political diarist start work for the woman he always referred to as 'the Lady'.

Despite his new office, Clark still gave his 'Shadow Cabinet' lunch a few days later. The theme for discussion was 'What the Government Should be Doing with Its Huge New Mandate'.[35] He noted how reserved his colleagues were in talking about the 'broad canvas': 'I fear that we all still suffer from a lack of confidence. Very deep-seated it is, running back as far, perhaps, as before the war and those Admiralty memoranda saying we couldn't even take on the Italian Fleet in the Mediterranean. So when we win something we can barely believe our eyes. There is no follow-through.' This was a good summation of traditional male Tory psychology, a state of mind which Mrs Thatcher never shared and always fought.

Although Ian Gow had rung his friend Clark about his new job, he was not, strictly speaking, the person to do so. His role had already changed. After his four extraordinarily successful years as Mrs Thatcher's parliamentary private secretary (PPS), she had promoted Gow to be minister of housing. Although she does not appear to have worried at the time, Gow's departure from her side did serious damage. No one understood her better, was more devoted to her or knew more about human frailty as exhibited by Conservative MPs. For the whole of the first term, Gow had worked from 7 a.m. in the office till late into the night in the Smoking Room 'with the wine flowing',[36] tirelessly absorbing the grumbles of backbenchers and then reporting to Mrs Thatcher and advising how best to handle them. He had advanced her causes, and protected her from her own innocence about the motivations of colleagues. He had also, because of his old friendship with Geoffrey Howe – the two men liked to smoke together and chat – helped keep relations between Mrs Thatcher and her Chancellor in tolerable repair. With Gow absent, and Howe translated to the more distant role of Foreign Secretary, there was no one to prevent the two drifting apart.

Gow's successor as the Prime Minister's PPS was Michael Alison.* He seems to have been appointed for the kindly but not well-thought-out reason that he had given conscientious service as a junior minister but was not now being offered another ministerial job, so had better have something else. Except for the fact that both Alison and Gow were utterly loyal to Mrs Thatcher, their characters could scarcely have been more different. Brought up in a rich, dysfunctional and somewhat bohemian family (his

---

* Michael Alison (1926–2004), educated Eton and Wadham College, Oxford; Conservative MP for Barkston Ash, 1964–83; for Selby, 1983–97; Minister of State, NIO, 1979–81; Department of Employment, 1981–3; PPS to the Prime Minister, 1983–7.

sister Barley was one of the many illicit girlfriends of Roy Jenkins), Alison had been converted to evangelical Christianity at Oxford and had adhered to it earnestly ever since. As Edward Boyle, Mrs Thatcher's Oxford friend and her predecessor as Conservative education secretary, put it, he was 'the last person on earth for whom the word "Protestant" is a trumpet call'.[37] While universally liked and respected, Alison was, in the view of Stephen Sherbourne, who shared an office with him, 'not that interested in politics' and therefore 'not really suited to the job'.[38] So godly was he that there were moments, sometimes during preparations for Prime Minister's Questions, when he absented himself without explanation and slipped off to prayer meetings from which he could not be fished out.[39]

Alison was undoubtedly a comfort to Mrs Thatcher. All secrets were safe with him. She trusted him, and benefited from his calm kindness. She was also interested in the religious perspective he brought to public affairs, and sought his advice on Church-and-state and moral issues and on Church appointments. He would receive and reassure the many people who wanted to see her about such matters ('I gave him Mary Whitehouse,'* Stephen Sherbourne recalled).[40] In his own prayers, Alison would seek divine guidance about which passages of Scripture would be most suitable for the Prime Minister. He would then read them to her on long car journeys, as well as improving books such as *The Screwtape Letters* by C. S. Lewis. He regarded Mrs Thatcher as 'the most religious Prime Minister since Gladstone' and, in the view of his daughter Rosie, served her almost like a private priest.[41] This gave her solace, and did something to mitigate the atmosphere of intrigue which tends to surround the 'court' of any prime minister.

But in terms of party-political management, Alison was almost useless. On one occasion, Matthew Parris† came to see her on behalf of Tory MPs like himself who wanted her to take gay rights more seriously. Since he was now leaving the House, he plucked up the courage to tell her that he was himself homosexual. Mrs Thatcher's only reaction, Parris recalled in his memoirs, was to say 'There, dear . . . That must have been very hard to say.'[42] Parris complained that, as he left the room, the 'cold, churchy' Alison asked him for the names of the other MPs for whom he spoke.

---

* Mary Whitehouse (1910–2001), educated Chester City Grammar School and Cheshire County Training College; freelance journalist and broadcaster; co-founder 'Clean Up TV Campaign', 1964; honorary general secretary, National Viewers' and Listeners' Association, 1965–80; president, 1980–93. Her autobiography, *Quite Contrary*, was published in 1993.
† Matthew Parris (1949–), educated Waterford School, Swaziland and Clare College, Cambridge; Conservative MP for West Derbyshire, 1979–86; presenter, *Weekend World*, 1986–8; author, columnist for *The Times*, 1987–.

Being a politician, Parris naturally assumed that Alison wanted the information to use against the men later. In fact, Alison told his secretary at the time, he had asked for the names so that he could pray for them.[43] He was too good for the world in which his job forced him to move.

As Mrs Thatcher's connection with opinion in Parliament and party now weakened, so the role of No. 10 in the direction of policy grew. Alan Walters, now knighted for his services to Thatcherism, left after a few months to take up an academic position in Washington, but he agreed to maintain an advisory role at a distance. As had been foreshadowed before the election by her anger about the CPRS leak, Mrs Thatcher was now determined to change the whole system of policy advice so that it could serve her more directly. In 1982, as we have seen (Chapter 2), she had strongly contemplated abolishing the CPRS but John Sparrow, whom she had just appointed to run it, persuaded her to think again. In April 1983, therefore, he had been startled by her writing 'No further long-term work of any kind from now on'[44] on a memo he sent her proudly setting out the CPRS's new work programme. Once the election was out of the way, she told Sparrow that she wanted the CPRS wound up after all. This was a 'shock' to him.[45] In his view, it was a mistake for her to want policy advice channelled to her alone rather than to the Cabinet in general; but this was certainly her purpose. She at last felt strong enough to close the Think Tank down and empower and expand her own Policy Unit. She told her new Cabinet that it was 'Better for work to be done under political control'.[46]

Ferdinand Mount, who ran the unit, naturally disagreed with Sparrow's view. In government, he believed, you could only inch forward in the right direction, and the best way for the Prime Minister to do this was through a policy unit which could be mandated only by her. It could 'tell her how badly some things worked in government (which no one else does)' and get close to important departments in order to make sure her ideas and wishes provided 'a course of injections into the Whitehall bloodstream'.[47]* The unit, which already contained John Redwood, now duly expanded, with additions in the course of the coming months which included Oliver Letwin from Keith Joseph's office, David Willetts† from

---

* For an entertaining account of the Policy Unit in Mount's time, see his memoir *Cold Cream: My Early Life and Other Mistakes*, Bloomsbury, 2008.

† David Willetts (1956–), educated King Edward's School, Birmingham and Christ Church, Oxford; No. 10 Policy Unit, 1984–6; director of studies, Centre for Policy Studies, 1987–92; Conservative MP for Havant, 1992–2015; parliamentary secretary, Office of Public Service, Cabinet Office, 1995–6; Paymaster-General, 1996; Shadow Secretary of State for Education

the Civil Service (where he had earlier been Nigel Lawson's private secretary), Bob Young* and David Pascall† from the Think Tank and Peter Warry‡ direct from industry. The Policy Unit, which had been growing in strength since its uncertain beginnings, now became central to the projection of Mrs Thatcher's will throughout government, particularly in all economic and industrial questions not led by the Treasury.

This was to have two consequences. The first was that ministers would sometimes become extremely annoyed at what they saw as *lèse-majesté*. Many stories are told, for example, of Norman Tebbit's rage when he felt that Mrs Thatcher was being influenced by Policy Unit advisers trespassing on his ministerial patch. By his own account, he was so infuriated to find her quoting against him from a unit briefing about the motor industry that he told her, 'Prime Minister, you have done me the honour of making me, as secretary of state, your principal adviser on this matter. I would be grateful, therefore, if you would take my advice. Good day.'[48] He then walked out. Norman Lamont recalled another meeting, also in relation to the motor industry, when Mrs Thatcher, Tebbit and he met alone. Mrs Thatcher started to press Tebbit very hard on the issue. 'Suddenly, Norman got very angry. He threw his papers on the floor and said to her: "If you think you can do my job better than me, you can have it." Margaret went very pale. It was the only time I'd seen her really crumple.'[49] This anger resembled that which Francis Pym had felt about the appointment of Anthony Parsons or which Nigel Lawson later exhibited about Alan Walters, or which most Cabinet ministers felt, from time to time, about Bernard Ingham. It arose from the sense that they were not allowed to be masters in their own house.

The second consequence was that, much more than in the past, policy action could be driven forward from No. 10. Original ideas therefore had more chance of being translated into action. This would be seen, mainly

---

and Skills, 2005–7; for Innovation, Universities and Skills, 2007–10; Minister of State for Universities and Science, 2010–14; granted a peerage in the Dissolution Honours List, 2015.

* Bob Young (1944–), educated Magdalen College, Oxford; principal, European Economic Research Ltd, 2004–14, now special adviser; member, Central Policy Review Staff, 1983; No. 10 Policy Unit, 1983–4.

† David Pascall (1949–), educated Queen Mary's Grammar School, Basingstoke and University of Birmingham; held various positions in British Petroleum, 1967–93; seconded by BP to the Central Policy Review Staff, Cabinet Office, 1982–3 and then to the No. 10 Policy Unit.

‡ Peter Warry (1949–), educated Clifton College and Merton College, Oxford; group managing director, Aerospace Engineering plc, 1982–4; special adviser and deputy head, No. 10 Policy Unit, 1984–6; chief executive, Nuclear Electric, 1996–8; chairman, the Royal Mint, 2012–.

to advantage, in the privatization programme and the conduct of the miners' strike, and also, much more controversially, in relation to European policy and the invention of the poll tax. The trend would help to Thatcherize the government Mrs Thatcher led, but also increased the resentments felt against her.

In the first full week of her second term, Mrs Thatcher found herself addressing a set of disparate and largely uncongenial problems. These included Hong Kong, where Howe reported that the Chinese had falsely claimed that Mrs Thatcher had already conceded sovereignty to them, and Zimbabwe, about which she had a long and uncomfortable meeting with Robert Mugabe discussing his increasingly tyrannical imposition of a one-party state, rigged trials of RAF officers (who were Zimbabwean citizens) and rumours of political murders. The seemingly endless question of Britain's budget contribution to the European Community appeared quite unaltered by electoral victory. Mrs Thatcher told the Cabinet that it was supposed to be solved by the upcoming European Council in Stuttgart, but there was 'no sign of that'.[50] When Cecil Parkinson ventured that the Germans were 'desperately keen to help', Mrs Thatcher added tartly, 'Short of producing the money.' There was inconclusive talk, as in the past, of Britain legislating to withhold its contribution.

The Stuttgart Council took place over the next two days. Although Mrs Thatcher gave and received the usual hard pounding, the meeting went better than she had feared. It had been 'v. difficult',[51] she told the Cabinet the following week, but 'We owe a fantastic amount to Kohl [the Germans held the EEC presidency at this time]. I don't know how he bettered Mitterrand, but he did.' Britain's position, urged on Mrs Thatcher by a 'pincer movement' of Foreign Office officials and Geoffrey Howe, Robert Armstrong and Robin Butler,[52] was to concede a readiness eventually to consider increasing the Community's 'own resources' (the percentage of taxes permitted to it by the member states) so long as fair budgetary mechanisms and controls on the Common Agricultural Policy (CAP) were agreed first. Thanks to Kohl's chairmanship, Mrs Thatcher also won agreement for another year of temporary rebate for Britain, pending permanent settlement. She wrote to Kohl with unaccustomed warmth, congratulating him on his 'well-deserved triumph'[53] in beating down French objections to this compromise. 'What I am really afraid of is next year,' she told the Cabinet. 'It will be very rough.'[54]

She was also persuaded to sign at Stuttgart the Solemn Declaration on European Union. This committed the signatories to bring about 'an ever closer union of the peoples and Member States of the European Union', a change from the original Treaty of Rome, which had spoken only of the 'peoples' being in ever closer union. 'I went along with it,' wrote Mrs Thatcher, because 'I could not quarrel with everything, and the document had no legal force.'[55] The customary Foreign Office approach, in which specific, detailed gains were considered more important than issues of principle which could be dismissed as theoretical, prevailed. As so often with these windy European generalizations, however, the Declaration was indeed as solemn as its name: its intent was to move towards something much deeper than anything Mrs Thatcher ever wanted. It would come back and hit her two years later.

In parliamentary affairs, Mrs Thatcher faced two thorny difficulties – the Speakership and MPs' pay. The first was of her own making. Having alienated Jack Weatherill by trying to get him to withdraw and having failed to ignite a spark in Pym, she sought an alternative candidate. She had greatly liked the incumbent Speaker George Thomas who, though Labour, had showed compliance, not to say servility, in favour of the executive and against backbenchers.* She feared, correctly, that Weatherill would be more independent-minded and, indeed, said as much to him: 'You won't look after us like George Thomas did.'[56] She tried to buy him off with the offer of a junior post at the Foreign Office, but he refused. She wanted to secure the Speakership for Humphrey Atkins,† about whose enforced resignation because of the Argentine invasion of the Falklands in 1982 she felt guilty. This too failed, however, because of what Weatherill called a 'peasants' revolt' in which the Labour Party combined with Tory backbenchers to indicate that they would support him. He became Speaker unopposed. So Mrs Thatcher began the new Parliament with a botched attempt to manipulate it and a Speaker chosen in defiance of her. Weatherill continued not to oblige her: 'If I was accused of favouring the Labour Party it was probably true.'[57]‡ He saw the House of Commons as a safety

---

* Mrs Thatcher rewarded Thomas by making him her second viscount. He took the title of Tonypandy. She also agreed to be interviewed by him for a soft television series he made called *George Thomas in Conversation*. For this, she so much liked the make-up she wore to see him ('Pressed powder – light – by Cosmetic a la carte ... Lipstick – Honey Raisin by Clinique Gloss') that her staff made a note of it for future reference (Wallace to Robilliard, 13 September 1983, CAC: THCR 5/1/5/215).

† Humphrey Atkins (1922–96), educated Wellington; Conservative MP for Merton and Morden, 1955–70; for Spelthorne, 1970–87; Secretary of State for Northern Ireland, 1979–81; Lord Privy Seal, 1981–2; created Lord Colnbrook, 1987.

‡ It remains to this day a fairly safe bet that a Speaker coming from the Conservatives will tend to favour Labour, and vice versa. This is partly because the Speaker understands the need for balance, and partly because, in politics, it is axiomatic that one's real enemies are to be found on one's own side.

valve for a frustrated opposition, and wanted to weaken the extreme left which was pushing the party to take to the streets.*

The matter of MPs' pay always arose after a general election, on the constitutional grounds that each new Parliament must decide its own salaries, rather than being bound by the last. Now MPs felt they had fallen behind in what was still an era of high inflation, and wanted more. Like the Speakership, this was ultimately a matter for Parliament, not for the government; but in this case Mrs Thatcher had more justification for intervening. It was hard for her to maintain a policy of public sector salary restraint if the Parliament ultimately enforcing that restraint was voting itself much larger rises. An official report commissioned from Lord Plowden suggested that MPs should be made comparable with a level of the Civil Service and recommended that their salaries should rise from £14,510 to £19,000 a year. This seemed quite out of the question to Mrs Thatcher, who suggested a 4 per cent increase. Eventually, a compromise, unfavourable to her wishes, was reached by which MPs' pay would rise gradually and, by the end of the Parliament, reach the Plowden recommendation plus a bit extra. As compensation for the lack of jam today, various allowances were made more generous – a slightly surreptitious means of handing out money which would eventually, in the twenty-first century, attain the proportions of a scandal. Even with these concessions, MPs still defied her wishes by voting that their pay be linked to that of a higher Civil Service grade than had been proposed. Mrs Thatcher probably had little choice but to resist the demands, but her approach – which adversely affected ministers' pay as well as that of backbenchers – added to the ill will among her parliamentary colleagues before the Parliament had really got going. Mrs Thatcher volunteered, as she had done since 1979, to take only the standard Cabinet minister's salary of £40,000 a year, forgoing the extra £10,000 to which she was entitled. Such self-sacrifice probably made her even less popular with her ministers, who would have felt the implied reproach.†

There was a grimmer matter on which the House of Commons staged

---

* In 1984, Weatherill made some outspoken comments about Prime Minister's Questions and said that Parliament should make life 'hell' for the government. When these comments were reported in the press he wrote a grovelling letter to Mrs Thatcher to 'apologise for the embarrassment I caused' (Weatherill to Thatcher, 7 June 1984, CAC: THCR 1/3/13 (http://www.margaretthatcher.org/document/136373)).
† Some also resented her self-sacrifice, saying that, since her husband was quite rich, she could afford it. There was some truth in this, though it is worth pointing out that Denis and Margaret kept their finances entirely separate, and he did not pay any of her bills. He did, however, pay the rent charged by the government for the flat they shared in 10 Downing Street.

yet another occasion which, by convention, the government could not control. On 13 July 1983, the House debated and voted on the return of capital punishment, which had been suspended since 1965. The subject was always treated as a matter of conscience, and was therefore unwhipped.* In theory, this debate, which Mrs Thatcher wanted, served her turn. She had always supported the death penalty, and this had done her no harm with potential Conservative voters, especially working-class ones. At the general election, Tory candidates who opposed the death penalty had been given a rough time by voters, even more so by their constituency associations. Now, with such an overwhelming Conservative majority, it even seemed possible that 'the rope' – always anathema to the 'chattering classes', the BBC and so on, but always strongly supported in opinion polls – could at last return. But whereas Margaret, the battling housewife and mother of two, could rage against detestable crimes and call for the ultimate deterrent, Mrs Thatcher, the Prime Minister, knew that actually bringing back capital punishment would be a legislative and political nightmare, setting her colleagues against one another. It was more important for her to be seen to be on the 'right' side of this question than for her will to prevail. She therefore let it be known that she did not think the vote would go her way.† This made it easier for fellow Tories to vote against her wishes without seeming disloyal.

Willie Whitelaw had always been an abolitionist and this had made restoration very hard so long as he had been Home Secretary. There was much speculation about the way his successor, Leon Brittan, previously an abolitionist too, would proceed. When he spoke in the House, Brittan continued to argue against capital punishment in most cases, but now said that he felt it was justified for terrorist murders. His argument was considered 'lawyerly' in the unflattering sense of that word and therefore not morally persuasive. The Commons rejected the death penalty for murder of a policeman by a majority of 81 and for murder plain and simple by a majority of 145. None of this could exactly be regarded as a defeat for Mrs Thatcher, who pronounced herself 'not surprised at the result'.[58] In practical terms this was probably what she wanted. But there was something inglorious about it.

---

* It is traditional in Parliament not to impose a whip on votes which are deemed a matter of conscience, such as abortion, fox-hunting, euthanasia.

† In the press it was reported that up to three Cabinet ministers – Walker, Prior and Heseltine – would resign from the government if the Commons voted to restore the death penalty. According to the *Daily Mail*, Ingham told Mrs Thatcher, 'This is reason [sic] you have suddenly washed your hands of any direct Government involvement' ('Press Digest', Ingham to Thatcher, 8 July 1983, CAC: THCR 3/5/25).

By July, the talk in Parliament and press was of Mrs Thatcher's 'banana skins' and 'lack of direction'. Mrs Thatcher felt it herself. She defended the government, telling the BBC's John Cole, 'I don't think it's been accident prone at all,'[59] but in a private interview that month she quoted an 'old Balliol phrase' (of Benjamin Jowett): 'Don't expect too much and don't attempt too little,' which, she said, she kept repeating to Cabinet colleagues.[60] She had to remind them, she went on, that they were not '22 miscellaneous heads of department, but custodians of a general strategy'. As always, though, she did not have what others would recognize as a general strategy. She had a purpose – the transformation of Britain from semi-socialism to a freer society and a liberal economy – but no programme for achieving it. She might have persuaded colleagues to readier collaboration if she had given them a bit more flattery and credit. Butler noted: 'She did not refer once by name to any of her Cabinet colleagues . . . I find this absolutely extraordinary.'[61]

Most of these difficulties were more atmospheric than substantive. Difficulties with the economy were more tangible. The need to win a general election had, as always, done damage to the public finances. On the morning of 7 July, *The Times* carried a leak about what was not far short of a spending crisis. At Cabinet that day, Nigel Lawson confirmed to colleagues, who were suspicious about the rush, that the PSBR was 'substantially higher than forecast for last 6 months'[62] and that there was 'considerable concern abt our commitment to [our] strategy . . . So something has to be done. Extremely difficult, and not happy politically.' The overall burden of tax in relation to GDP was now 38.75 per cent whereas, in Labour's last year, it had been only 34.75 per cent. More than £1 billion was needed off the PSBR, so the Chancellor demanded a 1 per cent reduction in money allocated for pay all round and 2 per cent off non-pay 'cash blocks'. 'We also have to increase the disposals programme,' he added. (His use of the favoured Treasury word 'disposals', rather than 'privatization', indicated his department's overwhelming concern for how much money could be raised rather than what would happen to the industries sold.) Lawson immediately encountered some resistance. Michael Heseltine complained that 'everyone will say there were secret plans.'[63] It was agreed that the Chancellor would have to make a statement to the House that afternoon, but he also promised to return to Cabinet a fortnight later to present his ideas in full.

In the intervening period, all those concerned with the long-term economic strategy begged Mrs Thatcher to stand firm. In a short, handwritten note, Alan Walters told her: 'This is the one non-repeatable opportunity to roll back public spending. If a Tory majority of 144 cannot do it, then there is little hope for Britain.'[64] Analysing the present discontents, Bernard Ingham complained to Mrs Thatcher that there had been no 'sureness of presentational touch'.[65] This must be sorted out before the recess. 'I have found it difficult to get a real "feel" for the Government,' he told her. He linked the capital punishment and the public spending issues: 'so far as <u>hanging</u> is concerned, the Lobby [that is, the lobby journalists] feel that this distraction has shown you in a less resolute light . . . if you had <u>really</u> wanted hanging restored you would have campaigned for it; you didn't and therefore you were part of the conspiracy to kill the issue for this Parliament.'

The public spending matter was 'more damaging': 'This is because the Chancellor is widely felt by the media to have been less than frank and to have bounced his colleagues into submission. They see him paying a longer-term price for a short-term gain.' This could damage Mrs Thatcher because 'potentially at least your priceless assets with the electorate – integrity and resolution – may have been compromised.' So the media would be watching the coming public expenditure Cabinet for evidence that 'rising damp in the Cabinet has become a surge' and the markets would want 'reassurance that the Government really is determined to keep on top of spending and exercise restraint as a way of life'. Mrs Thatcher underlined this passage vigorously. Fearing leaks and unhelpful briefing, Ingham told her he wanted a statement of the government's aims to be put out immediately after the key meeting: 'We must not allow others to get their oar in first.' Ingham's anxieties showed that Mrs Thatcher was by no means at one with all her colleagues.

At the public spending Cabinet on 21 July, Heseltine renewed his objections, and was joined by others, including Norman Fowler at the Department of Health and Social Security, who pleaded that 'We shd stick to our social aims.'[66] 'For the first time, it was absolutely explicit that the whole purpose was to cut spending to make room for tax cuts,' recalled Fowler. 'The old One Nation thing was swept aside. We hadn't remotely gone into the election saying this. For me, this was a major torpedo.'[67] Lawson's simple point, however, was that he was doing no more than insisting that ministers stick to spending totals already agreed. Setting out targets for the Parliament, he predicted that unemployment would soon 'peg' at a little more than 3 million, and demographic change would favour spending restraint, so better times were ahead. Mrs Thatcher backed him strongly and repetitiously – 'It is not possible to overrun totals on which we fought the Election . . . We cannot go out of this room without agreeing totals. Ch. has been very modest.' Ministers agreed to accept the totals for that year, but Heseltine called for a collective discussion at a later date of what would happen in the long term – just the sort of thing which Mrs Thatcher, always anxious that colleagues might conspire to frustrate her aims, wanted to avoid. Lawson said he welcomed Heseltine's suggestion: they should 'Agree we look at sacred cows'. Mrs Thatcher switched the animal metaphor: 'But not a hobby horse race', she warned.*

By his own account, Lawson, even as he began his new job, was having to adopt a more cautious stance than he would have liked. The panic caused by the CPRS leak the previous year had made it impossible to advance tax cuts through actual reductions in public spending. Instead, he developed the aim of 'holding the level of public spending steady in real terms while the economy grew',[68] and later 'refined' this to 'a slower rate of growth for public spending than the sustainable growth rate of the economy as a whole, with the result that public spending would steadily decline as a share of GDP'. For all the genuine economic radicalism of the Thatcher years – trade union reform, privatization, tax changes – the basic task of holding back the growth of state spending remained painfully hard, chiefly because little serious attempt was made to reform and reduce spending on social programmes. Public spending, as a whole, was never cut. The frontiers of the state were indeed rolled back from interference in a great deal of economic activity, but in terms of money spent, they ceded surprisingly little ground.

On 28 July, the by-election in Penrith and the Border caused by Willie Whitelaw's elevation to the House of Lords took place. It was won by the Conservative candidate, David Maclean, but the Tory majority fell from 15,421 to 552, confirming the prediction of Mrs Thatcher's loyal though irritated deputy. It was not the good note on which to begin the parliamentary summer recess that Bernard Ingham had wanted.

Mrs Thatcher herself was not quite on her top form. Although some, including Robin Butler, considered her enthusiasm undiminished by the election struggle, others thought she was badly in need of rest. Well-wishers, such as the Bishop of Ely, Peter Walker (not to be confused with the other Peter Walker), wrote to encourage her to take a respite. 'Alas, I have not time to "Go Slowly",' she replied.[69] John Coles, her foreign affairs private secretary, noticed that 'it was not quite the same Margaret Thatcher who

---

* Mrs Thatcher did, in fact, have her own hobby horse – the money spent on the intelligence services, which she was determined not to pare back. She was able to do this unobserved because, in those days, when the services were not publicly 'avowed', 'their budgets were secret too' (Interview with Lord Lawson of Blaby).

returned to No. 10'[70] after the 1983 election. There was some decline in her energy (though, by ordinary standards, it was 'still prodigious'): 'It became much rarer for her to work after midnight, much rarer for her to keep dinner party guests back for discussion into the small hours.'

One reason for this, obviously, was fatigue after the campaign, added to, in Coles's view, by the long backwash from her total commitment in the Falklands War the previous year. But there was something else as well. A couple of days after the 1983 victory she told Coles, 'I have not long to go.' He was very surprised, given the scale of her victory, and asked why. 'My party', she replied, 'won't want me to lead them into the next election – and I don't blame them.'[71]

This was an important part of Mrs Thatcher's psychology which hindsight, because of her victory in 1987, has obscured. In 1983, she knew that, well before the next general election, she would have served longer as party leader than any since Winston Churchill. Having herself performed the political assassination of a Tory leader (Heath), she understood how colleagues could rebel. She was aware that her trouncing of the Wets had made her more powerful, but not necessarily more popular with Cabinet colleagues. She recognized how ambitious people seek to displace one another, and she kept telling herself that she could not possibly expect her luck to hold. This helps to explain why she did not mellow in her dealings with her Cabinet. She did not feel much more secure than before her landslide victory: she was right not to.

Apart from all this, though possibly related to the strain caused by hard work, she was also suffering from a physical ailment. On the day following the Penrith by-election, while inspecting RAF Cranwell on her home turf in Lincolnshire, she noticed black spots in the field of vision of her right eye. At Chequers that weekend, they did not improve. She thought she was going blind[72] and consulted her private doctor John Henderson, who lived near Chequers. In fact, she had a detached retina. On Sunday evening Mrs Thatcher underwent laser treatment at King Edward VII's Hospital in Windsor, before returning to Downing Street. After further tests on Wednesday 3 August, her consultant decided that more extensive repair work was needed. She entered a private hospital in Windsor for an operation that evening.* Perhaps because of the general sense of her invulnerability,

---

* This is the occasion fictionalized in Hilary Mantel's controversial short story 'The Assassination of Margaret Thatcher' (included in the collection of that title published by Fourth Estate in 2014). In it, a local resident finds herself allowing an Irishman into her flat in Windsor because he says he wants to 'shoot' the Prime Minister and she assumes he is a photographer. When she discovers he is a terrorist, however, she still lets him stay and kill Mrs Thatcher as she leaves the hospital.

most of those close to Mrs Thatcher did not take the moment as seriously as they should have done. Robin Butler recalled that when she told him what was happening, he gave her a matter-of-fact, businesslike reply about the work arrangements made necessary by her treatment, and then realized, guiltily and too late, that 'what she really wanted me to say was "Poor you." '[73] He noted, too, that she was embarrassed at the thought that she might have to wear an eyepatch. Denis, who always had a horror of illness and hospitals, dutifully visited his wife during her three-night stay, and Mark, the attentive son, made several visits.[74]

To convalesce, Mrs Thatcher – and her husband – went to stay, as in the past, with Lady Glover at Schloss Freudenberg. For once, her state of health meant that she was forced to have a bit of real rest, although she did, on 5 August, sign a personal minute to all Cabinet ministers, urging them to work out with the Chief Secretary the longer-term trends in public expenditure, so that the Chancellor could have 'a solid enough basis' for his Medium-Term Financial Strategy throughout the Parliament.[75]* She was inundated with more than a thousand letters from well-wishers which she answered on her return from Switzerland. Most untypically for one usually so thoughtful towards her juniors, she lost her temper with the Garden Room staff (so called because they operated from two basement rooms looking on to the garden of No. 10) for not typing her replies fast enough[76] – a sign that she was still under strain.†

President Reagan telephoned on 3 August but found her still recovering, so he called again three days later to wish her his best. There were flowers from President Mitterrand, mangoes from President Zia of Pakistan, letters from Indira Gandhi‡ and Michael Foot, a 'posy' from the novelist Roald Dahl and a card from Jimmy Savile,§ the subsequently notorious

* The Medium-Term Financial Strategy had been Lawson's own invention in the previous Parliament. It spelt out in advance the government's planned borrowing, thus setting targets, and helping to restrain what could be spent. It was the best-known tool of the government's policy of monetary control. See Volume I, pp. 504–7.
† As late as September she told Alan Walters that her eye specialist, who had seen her on television, thought her eye looked inflamed and wanted to see her again. 'PM changed her working habits,' Walters recorded, '– now goes to bed early and gets up early in the morning to read papers' (Diary entry for Monday 5 September 1983, the diary of Sir Alan Walters, Papers of Sir Alan Walters, CAC: WTRS 3/1/5). Luckily, her retina did not detach again.
‡ Indira Gandhi (1917–84), Prime Minister of India, 1966–77 and from 1980 until her assassination in October 1984; daughter of the first prime minister of India, Pandit Jawaharlal Nehru; Minister of Information and Broadcasting, 1964–6; Minister for Home Affairs, 1970–73; for Atomic Energy, 1967–77, 1980–84; for Defence, 1980–82.
§ Jimmy Savile (1926–2011), educated St Anne's School, Leeds; TV and radio presenter of programmes including *Jim'll Fix It* and *Top of the Pops* (TV) and Radio One *Weekly Show*; charity fund-raiser; knighted 1990. After his death, allegations were made public that Savile

disc-jockey.* Ferdinand Mount sent a postcard: 'We have been trekking across Tuscany where P. Shore, R. Hattersley & N. Kinnock are all said to be on holiday. Luckily, so far we have only seen S. Botticelli & L. da Vinci.'[77] Replying to Cecil Parkinson's 'get well' note, she thanked him and added, 'We shall need to have a great new drive in September–October.'[78] She still had every expectation of keeping her favourite minister.

While Mrs Thatcher was still in hospital, Alan Clark dined with Ian Gow. 'To my horror he told me that he had not seen the Prime Minister since 14 June, which was the day that Michael Alison took over. How ruthless women can be – far worse than men.'[79] The two agreed that Michael Alison, 'although a pleasant and saintly man, could not possibly provide the Lady with the same alternating course of stimulus and relaxation'. And her position constantly needed securing:

> Ian told me that even the present Cabinet could only guarantee her a majority of two when the chips were really down – 'and supposing Geoffrey is away?' Is that margin of one constituted by Willie? I didn't ask, although his name has returned to the forefront with this ludicrous assurance that he is '. . . standing by at his farm in Cumbria' in case the Lady goes blind and the ship of state becomes rudderless.

'It should have been a celebratory dinner,' Clark reflected ruefully. '. . . Now we are both Ministers with a Government majority of 140 and no Opposition of any kind in sight. But there was a certain melancholy too. How often is it better to travel than to arrive.'[80]

During the recess, Cecil Parkinson became increasingly worried that his affair with his former secretary, Sara Keays, and the fact of her pregnancy, would become public knowledge.

On holiday with his wife Ann and their three daughters in August, Parkinson had finally decided – although he had sometimes in the past told Sara Keays that he would leave Ann and marry her – that he would

---

had used his celebrity status and free access to NHS hospitals where he was a volunteer helper to carry out acts of sexual abuse. A series of official investigations published in 2013 and 2014 concluded that he had sexually assaulted victims of all ages in NHS hospitals over several decades.

* Mrs Thatcher was keen that Savile should be knighted for his services to charity. In May 1983, she asked Robert Armstrong whether he thought this a good idea. He said he did not, because he had heard stories about Savile's misbehaviour with women (though not allegations of child abuse). 'I didn't know anything definite,' Armstrong recalled, 'but I told her I just didn't like the feel of it, the smell.' (Interview with Lord Armstrong of Ilminster). Mrs Thatcher later renewed her interest in a knighthood for Savile after Armstrong had ceased to be Cabinet secretary. He finally received the honour in 1990.

stay with his wife. This news pleased Mrs Thatcher, who had authorized Ian Gow (possibly the only other politician party to the secret) to tell him that 'the one thing Margaret is passionate about is that you should not leave Ann,'[81] but, strangely, it also made Parkinson more vulnerable politically. Sara Keays was now angry, and felt cheated.* She wanted a statement put out about the pregnancy; negotiations with lawyers were in progress. Parkinson feared an explosion, particularly at the party conference, and advised Mrs Thatcher to get a new party chairman as soon as she decently could, although he hoped to hang on to his Cabinet post.

Mrs Thatcher had intended to keep Parkinson in place as chairman until the party conference in October, so that he could take credit for the successful election campaign, but she bowed to the inevitable. To replace Parkinson she chose John Selwyn Gummer, the Parliamentary Under-Secretary at the Department of Employment.† Although only a junior minister, Gummer was well known to Mrs Thatcher because he often helped with her speeches. She also liked his interventions at the General Synod of the Church of England, where he was one of the few members who defended the government on moral, social and nuclear issues. As she put it, 'He used to make very good speeches on the basic philosophy of the party.'[82] She was worried that her own choices for the main departmental posts – Lawson, Howe and Brittan – were not good television performers, and wanted a youngish man out in front to counter David Steel, David Owen and Neil Kinnock, the forty-one-year-old favourite to succeed Michael Foot as leader at the coming Labour Party conference. She sought someone who would attack the Labour Party 'like a terrier'.[83] Gummer had the additional advantage, which she naturally could not explain to others, that he was sexually 'safe',[84] as he was securely married.

Nevertheless, it was a controversial choice, and an eccentric one. On hearing of it, Norman Tebbit, Gummer's departmental boss, 'came steaming into Downing Street, very angry', and told Mrs Thatcher that he 'wasn't having it'.[85]‡ His protest was in vain, but understandable.

---

* A change in social mores, already emerging in 1983, became clear in 1997, when Robin Cook, Foreign Secretary in the first Blair government, was told by Alastair Campbell, Tony Blair's communications chief, to make up his mind at once between his wife and his lover when his affair was about to be exposed in the press. He chose the latter, and stayed in post. It probably would have gone worse for him in the media if he had stayed with his wife.
† Gummer dropped the use of the name Selwyn, pleasingly ornamental in the Cambridge of his youth where he had attended Selwyn College, within days of attaining the chairmanship. Perhaps to make himself seem more ordinary, he made himself plain Gummer.
‡ There is a passage in Alan Clark's diary for 1 September 1983 in which Clark records Tebbit indicating that he would eventually like to be party chairman himself, but telling him that 'She wants to appoint a Parly Sec.' (Alan Clark, *Diaries*, Weidenfeld & Nicolson, 1993,

Traditionally, the chairman of the party was a senior figure. Gummer, who was in his early forties and lacked physical stature as well as Cabinet experience, was demonstrably no such person. His appointment felt like an affront to her senior colleagues, and seemed to disturb the chain of command. Besides, the role of party chairman after a general election was usually to repair the party organization more than take part in public debate. Mrs Thatcher's own view, in the retrospect of retirement, was that Gummer 'couldn't organise anything'.[86] For his part, Gummer considered that Mrs Thatcher herself allowed Tory organization and the party's base in local government 'to be destroyed – it did not interest her at all'.[87] Seen in terms of managing opinion to assist the leader – another role of the chairman – the choice of Gummer, a man of the party's pro-European, Heathite wing, was also odd. As was obvious at the time to those working for her, the godly combination of Gummer and Michael Alison would never do the business for her as the worldlier Parkinson and Gow had.[88] It also created a void in her life. Parkinson was the sort of man who greeted her by saying things like 'You're looking wonderful today, Margaret.' It is unimaginable that Gummer, fourteen years her junior, could have attempted such a thing.

Parkinson himself had not suggested and did not support the appointment of Gummer, whom he saw as 'a choirboy',[89] but he was in no position to interfere. He was involved in increasingly tense legal discussions about the joint statement, which Sara Keays wanted, revealing her pregnancy.

Matters were brought to a head in a strange way. In the first week of October, the satirical magazine *Private Eye* implied, in its 'Grovel' gossip column, that Parkinson might have had to leave the Tory chairmanship because of his 'marital difficulties', and reported that 'Parkinson's fun-loving secretary Ms Keays is expecting a baby in three months' time'. In the same piece, it falsely suggested that she was having an affair with another Conservative MP, Marcus Fox, whose name it deliberately misprinted as 'Fux'. At this time, for somewhat obscure reasons, the magazine's jokey euphemism for illicit sexual relations was 'discussing Ugandan affairs' (or variants on the word Uganda). The *Eye* said that Miss Keays 'had only recently returned from exploring the jungles of Uganda' with

---

pp. 37–8), without naming anyone. Clark advises Tebbit to talk her out of it. This suggests that Tebbit knew about, and hoped to frustrate, the Gummer idea well before it was announced on 15 September. On 8 September, he saw Michael Spicer privately, and put forward the idea that he (Tebbit) should be chairman of policy, with Spicer as chairman of the Central Office organization (Michael Spicer, *The Spicer Diaries*, Biteback, 2012, pp. 72–3). He seems to have been seeking more power for himself in the party in a way compatible with what Mrs Thatcher wanted.

Fox.[90] Robin Butler (who, as yet, knew nothing of the Parkinson affair) immediately showed this to Mrs Thatcher. 'Oh, that's really libellous,' she exclaimed.[91] The matter was further discussed during a meeting of ministers with her later in the day. Mrs Thatcher waved the magazine about: 'Robin's shown me this. I know it's untrue. Marcus told me he's never visited Africa.' It fell to Butler, as principal private secretary, to explain to the Prime Minister what the phrase meant, while Cabinet colleagues tried to contain their mirth.[92]

It was clear that Parkinson's affair could not be long concealed. Rather against his will, a statement agreed with Sara Keays's lawyers was put out late on the night of 5 October. It distracted media attention from the Labour Party conference, at which, three days earlier, Neil Kinnock had been elected his party's leader. In the statement, Parkinson admitted a long relationship with Miss Keays and said that she was expecting his baby in January: 'I am of course making provision for the mother and child.'[93] In the statement, Parkinson also admitted that he had promised to marry Miss Keays and had then changed his mind. He expressed his 'regret' for 'the distress I have caused to Miss Keays, to her family and to my own family'.

As she had done throughout, Mrs Thatcher stood by Parkinson ('Maggie says he will not have to quit Cabinet,' *Daily Express*). Bernard Ingham reported that at their weekly lobby meeting with him, the Sunday newspapers were trying to keep the story going. Would there be 'less talk of Victorian values'[94] now, they asked? Would she mention Parkinson in her party conference speech? Was it true that 'the Government is running into early trouble and that you are running out of luck'? What they wanted, Ingham told her, was a speech 'which conjures inspiration out of the essentially long-term task of rejuvenating Britain'.

The fate of Parkinson now lay in the hands of the party conference at Blackpool. The Tory rank and file, taking their tone from the leader, clapped whenever Parkinson's name was mentioned in speeches. The grandees were more tepid. Parkinson, who made his own platform speech on Thursday 13 October, noted that while the hall gave him a standing ovation, the platform stayed seated.[95] His potential departure was not displeasing to those who wanted Mrs Thatcher's power reined in. All went well with him throughout the conference, however, until late that night, the last of the conference and Mrs Thatcher's fifty-eighth birthday.*

She and her team were working on her next day's setpiece leader's speech

---

* Mrs Thatcher downplayed her birthday celebrations. She refused to have a cake presented to her in the conference hall. (Sherbourne to Thatcher, 4 October 1983, CAC: THCR 2/9/19.)

when, at about 11 p.m., Robin Butler was called out of her hotel suite to be told about the first edition of the following morning's *The Times*. In it, Miss Keays said that she had been so upset by a leading article in the *Daily Telegraph* advising her to have an abortion that she had decided to speak out.* She denounced Parkinson and went through exactly how often he had promised her marriage, withdrawn the offer, and then promised it once more.† The story, so carefully timed, was clearly her public declaration of a war which Parkinson was in no position to fight. The Prime Minister needed to be told. Butler wondered whether he should interrupt Mrs Thatcher in the always acutely tense period of last-minute speech preparation. He decided against it, and woke Denis instead, to seek his advice. Denis suggested telling Parkinson first. When he was informed, Parkinson said, 'I've had it, haven't I?' Denis agreed that he had. Ferdinand Mount, who was in the suite working on the speech, noted the 'strange grey deathmask colour' of Parkinson's face.[96] Ascertaining that Mrs Thatcher herself was no longer in the throes of composition, Denis, Parkinson and Butler broke the news to her.[97] Parkinson recalled her characteristic reluctance to make the key decision herself. 'It's up to you,' she said. He resigned.

In her party conference speech the next day, Mrs Thatcher paid tribute to 'the man who so brilliantly organised the campaign', but did not name him. One further duty remained. As trade and industry secretary, Parkinson had been booked to open an extension of Blackpool airport on the Friday. Having resigned, he did not do so. Denis Thatcher opened it instead. The commemorative plaque of the occasion, however, inscribed beforehand, still bears Cecil Parkinson's name.

The loss of Parkinson was a serious blow to Mrs Thatcher. She attracted little odium for having defended her straying Secretary of State, and indeed some admiration for her lack of censoriousness. It was a relief to many that this woman who, as David Wolfson put it at the time, 'never did anything she could not be photographed doing',[98] was not puritanical about others; indeed, she preferred 'naughty boys' to goody-goodies.[99] But Parkinson had been her favourite in the Cabinet and perhaps the only one whom she regarded as a private friend. He understood and shared her politics, and was uniquely good at cheering her up and handling her productively.[100] She 'adored the Cecil type of flattery',[101] and found no

---

* In fact, as the *Telegraph*'s editor, W. F. Deedes, wrote to *The Times* to point out, the article in question had argued the exact opposite, and praised her for not having an abortion, but Miss Keays seems to have been too angry to have noticed.

† Sara Keays's full story is told in her book *A Question of Judgement*, Quintessential Press, 1985.

replacement for it. Now she was like a queen who had lost her most loyal and dashing knight.

As well as making her government look a bit ridiculous and ill-starred, Parkinson's departure exposed her more clearly than before to the possibility of eventual challenge. In his stead, she promoted Norman Tebbit to the DTI, moving Tom King to replace him at Employment and putting her close ideological ally, Nicholas Ridley,* in the Cabinet for the first time at Transport. It was immediately noted that Tebbit now led the race, on the right at least, to succeed her. According to Parkinson, he had told Tebbit about Sara Keays's pregnancy for the first time while driving him back from a weekend visit to Chequers in September. 'Norman's first reaction was to say: "There were three of us. Now there are only two." He just couldn't stop himself.'[102]† Tebbit meant that Parkinson was now out of the race to succeed Mrs Thatcher. This left, in his opinion, only him and Michael Heseltine. It was the common observation of those surrounding Mrs Thatcher at this time that Tebbit was indeed a challenger, and that this made him surprisingly touchy and awkward.[103] He seemed, on the one hand, tough in his public rhetoric, in order to maintain a Thatcherite base, but, on the other, in his governmental capacity, unradical and 'amazingly uncertain about taking strong positions'.[104]

Tebbit did not, in later life, deny his ambition. Referring to the DTI, he thought that 'If Cecil was out of the picture, I was the natural to do that job.'[105] Second only to the Chancellorship, it was the post which had most work to do in the Thatcher revolution, transforming the supply side of British business and presiding over the bulk of the privatizations. In comparison, Heseltine, at Defence, lingered in impotent eminence. After he had succeeded Parkinson, Tebbit soon found that 'Relations with Margaret became quite bad across the waterfront.' The two had strong disagreements about the motor industry, he wanting a continuing British volume-car base and she thinking that 'the only thing was to close the whole thing down and stop the money leaking'.

Tebbit saw Mrs Thatcher as 'rather extreme' in her belief that markets must decide this matter, whereas he saw things rather more pragmatically

---

* Nicholas Ridley (1929–93), educated Eton and Balliol College, Oxford; Conservative MP for Cirencester and Tewkesbury, 1959–92; Financial Secretary to the Treasury, 1981–3; Secretary of State for Transport, 1983–6; for the Environment, 1986–9; for Trade and Industry, 1989–90; forced to resign after an interview criticizing Germany and the EEC in the *Spectator*, 14 July 1990; created Lord Ridley of Liddesdale, 1992.

† Tebbit had a different recollection, recalling (and recording in his memoirs) that Parkinson had told him during the general election campaign (Interview with Lord Tebbit. See also Norman Tebbit, *Upwardly Mobile*, Weidenfeld & Nicolson, 1988, pp. 204–5).

and was worried about Tory seats in the West Midlands. In his view, the difference between Mrs Thatcher and him was 'like that between the Vatican and a parish priest: I had to deal with the reality of human life.'[106] But it was also, he thought, 'a case of "Uneasy lies the head that wears the crown". She was conscious I was receiving a lot of press support.' At the Conservative conference, in the days before Parkinson fell, Heseltine and Tebbit were the two star turns on the platform. It was noticed that Heseltine, who had long made party conferences his speciality, received a rather more *pro forma* welcome than usual, whereas Tebbit's was more heartfelt.

On the Monday following Parkinson's resignation, Bernard Ingham's press digest drew Mrs Thatcher's attention to the headlines: '*Sun* leads with "Tebbit is the Man – 'worst enemy' Norman gets Parkinson's job".* Mr Tebbit is now just a heartbeat away from Tory leadership.'[107]

It would be wrong, however, to leave the impression that difficulties in the early months of the second term deflected Mrs Thatcher from her essential purpose. The scale of her victory had finally convinced the Civil Service that, as Ferdinand Mount put it, ' "This lot has an ongoing future: we must bend with its wind and learn its language." Obstruction very much dwindled and ambitious assistant secretaries came up with bright ideas.'[108] The global effect was similar. 'Thatcherism works' was the simple headline of a piece that Alan Walters wrote in the *Washington Post*.[109] This was a message that most of the world was now ready to hear. The concept of Thatcherism was simultaneously vague – in the sense that it had no agreed sacred text or statement of principles – and strong. It was opposed to big government, high taxes and high deficits, the political power of trade unions, and Communism. It was in favour of individual opportunity and choice, free markets, strict monetary control, nuclear weapons and a vigorous NATO alliance. Its emotional pull was that, after the weakness of the 1970s, it rejected the idea that the left must have everything its way. Instead of conservatism being a method of orderly retreat before the forces of socialist progress, Thatcherism saw it as a dynamic and creative force, the best way of advancing the prosperity and security of the many. Thatcherism set out to prove that the modern world could be shaped in the interests of greater liberty.

Things really had changed. As Ronnie Millar, her thespian speech-writer, wrote to Mrs Thatcher after the election,

I see poor old Foot keeps saying Labour lost because they failed to get their

---

* Parkinson was alleged to have described his former friend Tebbit as his 'worst enemy', at a private dinner in Blackpool. Parkinson always denied this. (Interview with Lord Parkinson.)

message across. Not so. They lost because they got their message across all too clearly – and the people cared not for it. Let's hope Kinnock takes over, because then the message will be virtually the same – and so will the people's answer. Which means, dear, you will have to go on forever.[110]

In fact, it was under Neil Kinnock that the great Labour rethink would at last begin, but at this stage his party was far too weak and far too embroiled in its own quarrels to produce coherent opposition.

On 8 June, the day before polling day, Ferdinand Mount had sent Mrs Thatcher a paper called 'The Next Fifteen Months', written by David Young. Young, a protégé of Keith Joseph, was making a great success of the Manpower Services Commission, the body charged with addressing unemployment. Young's innovations included a youth training scheme that aimed to provide 460,000 places for school leavers. Mount regarded him as 'a really energetic independent mind'.[111] Young now offered her related but wider thoughts about how to get business and government moving. He had a long list – privatizing nationalized industries, putting all local government operations out to tender, restricting the *functions* of the Civil Service rather than obsessing about numbers alone, stopping the Inland Revenue frustrating the tax allowances for business start-ups, inventing a training voucher scheme, getting residential house building going by extending capital allowances, overcoming regional policy's obsession with plant, and so on. As Young put it, 'The first term has above all else changed attitudes. What we now have to do is to change the real world.'[112] This was a capitalist echo, possibly unconscious, of Marx's famous phrase: 'Philosophers have only interpreted the world in various ways. The point, however, is to change it.'[113]

All this was closely linked, in the minds of Mrs Thatcher and her advisers, with employment. Later in June, Mount wrote to her to point out how lucky the Tories had been that unemployment had not been much of an issue in the general election. They would not be so lucky again, he went on, and must get it right by the second and third years of the Parliament. He proposed a mixture of measures – some, like 'interim retirement benefit' for workers over sixty, to massage the headline figure down; others, like attacking benefit traps, Wages Councils (which dictated wage levels in some trades) and excessive employment protection, to let new jobs grow.[114] Suggesting to Mrs Thatcher a device called 'a passport for a job', Lord Cockfield sent her a memo with two sentences encapsulating the key idea which governed Thatcherite thinking on the subject: 'Our objective is the creation of employment. This will lead to a reduction of unemployment: but it is not the same thing.'[115] The old idea of post-war planners and interventionists was that jobs had to be 'saved'. Mrs Thatcher's idea was that many old jobs were bound to go: the key question was whether the economy was free enough to create new ones.

Just before her seminar on the Soviet Union at Chequers in early September (see Chapter 5), Mrs Thatcher held a comparable event there, on two weekdays, on 'what the next steps should be in the Government's strategy for creating a more prosperous and enterprising British economy and thus reversing the growth in unemployment'.[116] This way of formulating the question was itself part of the answer: successful employment would come from successful enterprise.

She wanted the fact of the meeting, never mind its content, 'closely guarded'.[117] Contributions were invited not only from, first and foremost, Nigel Lawson, but also from Parkinson, Tebbit, Jenkin, Walker and Joseph – that is, Trade and Industry, Employment, Environment, Energy and Education. 'Mrs Thatcher particularly hopes that each paper will avoid generalities and will concentrate on the specific decisions that need to be taken.'[118] As well as the ministers and officials, Mount, Walters and David Young attended. Topics ranged over portable pensions, further reductions in union power, 'The Taxation system and Employment', housing and labour mobility, how to give workers and managers the 'Enterprising Approach they require'[119] and a dozen other subjects. Mrs Thatcher wrote separately to each departmental minister to ask for a personal (as opposed to official) paper, as well as circulating Walters's recent notes on employment, supplementary benefit and relative wages. Nineteen ministerial papers were on the agenda. This was what later came to be called 'joined-up government', with a vengeance.

Alan Walters kept rough notes of proceedings for his own benefit (headed 'Checkers', as if the name of the place were American). His summaries of Mrs Thatcher's interventions give the flavour of her way of talking and of jumping between subjects: 'Wage related pension burden', 'Defence exp – cannot go on increasing it', 'Orders from Mexico and Brazil for ships', 'L'pool [Liverpool] had more money and made things worse', 'DES dreadful – portrait of Lenin in one room', 'keyboard skills'.[120] Nigel Lawson's recorded interventions, reflecting his more orderly mind, tended to concentrate on tax reform. Although the conversations were almost absurdly wide-ranging, they did produce an effect rather like an orchestra in its first rehearsal of a new symphony. Those taking part were serious about getting the music right.*

---

* There was actual music as well. Michael Scholar soothed Mrs Thatcher by playing Bach, Mozart, Schubert and Schumann on the Steinway piano that Ted Heath had installed when prime minister. (Interview with Sir Michael Scholar.)

In her speech to the party conference the following month, Mrs Thatcher's economic message tried to advance her economic radicalism as a unifying idea. The Conservatives had discovered at the election, she said, 'where the heart of the British people lies'.[121] 'We have created the new common ground,' she said, echoing Keith Joseph, who had used this phrase in 1975 to urge the party to pursue policies with broad public appeal rather than tacking to the political centre. The people had utterly rejected state socialism and understood that 'There is no such thing as public money; there is only taxpayers' money.' Nigel Lawson would make sure that those taxes would be lower: 'Further action there will be.'

Before Christmas that year, Ferdinand Mount left the Policy Unit, feeling a little jaded by his 'holiday from irony' under Mrs Thatcher, so different from his normal literary and journalistic milieu.[122] John Redwood, the colleague he had chosen as his successor, was a very different character, more trained in economic questions and much more strictly committed to the Thatcher political project. He produced for Mrs Thatcher what Andrew Turnbull,* who handed it over to her, drily called his 'inaugural'. 'There is every opportunity for you', Redwood wrote,

> to dominate the popular ground of British politics. Your personal authority and commitment to . . . restoring individual freedom, responsibility and choice can be used to define what people want, and to find practical ways of giving it to them. Many of the things this Government wants to do or is doing have wide appeal far beyond the bounds of the Conservative Party.[123]

Redwood listed some of the best issues – home ownership ('We have won this argument'),[124] reducing crime, 'value for money' in defence procurement (surely aimed at Heseltine personally), denationalization ('We must press on'), portable pensions, simplified taxation, competitive buses and more. But he did also observe, without criticizing Keith Joseph directly, that the issue of education was not much further advanced, and that health held 'dangers for us'. The Tories' popular ratings remained 'abysmally low' on this subject, and there was, as yet, no policy way through. All this was a reasonable summation of the lop-sided situation of Mrs Thatcher's government – completely in charge of the economic agenda, but still uncertain about the social one. As Ferdinand Mount, who had tried without great success to integrate a family policy with the

---

* Andrew Turnbull (1945–), educated Enfield Grammar School and Christ's College, Cambridge; private secretary to the Prime Minister, 1983–5; principal private secretary, 1988–92; Permanent Secretary, Department of the Environment, later Department for Environment, Transport and the Regions, 1994–8; Permanent Secretary, Treasury, 1998–2002; Cabinet Secretary, 2002–5; knighted, 1998; created Lord Turnbull, 2005.

government's economic policies, put it, 'Social policy was not on the back burner, but it was on a neighbouring work surface.'[125]

'The work I am initiating', Redwood told Mrs Thatcher, '. . . is designed to help establish that domination over the debate through careful attention to public attitudes, to make the task of Opposition thankless and difficult, to write the concerns and views of your Government into the grammar book of politics.'[126] The metaphor was a good one. The strict, energetic, innovative schoolmistress was indeed teaching a new grammar, and even the most unruly pupils were having to learn it.

Quite a different, anxious, complicated task also awaited Mrs Thatcher after 9 June. In the unsettled question of the future of Hong Kong, her smashing election victory did not seem to strengthen her hand with the world's largest dictatorship. The very next day, the value of the Hong Kong dollar fell sharply. After nine months of hostile Chinese pressure, confidence trembled. At a meeting the following week, she aired the issues with Geoffrey Howe and others for the first time since she had made him Foreign Secretary. As the Chinese were insisting, she said, on what they themselves called 'red flag and yellow face' (that is, neither British sovereignty nor administration after 1997), this was all the more reason to have an 'umbilical cord . . . whereby the rights of the people of Hong Kong depended on the United Kingdom and were independent of Peking'. This need not be called 'British administration', but she hoped China could get 'little more than titular sovereignty'. 'Our major responsibility', she said, 'was to the 4 million* Chinese who had sought freedom from Communist rule.'[127] Howe, taking his new office's line, said he was worried about making any settlement conditional on being 'acceptable to the people of Hong Kong'. Mrs Thatcher retorted that she could not recommend the transfer of sovereignty if it were not acceptable to them. This exchange summed up a difference at the heart of the government.

Nevertheless, the difference worked, on the whole, creatively. Cradock was instructed by the Cabinet to negotiate with China about arrangements post-1997, arrangements between then and 1997, and 'matters relating to a transfer of sovereignty', in that order. Mrs Thatcher understood well enough what was happening. As she said privately to the US Vice-President George Bush the following week, she hoped 'it might be possible to find a

---

* Different figures for the number of people in Hong Kong are explained by the fact that they often refer to different things. There were native Hong Kong people and Hong Kong people who were refugees. Some of these held British Dependent Territory passports. There were also numerous foreign residents. The total inhabitants of Hong Kong at this time officially numbered 5.322 million.

solution which salvaged China's pride but preserved Hong Kong's system'.[128]*
What she did not add was that she wished to salvage her own pride too.

Negotiations of immense complexity ensued. Although the Americans
offered the British team informal advice and, according to US officials,
shared intelligence,[129] this was a purely UK–China bilateral affair.† Its
twists and turns were relayed to London with pellucid clarity and a brilliant, almost insane grasp of nuance by Percy Cradock. In total, Howe
calculated, the Foreign Office traffic about the negotiations amounted to
40,000 telegrams. The exact use of words became an art-form. Cradock
reported, in a half-suppressed boast, how, by demanding '*a transfer of
sovereignty*' and opposing his counterpart Zhou Nan's suggestion of '*the
transfer . . .*', he had left the way open for Zhou to introduce the wording
Britain secretly wanted – the use of the phrase 'transfer of sovereignty'
with no article, definite or indefinite.[130] 'He handled it very well,' wrote
John Coles to Mrs Thatcher. 'Wonderfully,' she responded.

Although Cradock and Howe often found Mrs Thatcher tiring to deal
with, they also appreciated her utility when they talked to China. She was
'marvellous', recalled Howe, 'as a card off-stage'.[131] She was the demanding
mistress, he the endlessly patient emissary. She reminded Cradock of Jorkins in Charles Dickens's *David Copperfield*. Jorkins is the largely absent
business partner of nice Mr Spenlow, who 'finds it convenient to turn him
[Jorkins] into a hard man, an ogre, to whom he can attribute refusals of
any inconvenient request'. 'We operated', Cradock went on, 'on the same
principle . . . with the difference that our Jorkins, in London, needed no
invention.'[132] The London ogress, Cradock believed, did understand that
'it was a matter of brute power,'[133] and that therefore China was much the
stronger party; but she also understood that she could increase Britain's
small supply of brute power by playing up to her role. In the view of Charles
Powell,‡ who succeeded Coles as her foreign affairs private secretary the
following summer, her 'original ridiculously unobtainable goals' made it
possible for Britain to demand and get more than anyone would otherwise
have dared.[134] ' "If the Chinese think you're being difficult," she told the

---

* The Chinese attitude was not completely dissimilar, from the other side of the fence. 'We
will enable the British to back down with grace,' Deng Xiaoping told Edward Heath (Youde,
telegram 1031, Hong Kong, 19 July 1983, Hong Kong, TNA: PREM 19/1056).
† In October 1983, officials debated internally whether it might be in the US interest 'to
involve ourselves directly in the ongoing talks' (Draft NSSD, 'US Policy Toward Hong Kong',
China-Foreign Relations-Hong Kong (9/16/83–10/29/83), Box 13, Laux Files, Reagan
Library). These ideas did not find favour and the US remained resolutely on the sidelines.
‡ Charles Powell (1941–), educated King's School, Canterbury, New College, Oxford; Private
Secretary to the Prime Minister (1983–91); created Lord Powell of Bayswater, 2000.

Foreign Office, "just tell them who can be really, really difficult." She was a tiger kept in a cage.'[135] According to one of those who accompanied Mrs Thatcher in Peking, the Chinese respected this: 'They felt great admiration for her because she was the Iron Lady. They were very impressed by how well she dressed: they thought of her as a proper, serious leader.'[136]

Mrs Thatcher's other crucial role was in maintaining the confidence of the people of Hong Kong. To the Foreign Office, and particularly to Percy Cradock, who had the perfectionist's dislike of any exterior interference, China was a subject only diplomats understood. The Foreign Office sinologists were a sort of priesthood, and Cradock was their high priest, the keeper of the sacred mysteries. He felt that Hong Kong people would simply get the wrong end of the stick and annoy China if they were even informed about, let alone allowed to take part in, the unfolding process. It was the job of Edward Youde, the Governor, to stand up for Hong Kong people, and this he did conscientiously. But since the British colony had always avoided introducing democracy, they lacked their own political champion. Mrs Thatcher was the nearest they had to one. She understood more clearly than colleagues that the confidence in capitalist Hong Kong which everyone, even the Chinese Communists, wished to maintain, depended much more on whether Hong Kong people believed in the future than on whether Britain and China could get all the sub-clauses right.*

At every turn in the negotiations, Mrs Thatcher could be found pleading these people's cause. In late September 1983, for example, when

---

* Mrs Thatcher's attention to Hong Kong views led her to take very seriously an accusation against Robin McLaren, the political adviser to the Governor. McLaren was accused by a naval commander and other Hong Kong residents of expressing pro-Soviet views at private parties, saying that the Falklands campaign had been 'a great mistake', and making other 'extreme left-wing comments' (Coles report, 5 September 1983, TNA: PREM 19/1057/1). Mrs Thatcher insisted on an investigation, but this was dropped on the grounds that the case was insubstantial. However Jill Knight, a Conservative MP, then raised the matter at a meeting with Mrs Thatcher. Further accusations against McLaren followed, including from Lord Cromer, the former Governor of the Bank of England, and although the Foreign Office remained convinced of McLaren's integrity, it recommended an MI5 inquiry. 'I see no alternative,' wrote Mrs Thatcher (Appleyard to Coles, 26 March 1984, TNA: PREM 19/1263). Nothing was found against McLaren, but it was deemed prudent to move him to a different posting. 'It was an unhappy and unfair story,' recalled Charles Powell. 'I'm afraid it rather blighted his subsequent career.' (Interview with Lord Powell of Bayswater.) McLaren went on to become ambassador to Beijing in the 1990s, however. Throughout this process, Mrs Thatcher never called for McLaren's head, but her extreme vigilance revealed not only her perennial anxiety about Communist penetration, but also her concern for sensitivities in Hong Kong.

Cradock's 'first finesse' (see Chapter 1) had not worked, the Hang Seng index had fallen by 15 per cent in a week. He was softening her up to make a further concession (the 'second finesse') on sovereignty. She told Howe that Cradock's talk of maintaining prosperity and stability was beside the point unless it was recognized that 'The prosperity is due to 1. Chinese character. Plus 2. British system & administration.'[137] In December, as Cradock pressed harder for Mrs Thatcher to concede that no link of authority between Britain and Hong Kong after 1997 would survive, Mrs Thatcher wrote, 'The most difficult thing is acceptability to the people of Hong Kong . . . If I were a Chinese in Hong-Kong I would be getting worried that we [that is, Hong Kong Chinese] were not involved in the negotiations.'[138] At roughly the same time, Mrs Thatcher was contemplating comparable problems about how much to consult the people of Northern Ireland about their own future. As will be seen (see Chapter 10), they were also kept on the sidelines. In both cases, she was the only important person in the British government who constantly (though often without success) bore this dimension in mind. She did so with greater determination over Hong Kong than over Northern Ireland.

She also made herself available, as often as she could, to see the 'Unofficials' – the non-governmental executive and legislative advisers to the Governor who, as much as anyone, represented Hong Kong opinion.* She tended to see things from their point of view and told them frankly that she feared the Chinese 'had no concept of a free society'.[139] In the spring of 1984, when Howe informed her that China was now seeking a say in running Hong Kong *before* 1997, she wrote, 'Until now EXCO have said "at least we have until 1997!" Under this, they haven't. And before long we shall be pushed further.'[140] On the same day, Sir S. Y. Chung,† the head of EXCO, protested to Youde that this was 'the last nail in the coffin. We had gained nothing from the process of negotiation and had been forced into constant retreat.'[141] Without the sessions in London in which Mrs Thatcher listened to the Unofficials for hours, sympathized with their woes and tried to reassure them that the government would not abandon them, it is doubtful whether their nerve would have held. It is also doubtful whether Britain would have fought so hard for the interests of Hong Kong people.

For the Chinese government, who regarded Hong Kong as inalienably theirs, the idea of Hong Kong people having a say over their future was a

---

* The various bodies involved were EXCO (executive), LEGCO (legislative) and UMELCO (the grouping of Unofficials from both the others).

† Sze-yuen Chung (1917–), Member, Hong Kong Executive Council, 1972–80; Senior Member, 1980–88; adviser to Government of People's Republic of China on Hong Kong affairs, 1992–6; Convenor, HKSAR Executive Council, 1997–9; knighted, 1978.

heresy, even a reward for being unpatriotic. Deng, in particular, felt this strongly. Although he genuinely wanted to preserve Hong Kong's capitalist success, he found it difficult to understand that this depended on confidence and continuity which could not survive too much Chinese bullying. He also feared that Britain was insinuating sovereignty for itself and was engineering runs on the Hong Kong dollar to frighten him. He could not credit the British government's repeated, truthful assertion that it got no profit from the colony.[142] In his mind, there were piles of gold lying around which Britain from time to time smuggled out. 'Deng himself is not only suspicious and ill-informed', wrote Cradock, 'but impatient.'[143]* In the early part of 1984, China applied maximum pressure. It insisted on Deng's inflexible deadline for agreement – September 1984. It demanded that a Joint Liaison Group to help China prepare for the handover be set up in the colony itself, thus frightening Hong Kong people who thought it would become 'an organ of power'. Unbending on its own definition of nationality, China seemed to threaten the 3 million Hong Kong people who carried British Dependent Territory passports with either capitulation or statelessness.

By early April 1984, Hong Kong nerves were strained almost to breaking point. At an emotional meeting in London with the Unofficials, Sir S. Y. Chung warned Mrs Thatcher that the colony 'would become ungovernable long before 1997'.[144] By the time Geoffrey Howe visited Peking for talks later in the same month, the Chinese had already rejected the British draft agreement as a basis for discussion. They also told Howe, to his dismay, that China would garrison Hong Kong with a detachment of the People's Liberation Army after 1997. When he returned to Hong Kong, he publicly announced – information which until then had been held privately – that the British administrative link would be broken entirely in 1997. This was, he later recalled, 'the most anxious moment of my life'.[145]

'It seems as if the <u>Unofficials</u> were <u>right</u> in their judgment of the Chinese,'[146] Mrs Thatcher wrote privately as this process unfolded. She felt with Hong Kong, and tended to berate Howe and the Foreign Office, though no one could say they had not warned her. She felt strongly, in a way that Percy Cradock did not, that, as S. Y. Chung put it to her after Howe's announcement, 'To transfer land was one thing. To transfer people was another.'[147] That she, the great Cold Warrior, might end up delivering a free people to Communism was an unbearable thought. That she, the

---

* These words appeared in Cradock's farewell despatch as ambassador to Peking, a job which he left at the end of 1983. His successor was Sir Richard Evans. Cradock returned to London, however, as Mrs Thatcher's principal foreign policy adviser (succeeding Tony Parsons), and also retained a senior position in the Foreign Office. He remained effectively the official in charge of the negotiations with China.

victor of the Falklands, should fail to help a pro-British colony was, if anything, even worse. But, however tempted, she never gave up on the negotiations. She reluctantly accepted Cradock's analysis that China was absolutely determined to win the full outward form of sovereignty and power, but would be flexible about almost everything else. His metaphor was of a house. China had to have the house, but had few ideas about how to furnish it: that was Britain's chance to make a difference.

Mrs Thatcher therefore overruled objections from Youde and the Un-officials and agreed that Britain should try to meet the Chinese deadline. She accepted the view of Howe and Cradock that Howe should go to Peking again in July and do everything decently possible to secure agreement there. To empower her Foreign Secretary, she wrote a secret letter to her counterpart, Zhao Ziyang. It expressed her desire to conclude the talks on time, but emphasized that there must be an agreement which she could honourably put to Parliament. The idea of the Joint Liaison Group located in Hong Kong, she said, 'particularly disturbed' her and threatened to undermine government in Hong Kong.[148] Progress could be made, she said, if the question of location could be put aside for the time being.

Howe arrived in Peking in late July, accompanied by Cradock. At a lunch with his interlocutor, Zhou Nan, on the first day, Cradock was told that the Chinese leadership were ready to concede delay in starting the Joint Liaison Group, to continue its work after 1997, and to accept the terms of reference for it that Britain wanted, so long as everything was settled in the next two or three days. The Chinese encapsulated what they wanted for Hong Kong after 1997 in the formula they had first conceived in relation to Taiwan – 'One Country, Two Systems'. Cradock considered this 'the moment of truth',[149] and agreed as much with Howe under a flowering tree in the garden of the government guesthouse, the location he chose to avoid being bugged. He duly cabled 'Jorkins' in London. She gave 'encouragement, but not *carte blanche*'.[150] In two days, questions that had stalled for years were suddenly settled. On 31 July, as a mark of the importance of the moment and perhaps of his victory, Deng Xiaoping himself arrived after a five-hour train journey from his seaside holiday resort. Agreement was reached. Now that the Chinese believed they had got the recognition of the sovereignty they had always claimed, they could be more flexible. As Howe's team reported it to Mrs Thatcher: 'Deng said this was very good. The Chinese side had the highest trust in the Secretary of State and the Prime Minister. They had come to that conclusion in the course of the Hong Kong negotiations. He was full of confidence that One Country Two Systems would work.'[151] Deng even invited the Queen to visit China.

In his telegram to Mrs Thatcher explaining everything, Cradock said that these three days in Peking had been 'make or break'. Britain had got a deal which would be legally binding. Its detail could therefore develop the Basic Law by which Hong Kong would be ordered. It would be an agreement, rather than a unilateral Chinese promulgation. Deng should now be flattered with 'undue credit' for the idea of One Country, Two Systems, which was not, in fact, his own. 'We shall be inept', Cradock concluded, 'if we cannot manage it now.'[152] Whatever critics said about Cradock, he was not inept. The Chinese had won the house, but the British were indeed ready to furnish it. With relief and generosity rare in her dealings with the Foreign Office, Mrs Thatcher wrote: 'Thank you – many congratulations to you both [that is, Howe and Cradock] – it was an excellent result – progress beyond all expectations.'

When Mrs Thatcher saw the Unofficials the following month, Sir S. Y. Chung told her that he could commend the Agreement to the people of Hong Kong 'in good conscience'.[153] Mrs Thatcher thanked him. That phrase, she said, had 'very deep significance' for her.

Mrs Thatcher agreed to fly to Peking for the signing of the Agreement – known as the Joint Declaration – in late December 1984. It formed part of an astonishing week in her life which began with giving lunch to the Soviet heir-apparent, Mikhail Gorbachev, in Chequers, continued in Peking and Hong Kong, and ended with President Reagan at Camp David (see Chapter 8). For her trip, she requested a book by Liu Shaoqi, who had been a comrade of Chairman Mao and president of China, until Mao turned against him for being a 'capitalist roader' and subjected him to torture which may have contributed to his death in 1969. The book did not express Mrs Thatcher's personal ambitions: it was called *How to be a Good Communist*. After Mao's death, Deng had rehabilitated Liu's reputation: she sought to understand how any Communist could be good – or at least, how some could be better than others.

Charles Powell was in the prime ministerial party, which arrived at Peking airport at night. In those days, he recalled, the city was virtually dark, with the road 'a single track between trees with lots of chaps wobbling about on bicycles'. Mrs Thatcher travelled into town with the Chinese Foreign Minister and an interpreter. 'Get in there,' Percy Cradock told Powell, pointing to the car's jump-seat, 'and tell us what they say to each other.'[154] 'It was very stuffy and slow,' recalled Powell, 'and I fell asleep. When we all got out, Cradock and Youde rushed up to me and asked, "What did they say to one another?" Not wanting to seem an idiot, I said, "To be honest, it's so secret, I don't think I can tell you."'

Before the signing the next day, Mrs Thatcher met Deng in the Great

Hall of the People. He was grown old and deaf, and 'There was a lot of shouting at him down an ear trumpet.'[155] Deng told Mrs Thatcher that the Agreement had 'historic significance' and that China would honour it.[156] Mrs Thatcher, following Cradock's advice, praised 'One Country, Two Systems' as a 'stroke of genius'. Deng said, 'The credit should go to Marxist dialectics or "seeking truth from facts" [one of his famous anti-Maoist slogans].' Socialism would not have been acceptable to Hong Kong or to the United Kingdom, he told her.*

Mrs Thatcher asked Deng why he had agreed to one of the most precious features of the deal, which was that One Country, Two Systems would last for at least fifty years from 1997. He answered that it was because China 'hoped to approach the economic level of advanced countries by the end of that time'.† For her part, she pressed on Deng the 'doubts' that Hong Kong people would naturally feel, and the need for China to reassure them. 'She was actually rather impressed by him,' Powell judged. 'Here was this tiny figure, who exerted absolute control over 1.3 billion people. He dominated the others, who were plainly in thrall to him. Did she warm to him as a human being? No. He was a Communist and a tyrant.'[157] Deng asked Mrs Thatcher for her impressions of Gorbachev from her meeting three days earlier. It reveals something of the dramatic nature of the week that she found herself discussing the potential leader of the Soviet Union with the leader of the largest Communist country in the world before she had had a chance to do the same with the President of the United States.

After this meeting, Mrs Thatcher signed the Hong Kong Agreement in what she described as 'a spirit of pride and of optimism'.[158] The next day, she flew to sell it to the anxious but mostly welcoming people of the colony she had just agreed to hand over.

Huge difficulties remained. The full detail flowing from the Agreement had to be worked out and the Basic Law secured. The question of nationality and British passports for Hong Kong people was extremely sensitive and would become more so whenever something went wrong in China. So was the matter of democratization. No one could really know how China, emerging under Deng from utter totalitarianism, would behave. Mrs Thatcher had not got what she had set out to attain in 1982, or

---

* She also remembered, though the notetaker did not reproduce this, that Deng had said that capitalism should exist only on the periphery of China because otherwise it would 'eat up socialism'. Mrs Thatcher relayed this to Vice-President Bush when she saw him in Washington four days later. (Butler to Appleyard, 23 December 1984, TNA: PREM 19/1502.)
† In fact, China was to achieve this early in the twenty-first century, roughly forty years ahead of schedule – at least as measured by total output rather than per capita.

anything like it. Those on the conciliatory side of the argument – notably Cradock and Howe – were therefore the more pleased. Howe regarded the Joint Declaration as the example of his relationship with Mrs Thatcher 'at its best',[159] whereas she, he noticed, felt that 'we could have done something better' for Hong Kong. Charles Powell thought that she was 'never really happy about it'.[160]

Powell also recognized, however, that it was 'a remarkable agreement given that the Chinese could just have walked into Hong Kong', and one that would stand the test of time. According to the Hong Kong Chinese Lydia Dunn,* a member of EXCO, who dealt frequently with Mrs Thatcher,

> She was perhaps alone among the British team in understanding that Hong Kong was a human issue, not just a diplomatic one. Those in EXCO were convinced of her genuine empathy and thus quickly came to trust her. This helped to overcome the widely underlying suspicion of the so-called 'British sell-out'.

She had 'instinctual sympathy' for Hong Kong people and their dilemma, and this made a crucial difference.[161]

Just after Geoffrey Howe reached agreement in Peking at the end of July 1984, Mrs Thatcher was sent examples of the largely favourable Hong Kong press reaction. One pro-Peking paper said that 'it took an Iron Lady to have the courage to end British colonialism'.[162] Mrs Thatcher underlined this and wrote an exclamation mark beside it. The paper's comment had been intended as a compliment, but it was not one she could cheerfully accept.

For Mrs Thatcher, who detested Communism, never thought ill of the British Empire and felt tenderly towards all those who liked British rule, the Agreement was bound to be bitter-sweet. In her memoirs, written before the handover and after the trauma of Tiananmen Square in 1989, she devoted little space to the subject, perhaps worrying that everything might yet go wrong. But capitalist Hong Kong did not collapse, and for that she deserves part of the credit. Flushed by her victory in the Falklands, she had dared to dream that Hong Kong could remain proudly British. In this she failed, and was bound to fail. But she also dared to dream that the free, capitalist society which Britain had brought into existence could be preserved from Communism, by agreement with Communists. In this, though it may still be too early finally to judge, she partially succeeded, with important results for China's attitude to freedom and to the outside world.

---

* Lydia Dunn (1940–), Member, Legislative Council of Hong Kong, 1976–88; Senior Member, 1985–8; Member, Executive Council, 1982–95; Senior Member, 1988–95; created Lady Dunn, 1990.

5

Reagan plays her false

*'If I were there, Margaret, I'd throw my hat
in the door before I came in'*

By winning the general election of 1983, Mrs Thatcher had also won a mandate for the deployment of US cruise missiles on British soil. Unilateral nuclear disarmament had been clearly offered to the electorate by the Labour Party, and clearly defeated. The actual arrival of the missiles remained controversial. The launchers and warheads reached Britain in November. Protests, led by women, at RAF Greenham Common where some of the missiles were sited, continued, but decreased in number: 'they had become an eccentricity,' Mrs Thatcher told Vice-President Bush that June.[1] By prevailing, Mrs Thatcher had won her only really difficult domestic Cold War battle. Her triumph – electoral, international and, in her view, moral – gave her the space to reflect. Calling to offer his congratulations, President Reagan, clearly delighted, had declared her victory 'a shot in the arm for all of us who have a kind of solid philosophy worldwide'.[2] In response Mrs Thatcher showed the way her mind was tending: 'she believed the result would strengthen the Western alliance and might encourage the Soviet Union to show more flexibility in disarmament negotiations.'[3]

Although always a hawk in relations with the Soviet Union, Mrs Thatcher was no absolutist. Even before her election victory, she had indicated an interest in negotiation. In July 1982, she had received the former US President Richard Nixon, whose foreign policy expertise she respected. 'The Soviets will listen to you before they listen to us . . .' Nixon told her. 'They know you've got a lot of clout with our, frankly, inexperienced White House. With your credentials you can bring a new realism into East–West relations.'[4] On the death of the long-time Soviet leader Leonid Brezhnev, in November 1982, Reagan had written to her expressing his hopes of a better relationship with the Soviets. She had replied warmly: 'I agree very strongly with all your views, in particular the need to make it clear to the new Soviet leaders that a more constructive East/West relationship is available if they are willing to adopt a new approach.'[5]

She had said much the same publicly in her speech at the Lord Mayor's Banquet three days later. As she grew in confidence in international affairs, she was readier to look for opportunities.

In March 1983, through the suasion of her former private secretary Bryan Cartledge,* now Ambassador to Hungary, Mrs Thatcher met József Marjai, the Hungarian Deputy Prime Minister, in London. Malcolm Rifkind,† the junior Foreign Office minister in charge of relations with the Soviet Union and Eastern Europe,‡ recalled: 'The first thing she said was, "So Mr Marjai, my officials tell me you have some rather unusual views on economic policy . . ." He said, "Yes, Madam Prime Minister. The biggest problem we have in Hungary is to convince the Hungarian people that the government has no money of its own." Her eyes lit up. "But that's what I'm always saying in this country!" It was a love-in from then on.'[6] Gradually, the idea grew in her mind that not all Communists were necessarily alike.

She was also spurred on by knowing that other European leaders had contacts with the Eastern bloc. As Nigel Broomfield,§ one of the Foreign Office's Soviet experts, put it:

Schmidt, Giscard spoke to the Russians and would talk about their exchanges when they met. She was out of that. The Embassy in Moscow kept her well informed, but at her level it is important to be able to say, 'Well, I said to him this. And he said that.' . . . If we wanted to be able to play a full role at the Great Power table we needed to have contacts at the highest level and the ability to judge for ourselves what these people were likely to do and to make them aware of our views.[7]

Mrs Thatcher's competitive spirit was aroused. She asked for a seminar of experts on the Soviet Union to be held at Chequers, the centrepiece of

* Bryan Cartledge (1931–), educated Hurstpierpoint and St John's College, Cambridge; head of East European and Soviet Department, FCO, 1975–7; diplomatic private secretary to the Prime Minister, 1977–9; Ambassador to Hungary, 1980–83; to the Soviet Union, 1985–8; Principal of Linacre College, Oxford, 1988–96; knighted, 1985.

† Malcolm Rifkind (1946–), educated George Watson's College and Edinburgh University; Conservative MP for Edinburgh Pentlands, February 1974–97; for Kensington and Chelsea, 2005–10; for Kensington, 2010–15; Secretary of State for Scotland, 1986–90; for Transport, 1990–92; for Defence, 1992–5; for Foreign and Commonwealth Affairs, 1995–7; unsuccessful candidate for leadership of the Conservative Party, 2005; knighted, 1997.

‡ The fact that Rifkind, a parliamentary under-secretary, and therefore on the lowest rung of the ministerial ladder, had this large role shows how little importance the British government ascribed to East–West links at that time.

§ Nigel Broomfield (1937–), educated Haileybury and Trinity College, Cambridge; diplomat; Ambassador to German Democratic Republic, 1988–90; Ambassador to Germany, 1993–7; knighted, 1993.

a broader review of the government's approach to international affairs. The process ran parallel to a similar desire in the United States to analyse the situation and work out how to bargain from strength. In July 1983, Geoffrey Howe, now Foreign Secretary, was received by Reagan. 'He agreed with you', the British Ambassador, Sir Oliver Wright, recorded for Howe, in words which Mrs Thatcher underlined, 'that we must <u>emphasise disarmament as well as defence and said he had never been more serious about anything in his life</u>. We could not go on as we were with nuclear weapons pointing at each other.'[8]

Although Reagan and Thatcher were as one in their hatred of Communism and their belief in the Western way of life, they did not, at bottom, agree about how best to defend it. Reagan had a strong antipathy to nuclear weapons which can be traced back to the US decision to drop atomic bombs on Hiroshima and Nagasaki in 1945.* Reagan, recalled one of his speech-writers, Peter Robinson, would tell a story from his undergraduate days. A friend had once said to him,

> 'When the next war comes along we'll just use airplanes and drop bombs on the other country.' Reagan said, 'I told him "Oh no. We could never do that. We are Americans. We could never bomb civilian populations."' And he looked down and fell silent . . . you could feel that 50 years later he was still shocked by the idea . . . Nuclear weapons were an offence against basic notions of decency.[9]†

Reagan was always looking for a means of getting beyond the dominant post-war nuclear doctrine, upon which the theory of deterrence rested, of Mutually Assured Destruction (MAD). On 23 March 1983, the President told a startled world that he thought he might have found it. Speaking directly to the nation from the Oval Office, the President asked, 'Wouldn't it be better to save lives than to avenge them? . . . I call upon the scientific community in our country, those who gave us nuclear weapons . . . to give us the means of rendering these nuclear weapons impotent and obsolete.' He announced a research and development programme 'to begin to achieve our ultimate goal of eliminating the threat posed by strategic

---

* For a fuller picture see Paul Lettow, *Ronald Reagan and his Quest to Abolish Nuclear Weapons*, Random House, 2005, ch. 1.

† For Reagan, a biblical Christian, a nuclear holocaust carried significant scriptural connotations. '[S]ome day people are going to ask why we didn't do something now about getting rid of nuclear weapons,' he once told his national security team. 'You know I've been reading my Bible and the description of Armageddon talks about destruction, I believe, of many cities and we absolutely need to avoid that.' (NSPG Meeting Minutes, 8 November 1987, NSPG 0165 09/08/1987, Exec Sec, NSC: NSPG Meetings, Box 91309, Reagan Library.)

nuclear missiles'.[10] This venture was known as the Strategic Defense Initiative (SDI), often referred to, usually derisively, as Star Wars. Reagan had developed the idea in almost complete secrecy, relying on a handful of trusted advisers. Its central premise was that the US would develop a defensive missile shield which would make MAD obsolete.

The world did not receive SDI rapturously. There was mixture of mockery that the notion was fanciful and wouldn't work, and fear that it wasn't and would. The Russians considered it a brazen attempt to undermine the Anti-Ballistic Missile (ABM) Treaty* and exempt the United States from deterrence. If the US could block Soviet missiles, reasoned Moscow, then it could launch a first strike with impunity. In Britain, the fear amounted to the same thing, though from a different point of view. Michael Heseltine, then Defence Secretary, recalled: 'I think that the reaction to the announcement was one of despair – Oh Lord! Here we go again, the next escalation in the arms race – and then *realpolitik* – Oh help! What's this going to do to Britain's independent nuclear deterrent[?]'[11] If the Soviets, too, could develop a shield sufficient to defend against Britain's very limited nuclear arsenal then the rationale for Trident, the new generation of submarine-launched nuclear missiles which were replacing Polaris (see Volume I, pp. 571–3), would vanish overnight.

Mrs Thatcher, who had known nothing of the run-up to the SDI speech, was given a few hours' notice by Reagan. In a message which clearly tried to anticipate the objections, he flattered her by saying that he and she had 'borne the responsibility to provide for our people's security against the most awesome threat in history'. Now they had to move from offensive to defensive technologies. Notions that his country would become 'fortress America', 'violate the ABM Treaty' or 'depart from our commitments to allies' were 'of course utter nonsense'.[12] The benefits of SDI would not come through 'in material terms until the turn of the century', and they would 'be shared with our friends and allies'.[13]

In later years, Mrs Thatcher tended to give the impression that she had welcomed SDI. She boasted that her scientific education, contrasted with 'Laid back generalists from the Foreign Office',[14] enabled her to grasp the concept and run with it. She was certainly not one of those who were appalled.

---

* The ABM Treaty between the US and the USSR placed strict limits on developing defences against nuclear-armed ballistic missiles. 'Strategic ballistic missiles' were considered the most potent weapons in a nuclear arsenal due to their rapid speed and ability to deliver a devastating nuclear payload anywhere in the world. They should be distinguished from 'cruise missiles' that travelled more slowly and had lesser ranges. The umbrella term 'Intermediate Nuclear Forces' (INF) covered non-strategic, land-based ballistic (e.g. Pershing) and cruise missiles with a range of 300 to 3,400 miles.

But the very scientific education which she mentioned led her to be 'dubious about the practicality', Robert Armstrong recalled. '... I think she instinctively doubted whether it would be as effective as Reagan seemed to think it would be.'[15] According to John Weston, the head of the Foreign Office Defence Department, 'She was saying things like, "Well ... the Star Wars thing is just a pipedream and like all dreams it will vanish with the dawning of the day." We all thought, "Good, she's being sensible." '[16] Her immediate reaction was to play for time by emphasizing that SDI was a programme of research and not deployment. 'There is a long way to go in research before we reach any development,' she told Michael Foot in the Commons a few days later. 'I believe in research, but the right hon. Gentleman obviously does not.'[17]

The difference between research and deployment was vital to her approach. It also enabled her to gloss over the fact that she disagreed with Reagan about nuclear weapons. She never departed from the view that nuclear deterrence had worked, keeping the peace since 1945. She naturally wished, if it was safe, to stop the arms race and cut weapons stockpiles, but she did not share the President's sunny vision of a world freed from nuclear threat. What had been invented could not be disinvented, she insisted. She also had a particular worry about where Britain stood in all of this. Mrs Thatcher was well aware that any talk of abolishing nuclear weapons risked making Europe 'safe for conventional war', something NATO had striven to avoid since 1949. If the United States now saw the future in terms of SDI, what would happen to its nuclear guarantee for Europe? Might not Reagan's policy end up serving the turn of the unilateralists? How could Britain justify Trident if its purpose was to be nullified? She did not make a great fuss about these points at this time, but she never abandoned them. They would bulk large later.

The Chequers seminar on 8 September 1983 was carefully prepared by the officials of the Foreign Office, who saw it as their greatest opportunity to influence the Prime Minister's thinking. They were conscious of Mrs Thatcher's suspicion that they might be too wet towards Soviet Communism. Howe, encouraged by his good relationship with the American Secretary of State, George Shultz,* who seemed to think along similar lines, was 'more in favour of engaging with the Soviets than Margaret'.[18] In a cross reply to FCO suggestions about who should attend the seminar, Mrs Thatcher wrote:

---

* George Shultz (1920–), US Secretary of Labor, 1969–70; Director, Office of Management and Budget, 1970–72; Secretary of the Treasury, 1972–4; Secretary of State, 1982–9.

This is NOT the way I want it. I am not interested in gathering in every junior minister, nor everyone who has ever dealt with the subject at the FO . . . I want also some people who have really studied Russia – the Russian mind – and who have had some experience of living there. More than half the people on the list know less than I do.[19]

Above all, Mrs Thatcher wanted to hear from experts from outside the government machine. The final list of academics and other invitees was not, in fact, displeasing to the Foreign Office,* nor were the papers which the academics submitted. What most worried Howe's officials was any serious advocacy of destabilizing the Soviet Union. No paper did this, though one, by Dr Ronald Amann, discussed it as a possibility. The FCO's own paper, probably thinking of Reagan's remark earlier in the year that the Soviet Union was an 'evil empire', counselled against 'statements which disparage the Soviet state or its leaders'.[20] Its main aim was to argue that 'the time is ripe for a more active policy' towards the Soviet Union aimed at a 'gradual evolution towards a more pluralistic political and economic system'.[21] Mrs Thatcher doubly underlined 'ripe' and 'more active policy', but scribbled 'by whom?'

Events appeared to conspire against the supporters of engagement. On 1 September 1983, the Soviets shot down a Korean civilian airliner (KAL 007), which had accidentally strayed into Soviet airspace. All 269 people on board were killed. Mrs Thatcher refrained from immediate public comment, but backed sanctions by the allies. Privately, she wrote to Reagan: 'I share your profound horror at what occurred . . . This incident has vividly illustrated the true nature of the Soviet regime. Its rigidity and ruthlessness, its neuroses about spying and security, its mendacity . . .'[22] But unlike some of the hawks in Washington, Mrs Thatcher did not believe that the West should automatically break off all contact with Moscow. 'I also very much agree that we must continue our search for balanced and verifiable agreements with the Soviet Union,' she concluded.[23] Howe went further. He wrote to her before the seminar, arguing that the atrocity, far from showing that dialogue with the Soviets was impossible, suggested 'the exact opposite': 'this incident proves how dangerous is the state of

* The eight academics present were Ronald Amann (Birmingham University), Archie Brown (Oxford University), the Rev. Michael Bourdeaux, Christopher Donnelly (Royal Military Academy, Sandhurst), Michael Kaser (Oxford University), Professor Alec Nove (Birmingham University), Alex Pravda (Reading University) and George Schöpflin (LSE). On the government side, Mrs Thatcher was accompanied by Geoffrey Howe, Michael Heseltine and Malcolm Rifkind as well as Hugh Thomas (then Chairman of the Centre for Policy Studies and an informal adviser to her on foreign affairs) and a range of officials.

affairs where the two superpowers talk to each other more across the floor
of the United Nations than they do on the Hot Line.'[24] Archie Brown, one
of the academics present, noted what happened when Howe tried to make
a similar point at the Chequers seminar:

> just before lunch Sir Geoffrey Howe finally got in a question he had had
> his mouth open to put half a dozen times which was whether the rhetoric
> in which Western comment on the Soviet Union's actions was couched made
> any difference ... Before the answer could be developed, however, Mrs
> Thatcher butted in to say but, of course, we must condemn them in the
> strongest possible terms when they do something like shooting down the
> Korean airliner. She then announced that we should adjourn for a pre-lunch
> drink.[25]

Mrs Thatcher had prepared for the seminar with a tough line. In what
appears to be an aide-memoire, written in her own hand, she said:

> The Soviet Union does not regard disarmament as an end in itself ... It
> seeks to use negotiations to maintain or achieve a degree of military supe-
> riority; to foster the impression that the Soviet Union is a peace-loving
> nation; to contain both western defence capability and its own defence costs
> and to seek visible endorsement by the US of its superpower status.[26]

She argued in this way at Chequers and, by Brown's account, 'the only
person on the government side of the table who ventured to contradict her
throughout the entire meeting' was Michael Heseltine.[27] But she did study
what the experts had written and listened to what they said. The drift of
their contributions was that Britain should, indeed, engage with the Soviet
leadership. She accepted this more readily from them than she did from
the Foreign Office.

She also, it seems, listened when Archie Brown developed what he had
written earlier about the next generation of leaders in the Kremlin. His
paper described the 'two best-placed contenders' as successors to the ailing
Yuri Andropov (who had replaced Brezhnev as general secretary of the
Communist Party) as 'Gorbachev (52)* and Romanov (60)'. He described
Gorbachev as 'the best-educated member of the Politburo and probably
the most open-minded'.[28] Mrs Thatcher underlined Brown's passage about
Grigory Romanov's 'extravagant lifestyle' but marked none of the remarks
about Gorbachev. In conversation at the seminar, however, Brown recalled
that he advanced the idea of Gorbachev as the best leader from both the

* Mikhail Gorbachev (1931–), General Secretary of the Communist Party of the Soviet
Union, 1985–91; President of the Soviet Union, 1990–91.

Soviet and Western points of view: 'Mrs Thatcher turned to Sir Geoffrey Howe ... and said: "Should we not invite Mr Gorbachev to Britain?" Howe concurred.'[29] This, it seems, was the first moment at which the name 'Mikhail Gorbachev' entered Mrs Thatcher's mind.* Her suggestion that Gorbachev be invited to Britain seems significant in light of later events, but at the time it was little more than her thinking out loud. It did not reach the level of a prime ministerial instruction.† An important seed had been planted, but it had yet to germinate.

All through the meeting, the Foreign Office officials were highly anxious, wanting to push the Prime Minister towards dialogue. One report shows how, from their point of view, things nearly went off the rails:

> The level and tone of the discussion had however deteriorated after lunch when the academics had departed. The Prime Minister made a great show of reluctance about accepting the present lack of channels to Moscow damaged our interests. She wanted to know what the purpose of a dialogue would be and what its content should be.[30]

If Mrs Thatcher had known that her interest in the purpose and content of dialogue was considered a bad sign, it would have confirmed her worst suspicion about the Foreign Office – that it wanted dialogue for its own sake. But in the event, what Rifkind observed to be her 'insatiable curiosity'[31] seems to have got the better of her:

> Nevertheless, she showed signs of interest in meeting Andropov, but not in Moscow. She agreed in the end that once the KAL crisis had died down there should be an improvement in links with the Russians so long as they did not involve herself and as long as it was understood that she had the right to veto these talks if they went too far.[32]

So sensitive were all involved about the seminar that John Coles, her foreign affairs private secretary, did something he could not recall doing on any other occasion.[33] He asked Mrs Thatcher to look at his records in draft. 'Her concern would have been that the party, particularly the right wing and a lot of her supporters in the country, would have been rather

---

* There is some dispute among those claiming the credit for first noticing Gorbachev in Britain. Rodric Braithwaite, later British Ambassador to the Soviet Union, has said: 'Archie Brown believes that he was the first person to notice Gorbachev, but people in the Foreign Office at the time disagree. They say that everybody noticed Gorbachev at the same time.' (Interview with Sir Rodric Braithwaite.) Nonetheless, Brown may well have been the first to draw Gorbachev to Mrs Thatcher's attention.
† Her comments on Gorbachev were not recorded in any official document, nor were they recalled by anyone other than Brown himself.

disappointed if she began to be open-minded about the Soviet Union,'
recalled Coles.[34] He asked her to make sure that he had got it right. She
said, 'You have.'[35] The conclusions of the meeting were hardly sensational.
They were 'very doubtful' whether much 'greater diversity' could be
expected from the Soviet Union, and so 'Our policy should . . . be based
on the assumption that any change in the system in at least the medium
term would not be fundamental.'[36] But some form of talking should start:
'It was agreed that the aim should be to build up contacts slowly over the
next few years,' but there would be 'no public announcement of this
change of policy'.[37] Dialogue would probably prove easier with Eastern
European states, especially Hungary, than directly with the Soviet Union,
but there should also be top-level Soviet contacts. These might include
arranging for 'senior members of the Politbureau, particularly potential
successors to Andropov, to visit London'.[38]

The Chequers seminar marked no dramatic reversal of Mrs Thatcher's
previous approach, but the Foreign Office was correct to see it as a moment
at which it pushed her further down its preferred path than she had travelled before. Charles Powell, who was to become the most important to
her of all her private secretaries, joined her the following year. He assessed
the Chequers seminar (which, of course, he had not attended) thus: 'I don't
think she was any less staunch a Cold Warrior, but tactically she thought
it would be wise to find ways to try to weaken them through the soft
underbelly of Eastern Europe . . . The overall aim remained that Communism had to be defeated, but the question really was what is the best
way to do it.'[39]

The seminar at Chequers also prepared the ground for Mrs Thatcher
and Mikhail Gorbachev to meet, in the same place.

At the end of September 1983, Mrs Thatcher flew to Washington. Her
own developing attitudes to the Soviet Union paralleled those of the US
President. Reagan had begun his presidency taking the line of Caspar
Weinberger, his Defense Secretary, that the Soviet Union was not only
immoral but unchangeable. But, by 1983, he was listening more to the
view of his Secretary of State, George Shultz, that the Soviets, while
immoral, would, if America stood up to them, be ready to make solid
agreements. In this shift, he was urged on by his wife Nancy, who, according to Reagan's aide Michael Deaver, 'was always bugging me about
"What are we doing about this Soviet thing?"' Deaver explained that he
thought Shultz had yet to be convinced that Reagan genuinely wished to
engage with the Soviets. 'And so Nancy said, "Well, we'll just have to have
him over to dinner."'[40] The dinner with Shultz took place on 12 February

1983 and proved 'the beginning of the beginning'.[41] Three days later, Reagan met Anatoly Dobrynin, the Soviet Ambassador in Washington, in conditions of great secrecy. That summer, personnel changes within the NSC staff favoured those who advocated dialogue. Although debate still moved to and fro on the subject in Washington – and the opponents of dialogue gained influence because of the shooting down of the KAL airliner – Reagan was now edging towards a new approach. So when they met in September, the two most hawkish Western leaders of the post-war era were, by the US administration's own stern standards, looking rather more like doves.

En route for Washington, Mrs Thatcher visited Canada. There, in discussion with the Prime Minister, Pierre Trudeau, she heard the name of Gorbachev once more. Trudeau had met him when he visited Canada earlier in the year. 'I did not at this time foresee the importance of Mr Gorbachev for the future,' she wrote later,[42] but, as John Coles recalls it, the Canadians 'thought he was a different sort of Russian and that the West should try to get to know him well. I know that made an impact on her.'[43]

On the morning of 29 September 1983, Reagan received Mrs Thatcher in the Oval Office. The friendship between the two was as warm as ever.* In his diary he wrote: 'PM Margaret Thatcher arrived. She & I had an hour's talk before lunch mainly about the Soviets & what it would take to get back into some kind of relationship ... I don't think U.S.–U.K. relations have ever been better.'[44] In their discussions, Mrs Thatcher gave Reagan a preview of what she would say in her speech that evening to the Winston Churchill Foundation: 'She would, of course, be emphasising that we must deal with the Soviets from strength,' but she felt that it might be time to engage. 'While she would not say so this evening, we must, she stressed, strive to establish normal relations ... The President replied that he shared her views.'[45]

Her speech that evening contained plenty of strong words about the Soviet Union that the press happily reported: 'Their creed is barren of conscience, immune to the promptings of good and evil,' she declared. 'To them it is the system that counts, and all men must conform.'[46] Less attention was paid to her other point that, however unpleasant it might be, 'We have to deal with the Soviet Union. But we must deal with it not as we would like it to be, but as it is. We live on the same planet and we have to

---

* In May, Reagan had mentioned, in a letter to Peter Hannaford, that Mrs Thatcher 'continues to be my favourite head of state' (Reagan to Hannaford, 3 May 1983, Kiron K. Skinner, Annelise Anderson and Martin Anderson, eds, *Reagan: A Life in Letters*, Free Press, 2003, p. 725). Mrs Thatcher was not, of course, a head of state, only a head of government, but it was the thought that counted.

go on sharing it. We stand ready therefore – if and when the circumstances are right – to talk to the Soviet leadership.'[47]

Interviewed in November, Mrs Thatcher complained that 'no-one took any notice of the part that I thought they would fall upon,' by which she meant the section about the need to talk. Instead of carrying this conciliatory message, 'so many of the papers said Maggie Slashes Moscow.'[48] At the time of the speech, though, she was not displeased by such coverage. Just after her Washington visit, she told George Urban,* who had helped with her speech, that her warning about the danger of thinking the Soviets shared Western morality was 'the most important thing I said in Washington'.[49] As was often the case in her interpretations of her own views and actions, she varied them considerably depending upon the moment and the interlocutor.

In essence, though, the strong words and the more conciliatory ones were not contradictory. They fitted the 'bargain from strength' idea. There was no formal collaboration between the United States and Britain on this subject at this time, but there was a common approach. As Shultz put it,

> The British and we bounced ideas off each other . . . Margaret Thatcher had a very clear view of the nature of the contest [in East–West relations], its importance and the interplay of strength with diplomatic efforts. This was always consistent with President Reagan's view . . . Since President Reagan always had a great deal of confidence in her judgement, whenever she went to the Soviet Union, or somebody visited London, or before our own visits, we always had a very full and complete exchange. President Reagan would say, 'Well, I see this is the cable that has come from the Foreign Office, but what does Margaret really think?' He was always very interested in what came directly from her.[50]

Mrs Thatcher was well pleased with her Washington visit. She now felt emboldened to make her readiness for dialogue with the Soviets more public. At the Conservative Party conference, speaking the day after her fifty-eighth birthday, and hours after Cecil Parkinson's resignation, she reasoned with her potentially sceptical audience: 'But whatever we think of the Soviet Union, Soviet Communism cannot be disinvented.' She repeated her Washington point about living on the same planet: 'and that is why, when the circumstances are right, we must be ready to talk to the Soviet leadership . . . But such exchanges must be hard headed. We do not want the word "dialogue" to become suspect in the way the word "détente" now is.'[51]

*

---

* George Urban (1921–97), Hungarian-born journalist, author and broadcaster.

The Soviet reaction to Mrs Thatcher's talk of dialogue was negative. According to Oleg Gordievsky,* the KGB officer who had been recruited as a double agent by SIS† in 1974, and from June 1982 worked in the Soviet Embassy in London, the Soviets disliked her as much as she disliked them. The Soviet leadership had a general belief that 'A Labour government would always be much better for the Soviet Union.'[52] They also had 'an instinctively positive attitude to Edward Heath' and would say 'Look what that woman has done to him.' Once she came into office, their 'hatred and respect for her grew'.[53] The task of the KGB was to discredit her politically. They were particularly eager to undermine her efforts to deploy US cruise and Pershing missiles in Europe. When Mrs Thatcher started to speak in less hostile tones, just as the missiles were about to be deployed, they reacted sceptically: 'The general attitude was that she was the Iron Lady. She's an imperialist. She's an American lackey. She's anti-Soviet. She's an enemy . . . there was not much of a belief that she would change.'[54]

There was also a more specific and dangerous Soviet anxiety, which Gordievsky's clandestine work for Britain revealed. Implausible as it might seem, there were growing Soviet concerns that the West might launch a pre-emptive nuclear strike against them. From 2 to 11 November 1983, NATO conducted a 'command post' exercise, known as ABLE ARCHER. This was designed to test what would happen in a gradually escalating conflict. According to John Scarlett,‡ Gordievsky's SIS case officer at the time, and much later the head of the Service, the exercise was part of an established pattern of annual 'war games', which tested procedures and communications without the involvement of weapons. But it 'came at a moment when tension between Moscow and the US was at a particular height and paranoia was dominant'.[55] The extent to which this infected Soviet thinking was made clear to SIS by Gordievsky. His high level of information was considered unusual, and his briefings struck home. In the words of Colin McColl,§ then Deputy Director of SIS and later its chief, it alerted the service to 'a very important thing to know which we

---

* Oleg Gordievsky (1938–), joined KGB, 1963; posted to London in 1982 and rose to the rank of colonel; a secret agent for SIS, 1974–May 1985, when he was recalled to Moscow by the KGB. In July 1985 he was exfiltrated and returned to the UK. He has lived in Britain since.

† The British Secret Intelligence Service (SIS) is often referred to as MI6 even though this name is formally obsolete.

‡ John Scarlett (1948–), educated Epsom College and Magdalen College, Oxford; Secret Intelligence Service, 1971–2001, serving in Nairobi, Paris and twice in Moscow; Chief of SIS, 2004–9; knighted, 2007.

§ Colin McColl (1932–), educated Shrewsbury and the Queen's College, Oxford; Chief of SIS, 1988–94; knighted, 1990.

didn't know'.[56] When SIS shared the information with the Foreign Office, it compared it with its wider sources, and agreed. Geoffrey Howe later wrote: 'Gordievski left us in no doubt of the extraordinary but genuine Russian fear of a real-life nuclear strike. NATO deliberately changed some aspects of the exercise so as to leave the Soviets in no doubt that it was only an exercise.'[57]* Moscow, however, remained suspicious. The Soviet intervention in Hungary in 1956 and the Warsaw Pact intervention in Czechoslovakia in 1968 had both taken place under cover of exercises. They feared, incorrectly, that Western planners might share their mindset. Towards the end of ABLE ARCHER, KGB headquarters despatched a 'most urgent' telegram to its residencies overseas. It reported, erroneously, that American forces had been put 'on alert' and provided a number of possible explanations, 'one of which was that the countdown to a nuclear first-strike had begun under the cover of ABLE ARCHER'.[58] Gordievsky, of course, reported this to his British handlers. 'I felt that this was a further and disturbing reflection of the increasing paranoia in Moscow,' he said later, 'but not a cause of urgent concern in the absence of other indications.'[59]

This moment gave birth to a controversy which rumbles on to this day:[60] did Moscow really think that the West might be on the verge of launching a surprise nuclear attack? Or were the Soviets, well aware that this was an exercise, merely responding in kind? Worse, was there an element of Soviet disinformation here, designed to confuse the West? Britain's intelligence analysts later concluded that 'we cannot discount the possibility that at least some Soviet officials/officers may have misinterpreted Able Archer 83 . . . as posing a real threat.'[61]

If Soviet paranoia was indeed genuine, the question became, what should be done about it? Rodric Braithwaite,† one of the Foreign Office Russian 'doves', recalled that 'What Gordievsky made clear was that the rhetoric that she and Reagan were using was terrifying.' The ABLE ARCHER experience 'gave an insight into the way officials and senior people in the Soviet system felt about the Western threat to them. Reagan and Thatcher had only ever thought the other way, about the Soviet threat to them.'[62] Oddly enough, Mrs Thatcher does not appear to have disagreed with this analysis. As is customary with intelligence work, she did not, at

---

* Originally the plan had been for Western leaders, including Mrs Thatcher, to take part in ABLE ARCHER. In the event, only officials participated. (Gordon Barrass, *The Great Cold War*, Stanford University Press, 2009, p. 298.)

† Rodric Braithwaite (1932–), educated Bedales and Christ's College, Cambridge; Ambassador to Russia, 1988–92; Prime Minister's foreign policy adviser, and chairman, Joint Intelligence Committee, 1992–3; knighted, 1988.

the time, know Gordievsky's name or position in the KGB, but she probably knew that there was a British 'mole' at the Soviet Embassy, and was certainly given the results of his espionage, first hearing about Gordievsky's warnings on 23 December 1982.[63] Always someone who studied intelligence carefully and believed in its value, she was strongly impressed with what Gordievsky reported, and worried by what it conveyed. She later directed her officials to share Gordievsky's revelations with the Americans.[64] In John Scarlett's view, the discovery of the Soviet reaction to ABLE ARCHER had a wider, slower influence on policy: 'It is possible that this set off a train of thought that Cold War stability wasn't so stable. We were misjudging the mentality and psychology of the rather old Soviet leadership.'[65]* The train of thought led naturally to an interest in a fuller conversation with the Soviet leadership. It fitted with the conclusions of the Chequers seminar.

Just as she was trying to get a better understanding of her Soviet enemies, Mrs Thatcher was confronted with a nasty shock from her American friends. Late in the afternoon of 24 October 1983, the Prime Minister was told to expect a cable from President Reagan. She saw it at 7.15 p.m. In it, Reagan explained that he was now so worried about the situation on the tiny Caribbean island of Grenada, whose leader, Maurice Bishop, had been murdered the previous week, that he was 'giving serious consideration' to a request from the Organization of Eastern Caribbean States (OECS)† for military assistance. In the cable, Reagan sought Mrs Thatcher's 'thoughts on these matters'. He also pledged to 'inform you in advance should our forces take part in the proposed collective security force, or of whatever political or diplomatic efforts we plan to pursue. It is of some assurance to know that I can count on your advice and support on this important day.'[66] The cable gave no hint (except, perhaps unintentionally, in the use of the phrase 'this important day') that invasion was imminent. Mrs Thatcher was just off to a farewell dinner given by Princess Alexandra for the outgoing US Ambassador, John Louis. She was 'strongly against intervention'[67] and left instructions for a reply to be drafted accordingly. Intuiting urgency, however, she also asked for a meeting to be arranged for her return. Mrs Thatcher hoped to extract some explanation from the guest of honour after the dinner. But when the ladies 'retired', the Prime

---

* It was considered important, in this context, that Andropov had never travelled outside the Soviet bloc, and therefore found it hard to imagine life in the West.
† The OECS comprised Antigua and Barbuda, Dominica, Montserrat, St Lucia, St Kitts-Nevis and St Vincent as well as Grenada and the Grenadines.

Minister, now increasingly 'edgy', was forced to make small talk with the wives while the men lingered over port and brandy at the table. 'Oh, I do wish they would come out!' she exclaimed.[68] When they finally emerged, she buttonholed the Ambassador only to discover he knew less than she did.

When Mrs Thatcher returned to No. 10 shortly after 11 p.m., a second message from Reagan was waiting. 'I have decided to respond positively to this [the OECS] request . . .' Reagan told her. 'Our forces will establish themselves in Grenada.'[69] He was invading without the consultation with Mrs Thatcher which he had promised little more than three hours earlier. 'We were both dumbfounded,' recalled Geoffrey Howe. 'What on earth were we to make of a relationship, special or otherwise, in which a message requesting the benefit of our advice was so quickly succeeded by another which made it brutally clear that that advice was being treated as of no consequence whatsoever?'[70] The Americans were not even acting against Mrs Thatcher's advice, but without it. Her drafted reply had not, at the time Reagan's second message was received, been sent.

Grenada was a strange story – as unusual, in its way, as the Falklands War the previous year. Like the Falklands, it exposed tensions between the United States and Britain which neither partner had quite bargained for. Unlike the Falklands, it did not end harmoniously.

Part of the trouble arose, as so often in Anglo-American difficulties, because of Britain's colonial legacy. In 1974, Grenada, until then a British colony, gained independence. As was fairly common, the Queen remained head of state, represented on the island by a governor-general. In 1979, the government was overthrown in a Marxist coup led by Maurice Bishop. The United States, always vigilant about Communist subversion in its backyard, noted a growing Cuban presence on the island, including a large workforce helping to construct a new airport with suspected military application. On 13 October 1983, hardliners in Bishop's government led by the military commander, General Hudson Austin, and the Deputy Prime Minister, Bernard Coard, overthrew their leader. The Americans feared for the fate of the thousand or so US students attending the St George's Medical School on the island who might be taken hostage. Anxiety deepened when, on 19 October, Austin's men put down a revolt by Bishop's supporters. Between thirty and forty Grenadians were killed and Bishop and his lieutenants executed by firing squad.

The Americans sensed danger, but also opportunity. On 20 October, the administration's Crisis Preplanning Group met and discussed a rescue plan for the students, but also the possibility of overthrowing the hostile

Grenadian regime. According to Lawrence Eagleburger,* the Under-Secretary for Political Affairs at the State Department, 'The prime motivation was to get rid of that son of a bitch [General Austin] before the Cubans got any further embedded . . . The students were the pretext . . . but we would not have done it simply because of the students.'[71] In the view of Robert 'Bud' McFarlane,† who had recently succeeded Judge Clark as National Security Advisor, there was a real fear of the Communists subverting the whole region: 'It was Reagan's sense that this was truly a strategic move by the Soviet Union. It had to be countered.'[72]

The British, recalled Howe, 'were aware of the long-standing US concern with Communists on Grenada, but we didn't really take it very seriously.'[73] And the Americans were not shipshape in communicating their concerns. McFarlane blamed his predecessor. 'It was very, very badly handled from our side,' he said, insisting that the administration's position should have been shared with Mrs Thatcher months earlier. 'I was surprised at Judge Clark.'[74] But there was some contact. According to an early draft of George Shultz's memoirs, in a passage excised before publication, 'A plan was floated after lower level British–American consultations that involved a small assault effort by a Special Air Services [SAS] Team, the elite British commando unit.'[75] Officials at the Embassy in Washington were involved in discussions about the extent of possible UK–US co-operation.[76] The plans did not get very far, however, because, when the Americans, on 21 October, sought a Foreign Office view about direct intervention, they were, in the words of Robin Renwick,‡ the Head of Chancery at the British Embassy in Washington, 'heavily brushed off'.[77] As Renwick saw it, 'The effect of this uncompromising response was to ensure that we were excluded from US planning.'[78]

Mrs Thatcher was not directly involved in this exchange, but the Foreign Office's attitude reflected her view. On the same day, 21 October, she received reports revealing that Tom Adams, the Prime Minister of Barbados, was trying to arrange 'a multi-national intervention'[79] in Grenada, involving the Americans, various Caribbean states and 'a British contribution'. Mrs Thatcher put her wiggly line of disapproval under the last

---

* Lawrence Eagleburger (1930–2011), diplomat; Under-Secretary of State for Political Affairs, 1982–4; Deputy Secretary of State, 1989–1992; Secretary of State, 1992–3; received honorary knighthood from the Queen, 1990.
† Robert ('Bud') McFarlane (1937–), counsellor, Department of State, 1981–2; Deputy National Security Advisor, 1982–3; National Security Advisor, 1983–5.
‡ Robin Renwick (1937–), educated St Paul's and Jesus College, Cambridge; Rhodesia Department, FCO, 1978–80; Assistant Under-Secretary, FCO, 1984–7; Ambassador to South Africa, 1987–91; to the United States, 1991–5; created Lord Renwick of Clifton, 1997.

phrase. The source indicated that Adams wanted Britain to know what he was up to, and that the British contribution he had in mind was that the SAS should secure the safety of the Governor-General, Sir Paul Scoon. These ruminations from the Caribbean were far from a formal request for British assistance and consequently had little standing in London. Mrs Thatcher's desire was to avoid military action of any kind against Grenada. She indicated this on John Coles's covering note.[80] Encircling the phrases 'American troops' and 'the SAS', she linked them with arrows and the words 'This seems most unwise' (underlined three times). Coles described the idea that the Governor-General's safety could be a pretext for invasion as 'dubious'. He told Mrs Thatcher that Geoffrey Howe, who was in Athens, was being consulted, and added, in words which Mrs Thatcher underlined, 'There is a just a chance . . . that one of the Caribbean Prime Ministers or perhaps even the Americans will try to get in touch with you over the weekend.'[81]

Ronald Reagan left Washington for a long-scheduled golfing break in Augusta, Georgia, on Friday 21 October 1983. By then US planning for the invasion of Grenada was well advanced. In the early hours of the following morning, 22 October, the President was awoken by news of a request from the OECS for 'assistance', in other words, to invade. Although the Pentagon approached the possibility of military action with great caution, Shultz and the NSC staff were strong advocates. Reagan readily agreed to the OECS request. His agreement was hardly surprising, since the formal OECS request had been engineered by his own Secretary of State.* The OECS nations were deeply concerned by the instability on Grenada with Eugenia Charles, the Prime Minister of Dominica, particularly vocal in asking Washington for support. As early as 18 October, Shultz (encouraged by Reagan) had asked her to generate a formal OECS request for military assistance. Miss Charles agreed. Meeting in Washington at 9 a.m. local time on the Saturday, the Special Situations Group (SSG), chaired by the Deputy National Security Advisor, John Poindexter, met to plan the invasion. According to Poindexter, consultation with the British 'wasn't a big deal to us',[82] but informing Mrs Thatcher was discussed and it was agreed to 'notify her at the last minute'.[83] The SSG

---

* Later, in conversation with Mrs Thatcher, Reagan's tongue slipped and he referred to the OECS 'request' as 'an offer' before quickly correcting himself (Memorandum of telephone conversation, Prime Minister Margaret Thatcher, 26 October 1983, Exec Sec, NSC Country File, UK Vol. V, Box 91331, Reagan Library. The Library has also released a tape of the call (RAC Box 53, White House Situation Room Records)). In fact, to the Americans it *was* an offer: a chance to invade with a justification for action.

produced a time chart for 'D-Day', the day of invasion, which provided that Mrs Thatcher be informed only on 'D-DAY MINUS ONE':

> 1500
>
> Eagleburger calls in UK Ambassador and provides him signed letter from President to PM Thatcher stating our concern for safety of foreigners, concerns of Caribbean leaders from threat from military regime on Grenada, formation of government, US interest to cooperate with provisional government and Caribbean leaders to restore democracy in Grenada. President will inform Mrs Thatcher when there is final decision.[84]

In short, by the Saturday morning, the Reagan administration had decided to keep Mrs Thatcher in the dark over Grenada until it was too late for her to do anything about it.

Some subsequent explanations by American participants suggested that it was simply the rush of events which made them forget their closest ally, or the need for complete secrecy, or the assumption that she would be all for the invasion. In fact, the expectation was not that Mrs Thatcher would agree, but that she would not. According to Duane Clarridge* of the CIA, who attended the SSG meeting, 'we anticipated that Mrs Thatcher would be unhappy. We . . . didn't want to give her any room for manoeuvre, either publicly or privately. We didn't want to lose control of the operation.'[85] This was the real reason that Mrs Thatcher was not consulted.

There is no record of an explicit order by Reagan or Shultz to keep Mrs Thatcher unsighted, but both were complicit. Ken Adelman† recalls hosting a dinner for Sir Anthony Kershaw, the chairman of the House of Commons Foreign Affairs Committee, who visited Washington shortly after the invasion. As Adelman told the story, Kershaw, when he met Reagan, had asked the President why he had not consulted Mrs Thatcher earlier. At first, Reagan 'says nothing. So he says, "And she considers you a close personal friend." Reagan is silent.' Kershaw asked again: 'Reagan then took off his glasses, which showed he was a little angry, and said, "Because I didn't want her to say no." '[86] This story has never been corroborated – it may be apocryphal – but, according to Jack Matlock‡ of the NSC, its point was correct: 'It might seem cowardly, but I had the feeling that Reagan knew he would have trouble psychologically

---

* Duane Clarridge (1932–), served in a number of positions in the CIA, 1955–87; Chief, Latin America Division, 1981–4.
† Kenneth Adelman (1946–), US Ambassador and Deputy Permanent Representative to UN, 1981–3; Director Arms Control and Disarmament Agency, 1983–8.
‡ Professor Jack Matlock (1929–), American academic and diplomat; US Ambassador to the Soviet Union, 1987–91.

authorizing the invasion if Thatcher objected . . . he decided it would be
best to confront the PM with a fait accompli.'[87] In Geoffrey Howe's view,
the deception was necessary because the friendship and 'sexual chemistry'
between Mrs Thatcher and Reagan was such that 'if Mrs Thatcher had
talked to Reagan [before the attack was under way] she'd have dissuaded
him.'[88] In the view of Howard Baker, later the President's Chief of Staff,
'Maggie Thatcher was the only person who could intimidate Ronald
Reagan.'[89]

   This assessment may exaggerate the power Mrs Thatcher had over her
most powerful ally, but the accurate belief on both sides that Mrs Thatcher
and Reagan enjoyed a relationship of trust does help to explain the actions
of those involved. For the Americans, it was a reason to deny her information. For the British, it was a reason to take things slightly for granted.
Certainly, British diplomats in Washington that weekend gained their
main information from sources which were not close to the action. In
particular, much store was set by a conversation between Robin Renwick
and Admiral Jonathan Howe, the Director of the Bureau for Politico-
Military Affairs at the State Department, which was reported to London
on the evening (London time) of Saturday 22 October. Howe had informed
Renwick that the NSC had decided that 'the US should proceed very cautiously'; 'Howe also assured us that there would be consultation if the
Americans decided to take any further steps.'[90] Explaining this to the
present author, Howe insisted that he 'wouldn't have tried to mislead
Robin' and that his view may have been 'reflecting the Department of
Defense's reluctance to act'. His comments were not intended as an official
statement of administration policy. Had he realized that the British
government would base its entire policy on these fateful words, Howe
confirmed that he would have been horrified.[91] It was indeed odd that so
much weight was put on the words of a single, middle-ranking administration official. British fears were too easily allayed.

   This was not so true of Mrs Thatcher herself, always more likely to
suffer from agitation than complacency. At Chequers that weekend, she
followed the situation closely. Informed that Geoffrey Howe, from Athens,
had authorized HMS *Antrim* to depart in the direction of Grenada, Mrs
Thatcher rang Richard Luce that Saturday afternoon. Luce had returned
to office after his resignation over the Falklands invasion, and now found
himself in the same role as then, deputizing in the absence of the Foreign
Secretary abroad. He was at home watching a Western on television when
the Prime Minister rang: ' "What are you doing sending ships?" she
demanded. "We don't want a war!" '[92] She calmed down only when Luce
explained to her that the ship was approaching the island (keeping below

the horizon) in order to be ready to rescue British citizens and with no belligerent intent. Luce soon discovered that Mrs Thatcher was worried by the threat of US action: 'She said that evening that she was "fearful of being dragged into an unwarranted conflict",' and of embarrassment that might be caused to the Queen.[93] He urged her to 'put her oar in in Washington. She said she would call a meeting the next day.'[94]

On the same day, Mrs Thatcher had learnt, as Tom Adams of Barbados had foreshadowed, that the OECS had resolved unanimously to use force to restore order on Grenada and to seek help from Britain and others in doing so. On the other hand, she was informed that CARICOM, the wider and more powerful organization of Caribbean states, had taken a cautious line, urging a diplomatic solution. She was also armed with information from Buckingham Palace which, despite the constitutional separation between the Queen's role as head of state of a Commonwealth country and the government of the United Kingdom, naturally kept in touch. At 9 a.m. (UK time) that morning, the Queen's assistant private secretary, Robert Fellowes,* had spoken on the telephone to the Governor-General. Scoon had 'assured Fellowes that there was no threat to himself or to Lady Scoon, and that they were both in good form'.[95] In the circumstances, it did not seem necessary or wise to agree to the OECS request, which had only been conveyed orally.† The British government chose inaction, masterly or otherwise.

The next day, Mrs Thatcher did not follow up Luce's advice to get in touch with Washington directly. She always disliked transacting business on the telephone, and took some comfort in the assurances relayed from Admiral Howe. She decided instead to discuss the whole matter in Cabinet committee (OD) the following day. She would have acted more swiftly – and angrily – if she had known that the OECS request had been encouraged by the Americans in the first place.

On that Sunday morning, 23 October, events in Lebanon provided a sudden and tragic distraction. The US Marine barracks in Beirut, part of a multinational peacekeeping force, were destroyed by a truck bomb (see Chapter 9). The eventual death toll was 241. This terrible event obviously made it harder for Mrs Thatcher, if she was still so minded, to get in touch with Washington about Grenada. For an America which had not seen

* Robert Fellowes (1941–), educated Eton; assistant private secretary to the Queen, 1977–86; deputy private secretary, 1986–90; private secretary, 1990–99; chairman, Barclays Private Bank, 2000–2009; knighted, 1991; created Lord Fellowes, 1999.
† It later emerged that a fax formally requesting British help had been sent by mistake to a London plastic-bag manufacturer rather than to the Foreign Office, but this error was not known that day.

full-scale military action since Vietnam, the combination of this attack with the perceived threat in Grenada was a powerful spur to action of some sort. Mrs Thatcher wrote in her memoirs, 'What precisely happened in Washington I still do not know, but I find it hard to believe that outrage at the Beirut bombing had nothing to do with it. I am sure that this was not a matter of calculation, but of frustrated anger.'[96] In fact, the evidence shows that the Grenada decision predated the Beirut atrocity. The only political effect of Lebanon was to brush aside any remaining American doubt about acting over Grenada. The practical effect was to allow the NSC to go into continuous session, making it impossible for the British, anxious for information about Grenada, to speak to their best contacts. When the NSC meeting ended, Robin Renwick reached a State Department contact, who told him that 'Grenada was now a subject on which there was "no cable traffic".'[97] As Renwick explained later, 'That could mean only one thing.'[98]

Nevertheless, that 'one thing' was not clearly or quickly conveyed by the British Embassy in Washington. At the OD meeting chaired by Mrs Thatcher the next morning, Geoffrey Howe reported that the US was not planning military action: 'The Prime Minister and colleagues endorsed our reasoning.'[99] It is remarkable, given her anxiety over the weekend, that Mrs Thatcher accepted the Foreign Office's reassurances so readily. She probably did so because of her trust in her closeness to Reagan. As Howe himself put it afterwards: 'The closer co-operation was the more one relied on it.'[100] That afternoon, Howe made a statement to the House of Commons in which he said that 'we are keeping in the closest possible touch with the United States Government . . . I have no reason to think that American military intervention is likely.'[101]* Mrs Thatcher kept her own copy of Howe's statement and noted down what was said in questions that followed as she sat beside him. She recorded Howe's answer when his shadow, Denis Healey, asked if the United States intended to invade: 'I know of no such intention.'[102]

It is strange that the government found itself saying such things. As the report of the Commons Foreign Affairs Committee into the fiasco emphasized, it had known by 22 October at the latest that the OECS were preparing for an invasion, so its reliance on (mistaken) evidence from Washington alone was curious. Another important clue came from a conversation with the Governor-General on the afternoon of 23 October.

* By this stage, a new telegram from the Embassy in Washington had reached London reporting that the Americans were close to taking military action. Due to bureaucratic fumbling, it did not reach Howe before he spoke. (Interview with Lord Renwick of Clifton.)

Visited by a British diplomat,* Scoon was asked if he would be prepared to support a US military intervention, backed by CARICOM forces. 'He replied, without any hesitation, that he would probably be <u>eliminated</u> if he made <u>any move that directly challenged</u> the authority of the <u>RMC</u> [the revolutionary government]. He doubted therefore that he could ask for outside help.'[103] It was on this telegram that Mrs Thatcher based her view of the Governor-General's position (the underlinings on it are hers). The interpretation she and her government seem to have put on Scoon's reported words was that he was not asking for help. But they probably suggested the opposite: by telling his visitors that his life was in danger, Scoon was explaining why he could not speak freely and hinting that he did, indeed, need assistance. Scoon's message was shared with Tom Adams, who saw it as the green light for action. The Americans, in close touch with the Caribbean leaders, took the same view. They made Scoon's 'request' central to the legality of their involvement and now concocted a rigmarole with the OECS – drafting a written request for help from Scoon, which would be presented to him for his signature only after he had been rescued.

On Monday 24 October 1983, the day of Howe's unhappy statement, the Americans followed the secret timetable drawn up by the Special Situations Group two days earlier. The first of the two Reagan messages for Mrs Thatcher was cabled at 14.47 hours, almost exactly as planned. Following his allotted task, Lawrence Eagleburger got in touch with the British Ambassador, Oliver Wright, that afternoon. 'What he was saying in effect', Wright reported, 'was that the US Administration would not understand if we actively lobbied against the course of action which they had almost but not quite decided upon.'[104] The first Reagan message to Mrs Thatcher suggested consultation. The second, which arrived before she had returned from the dinner with Princess Alexandra, was that the invasion was going ahead. There had been no consultation at all.

   Mrs Thatcher was seriously perturbed and affronted: 'She didn't see how the invasion of sovereign territory could be right.'[105] Only the previous year she had fought a war to carry that point. She was also mortified that a country of which the Queen was head of state was to be invaded. And above all, she was shocked by what she suspected was the duplicity of the Americans. At half past midnight, she sent a reply to Reagan's second cable, noting the shortage of time between one message and the other and stating, 'I must tell you at once that the decision which you describe causes

* David Montgomery, the Deputy British High Commissioner in Barbados.

us the gravest concern.'[106] She said she feared for the safety of US and British citizens on the island, and complained that the invasion put the Governor-General – 'the Queen's representative on the island' – 'in a very delicate position'. She also pointed out that Britain had never received a formal request from the OECS. She widened the argument. Invasion without agreement or consultation, she said, would undermine her case that America could be trusted to behave with restraint:

> This action will be seen as intervention by a Western democratic country in the internal affairs of a small independent nation, however unattractive its regime. I ask you to consider this in the context of our wider East/West relations and of the fact that we will be having in the next few days to present to our parliament and people the siting of cruise missiles in this country ... I cannot conceal that I am deeply disturbed by your latest communication. You asked for my advice. I have set it out and hope that even at this late stage you will take it into account before events are irrevocable.[107]

This message was written and sent after consultation with Howe, Heseltine, Antony Acland, the head of the Foreign Office, and her private secretaries Robin Butler and John Coles. Those present took the view that Mrs Thatcher should immediately follow it up with a telephone call to the President. According to Butler she was extraordinarily reluctant to do so, partly because she was 'not wanting to have a great row with Reagan about it'. 'I think the penny eventually dropped,' continued Butler. 'Indeed, I remember us saying to her, "You're going to have to say something about this in the House of Commons tomorrow. And you really must have made some effort to speak to Reagan about it."'[108]

So she did.

While Mrs Thatcher felt indignant, she was still working out how best to handle the situation. Her words to Reagan were not angry ones and the call lasted only three minutes.* Butler, who also listened in to the call, confirmed that it had 'barely any substance at all', and, in his eyes, became unintentionally comic:

> First of all, Reagan was very reluctant to come to the telephone. When he did eventually ... I can only describe his tone of voice as one of a naughty schoolboy who had been caught out doing something he shouldn't have been ... And then she said, and this was the funny thing, 'Well, er, Ron. I

---

* Some American witnesses recalled a much longer exchange in which Mrs Thatcher, who was 'just livid' (Interview with Bud McFarlane), had a great row with the President. This is not supported by other participants nor by the documentary record.

don't want to say too much on the telephone.' And he then said, 'But Margaret, we're speaking on our most highly encrypted line.' And she said, 'But never mind. You can never be sure about telephone calls.'[109]

At first Butler thought this showed extraordinary naivety on Mrs Thatcher's part about the technology, but 'In fact I think it was an excuse. She didn't really want to go into it very much. The call took place for the sake of the call taking place.'[110] Recording its main points, John Coles noted simply that Mrs Thatcher urged Reagan 'to consider her [cabled] reply very carefully indeed. The President undertook to do so but said, "We are already at zero." '[111]

Mike Deaver was with Reagan when he finished the call:

Reagan hung up and said, 'She's not with us. She's not going to be with us.' I could tell, knowing him, the pain for him of the conversation . . . He said, 'But we have to go forward. We've got to go forward anyway.' . . . It was clear from when he hung up and his shoulders kind of sagged that he was disappointed not to have his friends with him.[112]

Much later that evening, Reagan sent a third message to Mrs Thatcher, conciliatory in tone, but firm in content, sticking to his view that invasion was 'the lesser of two risks'. He sought the 'active cooperation of Her Majesty's Government' and, playing the legitimacy card, hoped that 'the Governor General will exercise his constitutional powers to form an interim government which would restore democracy and facilitate the rapid departure of all foreign forces'.[113] Two hours later, US forces began their assault on Grenada.

Although the Americans had not intended to humiliate Mrs Thatcher, they deliberately misled her. The Special Situations Group plan was followed throughout. Reagan's line in his first cable to Mrs Thatcher that he wanted her 'thoughts' was never true: they were deliberately sought only when it was too late for them to matter.* The system of messages was a charade, carefully worked out. In his memoirs, Reagan overlooks the messages altogether, suggesting – erroneously – that Mrs Thatcher got wind of the invasion from 'British officials in Grenada'.[114] The American

* Archival evidence suggests that, when US officials were preparing to send Reagan's first cable, they already had a final draft of the second one in front of them: 'send via CABO at 1500,' an official wrote on a note covering a draft of the first cable, '2nd cable later' (Hill to McFarlane, 'Grenada', 24 October 1983, Exec Sec, NSC: Country File, Grenada invasion October 1983 (1), Box 91365, Reagan Library).

deception may well have been justified from the administration's point of view, but a deception it was.*

It took a bit of time for the full import to sink into Mrs Thatcher's mind. From the start she was deeply worried, but the real anger came later. Her immediate reaction was simply to try to deal as fast as possible with the problems which arose. As she had predicted, critics used the invasion, and Britain's exclusion from the decision-making, to question US reliability over cruise missiles. Her claims to a close relationship with the President were widely ridiculed. The papers carried a flurry of bad headlines. 'Reagan's midnight snub for Maggie', said the *Sun*, '– stunning humiliation'. While the final outcome of the invasion could not be in much doubt, US forces met stiffer resistance than had been expected, and fighting on the island was continuing.† This circumscribed Mrs Thatcher's ability to make any final judgment or comment.

Speaking on the telephone Tom Adams, the Prime Minister of Barbados, told her that 'It had come as an enormous shock to him to discover that so little was known in London.'[115] Mrs Thatcher expressed both her disappointment and her caution. 'We naturally wondered whether we'd been kept in the dark,' she told Adams, but 'Whatever our feelings about the American attitude, the operation was now taking place. We hoped that it would succeed . . . We wanted to avoid harm to the Alliance.'[116] In response to a Foreign Office request that Mrs Thatcher speak to the Prime Minister of Jamaica to calm him down about Britain's failure to support the invasion, she scribbled: 'I don't think a phone call would help at the moment. He is not the only one with strong feelings. Least said soonest mended.'[117]

In the meantime, though, she was made to feel the embarrassment of her situation. She saw the Queen for her usual weekly audience on 26 October. There is no record of the Queen expressing her views on the invasion at the audience, but Buckingham Palace was mortified by the difficult position in which, as sovereign of Grenada, it put her.[118] Apart from anything else, the safety of her representative, the Governor-General, was not assured until 26 October, when he was rescued by US Navy Seals. This news reached London after Mrs Thatcher's audience. At the time at which she saw the Queen, Scoon could, for all she knew, have been dead. Always

---

* In his memoirs, George Shultz muddies the waters by suggesting that the US despatched a cable seeking British counsel as early as the Sunday. (See George Shultz, *Turmoil and Triumph*, Charles Scribner's Sons, 1993, p. 330.) No such cable existed.

† Fighting did not end until 29 October, by which time nineteen US servicemen had been killed.

extremely correct and rather tense about all dealings with the monarch, Mrs Thatcher was unhappy. Foreign Office officials noted that 'Mrs Thatcher understood that the Queen was upset and Mrs Thatcher was very disturbed by this.'[119] In the course of 25 and 26 October 1983, the full extent of British dismay was conveyed to Reagan. He 'felt badly about it', recalled Baker, and was advised to telephone Mrs Thatcher to 'kiss and make up'.[120]

Reaching her on 26 October, in the middle of the emergency Commons debate on the invasion, Reagan attempted to disarm the Prime Minister with a line which could have come from one of his 1940s movies. 'If I were there Margaret,' he said, 'I'd throw my hat in the door before I came in.'[121] 'There's no need to do that,' she replied primly. Reagan attributed his reluctance to consult her earlier to 'a nagging problem of a loose source, a leak here', not to any lack of trust in her. Secrecy had been vital, he said. In this Mrs Thatcher appeared to concur: 'I'm very much aware of sensitivities. The action is underway now and we just hope it will be successful.' This gave Reagan an opening to assure her that all was 'going beautifully' in the operation, though some fighting continued. Then Reagan flattered her: 'We know that you and through the Queen's Governor General there – all of us together – can help them get back to that constitution [he used the phrase 'that constitution' because he had earlier praised Britain for bequeathing it to Grenada] and a democracy.' He praised Eugenia Charles, the Prime Minister of Dominica and Tom Adams of Barbados, and, when Mrs Thatcher agreed with him, took this as his cue to draw her further in: 'They all feel – and dating from the days when they were under the Crown – she [Miss Charles] used the expression: kith and kin. I don't know if that's one of our expressions or one of yours.' 'It's one of ours,' said Mrs Thatcher. 'Well,' said President Reagan gallantly, 'we still use it here. We still have the heritage . . .' He was making a play for her sense of British cultural hegemony. Mrs Thatcher sounded a few warning notes about what might happen next – 'There's a lot of work to do yet, Ron . . . And it will be very tricky' – but raised no positive objection to anything he said. When he apologized for 'any embarrassment that we caused you', she said it was 'very kind of you to have rung'. When she closed by saying that she must go back to the debate in the Commons, Reagan urged her, 'Go get 'em. Eat 'em alive.' 'Goodbye,' she replied and hung up rather abruptly.[122]*

Mrs Thatcher had not yet forgiven Reagan and she was, as usual on

* In 2014, the audiotape of this call was released by the Reagan Library. In it, Reagan's tone

the telephone, guarded in her responses. Nonetheless, she was somewhat mollified by what he had said; and he, hearing no renewal of her earlier concerns, was greatly bucked up. Talking to the Australian Prime Minister, Bob Hawke, later that day Reagan referred to 'the pressures coming from England', but added, 'I'd be very much surprised if it doesn't let up.'[123] David Goodall told the US Embassy that the President's call had been ' "just the right move". It had helped assuage the PM's own feelings, and she had used the information provided to bolster the Cabinet at a critical juncture.'[124]

The invasion of Grenada was discussed in full Cabinet on Thursday 27 October. Despite her feelings, Mrs Thatcher chose to defend the US against a number of more sceptical colleagues. George Younger,* the Scottish Secretary, backed up by Whitelaw, was unconvinced: 'Have Americans been straight with us? There must have been something cooked up over the weekend,' he said. 'We have been ill served by our allies. We may have no constitutional position, but our Queen is Queen of Grenada.'[125] Mrs Thatcher refused to join the chorus: 'I am not surprised that US told as few people as possible,' she insisted, and made an effort to understand the American position: 'They are entitled to see things in a different perspective.' Her one strong criticism was about the wider effects of the crisis. She feared that the invasion would undermine 'US/NATO lore that NATO is only defensive' and that only the Soviets launched military action against independent nations. She thought there was now a greater 'danger that US pulls out of Europe to concentrate on her own backyard'.[126]

In Prime Minister's Questions in Parliament that afternoon, Mrs Thatcher maintained her protective public attitude to the United States. 'We stand by the United States,' she told Neil Kinnock, 'and will continue to do so in the larger alliances.'[127] She was clearly trying to bury the hatchet.

That was on the Thursday. On the following Sunday (30 October), she dug the hatchet up again and waved it in the air. As a guest on the BBC World Service international phone-in that afternoon, she faced a question from a New Yorker that could have been perfectly designed to provoke

---

is one of embarrassed, gallant conciliation, like that of a suspect boyfriend in a 1940s film. Mrs Thatcher's is one of correct and chilly politeness.

* George Younger (1931–2003) (4th Viscount Younger of Leckie), educated Winchester and New College, Oxford; Conservative MP for Ayr, 1964–92; Minister of State for Defence, 1974; Secretary of State for Scotland, 1979–86; for Defence, 1986–9; created life peer, 1992; KCVO, 1993; KT, 1995.

her. Americans, he said, were 'shocked and dismayed at Britain's implicit support of international terrorism' in its reaction to the invasion. Given US help over the Falklands, didn't Mrs Thatcher's government have a duty to support America now, or at least shut up? Mrs Thatcher could never bear the idea that anyone would think her soft on terrorism. Nor could she tolerate any inaccurate or unfriendly reference to the Falklands War. Off she went: in the Falklands, she said,

> Britain went to get its own territory back . . . That has no parallel whatsoever with Grenada . . . I am totally and utterly against Communism and terrorism. But . . . if you are pronouncing a new law that wherever Communism reigns against the will of the people . . . there the United States shall enter, then we are going to have really terrible wars in the world. I have always said . . . that the West has defensive forces in order to defend our own way of life and when things happen in other countries which we don't like, we don't just march in.[128]

It was a classic statement of her approach to armed conflict, national sovereignty and the rule of law, expressed with eloquent clarity.

It was also exasperating for the Americans, because it opened up the whole issue all over again in a highly contentious manner. She was 'rightfully pissed off but she overreacted', recalled John Lehman, the Secretary of the Navy; 'she hit us too hard.'[129] 'Margaret didn't support us,' George Shultz recalled. 'She undercut us, which we didn't appreciate. She was mad [that is, angry] . . . She was a big problem.'[130] There was a widespread feeling in Washington that she was being ungrateful, given US support over the Falklands. Bud McFarlane duly fired off a cable of protest to the Cabinet Secretary, Robert Armstrong. Britain's public reaction to the invasion had 'caused us profound disappointment', McFarlane declared, singling out Mrs Thatcher's remarks about marching into other countries as 'unusually harsh'. 'The infliction of such public criticism by one of our closest allies' after the 'national anguish' caused by the Beirut bombing was 'doubly wounding'.[131] His complaint, he explained, was not about private differences, but about public ones which 'only serve to diminish British–American solidarity which has served our mutual interests so well'. He was sending this message, he said, to 'clear the air' and appeal for British support.

Strongly worded as this message was, the final draft had been toned down several notches. An earlier draft had been more personal, suggesting that Mrs Thatcher's attitude had put at risk 'the solidarity which our respective heads of state have worked so hard to foster'.[132] Underlying McFarlane's message was a sense, not directly stated, that Mrs Thatcher had personally endangered her relationship with President Reagan by what she had said in public.

Armstrong sent Mrs Thatcher a copy of his proposed reply to McFarlane, which put the British counter-case in more restrained language. Mrs Thatcher disliked his tone of compromise, Armstrong was told: 'Mrs. Thatcher does not wish to give the impression that we were grateful for the advance notice of the Grenada operation (which she considered quite inadequate) nor that our views, private or public, would have been different if we had had more time or more knowledge.'[133] He was instructed to redraft his reply to make it less conciliatory.

Why was Mrs Thatcher so annoyed, and more so as time passed than she had been at first? Normal explanations must play a part. In early November a *Sunday Times* poll suggested that a little over a third of those asked believed she was good in a crisis, down from almost two-thirds before the Grenada episode.[134] The press and Opposition jibes that she was the humiliated poodle of the President obviously had to be countered. So did media attempts to drive a wedge between herself and Geoffrey Howe on the issue. She had suffered a week of bad headlines, and both experience and temperament told her that the best form of defence is attack. She also believed in the justice of her case against the invasion. But to understand the depth of her feeling about Grenada, one must look more at Mrs Thatcher's character, and perhaps her sex, than at the details of the issue itself.

Ever since Ronald Reagan had become president at the beginning of 1981, Mrs Thatcher had tried to forge an unbreakable friendship between the United States and Britain, based on common beliefs, common threats, common interests, and personal affection and trust. She had succeeded beyond expectation. When she had visited Washington in September 1983, following her second election victory that summer, she had been royally received. She was confident that INF deployment, for which she had taken so many risks, would go ahead in November. She liked Reagan for his gentlemanly charm, his courtesy to her as a woman, but above all because he inspired her trust. In her mind, there was no greater virtue than trust.

As she contemplated the saga of Grenada, a short month after her Washington triumph, she could not avoid the conclusion that the President had betrayed this trust. At first, she preferred to think that the trouble had come from his underlings, but, in the face of repeated evidence, she could not excuse him from blame. A full account from Robin Renwick entitled ' "Consultation" with the Americans about Grenada'[135] had reached her on 28 October, after her call from Reagan and before her World Service broadcast. It reiterated that a promise to consult had been given, and broken. It concluded that Reagan had more or less decided to invade as early as the morning of 22 October. In these circumstances, she considered Reagan's cables and the flattering words of his post-invasion telephone call dishonest. His emollient call had, one might say, rubbed sugar in her wounds, which was not much more healing than salt.

And so Mrs Thatcher, who, despite her great professionalism, always invested strong personal feeling in her relationships, and was susceptible to charming, well-dressed men who flattered her, was as disappointed as a two-timed girlfriend. 'My relations with President Reagan will never be the same again,' she told a senior official.[136] She felt she had been made a fool of. For a proud woman who had a slightly old-fashioned view of the relations between the sexes, this experience was even more mortifying than it would have been for most men. In this sense, her outburst on the World Service was uncalculated, a natural expression of pique and anger. One might conjecture that President Reagan, also fulfilling the stereotype of his sex, felt as deflated as does any professional charmer when his arts fail. It was surprising – and lucky for both sides – that the press did not pursue this rift much further. It had the potential to do real harm.

From the BBC World Service phone-in onwards, the bureaucracies of both countries struggled to get the relationship back on track. It was arranged that Kenneth Dam, the Deputy Secretary of State, would call on Mrs Thatcher for breakfast at Chequers on 7 November 1983. From the moment he arrived, Dam found her 'highly agitated about Grenada'.[137] He recalled: 'She invited me immediately after shaking hands to go to a sideboard where she took a grapefruit and I, in American fashion, chose some orange juice. She demanded to know why I had not taken grapefruit. The only thing I could say was that I preferred orange juice. She seemed displeased . . .'[138] Mrs Thatcher then launched into what Dam considered a tirade about Grenada, starting with the provocative question 'whether Grenada was unique or a replay of the Monroe Doctrine and Bay of Pigs that portended further similar moves'[139] in, for example, Nicaragua. The British official record largely confirms this, and shows Dam inserting the odd word of apology and polite, downplayed disagreement. Mrs Thatcher spent an hour and forty minutes venting her irritation about not only Grenada, but also INF deployment, Lebanon and possible American support for the supply of arms to Argentina.[140]

In Dam's view, the conversation 'ended on a very cordial note. She had just been blowing off a huge head of steam.'[141] Others were not so sure. Edward Streator, Chargé d'Affaires at the US Embassy in London, warned Washington of 'mounting problems with Thatcher'[142] and intervened informally with Howe and Carrington to 'try and persuade Mrs Thatcher to cool it'.[143] In her Mansion House speech on 14 November, Mrs Thatcher was prevailed upon to reiterate Alliance solidarity – 'it is the strength and resolution of the Western alliance which keeps the peace today' – but she remained grumpy, and was curiously unimpressed by the argument, which Dam had put to her, that polls showed 91 per cent of the people on Grenada pleased with the invasion.* As late as early December, Vice-President Bush, who had been 'inundated with pleas from the Brits to repair the schism',[144] wrote to Mrs Thatcher to say, 'I wish we could sit down and chat because I have been troubled by recent tensions and I know it hasn't been easy for you either.'[145]

It was the historian Hugh Thomas,† her informal and occasional adviser on foreign policy, who provided the most thoughtful summary of her problem, parts of which Mrs Thatcher underlined. Thanking her for dinner on 14 December 1983, Thomas wrote that he had found 'one part of our conversation disturbing. That related to yr. current view of the U.S.'[146] He counselled against 'drawing up a general indictment' of the US administration on the basis of Grenada 'unless there is some alternative general underpinning of our foreign policy with which you wish to experiment'. She herself had ruled out greater European defence collaboration, he wrote, so what alternative was there? There should therefore be 'a considered attempt to mend our fences with the US', and a clear preference for Reagan re-elected over any Democrat alternative. She should try to 'make a new start' after Christmas:

> You have such a fine reputation over there. Those of us who look to you to provide us with the kind of direction that de Gaulle gave France have always pointed out that yr strength, in comparison with the general, is that you do accept the essential part that the US has had since 1945. All US officials & politicians . . . except you from their general moans about European defeatism. You can surely rebuild on the basis of those facts.[147]

This letter was well expressed because, in the de Gaulle comparison, it played on Mrs Thatcher's temptation to define her national leadership by cutting loose from America – only in order to dismiss it. Under political

---

* Nor was her view much changed by news of the vast hoard of documents the Americans recovered from Grenada, illustrating the extent of Moscow's support for the original coup against Bishop.

† Hugh Thomas (1931–), educated Sherborne, Queens' College, Cambridge and Sorbonne, Paris; Professor of History, University of Reading, 1966–76; chairman, Centre for Policy Studies, 1979–90; author of *The Spanish Civil War* (1961); created Lord Thomas of Swynnerton, 1981.

pressure from the likes of Enoch Powell* and David Owen, she was worried that others might play the patriotism card better than herself, and she was still smarting from being, as she saw it, let down. She may briefly have harboured illusions, post-Falklands, that Britain could behave like Gaullist France, almost defining itself by independence from the United States. Thomas's words were accurately judged to remind her that a British version of Gaullism could work only if it were essentially pro-American. Although she would never admit that she had gone too far in her wrath over Grenada, she secretly knew that Thomas's argument was right.

Mrs Thatcher also understood perfectly well the significance of the fact that INF deployment had begun, as planned, by the end of November 1983. It was a triumph for the Western Alliance; but it also caused the Russians to walk out of the INF talks in Geneva, increasing East–West tension. She recognized both her own success and the accompanying need to look for dialogue. It was in this spirit that she began 1984.

* J. Enoch Powell (1912–98), educated King Edward's, Birmingham and Trinity College, Cambridge; Professor of Greek, University of Sydney, 1937–9; war service, rising to rank of brigadier, 1939–45; Conservative MP for Wolverhampton South West, 1950–February 1974; left Conservative Party before February 1974 election and advocated a Labour vote; Ulster Unionist MP for Down South, October 1974–1985 and 1986–7 (resigned his seat in December 1985 in protest at the Anglo-Irish Agreement; re-elected January 1986); Minister of Health, 1960–63.

6

The enemy within

*'If anyone has won, it has been the
miners who stayed at work'*

In her first term, Mrs Thatcher had tried to avoid direct confrontations
with the trade unions. Her approach had been to change the law 'step by
step' in order to reduce their legal immunities, rather than go to war. In
her second term, while she remained tactically cautious, she began to
believe she could actually win, and so was readier to fight. She was readier
for full-scale contests with public sector and nationalized industry trade
unions which would test both the strength of her new labour laws and the
political mettle of her government. In the case of the National Union of
Mineworkers, she had every reason to see such a contest as almost inevitable. The ground for her first confrontation, however, was not central
to her battle to overcome industrial chaos. It concerned trade union power
in a separate area, but one close to her heart – national security.

The Government Communications Headquarters (GCHQ) at Cheltenham was, for technological reasons, an ever more important part of
Britain's intelligence capacity. By the end of the 1970s, its glorious wartime
role of decrypting Nazi signals at Bletchley Park had been partially disclosed. It was also (and is even more so today) central to the relationship
of intelligence co-operation and trust with the United States which had
begun during the Second World War and continued in the Cold War.
GCHQ's operations were secret, but it was not, in a formal sense, part
of the secret services at that time. Its staff were members of the general
Civil Service and free to join trade unions accordingly. The Security Service (MI5) and the Secret Intelligence Service (SIS) stood apart from the
general Civil Service. Their staff were specifically denied the right to join
a union because unions, being national organizations reaching beyond
those services, could not be restrained by the necessary rules of secrecy.
MI5 and SIS staff were not permitted to strike.

The union presence at GCHQ worried Mrs Thatcher. During the 'Winter of Discontent' in early 1979, under the Labour government which she
was to defeat that May, strikes by unionized staff had seriously disrupted

GCHQ's work. The same happened in the Civil Service strike of 1981. One senior national union official crowed in the media: 'This [the GCHQ signals research station at Culmhead in Somerset] is the most crucial station we have hit so far. We are going to hit this Department "as hard as we can".'[1] Other union boasts specifically proclaimed how they had damaged Britain's secret communications surveillance network nationally and internationally. The unions' motivation was not Moscow-inspired subversion, but part of their desire to make life as difficult as possible for the government during the strike, right across the Civil Service. They probably did not understand the depth of alarm their actions provoked. The Director of GCHQ, Sir Brian Tovey, told staff that the strikes meant the services were losing confidence in GCHQ's ability to provide early warning of Soviet intentions. He added that the US National Security Agency (NSA) was also alarmed.[2] To Mrs Thatcher, he claimed that if not guaranteed a reliable supply of SIGINT (signals intelligence) by the British, the Americans would 'insist on supplying personnel' to man British stations.[3]

Mrs Thatcher was furious with the Civil Service unions. 'There was a sense of betrayal,' recalled Robert Armstrong. 'She never forgave them.'[4] She was a passionate believer in upholding national security and in the importance of the Anglo-American relationship. It was intolerable to her that these things could be put at risk by displays of union muscle. She was the first prime minister since Winston Churchill in 1941 to consider GCHQ worth visiting. She also held strong, old-fashioned views about the value of secrecy in security matters.* She wanted to prevent a repetition of such strikes by banning union membership at Cheltenham, and was supported in this by the top management of GCHQ. Although there is no evidence that the United States ever suggested a union ban to the British government or to her personally, the US agencies had certainly made known their anxieties about the disruption. By acting firmly, Mrs Thatcher believed, she would be serving the interests of the alliance as well as the direct national interest.

Change was complicated because of GCHQ's status and funding. It was part of what was called 'the hide', the device by which its budget was concealed inside those of conventional departments. It had no formal national security status. Only by 'avowing' GCHQ's SIGINT activities

---

* Throughout her time as prime minister, for example, Mrs Thatcher held back publication of the final volume of the official history of British intelligence in the Second World War, although it was written by Sir Michael Howard, whom she greatly admired. She thought it might reveal information about thought processes in the Security Service which, if made public, might put current intelligence operations at risk. (Interview with Lord Armstrong of Ilminster.)

for the first time could the government justify its removal from the general
Civil Service. As a formally secret organization it could then be excepted
from the Employment Protection Act and its union rights removed. So the
paradox was that, for GCHQ to be classified as secret, the nature of its
work had to be made public. Avowal would, however, have tricky consequences for SIS, which was, at that time, totally secret and not avowed.
Plans were drawn up, but the Falklands War pushed them to one side.
Besides, Mrs Thatcher was conflicted between her desire to delay avowal
and her desire to ban unions. 'I insisted that we play GCHQ long.'[5]

An unrelated event changed matters. In April 1982, a GCHQ employee,
Geoffrey Prime, was arrested for sexual assaults on young girls. It then
emerged that he had also been passing SIGINT secrets to the Soviet
Union. He was later convicted of both offences and sentenced to thirty-five
years in prison. There was no trade union issue in Prime's case, but his
conviction brought further public attention to the work of GCHQ. In
November that year, Mrs Thatcher explained the Prime case to the House
of Commons and in doing so effectively 'avowed' GCHQ's work.[6] Her
way now lay open, if she won, to make changes. She intended this, and
asked officials to put it in hand.*

The task fell to Robert Armstrong. He was, recalled Lord Gowrie,† who
was Civil Service minister at the time, 'very iffy about the whole thing'.[7]
Although happy in principle to execute Mrs Thatcher's aims, he was anxious about the means. As head of the Home Civil Service, Armstrong saw
his job as a pacific one, and 'wanted the usual channels to calm it all down.
She, by contrast, was on a Spitfire raid, propellers whizzing.'[8] In his many
memos to her on the subject, Armstrong tended to insert caveats and suggest compromises. Mrs Thatcher would scribble crossly in the margins.
When he told her, for instance, that 'in general civil servants are expressly
encouraged to join a union', she wrote, 'why? By whom?'[9] No one, however,
including Armstrong, advised Mrs Thatcher not to try to ban unions at
GCHQ. Just before Christmas 1983, Mrs Thatcher and those ministers
directly involved decided to put their plan into effect in the new year.

Because of the demands of secrecy, there was no consultation in advance

* Seeking to emulate US agencies the government had intended to introduce routine
lie-detector tests for GCHQ staff in tandem with the union ban. Mrs Thatcher's support
for this fell away after sceptial British experts appealed to her sense of herself as a scientist.
(Interview with Tony Comer.) She did not become deeply involved in the issue.
† Alexander Greysteil Hore-Ruthven, 2nd Earl of Gowrie (succeeded grandfather, 1955)
(1939–), educated Eton and Balliol College, Oxford; Minister of State, Department of
Employment, 1979–1981, Northern Ireland Office, 1981–3; Minister for the Arts, 1983–5;
Chancellor of the Duchy of Lancaster, 1984–5.

with those affected. The GCHQ staff and the trade unions were informed only minutes before Geoffrey Howe* announced the union ban to the Commons on 25 January 1984. The ban, Howe told the House, would be compensated by a one-off payment of £1,000 to each employee.[10] Robert Armstrong gave the news to the trade unions in person. There was 'outrage', he reported to Mrs Thatcher, and they 'protested bitterly' at not being consulted. They described the £1,000 as a 'bribe'; one official uttered the words 'Judas Iscariot'.[11]

In GCHQ itself, there was some anger at the ban and the payment among unionized members of staff. 'She thinks we can be bought,' said critics. If so, perhaps she was right: in the first twenty-four hours, 460 employees accepted the new status and the money, and only two rejected it. Twenty-four hours later, the number of acceptances had doubled and that of rejections had halved (since one of the two who had refused changed his mind).[12] Tony Comer, then a young GCHQ employee and later the official historian of the organization, recalled that significant numbers of the staff, who were appreciative of the benefits in terms and conditions of employment that trade union membership gave them, were nevertheless 'uncomfortable with the danger of their work in GCHQ being compromised to support somebody else's agenda'.[13]

The press and public reaction to the shock of the announcement was mostly negative. Some thought the measure was a slur on the loyalty of trade unions to the nation, and were deeply offended; others thought it too draconian. Many more simply thought it was being mishandled. The Cabinet, which, because of her worries about secrecy, Mrs Thatcher had not consulted, was grumpy at having been kept in the dark. 'If she had taken things to Cabinet,' commented Robin Butler, 'there might have been wiser heads to look at the problem.'[14] Always adroit in attack, Jim Callaghan told a TUC protest rally that although Mrs Thatcher was known for her interest in Victorian virtues, 'She seems also to have picked up some Victorian vices. For this arbitrary action is no better than that of a nineteenth-century mill-owner.'[15]

The consultation which, in a non-secret organization, would have taken place before the announcement, now happened after it. Mrs Thatcher did not like this but, given the public indignation, could not prevent it. Geoffrey Howe put Robert Armstrong in charge. Armstrong, who conducted painstaking discussions with the Civil Service unions personally, found that, for all their rage, the unions were 'desperate about it. They

---

* Howe made the statement because the Foreign Office was the lead department responsible for GCHQ.

would go to almost any lengths to keep their foot in the door.'[16] They offered to make no-strike agreements and to let negotiations be conducted by security-cleared union officials in Cheltenham rather than by their national officers. He told Mrs Thatcher that the 'relatively moderate men – the officials with whom I am dealing – heartily wish they had not [caused disruption in 1981] . . . There is a case for giving the unions a chance.'[17]

Mrs Thatcher did not think so. She was not disposed to accept the unions' concessions, but she did agree to Armstrong's request that she see their leaders, including Len Murray,* the general secretary of the TUC. She went into the meeting fortified by a note from Robin Butler written the night before:[18]

> Close of play score at Cheltenham
> Acceptances   4260   60.5 per cent
> Refusals   13

She was polite – 'She did not doubt the dedication of individual staff' – but she gave no ground on the 'inherent conflict of loyalty'[19] created by the needs of national security on the one hand and the nature of the trade union structure on the other. For Mrs Thatcher, the strike-induced disruption had been the symptom of the problem. She now wished to tackle the cause. The union leaders vented their wrath. Murray accused her of being 'dismissive of trade unions generally'. He regarded this meeting as the final signal that the closeness between government and the unions which had been the dominant feature of his era and his career was dead. He resigned from his job a couple of months later. 'For him,' Armstrong recalled, 'it was the last straw.'[20]

Although she had no personal animus against the amiable and decent Murray, Mrs Thatcher was not moved by the unions' protests. In the same meeting, Geoffrey Howe had explained that the GCHQ ban was a special case, not a criticism of unions as such. Mrs Thatcher did not endorse this view. When Howe sent her the draft of his speech in the debate on the subject to be held four days later, he included a sentence saying he did not want 'to cast doubt on the loyalty of the staff at GCHQ'. After 'loyalty of', Mrs Thatcher inserted 'individual members'.[21]† Although there is no

---

* Lionel ('Len') Murray (1922–2004), educated Wellington Grammar School and Queen Mary College, University of London; general secretary, Trades Union Congress, 1973–84; created Lord Murray of Epping Forest, 1985.
† There is no reason to doubt that Mrs Thatcher's admiration for the majority of the GCHQ staff was genuine. In early April, just after the Queen had visited Jordan, she wrote to Peter Marychurch, who had succeeded Tovey as the GCHQ director, to thank them for monitoring threats to the monarch and for the 'devotion and professionalism' they had shown through

evidence that she thought the unions were traitors working for the Soviet Union, she did indeed, after what had happened in 1981, doubt their loyalty to GCHQ. When he came to deliver his speech in Parliament, Howe ignored her inserted words and stuck to his original text. Although he was not outspoken with her about it at the time, he later regarded the GCHQ saga as an example of 'one of Margaret's most tragic failings: her inability to appreciate, still less accommodate, somebody else's patriotism'.[22] In his negotiations, Armstrong believed he achieved '97 per cent' of what Mrs Thatcher wanted. Howe would have been content with this. Mrs Thatcher was not. 'She wanted to get the unions out of GCHQ hook, line and sinker,' Armstrong recalled. 'She wanted everything.'[23] Numerically at least, she very nearly got it. By 2 March, 6,616 employees, almost 95 per cent of the Cheltenham staff, had accepted the new arrangements and only 45 had refused.

She also carried her point. She would not accept the so-called 'card in the pocket' solution, eventually conceded by the unions, which would have allowed GCHQ staff to remain members of national unions, without those unions having any negotiating rights at GCHQ. There could be a staff association, she agreed, but not one with any right to industrial action or any link with an exterior trade union. Once GCHQ's funding had been transferred to the 'secret vote', hidden from public gaze, it was easier to provide its staff with better pay and conditions. Mrs Thatcher wanted to make sure the staff positively benefited from not having a union: 'I saw to it that they did a damn sight better with the staff association than they had ever done with a Trade Union.'[24]

Throughout the almost year-long processes of consultation, parliamentary and public argument, and the judicial review which the government lost on appeal in July* but then won in the House of Lords in December,† Mrs Thatcher carefully worked through all the suggestions Armstrong made, but nevertheless resisted any compromise. In this, she was strongly supported by her principal private secretary, Robin Butler, who, in Lord Gowrie's phrase, was 'hawkier than thou'.[25] He often wrote on the margin of memos from Armstrong, urging Mrs Thatcher not to be lured into anything that could be represented as a climbdown, and he composed a

---

this time of 'personal difficulties and anxieties'. (Thatcher to Marychurch, 2 April 1985, Prime Minister's Papers, Security, The Funding, Status and Staffing of GCHQ, Part 3 (document consulted in the Cabinet Office).)
* The government won on three of the four main points, but lost on the issue that it should have consulted the unions before instituting the ban.
† At that time, in its Judicial Committee, the House of Lords was the highest court in the land. This function was taken over by the Supreme Court in 2009.

memo, enlisting Bernard Ingham's support, which set out the dangers. 'I probably thought Robert was too chummy with the Civil Service unions,' Butler recalled.[26]

Butler was also conscious of the wider accusations of drift from which Mrs Thatcher's government was suffering at the time. 'If you are not resolute about this,' he wrote to her, 'it will be taken as proof positive that you are not as resolute in your second Administration as you were in your first.' If she weakened now, 'the unions will have the Government over a barrel.'[27] 'There goes someone one who wants to be the next Cabinet Secretary!' Gowrie remembered thinking as he saw Butler at work;[28]* but if one looks at the issue from his boss's point of view, Butler was surely right. If she had blinked, she would not only have lost the first union battle of her second term which, up to then, she had been winning: she would also have disabled herself for the much bigger battles to come. The fact that an ambitious civil servant could see this showed how Mrs Thatcher really had got the better of establishment doubters by winning her second general election. 'The major mandarin resistance to her had gone,' recalled her private secretary Tim Flesher. 'GCHQ was the issue that symbolized this. It may have been a battle which was disproportionate, but once she got into this fight, she had to win it.'[29] Butler understood how she was changing everything. Armstrong either did not, or more likely did, but did not like it.

Six weeks after announcing the GCHQ union ban, and long before the issue was settled, Mrs Thatcher found herself engaged in the most titanic struggle with a single trade union ever known in Britain.

In February 1981 (see Volume I, Chapter 19), Mrs Thatcher had surrendered to the National Union of Mineworkers. In order to avert a strike for which her government was not ready, she had dropped the proposed programme of pit closures designed to put the coal industry on an economic footing. On that day of defeat, Bernard Ingham wrote her a rueful note about the assault he had suffered from the press lobby that morning. The journalists, he told her, had tried to establish that there had been 'a massive U-turn . . . without knowing the financial cost'. His response, he said, had to been to explain that 'no Government ever gets from A – B in a straight line.'[30] As he well knew, Ingham was making the best of an extremely bad job, but his answer was accurate. Mrs Thatcher did indeed intend to move from A to B. In her mind, the increasing government

* This prophecy was to be fulfilled in 1988.

subsidies demanded by the loss-making coal industry (which in 1983–4 reached £1.3 billion) left her little choice. By March 1984, she was ready.

The one merit of her 1981 capitulation was that it had been swift. Rather than drawing out a struggle she could not win, and thus suffering the fate of Edward Heath in February 1974, she had surrendered at once. 'I hugely admired the way she cut and ran very quickly in 1981,' Butler recalled. 'She reckoned she couldn't cut and run again.'[31] In almost every way – for her economic transformation of Britain and her reform of the trade unions, for her party's need to exorcize the ghosts of 1972 and 1974, for her personal pride and her very survival in office – it was essential that she should not be beaten again by the NUM. Mrs Thatcher did not, at that point, know how or – even more difficult – when a national coal strike would come. All she knew was that it would be decisive for her premiership. And so, unusually for a woman who tended to act more by instinct than strategy, Mrs Thatcher started to plan.

However complicated the politics, the plan itself was simple. What mattered most was called 'endurance': there had to be enough coal to survive a complete shut-down of production. Since nearly three-quarters of British coal was used in electricity generation, this meant, above all, having enough of it stockpiled both at pitheads and at power stations. It also meant being able to transport those stocks when and where needed. This, in turn, demanded trade union laws which restricted the ability of pickets to block coal movement, and police with enough authority and resources to enforce both these and the common law. Although many of the requirements for endurance were highly technical – Mrs Thatcher delighted, as a scientist, in showing off her knowledge of the ancillary chemicals, such as carbon dioxide to cool the turbines, required to keep the power stations functioning – it was really a question of organization and of political will.

In 1981, despite Mrs Thatcher's efforts to prod the lethargic Whitehall machine into action, coal supplies had been sufficient only for six weeks. This meant that no government could withstand a strike: the lights would soon start to go out. After this debacle, the government realized that endurance of at least six months was necessary. From July 1981, the civil servant in charge of putting things to rights was Peter Gregson* at the Cabinet Office who, as a young private secretary to Edward Heath, had witnessed and felt 'deep depression'[32] at the first capitulation to the NUM

---

* Peter Gregson (1936–), educated Nottingham High School and Balliol College, Oxford; Deputy Secretary, Cabinet Office, 1981–5; Permanent Under-Secretary, Department of Energy, 1985–9; Permanent Secretary, DTI, 1989–96; knighted, 1988.

in 1972. Gregson believed that better strategic oversight was needed to prepare for a strike. He insisted that government tactics over public sector pay should be linked with endurance. He chaired an 'official group' on strike preparation in the coal industry, and was also in charge of the Cabinet Office's work on trade union reform.

Mrs Thatcher had also begun the necessary political preparation by replacing David Howell as energy secretary with her rising star, Nigel Lawson, in 1981. According to Lawson, her brief to him was 'succinct': ' "Nigel," she said, "we mustn't have a coal strike." '[33] This suggests that, contrary to the view of many on the left, Mrs Thatcher was not going out of her way to pick a fight with the miners. However much she wanted to defeat union militancy, her attitude was essentially defensive. As Gregson explained the task: 'We were *never* spoiling for a fight. We wanted as much time as possible.'[34] Lawson knew that his brief from Mrs Thatcher was an instruction not to appease the NUM, but to prepare for when the government might be strong enough to resist them. In November 1981, over 70 per cent of NUM members voted for the left-wing extremist Arthur Scargill* to succeed the moderate Joe Gormley as president of the NUM when Gormley's term of office ended in April 1982. Scargill's political opposition to the Tory government was absolute. An attack was therefore expected.

It is surprising that more controversy did not surround the build-up of coal stocks. When Mrs Thatcher and senior colleagues discussed the matter, at Lawson's suggestion, in February 1982, Jim Prior had raised the traditional Wet objection that it would be seen as 'provocative'.[35] But in fact the stockpiling went smoothly. The high cost of the work could be concealed in the huge profits of the Central Electricity Generating Board (CEGB), rather than adding to the huge losses of the National Coal Board. 'I was astonished we got away with it,' recalled Peter Gregson. 'Everyone could see these mountains of coal at the power stations. Why didn't Scargill stop it?'[36] The extra production was good news for ordinary miners because it helped to keep otherwise threatened pits open, for the railway workers (whose 'sympathy' strikes were also feared) because they could earn more overtime moving the coal to the power stations, and for the moderate power-station workers. The build-up worked fast. In July 1983, with the Conservatives' election landslide won, Robert Armstrong reported to Mrs Thatcher that, by November, power-station endurance would be six months.[37]

---

* Arthur Scargill (1938–), educated White Cross Secondary School and Leeds University; president, Yorkshire National Union of Mineworkers, 1973–82; president, NUM, 1982–2002; honorary president from 2002.

The government gave thought to human resilience as well. Previous confrontations with the unions had proved how weak the leaders of the nationalized industries could be. Mrs Thatcher knew that this must change. In 1982, she strongly supported Lawson's choice of Sir Walter Marshall,* the chairman of the UK Atomic Energy Authority, as the new chairman of the CEGB. She admired Marshall's credentials as a scientist and his fierce commitment to the development of nuclear power which, if fully pursued, would get rid of dependence on coal for good. 'Marshall gave her confidence that he knew what he was talking about.'[38] She agreed with Lawson that Marshall would 'co-operate to the full with the Government in the preparations to withstand a strike'.[39] So it would prove. He would be much admired for his ingenuity once the strike began: 'He found ways of smuggling spare parts from one power station to another.'[40]

Even more important was the question of who should be chairman of the Coal Board. Sir Derek Ezra, the chairman from 1972 to 1982, was a classic example of the corporatist type against which Mrs Thatcher rebelled, always seeking maximum agreement rather than taking tough decisions, and allowing the union to manage much of the industry. He was blamed for feebleness in the debacle of February 1981. Ezra's term as chairman expired in 1982, and Lawson appointed the elderly but effective stop-gap, Norman Siddall, for a year. But for some time Lawson had been courting Ian MacGregor, the controversial (and also elderly) Scottish American whom Keith Joseph had appointed in 1980 to turn round British Steel. After the squashing of Joseph's idea that MacGregor should run both coal and steel at the same time, his appointment to the Coal Board was formally announced in March 1983. By the time he took up the post in September, Mrs Thatcher was securely in office for her second term. After the election victory, having made Nigel Lawson her new Chancellor of the Exchequer, she needed a replacement at Energy. She invited Peter Walker, the chief remaining Wet in government, to do the job. Although she mistrusted Walker, and disagreed with him on economic policy, she also had a high regard for his abilities. 'If Peter wants to be in every Cabinet of mine, he can be,' she told her private secretary.[41] By Walker's own account, he had intended to refuse office, but when Mrs Thatcher offered him Energy he realized that if he said no she would say 'Faced with Scargill, he went.'[42] So he accepted.

*

* Walter Marshall (1932–96), educated Birmingham University; Chief Scientist, Department of Energy, 1974–7; chairman, United Kingdom Atomic Energy Authority, 1981–2; chairman, CEGB, 1982–9; knighted, 1982; created Lord Marshall of Goring, 1985.

By the autumn of 1983, then, with all the key lieutenants in place, Mrs Thatcher felt ready to move forward. Peter Gregson advised her that stocks at power stations were now almost as great as was physically possible. If a strike came, therefore, it could be better resisted than in the past and 'there is no case for making a special effort to avoid a miners' strike this year in particular.'[43] It was time to push ahead with efforts to put the industry on an economic footing. The newly arrived Ian MacGregor produced his 'preliminary conclusions' on how to achieve this to which, he said, he did not want to be 'held'. Peter Walker, fearing leaks, unveiled these to Mrs Thatcher in a meeting whose record was not circulated beyond the private office. MacGregor, who, said Walker, 'was clearly handling the situation very adroitly',[44] saw a future for the coal industry which could be 'bright indeed'. He wanted continued investment in new, low-cost capacity to be 'presented to the workforce as a quid pro quo for closures'. Between then and 1985, he was minded to suggest that a further seventy-five pits would close, reducing manpower from 202,000 to 138,000.* Some areas would be badly hit by closures: in Wales, for example, two-thirds of miners would lose their jobs.

There is little evidence that Mrs Thatcher had strong views on the precise content of the MacGregor package as it developed. She trusted him to work out the details according, as far as was possible, to commercial principles. Her chief concern was to be ready for a strike. The first rumbles of confrontation were felt on 31 October 1983, when the NUM began an overtime ban in protest at the current pay offer and rumours of pit-closure

* Critics, such as the BBC's former industrial correspondent Nicholas Jones, have seized upon the record of this meeting as evidence of a 'secret plan to destroy the British coal industry', proving that, as Scargill claimed at the time, the government had a secret 'hit list' of over seventy pits earmarked for closure (http://www.cpbf.org.uk/body.php?id=3007; http://www.bbc.co.uk/news/uk-25549596). This document does not provide evidence of a government 'hit list'. What it does record is MacGregor's insistence, reported by Walker, that there be 'no closure list, but a pit by pit procedure'. (Record of a meeting in No. 10 Downing Street, 15 September 1983, TNA: PREM 19/1329 (http://www.margaretthatcher.org/document/133121).) The seventy-five-pit figure was merely MacGregor's early suggestion, which left ministers unconvinced. There 'would be considerable problems in all this', Walker concluded, and no decisions were taken. The policy was settled only at a meeting on 19 January 1984. This time there was no talk of a specific number of pit closures, but ministers focused on reducing manpower. MacGregor proposed to accelerate workforce reductions over the next two years from 28,000 to 45,000, aided by a generous redundancy scheme. Mrs Thatcher summed up the meeting by saying that 'the objective of a more accelerated run-down of coal capacity was accepted', as were the terms of the enhanced redundancy package. (Record of meeting in No. 10 Downing Street, 19 January 1984, TNA: PREM 19/1329 (http://www.margaretthatcher.org/document/133712).) The policy was to put the industry on a sustainable footing, not to destroy it. Two weeks later, Walker announced the investment of £400 million in new mines in the Vale of Belvoir. (For more details see http://www.margaretthatcher.org/archive/1984cac1.asp.)

plans. In a meeting of ministers two days later, which Mrs Thatcher chaired, it was agreed that the danger of a strike was 'likely to increase in the second half of 1984'.[45] Ministers assumed that the NUM would not be so foolish as to begin a strike in the spring just when demand for coal would fall. Preparations for the inevitable confrontation continued. 'The first priority', Mrs Thatcher told the meeting, 'should be to concentrate on measures which would bring benefit over the next year or so.'[46]

Despite the careful preparations, the actual moment when the strike began was a surprise. On 1 March 1984, the South Yorkshire Coal Board director announced, erroneously, that Cortonwood, a pit in South Yorkshire, would close in five weeks' time. On 6 March, MacGregor disclosed that 20,000 jobs in the industry would go in 1984. Mrs Thatcher's Policy Unit, however, minuted her office to say, 'we do not think that the Prime Minister should be unduly alarmed at this stage.' The Yorkshire and Scottish miners could strike with the approval of their executives and without a ballot, the unit's memo went on, but 'a national strike could not take place without a national ballot.'[47] At Cabinet on 8 March, Mrs Thatcher set up a ministerial group (MISC 101) of senior ministers to keep abreast of the situation. On the same day, the NUM executive declared strikes in Yorkshire and Scotland official, invoking the right to 'area action'. In a move that would assume tremendous significance, Rule 43, which demanded a ballot before any national strike, was not invoked, despite minority demands that it should be. Most miners in Nottinghamshire and Lancashire, in particular, did not want to come out on strike.

Mrs Thatcher was eager to make clear that her government's approach was different from that of her Conservative predecessors. She told the Cabinet that 'the dispute in the coal industry was strictly between the NCB and the National Union of Mineworkers and the Government should neither intervene nor comment on the issues. The Home Secretary should continue to ensure that the law was upheld.'[48] There was sense in this doctrine. Many of the disasters in the Heath era had come from the false idea that intervention by politicians would solve matters: in reality it had given the strikers exactly the political leverage they sought. Only if labour disputes were conducted between employers and employed, rather than becoming political confrontations, could sanity return to British industry. It is precisely because she did not want to become a party to these disputes that Mrs Thatcher had been so keen to appoint people like Ian MacGregor. On the other hand, the doctrine of non-intervention was a fiction. The government was paying for the enormous losses of the NCB. The government was ultimately responsible for the rule of law, for public order and for ensuring energy supply. And, in the case of the miners, if everything went wrong, the government would fall. It was therefore inextricably involved in any dispute.

Mrs Thatcher had to face this contradiction the very next day. Ian MacGregor came to see her, by long-standing arrangement, about the Channel Tunnel project in which he was, for non-NCB commercial reasons, interested (see Chapter 12). Before turning to the business on the agenda, the two discussed the miners' dispute, with Peter Walker also present. MacGregor explained that the NUM was trying to bring the union out on strike nationwide without a ballot. Flying pickets from Yorkshire were preventing men in Nottinghamshire from going to work, while the police did nothing. He emphasized Arthur Scargill's political purposes.[49] This, then, was Mrs Thatcher's first real test: where miners wished to continue working, could pits be kept open in the face of intimidation from those on strike elsewhere? Would the law be upheld? According to Andrew Turnbull, her response was 'a great explosion'.[50] The Prime Minister was 'deeply disturbed' that the disasters of the 1970s might be recurring. 'The events at Saltley cokeworks* were being repeated,' she declared. It was essential to 'stiffen the resolve of the Chief Constables'.[51] With MacGregor and Walker still present, she got Leon Brittan, the Home Secretary, on the line, and ordered him to urge the head of ACPO, the Association of Chief Police Officers, 'to tell the police that they must allow people to get to work rather than just maintaining order'.[52]

She then chaired a wider ministerial meeting. Mrs Thatcher told ministers she had just met MacGregor and had learnt that pickets were preventing men who wanted to work from doing so: 'at the start of the week 93 pits were open and 71 were closed,' but by then, Wednesday 14 March, 133 pits were closed. 'It appeared', she went on, 'that the Police were not carrying out their duties fully.'[53] Brittan replied uneasily that he was not satisfied with the police response, but 'He had gone to the limit of what the Home Secretary could do while respecting the constitutional independence of Police Forces.'

While Brittan was right, constitutionally, that the Home Secretary could not issue operational orders to the police, this was not quite the point at issue. There was a precedent for police forces stopping flying

---

* The confrontation at the Saltley cokeworks in 1972 proved a turning point in the struggle between Edward Heath and the NUM. Arthur Scargill, then one of the leaders of the Yorkshire miners, had succeeded, by mass picketing, in forcing the police to turn away coking lorries. Shortly afterwards, the government, as Douglas Hurd wrote in his diary, ended up 'wandering vainly all over the battlefield looking for someone to surrender to'. (Douglas Hurd, *An End to Promises: Sketch of a Government, 1970–74*, Collins, 1979, p. 103.) The miners won their fight over pay, and Scargill took much of the glory.

pickets out of area: this had been done during the dispute over Eddie Shah's* union-busting newspapers the previous year, when police in Bedford had interdicted pickets heading for Shah's offices in Manchester. The principles of 'mutual aid' were also well established between police forces. What the chief constables needed to know was that they would get the political and financial backing required. For all his careful, formal statement of the rules, Brittan understood this. He had noted Mrs Thatcher's extreme anxiety, and he shared it. He recalled putting it to Brian Cubbon,† the Permanent Secretary at the Home Office, thus: 'I know there's reticence in the police about enforcing the picketing law. I like operational independence, but if they don't do what's necessary to stop violence, that constitutional arrangement will not survive.'[54] Rather than saying this to Mrs Thatcher,‡ or directly to any police officers, he asked Cubbon to pass it on.

Cubbon agreed that some chief constables 'needed a prod'.[55] He sent them all what he called 'a stiffening letter'. He also got in touch with the Chief Constable of Nottinghamshire in particular, to encourage him. 'He was a tough man,' Cubbon recalled, 'but he needed help.'[56] The chief constables needed money too to defray the extra costs. As the dispute went on, they would get most of what they demanded via special subventions from the Home Office. In order to strengthen the central grip on the dispute, Brittan took advantage of the Home Secretary's power to 'call for reports'. The National Reporting Centre at New Scotland Yard, which had been used to co-ordinate information about the riots in 1981, became the nearest thing the British constitution would permit to a national command post. Later in the dispute, a secret centre in Leicester also co-ordinated all police intelligence. All forces in England and Wales and half of those in Scotland took part in mutual aid.

The messages from Cubbon to 'stiffen' the police had an immediate effect. On Monday 19 March 1984, Andrew Turnbull reported that forty-four pits were working that day, compared with only eleven the previous Friday. As a result, the Coal Board, which had won an injunction against the secondary picketing of Nottinghamshire§ by the Yorkshire

---

* Selim Jehan ('Eddie') Shah (1944–), educated Gordonstoun and Haywards Heath Grammar; Manchester-based businessman who launched the *Warrington Messenger*, in 1983, which was the first of a portfolio of sixty newspapers printed with new technology; founded *Today* newspaper, 1986.
† Brian Cubbon (1928–2015), educated Bury Grammar School and Trinity College, Cambridge; Permanent Under-Secretary, NIO, 1976–9; Home Office, 1979–88; knighted, 1977.
‡ Luckily for her political position, when leader of the Opposition during the Winter of Discontent Mrs Thatcher had argued that the Labour Home Secretary, Merlyn Rees, was entitled to give 'advice' to the police about how to deal with mass picketing round the country.
§ Under the 1980 Employment Act, picketing was made lawful only if conducted at or near

NUM, dropped its legal action for the time being.[57] As MacGregor had already informed Walker, 'all the actions he is taking on this front [legal challenge] can of course be changed if the Government so wishes.'[58] Turnbull, who worked on the miners' strike more closely than any other member of Mrs Thatcher's staff, believed that her angry reaction on 14 March was crucial to the course of the entire dispute. Commenting to Mrs Thatcher on the strike in retrospect, he argued that:

> The key point was possibly right at the start on Wednesday 14 March when, by chance, Mr. MacGregor came to see you to discuss Euroroute . . . At the meeting which immediately followed, you galvanised the Home Secretary, who in turn galvanised the police into keeping the entrances to the pits open. This led immediately to the activation of ACPO. If that first battle had been lost, the rest would have been academic.[59]

Mrs Thatcher underlined his last sentence approvingly.

The strike retained the same essential character throughout. During its entire course, the NUM refused a ballot, and Nottinghamshire and a few other areas, often under heavy police protection, went on working. At the lowest point, 20 per cent of normal national coal production was maintained, and at the highest point – towards the end – 50 per cent. Since government calculations of endurance had obviously not been able to factor in continued working, this 'scab' production was all gain from Mrs Thatcher's point of view. Looking back, one is tempted to see the strike as a war of attrition which – given the coal stocks built up – the government was bound to win. It did not feel like that at the time, however. Indeed, it was not so. At any moment, it was possible that trade union solidarity, or the effect of NUM violence, or legal disaster, or the mishandling of negotiations by the Coal Board, or a loss of political nerve would produce defeat. Even a national ballot, which Scargill refused and for which Mrs Thatcher repeatedly called, was full of risk for the government. Suppose the vote took place, and went the 'wrong' way. Then Scargill's actions would gain a democratic legitimacy which would be politically hard to resist. As Leon Brittan recalled: 'We never thought we'd definitely lose, but only two-thirds of the way through did we know that we would win . . . The miners' union was considered as unstoppable as the rain.'[60]

Mrs Thatcher and those close to her had it constantly in their minds that the miners' strike was 'a seminal event in British history'.[61] If it went

---

the picket's place of work. Under the 1982 Employment Act, trade unions were made financially liable for organizing unlawful picketing.

wrong, the ill-chosen, never properly answered question of the February 1974 general election, 'Who Governs Britain?', would be decided against the elected government which Mrs Thatcher led. As in a war, the picture could change dramatically each day, and on several fronts. A 'Daily Coal Report' was supplied to ministers and officials, listing statistics of tonnes produced, pits operating and miners working, injuries to police, legal actions proposed, and so on. Downing Street staff studied these details with almost as much anxiety and attention as they had devoted to the Falklands conflict. Instead of names like Bluff Cove, Goose Green and Mount Longdon, they became familiar with pits like Shirebrook, Manton and Bilston Glen. As Stephen Sherbourne, Mrs Thatcher's political secretary throughout the dispute, put it, 'Remember that nobody knew in 1914 it would go on for four years.'[62] The endurance required was not only that of coal stocks, but that of will, concentration and morale.

But Scargill's failure to call a ballot and the refusal of Nottinghamshire to do his bidding meant that the war, as well being a conflict between government and union leadership, was also internecine. Once the violent picketing had started, Mrs Thatcher was quick to tell the public: 'This is not a dispute between miners and Government. This is a dispute between miners and miners.'[63] This line never failed her throughout the dispute.

Also as in wars, there was a debate about command. In formal terms, the pattern was quickly established. MISC 101 was the rough equivalent of a war cabinet (although, unlike war cabinets, it included the Chancellor of the Exchequer). Ian MacGregor and the Coal Board were solely responsible for dealing with the NUM. The Department of Energy, as the sponsoring department, dealt with the Coal Board. It followed that it was not considered appropriate for Mrs Thatcher to meet MacGregor regularly. For a line into the Coal Board, she was reliant on Walker.

This all made theoretical sense, and no one doubted Walker's ministerial ability. But Mrs Thatcher's congenital anxiety to understand the detail of everything could not be satisfied by the arrangement; nor could her suspicion of Walker be allayed by it. According to Butler, she thought Walker and MacGregor, whose business toughness she respected but whose tactical abilities she increasingly questioned, would 'do a fudge, like Pym and the Foreign Office in the Falklands had tried to do'.[64] She was not alone. Memos from ministers and officials during the strike quite often refer to the opacity of what was happening and to tensions in MISC 101. The lingering fear was that Walker might concoct a deal which would 'solve' the strike on terms politically favourable to him but disastrous, in the minds of Mrs Thatcher and those who agreed with her, for her and her policies. There were constant efforts to prise more information out of Walker. A typical private office note to Mrs Thatcher before one important meeting informed her that Walker would have just spoken to MacGregor 'and will, therefore, have no excuse for not knowing or not telling what the NCB is planning'.[65]

In these circumstances, Mrs Thatcher liked to draw on other sources of information and advice. One of these was her Policy Unit, run by John Redwood. Particularly through two of its members, David Pascall and Peter Warry, and Redwood himself, it tried to maintain the aim of getting a slimmed-down, well-functioning coal industry to emerge from the dispute, rather than seeing a settlement as automatically desirable. Another important source of information was Bernard Ingham, who masterminded the narrative which was handed down to the public. Ingham was one of the few people close to Mrs Thatcher who knew the trade unions well. His contacts built up as labour correspondent of the *Guardian* in the 1970s enabled him to maintain informal links with union leaders during the dispute, and to interpret union behaviour to Mrs Thatcher. He could also make up for the inadequacies of the NCB's press department, a factor which was to become more important as the strike continued.

Once it had become clear that the working miners were to be central figures in the drama, the government obviously wanted to know much more about them. This was difficult. Until a very late stage, they had no clear organization.* Mrs Thatcher found that the working miners 'in many ways chimed with her view of the world'.[66] They seemed to represent everything she most admired: they wanted to work, they resisted left-wing union militancy and they faced intimidation and violence bravely. For the Coal Board and the Department of Energy, however, the working miners often seemed more like a complication. Both were used to operating a close, even cosy relationship with the NUM, and so did not welcome a new element in the game. Mrs Thatcher constantly tried to counter this and insist that the working miners' interests be considered at all times. But she lacked the information on the ground. It was here that her third and most eccentric source of advice came into play: a man called David Hart.† With a mixture of fantastical self-promotion and genuine knowledge and flair, Hart told her what he thought the working miners were up to.

Hart was the sort of insider/outsider for whom Mrs Thatcher had a soft

---

* The formal NUM leaders in Nottinghamshire were tepid supporters of the national union's line but quickly found that their writ did not run in their own area.
† David Hart (1944–2011), educated Eton; political adviser, novelist and property developer.

spot. 'She liked dangerous people, and he was one of them,' observed Tim
Flesher.[67] Intermittently rich (he had been bankrupt in the 1970s), Hart
was the son of a banker, very conscious of his Jewishness and fond of
wearing his Old Etonian tie, though he had been unhappy at Eton. A
libertarian, a Cold Warrior with several good contacts inside the Reagan
administration, Hart, known as 'Spiv' to his close friends, was a resource-
ful campaigner for the causes he believed in, often backing them with his
own money. He helped persuade the British-based American billionaire
and philanthropist John Paul Getty* to contribute large sums to help the
working miners organize. In particular, money went to assist their legal
actions against Scargill and the NUM. Hart had known Mrs Thatcher
through the Centre for Policy Studies since 1980, and liked to tell her
what, in his view, 'the street' (an American phrase of which he was an
early user in Britain) was thinking. He wrote her frequent reports from
the street as well as offering his semi-solicited advice. All this interested
her, and she gave him some access, despite the efforts of staff, who thought
him too disreputable, to keep him at bay.†

Hart was also a novelist. In one of his novels, the hero, Dov, a thinly
veiled, heroic autobiographical persona, says, 'I am an eagle over England
at last. In my highest flight. I look down and know that the Prime Minister
is mine.'[68] This accurately expressed Hart's longing. The miners' strike
brought him closer, though not really very close, to fulfilling it. As soon
as the strike began, and Nottinghamshire continued to work, he made it
his business to visit the pit areas, sometimes in a chauffeur-driven Mer-
cedes, to find out what was happening. Hart took snuff like many miners,
forbidden from smoking underground, who needed a cigarette substitute.
This served to confirm in his own mind his surprising impression that he
'fitted in' in mining communities.[69] From these forays, he would send Mrs
Thatcher vivid despatches. At the end of April 1984, for example, he
contrasted his visit to Nottinghamshire miners with his experience of a
Scargill rally in Sheffield. At the latter, he told her, 'I could not escape
thoughts of Nuremberg . . . The stink of fascism.' He warned her that
although at present the Notts miners were 'very angry with Scargill' for
trying to coerce them, if they were given the ballot they demanded they

* John Paul Getty (1932–2003), adopted British nationality, 1998; KBE, 1986.
† At the party conference in 1983, Hart sought to change the draft of her speech at a late
stage. Mrs Thatcher told Sherbourne that 'I've just seen David Hart, and he's got marvellous
ideas for the speech.' 'I was horrified,' Sherbourne recalled. 'I opened my door on to the
detectives in the hotel corridor and said, "If a man called David Hart comes looking for me,
I'm not here." "I *am* David Hart," said the man in the suit.' (Interview with Lord Sherbourne
of Didsbury.)

might vote for a strike.[70] Mrs Thatcher read such reports carefully, under-lining them throughout: 'he did have some real intelligence,' she later recalled.[71] As time went on, Hart, who had also worked his way into the favour of Ian MacGregor, was able to give him and Mrs Thatcher a good deal of information about the working miners, and also, less helpfully, to stir her up against Walker.

After the opening salvoes of the strike, the next crisis, from Mrs Thatcher's point of view, came when the question of a national ballot returned to the fore. Confident of his majority on the NUM national executive, Scargill pushed for a rule change by which the existing threshold of 55 per cent of those voting for a strike before one could be called should be reduced to 50 per cent. The government was extremely nervous about this. Not only would a yes vote halt production, it would also, by legitimizing the strike, make the other unions, notably railwaymen and steelworkers, feel bound to act 'in sympathy' with the miners. Aware of Scargill's unpopularity with TUC colleagues, the government was anxious not to encourage trade union leaders to make common cause with him. Early in April, it dropped its plan to reform the political levy by which union members had to pay money to the Labour Party. The plan had been to change it from a contracting-out system, whose inertia helped Labour, to a contracting-in one. Aborting this caused a rebellion on the Tory back benches, but the government was determined to avoid any confrontations which were not strictly necessary.

Scargill called a special delegate conference of the union in Sheffield for 19 April 1984 to approve his proposed rule change. The day before, John Redwood and David Pascall told Mrs Thatcher that, if Scargill were successful in lowering the voting threshold for a strike, the conference might 'recommend a strike ballot which they would expect to win'.[72] If that happened, and all movement of coal ceased, power-station stocks could last until the end of September, but supplies were already dropping and the public would 'go soft' if the dispute started to hurt them. In fact, the conference did vote for the rule change, but then rejected a proposal to call a national ballot at once. Scargill himself ensured that rejection because he was not sufficiently confident of victory in any national ballot and was over-confident about his ability to use mass picketing to coerce where he could not persuade. At Cabinet on 3 May, Brittan reported that Scargill had now 'taken personal charge' of the NUM tactics, trying to hit individual pits hard in order to achieve 'the maximum surprise'.[73] The day before, more than 8,000 pickets had appeared at Harworth colliery in Nottinghamshire. But Walker was nevertheless able to tell colleagues that the production and movement of coal now stood at its highest since the strike had begun.

Without the chance of settling anything via the ballot box, the physical fierceness of the dispute intensified. In his keenness to get his way, Scargill underestimated the fact that the NUM was a federation, with each area bearing a strong identity. The more his Yorkshire-based vanguard turned up to try to tell their Nottinghamshire neighbours what to do, the more Notts' loyalty to the central union waned. After all, in their own area ballot, 73 per cent of Notts miners had voted against a strike. People spoke of the return of 'Spencerism', named after George Spencer, the Nottinghamshire miners' leader who led a breakaway union after the failure of the coal strike in 1926. A demonstration of Scargill supporters mainly from Yorkshire, who arrived in Mansfield in Nottinghamshire in the middle of May, was violent, with 90–100 police injured, but it did little to stop the Notts men working. Walker reported to colleagues that Scargill had 'made two statements which he could later regret'.[74] He 'had claimed the downfall of the Government as an explicit objective of the strike', and he had made it clear to miners that the strike might have to continue until December. Mrs Thatcher reacted extremely strongly to the reports of violence against those trying to work and against the police. 'Most decent people are sickened by it,' she scribbled on the note of the meeting.[75] The level of violence hardened her attitude to any possible settlement.

As the violence grew, Mrs Thatcher began to feel anxieties about the Coal Board's readiness to settle on the wrong terms. Being a nationalized industry and 'unionized right up to Ian MacGregor's feet',[76] the NCB was naturally predisposed to think that almost any deal was better than no deal. This was less true of MacGregor than of most of his colleagues, but it gradually became apparent that though 'a remarkable man with very strong qualities, he was not very good at the negotiation of documents. He nearly signed away too much ... Mrs Thatcher was always suspicious.'[77] About two months into the strike, during widespread talk of a possible deal, Peter Gregson warned Mrs Thatcher:

> Ministers will not wish to wake up one morning to find that the NCB is in the middle of a negotiation about closures without their ever having had the opportunity to discuss what the Government would wish to see come out of this strike ... the Government has too much at stake to allow the NCB a completely free hand.[78]

It was lucky for Mrs Thatcher that each time possible concessions by the NCB seemed to be in the offing, Scargill rendered them impossible by refusing to budge from his position that no pit should ever be closed for economic reasons, but only if its seams were exhausted (or unsafe). A more skilled and less extreme union leader would have taken the trouble to work out the differences between the Coal Board, the Department and 10 Downing Street and exploit them.

Scargill liked to see himself in an ideological and heroic role. At the end of May, in an attempt to replicate his success at Saltley in 1972, he began a series of mass pickets designed to stop coke* being moved from the British Steel coking works in Orgreave, South Yorkshire. On 29 May, there was grave violence there, with darts and bricks thrown at police and sixty-nine people injured. Earlier that morning, Scargill, as Peter Walker put it privately, 'invited his own arrest'.[79] Mrs Thatcher reacted with genuine horror to the violence. Speaking at Banbury Cattle Market the following day, using the repetition which, in her, was usually a sign of vehemence, she said: 'You saw the scenes that went on in television last night. I must tell you that what we have got is an attempt to substitute the rule of the mob for the rule of law, and it must not succeed. It must not succeed.'[80]

As trouble continued at Orgreave, she also expressed her concerns privately. She wanted the British Steel Corporation to use the law against the NUM. It was disinclined to do so, since, despite the picketing, its lorries were getting their coke out successfully. 'You raised the question', Andrew Turnbull wrote to her, 'of whether it was right "to leave the police in the firing line" while no action was being taken in the civil courts. The key question is whether, apart from moral support, the police would be any less in the firing line.'[81] If there were a sequestration of union funds because of a court case, he told her, the police would have to enforce it: 'It must be doubtful whether this would help the police.'[82] It was probably not true that sequestration, which involved chasing funds not people, would create much work for the police, but Turnbull was looking for ways of holding Mrs Thatcher back. For him, as for several of those working closely with her, Mrs Thatcher's enthusiasm for invoking her own government's laws against the NUM came into the category of 'reckless ideas'[83] which she tended to produce.† In this, perhaps surprisingly, there was agreement between Peter Walker and Norman Tebbit, the Trade and Industry Secretary, both of whom argued that the NUM's fellow trade unions should not be provoked by any action they might see as high-handed. It

---

* In this context, 'coke' is the term for the high-carbon fuel derived from coal.
† Mrs Thatcher also fantasized about 'snatch squads', organized by members of local rugby clubs, or even involving the army, to go in to picketed mine-heads to get the coal out, but these notions were not pursued (Interview with Lord Turnbull).

was not that Walker, let alone Tebbit, the author of the 1982 Act, had doubts about the moral or practical merits of the laws. It was a matter of tactics. The ministers' line was: 'Keep the temperature down and don't give the unions any pretext.'[84] Mrs Thatcher 'railed against this, but took the advice'.[85] In her memoirs, she admitted that 'there was much to be said for emphasizing the point that it was the basic criminal law of the country which was being flouted by the pickets and their leaders, rather than "Thatcher's laws".'[86]

Mrs Thatcher was less ready to listen to anything that smacked to her of appeasement. While the picketing of Orgreave continued, talks took place between the Coal Board and the NUM. Peter Walker reported to Mrs Thatcher MacGregor's belief that the talks 'had begun to move towards a satisfactory discussion of the issues'.[87] Soon this reached the press as a story that MacGregor was going to come up with a new 'Plan for Coal'. Downing Street became agitated that something was being cooked up without its agreement. 'It was most important', Mrs Thatcher summed up at a MISC 101 meeting on 12 June, 'both that the NCB should continue to stand firm on the essentials of their case and that the Board's handling of the talks should not allow the NUM the opportunity to mis-represent the outcome.'[88] Luckily for her, Scargill quickly made any compromise impossible by putting out a ten-point programme demanding an extended lifespan for all pits, higher pay, earlier retirement and so on. He then pretended that the NCB had walked out of the meeting rather than discuss these ideas. The device had some media success and helped to promote a notion that Scargill and MacGregor were each as bad as the other. Turnbull expressed and fanned his principal's anxieties: 'What is surprising is not the outrageous nature of Mr Scargill's demands but the fact that it was reported to you last Friday that Mr MacGregor was detect-ing signs of realism.'[89] Doubts grew about the NCB's capacity to communicate clear messages. Unhappy with the text of a proposed letter from MacGregor to all striking miners, No. 10 toyed with the idea of insisting on another draft of its own devising, though Robin Butler strongly advised that it would be dangerous to submit another text for Walker to send on to MacGregor, even if it were 'anonymous'.[90] The desire to keep out of the fight clashed with the longing to exercise closer control.

On 18 June 1984, the climactic 'Battle of Orgreave' took place. The pickets, estimated at between 5,000 and 10,000 strong, confronted about 5,000 police. Conducted in a series of advances and retreats, in some of which police horses forced back the pickets, the battle was fierce, but the NUM never succeeded in preventing the lorries loaded with coke from leav-ing the plant. Twenty-eight police officers, and many more pickets, were injured and ninety-three arrests were made. Orgreave looked, Andrew Turnbull recalled, 'like the Wars of the Roses'[91] and it carried the implication of civil war which goes with that comparison.* The contest produced images of violence which could be deployed by both sides. Orgreave quickly became a talismanic name in the legends of trade unionism. It was later the subject of the Dire Straits song 'Iron Hand' (1991), and was re-enacted for Channel 4 television in 2001.† For the majority of the public at the time, however, it confirmed a growing view that the NUM, and Scargill in particular, were committed to unjustified violence. A Gallup poll in July showed that 79 per cent of the public disapproved of the methods used by the NUM. More important still, Orgreave proved that, in enormous confrontations, the police now had the numbers, the equipment and the will to prevail. The defeat of Scargill's pickets at Orgreave also emboldened miners who wanted to return to work. In the last full week in June, the number of those at work rose by 1,400 on the week before, bringing the total working to 53,000. This was not a seismic change, but it was clear that the attempt to break the will of the working miners had failed. Scargill at Orgreave exorcized for Mrs Thatcher the demon of Scargill at Saltley twelve years earlier.

It did not automatically follow, however, that the government would win. It remained possible that key trade unions would combine successfully against it. With so much unease in the air, there was the chance, on the one hand, that a longing for peace and moderation would undermine the Prime Minister and, on the other, that she would find herself conceding too much. In mid-June, the Conservatives lost the previously safe seat of Portsmouth South to the SDP–Liberal Alliance in a by-election. A few days later, immediately after the scenes at Orgreave, the *Daily Telegraph* reported that the Queen had been 'shocked' by the clashes.[92] There was a risk that Mrs Thatcher would be blamed for overreaction and thus be held responsible for the clashes. If public opinion came to see Mrs Thatcher's desire to defeat Scargill as personal and vindictive – with MacGregor as the agent of her wishes – then it would turn against her.

But those who believed that Scargill should be clearly defeated also felt

---

* David Willetts recalled that when working for Mrs Thatcher during the miners' strike the comparison with a civil war was apposite. 'You would be in a meeting with Mrs T on some other subject and messengers would come in with reports like "Kent is solid . . . Nottingham is with us . . . Yorkshire is in rebellion." It did feel like a scene from one of Shakespeare's history plays.' (Correspondence with David Willetts.)
† To this day, attempts are made, for example by the Orgreave Truth and Justice Campaign, to arraign the government and police via a formal judicial inquiry, almost as if the incident were like 'Bloody Sunday' in Londonderry in 1972.

demoralized. With NCB–NUM talks continuing, working miners were worried by the prospect of Coal Board concessions to Scargill: all such rumours discouraged new recruits to their cause, and they feared that they would be left unprotected by any settlement and subject to revenge attacks for having been 'scabs'. Conservative supporters could not really understand why the trade union laws which they had warmly supported were being shunned, and they hated the police being made to endure so much violence. The idea that, for the sake of temporary peace, Scargill might be allowed to live to fight another day was anathema to millions. Any sense of government weakness also reflected badly on Mrs Thatcher herself. Many were puzzled as to why she seemed to hold back. With a speech draft sent on 16 July, Ronnie Millar wrote a note expressing this frustration: 'I am sure the country is just waiting for you to take this gentleman [Scargill] apart.'[93] Luckily for Mrs Thatcher, there was no deep ideological difference within the Cabinet about the issue – Scargill's politics and personality brought the enemy into plain view. There was no faction in her own party against her. But there was a genuine dilemma about handling.

Just before Mrs Thatcher, Walker and MacGregor sat down to discuss all the issues, at the beginning of July, Peter Gregson sent her a wide-ranging memo. He reported the feeling of stalemate. It was 'common ground' in government that 'unless the NUM position is crumbling fast by the end of September, the prospect of winter will give Scargill a major psychological advantage.'[94] At present, 'We have not so far identified any initiative . . . which could be relied on to bring the matter to a head in our favour.' In these circumstances, Gregson proposed a three-pronged strategy. The government should get more men back to work; it should maintain public support by being reasonable about talks and showing Scargill as an 'anti-democratic bully with ulterior motives';[95] and it should do everything possible discreetly to prolong endurance into 1985. If this strategy failed, it might be necessary, by September, to change tactics, start closing pits, making strikers redundant and getting imported coal into power stations (something which the government had hitherto avoided in order not to alienate working miners). Gregson also touched delicately on the question of how to get the best out of Ian MacGregor: 'As he is so laconic, it is all too easy to put words into his mouth and it would be much better for you to hear from him at the outset how he thinks the battle is going.'[96] Between the lines, one can read an official's exasperation at Mrs Thatcher's tendency to talk non-stop.

All the problems of strategy and tactics suddenly deepened when, on 9 July 1984, a dock strike broke out almost without warning. The Transport and General Workers' Union claimed that the British Steel Corporation, by using contract labour to move iron ore from stockpiles in Immingham docks to its steelworks in Scunthorpe, was flouting the National Dock Labour Scheme, which protected dockers' privileges. The strike was not, on the face of it, concerned with the miners' dispute, but the TGWU leadership were close to the NUM, and Downing Street immediately understood what was going on. 'The extreme Left', wrote John Redwood, 'is mounting a major extra-parliamentary challenge to the Government on a number of fronts,'[97] including coal, the dock strike and local government. 'There is only one thing worse than presiding over industrial chaos,' he went on, in a passage which Mrs Thatcher underlined, 'and that is giving in <u>to the use of industrial muscle for unreasonable ends</u> . . . <u>it is dangerous to blow hot and cold, to be out of the fray one week and then in it another</u>.' Any 'fudged formula' on closures 'is defeat', said Redwood. There had to be a return to the 'war of attrition'.

The government's priority now was to keep the docks working, at all costs. On 15 July Mrs Thatcher and ministers discussed the possibility of deploying troops to keep dock traffic moving. The Ministry of Defence estimated that 2,800 troops could move 1,000 tonnes (fifty lorries) a day.[98] Ministers feared that these estimates were 'far too low' to make much of a difference[99] and there was, in any case, little enthusiasm for the idea. Mrs Thatcher realized that there would be no tactical advantage but considerable adverse publicity.* The government's focus was, in fact, not on breaking the dock strike, but on settling it. The political and economic stakes were much higher in the coal strike, Gregson reminded Mrs Thatcher. Therefore the government should 'end the dock strike as quickly as possible, so that the coal dispute can be played as long as necessary'.[100]

The fact that contingency plans were being discussed, however, does show the government's precarious position. It was made worse by the return of a quite separate union problem. On the same day as Mrs Thatcher's dock-strike meeting, judicial review of the union ban at GCHQ found that the government had acted beyond its powers in imposing the ban without prior consultation. Mrs Thatcher first saw the news on a newspaper hoarding as she and Robin Butler were passing in the car:

> She said to me: 'We'll appeal, of course, but if we go down, we'll have to accept this. The law is the law.' I admired her very much that this was her first reaction. Think of how defeat on this issue would have helped the miners. For her, the judgment of the courts should always be respected.[101]

* The release of the relevant government papers in 2014 led to misleading reports that Mrs Thatcher had 'a secret plan' to use the army 'at the height of the Miners' Strike' (see *Guardian*, 3 January 2014, http://www.theguardian.com/politics/2014/jan/03/margaret-thatcher-secret-plan-army-miners-strike). The possibility of using troops was, at this point, discussed only in the context of the dock strike.

So uncomfortable did the situation seem that President Reagan took the step, highly unusual in an ally's purely domestic political difficulty, of writing to Mrs Thatcher. In recent weeks, he said, 'I have thought often of you with considerable empathy as I follow the activities of the miners' and dockworkers' unions. I know they present a difficult set of issues for your Government.'[102] Sending his 'warm regards', he concluded, 'I'm confident as ever that you and your Government will come out of this well.' On 18 July 1984, the same day as Reagan sent his letter, the sky, at least as Mrs Thatcher perceived it, began to brighten. First, NCB talks with the NUM broke down over the question of whether uneconomic pits could be closed. 'I have to say I was enormously relieved,' wrote Mrs Thatcher in her memoirs.[103] This 'marked a new phase', she told the Cabinet: the government should increase pressure for a return to work and help 'in a sustained publicity campaign'.[104] The following day, the dock strike collapsed for lack of support from TGWU members. On 23 July, Mrs Thatcher wrote to thank Reagan for his letter, excusing her delay by saying she had been waiting for an end to the dock strike. As for the NUM strike, she told the President, 'I am confident that in due course firmness and patience will achieve a victory for the forces of moderation and common-sense which are Britain's traditional sources of strength.'[105]

The war of attrition resumed, but Mrs Thatcher felt less uneasy. She had been reassured by the trusted Walter Marshall that, on current trends, endurance would last until June 1985. The leaders of the various unions in the Central Electricity Generating Board (CEGB) 'had privately told him that their ability to provide moderate leadership would be totally undermined if the hard left leadership of the NUM were successful'.[106] She had also been spurred on by advice from Walker,[107] normally more cautious than she in this area, that the government should encourage two Nottinghamshire miners who were bringing a legal case claiming that the NUM attempt to embroil them in a strike was unlawful. She had constantly been advised that 'if she were in league with the working miners, that would undermine their position'.[108] Intellectually, she accepted this view, but emotionally she longed to do more for her heroes. The prospect of the court case cheered her up. So did some of the clandestine work by David Hart, who produced an itinerant co-ordinator of working miners codenamed 'Silver Birch' (who later became known as 'Weeping Willow' because of his lachrymose tendencies). At the beginning of August, Silver Birch gave newspaper interviews, and was revealed as Chris Butcher, a miner from Bevercotes colliery in Nottinghamshire.

Mrs Thatcher was inspired not only by her determination not to suffer the fate of Edward Heath, but also by her understanding of what Arthur

Scargill was up to. Ever since the 1970s, she had agreed with those who saw a serious, semi-organized attempt by the extreme left to subvert British parliamentary democracy. Fear of this phenomenon played a part in her attitudes on many issues – détente, local government, education policy, police reform, the Labour Party, intelligence, sanctions against South Africa, and IRA terrorism, as well as trade union militancy. After her landslide general election victory in 1983, the left turned away from the parliamentary politics which they had failed to capture. In his speech to the NUM conference in July of that year, Scargill had told his members that 'Extra-parliamentary action will be the only course open to the working class and the labour movement.'[109] The miners' strike was intended to be part of a wider phenomenon. Scargill's approach paralleled that of many Labour activists in local government, notably the members of the Militant Tendency, such as Derek Hatton in Liverpool, and Ken Livingstone,* the leader of the GLC. As the miners' strike proceeded, so did the government's legislation fulfilling its election promise to abolish the GLC and the metropolitan counties.† 'I was up to my neck with Scargill,' recalled Livingstone.[110] 'We broadly merged the miners' strike and the GLC campaign.' In August, Livingstone and three others resigned their seats in the GLC to fight by-elections in protest at the abolition. Scargill's local government allies did what they could to help the striking miners. Council funds, sometimes illegally, provided relief. In some areas, left-wing police authorities sought to punish the police for their fights with the mass pickets. In South Yorkshire, for example, the scene of the Orgreave battles, the police authority tried to have the Chief Constable suspended. The fact that Scargill had publicly justified the strike as necessary to overthrow the elected government gave Mrs Thatcher the permission she sought to have some of the strikers' activities monitored by the Security Service. Stella Rimington,‡ who later became the head of the service, classified Scargill, whose telephone had been tapped for years because of his links with the Soviet-backed Communist Party of Great Britain, as 'an unaffiliated subversive'.[111]

For Mrs Thatcher, all this showed what would happen to Britain if her policies did not prevail. At the traditional 'end of term' meeting of the 1922 Committee before the summer recess, when the Conservative leader

* Kenneth ('Ken') Livingstone (1945–), Tulse Hill Comprehensive School; member, Greater London Council, 1973–86; leader, 1981–6; Labour MP for Brent East, 1987–2001; Mayor of London, 2000–2008.
† For a full discussion, see Chapter 11.
‡ Stella Rimington (1935–), educated Nottingham High School for Girls and Edinburgh University; Director-General, Security Service, 1992–6; created dame, 1996.

Mrs Thatcher's notes for her speech to the 1922 Committee, July 1984. Her notations referring to the 'Enemy within' begin at the bottom of the left-hand page.

addresses the backbenchers, she gave full vent. The occasion is always a private one, but details of her speech quickly leaked. From Mrs Thatcher's surviving manuscript notes (there was no formal text), her drift is clear. Indeed, her short notes convey the essential Thatcher more than a full draft would have done. She was speaking the night after the NCB–NUM talks had collapsed, and she was fired up: '<u>Winter of Discontent</u> We were returned to Parliament Supreme Uphold Rule of Law,' the relevant passage of her manuscript notes began:

> Since Office
> Enemy without – beaten him
> & strong in defence
> Enemy within –
> Miners' leaders.
> Liverpool & some local authorities
> – just as dangerous
> in a way more difficult to fight
> But just as dangerous to liberty
> Scar across the face of our country.

Then she quoted Walt Whitman: 'There is no week, nor day, nor hour when tyranny may not enter upon this country if the people lose their supreme confidence in themselves and lose their roughness and spirit of defiance.'[112]

Her speech was noisily applauded by the traditional banging of desks (clapping being, by convention, forbidden in the Palace of Westminster); but not all Tory MPs present liked its tone. The phrase 'the enemy within' was taken up by critics as the epitome of her divisive approach.* Although she had spoken only of the miners' *leaders* (and the left-wing local authorities) as being the enemy within, this was quickly misrepresented by her opponents as her description of all miners, proof of her hostility to the organized working class. It would be used against her forever afterwards.

Yet what she actually said was not far from being a statement of plain fact, and was surely not something with which Arthur Scargill himself could have disagreed. The main miners' leaders were proud of being the enemy of the government and were declaredly set on bringing it down. They did consistently refuse their members the ballot for a national strike which their constitution demanded. And they did, by means of violence and intimidation, try to prevent other miners from working. In addition, some of them, most notably Scargill himself, were in alliance with revolutionary elements and, as later events were to show, in contact with foreign regimes hostile to Britain. They *were* the enemy within, though of course being a declared enemy of the government led by Margaret Thatcher did not of itself make anyone a subversive.

One reason which emboldened Mrs Thatcher to speak so fiercely was the agony of the Labour Party. From the start of the dispute, Labour had been torn between its hereditary, instinctive loyalty to trade unions – especially miners, especially against Tory governments – and its anxiety about the circumstances of the miners' strike. Early in the dispute, the veteran political commentator and expert on the Labour Party Alan Watkins noted that just as Labour people had spoken of 'a Michael problem'

---

* Chris Collins of the Margaret Thatcher Foundation has pointed out that the phrase 'enemy within' would have been familiar to Mrs Thatcher because of her Methodist background. The words are used, for example, in Wesley's Sermon 13, *On Sin in Believers*, and also in a number of Methodist hymns (http://www.margaretthatcher.org/archive/1984cac1.asp). In more recent times, the phrase had been used in a political context. The Labour Prime Minister Clement Attlee had spoken of an 'enemy within' when warning about Communist infiltration of the trade unions (*The Times*, 31 July 1950). Twenty years later, Enoch Powell had spoken about a 'hidden enemy within' to describe leftist agitators undermining British democracy. Mrs Thatcher was well aware of Powell's speech: she had endorsed his sentiments at the time (see Volume I, pp. 195–6). She presumably remembered Attlee's as well.

in the era of Foot's leadership, so they were beginning to talk about 'a Neil problem'.[113] Neil Kinnock, said Watkins, had already missed the chance to take a stand on the issue of the ballot. From the beginning, Kinnock had favoured a national ballot, and had publicly said so, but somewhat obliquely. When Scargill was about to embark on the strike in March, Kinnock recalled, 'I told him in terms that if there were no ballot there couldn't be unity . . . My deep regret was not to have been louder and more emphatic.'[114] As the child of a mining family from South Wales, Kinnock was emotionally committed to the NUM cause, but he was no friend of Scargill and was only too aware of the disastrous potential of the strike for the industry, for trade union solidarity and for his own party's unity. Once the strike got going, he sympathized with those in the coalfields and felt that publicly 'to attack the absence of strategy would have been an attack on them'.[115] He could not quite decide which line to take.

Mrs Thatcher played on this. The twice-weekly Prime Minister's Questions in the House of Commons, which should have been good moments for Kinnock to arraign her for all the problems with the strike, were often the other way round. It was Kinnock, not she, who was suffering internal political embarrassments over the strike, as she did not hesitate to remind him. She was particularly fond of throwing back at him a remark he had made on 12 April when he had welcomed a national ballot as 'a clearer and closer prospect'. By July, however, as the struggle had intensified and attitudes become more polarized, he said that 'There is no alternative but to fight.'[116] What had made him change his mind, she taunted him? Kinnock was therefore reluctant to go on the attack. Despite the provocation of her 'enemy within' speech to the '22, he did not raise it or the miners' strike at Prime Minister's Questions on the three occasions that remained to him before the summer recess. In those sessions, his preferred subjects were merchant shipping, the bid by an American company, Standard Telephones, for ICL, and mortgage-capping. Kinnock's visible evasiveness on the strike emboldened her. In the no-confidence debate* in the Commons on 31 July 1984, she accused him of 'appeasement' because he refused to call for a ballot.[117]

Her parliamentary victory over Kinnock that day, so soon after the

---

* The Opposition quite often exercised its right to put down a motion of censure or call a motion of no-confidence in Parliament. On this occasion the Opposition's motion condemned the 'economic, industrial and employment policies of Her Majesty's Government'. As Mrs Thatcher had a stable majority, such occasions were used as an opportunity to protest against the government or express disapproval of a particular policy.

crisis of the dock strike had loomed, put heart into her MPs as they left for their summer break.

For her customary but always unwelcome summer holidays, Mrs Thatcher went, as she had done several times before, to Schloss Freudenberg, the lakeside home of Lady Glover in Switzerland. She did not take advantage of her break, however, to stop thinking about the miners' strike. At the end of August, Peter Gregson was up a tree in his garden, tending to his apples, when the telephone rang. 'She's coming back!' wailed an official from No. 10. 'She'll be here by lunchtime. She's worried it's all going wrong. Come and reassure her.'[118] Gregson did so. It turned out that she had no very specific anxiety, just the unease she always felt if she was ever out of touch. She sought reassurance about endurance: 'I have to have it from Walter [Marshall], from his own lips.'[119]

Mrs Thatcher was right to be anxious. The return to work had slowed since July, and the season of conferences produced a plethora of peace plans. These tended to expose the Coal Board's vulnerability. As Peter Gregson recalled, Ian MacGregor was 'a very good manager, but he didn't understand the politics of the British coal industry.'[120] On 3 September 1984, the government's internal Daily Coal Report recorded that MacGregor had just confirmed that further talks were being arranged between the NCB and the NUM: 'He said that it appeared the NUM was taking "a more realistic" approach,' words which Mrs Thatcher marked with her wiggly line of scepticism.[121] She and many of those round her were suspicious of Peter Walker's game, and anxious about MacGregor's tendency to make mistakes. Andrew Turnbull suggested she ask them to explain 'the understandings on which the talks have been re-launched'.[122] Walker alleged, he went on, that Scargill now wanted to discuss the closure of uneconomic pits, but MacGregor's public statement had made no explicit reference to such closures: 'What is to stop a repetition of the last meeting? . . . The NCB offer last time was perilously close to going too far.'

The following day, Arthur Scargill announced that the NCB had cancelled the talks, though this was not the case. In a meeting with Walker and MacGregor that day, Mrs Thatcher insisted that a line be drawn – 'It was agreed that the NCB could make no further concessions on the principle of closing uneconomic pits,' although Peter Walker held out for the value, in terms of public opinion, of being seen to welcome talks. Mrs Thatcher was unconvinced, even suggesting that 'In future it might be better if such discussions were conducted on paper.'[123] Nevertheless, talks and meetings continued. One series of them between the NCB and the

NUM, which were supposed to be secret, took place in early September at the Norton House Hotel near Edinburgh. The press got wind of it, and when MacGregor came down the drive for the talks, he was spotted. Climbing out of the car, he covered his face with a green plastic bag. This was supposed to be a joke about the secrecy of the meeting, but the photographs and film in the media 'made him look divorced from reality'.[124] The pictures contributed to the public sense that MacGregor was a peculiar leader for the industry, and to Downing Street's growing dismay about his conduct of the dispute. It was 'ghastly', recalled Sherbourne.[125]

It was a Coal Board mishandling, indeed, which brought about 'the single most dangerous moment'[126] of the entire strike. In the completely unionized world of coal mining, there were other, minor unions as well as the mighty NUM. Of these, the elaborately named National Association of Colliery Overseers, Deputies and Shotfirers (NACODS) had an importance beyond its modest numbers. This was because its members were chiefly responsible for safety. If safety cover were not present, the pits would be legally obliged to close. Then Arthur Scargill would very likely win. In the middle of August, seemingly without thought for the possible consequences, the Coal Board issued a circular to NACODS members ordering them all to cross picket lines, on pain of losing pay. Until that point, policy had varied from area to area, with many NACODS men who were employed on strike-bound pits being allowed to stay away on full wages. Since the NACODS men, in a ballot in April, had voted for a strike (though not by the two-thirds required to trigger action), this was a dangerous move. The leaders of the union, Ken Sampey and Peter McNestry (known as 'Scampi and Chips'), were more sympathetic than most of their members to Arthur Scargill. Now they grasped their moment. They called a strike ballot for 28 September. The hard left saw their chance. 'I always thought the miners could defeat Thatcher,' Ken Livingstone remembered. 'I thought NACODS could do it.'[127]

For Downing Street, this mess confirmed the belief that the Coal Board was no good at running the dispute. MacGregor seemed too fierce against NACODS, too wobbly about the NUM. On 13 September, John Redwood minuted Mrs Thatcher with his view that the NCB senior management should pay much more attention to the NACODS problem: 'It is vital that they are not totally preoccupied by the current talks with Scargill, so that their eye is taken off the ball.'[128] MacGregor, under considerable strain, and not able to trust many of his colleagues, seemed bewildered. Even David Hart, who worked closely with MacGregor, told Mrs Thatcher that the NCB chairman was 'an acute business negotiator who has not yet fully understood that he has been cast in the greater role of statesman . . . He has his "wets" as you had yours. He is more likely to give in to them.'[129] 'This', Hart warned her, 'is the greatest danger for you.'[130]* The new Bishop of Durham, Dr David Jenkins,† a left-wing theological radical, caused a stir by using his enthronement sermon in the cathedral to declare that neither side must win a victory. He proposed that MacGregor should withdraw from his chairmanship and Scargill from his 'absolute demands': 'The withdrawal of an imported elderly American to leave a reconciling opportunity for some local product is surely neither dishonourable nor improper.'[131] His suggestion was not taken seriously by many, and provoked one of those uproarious public debates which are often a feature of political interventions by Anglican bishops. But its focus on the shortcomings of MacGregor and the 'moral equivalence' it set up with Scargill were part of a trend which was difficult from Mrs Thatcher's point of view. There was alarm at what could be presented as the intransigence of both sides. People cast around for compromises.

Robin Butler summed up the situation in a memo to his boss. Scargill had 'made headway' recently, he told her, with his argument that putting pressure on the NCB and the government was 'the best way of finishing the dispute quickly'. 'Most people,' he went on, 'including those in the unions, desperately want to see Scargill defeated but may be beginning to doubt that we have the means of doing it.'[132] As if to prove him right, two days later NACODS members voted overwhelmingly to strike.

The NACODS leaders demanded not only the withdrawal of the NCB's circular – a wish which was easily granted – but also their own solution to the question of uneconomic pits on which all talks with the NUM had foundered. They proposed a system of independent, binding arbitration when the closure of any pit was proposed. They would start a strike on 8 October – the day before the opening of the Conservative Party conference – unless they got their way. The government tactic in response was to get the Coal Board to string NACODS along in talks. As the Tories converged on Brighton, no agreement with NACODS had been reached.

---

* Hart continued to seek direct access to Mrs Thatcher. Stephen Sherbourne, having encountered Hart at the party conference the year before, remained wary of him. 'I told him that he can always feed intelligence through me but that visits to No. 10 can create dangers. He will be at Brighton [at the party conference] but I believe he really must keep his distance from you there because of the hot-house atmosphere of the Conference hotel.' (Sherbourne to Thatcher, 28 September 1984, CAC: THCR 2/6/3/56 (http://www.margaretthatcher.org/document/136253).)

† David Jenkins (1925–), educated St Dunstan's College, Catford and the Queen's College, Oxford; Professor of Theology, University of Leeds, 1979–84; Bishop of Durham, 1984–94.

The strike start was delayed, but the threat still hung in the air. The political atmosphere was one of extreme unease.

The Conservative Party conference at Brighton in 1984 is remembered for the IRA bombing of the Grand Hotel in the early hours of the morning of Friday 12 October. (For a full account, see Chapter 10.) Mrs Thatcher, who was staying at the hotel – she was awake and working on the final drafts of her conference speech when the bomb went off – survived unscathed, but five people were killed and many others were injured, some very seriously. Public sympathy, at a rather low ebb when she arrived in Brighton, switched at once to Mrs Thatcher's side. She was determined that the party conference should continue and she was widely praised for turning up at the conference as planned on the Friday morning. As the facts and therefore the mood changed, so too did her annual leader's speech.

Early drafts suggest that she had originally intended to make a 'different kind of conference speech . . . more of a single issue speech than normal'.[133] The 'speech that never was' was much more partisan and more provocative than the one she actually made, and much of it would have focused on the miners' strike. Mrs Thatcher had intended to start by warning the Conference of a 'shadow that has fallen across . . . freedom since last we met'.[134] Building on her summer theme of an 'enemy within' – though these words were not used in the text – the draft noted that 'organised groups of influential men and women question, even repudiate Parliament and the rule of law'.[135] These 'views and voices' were now to be found in the Labour Party,* which was 'so willing to trumpet the cause of the present NUM leadership in its extreme and uncompromising objectives'.

The version which she delivered, on the day after the bomb, moved the miners' strike well down the order of the speech, and got rid of the attacks on Labour. But while Mrs Thatcher pruned the most partisan elements, what she said about the miners' strike was still combative. She kept some of the strongest phrases – 'Scabs? They are lions!' she said of the working miners – and she even linked, by implication, the struggle against the terrorism she and her party had just experienced with the extremism of Arthur Scargill and his supporters. She spoke of 'the emergence of an organized revolutionary minority' prepared to exploit industrial disputes, and the threat of violence which lay behind their demands. She quoted Kipling: 'We never pay anyone Danegeld, no matter how trifling the cost / For the end of that game is oppression and shame / And the

* Mrs Thatcher highlighted the words 'Labour Party', and scribbled 'their natural home'.

nation that pays it is lost.' For her, what was going on was 'the battle to uphold the rule of law' and 'the right to go to work of those who have been denied the right to go to vote'. She concluded: 'The nation faces what is probably the most testing crisis of our time, the battle between the extremists and the rest ... This nation will meet that challenge. Democracy will prevail.'[136] The extremists at the top of people's minds were now, of course, the IRA, but she meant Arthur Scargill and his militants too.

As befits the self-absorption of industrial disputes, the miners' strike continued as if no bomb had gone off. Mrs Thatcher barely rested from her ordeal. From the government's point of view, things got worse. Over the weekend immediately after the bomb, while Mrs Thatcher was recovering at Chequers, there was much toing and froing with NACODS. The union saw the NUM and then met the NCB: 'it was a rough meeting, with NACODS taking on the role of NUM shock troops. They argued that they had a strong mandate for a strike and that their members could not be restrained much longer.'[137] So desperate was Ian MacGregor for some sort of settlement that he even agreed to consider the deletion of the word 'closure' from the text of any agreement. After anxious discussion with Peter Walker and Tom King, Mrs Thatcher rang MacGregor on the Sunday afternoon. Speaking with a voice still weak from the effects of inhaling dust in the Brighton explosion, she told him that he would have 'the full support of Ministers' in resisting such a deletion.[138] 'The call ended with the Prime Minister emphasising again that there could be no further movement.'[139] The government could agree to an independent colliery review body, but not one, as NACODS demanded, whose recommendations were binding. Ministers privately accepted that 'if necessary, the possibility of a strike by NACODS should be faced.'[140] The expected strike date was 25 October 1984.

The government was now seriously alarmed. It did not trust MacGregor to handle the negotiations right, nor to present them well. There was an awkward situation in which MacGregor seemed to the public too intransigent, but, to those who knew what was happening in the negotiations, too inclined to give in by mistake. Noting his own telephone conversation with Mrs Thatcher on 14 October, David Hart recorded: 'MAC SELLS PASS SANS REALISING WTHR THRU OLD AGE OR TOTAL LACK POLITICAL AWARENESS I DON'T KNO.'[141] The government knew that it had to make the ultimate decisions about NACODS, but was still nervous of getting more deeply involved. There was a flurry of activity. Peter Walker wrote to MacGregor to tell him that the work of the Coal Board's advertising agency, which it employed to influence public opinion over the strike and frame public communications to miners, was useless. MacGregor agreed to recruit a new one. There were internal presentational changes too. Michael Eaton, the genial, pipe-smoking North Yorkshire area manager, was made public spokesman for the Coal Board, so that he, rather than MacGregor, would put the case on television; but even this change was mis-presented, giving the impression that Eaton's appointment represented a softening of Coal Board policy. Tim Bell, who was already helping MacGregor, also drafted in Gordon Reece to assist him. Walker himself tried to get more involved in negotiations, which caused anxiety in No. 10. Everyone was blaming everyone else for the way things were going wrong.

Mrs Thatcher was also – unusually in the history of the strike – embarrassed in Parliament. At Prime Minister's Questions on 23 October, Neil Kinnock accused her of having a 'hit list' for closures and of blocking attempts at a reasonable settlement. Mrs Thatcher, wanting neither to give in nor to provoke NACODS by angrily resisting, had to take refuge in bland, procedural language. She looked both weak and obstructive at the same time.

But on 24 October, against the pessimistic expectations of government, the NACODS executive decided to call off the strike. The union's leaders realized that they did not have the necessary support from their members, who were less left-wing than they, now that their main demand had been conceded. The government's Daily Coal Report gloated in a rather unWhitehall sort of way: 'The news was announced this afternoon and represents a massive blow to Scargill.'[142] This was the case. NACODS had been the NUM's last hope of broadening the dispute and also – since the NUM had not dented the determination of the working miners – of shutting down the pits altogether. From now on, the NACODS formula became the benchmark for the reasonable settlement of the dispute, with the NUM steadfastly refusing to accept it.

With the NACODS problem out of the way, the legal net tightened on the NUM. Throughout the strike even Mrs Thatcher had reluctantly accepted that 'Tory laws' should not be at the centre of the dispute. The fear was that the use of such laws would unite the trade union movement and encourage it to try to destroy them, as had happened with Ted Heath's Industrial Relations Act. From early days, many supporters of Mrs Thatcher's battle had disagreed. In July 1984, Andrew Turnbull reported to Mrs Thatcher the view of Jack Peel,* the right-wing trade unionist with

---

* Jack Peel (1921–93), educated Ruskin College, Oxford; railwayman, 1936–47; trade unionist; special adviser to Secretary of State for Transport on long-term industrial relations strategy, 1983–4.

whom she was friendly, that the government had 'missed a trick by not invoking the civil law'.[143] Turnbull admitted to her that 'If we had known how solid the working miners would be, how much coal could be moved by road and how long the striking miners would hold out we might have come to a different judgement some weeks ago.'[144]

As the summer progressed, various actions had been brought against the NUM. At the end of July, the High Court found that the South-West Area of the NUM had been in breach of an earlier order banning unlawful picketing of two haulage companies carrying coal and coke for British Steel. The union was fined £50,000. At the end of September, the High Court upheld an attempt by two working miners, Robert Taylor and Ken Foulstone, to have the strike declared unlawful. A writ alleging subsequent contempt was later served on Scargill, who was defying the court. Scargill was personally fined £1,000 and the union £200,000 for the contempt, with the threat of sequestration of the union's assets if the fine was not paid. An attempt was made to kill Taylor at Manton in Nottinghamshire when he was visiting his mother after the death of his father, and the secretary of the local NUM was charged with 'threatening to kill'. Using money raised privately and by public appeal, David Hart helped the National Working Miners' Committee bring actions which, like 'Gulliver's ropes' as he put it, would tie down the NUM in litigation: 'Scargill had tremendous energy. The first goal of the legal actions was to sap that energy.'[145] An order sequestrating the NUM's assets was issued on 25 October. Eventually, the sequestrators found and froze £8 million of NUM money hidden in Dublin, Luxembourg and Zurich. Defiance of the court might be popular with enthusiastic strikers, but it drove the NUM into the position of an impoverished outlaw, and into the arms of dangerous friends.

On 28 October 1984, the *Sunday Times* revealed that Roger Windsor, the chief executive of the NUM, had visited Libya to solicit money to support the strike from the country's dictator Colonel Muammar Gaddafi,* whom he met. Later, the paper established that $200,000 reached the NUM from this source. This visit had been arranged with the backing of Scargill, but without the knowledge of the NUM executive. Given the nature of Gaddafi's regime this revelation was extraordinarily damaging. Libya was known to supply arms to the IRA, and in April a gunman inside

---

* Muammar Gaddafi (1942–2011), politician, soldier and revolutionary; seized power from King Idris of Libya in a bloodless coup in 1969 and ruled the country until the 'Arab Spring' uprisings of 2010–12. He died of injuries sustained in a NATO airstrike in his ancestral home of Sirte in October 2011.

the Libyan Embassy in St James's Square had opened fire on anti-Gaddafi demonstrators outside, killing WPC Yvonne Fletcher, who was policing the protest. British intelligence had known what Scargill was up to and how money was being moved.[146] Mrs Thatcher was aware of this, and of covert leaks to help the cause. There was an argument within the intelligence services, with MI5 arguing that the information should not be passed to the press, and SIS arguing that it should. SIS prevailed.[147] On 5 November, Robert Armstrong informed Robin Butler that 'Steps are being taken to prompt journalistic inquiries' about the NUM's connection with the Soviet Union and the Eastern bloc.[148] It duly emerged in the press that Scargill himself had visited Paris for a secret meeting to get money from the Soviet Union – $1.4 million was authorized to be paid across.[149] This cast a shadow over the first visit of Mikhail Gorbachev, the future Soviet leader, to Mrs Thatcher at Chequers the following month (see Chapter 8). The NUM also collected money from Czechoslovakia, Bulgaria and Soviet-occupied Afghanistan.* It would have been hard for anti-Scargill propagandists to have constructed a less favourable picture than the actual truth. Here was the miners' leader consorting secretly with the enemies of his country – the enemy within and the enemy without.

As the position of the NUM became more and more compromised, the working miners gained in confidence. The day after the Libyan story broke, Chris Butcher, alias Silver Birch, asked if he could bring a group of working miners to see Mrs Thatcher. Walker advised strongly against this. He was concerned about jealousy between Silver Birch and the Working Miners' Committee – he 'regards the latter as more formidable', Turnbull told Mrs Thatcher; '– in his view the Silver Birch Group is something of a publicity exercise financed by the *Daily Mail*.'[150] Mrs Thatcher, however, full of enthusiasm for the working miners, did not like this cautious, but probably sensible, advice. She was often being tempted by David Hart's suggestions that she should pay a visit to a working miners' community to show solidarity with them. 'It will be difficult to refuse,' she wrote on the memo. 'Could I not see representatives <u>of both</u>? – Separately.'[151]

In fact, she did not see Silver Birch.† It was easier to show her support

---

* Mrs Thatcher also won backing, though not of a financial kind, from behind the Iron Curtain. The *Sunday Mirror* quoted Lech Wałęsa, the leader of the Polish Solidarity trade union: 'With such a wise and brave woman, Britain will find a solution to the strike' (*Sunday Mirror*, 29 July 1984).

† In June 1985, Butcher wrote to Mrs Thatcher directly, offering to bring her evidence of continued intimidation of working miners (Butcher to Mrs Thatcher, 16 June 1985, CAC: THCR 2/2/4/26). The Department of Energy again set out its objections to the meeting. 'Not

for working miners by treating the issue in a humanitarian rather than a
political way. This she did by corresponding with, and receiving delega-
tions from, the wives of working miners. In the middle of September, she
met a group of three wives, from Wales, Derbyshire and Kent. (This last,
Mrs Irene McGibbon, made a strong impression when she spoke at the
Conservative Party conference the following month.)* Her visitors told her
about intimidation, the need for transfers from troubled areas when the
strike finished, the unhelpfulness of the BBC to their cause and the support
for the NUM among NCB managers in some areas. Mrs Thatcher's manuscript notes of the meeting reveal her strong reaction to what she heard:

> Fear
> Threat
> Hands knees – rocks
> ... Totally disillusioned
> ... NUM 'slush fund'
> Danger to life.
> Churches – money to miners
> Hoax 999 ...
> ... Picketing – outside home[152]

Such stories fed Mrs Thatcher's indignation against the strikers and her
solidarity with those who defied the strike. All through the dispute, there
were horrible attacks on working miners and their families – the wife of
a working miner who was held down by youths in Nuneaton while others
scraped her face with a Brillo pad (to remove the 'scab'); the miner who,
a fortnight after returning to work, committed suicide because of threats;
the mobs that beset the homes of working miners. Less than a week after
the Brighton bomb, the house of Mrs McGibbon was attacked with paint
bombs after the *Morning Star* had deliberately published her home address.
Perhaps because of her sex, Mrs Thatcher was more conscious of the effect
on the families of the working miners than were her male colleagues. The
government files on the dispute are full of her exclamations, underlinings
and expressions of disgust at their ill treatment, and that meted out to the
police, by Scargill supporters. Her thinking about the entire dispute was

---

the convincing dossier against Mr Butcher we had been led to expect,' wrote Robin Butler.
'But he is distrusted by the NCB and the Notts Miners Union.' (Butler comment on Dart to
Butler, 16 July 1985, CAC: THCR 2/2/4/26.) Mrs Thatcher agreed that Butcher could see
Michael Alison instead, but the meeting was deferred several times.
* In a letter to Mrs McGibbon in August 1985, Mrs Thatcher had scribbled, 'So good to
hear from you again. We will do all we can to help the three courageous people mentioned
in your letter' (Thatcher to McGibbon, 27 August 1985, CAC: THCR 2/6/3/75).

governed not only by her determination that the NUM should lose, but also by her desire that the working miners should win.

On 30 November 1984, the violence reached a dreadful climax. 'News has just reached us', wrote Bernard Ingham to Mrs Thatcher, 'of an incident in the coal dispute.'[153] A three-foot concrete garden post had been thrown from a roadbridge at a taxi carrying a working miner on the way to the Merthyr Vale pit in South Wales. The miner was unhurt, but the driver, David Wilkie, was killed. 'I have said', Ingham went on, 'that you are horrified and utterly condemn this murderous activity.'[154] Arthur Scargill, who had previously avoided any criticism of violence, was forced to condemn this attack. He did so on a platform shared by Neil Kinnock, and when he uttered the word 'condemn', Kinnock leapt up to applaud. This meant that Scargill's full words were drowned out. What he actually said was that he condemned such attacks when they happened 'away from picket lines'.* By chance, on the very same day as the attack, the High Court appointed a receiver to run the affairs of the NUM. The effect of Wilkie's killing – for which two miners were sentenced to life imprisonment, a sentence later reduced to eight years after the conviction ws changed from murder to manslaughter – was to lower the level of violence. This had risen as the strikers had become more desperate. By 4 December 1984, a total of 8,688 arrests had been made in the course of the dispute. Now the fight went out of them.

As well as disgusting wider opinion,† the violence did not stop the return to work. This picked up as soon as the NACODS strike was called off. By 7 November, 72,000 men were working, roughly 30,000 more than at the beginning of the strike. A further 6,000 returned in the course of the next week, with miners responding to a pre-Christmas deadline from the NCB for anyone wishing to qualify for back-payments of holiday pay. It now became clear to the government, for the first time, that it would almost certainly win. 'The miners were going to lose,' Neil Kinnock recalled thinking, but he comforted himself: 'I was dedicated to ensuring that Scargill would never avoid the blame.'[155] On 8 November, Mrs Thatcher told the US Ambassador, Charlie Price, that she believed 'the strike would end by "crumbling"; this would be the best result since it would dampen animosity between the working miners and those who were now drifting back.'[156] 'Ministers', said the Cabinet minutes for

* Lord Kinnock confirmed that 'I and Stan Orme [a member of his Shadow Cabinet] jumped up at once to clap it,' in order to make Scargill's condemnation as unqualified as possible (Interview with Lord Kinnock).

† An NOP poll published on 7 December showed a great majority of the public believing that NUM violence was planned. Labour voters split 49–41, with the majority saying it was spontaneous. ('Press Digest', Ingham to Thatcher, 3 December 1984, THCR 3/5/41.)

15 November, 'should avoid any appearance of gloating over the continuing return to work.'[157] On 13 November, Harold Macmillan, elevated by Mrs Thatcher to the House of Lords as the Earl of Stockton, made his maiden speech there, at the age of ninety. Lamenting the coal conflict, he declared that the miners were 'the best men in the world. They beat the Kaiser's army and they beat Hitler's army. They never gave in.'[158] Whether or not Macmillan was right in his history, it was already perceptible that the miners were not going to beat Margaret Thatcher.

Mrs Thatcher did not feel, however, that the way to victory lay plain before her. The drift back to work was not yet a flood, and it remained possible that the Coal Board might fall for an inadequate settlement. There was also a countervailing danger that any victory might be seen by the public as pyrrhic, with Mrs Thatcher blamed for harshness. Within the government, there were disagreements about tactics. Some, such as the Policy Unit, thought that matters should be brought to a head by withdrawing the promise of no compulsory redundancies to those still on strike. But Mrs Thatcher, despite her instinctive support for a tough line, could see the dangers. When Turnbull wrote to her that 'I don't agree that the time has come to switch from the carrot to the stick ... Withdrawing the job guarantee and the redundancy terms would represent a major change of course by NCB/ Government,' she scribbled, 'I agree with you.'[159] Nothing should be done which might threaten the industry's capacity to endure until the spring.

Desperate to bring the strike to a close without any obvious humiliation of trade unionism, the TUC, and some union leaders acting individually, tried to reach out to the government for deals. Bernard Ingham, well plugged in to the union movement, had a secret meeting with David Basnett, the fairly moderate head of the large General, Municipal, Boilermakers' and Allied Trades Union. Private discussions between Peter Walker and the TUC took place. But the government was conscious of the dangers. Mrs Thatcher told a meeting with Walker that 'nothing should be agreed which would undercut the position of the working miners,' and that it was 'essential to prevent the NUM from claiming that the programme of pit closures had been withdrawn'.[160] Besides, as Peter Walker pointed out, Scargill would not agree to anything anyway. At every twist and turn, the NUM's intransigence made things easier for the government. On 20 December 1984, the private office of the Department of Energy sent a letter to Mrs Thatcher's private office: 'Happy Christmas to all,' it said; '– the lights are still on!'[161] On 17 January 1985, the demand for electricity was higher than it had ever been at any point in British history. The CEGB met the demand with no difficulty.

In that month, yet more attempts at new negotiations between the NCB and the NUM were floated, some based on a TUC document. There were the usual posturings and the rumours of concessions that came to nothing. Mrs Thatcher wrote to Pauline Linton, one of the leaders of the working miners' wives, to reassure her: 'For my part, I have made clear that there can be no fudging of the central issue, and no betrayal of the working miners to whom we owe so much.'[162] In what Andrew Turnbull called 'A good letter for once',[163] the NCB wrote to the NUM to say that, since Scargill had not changed his mind on uneconomic pits, there was nothing to discuss.

In a characteristically highly coloured missive, David Hart summed up the situation in terms that were probably not displeasing to Mrs Thatcher, who underlined parts of it: 'Like the snow, the last few weeks of the dispute must be endured bravely. We are on the brink of a great victory. If we don't throw it away at the last moment. Much greater than the Falklands because the enemy within is so much harder to conquer.'[164] He was also, it seems, the first person to set out to her on paper 'the most likely' way the strike would end. 'The NUM will lead its men back to work with no settlement,' he foretold. 'It is the best option for us . . . an unequivocally clear victory,' which would prove 'the utter pointlessness of the strike'.

Hart's prediction was correct, including the suggestion that there were still a few weeks left to run. Mrs Thatcher agreed to meet the TUC in person on 18 February. But the aim was chiefly presentational – to demonstrate the government's willingness to find a good settlement. Bernard Ingham wrote her a note beforehand to point out the danger of entrapment and misrepresentation: 'the TUC will seize on the slightest sign of softening or weakening to suggest you are moving (and will blame you afterwards if there is a breakdown) . . . you cannot trust any one of those coming to see you.'[165] The main purpose, from a media point of view, was to 'carry our message to them, confidently and firmly'. To her speaking note for the meeting, Mrs Thatcher added her own thought about the nature of an agreement: 'language – such as is clear to the Ordinary Person – meaning clear & unambiguous'.[166] After the meeting, in which the TUC claimed signs of movement by the NUM and the government found none, the NUM national executive duly rejected the final position of the NCB. Neil Kinnock complained that it was 'foolish and divisive' of the government to seek a return to work by attrition rather than negotiation, but by this time 'attrition' was no longer the right word. On 25 February, 3,807 new faces – a record – presented themselves for work. Two days later, the Daily Coal Report noted that 'Over 93,000 NUM members – 50.25 per cent – are now not on strike.'[167] This was the first time that more men were working than striking.

On 3 March 1985, a special delegate conference of the NUM voted to return to work without a settlement. Scargill promised that 'guerrilla warfare' would continue. Men went back to the pits, some marching to the music of colliery bands. On 8 March, the Daily Coal Report said that 97 per cent of the men were now not on strike: 'Because the situation has settled down coal reports will no longer be issued on a daily basis.'[168] 'We shall miss you!' wrote Andrew Turnbull.

Mrs Thatcher had won the most important single victory of her career. Naturally she did not put it this way. 'If anyone has won,' she said outside 10 Downing Street, 'it has been the miners who stayed at work' and all those 'that have kept Britain going'.[169]

The internal post-mortem on the strike, conducted under the chairmanship of Peter Gregson and presented to Mrs Thatcher in late May, told the story in simple narrative form. The economic loss directly attributable to the strike in 1984–5 was 1.25 per cent of GDP, it said, and public expenditure had increased by £2.5 billion because of it. Coal stocks held up, and by the end of the strike an endurance of ten months, better than at the beginning, was assured. Twenty-six civil cases were brought against the NUM and forty-seven injunctions granted; remedies under the 'Tory laws' were used as well as under the common law. In England and Wales, 1,390 police officers were injured, and 10,372 criminal charges were brought. The report identified three main reasons for the defeat of the NUM: the provisions for endurance, the NUM's failure to get enough support from other unions and its own members, and the success of police 'mutual aid'.[170]

Passing it on to Mrs Thatcher, Turnbull commented that the report did not convey 'how near, on occasions, the Government came to disaster'.[171] Mrs Thatcher agreed, describing it as 'too turgid'. In her substantive points, she focused chiefly on the working miners. She wanted the government to 'instruct' the Coal Board that working miners who wanted a transfer to another pit (to escape retribution) should have one, expenses paid, and should not suffer financially in any way for having worked through the strike. In the aftermath of the dispute, it was this matter that absorbed most of her energies. She intervened with MacGregor who, she felt, did not care enough about the issue in general, to support the Fjaelberg family – Mrs Fjaelberg, one of the three wives who had visited No. 10, had been prominent in the working miners' wives group – who wanted a transfer from Wales to Nottinghamshire because of harassment. She attended a secret dinner at Woodrow Wyatt's* house in St John's Wood to meet the Nottinghamshire-based president of the Working Miners' Committee, Colin Clarke, and leaders from other regions.† They discussed how best to set up their own national union, which eventually, in December, became the Union of Democratic Mineworkers. Robin Butler, who also attended, remembered being introduced to a working miners' leader with another arboreal codename, 'Lone Pine'.[172]

Mrs Thatcher was extremely sensitive in later years to what she thought was a 'widespread belief that the Government had let the working miners down'.[173] In a sense, this belief was correct. The let-down was not intentional, and government documents all through the strike show numerous plans and suggestions for building a thriving coal industry once the war was over. But in the struggle to win the strike, no clarity had ever been reached about what ought to happen after it. Some of Mrs Thatcher's advisers, notably in the Policy Unit, had argued for bold new policies, such as a great increase in open-cast mining, and a break-up of the NCB, to create an era of modern, profitable and decentralized coal production. But Peter Walker and Ian MacGregor, who by this time had more or less lost confidence in one another, were in no mental state to think through a new business plan. Strange though it seems in retrospect, everyone was preoccupied with the idea that any bold move would provoke another strike. Immediately after the strike, Walker publicly scotched the idea of privatization.‡ Closures proceeded, but, in order to avoid Scargill mobilizing once more, not according to any discernible strategy.

Besides, the economics of the entire business were even worse than the government had earlier believed. In Turnbull's retrospective view, it was the collapse in the oil price to $10 a barrel in 1986 which finally discouraged serious efforts to maintain a big coal industry:

> Everyone wanted gas, and people could see that the social costs of mining are immense. Deep-mined coal is a kind of barbaric way of producing energy . . . Economics had to prevail. You couldn't fight for the principle of

---

* Woodrow Wyatt (1918–97), educated Eastbourne College and Worcester College, Oxford; journalist; Labour MP for Aston Division of Birmingham, 1945–55; for Bosworth Division of Leicester, 1959–70; chairman, Horserace Totalisator Board, 1976–97; created Lord Wyatt of Weeford, 1987.

† The guests at the dinner were Clarke, John Blessington and John Liptrot (Notts), Tony Ellis (Yorks), Tony Morris (Staffs), Roland Taylor (N. Derbyshire), Terry Hackett (Stoke-on-Trent) and T. Holdman and Ewan Thomas (S. Wales). There were 'no staff present so as not to impede conversation'. (Note to Mrs Thatcher, 28 March 1985, CAC: THCR 1/7/9.)

‡ Privatization eventually took place under the premiership of John Major in 1994.

economic pits and then keep uneconomic pits open because of a fondness
for the working miners.[174]

By the 1990s, Arthur Scargill's prediction that the coal industry would
be destroyed had more or less come true. What he could not acknowledge
was that, but for his total resistance to the idea of an economic pit and
the immense cost of his suicidal strike, this need not have happened. Much
of the destruction of mining communities, of which he complained and
which was real enough, could have been mitigated. Virtually all the bitter
divisions between working and striking miners could have been prevented
if he had agreed to a national ballot.

The political and psychological situation for Mrs Thatcher after the
end of the strike was a strained one. Even for the victors, there was a sense
of melancholy. The certainty, both moral and political, that Scargill must
be defeated did not remove sympathy for miners in general. 'It was the
most miserable thing I'd ever been involved with,' John Redwood recalled,
'because I could see that the miners had a point as well as the Coal
Board.'[175] Millions of people who had no time for Scargill had nevertheless
felt uneasy on behalf of the miners, and resented the divisive pressure to
take sides. There was also a problem of tone. Mrs Thatcher had won the
key industrial relations battle of the post-war era, but she felt she could
not say so publicly. Some of her staff, including Tim Flesher and Stephen
Sherbourne, thought this was a mistake. 'We need to find a way to say
clearly, but without sounding triumphalist, that the Government has won,'
Sherbourne told her.[176] In answers to questions after a speech in Malaysia
in April, Mrs Thatcher did say that the government 'saw off' the miners'
strike and that trade unions were at last 'learning the facts of life',[177] but
this was considered deplorably insensitive; she was particularly attacked
for making such remarks abroad. Writing to her after this, Bernard Ingham set out the dominant view of how to handle the matter. He was
'profoundly unconvinced', he said,

> that it would have been wise at the time to rub the NUM's nose in it, but
> we ought progressively to get over [that is, convey] the fact that the NUM
> lost . . . I also take the view that the Labour Party/TUC performance during
> the NUM strike will be a serious liability [for Labour] at the next election,
> provided the point of their performance is steadily and regularly registered
> with the public.[178]

The calculation was that the public were relieved by the defeat of Scargill, but also distressed by the amount of conflict which it had entailed.
Their feeling that Mrs Thatcher was too confrontational a figure would

only be exacerbated if she were to drive her victory home. There was sense in this view, but it probably underestimated the extent to which a failure to say something important in politics tends to be interpreted as evidence of self-doubt or divided counsels. Without a full explanation from Mrs Thatcher and her colleagues of what they had achieved, the field was open for the mythologizing of the strike by the left, something which achieved its apogee in the film *Billy Elliot*. Thirty years on, it was commonplace to find people talking about the strike who had no idea of its central, distinguishing feature – that it was called and continued without a ballot.

Besides, the miners' strike was not, in reality, an event which showed Mrs Thatcher's character in a bad light. She was not intemperate, as she often was in her EEC dealings, or vengeful, as she was accused of being over GCHQ, or uncollegiate with Cabinet ministers, or divisive of her party. Whatever her longing for dramatic interventions, she maintained personal and collective discipline throughout, listening carefully to Peter Walker and others and, more often than not, erring on the side of caution. She was in charge but not embroiled. To return to the metaphor of war which dominated the entire year, one could say that she fought a battle which she saw as necessary rather than welcome. 'She fought every skirmish like a good commander,' recalled Stephen Sherbourne, 'and she brought limitless energy to everything she tussled with.'[179] Even Ian MacGregor, with whom she had many disagreements, was in no doubt about her leadership. 'If you fight a war,' he told Tim Bell when it was all over, 'you want a great general. She was a great general.'[180] Tim Flesher concluded that 'No other British Prime Minister would have won the Falklands War or the miners' strike. She showed unique resolution and clarity. She was terrifically inspiring. If she hadn't won, we'd be like Greece.'[181] Even Peter Walker, who had little cause to love Mrs Thatcher, said that, in the miners' strike, 'I felt I had a PM who always backed me.'[182] Such points were not publicly made at the time. In some areas of policy – privatization, for example – Mrs Thatcher was given more personal credit than was really due. For the conduct of the miners' strike, she was given too little.

Mrs Thatcher's most passionate feelings in the whole saga had been engaged by the cause of the working miners. A month after the end of the strike, she wrote a remarkable letter to a Mrs Hackett, from Staffordshire, whose husband Terry had been one of those who refused to strike and who had met Mrs Thatcher at the dinner given by Woodrow Wyatt. She had already thanked Mr Hackett, she wrote, but she wanted to thank her as well because she knew 'how much he values the help and support which you have given him throughout this difficult time'.[183] She added 'how much

I also appreciate and admire your courage'. Her letter set out what she thought about people like Terry Hackett:

> The miners who stood up for their right to work in the mining dispute were defending a fundamental privilege of a free people. We can be very proud of them. They withstood, and continue to withstand, the most extreme threats and intimidations with a courage which is an example to us all. The nation owes them a debt of gratitude.

When Mrs Thatcher checked the letter and signed it, she had the imagination to consider the effect on the recipient of receiving a letter marked '10 Downing Street' in the potentially hostile territory of a mining community. With a thoughtfulness and attention to detail which is hard to imagine in a male prime minister, she wrote a covering note which said: 'Please send in Plain envelope.'[184]

7

Sales of the century

'Tell Sid'

Critics had attacked the 1983 Conservative general election manifesto for being too bland. Many of her closest supporters – and Mrs Thatcher herself[1] – considered it had been a wasted opportunity to set a clear direction for the second term. But in fact it had set out lucidly, though not in detail, the government's overall economic approach. This included tax reform, further union reform, removing barriers to job creation, and the sale of nationalized industries to the public. So great was the convulsion of the miners' strike that it is hard to remember that in the year over which it lasted, absorbing so much of Mrs Thatcher's time and energy, the government she led nevertheless embarked on further major tax reform, and on privatization on a grand scale. Nigel Lawson's 1984 Budget, indeed, was delivered to Parliament on 13 March, the day after the calling of the miners' strike.

Since the public spending row of the previous July (see Chapter 4), little had seemed to go right for the new Chancellor. He had immediately become associated in the public mind with the punitive rather than the aspirational side of Thatcherism. His speech at the party conference in October had been, in his own words, 'rather indifferent'.[2] To the British public, he seemed clever, but his cleverness caused other people to feel stupid, and therefore irritated. No one doubted his abilities, but he had little political following. And because he had to wait not far short of a year before he delivered his first Budget, he had had no opportunity to make a decisive mark.

Lawson used his time well, however. He began preparing his Budget, by his own account, on the aeroplane back from a conference in the United States on 28 September 1983. He later claimed that of the eight main tax reform ideas he jotted down on the flight, six found their way into his first Budget.[3] Although there was not complete agreement between No. 10 and No. 11 – Mrs Thatcher's people wanted a tighter PSBR than the Treasury, for example – the sense of common purpose between the two at that time was strong. As Lawson developed his tax ideas, John Redwood encouraged them, invoking the long-distance support of Alan Walters* from across the Atlantic to bolster his case. Writing to Mrs Thatcher, Redwood backed Lawson's plans to concentrate on business taxation, 'removing tax impediments to individual enterprise and initiative': 'This is the budget to be bold. It should stake out the radical tax measures of this Parliament.'[4] At the Department of Trade and Industry (DTI), Norman Tebbit, who admired 'the great determination' for reform which he observed at Lawson's Treasury, also weighed in on Lawson's side, arguing, for example, for the vital importance of getting rid of the job-damaging employers' National Insurance Surcharge (NIS) which Labour had imposed. 'I had, to a reasonable extent, the confidence of the PM, and I had the friendship of Nigel,' he recalled. 'So I could sweet-talk them.'[5] The Tebbit–Lawson combination was formidable. 'I couched my submissions along lines which supported Nigel's own intentions,' Tebbit recalled, 'knowing of course that they would probably be drawn to the attention of the PM.'[6] Jeffrey Sterling,† special adviser to all Mrs Thatcher's DTI secretaries of state, considered that 'If Norman and Nigel worked together, they would nearly always succeed in persuading her.'[7]

On most of the matters at stake in the 1984 Budget, Mrs Thatcher did not need a huge amount of persuasion. In Lawson's view, she did not share his interest in producing a more logical tax system: 'This idea of tax neutrality – the removal of special reliefs for this, that or the other . . . held no appeal for her.'[8] She did not care as much about undistorted markets as he did. Her natural inclination was to use the tax system actively to favour those with whom she sympathized, most notably homeowners, or potential homeowners, and pensioners. But she was also fervently in favour of reducing burdens on business and obstacles to job creation. She therefore supported her Chancellor's desire to cut the rate of corporation tax, while coppicing its forest of allowances and reliefs, and to get rid of the NIS. So long as income tax cuts were recognized as the ultimate, though not necessarily immediate, goal, she was happy to

---

* At this stage, Lawson did not find Walters's role in giving Mrs Thatcher economic advice oppressive. Indeed, when he wrote to Mrs Thatcher to argue for separate targets for the different measures of money, M3 and M0, he told her that Walters was 'very much in favour of the new range for narrow money' (Lawson to Thatcher, 20 February 1984, TNA: PREM 19/1197 (http://www.margaretthatcher.org/document/134139)).

† Jeffrey Sterling (1934–), educated Reigate Grammar School, Preston Manor County School and Guildhall School of Music; businessman; special adviser to Secretary of State for Industry, later for Trade and Industry, 1982–90; executive chairman, P&O, 1983–2005; knighted, 1985; created Lord Sterling of Plaistow, 1991.

enter into the spirit of Lawson's first Budget. In her first administration, Lawson told her, 'our major achievement was bringing down inflation', but they had not managed a 'radical structural reform of . . . business taxation . . . We now have a rare opportunity.' He had a plan for the Parliament, sequenced for electoral advantage: 'With a neutral Budget in 1984 and a large fiscal adjustment [partly due to asset sales] in prospect for 1985, this leaves room for desirable changes in personal taxation, provided we keep public expenditure flat.'[9] She underlined the words 'provided' and 'flat' many times, to encourage rigour.

Under the British system, the Budget is not a Cabinet decision, though the Cabinet is perfunctorily consulted and informed before it is unveiled to Parliament. It belongs exclusively to the Chancellor, and, 'The only person the Chancellor is obliged to consult is the Prime Minister.'[10] Lawson was more jealous of the Chancellor's rights in this area than the more conciliatory Geoffrey Howe had been. He made it clear, from the first, that he would be master in his own house. He ruthlessly squashed Mrs Thatcher's hope that Lord Cockfield, who, since the election, had been Chancellor of the Duchy of Lancaster and, in effect, adviser to Mrs Thatcher on fiscal and business subjects, could be an independent source of tax reform. He also did little to enlighten the Cabinet about his Budget thoughts, provoking irritation. It got back to Mrs Thatcher, via Bernard Ingham, that John Biffen* had been so annoyed by Lawson's attitude that he had briefed lobby journalists that 'Cabinet this morning [9 February] had been one of the most bland, miserably disappointing and boring meetings he had ever been at. It was absolutely awful; there was no lively debate, just unctious [sic] self-satisfaction. Things had been described as "going along nicely", although unemployment was still high.'[11] The incautious outburst of the increasingly and dangerously frank Biffen was untypical of the Cabinet, but he was probably reflecting colleagues' feelings of exclusion.

In fulfilling his duty to consult Mrs Thatcher over the Budget, Lawson was less punctilious than Howe. His preferred method was discussion after a Sunday-night supper in No. 11. Denis and Margaret and Nigel and his wife Thérèse would eat together, and then Chancellor and Prime Minister would retire to discuss Budget plans *à deux*.[12] This method avoided leaks, because, on such matters, Mrs Thatcher was utterly

---

* John Biffen (1930–2007), educated Dr Morgan's School, Bridgwater and Jesus College, Cambridge; Conservative MP for Oswestry, 1961–83; for Shropshire North, 1983–97; Chief Secretary to the Treasury, 1979–81; Secretary of State for Trade, 1981–2; Lord President of the Council, 1982–3; Leader of the House of Commons, 1982–7; Lord Privy Seal, 1983–7; created Lord Biffen, 1997.

discreet. Lawson also believed that it relaxed her, but in fact it made her somewhat uneasy because she preferred serious government business to be done on paper. Matters were not clearly argued through. As time went on, Lawson's preference for chat became a means of avoiding important differences and made Mrs Thatcher more suspicious.[13] This was not so in 1984, but already it caused muddle. Andrew Turnbull, for example, had to seek Mrs Thatcher's guidance after Lawson's private office made assertions about what had been agreed about extensions of value-added tax (VAT) at one of these tête-à-têtes: 'It would be very helpful if you could confirm whether this account is consistent with your account of the meeting.'[14] She said it was. Confusions in later years were not to be so easily dealt with.

In the preparation for the 1984 Budget, however, differences between Mrs Thatcher and Lawson mostly worked to their shared advantage. She qualified his reforming zeal with her political sense of what she called 'our people'. She advised him against the levy on consumer credit which he proposed (though Walters supported him),[15] and fretted about VAT extensions to house repairs. She agreed personally to soothe the feelings of Nissan, the Japanese car company whose entry into British manufacturing in the north-east had been sweetened by capital allowances which now stood to be reduced by the proposed reforms.[16] In particular, she followed the lead of Bernard Ingham, who warned that Lawson's idea of extending VAT to newspapers would spoil everything:

> It may be objected that Fleet Street could afford to pay VAT if only it would sort itself out [by taking on the print unions]. That is no doubt true and I have very little sympathy or patience left with Fleet Street. But that is still not a good reason for setting Fleet Street against you. Look what happened to Mr Macmillan.[17]

Fleet Street proprietors often owned the more estimable local press too, Ingham reminded her. He came on strong: 'I am profoundly concerned lest you set potential or actual supporters against you,' he said. 'Please show to N.L.,' wrote Mrs Thatcher beneath these words. She personally told the Chancellor not to spoil the 'wonderful reception' his 'wonderful Budget' would otherwise get.[18] VAT was not extended to newspapers. Politically, if in no other sense, Mrs Thatcher and Ingham were undoubtedly right, and Lawson wrong.

Despite the most comprehensive leak in Budget history, when the *Guardian* published a full early draft of the text almost two weeks before delivery,[19] Lawson's first Budget speech still came almost as a surprise. It confounded the expectations of the political market-place. Because of

Lawson's early difficulties as Chancellor, the media had forgotten his mastery of his subject and the strength of his ambition. 'This Budget will set the Government's course for this Parliament' were his first words.[20] He set out his two themes – the further reduction of inflation and his reforms of business taxation and how these would pave the way for tax cuts. The man who had invented the Medium-Term Financial Strategy (MTFS) seemed to carry authority as he gave the House the future narrative which he wanted.

Lawson set the PSBR, optimistically, at only £7.25 billion (Walters had been even more hopeful, recommending £6 billion),[21] though in the previous year it had hit £10 billion. It was his tax changes, however, which commanded the most attention. He halved stamp duty, withdrew all new life insurance premium relief, and got rid of the 'investment income surcharge', which taxed 'unearned' income at a higher rate. He changed capital allowances to discourage companies from hiding from tax in industrial buildings, machinery and plant, and he laid out plans for a phased reduction in corporation tax, lowering the rate over several years from 52 per cent to 35 per cent. The small companies rate fell to 30 per cent. Share options were taken out of income tax altogether and the NIS ('this tax on jobs') was abolished. He extended VAT to building alterations and hot take-away food, creating a press outcry about punishing fish and chips. In a little *coup de théâtre*, Lawson complained about a European ruling forcing him to tax beer as heavily as wine. He said he would obey it – largely by cutting the duty on wine. He held income tax rates at existing levels, but raised their thresholds well above inflation.

All this Lawson accomplished in a crisp, short speech, delivered with confidence and the suppressed excitement that a writer might feel when, after years of drafting his magnum opus, volume one at last appears. He gave the impression of knowing what he wanted and where he was going. Reviews like 'A Star is Born' (the *Spectator*),[22] 'a pyrotechnic display of economic and financial skills' (*Guardian*),[23] followed. A delighted Mrs Thatcher excitedly gatecrashed Lawson's thank-you party for staff in No. 11 afterwards. A week later, John Redwood was moved to write to Mrs Thatcher, 'The Government has now regained momentum, thanks to a strong Tory radical Budget.'[24] He argued that Lawson had successfully advanced the radicals without alienating the consolidators. The radicalism must continue, or there would be 'a lack of wind in the sails', but the Tories must also remember that 'vested interests' were often their essential supporters. The task of the government was to bring these apparent opposites 'behind purposes about which they could all unite'. It was a novel and pleasing experience for Mrs Thatcher to be presented with a Budget which was, in her view, right, and also popular. It was the first big achievement which made Nigel Lawson, in the word she was to use at a later, much less happy moment, 'unassailable'.

One important issue over which most radicals and consolidators could be persuaded to unite was privatization. The subject had also been well fore-shadowed in the supposedly overcautious manifesto for the 1983 election. The manifesto had boasted that 'We have returned to free enterprise many state firms, in order to provide better service to the customer and save tax-payers' money.' It listed the sales achieved so far and made much of employee share ownership as 'the truest public ownership of all'. More important, it promised to go much further. The word 'privatised' appeared, though slightly *sotto voce*, under the heading of 'The Nationalised Industries'. Their reform, the manifesto declared, was 'central to economic recovery'.

Big names were named. BT, Rolls-Royce, British Airways and substan-tial parts of the British Steel Corporation, British Shipbuilders and British Leyland were promised for sale. So were British Gas's offshore oil interests. The Tories said they would 'seek other means' of encouraging competition and capital in the gas and energy industries. They also stated: 'Merely to replace state monopolies with private ones would be to waste an historic opportunity.' There was a clear policy purpose and a clear agenda to get through. It was not 'a great ideological crusade',[25] more a determination to solve a collection of problems which government was peculiarly ill equipped to deal with, searching for 'a route out of this mess'.

In this, however, it helped very much that Mrs Thatcher and Nigel Lawson were ideological soulmates in most of the economic aspects of Thatcherism. Her relationship with Geoffrey Howe as Chancellor, though vitally important and, broadly speaking, successful, had been forged more by necessity than by shared zeal. Lawson, younger than Howe, and there-fore in the early days more of an acolyte than an equal to Mrs Thatcher, had seen himself as a proto-Thatcherite. He was a more systematic devel-oper of her own ideas than she was herself. He had also, both as financial secretary to the Treasury and as energy secretary, led privatization in the first term.

David Pascall, who moved over from the Think Tank when Mrs Thatcher closed it down, to join the Policy Unit, immediately felt this sense of common purpose at the heart of the government. 'This was the most creative period, and we [the Policy Unit] were custodians of the strategy.'[26] Although seconded from industry, and not politically engaged, Pascall was tremendously impressed by the Prime Minister. She had 'both strate-gic depth and attention to detail, and that curiosity which was never satisfied. She was in a league of her own.' Bob Young, who also joined the Policy Unit at this time, had a similar sense that they were witnessing a 'major shift in the way the economy and society were working'.[27] He described this time as 'the golden years'.

The 'big push', as the No. 10 unit saw it, was for a competition agenda, rolling back the state, popular share ownership.[28] Indeed, the Policy Unit was even more preoccupied with these themes than was Mrs Thatcher herself. Privatization was central. Mrs Thatcher had an 'abiding hatred'[29] of the nationalized industries because of the amount of government time and money they consumed, their appalling labour relations and their inability, in their existing form, to raise capital for proper investment. 'I do hope to be able to show to people that privatisation works,' she said shortly before the 1983 election. 'It is often more efficient because people know . . . they are on their own, whereas if they are nationalised they think, "Oh well, we can turn round and the taxpayer has got to subsidise us." '[30] She longed for 'decisions to be taken at a commercial and not a political level'.[31] According to Peter Warry, who joined the Policy Unit in the summer of 1984, having previously been chief executive of a British Leyland subsidiary, the DTI and, to a lesser extent, the Treasury 'were quite well captured by the nationalized industries'.[32] Mrs Thatcher was not: she regarded most of their managements as incompetent and weak. She was often very well informed about particular nationalized industries, especially the 'smokestack' ones. She was well advised, Warry believed, by Denis: 'When I was discussing BL with her, I found I was really on my mettle. She was very impressive. Sometimes she knew things I had not read.'[33] Tebbit agreed, from a different perspective: 'I had dark suspicions that Denis had given, informal, brutal advice on BL.'[34]

The Treasury, keen to sell off state assets, was primarily concerned with the benefit to the public finances from the proceeds.* Mrs Thatcher saw the issue more widely – in political, social and industrial as well as financial terms. This difference of emphasis between No. 10 and the Treasury was – on this subject – largely harmonious, one of function rather than ideology. Lawson, after all, had given more orderly thought to the whole philosophy of privatization than had Mrs Thatcher herself. 'We saw Lawson as understanding it all,' recalled Oliver Letwin. 'He was completely on the side of the market.'[35] John Redwood, who succeeded Ferdinand Mount as head of the Policy Unit at the end of 1983, was, as he immodestly

---

* The benefits, because the revenues were treated as negative public spending, were great for the PSBR as well as for straightforward receipts. Much later in the sequence came an even bigger Treasury benefit – the amount of tax paid by privatized companies.

but correctly put it, its 'guru on privatization'.[36] Mount had recommended him for the post partly because he saw the rising importance of this whole area of policy.[37] Under Redwood – much more than Mount, who had helped draft the 1983 manifesto – there was a sense within the Policy Unit that the manifesto had been 'too empty of actual policy'.[38] The unit's new, self-appointed role was to make government more 'pro-active', and less defined by its conflicts with the NUM or the 'loony left'.[39] All issues of ownership, above all privatization, contributed to this drive.

Part of Redwood's job was liaison with John Moore,* the Treasury junior minister chosen by Lawson to push through the privatization programme. Moore, a telegenic, young, self-made son of a factory bench-hand turned publican, was an example of Thatcherism in practice and was widely regarded as Mrs Thatcher's 'blue-eyed boy' of the time. He felt empowered by this, and by Lawson's own enthusiasm for privatization – 'a boss who really believed the same way'.[40] He saw the link with Redwood at No. 10 as 'very important for keeping in touch'[41] and in retrospect saw the period from June to December 1983 as the key one for the whole privatization programme. If it did not get off to a flying start, backed by all the relevant departments, too little would be accomplished by the next election. The Policy Unit felt the same way – 'If we did not push, everyone else would water it down'[42] – and found themselves in the congenial position not only of making policy, but, as Bob Young saw it, of 'getting things done'.[43] This was made possible by prime ministerial determination, her endless progress-chasing and her unique authority across the whole of government. 'Without her support,' Moore recalled, 'we could not have done any of these things.'[44]

It did not follow from any of this that Mrs Thatcher was either the most expert or the most confident member of her own government where privatization was concerned. The successes of the first term notwithstanding (see Chapter 2), she continued to harbour many doubts and fears. She worried that opinion polls suggested it would be electorally unpopular. She was immensely conscious of market and political difficulty, and the possible relation between the two. In the view of John Redwood, even into her second term Mrs Thatcher was almost a slow learner, failing to recognize 'my central point' that privatization would 'unlock the cornucopia at once' because it would give the businesses 'instant access to ready

---

* John Moore (1937–), educated LSE; Conservative MP for Croydon Central, February 1974–1992; Economic Secretary to the Treasury, June–October 1983; Financial Secretary to the Treasury, 1983–6; Secretary of State for Transport, 1986–7; for Health and Social Services, 1987–8; for Social Security, 1988–9; created Lord Moore of Lower Marsh, 1992.

cash'.[45] She was 'ready for it', he thought, 'but not an evangelist for it'. She liked to ask, 'That's all very well, but how do we do it?' As Redwood saw his role, 'I arrived in No. 10 to create a programme out of thin air.'[46] He was greatly exaggerating – Lawson had already thought the issue through much more than had Mrs Thatcher. It was a year, after all, since Geoffrey Howe had persuaded Mrs Thatcher to send out the personal memo driving forward privatization candidates for the next Parliament. But it was true that Mrs Thatcher was not leading the pack and had not organized any timetable. On the whole, this was to the good. David Willetts, who, at the Policy Unit, observed her methods closely, recalled that she was always 'very wary of grand strategy' and 'brilliant at moving between strategy and tactics'.[47] She had a way, 'rather like a camera in a film, of drawing back to get a panning shot and then focusing right in on a tiny detail'. The strategy was 'implicit in day-to-day decisions' rather than rigidly imposed. Instead of crushing objections unthinkingly, she listened carefully. She stuck to one of her favourite maxims – 'Time spent in reconnaissance is never wasted' – and proved its truth.

Mrs Thatcher's landslide victory in June 1983 naturally improved her confidence and made her keen to get on with things which had been impossible before it. It turned privatization from an experimental affair into something politically central and industrially and financially momentous. The government, regretted John Moore, had 'done the easy bits first'.[48] Rather than making the radical case for a massive shift of industrial power away from the state and the breaking up of monopolies, it had dealt with problems at the margins. As Nigel Lawson wrote to Mrs Thatcher in July 1983,

> Hitherto the companies we have sold have mainly been profitable and operating in competitive environments. Preparing them for privatisation . . . has involved relatively little change to their structure. But from now on we are increasingly working in the heartland of the public trading sector, where we shall have to deal both with the giant utilities and unprofitable companies.[49]

He called for a programme and timetable for each privatization.* She swung into action.

* Typically, though supportive of the idea, Mrs Thatcher, ever wary of leaks, was annoyed by some of Lawson's methods. She put a wiggly line under his sentence telling her that he was copying his note to all Cabinet colleagues. 'Further work on this a matter for E [Committee],' she wrote, '. . . and NOT to be invoked by MINUTE . . . I shall have to have a word with the Chancellor.' (Lawson to Thatcher, 25 July 1983, TNA: PREM 19/989 (http://www.margaretthatcher.org/document/128139).)

   The Redwood–Moore combination spent much of the summer and autumn acting upon this call to arms, touring government ministries. 'We went round from department to department,' Moore recalled, 'but they all said, "It's a political disaster." '[50] In October, Lawson summarized colleagues' responses: 'We cannot be satisfied with the overall picture that they show. Many of the candidates have been under consideration for much of the last Parliament. Yet, in several cases, points of principle still need to be resolved. We must accelerate the programme.'[51] He set out again why privatization mattered. There was 'a clear benefit to the PSBR' in the short term. 'But the major advantages to the economy as a whole arise if privatisation increases competition, improves resource allocation and helps eliminate inefficiencies.' Mrs Thatcher underlined all this approvingly. Lawson added that the government was not paying enough attention to getting rid of monopolies – an implied criticism of Peter Walker, at the Department of Energy, who wanted neither gas nor electricity broken up. After BT had taken up the first half of the Parliament, gas and electricity would be next, Lawson said. 'It is therefore vitally important that early decisions are taken about the future of these two industries.'

   On cue, Ferdinand Mount (at this stage still running the Policy Unit) wrote to Mrs Thatcher to commend Lawson's paper and urge her: 'It is now essential for you to put your full authority behind the privatisation programme.'[52] Less oblique than Lawson felt he could be, on paper, about a Cabinet colleague, Mount wrote: 'We cannot allow Peter Walker and others to get out of this exercise . . . We cannot agree a coordinated programme which omits the energy industries.' Mount attached an even franker memo from John Redwood, describing the DTI submission on the car manufacturer British Leyland as 'woefully inadequate'. Redwood urged that the whole of Jaguar (the elite car marque) should be sold in 1984. The prospectus, which envisaged a sale of Austin Rover (the volume car-maker) to investors after 1990, was 'bogus'. Both the DTI and BL itself showed 'a lack of commitment to the policy', and the dangers of delay were visible: 'We are heading for the worst trading year on record, and there is no sign of any relief.'[53] Here the unit's unnamed villain was Norman Tebbit who, despite his closeness to Mrs Thatcher, was thought to be suffering from 'producer capture'[54] in his love of British car production at a punitive rate of subsidy (estimated at £200 million in 1983).

   Ministers felt the pressure. By Christmas, Walker had permitted himself to be nudged forward a little. He wrote to Mrs Thatcher saying that the privatization of gas should come before that of electricity in the queue because it was easier and would create fewer problems with Arthur Scargill.[55] This did not buy off the watchful Redwood, however, who still believed that Walker was playing for time: 'The whole programme without firm decisions on the energy industries is like Hamlet without the Prince.'[56]

In mid-January, Lawson sent Mrs Thatcher the full programme of privatizations, with dates. There were twenty-three enterprises mentioned, including all those promised in the manifesto, plus, among others, the British Gas Corporation, the National Coal Board and Electricity (England and Wales and Scottish Electricity Boards). It was one of the most ambitious plans for legislation ever laid before a British Cabinet.* As the junior minister doing the detailed work, John Moore was invited to attend the Cabinet sub-committee meeting which Mrs Thatcher chaired to discuss and agree the Lawson programme. According to Moore, Mrs Thatcher stared at the wall-chart of what would be sold when and said: ' "This is marvellous. Isn't it? Isn't it? Are there any questions?" There was complete and absolute silence. The chart became the policy.'[57] Gerry Grimstone,† one of the main officials overseeing privatization, saw Mrs Thatcher's role at this meeting, and subsequent similar ones, as crucial. Unlike in her first term, privatizations were now 'intellectually conceptualized'[58] by the government conducting them. Lawson was extremely important because 'he understood markets', but Mrs Thatcher was the only one with the power to maintain the pace: 'She never saw herself as the captain of the team, but as the coachman flogging the horses.' Redwood, he added, 'put metal in the whips'.‡ Mrs Thatcher's role as coachman was particularly important because the number of privatizations was so large and the detail so complicated. These gave endless opportunities for officials to slow the pace, so the Thatcher lash was often needed.

British Telecom was the great test of the government's resolve and capacity. The company had nearly 250,000 (unionized) employees, but, allegedly, only one proper accountant. It was about six times bigger in value than anything sold before. It provided a service which almost every citizen used. It was the principal – indeed, in the era before mobiles and emails,

---

* Indeed, the programme of privatization was so extensive in legislative terms that there was a Treasury scheme to pass a single Enabling Act which would allow all of them to take place without separate Bills. This was turned down because the other government departments objected.

† Gerald Grimstone (1949–), educated Whitgift School and Merton College, Oxford; Assistant Secretary, Treasury, 1984–6; J. Henry Schroder Wagg, 1986–99; chairman, Standard Life plc, 2007–; knighted, 2014.

‡ This description of the roles is more accurate than Lawson's somewhat *parti pris* view that she did little about privatization herself, but 'left me to get on with it' (Interview with Lord Lawson of Blaby).

virtually the only – means of instant one-to-one communication (although liberalizing legislation in the first term had permitted the creation of one competitor, Mercury). Telecoms were also vital to the commercial and technological revolution which Mrs Thatcher sought to bring about, particularly in financial services, so the industry had to be properly capitalized and run. The company in its nationalized form could not keep pace with normal demand, let alone innovation.* If BT privatization succeeded, the way would lie open for virtually any other sale. If not, significant change would become almost impossible. The one thing the sale could not do was flop.

If it were not to flop, it was likely to err on the side of BT being sold as a monopoly. Mrs Thatcher had opposed this in the first term, but been forced to back down. The BT privatization Bill, which had fallen in 1983 for lack of time before the election, returned to the new House of Commons in 1984 unchanged in its essentials. The problem was crisply stated by Lord Cockfield. He wrote to Mrs Thatcher invoking the views of Lord Weinstock,† the great industrialist (and himself a shameless monopolist), 'that what we are doing is selling a monopoly: to the extent that we restrict that monopoly we are reducing the proceeds of sale: that the Treasury requirement for money is regarded as paramount: and that therefore we are doing everything we can to maintain the monopoly'.[59] In Cockfield's view, 'Weinstock's argument is quite right. There is an inescapable conflict here between competition and the Treasury . . . We shall face exactly the same problem when we come to privatize other monopolies such as gas and electricity.'

Mrs Thatcher and the relevant ministers were well aware of the problem. She had an uneasy conscience about it. Her scribbled interventions on memos about privatizations often complained about monopoly and its bad effects on prices and competition. In her approach to British Leyland, for instance, she consistently opposed a strategy of making BL a 'national champion' and trying to sell it off as one big thing – 'She believed that the good apples were affected by the bad apples in the basket.'[60] But the government had always to face both the need for money for the Exchequer

---

* In 1981, the present author bought his first house. It had no telephone and he wished to install one, but was told by BT that this would take six months because of a 'shortage of numbers'. The only way to speed this up was for his employer, the editor of the *Daily Telegraph*, to have a word with the chairman of the company, Sir George Jefferson. The device was installed in ten days. This was a classic example of how a nationalized industry would respond to string-pulling, but not to the ordinary customer's needs.

† Arnold Weinstock (1924–2002), educated LSE; managing director, General Electric Company plc, 1963–96, then chairman emeritus; knighted, 1970; created Lord Weinstock, 1980.

and the rush of 'Time's wingèd chariot'. Something as complicated as privatization could be forever postponed if ministers let the best be the enemy of the good. Mrs Thatcher had already confronted this conundrum in the previous Parliament when she had resisted an attempt to refer BT to the Monopolies and Mergers Commission in 1982. 'I take the view', she wrote to Ferdinand Mount, 'that denationalisation should not be jeopardised.'[61] As Cecil Parkinson, the new Trade and Industry Secretary, explained to the House of Commons at the second reading of the post-election BT Bill, the quickest way to bring accountability to BT was to move it to the private sector: 'That is one reason why I have decided against breaking up BT before offering it to the public. To do so would require a delay of many years in order to put British Telecom's accounts into a form which would make piecemeal disposals possible.'[62]

A similar pragmatism drove the notion that the reluctant senior executives of nationalized industries should be paid much more to take their businesses to market, even if these payments were not, in all cases, meritorious. When nationalizing health care in the 1940s, Aneurin Bevan had won over consultants by, as he later put it, having 'stuffed their mouths with gold'.[63] Now the Thatcher government used a similar method to achieve the reverse effect across a range of industries. It was important that 'Most of the interests involved thought there was something in it for them.'[64] In the case of BT, the chairman, Sir George Jefferson, saw his salary rise more than 70 per cent to £160,000 shortly after privatization.[65]

Although she had capitulated in relation to BT, Mrs Thatcher still hoped to avoid future monopoly sales, especially of gas and electricity. In the same week as Cockfield sent his letter, the *Financial Times* reported that 'It was agreed [by E Committee of the Cabinet] that British Gas should not be sold off as one block in its present form, though such a sale was urged by Sir Denis Rooke,* the British Gas chairman.'[66] This provoked Peter Walker to a rage. He supported Rooke, the brilliant engineer and born monopolist who ran British Gas as his personal fiefdom, in selling off the company as a whole, if at all. Now, he suspected, he was being bounced into a policy he did not agree with by No. 10, via press briefings. He was 'very shocked' by the story, he wrote to Mrs Thatcher, which was 'totally untrue'.[67] The Cabinet had agreed nothing on the subject, he protested. Clearly implying that she could control such leaks, he went on, 'I hope you will immediately inquire as to where these briefings

---

* Denis Rooke (1924–2008), educated Westminster City School, Addey, Stanhope School and University College London; chairman, British Gas plc (formerly the Gas Council, then British Gas Corporation), 1976–89; knighted, 1977; OM 1997.

were given, and point out the considerable damage that has been done.'
There was a certain piquancy in this complaint, since Walker was the
Cabinet minister most likely to leak against Mrs Thatcher, and the chief
reason why she disliked giving detailed information to full Cabinet.
Andrew Turnbull, her private secretary, duly reported to her the source
of the story (a Treasury briefing). He included a dig at Walker: the Secretary of State was, 'of course, correct in saying that there has been no
collective discussion on the privatisation of gas and electricity. D/En* have
still to make proposals.'[68]

To guard against the monopoly power which it had itself failed to break
up in the case of BT, the government turned to regulation. Lawson argued
strongly that a privatized monopoly was much better than a nationalized
one because there was 'a conflict of interest if the regulator and the business regulated is the same'.[69] A privatized industry could be independently
regulated. A state-owned agency, the Office of Telecommunications
(OFTEL), was established. Part of its remit was to prevent excessive charging. This was done by a simple formula invented by Professor Stephen
Littlechild, known as RPI − X, which would be used to determine future
BT price rises. RPI was the Retail Price Index (the measure widely accepted
as the rate of inflation) and X was the percentage decreed by OFTEL.
This was eventually settled, after much argument, at 3 per cent. The
idea was that these newly privatized industries should be able to achieve
productivity growth at a faster rate than the economy as whole. Lower-
than-inflation price rises could thus be afforded by efficiency gains: the
customer must get more for less. It was also true that the more efficiently
the companies operated, the more profit they would make (within the
constraints imposed by the price limit). This was not supposed to be the
ultimate answer to the monopoly problem, but was more of stop-gap
measure until sufficient competition developed. As matters turned out,
however, it stopped a great many gaps, and became a regulatory price
model for other privatizations. Mrs Thatcher liked it for the added reason
that it would, over time, help push the inflation rate figure down.

Much of the challenge of the BT sale was its sheer size. It was, at the
time, the biggest single equity issue anywhere in the world, ever. Partly
for this reason, it had always been agreed that only 51 per cent would be
sold in the first tranche. Even so, there was serious anxiety about whether
the City could handle something so big. Redwood considered the scale of
the task as an additional reason for making sure that shares were offered
to the general public. 'You won't get so much criticism', he told Mrs

* Walker's Department of Energy.

Thatcher, 'if the public buy it.'[70] He saw this as a chance to begin to create the 'society of owners' of which Mrs Thatcher increasingly spoke. He told her, 'This is the new council house sales.'

Enthusiasts in the City, such as Martin Jacomb* at Kleinwort Benson, which was handling the sale, saw the matter quite similarly. The sale of BT was 'an analogue for the British economy as a whole – a way of participating in a successful company',[71] and of opening up markets to the wider world, especially American investors. In the autumn of 1983, a year before the sale was due to take place, there was great scepticism in the City as to whether there would be enough demand for the shares which had to be sold. It became 'apparent that we couldn't raise enough capital without going to the retail investor'.[72] So there was a financial reason for seeking popular share ownership as well as an idealistic one. Indeed, the involvement of the retail investor was the answer, strongly driven by Redwood, to the threat from Kleinworts that the BT sale would have to start as a much more modest effort, offering much less than half of the business to investors, and therefore not constituting a true privatization.[73] 'It was only because we got personal investors in that we could sell so much,' recalled David Willetts. 'Besides, if we were selling only to City institutions, they had us over a barrel.'[74] The presence of the retail investor had a further effect. It ensured Mrs Thatcher's close involvement in the whole thing, because it was 'politically out of the question to sell shares to the public and then see them collapse'.[75]

A virtuous circle was created. If the sale of BT mattered so much, it must be backed by all the resources of everyone involved. The workforce and pensioners of the company must be able to benefit. The price must not be so low that the shares would all be 'stagged'† – sold on immediately after flotation for quick profits. Yet it was even more important that it should not be so high that the public either failed to take part or lost money on their investment. From this followed all sorts of marketing incentives, such as the voucher scheme which would discount telephone rental charges. The small investor was deliberately favoured in the allocation of shares, and was permitted to pay in instalments: as a broker in Chicago, Moore

* Martin Jacomb (1929–), educated Eton and Worcester College, Oxford; vice-chairman, Kleinwort Benson Ltd, 1976–85; chairman, Barclays de Zoete Wedd, 1986–1992; chairman, Postel Investment Management Ltd, 1991–5; deputy chairman, Barclays Bank plc, 1985–93; director, Bank of England, 1986–95; knighted, 1985.
† This had happened dramatically with the privatization of the radiochemical company Amersham International, in the first term, which was oversubscribed twenty-four times. Moore described this as 'a massive feast for the stags', but an event which had also 'made the City see that a market-place existed' (Interview with Lord Moore of Lower Marsh).

had learnt the 'psychology of mass ownership', and advocated a policy of 'the less you put in for, the more you get'.[76] A 'bill stuffer' went out with the quarterly bills in July 1984 announcing the pending sale. There were numerous public advertisements which avoided breaking stock market rules by not pushing the stock directly but promoted the idea of BT as a great telecommunications company ('The power behind the button'). These were extremely important in an era where the sale of shares was an arcane procedure and most people simply had no idea how to buy them: the BT sale inaugurated a new age in which share applications could be made simply by filling out application forms from the national newspapers, including tabloids. Attention was also given to the unique problems of scale. David Clementi at Kleinworts, for example, realized that special warehouses would be needed to handle the public's cheques in time. The building societies were warned to expect huge withdrawals as BT share-buyers drew on their savings. In all this, Jacomb worked with Mrs Thatcher. He observed her, and her co-operation with her Chancellor, very favourably: 'She really was at the height of her power – confident enough to listen and take advice. She was absolutely in charge, but not running a dictatorship.'[77]

The BT offer for sale was made on 20 November 1984, at a price of 130 pence, with the offer closing on 28 November. City institutions (such as pension funds) bought 45.8 per cent of the total offered, the public 34 per cent, overseas investors 14 per cent and employees 3.8 per cent. Defying the anathemas of their union, 95 per cent of BT employees bought shares. Everyone applying for 400 shares or fewer got 100 per cent of what they sought. Those who had applied for 100,000 shares or more got nothing. This was controversial in the City but good for the popular perception of the sale's purpose. The total proceeds of the sale were £3.615 billion. About 2.15 million people bought BT shares, roughly the same as the total number of British citizens who had owned shares of any kind when Mrs Thatcher first came into office. 'Just a few years ago, in Britain, privatisation was thought to be a pipe dream,' Mrs Thatcher declared, speaking to the US Congress in February 1985. 'Now it is a reality and a popular one,'[78] and, she could have added, the first of its kind in the world. The BT sale ended the previously prevailing scepticism about whether the City could do it. 'We are seeing the birth of people's capitalism,' said Nigel Lawson, happily conscious that a sale to so many made privatization 'irreversible'.[79] Mrs Thatcher was uneasy with the word 'people's' because it reminded her of Communist countries which were called 'the people's republic' of this and that. She preferred the phrase 'popular capitalism'.[80] But Prime Minister and Chancellor were at one about the concept.

*

Each privatization was different. There was an overarching common idea, but no template. As Mrs Thatcher herself put it, 'It is one of the disadvantages of being in the vanguard of reform – as the British who pioneered the industrial revolution know well – that the only experience you can learn from is your own.'[81] Realizing that the field was too big and varied for her to be useful in all circumstances, Mrs Thatcher intervened much more in some than in others. BT, though by a long way the biggest privatization yet attempted, had not, for some years, been losing the government money. Companies like British Leyland (BL) and British Airways (BA) were losing very large sums, often in politically controversial ways. It was these which excited her interest the most and where she felt she could make a difference.

The BA story is a good example of the thorny and circuitous path that privatization often had to take, and of Mrs Thatcher's striking methods of getting her way. It was one of the first privatizations legislated for by the Thatcher government (in the Civil Aviation Act of 1980), but an early sale became impossible when the extent of the company's losses was uncovered. The company had expected profits of £180 million over 1980–83, but an outside accountants' investigation revised this figure to a loss of £400 million.

In February 1981, the government appointed Sir John King* as chairman. He took the job only on the understanding that he would be able to sell the company. King was a ruthless, charming, buccaneering man with a gleam in his eye, an expert in most industries connected with wheels and wings, and the sort of individualistic and inspiring leader who endeared himself to Mrs Thatcher. A man of poor origins who successfully concealed the identity of his real father and lied about his age (so as not to be made to retire), King had started as a car salesman, and did well out of defence engineering work during the war. He later made a small fortune from manufacturing ball-bearings and became chairman of Babcock International in 1970. He was also a master of foxhounds, married to the daughter of a viscount, and famously good at building up a web of contacts. King had been so annoyed with the CBI's anti-Thatcher stance during the recession of the early 1980s that he took Babcock out of the organization and joined the more free-market Institute of Directors. Babcock gave a good deal of money to the Conservative Party and King, behind the scenes, helped organize a City–industrial Conservative

* John King (1917–2005), chairman, British Airways plc, 1981–93; president, 1993–7, then president emeritus; chairman, Babcock International Group plc, 1970–94; president, 1994–2005; master, Belvoir Hunt, 1958–72; knighted, 1979; created Lord King of Wartnaby, 1983.

fund-raising link. He was a long-time associate of other Thatcher supporters in business, notably Lord Hanson* and Sir Gordon White.†

In King's dealings with Mrs Thatcher in her first term as prime minister, his main link was her PPS Ian Gow, who had been his family solicitor.
King quickly learnt how, via Gow, to bypass any Cabinet minister who
was giving him trouble and see Mrs Thatcher herself. He also understood
that the chairman of BA had enormous influence over MPs by the simple
ruse of giving them free flights. This could be plausibly justified, in those
less rule-governed days, as a way of facilitating the work of legislators,
but it was widely abused by MPs of all parties demanding upgrades and
tickets to holiday destinations. The minor scandals that it caused, however, tended to damage not King but the MPs, who looked greedy. Perhaps
more than any other industrialist of the time, King built up a vital network
of parliamentary support for his company's interests. At the height of BA's
campaign for privatization, it gave what is thought to have been the biggest lobbying lunch in British history, entertaining 151 Tory MPs in the
River Room of the Savoy Hotel.

King presented to Mrs Thatcher a characteristic puzzle of privatization.
On the one hand, he was exactly the kind of man she wanted to sort out
a nationalized industry. He had the nous and gumption which she admired.
Indeed, he was known in the press – and she never complained of it – as
'Mrs Thatcher's favourite businessman'. On the other, he had the great
industrialist's natural desire to aggrandize his company and squash all
rivals, fighting as hard as possible for every sort of privilege that government could confer. So while he would accomplish the turn-round of the
company and the eventual sale which she wanted, he would do so at a
price.

In April 1982, King went to see Mrs Thatcher and told her that he
needed two more years to make BA a successful airline. He demanded
'freedom of action' – by which he meant the right to pay private-sector-style
salaries – to recruit the people to do it. The Trade Secretary, Lord Cockfield, on his second day in the job, objected that BA was a massive
loss-maker: overpaying managers would set a bad example in nationalized
industries. But Mrs Thatcher airily declared that 'Sir John should go ahead

---

* James Hanson (1922–2004), chairman, Hanson PLC, 1965–97; director, Hanson Transport Group Ltd, 1946–2004 (chairman, 1965–96); director, Hanson Capital Ltd, 2000–2004;
knighted 1976; created Lord Hanson, 1983.
† Vincent Gordon White (1923–95), educated De Aston School, Lincolnshire; deputy chairman, Hanson Trust Ltd, 1965–73; special commission to open Hanson Trust's opportunities
overseas, 1973–83; chairman, Hanson Industries, 1983–95; knighted, 1979; created Baron
White of Hull, 1991.

and look for the three people he had in mind.'[82] She doubted the alleged danger of the 'repercussive effect' in the public sector – look at the benefit, she said, of paying lots of money to Ian MacGregor at British Steel.

In the coming weeks, the Department of Trade continued to try to frustrate the increased salary proposals. King fought back and kept Gow informed. Gow wrote to Mrs Thatcher,

> Although I have considerable reservations about this salary [£55,000 a year for BA's proposed new finance director] (greatly in excess of that paid to the Queen's First Minister) I have the highest regard for John King and think we ought to let him run British Airways as he thinks best, with the earliest possible prospect of privatisation.[83]

King was allowed to get his new man. Two months later, Mrs Thatcher marked with approval Peter Gregson's suggestion that, although privatization might have to be postponed until late 1984, it 'might help to sustain the momentum which Sir John King appears to have created' if the provisional target remained late 1983.[84] E Committee agreed to this.

By September, however, Mrs Thatcher was appalled by BA's newly uncovered loss of £600 million on 'extraordinary items', and complained about its high redundancy payments (King was cutting the staff from the 51,000 with which he began to under 35,000). Then she pitched in: 'why any increase in pay? We cannot just agree to any request which private companies could not afford.'[85] In apparent contradiction of her earlier indulgence of King, she supported a pay cut, or at least freeze, and the minimum possible redundancy payments. Now it fell to Cockfield to defend BA's position: 'we cannot pick out BA to impose a pay freeze which we are not prepared to impose elsewhere.'[86] Mrs Thatcher underlined this phrase with her squiggly line of disapproval. 'Why not,' she metaphorically shouted back, 'when they are losing or have lost so much? . . . I feel we have been bounced.'

As it became clear that BA was most unlikely to be sold off before the general election, Mrs Thatcher also began to realize that the strengthening of BA for privatization would involve the weakening of its main British rival, British Caledonian (BCal). Would this not damage the competition dear to her heart? As her chief of staff, David Wolfson, put it to her, a privatized BA with 80 per cent of the market 'would be able to destroy British Caledonian whenever it chose'.[87] Sir Adam Thomson, the chairman of British Caledonian, begged her to let him have more BA routes. Although she often wrote expressions of anxiety about BCal's fate in the margins of government documents, she let herself be beaten down by John Redwood's argument that BA's real competitors were foreign airlines and so BA privatization 'is light years away from the substitution of a private for a public monopoly'.[88] She readily agreed to see King to discuss these matters, while fending off poor Thomson.

King lobbied her against the reallocation of routes to small airlines by the Civil Aviation Authority (CAA), and called in many favours by writing to all MPs in the same strain. There followed a heated battle in Whitehall and beyond, with Lord King* lobbying Mrs Thatcher hard through his connections with the influential family of Lord McAlpine, the Tory treasurer. Unusually, the Cabinet minutes for 1 August formally recorded that the Cabinet had been 'unable to make a decision' over the allocation of routes. Nicholas Ridley, the Transport Secretary and therefore the minister responsible, favoured more routes for BCal. So did Willie Whitelaw, whose son-in-law, David Coltman, was its chief executive. Lawson and Tebbit supported King. Mrs Thatcher, advised in favour of conceding the routes by Andrew Turnbull, but against by Redwood and the Policy Unit, wavered. At a ministerial meeting in September, she summed up the problem. The CAA review of routes 'touched on important elements of the Government's philosophy – its wish to encourage competition and enterprise and to reduce the boundaries of the public sector', she said, but then, with an untypical admission of ambiguity, added: 'Some of these objectives were in conflict with one another.'[89] The propaganda war now turned quite nasty. King annoyed Mrs Thatcher by threatening to resign. He also lobbied for the sacking of Ridley – an overreach for which he was rebuked by Cecil Parkinson on behalf of the Prime Minister.[90]

At last, towards the end of 1984, a compromise was patched together in which BA conceded and BCal accepted a 'route swap'. This was favourable to BCal, but much less so than the changes originally proposed by the CAA. It cleared this particular block to privatization without seriously hurting BA.†

Quite a different barrier, however, still stood in the way. At the Cabinet on 1 August 1984, ministers had been told that legal suits in the United States against British Airways, first mooted after the collapse of Laker Airways in 1982, might yet delay privatization. This issue proved astonishingly tough, but Mrs Thatcher proved even tougher.

In March 1982, the 'cheap and cheerful' Laker Airways had gone bust, following a price war with the big monopolistic carriers which it had been

---

* He had been ennobled the previous year.
† The deal was also ultimately fatal to BCal. The company was forced to sell out to British Airways for £251 million the year after the BA privatization.

set up to fight. The US Justice Department, rightly suspecting collusion between the airlines, was considering prosecuting BA under antitrust legislation. Civil suits also loomed. With this potentially ruinous threat hanging over BA, privatization seemed impossible.*

Mrs Thatcher went to war. She felt guilty, perhaps, that Laker had gone under. She had always supported Freddie Laker's emancipating, no-frills, transatlantic service which opened up flights to the United States to poorer people for the first time. She had praised Laker by name in her 1981 party conference speech. When the airline had started to go down, she had contemplated a rescue ('My passengers! My poor passengers!'),[91] until she discovered that the cost might be open-ended ('Oh dear! An open-ended situation! I couldn't wish that on my poor taxpayers').[92] Laker, like King, who had just ruined Laker's airline, was the sort of businessman Mrs Thatcher admired. She resented American claims to extraterritoriality. More important, she could not stand the thought of privatization being indefinitely delayed, which was tantamount, given the demands of the political timetable, to being dropped. As the then British Ambassador in Washington, Oliver Wright, put it, 'I think that BA were as guilty as hell, but Margaret intervened.'[93]

The US Justice Department answered, ultimately, to the President. Therefore, in March 1983, Mrs Thatcher wrote to Reagan, asking him 'personally and urgently' to prevent the imminent announcement of an official antitrust investigation and to handle the matter through existing aviation agreements. 'I am most disturbed about it,' she wrote.[94] His answer was no. Although technically possible, a presidential intervention would amount to interference in an accepted legal process. 'This gets us into Nixon territory,' administration officials complained to the British Embassy.[95] 'You know how highly I value our personal relationship . . .' Reagan told Mrs Thatcher. 'However in this case I feel I do not have the latitude . . .'[96]

Immediately after her election victory in June 1983, Mrs Thatcher retaliated, effectively banning British airlines from co-operating with the US investigation. The US administration became uneasy. 'Perhaps we can help put the brakes on Justice, who may have a tendency to overreact,' minuted one NSC staffer.[97] A compromise was agreed whereby the investigation would proceed more cautiously. But BA could not go forward to privatization while this cloud still lingered. Following efforts in the

---

* Being a nationalized bureaucracy, BA had been foolish enough to record its numerous telephone calls on this matter, so the evidence of misbehaviour potentially available to a court was there in cold print.

English courts by Laker's liquidators to counteract the ban on BA's co-operation, in July 1984 the House of Lords found against BA's position and declared that the case could be tried in the United States. A US Grand Jury was now considering a range of indictments against BA and its employees.

Mrs Thatcher mounted an attack on all levels. Ministers and messages were despatched to Washington. In London, a few days after Reagan had been safely re-elected president in November 1984, Mrs Thatcher herself saw the US Ambassador, Charlie Price, who was left shaken by his reception: 'She confirmed our worst fears about how she and her senior Cabinet ministers will react to an indictment decision . . . if there were any doubts before today about how seriously Thatcher herself views the matter, they surely have vanished.'[98] Price, who was a close friend of the President and always cultivated the Reagan–Thatcher relationship, urged the White House counsel to persuade the Justice Department to alter course but without success. Price's concerns were broadly shared within the State Department, where no one wanted to see a repeat of the sharp Reagan–Thatcher clash over the Siberian pipeline (see Volume I, pp. 576–8). The Justice Department, however, proved implacable.

On 16 November, the Laker arguments were laid before the President. George Shultz, the Secretary of State, argued in favour of dropping the indictments and Carol Dinkins, the Deputy Attorney-General, against. Bud McFarlane, the National Security Advisor, had briefed Reagan: 'This is a problem presenting two conflicting constitutional obligations of the President – your duty to enforce the laws and your obligation to conduct the nation's foreign affairs.'[99] McFarlane advised Reagan to side with Shultz and order Justice to drop the investigation.

At the meeting, Shultz put his case. Dinkins put hers. Jim Baker, the Chief of Staff, who later had presidential ambitions of his own, said, 'Mr President, this is one of those rare times that no one in this room wants to be sitting in your seat!' Robert Kimmitt, General Counsel of the NSC, recalled: 'The President had a quick laugh, paused for a second and said . . . "We live in a very dangerous world. We don't have any friends better than Margaret Thatcher. If this is important to her, even I, as a law and order man, am not going to proceed, in the interests of US national security.'[100] Fresh from his election victory, Reagan did not appear to find the decision particularly agonizing. 'P.M. Thatcher has really dug in her heels,' he wrote in his diary. '. . . Hearing both sides I came down on the side of foreign relations – case closed.'[101]

It was an astonishing, almost unprecedented decision for a president to turn down a formal recommendation from the Department of Justice for a criminal prosecution. It infuriated Justice, which felt it had wasted two to three years' work. Reagan's decision was testimony to the unique strength of his relationship with Mrs Thatcher.

He did, however, expect something back. Allen Wallis, the Under-Secretary for Economic Affairs, was despatched to London to inform Mrs Thatcher of the decision. He was instructed, disingenuously, to quote 'one of the President's aides' as saying that 'he has never seen the President more concerned in reaching a decision.'[102] Reagan, he was to tell her, had taken her side even though the allegations involved 'deliberate, knowing, repeated violations of fundamental requirement of the US anti-trust law'. The British should now concede greater flexibility in pricing and capacity in transatlantic routes and pledge to abide by US antitrust law in the future: 'The United States needs to be able to demonstrate that its act of extreme restraint has advanced the interests which strict law enforcement in this case would have served.'[103]

Mrs Thatcher had been expecting bad news, so when Wallis told her Reagan's decision she was 'positively effusive. She said that she was "thrilled" . . . and underscored her euphoria with gestures and movements showing genuine appreciation.'[104] She conceded nothing, however, on the substance: 'Simply stated, the UK did not accept our conclusions.'[105] She wrote to Reagan on the same day and in a similar strain ('I admire your courage'),[106] agreeing on the need to 'complete the negotiations' to mutual satisfaction.

In fact, however, the British offered virtually nothing in return for Reagan's generous decision. Instead, they made a further demand. If the Americans wanted any movement on pricing, capacity and so on, the US administration would have to seek British aviation's exemption from the so-called 'treble-damage provisions' which permitted injured parties in civil suits to sue for three times the value of the damage they had actually suffered. The US administration had dangled this idea in earlier talks with the British, but withdrawn it after Reagan dropped the indictments. This withdrawal allowed Mrs Thatcher to write to Reagan to say that she was 'very disappointed';[107] but it was the Americans who had cause to feel unsynthetic indignation. 'Since your courageous decision on indictments,' Charlie Price wrote to the President, 'we have been going backward rather than forward . . . They thanked us when we quashed the indictments – but so far we have nothing in hand but a bag of air.'[108] The issue now loomed uncomfortably as both sides prepared for Mrs Thatcher's visit to Camp David just before Christmas.

*

On the morning of 22 December, before leaving for Camp David, Mrs Thatcher was at the British Embassy in Washington. She had flown in from Hong Kong the day before (see Chapter 4). Her main preparatory discussions were about Reagan's Strategic Defense Initiative (SDI), but she nevertheless found fifty-five minutes to interrogate Roger Maynard, the Embassy's aviation and shipping counsellor, about the Laker case. 'She had a brief from London and she'd written all over it . . . At the end, she said, "Thank you very much, I'm going to talk to the President about this. I've got to stop this. The privatization has to go ahead." '[109]

At Camp David, the conversation between President and Prime Minister largely turned on East–West relations and SDI (see Chapter 8). This took up the whole morning. But when Reagan proposed lunch, Mrs Thatcher asked that they discuss civil aviation first, tirelessly making the familiar arguments. She thanked Reagan for dropping the Grand Jury and 'noted her relief that his decision did not result in a bad press for the President',[110] a fairly unsubtle hint that the decision had not been as difficult as the Americans had made out. Then she berated the administration for dropping their proposal to remove the treble-damages remedy, which hung over British Airways 'like a dark cloud': American action was 'denying her the ability to denationalize British Airways'. Reagan's tone was sympathetic, but he told her that Congress would reject a proposal to waive treble damages. 'You could see how fiercely she fought for British economic interests,' recalled George Shultz. 'She was absolutely fierce about it.'[111] Over cocktails and then lunch, Mrs Thatcher worried the issue like a dog with a bone: 'Noting it had just been discussed, Mrs Thatcher said she wished to return briefly to civil aviation.'[112] And off she went again. This time, Reagan said nothing, and Shultz and Price argued back. No progress was made.

When one remembers that, in the course of the previous six days, Mrs Thatcher had met Mikhail Gorbachev for the first time (at Chequers), flown to Peking to sign the Hong Kong Agreement, flown on to Hong Kong to sell it to the colony's people, and then flown to Washington via Honolulu; and when one further reflects that the Cold War issues at stake at Camp David were so important and demanding, it is well nigh incredible that she could have summoned the energy to argue the BA–Laker case again and again with her hosts. Almost any other British leader would have let himself be overcome by boredom, embarrassment, good manners or sycophancy towards his powerful hosts. But Mrs Thatcher was impervious to boredom if she thought a point mattered, especially a point about British trade advantage, and she almost never considered repetition a fault. 'I think Margaret Thatcher always expected what she wanted to be done,' said Charles Powell. 'One of her great strengths was her single-mindedness and her absolute refusal to see that there could be another side to any case.'[113] Her hosts – much more interested in what she had to say about the world-historical issues of the Cold War and SDI – were impressed and exasperated in equal measure.

Realizing that she could not prevail over treble damages, Mrs Thatcher changed tack. Instead of the legislative route, she sought more informal ways of settling the civil suits. In February, she asked for Reagan's help in agreeing a favourable settlement for BA out of court with Ex-Im Bank, its largest creditor. 'The President observed that the Exim Bank has autonomy of operation, but we were in communication with the Director. Ambassador Price . . . has been trying to work something out, and he (the President) would weigh in if necessary.'[114]

At last, the logjam broke. A settlement was agreed that saw Ex-Im Bank recoup its principal, but without the penalty interest originally sought.[115] In July 1985, a broader private settlement was reached covering most of Laker's outstanding claims for far less than the $1.1 billion potential liability. Thanks, in considerable part, to Mrs Thatcher's relationship with President Reagan, the privatization of British Airways could take place.

The company was finally sold to the public – 100 per cent and without a government 'golden' (or 'special') share allowing state buyback in emergency* – in February 1987. It was presented by BA as a proud moment for popular capitalism, which it was. People were keen to own a bit of the country's now successful airline. The sale raised £900 million and was underpriced, being eleven times oversubscribed. The whole process had taken seven years.

'The Treasury should be given encouragement to keep up the pressure on reluctant departments. In particular,' wrote John Redwood impatiently to Mrs Thatcher in July 1984, 'you should expect much more urgency from the Department of Energy in pursuing the ideas on British Gas.'[116] He called for a special progress-chasing meeting of the relevant Cabinet sub-committee to goad the laggards forward. The 1983 manifesto had pointed towards opening up the gas and electricity industries. The approaching sale of a quasi-monopoly, quasi-utility, British Telecom, showed that the government was prepared to attack public ownership of industry near its heart and ready to handle the vast financial scale of the

---

* The golden share was not considered a necessary protection for the public since British Airways was not a utility.

flotations involved. The Chancellor had long wanted British Gas (BG) to be broken up and sold once BT was done. So had the Prime Minister. Yet the whole issue was proving extremely difficult.

The problem, from Mrs Thatcher's point of view, began with the chairman of British Gas. Sir Denis Rooke was the classic nationalized industry chief of the successful sort. (Most were unsuccessful.) Rising through the industry as an engineer, he had been responsible for converting every household from the previously prevailing (and poisonous) 'town gas' to the large supplies of natural gas found in the North Sea from the 1960s. He was a bully and, according to Nigel Lawson, 'a megalomaniac'[117] who believed that he alone understood his trade, 'treating Ministers and officials alike with a mixture of distrust, dislike and contempt'.[118] Rooke had brought semi-related companies (for example, Britain's only onshore oilfield, Wytch Farm) under his wing, thus increasing his power. He had a famously short fuse, and had to take pills to prevent himself shouting at people.[119]* He was 'a big tree in whose shade no sapling ever grew'.[120]

After becoming energy secretary in 1981, Nigel Lawson had worked hard to, as he put it, 'weaken Rooke's empire',[121] by announcing the privatizations of the oil-producing business of the British National Oil Corporation (later Britoil) and British Gas's offshore oil business, and by abolishing BG's statutory monopoly on the purchase of gas and control of the onshore gas pipeline grid. He had tried, but failed, after well-organized opposition by Rooke and the trade unions, to arrange the sell-off of BG's gas showrooms. It had been Lawson's last act as energy secretary to sign a letter to Rooke enforcing the disposal of the offshore oil assets (which later became known as Enterprise Oil). He gave the letter to his private secretary for safe-keeping during the campaign, with instructions to send it on to the BG chairman if the Conservatives won. It was duly sent to Rooke the day before Lawson was made Chancellor of the Exchequer.[122]

Mrs Thatcher, however, had, for unrelated reasons, made Peter Walker Lawson's successor at Energy (see p. 145). Walker did not share his predecessor's views, or his closeness to the Prime Minister. He regarded Denis Rooke as 'the best nationalised industry chairman I met'.[123] Although not adamantly opposed to privatization in all its forms, he had little objection to BG's monopoly power. He stood with Rooke on the idea that the company should be a 'national champion', and indeed wanted it to become a European entity, rather in the way the French EDF much later became.[124] If it must be sold, he believed, it must be sold whole.

In principle, neither Lawson nor Mrs Thatcher agreed with this, but

---

* These were reported to be ineffective.

principle could not be the only consideration in the difficult circumstances in which they found themselves. On the memo from John Redwood quoted above, Andrew Turnbull wrote: 'I think John's judgment may be rather harsh. On gas, Mr Walker has broached the subject with Sir D. Rooke but given the controversial nature of the proposals feels he needs to move carefully. I doubt if a progress chasing meeting will do more than irritate Ministers. Mr Walker feels that the references to BGC privatisation are unhelpful to him in the tricky task he is engaged upon.'[125] Following her private secretary rather than her Policy Unit head, Mrs Thatcher wrote, 'No meeting at present.'

The 'tricky task' was the management of the alarming Rooke, who 'loomed over' everything and with whom Walker made a 'Faustian pact'.[126] Ministers believed Rooke had the capacity to undermine confidence in the privatization of the industry and so had to be handled with great care. Peter Gregson, who became permanent secretary of the Department of Energy in May 1985, remembered Mrs Thatcher 'sometimes sucking her teeth and saying how convenient it would be if we could get rid of Denis; but she saw that he was a force of nature.' John Redwood advised her to 'change the chairman'.[127] She did not want to take the risk. The tactic of humouring Rooke worked, in its own terms at least. Gregson noticed the chairman gradually coming to see that something might be made out of privatization 'so long as he could wield great power'.[128] Walker was skilled at handling Rooke, and, as a minister, 'decisive, and a good seller and deliverer of policy'.

Given the joint power of Thatcher and Lawson, it might, in more ordinary circumstances, have been possible to overrule what David Young called the 'unholy combination'[129] of Rooke and Walker; but the circumstances were extreme. BG privatization could not take place until BT's sale was well out of the way. BT was sold at the height of the miners' strike. Discussions of BG privatization began before the strike and finished after it. Mrs Thatcher felt that she could not afford to fall out with Walker, the minister in the front line of the conflict with Arthur Scargill, while the strike was in progress, or to punish him after its successful conclusion. She could not move Rooke against Walker's will. Walker advised that gas privatization would be doable but that, in the context of the miners' strike, electricity would not. He insisted that the sale must be of a single entity. Mrs Thatcher recognized that she did not have much choice but to accept Walker's advice, though it involved ignoring what Redwood and the Policy Unit told her. Although she saw Rooke as 'a huge tombstone in the way of what the Government wanted to do',[130] she felt she could not get rid of him once privatization was 'hurtling down the track'.

Andrew Turnbull recalled ruefully that when he was off work, suffering from shingles, in late March 1985, two momentous and unhappy decisions were made. The first was agreement, in principle, to the poll tax ('community charge') (see Chapter 11). The second was that 'The Treasury had settled the form of gas privatization with Peter Walker.' The thing was squared between Mrs Thatcher, Lawson, John Moore and Walker on 26 March 1985. BG would be sold off in full and as one unit, provided that this happened without delay. 'Walker's support was better than endless argument.'[131] In her memoirs, Mrs Thatcher defended the decision on the grounds that the sale had to take place before the next election, so that the most important reason for not breaking the company up was, 'curiously enough . . . the lack of parliamentary time'.[132] This was true, but not the whole truth. She was also scared.

There were secondary reasons, too, for not breaking the company up. More than he liked to admit, Lawson was – almost *ex officio* as Chancellor – keen on maximizing the proceeds. Mrs Thatcher was not immune to this either. After the success of the British Telecom sale, she had said to Gerry Grimstone, 'What can we do that's twice the size of BT?'[133] The stronger the monopoly, after all, the higher the price. The need to press on with the sale was genuine, and later became stronger as other privatizations, such as BA, BL, water and the Royal Ordnance Factories, for one reason or another were delayed or fell by the wayside. It was understandable to take the view advocated by Turnbull's successor as Mrs Thatcher's Treasury private secretary, David Norgrove, that 'It is better to give in, because you can always change the rules later.'[134]

Nevertheless, there was 'something disreputable' in this way of proceeding,[135] and something, by Mrs Thatcher's very high standards of due diligence, negligent. Martin Jacomb noticed that, in relation to BG (of which he was a director), Mrs Thatcher had 'perceptibly lost the desire to master the detail'.[136] The biggest problem was that the sale of a monopoly was not adequately compensated for by new regulation. Although the government recognized the need and legislated for a regulator, it did so rather cautiously because of fears of further explosions from Sir Denis Rooke. 'Walker said, "Don't pick someone too difficult as the regulator,"' Peter Gregson recalled.[137] The failure to regulate rigorously was to give rise to a great many difficulties in the years ahead and produce a certain disillusionment with privatization, so far, at least, as the utilities were concerned. Although sales of share issues continued to do well throughout this period, Turnbull noticed an odd, emerging phenomenon that 'each privatization seemed to be more unpopular than the last'.[138]

Once the sale of BG as a unit was agreed, however, the full energy of the government could at least go into getting the sale right. Great attention was given to tight pricing, and a huge effort was made to sell as many shares as possible to record numbers of the general public. Rothschilds, led by the great networker Michael Richardson,* handled the sale. The advertising company Young and Rubicam devised a famous campaign which cleverly exploited the rules restricting the puffing of a stock by inventing an invisible character called Sid, who might, or might not, learn about the sale. The advertisement concerned only the fact of the sale, not its details. 'If you see Sid, tell him,' was the catchphrase. 'Sids' became the name for all ordinary buyers of privatization stocks, and 'Siddery' the sometimes disparaging term for trying to lure the buyers in. Market research showed that 98 per cent of the adult population had heard of the BG offer.[139] The whole of BG (except for the government's golden share) was sold in November–December 1986. Its handling was a triumph for the new world begun only a few weeks earlier in the City's 'Big Bang' reform of the Stock Exchange. Over 4.5 million applications were received, which made BG the company with the largest number of shareholders in the history of the world. The sale raised £5.434 billion for the government. The stagging was not nearly as bad as in the past. Two million of the buyers had never before bought shares, so this was a giant leap for the policy of popular share ownership. Not coincidentally, it was also a good way of securing Conservative votes in the election pencilled in for the following year.

On 27 October 1986, the City of London experienced what was known as Big Bang.† On a single day, all the reforms of the Stock Exchange were implemented at once. The phrase was apt, because the changes which came into force that day were indeed explosive, but the phenomenon had small beginnings.

At first, the question had seemed almost technical. When she came into office in 1979, Mrs Thatcher had inherited from the period of Labour government a commitment by the Office of Fair Trading (OFT) to investigate the Stock Exchange for restrictive practices. The OFT estimated that there were more than eighty such practices,[140] but there were three

---

* Michael Richardson (1925–2003), educated Harrow; partner, Cazenove & Co., 1971–81; managing director, N. M. Rothschild & Sons Ltd, 1981–90; after Mrs Thatcher left office, Richardson had a hand in running Mark Thatcher's finances, while privately indicating that he was running hers, which was not the case; knighted, 1990.
† The first man who applied the name for the dominant theory about the creation of the universe to the City is thought to have been Douglas Dawkins, of the Bank of England. Although never official, the phrase at once became almost as universal as it was for the creation event itself.

that mattered. Membership of the Stock Exchange was severely controlled, and excluded all foreign firms; the members of the exchange operated on fixed commissions; and the 'single capacity' rule meant that brokers could not themselves trade in shares but must buy and sell shares for their clients via 'jobbers', who could. Single capacity had been introduced in 1911, on ethical grounds because it avoided conflicts of interest, but restrictive was exactly what these practices were. They maintained the Stock Exchange as a sort of old boys' club (it was heavily dominated and hereditarily filled by pupils educated at the major public schools) which did well by its members, but kept charges high and new entrants out.

Because the Conservatives were regarded as the friends of the City establishment, it was widely assumed that the new Tory government would reverse Labour's decision and exempt the Stock Exchange from the OFT's investigation. But, for precisely this reason, it was reluctant to do so. Indeed, the normal political situations were reversed. The Labour former Prime Minister Harold Wilson, who had chaired a committee reviewing the functioning of financial institutions, wrote to Mrs Thatcher in the autumn of 1980 asking her to lift the case against the Stock Exchange. She declined, arguing that 'propriety' made it difficult to remove a case from the legal process.[141] For the same reason, Mrs Thatcher did not get involved in policy discussions on the matter at this stage. Gordon Borrie,* the director-general of the OFT, also refused to countenance a deal with the Stock Exchange. So the investigation trundled on.

It began to become clear to many of those involved, however, that the court case which would inevitably result if no deal were done would be disastrous for the Stock Exchange. For as long as any case lasted, uncertainty about the system's future would damage the City. This would also be dangerous for the government, since the Exchange was the market for raising government debt. People like David Walker† at the Bank of England and Lord Cockfield, Mrs Thatcher's last Trade Secretary before the 1983 election, saw the danger. So did Nicholas Goodison,‡ the chairman

---

* Gordon Borrie (1931–), educated John Bright Grammar School, Llandudno and University of Manchester; barrister; Professor of English Law and director, Institute of Judicial Administration, University of Birmingham, 1969–76; Honorary Professor of Law, 1989–2010; director-general of Fair Trading, 1976–92; chairman, Advertising Standards Authority, 2001–7; knighted, 1982; created Lord Borrie, 1995.
† David Walker (1939–), educated Chesterfield School and Queens' College, Cambridge; joined Bank of England as chief adviser, then Chief of Economic Intelligence Department, 1977; a director, 1981–93; chairman and chief executive, Securities and Investments Board, 1988–1992; chairman, Barclays Bank plc, 2012–15; knighted, 1991.
‡ Nicholas Goodison (1934–), educated Marlborough and King's College, Cambridge; chairman, Stock Exchange, 1976–88; TSB Group, 1989–95; knighted, 1992.

of the Stock Exchange, who was concerned that 'the court would make a sudden-death decision and there would be chaos.'[142] 'He knew that the court might declare the Stock Exchange's rulebook illegal and not say what would be legal.'[143] Despite objections from many of his more conservative members, Goodison believed that the Stock Exchange should not resist outright, but should reform itself, rather than having change imposed upon it by a court. All these men argued that reform was not only unavoidable, but also desirable. The unreformed Stock Exchange was turning London into a backwater. The only foreign equities traded in London at that time were South African gold stocks and a few Australian mining shares.[144] The small British firms which composed the Stock Exchange had little access to capital. London dominated some markets, such as foreign exchange and commodities, but 'the securities business was the one weak link. There was not enough capital because of the old partnership system, and there never would be.'[145] New York, which had introduced stock exchange reform in the mid-1970s, was leaving London behind. In 1982, the turnover of equities in New York was more than fifteen times greater than that of London. As Jacob Rothschild* pointed out in a speech at the time reform was first announced, Salomon Brothers alone, in New York, made $500 million in 1982, while 'I think I am on fairly safe ground if I state that the combined profits of the London Stock Exchange came to less than this figure.'[146] Only seven UK financial services executives in the whole country received six-figure salaries. The pressure to adapt or die was becoming unstoppable.

Nothing was settled, however, before the 1983 general election. Indeed, the confusion of policy in the corridors of power had become clear only in 1982 when Treasury officials and officials at the Department of Trade discovered that the evidence attacking the Stock Exchange which they proposed to submit to the OFT ran directly counter to the evidence prepared by the Bank of England, which defended it.[147]†

Once Mrs Thatcher had won her landslide victory, things moved very fast to stop the OFT case going beyond the point of no return. It was clear to Nicholas Goodison, and to the new Chancellor, Lawson, that, if the matter went to court, 'the Stock Exchange would lose'.[148] Goodison wrote in longhand to Cecil Parkinson, now at the Department of Trade and Industry (DTI), and asked him to prevent the court case in return for a

---

* Jacob Rothschild (4th Baron Rothschild) (1936–), educated Eton and Christ Church, Oxford; chairman, RIT Capital Partners plc, 1988–; chairman, Five Arrows Ltd, 1980–2010; president, 2010–; chairman, National Gallery, 1985–91; OM, 2002.
† David Walker's views on reform were, at that stage, personal, and well in advance of the Bank's official view.

promise by the Stock Exchange to reform.[149] 'I said I couldn't guarantee the integrity of the market if the thing went to court.'[150] Parkinson was supportive of reform because of his own experiences as a young account-ant in the City in the 1960s when 'They could keep you out of the Stock Exchange if they didn't like the way your tailor cut your suit.'[151] Parkinson felt in a 'creative fervour'[152] – as he, with unintentional comedy, put it – because he knew he had the Sara Keays problem hanging over him and thought he might not survive in the Cabinet.

Parkinson also found in the new Chancellor, Nigel Lawson, a much more ardent bringer of change than Geoffrey Howe. As a former financial journalist, Lawson felt a certain cynicism about the motives of those who ran the City. As a well-instructed believer in free markets, he was, recalled David Walker, 'like a supersonic missile'[153] for reform. Michael Scholar, who was Mrs Thatcher's Treasury private secretary after the election, recalled being 'collared' on the subject by the newly appointed Chancellor in the summer of 1983, 'and I wondered what the hell he was talking about.'[154] Lawson had been the main intellectual driver for the abolition of exchange controls in 1979, and he understood and intended that this would lead to the end of the Stock Exchange's restrictive practices. The world would want to come to London, and should be encouraged to do so. Indeed, the problem with Lawson was that he wanted to go too fast, 'not quite trusting the Stock Exchange to deliver any promise it might make'.[155] He agreed, however, that it would be better to avoid snarling up change in a court case. He helped Parkinson persuade doubting Cabinet colleagues of the argument.

Mrs Thatcher herself was not deeply engaged in the issue and 'didn't descend into the details of how the City worked'.[156] 'It was a real struggle to get time in her diary to brief her on it,' David Willetts recalled.[157] She continued to worry that it looked bad for a Conservative government to interfere, seemingly in favour of the Stock Exchange, in a legal case. But she did have some strong, relevant prejudices which made her easy to win over. She had a distaste for monopoly and 'disliked the people in the City who were looking after themselves very nicely'.[158] Indeed, she had 'a bee in her bonnet (a good one) about breaking up the men in the City'.[159] She had some strong supporters in the Square Mile, including Michael Rich-ardson at Rothschilds, who, when at Cazenove, had arranged for that company to pay for her office as leader of the Opposition. But on the whole she doubted the positive economic contribution made by the City's club mentality, and she often felt slighted by City men. Parkinson recalled meeting her returning from lunch at a big bank before her first victory in 1979. 'They had given her hell. She was very depressed. I said: "Don't worry; they'll vote for you, and they'll forget it." "They may,' replied Margaret, 'but I won't.' '[160]

As with privatization, Mrs Thatcher herself does not seem to have been particularly quick to see exactly how City reform might serve her wider economic agenda, but advisers were more than ready to help her. John Redwood saw the opportunity and had the necessary City knowledge to deal with the technical issues, combined with a Thatcherite vision of 'popular capitalism'.[161] In his own mind, Redwood linked City reform with privatization, deregulation, wider ownership, a mass market in shares, personal 'portable' pensions, the rejuvenated London Docklands which Mrs Thatcher and Michael Heseltine had begun in the first term, and a more competitive, internationalized Britain. 'This was something I took to her,' he later claimed,[162] rather than something which she initiated. It was part of the 'massive enterprise revolution' which she sought.

In July, Mrs Thatcher supported Parkinson, who urgently wanted to accept the undertakings offered by Goodison to forestall the OFT action. She agreed to an immediate statement to Parliament stating the government's intention to exempt the Stock Exchange, by law, from the Restrictive Practices Act, so long as it reformed itself within an agreed period of three years. She was not interested in sheltering the City from change. Marking the draft of Parkinson's statement to the House, she wrote 'Why?' against his promise that 'single capacity' would be maintained.* 'Promote competition as well as investor protection,' she scribbled.[163]† In his Commons statement, however, Parkinson ignored Mrs Thatcher. He said that he hoped single capacity would be 'preserved in its present form for the time being'.

As the *quid pro quo* for the OFT dropping the case, Parkinson also publicly promised, before he resigned in October, that there would be a Financial Services Act to bring new law to the new world which Stock Exchange reform would create. John Redwood thought the situation, even though forced by the OFT threat, was politically advantageous, and a cause for celebration. 'We should claim more credit', he wrote to Mrs

---

* Oddly, it was the government, not the Stock Exchange, which clung to single capacity at this point. This was because single capacity had recently been introduced in the Lloyd's insurance market to reduce conflicts of interest, and so the government was frightened of looking inconsistent. The Bank of England also found it convenient for the gilts market. Goodison was more clear-sighted than Parkinson that single capacity would have to go because of the abolition of minimum commissions.

† In the opinion of Martin Jacomb, Mrs Thatcher 'readily understood' how restrictive single capacity was, because she was 'well briefed' by Denis on the subject (Interview with Sir Martin Jacomb).

Thatcher, 'for breaking a cosy cartel.'[164] She doubly underlined the last two words to show her approval.

Within No. 10, it was Redwood who gave Mrs Thatcher the most guidance. When the Stock Exchange set out its own detailed proposals, in April 1984, he counselled her in favour of liberalization: 'You should not be too worried about the possibility of foreigners coming in and buying up the British financial system . . . The Americans will undoubtedly make an entry to the market in due course,' probably through their banking businesses. '. . . This is a perfectly healthy development,'[165]* and would be natural as trading moved from the floor of the Stock Exchange to computer screens. With his advice in mind, her private office conveyed her views to the DTI: 'She welcomes the radicalism of the Exchange's consultative document, which fully justifies the decision to take the case from the OFT and has noted that [it] recognises that the end of minimum commissions will in the end mean that single capacity may not be sustained.'[166] She made the link between technological change and reform of the market: 'She has suggested that the Stock Exchange should now move as rapidly as possible to establishing suitable electronic systems for handling for dealing . . . in readiness for the move to dual capacity.' This would provide 'the best guarantee of investor protection after the demise of single capacity'.[167]

The end of the Stock Exchange's club-like existence would also, most people understood, require different, more formal systems of regulation. The new report by Professor Laurence Gower on investor protection moved in this direction. Redwood worried that this would blow back on government: 'People would expect the Government to offer them redress. People would expect the Government to make sure there were no crooked operators. It is not within the Government's power to ensure either of these things.'[168] Mrs Thatcher underlined these sentences approvingly. Redwood made a classic conservative case for protection by the common law rather than by government control, a view which Mrs Thatcher instinctively shared. Echoing his anxiety about the Gower report, she worried that 'ultimately the government could be blamed for any malpractice.'[169]

In fact, the Thatcher–Policy Unit view of regulation was not widely shared and did not prevail. The Bank of England and the DTI accepted

---

* It was also an extremely profitable one. Once the restrictions on membership of the Stock Exchange were ended, big companies, including foreign businesses, would be free to buy up stockbroking firms. This allowed 'almost any firm of any size to sell itself for ridiculously high prices' to American and other banks which thought, largely erroneously, that they needed these firms to get near the action (Interview with Sir Nicholas Goodison).

the thrust of the Gower report that there should be a statutory regulatory body, and persuaded the City to do the same. The Financial Services Act created a new Securities and Investments Board (SIB), whose first chairman Sir Kenneth Berrill, a former head of the Think Tank, was not seen by Mrs Thatcher as a kindred spirit. (The more congenial Martin Jacomb refused the job.) The SIB got off to a rather acrimonious start, until being later rescued by David Walker. In the view of Nigel Lawson, Mrs Thatcher 'did not really engage' with the issues of regulation.[170] David Norgrove, her Treasury private secretary at the time of Big Bang, thought that she was 'a bit out of her depth in the subject'.[171] It is clear from the government files that she sometimes learnt about the full proposals only after they were well in train. Her role in the details of City reform was seldom more than marginal.

In general, she was seeking to balance proper control of the risks involved with what she, Lawson and indeed almost everyone who cared about the financial competitiveness of the City of London regarded as inevitable change. In April 1986, with Big Bang fast approaching, Brian Griffiths* and David Willetts produced a report for which Mrs Thatcher had asked to update her on the whole subject. As well as pointing out the clear advantages, they flagged up dangers: 'Will we see boom and bust?', would there be 'more embarrassing fraud cases?'[172] They worried particularly about how, in bad times, the new firms might be tempted to 'dump their losses on to the client'. They pointed out the Glass–Steagall Act in the United States, which enforced the separation of clearing banks and investment banks,† and said: 'It is open to question as to whether we shall some day, after a nasty scandal, be forced in the same direction.' Mrs Thatcher marked this passage very heavily. The risk was acknowledged; but in a culture quite unused to regulation of this sort, such a level of legislative interference was considered undesirable.

On the whole, though, the government felt confident that it was going in the right direction. As early as the summer of 1984, Redwood was sufficiently pleased to present a sort of fairy tale about City reform to his Policy Unit colleagues. It was called 'Tilting at Castles'. He satirically imagined the Stock Exchange as a 'great big castle' occupied by a 'noble and chivalrous group of knights',[173] where brokers and jobbers lived together in 'fraternal enmity'. The knights had what they considered 'a

---

* Brian Griffiths (1941–), educated Dynevor Grammar School and LSE; Professor of Banking and International Finance, City University, 1977–85; head of No. 10 Policy Unit, 1985–90; vice-chairman, Goldman Sachs (Europe), 1991–; created Lord Griffiths of Fforestfach, 1991.
† This law was later repealed under the Clinton administration, a decision which was afterwards considered a major factor in the onset of the 2008 financial crisis.

very good rule which said that they were never allowed to cut their prices . . . [for] all the people outside the Stock Exchange', and so they could enjoy endless feasting and jousting. As a result, the tale continued, the OFT threatened the castle with its guns. But then the country, which had previously been badly governed, 'fell under a wise ruler' who sent her 'boldest champion' (Parkinson) to parley with the knights, while keeping the guns trained on their castle. Their champion was their 'most Parfait Knight, called Sir Nicholas', who agreed they would mend their ways.

Then the 'wicked old institutional barons' (commercial banks, pension funds) got interested in buying skills the Stock Exchange could offer and, because they 'weren't very bright',[174] paid the knights 'so much money [for their companies and their skills] that they could go on feasting forever'. But a few bold people realized that 'the best thing to do was to lead the peasants' (small investors) – 'Everybody had tended to forget about the peasants' – and the Stock Exchange knights began to think that they might have to let in 'foreigners and institutional barons and all the rabble they'd kept out for so many years'.

Then, Redwood admitted, 'The narrative of the chronicle now becomes frayed and torn. Several textual commentators have supplied different endings to the story.'[175] He proposed a short, happy ending:

> And so it became apparent to all the peasants that they had indeed been wisely governed . . . by being nice to everyone, the Government had wrought a great revolution . . . All agreed that it was much better to live in a world where the institutional barons now had to behave themselves and do what the peasants told them; and where the Stock Exchange knights no longer belonged to a special Order . . . but where people could choose for themselves what to do with their wealth.

Thus had popular capitalism triumphed, said Redwood. Mrs Thatcher herself saw a copy of his fairy tale. She was not naturally at ease with the genre, but this one quite faithfully epitomized what she wanted.

Was it what she got? Did the fairy tale correspond with reality? Even now, as Zhou Enlai is alleged to have said when asked his opinion about the effects of the French Revolution, it may be too early to say. Controversy swirls about Mrs Thatcher's unlocking of capitalism and has become, if anything, more turbid, as the seemingly effortless prosperity of the immediate post-Cold War era has been replaced by the West's debt crisis which began in 2007.

What is certain is that Mrs Thatcher's innovations of privatization and financial reform changed the world. The City 'club' really did disappear, and London really did become a centre for international markets and for banks as it had not been since before the First World War. It is a mark of the boldness of her government that, despite all the well-known disadvantages of nationalization, no one before her had really tried to unscramble the state grab for industrial power of the middle of the twentieth century. And it is a mark of the policy's success that no nation, once embarked on privatization, has yet seriously attempted to reverse it. Privatization became, and remains, the greatest policy export ever invented in Britain (unless one can describe parliamentary democracy or the rule of law as a policy).

Oliver Letwin, who joined Rothschilds after his time at the Policy Unit, found the world coming to London to discover what Mrs Thatcher's governments had achieved and ask how it could follow suit.* Thanks, in part, to Big Bang, City institutions now had the capacity to help answer these inquiries. Nationalization had seemed, in the middle of the twentieth century, to be a 'structural solution' to the problem of once-great heavy industries. It had run out of steam and money: 'Once someone had showed that the reverse was possible, this too was a structural solution.'[176] In his ten or so years at Rothschild, Letwin found himself advising the following countries on privatization – Canada, the United States, Colombia, Mexico, Chile, Honduras, Kenya, Tanzania, Congo (Brazzaville), Morocco, South Africa, Ivory Coast, Singapore, Malaysia, Australia, New Zealand, Spain, Italy, France, Ireland, Portugal, the Netherlands, Sweden, Finland, Ireland, Poland, the Czech Republic, Slovakia, Hungary, Moldova, Russia and even Cuba.[177] Mrs Thatcher noted the beginnings of this trend as early as 1986. 'People are no longer worried about catching the British disease,' she proclaimed. 'They're queuing up to obtain the new British cure.'[178] She does not deserve personal credit for inventing the policy, but only a government led by her could have seen it through. The world recognized this, more perhaps than did her fellow countrymen.

In a famous speech delivered in November 1985, about a year before British Gas was sold, Harold Macmillan, by then ninety-one years old, likened privatization to the unwilling sale of the contents of a once-noble house: 'First of all the Georgian silver goes, and then all that nice furniture that used to be in the saloon. Then the Canalettos go.'[179] It was wittily done, but it revealed Macmillan's paternalist way of looking at the

* As early as 1988, Letwin published a short book called *Privatising the World* (Cassell, 1988), showing people how it was done. In the preface, John Redwood described the book as 'the first bible of this new world-wide economic religion'. This sounds absurdly hyperbolic, but it is notable that Letwin's expectations in his book of the spread of the creed were considerably more modest than what actually happened.

phenomenon. In his mind, he – or his friends – had once owned the family silver, and now it was gone. Its departure was therefore a loss. Seen from a wider point of view, however, the silver had not been sold away. As Mrs Thatcher put it, she was 'selling the family silver back to the family'[180] – that is, the nation.* It was now better polished and better used. This was a gain. In the same speech, Macmillan for some reason fastened on Cable and Wireless and BT as 'the two Rembrandts' sold off. In both these cases, it was impossible to argue that the 'Rembrandts' were not in better hands after privatization. Indeed, his analogy with paintings, silver and furniture was inadequate because privatized companies not only had capital value, but also earnings and profits. In the great majority of cases, these rose, to the general advantage, not only of shareholders, but also of consumers who could benefit from the new profits reinvested in the businesses, and in more competitive prices and better services.

There was a radical transformation in the performance of almost all the companies privatized or opened up by the breaking of cartels. They became, and mostly remain to this day, 'properly functioning parts of the capitalist system'.[181] There were serious failings too. Some monopolies were not tackled. Even John Redwood admitted, 'We were weaker on competition than we should have been. It is competition which produces the magic.'[182] There were serious problems that were inadequately provided against, such as the merging, after Big Bang, of commercial 'high street' banks with merchant, later called 'investment', banks. The failure to prohibit the emergence of so-called universal banking, which Nigel Lawson described as 'my one regret' about reform of the City,[183] contributed to the disaster of the credit crunch in 2008. But it is nevertheless unimaginable that a Stock Exchange playing by the old rules could have survived, or that a nationalized British Telecom with monopoly power could possibly have presided over the telecoms revolution, or that a state-subsidized BL, unbroken up, could have brought about the situation obtaining in 2015 that Britain was exporting more cars than ever before in the nation's history.

The privatized companies were also now owned, in a real and not merely nominal sense, by millions of people. The campaign for wider share ownership was by no means an unqualified success, however. Although there were 3 million private shareholders in Britain in 1979 and 11 million when Mrs Thatcher left office in 1990, in many cases their ownership resembled those seeds in Jesus' Parable of the Sower which shoot up well at first but are then strangled by weeds. As John Moore put it, 'We didn't

---

* To some, this seemed reprehensible – why should the public buy what it owned already?

insist on creating a people's market-place. We allowed the City to fold back into its elitist attitudes.'[184] The institutions soon resumed their sway. In the view of Andrew Turnbull, who was much involved, the ownership of shares by Sid 'turned out to be a complete failure'.[185] This is unduly harsh. Most British people did not become serious long-term holders of equities, but it is clear that Mrs Thatcher's slogan of 'every earner an owner' acquired meaning in her time. Owner-occupied houses, shares, portable pensions, employee ownership, much greater opportunities to start up companies with small initial outlay, and even the highly controversial loosening of controls on personal credit, all helped create prosperity and greater financial freedom for classes of British citizens who had never known such things before. It was partly the success of privatization and the opening up of the City which emboldened Nigel Lawson to start Personal Equity Plans (PEPs) in 1986. These permitted owners of small but not insignificant amounts of shares to shelter them wholly from tax and add the same amount each year. These were reformed but not abolished by New Labour after 1997. In the form of ISAs, they remain an important part of many people's provision for their retirement. There is some truth in the accusation that Mrs Thatcher's policies, especially when oversold in the Lawson boom of the late 1980s, encouraged people to 'get rich quick', but most of the achievements did not melt away. Besides, getting rich, quick or otherwise, is broadly speaking better for a country than getting poor slowly, which was the situation Mrs Thatcher's policies sought to remedy.

Despite his ultimate quarrel with Mrs Thatcher, Nigel Lawson made the simple point that 'it has not sufficiently come out in most accounts that the great success of Mrs Thatcher on the economic front was the reform and transformation of the economy.'[186] In the end, this mattered more than all the later rows about interest rates and exchange rates. It is what made the difference.

PART TWO

Shocks

8

Glasnost in the Chilterns

'For heaven's sake, try and find me a young Russian'

The year 1984 had a symbolic significance in Western minds because of George Orwell's famous novel of that name. Writing in 1948 (and deliberately reversing its last two digits), Orwell had imagined a grim future in which the world was divided between a few, warring, totalitarian superpowers and freedom had been snuffed out. Although Orwell was on the left, he was much admired by many on the right, including Mrs Thatcher, for his vision of the evil of Soviet Communism. As the year itself approached, people naturally asked whether Orwell's warning had come to pass. Mrs Thatcher herself, thanking her political office for a Christmas present, wrote of the 'Orwellian year to come'.[1] It was a moment when people assessed the Cold War, and wondered who was winning.

For Mrs Thatcher, as for her American allies, there was a feeling of greater strength than at any time since the 1960s, but an accompanying sense that the onus now fell on them to make progress. The Soviets, who had walked out of the ongoing arms control talks in Geneva in protest at the deployment of Intermediate Nuclear Force (INF) missiles to Europe, offered little encouragement. Just before Christmas 1983, Mrs Thatcher, giving dinner to Henry Kissinger, complained that 'She could barely recall a situation where there was at once so much uncertainty and so little contact.'[2] She felt encouraged to try, however, by the attitude of Reagan himself. As Kissinger put it to her, the European perception of Reagan was 'totally wrong . . . He was not a monarchical cowboy but was in fact slightly softer than Nixon.'[3] Following her Chequers seminar the previous September (see Chapter 5), Mrs Thatcher made it her business to seek out the next generation of Soviet leaders. The year 1984 was to mark her first dramatic success in this search.

On 16 January 1984, President Reagan softened his rhetoric. Addressing the nation, he argued that, while deterrence remained essential, 'deterrence is not the beginning and end of our policy toward the Soviet Union. We must and will engage the Soviets in a dialog as serious and constructive as possible.'[4] This speech was seen as a turning point within the administration. Mrs Thatcher warmly welcomed it publicly, and wrote privately to Reagan,

> If I may say so, I thought you struck exactly the right note and at the right time. As we enter 1984, and against the background of public disquiet at the Soviet interruption of the arms control talks in Geneva and Vienna, it was good to put on record your willingness to establish a constructive and realistic working relationship with the Soviet Union. As you say, this is a long-term policy. We cannot expect rapid changes. The Soviet system is too rigid for that, as their initial public response to your speech has demonstrated. But I am sure that it is right to try: and that the best way is to engage the Soviet Union in a dialogue on a broad range of questions – bilateral and regional, political and economic.[5]

On 2 February, Mrs Thatcher travelled to Hungary, her first visit to a Warsaw Pact country (other than her 1979 stopover at Moscow airport) as Prime Minister. Her surprisingly successful meeting with József Marjai, the Hungarian Deputy Prime Minister, in 1983 (see p. 103) helped inform this choice. She had settled on Hungary because it had the greatest economic freedom of all the Soviet satellites: 'I think she began to sense that talking about "the Soviet bloc" wasn't quite the right approach. There were important differences that you had to recognise and deal with.'[6] She was also aware that the Hungarian leader, János Kádár, could be the conduit for messages to Andropov. The brief supplied by the Foreign Office offered various 'Points to use in private conversations in Budapest' and reflected many of Mrs Thatcher's views. The points included:

> How can we bring the Soviet leaders out of their isolation? Andropov is too ill to receive visitors, much less to travel to the West. [The Soviet Foreign Minister Andrei] Gromyko gives the impression of having made up his mind on all international questions ten years ago, if not twenty. Whom can we talk to, and how?[7]*

A covering note from Geoffrey Howe's office offered messages for Moscow that Mrs Thatcher might plant in Kádár's mind: 'after a period of relative inactivity in this field, Britain is once again playing a significant

---

* Another of the 'Points for use', predicting a problem which would, much later, enrage Mrs Thatcher, asked: 'Have the Hungarians noticed the emphasis Chancellor Kohl has been giving to the theme of German unity? It seems to us that the rest of the world would be no more able to prevent German reunification, if the Russians decided to permit it, than we can bring it about now, when the Russians are implacably opposed.' Subsequent history suggests that Mrs Thatcher paid too little attention to this line of argument.

role in East/West relations and has a particular contribution to offer, not least under the present Prime Minister because of our special relationship with the US.' The note suggested Mrs Thatcher stress that Reagan was 'a man of peace', signs to the contrary notwithstanding, and that 'the cause of peace requires the Russians to find a way . . . back to the negotiating tables in Geneva and Vienna.'[8]

Mrs Thatcher hastened to report her meeting with Kádár to Reagan. Kádár had told her 'with some conviction' that he 'believed the West could do business with the Soviet Union',[9] but he had also made clear that the Hungarian experiment

> is conducted within very strict limits: the single political party, the con-trolled press, the sham parliament, the state ownership of all but the smallest economic units, but above all the close alliance with Moscow. Kadar . . . made it perfectly plain that these things cannot change. I believe that it is realistic to formulate our policies on this assumption. It follows that for as far ahead as we can see we have to find a way of living side by side with the Communist system, repugnant as it is.[10]

On 9 February 1984, the day Mrs Thatcher's message landed on Reagan's desk, Andropov died. Two years earlier Mrs Thatcher had refused to attend Brezhnev's funeral, but she now made the trip to Moscow. 'The funeral is a God-send,' she told Vice-President Bush shortly before she set off. The question now, continued the notes of their meeting, was 'what to do next'.[11] Mrs Thatcher's mere presence created a good impression with her hosts. During the outdoor ceremony she endured Moscow's frigid temperatures stoically, helped by a hot-water bottle concealed about her person. There was also much excitement about her bodyguard, Detective Superintendent Parker:

> He was a large man and it was a very wintry occasion. He would shadow her everywhere with enormous bulging pockets. Russian security were deeply impressed by this heavily armed man. Then they got to the Kremlin afterwards to attend the reception. She took off her coat and then unzipped her boots – whereupon Detective Superintendent Parker produced a pair of high-heeled shoes from his pockets. The Russians were rather disillusioned.[12]

Once the obsequies had been concluded, Mrs Thatcher, like many other world leaders, was due to meet Andropov's successor, Konstantin Chernenko,*

---

* Konstantin Chernenko (1911–85), General Secretary of the Communist Party of the Soviet Union, 1984–5.

who was widely regarded as an elderly stand-in until the successor from the next generation could emerge. During the inevitable waiting around she turned down the offer of a rare behind-the-scenes tour of the Kremlin, insisting the time could be better spent studying her briefing papers. 'Do you think I've come here as a *tourist*?' said the woman who always preferred work over leisure.[13] When she finally saw Chernenko she found him a sick man. Tony Bishop, who interpreted for Mrs Thatcher, recalled that Chernenko:

> opened with a lengthy typed formal statement, delivered in a high-speed gabble and with the same stumbles, monotony and lack of coherence that we had heard in public earlier in the day during his eulogy to Andropov . . . In the brief extempore exchanges at the end of the short meeting there was perhaps a rare moment of fleeting warmth in Chernenko's voice, when he repeated his appreciation of Mrs Thatcher's gesture in attending Andropov's funeral. But it was, for her, like meeting an ailing member of her father's generation . . .[14]

Unlike Vice-President Bush, who reported rather optimistically to Reagan about his conversation with Chernenko, Mrs Thatcher was 'unimpressed'.[15] She 'treated him with every civility, trying hard to draw him out a little, but with no great success'.[16] She did, however, convey her plea for progress: 'They had a chance, perhaps even the last chance, of securing fundamental disarmament agreements enhancing security.'[17] In her Foreign Office briefing material, Mrs Thatcher had underlined the information about Mikhail Gorbachev, marking her interest, but she did not meet him.* On the plane home, discussing the trip with her small team of advisers, she made her frustration with Chernenko clear. 'For heaven's sake,' she exclaimed, 'try and find me a young Russian.'[18]

The Foreign Office was already at work on this task. On 2 February 1984, before Andropov died, an invitation had been sent to Moscow. To avoid problems of inter-government protocol, the Foreign Office had arranged

---

* Recent accounts have suggested that Mrs Thatcher *did* meet Gorbachev, even that to escape the cold he 'gallantly escorted her to a warm room' (Jonathan Aitken, *Margaret Thatcher: Power and Personality*, Bloomsbury, 2013, p. 478), and that she personally invited him to visit London (Richard Aldous, *Reagan and Thatcher: The Difficult Relationship*, Norton, 2012, p. 167). These claims are based solely on the testimony of Leonid Zamyatin, the former Soviet Ambassador to the UK, whose account has become increasingly embroidered over the years. Those who accompanied her, and who knew her mind, confirm that none of this ever happened. (Correspondence with Sir John Coles, Lord Butler of Brockwell, Archie Brown, Lord Powell of Bayswater.)

for the invitation to come from the Inter-Parliamentary Union (that is, from British Parliamentarians to their Soviet counterparts). It did not mention any Soviet official by name but merely suggested that a delegation might come to the UK.[19] The death of Andropov gave the search for a 'young Russian' added urgency. British officials developed a shortlist of three preferred invitees: Grigory Romanov, the mayor of Leningrad, Chernenko's close associate Viktor Grishin, and Mikhail Gorbachev.[20] They swiftly settled on Gorbachev who, under Chernenko, became the de facto number two in the Soviet hierarchy.* He also assumed the honorific position of chairman of the Foreign Affairs Committee of the Supreme Soviet. This made him the automatic person to invite to Britain as leader of a 'parliamentary' delegation. His invitation, which made clear that Gorbachev would meet senior government figures as well as backbench MPs, was sent in mid-June. For a long time, it received no reply.

In the same month, before a visit to Moscow, Geoffrey Howe suggested inviting Chernenko himself to London on behalf of Mrs Thatcher. Charles Powell wrote to his boss disapprovingly. He said it was worth inviting Gorbachev, and his youngish Politburo colleague Heydar Aliyev, who was to be asked for the following year, because 'there is a chance they will come and it would do them good,'[21] but the Chernenko suggestion looked like a 'routine gesture'. Worse, it came at a time 'when such gestures might seem rather offensive' since Mrs Thatcher was campaigning hard for the Soviet dissidents Andrei Sakharov† and Anatoly Shcharansky,‡ both of whom were suffering ill treatment, and in the latter's case imprisonment, at the time. Beside Powell's words, Mrs Thatcher wrote, 'Do not invite Mr Chernenko – it is much too soon.' When Howe arrived in Moscow, his request to call on Gorbachev was turned down.

In public, Soviet hostility to dialogue continued, chiefly because of resentment at the US Strategic Defense Initiative (SDI). But towards the end of the summer, the Americans received private signals that contacts

---

* Nigel Broomfield, then head of the Soviet Department at the Foreign Office, recalled that when he and his team made this choice they were entirely unaware of Archie Brown's earlier efforts (see Chapter 5) to draw Gorbachev to Mrs Thatcher's attention (Correspondence with Sir Nigel Broomfield).

† Andrei Sakharov (1921–89), nuclear physicist, Soviet dissident and human rights activist; winner, Nobel Peace Prize, 1975; internally exiled, 1980–86, following his public protests against the Soviet intervention in Afghanistan in 1979.

‡ Anatoly Shcharansky (later Natan Sharansky) (1948–), Soviet-born human rights activist and author; one of the foremost campaigners in the struggle of Soviet Jewry to emigrate to Israel; spent nine years in Soviet prisons (1977–86) for allegedly spying for the US. On release he went to Israel, where he served as a minister in four successive Israeli governments, 1996–2005.

might be resumed. Reagan duly invited Gromyko to the White House on 28 September 1984, the first such invitation since the Soviet invasion of Afghanistan. Gromyko accepted. Four days before the meeting, Reagan addressed the General Assembly of the United Nations. Edging further towards dialogue than ever before, he called for 'regular ministerial or cabinet-level meetings' with the Soviets.[22] He was trying to set the tone for the second term as president for which he was campaigning. Mindful of 'how deeply you feel about the need to improve US–Soviet relations', Reagan wrote to Mrs Thatcher two days later, his 'primary aim' with Gromyko would be 'to impress upon the Soviet Government my strong, personal desire to put our relations on a more positive track and, in particular, my commitment to negotiate agreements to reduce arms in a fair, balanced and verifiable manner'.[23] Mrs Thatcher wrote back the same day: 'I wholeheartedly endorse the approach you have outlined to East/West relations. I saw your speech on television and thought it superb.'[24]

Although Reagan made no major breakthrough with Gromyko, he felt pleased with the talks: 'I am personally hopeful that in time, some of the ideas and suggestions for an improvement in our dialogue that we have raised with Mr Gromyko over this past week will eventually be realized,' he reported to Mrs Thatcher. '. . . I am prepared to be patient,'[25] Mrs Thatcher replied, endorsing Reagan's belief in 'sober realism, firm resolve and patience' and characteristically adding the need for 'careful preparation'. She suggested that 'Even a change in leadership brought about by Chernenko's incapacity is not likely to have an immediate impact', but she was also convinced that 'progress will be possible only if there is direct communication at the highest level with the Soviet leadership.'[26]

In mid-October 1984, just after the Brighton bomb, Mrs Thatcher received a handwritten note from Charles Powell. 'Something which I think will interest you,' he wrote: 'GORBACHEV has just accepted an invitation to the UK and wants to come in December.'[27] When a letter arrived from the Foreign Office officially confirming the acceptance, Powell wrote on it: 'Will you see him here [Downing Street]? Or invite him to your dacha?' Mrs Thatcher preferred her dacha, writing 'Lunch at Chequers'.[28] Mrs Thatcher sat on the news until she spoke in the Queen's Speech debate in Parliament on 6 November 1984.

Not only the fact but also the timing of Gorbachev's acceptance worked very well for Mrs Thatcher. It clearly followed the Reagan–Gromyko meeting, showing that the rising generation of Soviet leaders saw Britain as the best place to explore Western attitudes. It also complemented Reagan's landslide victory in the presidential elections on 7 November.

1. Preparing for battle: Mrs Thatcher, in No. 10, makes sure her hair is in place for the 1983 general election campaign.

2. Denis listens attentively to one of his wife's election platform speeches. During her more informal 'stump' speeches, he was often to be found at the back of the crowd, shouting 'Hear, hear'.

3. The winning team launch the 1983 election manifesto: Mrs Thatcher
with (top, left to right) Norman Tebbit, Geoffrey Howe, Francis Pym
and (beside her) Willie Whitelaw. Pym said a landslide victory would be
a bad thing. After she won one, she sacked him.

4. Shouting down the hecklers in Salisbury, with the
Conservative candidate Robert Key, who won.

5. The 1983 Labour manifesto was even more useful to her than her own.
Here she reads out blood-curdling passages to a rally in Cardiff.

6. On the morning of victory on 10 June 1983, Mrs Thatcher, Denis and Cecil Parkinson
wave to supporters from the window of Conservative Central Office. She already knew
that Sara Keays, Parkinson's former secretary, was pregnant with his child.

7. Emerging from hospital in Windsor, in August 1983, after an operation for a detached retina. She had thought she was going blind.

8. Returning to Downing Street with shopping, October 1983. She liked to play up to the role of housewife-superstar.

9. Cecil Parkinson fights for his political life at the party conference in Blackpool, October 1983. John Gummer, his replacement as party chairman, is next to Mrs Thatcher. Behind him is Parkinson's wife, Ann. The next day, Parkinson resigned.

10. Helmut Kohl and Mrs Thatcher inspect a guard of honour during her visit to West Germany in November 1983. Even at this early stage, and despite their shared conservative politics, they were not close.

11. François Mitterrand and Helmut Kohl showing reconciliation on the battlefield of Verdun, September 1984. Asked if she found it moving, Mrs Thatcher replied: 'No, I did not. Two grown men holding hands!'

12. At Yuri Andropov's funeral in Moscow in February 1984, Mrs Thatcher meets his already ailing successor as Soviet leader, Konstantin Chernenko. Her dignified bearing at the freezing ceremonies made a powerful impression on the Soviets.

13. Mrs Thatcher receives the South African State President, P. W. Botha, at Chequers, June 1984. She urged him to consider releasing Nelson Mandela, but opposed isolating the white regime.

14. Neil Kinnock (right), Labour leader since 1983, with Arthur Scargill, the leader of the National Union of Mineworkers, at the Durham Miners' Gala in July 1984. Kinnock was torn between solidarity with the striking miners and dismay that Scargill would not call a strike ballot.

15. The Coal Board chairman, Ian MacGregor, plays a joke with the media as they catch him attending a secret meeting with the NUM in September 1984. His behaviour was considered embarrassing.

16. Lines of police confront the NUM pickets at the Orgreave coking works on 18 June 1984. The controversial defeat of the pickets' attempt to prevent supplies leaving the plant was a turning point against Arthur Scargill in the strike. The NUM were incensed by police tactics.

17. Speaking at Banbury market, 30 May 1984, Mrs Thatcher passionately condemns picket-line violence at Orgreave: 'an attempt to substitute the rule of the mob for the rule of law'.

18. The Energy Secretary, Peter Walker. He and Mrs Thatcher neither liked nor trusted one another, but she respected his abilities. Between them, they ran the politics of the miners' strike successfully.

19. Miners in Armthorpe, South Yorkshire, vote to return to work without an agreement, March 1985. Scargill's intransigence prevented any deal being done and helped ensure the government's complete victory that month.

20. Mother and daughter. Mrs Thatcher takes six hours off over the Bank Holiday weekend, May 1984, to help Carol decorate her new house – a rare moment of shared domesticity.

21. Mother and son. Mrs Thatcher, suitably dressed for her holiday at Imlau, Austria, in August 1985, receives a slice of cake from Mark to celebrate his thirty-second birthday.

22. Mark's wedding reception at the Savoy Hotel, February 1987. He married Diane Burgdorf, a Texan. The couple, who had a son and a daughter, were to divorce in 2005.

23. The very special relationship: President Ronald Reagan is welcomed by his greatest ally at the London Economic Summit, June 1984. Nancy Reagan stands between them.

24. Mrs Thatcher turns away from European partners at the Fontainebleau European Council, June 1984. It was here that she at last prevailed in the five-year row about the British contribution to the European Community. The other member states would get their own back on her later.

25. Denis and Margaret dressed up for the Conservative Agents' Ball at the party conference in Brighton, October 1984. A few hours later, an IRA bomb went off in their hotel.

26. Still dressed in her ball-gown, Mrs Thatcher is driven with Denis (in pyjamas) from the Grand Hotel after the bomb went off at 2.54 a.m., accompanied by her assistant Cynthia Crawford ('Crawfie').

27. Sir Keith Joseph, the Education Secretary, stands with police on the Brighton seafront in his silk dressing-gown after the bomb.

28. Norman Tebbit, the Trade and Industry Secretary, is dragged from the wreckage of the Grand by firemen. He was seriously injured. His wife, Margaret, was paralysed for life by the bomb.

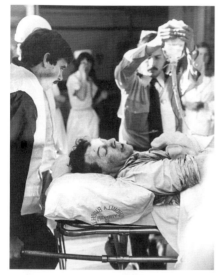

29. John Wakeham, the Chief Whip, is taken to hospital. His legs were severely injured. His wife, Roberta, died in the blast.

30. The bathroom in the Thatchers' hotel suite after the bomb. Luckily for them both, the damage to bedroom and sitting-room was much less.

31. The front of the Grand Hotel after the explosion. Only one vertical section of the building's construction, which did not include Mrs Thatcher's suite, was destroyed.

32. In memory. The Prime Minister, flanked by Willie Whitelaw (left) and the Home Secretary, Douglas Hurd, observes silence at the conference to honour the victims the morning after the bomb. Later in the day she delivered her platform speech.

33. With Indira Gandhi, the Prime Minister of India, at the Commonwealth conference in 1983. The two women were on good terms. Less than a month after Mrs Thatcher had survived the Brighton bomb, Mrs Gandhi was assassinated by two members of her own bodyguard in Delhi.

34. **All in one week** (i): The man she could do business with. Mrs Thatcher stands at the door of Chequers with Mikhail Gorbachev, then the Soviet heir apparent, in December 1984, their first meeting. The two became so engrossed in their astonishingly frank discussions that he was two hours late for his next appointment.

35. (ii): On the way to Peking with Geoffrey Howe to sign the Hong Kong Agreement. On this subject, her grit and his emollience proved an effective combination.

36. (iii): Within spitting distance (note the bowl), Mrs Thatcher and the Chinese leader, Deng Xiaoping, discuss the future of Hong Kong much more amicably than when they had met two years earlier. Their interpreters, and William Ehrman (right) of the British Embassy, sit behind.

37. (iv): Mrs Thatcher flies on to Hong Kong from China. Her headphones are upside down to avoid disturbing her hair.

38. (v): With Sir Edward Youde, the Governor of Hong Kong, Bernard Ingham and Howe, Mrs Thatcher attempts to explain the agreement to the Hong Kong people. It was not an easy sell, but the deal survived.

39. (vi): Charles Powell carries her despatch box onto the plane from Hong Kong to Washington. She stayed awake for the entire journey to be prepared for her meeting with Reagan.

40. (vii): The President steers his guest in a golf buggy round Camp David. She was terrified of his driving but successful in their talks.

41. (viii): Ready to celebrate, Mrs Thatcher and Bernard Ingham pull a Christmas cracker on the flight home.

42. (ix): On the same flight, a rare moment of clowning with the press.

43. Anti-Thatcher protesters gather in Oxford, January 1985. Senior members of the university voted to refuse its most famous living graduate an honorary degree. Denis said that nothing hurt her more in her whole time in office.

44. Buckingham, the first independent university, treated her more generously. Here she receives its honorary doctorate in 1986.

45. In May 1985, Mrs Thatcher addresses a joint session of both Houses of Congress, the first British prime minister to do so since Winston Churchill. Behind her are the Speaker, Tip O'Neill, and the Vice-President, George Bush.

Mrs Thatcher was not slow to exploit the moment. 'What a victory! I cannot tell you how delighted I am,' she wrote to him the next day. '. . . My fondest hope is that we can continue to work as closely together as we have over the past four years and consult privately and with complete frankness on all major international problems.'[29] She slipped in a request: she would be in Peking on 20/21 December to sign the Hong Kong Agreement: 'if you happened to be in California then, I could stop over for an hour or two on 22 December on my way back to London.'[30]

In this request, the geography supplied by the Foreign Office was defective (the return route from Hong Kong to London does not include California), and so was its information about Reagan's whereabouts. He would not be in California, but at Camp David. 'I believe we should not encourage her to come to Washington at that time,' McFarlane advised Reagan,[31] who politely declined her request. Feelers were put out by the British about whether Mrs Thatcher could come to Camp David. 'Frankly we on the staff were horrified,' recalled Jack Matlock, a senior NSC staffer:

> normally that was private time for the Reagans. They never invited outsiders to Camp David. But it went in to Reagan and he was delighted . . . so it became almost a family visit in a way. That told us that it was more than just politics. The couple really did like the Thatchers.[32]

Needless to say, although the friendship was genuine, Mrs Thatcher had no interest in a purely 'family' visit. She had two goals for the Camp David meeting. The first was finding the best way of dealing with the question of SDI so as to support Reagan while persuading him to try to ease European concerns. The second was to report to the President on her meeting with Gorbachev which was to take place a few days earlier.

The importance of the Gorbachev visit, and thus of the Camp David trip, was increased later in November by a strong sense that the Soviets were ready to come out of the cold. Moscow now proposed that Shultz and Gromyko meet in January 1985 to agree terms for a wide range of nuclear negotiations. It was the perfect moment to help shape the emerging US approach. Mrs Thatcher had now achieved greater salience in East–West affairs than at any time in her premiership.

Mrs Thatcher's intensive preparations for the Gorbachev visit included another briefing seminar with academics, held at No. 10 the day before he arrived in Britain.* As if to guard against their own excitement and

---

* For this less formal gathering four academics were on hand to brief Mrs Thatcher and Geoffrey Howe. Archie Brown, Michael Kaser and Alec Nove, return guests from the

hers, Mrs Thatcher's advisers constantly reminded her that Gorbachev, for all his interest in reform, was still a chip off the old, Soviet bloc, and was not yet certain to be the next leader. Mrs Thatcher underlined parts of her Foreign Office briefing that described Gorbachev as 'intelligent and confident', while noting there was 'nothing to suggest he is not a convinced communist or that he intends (or would be able) to make fundamental alterations to the system itself'.[33] Any publicity for him as the next leader might damage him with his colleagues, it warned: 'We should treat him as he is, and not refer publicly to what he might become.'[34] The general objectives included 'to teach him something about how a Western democracy works and what a free market economy can achieve'. The 'specific' objectives were chiefly to emphasize 'the sincerity and willingness of the West in general and President Reagan' in wanting to negotiate over arms and to set out the areas – nuclear, chemical, outer space – where progress could be made. Under Charles Powell's guidance, a lunch at Chequers was organized which would permit the maximum freedom of discussion.*

For their part, the Russians saw Mrs Thatcher as the most useful ally of the United States with whom they could communicate. Gorbachev also realized the opportunity in an invitation to Britain. It was a 'dress rehearsal for his future diplomatic role', recalled Andrei Grachev, who would later become Gorbachev's spokesman. 'Gorbachev singled out Thatcher as the shortest way to send a message to Washington. He was well aware of her reputation . . . as a "hard-liner" vis-à-vis the Soviet Union . . . and he believed this to be an advantage rather than a handicap.'[35] Gorbachev himself met Sir Iain Sutherland,† the British Ambassador in Moscow, and told him that he wanted (Mrs Thatcher's underlining) 'frank political discussions with the Prime Minister, with no diplomatic formalities'. He also 'spoke of his interest in English history and the English legal system, which he had studied'.[36] Percy Cradock, who had succeeded Anthony Parsons as Mrs Thatcher's foreign policy adviser, tried to read Russian intentions for her: 'for the Russians space [that is, SDI] will be the key . . . In return for assurances on space they may be ready to negotiate on

---

1983 Chequers seminar (see Chapter 5), were joined by Professor Lawrence Freedman (King's College London).

* Originally, Gorbachev's wife, Raisa, was excluded, but when Denis intimated that he would be at Chequers, and therefore at the lunch, Mrs Thatcher directed Powell to invite Mrs Gorbachev as well (Powell to Thatcher, 7 December 1984, TNA: PREM 19/1394 (http://www.margaretthatcher.org/document/134716)).

† Iain Sutherland (1925–86), educated Aberdeen Grammar School, Aberdeen University and Balliol College, Oxford; Ambassador to Greece, 1978–82; to Soviet Union, 1982–5; knighted, 1982.

offensive missiles.'[37] He counselled against allowing the Soviets to drive a wedge between the British and the Americans: 'it encourages them to think that they can divide and rule.'

The British also used their mole, Oleg Gordievsky, to assist. Ever since he had provided important information about ABLE ARCHER (see Chapter 5), Gordievsky had been taken very seriously in Whitehall. This was partly because Mrs Thatcher herself had a great respect for British intelligence, dating back to her time as leader of the Opposition. Airey Neave, her campaign manager in the 1975 leadership election and subsequently her chief of staff, had good intelligence links, deriving from his own work in the Second World War. Neave had arranged for Mrs Thatcher to meet former intelligence officers, including Nicholas Elliott,* an eccentric officer from SIS, who later published books dropping hints about his work with facetious titles like *With my Little Eye*.[38] Elliott and others briefed her about the work of the intelligence services and tended to confirm her fears, which the Foreign Office liked to play down, about the extent of Soviet penetration of the West.

The Labour government which Mrs Thatcher's administration replaced had kept intelligence at a distance, particularly because of the paranoid fear of the services harboured by Harold Wilson, Prime Minister until 1976. But for Mrs Thatcher, who combined suspicion of the Soviet Union with a desire to know more about what it was up to, intelligence furnished the sort of information which diplomacy, in the frozen periods of the Cold War, was ill equipped to provide. It also, through MI5 on the home front, kept watch on the Communist subversion which was a significant factor in industrial disruption. She was so concerned about this that, early in her term as prime minister, she called together the heads of the two intelligence services to try to persuade them to amend the 1952 Security Service Directive to allow MI5 to engage in stopping 'wreckers' in industry[39] as well as those actively engaged in the subversion of the state. When Sir Howard Smith, the Director-General of MI5, refused, Mrs Thatcher and Robert Armstrong pursued the aim by other means, cutting Smith out of the planning, and moving a senior MI5 officer, John Deverell, to the Cabinet Office to keep an eye on industrial subversion.[40]

In general, Mrs Thatcher saw the intelligence services as robust and accurate. According to Sir Colin McColl, head of SIS from 1988, 'She thought of us in the same way as she thought of the armed forces – part

---

* Nicholas Elliott (1916–94), educated Eton and Trinity College, Cambridge; Acting Lieutenant, Intelligence Corps, 1940–45; Head of Station, Secret Intelligence Service, Berne, 1945–53; Vienna, 1953–6; Beirut, 1960–62.

of the national defence. That was wonderful for us. We knew we had her support.'[41]* When McColl first met her in the early 1980s, he noted what he saw as her charming simplicity in preaching to the converted: 'Here's this lady, running a very complicated country. She spent a large part of the meeting telling us that Communism was a very bad thing. Lovely.'[42] She was also not above being excited by secrecy in itself and by the romance of espionage. So when Gordievsky started to report, his revelations, conveyed 'for her eyes only' via her foreign affairs private secretary (first John Coles and then Powell), fell on fertile ground. In the past, British agents recruited from the KGB had been valued chiefly for their counter-intelligence, but what excited Mrs Thatcher even more about Gordievsky was 'the value of his *political* information. It was a big event.'[43] Gordievsky's despatches also conveyed to her, as no other information had done, how the Soviet leadership reacted to Western phenomena and, indeed, to her. He reported that the Politburo had been greatly impressed by her demeanour at Andropov's funeral – 'smart, serious, dignified, properly dressed, and more than just the Iron Lady'.[44] As Gordievsky himself put it, 'Because she knew of me from an early stage, she started to think of them [the Russians] not as robots but as human beings.'[45] The main human being who started to feature in his reports was Mikhail Gorbachev.

As Gorbachev's visit approached, Gordievsky was ordered to write a report for Moscow on what the British were likely to raise at the meetings with their visitor. Gordievsky recalled that he 'had no idea. So I went to the Friends [SIS] and said, "Help!"'[46] Here was an important opportunity to prove his worth to his Soviet superiors. The British decided to furnish Gordievsky with the briefing points which Howe would have in front of him during his meetings with Gorbachev. Gordievsky later came to believe that the high quality of his report aroused the KGB's first suspicions about him: 'When I wrote the report, my number one, a very clever counter-intelligence officer, said, "Mmm, very good report about Geoffrey Howe. It sounds like a Foreign Office document." I felt my heart ache. It was too good. Really too good.'[47]

Apart from all the expected anxieties about a meeting which was both so important and unprecedented, there was also a subversive sub-theme. Gorbachev's visit came some nine months into the miners' strike. As

* One way in which she demonstrated this support was through visiting the offices of the intelligence services. During her first visit to SIS, early in her career as prime minister, she asked the man sitting next to her, 'Do you employ forgers?' He told her that they sometimes did. 'How do you know', she asked, 'whether their references are genuine?' (Private information.)

matters had grown more difficult, legally and financially, for the strikers, Arthur Scargill, the NUM leader, had sought help from foreign countries hostile to the UK government. First, contacts with Libya were exposed. At the same time, Gordievsky was reporting that NUM lines to the Soviet Union had been opened up. MI5 reported that in early November the Soviet Foreign Trade Bank had tried to pay approximately $1.2 million to the NUM via banks in Switzerland and London, but the operation had been abandoned when the Swiss bank had grown suspicious.[48] Gorbachev himself had signed off the effort to provide the NUM with $1.4 million back in October (see Chapter 6). Mrs Thatcher wanted advice on how to 'discourage the Russian Government's provision of funds indicated in that Report, perhaps by using the evident wish of the Russians to avoid publicity'.[49] Should she raise the matter with Gorbachev?*

Mikhail Gorbachev and his wife Raisa arrived for lunch at Chequers on Sunday 16 December 1984. Present were Mrs Thatcher and Denis, and Whitelaw, Howe, Heseltine, Malcolm Rifkind, Paul Channon† and, because Gorbachev had supervised agriculture for much of his career, the Minister of Agriculture, Michael Jopling. At the drinks beforehand, Gorbachev 'wanted solely to talk about agriculture' which rather nonplussed the very unagricultural Mrs Thatcher,[50] but as soon as they sat down to lunch 'our conversation', as Gorbachev remembered it, 'took a rather polemic tone'.[51]‡ According to the British interpreter, Tony Bishop, Mrs Thatcher 'deliberately and breathtakingly . . . set about serially cross-examining him about the inferiority of the Soviet centralised command system and the merits of free enterprise and competition'.[52] The contemporary record bears this out. Mrs Thatcher asked Gorbachev how people could possibly better themselves 'in a centralised and rigid economy'.[53] He replied that, in the Soviet Union, the availability of jobs was 'already solved'. Mrs Thatcher then attacked Soviet five-year plans: 'She herself did not wish to have the power to direct everyone where he or she should work and what he or she should receive.' Gorbachev said

---

* The Soviet involvement in the miners' strike was further emphasized by the presence in Gorbachev's delegation of Ivan Strelchenko, a coal-pit foreman from Donetsk, designed to show solidarity with the NUM.

† Channon was standing in at Trade and Industry because of Norman Tebbit's Brighton bomb injuries.

‡ Bernard Ingham often related (including to the present author) that one of Mrs Thatcher's very first remarks to Gorbachev was 'I hate Communism.' While this was certainly the spirit of what she said, neither the written record nor other recollections of the encounter support Ingham's claim.

he understood that the British system was different, but 'the Soviet system was superior.' He invited Mrs Thatcher to come and have a look for herself: 'She would see how Soviet people lived – joyfully.' Reading the record later, Mrs Thatcher underlined this last word and wrote '!' beside it.

Next the Prime Minister complained about the Soviet treatment of dissidents like Andrei Sakharov and Anatoly Shcharansky and of *refusnik** Jews in general. Gorbachev declined to answer, reminding her that 'they had not completed their discussion of the two economic systems'.[54] Mrs Thatcher took this as her cue to start on the miners' strike. There had been much intimidation and violence, she said, 'and even recently a murder'.† 'Communism', she went on, 'was synonymous with getting one's way by violence. Its slogan was: "Brothers – when you are free, you will do as you are told." ' She said that people like Scargill, and his Communist vice-president, Mick McGahey,‡ 'gave Soviet Communism a bad name'.[55] She accused Communists in Britain of taking over the trade unions 'under Labour colours' and infiltrating the Labour Party because they could not win parliamentary seats under their own banner.

Gorbachev took this, rightly, as an attack on the Soviet Union: 'this was the first he had heard of this.' Did the Prime Minister really think, he asked, that his country could run a miners' strike or manipulate British public opinion? It was the Soviet Union's 'firm policy' that there should be 'no export of Revolution and no export of Counter-Revolution'. Mrs Thatcher replied that she didn't mind foreign propaganda because 'She could prove that the British system was better. But the Soviet Union's fellow-Communists who could not get their own way through the ballot box were opting for violence.' Then she challenged him almost directly: 'They were also being helped with finance from outside.'[56] Gorbachev stoutly and mendaciously denied the accusation: 'The Soviet Union had transferred no funds to the NUM.' At this the official record added, '(After a sideways glance from Mr Zamyatin [the Central Committee's chief of international propaganda, who was part of the Soviet delegation], he amended this to "as far as I am aware")'.[57] He went on the offensive: 'The Prime Minister should blame Britain and not foreign Communists for the situation. *Das Kapital* had been written in London.' Mrs Thatcher 'interjected that in a free society it was entirely possible to do so and get

---

* *Refusnik* was the Russian word for Jews who wished to emigrate to Israel but were forbidden to do so by the authorities.

† She was referring to the killing of David Wilkie, a taxi driver carrying a strike-breaker to work in Wales (see p. 175).

‡ Mick McGahey (1925–99), miner and trade unionist; vice-president, NUM, 1974–87.

it published'. Gorbachev said that he was aware 'that the Prime Minister was capable of defending herself. But the Second Congress of the RSDRP* had also been held in London.' Unquenchable, Mrs Thatcher asked Gorbachev 'when she might contemplate the holding of British Party Congresses in Moscow. Lenin had set a tragic example of resorting to violence when unable to win through the ballot box.' Equally defiant, Gorbachev told Mrs Thatcher to 'deal with realities': 'He recalled that Mr Churchill, a "dyed in the wool anti-communist"', had wisely joined forces with the Soviets.

At one point, Gorbachev later recalled, the conversation became so heated that he and Mrs Thatcher turned away from each other: 'Then I caught Raisa's eye across the table, and her lips moved to say "It's over!", and for a moment I wondered if we should leave.'[58] But suddenly Mrs Thatcher changed tone: 'The Prime Minister said that the difficult part of their discussion was now over.'[59] In Tony Bishop's view, she was signalling to Gorbachev 'that he'd passed the first audition'.[60] He responded in kind, welcoming her remarks and recalling 'good examples of cooperation between the two countries, including the honouring of contracts in the energy field [a reference to her fight with Reagan over the Siberian gas pipeline]'. He proposed a toast, celebrating the '"domestic ambience" and the good atmosphere prevailing around the table'.[61] Lunch ended, the principals adjourned for a smaller and more informal meeting in the main sitting room. Denis left and Raisa enjoyed a tour of the house with officials.†

The lunchtime conversation between Mrs Thatcher and Gorbachev had been one of the most remarkable ever to have taken place across that dining table. It defied all diplomatic norms. It produced almost nothing but disagreement, and the sharpness of its tone exceeded all the usual Foreign Office euphemisms for rude and quarrelsome meetings, such as 'frank' or 'candid'. Each side appeared to stay inside its ideological trench, firing hard. Yet the occasion was, quite clearly, a success, and was immediately recognized as such by both sides. Gorbachev's Marxism, thought Mrs

---

* The Second Congress of the Russian Social Democratic Labour Party met in Charlotte Street, London, in August 1903. At this congress, the party split. The Bolshevik faction, led by Lenin, was ultimately victorious in the Russian Revolution of 1917.

† A graduate of the Philosophy Faculty of Moscow University, Raisa 'wanted us all to know that she wasn't just another dumpy, head-scarved wife', recalled Martin Nicholson, the Foreign Office official who interpreted for her. ' "I know where my own country is," she snapped when our guide helpfully pointed out Russia on an ancient globe in the Library.' (Martin Nicholson, unpublished manuscript, kindly made available to the author by Martin Nicholson.)

Thatcher, was standard stuff. 'But his personality could not have been more different from the wooden ventriloquism of the average Soviet *apparatchik*.'[62] By his own account, Gorbachev paid a similar compliment to Mrs Thatcher, although the official record does not confirm this:* 'I told Mrs Thatcher: "I know you are a person of staunch beliefs . . . This commands respect. But please consider that next to you is a person of your own ilk. And I can assure you that I am not under instructions from the Politburo to persuade you to join the Communist Party." After that statement she burst into a hearty laugh . . .'[63] Those present on the British side were struck by Gorbachev's physical vitality. 'He was so visibly not one of the older men,' recalled Charles Powell, who noted 'this short, energetic man bouncing on the balls of his feet': 'I think everybody was caught by surprise. She certainly was.'[64] Without excessive overconfidence, Gorbachev was acting as if he were all but certain to be the next Soviet leader. He spoke with the ease of the man at the very top.†

From neighbouring armchairs in the sitting room, and joined only by Howe, Powell and Bishop on the British side, Mrs Thatcher and Gorbachev got down to a less argumentative discussion about arms control. They sat in front of the fire. Occasionally Mrs Thatcher herself would approach the hearth and toss on a new log to revive the flames. Putting aside the polemics of lunch, both sides agreed to discard their briefing papers and talk.[65] Mrs Thatcher explained that, following her seminar at Chequers fifteen months earlier, she had decided 'that she must try to do something' to engage with the Soviet Union.[66] There was no point in one system trying to convert the other, she said: the point was 'to diminish hostility and the level of armaments'. In making these arguments, she boasted, Britain had a bigger influence with the United States than any other NATO member. When he met Gromyko at Geneva, George Shultz would be looking for balance, not unilateral advantage. She was worried that 'unless the two sides could agree on how to deal with the problem of weapons in outer space, there would be a new spiral in the arms race.'[67]

---

* It is possible that some parts of the conversation did not make it into the official record. Charles Powell did his best to take notes but had difficulty hearing everything given that this was all taking place over lunch (Lord Powell of Bayswater, British Diplomatic Oral History Programme, Churchill College, Cambridge (https://www.chu.cam.ac.uk/media/uploads/files/Powell.pdf)).

† Tony Bishop, the interpreter, noticed that Gorbachev's language was 'irreproachably sound' in Soviet terms, but used refreshing colloquialisms, such as '*chepukha* (nonsense/twaddle)' (Gorbachev, A Personal Assessment of the Man during his Visit to the United Kingdom, 15–21 December 1984, TNA: PREM 19/1394 (http://www.margaretthatcher.org/document/134739)).

This enabled her to make her point, which she so often put to bridge the gap between Americans and Europeans, that SDI research was fine, but translation into weapons production was another matter altogether.

Gorbachev replied rather more luridly, speaking of 'avoiding a holo-caust', and raising the spectre of 'nuclear winter' after an exchange of missiles. He produced a diagram from the *New York Times* illustrating the vast destructive capacities of the world's nuclear arsenals. It had been difficult for the Russians to contemplate returning to negotiations (at Geneva), he complained, because, in four years of Reagan, 'not a single step forward had been taken in Soviet/US relations'. He was particularly concerned about 'the activities of the group round Mr. Weinberger and Mr. Perle'.* How could Mrs Thatcher tell that her assessment of the United States was right? Mrs Thatcher came back with a staunch but nuanced defence of Reagan. The Americans did not want to dominate the world, she said: the freeze in relations had more to do with the Soviet invasion of Afghanistan. Reagan 'saw the Soviet Union as a country com-bining immense patriotism with the aim of the world-wide victory of the Communist system'. Naturally, he felt fearful and suspicious, but 'The last thing he would ever want was a war.' He had wished only to restore America's confidence and make her 'strong enough to defend her way of life'. She said how disappointed Reagan had been by Brezhnev's lack of friendly response to the handwritten letter he had sent early in his presi-dency asking for a meeting. Now he was ready 'to have another go'.

Then Mrs Thatcher took a risk. Reagan also 'had a dream', she said, 'expressed through the Strategic Defence Initiative, of being able to rid the world of nuclear weapons. Sadly, it was not a viable dream because the process of acquiring a ballistic missile defence would inevitably lead to a fresh twist in the arms race spiral . . . In any case, the knowledge of how to build nuclear weapons could not be disinvented.'[68]

Gorbachev replied that he disagreed with Mrs Thatcher's friendly account of US intentions, but agreed with her about the value of talking. Spotting the gap between American views on SDI and her own, he tried to flatter her sense of British independence by quoting Lord Palmerston's dictum about England having no permanent friends, or permanent ene-mies, only permanent interests.† He implied that Britain could be friendlier with Russia and less close to the United States. Gorbachev told her he was

---

* Richard Perle, then Assistant Secretary for Defense and close to Weinberger, was well known as one of the Pentagon's leading anti-Soviet hawks.

† Mrs Thatcher noted this remark on her briefing paper, misspelling the nineteenth-century Prime Minister's name as 'Palmerstone'.

'worried by what the Prime Minister said about President Reagan's day-dreams in connection with space-based systems'. Trying to drive the wedge still deeper, he told her that 'The United States' position, vis-a-vis Western Europe, on the Strategic Defence Initiative was an egotistic one.'[69] The point had been made and the meeting drew to a close. 'What we need now is a process,' said Gorbachev, suggesting that their dialogue should continue. This, according to Tony Bishop, was 'music to the PM's ears'.[70] Her efforts to engage with the Soviet Union appeared to be bearing fruit.

The post-lunch meeting so exceeded its allotted time that Gorbachev did not leave for London until six, making him nearly two hours late for a reception at the Soviet Embassy. Mrs Thatcher lingered briefly with her officials before exclaiming, ' "Tomorrow it's China, and I haven't had my hair done!" She ran upstairs and was gone.'[71]

Those with Mrs Thatcher that day noticed her excitement. 'At the end, she felt very elated: this really was something new,' recalled Charles Powell.[72] Tony Bishop registered the 'palpable human chemistry at work between them'.[73] He looked upon the occasion with his interpreter's eye: 'It struck me – not just as an observer but as one who had to be her voice and reflect her tone – that at such times I was witnessing something akin to a flirtation between two people with much to gain from and offer to each other: a flirtation that was pleasurable and stimulating but ultimately "safe" and platonic.'[74]*

After Gorbachev had left, Bernard Ingham came and asked Mrs Thatcher how he should brief the press. As Charles Powell remembered it, 'she was going on about how different he was from previous generations and how she could have a good discussion with him. I maintain that I said, "Yes, he's the sort of guy you can do business with." Bernard said, "That's it. A man to do business with." '[75] Ingham, however, insisted that he, not Powell, came up with the words while listening to Mrs Thatcher's account of their talks and then persuaded her to use the phrase with the media.[76] Whatever the parentage of the famous phrase, Ingham duly put

---

* Mrs Thatcher, who rarely had much time for the wives of her fellow world leaders, paid slightly beady attention to the well-dressed Mrs Gorbachev. She keenly scrutinized a report from Miss Horner, the Foreign Office official who accompanied Mrs Gorbachev on her shopping and cultural expeditions in London, underlining references to 'the jewelled drop-earrings' she bought for £750 at Mappin and Webb which revealed her 'as someone accustomed to living life on that level'. Mrs Thatcher was always very alert to the fact that the Soviet leadership lived in conditions of privilege, whereas the Soviet people went without. (Appleyard to Powell, Summary of Miss Horner's minute, 21 January 1985, Prime Minister's Papers, Soviet Union, UK/Soviet Relations, Part 4 (document consulted in the Cabinet Office).)

it out that night. Mrs Thatcher repeated it herself in interviews the next day.

Gorbachev himself took an almost identical view of what had happened. Talking to Richard Luce at the Speaker's dinner in his honour that followed the Chequers meeting, he pronounced himself 'very satisfied indeed with his talks with the Prime Minister. He had arrived with preconceived ideas about her attitude towards the Soviet Union. These had been proved wrong, and, to his great pleasure, he had established a good understanding with her.'[77] She had what he considered good ideas about each country defending its own interests: 'On such a basis, people could do business.'* The visit also helped Gorbachev's standing domestically. He had passed what Grachev termed the 'Thatcher test'. Given her reputation as a staunch anti-Communist, there was a feeling that if Gorbachev 'could make it in London, he could make it anywhere'.[78]

From his unique position in the Soviet Embassy, Oleg Gordievsky was critical of Mrs Thatcher's enthusiasm for Gorbachev. He felt at the time that 'The British were dreaming about a change, and grossly exaggerated what was coming.'[79] Mrs Thatcher found Gorbachev 'attractive and charming', but in Gordievsky's view, he seemed to most Russians, with his 'Tartar eyes', to be 'an oriental monster'. He was 'an apparatchik listening to himself with great pleasure'. He later came to think that 'the British intuition had been correct'[80] because Gorbachev was surrounded by genuine reformers such as Alexander Yakovlev,† who accompanied him to Chequers. Gordievsky's reports from the Embassy did, however, bring out the fact that Soviet officials themselves were excited by Gorbachev. Although no longer Gordievsky's case officer by the time of Gorbachev's visit, John Scarlett recalled that the Soviet hierarchy had conveyed 'an inchoate sense of weakness and vulnerability because of being left behind by American power: it was not clear how much the

---

* A curious incident indicates something of Gorbachev's own excitement about his British visit. On 19 December 1984, David Barclay, one of Mrs Thatcher's private secretaries who had remained in London when she flew to China, reported that at five o'clock that afternoon Gorbachev and his entourage had passed Downing Street on their way from Parliament to the Soviet Embassy. He had suddenly 'expressed a wish to see the outside of No. 10'. Special Branch had negotiated with the policeman at the barrier '(without informing us)', and he had been let in and then allowed to enter the front hall. 'They were gone before any private secretary had reached the spot – reportedly in good humour.' (FCO telegram 2520, 19 December 1984, Prime Minister's Papers, Soviet Union, UK/Soviet Relations, Part IV (document consulted in the Cabinet Office).)

† Alexander Yakovlev (1923–2005), joined the Communist Party in 1944; head of Department of Ideology and Propaganda, 1969–73; Soviet Ambassador to Canada, 1973–83; member of the Politburo, 1987–91; one of the main proponents of *perestroika* (restructuring).

gerontocracy understood. It was always clear that Gorbachev was the liberal, the reformer. He seemed different.'[81] Gordievsky also reported the enthusiastic Moscow feedback from the Chequers meeting. 'The phrase that Gorbachev always used [about the nuclear confrontation] was "We can't live like this." '[82] The Thatcher meeting made him feel that both sides could move towards the change required.

Buoyed up by these reactions, and enthusiastic press coverage, Mrs Thatcher had only one immediate problem about the Gorbachev visit – how it would go down in Washington. She probably had a slightly guilty conscience about her remarks to Gorbachev on SDI. In her memoirs, she makes much – too much – of how she reiterated her staunch support for America: 'My frankness on this was particularly important because of my equal frankness about what I saw as the President's unrealistic dream of a nuclear-free world.'[83] Her 'equal frankness' to Gorbachev about Reagan's 'unrealistic dream' gave ammunition to the enemy. The day after the Chequers visit, Powell wrote to the Foreign Office to advise that the report of the meeting offered to NATO allies should be kept fairly general, holding back specifics for Mrs Thatcher's meeting with Reagan on the coming Saturday. He added: 'Particular care should be taken in dealing with any suggestions that the Prime Minister distanced herself from President Reagan over the question of arms control in space.'[84] The 'particular care' was required because that is exactly what she had done.

Washington, where the administration was itself divided – Shultz on one side, Weinberger on the other – about whether the US should even agree to discuss SDI with the Soviets, was buzzing with rumours that Mrs Thatcher had gone too far. According to the *Washington Post*, 'President Reagan fervently hopes that during their meeting in Camp David this weekend his straight-talking conservative ally from London will get off the gee-whiz kick about the Kremlin's personable heir apparent . . . What shook White House insiders was the juxtaposition of Thatcher's "can-do-business" pledge and Gorbachev's assertion that killing Star Wars is the precondition for serious arms control negotiations.'[85] Both Shultz and McFarlane warned the President of differences between himself and Mrs Thatcher on SDI. The US Ambassador in London, Charlie Price, also weighed in with Reagan. 'During my first year in London, I have met with the PM perhaps 15 times,' Price wrote. 'In every meeting, she does most of the talking. On SDI, it's time she did some listening.'[86]

On 22 December 1984, Reagan received Mrs Thatcher's own report about the Chequers meeting. Using the already familiar phrase, Mrs Thatcher wrote, 'I certainly found him a man one could do business with. I actually rather liked him,'[87] but added, 'I got the impression that in some ways he was using me as a stalking horse for you . . . At the same time, he was on the look-out for possible divergences of view between us.' She downplayed talk of SDI but reported that Gorbachev had made the ABM Treaty a 'key stone' of his approach. 'I warned him of trying to drive wedges between the Allies.' She described the Russians as 'genuinely fearful' of the costs of technological advance in any arms race and 'therefore prepared to negotiate seriously on nuclear weapons if they believe that you are politically committed to reductions'.[88] She did not repeat what she had told Gorbachev about Reagan's 'dream' of a nuclear-free world.

If one looks at the week leading up to Christmas 1984, one can see how prodigious were Mrs Thatcher's powers of mental and physical endurance. On Sunday 16 December, she met Gorbachev at Chequers, a six-hour encounter which had required heavy preparation. On Monday evening, she set off for Peking to sign the Hong Kong Agreement with China on Wednesday 19 December, and went thence to Hong Kong itself to encourage a favourable reaction in the colony. Sending Geoffrey Howe back to London (she always travelled more happily without him), she then flew to Washington for the Camp David meeting on Saturday 22 December, returning to London in the early hours of the following day.

The flight from Hong Kong to Washington lasted twenty-four hours and included two stops and a twelve-hour time change The VC-10 in which they were travelling was far from luxurious, but it did have a bed for Mrs Thatcher in a curtained-off area. Some time into the flight Robin Butler announced his intention to get some sleep. 'Well, I'm not going to,' Mrs Thatcher replied. 'I'm going to stay awake for the 24 hours. And I'm going to study the ABM Treaty and Cap Weinberger's statements on the SDI.'[89] And so she did, staying in her seat for the entire journey.* The plane touched down in Honolulu in the early hours of the morning to refuel. The prime ministerial party were received by the base commanders, including one 'very sleepy admiral'. Mrs Thatcher, always eager to put her time to good use, said how sorry she was that she could not stay long enough to visit Pearl Harbor. It was still dark and her hosts seemed somewhat relieved. Pearl Harbor was just the other side of the airfield, they told her, but it was a long drive, all the way around the base perimeter, to get there. Mrs Thatcher's eyes lit up. 'Oh well,' she said, 'if it's just the other side, why don't we walk across?' 'Well, it's dark,' came the response. 'Ah,' she replied, 'but I have a torch in my handbag' (something she always

---

* Butler, meanwhile, persuaded the RAF crew to allow him to sleep on the floor of the plane on an inflatable mattress.

carried after the Brighton bomb that October). So the party set off, recalled Butler, 'She in her high-heeled shoes and this admiral and this air force commander dragging along. And we got to the edge of the airfield [by this time, it was dawn] and looked out over Pearl Harbor.' Mrs Thatcher's inspection complete, the party marched back whence they came. 'We got back on the plane and she resumed her study of the ABM Treaty and Cap Weinberger's speeches.'[90]

When she arrived at the Washington Embassy Mrs Thatcher ordered a briefing meeting at 11 p.m. She got up at six the next morning for a hairdressing appointment, which was followed by another briefing meeting, and then breakfast with Vice-President Bush. She reached Camp David, some 60 miles away, by helicopter at 10.30 a.m. She had been briefed by the Embassy that 'the President will be wearing an open-necked shirt, sweater and slacks . . . We have said that, since the Prime Minister will be giving a press conference immediately after Camp David, we doubt that she would wish to dress casually.' Mrs Thatcher was also warned to expect rather colder weather at Camp David than in Washington: 'the Prime Minister will wish to dress accordingly particularly because the President will meet the Prime Minister at the Camp David heli-pad in his golf cart . . . the reason for the golf cart is that the White House are keen to have a memorable and informal pre-Christmas photo opportunity.'[91] Mrs Thatcher stepped off the helicopter dressed, as predicted, formally. She wore a smart beige tweed suit for the ride in the cart with the casually dressed President.

As the Thatcher party flew round the world, Charles Powell had scribbled the key thoughts for the meeting on the back of his official programme for the visit to China. Headed '<u>President</u>', they began with 'E/W – Gorbachev' and then listed six points about arms control. It was, he scrawled, the 'Last chance to lodge ideas before Geneva meeting [when Shultz and Gromyko would reopen negotiations]. Need more links between various negotiations . . . Key quality is readiness of US to talk about blocking off some elements of SDI.'[92] This was, in essence, Mrs Thatcher's agenda.

Mrs Thatcher's Camp David meeting began tête-à-tête with Reagan, joined only by notetakers, and then moved into a wider gathering, including Shultz, McFarlane and others – but not, significantly, Weinberger* – which continued into a working lunch. At the private meeting with Reagan, Mrs

---

* Weinberger had been deliberately excluded. 'Colin Powell [his military assistant] tells me Cap is very desirous of attending,' one NSC staffer minuted McFarlane ahead of the meeting

Thatcher relayed her impressions of Gorbachev. She said 'he was an unusual Russian in that he was much less constrained, more charming, open to discussion and debate, and did not stick to prepared notes. His wife was equally charming. The Prime Minister noted that she often says to herself the more charming the adversary, the more dangerous.'[93] She reassured Reagan and the wider meeting that she 'had emphasized to Gorbachev that it would be a futile effort to try to divide Great Britain from the US'.[94]

At the private meeting, it was Reagan, not Mrs Thatcher, who broached SDI. He said he saw Soviet attacks on it as part of their propaganda preparations for the Geneva talks. He defended SDI: 'Its aim would strictly be to strengthen deterrence . . . if it [research] proves successful he would be willing to put this new technology into international hands. The President said we were not violating the ABM Treaty . . . The new Strategic Defense Initiative also has a moral context. We must search for ways to build a more stable peace. Our goal is to reduce, and eventually eliminate nuclear weapons.'[95] 'These remarks made me nervous,' Mrs Thatcher later wrote,[96] but she kept her peace for the time being and made it clear that she had let Gorbachev know that 'Britain supports the SDI program and told him it was not linked to a first strike strategy,'[97] which was the truth but not the whole truth. She also reported that Gorbachev had asked her to 'tell your friend President Reagan not to go ahead with space weapons'.[98] In doing so, she was not endorsing Gorbachev's comment but wanted Reagan to understand the impact SDI had made on the Soviet leadership. Unlike Gorbachev, she did not wish Reagan to abandon his efforts. Instead, as the British record made clear, she stressed the distinction between research, which she supported wholeheartedly, and deployment, for which she 'foresaw grave difficulties'.[99]

At the larger meeting, Mrs Thatcher reiterated her support for SDI research, but expressed her desire to know more about the subject, asking for an expert to be sent to London to brief her. She went quickly to the heart of her anxieties: 'She . . . understood that we will not know for some time if a strategic defense system is truly feasible. If we reached a stage where production looked possible we would have some serious and difficult decisions to take. There were ABM and outer space treaties . . . possible countering strategies must also be considered . . .'[100] According to Powell, she found 'the depth of Reagan's anti-nuclear sentiments . . . a very tricky issue for her to navigate: first, because she disagreed

(Untitled memo, CO 167: 270790–289999, WHORM File, Reagan Library). This plea went unheeded.

profoundly with it. Secondly, because it was capable of causing her immense embarrassment in the UK in the debate with CND and Kinnock over unilateral disarmament.'[101] She set out her own, unchanged view about nuclear weapons: 'Nuclear weapons have served not only to prevent a nuclear war, but they have also given us forty years of unprecedented peace in Europe. It would be unwise, she continued, to abandon a deterrence system that has prevented both nuclear and conventional war.'[102] 'We have some real worries,' she continued, 'especially about SDI's impact on deterrence. The wretched press has tried to make out that we have major differences. This is simply not true, but we do feel it is unwise to conclude where we will go on SDI, before the research programme is completed.' She had her doubts about whether the programme would be feasible: 'In the past, scientific genius had always developed a counter system. Even if an SDI system proved 95 per cent successful . . . over 60 million people would still die from those weapons that got through.'[103]

All this had quite an impact. 'Reagan was taken aback,' said Bud McFarlane. 'He had heard it through us, but it was palpable across the table from the Prime Minister. This was not a *pro forma* position at all. This was the first time he had grasped that the person he respected above all others was making a very compelling case. It was passionate. He was very sobered by it.'[104] He conceded that many of Mrs Thatcher's points needed to be addressed, but stuck to his vision. The argument then got more detailed and eventually more circular, with Reagan's lieutenants taking it up as their chief's attention began to wander. Bernard Ingham, who was present, noted that 'There were times in the log cabin when he didn't seem engaged at all.'[105]

At drinks before lunch, Mrs Thatcher seized the moment. 'Put these points down, the points we've been discussing, on a bit of paper,' she said to Powell, 'and we can see if we can't get them agreed.'[106] Powell and John Kerr,* the Head of Chancery, disappeared to a side room and got to work.† They produced a draft press statement, culminating in four points said to have been agreed by both the UK and the US. In Powell's view, this statement was not intended 'to be very very clever . . . It reflected

* John Kerr (1942–), educated Glasgow Academy and Pembroke College, Oxford; principal private secretary to Chancellor of the Exchequer, 1981–4; Head of Chancery, British Embassy, Washington, DC, 1984–7; Assistant Under-Secretary, FCO, 1987–90; Ambassador and UK Permanent Representative to EU, 1990–95; Ambassador to the United States, 1995–7; Permanent Under-Secretary, FCO, 1997–2002; created Lord Kerr of Kinlochard, 2004.
† Powell and Kerr dictated while Nigel Sheinwald, himself much later Ambassador to the US, hammered out the text on an old-fashioned typewriter.

principally what she said, but also what Reagan had not objected to.'[107] The draft said that Reagan and Mrs Thatcher, in relation to arms control negotiations and SDI, 'see matters in very much the same light', and warned the Soviet Union that 'Wedge-driving is just not on.' It had Mrs Thatcher saying, 'I told the President of my firm conviction that the SDI programme which at present is solely a research programme should go ahead.' Then it stated the four points of agreement. The first was that the US and the West aimed for balance, not superiority. The second said that 'SDI-related testing and deployment would, in view of treaty obligations, have to be a matter for negotiation.' Point 3 stated that 'The overall aim should be to maintain, not undercut, deterrence.' The fourth point said that the aim of resumed US–Soviet arms control negotiations would be 'to achieve security with reduced levels of offensive systems on both sides'.[108] Points 1, 3 and 4 essentially reflected American points with which the British agreed. Point 2, however, represented a British push which the Americans had been resisting. At no stage in the discussions had the Americans conceded that SDI was bound by treaty obligations. Point 2 was an important reassurance for Mrs Thatcher and for allies more generally.

Powell passed Mrs Thatcher the draft before the party had gone in to lunch. 'She read it and said, "That's fine." She handed it to the President who appeared to read it and nodded. He then handed it to George Shultz. This was the first time they had seen it.'[109] McFarlane and other US officials now looked at the draft, and quickly came back with minimal changes. They removed Powell's description of SDI as 'solely' a research programme. For Point 2, they took 'testing' out, leaving only 'deployment' as 'a matter for negotiation'.

The Four Points were a triumph for Mrs Thatcher. She had something clear to say at the press conference which would quell reports of differences between herself and Reagan. Much more important, she had an all-purpose form of words. As Powell put it, 'The Camp David points became the Bible. They were the basic text, the constitution. It did produce a position which could command broad support in the alliance as well, at a time when a lot of Europeans were throwing their hands in the air (in Britain too) and saying [SDI] would mean an end to arms control.'[110]

Nothing in the Four Points required Reagan to back away from SDI. But 'the Treaty of Camp David', as it was sometimes referred to in Washington, did alter the balance of forces within the administration. It upset the Pentagon and pleased the State Department as it geared up for negotiation. As Shultz put it in his memoirs: 'It was an excellent statement: it differentiated between research and deployment of space-based defense and gave me some running room in Geneva. Since the president had signed on, my instructions would reflect what had been agreed upon. The argument coming from Cap [Weinberger] and others at the Defense Department that we should not be willing to discuss SDI in any way was bypassed.'[111] Richard Burt, one of the State Department officials present at the meeting, explained the effect of the treaty: 'Nobody could come back and say "How could you have done this?" You'd just say, "The President and Mrs Thatcher did it." '[112]

As for Mrs Thatcher's views on Gorbachev, these too aroused anxieties in Washington, while at the same time influencing the administration. Many feared that she had been taken in or had even developed a 'schoolgirl crush on The Russian With A Smile'.[113] They believed, as Henry Kissinger put it, that 'Margaret may have fallen too easily into the British role, the Macmillan role, of mediating between the two sides.'[114] Richard Perle, at the Pentagon, described the danger as he saw it: 'There were people who were eager to change US policy fundamentally from the President's policy – of bringing the Soviet Union down – to more of a détente. So they would seize on the "do business" statement for their own purposes. It wasn't the statement so much as the way that it was likely to be viewed.'[115]

On the other hand, the person who has actually met someone in whom others are interested immediately acquires an advantage. The Americans were painfully badly informed about the Soviet leadership. 'We knew Gorbachev principally because he had this big red spot on the top of his head [his birthmark],' recalled Art Hartman, the US Ambassador in Moscow. 'I can't say that any of us on the outside knew a lot about what the hell was going on in the Politburo.'[116] They were deeply interested, therefore, in what Mrs Thatcher had to report. Reagan, already considering the possibilities for dialogue, listened to her with respect. As he later recalled: 'She told me that Gorbachev was different from any of the other Kremlin leaders. She believed that there was a chance of a opening. Of course, she was proven exactly right.'[117] Mrs Thatcher's views, and Reagan's willingness to listen to them, gave heart to those in the administration arguing for greater dialogue with Moscow. 'It was fundamental to be able to wrap ourselves in the support of Margaret Thatcher and Ronald Reagan,' said Roz Ridgway, who headed the State Department's European Bureau from 1985.[118] And precisely because Mrs Thatcher was the only foreign leader whom Cold War hawks regarded as sound, 'her opinions', as Shultz put it, 'had weight even with those who were dubious about the

merits of dialogue.'[119] As Colin Powell,* at that time serving as Weinberger's military assistant, later described it: 'along comes Gorby – he's
like none we've ever seen before – with his beautiful suits, his French ties
and a stunning wife who is every bit as smart as he is. And the first statement he got of acceptability was from Margaret . . . before he was even
General Secretary. The feeling was "Jesus, if dear old Margaret thinks
there's something here we'd better take a look." '[120]

A comparison between Mrs Thatcher's unhappiness in the aftermath
of Grenada and the strength of her position after Camp David showed
what an enormous difference the year 1984 had made. She had begun with
ill feeling towards her most important ally and a sense of gloomy stasis
in relation to the Communist bloc. Now both those things had changed.
In a single week, she held profoundly important conversations with the
likely future leader of the Soviet Union, contracted a treaty with Communist China, and persuaded the President of the United States to adopt
a new public stance on arms control. She had also weighed in powerfully
on the inter-agency debate in Washington over the merits of increasing
dialogue with Moscow. In her meetings both with Gorbachev and with
Reagan, she had combined courtesy with frankness, and even a certain
daring. Her interventions about SDI could have gone disastrously wrong
and her enthusiasm for Gorbachev could have made her look like a Soviet
dupe. In fact, her tactics had paid off. As she got home for Christmas after
a week circling the earth, she was entitled to tell herself that her country's
global influence rivalled anything Britain had enjoyed in the post-Suez era.

The New Year marked the 200th anniversary of US–UK diplomatic relations following Britain's defeat in the War of Independence. The US
government gave Mrs Thatcher replicas of a pair of silver candlesticks
which had belonged to John Adams at the time when the Treaty of Paris
established diplomatic links. 'The Prime Minister proposes that the candlesticks should stand on the Cabinet table with those already there,'
wrote Charles Powell to the Foreign Office, '(but don't tell anyone this
until we have had a look at them and made sure that they are not an eye-
sore).'[121] Despite the proximity of her Camp David visit, Mrs Thatcher
stuck to the earlier plan that she should visit Washington in February to
mark the occasion. On 20 February 1985, she stood on the White House
lawn while President Reagan paid tribute to the 200 years just

---

* Colin Powell (1937–), Senior Military Assistant to US Secretary of Defense, 1983–6;
Deputy National Security Advisor, 1986–7; National Security Advisor, 1987–9; General,
1989; chairman, Joint Chiefs of Staff, 1989–93; Secretary of State, 2001–5.

commemorated: 'Over the years these relations have taken on a very special quality. In fact, they're quite extraordinary. We as Americans are proud of our relations with our allies the British and I am personally proud of my close collaboration with my friend Margaret Thatcher.'[122]

Along with the genuine goodwill, his friend had prepared for her visit with her usual exacting thoroughness. The biggest formal occasion of the visit was Mrs Thatcher's Joint Address to Congress, an honour which had not been accorded to any British prime minister since Winston Churchill. Even by her own standards, Mrs Thatcher's rehearsal was exhausting. 'I remember that a lot of the visit was concerned with the blasted speech,' said Charles Powell. She was using a teleprompter for the first time and so she 'practised it until about five in the morning and we got an hour's sleep before she was doing the morning television programmes ahead of a full day – having flown in late the night before. It was one of the least attractive nights of my time.'[123] Mrs Thatcher's speech was naturally flattering to her hosts: 'The debt the free peoples of Europe owe to this nation, generous with its bounty, willing to share its strength, seeking to protect the weak, is incalculable.'[124] But when she invoked Churchill she did so not just out of piety, but to serve the purpose of her argument. 'No-one understood the importance of deterrence more clearly than Winston Churchill,' she declared,

> when in his last speech [in 1952] to you he said: 'Be careful above all things not to let go of the atomic weapon until you are sure and more than sure that other means of preserving peace are in your hands!' Thirty-three years on, those weapons are still keeping the peace, but since then technology has moved on and if we are to maintain deterrence – as we must – it is essential that our research and capacity do not fall behind the work being done by the Soviet Union [applause]. That is why I firmly support President Reagan's decision to pursue research into defence against ballistic nuclear missiles – the Strategic Defence Initiative [applause].[125]

Her declaration was rapturously received. Newspapers immediately took up her words as an endorsement of SDI, which is what she had intended; but she framed SDI as being crucial for the maintenance of deterrence, not as the means to a nuclear free world. As ever, she focused her supportive words on 'research' rather than 'deployment'.

She developed her argument in an arms control 'seminar' with Reagan after lunch at the White House.* In the period between the Camp David

---

* Most authors (including Aldous, *Reagan and Thatcher*, p. 201; Aitken, *Margaret Thatcher*, p. 490; and John Campbell, *Margaret Thatcher: The Iron Lady*, Jonathan Cape, 2003, p. 292) have followed Geoffrey Smith (*Reagan and Thatcher*, Bodley Head, 1990, p.

meeting and this session, there had been a good deal of transatlantic traffic. In early January, Reagan had sent Bud McFarlane to brief Mrs Thatcher in greater detail on SDI. McFarlane brought with him General James Abrahamson,* the Director of the SDI Programme. Despite the Four Points, Reagan was still uneasy about Mrs Thatcher's attitude. It was a clever move by the Americans to bring Abrahamson along. Mrs Thatcher liked 'General Abe' and his presence flattered her pride. 'She thought as a scientist she understood those things better than others,' Charles Powell recalled. 'She loved all the talk of "garages in space" and "brilliant pebbles".'[126] After their meeting in early January, the two began to correspond and meet. McFarlane had also used the visit to plant the idea that SDI research could bring business to British companies. This excited Mrs Thatcher and helped to make the Ministry of Defence in London more supportive. The US was trying to bind her in.

The fact remained, however, that her approach to SDI and nuclear weapons was still no closer to Reagan's. Worse, Reagan continued to speak out against accepted nuclear doctrine. '[We] must seek another means of deterring war,' the President wrote just days after the meeting at Camp David. 'It is both militarily and morally necessary.'[127] This talk of morality worried Mrs Thatcher because it gave succour to the unilateralists back in Britain. On the handwritten speaking card she had prepared for the meeting, Mrs Thatcher noted (with seemingly random inverted commas):

Watchful of where 'nuclear immoral could lead'
a) Unilateral disarmament
b) Why deploy cruise – just when we need to.
c) why modernise Polaris to Trident.
Have to rely on nuclear deterrent for many years to come.[128]

At the White House 'seminar', she argued that the Soviets would probably hold reductions in nuclear arms hostage to limiting research on SDI and suggested that the West turn the tables: the Americans should warn Moscow that unless it agreed to such reductions, work on SDI would

---

165) in dating this seminar to July 1987. In fact, during her visit to Washington that summer Mrs Thatcher did not meet Reagan, who was recovering from surgery.

* Lieutenant General James Abrahamson (1933–), educated Massachusetts Institute of Technology and University of Oklahoma; lieutenant general (retired) US Air Force; astronaut with the Manned Orbiting Laboratory Program, 1967–9; Associate Administrator at NASA, responsible for the US space shuttle program, 1981–4; Director, Strategic Defense Initiative 1984–9.

proceed apace.* Then, following her speaking notes, she explained how difficult it was to present SDI in Europe because of the need to maintain public support for cruise and Pershing and modernize Britain's own nuclear missiles: 'We must not get into a situation where people were told that nuclear weapons were wicked, immoral and might soon be rendered unnecessary by the development of defensive systems.'[129]

Reagan reassured her that the United Kingdom could 'rely on the over-all protection of the Alliance and NATO nuclear weapons', but he noted that SDI was 'designed to render obsolete a strategy based on the nuclear destruction of populations. It was not a bargaining chip.' Back came Mrs Thatcher with her belief that, for the foreseeable future, nuclear weapons would remain 'the essential deterrent of war'. Reagan did not argue with this. Although his ultimate goal was to render nuclear weapons obsolete, before this day came he had no intention of letting the Soviets gain the upper hand in the arms race. 'The United States was determined to bring its strength up to balance with the Soviet Union . . .' he reminded Mrs Thatcher. 'It was the realisation of this which had persuaded them to negotiate.'[130] On this they agreed.

Mrs Thatcher's public statement on departure spoke of 'a real meeting of minds'.[131] But, in personal terms, the meeting was rather unsuccessful. Mrs Thatcher seemed somewhat ill at ease, which Charles Powell attrib-uted to the fact that 'she had been manoeuvred into taking Geoffrey Howe and Michael Heseltine. They attended the plenary session and had the impertinence to say something! Not what she wanted. She regarded herself as the only true spokesman of her government with the President.'[132]† By this time, she already felt the hostility towards Heseltine which was to overflow in the Westland crisis at the end of the year. She reacted, as she so often did when feeling anxious, by being repetitive and strident. On and on she went. After about ten minutes of this, Ken Adelman noticed Reagan 'kind of inhaling and ready . . . to talk, and Margaret Thatcher says, "One minute Ronnie, I'm almost finished." And she goes on.'[133] After the meeting broke up, Adelman observed 'someone turning to Reagan as we walked down the hallway, and saying, "Boy, she's not a very good

---

* This 'reverse hostage' concept was first suggested to Mrs Thatcher by Charles Powell.
† George Shultz observed this tendency. An early draft of his memoirs contained a passage, removed before publication, noting that Mrs Thatcher had 'a wonderful Foreign Secretary, Sir Geoffrey Howe, who I saw a great deal of and came to admire. But Margaret Thatcher seemed to pay little attention to him . . . It was always a puzzle to me how one could do it this way. I know that, if I had been in Geoffrey's shoes I simply wouldn't have stood for it.' (Unpublished draft, 'G. P. Shultz – Great Britain', Box 61, Papers of Charles Hill, Hoover Institution.)

listener, is she?" And Reagan, face lights up, turns to this person and says, "No, but she's a marvellous talker!" '[134]

No sense of frustration at Mrs Thatcher's seminar performance, however, permeated the atmosphere at the British Embassy dinner that night. On an occasion packed with sentiment but also genuine affection, guests dined on poached salmon 'Nancy', fillet of veal 'special relationship' and raspberry mousse 'Margaret'.[135] Ronald and Nancy Reagan insisted on attending, ignoring the general rule that the President did not dine out in foreign embassies. They were keen to come because, as McFarlane put it, 'This was family. That's the way he felt about it. Mrs Reagan too. They liked Denis. They liked the Prime Minister.* To him this was kind of a child of Churchill. This was the person above all others whom he was privileged to know in his presidency and he was confident would have an enduring place in history. Any occasion that offered a chance to elevate the standing of Prime Minister Thatcher he would do.'[136]

---

* It may be doubted whether Mrs Reagan was quite as close to Mrs Thatcher as her husband was. That evening, Mrs Reagan was seen to be irritated by her husband's desire to stay late and go on talking to Mrs Thatcher (private information). In the view of Charlie Price, without their mutual admiration for Ronald Reagan, Mrs Reagan and Mrs Thatcher 'wouldn't ever have been close personal friends' (Interview with Charles Price).

9

Arms and the Woman

'Your Majesty, who do you trust –
Mitterrand or Mrs Thatcher?'

On 11 March 1985, just after the miners' strike had collapsed, the death of Konstantin Chernenko was announced in Moscow. His short reign had been a nullity. Within four hours, Mikhail Gorbachev was proclaimed his successor. As with Andropov's funeral the previous year, Mrs Thatcher decided to attend;* she left London the following day. Very unusually, she wrote a manuscript account of her visit. It was entitled 'Return to Moscow' and was composed as soon as she returned to London.[1]† Mrs Thatcher noted her memories and impressions with an almost schoolgirl innocence, rather like a 'What I did in the holidays' essay, an impression added to by her only intermittent punctuation. 'On the plane', she recorded,

> I read and analysed Mr. Gorbachev's Acceptance speech – (no deviation from settled policies but more initiative needed – their fundamental dilemma!) – and also a speech he had recently made at Kiev. All confirmed the impression gained at Chequers the previous December, that even if he wished to change matters he wouldn't know how to, because a rigid Communist system was the only one he had ever known.[2]

When her party reached Moscow, they were greeted by a fleet of cars: 'They gave me a very large one and as the Ambassador [Sir Iain Sutherland] climbed in beside me I signalled to him circling my hand in the air, was the car likely to be "bugged". He nodded and the conversation proceeded carefully!' Mrs Thatcher was struck by the lack of lights in the shops and the dirtiness of the streets. When they reached the Ambassador's residence, the motherly Prime Minister presented the staff with 'masses of fresh vegetables and fruit and English cheese because that is

---

* President Reagan, however, decided otherwise: 'My gut instinct said no' (11 March 1985, Ronald Reagan, *The Reagan Diaries*, HarperCollins, 2007, p. 307).
† It is not clear why Mrs Thatcher kept this account. It contains little political analysis, and ends without recording her substantive conversation with Gorbachev. It is possible that she intended to write up the entire trip, but never found time to finish it.

what they wanted most'. She was much impressed by the architecture and opulent decoration of the residence – 'a magnificent house, built by a sugar baron who married into the aristocracy and built a suitable house for such a bride'.[3]

At the funeral the next day ('Funerals are great occasions for meeting other heads of government'), Mrs Thatcher laid a wreath and then met Chernenko's family:

> some in tears and all deeply grieved. It is really a terrible ordeal for them. Mrs Chernenko is such a nice woman. I shook hands with her and she pointed to her neighbour who was crying, saying in English 'his sister', and then 'daughters'. Even the head of a communist country who has no sympathy for those who disagree, nevertheless has a family who sorrow for him.[4]

Then, with her usual attention to dignity and presentation, she stood still and erect for the speeches and march-past. According to her interpreter Tony Bishop, Mrs Thatcher 'acquired heroic status in the eyes of the Russian TV audience by standing, unflinching, on Red Square ... while the ceremonies slowly unrolled in an air temperature of minus 12'.[5] The weather 'felt very raw', she wrote. 'I do not possess a fur coat so make myself as warm as possible in a wool coat and fur-lined boots. In my pockets I carry warm packs which help a little.' She remembered how, at Andropov's funeral, she had bumped into Mrs Gandhi as they arrived: 'Alas, neither of us could have foreseen that she would no longer be with us because of the assassin's bullet.'[6]*

As was often the case when she saw parades, Mrs Thatcher was much taken with the soldiers – 'very fine young men, superbly tailored grey greatcoats, white gloves, black boots, grey fur hats. They didn't move a muscle.' But although she remarked on the good order of the occasion, she noticed what it lacked:

> When I first attended a Communist funeral (Tito's) it had been a shock to realise that it contained no religious element whatsoever. Of course one knew that intellectually but just a final political ceremony – it seemed comfortless and matter of fact. Mr Chernenko's funeral had a let's get it over conveyor quality about it.[7]

'The speeches began,' she went on. 'The voice and command of Mr Gorbachev in such striking contrast with the hesitancy and muffed words of

---

* Mrs Thatcher was probably comparing Mrs Gandhi's fate – she had been assassinated on 31 October 1984 – with her own good fortune in surviving the Brighton bomb in the same month unscathed.

Mr. Chernenko's a year previously at Mr. Andropov's funeral.' Once the funeral was over 'the mood changed sharply as the band struck up for the march past – and very impressive it is – all officers marching in goose step (which we hate because of its connections but which they still adopt) each row matched perfectly in height.'

Then the guests were moved to St George's Hall for the reception. Mrs Thatcher was much impressed:

> St. George's Hall is unbelievably beautiful. Lofty, all in white with the most magnificent chandeliers augmented by hundreds of electric candle lights marching in continuous line just below the cornice. And not a single bulb had gone! Every one was working! The file climbed slowly up the long staircase passing a rather wonderful picture of Lenin addressing a Youth Congress at the top.

Luckily, Mrs Thatcher did not have to wait too long contemplating Lenin because the protocol officer presented himself and said, ' "Ladies first" – come along Mrs. T we must move you forward.' Accompanied by the similarly favoured Imelda Marcos of the Philippines, she ' "queue jumped" right into St. George's Hall feeling a little guilty for we British don't like queue-jumping. We all shook hands with the reception party, Mr. Gorbachev, the Prime Minister and Mr. Gromyko.'[8] At this point, she said nothing more to Gorbachev than the formalities of condolence and congratulation. She would see him again that evening.

Their encounter, scheduled for fifteen minutes, lasted nearly an hour. The speaking note for the meeting, prepared by Charles Powell, sought to counter the Soviet belief that she had hardened her support for SDI since the Chequers meeting. The Powell line read, 'As I said to you at Chequers, it is a dream which he [Reagan] has: and like all dreams no one can know whether it is capable of being realised.'[9] She should emphasize that Reagan saw SDI as replacing nuclear weapons in 'both East and West' and had promised to negotiate deployment under the ABM Treaty.* On this paper, Mrs Thatcher wrote, 'New occasions teach new duties,' a quotation from one of her favourite hymns, by James Russell Lowell, which begins 'Once to every man and nation comes the moment to decide / . . . for the good or evil side.'

Sure enough, Gorbachev brought up SDI almost as soon as their meeting began, complaining of the 'enormous danger' of transferring nuclear weapons to space. This was an empty charge as SDI did not envisage such

---

* In fact, SDI deployment would have required some renegotiation (if not complete abrogation) of the ABM Treaty.

a transfer. But Mrs Thatcher, keen to point to her own pivotal role, ignored this and explained that the Camp David agreement had changed matters; it 'was the first time that the Americans had been persuaded to put publicly on record that any deployment would require negotiation'.[10] Each leader emphasized the importance of future personal dialogue. Mrs Thatcher said that 'If Mr. Gorbachev ever wished to send a message to her, she would be very ready to receive it.' Gorbachev acknowledged this invitation and said that 'the general trend of his discussion with the Prime Minister . . . was something which he took a liking to.'[11] He wanted an 'expanded dialogue'. Tony Bishop noted that 'When Gromyko chipped in that this could perhaps best be done by exchange of messages, Gorbachev pointedly went on to say that . . . he had been impressed by his discussion with the Prime Minister . . . "We must continue to meet, talk to each other and exchange views." '[12]

Mrs Thatcher turned on all possible charm. The Russian interpreter, Sukhodrev, gave his version of the meeting to Gorbachev's aide Anatoly Chernyaev:

> [she] was all over him, charming him, fascinating him and he responded in kind. That's evidently the way she 'does politics' and with the help of M. S. [Gorbachev] she wants to outflank the likes of Kohl and Mitterrand – even Reagan himself – in world affairs. And she likes to use her woman's wiles to play games with Gorbachev in particular.[13]

As an analysis of Mrs Thatcher's methods and mindset, this was perceptive, but, whatever her search for personal power, she was certainly not so foolish as to try to cut the Americans out of anything. Before seeing Gorbachev, she had met Vice-President George Bush, representing the US at the funeral, to co-ordinate their approaches. Bush had told her in confidence that he would give Gorbachev a letter from Reagan suggesting that the two men meet, his first proposal of a formal summit since he had entered the White House. George Shultz, who was present, had told her that their focus on Gorbachev had originated with her. He had also suggested that, when Gorbachev threw SDI at her in their meeting, she should emphasize the Four Points from Camp David: 'This was firm ground.'[14] She had given her own view of Gorbachev to the Americans. 'He was formed by the system,' she had said. '. . . He would probably go the same way as Andropov in trying to make the existing system work better.' But, she added, he dominated the Politburo: 'he had the ability, the personality and the will.'[15]

There is no doubt that, in terms of Anglo-American relations, and of wider prestige among the allies, Gorbachev's emergence as the Soviet leader greatly helped Mrs Thatcher. Charles Powell believed that 'The key to understanding Mrs Thatcher and Gorbachev is that she felt, from quite early on, that she was investing hugely in him. She was like a hedge fund manager. She had decided that she was going to buy Gorbachevs and profit from them. She was very keen to keep him in play.'[16] Gorbachev seemed equally keen. A couple of months later, the Ambassador, Sutherland, reported a conversation he had had with an official in Gorbachev's office: 'Mrs Thatcher had made a great impression on Gorbachev. He was always speaking about her. It was true that there were many problems where Britain and the Soviet Union differed . . . but this was an instance where a personal relationship could have an effect upon the course of history.'[17]

It was not necessarily easy, however, for Mrs Thatcher to sustain the personal relationship, or her prominent role, once she returned from Moscow. Although the East–West mood was improved, Britain played no direct part in negotiations over nuclear weapons. The Soviets remained highly suspicious, and the Americans uncertain. No Western power, including Britain, had good lines of communication to the Soviet hierarchy.*

The Soviets, however, recognized that their ties to London were now far stronger than their ties to Washington. Herein lay a significant part of Mrs Thatcher's appeal. There was a danger that she would either try to exercise a greater influence than she truly possessed, thereby irritating at least one of the two great powers, or, on the other hand, fail to develop her own strengths. After all, if she were successful in persuading Reagan to deal with the Soviets, the logic might be that Britain would be redundant: having effected the introduction, Mrs Thatcher might find herself being asked to leave the party. Although a leader who always sold herself in public as a 'conviction politician', Mrs Thatcher was, in her approaches to the Soviet Union and in her role of persuader in Washington, displaying the skills which, in theory, she disparaged – those of a diplomat. These would be tested over the coming months.

---

* An indication of the detail with which anything emanating from Moscow was studied can be seen in the reaction to an intentionally comic letter sent by Mrs Gorbachev to Michael Jopling, the Minister of Agriculture, more than seven months after they had met at Chequers: 'Esteemed Mr Jopling, At Chequers, I told you that in Byelorussia we had 300 recipes for potatoes . . . My apologies for being somewhat inaccurate: in fact, there are 500, rather than 300, recipes to cook potatoes.' Mrs Gorbachev enclosed the recipe book. Charles Powell forwarded the note to Mrs Thatcher with the words 'Fascinating evidence of a new style!' (Raisa Gorbachev to Jopling, 19 July 1985, Prime Minister's Papers, Soviet Union, UK/Soviet Relations, Part 4 (document consulted in the Cabinet Office).)

It did not help that her own Foreign Secretary broke ranks. On the way home from Moscow, Charles Powell was shown the text of a major speech to the Royal United Services Institute (RUSI) which Geoffrey Howe was about to give. Powell's task was to vet it for No. 10's approval, but as he put it: 'I'm ashamed to say that two pages into it I dropped asleep and never read any more.'[18] He sent a *pro forma* letter to Howe saying that the Prime Minister had 'seen and approved' the speech. Unfortunately, for Powell, the content was not, in fact, soporific. Howe had decided to attack SDI.

Perhaps irritated by Mrs Thatcher's tendency to ignore him, Howe warned that, even if SDI worked exactly as planned in stopping all ballistic missiles, it would not deal with the other sorts of nuclear weapons. Howe's memorable phrase was that 'there would be no advantage in creating a new Maginot Line* of the 21st century liable to be outflanked by relatively simpler and demonstrably cheaper countermeasures.'[19] Howe's views were not, in themselves, completely at odds with Mrs Thatcher's, but his decision to express them publicly, after the agreement of the Four Points at Camp David, 'appeared to undercut her deal with the President'.[20] American suspicions of British sincerity were naturally aroused. Richard Perle, attending a conference in London, was furious. 'It was a kind of furtive undermining', he recalled, '. . . which struck me as wrong and even cowardly.'[21] Without clearing anything with Washington, Perle redrafted his conference speech, adding the memorable riposte that Sir Geoffrey's speech 'proved an old axiom of geometry that length is no substitute for depth'.[22]

Mrs Thatcher, too, was furious with Howe and dressed down Charles Powell so severely that he thought he might be sacked.[23] *The Times*, whose editor Charles Douglas-Home and contributor David Hart knew Mrs Thatcher's mind, branded Howe's intervention 'mealy-mouthed, muddled in conception, negative, Luddite, ill-informed'. So helpful was the speech to the Soviets, the paper continued, that it might best be described as 'the Gorbachov [sic] amendment'.[24] In a letter to Reagan reporting on Chernenko's funeral, Mrs Thatcher added a final paragraph: 'I look forward to keeping in the closest touch with you as the talks proceed. I can assure you of our continuing support. Our position has <u>not</u> changed, <u>whatever</u> you may have heard or read.'[25] The underlining was in her own hand, a point made very clear to the Americans.[26] Reagan obligingly told a press

---

* The Maginot Line was France's means of defence against Germany in the 1930s which proved quite useless when Hitler went round the fortifications and entered France through Belgium in 1940.

conference that, though surprised by what Howe had said, 'I do know we have the support of Prime Minister Thatcher and therefore the English [sic] Government in our research for the Strategic Defense Initiative.'[27] Only a little damage was done, and the incident helped make it clear once again that it was Mrs Thatcher herself, rather than any of her ministers, who was the architect and executor of British policies. It therefore did her no harm in Washington.

In continuing to pursue her search for dialogue with the Soviets, Mrs Thatcher had greater difficulties with the US administration than with her own. Under pressure from those who worried he was going too fast, Reagan looked as if he might slow down moves towards a summit with Gorbachev. He told Shultz he thought November was too early for any summit anywhere. In June 1985, after being urged by the Russian-American oil wheeler-dealer Armand Hammer that he should meet Gorbachev 'one-to-one' in Moscow, Reagan noted in his diary: 'He's convinced "Gorby" is a different type than past Soviet leaders & that we can get along. I'm too cynical to believe that.'[28] There seems little doubt, however, that Reagan did consistently want the meeting to take place. Mrs Thatcher's role was to push him a bit further in the direction he anyway sought, helping to ease his position with his own conservative backers. As Henry Kissinger put it, 'Reagan was determined to have a meeting with the Soviet leader. Mrs Thatcher's views gave him the moral strength, the encouragement to do it. Shultz undoubtedly also wanted a meeting. So you can't say she shifted the debate from "no" to "yes". But on a continuum, a swing of the pendulum, she pushed him closer to a meeting.'[29] On 3 July, a Reagan–Gorbachev summit was announced for November, in Geneva.

At the same time, Gorbachev was keen to take up Mrs Thatcher's open invitation to send her messages. On 7 May 1985, the fortieth anniversary of VE Day, he wrote to her recalling the 'gigantic efforts' of his own country against 'fascist tyranny'. The Soviet people, he said, 'harbour feelings of respect for the gallantry of the British people who made a sizeable contribution to achieving the victory'.[30] Now, he went on, it was essential to stop a new war by 'preventing the militarization of space' (Soviet parlance for SDI): 'The Soviet Union is prepared to cooperate with Great Britain – its former ally in the anti-Hitlerite coalition – in achieving these noble goals.' It was not hard, of course, for Mrs Thatcher to spot – and resist – such a blatant piece of wedge-driving, but the message was evidence of the danger inherent in leading the field for engagement with Gorbachev. There was a thin line between being a pioneer for peace and being a 'useful idiot'.

In fact, though, Gorbachev's message coincided with Mrs Thatcher's growing enthusiasm for SDI, and did nothing to counteract it. The Americans' policy of flattering her by briefing her on the scientific aspects of the programme was working. So was their offer that British companies might share in the research contracts that would emerge. Her first meeting with General Abrahamson in January had been very successful. In late July, she visited Washington again. She was not able to see Reagan because he was convalescing from a second operation for cancer. This contributed to a sense that his presidency was weakening. The British Ambassador, Sir Oliver Wright, reported on the eve of her visit that 'There is a curious disparity between the President's popularity, and the way he discharges with grace and general approval his role as head of state, and <u>his inability as head of government to make his policies prevail</u>.'[31] Mrs Thatcher underlined the second half of the sentence. She spoke to Reagan on the telephone while visiting Vice-President Bush. 'His voice sounded strong, very strong,' she told the press afterwards.[32]* But business had to be transacted elsewhere.

She saw Abrahamson and Caspar Weinberger. The meeting with Abrahamson was a 'highly restricted' briefing; its effect was to increase Mrs Thatcher's excitement. Abrahamson remembered it with pleasure:

> Mrs Thatcher responded to our meeting both with understanding and great curiosity about where SDI could go and how fast it could go, right from the beginning. Sure, she had some doubts. But she was delightful. She asked very good questions that would range from the deterrence basis to how are we going to get there? She loved the latter. At the end of the briefing she said, 'I would like for you to plan for us to meet at least three times a year. I want to hear about this.'[33]

Weinberger and Abrahamson were only too happy to oblige. They could see how it would help:

> She set up a paradigm for all our meetings. She let it be known that I was coming with my one CIA guy – that was our whole briefing team – and then she would never invite anybody from the MOD (or elsewhere in the government). You can imagine that afterwards I was the most popular guy

---

* Privately, Charles Powell reported, 'The Prime Minister commented that the President's voice sounded firm and he appeared in good spirits. Mrs Reagan, who also spoke, sounded by contrast careworn and under strain.' Bush confirmed this: 'he was worried about her. She had nagging doubts as to whether the President's cancer had really been eliminated. She also thought that the President's staff were "bearing down" on him unnecessarily and pushing him to get back to work.' (Powell to Appleyard, 29 July 1985, Prime Minister's Papers, USA: Prime Minister's Visit to the USA on 25/26 July 1985 (document consulted in the Cabinet Office).)

in town. She did that deliberately. She never said it, but it was very clear that she understood her own bureaucracy very well.[34]

Her own bureaucracy could only, ruefully, agree. As John Weston, from the Foreign Office, put it:

> The Americans sensed the various attitudes at work in the system. So they decided that the way to do this was to get round the political blockages in the FCO, cut them out and go straight to her. They felt that if they could get Abrahamson (a charming, starry fellow) in with Mrs Thatcher, then he could fill her up with all this stuff until it was coming out of her ears.[35]

In Mrs Thatcher's own mind, the briefings also gave her more power behind the scenes with the Americans. 'She wanted to understand it and shape it,' Abrahamson recalled. 'I absolutely valued her input and so did the President. I met with the President quite often. I would always use those occasions to say ". . . and Mrs Thatcher made these points." And he would say, "Awww. That's interesting." '[36] Probably Mrs Thatcher, always proud of her Oxford science degree, was inclined to exaggerate her own grasp of the technicalities and therefore her effect on the shape of the project. Certainly it served Reagan and his colleagues to say 'Awww. That's interesting' about something she had said, even if they thought it wasn't. It made it easier for them to bring her with them. But the Abrahamson conversations were part of a wider process by which Mrs Thatcher was placed in a position of trust and knowledge, thereby attaining far more political influence than any other non-US citizen.

At her Washington meeting with Weinberger, the Defense Secretary informed Mrs Thatcher that, in SDI research, 'The barriers were crumbling.'[37] There was a list of areas where Britain could get involved in the research work. Emboldened, perhaps, by her relationship of mutual admiration with Weinberger, Mrs Thatcher adopted an almost peremptory tone. Britain 'would not be fobbed off with a few small contracts', she said; '. . . it should be clear that Britain was in a different category to other countries.' Weinberger answered drily that 'there might be some unenlightened people in Congress who failed to recognise this. The Prime Minister replied that it was the Administration's task to tell them.'[38]* Weinberger also expressed caution and anxiety about the summit. The Soviets, he said, wanted to restrict SDI research solely to ground-held ABM systems, offering reductions in offensive strategic weapons in return.

---

* Despite Mrs Thatcher's admonition, by 1990 British SDI research contracts totalled just $81.9 million, a very small share of a multi-billion-dollar pie (cited in Stanley Orman, *Faith in G.O.D.S: Stability in the Nuclear Age*, Elsevier, 1991, p. 96).

This would be highly disadvantageous, but he was frightened Congress would grab it. He told Mrs Thatcher that he thought the Reagan–Gorbachev summit would have no great developments but would be 'a "feel" meeting'. Mrs Thatcher thought this inadequate. Problems at the current negotiations made it 'all the more important to ensure that the summit itself was a success and gave them a fresh impetus'.[39]

The formal purpose of Mrs Thatcher's Washington visit was to attend the conference of the International Democrat Union, which she and Reagan had founded 'to bring together Conservative parties from different parts of the world and to balance the European Democrat Union (EDU) which was mostly Christian Democrats and not – in her view – really Conservative'.[40] She used her public speech at the gathering to warn about how the build-up to the summit could go wrong:

> Mrs Thatcher noted that Mr Reagan and Mr Gorbachev are to meet in Geneva in November, and she asserted that this fall 'our peoples will be presented with alluring prospects' – if the United States will give up President Reagan's Strategic Defense Initiative . . . and if the French and British will give up their nuclear deterrents. The Prime Minister drew her loudest applause when she asserted: 'This we will not do.'[41]

For most of 1985, then – especially once the Geneva summit was set for November – Mrs Thatcher saw it as her task to continue to engage with the Soviet Union. During the summer these efforts faced their stiffest test to date as Mrs Thatcher became embroiled in the most important espionage confrontation of her time in office. At the end of April, Oleg Gordievsky was appointed KGB resident-designate in London, but, on 16 May, he was suddenly called to Moscow, ostensibly for high-level briefings, but actually to be interrogated as a suspected British agent.* Despite interrogation by the KGB, assisted by the use of drugs, Gordievsky did not confess, and was told to take some time off (while the KGB kept an eye on him). British intelligence realized this offered the only opportunity. Thanks to a carefully prepared plan, he escaped his KGB minders and was 'exfiltrated' over the Finnish border, though without his wife and children. He arrived at Heathrow on 22 July 1985. He then underwent a two-month debriefing session. The news of his defection was not

---

* It is still not known what prompted Moscow's suspicion. Some believe Aldrich Ames, a Soviet mole in the CIA, was the first to give Gordievsky away. Gordievsky, however, insists that his cover was blown by 'another, as yet unidentified source outside the British intelligence community'. (Christopher Andrew, *The Defence of the Realm: The Authorized History of MI5*, Allen Lane, 2009, p. 726.)

immediately known to the Russians, and the KGB suspected he had committed suicide.[42] On 15 August, Moscow was officially informed of Gordievsky's
defection, but it was not publicly announced, in the hope that this would
make it possible for the Soviet authorities to allow his wife and children to
join him. As was usual KGB policy in such cases, this request was refused.

To date, there had been no communication at all between Mrs Thatcher
and Gorbachev on the issue. But in late August, while on holiday in the
flat she continued to rent at Scotney Castle in Kent, Mrs Thatcher was
informed that the Soviet Chargé d'Affaires had an 'urgent and personal
letter' for her from Gorbachev, which he wanted to deliver in person.[43]
The context, of course, heightened the drama. With Gordievsky on British
soil, what 'urgent and personal' missive did Gorbachev wish to impart?
Mrs Thatcher pronounced herself amenable to this meeting and soon
afterwards, as was usual practice, she received an advance copy of Gorbachev's message. She promptly discovered that the letter was neither
particularly urgent nor particularly personal. It was a message with intentions similar to those of his letter on VE Day: to drive a wedge between
London and Washington. The issue this time was nuclear testing, on which
Gorbachev had recently called for a moratorium. He sought a positive
response from the US and now appealed for Mrs Thatcher's help.[44] She
did not reply to Gorbachev's message and, hearing that the British Ambassador in Moscow had been told to expect a summons from Gorbachev
himself, went back on her original readiness to meet the Chargé. The
British came to realize that these manoeuvres were part of a scheme to
delay, embarrass and confuse the British government while the Soviets
worked out how to handle the Gordievsky defection. Bryan Cartledge,
the British Ambassador, was kept waiting for several days for the promised
summons from Gorbachev which never came.[45]

To some in the British foreign policy establishment, including Cartledge, Gordievsky was an irritating distraction, but Mrs Thatcher believed
strongly in his importance and was passionately committed to his welfare.
She understood, as Christopher Curwen, the then 'C' (head) of SIS, put
it, that 'It's almost unique that the Prime Minister has a source who tells
her what the Russians were up to,'[46] and she valued Gordievsky accordingly. It was she personally, rather than, as was more usual in such matters,
the Foreign Secretary, who authorized Gordievsky's exfiltration. Despite
the difficulties she knew this would cause in her relationship with Gorbachev she agreed the plan without hesitation. 'We never thought for a
minute that Mrs T would stop us,' recalled Colin McColl,[47] who at that
time was Curwen's deputy. In August, during his debrief at a fort in southern England, while in very low sprits, Gordievsky received a personal letter

from Mrs Thatcher telling him to be cheerful and not give up hope that his wife and children would get back to him.[48] In all her subsequent meetings with Gorbachev, she always pleaded vigorously for the release of the Gordievsky family, and she constantly urged Reagan, in his meetings, to do the same.* In her August letter to Gordievsky, Mrs Thatcher told him, 'You know what kind of people we are dealing with.'[49] He was impressed by this, because it proved to him that she was not starry-eyed about Gorbachev.

In early September the government prepared to make Gordievsky's defection public and simultaneously expel all those Soviet officials known to be spies, sparing only the KGB's security officer.† There were twenty-five of them. When the time came for Mrs Thatcher to authorize this plan, she was staying with the Queen at Balmoral. Because of the secrecy involved, a phone call was out of the question and so Charles Powell had to fly up to Scotland and intrude upon the sanctity of Mrs Thatcher's royal retreat. 'I drove to Balmoral and spent about an hour arguing with the Equerries as to whether I should be admitted at all,' Powell recalled. 'I finally fought my way through to Mrs Thatcher's bothy‡ to get her authority and then set off back to London.'[50] Rehearsing the plan just before its execution, Robert Armstrong reminded Mrs Thatcher that relations with the Soviet Union were bound to worsen because of the expulsions but 'it would not have been right or understandable to respond less vigorously'.[51] The defection was, he said, 'a great coup for our security and intelligence services'. The following day, the defection (though not Gordievsky's presence in Britain) was publicly announced. The Soviet media did not mention the defection, but reported the expulsions. As Armstrong had predicted, the Soviets hit back at once, expelling twenty-five British nationals from Moscow, not all of whom were intelligence officers. On 15 September 1985, Mrs Thatcher met Geoffrey Howe and the new Home Secretary, Douglas Hurd,§ to decide what to do next. Howe pleaded with her to expel only four more Russians, but Mrs Thatcher thought that 'a further four expulsions on their own did not constitute an adequate response,'[52]

* The Gordievskys were finally allowed to leave Russia for Britain in September 1991, nearly a year after Mrs Thatcher had left office.
† Most assumed that this information had come directly from Gordievsky, but he insists SIS already knew the identities of the KGB's agents. 'They used me as an excuse,' he said, 'because of the political situation after my escape.' (Interview with Oleg Gordievsky.)
‡ A little hut on the estate.
§ Douglas Hurd (1930–), educated Eton and Trinity College, Cambridge; Conservative MP for Mid Oxon, February 1974–1983; for Witney, 1983–97; Secretary of State for Northern Ireland, 1984–5; Home Secretary, 1985–9; Foreign Secretary, 1989–95; contested Conservative leadership unsuccessfully, 1990; created Lord Hurd of Westwell, 1997.

and kicked out six, a figure which Moscow again matched. She also refused a Foreign Office suggestion that she send a letter of congratulation to the newly appointed Soviet Prime Minister because 'in the present climate of relations a message would be out of place.'[53]

Many feared that the Gordievsky row would sink Mrs Thatcher's capacity to 'do business' with Gorbachev. Bryan Cartledge wrote a despatch from Moscow, which he himself described as 'a little downbeat'. He said that relations could not now go beyond 'damage-limitation', and quoted a Central Committee member as complaining that 'Your Prime Minister thinks she can treat us as if we were Argentina.'[54] Mrs Thatcher herself was aware of the problem. In Gordievsky's view, she showed a good sense of 'balance', because, though wanting engagement with Gorbachev, she was prepared, for the sake of the defection, 'to put everything on ice'.[55] In fact, however, although the affair did cool relations and 'give her a bloody nose'[56] in her attitude to Gorbachev, it also enhanced her reputation, and the salience of Britain in the development of the Cold War. It helped confirm the view, as John Scarlett put it, that Mrs Thatcher was 'our key card to play – the outstanding Western leader outside the United States'.[57] The Americans were extremely excited by Gordievsky's defection. Only four days after its public announcement, Gordievsky later wrote, 'who should come skimming into the fort by helicopter but Bill Casey, veteran head of the United States' Central Intelligence Agency (CIA), who wanted to brief President Reagan for his first meeting with Gorbachev, due [in Geneva] in November.'[58] Casey carefully tape-recorded Gordievsky's answers to his questions, some of the most important of which concerned SDI. Gordievsky told Casey that the Russians would never agree to share the technology, because they would see it as a trick. He added that if the Americans were to drop SDI, they would win big concessions from the Soviets on arms control. Casey said that this would never happen because SDI was 'the President's pet'. 'All right,' replied Gordievsky. '. . . I think that in the long term SDI will ruin the Soviet leadership.'[59]

Mrs Thatcher chose 12 September 1985, the same day as the announcement of Gordievsky's defection, to send a long letter to President Reagan. Presumably her timing was intended to make clear that the 'engagement' show was still on the road. The letter concerned the run-up to the Geneva summit. She was worried that Gorbachev, rather than Reagan, might gain the upper hand:

> As we both expected, Gorbachev is showing himself to be a deft operator. He is playing Western public opinion skilfully and for all it's worth . . . And

his performance is spoiled only by the arrogance which he cannot always conceal. His purpose is, of course, to set opinion in Europe against the United States, to give the impression that the Soviet Union is full of initiatives and original ideas while the United States is flat-footed and unimaginative.[60]

Even more important than countering Gorbachev's offensive, she argued, was for the US to show that 'it has appealing proposals of its own on which you will be prepared to begin the process of negotiation when you and Gorbachev meet.' She wanted the Geneva meeting to be one of substance: 'I am troubled, in particular, by the notion which is gaining ground that you see the meeting as little more than a "getting to know you session" . . .'[61]

The main substance in which Mrs Thatcher was interested was arms control. Using the mandarin locutions employed by people like the Cabinet Secretary when advising her how to guide a meeting, she advised Reagan: 'You will certainly want to explain to him [Gorbachev] personally the rationale behind your Strategic Defense Initiative,' and she urged him to base his exposition on the Camp David Four Points. She never suggested that the President should offer to give up SDI, but she did recommend limiting its freedom of action as a sweetener for Soviet concessions. This could lay the basis for detailed talks. She also gave Reagan the benefit of her experience of where conversations with Gorbachev tended to go wrong. When she had raised the subject of human rights:

> We found that he reacted most often by hitting back with allegedly bad features of life in the West. This can too easily lead to an argument about the fundamentals of our two systems, or the trading of particular accusations, neither of which in my own experience is likely to get us anywhere in terms of better Soviet behaviour. I found the best tactic was to concentrate instead on putting across to Gorbachev two parallel convictions[:]

> that we in the West are not in the business of undermining the Soviet state . . .

> [and that] nevertheless, human rights in the Soviet Union are our business: not just because both East and West have committed themselves to them at Helsinki:* but also because justice at home is more likely to produce stability and responsible behaviour abroad.[62]

She ended by trying to instil a sense of urgency:

---

* In return for a commitment to respect human rights within the Soviet bloc, the Helsinki Final Act (1975) had recognized Soviet domination of Eastern Europe. At the time Mrs Thatcher had been suspicious of the deal, but she now intended to hold the Soviets to their part of the bargain (see Volume I, Chapter 12).

I am convinced that we must stop Gorbachev's bandwagon from gaining
too much speed before your meeting by making clear now that the US is
utterly serious about making the maximum progress at Geneva; and that
we must set clear goals for the meeting itself with which our people on both
sides of the Atlantic can identify.[63]

The fact that Mrs Thatcher could write such a detailed letter of opinion
and advice to the President, unsolicited, was itself unique. Other allied
leaders would usually write only when asked, and not in such substantive
terms. Such letters were evidence of her confidence and her intimacy with
Reagan. Officials recalled that Reagan would always read her messages in
full rather than relying on a précis, as he did with most other correspondents.[64] In this case, Reagan responded warmly and quickly. 'As always,
your views captured not only the immediate challenges and opportunities,
but expressed as well how these meetings can set us on a course towards
long-term stability.'[65] He maintained his dedication to SDI – 'I cannot, and
will not, endanger this research program which means so much to all man-
kind' – but took her point about the handling of human rights issues and
endorsed her desire for making real progress at the summit and being able
'to set in motion the resolution of specific problems'.[66]

Reagan subsequently composed and wrote out in longhand his strategy
for Geneva. The document survives and shows that he had adopted most
of Mrs Thatcher's points. He wrote that Gorbachev's 'major goal will
continue to be weaning our European friends away from us. That means
making us look like a threat to peace.'[67] And he accepted her call for substance: 'Those who think the Summit can be made to look successful if
we get agreements on cultural exchanges, the consulate we want, fishing
and trade matters are dealing with window dressing'[68] – the 'main events'
were 'arms control, the regional areas of conflict and the prevalent suspicion and hostility between us'.

In a separate letter, Reagan also wrote to Mrs Thatcher to congratulate
her over the Gordievsky affair. 'I admire the strong action you took last
week . . .' he told her, and he agreed with her on the need to balance
'intolerance of Soviet hostile international activities' with 'our desire to
build a constructive relationship with the Soviet Union'.[69]

The groundbreaking summit at Geneva was now just a month away, and
Mrs Thatcher's relationship with Reagan as productive as it had ever been.
At the same time, the previous difficulties in her relationship with Gorba-
chev now seemed to evaporate. The Soviet leader chose the occasion of
Mrs Thatcher's sixtieth birthday, 13 October 1985, to send her his

congratulations. Their discussions at Chequers and in Moscow, he said, 'took a correct political tone'. He wanted their mutual understanding at those meetings to 'remain in force', but for this 'much effort, political wisdom and goodwill will be needed.'[70] Mrs Thatcher could feel well pleased at her navigation of these difficult shoals and currents. Business could still be done.

In her annual speech to the Conservative Party conference two days earlier, she expressed her confidence publicly: 'Our wish is to see substantial reductions in nuclear weapons, provided they are balanced and verifiable. I know that will be President Reagan's objective at his meeting with Mr Gorbachev, and he has our full support and good wishes as he goes to Geneva. The West could not have a better or a braver champion.'[71] Although, for quite other reasons, she was in choppy waters at home, she was navigating the oceans of world diplomacy with a sure touch.

At the same time as Mrs Thatcher was coaxing Reagan towards a different approach to the Soviet Union, she began modestly to attempt something similar in relation to the Middle East. Pro-Israeli though she instinctively was, she grew impatient with the lack of movement on the question of Palestine, and felt that America needed nudging. In this, she was influenced chiefly by her admiration for King Hussein of Jordan,* the Middle Eastern ruler with the closest links to Britain.† In her mind, Hussein was 'the gallant little King'.[72] In 1985, her support for him briefly took dramatic form.

When she entered office in 1979, Mrs Thatcher had been chiefly motivated by two related views in her approach to the Arab–Israeli conflict. The first was her strong belief – reinforced by her Jewish connections in her constituency of Finchley – that the story of the Jewish nation was heroic and that Israel was pro-Western. The second was her hatred of terrorism, and therefore her extreme suspicion of the Palestine Liberation Organization, led by Yasser Arafat.‡

She quickly clashed with the long-standing Arabism of the Foreign Office. Lord Carrington, her first Foreign Secretary, embodied this and acknowledged that 'her views were not mine.'[73] From the first, he pressed her to make some move in favour of the Palestinians, and in August 1979 urged her to support a UN Security Council call for Palestinian

---

* King Hussein of Jordan (1935–99), educated Harrow School and RMA Sandhurst; King of Jordan, 1952–99.
† Mrs Thatcher also felt gratitude to King Hussein because during the Falklands War he had written to her to offer 'our total support of your position' (Hussein to Thatcher, 19 May 1982, CAC: THCR 3/1/21 (http://www.margaretthatcher.org/document/123328)).
‡ Yasser Arafat (1929–2004), chairman, Palestine Liberation Organization, 1968–2004.

self-determination, if the words could be moderately framed. On the back of the Foreign Office note setting this out, Mrs Thatcher wrote a summary of her own approach. 'I will leave Lord Carrington a free hand in this,' she began, but 'I remain concerned at the proposed course of action.'[74] The fact that the Palestinians might be considered as a people should not be 'the sole determinant of the way we vote', she went on.

> Suppose that because of the acts or omissions of the United States, or the East Germans [who were often Soviet proxies for action in the region] . . . the oil-bearing states cease to be in present hands and come directly or indirectly under Soviet control. There is only one nation there that would really stand & fight and that is Israel. If there is an ultimate East–West battle she will be our ally . . . The problem with Israel at the moment is Begin [the Israeli Prime Minister]. Further – has anyone really thought through a new Palestinian 'homeland'?

Even more than in relation to the Cold War, Mrs Thatcher was conscious that the United States bore the security burden of the Middle East problem. She was therefore suspicious of EEC or even British diplomatic interventions. When Carrington pushed the idea of a European policy towards the Middle East, arguing for a Palestinian entity, she wrote, 'Am very unhappy with this approach. It seems to me that if we are to take a major part in negotiations we shall have to take a major part in the Security of the region. As it is, we expect the Americans to do that in large part while we nevertheless negotiate. It doesn't add up.'[75]

Her concerns expressed, Mrs Thatcher nonetheless deferred to the much greater knowledge of Carrington and the Foreign Office in this area (hence his 'free hand'), and allowed herself to be dragged slowly in their direction, without ever going all the way. Government papers of her first six or seven years in office show her constantly resisting moves to meet PLO representatives but, quite often, in the end, compromising. As early as June 1980, when the European Council met in Venice, it approved, with Mrs Thatcher's reluctant agreement, a statement calling for self-determination for the Palestinians, along with the recognition of Israel's right to live within secure borders. The unstated logic of this stance was that contact with Palestinian representatives should be made. It was almost impossible to do this without dealing with the PLO. Within five years, Mrs Thatcher would be encouraging direct official and even political contact with 'moderate' members of the organization.*

---

* Mrs Thatcher was, in fact, the first senior British politician to meet Yasser Arafat, but this was by mistake on her part, though not on his. He tapped her on the shoulder at the funeral

Luckily for the Foreign Office, Mrs Thatcher's dislike of terrorism cut both ways. She was extremely prejudiced against Menachem Begin,* the Israeli Prime Minister when she came into office, and his Likud successor, Yitzhak Shamir,† because both had been involved in terrorist attacks on British forces during the period of the British Mandate in Palestine which ended in 1948.‡ In the same month that she became prime minister, she received Begin in Downing Street. He upset and offended her by attacking the Western allies for their 'failure . . . to bomb the railways leading to Auschwitz at the end of the war . . . Israel had a valiant army which would fight if necessary.'[76] To Vice-President Mubarak§ of Egypt, Mrs Thatcher described her meeting with Begin as 'one of the most difficult she had experienced'.[77] According to her principal private secretary, Clive Whitmore, 'She hated Begin.'[78] In discussions with the Canadian Prime Minister, Pierre Trudeau, in 1981, she described how Zionist terrorists in the 1940s had booby-trapped the bodies of two British soldiers, and broke down in tears.[79]

In Israeli politics, therefore, Mrs Thatcher did not, as she usually did in other countries, support the more right-wing party, but favoured the Labour Party of Shimon Peres,¶ whom she liked. When Israel, under

---

of Marshal Tito in Belgrade in May 1980, and she shook hands with him politely before realizing who he was. Her dislike of Arafat was added to by the fact that he did not, in her view, shave properly. (Interview with Sir Dennis Walters.) 'He *looks* like a terrorist!' she would exclaim (Interview with Lord Luce).

* Menachem Begin (1913–92), born Poland; commander, Irgun Zvai Leumi, 1943–8; Leader, Herut Party, 1948–73; of Likud Party 1973–83; Minister without Portfolio, 1967–70; Prime Minister of Israel, 1977–83; joint winner, Nobel Peace Prize, (with Anwar al-Sadat), 1978.

† Yitzhak Shamir (1915–2012), born Poland; elected to the Knesset as a member of the Herut Party, 1973; Foreign Minister, 1980; Leader of Likud Party, 1983–92; Prime Minister of Israel 1983–4. After 1984 elections he alternated posts with Shimon Peres of the Labor Party, serving as Foreign Minister, 1984–6 and Prime Minister, 1986–92.

‡ Begin had been in charge of Irgun, the organization which blew up the King David Hotel in Jerusalem in 1946, killing ninety-one people, many of them British soldiers. Shamir planned the assassination of Lord Moyne, the British Minister for Middle East Affairs in 1944, and also of the UN envoy and rescuer of Holocaust victims, Count Bernadotte, in 1948.

§ Hosni Mubarak (1928–), Vice-President of Egypt, 1975–81; Prime Minister 1981–2; President, 1981–2011. He stepped down in February 2011 following mass protests in Cairo and other Egyptian cities. After a series of trials, Mubarak and his sons were convicted of corruption and given prison sentences.

¶ Shimon Peres (1923–), born Poland; member of Israeli Knesset, 1959–2007; Minister of Immigrant Absorption, 1969–70; of Transport and Communications, 1970–74; of Information, 1974; of Defense, 1974–7; Chairman of Labor Party, 1977–92 and 1995–7; Acting Prime Minister, 1977; Prime Minister, 1984–6 and 1995–6; Vice Premier, 1986–90; Minister of Foreign Affairs, 1986–8 and 1992–5; Minister of Finance, 1988–90; President of Israel, 2007–14; joint winner Nobel Peace Prize (with Yasser Arafat and Yitzhak Rabin), 1994.

Begin, bombed the Iraqi nuclear reactor at Osirak in 1981 and invaded Lebanon the following year, she was disinclined to cut it the slack she might well have allowed to a Peres government or to other friendly countries when confronted with severe security threats. Her preferred interlocutors in the Middle East were Mubarak, who became president of Egypt after the assassination of Anwar Sadat in 1981, the rulers of Saudi Arabia, the Gulf States and Oman, and above all King Hussein.

Unlike in areas of policy more central to her, such as the Cold War or trade union reform, in Middle East questions Mrs Thatcher was not assisted by the small bands of 'irregulars' whom she used to challenge official views. Her strong Jewish connections – most notably Keith Joseph in the Cabinet and David Wolfson in her own office – kept her well in touch with Jewish feeling, as did her Finchley constituents. But none contributed sustained intellectual and policy input. The occasional essay by distinguished Jewish academics like Elie Kedourie, sent to her by Hugh Thomas, or Leonard Schapiro, sent by Joseph, was not nearly enough to counteract the official orthodoxy, especially after she had made the arch-Arabist Sir Anthony Parsons her first foreign policy adviser in No. 10 in 1982. Even less than over the question of Northern Ireland (see Chapter 10), where Mrs Thatcher's instincts were also different from those of officialdom, did she have, or seek, outside aid. In David Wolfson's opinion, this was because 'It was not really a major issue: everyone knew her view':[80] Mrs Thatcher could be trusted by friends of Israel. In terms of her heart, this judgment was correct, but was perhaps not so true of her head.*

Mrs Thatcher's chief aims across the Middle East were to assist and, where necessary, restrain the United States, to be vigilant against the Soviet Union and to improve British export markets with Arab countries. This meant gently chiding America for not being tougher on Israel, but also siding firmly with the United States when solidarity was required. Under the Camp David agreement between Egypt and Israel,† for example, a

---

* Wolfson could recall only one instance when she used her informal Jewish connections in the Middle East. In 1982, the Israeli government was minded to make Eliyahu Lankin its new ambassador in London. Lankin had a terrorist record against the British. Mrs Thatcher asked Wolfson to visit Begin in Israel and request informally on her behalf that Lankin should not be sent to London. This he did, successfully. (Interview with Lord Wolfson of Sunningdale.)
† These accords, brokered by President Jimmy Carter in 1978, led to Egypt and Israel agreeing 'land for peace', the former recognizing the latter, and Israel withdrawing from Egyptian land occupied after the Yom Kippur War of 1973.

multinational force (known as MFO) was required to supervise the agreed withdrawal of Israel from the Sinai peninsula in 1981. It was not UN-sponsored, because Camp David had enraged the other Arab nations, but the United States did not want to do it alone. In what Carrington called 'the dirtiest of tricks', the United States asked Britain to take part in the force, without, at that stage, asking other European nations too. Reagan personally wrote to Mrs Thatcher to seek her help, causing Sir Nicholas Henderson,* the British Ambassador in Washington, to set out the Foreign Office view in a letter to Carrington: 'The difficulties for us in accepting arise from the association with the Camp David process and with an American regime that has been looking increasingly pro-Israeli: and these are particularly worrisome when you are hoping to have dealings with the Saudis and to get on to terms with Arafat.'[81] Although, unlike Carrington, she had no desire to get on terms with Arafat, Mrs Thatcher did not welcome Reagan's invitation: she wanted to avoid damaging relations with Arab states which were often good customers for British defence equipment. She also feared the overstretch of British military commitments.

Reagan tracked her down on the telephone to the Imperial Hotel in Blackpool, where she was attending the annual Conservative Party conference and facing revolt over public spending from Cabinet colleagues. With a good deal of 'Oh Lord, and I'm interrupting you' and 'I'm going to be a pest again,' he begged her to take part in the MFO, in order to get Continental Europe, Australia and Canada to do the same. Mrs Thatcher told him it was all most unfair that Britain had to go first: 'I saw Crown Prince Fahd† [of Saudi Arabia] myself – I had him to lunch at No. 10 – and asked him flat out what would be the effect in the Arab world . . . He thought it would be very adverse indeed . . . I simply cannot afford to lose the business.'[82] If she were to agree, 'France would then get the whole lot, and I'd get the unemployment.' Perhaps conscious that, given Sadat's assassination a few days earlier, Mrs Thatcher would anyway feel strong moral pressure eventually to give in to his request, Reagan elegantly withdrew at this point. In due course, Mrs Thatcher did agree – with France and Italy also contributing – that Britain should provide a very small headquarters unit to the MFO. To general surprise, this proved largely uncontroversial. In her dealings with the Reagan administration, Mrs

---

* Nicholas ('Nicko') Henderson (1919–2009), educated Stowe and Hertford College, Oxford; Ambassador to Poland, 1969–72; to Federal Republic of Germany, 1972–5; to France, 1975–9; to the United States, 1979–82; chairman, Channel Tunnel Group Ltd, 1985–6; knighted, 1972.
† Fahd of Saudi Arabia (1921–2005), Crown Prince of Saudi Arabia, 1975–1982; King, 1982–2005.

Thatcher much preferred to grant favours and bank them to gain new ones in return, rather than refuse them point-blank.

A similar motive governed Mrs Thatcher's reluctant agreement to a much more dangerous venture. After the Israelis had invaded Lebanon in June 1982, in order to punish the PLO, they surrounded the organization's headquarters in Beirut, effectively holding it hostage. Israel was eventually persuaded to let the PLO evacuate under the supervision of a new multi-national force formed explicitly for this purpose. This force, known as the MNF, was led by the US, with French and Italian help and without British. But the day after the PLO had left, the Lebanese President-elect, Bashir Gemayel, was assassinated, and the MNF returned at the request of the Lebanese government. This time, the United States asked Britain to take part, on a small scale. Once again, Mrs Thatcher was most reluctant, but once again she gave in. Matters got worse in 1983, because, although Israeli forces eventually agreed to withdraw, Syrian forces refused. By August, the MNF had become so closely identified with the Lebanese government that it came under fire from pro-Syrian factions. As the killing worsened, Mrs Thatcher became more concerned not to get deeper in and said as much to Reagan when visiting Washington in September. On 23 October, a huge truck bomb blew up the US Marine barracks in Beirut, killing 241 US personnel. A simultaneous attack on the French barracks killed 58 people. The US invasion of Grenada (see Chapter 5) followed two days later.

Naturally, the United States was tempted to retaliate. Equally naturally, Mrs Thatcher wanted to avoid this. The British contingent had not been bombed, but she was fearful that it would be, all in furtherance of what she saw as a pointless internecine dispute. She told Reagan's envoy, Kenneth Dam, that 'the MNF did not have purposeful objectives at the moment'.[83] The implication was that she wanted to get Britain out. She was also, because of the invasion of Grenada, particularly jumpy. After George Shultz had met Geoffrey Howe to discuss the matter, she wrote to Reagan: 'I was somewhat relieved to note that George Shultz made it clear that there would be no hasty reaction on your part by way of retaliation for the attacks on your Marines. I know you will think twice and three times before doing anything that could damage the process of reconciliation and put in further danger the contingents in the MNF.'[84]

Because of the Grenada embarrassment, the Americans felt compelled to consult Mrs Thatcher, but not to follow her advice. Invoking 'self-defence', Reagan signed an order to bomb the Sheikh Abdullah Barracks in Lebanon, which were run by the Iranian Revolutionary Guard, and may have been the headquarters from which terrorism was directed. But then, paralysed by disputes within the administration, his order was not executed and it was left to the French to carry out the attack alone. The MNF stayed on, uneasily. In early February 1984, the Lebanese government fell apart, and Reagan was persuaded to deploy the Marines offshore, keeping them in the relative safety of US ships. Mrs Thatcher told him she had had enough: 'The latest advice from our people on the spot . . . is that it is now virtually impossible for our contingent to play a useful role and that there is a greatly increased risk of their incurring casualties.'[85] She was prepared to co-ordinate timing of withdrawal with the United States so that no one could 'drive wedges between us', but that was all.

The thing ended in farce. On the same day she wrote to Reagan, he informed her that he would redeploy offshore that evening. Britain therefore got ready to withdraw simultaneously. Then Reagan changed his mind, and asked Mrs Thatcher to hold off. Mrs Thatcher cabled him politely but firmly. She understood how difficult it all was but had 'decided that we must go ahead' in the course of the next twenty-four hours. 'I am sorry that we cannot meet your request to "go into neutral" but frankly it came too late.'[86] Reagan's self-countermanded decision to redeploy leaked to the media, so he redeployed anyway. 'Our troops left in a rush, amid ridicule from the French and utter disappointment and despair from the Lebanese,' wrote George Shultz in his memoirs.[87] In what was literally a parting shot, US forces shelled pro-Syrian positions from USS *New Jersey*, causing widespread condemnation, but none from Mrs Thatcher. She was relieved to be out, and suppressed whatever irritation she may have felt against the President she had tried to help.

As the years passed, Mrs Thatcher's confidence grew and her views about the Middle East gradually changed. From merely reporting moderate Arab concerns to the Americans, she began to develop some policy of her own. In 1981, she passed on to Reagan comments made by Crown Prince Fahd of Saudi Arabia, and the rulers of Kuwait and Bahrain:

> the dominant strand in all they said to me was of grave disappointment with and alienation from the United States. I found this most upsetting but felt that I must let you know. I have the feeling that these moderate Arabs hesitate to express the strength of their feelings directly to you and your Government. You may, therefore, not have the whole picture. Those to whom I talked argue that your Government is so wholly committed to Israel that it ignores the rightful claims of the Palestinians. It thereby creates acutely difficult problems for the moderate Arab leaders.[88]

Increasingly, she tried to make herself the Western champion of these moderates, especially King Hussein.

In choosing Hussein as her main interlocutor on the Middle East, Mrs Thatcher was in the mainstream of British policy. Jordan itself, and the Hashemite monarchy which ruled it, were creations of the British colonial era, and the country's security was closely bound up with British protection. Mrs Thatcher also had a strong personal fondness for the man himself. Hussein, one of whose wives was British, had been educated (like Mark Thatcher) at Harrow, and had been an officer cadet at Sandhurst. He was very pro-British, and spoke the English language in an English idiom. Often Western leaders found conversation difficult with Arab rulers; with Hussein this was not a problem. Like Mrs Thatcher herself, he maintained a courtly protocol without being haughty. He had man-of-action charm (he was an accomplished pilot), a courage which had helped him survive numerous plots against him and a sense of honour, all of which she admired. He was extremely respectful towards her. According to John Coles, her foreign affairs private secretary who went on to become ambassador to Jordan in 1984, she was also 'intrigued by the accounts he could give her of what was going on',[89] since he maintained relations with leaders who, for her, were largely beyond the pale, such as Hafez Assad of Syria and Saddam Hussein of Iraq. King Hussein, for his part, understood Mrs Thatcher's closeness to Reagan and saw her as his best conduit through the Washington labyrinth to the top.

From her early days as prime minister, Mrs Thatcher had cultivated Hussein's friendship. When, in 1981, he gave her a paper setting out his ideas for the region ('Total withdrawal for total peace'), she wrote on top of it, 'This is the most <u>cogent</u> argument that has ever been presented by the Arab world in that it deploys concepts fundamental to American thought,'[90] and she commended it to Reagan. After winning her landslide victory in the 1983 general election, she took time to think through her Middle East policy and held a meeting at Chequers in September to discuss it. Under the general conclusion that 'It was more important to concentrate on the realities of the situation than to think in terms merely of improving our posture,'[91] the meeting agreed several aims. These included that it would be hard to get much out of the United States until the presidential election of 1984 was finished, that Mrs Thatcher herself should get more involved with President Reagan on the subject, that the Gulf needed more attention and that 'the stability of Jordan was ever more important'.

Mrs Thatcher's actions in the ensuing years usually followed these priorities. In June 1984, she wrote to tell King Hussein that she had privately asked Reagan to consider a fresh initiative in the Middle East once re-elected – as it was widely (and correctly) predicted that he would be – in November. When Shimon Peres replaced Shamir as prime minister of Israel in September 1984, she thought this change presented an opportunity, and she so advised Reagan at Camp David in December.[92] In February the following year, she opposed the suggestion of an EEC initiative. She was more interested in the news, which she received before it became publicly known, of an agreement between Hussein and Arafat. For the first time, the PLO committed itself to working with Jordan for 'a just and peaceful settlement' of the Israel–Palestine dispute.

Mrs Thatcher threw herself into supporting Hussein's initiative. When she saw Reagan in Washington at the end of February, she spoke publicly and privately in favour of it, and wrote to Hussein to say that the President's attitude had been 'very encouraging'.[93] Hussein, who usually copied his letters to and from Reagan to Mrs Thatcher, wrote a passionate appeal to the US President: the 'very credibility of the United States in the entire Arab world' was at stake, and the moment was now. 'It [a solution] could conceivably only come in the second term of office of President Ronald S. Reagan.'[94]* Mrs Thatcher backed him up. 'The King', she wrote to the President, 'is clearly under considerable pressure and feels it ... He is looking for evidence of your personal support for his initiative.' The next step, she argued, would be for the relevant United States Assistant Secretary, Richard Murphy,† to agree the membership of a Jordanian–Palestinian delegation which could be received in Washington, in order to put the Palestinians under pressure to negotiate along lines acceptable to the US. This was a bolder version than Reagan's, who wanted the 'Murphy meeting' to take place only in Amman, Jordan's capital. 'We must all keep in mind the importance of weakening the influence of those Arab states who would all too readily look to the Soviet Union for help,'[95] Mrs Thatcher concluded.

At first, everything seemed to go well. Hussein had what he told Mrs Thatcher were 'very fruitful talks'[96] with Reagan. The first Jordanian–Palestinian delegation meeting would take place in Amman, he said, and this would lead to a Jordanian–explicitly-PLO delegation being created which would publicly accept the key UN Security Council Resolutions 242 and 338.‡ She did hesitate, however, at Hussein's suggestion that a

* Reagan's middle initial was actually W (for Wilson).
† Richard Murphy (1929–), US Ambassador to Mauritania, 1971–4; to Syria, 1974–8; to the Philippines, 1978–81; to Saudi Arabia, 1981–3; Assistant Secretary of State for Near Eastern and South Asian Affairs, 1983–9.
‡ These two resolutions, the first after the Six-Day War of 1967, the second after the Yom Kippur War of 1973, called on Israel to return to its 1967 borders, but also upheld the need

Jordanian–PLO delegation should be received in London. Such a move would, of course, confer considerable legitimacy upon the delegation and she hesitated to do this without US support. She thus argued that the delegation, however composed, should be received in Washington first, London second. She told Hussein – and then told Reagan what she had told the King – that his idea that the United States might soon meet a Jordanian–PLO delegation was 'running ahead of the game'.[97] No British meeting should 'short-circuit' anything between Reagan and Hussein.

Charles Powell quickly reinforced her caution about the suggested encounter in London. 'Such a meeting is our high card,' he told her, 'and it is a great mistake to play it too early.'[98] He added that the Foreign Office was ignoring the difference between a delegation of Jordanians and Palestinians and one of Jordanians and the PLO. Mrs Thatcher repeated Powell's 'high card' phrase to Geoffrey Howe, but herself suggested the idea that the two moderate PLO men whom Hussein had proposed to her – a West Bank mayor and an Anglican bishop – could be received as private individuals rather than as PLO representatives. Two drafts of a letter to Hussein, one from the Foreign Office and one from Powell, were composed. 'I much prefer yours,' Mrs Thatcher scribbled on the latter's,[99] and it was sent. The Powell version told the King that if his chosen PLO men would publicly reject violence while in London and sign up to resolutions 242 and 338, Mrs Thatcher would be happy for Howe to see them as part of the delegation.[100]

As the summer progressed, the White House became more nervous about what Hussein was proposing. The Americans continued to insist that the delegation he was putting together remain free of PLO representation. Reagan also told Hussein he would not authorize any Murphy meeting anywhere without 'assurances of prompt and tangible movement towards direct negotiations' with Israel.[101] Hussein replied angrily that the United States had been 'unresponsive or negative to every single item contained in my proposal': 'with a heavy heart', he could not accept the new conditions for the Murphy meeting.[102]

The American rejection came shortly before Mrs Thatcher's proposed visit to Egypt and to Jordan, the first to the latter by any sitting British prime minister. She had agreed to the trip partly because John Coles, her private secretary for foreign affairs until mid-1984, had just become the ambassador there, and also because she felt fired up by Hussein's cause. When she met

for 'secure and recognised boundaries' of all states in the region to be respected (UN Security Council Resolution 242, 22 November 1967 (http://unispal.un.org/unispal.nsf/0/7D35E1F 729DF491C85256EE700686136)).

the King at the Nadwa Palace in Amman on 19 September 1985, she found
him in an emotional state. Everything had 'come to the end', he told her.
The Americans were unreasonable to expect independent Palestinians since
'one could not find a Palestinian who was not selected by the PLO': all the
others 'feared for their lives'.[103] The White House condition of 'direct and
visible contacts with the Israelis' at this stage was simply impossible, he went
on. Mrs Thatcher shared his mood. She would confront President Reagan
with the 'enormity' of the consequences of the failure of Hussein's initiative,
she told Hussein, and would speak out in her press conference in Amman
the following day: 'It was no good her coming here and calling on others
to take risks for peace unless Britain was prepared to do its part.'[104] She
would try to press ahead with the Hussein initiative herself.

The dinner that evening in the British Ambassador's residence for the
King and Mrs Thatcher turned into a dramatic occasion. The Jordanian
Prime Minister, Zaid Rifai, 'spent the bulk of the time', recalled the host,
John Coles, 'moving between the dinner table and the phone in my study'.
He was trying to persuade the Palestinian members of the proposed dele-
gation, themselves PLO members, to agree a statement about their visit
to London and 'make clear their commitment to peaceful negotiations'.[105]
'When we sat down to dinner there was no agreement that the delegation
would be received in London. By the coffee, there was.'

Immediately this was settled, Mrs Thatcher cabled Reagan to inform
him. She wanted, she began bluntly, 'to let you know how worried I am
by the absence of progress following up King Hussein's peace initiative'.[106]
Everything had been going well, she continued, until 'your people' set the
conditions of direct, visible Jordanian–Israeli contact. She reminded the
President of the assassination of the King's father Abdullah, in 1951. Failure of Hussein's scheme now 'could again prove fatal for this courageous
and steadfast family': 'I do not see that anything is lost by a meeting with
the joint delegation.' The British government would be ready to meet it in
London, with the Palestinians represented by 'two well-known moderates', who would make the statements agreed over the telephone at dinner
'publicly when they come to London'. She told Reagan that she proposed
to announce all this at her press conference the next day. This she did.

For Mrs Thatcher to agree to the delegation was, in Charles Powell's
view, 'a big concession'. She was, in effect, accepting that a senior British
minister should meet the PLO, which she had always said would not happen. She did it for Hussein. Her romantic nature was engaged. 'She had
stars in her eyes about the gallant little king.'[107] John Coles agreed, and
indeed had intended this: 'My main aim was that she should come to support the King.' Hussein took Mrs Thatcher to the ancient, deserted city

of Petra and flew her alone in his helicopter over the vast extent of the spectacular ruins, dipping into its rose-red ravines for forty minutes. 'When she got out, she was white as a sheet,' recalled Coles, but this contributed to her sense of excitement.[108] In her letter of thanks to Coles afterwards, she told him that she and Denis 'think that Jordan was quite the nicest tour we have ever made'.[109] 'If she hadn't paid a visit to Jordan, I wonder if any of this would have happened,' said Coles.[110]

'Not welcome' was the headline of the leading article in Rupert Murdoch's *Sun*,[111] which normally supported Mrs Thatcher ardently. Conservative Friends of Israel criticized her[112] and so did Israel itself, both Peres and Shamir. In response Bernard Ingham, taking note of what he described as Mrs Thatcher's 'constituency interest', encouraged her to give an interview to the Israeli press to 'set out clearly for the Jewish reader, listener and viewer your case in your own terms'.[113] The Americans were not pleased, although Richard Murphy himself 'felt hopeful that it might work'.[114] Events also conspired against her. Palestinian terrorists killed three Israelis in Cyprus and on 7 October the Palestine Liberation Front (PLF) captured the cruise ship *Achille Lauro* and murdered a disabled American Jewish passenger named Leon Klinghoffer. On 1 October, in reprisal for the Cyprus killings, the Israelis bombed the PLO headquarters, newly established in Tunis. Arafat escaped, but seventy-one people died. Charles Powell warned the Foreign Office that Mrs Thatcher was worried about *exactly* what the two Palestinians in the joint delegation would say when they arrived in London. He produced a text for them to adhere to. In a rare intervention, David Wolfson sent Powell a short note with background material which claimed to show that the two Palestinian delegation members were supporters of terrorism. He warned that if the government thought 'Arafat's "wing"' of the PLF had not been involved in the *Achille Lauro* attack, 'we may well be proved very wrong. Or very naïve, or both. My main concern is no more egg on faces than necessary.'[115]

Egg on faces was not completely avoided. 'A major setback', Powell informed Mrs Thatcher on 13 October. One of the two Palestinians (Mayor Mohammed Milhem), in London for the promised meeting, had now demanded the removal of any reference to Israel from his public remarks. 'This is clearly completely unacceptable,' Powell went on:[116] the meeting would not now take place at all. Desperate efforts were made to inform King Hussein, who was staying on the estate of the Duke of Roxburghe in Scotland. If the meeting had gone ahead, he would have been well placed to enjoy a considerable triumph. 'I am <u>deeply disappointed</u>,' Mrs Thatcher wrote to him the next day.[117] Her rather quixotic attempt to bring change in the Middle East had failed. In February of the following year, Hussein announced that he was giving up on the PLO altogether.

Mrs Thatcher's relations with the United States, or even with Israel, were not damaged in the long term by this adventure. Her goodwill was recognized. From this point onwards until the general election of 1987, her involvement in the search for a solution to the Arab–Israeli conflict was more limited. She did, however, visit Israel in May 1986 – also, as in Jordan, the first serving British prime minister to do so. Her motives, according to Charles Powell, were partly 'to respond to pressure from the Jewish community, who were keen for her to go',[118] and partly to show her support for Peres.

Arriving not long after she had given the United States permission to use British bases to bomb Libya in response to Colonel Gaddafi's terrorism (see Chapter 15), Mrs Thatcher was warmly received. In her setpiece speech at dinner in the Knesset (the Israeli parliament), however, she maintained her position on Palestine. She praised Israel's 'love of liberty and justice', but turned this to serve her case: 'Because of your own high standards, more is expected of Israel than of other countries, and that is why the world looks to Israel . . . A future in which two classes of people have to co-exist with different rights and different standards is surely not one which Israel can accept.'[119] She also met Palestinian leaders – not PLO people; this was the first time that a Western leader had used a visit to Israel to do this.* She called for West Bank elections.

None of this impaired relations with Peres, with whom she had four hours of talks. According to his adviser Nimrod Novik, his relationship with Mrs Thatcher 'was unique since the discussions with her were more intimate than those she held with Kohl, Mitterrand or anyone else'.[120] Charles Powell had a similar impression: 'I have a happy memory of driving back with her from the Negev towards Tel Aviv . . . with her and Peres on the back seat. They gradually fell asleep with her head resting on his shoulder. It was rather touching.'[121] William Squire, the British Ambassador to Israel, cabled the Foreign Office in almost ecstatic terms: the warmth of Mrs Thatcher's welcome from the public had been a 'personal triumph'. 'The emotion that the Prime Minister displayed on the first morning at the visit to the Holocaust Memorial and to the Commonwealth War Graves Cemetery struck a real chord.' Israelis believed her to be 'a bona fide interlocutor', he said, and, thanks to her, had got over the long-standing

---

* The guests included Haj Rashad Shawwa (the deposed Mayor of Gaza), Elias Freij (Mayor of Bethlehem), Izzat al Alloul (Acting Mayor of Nablus), and a number of lawyers and journalists (Dinner in Honour of the Prime Minister, 26 May 1986, CAC: THCR 1/10/104).

'psychological hump' caused by her ill feeling over the period of the Mandate. Anglo-Israeli relations were at 'an all-time high'.[122] For someone known for taking strong positions, Mrs Thatcher was skilful in not being exclusively identified with one Middle East faction. Shortly before the 1987 election was called, Charles Powell wrote to the Foreign Office rebuking it for trying to support a new initiative by the UN Secretary-General and considering joint action with the French. Nothing should be done to 'lose us the carefully balanced position which we have created over the last two years or so, as a result of which she stands quite well with both sides'.[123] Mrs Thatcher knew her power in the region was marginal; on the whole she used it astutely. This was an area where her growing global, personal prestige counted for more than the conventional assertion of British interests.

The other factor which weighed heavily with Mrs Thatcher in her dealings with the Arab and Muslim world was British trade, particularly sales of defence equipment. She was the most tireless saleswoman for British companies. 'Tell Treasury & Defence not to argue – just go and get the contract' was a typical injunction scrawled on a letter about sales to the United Arab Emirates (UAE).[124] Customers, actual or potential, included allies like Jordan (which, not being an oil state, had little money), Egypt, the mostly rich Gulf states (Kuwait, Bahrain, Qatar, the UAE, Oman) with all of which Britain had historic connections, and then, much more problematically, Iraq and Iran (which were fighting each other) and Syria.* Following the invasion of Lebanon in 1982, Britain had frozen its limited arms sales to Israel. By far the largest player in the market was Saudi Arabia.

Mrs Thatcher's attitude to these matters was simple, arguably simplistic. Her view was that if countries wanted to be armed, better that they should be armed by the British. Then they would have better relationships with Britain and create more British jobs. This rule could apply even to potentially hostile countries: how did it help Britain if they were dependent for weapons on the Soviet Union? She also well understood that, in the Arab world, where personal relationships were much more important than bureaucratic ones, the sales impact of a dynamic prime minister cultivating the rulers could be mighty. She counter-intuited that her sex, far from being a disadvantage in the completely male-dominated Arab world, helped her: it made her an object of fascination. She suffered from none of the traditional ruling-class British embarrassment about selling things hard. Her papers are stuffed with correspondence and records of meetings in which she tries, often successfully, to sell kit to Arab potentates.

---

* Discussion of arms sales to Iraq and related matters will appear in Volume III.

Although, geo-politically, Mrs Thatcher was worried about Soviet influence, what personally upset her more was when Western allies, particularly
the French, did better in Middle Eastern markets than Britain. In 1980, the
junior defence minister, Geoffrey Pattie,* sent her privately an internal MOD
report about French defence sales in the region. It quoted from an encounter
between the Head of Defence Sales and a potential customer in the Gulf the
previous year. 'When we were poor', the sheikh had told him, 'you were here;
you even taught us English so that we could understand you. Now we are
rich, we never see you, and we are having to learn French.'[125] Mrs Thatcher
scratched dark lines of emphasis beside this quotation.

The biggest British pitch was to Saudi Arabia. In February 1981, the
relevant Cabinet committee (OD) had agreed in principle that Britain
should sell Tornado combat aircraft – which British Aerospace (BAe) had
developed with the Germans and the Italians – to overseas customers. At
first, sales efforts centred on Jordan, but these failed. By September 1983,
the MOD told Mrs Thatcher it was ready for the greater prize of Saudi
Arabia. The Saudis were interested because they feared attack from Iran
and wanted the necessary 'punch' to repel it.[126] The Defence Secretary,
Michael Heseltine, asked Mrs Thatcher if they could go ahead. 'Agreed,'
she wrote, 'and hope we succeed.'[127] In his memoirs, Heseltine confines
his description of Mrs Thatcher's role in the search for this deal to one
sentence: 'Mrs Thatcher played her part in the process.'[128] That is one of
the greater understatements of history.

The MOD thought it would probably win the Tornado sale. In the
autumn of 1983, Heseltine attended a dinner given by Jonathan Aitken†
for the former US President Richard Nixon. Aitken seated Heseltine next
to Wafic Saïd,‡ the Syrian-born *homme d'affaires* for many of the Saudi
royal family's business dealings. ' "I've just been to Saudi," Heseltine told
me,' Saïd recalled. ' "We're securing a project there very soon." I knew
from the grapevine that Prince Sultan was in negotiation with the French
and wasn't so sure. I told him, "I very much advise you not to take it for
granted." He looked at me as if to say, "Who are you?" '[129] But not long

---

afterwards Saïd was contacted by James Blyth,* the Head of Defence Sales at the MOD, who asked to see him. Saïd knew that Prince Sultan, the Saudi Defence Minister, favoured the French and that discussions were in progress. This news 'took us by surprise', recalled Clive Whitmore,† the Permanent Secretary at the MOD.[130] Saïd subsequently consulted his close friend Prince Bandar,‡ the Saudi Ambassador in Washington, who confirmed that a deal for his country to buy Mirage 2000s from the French was well advanced. Despite being the son of Prince Sultan, Bandar was not in favour of the sale, which he told Saïd was 'mad'.[131] He preferred the British. Back in London, Saïd reported this to Blyth, who had brought Richard Evans§ of BAe with him. Alarmed, Evans arranged for Saïd to meet Mrs Thatcher informally. Saïd told her that the Saudi government was inclined to go for the French Mirages. She was 'very angry' at the French advance. 'Have the Saudis misled me?' she asked Saïd, and reminded him of how Britain had supplied Saudi Arabia with Lightnings in 1959 and taught the Royal Saudi Air Force how to use them: 'We trained your pilots, Mr Saïd. This is our key national interest. For your country, it is a matter of trust: we will prove a loyal ally.'[132] Saïd advised Mrs Thatcher that she should discuss the matter with Prince Bandar. As soon as Heseltine heard the news that 'the French were much further advanced than we had known, he announced, "We'll go to Saudi this weekend, and put things right." '[133] When he flew to Riyadh, he carried with him a letter from Mrs Thatcher for King Fahd encouraging the sale. In the whole saga of the deal, despite the bitter falling-out which led to Heseltine's resignation over Westland in January 1986, his relations with Mrs Thatcher on this matter were 'completely harmonious'.[134] But although Heseltine was dynamic in pursuing the contract, ultimately the MOD 'depended a great deal on

---

* James Blyth (1940–), educated Spier's School and Glasgow University; businessman; Head of Defence Sales, MOD, 1981–5; knighted, 1985; CEO, Alliance Boots Holdings Ltd, 1987–98; chairman, 1998–2000; chairman, Diageo plc, 2000–2008; created Lord Blyth of Rowington, 1995.

† Clive Whitmore (1935–), educated Sutton Grammar School, Surrey and Christ's College, Cambridge; principal private secretary to the Prime Minister, 1979–82; Permanent Under-Secretary, MOD, 1983–8; Home Office, 1988–94; director, N. M. Rothschild & Sons Ltd, 1994–; knighted, 1983.

‡ Prince Bandar bin Sultan (1949–), fighter pilot, trained RAF Cranwell; Saudi Arabia's Ambassador to US, 1983–2005; Secretary-General, National Security Council, 2005–15; Director-General, Saudi Intelligence Agency, 2012–14; King Abdullah's special envoy, 2014–15.

§ Richard Evans (1942–), educated Royal Masonic School; chief executive, British Aerospace plc, 1990–98; chairman, 1998–2004; knighted, 1996.

her'.[135] The process of negotiation was immensely long and complicated, and the Saudis expected engagement at the highest level.

Prince Bandar was an exceptional character. He was the son of Prince Sultan, but born of an unmarried African mother who had been a maid in the royal palace. For that reason, Bandar was looked down on by other members of the Saudi royal family. Until the age of eight, he was brought up without regular contact with his father. So great were his own abilities and drive, however, that, despite the gerontocratic customs of the House of Saud, he was made ambassador to Washington at the age of only thirty-four. He was also a trained pilot with a particular interest in military aircraft. He had perfected his flying skills at RAF Cranwell in Lincolnshire – the base, by chance, with whose pilots the young Margaret had danced during the war. His flying career was cut short by a car-crash: 'He was a light-hearted young man. He used to tell us "I'm just a retired injured fighter-pilot,"' recalled James Blyth.[136] Unlike his francophile father, Bandar was also extremely pro-British. He had little time for the French, who he felt were 'all like Inspector Clouseau'.[137]

There was also a generational difference: 'Sultan was oldish, inscrutable, not obviously accessible to us. Bandar was open and Westernized, so we cultivated him.'[138] As an expert on aircraft, he believed that the Tornado, 'with its longer range and heavier payload',[139] was superior to the Mirage. As a rising figure in Saudi court politics, he knew that it would improve his influence if Saudi Arabia were to buy British rather than French. He also saw the matter strategically. He considered that there was a 'trilateral relationship – not just a bilateral one between Saudi Arabia and the United States. Reagan, King Fahd and Mrs Thatcher had an informal meeting of the heart and agreement on the strategic outlook. We were all fighting Communism together.'[140] He was also conscious that Fahd, four years Mrs Thatcher's senior, considered her a very beautiful woman and, for that reason as well, the King was keen to do business with her.[141]

The young Prince was in a delicate position because of his father Sultan's views, but he was aware that King Fahd, who had come to the throne two years earlier, felt resentful of the total power over defence issues which Prince Sultan had been given by his predecessor, King Khaled. Fahd wished to wrest control of defence from Sultan, and Bandar saw a way to help him do this. He knew that Fahd had no personal love for the French.* At same time, because of his position in Washington, Bandar had a better

---

* When Fahd had met François Mitterrand, he asked him to let him build a mosque in France, and was irritated by Mitterrand's reply: 'Your Majesty, if you permit one church to be built in Saudi Arabia, I shall let you build a hundred mosques in France' (Private information).

understanding of American attitudes than any other Saudi. Indeed, he had been put there because King Fahd, who was strongly pro-American, wanted him to get as close to the Reagan administration as possible. Bandar knew that Congress, because of its support for Israel, was likely to block the sale of American F-15 Strike fighters to Saudi Arabia. In Bandar's view, the purchase of French Mirages depended on the F-15 Strike deal, because the combination of the two planes would give Saudi 'the right low–high airforce structure'.[142] Once the American option was removed from the equation, the French chances would fade and the British opportunity grow.

Bandar went to see Mrs Thatcher for the first time in December 1984. She was impressed by the energetic and handsome young Prince,[143] who had 'lots of charm and dash'.[144] He was equally taken by the blonde states-woman. Mrs Thatcher insisted on meeting Bandar at the door of No. 10 and curtsied to him: 'I thought she'd slipped.'[145] But her deference to his royal blood did not make her servile: 'She had such a powerful per-sonality. She liked to give you a taste of it, to help you get to know her. She was a hell of a man!' At the end of the conversation, Mrs Thatcher insisted on bringing Prince Bandar down to be photographed with her beside the No. 10 Christmas tree. Bandar presented her with a rock-crystal model of a bulldog with sapphire eyes in recognition, he told her, of the British fighting spirit. After she had said goodbye to him, she said to James Blyth, who had been in the wings, 'Isn't that a lovely present!' 'Yes, Prime Min-ister,' said Blyth, 'but unfortunately that's a French bulldog.' 'If he buys aeroplanes from us, I don't care where he buys his bulldogs,' Mrs Thatcher exclaimed.[146]

It was the beginning of a beautiful friendship. While in office, Mrs Thatcher had twenty-three meetings with Bandar, probably more than any other foreigner (apart from the US Ambassador, Charlie Price) who was not a head of government. Their diplomacy was almost completely private. In most cases, 'to the rage of the Foreign Office', the only other person present was Charles Powell.[147] With Bandar's encouragement, Mrs Thatcher started to write personal letters to King Fahd, often more than once a month, commenting on world events and Middle Eastern affairs and reporting to him her conversations with world leaders. Sometimes, Bandar himself would carry these messages by hand.*

---

* The typed correspondence survives, but a few of them, it seems, were handwritten (and were not copied). When King Fahd first received one of these, he was surprised. 'Does the lady not have someone to type letters for her?' he asked. It was pointed out to him that, in British culture, a handwritten letter was a mark of personal attention. (Private information.)

In their first encounter, and in a longer meeting in early January, Mrs Thatcher and Bandar discussed the prospects for the Tornado purchases, and debated tactics. By Bandar's account, he informed her of President Reagan's view that Congress would want to block the sale of F-15s to his country. 'She was so sharp: she was thinking all the time.'[148] She suggested that she herself should lobby Reagan to go ahead with the sale and also ask his agreement for her to lobby Congress for the same result, knowing that this would not work and the F-15s would be blocked: 'Then I will say to the Congressmen that contracts must not go to the Soviet Union or China [with which Saudi Arabia was threatening to trade], but to us.' She greedily sucked up all information which Bandar had about what Saudi might want: 'Give me the numbers. And? And? And?'[149]

Invigorated by his Thatcher meetings, Bandar argued the British case to King Fahd. Both the Mirage and the Tornado are 'good aircraft', he argued, 'but the important question, Your Majesty, is, "Who do you trust – Mitterrand or Mrs Thatcher?" "Mrs Thatcher," he said. "Well," I said, "that solves the problem." '[150] Fahd agreed that Saudi Arabia would now negotiate with Britain for the Tornadoes. Mrs Thatcher met Bandar once more, on 18 February 1985, just before she flew to Washington to see President Reagan. After her visit, Mrs Thatcher wrote to Fahd. She told him that Bandar had informed her about the King's recent talks with Reagan. She added, artfully: 'I left the President in no doubt of my concern about the situation in the Middle East. I raised the subject by referring to the importance of the joint communiqué you issued after your visit to Washington and said that Britain supported it.'[151] Mrs Thatcher was also aware, thanks in part to Bandar, that Reagan himself was on her side. If Congress would not let him sell his own country's aircraft to Saudi Arabia, he would much rather Mrs Thatcher should get the benefit than François Mitterrand. Reagan privately advised King Fahd to buy British.*

At the end of March, Bandar rang Mrs Thatcher to pass on an invitation from King Fahd. Since she would soon be passing his way on her return from a visit to Malaysia, Singapore, Brunei, Indonesia, Sri Lanka and India, please would she drop in on Riyadh for dinner on the way

---

* According to Bandar, Mitterrand got wind of the British counter-attack and sent his brother, General Robert Mitterrand, to plead with King Fahd. 'Those French have the gall,' Fahd said to Bandar. 'The letter from President Mitterrand his brother was carrying told me to hurry up and sign the Mirage contract because it is important for French interests!' The King told the General, 'Last year your country cancelled 50 per cent of our oil contract with the French without informing us, and that was important for our interest. However, we did not object, because it was a sovereign decision just like this is our sovereign decision.' (Interview with Prince Bandar bin Sultan.)

home? She duly agreed to join the King on 15 April. Robin Butler, who accompanied her, remembered the occasion with pain, because 'Fahd talked and talked and talked way beyond the scheduled time' and her exhausted entourage were all desperate to get on with their flight.[152] But the dinner was worth while for Mrs Thatcher. In the course of it, King Fahd turned to her and said, 'Prime Minister, the deal is yours.'[153]

The details were as laborious as the deal itself. It was a question whether BAe, which already had heavy commitments supplying Tornadoes to the RAF, would be able to produce the aircraft required in time and in the number that Saudi Arabia wanted. Mrs Thatcher was so determined to do this that she ordered the first aeroplanes to be taken out of the queue intended for the RAF and sent quickly to Saudi Arabia.*

In August, Bandar wanted to see Mrs Thatcher. She was on holiday, but agreed to meet him in Salzburg, just before she returned to England. Bandar told her that King Fahd wanted forty-eight Tornado IDS (interdictor/strike) aircraft, thirty Hawk fast-jet trainers, thirty Pilatus PC-9 training planes and an ongoing programme of technical training. Prince Sultan, calling with Bandar on Mrs Thatcher at the end of September, confirmed the agreement, which was formally signed by Michael Heseltine. The knowledge that this deal would be forthcoming probably helped Mrs Thatcher to act as boldly as she did in relation to Hussein's Jordanian–Palestinian initiative. She knew she stood high with non-militant Arabs, and had some advantage over the Americans because of this. The contract was initially worth £5.2 billion, but provided for its own renewal and for associated services in the future, including construction. It assured the future of BAe's facility at Warton in Lancashire and the capability of BAe eventually to produce the Eurofighter. A second stage of the contract was signed in October 1987. Over more than twenty years, the deal is estimated to have amounted to £42 billion.† There were also various 'off-set' British–Saudi joint ventures in projects in the kingdom. It was, judged James Blyth, 'the biggest single deal anybody has ever done for the United Kingdom. It was Mrs Thatcher who pulled the mutton over the threshold so far as the King was concerned.'[154]

At his meeting with Mrs Thatcher, Prince Sultan told her that King

---

* In Jonathan Aitken's full and revealing account of Al-Yamamah (Aitken, *Margaret Thatcher*, ch. 25), he asserts that Mrs Thatcher authorized sending these planes to Saudi Arabia, though 'nuclear-wired', after extracting a promise from the King not to try to find nuclear bombs for them. This story is adamantly denied, both by James Blyth and by Charles Powell, who say that it would not even have been possible, since such wiring did not exist.
† It was financed through a carefully negotiated oil-for-aircraft arrangement.

Fahd had wanted the contract because of his 'great respect for the Prime Minister': the deal should be seen not only materially, but as a contribution to 'peace and stability'.[155] He congratulated her on her initiative with King Hussein: the prospect of a Jordanian–Palestinian meeting in London had been 'very well received in the Arab world'. In January of the following year, the commercial terms were settled and the contract was given a name – Al-Yamamah, the Arabic for a dove (of peace). The first Tornadoes were delivered in March. In May 1986, Mrs Thatcher felt able to write and thank King Fahd for his 'deep personal interest' in the deal.[156]

Mrs Thatcher had now established for Britain a relationship both of trust and of profit with the most important oil state. It would greatly assist her future contacts in all sorts of international diplomacy, and prove important in the Gulf War at the end of the decade. Al-Yamamah helped confirm the unique salience in world affairs which she had now achieved. In Prince Bandar's view, 'Before her, no one really cared what Britain thought or did. In her time, all over the world, they asked: "What does Thatcher think? Where will Britain be?"'[157]

Given the scale of her achievement, of which Mrs Thatcher was proud, it might seem surprising that, both then and later, she said almost nothing about it. Her memoirs make no mention whatever of Al-Yamamah or of Tornadoes. They devote three pages to her visit to Malaysia, Sri Lanka and so on in March–April 1985, but are silent about her visit to Riyadh on the same trip.* There are two probable reasons for this. The first is the extreme discretion Mrs Thatcher always exercised in relation to matters like intelligence, defence equipment and personal diplomacy. Her creed of loyalty put great emphasis on trust, and she knew that Saudi culture felt the same way: boasting would have been dangerous to the relationship and have created controversy at home.† The second reason was more difficult for her. It was to do with her son.

Mark Thatcher was often accused of seeking to profit from his mother's position. In principle, this was not something Mrs Thatcher condoned.

---

* It is notable that Al-Yamamah, Tornadoes, Prince Bandar, King Fahd and indeed Saudi Arabia itself do not feature in Geoffrey Howe's memoirs. This is evidence of discretion, but also of how much Mrs Thatcher excluded the Foreign Office from the subject.
† In the twenty-first century, it was alleged that Al-Yamamah had been a highly corrupt contract, with large rake-offs for Saudi princes, including Bandar himself. If this was so, it is unlikely that Mrs Thatcher would have known about it, since no such arrangements would have been made with the British government. In those days, unlike today, the rules governing defence sales permitted the payment of agents. Indeed, sales in the Arab world could not be achieved without them.

On one occasion, Carol recalled, 'she gave us both a little lecture about freebies. She was very against cashing in.'[158] But the issue was not always so black and white. It arose with particular virulence in 1984 when the *Observer* newspaper revealed, rather belatedly, that Mark had been involved in a contract to build a university in Oman in 1981. The circumstances, the paper alleged, had been scandalous.[159]

In November 1980, Mrs Thatcher, unwisely and unbeknown to her principal private secretary,[160] gave her son, then aged twenty-seven, a handwritten letter of introduction to Sheikh Zayed,* the President of the United Arab Emirates.[161] Through the sheikh, Mark was employed in Abu Dhabi by a company called Galadari. His work for Galadari was not in itself controversial, but Zayed's role in his advancement aroused criticism. At the same time, Mark also benefited from Mrs Thatcher's close acquaintance with Lord (Victor) Matthews,† chairman of the *Daily Express* and group managing director of the British construction, property and engineering conglomerate Trafalgar House. He acquired a consultancy with Cementation International, Trafalgar House's subsidiary in the Arab world. Through Zayed's recommendation and because of whose son he was, Mark was granted an audience with the pro-British Sultan Qaboos‡ of Oman. From this introduction, Mark was eventually able to lobby for Cementation to be given the contract to build the new university in Oman.

In April 1981, Mrs Thatcher went on a trade mission to India, accompanied by Denis and by Carol, who came along for the fun. The trip included a visit to Abu Dhabi, where Mark was working. There, apparently without warning, he joined his mother for a party. She went thence, via Dubai, to Muscat, the capital of Oman, where Mark was also already working. Again, he joined her. 'Bloody Mark has turned up,' said Carol as she sat beside the swimming pool with Tim Lankester, Mrs Thatcher's Treasury private secretary.[162] Because Mark had arrived separately, he managed completely to evade the attention of the press, who did not know he was in the country. There was consternation among the private secretaries, who feared that he was there to advance his commercial interests via his mother. Earlier, hearing that Mark was likely to join them in Muscat, Michael Alexander, then her foreign affairs private secretary, had seen Mrs Thatcher privately and remonstrated with her about Mark's presence, but 'She blew him off. He came out very annoyed.'[163] In

* Sheikh Zayed (1918–2004), President of the United Arab Emirates, 1971–2004.
† Victor Matthews (1919–95), educated Highbury School; chairman, Express Newspapers plc, 1977–85; created Lord Matthews of Southgate, 1980.
‡ Qaboos bin Said (1940–), educated Bury St Edmunds and RMA, Sandhurst; overthrew his father as sultan with British support in 1970; Sultan of Oman, 1970–.

September of the same year, the government of Oman awarded the construction contract to Cementation. The other bidders complained that they had not been given a fair chance.

The accusation was that Mrs Thatcher had used her influence with the Sultan to get the contract for the firm for which Mark was working. Following up the *Observer*'s story, in March 1984 the *Sunday Times*, using subterfuge, got Mark's bank details and revealed that Denis Thatcher was a co-signatory to one of Mark's accounts. The paper implied that Denis was also profiting from Cementation. 'Denis shares Mark's Oman account' was the headline.[164] Although the story about Denis did not really go anywhere,* the two combined presented Mrs Thatcher with considerable difficulties, which went on for months.

The *Observer* story was not easy to shrug off because it came in part from the ranks of officialdom. Mark's actions had ruffled many a feather in the British Embassy in Oman, and Ivor Lucas, the Ambassador, had warned Whitehall that his presence was 'a potential embarrassment'.[165] This unease had only grown when, without warning, Mark had arrived to join Mrs Thatcher, Denis, Carol and others for a private lunch at the Sultan's perfume-filled Salalah summer palace on the beach, 700 miles from the capital. After lunch, Mrs Thatcher retired for a private tête-à-tête with the Sultan. In the course of this, as she said publicly after the *Observer* story broke, 'I was advised to raise the matter of the whole university contract with the government of Oman. I did it. I believed in it very forcefully because I wanted the business to come to Britain.'[166] She did not distinguish between British companies, she said: 'I bat for Britain.'[167]†

The *Observer* story was not a knock-down blow. No iniquity was proved. Mark Thatcher insisted he was doing nothing wrong: 'So what? I was at least working for a UK company. Dad always told me to take care only to work for UK companies. Would those who sought to criticize this have preferred me to work for a German or Cypriot company? In such a case there would have been more criticism, of course, and rightly so. It was a no-win situation. At least I was working for the benefit of the UK economy.'[168] He turned down the chance of working in the Sultan of Oman's palace office, preferring his work in the UAE.[169] It is true,

---

* Mark Thatcher maintained that the purpose of Denis's signature was to sign cheques in Mark's frequent absences abroad and that the account was not related to Cementation. (Interview with Sir Mark Thatcher.)

† Mrs Thatcher took her role in the promotion of British trade extremely seriously. During her visit, Lucas introduced her to staff in the Defence Attaché's office, explaining that they were responsible for the promotion of arms sales. 'Oh no, they aren't,' she replied loudly; 'they are so bad at it that I have to do the job for them.' (Correspondence with Ivor Lucas.)

however, that Mark had close links to Brigadier Tim Landon,* the Sultan's closest confidant, who sometimes came with Mark to see Mrs Thatcher at Chequers. Mark once also brought Landon to lunch with her when she was on holiday in Austria in August 1985. Such connections were bound to make people suspect abuse of his mother's position. Mrs Thatcher's private office tried unsuccessfully to convey to Mrs Thatcher the risks involved. 'She really didn't understand conflicts of interest', recalled Tim Lankester, 'if they came under her category of batting for Britain.'[170]

Clive Whitmore, Mrs Thatcher's principal private secretary from 1979 to 1982, did not travel on the Oman trip. But he did quite often have to deal with problems of Mark 'trying to exploit his mother's name', particularly in the Middle East, 'where family and government is usually muddled up, and therefore the son was seen as the extension of the mother. Mark was not slow to take advantage of this.'[171] On one occasion, the chairman of BP came to see him, threatening to go public with a statement that Mark's activities with oil deals were endangering the company's established relationships. Whitmore took the matter to Mrs Thatcher: 'I told her. She said, "Would you see him?" I did. I said: "You cannot damage the reputation of your mother. It's got to stop." Mark accepted this.'[172] The problem recurred in different forms, and with different enterprises, however, because, Whitmore believed, 'Mark was driven by greed and reluctant to pass up any opportunity.' A pattern developed in which Mrs Thatcher had 'an air of resignation about it all, but was indulgent towards Mark. The rational PM knew well what he was up to. But the mother found it difficult to be tough with him.'[173] She felt guilty both about not having had enough time for her children and because, as she saw it, her job made it harder, not easier, for Mark to pursue a business career. Mark disagreed: 'I never thought my mother's career impeded my own in any way.'[174] But the whole subject made her tense and irresolute. Mark himself considered that Mrs Thatcher 'felt her maternal instinct with the same fervour as she deployed her political arguments'.[175] This was true, but she was much less adroit in working out how to act upon her maternal instinct successfully. Sometimes she would pass the task of reprimand to Denis, who would exclaim, 'The bloody young fool!'[176] 'Denis did his best,' thought Whitmore, but was no more successful than Mrs Thatcher.

Robin Butler, Mrs Thatcher's principal private secretary when the Cementation story broke in the *Observer*, was still more severe. He

---

* Timothy Landon (1942–2007), educated Eastbourne College and RMA, Sandhurst; soldier and businessman; served in the armed forces of Britain and Oman; holder of Canadian passport; appointed honorary KCVO, 1982.

thought that Mrs Thatcher's behaviour in Oman 'had conveyed a whiff of corruption, though she might not have regarded it as such. She had wanted to see Mark right. She sought the deal for Mark. She excluded everyone from her talks with the Sultan. Mark was dealing with Brigadier Landon who was the Sultan's go-between. She behaved in a most peculiar way. I suspected the worst.'[177] Nigel Wicks,* who succeeded Butler as principal private secretary in 1985, also had to deal with problems over Mark, and eventually told him that he should stop working in business 'because I was damaging my mother's interest'.[178] Mark did not believe that Mrs Thatcher knew of Wicks's approach: 'I am sure she would have raised it with me if she'd been concerned.'

When the nature and dimensions of the Al-Yamamah deal gradually emerged, allegations against Mark Thatcher began again. In their 1995 book, Paul Halloran and Mark Hollingsworth claimed that Wafic Saïd used Mark as a conduit to his mother, and suggested that Saïd had some sort of financial relationship with him, possibly helping him buy a house, for example.[179] Saïd always categorically denied this,[180] and indeed it is not easy to see what access Mark could have brought him that he did not have by other means. He had a good relationship with Charles Powell, who was to work for him in the 1990s, and he used frequently to lunch with Denis at the Connaught Hotel when Mrs Thatcher was prime minister: both men had daily contact with Mrs Thatcher, more than Mark did. Prince Bandar also denied that Mark had anything to do with Al-Yamamah and said that he had met him only twice.[181] Saïd believed that Denis played 'a fantastic, patriotic role' and kept his son at a distance from the deal.[182] Mark denied, almost wistfully, that he got money out of the contract: 'If I had been involved in it, I wouldn't be sitting here.'[183] One source close to the family considered that Mark was 'buzzing around' Al-Yamamah, looking for money, but did not get any. It was thought possible that Mark had been retained by powerful Saudis not to pursue any specific interest but just 'to keep in with the Thatchers'.[184]

In summary, no wrong was proved against Mark in relation to Al-Yamamah, but it is also clear that there was pervasive unease about the son's business dealings in areas where the mother's influence was high and about her reluctance to do anything decisive about the issue. What can also be said is that her Saudi friends remained loyal to her. In her retirement, Wafic Saïd gave her free use of the Clock House on his estate in

---

* Nigel Wicks (1940–), educated Beckenham and Penge Grammar School and Portsmouth College of Technology, London University and Cambridge University; private secretary to the Prime Minister, 1975–8; Economic Minister, British Embassy, Washington, DC, 1983–5; Principal Private Secretary to the Prime Minister, 1985–8; knighted, 1992.

Oxfordshire, where she used to go to rest. Saïd also employed Bob Kingston, one of her most faithful detectives when she was in office, as the head of security on Prince Bandar's nearby Glympton estate which he managed. And when, in 2005, Mark was convicted in South Africa for helping plot an unsuccessful coup against the government of Equatorial Guinea, Prince Bandar, who was a friend and supporter of Nelson Mandela, interceded informally with the South African government on Mark's behalf. Mark was permitted, on payment of a fine, to leave the country.[185] Bandar's involvement probably did not alter the rulings of the South African justice system, but it was evidence of his ongoing concern for Mrs Thatcher.

To be fair to Mark – which few were inclined to be – any attempt by him to pursue a business career was constantly harassed by a hostile press. In the early 1980s, when he was Mrs Thatcher's only child in Britain (because Carol was working in Australia), he was the object of much media attention. In addition, he had a problem of security. At the time of the 1981 hunger strikes, it was secretly reported that the IRA were contemplating kidnapping him in Britain and then starving him to death. From then on he was given permanent protection. The costs of altering the house in Flood Street (where the Thatchers lived before she entered Downing Street in May 1979) to make it secure were considered too high, and it was deemed safer for Mark to live in No. 10 Downing Street.* This had a somewhat imprisoning effect. Mark recalled: 'I was happy to make the move for the greater good, but it inevitably drew more attention to my life. Some people complained it was a benefit to me, but really it was a sacrifice.'[186] He was criticized for self-aggrandizement when he gave 10 Downing Street as his home address, and yet he was not really permitted to live anywhere else.

After the Cementation story in 1984, it was decided that it would be best for all concerned if Mark were to leave the country. It was Denis who advised this, and suggested his son go to the United States, where he had a work permit, and employment offers that arose through his father's connections, not his mother's. 'I would have preferred to stay in England,' Mark recalled, and the whole thing was 'extraordinarily painful for my mother',[187] but it happened. Mark left Britain towards the end of 1984, and based himself in Dallas, Texas.

Problems about Mark's security almost immediately cropped up. *Irish American Voice*, the paper of IRA sympathizers in the United States, published his rough whereabouts. His mother was naturally upset. 'It is

---

* By November 1982, the accumulated cost of Mark's police protection was officially computed, but not publicly revealed, as having been £113,485.

his flat that I am most worried about,' she wrote to her private office. 'There is <u>no</u> back way out and no means of getting help.'[188] The exacting duty of looking after Mark fell to John Kerr, the Head of Chancery at the British Embassy in Washington. Kerr quickly came to the view that Mark felt he was 'entitled to have protection officers with him at all times, probably primarily to book tables in restaurants'.[189] Care of Mark was complicated. 'One of the problems with Mr Thatcher', wrote an official from the British Consulate in Dallas, 'is that he does not let anyone know about his movements.'[190] Kerr represented to the American authorities that Mark's security was necessary not only in itself (though the risk was not judged high), but 'for Mrs Thatcher's peace of mind – and therefore in the interests of the alliance'.[191] Mark was assured by Charlie Wick, former Director of the US Information Agency and a close associate of President Reagan, that 'The President is never going to allow himself to be put in a situation where he has to telephone your mother to say that her son has been injured on US soil.'[192] So both the American and British authorities shared the burden.

It was quite heavy work. One State Department official wrote drily to a colleague that Mark's sports car, 'a bright red Lotus [part of Mark's work was to promote the Lotus brand] was hardly the type of vehicle required to preserve or promote anonymity'.[193] Letters flew back and forth complaining how hard it was to find Mark, especially when there were complications in his love life, and how rude he was when he was found. Mandarin phrases like 'not altogether satisfactory' and 'silence reigns' conveyed the flavour of disgruntled officialdom.

After the American bombing of Libya from British air bases in April 1986, Mrs Thatcher became alarmed once more. 'Nigel,' she wrote to Wicks, '. . . after yesterday's terrible news [three employees of the American University of Beirut – two British and one American – had been murdered by Islamic terrorists in retaliation for the US attacks on Tripoli], I fear he may be a priority target – and so may <u>Carol</u> . . . he is alone in the flat.' He was going to stay with the Annenbergs that weekend,* she went on: 'I thought the security people over there would <u>automatically</u> [underlined three times] think of giving him special protection but nothing has happened.' Then she turned to her daughter: 'Fortunately <u>Carol</u> has alarms in her house but I will ask my detectives if they can arrange for the local police to be especially watchful during the coming weeks. I will also remind her to <u>watch her car</u> for <u>explosives</u>. Indeed it may be best to keep it parked outside No. 10 for the time being.'[194]

---

* Walter Annenberg (1908–2002), businessman and philanthropist; US Ambassador to Britain, 1969–74.

This letter was expressive not only of a mother's natural concern, but of guilt. Mrs Thatcher was conscious that her policies had increased the risk to her children. This feeling was probably stronger in her than it would have been in the more compartmentalized mind of a typical male political leader. Perhaps sensing this, Nigel Wicks wrote back immediately with particular solicitude. He reassured Mrs Thatcher that, once returned from the Annenbergs, Mark would have security men with him at all times, and added: 'Please, please let me know at any time of day or night if you think there is anything more that we can do to help you.'[195] Despite Wicks's efforts on Mrs Thatcher's behalf, however, Carol asserted her independence and steadfastly refused personal protection, though the security of her house was improved. She was following the example of her father, who declined to have permanent protection throughout the nearly thirty years of his life that it was accorded to his wife.

There was still trouble about Mark. Some of the neighbours in his apartment block complained about the disruption caused by his level of security, and also, to the rage of the more pro-British residents, wanted Mark out of the block for the sake of their own safety. Mark was asked to leave his apartment, and this was widely reported. For a while he took refuge with the Perots,* but reports came to the British Embassy from the US Chief of Protocol that all was not well in the Perot household: 'she formed the impression that he was exploiting his position there and that the Perots would be greatly relieved if and when he moved out in July to the new house. She feared there was a risk of a non-terrorist explosion!'[196] It was essential, said Kerr, that a new home be found for Mark quickly: 'one well-publicised eviction is excusable, but two might provoke comment from the Lady Bracknells, not to mention the Fleet St newshounds.' All through the summer, there was wrangling about Mark's accommodation. 'I think all concerned, possibly including the Prime Minister, ought to be explaining to Mark that he simply <u>must</u> choose his permanent Dallas home,' noted Kerr. 'We shall do that as soon as we can get hold of him . . .'[197]

Then there was the question of money. Who would pay for Mark's security? The Cabinet Office would not contribute unless Mark had permanent accommodation, as Wicks, not wanting to bother Mrs Thatcher, explained to Denis ('if there is anything you can do to encourage him in his search . . . that would be very helpful').[198] And the State Department threatened to drop his protective detail. Mark was reluctant to settle

* Ross Perot (1930–), who was courting Mark to work for his firm, Electronic Data Systems, was a prominent Texas businessman who later ran twice as independent candidate for the presidency of the United States. In the 1992 contest, he won nearly 20 million votes.

down, however, because he calculated that Dallas property prices were falling and so it would be better to buy later.[199] Denis sympathized with Mark about property prices, but not about protection. If the authorities withdrew protection in Dallas 'we should not object,' Denis said. He told Wicks, who reported this to Mrs Thatcher herself, that he thought there would be an outcry if British public funds were used to make their son's home more secure.[200] An agitated Mrs Thatcher asked to speak to Mark on a secure line about this. This was not possible in Dallas, however, and so the message was conveyed to Mark by the Embassy that his protection would be withdrawn. But Mrs Thatcher insisted that the withdrawal should not be abrupt.[201] So Mark was put on notice, but not, in fact, left unprotected.

It was not until December that Mark finally decided to get a house of his own in Dallas. He sought government money to have it made secure. He told Wicks that he thought this would cost $25,000,[202] causing Mrs Thatcher to write, 'May I first have a realistic estimate? The sums seem enormous – way beyond what I could reimburse.' A survey was duly conducted and a British Embassy official reported from the scene:

> Mr Thatcher [Mark] was present for the survey and his attitude was that the exercise should be done properly or not at all. At one point when I raised a query on the specifications for the proposed safe haven he remarked that if I was adopting that attitude I might as well get on the next plane back to Washington ... In Mr Thatcher's view there would be no difficulty in obtaining the necessary funds – he added that £160,000 had recently been spent on the Prime Minister's house.[203]

In the end, the cost was estimated at $61,618, and the Cabinet Office felt, despite Denis's anxieties, that it could bear the cost up to $30,820. 'I gratefully accept the Cabinet Office proposal,' wrote Mrs Thatcher. 'Mark's security is endangered because of my actions as Prime Minister and these safeguards are I believe justified.'[204] After this, things calmed down. In the following month, Mark married his Texan girlfriend Diane Burgdorf at the Savoy Chapel in London, a pre-wedding party having been given in their honour by Denis and Margaret at 10 Downing Street. The couple spent their honeymoon in Australia, where they travelled under the name of 'Mr and Mrs Green',[205] and were given personal protection.

Mark had experienced genuine difficulty, because risk did exist and he was effectively forbidden to live in Britain, but, as John Kerr remembered, 'He was jolly hard to help.'[206] Mrs Thatcher found this too. The supremely powerful, decisive and determined Prime Minister, courted by the great statesmen of the world, could never quite work out how to deal with her son.

IO

Irish Agreement, Brighton bomb

'The day I was not meant to see'

When he heard that he would become prime minister for the first time, in 1868, William Gladstone said, 'My mission is to pacify Ireland.' Mrs Thatcher never entertained such a grandiose idea. For her, the subject of Northern Ireland was always a distraction from her great task of restoring British economic liberty and success. It did engage her passions, however, because she was instinctively protective of anything and anyone who, as she saw it, was assailed for being British. She felt especially emotional about the fact that hundreds of British soldiers and members of the Royal Ulster Constabulary (RUC) were killed and injured in terrorist attacks, mainly committed by the IRA. She was determined to fight terrorism and was acutely aware of the threat to her own life (and the lives of her friends) presented by Irish Republican terrorists. In the view of politicians from Northern Ireland, Mrs Thatcher was well briefed on the affairs of the province but she had little 'feel' for the problem.[1] She had no personal vision of how Northern Ireland could be governed more successfully.*

In her first term as prime minister, Mrs Thatcher had bravely faced down international anger in her resistance to the IRA hunger strikes (see Volume I, Chapter 21), but no political initiative in Northern Ireland had borne fruit. Enraged by the mischief, even malice, displayed by Charles Haughey's† government in Dublin during the Falklands War, she had

---

* One piece of evidence for her lack of 'feel' was her failure to master the normal terms of the discussion. She never had clear in her mind the difference between Irish Nationalists (such as the Social Democratic and Labour Party (SDLP)) and Republicans (such as Sinn Fein), and she could not pronounce or remember the name of the Irish parliament, the Dáil (pronounced 'Doil'). She sometimes, in conversation, would refer to the 'United Kingdom', when she meant Great Britain without Northern Ireland.

† Charles Haughey (1925–2006), educated St Joseph's Christian Brothers' School, Fairview, Dublin, University College Dublin and King's Inns, Dublin; Fianna Fáil TD, 1957–92; Minister for Finance, 1966–70 (dismissed from government because of alleged involvement in an attempt to import arms for the IRA); Leader, Fianna Fáil, 1979–92; Taoiseach, 1979–81, March–December 1982 and 1987–92.

frozen the rather tentative connections between the British and Irish governments. While privately telling officials that she wanted to 'do something about Ireland', she had no idea of her own what that 'something' might be, and no machinery of her own to develop the appropriate ideas. Initiatives came from the most pro-Nationalist officials in the Whitehall machine, notably the Foreign Office, whose standing in her eyes, after the debacle of the Argentine invasion of the Falklands, was low. 'People would speak to me of the necessity of having an initiative, and I would say "What?",' she recalled,[2] as if expecting no useful suggestion to follow.

It was in this state of angry immobility that Anglo-Irish relations stood when Garret FitzGerald* became taoiseach† (prime minister) of the Irish Republic for the second time in December 1982. FitzGerald was keen, despite the difficulties, to resume progress towards a settlement between Britain and the Republic over the question of Northern Ireland. One of his officials set out the situation bluntly:

> Anglo-Irish relations have been very bad since May last. The differences over the Falklands . . . confirmed the British Prime Minister in her feeling that she should have followed her personal instincts and natural supporters in the Tory party and been much more cautious in her involvement in Anglo-Irish approaches . . . Her distrust of the Foreign Office . . . will not promote a favourable attitude to the resumption of the Anglo-Irish process.[3]

The official recommended a security-led approach to the problem. The Irish government should 'strike hard at the terrorists' – 'tougher action would be welcome to the British Government and would help to lay the basis for a resumption of an Anglo-Irish process.'[4]

This was a good reading of Mrs Thatcher's state of mind. For her, security came first, and she was perpetually and often justifiably dissatisfied with the Republic's contribution to it. From time to time, she would put forward the idea of a fence, built all along the border, with what she called an 'access corridor'.[5] No colleagues ever gave countenance to her notion, but it frequently recurred. In private conversation, Mrs Thatcher was particularly preoccupied by what she considered the inglorious role of the Republic of Ireland in the Second World War. 'The Irish were worse

---

* Garret FitzGerald (1926–2011), educated Coláiste na Rinne, Waterford, Belvedere College, University College and King's Inns, Dublin; PhD; Fine Gael TD, 1969–92; Minister for Foreign Affairs, 1973–7; Leader, Fine Gael, 1977–87; Taoiseach, June 1981–March 1982, December 1982–March 1987.
† Pronounced 'Tee-shock'.

than neutral,' she said[6] – their formal neutrality had effectively given comfort to the Germans.*

In her memoirs, Mrs Thatcher was rather unkind about Garret FitzGerald, making sarcastic remarks about his loquacity and inability to understand Unionist fears. She compared him unfavourably to Charlie Haughey, saying privately that 'Haughey was a tough guy . . . often it is easier to deal with a tough guy.'[7]† This was not how she felt about FitzGerald when she was in office. It was true that she considered him 'a man of many words',[8] a significant proportion of which she could not hear because of his quiet voice and rapid flow.‡ She remembered him as an 'Irish Geoffrey Howe'.[9] One of FitzGerald's officials recalled that 'before each meeting with Mrs Thatcher, I'd urge him to "speak slowly, speak slowly" . . . he'd start quite slowly and intelligibly, but then the ideas started to crowd in and he'd speed up. He couldn't vocalize his thoughts quickly enough.'[10] On one occasion, she fell asleep in his company.§ But her published complaints probably reflect her retrospective sense of unease about the whole Anglo-Irish process. At the time, Mrs Thatcher did recognize that FitzGerald was not anti-British, and was genuine in his desire for better relations between the two countries and for peace in Northern Ireland. FitzGerald's sincerity commanded her respect. 'He was very easy to get on with,' she recalled.[11] 'He did have a wider view.' Robert Armstrong, who led the British side of the negotiations for an Anglo-Irish agreement throughout, noted: 'She liked FitzGerald and thought he was an honest, decent man. I think she felt motherly towards him: she wanted to stroke his curly hair.'[12]¶ Mrs Thatcher believed that she owed FitzGerald a hearing and she was very conscious of the watching world, particularly in the United

---

* Garret FitzGerald believed Mrs Thatcher was not alone in taking this view. 'All [British] politicians up to and including Margaret Thatcher, who retained a memory of the war . . . had a problematic attitude to Ireland, which made it difficult [for us]. That included her, but it also included Jim Callaghan.' (Interview with Garret FitzGerald.)

† Martin Mansergh, an official who was close to Haughey, felt there was mutual respect between them because 'despite often sharp differences and considerable distrust, she recognized Haughey as a fellow professional politician. Neither of them always saw Garret in that light' (Interview with Martin Mansergh).

‡ Mrs Thatcher was not alone in this. The Queen was known to complain, 'I'm glad that Mr FitzGerald isn't one of my prime ministers. I can't understand a word he says' (Private information).

§ When he noticed that Mrs Thatcher was asleep, FitzGerald paused. 'Just keep talking,' said Charles Powell encouragingly. 'I'll write it all down.' (Interview with Lord Powell of Bayswater.)

¶ In spite of this motherly instinct, Mrs Thatcher often confused FitzGerald's name and called him 'Gareth' (Interview with Michael Lillis).

States. She did not want to be seen to be hostile to the cause of peace and reconciliation.

FitzGerald felt a greater sense of urgency than Mrs Thatcher. He was preoccupied with the idea that Sinn Fein, the political wing of the IRA, might overtake the more moderate nationalists of the Social Democratic and Labour Party (SDLP), who were led by John Hume.* This, he believed, would destabilize not only Northern Ireland, but also the Republic. He wanted to bring the Nationalist parties together to work out a common approach to the Northern Ireland question which would bolster the SDLP. To this end, without support from Mrs Thatcher, who was suspicious of all-Ireland solutions, he set up the New Ireland Forum in May 1983.

After her famous victory in the general election of June 1983, Mrs Thatcher found that FitzGerald's agenda dominated discussion of Northern Ireland's future.† Although she did not much like the 'Irish dimension', she had few friends, advisers or political colleagues who gave her creative advice about Ulster's future from a Unionist point of view. After the election, she had promoted her closest Unionist associate, her PPS Ian Gow, to be minister of housing, so he was no longer at her side. She had little personal relationship with the Ulster Unionist leader James Molyneaux‡ ('he was perfectly all right . . . he was not a strong person') – and was uncomfortable with the 'arch-Unionist' Ian Paisley ('he was not easy').[13]§ Although she retained respect for Enoch Powell who, since October 1974, had sat as an Ulster Unionist MP, she could not countenance his anti-American conspiracy theories. 'Enoch thought', she privately recalled,

* John Hume (1937–), educated St Columb's College, Derry and St Patrick's College, Maynooth; Leader, SDLP, 1979–2001; MEP for Northern Ireland, 1979–2004; SDLP MP for Foyle, 1983–2005; joint winner, Nobel Peace Prize, 1998.

† Sinn Fein did not perform as well as expected in the general election – it received 13.4 per cent of the overall vote, coming in fourth place behind the SDLP (17.9 per cent). The election of Gerry Adams as MP for Belfast West, however, was seen as a vindication of the 'Armalite and ballot box' strategy associated with the younger generation of Republicans (see Volume I, p. 616). Adams became president of Sinn Fein later in the year.

‡ James Molyneaux (1920–2015), educated Aldergrove School, Co. Antrim; Ulster Unionist MP for Antrim South, 1970–83; for Lagan Valley, 1983–5 and 1986–97 (resigned seat in protest over Anglo-Irish Agreement, December 1985; re-elected, January 1986); Leader, Ulster Unionist Party in House of Commons, 1974–9, and Leader of the party, 1979–95; created Lord Molyneaux of Killead, 1997.

§ Ian Paisley (1926–2014), educated Ballymena Technical High School, South Wales Bible College and Reformed Presbyterian Theological College, Belfast; ordained, 1946; moderator, Free Presbyterian Church of Ulster, 1951–2008; Democratic Unionist MP for Antrim North, 1974–2010 (resigned seat in protest at Anglo-Irish Agreement in December 1985; re-elected January 1986); MEP for Northern Ireland, 1979–2004; Leader, Democratic Unionist Party, 1972–2011; Member, Northern Ireland Assembly, 1998–2011; First Minister, Northern Ireland, 2007–8; created Lord Bannside, 2010.

'that some of the violence in Northern Ireland had been carried out by the American secret service – it was absolutely mad.'[14] To general surprise, she kept Jim Prior on as Northern Ireland secretary after the 1983 election.

Mrs Thatcher's Unionist instincts faced an even more formidable obstacle than Dublin – Robert Armstrong and his Cabinet Office colleagues, most notably David Goodall.* Worried by the idea that the Foreign Office should take the lead in discussions with the Republic about a part of the United Kingdom, Mrs Thatcher had much earlier decided that the Cabinet Office should be in charge (see Volume I, Chapter 21). Armstrong, the Cabinet Secretary, had urged this course, but his own views were even more 'green' (sympathetic to Irish nationalism) than those of the Foreign Office. Armstrong's counterpart in Dublin was Dermot Nally,† whom Armstrong had known since 1979. The two men had a 'mutual respect and friendship' and found that they agreed about the need to improve relations between the two governments.‡ It was the 'Armstrong–Nally process' – formally known as the steering committee of the Anglo-Irish Intergovernmental Council (the apparatus set up by Mrs Thatcher and FitzGerald in 1981 to consider matters of mutual concern to both governments) – which kept contacts between London and Dublin alive in the most difficult days.§ Goodall, a cerebral and almost saintly Roman Catholic of partially Anglo-Irish Protestant descent, was deputy secretary at the Cabinet Office. 'I was always thinking about Ireland,' he recalled. 'So was Robert Armstrong,'[15] although at this stage Goodall had never visited Northern Ireland. He took part in even more negotiations than his boss. Both men were far more expert in the subject than Mrs Thatcher. They were highly professional civil servants who knew how to observe the proprieties, but they never agreed with her. 'Robert never definitely overstepped

---

* David Goodall (1931–), educated Ampleforth and Trinity College, Oxford; diplomat; head of Western European Department, FCO, 1975–9; Cabinet Office, 1982–4; Deputy Under-Secretary, FCO, 1984–7; High Commissioner to India, 1987–91; knighted, 1987.
† Dermot Nally (1927–2009), Deputy Secretary to the Department of the Taoiseach, and head of Northern Ireland Affairs, 1973–80; Secretary-General to the Department of the Taoiseach (and Cabinet Secretary), 1980–93.
‡ Contrary to what some accounts suggest, Armstrong had not been at the talks at Sunningdale but, in December 1973, he was at a dinner at 10 Downing Street for the participants in the talks, and he met and talked with Nally then (Correspondence with Lord Armstrong of Ilminster).
§ The two sides of 'Armstrong–Nally' were so close that the Irish side even invented two ties, dark green for the Irish, maroon for the British, with the letters 'NA' (reflecting the Irish order of the two names) on them, and gave both to each side. Members of this unofficial club would wear them for reunions.

the mark,' said Charles Powell, 'but they were all going behind her back. Their meetings were principally to discuss how to handle her.'[16]

So it was Robert Armstrong who wrote to Mrs Thatcher after her election victory in June 1983, and urged her to get back on terms with the Republic, using the summit with the Taoiseach which had recently been agreed for November. It was precisely because the report of the New Ireland Forum would be unwelcome, Armstrong explained, that the governments should re-engage: 'It will help to give it [the Forum report] a lower profile if there is already an established dialogue between Dublin and London on other, less contentious, subjects.'[17] He wanted a 'measured resumption of business' after the Falklands froideur. Mrs Thatcher smelt a rat. 'I don't like this at all,' she wrote. 'The truth is that we haven't anything to talk about save security and E.E.C. matters . . . This is how we get into difficult situations with the Unionists.'[18] She never forbade the process, however, and so Armstrong had, in effect, permission to press forward.

Over the next few months, Irish officials took the initiative, and discussed how best to approach the British. 'It was clear', recalled FitzGerald's close adviser Michael Lillis,* 'that there was no possibility of having negotiations with Mrs Thatcher which focused on anything except security. She had no interest in what nationalists would call political progress or any of those ideas.'[19] The trick was to think up something sufficiently enticing for Mrs Thatcher to accept some ideas of political progress as trade-offs for security co-operation. In September, while visiting Dublin, David Goodall had found himself invited by Lillis for a walk along the Grand Canal. As they walked, Lillis conveyed to him ideas which Goodall considered 'far-reaching'.[20] FitzGerald, he said, would be prepared to support formal recognition of the Union in return for the 'participation of Irish security forces in operations in the North and of Irish judges in terrorist trials there'.[21] This later grew into the idea that the Republic would repeal Articles 2 and 3 of its 1937 Constitution which laid claim to Northern Ireland. Such a repeal would have to be approved in a referendum. No formal offer of a constitutional amendment was made, but the idea was now dangled before Mrs Thatcher.† It was, perhaps, surprising that British officials set so much store by the idea of changing the 1937 Constitution. The idea had come up previously, and was not quite

---

* Michael Lillis (1946–), educated University College Dublin; Irish diplomat; head of Anglo-Irish Relations, Department of Foreign Affairs, 1982–5; Irish head of the Anglo-Irish Secretariat, Maryfield, Belfast, 1985–6; Ambassador to the UN in Geneva, 1986–8.
† The Irish records of these meetings show that it was Goodall who raised the question of constitutional change (Note by Michael Lillis, 29 September 1983, NAI: DFA/2013/27/1589).

as momentous as it seemed. Articles 2 and 3 meant little in international law since, in 1925, the treaty between Ireland and Britain had recognized the partition of Ireland. If Articles 2 and 3 had significance, it was an emotional and political rather than a legal or practical one.[22]

Shortly before the November summit, Armstrong wrote to Mrs Thatcher to report on his latest meeting, in Dublin, with Nally. FitzGerald, who liked to flatter visiting British officials by seeing them in person, had also summoned Armstrong to a private meeting. Armstrong now reported to Mrs Thatcher what he had said. Using a word which, did he but know it, was a red rag to Mrs Thatcher, who saw it as Marxist jargon, FitzGerald said that the minority in Northern Ireland suffered from 'alienation': 'What was needed was to create something upon which the loyalty of the minority in Northern Ireland could form.'[23] The Irish might be prepared to express publicly the fact that the Union would not be overturned in the foreseeable future. 'In exchange for that,' Armstrong reported FitzGerald as saying, 'the minority should be given law and order institutions on which it could focus confidence and loyalty (his word).'[24] Against this, Mrs Thatcher drew her series of disapproving wiggles.

Armstrong conveyed to Mrs Thatcher FitzGerald's desire to handle matters in a special way – at Chequers 'he would be suggesting that it would be very useful if there could be private discussions of these matters between his people and your people.'[25] By this he meant not the Foreign Office, but Michael Lillis and Nally and Armstrong and Goodall. Although Armstrong did not mention the point, such talks threatened to go against the public statement by Jim Prior that no secret deals would be contemplated.

On 2 November, Mrs Thatcher received reports of FitzGerald's state of mind. FitzGerald believed, the source reported, 'that the main obstruction to progress on the issue of Northern Ireland did not take the form of constitutional restraints, but was the Prime Minister herself'.[26]

As the November summit approached, Mrs Thatcher began to worry that the Irish were expecting more of a *quid pro quo* for security co-operation than she had wanted.[27] The meeting on 7 November was uneasy. 'It was electric the sensation that Mrs Thatcher exuded,' recalled Michael Lillis. 'I think it had to do with the issues . . . her sense of protecting British sovereignty against the ambitions of these mad nationalists but also the issues of loss of life of service people as well as of the population, including, let me say, the Catholic population.'[28] When FitzGerald used his favoured word 'alienation' to describe the feelings of the Nationalist community, Mrs Thatcher cut him short: 'I do wish you would stop using that dreadful word, Garret.'[29] FitzGerald spoke of the threat from Sinn Fein, and aired the New Ireland Forum's emerging suggestions of federation, confederation or joint sovereignty.* 'The Prime Minister said that she noted the Taoiseach's concern'[30] is all that the record betrays of Mrs Thatcher's thoughts. FitzGerald was clearly somewhat deflated.

But, as so often in the Irish story, power accrued to those who made sure that a process remained in place and then took charge of that process. After FitzGerald had left, the British team gathered round the fire with the Prime Minister and extracted from her what they really wanted, her consent for a formal British response to the Irish proposals. They developed what they called a 'basic equation'. Britain would agree to offer the Dublin government 'some form of political involvement in Northern Ireland in return for formal recognition of the Union'.[31] Anxious, however, about any accusation of 'secret negotiations', Mrs Thatcher now closed down the Lillis–Goodall channel. This made virtually no practical difference, since all further discussions could take place under the auspices of the Anglo-Irish Intergovernmental Council. The meetings were therefore publicly acknowledged. But their true subject matter remained secret.

The year 1983 ended with several dreadful terrorist incidents, including the assassination of a rising young Unionist politician, Edgar Graham, the killing by the IRA of two members of the Irish security forces – the first such incident since the beginning of the Troubles – and the IRA's bombing of Harrods, in London, in which six people died. On balance, these atrocities helped FitzGerald's cause. He wrote in *The Times* that both governments shared an interest in fighting terrorism: 'the next step must be that we all do it together.'[32] Mrs Thatcher responded in kind. Paying a surprise visit to the province just before Christmas, she combined a robust condemnation of terrorism ('We do not surrender to bullets or bombs') with friendly words for FitzGerald: 'I warmly welcome and accept the invitation of the Taoiseach to step up even further our co-operation in the battle against terrorism.'[33]

Early in the new year 1984, Mrs Thatcher brought Jim Prior and Geoffrey Howe to Chequers to discuss the situation in Northern Ireland. Airing her frustration about terrorism, she put forward various ideas which, from time to time, she liked to bring up and which everyone else tried to squash. David Goodall recorded:

> The Prime Minister asked why arrangements could not be made to transfer those members of the minority community who did not wish to remain

---

* All three Forum possibilities were unwelcome to Mrs Thatcher. FitzGerald recalled that she was particularly cautious about joint sovereignty because she wanted to be able to say truthfully afterwards that it had not been discussed (Garret FitzGerald, *All in a Life: Garret FitzGerald, an Autobiography*, Gill & Macmillan, 1991, pp. 476–7).

under British rule to the Republic. After all, she said, the Irish were used
to large scale movements of population. Only recently there had been a
population transfer of some kind. At this point the silence round the fire
became transfused with simple bafflement. After a pause, I asked if she
could possibly be thinking of Cromwell. 'Cromwell: of course.' 'Well Prime
Minister, Cromwell's policy was known as "To Hell or Connaught" and it
left a scar on Anglo-Irish relations which still hasn't healed.' The idea of a
population transfer was not pursued.[34]*

However startling Mrs Thatcher's 'thinking aloud' might be, the consequences of the meeting were, once again, satisfactory for those who
wanted negotiations. On 16 February, the Anglo-Irish proposals were
brought before Cabinet for the first time, with Mrs Thatcher, suffering
from laryngitis, speaking less than usual. She explained that a motive for
pushing forward with British proposals was to get ahead of the forthcoming Forum report. Her aim, though advanced with tough qualifications – 'We
need an acceptably binding commitment'[35] – was to encourage her colleagues towards talks rather than to express doubts. When Tom King,
who, much later in the process became Northern Ireland secretary himself,
objected that the Irish might not vote to amend Articles 2 and 3 and so
matters would stand worse than before, Mrs Thatcher replied, 'You can't
make it worse; you can't do nothing.'[36] The mood of the meeting was
cautious. Willie Whitelaw said, 'I strongly support the plan, to preserve
the Irish Govt's cooperatn [Armstrong's shorthand] in security,' but then
characteristically undercut himself by adding that he was 'Not optimistic
about outcome'.[37] The Lord Chancellor, Lord Hailsham,† the most Union-

---

* There was some precedent for the idea of redrawing the Irish border. It seems likely that
Mrs Thatcher was actually thinking of the Boundary Commission which was established
after the Anglo-Irish Treaty of 1921 to determine whether areas with large Catholic population should be transferred to the Free State. In the end no changes were made. 'Mrs Thatcher
was conscious of the Boundary Commission initiated by Lloyd George, which came to
nothing . . . she seems to have thought it was a mistake not to allow troublesome townlands
to be exchanged. She didn't understand what dynamic that would have set off' (Interview
with Martin Mansergh). (For a discussion of the role of the border in Irish politics, see Henry
Patterson, *Ireland's Violent Frontier: The Border and Anglo-Irish Relations during the
Troubles*, Palgrave Macmillan, 2013.)
† Quintin Hogg (1907–2001) (succeeded his father as 2nd Viscount Hailsham and 2nd Baron
Hailsham, 1950, but disclaimed his peerages for life in 1963); educated Eton and Christ
Church, Oxford; Fellow of All Souls College, Oxford, 1931–8; Conservative MP for Oxford
City, 1938–50; for St Marylebone, December 1963–70; First Lord of the Admiralty, 1956–7;
Chairman of the Conservative Party, 1957–9; Leader of the House of Lords, 1960–63; Lord
Privy Seal, 1959–60; Secretary of State for Education and Science, April–October 1964; Lord
Chancellor, 1970–74 and 1979–87; created Lord Hailsham of St Marylebone, 1970; Knight
of the Garter, 1988.

ist member of the Cabinet, warned that no referendum in the Republic would get through. But Mrs Thatcher felt able to sum up the meeting, as noted by Armstrong, thus: 'Cab. approves probe, in utmost secrecy.'[38]

Preoccupied with the New Ireland Forum, the Irish did not formally engage with the British proposals until the Forum published its report on 2 May 1984. Although praised by FitzGerald as acknowledging for the first time the feelings of the majority in Northern Ireland who considered themselves British, the report was not at all comforting for Unionists. It gave a highly unflattering account of the British role in Ireland, and out-lined three futures – the creation of a unitary Irish state, a federal or confederal Irish state, or some form of 'joint authority' over the province administered by London and Dublin – all of which would have abolished or undermined the Union. Of these, the Irish government favoured joint authority, which FitzGerald considered different from the joint sovereignty which was unacceptable to Britain.* Joint authority meant, in practice, that Britain and the Republic of Ireland would rule Northern Ireland together, with equal recognition of the symbols and citizenships of the two states. To Mrs Thatcher, this was out of the question. It included joint command of the security services and the establishment of an all-Ireland court and criminal justice system. 'We had to rule out joint authority', she later recalled, 'because it was really a form of joint sovereignty.'[39]

Once again, however, Mrs Thatcher did nothing to prevent further negotiations. In public, she refrained from attacking the Forum report, confining herself to sounding unspecifically positive. 'If you look at the numbers of people in our security forces who have given their lives for this,' she told the BBC, 'if you look at the number of deaths in Northern Ireland, you look at the terrorism and you think: "This can't go on for-ever." Therefore, we must find something.'[40]

Privately, however, Mrs Thatcher was angry at the pressure from the Forum: 'I felt it was trying to coerce us.'[41] When she met ministers and officials to discuss the latest Armstrong–Nally proposals on 24 May, her reaction was strong: 'the starkness of the Irish bid for joint authority savoured of effrontery . . . and stung her into more than usually unguarded outbursts of irritation.'[42]

An important consideration in Mrs Thatcher's mind was the need to keep relations with the United States, only recently recovered from the spat over

---

* At this stage, the negotiations with China over the future of Hong Kong were reaching a critical stage (see Chapter 4). Mrs Thatcher was therefore unlikely to be well disposed to any concessions on 'joint sovereignty' or 'joint authority' over Northern Ireland.

Grenada (see Chapter 5), in good repair, particularly as President Reagan was about to visit the Republic in June. The Irish government, which prided itself on having an 'extremely close relationship with Reagan – in ways even more intimate than she did',[43] saw the Forum report as an opportunity to influence American opinion. It exploited the fact that Reagan needed the help of 'Tip' O'Neill, the Democratic Irish American Speaker of the House, to get legislation passed. O'Neill 'actually traded domestic issues with Reagan to make sure that Reagan put a little pressure on her'.[44]

In reality, Reagan's 'Irishness' was not very strong. According to Judge William Clark, Reagan's National Security Advisor, the President did have 'to remind Mrs Thatcher a few times that his own life might go better, considering the Irish influence in the Congress, if London treated its counterparts in Dublin with a little more dignity. But the President didn't feel very strongly about the Irish issue. I know he was suspected of this . . . but in spite of his Irish name and his visit to his ancestral home, he didn't feel that strongly.'[45] American pressure was extremely gentle. Before Reagan left for Ireland, his Secretary of State, George Shultz, briefed him on the Forum report:

> FitzGerald may ask you to use your good offices with Mrs Thatcher to 'be more forthcoming'. Without commenting on the merits of the report itself, your best course of action is to reaffirm your support for all efforts, of both the British and Irish governments, to find a peaceful and constitutional solution to the problems of Northern Ireland.[46]

Certainly Mrs Thatcher had few complaints about this emollient position: 'Ron Reagan was very helpful in totally and utterly condemning terrorism. He understood everything,' she recalled.[47] But, in return, she was keen, as Charles Powell put it, on 'keeping that old Irishman Reagan on side',[48] and the best way to give herself some cover was to be seen to be talking to the government of the Republic. She feared criticism from America that Britain was 'doing nothing' to address the 'genuine grievances' of the minority in Northern Ireland: 'that is not a reputation that I could have endured.'[49]

Exchanges now focused on what Mrs Thatcher might agree to in return for the Irish doing away with Articles 2 and 3 of their Constitution. Before Mrs Thatcher and FitzGerald met on 3 September 1984, David Goodall set out for Mrs Thatcher where matters stood. The Irish had proposed a new, unarmed police force drawn from the Nationalist community to police minority areas, and a new joint 'security force'. These ideas were 'unrealistic' and the consequent disarming and break-up of the RUC would have 'disastrous consequences'. As for constitutional change,

Britain would not concede joint anything, he wrote. 'What we are prepared to offer, however, is a means of exercising direct influence over the
affairs of the province through institutionalised consultative arrangements
about police and security matters.'[50] Mrs Thatcher should make FitzGerald see just how big this was 'in that it would involve for the first time a
formal British acknowledgement of the Irish Government's right to a say
in Northern Ireland's internal affairs'.[51] Mrs Thatcher did not like the
phrase 'right to a say' and put a wiggly line under it, but she did not jib
at the essential deal being floated.

When they met, in Downing Street, FitzGerald told her, with a
self-sacrificial air, that it was difficult to see how his government could
survive defeat in a referendum on Articles 2 and 3, 'But, he had consulted
his Ministers, who were ready to take the risk.'[52] Mrs Thatcher responded
with a piece of worldly wisdom. 'She had been in politics long enough to
know that often one started off with an idea but the real difficulty came
in translating it into practical politics.'[53] What FitzGerald was suggesting
would be fine in a world of common sense, 'But in Northern Ireland one
was dealing with folklore, resentment and suspicion.' His instinct was to
play up the principles involved in their negotiations and announce to the
world a new vision. Hers was to play them down.

Nothing new was agreed at this meeting, except, as usual, that
Armstrong–Nally should keep going. In the ensuing month, officials on
both sides entered a 'mildly euphoric phase'.[54] This optimistic atmosphere,
however, was soon, almost literally, exploded.

The Conservatives' annual party conference performance took place in
Brighton. As always, Mrs Thatcher prepared her setpiece leader's speech
exhaustively. Late into the night of Thursday 11 October 1984, she was
working on the draft in the Napoleon Suite on the first floor of the Grand
Hotel, still in full evening dress after the party's Agents' Ball. Denis had
gone to bed. At about 2.50 in the morning of 12 October, when she had
just finished her amendments to the draft and handed them over for typing
up, Robin Butler gave her a document about the Liverpool Garden Festi-
val, to consider overnight. 'I'll look at it now,' she said.[55] 'I was feeling
drowsy,' Butler recalled. 'Suddenly, there was this boom. I said, "There's
a bomb. You ought to come away from the windows." "I must see if Denis
is all right," said Mrs Thatcher,' and opened the door to the bedroom.
She plunged into the darkness and came out with her husband, who was
in his pyjamas, dazed from sleep. The bathroom was badly damaged. If
she had been in it at the time, she would have been severely injured.

Immediately across the corridor, in the room set aside for typing and photocopying, Amanda Colvin and Tessa Gaisman, who were enacting Mrs Thatcher's changes to the speech, immediately knew it was a bomb 'because we had both, by chance, been in the Harrods bomb the previous December'.[56] Stephen Sherbourne, who was with them, thought otherwise. He had heard the sound of breaking glass and wrongly guessed that striking miners, who had been besetting the conference, had broken into the hotel.[57] John Gummer, the party Chairman, was also in the typing room, fiddling with the speech. After the blast, he told everyone to lie on the floor. Then, gingerly, he crawled to the door and opened it. Oddly, the corridor lights were still working. He was surprised to be confronted by Mrs Thatcher, also on her hands and knees, and shoeless, on the other side of the door.[58] She came into the room. 'That was meant for me,' she said. 'Are you all right, dears?'[59] Then she noticed that a Garden Room girl, also helping with the typing, was rather tearful, so she went over to her: 'It's probably a bomb, but don't worry, dear.'[60] When Denis emerged, Bob Kingston, her detective, noticed that he was rather shaken, but that Mrs Thatcher was calm and composed.[61] Butler told them they must return to Downing Street at once, for the sake of her security. Mrs Thatcher said, 'I'm not leaving.'[62]

There followed about twenty minutes of confusion in which people debated where the Prime Minister should go in Brighton for her protection. It was considered risky to leave because of fears of a second bomb, and of snipers. At one point, indeed, there was a further loud explosion. 'It sounded like a second bomb,' Mrs Thatcher recalled.[63] In fact, it was the sound of falling debris from the blast. There was only one bomb, which had been planted with a long-delay timer by an IRA operative, Patrick Magee,* several weeks earlier under the bath in the sixth-floor room in which he stayed. Magee had worked out where Mrs Thatcher would stay, and had placed the bomb so that its force would blow down the vertical section of the building in which she would be situated. As it turned out, Mrs Thatcher was put in a suite away from the section that Magee had targeted, and so others took the force of the blast. None of this, of course, was known at the time.

Mrs Thatcher played little part in the discussions about where to go next, but busied herself worrying about Geoffrey and Elspeth Howe in the suite next door to hers. What looked like smoke, but was actually dust, was coming out from under their door. They were trapped in their room

---

* Magee was given a life sentence for murder in 1986, but was released under the provisions of the Belfast Agreement, in 1999.

because the door would not open. Their cries could be heard. Eventually, they were released from captivity, unharmed.

The police, in John Gummer's view, did not know what to do, so various people made helpful suggestions. Gummer himself proposed taking Mrs Thatcher to the nearby house of a doctor he had known when his father was a vicar in Brighton.[64] Someone else rang Ian Gow and secured an offer of his house at Hankham, near Eastbourne.* Eventually, the police rejected these ideas and decided to take Mrs Thatcher and her party to Brighton police station. They were escorted down the main stairs of the hotel by firemen, past the pile of rubble that had fallen into the hall and out to a cul-de-sac at the back, with Mrs Thatcher trying to check which people had been accounted for. 'The cement dust got in your mouth,' Mrs Thatcher remembered.[65] Butler and Bob Kingston packed some of the Thatchers' clothes and her No. 10 papers and brought them down to the vehicles. Mrs Thatcher herself had 'dashed into the bedroom to get clothes for the next day – a navy suit, two blouses and shoes'.[66] 'Don't worry, Prime Minister,' said Amanda Colvin, 'I've got the speech,'[67] and she put a copy of the latest draft into Mrs Thatcher's bag – evidence of the working assumption that the conference would go on and the speech be delivered.[68]† Mrs Thatcher's own secure car had been locked up for the night in the police station and so another vehicle had to be found from the hotel car park. David Wolfson offered his, and drove it. Mrs Thatcher, Denis and her long-standing assistant Cynthia Crawford (Crawfie) travelled with him. The rest of the entourage followed in a bus, including John Gummer's wife, Penny, shivering in her nightdress. Later Peter Morrison,‡ at that time a junior minister, turned up at the police station. Always one to drink copiously, he had only half woken when the bomb went off, assumed that the noise came from Young Conservative revellers, and gone back to sleep. The Howes, and their dog Budget, who was uninjured, were also brought to the police station.

Those involved did not, at the time, fully understand what had

---

* It was just outside this house, in July 1990, that Ian Gow would be blown up and killed by an IRA car bomb.

† The saving of the speech much impressed Mrs Thatcher. She later wrote to Amanda Colvin's father, recalling that 'Amanda was absolutely marvellous throughout – cool, calm and very good-humoured. <u>And</u>, she & Tessa remembered to bring out the speech. You can be very proud of her.' (Thatcher to Colvin, 30 October 1984, CAC: THCR 1/2/23 (http://www.margaretthatcher.org/document/136349).)

‡ Peter Morrison (1944–95), educated Eton and Keble College, Oxford; Conservative MP for Chester, February 1974–92; Minister of State, Department of Employment, 1983–5; of Energy, 1987–90; Deputy Chairman, Conservative Party, 1986–9; PPS to the Prime Minister, 1990; knighted, 1990.

happened. When she left the hotel, Mrs Thatcher was not aware that anyone had died.[69] In the days before mobile phones, emails and twenty-four-hour news, there was an acute shortage of information. It was only when being bussed back to the conference centre after daybreak that morning and hearing the news on the driver's radio that 'An attempt has been made to murder the Prime Minister and her Cabinet' that Stephen Sherbourne realized the full dimensions of what he had just been through.[70] In the police station, rumours started to come in about who might or might not have been hurt. The best-informed person was the US Ambassador, Charlie Price, who sat behind the Chief Constable's desk and got on the phone to his Embassy.[71] On the seafront, ministers, MPs and party representatives wandered around in a shocked state, some still in dinner jackets from the ball, others in their pyjamas. Sir Keith Joseph, resplendent in a Noël-Coward-style silk dressing-gown, conscientiously took his ministerial red box with him. Alistair McAlpine, the Tory Treasurer, rang the chairman of Marks and Spencer and persuaded him to open his Brighton branch early in the morning so that the victims could reclothe themselves in time for the conference. While at the police station, Mrs Thatcher spoke briefly to the BBC. 'The conference will go on,' she said. 'The conference will go on, as usual,' emphasizing those last two words.[72]

At 4.40, much against the will of John Gummer, who realized that Mrs Thatcher would be 'out of touch, which she hated',[73] the police drove the Thatchers to Lewes Police College several miles out of Brighton. There they spent the remainder of the night. After saying prayers with Crawfie, who shared her makeshift room, Mrs Thatcher slept for about an hour and a half in her clothes. While she was asleep, Gummer rang the college with the news that the consequences of the bomb were much more serious than had first been supposed. Some people were dead, and the firemen were digging people out of the rubble. Robin Butler decided not to wake her.[74] When she did wake, and appeared, dressed in new clothes for the conference, Butler gave her the news, including the fact that rescuers were still trying to extricate the Chief Whip, John Wakeham, from the debris: they could hear him calling beneath it. Crawfie turned on BBC breakfast television and called out to Mrs Thatcher, 'Look! They're getting Norman Tebbit out.'[75] Tebbit, in his pyjamas, was trapped under rubble, and firemen were trying to work him free. For once in her life, Mrs Thatcher was grateful for the television cameras: their bright lights were trained on the ruins to help the firemen operate.[76] Mrs Thatcher was shocked by what she heard and saw, but would not contemplate the suggestion that, in view of the deaths, the conference should not go ahead. 'We must be in the conference centre in time to start the conference on time,' she said. 'We must show that terrorism cannot defeat democracy. It's what they [the victims] would have wanted.' 'I was hugely moved,' Butler recalled.[77]

The conference did start on time, and Mrs Thatcher walked on to the platform with the party Chairman. The only departure from the schedule caused by the bomb was a short service and a two-minute silence in memory of the victims.* Then the debate – which, by chance, was on Northern Ireland – proceeded as usual.

Meanwhile, a makeshift office for Mrs Thatcher was set up in the conference centre, and her team got to work altering the speech. It was airless, and there was so little room that the secretaries had their typewriters on their knees.[78] All the party-political knockabout which normally formed a portion of the conference speech had to be jettisoned, and a new introduction, about the bomb, had to be composed, with most of the work done by Michael Alison and Ronnie Millar. At about eleven, the flow of composition was broken by the arrival of the Anglican Bishop of Chichester, Eric Kemp, and the Roman Catholic Bishop of Arundel and Brighton (the future Cardinal Cormac Murphy-O'Connor), who conducted a private service of prayers in the temporary room, which Mrs Thatcher attended. In the course of the morning, rumours ebbed and flowed, with hopes raised and dashed. Those in the room were told, for example, that Roberta Wakeham, wife of John, was recovering.[79] In fact, she died. Mrs Thatcher, famous in her inner circle for her pre-speech nerves, was almost serene, distracted from her usual worries by the sufferings of others: 'She was much calmer and less agitated than she normally was before a big speech.'[80]

Mrs Thatcher delivered her speech after lunch, as was customary. Dressed neatly and with her hair as well in place as ever, though not, as would normally have been the case, attended to by the hairdresser that morning, she was calm. She said that the 'inhuman' bomb had been 'an attempt to cripple Her Majesty's democratically elected government . . . the fact that we are gathered here now – shocked but composed and determined – is a sign not only that this attack has failed, but that all attempts to destroy democracy by terrorism will fail.'[81] Then, after thanking the police, emergency services and party workers, she turned to what she called 'business as usual'. After addressing the ongoing miners' strike,† Mrs Thatcher reached her peroration. 'The nation faces what is probably

* The police received a bomb warning just before the service was about to start, but Gummer, as chairman, decided not to evacuate the building and not to tell Mrs Thatcher. The alarm was, as he suspected, a hoax. (Interview with Lord Deben.)
† For a full discussion, see Chapter 6.

the most testing crisis of our time, the battle between the extremists and the rest . . . This nation will meet that challenge. Democracy will prevail.'[82] While her standing ovation was deafening, not everyone felt her speech rose to the occasion. 'Not particularly good,' Douglas Hurd wrote in his diary, 'but she had had no sleep and is tearfully applauded for what she is.'[83]

After her speech, Mrs Thatcher and Denis visited the injured in the Royal Sussex Hospital in Brighton, passing on to the patients the flowers that had been sent to her by well-wishers. John Wakeham was unconscious and Norman Tebbit scarcely able to speak, with 'his face so swollen that I could barely recognise him'.[84] She could see Wakeham only through the internal windows of the hospital. But she did speak to Tebbit's wife, Margaret, who told her, 'Margaret, I can't feel a thing below my neck.'[85] Mrs Thatcher also chatted to Harvey Thomas, the conference organizer, who had fallen two floors and been trapped for a couple of hours up to his waist in water from burst tanks. In Thomas's view, Mrs Thatcher felt guilt: 'She felt huge responsibility for all the deaths and injuries. It was this sense of loyalty.'[86]

The Thatchers were then driven, at speed, to Chequers, in time for her fifty-ninth birthday the next day. It was only at church near by, two days after leaving Brighton, that Mrs Thatcher gave way to tears: 'as the sun came through the stained glass windows, I thought – "this is the day I was not meant to see" – And then I remembered my friends who cannot see it. I have never known such a blend of gratitude and sorrow.'[87] 'Not long after the bomb, Denis bought his wife a watch and gave it to her with a note which said "Every minute is precious".'[88]

The final statistics were that five people died* in the Brighton bomb and thirty-one people were treated for injury.† Norman Tebbit made a slow, and in the view of some, incomplete recovery from his injuries. John Wakeham's legs were saved after prolonged treatment. Margaret Tebbit never escaped her paralysis and was to be in a wheelchair for the rest of her life. Those close to Mrs Thatcher believed that, as well as being physically unscathed, she suffered no serious mental problems either. There

---

* Sir Anthony Berry MP, Eric Taylor, Lady (Jeanne) Shattock, Lady (Muriel) Maclean and Roberta Wakeham.
† Peter Walker, the Energy Secretary, was not at Brighton that night because he had decided to stay in London to deal with the NACODS dispute. He gave his room in the Grand Hotel over to Sir Anthony Berry, the MP for Enfield Southgate, who was killed in that room by the blast (see Francis Beckett and David Hencke, *Marching to the Fault Line: The 1984 Miners' Strike and the Death of Industrial Britain*, Constable, 2009, p. 140), so it could be said that the miners' strike saved Walker's life.

were a few small changes – from then on, 'I always kept a torch beside my bed in a strange house,'[89] and at her summit with Garret FitzGerald at Chequers the following month, she insisted on leaving her bedroom door open to avoid the Howes' fate of being trapped inside.[90] The main practical consequence for her was a much greater isolation from the public, as she was even more intensely protected than in the past.* She may also have felt 'like the Royal family in the Blitz, that she and those around her were now part of the national struggle'.[91] 'We shall remember – not the bomb or the ruined building – but your courage, calm and nobility in the aftermath,' wrote John Coles. 'Not for the first time Britain has come to be deeply grateful to you.'[92] The IRA statement claiming responsibility for the bombing contained the famous and chilling phrases: 'Today we were unlucky, but remember, we have only to be lucky once. You will have to be lucky always.'

A day before the Brighton bomb, Robert Armstrong had sent Mrs Thatcher his proposed speaking notes for her planned November meeting with FitzGerald. She did not read the notes until after the bomb. When she did, she did not like what they contained. They included a draft joint declaration on Northern Ireland which stated that both communities should be entitled to give their identities 'appropriate public, political and social expression'.[93] '?? What is this meant to mean?' Mrs Thatcher wrote. On the top of the page on which the draft declaration appeared, she added: 'I could not possibly agree to this. It would strike fear into the Unionists.' On Charles Powell's covering note, she wrote: 'The events of Thursday night at Brighton mean that we must go very slow on these talks if not stop them. It could look as if we were bombed into making concessions to the Republic.' A few days later, she noted, for Powell's eyes only, that ' "The bomb" . . . may in the end kill any new initiative because I suspect it will be the first of a series.'[94]

What seems extraordinary in retrospect, however, is how little the policy on Northern Ireland actually changed in the light of the Brighton bomb. Despite a very nearly successful attempt by the IRA to destroy the entire British government, and the moral prestige which attached to Mrs Thatcher for her courageous behaviour in the face of the attack, no attempt was made to take political advantage of the situation. Unionists hoped that

---

* At the end of October a MORI poll gave Mrs Thatcher a popularity lead over Neil Kinnock of 18 per cent. This was put down to admiration for Mrs Thatcher's courage during the Brighton bombing. ('Press Digest', Ingham to Thatcher, 31 October 1984, THCR 3/5/59.)

Mrs Thatcher would call off the upcoming summit with the Taoiseach and that talks between the two governments would be ended. No one in government took this view. There is no evidence that anyone suggested to Mrs Thatcher that she seize the moment to insist on stronger security measures. There was no campaign to use the bomb to show the world that the IRA was the common enemy. Instead, after the slightest of pauses, the machine of negotiation rolled on as before, almost as if nothing had happened. The only person trying seriously to slow it down was Mrs Thatcher herself. She felt that she was confronted with extremism on two fronts: on 28 October came the revelation that Arthur Scargill's NUM had been getting money from the Libyan dictator, Colonel Gaddafi, to help finance the miners' strike (see Chapter 6). She was in no mood to concede to either enemy.

Less than three weeks after the attempt on Mrs Thatcher's life, assassins succeeded in murdering Indira Gandhi, the Prime Minister of India. Although she was not close to Mrs Gandhi in political views, Mrs Thatcher had always liked and respected her as a leader. Both women were graduates of Somerville College, Oxford (though they were not contemporaries), and each had a fellow feeling for the only other woman in executive charge of an important country. They used to take comfort in private conversations about their difficulties with their children.[95] Mrs Thatcher was shocked by Mrs Gandhi's death, and duly flew out to her funeral in Delhi. There she received from Geoffrey Howe passages of the draft communiqué for her forthcoming summit with Garret FitzGerald. In deference to the patently high threat to Mrs Thatcher from another terrorist attack, the venue of the summit had been moved from Dublin to Chequers,* but the date – 18 November – was unchanged.

Fired up by her ordeal, Mrs Thatcher wrote 'No' beside several of the proposed passages which Howe had sent her. She did not like the suggestion that a British government would endorse a pro-united Ireland vote in the North, or that the different communities in the province should be 'reflected' in the institutions.[96] Charles Powell noticed her different mood after the bomb: 'It was no good talking to her about Ireland for quite a long time afterwards. She would say, "If we appease them, it will be worse." '[97] When the British Ambassador in Dublin, Alan Goodison, reported that 'Dr FitzGerald cannot afford to come away from the summit empty handed,' she wrote coldly, 'That is not my problem.'[98]

---

* Arguing for the change of venue, Mrs Thatcher said: 'The IRA will probably get me in the end, but I don't see why I should offer myself on a plate' (Sir David Goodall, unpublished manuscript).

SECRET AND PERSONAL

The events of Thursday night at Brighton mean that we must go very slow on these talks if not stop them. It would look as if we were bombed into making concessions to the Repub.   33.

PRIME MINISTER
_____

ANGLO-IRISH RELATIONS: NORTHERN IRELAND

Attached are Robert Armstrong's proposed speaking notes for his
further secret talks with the Irish Government next Monday
and Tuesday.

I have been through them carefully and believe they are
generally within guidelines already agreed.   You will want
to look in particular at:

    Note 1. Mixed Law Courts.   This examines a number
of suggestions for allowing Irish judges to sit in
Northern Ireland courts and finds difficulty with all
of them.   It must be right to take a very restrictive
view of the possibilities here.

    Note 4. Practical Policing Measures. Using the
Regional Crime Squad model for an anti-terrorist force
to operate both sides of the border is an idea worth
exploring.

    Note 5. Institutionalized Consultation. This is
heavily qualified by Note 6 on Devolved Government, and
leaves pretty restricted scope for such consultation.

    Note 10. Draft Communique for the Anglo-Irish Summit.
This seems fine as a starting point, although the Irish
will inevitably want more.   *I could not poss.bly accept this. See Paper 10*

Taken as a whole, the speaking notes should continue the
process of scaling down Irish expectations.

October 1984. After the Brighton bomb, Mrs Thatcher calls a pause in Anglo-Irish negotiation. She does not want it to look 'as if we were bombed into making concessions to the Republic'.

At a meeting with officials before she left for India, Mrs Thatcher had thrown up all sorts of reasons against continuing the negotiations. She objected strongly to the idea that the Republic should have a representative in Belfast. 'Why should the Irish have such a thing?' she challenged David Goodall. 'How would you like it if there was a Russian representative in London who had to be consulted about everything?' To this Goodall replied: 'Well, Prime Minister, 30 per cent of the population of the United Kingdom aren't Russians. 'I see,' retorted Mrs Thatcher. 'It's like the Sudeten problem.'[99]*

On 14 November, with only four days left before the summit, Mrs Thatcher gathered officials, including Armstrong and Goodall, and told them that the Irish speaking note for the summit was making 'a number of unacceptable demands',[100] and showed that Dublin still did not understand that it could not have joint authority. She even raised the question of 'whether the present talks could usefully continue'.[101] After the meeting, Armstrong telephoned the Irish Ambassador, Noel Dorr, and asked him to call on the Cabinet Office the following day. Dorr found Armstrong 'quite gloomy'. He reported Mrs Thatcher's misgivings to Dublin: 'There is a good deal of concern (translation: Mrs Thatcher didn't like it at all) and we shall have to do some fence mending.'[102] Armstrong told Mrs Thatcher that Dorr had reassured him that the Irish speaking note was 'not intended to represent a hardening of the Irish position or preparation for failure' at the summit. It was not a 'bottom line'.[103] This made Mrs Thatcher suspicious. 'A strange visit,' she wrote on top of Armstrong's message, '– how did he know?' She guessed correctly that Armstrong had contrived for Dorr to convey his conciliatory message to Mrs Thatcher via him. Although it could be argued that Armstrong was helping clear up misunderstandings, it could also be said that he was trying to frustrate Mrs Thatcher's intentions. In Charles Powell's view, 'She did not have great faith in Robert on this. He was a Heath man.'[104] Similar doubts applied to Goodall: 'David she always suspected because he was a Roman Catholic.'[105] Yet she never, throughout the process, made any attempt to wrest the negotiations out of the hands of Armstrong and Goodall, and she generally expressed a high opinion of their abilities.† One of her skills, though she never admitted it, was to permit others to do things of which she in theory disapproved.

Rather surprisingly, Mrs Thatcher found something of an ally in her doubts in Douglas Hurd who, in September 1984, she had made Northern Ireland secretary. Despite his Foreign Office background and views, Hurd was, by conviction, a moderate Unionist, and was more attentive than Howe or Armstrong to the fears of the Unionist majority in Northern Ireland. The Northern Ireland Office (NIO), now brought into the British

* Mrs Thatcher was making a deliberately provocative comparison with the Sudeten Germans in Czechoslovakia in the 1930s, whose nationalism was supported by Hitler.
† She referred to Goodall affectionately as 'my favourite churchman' (Goodall, unpublished manuscript).

negotiating team, had a realistic view of the problems on the ground, and Hurd, on his first visit to Dublin on 25 October, floated the idea of a more modest set of measures to improve security co-operation rather than a constitutional referendum.*

As the Chequers summit approached, Dublin expected trouble: 'We are aware of the enormous impact of both Brighton and the assassination of Mrs Gandhi . . . The Prime Minister's cast of mind is strongly negative and this could create a real difficulty for the Taoiseach.'[106]

Garret FitzGerald and his party arrived at Chequers before dinner on Sunday 18 November 1984. It was one of those cold and foggy days in which that part of England, at that time of year, specializes. Mrs Thatcher and FitzGerald began with a tête-à-tête in which they argued, without much meeting of minds. Mrs Thatcher asked FitzGerald why Catholics in the North were still disaffected although they were no longer persecuted. He replied that it was because the minority had no part in decisions. This was 'not uncommon internationally', Mrs Thatcher pointed out. She compared it with the Ndebele in Zimbabwe or Muslims in India: sadly, 'it was inevitable when political parties were based on confessional or racial groups.' It would be better for voters 'to join more widely based parties'.[107]† FitzGerald countered by arguing for power-sharing, but Mrs Thatcher did not take up the suggestion. Both leaders briefed their teams afterwards. Mrs Thatcher's briefing, Goodall recalled, was 'aggressively negative'.[108]

The following morning, the battle continued. Mrs Thatcher questioned whether there was a realistic chance of amending the Irish Constitution to recognize the border. If not, it would be better to work for less ambitious objectives, especially security co-operation. FitzGerald disagreed: without greater political progress, Sinn Fein would overtake the SDLP at the local elections the following May. He even warned of the possibility of civil war if the chance were missed. Mrs Thatcher got increasingly

* Although the Northern Ireland Office was brought into the negotiations, officials from the Belfast-based Northern Ireland Civil Service were entirely excluded from the process for fear that they might offer 'inconvenient advice' (see Kenneth Bloomfield, *A Tragedy of Errors: The Government and Misgovernment of Northern Ireland*, Liverpool University Press, 2007, p. 60).

† Mrs Thatcher disapproved of the sectarian nature of the Northern Ireland party system, and she was sympathetic to those in Ulster who saw themselves as Conservative. Since 1972, Ulster Unionist MPs no longer took the Conservative whip at Westminster, though formal links remained until the late 1980s. Mrs Thatcher was reluctant to sever these links and expressed the hope that the two parties could be reconciled. (Whittingdale to Thatcher, 14 February 1990, CAC: THCR 2/6/4/68.)

irritated by what she saw as the problem of loyalty: 'what the Taoiseach seemed to be saying was that the minority in Northern Ireland wanted to make its living there but owe its allegiance to the Republic':[109] 'what was being sought was to achieve the effect of repartition without actually doing it in geographical terms.' When FitzGerald argued that the minority could not identify with the local police, she responded that she was 'worried by the trend of the conversation. The Taoiseach seemed to be saying that he wanted a Republican enclave in Northern Ireland.'[110] He replied angrily that 85,000 Catholics had been driven out of their homes in mixed areas – 'the biggest forced population move in Europe since World War Two'. Might not the IRA infiltrate the police if more Roman Catholics joined? asked Mrs Thatcher.

Mrs Thatcher then raised a point which struck at the heart of the whole process. Whatever emerged as the best way of governing Northern Ireland, she said, must arise from agreement between the two communities, rather than by intergovernmental fiat: 'the Anglo-Irish consultations were not the appropriate place to try to establish a structure of Government in Northern Ireland.'[111] The prospect of devolved government gave the communities strong incentive to agree, she went on. 'But one had to ask oneself seriously: was the animosity so fundamental that agreement would never be attained?' There was no meeting of minds between the two prime ministers. As Mrs Thatcher put it, in retirement, 'What we wanted they couldn't have, and what they wanted we couldn't have.'[112] All they could share was a general expression of the need for progress. 'The essence was to take a step forward,' Mrs Thatcher said, even if this was a more modest one than the Republic wanted.

In its combative frankness, the meeting was not unlike the famous one with Mikhail Gorbachev which was to take place, also in Chequers, less than a month later (see Chapter 8). And although FitzGerald described himself as 'rather depressed'[113] by the discussion, it may in fact have helped clarify the positions of both sides. Little noticed because of the heat of the prime ministerial discussions, the official British response to the Irish speaking note of 11 November made some concessions that were useful to Dublin. It abandoned the idea that devolution would have to be the prelude to any Anglo-Irish deal, thus removing the Unionist power of 'veto'.* The right for the Irish government to be consulted in the formulation of policy in Northern Ireland, in return for amendment of their Constitution, remained on offer. At the plenary session later in the day, Mrs Thatcher ended the conversation positively. 'We like you,' she told FitzGerald. 'We're

---

* The Unionists had a permanent majority. Those who disliked this called it a veto.

now tackling the problem in detail for the first time.'[114] The parties broke up agreeing, as always, that Armstrong–Nally would continue. There was certainly no euphoria, but neither was there despair.

The drama arose because of the press conference. It had been decided that each prime minister would give a separate one in his or her own country. FitzGerald was therefore flying back to Dublin while Mrs Thatcher was speaking. Irish television asked her whether she had ruled out the recommendations of the Forum report. Mrs Thatcher answered with her customary bluntness:

> a unified Ireland was one solution [in the report] that is out. A second solution was confederation of two states. That is out. A third solution was joint authority. That is out. That is a derogation from sovereignty. We made that quite clear when the report was published. Northern Ireland is part of the United Kingdom.[115]

Strictly speaking, Mrs Thatcher was saying nothing which she had not said in public before. By restating it, she was not attempting to embarrass FitzGerald. But her emphatic style and her love of repetition – 'out . . . out . . . out' – were too eloquent not to provoke a frenzy of reaction. As Douglas Hurd, who noticed a similar effect at numerous summits, observed, 'It wasn't what she said to the foreigners. It was what she said when she got out into the open air . . . It was like the Grand National: a certain excitement took charge.'[116] In the view of Richard Ryan* of the Irish Embassy in London, the fault lay not with Mrs Thatcher but with her minders.

> If Prior, and not Hurd, had been sitting beside her, she would have been kicked on the ankle after the first of her 'Out . . . Out . . . Out' sequence. She <u>can</u> be handled, but there is none around her at present to do it. We [the Irish side] should try to build into the next stage a mechanism between officials in order to get her statements framed with a measure of care . . . What about recruiting Howe to work on her?[117]

Poor FitzGerald returned to a storm in Dublin. The *Irish Times* said: 'She is as offhand and patronising as she is callous and imperious.'[118] Michael Lillis, who acknowledged Mrs Thatcher's lack of malicious intent, considered that she 'created a horrific problem for FitzGerald . . . it nearly ended his leadership.'[119] The episode reinforced Irish doubts about

---

* Richard Ryan (1946–), educated Oatlands College and University College Dublin; Counsellor, Irish Embassy, London, 1983–8; Minister-Counsellor, 1988–9; Ambassador to Korea, Spain, the UN, the Netherlands and the Czech Republic in later years.

FitzGerald's ability to deal with Mrs Thatcher. 'There was a sense in the Irish electorate that he wouldn't be tough enough for Thatcher . . . to the outside observer we had been beaten up.'[120] The British Ambassador in Dublin reported 'the widespread impression that Dr FitzGerald has been subservient to the Prime Minister and has failed to achieve anything by it'.[121] Needless to say, the Unionists were delighted by this turn of events, and Enoch Powell wrote to Mrs Thatcher to congratulate her on her handling of the summit. Back in London, Robert Armstrong was in despair: 'I really thought "This is it." '[122] Inevitably, the Taoiseach hit back. In remarks which, he said, were misrepresented, FitzGerald was reported as telling his parliamentary party in private session that Mrs Thatcher's words had been 'gratuitously offensive'.[123]* Now it was her turn to get annoyed.[124] She refused to send a conciliatory letter to FitzGerald which the Foreign Office had drafted for her.

FitzGerald wrote to Mrs Thatcher a pained but courteous letter, more in sorrow than in anger. He begged her to acknowledge the Forum report's virtue in recognizing the needs of Unionism and to admit the problem of 'alienation' of the minority, the concept she so much disliked.[125] A few days later, Robert Armstrong followed up these demands, taking FitzGerald's part and suggesting that she write to him to say that she regretted if her manner at the press conference 'has created difficulties for him at home'.[126] On this Mrs Thatcher, who was always acutely aware of the danger of apologies in politics, wrote 'Certainly NOT': 'The whole proposal is too <u>contrived</u> and apologetic. Why?'

Such was the pressure from officials and ministers alike, however (Charles Powell recalled that Geoffrey Howe remained 'very reproachful' for years to come),[127] that Mrs Thatcher bent slightly with the wind. On 29 November, she sent a letter to FitzGerald. 'I share your concern', she told him, 'that my references to the Forum Report and the situation of the minority community in Northern Ireland have been taken totally out of context.'[128] She still refused to accept the word 'alienation', but she agreed that some in the minority community 'do not have confidence in the system of authority and law and order . . . and therein lies the problem which both of us are trying to resolve.'

Rather against her will ('I will if he wishes – but I really think the less said the better'),[129] she agreed to meet FitzGerald in the margins of the European Council on 3 December, in Dublin Castle. There she told him

---

* In Britain the press strongly defended Mrs Thatcher, especially the *Sun*. Bernard Ingham summarized its position: 'The sooner Dr FitzGerald accepts reality the better for all of us' ('Press Digest', Ingham to Thatcher, 23 November 1984, CAC: THCR 3/5/40).

that 'she found it difficult to understand the reaction in the Republic to her press conference'.[130] As Charles Powell acidly recorded, FitzGerald 'continued that there was no point in going back over what had happened at the press conference. He then proceeded to do precisely that.' In response, according to Powell's account, Mrs Thatcher said that 'one thing was clear, one had to develop an extra sensitivity for commenting on the Irish problem. Her own style was to give a direct answer to a direct question.' FitzGerald again begged her, for her scheduled press conference at the end of the summit, to say something nice about the Forum report and to recognize the problems of the minority in the North. She refused, saying that she did not want 'to give the impression of backing down',[131] but the two parted amicably.* Dermot Nally thought: 'She was feeling rather guilty about the damage she felt she had done and did her best to make it up to him. When she came over she told him, "Garret, I am doing the best I can. I have been going around all day with a smile on my face." '[132]

In retrospect, FitzGerald came to the view that Mrs Thatcher's 'out . . . out . . . out-burst' (as some wit called it) had actually been helpful to him. He told Geoffrey Howe that it had helped him convince his Cabinet just how great the difficulties were.[133]

David Goodall agreed. This moment, he believed, had been 'a watershed'. Until then, the Irish had thought they would succeed in getting joint authority. After it, they knew they must settle for less.[134] There is also a psychological point to be made. Mrs Thatcher was one of those people who hate directly admitting error. She believed, probably correctly, that if she did so, her male colleagues (she had no female ones) would seize on it as a sign of weakness. But this does not mean that she was always unaware when she had made mistakes. Her actions after 'out . . . out . . . out' suggest that she did inwardly recognize that she had gone too far. From then on, she was never as strident on the subject again. It became more likely that there would be an Anglo-Irish agreement.

It may not have been a complete coincidence that Mrs Thatcher's reconciliation with FitzGerald occurred in the same month as her visit to Camp David to see President Reagan (see Chapter 8). Although the East–West debates bulked much larger in her mind than the problems of Northern Ireland, she was conscious of American interest in the subject. She also knew that she would be returning to Washington in February 1985, where

---

* The Irish notes on the meeting record a slightly different response from Mrs Thatcher: 'I am frightened to death of saying anything about Nationalists in Northern Ireland' ('Taoiseach's Meeting with Mrs Thatcher', European Council, NAI: DFA/2014/32/2059).

she had been given the honour of addressing both Houses of Congress. While her central theme would be her support for SDI research, she understood that some conciliatory words on Ireland would be expected.

In advance of the Camp David meeting, Reagan came under pressure from his own Irish lobby. Speaker Tip O'Neill wrote to Reagan asking him to 'encourage Mrs Thatcher to renew the Anglo-Irish dialogue over the Forum Report', citing strong support for this in Congress.[135] Reagan always paid careful attention to O'Neill, whose support he needed for bipartisan purposes, but there is little evidence that he actually did anything very much in this case.* Reagan's own officials' note of their encounter shows that it was Mrs Thatcher, not the President, who raised the matter:

> Mrs Thatcher said she wished to address the situation in Northern Ireland. Despite reports to the contrary, she and Garret FitzGerald were on good terms and were making progress . . . The President said making progress is important, and observed that there is great Congressional interest in this matter. Indeed, Tip O'Neill had sent him a personal letter, asking him to appeal to Mrs Thatcher to be reasonable and forthcoming.[136]

By mentioning O'Neill's letter, but not endorsing it, Reagan did what O'Neill had asked, but distanced himself from it.

In the run-up to her speech to Congress two months later (see Chapter 8), Mrs Thatcher was urged by British Embassy officials in Washington to 'introduce America . . . to the fact that there was a new era of co-operation between the Irish government and ours'.[137] She also saw Reagan again, and at lunch in the Oval Office linked her good relations with FitzGerald with their common purpose against terrorism:

> The Prime Minister said that she greatly admired the way in which Dr FitzGerald was fighting the IRA. He had the day before put through emergency legislation to seize IRA funds. She intended to continue her dialogue in Northern Ireland based on consent . . . The Prime Minister thanked the President warmly for the United States' readiness to negotiate to remove the political offence exception from extradition legislation.[138]

---

* In his biography of Mrs Thatcher, John Campbell quotes a letter drafted for Reagan which expressed anxiety that American perceptions of the Chequers summit were 'not favorable' and asked Mrs Thatcher to assure the American public that progress was being made, as evidence of the strength of the pressure brought to bear (see Campbell, *Margaret Thatcher: The Iron Lady*, p. 434). In fact, this letter was never sent. The briefings on the subject which Reagan received before Camp David from George Shultz and others were much more judicious.

When she addressed both Houses after lunch, Mrs Thatcher did as she had been advised, and emphasized the common front between Britain and the Republic: 'Garret FitzGerald and I will continue to consult together in the quest for stability and peace in Northern Ireland and we hope we will have your continued support for our joint efforts to find a way forward.'[139] This was not a central part of her extremely successful speech, but it was, of course, well received. It made it that much harder for her to break out of the process of Anglo-Irish negotiation. Expectations were rising.

Meanwhile, after what David Goodall called the 'merciful pause' of Christmas 1984, British officials had reassembled to take matters forward. The greater sense, post-Chequers, of realism on both sides now meant that the British were readier to accept that a referendum on revising Articles 2 and 3 was unlikely, and the Irish were less pressing about joint authority. But dangers remained from the British point of view, partly because the Irish, to whom the whole business mattered more, were more fertile than London in coming up with ideas. Mrs Thatcher did not bend her mind to the right alternative form of words about the Union which the Irish should concede in any agreement.

The Irish were more focused. The Republic wanted to alter what it saw as a Protestant bias in the RUC and the Ulster Defence Regiment,* and promoted the idea of 'mixed' or 'joint' courts. Because of the problems of intimidation in Northern Ireland, terrorist cases were heard by 'Diplock' courts (established after a report recommending them by the law lord Lord Diplock), in which a judge, without a jury, sat alone. FitzGerald wanted these replaced by courts with a panel of judges, at least one of whom would be drawn from the Republic. Another notion emerging from the Irish side was that, if an agreement was signed, there could be an early release of some terrorists from prison. Even Geoffrey Howe, of all senior ministers the most enthusiastic for an agreement, returned from a trip to Dublin with Douglas Hurd and reported to Mrs Thatcher that 'there is still a significant gap to be bridged.'[140] Frightened about rising newspaper speculation, he asked Mrs Thatcher to point out to FitzGerald 'the need for great caution if our dialogue is not to create more problems in Northern Ireland than it solves'.[141] She duly did so, but by this time, despite all the

* The UDR was a regiment of the British army which was recruited locally during the Troubles in Northern Ireland. Its membership was overwhelmingly Protestant and failed to attract cross-community support. In 1992 it was merged into the newly formed Royal Irish Regiment.

anxieties, the process towards an agreement was beginning to seem ineluctable.

On 24 April, the Cabinet sub-committee OD (I) met to discuss the suggestions now put forward by Howe and Hurd. A basis of agreement was 'now discernible',[142] and a working text existed. The Irish had come to recognize, said the Howe–Hurd paper, that they could not have an executive role in the government of Northern Ireland, but could be 'consulted on a formal basis though because of Irish sensitivities, the proposed text does not use the term "consultative"'. Mrs Thatcher put an angry squiggle underneath this very Irish ambiguity. The Irish would not formally amend their Constitution, but, as part of any agreement, would make a 'constitutional declaration' about the status of Northern Ireland changing only by consent. The combination of the consultative role in return for the constitutional declaration was the 'basic equation' about which both sides had talked for so long, though both elements remained pretty vague.

The Agreement, said Howe and Hurd, would bring Britain 'important gains on four fronts' – in dealings with the SDLP, with the Unionists, in security co-operation and in international image, especially in 'American goodwill'.[143] Unless there was an 'Irish dimension', the SDLP would go on 'resisting participation in the political institutions of the province'. The document stated that 'We gain nothing if we secure the support of the SDLP only at the price of losing the Unionists.' Mrs Thatcher put an arrow of emphasis beside this. But it then went on to argue that if the Unionists did not give anything to the minority, 'the alternative may be further development of the inter-governmental relationship' – a move which would surely 'lose' the Unionists completely.

In a note covering the Howe–Hurd paper, Charles Powell told Mrs Thatcher that she would need 'a firm undertaking from the Irish Government that John Hume and the SDLP will cooperate in moves towards devolution [after any agreement was signed]. (This may be the most difficult, but I don't see how you can go ahead without it.)'[144] The trouble was that the Irish government, despite its closeness to John Hume, was in no position to give such an undertaking, so the main political premise of a possible agreement was insecure. OD (I) went ahead all the same, however. The next day it agreed that the British document be put to the Irish.

Mrs Thatcher continued to worry about the obvious asymmetry in the process. Early in June, she pointed out to Douglas Hurd how dangerous it would be to be locked into an agreement if it started to function badly: 'This was particularly important in that the United Kingdom concession – a consultative role for the Republic – was incorporated in the agreement, but the potential benefits for the United Kingdom – improved security cooperation and SDLP participation – were not.'[145]

At the same time, British worries about the possible reaction of the Unionists grew. They had been deliberately excluded from the process, whereas the SDLP had been kept informed by the Irish government. The record suggests that there was remarkably little discussion about this: it is as if the two governments naturally assumed that it should be so. FitzGerald initially disliked negotiating over the heads of Unionists. He saw them as fellow Irishmen, but believed that they 'were totally intransigent . . . They never identified their own interests.'[146] In Robert Armstrong's view, the Unionists were 'not affected'[147] by the proposed agreement, by which he meant that the Union itself was not affected. It was an intergovernmental agreement that was being discussed. Therefore it was none of their business. According to Charles Powell, their exclusion worried Mrs Thatcher,[148] but even she seems not to have wanted to take the Unionists into her confidence. She knew, of course, the reaction she would encounter if she did, and the certainty of leaks. Besides, for her, 'The concept of the Union mattered more than the people':[149] she believed that she could defend the Union herself without the tiresome Unionist leaders. Her reluctance to talk to them partly stemmed from her surprisingly strong dislike of unpleasant scenes, but the decision to keep the Unionists almost completely in the dark was pregnant with trouble. As David Goodall – just as 'green' as Armstrong, but less ruthless – put it, the exclusion of the Unionists was 'uncomfortable and indeed unfair'.[150] It was bound to come back and bite the British government later.

It was Douglas Hurd and the Northern Ireland Office who insisted that more thought should be given to the Unionists. Hurd pressed Mrs Thatcher to override the Irish view that the Unionists should be told 'as little as possible'.[151] Later, he offered to tell Jim Molyneaux more about the negotiations on Privy Council terms,* but Molyneaux, warned against this by Enoch Powell, refused. Hurd did, however, see both Molyneaux and Ian Paisley (who was not a privy councillor) to outline the progress of the talks. Both declared themselves totally opposed to what they gathered was happening. Mrs Thatcher became increasingly anxious about anything which conceded any judicial or security power to the Republic.

When she met FitzGerald in the margins of the Milan European

---

* 'Privy Council terms' mean that those briefed – member of the Queen's Privy Council, denoted by bearing the title 'the Right Honourable' – are briefed only in confidence. Opposition parties therefore sometimes refuse such briefings on the grounds that they tie their hands when they need to criticize later.

Council at the end of June, she poured out her heart to him. 'She and the Taoiseach both had the same problem in mirror image . . . She was fearful of the reactions of the Unionists to the proposed agreement.'[152]

FitzGerald unwisely started to report to her how some judges in Northern Ireland did not agree with their own Lord Chief Justice, Lord Lowry, who had privately expressed his vehement opposition to joint courts a few days earlier. Mrs Thatcher brought him up smartly. These discussions, she said acidly, 'would run into acute difficulties if he purported to tell her about what went on in judges' meetings in part of the United Kingdom'. FitzGerald told her that he would not sign an agreement without joint courts. He was willing for the Republic to accede to the European Convention on the Suppression of Terrorism (ECST) of 1977. This had both symbolic and practical importance, because of its provisions relating to the extradition of terrorists between contracting states.* She said that she absolutely could not offer anything beyond a readiness to look at the possibility of joint courts; she then repeated this 'with great emphasis'.[153]

Now it was FitzGerald's turn to get passionate. 'Speaking with considerable emotion the Taoiseach said that he wanted the Prime Minister to understand that the Irish government and people did not want a role in Northern Ireland.' He was doing what he was doing because of his fear of the rise of Sinn Fein, helped by Colonel Gaddafi of Libya. He spoke of the danger of Ireland 'coming under a hostile and sinister influence'. Then he made a personal appeal: 'He and the Prime Minister were the only two people able to reach an agreement.' They *must* do so. Mrs Thatcher politely assured him that she 'shared the Taoiseach's aim of preventing Ireland coming under hostile and tyrannical forces',[154] but the key to building confidence would be prompt implementation of whatever agreement they ended up signing.

The underlying common purpose behind the fierce words on both sides was shown by the fact that they ended up discussing the date for the signing of the Agreement, and the best location. On 25 July 1985, the British Cabinet approved the draft Agreement. Although few Cabinet members were later willing to defend the Agreement in public, there was hardly any dissent at the meeting. Douglas Hurd was surprised to find support from Norman Tebbit and this, Hurd felt, persuaded Mrs Thatcher. 'He took the line that we started this negotiation and we might as well finish it. He was not enthusiastic, but he dismissed the idea that we should change our

---

* The ECST sought to limit the number of terrorists escaping extradition on the grounds that they had committed a 'political offence'.

policy because his wife had been crippled and he himself had been attacked. And that settled it.'[155]*

Although the two sides were now close, the ensuing period was as tense as any in the entire process. There were fears of leaks, backslidings and Unionist sabotage. The Irish were trying to get more 'associated measures' and enticing aspirations attached to the Agreement. Mrs Thatcher wanted fewer. Robert Armstrong was pushing for British concessions. As soon as the Cabinet had approved the draft Agreement, he acted. Following the Republic's desire to flesh out the Agreement with explanatory documentation, he sent Mrs Thatcher a 'Draft Passage for a Communiqué' to appear when the Agreement was signed and a form of words which she could use in the House of Commons to disclose that terrorist prisoners would be released if there were 'a real and sustained reduction in the level of violence'.[156] He wanted her to promise quick progress 'with a view to enhancing the confidence of all the people of Northern Ireland in the institutions of law and order' and to 'reinforcing' the even-handedness of the RUC. Mrs Thatcher peppered his note with '<u>NO</u>' and 'The tone is wrong': 'I am utterly astounded by this minute. I am not prepared to go ahead with either of these things.' At the bottom of his note, Armstrong had added: 'This proposal has been agreed with the NIO.' '<u>Not with me</u>,' scrawled Mrs Thatcher, underlining it three times. Reflecting opinion in Cabinet, she emphasized the need for parliamentary approval of the Agreement itself before anything could be added: 'The whole thing has to be debated first.'

In his reply to Armstrong on Mrs Thatcher's behalf, Charles Powell set out her criticisms sternly, but he did add his own gloss of her thoughts. She was saying, wrote Powell, that it would be 'counter-productive' to link the release of Irish prisoners to the Agreement: 'I interpret this to mean that she would not exclude some private assurance to the Irish government at a later stage.'[157] There is no evidence that such a private assurance was given, and Powell, when questioned by the present author about his note, said he could remember nothing about it. But for such a trusted official to write as he did on his mistress's behalf suggests that she was prepared to concede more behind the scenes than she liked to disclose in public, as she had also done during the hunger strikes. In the Northern Irish 'peace process' of the 1990s, the release of terrorist prisoners would become a

---

* The only serious doubts about the Agreement in Cabinet were expressed by John Biffen, the Lord Privy Seal. Although Biffen was liked by colleagues, he was discounted by Mrs Thatcher.

key issue. It is interesting to find it foreshadowed in the much tougher circumstances of the 1980s.

Back and forth through the summer came messages of doubt, hesitation and pain. Here Lord Hailsham, the Lord Chancellor, insisting that mixed courts were out of the question; there Robert Armstrong suggesting that mixed courts could be dealt with in a side-document to the Agreement ('This would probably leak and anyway be rather dishonest,' Powell told Mrs Thatcher).[158] Here were the Unionist leaders coming to see Mrs Thatcher and complaining of a sell-out. There were the Irish, denied mixed courts, threatening to withdraw their readiness to sign up for the European Convention on the Suppression of Terrorism, thus undermining the promise of better security co-operation – a key component of the Agreement from Mrs Thatcher's point of view. In a flurry of meetings, Armstrong–Nally went through point after point of language and detail. No one was guiltier of backsliding than Mrs Thatcher herself, always anxious about what she might have conceded. 'Having read the Agreement again,' she wrote on a Charles Powell memo of 26 September, '– I fear it does <u>not</u> accurately convey our meaning. The fact is that this committee is no more than <u>consultative</u>. We have made it sound as if we have given the Republic some <u>authority</u> in our affairs. We haven't and we don't intend to.'[159] In the end, the Agreement created a mechanism by which the Republic could put forward 'views and proposals' about the running of Northern Ireland. The Irish role was only consultative, but that word was avoided.

At the beginning of September, Mrs Thatcher had reshuffled her Cabinet. She promoted Douglas Hurd from Northern Ireland to the Home Office, and replaced him with Tom King.* (See Chapter 13.) Although the Irish had nothing against King personally, they regarded the change as an insult. With the Agreement imminent, changing the relevant minister implied that Mrs Thatcher did not really give much thought to Ireland, and moved her pieces round the chess board for other reasons. King, who admitted that he had not previously been familiar with the details of the negotiations,[160] asked Mrs Thatcher when she offered him the job whether she was determined to push the Agreement through. 'Yes, I am,' she said.[161] He was alarmed, when he took up the reins, to find how completely the Unionists were being ignored, when John Hume and the SDLP had been fully involved by the Dublin government. 'The presentation, the secrecy – they stirred up the Unionists. I had to deal with this problem.'[162]

On 27 September, Charles Powell passed on to Mrs Thatcher what he

---

* Like Jim Prior's previously, King's move from Employment to the NIO was regarded as a demotion.

described in his covering note as 'a bit of a bombshell'.[163] King had sent Mrs Thatcher a memo which, in Powell's words, 'is, in effect, a declaration of no confidence in the present negotiating team'. Although prefacing his remarks by saying that an agreement should be sought, King warned of 'unwelcome and unmanageable consequences, particularly in handling the unionist reaction'.[164] The Agreement as drafted 'strikes me as offering considerably more to the Irish than it does to us': he believed that they were getting 'an unprecedented foothold in the internal affairs of part of the United Kingdom'. Unionists would see the Agreement as breaching the undertaking that any arrangement for governing Northern Ireland must command widespread acceptance. A proposed reference to controlling parades and processions would be 'a red rag' to Unionists. The idea of locating the Irish secretariat set up by the Agreement in Belfast (Stormont itself, the seat of the former Ulster government and parliament, had been suggested) was 'asking for trouble'. The Unionists would physically impede it. And now the Irish, wrote King in exasperation, were even saying they would not accede to the terrorism convention after all.

Mrs Thatcher was stirred by what she read. 'This could be the end of the agreement,'[165] she wrote, and added, 'no prospect of devolution'. She endorsed King's argument that the Agreement was heavily in favour of the Irish – 'At present, it is.'[166] Sensing a danger that Mrs Thatcher might waver, Howe and Armstrong moved fast to counter what King had said. Howe, who was at a conference in Ottawa, wrote plaintively to her, pointing out that only a month ago he had phoned the Irish Foreign Minister, Peter Barry, 'at your express request'[167] to assure him that King's appointment had not changed the policy. It would be a terrible missed opportunity to drop everything now. Mrs Thatcher was not, in fact, intending to cancel the Agreement. Although she liked King, she found him 'too garrulous',[168] and his rather scattergun approach no match for the more intellectual and experienced people like Howe and Armstrong ranged on the other side. Besides, she was 'far too far down the road to go back'.[169] She saw King's warnings more as an opportunity to strengthen the British hand. 'I fear they [the Irish] have "fudged" some of the language,' she wrote on Howe's letter, 'so that our meaning and theirs is different and the words themselves unclear . . . We must look at the text afresh.'

She assembled Howe, King and Armstrong to discuss King's doubts and work out where the whole process had got to. On one side, the meeting argued that the Irish were 'likely to prove not just a thorn in the flesh but a positive thicket of brambles',[170] and there was no clear commitment from the SDLP to co-operate with devolved government. Against this, however, was the danger of strengthening Sinn Fein and 'the downside risks of failing to complete the Agreement'. The British must secure Irish accession to the terrorism convention, the meeting decided, and change the text of the Agreement to emphasize that national responsibilities were to be retained in their existing jurisdictions: 'The Prime Minister stressed that in public comment after an agreement was reached, we must be able to make crystal clear that the Irish Government would have no executive role in the North.'[171] She followed up the meeting with a letter to Garret FitzGerald telling him she was nervous of a 'violent reaction'[172] wrecking everything. She also asked FitzGerald to reconsider his government's refusal to accede to the terrorism convention. Eventually, a compromise was worked out in which the Irish 'intention' to accede echoed the British readiness to look at the 'possibility' of mixed courts.

Feelings were running high. The Unionists complained that the Pope knew more about what was happening in the negotiations than they did (which may well have been true). But the process tottered on, and discussions about a date and a place for signature neared completion. The Irish kept wanting to bring the date forward, the British to push it back. In the end, 15 November was agreed. All sorts of ideas – Dublin, the Irish Embassy in London, the Temple of Peace in Cardiff, even (an Irish suggestion) New York – were proposed for the great day, but gradually, despite anxiety about security and politics, both sides settled on Hillsborough Castle, the seat of British power in Northern Ireland.

At the end of October, the Agreement came to the Cabinet once more. This was the moment of real decision. Charles Powell set out for Mrs Thatcher what had gone wrong – the doubts of Tom King, the rise of Unionist opposition, the fact that the package had 'deteriorated'[173] because of the weakening of security co-operation and the dilution of the Irish commitment to signing the ECST, and the lack of any commitment from the SDLP. There was also a risk of misunderstanding with the Irish about the consultative nature of their role. On the other hand, the Agreement was 'defensible': 'it concedes nothing significant, though we shall be honour-bound not to make this too obvious.' Reports suggested that the Unionists would have more difficulty than in the past in getting strikes and protests going. Failure to go ahead would disappoint the Americans. 'You told President Reagan last week', Powell reminded her, 'that an agreement was likely.'[174] If the Cabinet did decide not to go ahead, 'we must leave ourselves with a good reason for terminating the negotiations.' In Powell's view, this would be the Republic's failure to accede to the ECST. But in Cabinet there was no trouble. On 31 October, it accepted the Anglo-Irish Agreement in principle, while inviting 'improvements'.

Once the Cabinet had decided, Mrs Thatcher was keen to get on. She refused, for example, Tom King's eleventh-hour attempt to get mixed courts out of the Agreement altogether. Of the two leaders, it was FitzGerald who became the twitchier. The day after the Cabinet decision, he deputed Richard Ryan of the Irish Embassy in London to call on Charles Powell. He was made 'nervous', Ryan told Powell, by Mrs Thatcher's recent remarks in New York in which she had reiterated that decisions about the North would continue to be taken in London, as those about the South were taken in Dublin: 'the line . . . woke memories of "out, out, out".'[175]

FitzGerald feared that what he regarded as great achievements would be allowed to trickle away. On 7 November, he wrote to Mrs Thatcher to say how worried he was about the location and timing of the Intergovernmental Conference (IGC) which the Agreement would create. It must be in Stormont, headed by representatives of high and equal rank on both sides, and it must not be delayed. Mrs Thatcher told Armstrong, Howe and King that she was 'perturbed by the tone of the Taoiseach's remarks about the location'.[176] It would send the wrong political signal to put the IGC secretariat in Stormont. The Northern Ireland Office started desperately scrabbling round for premises, and eventually found them in government buildings at Maryfield, just outside Belfast, which had no emotional political associations. In her reply to FitzGerald, she therefore gave him a rather dusty answer, emphasizing the importance of security co-operation 'in its own right' and pointing out that it would take time for people 'to get used to there being a presence of your government in Belfast'.[177] The draft of the letter supplied by Armstrong ended on an upbeat note about how Britain and the Republic were embarking on 'something entirely new and exciting'. Mrs Thatcher cut this out.

On 11 November, FitzGerald gathered the leaders of the SDLP to brief them on the full contents of the Agreement. The meeting ended with an emotional singing of the Irish national anthem. The mood in Ulster was quite different. Unionist newspapers and politicians sounded dire warnings. In the House of Commons, at Prime Minister's Questions a day before the signing of the Agreement, Enoch Powell asked Mrs Thatcher, 'Does the right hon. Lady understand – if she does not yet understand she soon will – that the penalty for treachery is to fall into public contempt?'[178] Richard Ryan was sitting in the public gallery: 'Powell blew it. She just looked at him with the most ferocious, cold, hardened face, and I think that is where his influence snapped.'[179] In terms of any personal relationship while she remained in office, this may well be true, although in after years Mrs Thatcher generally spoke respectfully of Powell. In the Commons, she replied that Powell's jibe was 'deeply offensive', and she meant it. But his words were telling all the same.* They played on her biggest anxiety about what she was doing, an anxiety which was never completely stilled.

Oddly, it was Bernard Ingham, normally keen that his boss should stand up to foreigners, who told her most clearly to put her heart into what was about to happen. He wrote to her to prepare for her joint press conference with FitzGerald: 'I believe that, in my [that is, media] terms, some resignations might be helpful in the sense that you will be seen to be standing up to the Unionists about whom you are perceived to be wobbly.'[180] Aware that her old friend Ian Gow was likely to resign (Gow saw her that very day to warn her of his intention), he added, '. . . you will need to deal firmly in public with those who resign.' 'The media', he went on, 'will be looking like hawks for signs of a lack of resolve.' He suggested a question which might be thrown at her – 'Is this a historic agreement . . . And if it doesn't mean much, why spend all the time and energy on getting it?' In her own mind, Mrs Thatcher did not have a confident answer to this question.

Early the next morning, Friday 15 November, Mrs Thatcher flew into RAF Aldergrove in Northern Ireland and was transferred by helicopter to Hillsborough Castle. Already Ian Paisley and his crowd of supporters were gathering outside the gates to protest. Inside, there was an atmosphere of 'nervous cheerfulness'[181] among British and Irish officials. Mrs Thatcher, always soothed by domestic detail, busied herself moving the flowers about and rearranging the furniture, making FitzGerald and Geoffrey Howe help her. She carefully 'checked [that] the picture on the wall behind the table at which she and the Taoiseach would sit [for the signing] had no overtly green or orange connotations'[182] and was relieved that it was an eighteenth-century view of Windsor Castle. Shortly after this, Ian Gow's letter of resignation arrived and was passed immediately to Mrs Thatcher. In it, he told her that 'the change of policy in Northern Ireland, including the involvement of a foreign power in a consultative role in the administration of the province, will prolong, and not diminish Ulster's agony. I cannot support this change of policy; it follows that I cannot remain in your Government.'[183] Mrs Thatcher went upstairs and spoke to Gow on the telephone for a long time, still hoping to dissuade him. She failed. The departure of such a close colleague on an issue of principle

---

* Powell had a masterful ability to capture the mood of the moment. In 1982, just after the Falklands War, he had praised Mrs Thatcher's leadership abilities, saying that she was made of 'ferrous matter of the highest quality' (playing on her reputation as the 'iron lady') (see Vol.1, pp. 750–5). These words had given Mrs Thatcher great pleasure, a fact that made Powell's later accusation of treachery all the more insulting.

with which she instinctively sympathized made her mood even more anxious. 'It seriously upset and rattled her,' recalled David Goodall.[184] Howe, who was present at Hillsborough, had particular cause to mourn. Gow was one of his greatest and oldest friends (he had been his election campaign assistant in the 1959 election), and his closeness to Mrs Thatcher had enabled many problems between Howe and her to be smoothed out. 'It was a blow to us and a blow to the whole relationship,' he recalled.[185]*

Those present noticed that her mood had changed. Watching from the Irish side, Michael Lillis observed:

> When she was getting ready to go down and sign the Agreement, I sensed the most intense tension. And I wonder subsequently, did she know what a difficult thing this was going to be for her? It sort of reminded me of the famous remark of Michael Collins [the Irish Republican leader] when he was leaving Downing Street in 1921 – 'I have signed my death warrant' . . . If that's true, I give her all the more credit for taking this tremendous risk, which, I believe, paid off. She did a very courageous and extremely valuable thing and I am sorry that she came to dislike it.[186]

She signed. The Taoiseach followed, using the Irish version of his name, Gearóid Mac Gearailt.†

After the signing, Mrs Thatcher went back upstairs with officials to prepare for the press conference. She was agitated, and began scribbling on scraps of paper and reading aloud sections of the agreed text. She recruited Dermot Nally to assist her and instructed Robert Armstrong to help FitzGerald: 'Dermot, you ask me the questions I might have to face. Robert, you ask Garret.'[187] She was trying to rehearse the lines which both sides wanted. With her usual slight muddle about the right terms to use in Irish matters, she kept referring in this practice session to the Anglo-Irish 'Treaty'. David Goodall pointed out the unfortunate historical associations for the Irish of that word, and reminded her to stick to 'Agreement'.[188] She then descended for the press conference, which was very hot and crowded. The 'frightful hammering noise'[189] from the Paisleyites beyond the gates was audible. Mrs Thatcher spoke first. She started with the rejection of violence and the mutual recognition of 'the validity of both traditions in Northern Ireland',[190] and placed only third in her order of

---

* In the *Daily Telegraph*, T. E. Utley wrote that 'Gow's resignation has done something to improve the moral health of public life.' On the whole the press supported the Agreement and had little sympathy with Unionist defiance ('Press Digest', Ingham to Thatcher, 18 November 1985, CAC: THCR 3/5/50).

† An Irish-language version of the Agreement was issued by the Irish government, though it had no standing in domestic or international law.

priority the most controversial aspect – the intergovernmental conference which allowed the Irish government to put forward 'views and proposals' about the province. Using clumsy nomenclature, Mrs Thatcher described herself as 'a unionist and a loyalist' and FitzGerald as 'a nationalist and republican'. FitzGerald began with a few words in Irish, 'A Naisiúntachtai Uaisceart Eireann, tógagaí bhur gceann,' roughly translated as 'Nationalists of Northern Ireland, lift up your heads!'* Tom King thought this was 'a pretty insensitive thing to have done without any warning to us, when neither Margaret nor Geoffrey nor I had the slightest idea what he was saying'.[191] Otherwise FitzGerald stuck carefully to pre-agreed lines. He spoke of himself and Mrs Thatcher coming to the negotiations 'with different historical perspectives and, as it were, different title deeds', but agreeing about the future. The press conference passed off without untoward incident.

The wider world welcomed the Anglo-Irish Agreement. Helmut Kohl extolled its 'historical significance'.[192] President Reagan produced a statement, supported by Speaker O'Neill, offering US assistance: 'We applaud its promise of peace and a new dawn for the troubled communities of Northern Ireland. I wish to congratulate my two good friends – and outstanding Prime Ministers – who have demonstrated such statesmanship, vision, and courage.'[193] As Mrs Thatcher herself put it, 'The Anglo-Irish Agreement put us on side with Americans.'[194] There was a wide welcome in the House of Commons too, which eventually voted for it by 473 votes to 47, though since the Labour Opposition praised the Agreement as a means of advancing a united Ireland, this was not wholly helpful to Mrs Thatcher. In the Republic, Charles Haughey immediately opposed the Agreement as compromising Irish claims on Northern Ireland, but there was a general mood of triumph, and he was soon forced to soften his opposition. Garret FitzGerald – deservedly, given his immense efforts – had won his place in history.

But, as Mrs Thatcher told FitzGerald when she met him on the margins of the European Council in Luxembourg at the beginning of December, 'You've got the glory and I've got the problems.'[195] Among the Unionists, there was rage. In a special session of the Northern Ireland Assembly the day after the signing, they denounced it. A week later, a huge rally in Belfast demonstrated a united Unionist front. In a sermon at his Martyrs'

* According to Michael Lillis, who drafted these words, the point FitzGerald was trying to convey was that this event should portend an end to the humiliation for successive generations of Nationalists (Interview with Michael Lillis).

Memorial Church, Ian Paisley prayed that God would 'this night . . . deal with the Prime Minister of our country. We remember that the apostle Paul handed over the enemies of truth to the devil that they might learn not to blaspheme. O God, in wrath take vengeance upon this wicked, treacherous, lying woman.'[196]*

The Almighty did not intervene as Paisley ordered Him, but He certainly did not hurry to Mrs Thatcher's aid either. Failing in their demand for a province-wide referendum on the Agreement, all Unionist MPs resigned their parliamentary seats, standing in by-elections with each of the Unionist parties giving the other a clear run in seats which it had previously held.† The slogan for the campaign was 'ULSTER SAYS NO!' In Tom King's view, Mrs Thatcher 'didn't anticipate the strength of Unionist opposition, and the position in which ministers found themselves'.[197] He was jostled and spat at, and the Unionist MPs boycotted him completely, though they went on seeing Mrs Thatcher.‡ A Unionist protest march descended on Maryfield, where the Anglo-Irish secretariat had been sited, and tore the gates down. Some Unionist politicians incited revolt, urging RUC officers that the Agreement was contrary to their oath of allegiance to the Crown. But the Chief Constable, Sir John Hermon, stood firm and the security situation, though tense, never ran out of control. 'I find it difficult to believe that there is an incipient crisis of confidence amongst the Royal Ulster Constabulary in the Chief Constable, the NIO and Government,' Mrs Thatcher told the Conservative MP Sir Eldon Griffiths. 'The loyalty and dedication of the Force is not in question and, as Tom King and I have made clear on many occasions, the Chief Constable enjoys our full confidence.'[198]§

On 3 March 1986, the Unionists ordered a 'Day of Action' in Northern Ireland, in effect, a general strike. It was widely observed.

---

* Mrs Thatcher, it appeared, did not take this to heart. Paisley might be a 'hardliner', she told President Reagan several months later, 'but not a terrorist; his bark is worse than his bite'. (Memcon, 4 May 1986, Exec Sec, NSC System I, #8603593, Reagan Library.)

† They all retained their seats by this process, except for one seat, gained by Seamus Mallon of the SDLP.

‡ After the Agreement had been signed, King worked hard to implement it. 'He was a loyal trouper,' recalled Richard Ehrman, then King's special adviser. 'He managed to keep the lid on the Unionist reaction . . . He won back Thatcher's respect because she realized what a hot potato the Agreement became.' (Interview with Richard Ehrman.)

§ Mrs Thatcher received letters from wives and mothers of RUC officers who were worried about security. 'I can well understand the anguish you must feel as a mother of three police officers in the Royal Ulster Constabulary,' she replied to one. 'I have nothing but the deepest admiration for their courage and fortitude in carrying out their duties in the most difficult circumstances.' (Thatcher letter, 7 May 1986, CAC: THCR 3/2/190.)

Being the sort of person who, once she has decided something, does not budge, Mrs Thatcher was not moved by these protests, except to anger. 'I was not prepared for the depths of the hostility,' she later recalled, 'but we get these things in Ireland.'[199] Anxiety in the Republic that she might resile from the Agreement was unfounded. Michael Lillis, who led the Irish delegation in Maryfield, and watched the assault on the Maryfield gates on television, was impressed by her resolve: 'It was a tremendous hurricane of fury, and she didn't back down. She confronted it. The RUC were put in a position of having to deal with it, and they did.'[200]

Provoked to justify her position over the Agreement, Mrs Thatcher started to take up arguments about Unionist misbehaviour over the years. The present author met her (for the first time) at a private dinner in the House of Commons at the end of November:

> She went on about Ulster and how the Unionists had persecuted the minority and how she couldn't send 'wave after wave' of young men to look after the place. She imagines she can win the Unionists over by offering power-sharing. She was sparky. She referred to matters of Ulster as 'foreign affairs'. I asked her how her devotion to the British nation could justify her sort of behaviour. She said human rights mattered more than anything else. I did my best to needle her and she became gratifyingly angry.[201]

She particularly reproved the Unionists because some of their local councils had allegedly refused to empty Roman Catholic dustbins.

However crossly Mrs Thatcher felt towards the Unionists, however, she did not feel correspondingly closer to the Nationalists. She had no desire at all to bring about any further constitutional shift in favour of the Republic. So she found herself effectively without allies on the ground in moving matters forward in Northern Ireland. She had persuaded herself that the Agreement might promote devolution. In her mind, it was 'a very important clause'[202] in the Agreement that once devolution returned to Northern Ireland, the powers the Republic had gained under it would return to a power-sharing government in Northern Ireland. But this was not a convincing defence of the Agreement, especially as Mrs Thatcher had not pushed for a devolution settlement while the negotiations were going on. The SDLP, in whose name so much of the Agreement had been negotiated, did not, after all, agree to take part in devolution or to urge its supporters to join the police or the UDR. A key premise of the Agreement fell away. Far from boosting the SDLP, the gradual effect of the Agreement was to strengthen the more extreme parties on both sides of the sectarian divide. In the summer of the following year, the Cabinet decided that the existing Northern Ireland Assembly was serving no useful purpose, and so no further elections were held. The Anglo-Irish Agreement did not regenerate the political life of the province, but produced, for quite a long period, complete stasis.

Worse, from Mrs Thatcher's point of view, was the failure of the Republic to deliver the security improvements which had been held up to her by British officials as the great prize of the Agreement. As she wrote in her memoirs, the Agreement's concessions 'alienated the Unionists without gaining the level of security co-operation we had a right to expect'.[203] Even Robert Armstrong accepted that the security results were 'disappointing'.[204] The trade-off between mixed courts and accession to the ECST fell to the ground, although the Republic did eventually ratify its accession after FitzGerald had lost office and eleven people had been killed in the Enniskillen Remembrance Day bombing of November 1987. The cross-border links between the RUC and the Garda Síochána (the Irish police) did not markedly improve, and Mrs Thatcher was particularly disappointed that greater intelligence co-operation did not result either: 'We received far better intelligence co-operation from virtually all other European countries than with the Republic.'[205] Speaking in 2012, Michael Lillis admitted that the Irish side did not do enough to tackle the security problem: 'I think we should have tried harder.' FitzGerald tried 'very hard', but he was faced with internal resistance particularly from the Garda Commissioner Larry Wren to some of Chief Constable Hermon's proposals.[206] Mrs Thatcher was naturally inclined to ask whether the game was worth the candle. The rather scratchy chapter about the Agreement in her memoirs concluded with the words: 'In the light of this [negative] experience, it is surely time to consider an alternative approach.'[207] She felt unease about what she had herself conceded. She knew, before she signed the Agreement, that the Irish might not deliver on the original promise of better security co-operation.*

Was Mrs Thatcher too harsh in her retrospective judgment? Many of those who worked with her on the subject thought so. People like Armstrong and Goodall, who had invested so much in the negotiations, felt proud of their work, and admired Mrs Thatcher for the way in which, as they thought of it, she had swallowed her prejudices to get the Agreement. They counted it a success. They saw the Anglo-Irish Agreement as the forerunner of the 'peace process' (the phrase was not in use at the time of the Agreement) which reached its climax in the Good Friday Agreement of 1998. 'Indeed, from some Irish diplomats' point of view, the later

---

* Notably, she had been told of FitzGerald's difficulties signing up to the ECST.

Agreement may have been seen as something of a comedown.'[208]* This, though it may be true, did not comfort Mrs Thatcher much.

As she considered the Anglo-Irish Agreement in later years, she came to look upon it more and more unfavourably.† This attitude found its final expression in her review of Simon Heffer's biography of Enoch Powell which appeared in 1998. 'On the matter of his [Powell's] objections to the 1985 Anglo-Irish Agreement,' she wrote, 'I now believe that his assessment was right, though I wish ... he had been less inclined to impugn the motives of those who disagreed with him.'[209] She meant that Powell's criticisms of the Agreement for its encroachment on British sovereignty were well founded. Unionists welcomed these words of repentance. After her death, they spoke of their admiration for Mrs Thatcher's willingness to confront terrorism and to stand up for the British nation.[210] But it was she, more than any other prime minister, who succeeded in overriding what pro-Nationalists called the Unionist 'veto'. She was not proud of this achievement. Political change had been imposed on Northern Ireland from outside. In this sense, Mrs Thatcher began something which she did not want and went against principles which she held dear. Speaking after her death, Charles Powell said that Mrs Thatcher's regret at signing the Anglo-Irish Agreement was comparable to Queen Mary I of England's terrible sadness at the loss of Calais. 'Queen Mary spoke of having "Calais" inscribed on her heart. Mrs Thatcher will have "Anglo-Irish Agreement" inscribed on her heart.'[211]

Where she did achieve something more positive, however, was in changing the attitudes of Irish and British governments to one another. The experience of the Thatcher–FitzGerald encounters was often bruising, but Mrs Thatcher did succeed in bringing the Irish government to a more realistic assessment of what it was possible for it to achieve. The old assumption of Irish politics, that it was always a good idea to be seen to be attacking Britain, was consigned to history. Not for nothing was the Agreement called the Anglo-Irish Agreement. It was a deal between governments, negotiated in good faith. It did not, in itself, greatly help the

---

* See the reflections of Michael Lillis and David Goodall on the Twenty-Fifth Anniversary of the Anglo-Irish Agreement, in 'Edging towards Peace', *Dublin Review of Books*, issue 16, Winter 2010 (http://www.drb.ie/essays/edging-towards-peace). The view that Mrs Thatcher paved the way for the Good Friday Agreement was repeated by many commentators after her death. See, for example, the *Irish Times*, 9 April 2013.

† In private, she cast around for someone to blame for a decision she now regretted. 'It was the pressure from the Americans that made me sign the Agreement,' she told Alistair McAlpine. (Alistair McAlpine, *Once a Jolly Bagman: Memoirs*, Weidenfeld & Nicolson, 1997, p. 272.) In fact, while American views mattered, there is precious little evidence that they ever came close to being decisive.

object of all its labours – the people of Northern Ireland. Even the Irish government recognized this. 'For the average person living in West Belfast or Derry nothing changed, and the war continued.'[212] From a Unionist point of view, the Agreement established the bad precedent that the future of a part of the United Kingdom could be a matter of international negotiation. But it did permanently improve the relationship between the two nations whose leaders signed it. In her somewhat ungenerous writings about Garret FitzGerald – a man whom she did, in fact, respect and like – Mrs Thatcher did not do justice to his patience, decency and lack of sectarian bitterness. She also did an injustice to herself. FitzGerald had been right when he told her that only he and she between them could strike a deal. She saw this and acted on it bravely. The Agreement was not the breakthrough of which FitzGerald dreamed, but it was a remarkable moment in the history of Britain and Ireland.

There is another way of looking at the story of the Anglo-Irish Agreement. Ignore, for a moment, the content of the whole process, and instead study its methods. If one does this, one is bound to conclude that the essential aim of both the British and Irish official machines was to persuade Mrs Thatcher into doing what she did not want to do. As Garret FitzGerald recalled in retirement, the whole process was 'extraordinary': 'Ultimately it was not a negotiation. Ultimately everybody was convinced that something should be done. "How do you persuade the Prime Minister?" was the question.'[213] 'Armstrong–Nally' was not symmetrical between the two countries. The sympathies of Armstrong were with FitzGerald in a way that those of Nally – or indeed of Armstrong himself – were never with Mrs Thatcher. The same applies to David Goodall. The pattern of business was that senior British officials were always received at the highest levels in Dublin. The same thing did not happen the other way round in London. Although the British members of Armstrong–Nally faithfully represented the points of view of the British government in negotiation, they were on extremely close terms with their Irish counterparts, whom they regarded as 'civilized'. They were desperate for an agreement in a way that Mrs Thatcher never was: 'We did have our hearts in this thing.'[214] Between them, Armstrong–Nally created a structure which was bound to frustrate the beliefs with which Mrs Thatcher instinctively approached the subject.

Geoffrey Howe, too, saw the issue from FitzGerald's point of view and 'kept an eye on things throughout'.[215] Hence, presumably, Richard Ryan's suggestion that he be 'worked on'. In his memoirs, Howe speaks of the Taoiseach's 'statesmanship' in contrast to Mrs Thatcher's 'intemperance'.[216] She was seen as the problem: 'It took a gigantic effort by many far-sighted people to persuade her.'[217] Robert Armstrong, one of those 'far-sighted' people, credited FitzGerald's 'extraordinary patience in dealing with her outbursts',[218] rather than praising his own Prime Minister for standing her ground. David Goodall, who, of all the participants, probably gave the greatest intellectual attention to the entire subject and recorded it most fully, conceded that 'It is very fair to say that we were all trying to persuade her . . . We did a bit conspire . . . We did have moments when she was being terribly difficult and unreasonable.'[219]

There is something tragi-comic about this image of the massed ranks of the British state behaving towards the Prime Minister almost as if she were a slightly mad, rich old lady who might cut them out of her will at any moment. As with many subjects – Rhodesia, Hong Kong, some aspects of the Cold War, the EEC – some of the cleverest men in the realm had real difficulty in understanding that they faced a Prime Minister who truly did not share their beliefs about the virtues of internationalism and consensus or their instinctive aversion to asserting the claims of Britishness. They went to great lengths to oppose what they saw as her mistaken will. More often than not, their version of *raison d'état* prevailed over her instincts. It would be absurd, however, to argue that Mrs Thatcher was their prisoner, and paranoid to suggest that they cheated her. She was too formidable for that. She was reluctant, but not deluded. As Charles Powell put it, 'They were all plotting to persuade her. She was tugged along. But she knew what it was about.'[220] Why, then, did she do it? Surely because, although she never liked what was being proposed, she did not have enough knowledge and backing to frame an alternative. She felt she had to do *something* and she allowed herself to be persuaded of the likely benefits of most of it. The subject did not matter to her so much that she was prepared to fight to what would certainly have been a bitter end.

II

Poll tax

'Voter & payer'

Because Mrs Thatcher believed in property, she did not like property taxes. To get rid of them, she embarked on a quest which reached its goal in her second term. The replacement she eventually chose turned out, once put into practice in her third term, to be the most unpopular domestic measure of her premiership. Although she adamantly refused to use the name, it became notorious as the 'poll tax'.

When she came into office in 1979, local government in Britain was, in principle at least, funded chiefly by the rates – business and domestic. The rates were property taxes, levied on the notional rental value of the property in question. Business rates upset Mrs Thatcher, because they were a form of taxation without representation.* Domestic rates seemed to her to punish the property-owning instinct which she so admired. 'Any property tax', she wrote in her memoirs, 'is essentially a tax on improving one's own home.'[1] Worse, domestic rates fell chiefly upon such improvers, and often did not tax other, non-property-owning voters – because of a system of rebates – in local elections at all. Those who made the greatest use of local government services – social services, for instance – were the least likely to pay for them. 'The people who benefit don't pay. The people who pay don't benefit' was how Mrs Thatcher encapsulated the problem.[2]

Rates also punished the sort of poor with whom Mrs Thatcher was most sympathetic: her favourite example was the elderly widow living alone, next door to a family of four workers in a similar house. The two households would face a similar rates bill and so the widow ended up paying four times as much as each of the workers. Non-ratepaying voters could, and often did, elect high-spending Labour councils, secure in the knowledge that they would not have to put their money where their vote was. These Labour councils increased the rates year after year – rises of

---

* The old business vote in local elections had long been abolished.

30 per cent were not uncommon in the early 1980s – confident that the non-paying voters would not mind, and that higher spending could, thanks to the curious system of 'rate support' invented in the 1920s by John Maynard Keynes, attract higher central government grants. Increasingly, hard-left Labour councils exploited the system not only to win local elections, but also to build socialist 'republics' (as they were often referred to) at the expense of their ratepayers and to the detriment of ratepaying, non-voting businesses. By the time Mrs Thatcher came into office in 1979, the central government Rate Support Grant accounted for over 60 per cent of total local government spending. Rates assailed those whom Mrs Thatcher liked to call 'our people', and their deficiencies had to be made up, on a grand scale, by general, national taxation. Local government spending was ultimately, in financial terms, the responsibility of the Treasury. It could have a major effect on the PSBR. If it went awry, therefore, her national battle against excessive public spending could not be won. She hated rates for both ideological and political reasons. It was her dream to abolish them. She also considered it her promise, first made in October 1974.

In the run-up to the 1983 general election Mrs Thatcher had struggled to advance this cause but failed (see Chapter 2). The Tory manifesto merely promised legislation to 'curb excessive and irresponsible rate increases by high-spending councils' and the introduction of 'a general scheme for limitation of rate increases for all local authorities'. It also pledged, rather at the last minute, to abolish the Greater London Council and the metropolitan counties – such as Greater Manchester and the West Midlands. These overarching bodies – particularly the GLC – had relatively few duties: the real work was done by the London boroughs and the city councils. But they did have considerable prominence and considerable sums of ratepayers' money which they liked to use in political campaigns. They – especially the GLC – became well known for promoting the causes of what the papers called the 'loony left', such as supporting Sinn Fein–IRA and undermining the police. They sought to fight the government, with ratepayers' money. It seemed to Mrs Thatcher and her supporters that they could be abolished with financial and political advantage and without affront to the constitution.* Some of her colleagues doubted this.

---

* An additional irritation for the government was that the bills from the GLC and the metropolitan counties were not separately received by ratepayers, but were 'precepts' – sums added to the rates bill sent out by the lower-tier councils (in London, the boroughs). This meant that voters were often confused about which extravagant authorities were hitting their pockets. Conservative boroughs could, and did, see their rates shoot up because of profligate Labour metropolitan county councils.

Michael Heseltine, recently promoted from environment to defence secretary, predicted in Cabinet in May 1983 that 'In some cases, the possibility
of confrontation will not be a threat, but an incentive.'³ This was prescient.
The manifesto said nothing about reforming the rates themselves.

So, early on in her second term as prime minister, Mrs Thatcher set to
work to enact these pledges, but the path to more fundamental reform
remained unclear. Stephen Sherbourne, the head of Mrs Thatcher's political office, bumped into Terry Heiser,* the Deputy Secretary at the
Department of the Environment (which had responsibility for local government), at a reception at No. 10 shortly after the 1983 election victory.
'I'd love to know what she wants to *do* with local government,' Heiser
said.⁴ Sherbourne felt he did not know the answer.

Nor, perhaps, did Mrs Thatcher herself. It has often been claimed that
she was hostile to local government. Some have tried to explain this
psychologically, as being a reaction against her father, the Grantham
alderman, or against the way he was thrown out of office by Labour
councillors,⁵ or both.† But there is no real evidence for this. She liked
municipal pride and municipal competence. What she always disliked,
from her earliest political days, was a lack of relationship between who
votes and who pays. She felt that Labour had weakened this link, removed
powers from local government and thus undermined its quality. In 1949,
when a parliamentary candidate in Dartford for the first time, she contributed an article on local government to a magazine called *Conservative
Oxford*. In it, she complained that nationalization had removed councils'
revenue-raising powers by taking utilities out of their control and by
grabbing entities such as hospitals from council management. There was
a 'loss of local responsibility'.⁶ Councils were left to deal only with little
things, she said, and so 'Civic pride . . . will disappear.' This remained
her view, and the rise of politically extreme, financially irresponsible
Labour councils in the 1970s and early 1980s seemed to confirm it. If only
local government could be largely self-financing (as late as the early 1960s,
the Rate Support Grant had been only about 35 per cent of its total spending), and if only most voters understood the cost because they would have

---

* Terence ('Terry') Heiser (1932–), educated Windsor County Boys' School and Birkbeck
College, University of London; joined Civil Service, 1949; various posts culminating in permanent secretary of the Department of the Environment, 1985–92; knighted 1992. As
permanent secretary he was the most senior civil servant dealing with the poll tax.
† The sanest version of these ideas appears in John Campbell's biography. He speaks of
'delayed revenge for her repressed and joyless childhood'. (Campbell, *Margaret Thatcher:
The Iron Lady*, p. 375.)

to pay it, then sanity would prevail, and Conservative votes would accumulate. These truths seemed so simple to her that she found the complications of actually reaching the happy state she sought intensely frustrating.

The manifesto policies on local government were scarcely more tractable to implement than the replacement of rates themselves. After some three months of argument following her electoral landslide, Mrs Thatcher's new Secretary of State for the Environment, Patrick Jenkin, sent her a warning. Local government issues, he predicted, are 'going to cause the Government lots of trouble over the next few years . . . I am not sure that senior colleagues yet appreciate the rows which, starting this autumn, are going to continue right up to the next election and beyond.'[7] He was understating the case.*

The rows were almost as great among Conservatives as with Labour opponents. Except for a few bold reformers, mainly in London, Conservatives in local government were conservative. They did not see much wrong with the system so long as they were in charge, and they were as proud as Labour about extracting money from Whitehall for local purposes. They knew, from bitter experience, that complicated, centrally devised formulae designed to restrain spending often had perverse effects, making the prudent subsidize the profligate. So they were cynical about change. Councillors from Barnet, which included Mrs Thatcher's own constituency of Finchley, made a point, from time to time, of reminding her of these uncomfortable realities. As for the GLC abolition, to many it just did not feel right. Much as they disliked Ken Livingstone, many Tories had constitutional objections. Mrs Thatcher herself, who always put a much higher value than most of her party on political warfare with the left, had discussed abolition in Cabinet committee in 1982 but, for fear of leaks, did not widen the discussion until just before the general election,[8] so the pitch had not been rolled.

Besides, the more pragmatic, pessimistic strain of Tories – locally, in Parliament and in government – foresaw too much trouble. This, in essence, was the Willie Whitelaw position. From his new perch leading the House of Lords, Whitelaw continued to advise Mrs Thatcher on all major policy issues. He was not so interested in whether or not, in principle, it was right for central government to intervene to improve local.

---

* In July of the same year, Jenkin had written to Mrs Thatcher arguing for a rate revaluation in England 'now that we have decided that rates are here to stay' (Jenkin to Thatcher, 27 July 1983, TNA: PREM 19/1565 (http://www.margaretthatcher.org/document/141600)). The fact that her own Secretary of State thought the government had abandoned rate reform for good shows that Mrs Thatcher had not made her mind understood.

He was simply worried about what would actually happen. Oliver Letwin, Mrs Thatcher's main Policy Unit adviser on rates and local government, recalled a meeting in which Mrs Thatcher and others discussed whether or not to send government commissioners in to Liverpool, which was deliberately proposing to set an illegal budget. 'Well, Margaret,' said Whitelaw, 'of course you can send commissioners in. Of course you can. But how will you get them OUT?'[9] His pragmatic argument prevailed in that case, but more generally it did not. Central government started to go in, often without safeguarding its passage back.

Whitelaw was so worried, indeed, that he acted out of character and explicitly (though not, of course, publicly) opposed Mrs Thatcher's policy. In the autumn and winter of 1983, ministers had debated all sorts of half-considered consequences, even as they published the White Paper on GLC abolition (7 October) and introduced the rate-capping Bill (21 December). Which bits of the GLC would be run by 'residuary bodies' and which would pass to the London boroughs? When, if at all, would they abolish the Inner London Education Authority (ILEA), which employed more non-teaching staff (over 20,000) than teachers, and was as great a force for the left as the GLC from which it sprang? Would much money really be saved? Shouldn't there be a 'voice for London' of some sort? (Mrs Thatcher's eccentric answer to this last was that the Lord Mayor of London, who was chosen only by and for the old City of London, and not through any democratic process, 'already provided the necessary representative office'.)[10] Even the politics of the matter – attacking the 'loony left' – began to look less good as it became clear that the mild, unpolitical Patrick Jenkin was no match for his Labour local government opponents. In December, Bernard Ingham wrote to him to protest that 'we cannot allow the Opposition to dictate the game for much longer.'[11] 'I was in dead trouble,' Jenkin recalled.[12]

In February 1984, Whitelaw came to see Mrs Thatcher. He was already shaken by how hard it was proving to get the privatization of British Telecom through the House of Lords; but in this case, he explained, his anxiety was not just about parliamentary tactics: 'His concern was not that the Bills could not be got through Parliament, but that the proposals themselves might be defective.'[13] On the matter of the GLC, in particular, he felt that the government did not have proper answers to all the questions raised.

Mrs Thatcher listened – she always treated Whitelaw respectfully – but did not back down. Having said his piece, Whitelaw resisted no longer. But Mrs Thatcher acknowledged, tacitly, at least, the amount of political and policy work still needed. Because 'she increasingly lost confidence in

Jenkin's ability to deal with Ken Livingstone',[14]* she began to rely more heavily on her Policy Unit to drive change through. She was, according to her Treasury private secretary, Michael Scholar, 'in a bullying mood with ministers'.[15]

Her mood was not improved by the growth of revolts against the proposed rate-capping. In Liverpool, where the Labour city council was now, in effect though not in name, controlled by the hard-left Militant Tendency,† the game got going. The council, claiming that central government forbade them the money they needed to fulfil their election promises, announced their illegal budget plan. 'It is better to break the law than break the poor' was their slogan. The councillors involved knew that this threat, if enacted, would make them liable to personal surcharge and disqualification, but they also knew that the government would be gravely embarrassed at being blamed for the breakdown of local services. Jenkin offered the council more money (out of a pot for housing), allowing Militant to declare that they had Mrs Thatcher on the run. The cocky, charismatic deputy leader of the council, Derek Hatton,‡ who was part of Militant and effectively ran the council, started to become a household name. '[Tony] Benn appears alongside Liverpool's Hatton at rally in support of illegal budget,' Bernard Ingham's press digest informed Mrs Thatcher, '– says Liverpool is graveyard of capitalism and birthplace of socialism: Council committee votes to set illegal rate.'[16] Like Livingstone, Hatton acquired a popular following, though he was demonized by much of the press.

At the No. 10 Policy Unit, Oliver Letwin, working under its director, John Redwood, was clear that Mrs Thatcher's dislike of what was happening in local government was motivated even more by the behaviour of left-wing extremists than by concerns about financial control. She saw

---

* Stephen Sherbourne, who had been Jenkin's special adviser in the previous Parliament, when he was Industry Secretary, remembered a meeting before the 1983 general election in which his boss saw, for the first time, the policy of GLC abolition expressed in the manifesto. Jenkin 'showed surprise and a touch of shock'. (Interview with Lord Sherbourne of Didsbury.)

† The Militant Tendency was a long-standing Trotskyist entry group in the Labour movement. Although it was forbidden to affiliate to Labour in 1982, and several of its leading figures were expelled from the party the following year, it continued to play an important subversive role in Labour, particularly in local government, for most of the 1980s. *Militant* was the name of its journal, allowing members to say, when challenged, '*Militant* is not an organization: it's a newspaper.' This, said Ken Livingstone, who, despite his own left-wing views, hated Militant's ideological rigidity, was 'always a lie'. (Interview with Ken Livingstone.)

‡ Derek Hatton (1948–), educated Liverpool Institute for Boys; deputy leader, Liverpool City Council, 1983; expelled from the Labour Party in 1986 for belonging to Militant.

them as threatening the 'stability of the United Kingdom'.[17] Since the smashing defeat of Labour in the 1983 general election, the hard core of opposition to 'Thatcher' prided itself on being extra-parliamentary. It hoped, by strikes, disruption, street protest, declaring 'nuclear-free zones', suborning parts of the public services and the building up of local centres of power, to be able to challenge the government. Much of this was mocked for its politically correct* posturing but, mad though some of it was, it was also powerful, and good at exploiting the divisions within the Labour Party. There was a close relationship in this enterprise between the left of the trade union movement and the left in local government, which the *Daily Mail* described as the 'Fascist Left'.[18] From the start of the miners' strike in March 1984, this semi-revolutionary struggle acquired sharp focus.

Despatched by Mrs Thatcher to visit Hatton and his cohorts in Liverpool alone, Letwin felt 'physically frightened' by the gang rule he observed in City Hall. He also noted how local government finance 'intersected with this. Underneath, there was no real accountability or democratic check.'[19] 'I got interested in this,' Letwin recalled, 'and I discovered that no one knew how it worked.'[20]†

From the late spring of 1984, it was Letwin who did most of the unit's work on the subject and Mrs Thatcher 'put a surprising amount of trust in him'.[21] His memos had an urgency and contained a level of detail and intellectual power which answered Mrs Thatcher's needs. Writing to Mrs Thatcher's office about rate-capping, for example, at the end of May, he protested that the relevant Cabinet sub-committee had 'sanctioned a near-absurdity'.[22] Under its proposed 'solution', some councils – Brent, Sheffield and Merseyside – would be rate-capped and yet their rates would rise sharply.‡ There might be 'respectable technical reasons for this', but 'Any Minister who is sufficiently foolhardy to attempt a complicated explanation of such results on a TV programme will be torn to shreds by an Opposition spokesman.' Couldn't the government adjust to avoid 'making a laughing stock of our entire rates policy'? 'The answer', said

---

* Although the phrase 'political correctness' was not yet current.

† Letwin admitted that 'One of the many people defeated by the complexity of the system was me.' He remembered a meeting chaired by Whitelaw in which his own computer's projection, happily accepted by those present, later turned out to be wrong by £10 billion. He had to apologize to Mrs Thatcher for this. She was indulgent of what she called 'computer error'. (Interview with Oliver Letwin.)

‡ This arose from a trick of accounting by which councils could transfer money from rate funds into 'special funds'; and then, in the following year, transfer it back again into 'rate funds' thus classifying it as 'negative public expenditure'.

Letwin, 'is to recoup our losses by being tough on the GLC and ILEA.' 'Agreed,' wrote Mrs Thatcher.

At this time, Letwin recalled, he 'wasn't thinking about the promise to get rid of the rates'.[23] In the course of 1984, however, as the problems of reforming the existing system became ever more apparent, it was natural to do so.

The incentive grew as the politics got worse. Ken Livingstone advanced his case for the GLC under the slogan 'SAY NO TO NO SAY'. The media consensus was that the government was being 'outspent, out-sloganised and out-advertised by Ken Livingstone'.[24] At the end of June, Bernard Ingham was so worried that he wrote to Whitelaw about the need to 'regain the initiative'.[25] On the same day, the government was defeated in the House of Lords on the 'Paving' Bill for GLC abolition. Peers complained that abolition was being pushed through without the new governmental arrangements to replace the authorities having been worked out. It looked bad for Mrs Thatcher that she was abolishing something for which people had voted, and trying to remove from elected office those who had been voted to it. Indeed, she herself had originally opposed this idea, preferring to keep elected councillors in post after abolition, but had eventually let herself be persuaded by Jenkin's unpolitical arguments about efficiency. Many of the peers had been ferried to and from the Lords, and fed and watered within it, by a well-organized GLC campaign.[26] There was a feeling, Ingham feared, that the government was 'losing out with the public; that the devil has all the best tunes'. The press secretary sketched out the main arguments in best Ingham style – 'London has no need of GLC representation when the Lord Mayor of London has not looked back since Dick Whittington.' 'I believe that we need a new speech written by someone – eg me – who is not too close to it all [an implied criticism of Jenkin], which takes on frontally all the arguments.'[27] The GLC and the mets were spending £3 million on politicized advertising in favour of themselves, so it was urgent for ministers to hit back.

Reconvening after her August break, Mrs Thatcher tried to get a grip on the problem. She invited leading ministers to a lunch at Chequers on 2 September to discuss the forthcoming annual party conference. In preparation for this, John Redwood set out all the issues her guests should consider. He told her that, even with rate-capping and abolition of the GLC achieved in the course of the year, the unfairness of the rates remained and the attempt by the left to break government policies had not been properly confronted. This 'remains for us a very vulnerable area of policy', he concluded.[28]

At Chequers, Patrick Jenkin urged Mrs Thatcher to order a review of the whole system of local government finance. She was not terribly pleased at the idea: 'there had been two previous reviews . . . and only the most modest of mice had emerged.'[29] At the end of the month, she held a more formal meeting of ministers and officials concerned. Briefing her for it, John Redwood argued how disastrous it would be if yet another review recommended no change, or change so radical as to be unworkable. 'Of all the options on offer,' he wrote, 'some kind of poll tax which is paid by every elector is the most likely to meet the requirements of accountability and visibility.'[30] There is no sign that Mrs Thatcher was immediately struck with this suggestion as the idea whose time had come. At the meeting, she let Jenkin begin proceedings with an extremely gloomy account of the situation: 'the whole system of local government finance was suffering severe strains and present policies could not hold the position very far into the life of the next Parliament.'[31] He wanted to be able to announce a review at the party conference in two weeks' time.

Nigel Lawson strongly disagreed. As Chancellor, with responsibility for national but not local taxes, he had an innate disinclination for major tax reform not led by him and his department. 'Rather than launch a review which would wrongly hold out hopes of a totally new system the emphasis should be on improving the working of existing arrangements where they were most inequitable.'[32] Lawson would not countenance any root-and-branch reform at all.

Looking for the sort of consensus which, despite her rhetoric, she often sought when in a tight spot, Mrs Thatcher said that Jenkin should be allowed to have his review and to announce it at the party conference. On the other hand, it should concentrate – this was her nod to Lawson – only on 'serious inequities'. It should not be called a review – the eventual preferred term was 'studies in the field' – and there should be no fanfare about it.

A week later, with the conference now a few days away, the Treasury tried to throw a spanner in the works. Peter Rees, the Chief Secretary, wrote to Mrs Thatcher, 'concerned' that Jenkin's speech might 'raise expectations of major change in the system of financing local government. I think this would be a mistake . . . It is not clear that we will be able to devise and deliver a solution to the intractable problems of the rating system.'[33] Nigel Lawson's department did not think much of Jenkin's officials. (They were 'useless', Lawson recalled thirty years later.)[34] It flatly opposed reform of the financing system. Perhaps because local government was not a Treasury responsibility, no one noticed the storm cone being hoisted. Mrs Thatcher did not answer Rees's letter. Perhaps if Lawson himself, rather than his deputy, had written, she would have given the matter more thought.

As it turned out, whatever was said at the party conference was instantly forgotten because of the Brighton bomb. Jenkin's speech, in which his field studies were announced, was little noticed. In the original draft of Mrs Thatcher's setpiece speech, the issue of local government had been an important part of her argument. Mrs Thatcher had planned to denounce the violence and intimidation of the miners' strike and all – especially at the previous week's Labour Party conference – who supported these things. Her draft extended this argument to the 'high spending Town Halls', where 'the new left seeks to use Councils to burst apart our carefully established programme for rational economic recovery'.[35] They were 'using public money to poison the public mind', and she directly quoted Livingstone and named Labour MPs who seemed to condone breaking the law and were ready to 'defy Parliament'. As she had told the 1922 Committee just before the summer recess, she considered the hard-left council leaders as well as Scargill's NUM leadership part of 'the enemy within'. As the miners' strike reached its climax, and the campaign against her reforms to local government gained strength, she fully intended to meet fire with fire.

After the bomb, she reduced her mention of local government issues to a couple of paragraphs. She reiterated (without explanation) the planned abolition of the GLC and the mets, praised Conservative councillors and competitive tendering, and left it at that. But while the IRA's carnage had made her change her partisan tone, it strengthened, if anything, her determination to defeat what she saw as a coalition against freedom.*

After a brief collective convalescence from the shock of the bomb, normal business resumed. At the end of October, those most closely involved in Jenkin's field studies – William Waldegrave, the number-three minister at the Department of the Environment, Terry Heiser, Letwin and Andrew Turnbull, Mrs Thatcher's Treasury private secretary – gathered at Chequers to give Mrs Thatcher a 'teach-in' (the phrase used) on how local government finance worked, or didn't. No new form of local tax was argued for (or against) at the meeting, but the deficiencies of the existing

---

* Indeed, in her Carlton Lecture at the end of November, Mrs Thatcher advanced many of the points she had removed from her Brighton speech: 'At the one end of the spectrum are the terrorist gangs within our borders, and the terrorist states which finance them and arm them. At the other are the Hard Left operating inside our system, conspiring to use union power and the apparatus of local government to break, defy and subvert the law' (The Second Carlton Lecture, 26 November 1984 (http://www.margaretthatcher.org/document/105799)).

system were fully aired. Waldegrave, who was enthusiastic for change because 'I thought the problem was soluble and would make my name,'[36] asked for six months to work with Heiser and a small team of independent minds on 'ground-clearing' before opening their ideas up to Cabinet consultation and later to the public.*

Mrs Thatcher herself suggested that the independent team be run by Lord Rothschild,† the former head of Ted Heath's Central Policy Review Staff (the Think Tank). In this she was prompted by Waldegrave,[37] who had worked under Rothschild there and had been engaged, at one time, to marry his daughter Victoria. Waldegrave was fond of Rothschild, and realized that his involvement would provide the clout which, as a very junior minister, he would lack if acting alone. Mrs Thatcher 'liked Victor being a scientist and she liked him being a Rothschild'.[38] She wrote to Rothschild two days after the meeting, explaining that she had asked Jenkin 'to have another look, starting from first principles, at the whole vexed subject of local government finance',[39] and inviting him to give the subject 'a really fresh look': 'We need sharp advice from the outside.' She did not ask, however, for a replacement for domestic rates to be dreamed up. This was not yet clearly envisaged. The initial task of the team was to look at taxes that were supplementary to the rates, not alternatives to them.[40]

Rothschild accepted Mrs Thatcher's invitation. He loved what later came to be called 'thinking outside the box', but, according to Robin Butler who, like Waldegrave, was a Rothschild Think Tank product, 'he never did it himself. He always had some brilliant source.'[41] For this task, Rothschild duly roped in a small band of allies, including Lennie Hoffmann,‡ a leading barrister. His motives, thought Butler, were 'mischief, fun, influence and being in on the act. He had a short attention span and his political judgment was nil, but he had originality.'[42] Always excited by bright ideas, Letwin was delighted by the Rothschild world in which clever people bathed difficult problems in the light of reason and ate good lunches at

* Only one Treasury civil servant, Jill Rutter, worked on the studies. Although highly regarded, she held quite junior rank at this time. According to Nigel Lawson, the only reason for her presence was 'so that we could know what was going on'. (Interview with Lord Lawson of Blaby.) It was 'my initiative' to join the team, Rutter insisted. 'The Treasury didn't want the thing at all.' (Interview with Jill Rutter.)

† Nathaniel Mayer Victor Rothschild (3rd Baron Rothschild) (1910–90), educated Harrow and Trinity College, Cambridge; scientist; chairman, N. M. Rothschild & Sons Ltd, 1975–6; director-general, Central Policy Review Staff, Cabinet Office, 1971–4; chairman, Rothschilds Continuation Ltd, 1976–88.

‡ Leonard 'Lennie' Hoffmann (1934–), educated South African College School, Cape Town and the Queen's College, Oxford; judge; served as a Lord of Appeal in Ordinary, 1995–2009; knighted, 1985; created Lord Hoffmann, 1995.

the Capital Hotel to discuss them: 'I fell rather in love with it all.'[43] The same can be said of Mrs Thatcher, who relied heavily on the twenty-eight-year-old Letwin. 'Because I was learning on the job,' Letwin recalled, 'so was she.'[44]

While Waldegrave and his advisers got on with ground-clearing, the politics of local government grew hotter. As well as advising closely on the policy, Letwin gave Mrs Thatcher extensive reports from the battle-fields. The opposition to rate-capping and GLC abolition was becoming 'ever more vigorous and intelligent', he warned her in the middle of November.[45] A mole within the advertising company Boase Massimi Pollitt (BMP) informed the Policy Unit about the propaganda films the firm was making for the GLC. The Local Government Campaign Unit, founded by David Blunkett,* the leader of Sheffield Council, was disseminating information about 'successful methods of attack'. Islington Council was paying 'Short Life User Groups' made up of 'politically aware squatters' to occupy its many empty houses.[46] Yet there was not enough urgency: 'The rate-capping revolt is just about to begin in earnest; but there has not yet been a clear statement of Government policy. Experience with the miners' strike shows that a clear line needs to be established from the start.' Letwin recommended that officials prepare for the revolt and for co-operation with the government's Civil Contingencies Unit. The tactic he urged in face of the revolt was 'brinkmanship': 'if services break down, do nothing for as long as possible, explaining constantly that the council has the remedy in its own hands'.[47]†

This sense of political siege drove Mrs Thatcher faster towards root-and-branch reform. A few days after Letwin's note, the Cabinet Office made the subject of the local government finance studies more explicit for Mrs Thatcher. There were problems of excessive local government expenditure and of central government intervention. There was also a disconnect between rating and voting inherent in the existing tax system, and the relationship between central and local government.[48] Beside this, Mrs Thatcher wrote 'Voter & payer'.

The controversies about local government issues dogged Mrs Thatcher wherever she went. In the astonishingly busy week in December 1984 in which Mrs Thatcher met Mikhail Gorbachev for the first time at

---

* David Blunkett (1947–), educated Shrewsbury College of Technology and Richmond College of Further Education; leader, Sheffield City Council, 1980–87; Labour MP for Sheffield Brightside, 1987–2010; for Sheffield Brightside and Hillsborough, 2010–15; Secretary of State for Education and Employment, 1997–2001; for Home Department, 2001–4; for Work and Pensions, 2005; granted a peerage in the Dissolution Honours List, 2015.

† This approach became known as the doctrine of 'quarter past twelve'.

Chequers, and then flew to China to sign the Hong Kong Agreement, a telegram reached her in Peking informing her of trouble. 'The Environment Secretary's statement on local authority capital spending went very badly today. In addition to the expected Opposition uproar, there was a consistently hostile reaction from Government backbenchers.'[49] There was a three-line whip (the severest form of whipping) for the debate the next day: 'The consequences of a defeat for the Government's economic strategy and for the international image of the Government are being strongly emphasised.'

So ended the year.

The new one began for Mrs Thatcher with a typically challenging letter from Lord Rothschild. Under the heading 'The Local Authority Problem Viewed by an Outsider', he told her that 'the outsider is most forcibly struck by the lack of harmony and ill feeling among those concerned'.[50] He complained of the low quality of Department of Environment officials and of the 'incredible complexity of the arrangements which the Government has allowed to develop'. Deliberately undercutting his own *raison d'être* and methods of working, he wrote that 'The malaise underlying these symptoms will not be cured by a small group of Officials and Consultants supervised, part-time, by a Minister or Ministers, with the odd Oxbridge seminar thrown in for good measure.'[51] This remark was really a means of putting Mrs Thatcher on her mettle: 'Has the time not come for the Prime Minister to say "Stop it"? . . . A new and ruthless broom is needed.' It was exactly as a new broom, and a ruthless one at that, that 'Maggie', the housewife-superstar, liked to see herself.

Kenneth Baker, much more political than his senior, Patrick Jenkin, also pushed a message of urgency. Having favourably impressed Mrs Thatcher as minister for information technology in her first administration, he had joined Environment, as minister for local government, the previous year. Although originally a Heathite, he had started to prosper under Mrs Thatcher because of two qualities which she liked: he was 'hugely enthusiastic and positive' about whatever he was doing, and he 'carried his ministerial responsibilities lightly'.[52] He and Waldegrave, thought Stephen Sherbourne, were 'terribly keen to curry favour with the Prime Minister', and Baker's way of doing this was to incite her to battle. He tapped into what he called her 'Grantham-speak'.[53] He tried to raise awareness within government of 'The Developing Political Crisis in our Cities'.[54] The hard-left councils – Liverpool, Hackney, Lambeth, Islington, Greenwich, Southwark and Manchester – he wrote, were using 'municipal control of all activities' as 'the bedrock of their policies'. The hard left 'really do hope', Baker went on, 'that the Government can be brought down by widespread action in the inner cities'. He quoted Ken Livingstone, speaking earlier in the month: 'We will effectively operate within the State in defiance of the State. That will prove the most dramatic challenge, apart from the challenge of the miners, that this Government has faced since 1979.' It was vital, Baker argued, to set local government policy within this political context.[55]

At the same time, a northern front opened up. Because of its different legal framework, Scotland was now compelled to have a rating revaluation. (England and Wales were overdue for one, but were freer, in law, to postpone. Michael Heseltine, as environment secretary, had done this. So had Patrick Jenkin, at Mrs Thatcher's insistence.) Its results were announced on 13 February 1985. The next day, the Chairman of the Scottish Conservative Party, Sir James Goold, came to tell Mrs Thatcher exactly how bad things would now be. There would be a 170 per cent increase in domestic rateable values,* he said, and 'only 20 per cent of Scottish householders were liable to pay full rates, and most of this small residue of householders were Conservatives'.[56] Jenners, the big department store in Edinburgh, would now pay twice the rates of Harrods in London though it had only one-tenth of the floor space. In Tory Perth and Kinross, rates would rise by 70 per cent. Mrs Thatcher shuddered at the political thought and told Sir James that the implementation of the revaluation should be postponed.[57]

In fact, delay was not in her legal power, as the Scottish Secretary, George Younger, later explained to her. The 'only course',[58] he claimed, was for the Treasury to hand him another £64 million which he could pass on to Scottish councils, thereby halving the domestic rate increases. The Treasury resisted, and eventually Younger was forced to settle for £38.5 million. The politics looked awful for the Tories in Scotland. 'I've never seen anyone more worried about anything,'[59] Letwin recalled. Sir Hector Monro, a senior Scottish Conservative MP, told Mrs Thatcher that she must prevent a 'complete loss of confidence amongst Conservatives in Scotland'.[60] She herself was exasperated that this crisis had broken without warning. 'It is pretty <u>pathetic</u>,' she wrote on a begging letter from Younger, referring to the money from the Treasury, 'but Scotland must

---

* It may be asked why an increase in rateable values automatically produced an increase in rates. After all, it was open to councils to charge a lower rate in the pound. The answer – apart from the perennial desire of local government, especially Labour local government, to get more money whenever it could – lay in the fact that revaluation put some values down when it put others up, so payments were bound to alter to reflect this. This created new winners, and new losers.

carry the can for not remedying the situation in time.'[61] It was apparent to her, as she struggled with the wider issue of local government finance, that she would have to carry the can in the rest of the United Kingdom if the problem could not be remedied in time to prevent electoral punishment. This lent urgency to the meeting of the Waldegrave–Rothschild studies team planned for the end of March at Chequers. Mrs Thatcher and many of her ministers were yearning for a big idea. Rothschild and his band of bright young brains did not intend to disappoint.

Even more important, perhaps, was Willie Whitelaw. Rudely heckled about the rate revaluation by a normally loyal Conservative audience in Bearsden, the prosperous Glasgow suburb where he had cut his political teeth, Whitelaw returned to London, badly shaken, to warn Mrs Thatcher of looming disaster. His fear of the effect of the revaluation made him cast aside his habitual dislike of radical reform. The man normally most likely to persuade Mrs Thatcher to hold back was ardent for change.*

Rothschild got to work on Mrs Thatcher. He was coming to see her, warned Robin Butler, to ask her a question about the review. 'He has been characteristically mysterious [Mrs Thatcher underlined these words and the ones following] about the question . . . I suspect that he wants to ask you whether you would like to abolish domestic rates completely.'[62] Butler then permitted himself a comment: 'He hankers after this, partly (I suspect) because it would be a dramatic solution to the problem. But abolition would involve a larger poll tax' (than the idea of a combined poll tax and rate which was also being canvassed). This would 'fall more heavily than the rates on people with low incomes'. The Thatcher–Rothschild encounter was not recorded, but it seems that he did indeed make such a suggestion. She was being softened up for the full-dress presentation of the big idea.†

In the run-up to the Chequers meeting, Andrew Turnbull had made a strenuous effort, supported by Mrs Thatcher, who always disliked large meetings, to keep out what he called 'gate-crashers'. At that stage,

---

* Whitelaw was held in great respect by both officials and ministers for his shrewdness, and this led Cabinet committee colleagues to disbelieve his self-deprecation when he told them in meetings that he did not understand the complex system of rates and grants in Scotland. They gradually realized that he was telling the truth: 'They thought he was fooling. He wasn't. He didn't really understand it at all' (Interview with Sir Brian Unwin). Whitelaw was not alone in his incomprehension.

† Those involved disagreed about Rothschild's personal influence on Mrs Thatcher. Robin Butler and Charles Powell believed that it was small, and even, in Powell's view, that she 'did not like him much'. (Interviews with Lord Powell of Bayswater and Lord Butler of Brockwell.) Others – Waldegrave, Letwin – put his influence much higher. It is true that Rothschild was not close to Mrs Thatcher, but it is also true that he carried intellectual and social prestige, and this weighed with her.

however, the name of the Chancellor of the Exchequer was firmly on the list, along with about half the Cabinet. Later in the month, it was not. The Treasury noticed this and asked to be represented at the meeting. 'I suggest we press hard to have the Chancellor himself,' Robin Butler wrote to Mrs Thatcher. To which Mrs Thatcher replied, 'Yes.'[63] According to Butler, no one had deliberately tried to exclude the Treasury from Chequers.[64] In the event, and at this very short notice, Lawson refused the invitation, 'being bolshy about it because it was on a Sunday'.[65] He may well have been tired, and felt politically weak, having just delivered a lacklustre Budget (see Chapter 13). Besides, he thought the meeting would be 'exploratory' rather than decisive.[66] 'I regret not attending,' he told the present author. He did not think that Mrs Thatcher had behaved wrongly in holding such an important meeting in the rather informal way she did: 'It was not impropriety, just folly.'[67] In Lawson's stead went Peter Rees, the Chief Secretary to the Treasury, who arrived without any brief from Lawson to speak against what might be proposed.[68]

Confusingly, just before the Chequers meeting, Rothschild reported to Butler that his brilliant friend Lennie Hoffmann did *not* think that the 'Community Charge (Poll Tax)' could be a 'complete substitute'[69] for domestic rates, although Waldegrave thought it might be. This is the first known instance where the phrase 'community charge' – the name eventually adopted for the new tax – appears in official records.

The meeting was held at Chequers on Sunday 31 March 1985. 'William [Waldegrave] has done a first-rate job,'[70] Redwood and Letwin minuted Mrs Thatcher in advance. They agreed with him that 'rates should be replaced by [a] poll tax.' They raised questions about some aspects of the proposals and called for extensive consultation, a Green Paper and then a White Paper.* But they argued strongly that this was the moment for Mrs Thatcher to seize:

> We believe that this review offers the only real hope of winning back the confidence of the Party. We also believe that it offers the prospect of a lasting change for the better in local Government. After years of half-remedies, you should now attempt a fundamental reform on the lines proposed.[71]

It is evidence of the importance attached to the Chequers seminar and the likely incendiary effect of what was discussed that only five copies,

---

* A Green Paper is the Whitehall phrase for an official document which sets out government plans for a piece of legislation in an early, relatively tentative version, offering them for consultation. A White Paper, which always comes after the Green, is the final version of the plans before they take actual legislative form.

each numbered, were made of Robin Butler's record of it. In acknowledgment, perhaps, of the potentially pivotal and potentially unfriendly
attitude of the Treasury, one of the five copies went to Peter Rees. No other
minister, except, of course, Patrick Jenkin, received one.

According to that record, Kenneth Baker and Waldegrave both spoke,
to complementary effect. Baker concentrated on the defects of the rating
system. Waldegrave then set out the proposed solution. This, he said,
included 'abolishing domestic rates and replacing them with a local residents' or community charge,* falling equally on all adults in each local
area. This would achieve the objective of accountability better than any
alternative tax.' There would need to be rebates for those on low incomes
'but not such as to insulate them from increases in the community charge
by high-spending councils'.[72] The likely cost of the charge per head per
year was guessed to be £50.[73] Although Waldegrave's last words were not
reported in the official account, some of those present remember him
ending with a flourish: 'So, Prime Minister, you will have succeeded in
abolishing the rates.'[74] Waldegrave was 'persuasive and sensible and
charming', recalled Letwin, and Mrs Thatcher was 'purring at all this'.
She had 'a weak spot for Fellows of All Souls'.[75]† 'The presentation',
recalled Terry Heiser, 'swept the board.'[76]

Mrs Thatcher, in Butler's memory, 'greeted it [the community charge
idea] enthusiastically'.[77] He regarded the meeting as 'the decisive moment'.
Waldegrave did not consider that Mrs Thatcher herself was blazing the
trail, but she did respond very positively: 'This was a phase of the world
when we were trying to bring people back to reality, as we had with trade
unions and with inflation. The idea that people have to pay for the services
they want was a strong part of her ethos.'[78]‡ She formally summed up the
mood of the meeting as supporting reform: 'It was increasingly difficult
to justify the retention of domestic rates and the group welcomed the
proposals which recognised the need to strengthen local accountability
and introduce fairer arrangements.'[79] More work would be done on the
proposals for a discussion in the second half of May with the aim of

---

* The word 'charge' was favoured by supporters of reform, including Mrs Thatcher, because
it reflected the costs of local government to those who used its services, rather than being a
'tax' for general purposes. Nigel Lawson regarded this argument as 'completely bogus'.
(Interview with Lord Lawson of Blaby.)

† Waldegrave had been a Fellow of All Souls College, Oxford, since 1971.

‡ Waldegrave writes a clear and amusing account of the poll tax story in *A Different Kind
of Weather: A Memoir*, Constable, 2015. It begins, 'The poll tax is the issue to which most
people attribute Thatcher's fall; and I was central to it' (p. 218). Oddly, he makes no mention
of the Chequers meeting, which was his moment of greatest triumph in the saga.

producing 'a predominantly White Paper with some green edges' in early autumn if the Cabinet agreed to go ahead. 'Some material' would be slipped to George Younger so that he could give a little comfort to the annual Scottish Conservative Party conference in Perth in May.

After the Chequers meeting, Mrs Thatcher wrote to Lord Rothschild to thank him for his contribution. The discussion had been so valuable because it had 'gone back to fundamentals':[80] 'As a result I think we have the best opportunity for a long time to find a lasting solution to this perennial but increasingly acute problem.' She asked him to 'keep a fatherly eye on the infant's development'.

There had been little political discussion at Chequers of the war with the hard left in local government, but the hopeful mood of the meeting was closely related to its timing. At the beginning of the month, the miners' strike had collapsed, giving Mrs Thatcher the greatest of all her industrial victories. With the strike ended, 'the focus switched to the municipal socialists' revolt'.[81] Very shortly after the defeat of the NUM, the GLC decided not to set an illegal rate, with Ken Livingstone, who 'knew it couldn't be done',[82] having to hold back his even more hardline comrades. A big march in London had been organized to 'give real hope of turning the tide' by helping create 'a joint strike against Local Government legislation *and* Pit Closures'.[83] The march was advertised under the banner 'one year!' (of the miners' strike), but it had now lost the purpose of its slogan. It seemed that the left was crumbling. Having achieved what no previous Conservative prime minister had managed, Mrs Thatcher had become very hard for colleagues to gainsay.

In a note to Robin Butler shortly after the Chequers meeting, Rothschild said, 'The community charge is, I believe, a winner. But I am nervous lest it is accidentally or deliberately misinterpreted, for example: "Tories hit the poor once again . . ."'[84] The question was whether the charge could 'avoid hardships and still collect what is necessary'. 'Only the figures', he went on, 'can provide the answers . . . and as, for some reason beyond my comprehension, they do not exist, they will have to be got.' He said he was going off to get his own ones from Cambridgeshire, the local authority where he lived.

Rothschild had put his finger on a key point which was to dog the development of the poll tax, as it had dogged all government attempts to control local government spending. Without knowing how the figures would work out, it was impossible to calculate who would gain and who lose. On such calculations would hang the success of the entire policy. Yet no one at the Department of the Environment, which was supposed to understand these matters, seemed to do so. To be fair, no amount of ingenuity could have made sums accurate. There were too many unknown quantities, because the change was so complete. Although Mrs Thatcher herself was, as always, interested in the figures, and sometimes scribbled sums on the relevant documents, she does not seem to have focused on the key point that the ultimate results were – literally – incalculable.

By the middle of May, Environment officials had produced their 'Specification Report' on the Local Government Finance Studies. It predicted that 7,450,000 people would lose as a result of the proposed reforms and that 9,250,000 would gain. Given the natural propensity of those who lose to make much more noise than those who gain, this figure was immediately recognized as dangerous. The calculations suggested that people living in inner London or parts of the northern industrial areas would suffer the most, especially those earning between £5,000 and £12,000 per year, the middle-income bracket at that time. Redwood and Letwin reported to Mrs Thatcher, with a certain nervousness, on these problems: 'Unless some of them can be sorted out this reform is unattractive.'[85] Yet how *could* they be sorted out? The Cabinet Office brief to Mrs Thatcher estimated that the poll tax itself would work out at an average of £160 per year,[86] over three times the figure imagined at the Chequers meeting just six weeks earlier.

Attached to this memo was one from Nigel Lawson which subsequently became famous. The Specification Report's own evidence, said Lawson, gave 'a horrifying picture of the impact. A pensioner couple in inner London could find themselves paying 22 per cent of their net income in poll tax, whereas a better off couple in the suburbs would pay only 1 per cent.'*[87] He did not think that efforts to correct these imbalances would work: 'We should be forced to give so many exemptions and concessions (inevitably to the benefit of high-spending authorities in Inner London) that the flat-rate poll tax would rapidly become a surrogate income tax. That is what a "graduated residents' charge" is.' 'This is not simply a hideous political problem,' he went on: 'local authorities would seize the opportunity to bump up their spending and revenue and blame it all on the imposition by the government of an alien system of taxation . . . the proposal for a poll tax would be completely unworkable and politically catastrophic.' He felt that the rule by which some people paid nothing no matter how high rates rose could be mitigated by limiting rate rebates rather than by inventing a new tax. 'This [Lawson's] scheme is certainly

* Lawson's memo of 16 May 1985 is extensively quoted and his views on the poll tax fully recorded in his memoirs *The View from No. 11*, chs. 45 and 46.

a runner,' Redwood and Letwin acknowledged, and it contained 'less political risk' than the poll tax, which would be attacked 'as "a tax on votes" and for its regressive nature'.[88] They repeated their view that nothing should be rushed.

It is a puzzle that Lawson's objection to the whole idea – trenchant even by his standards – should not have made more impact. For the man in charge of the nation's money to be so opposed to a new tax was a very big thing. In the twenty-first century, it would certainly have leaked and made huge headlines.* So successfully was the Thatcher–Lawson combination seen to be working for economic recovery that the media were not looking for a story pointing in a different direction.

Besides, Lawson himself did not fight the internal battle for all it was worth. Since local taxes were the one form of public revenue over which the Treasury did not hold sway, he had limited power to intervene. His attitude was that he was 'very happy' if local government tax reform was 'not getting anywhere'[89] since it bore no relation to the purposes of his own tax reforms. If asked, he would give his opinion, but he did not consider making this an issue of resignation. After finding himself isolated on the poll tax at the Cabinet committee meeting on 20 May, he did work up, at Mrs Thatcher's request, his own reform of rates which suggested basing them on capital values rather than putative rental ones; but on the whole he did not much mind colleagues making fools of themselves, with him 'sniping from the sidelines'.[90] His main task, as he saw it, was to carve out and protect his own sphere of operations, so he almost washed his hands of the whole subject.

Lawson also felt that he had enough matters to argue about with Mrs Thatcher without adding another. 'I got the impression she was fixated on the subject,' he recalled,[91] and he did not want to waste his breath. This attitude helps explain why, unlike Michael Heseltine over Westland, he did not seek confrontation and never, at the time or later, complained about Mrs Thatcher's methods of arriving at the decision. Furthermore, Lawson recalled, 'I had no personal reason for arguing with her about it.'[92] Often, without the spur of a personal quarrel or a turf war, politicians are not very energetic in pursuing their views.

In the later stages of the battle, Lawson was in an uneasy position, for other reasons. He had failed to persuade Mrs Thatcher that Britain should join the ERM in November 1985 (see Chapter 13), and so was grumpy.

---

* The press did later run some stories (*The Times*, for example, on 23 September) that the Chancellor did not support the poll tax. But they did not attract much attention. Internal discipline kept the disagreement subterranean.

He could not afford to fight on the front of the poll tax as well. Those involved in the policy believed that if she had felt able to trust Lawson, many errors would have been avoided.[93]

As for Mrs Thatcher, she also seems to have had some idea of demarcation. Here was a tax issue – the only one, in fact – where she did not have ultimately to defer to the Treasury. Although she naturally listened to Lawson attentively, none of her officials or colleagues remembered her putting his objections centre-stage. This was her subject, not his.

Where the attitude of the Treasury did make a serious difference, however, was not so much in its opposition to the poll tax as in its absence from the detailed deliberations. Although Waldegrave made it an 'absolute condition'[94] of his unit's work that nothing be kept from the Treasury, Letwin recalled that Lawson told his officials: 'I don't want you to be working on it.'[95] As Lawson himself conceded, 'We made no positive contribution to the subject.'[96] This meant that there was a lack of intellectual power because 'Half of the intellect of the government is in the Treasury.'[97]* It was certainly a very risky thing to create a new tax without the active help of the department whose grasp of the subject of taxation is unique.

Anyway, the issue of local government finance could not be considered with cool-headed policy reflection alone. The Scottish situation was politically desperate for the government. George Younger, whom Lawson considered 'a delightful man but very stupid on this subject',[98] seized upon the poll tax as the answer to his prayers. So desperate was he to push forward with it at his party's conference in May that Stephen Sherbourne felt he must caution Mrs Thatcher about rushing. Just before a crucial meeting with Younger on 1 May, Sherbourne complained to her that the Scottish party organization had been 'fanning the flames on rates so that the position is even more explosive politically'.[99] They were demanding a replacement of rates on the statute book by the next general election. The choice, therefore, was either to 'commit ourselves now to having a new source of local government finance passed through Parliament ... even though we have not decided what, OR we have a rough Party Conference'. His advice was clear: 'Better a bad conference in 1985 than a bad election in 1987'. Mrs Thatcher seemed to accept this view, and gave no promise about timing when she spoke to the Scottish party on 10 May; but she did

---

* This was not a universal view. William Waldegrave considered Department of the Environment officials such as Robin Young and Anthony Mayer, who worked for his unit, as among the very best he had ever met. He did not take refuge later in the excuse of poor-quality advice: 'I don't know an occasion when more firepower was produced.' (Interview with Lord Waldegrave of North Hill.)

authorize Younger, in his speech to the same gathering, to say that 'the status quo is not an option'.[100] This gave a clear signal. The political impetus, if not the precise legislative plan, was becoming hard to stop.

This applied nationwide. If it was true – which it certainly was – that the rate revaluation in Scotland was unbearably unpopular, especially with natural Conservative supporters, the same must apply to England and Wales. Indeed, it applied much more strongly, because revaluation had been so long delayed. So although it remained theoretically possible, at this stage, to stick with the rates, their potential future levels had already made revaluation seem politically out of the question. A poll tax looked ever more likely.

In the course of the summer of 1985, the government's tactics seemed to be paying off in its rate-capping battles against councils controlled by the extreme left. At the end of June, the district auditor issued notices of surcharge against forty-nine Liverpool Labour councillors who had voted to set an illegal rate. Shortly afterwards, Lambeth Council, led by the ultra-revolutionary 'Red' Ted Knight, capitulated. In late August, Edinburgh Council, also Labour controlled, wavered and decided to prepare a legal budget. In early September, Liverpool, still hoping to frighten the government into intervening by operating a 'deficit budget', found itself obliged to put its entire council staff on three months' notice. The new Secretary of State for the Environment, Kenneth Baker, refused its request to be allowed to borrow an extra £25 million. Some of the redundancy notices had to be delivered by taxi in order to reach their recipients within the time-period legally required. The council quickly ran into conflict with the previously supportive public sector unions. At the beginning of October, Liverpool's famously left-wing Anglican and Roman Catholic bishops, David Sheppard and Derek Warlock, furious with the extremists, wrote an article in *The Times*[101] headlined 'Stand Up to Liverpool's Militants'.* Mrs Thatcher was winning what Letwin called the 'war of nerves'.

The hard left's rate-capping revolt deeply embarrassed the Labour leadership. Neil Kinnock was conscious that his position during the miners' strike – criticizing Arthur Scargill, yet not demanding a ballot or breaking with the strike completely – had done him and his party great damage. Although he had just about held the Labour movement together, his stance had made him look weak, and under the thumb of the extremists. He did not want to repeat this mistake in the sphere of local government.

_____

* Kenneth Baker wrote to Mrs Thatcher: 'When I met them last week David Sheppard called Hatton "wicked". That is quite something from a Bishop' (Baker to Thatcher, 1 October 1985, TNA: PREM 19/1562).

In his speech to his annual party conference in Bournemouth at the beginning of October Kinnock aimed his fire at the extremists in his own party, taking the example of Liverpool. 'You start with far-fetched resolutions. They are then pickled into a rigid dogma ... and you end in the grotesque chaos of a Labour council – a <u>Labour</u> council! – hiring taxis to scuttle round a city handing out redundancy notices to its own workers.'[102] He was duly heckled by Militant and widely cheered in the country. Kinnock's eloquence and courage on this occasion did a great deal for his reputation. By turning on his internal foes, however, he ensured that resistance to the Tories' local government reforms was seen as merely a left-wing cause. It was not in Kinnock's interest to assail the emerging plans for a poll tax. By doing so, he would empower the very people in his own party he was trying to defeat. He gave Mrs Thatcher an almost free pass on the subject. As so often in her career, the left's hatred of Mrs Thatcher caused far more trouble for Labour than for the Conservatives. She could develop her new ideas in what was almost a vacuum of mainstream opposition.

The Local Government Finance Studies had been refined and returned for consideration in mid-September. Redwood and Letwin now advised Mrs Thatcher that Nigel Lawson's ideas for rate reform would be 'politically suicidal'.[103] Capital valuations as the basis for rates would be seen by 'your supporters ... as a wealth tax'. The notion that a property tax should remain in some form, however, was favoured even by some who supported a poll tax, notably Kenneth Baker. It helped deal with the 'regressive' aspect of the proposed reform.* 'If I'm on *Question Time*,' Baker was heard to protest, 'and I'm asked "Why do the Duke and the dustman have to pay the same?", there's no answer.'[104] Over the summer, Rothschild invented what he called, with his love of learnedly obscure jokes, 'Operation Gynandromorph' (ancient Greek for 'woman/man shape', the term often being used to describe butterflies or moths which exhibit male and female characteristics). This would mix a poll tax with a property element based on floor-space rather than rental valuation. Mrs Thatcher, seeing things, as always, from the point of view of the proud house-owner, objected: 'it would have the adverse effect that any <u>extension</u> would need an increase in rating.'[105] But Baker and Waldegrave took up the basic suggestion that a property element should remain.

Mrs Thatcher's Cabinet Office brief also re-emphasized, as did the

---

* A tax is 'progressive' if the proportion of tax paid rises as the income rises, 'regressive' if it is the same proportion for everyone. These are not terms of praise or blame (necessarily), simply of fiscal description.

Policy Unit, the fundamental purpose of the whole thing: 'Virtually all [Baker's and Waldegrave's] proposals are informed by the thrust towards disengaging central government and establishing automatic systems instead, and towards putting the control of local expenditure with the local elector.'[106] This point was made again and again throughout the process and was agreed by all the participants, so the many subsequent attacks which claimed that the Thatcher government wanted to 'destroy local government' by introducing a poll tax were untrue, indeed the opposite of the truth.*

What is true, however, is that Mrs Thatcher herself had low expectations of what local government could, in practice, deliver. When, as part of her consultation with interested parties in the summer of 1985, she met leaders of Conservative local government organizations, she set out her overall view: 'Britain was a unitary state with a strong tradition of national standards for the different services set by Government . . . local government could not be seen as a separate sphere of Government, but as a means of delivering statutory services combined with some degree of local discretion.'[107] It may be that she was instinctively happy with the conventions which had prevailed until the 1960s, by which local government concentrated on essentially uncontroversial services and was not very political. Her own father, in Grantham, had been a classic figure of this era – essentially, in his later years at least, a Conservative, but never using a party label, and resenting the gradual politicization of the council by Labour. She felt that the left had smashed the old conventions, thus creating conflict and threatening the power of the national elected government.†
So although she was genuine in her desire to bring taxation and representation into balance, thus empowering local electors, she did not want arrangements which, overall, made local government a greater power in the land. There was a contradiction here which she never resolved. The same point really applied to the rates themselves: they were not such a bad

---

* The fullest and best account of the poll tax story is *Failure in British Government: The Politics of the Poll Tax*, by David Butler, Andrew Adonis and Tony Travers, Oxford University Press, 1994. Many of its criticisms of the policy are right, and well evidenced. It suffers, however, from being so certain of Mrs Thatcher's malice towards the very idea of local government itself that it does not do justice to the seriousness of her government's quest for better accountability. If the government had not sought better accountability, it would never have chosen the poll tax.
† An important part of the politicization of councils which she resented was the tendency of Labour members to be elected representatives on one council and salaried employees of another. She saw this as an abuse of public money and also of power. This was a subject on which Denis Thatcher particularly liked to fulminate.

form of tax, so long as they were not pushed too hard. By the end of the 1970s, they had been.

In any event, the Cabinet committee – E (LF) – agreed that the Baker–Waldegrave proposals should go forward, and ignored Nigel Lawson. By early November, a chirpy Oliver Letwin felt able to write to Mrs Thatcher and tell her that everything was now resolved – including the plans to protect business ratepayers by creating a uniform, national business rate. 'The only remaining major issue', he advised, 'is the replacement of domestic rates by another form of taxation.'[108] She put a wiggly line under 'The only remaining major issue' and an exclamation mark beside it. Although she placed great faith in Letwin, Mrs Thatcher was by nature less blithe. His remark was a bit like 'Apart from that, Mrs Lincoln, how did you enjoy the play?' She had a strong sense of how difficult the subject remained. Indeed, she herself was a creator of the difficulty. As David Norgrove, who had replaced Andrew Turnbull as Treasury private secretary that month, put it: 'It all got more and more constrained because Mrs Thatcher was determined that there shouldn't be a property tax, yet all the options pointed to a property tax.'[109]

The Policy Unit could see the disadvantages of moving directly to a pure residence charge. It would produce 'too many big losers', said Letwin[110] – he and Redwood were now seriously worried by the loser calculations. On the other hand, a mixed tax would be seen in the media as two taxes. This could be unpopular, and would undermine the beautiful simplicity of the 'residence charge'.* If proposed in the forthcoming Green Paper, a mixed tax might look like a climbdown. 'We believe', wrote Letwin, 'that George Younger may be offering a way out of this dilemma. He is clearly extremely keen to use Scotland as a trail-blazer for the pure residence charge . . . If the Scottish experiment worked, it could make a pure residence charge look sensible rather than extreme.'[111] This was the start of the idea that Scotland might be what critics later called the 'guinea pig' for the poll tax. It is worth bearing in mind, however, that a guinea pig has no say about experiments conducted on him. Scotland, on the other hand – as judged by public and political opinion at the time – was fiercely hostile to increased rates and eagerly demanding a different form of local taxation.†

The eventual compromise between the Environment ministers, Baker

* The term 'residence charge' (or 'resident's charge' or 'residents' charge') was, at this stage, still competing with 'community charge'.
† The only important Conservative who wanted Scotland to go first precisely because the poll tax was damaging (though not because he bore ill will to Scotland) was Nigel Lawson: 'I thought, "If Younger is so keen, let him introduce it." I hoped it would then become clear

and Waldegrave, who wanted the mixture of taxes, and poll tax purists was a transitional scheme, known as 'dual running'. In England and Wales, this was intended to last for ten years. Part of the rates would be replaced by a community charge, and the remainder would never increase and would gradually wither away. One effect of the temporary retention of rates was to still objections from Nigel Lawson. But it also meant that the reforms themselves were threatened with incoherence. It was vital, argued Oliver Letwin, with supportive double underlining from Mrs Thatcher, that the change be presented as 'a phased <u>replacement</u> of <u>rates</u> by the community charge'.[112] After all, there would be little point in the whole exercise if Mrs Thatcher could not say, at the end of it, that she had got rid of the rates.

What remained, however, was the difficulty at the heart of the new tax. It was expressed by a senior official, Brian Unwin,* in his Cabinet Office brief to Mrs Thatcher. Although Unwin preserved the judicious, mandarin tone insisted on for such documents, the reader can detect a note of real anxiety. Indeed he was, according to David Norgrove, 'very concerned',[113] and he and his colleagues 'felt we ought to put our anxiety into the brief'.[114] On the same day as Letwin was crying 'Forward!', using Scotland as the battering ram, Unwin wrote to Mrs Thatcher:

> There is a fundamental problem that if local accountability is to be effective the consequences of excessive spending must be painful for the electorate. Moreover, if the tax base is to be expanded, some people will have to pay who have not done so before. The local charge will therefore almost by definition have to be unpopular, at least in high-spending areas.[115]

When confronted with this point in later years, Oliver Letwin said, 'That was the idea!'[116] This was a strong argument of principle, but it was hard to reconcile with the search for electoral popularity which was driving part of the longing to get rid of the rates. In retrospect, Waldegrave criticized himself for putting 'clever-silly' arguments[117] against this basic objection. How could a tax which extended itself, by some calculations, to potentially millions of people who had not paid local tax before, ever expect to be welcomed by them? Unwin's point was not answered.

Feeling, as he put it, 'self-protective',[118] William Waldegrave made sure

---

what a disaster it was. At least this would prevent it being done across the nation.' (Interview with Lord Lawson of Blaby.)
* Brian Unwin (1935–), educated Chesterfield School, New College, Oxford and Yale University; civil servant; Treasury, 1968–85; seconded to the Cabinet Office, 1981–3; Deputy Secretary, Cabinet Office, 1985–7; knighted, 1990.

throughout that he saw Cabinet ministers individually to explain his ideas to them. It was most unusual, in the hierarchical system of government, for such a junior minister* to find himself in such an important position, so he was as diplomatic as possible. On the whole, he was supported by his seniors. He remembered George Younger telling him, 'This is what I have been waiting for all my life.' Even the cautious Whitelaw, shocked by the anger against rate revaluation in his native Scotland, was 'thoroughly supportive'. Douglas Hurd, who had succeeded Leon Brittan as Home Secretary in September 1985, was quite seriously concerned that the poll tax would deter people from voting, since they would imagine (falsely) that the voting register and the register required by the new tax would be the same. He pointed out that the only existing poll tax – the television licence – was widely evaded, and, in bad areas like West Belfast, hard to collect. Evasion would 'bring the new system quickly into disrepute'.[119] Norman Tebbit was robust in dismissing the fears about a register ('Why shouldn't we be able to know who lives where in our own country?'), and said, 'At last we're doing something for our own people.' Only Michael Heseltine and Nigel Lawson were full-throatedly opposed. The former 'thought it was all nonsense',[120] but by the time the decision approached, he was deeply embroiled in the Westland affair (see Chapter 14) and unable to open another front in his struggle with Mrs Thatcher. The latter was rather sullen. 'I'm going to call these the Waldegrave reforms,'[121] Lawson told the young minister with baleful humour. As Norgrove put it, 'Lawson took his bat home.'[122] Lawson criticized colleagues – Hurd, for example, 'was not prepared to stick his head above the parapet'[123] – but also criticized himself: 'I was singularly unsuccessful in persuading them.'

By the time E (LF) had agreed the whole package in mid-December, the balance of forces within the Cabinet was narrowly in favour of reform. Oliver Letwin enumerated and named the different groupings for Mrs Thatcher.[124] Only five – Whitelaw, Younger, the Welsh Secretary Nicholas Edwards, Ridley and Baker – were fully in favour. Four – Hailsham, Lawson, Hurd and Heseltine – were 'probably against', and the rest in various states of mostly favourable wavering. At the turn of the year, Letwin followed up: 'This Green Paper is now about as good as it will ever be. The aim should be to get it through Cabinet and out into the world as soon as possible – otherwise, the rats will start nibbling.'[125]

---

* Waldegrave succeeded Baker as minister for local government in September 1985, but at the time when he took on the Local Government Finance Studies he was only the Parliamentary Under-Secretary in the department.

Although Letwin himself encouraged the idea that the paper was 'only Green, and that the Government seriously wants to know whether there are any undetected gremlins lurking in the proposals',[126] Mrs Thatcher put a wiggly line under this, and scribbled to Norgrove to stress that the Green Paper was 'green only in detail'.[127] She considered the decision of principle made. When it was suggested that Kenneth Baker should give a separate presentation to Cabinet about what was wrong with the rates, she grew nervous about the likely consequences. 'You were concerned that too extensive a discussion of this would give an opportunity for sceptics to question the need for any reform at all,' David Norgrove wrote to her.[128] 'Yes,' Mrs Thatcher confirmed. If Baker were allowed his presentation, 'Others would want to do the same.' She was thinking of Heseltine in relation to Westland. She wanted the Green Paper to be as White as possible. She wanted to get on.

On 9 January 1986, the Cabinet approved the Green Paper which launched the community charge. By a strange stroke of fate, this was the meeting at which Michael Heseltine stormed out over Westland and resigned. The community charge was the first substantial item of business after he had left the room, so he was not present to oppose it. No doubt it would have been counter-productive for his case if he had been because he was, at this point, so unpopular with colleagues and above all with Mrs Thatcher herself.

The discussion of the subject by the shell-shocked gathering was quite long, and contained several passages of debate where the 'rats', as Letwin had described them, did a bit of nibbling. According to Robert Armstrong's scribbled, semi-shorthand record,[129] critics on at least some points included Howe, Joseph, Hurd, Brittan, Biffen, John MacGregor (who had replaced Peter Rees as chief secretary to the Treasury the previous autumn), and the Energy Secretary, Peter Walker. The last was the most vocal and vehement. 'I don't think this is going to be positively attractive – the opposite,' Walker said. 'We are going to say to more than half of ratepayers you are going to pay more than before.' He spoke of the 'unbelievable complication' of the register, of tracing people and of rebates, and he warned of the political consequences: 'The disadvantaged will howl; the advantaged will keep quiet.' In a phrase presumably designed to stir Nigel Lawson, he said that 'If Ch Ex was thinking of a new tax, he wouldn't think of a poll tax, for sound reasons.' The real live Chancellor, however, did not weigh in, and confined himself to short, secondary points.

Kenneth Baker, who introduced and argued strongly in favour of the proposals, nevertheless expressed doubts about the Scottish desire to rush forward. It was the Scottish point of view, however, which came through most strongly. George Younger (whom Armstrong noted as 'SS Def (Scot)', because he had been promoted to defence secretary during that meeting) declared: 'It is essential for us in Scotland that we cannot rest just on a manifesto commitment,'[130] but must legislate before the general election. The community charge should begin in Scotland on 1 April 1989 and take three or four years to phase in. Willie Whitelaw argued that, contra Baker, there was 'a strong case for doing nothing', but that this case was over-whelmed by 'the full weight of Scottish feeling'. He supported Younger's call for immediate legislation as a 'political imperative'. If wise old Willie was for pressing forward, and Mrs Thatcher was firmly in favour, who could hold the line against them? What Mrs Thatcher wanted, Mrs Thatcher would get. The Green Paper would be published. Although this theoretically allowed time for second thoughts before legislation, the Scot-tish factor made the reform all but certain. Besides, no one could face a second row on the morning that Heseltine had just stormed out. The poll tax – as they were never allowed to call it – was agreed.

Given the weakness of Mrs Thatcher's political position after the Westland crisis it is striking to note how little trouble from colleagues she encoun-tered over the poll tax in the ensuing weeks and months. Her Tory critics, massing against her over issues like selling off British Leyland, more or less left her alone on the rates. The Green Paper, *Paying for Local Gov-ernment*, was published only the day after she had survived the last full-scale parliamentary assault over Westland. Kenneth Baker's statement in the House went well. The fact that there was now time for consultation (until October) and that the new arrangements would not begin to apply until 1989 in Scotland and 1990 in England and Wales, soothed anxieties. Criticisms in the press were quite strong, but the parliamentary reception, on the Tory side, was mostly good. Baker did record, however, that Nigel Lawson reached over to him and whispered: 'It will be her King Charles's head.'[131]* Except in the case of Scotland, the community charge would not be legislated for before the general election and, even in Scotland, would come into being after it. So the matter became more the subject of election planning than of heated parliamentary dispute.

With the drama shifted away from rates and their reform, public atten-tion reverted to the abolition of the GLC. This appeared to be a

---

* Lawson, untypically, was muddling his reference. 'King Charles's head' is a phrase from Charles Dickens's *David Copperfield*. The amiable Mr Dick has a mental quirk which always returns his conversation to the subject of King Charles's head. Lawson seems to have used the phrase to suggest her nemesis or fatal flaw. Perhaps he meant 'Achilles heel'. (Or perhaps Baker misremembered it.)

straightforward triumph for Mrs Thatcher. She had attacked the council
ever since Livingstone's coup the day after Labour's victory in the GLC
elections of 1981. With the collapse of the miners' strike and the
rate-capping revolts, Livingstone's dream of an extra-parliamentary campaign to bring down the Thatcher government had completely failed. Now,
on 31 March 1986, abolition took place. The huge sign which Livingstone
had erected years earlier on the roof of County Hall, the GLC headquarters across the river from Parliament, so that MPs could constantly be
reminded of the rising number of unemployed, now came down. County
Hall, as Mrs Thatcher wished, eventually found various private sector
uses, including as two hotels.

    Mrs Thatcher's victory, however, was perhaps too complete for people
to feel happy about it. Livingstone had been a bogeyman so long as he
seemed to be on top, but sympathy turned his way at the idea that an
elected body could be abolished by a government because it happened to
dislike its political complexion. Using £250,000 of money carefully harboured by various ingenious accounting tricks, the GLC spent its last days
celebrating itself, including a magnificent display of fireworks on the
Thames so that it literally went out with a bang. Many participants wore
badges saying 'We'll meet again'.* Mrs Thatcher herself made only two
references to the GLC in her memoirs, perhaps conscious that her policy
had not been the hit she had expected.

Although the politics went relatively quiet, the problems of the poll tax
within government continued throughout 1986. The essential difficulty
was that the pure, beautiful idea of leaving local government alone to do
the right thing when confronted by the wishes of newly empowered electors was constantly being compromised. In the real world, it just seemed
too frightening for central government to stand right aside, without granting exemptions and retaining powers to intervene and enforce.

    As, in February, 121 local authorities were rate-capped under the new
legislation, Mrs Thatcher was immediately confronted with cries of
unfairness about some of the consequences, and was naturally most alive
to these in councils which were Conservative controlled. She declared that
there would have to be a legal facility for the central government to cap
the community charge.[132] In her memoirs, she recorded that she did not

---

* In 2000, Ken Livingstone became the first directly elected mayor of London. In a curious
way, he felt grateful to Mrs Thatcher: 'The abolition of the GLC became an issue of democracy and people's rights. If she'd just ignored me, I would never have become a public figure'
(Interview with Ken Livingstone).

believe the 'optimistic suggestion' of her colleagues at Environment 'that enhanced accountability would make it possible to abandon "capping" altogether'.[133] She worried that left-wing councils would find ways of making trouble: 'indeed, before the end I would find myself pressing for much more extensive community charge capping than was ever envisaged for the rates.'[134] As so often, she was right in her instinct about what was politically likely. She was less attentive to the illogic she was importing into her own policy.

And although the community charge was intended to be decentralizing, other, related measures were intended to centralize. The non-domestic rate, paid by business, was now to be made uniform and set centrally. This presented Whitehall with a temptation (to which, over time, it has succumbed) of increasing the burdens on businesses rather than relieving them from those imposed by 'loony' Labour councils. Besides, Nicholas Ridley, who became environment secretary in May 1986, was conscious of the dangers inherent in the community charge 'even at present likely levels',[135] and so wanted the business rate to bear as much as possible of the strain. The uniform business rate meant that local government now had a much smaller proportion of its total finance to raise itself.

The problems of who should have to pay and how they could be made to do so were manifold. What of the need to impose a duty of registration on all citizens? What of the perplexing relationship between rebates on the community charge and social security payments? What about the mentally handicapped or the senile elderly? What of students, who, in a looser sense, were thought to lack responsibility? Nicholas Ridley was stern on these last: 'British students are one of the groups that most need to appreciate that public services cost money.'[136] Yet there was not much point running round trying to gouge money out of this naturally impecunious and disobedient group. 'The virtue of the community charge', Ridley wrote, 'is its universality.' But that was its vice as well. It did not fit all cases, and could not easily be collected from all its victims.

If, as planned, no person deemed responsible could avoid contributing at least 20 per cent of the standard community charge, how would you actually get it out of the poorest? Norman Fowler, the Social Services Secretary, thought there was 'no politically sustainable course short of increasing the planned income support level across the board (i.e. including the unemployed as well as the disabled etc) by the average cost of the new liability to pay 20 per cent'.[137]* 'I do have to warn colleagues', wrote

---

* Michael Ancram, who had to help get the Scottish reform through the House in late 1986,

Fowler to Mrs Thatcher, by way of follow-up, 'that the public debate will focus sharply on almost 4 million losers in real terms.'[138]

All the difficulties and objections applied, of course, to Scotland, which was pressing ahead first. Michael Ancram,* the Scottish local government minister, was concerned by the effects of 'asking everyone to pay the same', and argued for reductions for pensioners, exemptions for students and exemptions for most non-working wives.[139] This last group – quite possibly a larger number than the widows who suffered under the rates – also worried Stephen Sherbourne. It was the first time many of them had been directly taxed, and they were likely to feel ill used.[140] Such objections, however, were overruled, with the Treasury being tough. In Ancram's opinion, 'The Chancellor decided that the best way to ruin the tax was to make it as unpopular as possible.'[141]

On 26 November, the Bill to abolish domestic rates in Scotland was introduced in Parliament. At Cabinet two weeks earlier, Mrs Thatcher had emphasized that 'speedy enactment . . . was of the greatest importance.'[142] No parliamentary impediments were thrown in the way. Labour, which did not want to be seen to be fighting for the rates, mounted a half-hearted opposition. When it was voted on, Michael Heseltine, despite his declared opposition to the poll tax across the country, voted for it. Such controversy as there was concerned the transitional period. In February 1987, Malcolm Rifkind, by now Scottish Secretary, complained to Willie Whitelaw about 'sustained opposition'[143] to dual running, so complicated were the details and so eager were his fellow Scots to have the poll tax and nothing but. He decided to abolish domestic rates entirely and bring the Scottish poll tax into full operation on 1 April 1989.

The Scottish Bill effectively decided matters. Once the House of Commons had introduced the poll tax in Scotland, failure to proceed as promised with the same thing in England and Wales would have been a humiliating and unnecessary defeat. The mood was almost all the other way, the opposition weak. The government felt pleased that the ground for the general election was now prepared. It saw the new tax as a vote-winner. At the Scottish Conservative conference in Perth shortly

---

disparaged this as 'paying people to pay a tax', but was overruled. (See Butler, Adonis and Travers, *Failure in the British Government*, p. 102.)

* Michael Ancram (13th Marquess of Lothian) (1945–), educated Ampleforth, Christ Church, Oxford and Edinburgh University; Conservative MP for Berwick and East Lothian, February–September 1974; for Edinburgh South, 1979–87; for Devizes, 1992–2010; Parliamentary Under-Secretary, Scottish Office, 1983–7; NIO, 1993–4; Minister of State, NIO, 1994–7; Chairman, Conservative Party in Scotland, 1980–83; Chairman, Conservative Party, 1998–2001; created life peer, 2010.

afterwards Mrs Thatcher said that Scotland had suffered 'more than most' under the old system of rates. 'Indeed it was in response to your needs in Scotland that we finally decided on the introduction of the community charge.'[144]

The outcome of the poll tax is a matter for the final volume of this book. What can be said here is that the tax was not created on a whim of Margaret Thatcher, although it would certainly never have happened without the force of her will. It was a serious, long-considered attempt to get to grips with several genuine problems – distorted property taxes and central grants, lack of local accountability, left-wing profligacy and extremism. Although it drew heavily on ideas from 'irregulars' rather than emerging solely from the Whitehall machine of career civil servants, there was nothing unusual or necessarily wrong about that. It was very carefully considered by the machine: 'We did it so carefully, with *so* many papers,' recalled Terry Heiser.[145] At least three problems, however, were observable in the early stages, and were not resolved.

The first was extreme complication. No one, however brilliant, fully understood what was being done. The second was a defect in the principle itself. What, exactly, was the justification for the idea that everyone should pay the same? The argument at the time was that 'It is the same as a loaf of bread – you pay the same regardless of whether you are rich or poor.'[146] This was related to the idea that councils should be accountable to all voters. But in fact the loaf of bread analogy did not work. Customers can pay different prices for bread, and buy more or fewer loaves, and there is no law that puts them on a bread register and forces them to buy the stuff whether or not they have done so in the past. Besides, the poll tax cost a lot more than a loaf of bread each week and, in matters of tax, the amount demanded is almost always crucial. Somehow, the great minds who thought up the poll tax never quite confronted the flaws in their analogy. In the view of Stephen Sherbourne, the Prime Minister's Policy Unit and other advisers were too like 'clever schoolboys in science laboratories'[147] and therefore were not alert to political reality.

The third problem lay with Mrs Thatcher herself. Her instinct that getting rid of the rates could be like council house sales in securing her support was not foolish, but it led her to dismiss any virtue in property taxes and not to pay enough attention to the difficulties with the alternative she preferred. As Sherbourne put it, 'It was the beginning of her losing touch with people, with a real electoral base.'[148]

Perhaps she was too driven by anger that her 'promise' to get rid of the rates had been so long unfulfilled. David Norgrove remembered, one night in 1986, raising with her, while eating scrambled egg (cooked by her) in her flat, the problem of the number of losers from the poll tax. She acknowledged the danger and 'seemed to be rather regretting' what she was doing, but insisted, 'I have made a commitment to abolish rates. I have to do it.'[149] Bernard Ingham reported a sense from the lobby that the poll tax would be very difficult to collect and was fundamentally unfair. Quoting from the hymn 'All Things Bright and Beautiful', he emphasized the difference between 'the rich man in his castle' and the 'poor man at his gate'. Mrs Thatcher 'exploded'. 'The rich man in his castle is already paying through the nose in tax!' she exclaimed. She conceded that the tax might be difficult to collect in 'bedsitter-land', but not generally. Above all, 'she thought there *had* to be democratic control of local spending.'[150] So strongly did she believe this that she did not think through the consequences.

A single European

'How dare they! We saved all their necks in the war'

From the day she first came into office in May 1979, Mrs Thatcher had been arguing that Britain should get 'our money' back from the European Community (see Volume I, Chapter 18). The level of British contributions, negotiated at the time of entry by the Heath government, was, she believed, grossly excessive. What had begun as a net contribution of £102 million in 1973 had grown to £947 million by 1979[1] and, but for the series of temporary solutions negotiated during Mrs Thatcher's first term in office, would have increased further. She refused to allow the Community to embark on new endeavours until the imbalance had been rectified. More than five years later, on 26 June 1984, she finally succeeded. At the European Council in Fontainebleau, she secured a budgetary rebate of 66 per cent of the net British contribution. In addition, the terms satisfied her demand that 'the solution should be as long as the problem': the rebate would continue for as long as member states continued to fund the Community through the newly increased 1.4 per cent of their VAT receipts (own resources). There would be no more *ad hoc* deals, no more haggling. It was settled.

Almost until the last minute, success had not been assured. There had been talk, serious though not fulfilled, of withholding Britain's EEC budgetary contribution. At the previous Council in Brussels in March 1984, agreement had been widely expected, but had been prevented. According to Pierre Morel,* one of President Mitterrand's senior advisers, who was present, 'All the leaders were exasperated with Mrs Thatcher with an intensity that was striking. [Helmut] Kohl told her that she and he should follow the example of Churchill and Adenauer [the great

---

* Pierre Morel (1944–), diplomatic adviser to French President, 1991; French Ambassador to Georgia, 1992–3; to the Russian Federation and, at the same time, to Turkmenistan, Mongolia, Tadjikistan and Moldova, 1992–6; to Kirghizstan, 1993–6; to the People's Republic of China, 1996–2002; to the Holy See, 2002–5; EU Special Representative for Central Asia since 2006; for the crisis in Georgia since 2008.

post-war German Chancellor] and "think of the future". He was excited, out of himself. She just said, "No. Sorry. I want my money back." It was becoming dangerous: it was clear that she had gone too far.'[2] 'Everyone was furious with Margaret Thatcher,' Kohl later wrote. 'François Mitterrand . . . whispered to me at a meal, "I have had just about enough of these endless discussions . . . I think we should agree between ourselves that we will offer her nothing, nothing, nothing." '[3] Mitterrand and Kohl became determined that this row would go on no longer. So they worked for a final result at Fontainebleau, plotting with allies to isolate her if she would not agree. British diplomats got wind of some of this, and indicated to the French that Britain, too, was looking to settle the matter.[4] In a bilateral meeting with Kohl, at Chequers on 2 May, Mrs Thatcher confirmed, by hints, that Britain was prepared to give a bit in negotiations in order to get a deal. She repudiated the idea that Britain lacked loyalty to Europe. The note of their conversation reports her as saying: 'We were passionate Europeans. We joined the Community so that the conflicts that had occurred in the past could not recur in the future.'[5] All the 'big three' – Kohl, Mitterrand and Thatcher – were currently in strong electoral positions, she pointed out. Let them unite to get a budget settlement and go forward to a new phase in the development of the Community.

British officials such as Robin Renwick decided to try to deal with the French, who wished to bring things to a climax during their six-month presidency of the EEC. When Roland Dumas,* who later in the year succeeded his then boss, the much more anti-British Claude Cheysson,† as foreign minister, met Geoffrey Howe in Paris, he told British officials that they needed to find a new approach. Without the involvement or indeed knowledge of Mrs Thatcher, they and their French counterparts secretly cooked up the beginnings of a deal.[6] The rebate would be a straight percentage with the whole thing 'abated as we paid' (rather than refunded later) and enshrined in Community law.[7] Although British officials were by no means certain of success at Fontainebleau, almost their biggest worry was 'Thatcher handling'[8] rather than beating down the French. Would she go for the deal which they had prepared?

The Fontainebleau European Council meeting was one of the very few events in Mrs Thatcher's career as prime minister of which she wrote a

* Roland Dumas (1922–), French lawyer and Socialist politician; Minister for European Affairs, 1983–4; government spokesman, 1984; Foreign Minister, 1984–6 and 1988–93; President, Commission for Foreign Affairs, National Assembly, 1986–7; Chairman, Constitutional Council, 1995–2000.
† Claude Cheysson (1920–2012), French Socialist politician; European Commissioner, 1973–81; Foreign Minister, 1981–4; Member, European Parliament, 1989–94.

personal account afterwards.* Her exact reasons for doing so are not known, but once out of office she declared that she had put pen to paper 'shortly after the event with the aim of refuting misinterpretations'.[9] Her desire to record her recollections probably reflected both her pleasure at ending the long quarrel and anxiety that Eurosceptic critics might think she had given too much away. Her short, handwritten memoir recounted that she arrived at the summit unsure of what was likely to happen. She thought that Mitterrand (whom she always spelt, wrongly, with one 'r') had not decided which course of action to pursue. His choice lay between '1 – a solution & ∴ a triumph for France in the chair' and '2 – a failure – all due to Britain!'[10] The mood at the meeting was 'superficially cordial'. Mrs Thatcher put forward her budget proposal and its details were, at her suggestion, remitted to the foreign ministers, who were invited to report to the heads of government at the end of dinner. The dinner was held at the Hôtellerie du Bas-Bréau, the former hunting lodge in the village of Barbizon where Robert Louis Stevenson wrote most of *Treasure Island*. Mrs Thatcher was annoyed to notice all the foreign ministers, led by their French host Cheysson, drinking their coffee outdoors and swapping funny stories instead of settling the details of the budget problem and reporting, as arranged, to the heads of government inside. 'How dare they!' she exclaimed. 'We saved all their necks in the war.'[11] Renwick and David Williamson† chose this perilous moment to reveal their until then concealed plan of negotiation with the French. They left the actual percentage on which Britain would settle blank so that she could feel she had decided it: 'She glared, but gave us silent permission.'

According to Mrs Thatcher, whose account does not mention her diplomats' preparations, 'The President's displeasure [with the foreign ministers] was made plain,'[12] and at 11.30 in the evening Cheysson joined the heads of government with a proposed refund so low that Mrs Thatcher found it insulting: 'I was in despair and said we had never been treated fairly and if that was the best they had to offer Fontainebleau would be a disaster.'

Renwick had told his French opposite number that the British would not settle for less than 66 per cent – over 70 per cent being the figure which Mrs Thatcher had come to Fontainebleau demanding. The French were nominally demanding 50 per cent, hoping to stick at 60 per cent, but actually ready to go further. (They did not tell the Germans, who were sticking solidly at 60 per cent, about their game with the British.) So the

---

* Another came when she visited Moscow for Chernenko's funeral in 1985 (see Chapter 9).
† David Williamson (1934–2015), educated Tonbridge and Exeter College, Oxford; Deputy Secretary, Cabinet Office, 1983–7; Secretary-General, European Commission, 1987–97; knighted, 1998; created Lord Williamson of Horton, 1999.

next day had an element of play-acting, possibly even on the part of Mrs Thatcher, though play-acting was something she never, ever admitted to, even in private. As no agreement was reached round the table, Mitterrand suggested breaking into bilaterals, and Mrs Thatcher saw him and Kohl separately. 'I told Kohl we would accept 2/3 refunds . . . and we accordingly told Dumas. Kohl offered 65%.'[13] As Kohl recalled it, Mrs Thatcher 'became very vehement towards me. In essence, she said that the Federal Republic had to support Great Britain on the grounds that there were British soldiers stationed in our country.'[14] She then called a 'time out' to consult her officials. David Williamson said to Michael Butler,* who was tasked with 'Thatcher handling', 'Tell her she's got to settle now,' but Butler thought it better for her to have the thought unprompted, so he remained silent. 'I think we've almost got as much as we can,' she said, to his great relief,[15] adding, 'If I've got it to 65 per cent, I can add one more per cent.' Returning to the full session, she asked for this, and Mitterrand duly conceded it, with gallantry: 'Of course, Madame Prime Minister, you must have it.'[16] Butler recalled the 'huge, furious figure of Helmut Kohl' buzzing for his officials to prevent what would be financially disadvantageous to Germany. But the Germans, who also needed a favourable Common Agricultural Policy settlement for their farmers, did not dare gainsay the French presidency, and so the thing was done.

'After a very late lunch – by this time very good humoured,' wrote Mrs Thatcher, there was a press conference with 'the customary carping questions(!) and then home.'[17]† She had gained what she called the 'essential points' – the percentage rebate, acceptance that the deal would 'last as long as the problem', and that the rebate payments would be handed over automatically each year rather than being subject to a vote in the European Parliament.

Fontainebleau was the sort of deal that delights diplomats. Many years later, its progenitors would dwell on the famous victory. The official Treasury figure for the amount of money cumulatively saved for Britain by 2015 is £78 billion. Robin Renwick claimed it as 'the most valuable financial agreement this country *ever* negotiated'.[18] There were, however, other ways of looking at it. Mitterrand's officials claimed it as *their*

---

* Michael Butler (1927–2013), educated Winchester and Trinity College, Oxford; Ambassador and UK Permanent Representative to EEC, 1979–85; knighted, 1980.
† All matters having been settled, Pierre Morel put the first samples of the projected EEC/national passports on the lunch table for the leaders to peruse (Interview with Pierre Morel). These were unpopular in Britain and disliked by Mrs Thatcher, so it was perhaps fortunate for her mood that Morel saved this gesture for after Britain's rebate had been agreed.

country's triumph. Hubert Védrine,* Mitterrand's right-hand man, regarded it as the moment when the Kohl–Mitterrand axis forced Mrs Thatcher to accept compromise. He noted that she was 'terrifying to look at' as she capitulated: 'She did not see it at all as a victory.'[19] What would become an unbreakable relationship between Mitterrand and Kohl had been forged, Védrine believed, when the French President addressed the Bundestag in January 1983. Fontainebleau was 'le point de départ' for their active alliance to shape the future of Europe which lasted until the Maastricht Treaty in 1992: they had finally settled the British problem and got Britain, as part of the deal, to agree to a higher Community budget (the increase from 1 per cent VAT receipts to fund the Community's 'own resources' to 1.4 per cent). At last the stalemate was ended, and they could get on with European integration, whether Mrs Thatcher liked it or not. According to Jacques Attali,† who was not present, Mitterrand told him that he had been surprised to see that Mrs Thatcher 'was almost in tears' when she made the deal.[20]‡

Allowing for national exaggeration on both sides, it is fair to say that Fontainebleau was, indeed, a good financial deal for Britain. As the Europhile British diplomat David Hannay,§ who took part in the negotiations, conceded, 'no British Prime Minister for whom I worked would have got a better deal than Margaret Thatcher and several would probably have settled for something inferior.'[21] Her ability to master the detail and sustain the fight for so long in a ten-sided battle in which she had no reliable friends was astonishing. She carried with her into negotiation not only the conventional official speaking note, but also what were called 'handbag points' about particular issues which she would suddenly produce to confound her opponents, and 'stilettoes' which proved their

* Hubert Védrine (1947–), diplomatic adviser to President Mitterrand, 1981–6; Secretary-General, Office of the French Presidency, 1991–5; Minister of Foreign Affairs, 1997–2002.
† Jacques Attali (1943–), economist and senior civil servant; Member, Council of State, France, 1981–90 and since 1993; special adviser to President of French Republic, 1981–91; founding president, European Bank for Reconstruction and Development, 1991–3; president, Commission for Liberation of French Economic Growth, 2007–8.
‡ Attali's tale improved in the telling. For an interview with the BBC in 2009, he said that Mrs Thatcher twice had to ask for the percentage she finally got and actually burst into tears: 'It was an embarrassing begging for a tip and then we give them half the tip that she was requesting and we went on to very more [sic] serious issues' (Jacques Attali, Interview with the BBC, 6 July 2009, http://news.bbc.co.uk/1/hi/uk_politics/8136326.stm).
§ David Hannay (1935–), educated Winchester and New College, Oxford; Assistant Under-Secretary of State (European Community), FCO, 1979–84; Ambassador and UK Permanent Representative to European Communities, 1985–90; Ambassador and UK Permanent Representative to UN, 1990–95; knighted, 1986; created Lord Hannay, 2001.

hypocrisies, backslidings and evasions. She was the superior of all her counterparts in knowledge, argumentative skill, force of personality and perhaps even in raw intelligence, though not in diplomatic finesse. The budget saga proved how formidable she was in fighting for British national interests. But the French officials were not wrong to detect in Mrs Thatcher herself some anxieties about whether she had really got what she wanted. At the simplest political level, she had wanted a higher percentage than she achieved.* She was also conscious of strong Eurosceptic feeling at home. The hard core of twenty-five or so Eurosceptic Tory MPs, and the larger number of Labour counterparts, picked up on the fact that Fontainebleau won a financial benefit at the cost of acquiescence in higher European expenditure, no reform of the CAP and further European integration. In the Commons, the future Cabinet minister Peter Lilley† compared the deal to trying to 'dissuade an alcoholic from drinking by offering him unlimited whisky if he signed the pledge',[22] the alcoholic in this image being the EEC. As the *Spectator* put it in the week after the deal was made, Mrs Thatcher had 'passed up the only chance of real change by agreeing, before she had to, to more than she had to. We shall now return to the era of complacent Euro-pieties . . . and the relentless rise of costs.'[23] Detecting her anxiety, Bernard Ingham advised her before her post-Council press conference, 'You must present a successful outcome as a success and not grudgingly.'[24] Mrs Thatcher obeyed him, but she had her doubts. In her own written account, she celebrated the fact that the matter was well settled but added that, with regard to control of expenditure, 'the battle continues':[25] 'at least now we can reassess our European strategy. So much will depend upon its cohesion in the coming years.'

Sceptical though she was about closer European political links, Mrs Thatcher was interested in physical ones. Since the early 1800s, the idea of an underwater tunnel linking Britain with France had been promoted

---

* Documents show that the 66 per cent which pleased officials so much when they reached it was actually only their minimum aim at Fontainebleau. 'The real crux', wrote David Williamson to Geoffrey Howe, just before the Council, '. . . is how far, if at all, we can get them above the refund of the two-thirds of the VAT share/expenditure gap' (Williamson to Howe, 22 June 1984, Prime Minister's Papers, European Policy, European Council Meeting in Paris, Part 18 (document consulted in the Cabinet Office)).

† Peter Lilley (1943–), educated Dulwich College and Clare College, Cambridge; Conservative MP for St Albans, 1983–97; for Hitchin and Harpenden, 1997–; PPS to Chancellor of the Exchequer, 1984–7; Economic Secretary to the Treasury, 1987–9; Financial Secretary to the Treasury, 1989–90; Secretary of State for Trade and Industry, 1990–92; for Social Security, 1992–7.

by enthusiasts on both sides of the English Channel.* After the Second World War, the British and French governments began to take the idea more seriously.[26] In 1964 a joint tunnel project was agreed in principle, but proceeded very slowly because of concerns over financing.† When she came to power, Mrs Thatcher had neither the resources nor the inclination to commit taxpayers' money. She found the idea appealing, however, provided that a suitable private enterprise scheme came along. In 1981, through the ever persuasive recommendation of Ian Gow, she was introduced to a scheme dreamed up by her hero of the moment, Ian MacGregor, whom she had made chairman of the British Steel the previous year.

MacGregor, leading a group called EuroRoute, came to Mrs Thatcher with a new idea. Rather than a traditional bored tunnel, he envisaged a 'combined viaduct bridge and immersed tube for road and rail' with artificial islands for frontier controls.[27] It was based on the Chesapeake Bay crossing in the United States which, said Mrs Thatcher's briefing, 'is not thought to operate profitably'.[28] 'Can we check,' she wrote beside this (as usual she omitted question marks). She and MacGregor met and she 'acknowledged the attractions'[29] of the scheme.‡

MacGregor's ambitions accorded with Mrs Thatcher's ideology, which feared exclusive reliance on rail because it was both nationalized and wholly unionized, and preferred the freedom of the road and the power of the private sector. He was so well connected that he could personally lobby numerous Cabinet ministers. He also dangled the idea that Euroroute would create work for British Steel – 'approximately 250,000 man years of employment' over five years, he claimed.[30] But the prevailing view of the Departments of Transport and of Industry was that a pure rail link was better. In addition, the new French Socialist-led coalition government, whose Transport Minister, Charles Fiterman, was a real, live Communist, demanded a 'political cancellation' arrangement by which each

* Over the years, a number of elaborate schemes had been proposed, mainly by private investors, which included various combinations of tunnels and bridges.
† Edward Heath's government pressed ahead with plans for the tunnel but, when the Conservatives returned to opposition, Mrs Thatcher raised concerns about rising costs (Hansard, HC Deb 30 April 1974, 872/969–72 (http://hansard.millbanksystems.com/commons/1974/apr/30/channel-tunnel-bill)). The government plan was abandoned in 1975, but the idea was kept alive by interested private sector groups in subsequent years.
‡ Again through Gow, MacGregor tried to use Mrs Thatcher to gain an audience with President François Mitterrand, implying her support. She was happy to introduce him to the President, but aware that she must stay above the fray: 'he cannot say that I endorse his particular plan.' (Gow to Alexander, 25 November 1981, Prime Minister's Papers, Transport, The Channel Tunnel, Part 1 (document consulted in the Cabinet Office).)

government, once signed up to endorse a scheme, would be liable if it backed out. Mrs Thatcher's free-market guru Alan Walters, who was a transport economist and disliked railways, warned her that the public's 'growing expectations about the Chunnel/Brunnel [part-bridge, part-tunnel]' were worrying.[31] A rail tunnel would require unacceptable government guarantees, so the government should not allow people to get the impression that it might give them. The Trade Secretary, John Biffen, reminded colleagues of the vast losses made on the Anglo-French Concorde aeroplane and the danger of being 'generally at the mercy of the French'.[32]

Mrs Thatcher was cautious, but because of Mitterrand's helpful attitude during the Falklands War, she agreed with the Foreign Office line that Britain should find 'a way of keeping the French in play and out of mischief'.[33] So when she saw Mitterrand's Prime Minister, Pierre Mauroy,* in Edinburgh in May 1982 and he expounded his Channel vision, she agreed with him: 'She too harboured a dream of a fixed link.'† But she made no commitment of public money and added that 'she did not think [private] finances would be available for a rail link alone.'[34] It was up to the private sector to come up with interesting suggestions: when they had done so, the government would decide which scheme would be its best 'chosen instrument'. Politically, the matter then went quiet for eighteen months. At the 1983 general election, it suited the Conservatives, who had several Kent seats whose residents did not want the noise and bother of a Channel tunnel, to play the issue down. Nicholas Ridley, whom Mrs Thatcher made transport secretary in October 1983, was a tunnel sceptic, especially if the spending of public money was involved.

Early in 1984, Gow again asked Mrs Thatcher to see MacGregor, who was still pushing forward with his EuroRoute scheme. This meeting was partly a cover so that Mrs Thatcher and MacGregor could talk about the coming miners' strike without being seen to do so (see Chapter 6), but it was also an opportunity for him to attach the appeal of his project to the political preoccupation of the hour. Rail-only tunnels, he told Mrs Thatcher, 'would perpetuate and even enhance the monopoly power of rail unions on both sides of the Channel'. Rail unions were much on her mind, because there was a threat that they might come out in solidarity

---

* Pierre Mauroy (1928–2013), French Socialist national and local politician; Mayor of Lille, 1973–2001; Member of the National Assembly for Nord, 1973–81 and 1986–92; president, Regional Council for Nord, 1974–81; Prime Minister of France, 1981–4.
† The phrase 'Channel tunnel' was problematic, since it assumed there was no other possible built means of crossing the 22 miles between England and France. The wider term, adopted by the government, was 'fixed link'.

with the striking miners.[35] Although Mrs Thatcher continued to prefer a road element to a conventional rail link, she still did not give MacGregor her endorsement. Her Policy Unit advised her that the fixed link was in the category of 'would be nice' rather than 'must have',[36] and was therefore a matter for the private sector alone.

The situation, however, was unsatisfactory and gave rise to a private–public Catch-22. Several private promoters were now ready and eager to push their case, but could not do so without any government lead. The French wanted to move forward. The British did not want to be blamed for delay. President Mitterrand came to Britain for a state visit in October 1984 and mischievously told a press conference that he and Mrs Thatcher had discussed the Channel project 'all the time' during his visit and that it was her 'obsession'.[37] This tease pushed Mrs Thatcher towards action: she did not want to deny that she supported the project. Mitterrand was also conscious that she was coming to see him a month later for the Anglo-French summit in Paris.

These two occasions for the leaders to meet forced the government to think harder about what it really desired. Nicholas Ridley, who was off to see his French counterpart, wanted a steer from Downing Street. Even now, though, he did not really get one. Mrs Thatcher followed the advice of her Policy Unit and told Ridley that he should simply reiterate the 'existing position without sounding either bullish or bearish'.[38] The government was terrified it would have to end up supporting bids with public money. There was always a fear that a Channel fixed link could end up being the largest white elephant ever imposed on the British Exchequer.

After Mrs Thatcher's summit dinner with Mitterrand on 29 November 1984, Mrs Thatcher gathered ministers and officials in the British Ambassador's residence in Paris for drinks. Perhaps intoxicated by Mitterrand's Gallic charm towards women, for which he was famed, Mrs Thatcher suddenly became animated about the fixed link. She seemed to share the President's love of *grands projets*. 'It would be nice to have something exciting getting under way,' she said.[39] In her view, 'exciting' meant a scheme involving road: the alternatives did not interest her. 'I don't want the rail tunnel,' she declared, 'I want EuroRoute,'[40] as did Mitterrand. Bernard Ingham, who was present, was amazed by Mrs Thatcher's new-found enthusiasm for something about which she had for so long been so hesitant: 'I passed a note to Robin Butler which said: "When did this conversion on the road to Damascus take place?" "About 17 minutes ago," Robin replied. Mitterrand really did flirt with her.'[41] The following day, the two leaders announced their amity on the fixed link (though without stating which scheme), and promised to pursue the project with 'real urgency'.[42] Mrs Thatcher conveyed her excitement to the BBC: 'many people have a great dream that they would like to get in their car at Dover and drive all the way through to Calais.' In a separate BBC interview, she said that such a European link would 'make us confident in the future and as forward-looking as some of those of our forbears [sic] who built the first industrial revolution'.[43]

Despite Mrs Thatcher's new-found zeal, her vision did not, in fact, prevail. As John Wybrew in the Policy Unit complained to her, 'Ironically, the French team [the Socialist government] are embracing the positive spirit of the Thatcherite private enterprise formula . . . with more inspiration and enthusiasm than the British.'[44] Britain, not France, was the problem: there were 'too many hang-ups about rabies, plant health and terrorists'.* The project was now almost certain to go forward – the 'Invitation to Promoters' was issued in April 1985 – but the institutional forces in favour of a rail link were stronger and wilier. Sir Nicholas Henderson, hero of British diplomacy with the United States during the Falklands War and a former ambassador in Paris, was chairman of the Channel Tunnel Group which, with its French partner, Trans-Manche, was bidding for a rail tunnel. 'I am concerned', he wrote silkily to Mrs Thatcher, 'by the extent to which your views are being taken for granted . . . When I was in Paris recently I was told in the Prime Minister's office . . . that it was assumed in France that the British Prime Minister was in favour of Euro-Route.'[45] Could he come and see her? And by the way, his company could even offer a drive-through tunnel in addition to the rail one they had already planned.

It was Bernard Ingham who detected and neatly encapsulated which way things were going. The Cabinet committee set up to consider the different Channel 'fixed link' projects, he wrote to Mrs Thatcher, 'fails to address itself to which side of the road vehicles would drive. This may be a significant pointer to the ultimate choice.'[46] He meant that if the committee was not thinking about whether cars would drive through on the left- or right-hand side this was because it wanted a rail-only tunnel.

---

* Helmut Kohl, for one, believed that Mrs Thatcher shared these traditional British anxieties about Continental invasion. Richard Burt, the former US Ambassador to Germany, recalled the Chancellor's account of Mrs Thatcher's remarks on the subject: 'She started talking about her concerns that rats and animals with rabies would come through the Chunnel and spread rabies in Britain. Kohl saw this as a metaphor for her relationship with Europe. He said he'd never heard anything more stupid in his life.' (Interview with Richard Burt.) The British press was full of the sort of fears Kohl found 'stupid', including drug imports and damage to the ferry companies. Oddly, opportunities for illegal immigration, considered the great problem in the twenty-first century, were little mentioned.

In November, four plans were submitted, including those of EuroRoute and the Channel Tunnel Group. An effective deadline for decision was set by the fact that Mrs Thatcher and Mitterrand had agreed to meet in Lille on 20 January 1986 for a ceremony to announce their 'chosen instrument' for the project. Despite considerable pressures, Mrs Thatcher followed Charles Powell's advice that she must stand aside from the process of selection in order to avoid 'later accusations of trying to manipulate the outcome',[47] although Mitterrand, through a private intermediary, urged her to weigh in in favour of EuroRoute.[48] The Policy Unit thought the same way. 'Put your vision of what Europe is capable of achieving to the test,' urged John Wybrew. 'Challenge the private sector to undertake the EuroRoute scheme.'[49] She did not.

After much toing and froing, the decision was made for the bored-tunnel scheme of the Channel Tunnel Group/Trans-Manche. As Nicko Henderson had calculated, the vague offer of an eventual road tunnel in addition to the rail one made it much easier for everyone to accept. Mrs Thatcher's enthusiasm for MacGregor's more dashing idea had been overcome by her persistent caution about money, and the Channel Tunnel Group's superior acquaintance with the corridors of power on both sides of the Channel. It was all rather a rush. Charles Powell brought back from the ceremony at Lille a piece of paper on which he had written out:

> This – believe it or not – is a historic document. It is the PM's statement announcing the choice of the Channel Tunnel Fixed Link project . . . please file:
>
> THE UNITED KINGDOM AND FRANCE HAVE DECIDED TODAY, ON THE BASIS OF A REPORT BY EXPERTS, TO LINK THEIR TWO COUNTRIES BY A TWIN-BORE TUNNEL UNDER THE CHANNEL FOR RAIL TRAFFIC AND MOTOR VEHICLE SHUTTLE TRAINS.
>
> LATER A DRIVE-THROUGH LINK SHOULD BE BUILT.[50]

On this scrap of paper, François Mitterrand and Margaret Thatcher had appended their signatures.

The following month, on 12 February, Mrs Thatcher greeted Mitterrand at Manston airport in Kent and drove with him to Canterbury. 'He kept staring at her legs in the car,' recalled her detective, Barry Strevens.[51] They signed a treaty to formalize the deal in the Chapter House of the Cathedral. Thirty years on, the Channel Tunnel is extremely popular, although the high-speed rail link eventually installed had to be paid for by government, not the private sector. Of the drive-through link, there is no sign.

*

Through collaboration with a French socialist government, Mrs Thatcher had succeeded in bringing Britain and the Continent much closer, physically, than ever before. For all this, she remained uneasy about the future direction of the European Community. She did, at this stage, believe in the Community as an embodiment of Western democracy and an aid to peace in Europe. She was therefore pleased that Spain and Portugal, which had sloughed off dictatorships in the 1970s, were to be permitted to join (at the beginning of 1986). She did have an agenda of bringing Thatcherite freedoms and disciplines to the economic affairs of the EEC. In particular, she wanted what the British still usually called the 'Common Market', but was now being rechristened the Single Market,* to live up to its name. But she was scarred by the experience of European Councils over five years, and had developed almost measureless contempt for their endless dinners: 'It all proved so bloody difficult that it did sour her.'[52] 'These men!' she exclaimed to Bernard Ingham after attending the formal dinner at Fontainebleau. 'All they do is anecdote away. Never get down to business. So unbusinesslike!'[53]† Mrs Thatcher's Continental counterparts felt similarly annoyed. The fight had often been so fierce that it had permanently bruised them: 'in the process, she had alienated the others.'[54] 'These men' were fed up with 'that woman'.

Mrs Thatcher was already anxious about the different way in which her main European partners saw the future of the Community. Her Foreign Office brief for her meeting with Kohl a few weeks before the Council in Brussels in March 1984 had suggested that she argue 'There cannot be a Renaissance without a Reformation.'[55] This was not terribly good history – the Renaissance began long before the Reformation – but, for Mrs Thatcher, there was a further doubt. She certainly wanted a Reformation – the breaking down of bureaucracy, protectionism, the state direction of the economy, inefficiency and cronyism – but did she actually want the sort of Renaissance that gleamed in the eyes of all these foreigners? Her failure to share the deep emotions which underlay the drive for European Union is illustrated by a vignette three months after Fontainebleau. On 22 September 1984, on the field of the terrible First World War battle of Verdun, Kohl and Mitterrand stood together, hand in hand, to symbolize the reconciliation of France and Germany. Mrs Thatcher watched it on television.

---

* It was sometimes referred to as the 'internal market'. Mrs Thatcher did not like this phrase, though she did sometimes use it, because it implied that the EEC was an embryonic United States of Europe rather than a trading bloc.

† Her private manuscript account of Fontainebleau spoke of 'weak rather futile anecdotes' at dinner ('Fontainebleau', Thatcher Memorandum, undated, CAC: THCR 1/20/4 (http://www.margaretthatcher.org/document/139100)).

Wasn't it moving, she was privately asked afterwards? 'No, it was *not*,' she answered. 'Two grown men holding hands!'[56] She was often in favour of EEC developments, but she never shared the religion of Europeanism.

Like all religions, Europeanism needed its dogma. And Mrs Thatcher often found herself with little option but to accept the expansive language favoured by her European partners. The 'Solemn Declaration' that Mrs Thatcher had agreed to during the European Council at Stuttgart in June 1983 (see Chapter 4) provides a classic case of how the cause of European integration advanced despite Mrs Thatcher's resistance at every point.

The Declaration arose from the so-called Genscher–Colombo Plan of 1981, in which the foreign ministers of Germany and Italy had argued for greater European political integration, laying the ground for the creation of a European state and calling for a 'European Act' to advance it. In November 1981, the then Foreign Secretary, Lord Carrington, wrote to Mrs Thatcher soothingly to say that Genscher–Colombo would not need parliamentary ratification, because it was not a treaty. 'A tactical point,' he added: 'Our overriding aim in Europe at the moment is a satisfactory outcome on the Community Budget. For this, we need German cooperation. We shall find it easier to persuade our partners to make the substantial moves we need from them if we can provide them with evidence of simultaneous progress on the wider, vaguer and more theological issues addressed in the German proposals.'[57] Mrs Thatcher wrote uneasily on the note, 'We can't get away with this without reference to <u>Parliament</u>,' and added, 'This will reopen all the old wounds in the Tory Party and create <u>another</u> split. We <u>just</u> <u>can't</u> do it.'[58]

But do it they did. In February 1983, Carrington's replacement, Francis Pym, wrote to Mrs Thatcher encouraging her to sign up to the Genscher–Colombo proposals at the forthcoming European Council. Her private secretary, John Coles, deployed the classic line of tactics over long-term view in Pym's support: 'I do not think it will do any harm to sign this verbose document and Kohl will be upset if we make difficulties.' Mrs Thatcher wrote: 'I dislike it intensely.'[59] Three days later, she wrote, 'Do we have to sign it. Can't we just adopt it. It is a <u>dreadful</u> document.'[60] At the end of the month, Pym insisted that Britain would be isolated if she resisted signing. Like Carrington, he argued the tactical course: 'The appearance of the document will doubtless prompt some discussion but I do not think we should have much trouble in demonstrating that it has little real content.'[61] And he followed this up with a magnificent piece of King Charles Street ingenuity: 'If, on the other hand, we were to refuse to sign, we would run the risk of appearing to attach more credibility to the document than it either warrants or deserves.'[62] In other words, Britain should sign in order not to attach credibility to the document. 'Do you agree to sign?' a private secretary wrote on Pym's letter. 'Yes,' wrote an exhausted Mrs Thatcher.

British officials tried to reassure Mrs Thatcher that a Declaration – even a Solemn one – was much less than an Act. They were proud of a form of words in the Declaration which described European unity as a 'process' rather than a 'destination' point;[63] but its overall effect went strongly against Britain's pragmatic and modest approach. By it, the Community was committed to 'Strengthening of the European Monetary System . . . as a key element in progress towards Economic and Monetary Union' and to decide within five years 'whether the progress achieved should be incorporated in a Treaty on European Union'. Mrs Thatcher was almost always advised that what officials characterized as the 'windy rhetoric' or 'theology' of European declarations was worth putting up with in order to secure concrete advantages. Sometimes this was good advice, but the trouble was that the windy rhetoric usually meant something important to the men who uttered it. Theology always matters to a priesthood. The high priests of Europe would be sure – quite reasonably from their point of view – to use it later. That happened in this case: what was conceived by Genscher–Colombo in 1981 and solemnly declared at Stuttgart in 1983 would be framed as a treaty obligation at Luxembourg in 1985, included in the Single European Act of 1986, set in train at Hanover in 1988, confirmed at Madrid in 1989 and Rome in 1990, and implemented in the treaty which followed after the Maastricht Intergovernmental Conference of 1991. Because the builders of Europe saw the EEC as a continuous progress in one direction, they used each treaty, declaration, protocol, directive and so on as the building block for the next. Mrs Thatcher was very suspicious of this, both as a method of proceeding and because of the nature of the goals. But she was also trapped in it: it was a condition of membership.

There was a strong contrast in underlying attitudes, if not in explicit philosophy, between Mrs Thatcher and her European colleagues. In May 1984, for example, after visiting Mrs Thatcher at Chequers, Helmut Kohl delivered the Konrad Adenauer Memorial Lecture in Oxford. There he argued that European integration must be 'irreversible' and asked, 'Are all members prepared to work for the political union of Europe?', a question which implicitly challenged Oxford's most famous living female graduate. Mrs Thatcher was never committed to political union – as opposed to political co-operation – indeed she was adamantly opposed to it. Her way of putting this tended to have a guise of pragmatism, but underneath her views were hard: 'I do wish someone would define it [political union] first . . .' she told *Die Welt* in October 1984. 'I do not know what European political union means . . . I do not believe that we shall have or can have a United States of Europe.'[64] She could hardly comprehend the federalist ambition: 'It simply did not occur to me that they would want to bury the Mother of Parliaments in a United States of Europe.'[65] Her own thoughts about the EEC were limited, caustic and practical. Their flavour can be tasted not only in her own comments, but in those provided to her by Charles Powell. Powell, though seconded from the Foreign Office, was always clear that in his job as private secretary he owed loyalty to her alone. He therefore almost always projected, and even sometimes hardened, her view of the world in his communications, and relished it when she clashed with departmental orthodoxies. He often sent her sarcastic notes about European affairs to stir her up. One, entitled '59 New Regulations in 1984', mockingly mentioned 'sewage sludge in agriculture', 'the market in goatmeat' and laws on 'Boat Fittings'. 'They'll try to Harmonise Nursery Rhymes next!' he added.[66]

Some of the most consequential decisions Mrs Thatcher took in relation to the future of the EEC concerned appointments to the European Commission, the bureaucracy which runs it. Given her own vision of a largely economic Community, the choices she made were striking. So was the advice she received. Even among her ministers, there was a failure to understand – or sometimes a desire to avoid understanding – just how little Mrs Thatcher bought in to the European ideal. In 1984, for example, when discussion began about who should succeed Gaston Thorn as the head of the European Commission, Geoffrey Howe canvassed the cause of the Belgian Vicomte Étienne Davignon,* the Vice-President of the Commission, whom Mrs Thatcher did, in fact, favour. By way of praise, Howe wrote to her that 'in the last resort, he [Davignon] is less a Belgian than a European.'[67] Mrs Thatcher marked this sentence with her wiggly line of distaste: it was never a recommendation in her eyes that someone was a 'good European'. Even being a Belgian was better.

When it became clear that Davignon was not a runner, and that the Germans were unlikely to put forward their own candidate, the Foreign Office saw that the French would probably produce the new man. They wished to steer the choice away from the left-wing, anti-British Claude Cheysson and towards Jacques Delors,† Mitterrand's Finance Minister,

---

* Vicomte Étienne Davignon (1932–), Belgian diplomat, politician and businessman; Vice-President, European Commission, 1981–5.
† Jacques Delors (1925–), Minister of the Economy and Finance, France, 1981–3; Minister of Economy, Finance and Budget, 1983–4; President, European Commission, 1985–95.

whom they saw as more responsible. There is no record of Mrs Thatcher and British ministers discussing the appointment in terms of the candidates' attitudes to European integration. Mrs Thatcher knew relatively little about the characters on offer and so relied to a great degree on advice from the Foreign Office. Seeking to promote his own choice of Delors, Howe wrote to Mrs Thatcher that he 'would be likely to take a far more serious interest in the management of the community's finances'.[68] The following week, Mrs Thatcher met Howe's close ally Roland Dumas and discussed the appointment. Dumas commended Delors to her on the grounds that 'M. Delors was very strict in budget matters'.[69] These formulations are so similar, and occur so closely together, that it is hard to resist the idea that Howe and Dumas colluded to persuade Mrs Thatcher in the matter. Delors himself noted that Mrs Thatcher liked his determination to sort out the finances of France after the failure of Mitterrand's initial socialist version of a dash for growth: 'She was the daughter of the grocer, a hard-working man ... She demonstrated a sort of revolt against the old British system with their tea breaks. I had respect for that. Mrs Thatcher appreciated that I was operating in a difficult climate in France and she liked my methods. I think that may have played some part in her "yes".'[70] In terms of ability and experience, Jacques Delors was indeed eminently qualified to run the Commission, but he was also certain to try to use it to move Europe in a direction which was anathema to Mrs Thatcher. No one pointed this out to her. In the end, she supported Delors' candidature.

A similar attempt to make the system work for her rather than question its overall direction lay behind Mrs Thatcher's appointment of Lord Cockfield as the new European commissioner for the internal market and services. Here, Mrs Thatcher relied not on the advice of her ministers but on her own instincts. As a tax expert and believer in making markets operate efficiently, Cockfield had always impressed her, although, as a minister, he had been successfully marginalized by Nigel Lawson. Half-admiringly, half-teasingly, she used to say, 'Arthur can't walk past a row of pigeon-holes without wanting to fill every one of them.'[71] She thought that he would bring his formidable energies to bear to force the European Single Market to come into full existence. Charles Powell warned her that Cockfield, being a technocrat, would not make the political alliances she would find she needed, and recommended the more overtly pro-European Michael Butler for the post,[72] but she thought that Cockfield would be more 'one of us'. When she saw him on appointment, she told him that he must bring financial discipline to the EEC, and 'see the internal market completed and the proliferation of directives on industry drastically reduced'.[73]

Cockfield agreed enthusiastically, but once in harness he decided that the Single Market meant much more than Mrs Thatcher was prepared to countenance. Visiting her in May 1985, he said that, in order to create the Single Market by 1992, as planned, the Community must get rid of all fiscal barriers. 'The Treaty of Rome', he went on, 'provided for the harmonisation of indirect taxes.'[74] This provoked Mrs Thatcher into a learned dispute about the precise wording of the treaty, and then a fulmination: 'There was absolutely no question whatsoever of the UK accepting tax harmonisation. It would strike at the root of Parliament's powers . . . She was not going to be told by anyone outside the United Kingdom what rate of tax was to be charged here.'[75] But that was exactly what she *was* going to be told, including by people she had thought shared her view. Jacques Delors recalled Cockfield admiringly as 'quite inflexible, especially on difficult matters such as the harmonisation of indirect taxes'.[76] New directives poured out of the man, to Mrs Thatcher's extreme displeasure. When Cockfield came up for reappointment in 1988, she was determined not to keep him, but to replace him with Leon Brittan, a strange choice because he was quite possibly the most ardent Europhile to have served in any of her Cabinets. Even at that late stage, she was surprisingly unaware of the ideological nature of the struggle in the EEC. She would often promote people who were allies in other fields, only to be shocked by their adherence to a European creed which was almost completely at variance with her own.

When she met Delors for the first time after his appointment as president of the Commission, Mrs Thatcher emphasized to him that it was 'necessary to be practical' and to avoid vague idealism: 'For instance, these constant references to European unity, something which could never come about.'[77] Delors, who was to work unremittingly for just the sort of European unity which she opposed, did not disclose his own hand, but diplomatically observed that there were two trends in the community – one of 'practical improvements' and the other 'those who aspired to a new treaty'. Mrs Thatcher declared that the idea of a new treaty was 'absurd'. Yet Delors wanted new treaties. Before he had finished in office, he would have carried through two such, of huge importance. In such encounters, there was, no doubt, wishful thinking on both sides. The pro-Europeans wanted to think that Mrs Thatcher must really share their beliefs if only they could avoid irritating her too much; Mrs Thatcher wanted to believe that if she could only expose the Continentals to a bit of British common sense, all would be well. But, broadly speaking, Mrs Thatcher was more deceived than deceiving. Europe was not, for the most part, going her way, and it was never at any time likely that it would. This her officials and, with a very few exceptions, her ministerial colleagues did not tell her.

Instead, they tended to try to make her feel better about everything. Not long after Delors had taken up his post, Geoffrey Howe's private office passed on the following piece of indirect flattery: 'Delors is reported to have told some of his associates earlier this week that there was only one Member State which had a clear idea of where it wanted the EC to go, and was organising its efforts to that end effectively. No, he said, it was not France. It was the UK.'[78] In reference to the Single Market, his compliment to Britain was just; in reference to longer-term and deeper European aims, it was not. There was no British strategy for Europe, no sense of destiny to match – or rival – that of the Germans or the French.

As well as being deceived, Mrs Thatcher must also have been self-deceiving. For the Single Market to function, which she wanted, individual states could not be allowed to impose their own regulations on imports from the rest of the EU. Instead decisions had to be taken at a European-wide level by majority voting (and not subject to a national veto). Mrs Thatcher understood this, and consciously supported the biggest ever extension of majority voting in the Community in order to bring the Single Market about. So when she complained later, she was in effect repudiating what she herself had driven forward.

It was true, however, that, post-Fontainebleau, Mrs Thatcher's public prestige in Europe, if not her popularity among the elites, stood high. She had won a war in 1982 and a second, resounding electoral victory in 1983. She seemed to be presiding over an economic recovery at home as the result of her policies. Even her struggle with the National Union of Mineworkers, then at its height, reminded everyone of her strong will and her determination to bring about economic reform. She was the most arresting figure on the European, perhaps on the entire global stage. She had 'indisputable star quality'.[79] European leaders generally resented her success in the battle of the EEC budget but felt the need to be seen to listen to her, and all hoped that she could be persuaded to go along with Community development rather than oppose it. Some of them – some Dutch, some Danes and, now and again, Helmut Kohl – even agreed with a good deal of her free-market economic agenda. So, after Fontainebleau, serious efforts were made to keep Britain on side.

For her part, Mrs Thatcher was anxious to seem positive without ceding the national independence she prized. To all those attending the Fontainebleau Council, she had sent a copy of a short British document entitled *Europe – The Future* which set out a programme for making sure that 'internal barriers to business and trade come down'[80] so that 'the genuine common market in goods and services which is envisaged in the

Treaty of Rome' could be created. The document was deliberately focused on liberalizing markets and was modest or silent on the reform of EEC institutions which tended to obsess the builders of Europe. It should be contrasted, for example, with the 'Spinelli Treaty', approved in draft by the European Parliament in February 1984, which sought to bring about European Union, or with the work of the Dooge Committee, established at Fontainebleau, to advance the EEC's institutional development and encourage a treaty on European Union.

Britain was certainly seeking to mobilize the power of the EEC to bring about economic change, but it was not seeking to increase that power more than was necessary for that change. It therefore played a curious, though not wholly inconsistent double role – urging Europe onwards towards some reforms while working hard to prevent others. Malcolm Rifkind, then a junior Foreign Office minister who was Britain's representative on the Dooge Committee, recalled that he had to object to all calls by other member states for what he called 'Great Leaps Forward', especially in relation to European Union. He feared having to issue a minority report, but instead 'I succeeded but in a very EU way. I got agreement that for each proposal I did not like there would be an asterisk with a footnote that the UK representative did not agree.'[81] He had, under close Downing Street supervision, to stick in references to the Single Market and take out references to qualified majority voting (QMV)* and to European Monetary Union (EMU), the long-contemplated move to create a single European currency and central bank. None of this prevented the drift of the Dooge Committee from going firmly against Britain.

As this process of debate continued through 1984 and 1985, it was not always easy, even for the participants, to work out who was winning. Britain was succeeding in putting the Single Market at the top of the agenda. On the other hand, Britain was at odds with the ultimately much more powerful Franco-German axis which was determined (though Germany was more enthusiastic than France) to further the process of European integration. The situation was also complicated by the fact that, despite being fellow conservatives and allies in the Cold War and on most matters regarding spending, Helmut Kohl and Margaret Thatcher did not get on.

Having just taken up his post as British ambassador to Germany, Sir

---

* Those who favoured greater European integration wanted the EEC to get rid of unanimity requirements in most of its votes and replace them with 'qualified' majority voting. This was so called because a straight majority was not good enough: it had to be additionally qualified by the right balance of voting 'weights' accorded in proportion to population, and a sufficient spread of different member states.

Julian Bullard summed up his first impressions to Charles Powell in September 1984: 'the Anglo-German relationship at the highest level is not all that it should be.'[82] He had given Mrs Thatcher's message of greeting to the Chancellor, but 'his response was perfunctory . . . the Foreign Secretary may have been right when he remarked to me the other day that Mrs Thatcher and Herr Kohl [would probably] not be particularly close friends even if Kohl spoke English.' Couldn't John Gummer, the Chairman of the Conservative Party, who was calling on Kohl anyway, take a message from Mrs Thatcher 'saying something warm and special'[83] to the great man, Bullard suggested? Powell seconded the idea and put it up to Mrs Thatcher. She could send a speaking note for Gummer to use, 'but I think a letter would be more effective (particularly if you can bring yourself to put "Dear Helmut").'[84] Mrs Thatcher obliged by signing some words about Kohl's 'vision and statesmanship', but she felt quite incapable of supplying the personal warmth pleaded for: the letter began 'My dear Chancellor'.[85]

As well as the lack of personal rapport, there was a doubt on the British side about Germany's intentions. The 'German Question' – the existence of an artificially divided Germany – remained. Mrs Thatcher never doubted for a moment that the Berlin Wall was an abhorrent symbol of Soviet oppression, but equally she was never happy with the idea of Germany united and strong. The very fervour of West German expressions of Europeanism made her suspicious. Since she could not imagine her own great country seeking its salvation in the extinction of its sovereignty, she did not believe another great country when it protested that this was exactly what it wanted to do. Kohl's endless pleas for 'a European Germany' to avoid 'a German Europe' sounded almost like a threat in her mind. Julian Bullard sent a despatch on this subject in early October 1984, shortly after the hand-holding ceremony at Verdun. 'The statesmen of Europe', he wrote, 'will . . . one day have to address themselves to "The German Question" in a very concrete form, namely the question of what adjustments to the post-war political order in Europe might need to be considered in order to give a political shape to the common aspirations of the divided German people.'[86] Charles Powell drew it to Mrs Thatcher's attention and wrote: 'German reunification is an area where we have to say one thing and think another.'[87] Mrs Thatcher underlined these words, but saying one thing and thinking another was not her greatest skill. She tended to say what she thought, and what she thought about German reunification was already uncomfortable, and would later become unprintable. Even in 1984–5, her thoughts were rather dark. In February 1985, Powell passed to her another analysis from Bullard, with the words, 'An interesting letter . . . but it doesn't . . . answer your question: what are the implications of greater German consciousness of being German, and their growing tendency to throw their weight about in Europe?'[88] German reunification was, to use an expression not then employed, the elephant in the room. Helmut Kohl's elephantine person reminded Mrs Thatcher unpleasingly of this fact.

These difficulties, though real, were usually kept in the background. Both sides did make genuine efforts to foster a co-operative relationship. Rather surprisingly – for he usually tried harder than she did to be pleasant – it turned out to be Kohl, not Thatcher, who played a bit of a dirty trick.

With pressure for a new treaty on European Union building, it gradually became clear that the Milan European Council of June 1985 would settle the question of whether such a treaty, a significant step forward for those who favoured greater integration, would come to pass. Under Community rules, a new treaty would require an Intergovernmental Conference (IGC) of the member states to frame and agree it. Euro-integrationists loved treaties because only they could be enshrined in the domestic law of every member state and thus enforced in the courts. Since Britain did not want such a treaty, it did not want an IGC. Mrs Thatcher preferred Community agreements and conventions which were not legally binding and did not turn up as tiresome Bills in the House of Commons.

Seeking to avoid the 'isolation' which, in the diplomatic mind, is always the worst result of any negotiation, the Foreign Office advised Mrs Thatcher to get in ahead of France and Germany and develop her own ideas for Milan, sharing them with Kohl in advance. The opportunity presented itself because, as Charles Powell put it to Mrs Thatcher, 'You invited Chancellor Kohl (or to be more accurate agreed to his suggestion to be invited) to Chequers in May/June.'[89] Possibly Kohl had his own anxieties about the meeting: he conveyed through Julian Bullard his wish that the menu should 'not repeat not . . . include game or lamb (especially with mint sauce)'.[90]* Powell set out for his boss the purpose of the occasion. It was necessary to move towards 'sensible conclusions' on the future of the Community: 'On the one hand we have to convince the Euro-enthusiasts if not the Euro-fanatics that Britain is prepared to move ahead. On the other hand we don't want to succumb to the drivel about European union.'[91] The agenda should therefore consist of the completion of the internal market, 'no more powers for the European Parliament', more

---

* Mrs Thatcher had a reciprocal distaste for the national cuisine which the Chancellor offered her, much disliking the various stuffed bits of pig in which Kohl delighted. In this case, the German Chancellor's wishes were granted: they ate beef.

majority voting (subject to the Luxembourg Compromise being formalised),* and formalizing the existing arrangements for political co-operation ('PoCo'), which meant a closer approximation to a common foreign policy. Mrs Thatcher had always been in favour of PoCo, because of her belief that Europe should speak up for Western ideas with a stronger voice in the Cold War. Powell attached a draft on PoCo and explained, in a phrase which might have made Kohl, with his hostility to lamb and mint sauce, queasy, 'It does not restrict our national independence of action. In short, it is dressing up mutton to look like lamb.' 'The experts will not be convinced,' Powell went on, 'but I think you could sell it politically to Chancellor Kohl and to wider Community opinion as a British initiative, stake out a strong position, and make it impossible for others to put us in the dock as being a back marker on European union.'[92] 'Yes,' wrote Mrs Thatcher, 'it seems fairly reasonable.'

Mrs Thatcher would present her initiative to Kohl as 'witness to the Community's determination to speak and act as a single body in external affairs'.[93] A text in German was prepared for his convenience. Despite Foreign Office pressure, Mrs Thatcher was determined that the document she proposed should not aspire to the status of a treaty, but remain an informal agreement. The plan was to hand it to Kohl at their Chequers meeting. If he liked it well enough, it should also, after informing Kohl of this intention, be handed to the French.

When the two leaders met, on 18 May 1985, Kohl described his response to the British document as 'basically positive'[94] and said, in answer to Mrs Thatcher's anxieties about what might happen in Milan, that he did not want an IGC 'for its own sake'. He agreed that the British ideas should be passed to the French. Apart from a clear disagreement about increasing the powers of the European Parliament, the meeting was harmonious. 'During the flight home,' reported Bullard, 'Kohl was in excellent spirits, rhapsodising about Chequers and talking mainly about 19th century European history.'[95] It was true that, both publicly and privately, Kohl reiterated his desire that PoCo should take the form of a treaty which should also, he wrote to Mrs Thatcher, 'stipulate the goal of establishing European Union',[96] but Geoffrey Howe assured her that 'it looks as though we have persuaded Delors and the presidency [the Italians] to present matters at Milan in terms of options: either Treaty amendment or our approach.'

* The Luxembourg Compromise was the informal convention that each member state was free to veto any measure which it considered 'a very important national interest'. This, in theory at least, could override majority voting. The only time that Britain invoked the Compromise was at the Agricultural Council of 16 May 1982. The Community ignored it – hence the British demand that it be formalized.

Howe boasted that Britain had 'taken the wind out of the sails' by making its own proposals. 'This has come as something of a shock to those who had expected us to place the emphasis on what we cannot accept – rather than on what we think can and should be done.'[97]

But the shock was on the other side. Two days later, Horst Teltschik,* Powell's counterpart in Kohl's office, rang Powell to tell him, for the first time, that the French and Germans had prepared a draft treaty on European Union. Kohl would table it in Milan the following day. Powell reported his own outraged reaction: 'I said I took an extremely dim view of this message. The Prime Minister had taken the Chancellor into her confidence at a very early stage,' but now he and the French had stitched Britain up,[98] 'producing a text behind our backs . . . Speaking personally, I thought it was a black day for our cooperation.' In a way, it was even more humiliating than that. The text produced 'behind our backs' was actually little different from that originally drafted by Britain. It was simply, as Charles Powell later put it, that Kohl and Mitterrand stole what Britain had given them and 'then called it "Treaty on European Union"', creating the very thing that Britain had sought to avoid.[99] This effort had been carefully concerted. At the end of May, following his visit to Chequers, Kohl had a meeting with François Mitterrand on Lake Constance. Kohl had gathered 'not at all a good impression' from his Chequers meeting with Mrs Thatcher, he told Mitterrand. 'She is moving away from Europe.'[100] Mitterrand agreed – 'Le pb [problème] c'est le GB.' A week later, Horst Teltschik (for Kohl) and Jacques Attali (for Mitterrand) went to Rome to square the Milan summit in advance with their Italian counterpart, Renato Ruggiero. Their discussion centred on how to get round Mrs Thatcher: 'For Mr Ruggiero, it was not conceivable that the heads of state and government would give the impression of giving in to . . . the reservations of Mrs Thatcher.'[101] Teltschik and Attali proposed that their countries, with the Italian presidency, should pre-agree a plan which the Italians could then present to the summit. The plan must avoid any proposal which would require unanimity. A 'significant political advance' could thus be made 'between only those states who have decided to go forward'. Ruggiero agreed: 'Thus we will see how far the British are ready to go.' Attali 'underlined the . . . absolute secrecy obviously required to safeguard these ideas'.[102]

---

* Horst Teltschik (1940–), Chief of Staff, CDU/CSU Parliamentary Group, 1977–82; Ministerial Director, Federal Chancellery, and Head, Directorate-General for Foreign and Intra-German Relations, Development Policy, External Security, 1982–90; Deputy Chief of Staff, Federal Chancellery, 1983–90; president, Boeing Germany, 2003–6.

At the Milan Council meeting for which Mrs Thatcher had prepared so hard,* the Italian presidency in whom Geoffrey Howe had reposed confidence acted according to its secret agreement with the French and Germans: it suddenly took advantage of the rules. Although no treaty could be ratified without unanimity, the decision to call an IGC required only majority support. So the Italian Prime Minister, Bettino Craxi,† proposed an IGC and pushed it to the vote, the first ever taken in a European Council. An IGC was duly called for the end of the year, against Britain's wishes. A pained Howe wrote to Mrs Thatcher, saying that the Italians had 'worked throughout for <u>disagreement rather than agreement</u>'[103] (words which Mrs Thatcher underlined) and had been enabled to do so by Kohl's backing. Because they had given way to Mrs Thatcher on the European budget at Fontainebleau, he went on, Kohl and Mitterrand were 'determined to show themselves ready to go further than us'. Howe's view was that 'Any reasonable German government should see that it is in their interests to go for things which we can agree. One's faith that the Germans may have a clear perception of their interests . . . cannot be great after Milan.'

Was that actually so? Howe did not care to contemplate the possibility that the German (and French and Italian) trick made perfectly good sense to its perpetrators. They had a very clear perception of their own interests. They had studied revenge on Mrs Thatcher for Fontainebleau; they had got it, and now, after years of being blocked, they had found a way of going forward which she could not resist. The Foreign Office policy of reining in Mrs Thatcher so that confrontation with other member states could be avoided had failed. Indeed, it had been mocked. Britain had been, despite so many clever calculations and so much diplomacy, isolated. 'There was dismay in the Foreign Office,' recalled Stephen Wall;‡ 'we felt "We should have spotted this." '[104] Howe felt rueful about it ever afterwards: 'Margaret

* Although always affecting to be monoglot, Mrs Thatcher had clearly read, in French, the French memorandum 'Pour un Progrès de la Construction de l'Europe'. Next to the bit which advocated 'la consultation systématique des partenaires sociaux', she wrote 'No'. (French memorandum undated, Prime Minister's Papers, European Policy, European Council Meeting in Milan, 28–29 June 1985, Part 22 (document consulted in the Cabinet Office).)

† Benedetto ('Bettino') Craxi (1934–2000), head of the Italian Socialist Party, 1976–93; Prime Minister of Italy 1983–7; ended his days in judicial exile in Tunisia, under suspicion of handling bribes worth more than £100 million.

‡ Stephen Wall (1947–), educated Douai and Selwyn College, Cambridge; First Secretary, Washington, DC, 1979–83; Assistant Head, later Head, European Community Department, FCO, 1983–8; private secretary to Foreign and Commonwealth Secretary, 1988–90; to the Prime Minister, 1991–3; Ambassador to Portugal, 1993–5; Ambassador and UK Permanent Representative to EU, 1995–2000; head of European Secretariat, Cabinet Office, 2000–2004; official government historian, 2007; knighted, 2004.

worried about opening Pandora's box. I was more optimistic that we could play a trick on the Community and persuade them to develop conventions rather than have an IGC and a new treaty, but the wretched Craxi and Andreotti [at that time the Italian Foreign Minister] turned it upside down.'[105] Howe himself, however, was part of the reason for the behaviour at Milan which he disliked. According to Teltschik, 'from summit to summit . . . there was a common strategy to isolate her.' The Germans felt emboldened in this because 'We knew the Foreign Office didn't agree with her. We knew this from Genscher [Hans-Dietrich Genscher, the German Foreign Minister], who knew it from Howe.'[106]

Now Pandora's box was opened. Milan helped confirm Mrs Thatcher in her Eurosceptic instincts. She told the Cabinet that the meeting had been 'the worst chaired international meeting she had attended'.[107] In private, she said that the actions of the French and Germans had been 'the sort of behaviour that would get you thrown out of any London club'.[108] In public, she was fairly restrained, following Foreign Office advice that she should not absolutely rule out treaty change and complaining only that the vote for an IGC had delayed and complicated changes which could have been made at once without a new treaty. In an odd way, however, Bernard Ingham's press briefing brought out what she really felt. He admitted to journalists that Mrs Thatcher was 'irritated' by the result of the Council, but complained that the press always reported her in the same way: 'The media allow her but one emotion – fury. The Richter scale ceases to operate. She is not permitted to be irritated. Irritation becomes a volcanic eruption. Krakatoa has nothing on it.'[109] In the report in *The Times*, this characterization of the media was misunderstood (thereby making Ingham's own point for him), and was represented as being his account of Mrs Thatcher's actual views ('fury' and so on). The comparison with Krakatoa was included. Ingham wrote to the editor of *The Times* to say that the paper had got the whole thing back to front, which it had.* But in a deeper sense, though the paper had misunderstood Ingham's remarks, its report was accurate. Mrs Thatcher's reaction to Milan had, indeed, been little short of Krakatoan. She felt that Kohl, in particular, had shown himself in his true colours. At his post-Milan press conference, he declared that 'The hour of truth had struck. He could not accept that Europe should degenerate into an elevated free trade zone.'[110] He and Mitterrand, he trumpeted, were now the motors of change – 'the mission of the founding fathers had been to slowly dismantle

---

* Other press headlines also made Ingham's point – *Sun*: 'Maggie's rage at EC'; *Express*: 'Angry Maggie'; *Guardian*: 'Thatcher fumes over Summit setbacks' ('Press Digest', Ingham to Thatcher, 1 July 1985, CAC: THCR 3/5/47).

national sovereignty . . . At the end a European federal state could arise.'
For Mrs Thatcher, the enemy was in plain view.

Mrs Thatcher did not, however, take the chance offered by the humiliation
at Milan to alter her policy fundamentally. Nor did the Foreign Office,
despite the setback, question the underlying logic of its own position. The
biggest fear in Whitehall was still that of being 'left behind', and so the
remedies sought included better co-operation with France and Germany
(though they had just done Britain in) and a reluctance to oppose treaty
amendments unless absolutely necessary. The ultimate direction of the
European Community, and the problems this created for Britain, were not
discussed in those terms within government. Instead, the differences were
suppressed and the British government coalesced still further round the
project of the Single Market.

Government unity on the Single Market was, in fact, entirely genuine,
supported just as strongly by the Europhile Howe as by the sceptic Mrs
Thatcher. The whole issue of 'the free movement of goods, services, persons and capital' (as Article 8A of the treaty was to put it) between member
states was central to making the EEC live up to its name of being an
Economic Community. There were hundreds of small ways – the difficulty
of selling insurance in Germany, say, or the lack of mutual recognition of
professional qualifications – which impeded this general principle. The
attempts to address these, and the focus given by the target date of 1992 for
the completion of the Single Market, gave Mrs Thatcher hope that the
Community was at last concentrating on those practical areas which she
valued so highly. She also felt that it would challenge Britain to improve
its own economic performance. The openness of competition would be a
salutary 'cold shower for the British economy'.[111] The trouble was that
these gains tended to come at a cost in other areas which was not fully
debated or acknowledged by the British government itself. They also,
thanks to the operation of bureaucracy and the enthusiasm of Delors'
Commission for taking charge of the process, tended to create yet more
rules rather than just stripping away old ones.

The IGC at which the future direction of the Community would be
resolved was to be held in Luxembourg in December 1985. The British
tactic was the opposite of the one which had failed at Milan. Britain would
not show its hand, but would wait to see who proposed what. So, this
time, when Mrs Thatcher saw Kohl in advance of the summit, she had
nothing in her handbag to give to him. Just before they met on 27 November, Charles Powell advised her 'to let Kohl out of the penalty box for his
behaviour at the Milan European Council: but to play on his guilty

feelings (so far as anyone so thick-skinned has them) to induce him to pay particular attention to your points of view this time round'.[112]* She should tell him that she did not intend 'to be bounced by another Franco-German ganging up . . . You will in particular want to nail him down tight to opposing monetary amendments to the Treaty.'

At the same time as Kohl and Mrs Thatcher were meeting in London, in Brussels David Hannay, by now the UK Ambassador to the Community, was meeting Jacques Delors. Delors, he reported, was making 'emotional appeals'[113] in favour of the abolition of frontiers and the introduction of a single currency, and Hannay was replying that 'We were simply not prepared to give treaty force to a concept like EMU which no one was capable of defining or describing and which appeared to imply a fundamental shift in the relationship between the member states and the Community.' The next day, Nigel Lawson, the Chancellor of the Exchequer, wrote cheerfully to Mrs Thatcher that 'Your Summit discussions with Chancellor Kohl yesterday confirmed that the Germans, like us, are totally opposed to amendment of the monetary provisions of the Treaty of Rome.'[114] 'Totally' was not the right word. West Germany was torn on this subject at this time – on the one hand wanting to keep the Deutschmark, its proudest single creation of the post-Nazi era, on the other wanting never to compromise its devotion to European Union. Kohl had given Mrs Thatcher the impression that, so far as a new treaty went, his dedication to sound money would prevail.

Yet when the European Council actually met, and there was the expected push for EMU to appear in the new treaty, on the second day Kohl asked for a private meeting with Mrs Thatcher. Hannay, who was not permitted to attend the meeting, wrote that 'to my considerable astonishment, they emerged to say that the two had agreed to accept the symbolic reference to EMU . . . so long as it was accompanied by a binding provision requiring the negotiation of a new treaty (and thus separate national ratifications) before any progress towards implementing it could be made.'[115] In her memoirs, Mrs Thatcher says that she was 'dismayed that the Germans shifted their ground',[116] but takes credit for persuading Kohl to accept a form of words which spoke of EMU in terms of

---

* Powell went on in the same note to satirize Kohl for Mrs Thatcher's diversion: 'The first three or four hours – if you let him – will be devoted to gloating over the latest opinion polls in Germany, the state of the German economy, the fantastic sales of the latest biography of him (I am arranging to supply you with a copy. You might ask him to autograph it. He would never suspect a tease)' (Powell to Thatcher, 22 November 1985, Prime Minister's Papers, Germany, Chancellor Kohl's Visit to the UK, Part 9 (document consulted in the Cabinet Office)).

'co-operation in economic and monetary policy'. The word 'co-operation', she and her advisers believed,[117] avoided any commitment to the creation of a single currency. It was never made clear by Mrs Thatcher or by Geoffrey Howe, the only other British minister present at the meeting with Kohl, why Britain accepted Kohl's wish to gainsay what he had previously promised. It may have resulted from a desire to avoid being blamed for any possible breakdown of the Council, combined with the sense that the words chosen were sufficiently anodyne. Probably Mrs Thatcher did not want to admit the weakness of her own position, and she did want to ensure that her Single Market agenda was not acrimoniously derailed. Stephen Wall states it fairly when he writes that 'If, as she did, Mrs Thatcher subsequently felt that she had been double-crossed by Kohl, she was not double-crossed on the basis of official Foreign Office advice.'[118] Mrs Thatcher's account of her heroic role in moderating Kohl's wishes is not really borne out by the facts: it is more that Kohl's power forced her to compromise. But British officials had helped create an atmosphere in which the pressure to concede something to avoid isolation was too great to resist. Michael Butler, like most other officials, spoke with satisfaction of the process by which Mrs Thatcher's 'reason overcame her prejudices'.[119] It is not surprising that the belief gradually took root on the Continent that 'Mrs Thatcher always complains, but always comes along in the end.' This was an unflattering but correct formulation of the result, if not the intention, of British government policy.

There was a case for saying – as did those, like Hannay and Williamson, who favoured greater European integration – that the concession on EMU was a small and chiefly symbolic price to pay for the more concrete gains of the Single Market. But the trouble for Britain and Mrs Thatcher was that symbols were extremely important in the development of the Community. The reiteration and expansion in all documents, over the years, of the aim of EMU made it harder to resist and easier to throw in Mrs Thatcher's face. Sure enough, although he complained bitterly that the proposal for the 'Single European Act' agreed by the Council at Luxembourg was 'une grande déception' (which means 'disappointment', not 'deception') and 'a compromise of progress', Jacques Delors emphasized that EMU was now to be considered as 'a treaty objective'.[120] This went flatly against what Mrs Thatcher had said in her opening intervention in Luxembourg, when she accepted EMU as an 'aspiration', but added that 'for it to be a specific treaty objective is a different matter'. She had also warned that its inclusion in the treaty would have 'juridical consequences'.[121] In his note to her before the Council, Nigel Lawson had advised that 'the better course by far looks to be not to get caught up in this whole exercise.'[122] Given Mrs Thatcher's wishes in the matter, he was surely right. From now on, EMU would gather pace, and its prospect would make life extremely difficult for all remaining British governments of the twentieth century.

Bernard Ingham, advising her on what to say at her press conference at the end of the Council, reported that 'a large number of popular newspapers yesterday urged you to go to Luxembourg to sort out the Europeans and have no truck with their expensive ambitions.'[123] She would need to present very carefully, highlighting the completion of the internal market. And he warned her to watch out for:

> – the extent to which you are permitting majority voting (which the press see as a weakening of our sovereignty);
> – the animal and plant protection (the 'rabies clause') and frontier controls over drug traffickers, terrorists, etc;
> – the monetary issue which is arguably the most politically sensitive for you.[124]

At her press conference, Mrs Thatcher did more or less what she was told. She emphasized the importance of completing the internal market and justified moves to majority voting in that area. On the other hand, changes in taxation would require unanimity. She played down the text on monetary co-operation: 'it does not represent anything new at all, but describes the existing position.'[125] Britain's special animal and plant health provisions stayed.* She boasted that the gruelling twenty-seven hours of intensive conferring over two days had been made necessary by Britain's insistence on getting everything right. She glossed over the fact that the treaty, against her wishes, not only increased the standing of the European Parliament but also insisted that it be so called, rather than known, as stated in the Treaty of Rome and as she had always preferred, as the mere European Assembly.† And she emphasized that the 'reserves' (those areas

---

* It is an example of Mrs Thatcher's unusual way of doing business that when, after three hours of argument over phytosanitary controls on agricultural products, Geoffrey Howe came up with a solution and the chairman asked if anyone disagreed with it, the only person who said 'Yes, I do' was Mrs Thatcher. After embarrassing her own Foreign Secretary in front of others, she was eventually won round to his point of view. (See Stephen Wall, *A Stranger in Europe*, Oxford University Press, 2008, p. 68.)

† This matter of nomenclature was a test of Euroscepticism. The European Parliament always referred to itself as such, but, until the Single European Act, it was named in the treaties as the European Assembly. The Foreign Office always used the term 'Parliament'. Mrs Thatcher always preferred the term 'Assembly'. When the Conservative MEP Lord Bethell wrote to her to complain about this usage, she sent him a formal letter confirming his assertion that the word 'Parliament' was correct, but added a sort of snub in her own hand: 'I do not understand your antipathy to being an elected Member of a Treaty Assembly.' (Thatcher to Bethell, 8 August 1983, Prime Minister's Papers, European Policy, Confusion

where any individual member state had not yet agreed to a particular point) came from other countries as well as Britain. When one journalist incautiously remarked that all these reserves made the agreement 'rather like a Cheshire cheese, full of holes', Mrs Thatcher retorted: 'A Cheshire cheese is not full of holes – that is Gruyere! A Cheshire cheese has got no holes in it – it is British!'[126]

The one reserve which Britain had entered was in an area which would prove troublesome later. The other member states wanted qualified majority voting over matters concerned with health and safety at work (Article 21), but Mrs Thatcher was concerned that rules made in this way would impose heavy burdens on small businesses. Her colleagues and officials calmed her fears, and Britain belatedly signed up, but in fact, as some of the same officials later admitted, she was right: 'She was suspicious that it would extend into other areas. It turned out that QMV on health and safety was abused to impose social legislation which Britain did not want.'[127] 'We didn't deliberately mislead her,' recalled Stephen Wall, 'but we didn't want to see its consequences.'[128] This Trojan-horse effect would contribute greatly to Britain's sense of being imposed upon by European legislation in future years.

Returning to Britain, Mrs Thatcher encountered no serious political opposition to what she had achieved at Luxembourg. The press, with the solitary exception of the *Spectator*, was in favour. In Parliament, the Labour MP Bryan Gould made the point that Mrs Thatcher had just returned from 'a meeting which she did not want to take place, on an agenda which she did not want to discuss, and on agreements which she did not want to make'.[129] But because Mrs Thatcher put her own name to the resulting parliamentary Bill, rather than leaving it to Geoffrey Howe alone, she was able to quell all but a tiny group of opponents in her party, and turn the Bill into law. Only seventeen Conservative MPs rebelled against the Single European Act. The fact was that Margaret Thatcher, alone of all leading British politicians, was capable of carrying pro-European legislation without much difficulty in the country or her party. Being a sceptic herself, she could marginalize the sceptics: if she said it was all right, who would listen to their objections? In that sense, if in no other, Mrs Thatcher was the most effective promoter of European integration Britain has ever known.

The Single European Act (SEA), which was formally signed by the European member states in February 1986, marked the high water mark of this phenomenon. The first major revision to the 1957 Treaty of Rome, the Act established the goal of creating a single European market by the

over the terms 'European Parliament' and 'European Assembly' (document consulted in the Cabinet Office).)

end of 1992 and provided for the extension of qualified majority voting to achieve this. In rhetoric, if not in institutional reality, the EEC had now acquired a Thatcherite tinge. David Young, at that time the Secretary of State for Employment, and, from June 1987, for Trade and Industry, became evangelical about turning the Single Market into a practical reality, getting rid of all the 'non-tariff' barriers which hindered EEC free trade. He spoke, oddly but arrestingly, about how he wanted to be able to travel to Paris and there screw in a light bulb which he had brought from London for the purpose. There were undoubted British successes which resulted from the SEA – the freeing up, for example, of the European airline market – but it gave much greater power to Jacques Delors and his team than it did to Mrs Thatcher and hers. They were working full time on advancing their European control, whereas she had to fight on countless other fronts as well. Delors was able to devote a great deal of energy to using the extended QMV to get round whatever restrictions the SEA might appear to place on his ambitions for the Commission. The supposed costing of every future regulation before it was introduced – a measure agreed at Luxembourg – was evaded. 'Did anything happen?' Robin Renwick asked himself a quarter of a century later. 'Not at all! There was never any effective deregulation.'[130] Young's own eventual assessment was that the SEA was not a success for Britain. Its effects, in trade terms, were 'at best neutral . . . Movement of labour is far more open than it used to be . . . but I doubt that France has changed at all.'[131] And its political effects were dire.

As for Mrs Thatcher's own attitude, Young felt that she had a 'love-hate relationship' with the SEA. She loved 'the commercial aspect of Europe', but she hated 'the political aspects . . . The only aspect of the EC which Margaret was comfortable with was trade.'[132] Although this assessment is essentially correct, it should be added that the 'hate' bit of the relationship mostly came later. At the time, as David Williamson recalled, she 'positively wanted the Act', and although she was worried about the political and constitutional aspects, 'she felt that she was sufficiently protected.'[133] In his view, the years of Fontainebleau and the SEA were 'the golden years' in which Mrs Thatcher really did achieve what she intended, redirecting much of the Community's energies on to her agenda. Having worked closely with her throughout the relevant negotiations, he never countenanced the idea, later put about, that Mrs Thatcher did not understand the implications of the Act: 'I totally disagree that she was misled.'[134] He remembered her walking down the stairs in No. 10 early one morning at the time of ratification and saying, 'I've read every single word of this treaty, and I am happy with it.' Charles Powell, though approaching the matter with a less Europhile view than Williamson, also believed that Mrs

Thatcher was genuinely, consciously in favour of the SEA: 'In relation to the EEC, she had different periods – like Picasso in his painting. The first period was the budget row; the second was that of the SEA; the third – the violent stage – came on with the rising power of Delors and the issue of EMU.'[135] During the SEA stage, 'She was *not* a profound sceptic.' Her mistake, he considered, was not that she went for the Single Market, but that she failed to realize how hostile most Continental politicians secretly were to it because of their protectionist instincts, and how they would therefore try to frustrate its intentions.[136]

In her memoirs, Mrs Thatcher wrote that she had been 'wrong' to think, as she told the House of Commons at the time, that 'European and political union . . . mean a good deal less than some people over here think they mean':[137] she had underestimated the potency of the words and the political direction in which they pointed. She maintained nevertheless that 'I still believe it was right to sign the Single European Act, because we wanted a Single European Market.'[138] Those words were published in 1993. By that time, Mrs Thatcher was so upset with the pace of European integration that she had already moved further than her own words had suggested. In private conversations from that period onwards, including more than one with the present author, she said that she had been wrong to sign the SEA because it had pushed on towards the European Union which she feared. She remained circumspect, however, about saying such things in public, perhaps aware that if she were to trash her own achievements she would give licence to others to do the same. She certainly never gave credence to the idea that she had been fooled by her officials. It was true that most of them – notably, at this time, Butler, Williamson and Hannay – were strongly in favour of European integration and she, of course, was not. But neither side tried systematically, at this stage at least, to fool the other. It would be nearer the truth to say that each strove to push potential problems to one side and maximize areas of agreement. Williamson recalled: 'It was not in the British interest, I told her, to express general views,'[139] presumably because her general views, he knew, would spread alarm and despondency on the Continent. Throughout the years of tumultuous European negotiations which began in 1979 and culminated in the Single European Act of 1986, Mrs Thatcher never made time to develop systematically her own vision of Europe. She therefore stuck, in principle at least, to the inherited pro-European doctrines which the Conservatives had made their own under Heath and which had helped them against a Labour Party divided on the issue. It was only later that she worked out – and publicly declared – what she thought. The result would cause delight and dismay in roughly equal measure.

13

The death-knell of monetarism

*'She's a moral coward when it comes
to dealing with people'*

At the same time as Mrs Thatcher was negotiating the Single European Act, her Chancellor of the Exchequer was changing the basis of British economic policy. Issues which at first appeared technical gradually disclosed themselves as fundamental, altering Mrs Thatcher's relationship with Nigel Lawson and her ultimate political fate.

Despite the economic recovery, which had begun in the wake of the 1981 Budget and continued ever since, Nigel Lawson was not happy: 'Inflation seemed particularly difficult because monetary aggregates were all over the shop.'[1] Of all Mrs Thatcher's senior ministers, Lawson was the most technically accomplished advocate of 'monetarism'. It was he who had first articulated the Medium-Term Financial Strategy (MTFS), and by 1984 he could point to its success. Inflation, which had stood at more than 20 per cent in 1980, was now steady at around 5 per cent; markets had faith in the government's sense of direction; economic growth was recovering and was expected to reach 3 per cent over the course of the year.[2] Yet the explosion of economic activity which came from liberalization made it hard for policy-makers to read the dials they had chosen to study. How did the abolition of exchange controls and the expansion of credit affect the money supply? How much did necessary financial innovation make the monetary aggregates impossible to interpret? How much were these phenomena one-off or permanent changes in the landscape? In November 1984, to take one example, there was a surge in personal borrowing caused by the huge oversubscription of the British Telecom privatization. This was a vote of public confidence in Thatcherite plans to spread the ownership of wealth. But it also produced a large increase in sterling M3 (£M3), the chosen measure of money supply. This, in turn, weakened the value of sterling. The monetarist doctrine was that the government should control the quantity of money, not its traded price. So it should, to use the favoured term, 'let the exchange rate go where it will'. Lawson began to think otherwise.

His character was a complex mixture. On the one hand, he was restless, risk-taking, brilliant. On the other, he was preoccupied with the importance of rules – hence the MTFS and his famous dictum 'Rules rule, OK?' Temperamentally, perhaps, he was like an alchemist, seeking a scientific formula which would produce gold out of the dross of ordinary life. Mrs Thatcher greatly admired Lawson: 'She thought he was very clever and rather gutsy.'[3] She relied heavily on his intellectually self-confident advocacy of economic reform against the massed ranks of academic and media experts. She believed in his ability and his ideological soundness. But, as someone who saw economics much more in terms of moral wisdom than prestidigitation, she felt she inhabited a different mental universe from that of Lawson. 'Brian, he's a gambler,'[4] she complained to Brian Griffiths, who became head of her Policy Unit in September 1985, just before the Prime Minister and her Chancellor had their first major clash. As the years passed, she gradually came to believe that Lawson was gambling with the success of her entire economic and political project.

Equally gradually, though starting earlier, Lawson had come to the view that Britain would be better off inside the Exchange Rate Mechanism (ERM) of the European Monetary System (EMS). Unlike most ERM supporters, he was firmly opposed to the eventual aim of European economic and monetary union. He saw the ERM not as part of a grand political project for an entire continent, but as a possible guiding star for the management of sterling and hence the control of inflation. The ERM, which linked the values of member EEC currencies within slightly variable bands, had come into being early in 1979. It was declaredly designed as a forerunner of a single European currency, but was rarely discussed in British politics in those terms. Britain, while reserving the right to enter later, had refused to join (see Volume I, Chapter 18). By his own account,[5] Lawson had believed since 1981 that ERM membership was a good idea, but had waited till 'the right opportunity'.[6]* He meant not only the favourable economic conditions, but the right moment to persuade the person who, he correctly believed, would be least persuadable – Mrs Thatcher. In reality, however, the first move was not really an act of persuasion, more an accident.

In January 1985, there was a run on the pound. On Friday 11 January,

---

* One of Lawson's motives, in 1981, for favouring ERM membership was political. He thought that if he could link financial discipline with the European project this would outflank Wet critics of Mrs Thatcher's economic policy, who felt bound to support almost anything which they considered pro-European. (Interview with David Willetts.)

it fell to $1.12, less than half where it had been in 1981. Over the ensuing weekend, an atmosphere of panic set in after Bernard Ingham, for once incorrectly interpreting his boss's wishes, briefed the Sunday papers that the government did not propose to do anything about the falling pound. Whatever Mrs Thatcher might say in theory about leaving the market alone, she would have found pound–dollar parity politically intolerable. She also tended to see a weak pound as an affront to British pride and self-confidence. So worried was she that it was she, rather than Lawson, who proposed dramatic action. Rachel Lomax, serving her very first week-end as Lawson's private secretary, recalled listening in, in the approved official manner, to a telephone conversation between Lawson and Mrs Thatcher: 'She was berating him for not joining the ERM. It was such an odd conversation. It was not quite true that he seized the moment to persuade her. He was not yet stuck on the exchange rate: it was she that was pushing for change.'[7] Lawson nonetheless took the opportunity. Invoking the existing policy that Britain should join the ERM 'when the time was right' (or, sometimes, 'ripe'), he proposed to her that the government should look at the subject again. Mrs Thatcher duly called a meeting of senior ministers and officials for 13 February. By the time they met, Lawson had raised interest rates from the previous 9 per cent to 14 per cent.

In the meantime, on 15 January, Mrs Thatcher sent a secret message to President Reagan appealing for his help to bolster sterling. 'I have done as much as can be asked to tighten policy,' she insisted. 'But we are faced with continued dollar strength.' Noting that Lawson would be travelling to Washington shortly for a meeting of the finance ministers of the world's five leading industrialized nations (the G5), she asked whether the US would consider joining a 'collective attempt to restore reality to the markets'.[8] Throughout Reagan's first term in office, his Treasury Secretary, Don Regan,* had resisted intervention, insisting that only the market could determine exchange rates. British pleas, therefore, fell on somewhat stony ground. Talking points, drafted for Regan's meeting with Lawson, prepared the Treasury Secretary to dismiss the notion of a 'dollar problem', stressing that blame lay with the British economy. 'In sum', Regan was advised to tell Lawson, 'causes of weak sterling under your control, not mine.'[9]

But this was not the whole story. President Reagan's response to Mrs Thatcher was far more constructive: he reassured her that the US stood by its pledge at the 1983 Williamsburg summit to consider 'coordinated

* Donald ('Don') Regan (1918–2003), chairman and CEO, Merrill Lynch, 1971–80; US Secretary of the Treasury, 1981–5; White House Chief of Staff, 1985–7.

intervention where it was agreed such intervention would be helpful'.[10] When the G5 finance ministers met on 17 January, Don Regan remained, in Nigel Lawson's view, 'tiresomely condescending',[11] but he did agree to consider measures to address the strength of the dollar. The G5 subsequently took the unprecedented step of issuing a communiqué pledging co-ordinated intervention 'as necessary'. This sent a clear signal to the markets and, in time, helped alleviate the pressure on sterling. It was against this backdrop of growing willingness to intervene in currency markets that Mrs Thatcher's ministers and officials gathered to discuss the ERM.

Those present on 13 February included Mrs Thatcher, Lawson, Geoffrey Howe, Robin Leigh-Pemberton, the Governor of the Bank of England, Eddie George,* the Bank's expert on markets, and Peter Middleton and Terry Burns from the Treasury. This would be the main cast of characters in all subsequent discussions of the subject. There was one other important player – the inveterate opponent of the ERM, Alan Walters – but he was not present at any of the meetings. He was working in the United States at the time, and had no formal role in Downing Street but a constant line in to Mrs Thatcher. He was the ghost at every feast.

The official record shows no falling out.[12] Lawson put his case that the government 'should not close the door'[13] on the ERM, but was also clear that Britain should not enter at such a turbulent moment. Geoffrey Howe spoke in very similar terms. Mrs Thatcher summed up in a way which, Lawson later wrote, irritated him[14] by emphasizing the common view that this was not the right moment to join, rather than recognizing the important change of opinion among colleagues, which was of growing support for entry soon. It was agreed that the government should improve its foreign exchange reserves, to make its money market interventions more effective. But a contemporaneous note, in rather abbreviated style, kept by Burns, shows how clearly the two camps divided. Burns himself ('EMS . . . is a rigid system')[15] and George ('EMS will aggravate speculative flows') expressed scepticism. So did Mrs Thatcher. She did not blame the vagaries of the market, but the infirm purpose of her own government: the 'exchange rate clearly signalled what we ought to have known earlier. That policies were lax.'[16] She doubted Lawson's case: 'Superficially membership attractive but when looked into in detail it looks less attractive,' and she even protested against the existing policy itself: 'wonder if we

---

* Edward ('Eddie') George (1938–2009), educated Dulwich College and Emmanuel College, Cambridge; Deputy Governor of the Bank of England, 1990–93; Governor, 1993–2003; knighted, 2000; created Lord George, 2004.

should drop that line that we will go in when the time is ripe'.[17] The key point, however, not expressed in either record, was that now, for the first time, Mrs Thatcher was confronted by agreement in favour of ERM entry (though not yet) from the three most important people concerned – the Chancellor, the Foreign Secretary and the Governor.

This was part of the rather unhappy context for Nigel Lawson's 1985 Budget. 'High interest rates and the weakness of sterling have upset Budget plans,' John Redwood wrote to Mrs Thatcher.[18] He feared backsliding: 'A PSBR which is not credible means tearing up the rhetoric and ambitions of many years.' Mrs Thatcher underlined this heavily. 'We would stress', Redwood concluded, 'that the events of the last 4 weeks should not allow the Budget to become timorous or unimaginative. It has never been more vital for Chancellor and the Government that the Budget should be clear, purposeful, addressed to jobs, and pledged to lower interest rates and lower taxes.' On the same day, Andrew Turnbull informed her that the PSBR forecast was not good, and so 'On the reform of personal taxation he [Lawson] is stymied this year as he does not have enough revenue to give away to ease the transition to any new system.'[19]

On the night of Sunday 3 February, seeking to take advantage of Mrs Thatcher's habitual good mood after a weekend away at Chequers,[20] Lawson discussed his Budget plans with the Prime Minister. He told her that the PSBR for 1984–5, at an expected £10.75 billion, would represent an overrun of £3.5 billion, of which £2.5 billion could be attributed to the coal strike. The medium-term fiscal position was deteriorating: it 'could be a particularly difficult year'.[21] The two agreed that the PSBR for 1985–6 had to come down to £7 billion, but disagreed on the way to achieve this. Lawson's preferred package included extending VAT to newspapers. Mrs Thatcher had vetoed this the previous year on the straightforwardly presentational grounds that this would guarantee a rotten press for the entire Budget. This year, she was armed with a note from Bernard Ingham which warned: 'I understand the Chancellor's desire to broaden the VAT base. But I am bound to repeat: to impose it on newspapers will set against the Government a powerful and generally supportive medium.'[22]

Lawson also sought to confine mortgage interest tax relief to the basic rate of tax, introduce a tax on consumer credit (including mortgages) and tax pension lump sums.[23] These ideas did not find favour. Mrs Thatcher disagreed particularly strongly with any reduction of mortgage interest relief. She regarded this as one of the best ways of helping young people get on the housing ladder, however much economists urged her that it merely led to higher house prices. Shortly before the 1983 election she had pressed for the ceiling to be raised from £25,000 to £35,000 but, facing resistance from Geoffrey Howe, had grudgingly agreed to a £5,000 rise.[24] She wanted the ceiling for relief raised again. Prime Minister and Chancellor compromised by leaving the rate where it was.

Before the pre-Budget discussion in Cabinet the following week, Lawson circulated a paper on the economic strategy which Mrs Thatcher, scribbling on it, described as 'very thin – and a little on the complacent side'.[25] On 13 February, he had a still gloomier meeting with Mrs Thatcher, at which he told her that overspending in 1985–6 and in later years was now looking 'increasingly evident'.[26] John Redwood was almost beside himself at the figures that were emerging: 'Taxes up, public spending up, interest rates up, unemployment up, even Income Tax and National Insurance up (as a percentage of earnings). That is the story since 1979 told in these dismal documents.'[27] Mrs Thatcher thrice underlined '1979', as if in pain at what her governments were failing to achieve. 'You never give in,' Redwood urged her. 'Don't let others give in for the government at such a vital juncture.'

At the Cabinet meeting itself, the consensus was in favour of caution: 'There was a widespread feeling that this was not the year in which to embark on radical changes in the tax structure which would attract the hostility of powerful interest groups [ministers particularly had the pensions industry in mind] or increase the general price level.'[28] Fairly bloody discussions about cuts inevitably ensued ('Mr Fowler [the Social Services Secretary] has returned wounded to his tent').[29] The feeling of new opportunity which had suffused Lawson's Budget the previous year had faded.

The Budget which Lawson presented to the House of Commons on 19 March was considered rather drab. VAT was extended only to newspaper advertising and, to fend off anxiety, the Chancellor felt he had to promise no further extensions in the Parliament. Lawson described the tax-free treatment of pension lump sums as 'anomalous but much-loved', and left it alone.[30] He did, however, alter the income tax burden to favour the low-paid by increasing the personal allowance by double the rate of inflation, and he hit the better off by removing the ceiling on employers' National Insurance contributions. He also committed large sums in this 'Budget for jobs' to the Youth Training Scheme and the Community Programme.

His reviews were mostly tepid. His Budget attracted criticism not only from Wets like Ted Heath and Jim Prior, but also from Thatcherites. Lawson's old friend and former ministerial colleague Jock Bruce-Gardyne wrote in the *Spectator* that the Budget had been forced on him by his own backbenchers and was a 'lobbyists' victory'.[31] Bruce-Gardyne lamented that 'This was actually the last ideal year for radicalism' before the next general election. The paper's editor, however, did note that the Budget was consistent with Lawson's own doctrine about what in 1979 he called 'the Thatcher experiment' but had quietly renamed in 1984 'the British experiment'. Lawson had given classic expression to this in his Mais Lecture of June 1984. The theory of the experiment was that the normal rules of 'macro' and 'micro' would be reversed. Inflation would be controlled not by 'micro' prices and incomes policies, but by 'macro' measures on the money supply. Unemployment, on the other hand, would not be brought down by the orthodox 'macro' measures, but by 'micro' efforts to remove barriers to job creation:

> this is a micro-Budget, part of Thatcherism's answer to the grand certainties of the 1944 White Paper on Employment. It is the forerunner of a series of measures which will emerge from the Departments of Education, Trade and Industry, Employment, and Health and Social Security in the next two or three months.[32]

This Budget, though cautious, was not, despite Redwood's alarm, a U-turn. There was no panic in the markets. But the situation was inglorious. The government had not lost direction, but it was losing pace.

The mood was dour. Lawson felt it himself. After his 1984 Budget, Mrs Thatcher had arranged to gatecrash his post-Budget party. She had been 'ecstatic'[33] (see Chapter 7). After the 1985 Budget, Lawson gave a small party with a sense of 'anticlimax', and went to bed very early. He was woken at 11 o'clock by the doorbell of the No. 11 flat:

> I got out of bed, shoved on a pair of trousers (I always sleep naked), and went downstairs to open it. There was Margaret, with a sheepish Ian Gow* behind her. He had not tipped me off: it appears the decision had been taken on the spur of the moment. Margaret was very chic in a black, frilly dress, and had obviously come on from somewhere to look in, as she thought, on our post-Budget party. She was naturally somewhat taken aback to find me barefoot and naked from the waist up . . . After a very brief and somewhat stilted chat in the doorway about the immediate reaction to the Budget, she returned to Number 10.[34]

It was not until the end of the summer that Lawson returned to the ERM charge. He was now clearer in his own mind. The pound, the reserves and

---

* It seems more likely that it was not Ian Gow who escorted Mrs Thatcher to either occasion, but Michael Alison, who had replaced Gow after the 1983 general election as her parliamentary private secretary, or possibly a civil servant from her private office.

interest rates were in better shape. He had beaten down official resistance to his ideas; and he had taken part in an important change of international approach. On 22 September, in a special meeting of the G5, Lawson had signed the Plaza Agreement (so called after the Plaza Hotel in New York City in which it was negotiated), promoted by Reagan's new Treasury Secretary, James Baker.* Building on the G5 communiqué that January, it was designed to lower the value of the US dollar and move away from the previously prevailing doctrine of 'free-floating' exchange rates by accepting that serious imbalances required co-ordinated intervention. As Baker recalled it, the UK and the US were 'on the exact same wavelength' at the Plaza. 'Nigel was particularly enthusiastic.'[35] Knowing Mrs Thatcher's much greater respect for American decisions than for EEC ones, Lawson believed that the Plaza Agreement would soften her up: 'she remarked to me that the agreement created a favourable prelude to ERM membership.'[36] She consented to a meeting on 30 September.

The Treasury paper in advance of the meeting expressed itself in terms more of presentational advantages than of any fundamental change of course. 'We thought that people could understand a link to the Deutschmark more readily than all those Ms,' Lawson recalled,[37] referring to the various measures – M0, M2, M3 – of money. But the paper ended by drawing itself up to its full official height and making a major statement of intent: 'It is the considered view of the Chancellor and the Governor that we should become full members of the EMS, joining the ERM at the earliest practicable opportunity.'[38] Before the February meeting, Mrs Thatcher's close advisers – including Alan Walters – had warned her against joining the ERM. This time, their objections of principle were sharpened by the sense that Lawson was lining up the whole establishment against the Prime Minister, and perhaps that she herself had not been sufficiently clear on the subject. 'The Treasury, Bank and City are uniting behind a new fashion,' John Redwood wrote to Mrs Thatcher, just as he stepped down as head of the Policy Unit. He advocated a 'more pragmatic approach' which 'keeps our destinies in our own hands and not in those of the Germans; and still leaves us free to try and track the DM exchange rate if we wish to do so'.[39] Mrs Thatcher underlined the word 'fashion' three times.

David Norgrove, her new Treasury private secretary, firmly drew her attention to the high stakes:

---

* James A. Baker III (1930–), White House Chief of Staff, 1981–5; US Secretary of the Treasury, 1985–8; Secretary of State, 1989–92; White House Chief of Staff and senior counsellor, 1992–3.

joining the ERM could turn out to be the most important economic decision of this Parliament and quite possibly of your Administration . . . Your
discussions with the Chancellor have moved this question to the point where
it may look to the Treasury that it is a foregone conclusion that we shall
join.[40]

David Willetts of the Policy Unit linked the economic and political
aspects of the problem:

If God had intended us to join the Exchange Rate Mechanism, we would
be as productive and as moderate in our wage demands as the Germans . . .
Will the average home-owner happily accept a rise in his mortgage rate once
he knows its purpose is to maintain the £'s value against the German
Mark?[41]

Always preoccupied with housing aspirations, Mrs Thatcher doubly
underlined the word 'home-owner'.

The 30 September meeting, billed as a 'seminar', was much fiercer than
its February predecessor. Mrs Thatcher was by now fired up against joining. 'Need to prove the case for change'[42] are her challenging words which
begin Terry Burns's record. As each grandee – first the Chancellor, then
the Governor and then the Foreign Secretary – said his emollient and
stately piece in favour of entry, she would jump in with objections:

Frightened about what proposing. Scared to death – don't think can do
it . . . Not impressed by need to reinforce strategy . . . Up go interest rates
months before election . . . Divide own side . . . Forfeit capacity to do our
own thing . . . Don't like hitching to fixed exchange rate like 1960s and
70s . . . [people would] say 'u-turn' . . . Have to devalue . . . Build up credibility without selling soul to EMS . . . cannot fix exchange rate . . . gift to
speculator . . .

At no point in the discussion did she concede anything to the Lawson
thesis. When Burns suggested that her criticisms amounted to 'arguments
for not joining ever', she baldly answered 'Yes.'[43] To this, Geoffrey Howe
replied, in what amounted to a four-word summary of all his European
attitudes, 'Can't be independent indefinitely.' 'Why limit manoeuvre?
Argument of weakness,' said Mrs Thatcher, exemplifying all hers.

At the end, Brian Griffiths, newly arrived as the head of the Policy Unit,
was the only person present to support Mrs Thatcher's view. He suggested
that, rather than joining the ERM, the government could have an informal
exchange rate target, unannounced. Lawson objected that such a target
would soon be discovered. As Terry Burns abbreviated it, Mrs Thatcher

said, 'Know who to blame if went wrong',[44] which was her unnerving way of giving implied permission, but not support. With these tart, even menacing words, she closed the meeting. The official record was more decorous: 'Bringing the discussion to a close, the Prime Minister said she was not convinced that the balance of the arguments had shifted in favour of joining.'[45]

Only too aware of her isolation, Mrs Thatcher called for yet another meeting, a full ministerial discussion in which she might be able to bring in a few allies. This was arranged for 13 November. In the meantime, Lawson made part of the argument public. In his annual Mansion House speech, he announced that he was dropping the £M3 target and mocked the debate about 'the intricacies of the different measures of money'.[46] Though not announced as such, this was the death-knell of monetarism in British government policy. 'At the end of the day,' he concluded, 'the position is clear and unambiguous. The inflation rate is judge and jury.' It was a rash thing to say without offering some mechanism, such as an independent central bank, to oversee inflation-rate targeting: the 'judge and jury' would try Lawson in front of its kangaroo court in the years to come.

For her part, Mrs Thatcher fired off a series of questions about ERM entry to be sent to the Treasury in advance of the meeting. Lawson referred to them disdainfully as 'a rag-bag'.[47] This was not an unfair description. The record discloses what No. 10 called 'a draft exam paper for the Treasury and Bank'.[48] On it, Mrs Thatcher added some questions in her own hand, omitting, as was her habit, any question marks – 'What turbulence would you expect if we were to join' and 'What rate against the DM. No use to say whatever is the market rate on the day – that begs the question'. When the Treasury sent its reply two days later, Mrs Thatcher peppered it with exclamation marks and cries of 'No', 'u-turn' and 'encourage specln'.[49]

Lawson's own paper took its stand on the paradoxical argument that because the government had maintained the same policy for so long, there was 'a growing problem of presentation'.[50] He was trying to reassure Mrs Thatcher by saying that the government had done the right thing, while at the same time trying to convince her that it ought to be doing something else: 'there is a need for a shot in the arm – a touch of imagination and freshness.' Then he gave her an ultimatum. Not only the Governor, but also senior officials in the Treasury and the Bank (a reference to Burns, Middleton and George) had come round to his view,* and so, he implied,

---

* This was true. Lord Burns slightly regretfully recalled that 'Peter and I had persuaded ourselves that it was doable' (Interview with Lord Burns).

she was without allies. The decision not to join now, he said, would be 'a historic missed opportunity which we would before very long come bitterly to regret'.[51]

Before the meeting, David Norgrove warned Mrs Thatcher that Lawson had 'seen separately all the Ministers who are coming to this subject for the first time',[52] and had encouraged them to defer to the judgment of Chancellor and Governor. He had 'blinded them with science', leading them to think only of economic considerations, 'narrowly defined', and ignore the political disadvantages which she saw, 'particularly in the weeks before an election'. The prospect of a Labour government might subject the pound to intolerable exchange rate pressure within the ERM. Mrs Thatcher's supporters had not made any equivalent push to win ministerial opinion. In particular, Willie Whitelaw, usually the man called on by Mrs Thatcher to sort out disputes, had not been squared. John Wakeham, the Chief Whip, was also asked to the meeting, to lend support to Mrs Thatcher, but 'There were no briefings for Willie or me'[53] about what was at stake. Not for the first time, Mrs Thatcher was strangely innocent of Cabinet-level politics in her preparation for the meeting. By ill chance, her main advisers and officials – Nigel Wicks and David Norgrove in her private office, and Brian Griffiths in her Policy Unit – were all new to their jobs. None yet had the relevant experience to fight the Whitehall battle in the right way. Despite her astonishing personal dominance, hardly anyone was working the system to get her what she wanted.

The meeting of 13 November contained almost all the important ministers in the government – Mrs Thatcher, Lawson, Howe, Whitelaw, plus John Biffen, Leon Brittan, Norman Tebbit as party chairman and John Wakeham as chief whip. According to Nigel Wicks, who was in attendance, 'They all arrived in a gaggle, having come from No. 11. It was a very silly thing to have done.'[54] In substance, the argument did not add much to the debate of 30 September. Its significance was political and personal. Of those politicians present, only Biffen, a long-standing 'free floater' and Eurosceptic, opposed ERM entry. No one listened seriously to him because, as Leader of the House, he had little standing in the matter. Despite his Thatcherite reputation, Norman Tebbit supported Lawson. He recalled many years later that he had been swayed by his anger at Mrs Thatcher's attempt to follow the counsel of an adviser rather than the minister responsible (him) over British Leyland (see Chapter 15). He felt that Mrs Thatcher should either take the advice of the minister responsible in this case (Lawson) or move him.[55]

Lawson addressed Mrs Thatcher's political objection about pressure on the pound within the ERM in the run-up to a general election, and suggested a way out. The government would temporarily suspend membership until after an election victory. Mrs Thatcher argued 'strongly against' this curious notion,[56] saying that such a move would 'be taken as an indication of its [the government's] lack of faith in its own policies'. 'Don't want to be behind bars,' she said, according to Terry Burns's personal record. She was not speaking of prison: she meant she did not want to be locked into a policy. She repeated a phrase which she had used years before when objecting at first to the MTFS – the government would be 'in a graph paper position'.[57] She hated the idea of being trapped. 'She batted everything off in her best style.'[58]

After most of the argument had been heard, Willie Whitelaw spoke: 'We have said we will join when the time is right. Now we are told it is right. If CX [the Chancellor] and Governor say time is right then that is OK for my money.'[59] Mrs Thatcher responded, in words differently reported by different witnesses, that she could not accept this, no matter who was against her. Burns's version of what she said was: 'I'm not going in on run-up to election and put interest rates into someone else's hands.' Leigh-Pemberton remembered her saying: 'I'm afraid we're not going to do this. I'm sorry.'[60] Whatever her exact words, the bald truth of the situation was exposed: almost everyone wanted to join the ERM, but nothing would persuade the Prime Minister to do so. 'It was clear', recalled Norgrove, 'that she would resign rather than join.'[61] In this impasse, the only thing to do was to agree not to talk about what had happened and, as the official record expressed Mrs Thatcher's summing up, 'to maintain rigidly the line which had been taken so far that the UK would join when the time was right'.[62]

This outcome was a disaster because, oddly enough, it flummoxed all those taking part. Even Whitelaw had not played his customary role of smoothing Mrs Thatcher's path. According to Terry Burns, the expectation had been that Mrs Thatcher would agree to look at ERM entry further, but 'she brought the trap door down sharply'.[63] Neither side had prepared the ground with the other. 'I became aware of more personal animosity than I had realized,' John Wakeham recalled.[64] As a result, it was 'a bitter, nasty, unpleasant meeting'.[65] Foolishly, 'The bunch of conspirators went next door to No. 11 afterwards and asked "What do we do now? How do we bell the cat?" I stayed outside while the politicians talked,' recalled Burns.[66] From the officials' point of view, the disagreement was much worse than if the matter had not been discussed at all. 'It was the end of the consensus since 1976,' recalled Peter Middleton, 'a setback on the road to respectability.'[67] For Nigel Lawson, it was 'the saddest event of my time as Chancellor'.[68]

His choice of words reflected the importance of the issue, but also the effect that the meeting had on his relations with Mrs Thatcher. They never fully recovered. 'How do I stand as Chancellor when I've had a big meeting like that, won the argument, but lost the battle?' he asked himself. 'I did think of resignation.'[69] For his part, recalled David Norgrove, Nigel Wicks 'was determined that there shouldn't be another meeting like that, and therefore policy was never really discussed again between the two. As for Mrs Thatcher, she never wanted to discuss it with Nigel Lawson again if she could avoid it. He tried to raise it now and again with her in bilaterals, but she would quickly cut across him to stop the discussion.'[70] In this strange vacuum, Lawson decided to pursue his own policy.

Mrs Thatcher herself subsequently attributed less importance to the meeting than it deserved, and than she had felt at the time. This may have resulted partly from her general desire to conceal moments of humiliation. There was no doubt, in the minds of those closely involved, that the showdown upset her, although she was buoyed up by the adrenalin of arguing so fiercely. She invited Whitelaw and Wakeham up for coffee afterwards and complained to Whitelaw: 'I do think you and John might have waded in to help me a bit more.'[71] Whitelaw and Wakeham protested that no one had briefed them in advance on what would be needed: 'We would have supported her if we'd known she was in difficulties.'[72] Her own officials were acutely conscious that things had gone wrong. 'Nigel Wicks felt it had fundamentally undermined his relationship with her.'[73] In her memoirs, Mrs Thatcher treats it as only one in a series of encounters in which she had to fight against collective error. She sees it as a battle over an important particular issue, but does not recognize how it was bound to affect her general capacity to lead her own government. She does not mention, for instance, Whitelaw's role in the meeting at all. Nor does she see the significance of her own remark that the arguments which had by this time persuaded her against ERM entry 'applied to the principle – not just the circumstances'.[74] The policy was to enter 'when the time is right'. If she now rejected the principle, she was effectively opposed to her own government's policy – the time could never be right. History later showed that, as Terry Burns put it, 'she was fundamentally correct about this issue all the way through',[75] but being right is not necessarily the same as governing well. The Thatcher–Lawson clash made it increasingly difficult to run the British economy, and the British government, properly.

The fateful ERM meeting came towards the end of a year when politics, for reasons partly related to disappointing economic performance, had persistently gone badly for the government and especially for Mrs Thatcher personally. Although her defeat of Arthur Scargill was arguably the most important single achievement of her entire career as prime minister, it brought her no immediate political benefit. Indeed, public opinion seemed to feel that the great argument for Mrs Thatcher – dire necessity in a crisis – no longer applied. Tired of conflict, voters cast about for something softer. Many thought they might find it in the SDP and their Liberal allies who, in the local elections in early May, gained 302 seats; Labour lost a few and the Tories many. Opinion polls gave strong backing to the SDP leader, David Owen. Even Labour, under Neil Kinnock, and with the miners' strike out of the way, was starting to look less fractious and less extreme. People spoke of Kinnock's 'decency', contrasting it favourably with Mrs Thatcher's harshness.

As the external threats to the Conservatives looked more formidable, so internal discontent with Mrs Thatcher naturally grew. The terminology of Wets and Dries now sounded obsolete. People talked instead of 'consolidators' and 'radicals'; but the faultlines were the same. Peter Walker, for example, now politically strong because of his success during the miners' strike, delivered the Iain Macleod Memorial Lecture on polling day in the local elections. He spoke in favour of full employment. It was well understood – with total unemployment, at 3,272,565 in April,[76] still higher than the previous year – that he was criticizing Mrs Thatcher. A little later in May, Francis Pym and other senior Tories displaced by Thatcherism, such as Ian Gilmour and Geoffrey Rippon, launched a grouping called Centre Forward to promote their ideas. This was mocked for its outdated feel* and its disorganization, but it was a symptom of something. The tactic of Centre Forward and of many other critics was to bank Mrs Thatcher's achievements, praise her courage and determination, but then to look for a more 'compassionate' style and a change of tone. There was less outrage against her than in the first term, but more of a sense of being bored. If she was no longer necessary, they implied, she was unnecessary.

Perhaps more worrying for Mrs Thatcher was the lack of stirring support from the new generation of Conservative MPs. She had passed her tenth anniversary as party leader in February 1985, so the number of those backbenchers who had been with her from the first now constituted quite a small minority. With the passage of time and the departure of Ian Gow from her side,† the pool of reliable supporters was not well replenished.

---

* The centre forward in football was a position already supplanted by the more modern concept of the 'striker'.

† Though an invaluable adviser and confidant while at No. 10, Gow had disappointed Mrs

This also tended to mean that able Thatcherites were not recognized and given office because, without Gow, they did not have many friends at court. This was a source of growing resentment. Mrs Thatcher found it hard to strike the right balance. She was aware of the dangers of promoting only her supporters: 'If you just put your own people in . . . you have all the opposition on the back benches.'[77] Reminded in retirement how she had given advancement at this time to Richard Needham,* an inveterate opponent, she said, 'Did he go in [to government]? Some of them, you see, you put in to shut up.'[78] She was actually less good at accommodating her friends than her foes. Oddly, for one who valued ideological affinity highly, she was not skilful at identifying and promoting those who showed it.†

At the beginning of the Parliament, in 1983, those on the back benches who shared Mrs Thatcher's ideological zeal had begun to organize. Lord (Ralph) Harris of the Institute of Economic Affairs (IEA) had already set up a Repeal Group in the House of Lords to try to get rid of anti-market legislation. Like-minded men in the Commons followed his lead. These included Michael Forsyth,‡ Michael Fallon,§ Francis Maude,¶ Neil

---

Thatcher as minister for housing. 'This man wanted more money for local authority housing,' Mrs Thatcher later recalled. 'This man had been my right hand as a right-winger. IAN! IAN! IAN! MAD!' (Thatcher Memoirs Materials, CAC: THCR 4/3).

* Richard Needham (6th Earl of Kilmorey) (1942–), educated Eton; Conservative MP for Chippenham, 1979–83; for Wiltshire North, 1983–97; Parliamentary Under-Secretary, NIO, 1985–92; Minister of State, DTI, 1992–5; knighted, 1997.

† One of the best examples of this came with the promotion of John Major, who entered government for the first time in the 1985 reshuffle. For quite some time she considered Major a true believer, but events would later prove her wrong. 'We thought he had a better brain than he had' was how she (unfairly) put it later. (Thatcher Memoirs Materials, CAC: THCR 4/3.)

‡ Michael Forsyth (1954–), educated Arbroath High School and St Andrews University; Conservative MP for Stirling, 1983–97; Chairman, Scottish Conservative Party, 1989–90; Minister of State, Scottish Office, 1990–92; Department of Employment, 1992–4; Home Office, 1994–5; Secretary of State for Scotland, 1995–7; knighted, 1997; created Lord Forsyth of Drumlean, 1999.

§ Michael Fallon (1952–), educated St Andrews University; Conservative MP for Darlington, 1983–92; for Sevenoaks, 1997–; assistant government whip, 1988–90; Parliamentary Under-Secretary, Department of Education and Science, 1990–92; Minister of State, Department for Business, Innovation and Skills, 2012–14; Department of Energy and Climate Change, 2013–14; Secretary of State for Defence, 2014–.

¶ Francis Maude (1953–), educated Abingdon School and Corpus Christi College, Cambridge; Conservative MP for Warwickshire North, 1983–92; for Horsham, 1997–2015; Minister of State, FCO, 1989–90; Financial Secretary to the Treasury, 1990–92; Chairman, Conservative Party, 2005–7; Minister for the Cabinet Office and Paymaster-General, 2010–15; Minister of State for Trade and Investment, 2015–; created Lord Maude of Horsham, 2015.

Hamilton,* Peter Lilley and Richard Ryder.† They were a sort of counter to the Blue Chip group (see Volume I, pp. 646–7), including Chris Patten and William Waldegrave, which had been a thorn in Mrs Thatcher's side in the previous Parliament. They wanted to keep up the pressure for Thatcherite market reform and were, according to Gerald Howarth,‡ their convenor, 'very much designed to help her'.[79] After inconclusive discussions about what to call themselves, they noticed that there were twelve of them, and so privately took the title of The Disciples. Disciples of whom, they debated? They eventually agreed that members could choose to be the disciples of 'Hayek, Friedman, Adam Smith or any other compatible life-force', rather than explicitly of Mrs Thatcher herself.[80] They campaigned for contracting out, privatization, the freeing of rent controls, parental choice in schools and so on. On 18 June 1985, they met Mrs Thatcher in her room in Parliament to explain what they were up to. They were not a party within a party, they told her, but people who had come together to promote the market economy and did not accept that the Thatcher government was running out of steam: 'The goodwill is with reform, not with consolidation.'[81]

Later in the year, in November, The Disciples (not using that name publicly) brought out a pamphlet entitled *No Turning Back*, which called for 'a revolution of choice, a revolution of opportunity'. This literally made their name: from then on they became known as the No Turning Back Group. Mrs Thatcher treated them in a friendly manner, but nevertheless 'failed to secure the supply line'[82] with her supporters. At a later dinner with the group at the IEA's offices, Mrs Thatcher turned to Eric Forth,§ the group's leading eccentric, and said, 'Eric, you've been untypically silent. What do you have to say?' 'Well, Prime Minister,' said Forth, 'since

---

* Neil Hamilton (1949–), educated Amman Valley Grammar School, University College of Wales, Aberystwyth and Corpus Christi College, Cambridge; Conservative MP for Tatton, 1983–97. In 1997, while still an MP, Hamilton became involved in a political scandal known as the 'cash for questions' affair in which he was alleged to have accepted bribes for tabling parliamentary questions on behalf of the Egyptian owner of Harrods department store, Mohamed Al-Fayed.

† Richard Ryder (1949–), educated Radley and Magdalene College, Cambridge; Conservative MP for Mid Norfolk, 1983–97; Government Chief Whip, 1990–95; vice-chairman, BBC, 2002–4; created Lord Ryder of Wensum, 1997.

‡ Gerald Howarth (1947–), educated Bloxham School and Southampton University; Conservative MP for Cannock and Burntwood, 1983–92; for Aldershot, 1997–; PPS to Margaret Thatcher, 1991–2; Parliamentary Under-Secretary, MOD, 2010–12; knighted, 2012.

§ Eric Forth (1944–2006), educated Jordanhill College School, Glasgow and Glasgow University; Conservative MP for Mid Worcestershire, 1983–97; for Bromley and Chislehurst, 1997–2006; Conservative MEP for North Birmingham, 1979–84; Minister of State, Department for Education, 1994–7.

you ask, when are you going to appoint some decent people to your government?'[83] She seemed a little surprised by this thought. At the end of the dinner, a perplexed Michael Alison, never at ease with political nuance, went round politely asking the guests who these decent people might be.

From May, then, Mrs Thatcher's unideological counsellors began to plan her administration's recovery. Stephen Sherbourne urged her that it was not too early to think of the election manifesto. He reminded her that it had been drafted last time by Geoffrey Howe. Who did she want to do it this time?[84] The fact that there was no obvious answer implied a problem. So did the unspoken thought that putting Howe in charge of the task which he had performed well in 1983 now seemed unimaginable. Plans for a Cabinet reshuffle had also begun, with Willie Whitelaw and John Wakeham pushing for changes in July. They had supper with Mrs Thatcher for what they called the 'second reading' of reshuffle ideas. They were looking for reliability and better presentational skills, not radicalism – George Younger and Kenneth Baker moving up, Patrick Jenkin, Peter Rees and Tom King moving out. 'My impression', wrote Robin Butler, who noted the meeting for her, 'is that the Lord President [Whitelaw] has reservations about a "Night of the Long Knives".'[85]* At this stage, there was no plan to shift any of the most senior ministers. The most controversial thought was the return of Cecil Parkinson to his old job at the DTI. Tebbit, its incumbent, would then displace Gummer as party chairman to fight the presentational battle and prepare for the next election, whenever it might come. Mrs Thatcher went along with the drift of her lieutenants' preliminary thinking. She disagreed with them about the timing, however. It was one of her pet theories that it was kinder to reshuffle colleagues in September rather than July, 'bearing in mind that they would leave my office without a ministerial salary, without a car and without the prestige'.[86] Then they would earn the money for longer, and have less of a media frenzy surrounding them than when Parliament was sitting.

As Mrs Thatcher and colleagues continued to mull over possible changes, a controversial issue arose. Her normally efficient political radar failed to pick up the threatening signals. Lord Plowden, the chairman of the Top Salaries Review Body (TSRB), reported. Looking across the whole range of public pay at the highest levels, he recommended extremely large

---

* A reference not to Hitler's purge of the SA in 1934, but to Harold Macmillan's sacking of a third of his Cabinet in 1962, which had been satirically named after the original Nazi event. Macmillan's act had been intended to revive his government, but in fact caused ill feeling which hastened its disintegration.

increases including, for the top two dozen civil servants, rises of between 32 and 46 per cent. He told Mrs Thatcher that by 'pulling out the concertina' of permanent secretaries' salaries (that is, paying more to some than to others), he would 'improve motivation by giving those lower down something to aim at'.[87] Believing that Plowden's recommendations righted historic anomalies and that his 'range pay' concept 'would make an important contribution to better motivation and management of the Higher Civil Service',[88] Mrs Thatcher seemed to dismiss Nigel Lawson's obvious objection that the rises were simply much too large for the public to swallow. It was not in the interests of the senior civil servants advising her, all of whom would do well out of Plowden, to warn her of any political dangers; but they betrayed a certain unease by arranging that the government's favourable response to the TSRB report be put to Parliament only in the obscure form of a Written Answer to a Member's question.

Sure enough, when the report was published and the Written Answer sneaked out on 18 July, there was political outcry both at its content and at its surreptitious presentation. The following day, the *Sun* put the story on its front page with the headline '£25,000 rises for top people'. The story claimed that there would be 'massive pay rises' for 'judges, civil servants and military top brass', and named Sir Robert Armstrong as one of the main beneficiaries.[89] As Nicholas Owen in Mrs Thatcher's Policy Unit rather bravely put it to her, 'The proposals seem outrageous to the many people who look to the Government for a one-nation, even-handed approach to the higher and lower paid. How, they ask, can the Government give the Permanent Secretary of Education a pay rise considerably greater than the salaries of most of the teachers he is in dispute with?'[90] The choice of the Education Permanent Secretary was a pointed one, not only because there was an intermittent teachers' strike in progress, but also because, as Owen well knew, Mrs Thatcher was frustrated at that department's inability, under Keith Joseph, to secure the improvement of standards she wanted. Owen banged his point home: 'The Government cannot go into an Election having denied most of its employees any share of the increased prosperity on which the Government stakes its popularity.'[91]

Despite the huge fuss, Mrs Thatcher did not really back down. When alarmed officials wanted her to indicate to Lord Plowden that the government was not endorsing his 'range pay' notion as much as he thought, Mrs Thatcher refused, writing, 'the range pay proposal is <u>crucial</u> and I endorse it <u>warmly</u>.'[92] 'There was no doubt in my mind', she wrote in her memoirs, 'that we could not retain the right people in vitally important posts . . . unless their salaries bore at least some comparison with their counterparts in the private sector.'[93] This showed that she was not, in practice, as hostile to civil servants as she generally gave the impression of being. But it was surprising that she did not see the inconsistency of applying principles of comparability to the pay of top people employed by the government when she had so profitably (though belatedly) abandoned those principles across the public service by stopping the work of the Clegg comparability commission in 1980 (see Volume I, p. 458). As Nigel Lawson put it, arguing for the abolition of the TSRB, 'Whatever the advantages claimed for having the TSRB or something like it, experience shows that we do not get them. Its existence does not take the pay of these so-called "top people" out of politics; on the contrary it makes the issue even more "political".'[94] All she would concede, in public retrospect, was that the presentation of the salary announcements had been inept.[95] Privately, she suggested to the relevant ministerial committee that Lord Plowden 'might be sent on a sabbatical'.[96]

The pay row had come on top of a by-election which had made matters worse. On 4 July, the Conservatives fell to third in the previously safe Tory seat of Brecon and Radnor. The Alliance candidate (a Liberal) won and the Conservative share of the vote dropped by 20 per cent. 'At one point,' recalled Stephen Sherbourne, 'I thought we might become the third party in the national polls.* I even thought this could happen at the general election, if the Alliance secured second place in the opinion polls and then got a bandwagon rolling. We were coasting a bit.'[97] Conservative MPs had what Mrs Thatcher described as 'a bad case of the wobbles':[98] there was 'an unmistakeable whiff of panic'. Before rising at the end of July, the Commons rebuked the Prime Minister by cutting the government's huge majority to seventeen over the TSRB proposals. In the Lords, on a motion on the same subject without legal force, the government was actually defeated. For Mrs Thatcher this marked an unhappy end to an unhappy episode. 'I found the outcry was most upsetting and totally unjustified,' she remarked. 'And now the House of Lords has joined in.'[99]

Mrs Thatcher was duly inundated with end-of-term advice from her worried colleagues and officials. Bernard Ingham offered her his thoughts 'at the end of a rather difficult political year'.[100] People still said, he reported, that the government was 'arrogant' and 'insensitive' and 'We have manifestly not disposed of those charges.' He complained that the government's obsessive fear of leaks meant that it could not organize its case in advance of going public. He cited the TSRB affair, in which he had learnt the news

* Indeed, one or two polls did briefly show this.

only half an hour before he had to present the report to the press lobby. 'My 18 years in the Government service have taught me not to take criticism of presentation too seriously, but I think we must now do so.' This would require Ingham himself being 'privy to the sensitive issues before decisions are taken,' he said. Then he could prepare a presentational plan. He strongly advised her against making anyone in the Commons responsible for presentation. His stated reason was that the person entrusted with the task had 'to face questioning on the floor of the House', but the unspoken one was that Ingham did not want any centre of presentational power outside Downing Street. He applied his argument to the coming reshuffle: 'For real impact . . . personalities count. The media will be watching to see how you dispose of your presentational resources. Your actions cannot be ruled by presentation; but they must, in my judgment, be seen to recognise its importance.'

Although what Ingham wrote was self-serving, it was also true. In some ways an excellent public presenter herself, Mrs Thatcher was nevertheless more interested, when deciding what to do, in the issues themselves. She often held them too close and gave little thought in advance to how to introduce them to the world. If she were to take up Ingham's recommendations, this would obviously bring her press secretary much nearer to the heart of government, thus earning him the jealousy and suspicion of Cabinet members. It would also ensure, however, that the actions of government could be rendered more coherent in the minds of the public and of Conservative backbenchers who often felt bewildered and kept in the dark. In essence, though not in every detail, she accepted Ingham's suggestions. She thus gave him greater power which was bound to be controversial, and made him, in effect and for the first time, a forerunner of the modern 'spin-doctor'* rather than just a press officer.

John Redwood, before leaving the Policy Unit, also tried to sum up the difficult politics of that summer and turn them into a way of planning to win the next election. In a long memo, he threw at Mrs Thatcher the various unkind phrases widely used about the government – 'Uncaring Britain', 'class-ridden Britain', 'Tatty Britain' (with developers 'raping the countryside'), and the feeling of 'Time for a change'.[101] He sketched out a possible, even likely state which would ensure victory at the next general election – low inflation, unemployment falling for at least six months before the poll, seven years of continuous growth, transformed industrial relations, 'every earner an owner', strong defence. Redwood sought to link, rather than contrast, economic reform with concern for the social

---

* The term was not then current in Britain.

fabric. The charge that she did not care about public services like health and education should be countered by her commitment to patient and parent power. Jobs should be tackled squarely: 'You should not ignore unemployment policies. You do need further measures, and they are needed this autumn ... A generous Family credit accompanied by a cut in income tax rates, is probably the best run in to the Election, spending the asset sales money. This really is the last chance.'[102]

Because she believed that her government was fundamentally on the right track, Mrs Thatcher was more disposed to follow Ingham's advice, and reshuffle with presentation in mind, than to review policy. Having spared her colleagues from July executions, she spent much of August pondering her September reshuffle. This was a process which she protested that she hated. She was speaking the truth. Politically ruthless though she was, she had a vivid sense of how shattering it could be for ministers to lose office. She understood but resented the fact that good people sometimes had to be moved just to let new blood through the system. She also realized that she would be creating enemies.* Reshuffling was 'the worst and rottenest job a prime minister ever has to do', she thought.[103] When she returned from holiday in Austria, where she and Denis had been staying with the British Honorary Consul, the Austrian timber merchant Martin Kaindl, at Imlau, near Salzburg, she settled down to making some decisions.

One change she had hoped for was immediately frustrated. On the day after her return, she took the starring role in a plot organized by the Arts Minister, Lord Gowrie, and by Jacob Rothschild. Gowrie had ascertained that Paul Getty, the oil heir, was disposed to give a large sum of money to the National Gallery (of which Rothschild was the chairman), but hoped he would get a knighthood in return. Gowrie explained this to Mrs Thatcher and persuaded her to visit Getty to indicate to him, without stating as much, that the 'gong' would indeed be his. This she was happy to do. She loved raising private money for the arts, partly to show that it could work better than public money, partly because of her desire to maintain the prestige of Britain's greatest cultural institutions.

The reclusive Getty had been what Gowrie described as 'an A-grade smack addict'[104] and was still living full-time in the London Clinic recovering from his addiction and drinking 'eighteen cans of lager a day'. 'What

---

* Mrs Thatcher was only too aware that those who lost office could become bitter and 'treacherous': 'It all goes back to the fact that one sacked them' (Thatcher Memoirs Materials, CAC: THCR 4/3).

am I going to say to her?' asked Getty nervously. 'Don't worry,' replied Gowrie. 'She'll take over your case.' So it proved. Getty received Mrs Thatcher in his dressing-gown. She was flattering and briskly helpful: 'Oh, Mr Getty, we must get you out of here.' He happily received the implied promise of the knighthood, and soon afterwards gave the National Gallery £50 million. 'It sort of cured Paul,' Gowrie recalled. 'He remade his marriage and became a pillar of society.'

As Gowrie left with Mrs Thatcher, he asked to see her later that day at No. 10. After more than six years on a peer's ministerial wages, he 'felt very broke'* and wanted to accept an offer from Sotheby's to become its chairman. He told Mrs Thatcher that he would like to leave the government at the next reshuffle. 'But I really want to offer you Education,' she revealed.[105] She had finally plucked up the courage to contemplate retiring her beloved but increasingly ineffective Keith Joseph. Gowrie refused, telling Mrs Thatcher that people would not accept someone from the Lords running one of the main social departments of government. But it was rarely a bar in Mrs Thatcher's mind that a minister was a peer, since this meant that he would be one of the 'eunuchs in the seraglio'[106] and could be no rival to her. 'I think peers as Ministers should be able to answer for their policies at the bar of the House of Commons,'† she said, revealing a shaky understanding of the constitution.[107] She was greatly enamoured of Gowrie, whom she considered 'very lucid with an excellent mind'.[108] She thought that, with his 'great personality', he would 'electrify' Education. But it was not to be. She came to regard Gowrie's refusal of the job and departure from the government as 'the greatest loss'.[109] Poor Keith Joseph, unknowing of his near-dismissal, soldiered on.

Mrs Thatcher's other appointments came about in a less eccentric manner, though not easily. The changes she was about to make, John Wakeham warned her, were 'some of the most difficult you will ever have to do'.[110] With a Chief Whip's caution, his note of recommendations named no names, but only the proposed jobs reshuffled, so that Parkinson was referred to as 'the Secretary of State for Trade and Industry' and the

---

* Gowrie caused media mockery by saying that could not afford to live in London on the £33,000 salary paid to peers in the Cabinet. Ministers in the House of Commons received more than peers because of an extra consideration for being an MP.
† The bar of the House of Commons is not a drinking den (though these exist too), but a white line on the floor of the House beyond which only MPs may tread. Under certain rare circumstances, people guilty of an offence against the dignity or authority of Parliament can be called to the bar of the House as a form of admonishment. Peers cannot appear there, any more than MPs can appear in the House of Lords.

millionaire novelist Jeffrey Archer,* who, though neither an MP nor a peer, was gathering momentum, as the proposed 'Minister for Sport'. Wakeham was warning against both. Parkinson's return would look like 'going backwards'; Archer did not seem 'right'. In the case of Archer, a peerage would have been required, and this would have been controversial because of his chequered business career, which had forced him to leave the Commons when Parliament was dissolved ahead of the October 1974 election. Stephen Sherbourne also warned against Parkinson because he was 'unpopular with many women in the Party' and 'the real fear is that there would be further revelations from Sarah [sic] Keays and this time they would rebound on you and not just him.'[111]† Sherbourne's overall case was that the government's policy direction was good and the presentation wasn't. With that in mind, he recommended that Norman Tebbit replace Gummer as party chairman, that Jeffrey Archer come in as deputy chairman (a post for which membership of neither House was required), and that communicators – Kenneth Baker, John Moore, Kenneth Clarke – be chosen for key posts. Mrs Thatcher gave red ticks to all these names, except for Clarke's.‡ Worried by Nigel Lawson's lack of communicative gifts, Sherbourne described the Chancellor as 'clearly unmoveable' but 'he does need some confidant who can advise him regularly on PR'.

Other advice tended to concentrate on presentational questions and be more alive to risk than to opportunity. David Wolfson, himself Jewish, told her that she should get rid of Keith Joseph, though he was 'certainly the nicest person I have met in politics', because he was unsuccessful and there were 'already enough Jewish Members of the Cabinet'.[112] He also counselled that Parkinson's return was too risky and that the elderly Lord Hailsham should be removed from the Lord Chancellorship because his presence was 'a clear sign of weakness'. She should promote those who 'are seen to care about unemployment'. People like the Thatcherite Nicholas Ridley were not good for election victory, he thought. So worried was Wolfson about the narrowness of Mrs Thatcher's political

---

* Jeffrey Archer (1940–), educated Wellington School and Brasenose College, Oxford; best-selling author; Conservative MP for Louth, December 1969–October 1974; Deputy Chairman of the Conservative Party, 1985–6; political career ended with his conviction and subsequent imprisonment (2001–3) for perjury and perverting the course of justice; created Lord Archer of Weston-super-Mare, 1992, by John Major.

† There were. Miss Keays's book *A Question of Judgement* was published to coincide with the Tory conference and attacked Parkinson once again.

‡ Nonetheless, she commented on a contemporary note that Clarke had 'outstanding ability' and 'deserves promotion' ('Action for Sunday', Thatcher's handwritten notes on reshuffle, undated, CAC: THCR 1/14/14).

base and appeal that he actually recommended that 'Prospective Cabinet Members should have one particular qualification. They must not be "one of us"!'

Norman Tebbit also submitted his thoughts. By this time, he knew that he was Gummer's likely successor as chairman. His relationship with Mrs Thatcher was a complicated one. He was close to her ideologically, and famous for his bruising political rhetoric. He revelled in the satirical television programme *Spitting Image*'s depiction of him as her loyal skinhead.[113]* He was also grateful for her personal kindness after the Brighton bomb. Because his wife Margaret had been lying paralysed by her Brighton injuries in Stoke Mandeville hospital near Chequers, Mrs Thatcher had invited him to stay in her country house for several weeks, so that he could easily visit 'his Margaret'. Indeed, his private office was set up in the hospital so that he could continue with his DTI work, a move partly intended to show to the world that the IRA had not beaten him. Tebbit himself still needed medical attention, which he received at the hospital. He had lost a chunk of one side of his stomach and needed frequent skin grafts. He was in 'constant, managed pain'.[114] According to Andrew Lansley,† Tebbit's private secretary at the time, Mrs Thatcher was 'utterly charming and supportive' to Tebbit, 'beyond what convention demanded'.[115] She asked friends to rally round, and got the Duke of Westminster,‡ London's biggest residential property owner, to offer the Tebbits the special accommodation which they now needed. In Tebbit's own view, his presence near Mrs Thatcher provoked in her:

> not a guilty conscience, but a feeling that somehow she was responsible. She had been the target but others had paid the price. Every time I walked into the room, she remembered how narrowly she'd escaped death. Because she *was* a good woman, there was an element of feeling bad about this.[116]

Thus did her very sympathy for her injured minister make her feel that his presence was almost unwelcome.

At the same time as Mrs Thatcher felt sympathy and guilt, she also felt anger. The rumour spread that Tebbit was organizing his own leadership plans from his hospital bed,[117] and she seems to have believed this.

---

* Mrs Thatcher's depiction on *Spitting Image* is discussed in greater detail in Chapter 19.
† Andrew Lansley (1956–), educated Exeter University; private secretary to Secretary of State for Trade and Industry, 1984–5; Conservative MP for South Cambridgeshire, 1997–2015; Secretary of State for Health, 2010–12; Lord Privy Seal and Leader of the House of Commons, 2012–14; granted a peerage in the Dissolution Honours List, 2015.
‡ Gerald Grosvenor, 6th Duke of Westminster (1951–), educated Harrow; succeeded father, 1979; chairman of trustees, Grosvenor Estate since 1974.

According to Tebbit's special adviser, Michael Dobbs,* she was mis-informed. Tebbit had 'completely ruled himself out of any leadership bid since the bomb'.[118] Not long after he became chairman, indeed, he confided in Dobbs that he would give up all ministerial office at the next election in order to look after his wife. Mrs Thatcher, of course, did not know this. In her memoirs, she wrote of making Tebbit chairman, 'I thought he might one day succeed me if we won the election,' adding: 'better than an inspiration: he was an example.'[119] But in reality there was some sus-picion. 'He wanted the chairmanship', she recalled privately, 'as a springboard to take over from me.'[120] She also came to doubt his admin-istrative skills.

There was perhaps some truth in Mrs Thatcher's perception of his ambition, despite Dobbs's account. Senior politicians are rarely absolutely unequivocal in their refusal to contemplate becoming prime minister. In fact, though, Tebbit had not really wanted the chairmanship. He had enjoyed the DTI and would have preferred to remain a departmental min-ister, but he also found the strain of the work too great. When he returned to his office in January 1985, 'I thought I was more recovered than I really was. It was not only the shock, but I was physically quite weak. I concealed the extent of my own injuries.'[121] The chairmanship, having no depart-mental duties, was a much less heavy burden, as well as being obviously suited to Tebbit's gifts of political attack and communicative clarity. In Andrew Lansley's view, the effect of the Brighton bomb on Tebbit was extremely painful psychologically. He realized two incompatible things at the same time – that he had the ability and possibly the party backing to become leader, but that his own health, and even more that of his wife, made it impossible. This 'added a bitter edge. He had a sense of lost ambi-tion afterwards, without having fully had that ambition before.'[122] None of this made for the sort of harmonious relationship between Chairman and Prime Minister which had been such a feature of the Parkinson period. Besides, 'Norman and Margaret Thatcher were never friends. He didn't have the charm with women that Cecil had.'[123] From the very start, Dobbs came to believe, Mrs Thatcher was uneasy about Tebbit in the chairman-ship, and therefore inclined to permit 'a parallel operation' to intervene in party matters without consulting him.

In his note to Mrs Thatcher about the reshuffle, Tebbit assumed no

---

* Michael Dobbs (1948–), educated Christ Church, Oxford and Fletcher School of Law and Diplomacy, Tufts University; government special adviser, 1981–6; chief of staff, Conservative Party, 1986–7; deputy chairman, Saatchi & Saatchi, 1983–6, 1988–91; Joint Deputy Chair-man, Conservative Party, 1994–5; author of *House of Cards* and other political novels; created Lord Dobbs, 2010.

change in the very top jobs, and said he took it 'for granted' that Mrs
Thatcher would not feel she could sack Michael Heseltine or Peter Walker.
He was unequivocal, however, in his view of the former. 'Defence is in a
mess and we cannot afford things to get worse,' he wrote, continuing with
characteristic acerbity, '. . . Michael is not really thinking things through
and although I would like to see him carry the can for the errors he has
made you may feel that he should be moved.'[124] If so, Tebbit proposed his
great rival be given Energy* and Walker be sent to Health and Social
Security. Parkinson ('If he doesn't come back now, he never will') should
go to Defence.

On re-reading this note from Tebbit while composing her memoirs, Mrs
Thatcher was moved to comment on the character of Michael Heseltine.
She thought him lazy. 'At Defence he didn't take work home . . . He did
actually give quite a lot of luncheon parties at his large house. It is usually
a sign.'[125] She had in her mind a long list of minor incidents in which
Heseltine had not endeared himself to her – how, when she was at Education, he had ordered her officials, without asking her, to come and brief
him on which were the best schools for him to send his own children to;
how, at the fortieth anniversary of D-Day in 1984, he had failed to ensure,
until she intervened, that war widows could be flown out for the ceremony;
how, at Defence, he had, despite being a famed manager, failed to get a
grip of procurement. She also remembered a story told her by her PPS in
the late 1970s, John Stanley,† which she apologized for relating because
it involved repeating 'a word I hate . . . a four-letter word'. Heseltine had
told Stanley that the secret of his own advancement was that 'I have only
got on in life by being an absolute shit.'[126] All this, of course, was said by
her after Heseltine had brought about her fall. As Mrs Thatcher contemplated the reshuffle at the time, however, none of these thoughts stirred
her to action. Perhaps she preferred Tebbit's hint that if Heseltine stayed
at Defence he would have to 'carry the can' for that department's failings.
She dared neither promote nor demote him. He stayed in post.

Her most striking decision, not foreshadowed in the written communications she had received, was driven by her desire for better presentation.
At the beginning of September, she invited Leon Brittan to Chequers, in

* Tebbit would almost certainly have known that Heseltine had refused Energy when offered
it in 1979, holding out for Environment (see Volume I, p. 429), so he may well have calculated
that he would have rejected such a demotion if offered it and left the government.
† John Stanley (1942–), educated Repton and Lincoln College, Oxford; Conservative MP
for Tonbridge and Malling, February 1974–2015; Minister for Housing and Construction,
1979–83; Minister of State for the Armed Forces, 1983–7; NIO, 1987–8; knighted, 1988.

order, he supposed, to get his reshuffle advice. Instead, she sacked him from the Home Office, offering him the Department of Trade and Industry instead. Her reasoning was that the three men holding the great offices of state were all bad public communicators. Brittan 'had a first-class brain but he just couldn't get his point over at all'.[127] To Bernard Ingham, she was blunt: 'I've got Geoffrey at the Foreign Office, Nigel at the Treasury and Leon at the Home Office. Between them, they can't sell anything.'[128] She still considered Lawson vital to her government, and had no proper excuse for moving Howe, so Leon Brittan was the weakest link.*

Despite his undoubted ability, and his importance in the miners' strike, Brittan had never won a parliamentary following. He was seen as too much the lawyer, and was the victim of some behind-the-hand backbench anti-Semitism. He also suffered from rumours that, though married, he was homosexual, and even that he had been a child abuser (too often in those days the two were conflated in the minds of many). No one produced actual evidence for either accusation. Michael Jopling who, in his role as chief whip through the whole of Mrs Thatcher's first Parliament, was the recipient of most unsavoury stories and rumours about colleagues, recalled, 'I never heard a whisper about Leon at the time: and I knew him very well because he was the MP in the Yorkshire seat where I lived.'[129] Those involved in the reshuffle – Wakeham and Ingham – denied that the rumours affected Mrs Thatcher's decision.[130] But they did reinforce prejudices against Brittan and therefore weakened him politically. 'He always seemed quaint as a coot to me,' recalled Ingham, though admitting he had no evidence about anything.[131] Mrs Thatcher seems not to have had any personal suspicions of Brittan, or anxiety about his sexuality, but she did pick up his lack of standing among backbench colleagues.

She knew some of the background to the rumours. On 21 June of the previous year, 1984, a story had appeared in *The Times* denying rumours of a scandal involving a Cabinet minister. Robert Armstrong reported to her what had happened next. On the evening of the day the *Times* story appeared, Richard Ryder, who, as a former journalist, had good links with the press, had met Jonathan Holborow, the associate editor of the *Mail on Sunday*. Holborow, Ryder told Armstrong, had informed him that the paper was 'on to a very good thing' (as Holborow put it) about Leon Brittan's private life.[132] Neither Armstrong's report nor any of the press

* In retirement, Mrs Thatcher blamed herself for giving 'too much importance' to the job of chief secretary to the Treasury and therefore over-promoting men who had occupied that post well. Brittan was one such in her mind; John Major was another. (Thatcher Memoirs Materials, CAC: THCR 4/3.)

coverage at the time said what the stories were, but they seem to have involved accusations of child sex abuse, including an alleged relationship with a boy in his early teens said to live in Brittan's constituency.[133] Its source was a reliable one, Holborow said, but 'their investigations had run into the sand, and they really had no usable evidence.' The paper did have one remaining allegation, however, which was 'that the Security Services were putting it about that Michael Bettaney [the MI5 officer who had been caught trying to spy for the Russians in 1984] had said in the course of his interrogation that Moscow had information about Mr Leon Brittan's life that laid him open to blackmail'. Acting on this, Armstrong told Mrs Thatcher, he had checked the story with MI5 who assured him that Bettaney had said no such thing. Besides, 'The story was inherently improbable: Bettaney had been unable to establish contact with Russian intelligence service in London.'*

Armstrong explained that he had passed all this on to John Wakeham. Richard Ryder's opinion was that the *Mail on Sunday* was looking for a way of using the MI5 angle to carry a Brittan story: he thought the paper might turn it into a piece about how the Security Services were not accountable to ministers.[134] Armstrong said he had then talked to Bernard Ingham and agreed 'if any signs of allegations of this kind manifested themselves over the weekend, he should make it categorically clear that they were absolutely without foundation.' In fact, no Sunday papers went with the story, but *Private Eye* took refuge in announcing the untruth of the rumour in order to be able to repeat it, to suggest bad behaviour by disgruntled MI5 sources, and to name Leon Brittan.[135] Bernard Ingham then briefed about 'assassination by gossip' and the *Guardian* ran a story with the headline 'Brittan named in sex scandal rumours'.[136] Brittan issued a denial via the Press Association. A Labour MP, Harry Cohen, wrote to Mrs Thatcher demanding that she investigate the accusations against renegade MI5 officers.[137] She replied to Cohen, refusing his request on the grounds that, as 'the rumours to which you refer are totally unfounded, I see no need for any further statement'.[138] She did not answer Cohen's follow-up invitation to correspond further on the matter.

In short, Mrs Thatcher knew that stories were circulating about Brittan, did not believe them, and knew for a fact that at least some aspects of them were untrue. She would have been conscious that the circulation of such stories about a Home Secretary was particularly troublesome because

---

* Bettaney's pathetic failure to get to first base as a traitor and persuade the KGB to accept his proffered secrets is described in Christopher Andrew's authorized history of the Security Service (Andrew, *The Defence of the Realm*, pp. 714–22).

the Home Office was the department in charge of MI5, but she did not see this as a good cause to get rid of her Home Secretary.*

While the rumours were not the cause of Brittan's move, they did make him more moveable. Mrs Thatcher had quite other criticisms of Brittan of her own. She had not considered him adroit in the battle with the BBC over a documentary in a series called *Real Lives* in which the Corporation had outraged her by offering airtime to the IRA chief of staff, Martin McGuinness. She was also concerned, naturally, that her ministers should be good on television. Since she hardly ever watched television herself, her views on this subject tended to be formed by those who wished to influence her choice.[139] In this case, they were right. Brittan was a poor television performer, seeming supercilious. In Brittan's own view, which was also not wrong, he was the 'fall guy' for the government's unpopularity, set up chiefly by Mrs Thatcher's main window on the media world, Ingham.[140] John Wakeham probably also influenced Mrs Thatcher against Brittan. He considered that Brittan had been 'promoted a bit high and a bit quick' and 'wasn't really up to the job'. The impression he had given in the capital-punishment debate that he was supporting the death penalty insincerely counted against him too.[141]

When Mrs Thatcher had discussed her proposed changes with the Chief Whip, John Wakeham, at Chequers, he had predicted that if she tried to move Brittan the first thing he would ask her was 'What will be my

* As Mrs Thatcher prepared for the reshuffle announcement, she scribbled a few points on the back of a document outlining the changes, such as 'Cecil – not returning' and 'Announcements tomorrow evening'. This document survives among the papers she lodged at Churchill College. From the context it seems that these jottings related to a conversation she had with Bernard Ingham on the evening of Sunday 1 September. She also wrote '13 years old' (Thatcher notes on reshuffle, undated but from context 1 September 1985, CAC: THCR 1/14/14). Given the later speculation that one of her motives in reshuffling Brittan may have been rumours about child-abuse accusations, the possibility has to be considered that, in these three words, she was referring to these. This seems unlikely, however, since there is no evidence that any new accusations against Brittan had reached her since those of the previous year, so she would not have needed to write one down on a piece of paper just before the reshuffle. (She would also have been most reluctant, given her habitual caution, to commit any such thing to paper.) There is a much more likely explanation. On 22 August, there was a terrible air disaster at Manchester airport, in which fifty-four people died. Returning from holiday in Austria, Mrs Thatcher diverted her plane to visit the crash site and meet the survivors. They included three seriously injured thirteen-year-olds – two girls, both of whom had lost parents and other close relatives, and one boy. The press continued to carry reports about these children (and other victims) through the ensuing fortnight. On the day before the reshuffle took place, a commemorative Mass was held in Manchester. In that context it would not have been surprising for Mrs Thatcher to have asked for, or received news of, the three children from Ingham and for her to have scribbled a reference to them. (The author gratefully acknowledges the assistance provided by Chris Collins on this issue.)

position in the pecking order?' Ever innocent of such hierarchical ideas, Mrs Thatcher said, 'The pecking order? What's that?', as if unfamiliar with the phrase. When she spoke to Brittan, she reported to Wakeham afterwards, he did exactly as the Chief Whip had predicted: 'John, you were quite right. That is all he asked.'[142] Mrs Thatcher assured Brittan that his seniority remained unchanged, but he was insecure about his status and felt ill used. Although the DTI was undoubtedly a job more central to Mrs Thatcher's reforming mission in government than the Home Office, it was traditionally lower in the hierarchy.* Douglas Hurd – whom Mrs Thatcher thought 'a very calm person of great stature',[143] though in no sense a Thatcherite – became Home Secretary in Brittan's stead. He was replaced as Northern Ireland secretary by Tom King, who, contrary to the advice from Whitelaw and Wakeham, remained in the Cabinet.

As foreshadowed, Norman Tebbit became party chairman. Jeffrey Archer was not elevated to the peerage, and therefore could hold no ministerial office. He was made Tebbit's deputy chairman, however, with a brief to revive the party's grass-roots enthusiasm. This made Tebbit, who had not been consulted, 'a bit miffed'.[144] According to Michael Dobbs, Mrs Thatcher had also put Archer into the post 'to keep an eye on Norman for her',[145] part of the parallel operation.

Cecil Parkinson was not brought back. The justified fear of a further assault from Sara Keays prevented this, and although Mrs Thatcher allowed Parkinson to think that Wakeham and others were blocking his return, in truth she shared their anxieties and thought it was 'a little bit soon'.[146] Similar caution prevailed in the case of Lord Hailsham. He would have been succeeded as lord chancellor by Sir Michael Havers and that would have provoked a by-election when Havers moved from the Commons to the Lords. After the fright over nearly losing Willie Whitelaw's former seat in 1983 ('That really taught me a lesson'),[147] Mrs Thatcher would not risk this, and decided to keep the seventy-seven-year-old Hailsham in place until the next election.

Mrs Thatcher had come to believe that right-wing ministers were particularly poor at presentation compared with those on the left of the party. Ridley, for example, was one of the 'best brains' in government, but 'he couldn't get on with television.'[148] Concerned, in this exercise, more by

---

* In a moment that could have come from *Yes, Minister*, one of Brittan's first acts as DTI secretary was to write to oppose a levy on blank audio-cassettes which had recently been proposed in a letter from the then Home Secretary – himself (Interview with Andrew Lansley).

presentation than by ideology, she made Kenneth Baker environment secretary to take forward the 'community charge' and take on the left-wing Labour councils. For this, she sacked Patrick Jenkin. She also made Kenneth Clarke, who was Wet in politics but strong in personality, paymaster-general, with a seat in the Cabinet. He was, in effect, the Department of Employment's main representative in the House of Commons, because, doing for Employment what Gowrie had not let her do for Education, she had made a peer, Lord Young of Graffham, secretary of state.

David Young, whom Mrs Thatcher had made employment secretary, was promoted to do by stronger means what he had already been doing, originally at the Manpower Services Commission, and then as a minister. In August 1984, he had been sounded out for the chairmanship of British Petroleum. Rather than pursuing this, Young had gone to see Mrs Thatcher, using the possible BP job offer for leverage. He asked her to make him either her chief of staff or a peer and a minister.[149] She decided on the latter and made him (unpaid) minister without portfolio. Young, the legendary job-creator, was busy creating his own. Ministerial colleagues instinctively resented him, since he was not a professional politician. Mrs Thatcher was often quoted, although there is no record of anyone ever having heard the words from her lips, as saying that 'Other people bring me problems, but David brings me solutions.'[150]* This naturally enraged his fellow ministers, who thought of him as 'teacher's pet'. Tom King, who had cause to feel particularly threatened, complained to Alan Clark that 'David Young was not a member of the club, never fought an Election, always wheedling away . . .'[151] Young later admitted there was some truth behind these suspicions. Before he succeeded King, for example, he 'would occasionally go behind his back, to my shame, to No. 10 to make sure things were going properly'.[152] Indeed, this is what Mrs Thatcher had encouraged him to do: 'She was asking me to double-check on her Employment Secretary,' recalled Young; 'she's a moral coward when it comes to dealing with people.'

Now Mrs Thatcher put Young in full charge. Showing further disregard for Leon Brittan, she ceded to Young extra areas of responsibility from the DTI, such as tourism and small firms, which he had requested. Young's

---

* This quotation has been significantly embroidered over time. It seems to have originated in a 1984 profile of David Young written by Alan Pike, the industrial correspondent of the *Financial Times*. Young was then chairman of the Manpower Services Commission, not a minister. Pike quoted Mrs Thatcher as saying: 'Other people come to me with their problems. David Young comes with his achievements.' (See Alan Pike, *Financial Times*, 7 April 1984; letter to editor, 24 November 2010.)

attitude differed radically from the tradition of the Department of Employment which had, historically, been the department for dealing with the
trade unions. Rather than merely ameliorating the lot of the unemployed, he
wanted to reduce their number. He addressed everything which tended to
make getting a job difficult or undesirable – the benefit trap (tackled with
his Restart programme), poor technical and vocational training, and the
tax and regulatory difficulties which discouraged the creation and growth
of small businesses. When Mrs Thatcher made Young employment secretary, she told him, 'I want you to deal with unemployment by the next
election.'[153] He strongly believed in what Mrs Thatcher was trying to
achieve, and greatly admired her leadership because she was 'wonderful
at focus and follow-through'. She came to be more than satisfied with her
choice.* Indeed, his was one of her few important appointments which
she did not partially regret. As she later put it: 'I reckon he won the
'87 election for us because of his employment policies.'[154]

Perhaps because of the new faces brought in by the reshuffle, the Conservatives received rather more favourable media coverage during the conference
season than they deserved. At Labour's gathering in Bournemouth, Neil
Kinnock scored a palpable hit with his attack on the behaviour of the
Militant Tendency in Liverpool (see Chapter 11). The Tories had no comparable message of change or sense of direction. To great embarrassment,
the newly appointed Jeffrey Archer attacked 'the workshy young' in a
conference interview and compared his own return to wealth after
near-bankruptcy favourably with their failures. As Norman Tebbit left
the conference, which he had himself, as chairman, orchestrated, he said
to Michael Dobbs: 'That conference was a terrible balls-up: we were lucky
to get away with it. It had no theme.'[155]
    In her leader's speech at Blackpool, Mrs Thatcher attacked the 'courage'
Kinnock had shown at Bournemouth, by saying that it had come 'long
after the event'.[156] She contrasted it with the 'real courage' shown by working miners, lorry drivers, steel men, railwaymen and dockers during the
miners' strike. She tried to make a virtue of her government's lack of
startling economic progress by speaking of 'the realities of power exercised responsibly' and 'idealism tempered by realism'. And she was at pains

---

* Alan Clark, who found himself one of Young's junior ministers, and had previously been
much opposed to him, recorded their first meeting after Young's appointment: 'He is pleasant, charming almost, and fresh . . . He talks at twice the speed of Tom King, but listens too,
cracks jokes, is full of bright ideas. I can quite see why the Lady fancies him. He is utterly
different from the rest of the Cabinet – yet without being caddish.' (Clark, *Diaries*, 3 September 1985, p. 119.)

to emphasize her commitment to dealing with unemployment. 'No problem ... occupies more of my thinking,' she said, almost truthfully. She boasted that the millionth recruit would join the Youth Training Scheme by Christmas and that, in the last two years, 650,000 additional jobs had been created in Britain. She invited her audience to recall how they had supported her enthusiastically in the same hall when she had made her rousing first party conference speech as leader ten years earlier. She was applauded loyally, but not rapturously.

In political terms, it was perhaps a grim form of luck for Mrs Thatcher that riots had recently broken out in several black inner-city neighbourhoods. Although related to inner-city poverty and racial discontents in general, they were sparked by specific incidents with the police. In September, there were disturbances in Brixton and in Handsworth (in Birmingham); in early October, in Tottenham, north London. Although not nearly as extensive as their predecessors in 1981, the riots were fierce, some even bestial. In Broadwater Farm, Tottenham, an enormous modern 'sink' estate, whose walkways and dark stairs made crime easy, rioters protesting at the death of a black woman in a police raid attacked the police, who were trying to protect firemen fighting the effects of petrol bombs. One officer, PC Keith Blakelock, slipped as he emerged from a stairwell and was set upon by the mob. He received forty injuries from cuts or stabs. A six-inch knife was buried in his neck. He died shortly afterwards, the first policeman killed in a mainland British riot for more than 150 years. Bernie Grant, the black local Labour leader of Haringey Council,* said: 'The youths around here believe that the police were to blame for what happened on Sunday and what they got was a bloody good hiding.'[157] This was widely taken as excusing the murder. 'Maybe it was a policeman who stabbed another policeman,' he also said.[158]

The sheer savagery of PC Blakelock's murder gave the Tories, who were gathering for their conference when it happened, a new solidarity. Bernie Grant's comments created a political problem for the Labour Party, although Neil Kinnock quickly condemned his words. Norman Tebbit was characteristically laconic: 'I do not think one can say unemployment is the cause of a gang of 100 people falling upon a single policeman and murdering him. If so, we could have been singularly short of policemen during the 1930s.'[159] Mrs Thatcher herself was able to turn the traditional Tory subject of law and order into the centrepiece of her speech. She attacked 'crime masquerading as social protest', won her biggest applause

* Bernard ('Bernie') Grant (1944–2000), council leader, London Borough of Haringey, 1985–7; Labour MP for Tottenham, 1987–2000.

for saying that most British people 'regard the police as friends' and identified the hard left – 'socialism in action' in the council chambers of
Liverpool, Lambeth (home of the Brixton riots) and Haringey – as subverting the law. Into this, rather than merely asserting authority, she injected
a note of compassion: 'We are all involved. We cannot pass by on the other
side.'[160] She displayed concern for the decay of inner cities, which had
happened, she said, because local institutions and the power of church,
family and school had given way to the chill hand of the state. Mrs
Thatcher was appalled by the details of PC Blakelock's death and sent a
handwritten sympathy letter to his widow. 'The agony will be almost
unbearable, and words of little comfort,' she wrote. 'But I want you to
know that without the bravery of your late husband and others like him
Britain would not be the country we know and love. This new terrorism
in our midst is like a cancer – and similarly it must be overcome.'[161]

As was generally the case in moments of disorder, Mrs Thatcher was much
more concerned than most politicians by the details of what had actually
happened, especially to the victims of riot, and less inclined to move
straight into discussing policy changes. When the Home Secretary, Douglas Hurd, reported to her, in Blackpool, on the riots in Tottenham, she
gave a sort of stream of consciousness reaction:

> the ferocity of the night's events and the weapons used was evidence of a
> new situation . . . It was a great pity that so few arrests had been made . . .
> it might even be necessary to demolish houses in different estates in order
> to help policing. Extra search lights might be employed. Above all, the
> Government should stand up for the police.[162]

When the Police Federation privately told her Policy Unit that they
wanted to brief Mrs Thatcher in detail on the appalling injuries suffered
by PC Blakelock, the unit discouraged the idea, to spare her feelings. 'We
believe unless you request this information that you should not be troubled,' Hartley Booth, of the unit, told her.[163] Booth also informed her,
from what he said were police sources, that 'the ingredients of Napalm . . .
have been supplied to individuals in the Tottenham area.' If so, the police
would need protective clothing and plastic bullets. Concerned and perhaps
over-credulous, Mrs Thatcher rose to the bait. 'This is <u>most disturbing</u>,'
she wrote. 'Is everything possible being done to assist the police in their
duties?'[164] It was left to a civil servant, her private secretary David Norgrove, to point out gently that rumours were 'flying around'. There was
always a danger that Mrs Thatcher's concern for detail could be misdir-
ected if her advisers did not exercise enough restraint. Stephen Sherbourne

recalled that, in her middle period in office, Mrs Thatcher's authority was considered so great that it was important to invoke her name very sparingly in Whitehall: people would respond excessively to whatever they thought might be her will.[165] What the Prime Minister seriously wanted, in terms of policy, had to be distinguished from what she might say on the spur of the moment: her true wishes were sometimes different from her whim. She herself knew this, as is evidenced by her preference for government conducted more through work on paper than through sofa conversations.

The broad fact was that Mrs Thatcher was very interested in the state of the inner cities, and had been thinking about them increasingly for some time. 'I got fed up with [the state of] inner cities. There was no one responsible for them.'[166] This was part of the reason she had made David Young employment secretary. Instead of seeing the inhabitants of what were called Urban Priority Areas as passive victims of a bad system or government neglect, she wanted them to be participants in shaping a better future. For this to happen, business opportunities had to be made easier and, she believed, local government finance had to be reformed. If, for example, left-wing councils could set their business rates prohibitively high without suffering electoral retribution, they would, and jobs would leave their areas. This contributed to her thinking about the poll tax (see Chapter 11).

The official papers on the subject of inner cities at this time show Mrs Thatcher confronted with a piquant contrast. As bad news poured in about riots, so did good news about her largest urban regeneration project. 'Yesterday,' Kenneth Baker wrote to her on 3 October 1985, 'I met the American bankers and developers who want to build a huge new financial centre in London's Docklands.'[167] They would put £1.5 billion into the regeneration of Canary Wharf, involving 45,000 financial jobs and about the same again in supporting employment. The plans were 'visually stunning'. This huge development remains central to the financial success of London to this day. The London Docklands Development Corporation (LDDC), invented by Mrs Thatcher and Michael Heseltine in 1981, was achieving these results because it had the power to overcome local government objections and grant planning permission for commercial development and private housing. At this time, there were about 30,000 unoccupied private sector dwellings in Greater London, often sat on by Labour councils unwilling to sell but unable to afford to renovate. The LDDC also bought up public sector land which was lying idle and helped improve transport links. It was often harder to extend such opportunities to other inner cities, most of which were less depopulated than the London Docks and therefore more difficult to transform physically.

More broadly, Mrs Thatcher's government was not united on its approach to the inner cities. In departmental terms, too many cooks were spoiling the broth. From an ideological perspective, there was a half-stated disagreement between the more 'One Nation' Conservatives who thought that government money would do the work, and the Thatcherites, who were more interested in economic opportunity, non-state institutions and individual human character as means of transforming the inner cities. Booth and Letwin, the idealistic young moralists at the Policy Unit, wrote to Mrs Thatcher to point out that ministers wanted all sorts of different things – black middle-class entrepreneurs for Lord Young, refurbished council blocks for Kenneth Baker, a reduction in youth alienation for Douglas Hurd. But none of this reached the root, they declared:

> when things were very bad in the great depression of the 1930s, people in Brixton went out, leaving their grocery money in a bag at the front door . . . Riots, criminality and social disintegration are caused solely by individual characters and attitudes. So long as bad moral attitudes remain, all efforts to improve the inner cities will founder. David Young's new entrepreneurs will set up in the disco and drug trade.[168]

There was a related problem of who would make the best local partners, with subsidy backing the wrong people. 'Liverpool's catastrophic black activist, Samson Bond [a London leftist brought in to deal with race issues by Militant], is funded by the Home Office,'[169] a point which Mrs Thatcher underscored with her pen several times. Argument went back and forth within government about what should be done. Mrs Thatcher wanted more focus on inner-city youth, but still cogitated uncertainly about who should be in charge of it.

Into this discussion broke the Church of England. At the end of November, the Archbishop of Canterbury, Robert Runcie, sent a handwritten letter to Mrs Thatcher enclosing a copy of *Faith in the City*, the large-scale report of his Commission on Urban Priority Areas, which offered, by its own account on its back cover, 'a disturbing picture' of those major cities 'where economic, physical and social conditions are at their most acute and depressing'. 'It is not, of course, a comfortable read for Archbishops or for Prime Ministers,' wrote Runcie, but, 'despite some reservations which I have about certain sections, I believe the contents have to be taken seriously.'[170] The commission to which Runcie gave this somewhat tepid endorsement was made up almost exclusively of leading figures of the Anglican liberal-left of the era, sometimes known as 'South Bank religion', because of the influence of the Southwark diocese in the 1960s. It was chaired by Sir Richard O'Brien,* whom Mrs Thatcher had edged out of the Manpower Services Commission in favour of David Young. It included David Sheppard, Bishop of Liverpool,† Canon Eric James,‡ the director of Christian Action, and Professor A. H. Halsey,§ the leading socialist sociologist and former Reith lecturer.

Runcie himself was, according to his chaplain at that time, John Witheridge, 'a bit of a Tory Wet' who was 'quite confused politically'.[171] He had 'a quiet respect for Mrs Thatcher' and had not intended a political onslaught, but his own political confusion meant that he had left the field open for his more ideological fellows to launch an attack on Mrs Thatcher (though without naming her) and all her works. The report put forward an unreconstructed 1945-style programme of neo-Keynesian government-sponsored works and dressed it in ecclesiastical vestments. Describing the Church as 'the conscience of the nation', the report declared that 'too much emphasis is being given to individualism, and not enough to collective obligation.'[172] It referred respectfully to Marx and to Liberation Theology (the quasi-Marxist thinking popular with some South American clergy at the time), disparaged the Protestant work ethic and 'comfortable Britain', and quoted with approval one submission which said: 'The exclusion of the poor is pervasive and not accidental.'[173] When she read this, Mrs Thatcher put two large question marks besides it and heavy lines below 'not accidental', well aware that she stood accused.¶ In the view of Richard Chartres, later Bishop of London,** who was Runcie's chaplain

---

* Richard O'Brien (1920–2009), educated Oundle and Clare College, Cambridge; chairman, Manpower Services Commission, 1976–82; chairman, Archbishop of Canterbury's Commission on Urban Priority Areas that published the *Faith in the City* report in 1985; chairman, Policy Studies Institute, 1984–90; knighted, 1980.

† David Sheppard (1929–2005), educated Sherborne, Trinity Hall, Cambridge and Ridley Hall Theological College; Bishop of Liverpool, 1975–97; vice-chairman, Commission on Urban Priority Areas, 1983–5; created Lord Sheppard of Liverpool, 1998.

‡ Canon Eric James (1925–2012), educated Dagenham County High School and King's College London; director, Christian Action, 1979–90; a chaplain to HM the Queen, 1984–95.

§ A. H. (Albert Henry) Halsey (1923–2014), educated Kettering Grammar School and LSE; Reith lecturer, 1977; Professor of Social and Administrative Studies, Oxford University, 1978–90; Professorial Fellow of Nuffield College, Oxford, 1962–90.

¶ Mrs Thatcher was also not pleased to discover that the secretary to the report had been seconded by the Department of the Environment for two years at public expense and promoted within the civil service while away.

** Richard Chartres (1947–), educated Hertford Grammar School, Trinity College, Cambridge, Cuddesdon Theological College, Oxford and Lincoln Theological College; Bishop of London, 1995–; preached the address at Lady Thatcher's funeral at St Paul's Cathedral, 17 April 2013; Archbishop of Canterbury's chaplain, 1980–84.

when the report was first conceived, the recommendations and data about
the life of the urban Church were valuable, but its theology was 'pathetic'.[174]

All twenty-three main public policy recommendations of *Faith in the
City* involved increased government spending. The report opposed council
house sales, the private rented sector in housing, private schools, and
university cuts. It attacked the government for a 'dogmatic and inflexible
macro-economic stance' and declared that 'for most low-income city residents, freedom of choice is a cruel deception.' It also, in a section entitled
'Order and Law' – a deliberate inversion of the usual phrase so beloved
of Tory conferences – questioned the idea that obedience to the law was
necessarily important and concentrated on how law enforcement could
be used to marginalize the poor. This chapter provoked the rather excit-
able Hartley Booth to warn Mrs Thatcher that the report 'could play a
dangerous role in subverting support for the hard-pressed forces of law
and order, and in whipping up racial tension'.[175]

Brian Griffiths, as well as being an academic economist, was a
well-instructed churchman. He wrote the Policy Unit's 'critical evaluation'
of the report for Mrs Thatcher, advising her to welcome it as 'a serious
investigation of a real problem', but be ready to 'express surprise' at certain omissions and presumptions. 'Express surprise', he counselled, 'that
the recommendations of the report lay far more emphasis on central and
local government than they do on the family.'[176] Writing on top of all this,
David Norgrove advised her: 'This seems right to me. Kill it with kindness.
A Church–Government row would keep the Report on the front pages.'
Even the combative Ingham advised against 'a pre-emptive strike' since
this would 'draw more attention to the report'.[177] One unnamed minister,
however, speaking to the *Sunday Times*, described the report as 'pure
Marxist theology',[178] thus lighting the blue touch-paper.* This was the
sort of subject, beloved of newspapers, on which everyone could pitch in,
along almost wholly predictable lines. The general effect was to amplify
the idea that the government in general, and Mrs Thatcher in particular,
were 'uncaring'.

Mrs Thatcher did not welcome the controversy. Despite her combative
nature, she never wanted a fight with the Church. John Gummer, who
discussed the report with her, noticed that she felt 'hurt' by it. There was
a strong moral and religious base to her politics, and she 'saw the Church

---

* It has been frequently stated that the anonymous minister was Norman Tebbit. He denied
it: 'It was not Marxist. I am not at all sure that any minister did describe it as such. More
likely it was a BBC or Guardianista thinking that was what a Thatcherite minister would
have said' (Interview with Lord Tebbit).

as an important part of the stability of society'.[179] 'She didn't like its implication that she didn't care: she did.' She felt inhibited in disagreeing with Runcie himself, both because of his office and because he had 'had a good war'.* It was a pity, thought John Witheridge, that Runcie did not see her privately to talk matters over: 'If he'd had more confidence, he might have exerted more influence.'[180]† On the whole, the Church was more uncharitable to Mrs Thatcher than she to the Church: 'She was politer than we might have been.'[181] Privately, she was irritated by the 'unbelievably woolly'[182] passages of the report and the fact that it showed no understanding of how an economy works. She also disliked, of course, any passages which seemed left wing. Gummer admitted inciting her to particular outrage by pointing out to her the report's suggestion that churches in Urban Priority Areas should use 'banners designed and made locally'[183] for their worship. The report probably had in mind depictions of Christian scenes and symbols in contemporary settings, but she thought of banners as things carried by activists on protest marches.

In Gummer's view, Mrs Thatcher's was 'what my father [a clergyman] called a cut-flower religion' – neatly preserved and presented, but no longer alive. She had absorbed the precepts of Grantham Methodism and not continued from there: 'I never detected any religious influence afterwards.'[184] This was not right, although it was true that Mrs Thatcher was utterly uninterested in churchy controversies, or in theology. She continued to think hard about the Christian's duty to God and consequent duty to his or her neighbour. She was not one of those who thought Christianity should be merely private, with nothing to say about the life of society, but she was frustrated by the sense that the Church was trading on its spiritual and moral prestige to pronounce on economic matters which it failed to understand.

Casting about for backing for her views from other religious authorities, Mrs Thatcher was pleased by the writings of the Chief Rabbi, Immanuel Jakobovits.‡ He wrote a commentary on *Faith in the City*, entitled 'From Doom to Hope'. The two had first met when Mrs Thatcher was Education

---

* Runcie won the Military Cross in Willie Whitelaw's regiment, the Scots Guards, in 1945, for his acts of courage as a tank commander. He was the only archbishop, at least since the Middle Ages, known deliberately to have killed his fellow men.

† Runcie did occasionally try private communication with Mrs Thatcher. On one occasion, he slipped a personal letter into her handbag at a drinks party. She then forgot about it and it lay there unopened for ten days until a secretary found it. (Interview with Sir Mark Lennox-Boyd.)

‡ Immanuel Jakobovits (1921–99), educated University of London and Jews' College and Yeshivah Etz Chaim, London; Chief Rabbi of the United Hebrew Congregations of the British Commonwealth of Nations, 1967–91; knighted, 1981; created Lord Jakobovits, 1988.

Secretary. She had been impressed by Jacobovits's remark that her job meant that she was 'really the Minister of Defence'.[185] She admired his emphasis on education and effort as the means of conquering poverty and prejudice. In 'From Doom to Hope', the Chief Rabbi argued that Jews had broken out of the ghetto because 'we worked on ourselves, not on others' and 'hallowed our home life'. He thought it sad that *Faith in the City* 'falls short of hailing work as a virtue in itself' and declared that 'Cheap labour is more dignified than a free dole.' He quoted a medieval Jewish teacher who had made his point with a Hebrew pun: 'He who is poor (*rash*) is going to be a leader in the future (*rosh*).' She is supposed to have told Jakobovits that she wished she could make him archbishop of Canterbury. Since she could not, she made him a peer in 1988, the first chief rabbi to enter the House of Lords. It could be said that *Faith in the City* pricked her conscience, but not in the direction the report intended.

Perhaps not wholly coincidentally, Mrs Thatcher came to the view that Jakobovits's co-religionist, David Young, should be put in charge of inner-city initiatives, driving private sector 'task forces'. Rather than fretting about 'black alienation' and entering into identity politics, these would 'develop a viable private sector base in the inner cities'.[186] Mrs Thatcher preferred ideas which she thought came from the bank of the Jordan in biblical times than those from the South Bank of the Thames in the 1960s.

In a scribbled note to Mrs Thatcher, Robert Armstrong suggested that the task-force plan be announced soon to 'pre-empt . . . the Member for Henley (Mr Heseltine) [who had resigned from the government over the Westland crisis three weeks earlier (see Chapter 14)] who – Lord Young suspects – may before long turn his restless energies to the problems of inner cities and (especially) Liverpool'.[187] Mrs Thatcher acted accordingly.

14

Helicopter crash

'Her hands were not entirely clean'

When she came to compose her memoirs in the early 1990s, Margaret Thatcher was heard to remark, 'I can't even remember what the actual Westland thing was about now.'[1] She was not alone. To many, both at the time and subsequently, it seemed mysterious that an argument over the future of a West Country helicopter company, then worth about £30 million, should have convulsed a successful government with a parliamentary majority of 140. Yet that is what happened, and by the end of it all much would be revealed about how her government worked – or did not work. For the first time, Mrs Thatcher would find her personal reputation assailed not only by her political opponents – she was used to that – but by at least one 'enemy within', and even by allies. Her methods of exercising power would be exposed and her integrity seriously questioned.

The immediate cause of the explosion was not so much the issue of Westland itself, but the character of the Defence Secretary, Michael Heseltine. Said to dislike working for a woman, Heseltine had never been close to Mrs Thatcher, personally or politically. In spite of Mrs Thatcher's own reservations about Heseltine's character (see p. 434), he had performed well for her politically at Defence, notably by his vigorous prosecution of the campaign against CND over the installation of US cruise missiles in Britain. When, in July 1984, one of his own civil servants, Clive Ponting, had leaked to the Labour MP Tam Dalyell* papers which he thought showed government duplicity over the sinking of the *Belgrano*, Heseltine had been fiercer than she† in supporting Ponting's prosecution under the

---

* Sir Thomas ('Tam') Dalyell of the Binns (1932–), educated Eton and King's College, Cambridge; Labour MP for West Lothian, 1962–83; for Linlithgow, 1983–2005; Member, European Parliament, 1975–9. He never called himself Thomas nor used his title.

† When Ponting first came under suspicion for the leak, and was suspended without pay, Mrs Thatcher sent a message while on holiday: 'I think this is a bit rough. He and his family will have to live on something. We should, I believe, wait for the verdict ...' (Thatcher to Barclay, 18 August 1984, Prime Minister's Papers, Security, Investigation ... into documents

Official Secrets Act. (To the government's embarrassment, the prosecution failed.) But Heseltine always maintained markedly different views from Mrs Thatcher – more pro-European, more corporatist, more enthusiastic about regional policy. By 1985, seeing no prospect of further advancement for himself under the existing dispensation, he was chafing at the bit. Mrs Thatcher was not blind to these warning signs. At the end of her visit to Washington, DC, that February, on which Heseltine accompanied her, she pulled aside David Hannay, then working at the British Embassy there: 'I remember her quizzing me quite strongly as to what Heseltine had got up to while he was there, in terms that implied she had total distrust in him.'[2]

It was Heseltine who first alerted Mrs Thatcher to the growing problem with Westland, Britain's only helicopter manufacturer. Signs of trouble had appeared late in 1984. At the end of April 1985, he informed her that the company was running out of work, due to the collapse of a big order from India which she had done much to promote. He said he favoured a 'market solution' with new management, and thought this might come from an entrepreneur called Alan Bristow. He found it hard to see 'a single British specialist helicopter company competing in worldwide markets in the longer term'.[3] He did not think the United Kingdom should place extra orders to rescue Westland.

Nevertheless, government minds now bent to finding more work for the company. Mrs Thatcher jumped at an eccentric request from Kenneth Kaunda, the President of Zambia, who wrote asking for twelve Westland helicopters paid for out of the British overseas aid programme to check on poachers of elephants and 'the rhino, the eland, the leopard, cheetah and the black lechwe'.[4] 'I hope this can be done <u>very quickly</u>,' Mrs Thatcher scribbled on the covering letter. 'It may help Westlands.'* Concerned about the propriety of the aid programme, the Foreign Office intervened against the Kaunda request which, Geoffrey Howe told Mrs Thatcher, 'verges on the ludicrous'.[5] The High Commission in Lusaka intercepted her encouraging reply to Kaunda and made sure it was not delivered.

Other ideas were not much more successful. In the course of the early summer, the Bristow offer went awry because the government refused the backing he sought. Ministerial meetings, in which Mrs Thatcher took a part, were hastily called to try to stave off receivership and the consequent loss of 1,700 jobs in Yeovil in Somerset.† Foreign interest was not ruled

---

relating to the sinking of the *General Belgrano*, Part 1 (document consulted in the Cabinet Office)).

* Although the company was correctly known as 'Westland', this plural version was commonly used by ministers and officials.

† Yeovil was of particular concern to the Conservative government, because a Liberal, Paddy

out, although the Trade and Industry Secretary, Norman Tebbit,* discouraged an approach from Marmon Inc. of Chicago because 'I do not find the prospect of American ownership welcome.'[6] No. 10 had good links with Sir John Cuckney,† the chairman of Westland recently appointed to sort matters out, who came from an MI5 background. He had a high reputation as a 'company doctor', and had impressed Mrs Thatcher with his rescue of John Brown Engineering, the company for whose interests in the Siberian oil pipeline she had fought so strongly against President Reagan (see Volume I, pp. 582–3). One of Cuckney's early acts as chairman was secretly to hire Gordon Reece to advise him on political relations and PR.‡ From the first, Cuckney was interested by the pre-existing possibility that Sikorsky, the helicopter division of the American company United Technologies, might buy a big minority stake in Westland.

The No. 10 Policy Unit, keen to advance Thatcherite ideas of open competition, disliked any thought of state rescue. As early as 5 July, it urged that foreign owners should not be ruled out: 'From a defence and industrial point of view, a bid from Sikorsky might be far better [than another Bristow bid].'[7] In this spirit, Mrs Thatcher's office informed the DTI that 'While she has noted the general arguments against an American takeover, she believes that a different American offer would have to be judged on its merits.'[8] At this stage, there was not much overt politics involved. But already Cuckney was somewhat irritated by Michael Heseltine. He had been to see him at the end of June, and found him 'pretty arrogant and laid back . . . He was sitting in a jumper on a full-length sofa and didn't get up. He was not frightfully interested and told me to see Clive Whitmore [the Permanent Secretary].'[9]

The Cabinet reshuffle that September had significant consequences for

---

Ashdown, had gained the seat from the Tories at the previous general election. They wanted to win it back. The seat remained in Liberal hands until 2015.

* The Department of Trade and Industry was the lead or 'sponsor' department in the Westland affair, because the Ministry of Defence, as an actual and potential customer of Westland, had an interest to declare. This involvement of two departments, though inevitable, was to prove incendiary.

† John Cuckney (1925–2008), educated Shrewsbury and St Andrews University; appointments with various industrial and financial companies including chairman of Westland, 1985–9; knighted, 1978; created Lord Cuckney of Millbank, 1995.

‡ This hiring was so well concealed that, even at the height of the drama just after Christmas, when the Sunday papers were threatening to run the story that Reece was advising Westland and spending Christmas Day at Chequers, Bernard Ingham had to write to ask Mrs Thatcher whether any of this was true. It was. (Reece was divorced, and on his own for Christmas: Mrs Thatcher probably invited him more out of friendship than policy.) She sent no recorded reply. (See Ingham to Thatcher, 28 December 1985, Prime Minister's Papers, Aerospace, Westland Helicopters, Part 2 (document consulted in the Cabinet Office).)

the Westland story. While Heseltine stayed at Defence, Leon Brittan now replaced Norman Tebbit at the DTI. Brittan's demotion from the Home Office – for such, whatever the formal position, he rightly understood it to be – hit him hard. To observers in No. 10, he seemed 'a slightly changed character'.[10] It was in this grumpy and uneasy frame of mind that he now confronted the problem of Westland.

Michael Heseltine was not disposed to make matters easy for him. He had always hankered after the job which Brittan had just reluctantly accepted, and he liked to think that, in Defence, 'I can have my own industrial policy.'[11] In his view, he 'offered to help' the new Secretary of State: he felt that he had built up a great deal of relevant expertise in his dealings with the Europeans over the European Fighter Aircraft.[12] Brittan saw it otherwise: 'To him, I was the jumped-up minor person, and he was the big frog.'[13] Although Heseltine did not enter the Westland issue with strong views on the company's future, he did have earlier experience of dealing with Mrs Thatcher on industrial matters. He had claimed a role in industrial policy by circulating a paper to the E Committee of the Cabinet, setting out his interventionist views. She had reluctantly permitted him to do this. Although he had found little support among colleagues, it had made her 'pretty furious'.[14] Heseltine had also been hardened by a battle at the end of the previous year with Norman Tebbit and Mrs Thatcher about the building of two new Type 22 naval frigates. Tebbit had wanted them both built at Swan Hunter on Tyneside. Heseltine, who always pushed the cause of Liverpool, felt differently. In his view Tebbit unfairly changed the rules of competition by insisting that Cammell Laird, based on Merseyside, be allowed to bid for only one of the two frigates, whereas Swan Hunter was free to bid for both. Heseltine intimated that he would resign if he did not get his way. 'Margaret backed me,' he recalled;[15] but she did this only because she felt he was threatening resignation, and was left 'seething' at Heseltine's tactic.[16]

Norman Tebbit was also a significant figure in the drama, but a somewhat uncertain ally for Mrs Thatcher at this time: he had quarrelled with her over policy towards British Leyland (see Chapter 15). He, like Heseltine, felt he had learnt from the argument over Cammell Laird. Tebbit was close to Willie Whitelaw, the Deputy Prime Minister. Whitelaw had advised Mrs Thatcher to give Heseltine what he wanted over Cammell Laird, but had also confided in Tebbit that he felt Heseltine had been a 'bloody shit' in the affair.* Tebbit and Whitelaw watched Heseltine's

---

* Heseltine believed that Whitelaw 'never approved of me', for reasons that he never exactly understood. It may have been something to do with Whitelaw's view of business, which he

behaviour over Westland together, and recognized certain symptoms. They concluded quite early on, Tebbit recalled, that he was 'fishing for an issue on which to resign'.[17]

In early October, when Leon Brittan first wrote to Mrs Thatcher about the future of Westland, the tone of discussion was rational on all sides. He explained that either the Sikorsky bid, or an emerging joint European bid of the German MBB, the French Aérospatiale and the Italian Agusta, was possible. He opposed John Cuckney's suggestion that the government should underwrite the sales of forty-five W30-160 helicopters, and argued that Westland was 'not central to the aerospace industry'. He thought that Sikorsky was the most likely buyer, but also that Westland 'should be encouraged to pursue the possibility of a European solution'.[18] Charles Powell, informing Mrs Thatcher that Brittan wanted an early meeting to discuss it all, did not see a great urgency, given her crowded diary: 'You simply can't do this.'[19] Heseltine, who would later make much of Brittan's suggestion that a European solution should be encouraged, set to work. Brittan recalled that he had no personal preference in the matter and that his attitude to Heseltine's interest in a European solution was ' "Good luck! But it's an industrial matter, not a defence matter." The Government shouldn't force anyone: it didn't own the company.'[20]

It was true (and would become truer) that Heseltine instinctively pre-ferred European projects and Mrs Thatcher instinctively favoured American ones. Heseltine, for example, was proud of his role in advancing the European Fighter Aircraft: European defence co-operation was the sort of 'seat-at-the-top-table' corporatism which he favoured. It was also true that Mrs Thatcher thought in terms of free markets and Heseltine in terms of government intervention and 'picking winners'. They were always philosophically at odds. But the Westland issue was not framed in pro- or anti-European terms, or even much in terms of market theory, at this time. In this, the year before the Single European Act, Mrs Thatcher was not invariably suspicious of European projects, especially when they involved strengthening defence. Nevertheless, a difference of emphasis began to emerge. Tebbit, Charles Powell and – most important – Cuckney suspected the motives of the European bid. Cuckney told a DTI official that 'The interest of all three [European] companies was totally negative: they were only interested in blocking Sikorsky.'[21] Throughout the saga, he knew he must take a real European bid seriously, but 'we [the Westland board]

---

once expressed to Heseltine thus: 'I hate businessmen. I hate businessmen. I hate business-men.' 'Willie,' Heseltine replied, 'I am a businessman.' (Interview with Lord Heseltine.)

were put off by the lack of cohesion displayed by the so-called consortium'.[22] Heseltine, on the other hand, pressed on with European discussions. He came to believe that Sikorsky wanted Westland solely to turn the company into a vehicle for selling their own Black Hawk helicopters to the Ministry of Defence.

Emboldened by his victory over Cammell Laird, Heseltine now sought a new one over Westland. By his account, he told Charles Powell early in the struggle that it was like when Tebbit was trying to 'fix the competition' during the row over the new naval frigates.[23] In Powell's version, when he encountered Heseltine sitting outside the Cabinet Office, he said: 'She's not going to beat me on this one.'[24] So Powell prepared her for battle.

On 29 November 1985, two separate but closely related meetings took place in London, both organized by Heseltine and held at the MOD. One was of the European companies and their bid's bankers, Lloyds Merchant Bank; the other was of the National Armaments Directors (NADs) of the four countries involved, previously obscure functionaries whom Heseltine now decided to mobilize on behalf of his European idea. Although the meetings concerned the future of Westland, no one from the company was present. What Heseltine brilliantly, if precariously, cobbled together at speed was an agreement for a European bid for Westland, combined with an understanding among the NADs by which European governments would buy helicopters only from European companies. If this were to stand, a European defence cartel would be established and the Sikorsky bid would have no chance.

Cuckney had for some time been worried by disagreement over Westland between the MOD and Brittan's DTI. Well connected, and supported by Gordon Reece's advice, he decided: 'The monkeys are squabbling. I must go to the organ grinder' in No. 10.[25] Before the Heseltine meetings had even taken place, Charles Powell reported to Mrs Thatcher that Cuckney felt uneasy about what was going on, worrying that Sikorsky might 'take umbrage and withdraw their bid, while the European offer goes the way of the Cheshire cat's smile'.[26] After the meetings, Cuckney felt double-crossed: 'Heseltine hadn't explained to me *why* he was attracted to the European bid.'[27] With the Defence Secretary playing like a god with the future of his company, Cuckney appealed to a higher deity. He wanted Mrs Thatcher on his side.

Whitehall battle was joined. John MacGregor, the Chief Secretary to the Treasury, informed Heseltine he was disturbed by the recommendations of the NADs: 'Such a departure from our policy of competition would be questionable in any circumstances.' It had 'placed Westland in an impossible position'.[28] Leon Brittan agreed with this, and Mrs Thatcher supported him. Her Policy Unit summed it up in the way best calculated to rouse her ire against Heseltine, comparing it to Harold Wilson's reconstruction of the motor industry in the 1960s.

> Michael Heseltine is proposing that a Conservative Government should intervene to kill a private sector rescue of Westlands – which amazingly costs the Government nothing – in order to promote a European deal which will reduce competition and result in the stripping of Westlands, such that it will only survive long term with state subsidy. This surely isn't on.[29]

Mrs Thatcher strongly agreed.

As the government geared up to settle the matter collectively, Heseltine rushed round trying to inject new elements into his European bid. On 5 December came a note from Heseltine 'revealing that he has just (?) discovered that BAe would be ready to join a European consortium, thus making it less "foreign"' – as Charles Powell put it with sarcastic quotation marks.[30] When ministers met to discuss the matter next day, Heseltine presented the issue as whether Westland should come under 'foreign control' (that is, Sikorsky) or be rescued by a European consortium 'ready to return control to United Kingdom hands at any time',[31] which was a rather fanciful way of putting it. Mrs Thatcher, chairing the meeting, said that a 'clear majority' was 'ready to decide there and then that the Government should reject the recommendation from the National Armaments Directors',[32] but a minority 'strongly opposed' this view. The minority included Geoffrey Howe and Norman Tebbit, who could see merit in the European bid, and did not agree with Mrs Thatcher's demand that the meeting rule out the NADs' recommendation at once. Tebbit later claimed that his motive in supporting delay was to 'give Michael enough rope to hang himself', but Mrs Thatcher herself was not aware of this reasoning and held the incident against him. 'She thought Tebbit was a traitor,' recalled Heseltine, 'and was very rude to him.'[33] Given the differing views, Mrs Thatcher decided, with an ill grace, not to insist on a decision about the NADs' recommendation that day, but to refer it to a full meeting of E Committee on Monday. John Cuckney and his colleagues were invited by Mrs Thatcher to attend to explain their views, a highly unusual device which, she believed, would assist his cause. Tension now ran high.

'The struggle has continued over the weekend,' Charles Powell minuted his boss.[34] Heseltine was firing off new ideas – a French promise for sub-contracts, a deal about money in the space programme – to sweeten the European bid. Powell believed that Leon Brittan was not countering him robustly: 'In the face of all this figure skating, DTI look positively flat-footed.'[35] The latest was that the Westland deadline 'is not quite so dead as was alleged', and might now not come until shortly before Christ-mas,[36] a delay which would weaken Brittan and strengthen Heseltine by giving him more time to firm up and lobby for his rushed European bid. Knowing that some ministers were sympathetic, the Defence Secretary might now try to refer the matter to full Cabinet. Powell, who kept in close touch with Cuckney, was driving the DTI to do the same, because a decision had to be made and he was confident that Mrs Thatcher could prevail.

Seen from Heseltine's office, this ever greater No. 10 engagement was a provocation. Richard Mottram, Heseltine's private secretary,* believed that the problem of Westland was 'solvable so long as No. 10 acted for the proper conduct of government rather than taking a highly partisan view . . . Unfortunately, they decided they'd make it a big issue.'[37] It was particularly noticeable that Powell, who felt that Westland came within the defence aspect of his remit, had, in his own words, 'seized' the sub-ject.[38] Despite his seniority as principal private secretary, Nigel Wicks was 'squeezed out',[39] as was the new Treasury private secretary, David Nor-grove, who might have been expected to cover this territory. Powell's self-justification was that Wicks 'was a bit timid' and 'someone had to do it'. He felt No. 10 was 'so isolated'. Mrs Thatcher 'wanted a robust counter-offensive and Leon Brittan was bad at this'.[40]† Powell was an effective – perhaps too effective – projection of his principal's combative personality, bringing out the conflict between Prime Minister and Defence Secretary inherent not only in their views but in their characters. In the past, meeting by chance in the Lobby of the House, Mrs Thatcher had once remarked to Heseltine: 'You must realize, Michael, you and I are quite similar people.'[41] Both knew what they wanted and, in Heseltine's words, 'drove from the front to get it'. Her crisp analysis helps explain the Westland debacle. A collision between these two was becoming almost inevitable. Charles Powell believed that Heseltine, seeing no further advancement for himself under Mrs Thatcher by conventional means, had 'made up his mind early: it was win or leave'.[42] The same 'win or leave' mentality well describes Mrs Thatcher – and she had absolutely no inten-tion of leaving.

---

* Richard Mottram (1946–), educated King Edward VI Camp Hill School, Birmingham and University of Keele; private secretary to Secretary of State for Defence, 1982–6; Permanent Secretary, Office of Public Service and Science, 1992–5; MOD, 1995–8; Department of the Environment, Transport and the Regions, 1998–2002; Department for Work and Pensions, 2002–5; Intelligence, Security and Resilience, 2005–7; knighted, 1998.
† The alternative view, held by some inside the No. 10 private office, was that Powell was becoming 'a bit of an empire-builder' (Correspondence with David Willetts).

The E Committee meeting of 9 December did not go as well for Mrs Thatcher as she had hoped, even though Cuckney, who was present for the first half of the meeting, explained the threat to market confidence of delay (Westland's terrible accounts, showing losses of £98 million, were due to be published on Wednesday 11 December). He was considered to have performed well, but ministers were irritated that he was there at all. They felt Mrs Thatcher was putting them under undue pressure, and they therefore inclined to sympathize with Heseltine. As Nigel Lawson put it, 'While the balance of argument was clearly against Michael, sentiment was with him.'[43] This meeting took place only a few days after the one (see Chapter 13) in which Mrs Thatcher had found herself isolated among colleagues over ERM entry: there was a lack of friendly feeling. Cuckney was 'very impressed by the copious notes she took in large writing on foolscap',[44] but felt that things deteriorated when there started to be a disagreement. 'It was rather like a battalion commander finding a squabble between company commanders. She got a bit rattled by it.'[45] There was no groundswell of support for the European bid, but it was considered important that the bid have time to be put together and presented to Westland. The board could then decide whether to recommend the bid to shareholders by 4 p.m. that Friday (13 December), and should be left alone to take its own view. If the board did not endorse the European bid, ministers would reject the NADs' recommendation, leaving the way clear for Sikorsky. Heseltine did not dissent but, in a rather desperate gamble, asked for a special meeting after the Westland board decision on the Friday afternoon, when ministers were normally scattered across the country. His request was based on his belief in his own persuasive powers once the European bid was better developed. As on 6 December, Mrs Thatcher had to settle for compromise, rather than a final decision at once.

It was the results of these two meetings which enabled Heseltine later to say that 'I suppose she was pretty unnerved by the fact that she'd lost to me twice with colleagues.'[46] She had not lost – on both occasions she was in a clear majority – but she was certainly given pause. She deemed it more prudent not to force the issue. The following day, Westland shares were suspended, pending announcement of a deal.

Without realizing it at the time, ministers departed with different views of what exactly had been agreed about the next steps – an issue that would come to assume great significance. Heseltine 'believed (or affected to believe)'[47] – as Robert Armstrong put it – that a further meeting of the committee had been promised. Mrs Thatcher believed that a meeting had merely been provided for if the circumstances surrounding the European bid had changed sufficiently to warrant a further discussion. Initially, the

Cabinet Office had begun to ring round, lining ministers up for a meeting on Friday the 13th, but then pulled the plug. When Heseltine professed outrage, Mrs Thatcher claimed that the ring-round had been only to check availability rather than set a definite meeting. But it was her office that had stopped the ring-round, so suspicion lingered. Heseltine raised the matter at Cabinet on Thursday 12 December, and the difference of opinion about the ring-round was pointed out. According to Robert Armstrong's scribbled note of proceedings, out of which formal Cabinet minutes were later composed, Heseltine then said, 'Can I say what I have to?', and Mrs Thatcher replied, 'You might give notice,'[48] effectively ruling him out of order. According to Heseltine, he made a protest at this point, although none is recorded in Armstrong's contemporaneous note. Robert Armstrong's failure to record in the official minutes the protest which Heseltine believed he had made would be later added to his charge-sheet against Mrs Thatcher's corruption of Cabinet government. 'There was some force in Heseltine's claim that there wasn't a full Cabinet discussion,' Leon Brittan recalled. 'I thought he had the right to refer it to the Cabinet.'[49]

Heseltine had begun to attribute overwhelming importance to the Westland issue. On the assumption (or at least in the hope) that a meeting would take place on the 13th, he had already sent a passionate last-minute appeal – without informing Leon Brittan – to his three European counterparts, explicitly urging that they should help him go against the Sikorsky bid: 'Can we let it be said that in so fundamental a matter we are unable to match such resolve [meaning the resolve of Sikorsky]?'[50] He also obtained a letter offering GEC's financial support from his former Cabinet colleague and anti-Thatcherite Jim Prior, now the company's chairman, for the European bid. GEC's involvement added to the notion that the European bid was 'British'. The idea was to get a European bid in, higher than Sikorsky's, in time to impress colleagues on Friday. Heseltine could see, from everything Cuckney had said, that it was highly unlikely that the Westland board could be persuaded to accept the European bid on Friday. But he felt that if Cabinet colleagues were convinced of the bid, it would be clear that Westland's future contracts would be assured only by the European option. Then shareholders might be persuaded to reject the board's likely Sikorsky recommendation. And of course, if the Cabinet came down on Heseltine's European side, this would be a mighty defeat for Mrs Thatcher. Heseltine was also playing for time: if it had been clear that ministers had already rejected the European bid then it would have stood almost no chance with Westland shareholders. In Heseltine's mind, 'If I had accepted the cancellation of the meeting, I would have been finished.'[51] Brittan thought this view was correct: 'It was the only thing he had.'[52]

Charles Powell obtained a copy of a Cabinet Office memo which complained that at the Cabinet meeting of 12 December Heseltine had 'sought . . . to re-open' the E meeting of 9 December by protesting about the 'cancelled' meeting of 13 December. The officials said that the meeting had not been cancelled: it had never been arranged.[53] He showed it to Mrs Thatcher: 'Although not strictly for your eyes, you might like to glance at this helpful account of the lengths to which MOD are going.'[54] He urged her to press on: 'Agree that we should have no inhibition about going public on our rejection of the NADs' recommendation after 4 p.m. on Friday?' Mrs Thatcher wrote 'Agreed,' but then thought better of it and wrote words that cleaved more closely to the formally correct answer: 'I think the decision hinges on whether the European deal is acceptable to Westlands.'[55] The desire for a fight with Heseltine and the desire to observe the proprieties clashed in her mind.

On the day of the Westland board vote, John Cuckney rang Charles Powell just before the meeting. He warned that, if the board voted for the Sikorsky bid, he would then write Mrs Thatcher a letter complaining about 'the hostile and harmful actions taken against them by the Ministry of Defence'.[56] Cuckney said he had 'detailed evidence of disgraceful behaviour by the Ministry of Defence . . . including delayed payments, cancelled or postponed orders and instructions to contracts staff at the Ministry of Defence to treat Westlands as a company about to go into receivership'.[57] After the board meeting, Cuckney immediately informed Powell that it had decided not to recommend the European bid to shareholders. A version of his original letter, toned down at Powell's urging, arrived for Mrs Thatcher. It spoke of several attempts by the MOD (Heseltine was not named) to 'block a solution to Westlands problems' and asked that 'no UK Government statement is made to the effect that Her Majesty's Government will never purchase the Black Hawk',[58] since to do so would be inconsistent with the policy of full and fair competition.

So ended the first full week of more or less explicit hostilities. Heseltine was, on balance, losing. It was still not impossible, however, that the European bid, constantly topped up with new money, promises and implied understandings, might ultimately prevail with the Westland shareholders. And it was clear that Mrs Thatcher had allowed herself to be dragged into something disagreeable. Her private office – really Charles Powell – increasingly took control of the issue because it was not going well in the hands of the DTI. This behaviour was understandable, but it was likely that Mrs Thatcher would be touched with pitch as the fight got nastier. She was as tough as anyone in politics, but not a good Machiavellian.

The dispute over the meeting which Heseltine accused her of cancelling

was a case in point. It was almost certainly not true that she had deliberately misled Heseltine about the meeting, but it was the case that Nigel
Wicks, her principal private secretary, had quickly countermanded Cabinet Office officials who had begun to ring round to make provisional
arrangements for setting one up.[59] Wicks had been doing her will, which
was to make the meeting as unlikely as possible. She would have done
better to have made sure that Heseltine could have his meeting – and make
equally sure that he would not prevail in it. In Heseltine's view, her behaviour over the meeting ensured that 'the disaster was cast in steel.'[60]

By this time, the press was excited about the Westland affair, and the disagreements between ministers were exposed to the public. 'This has been
one of the most extraordinary episodes in British government in recent
years,' wrote Geoffrey Smith in *The Times*. 'The public battle that has
raged between ministers was the sort of thing that one expects with American administrations, but not with British governments.'[61] Leon Brittan
made a statement to the Commons on Monday 16 December, explaining
government policy. The government was not taking sides over bids for
Westland, he said, and was leaving matters to the market. Sitting on the
front bench with him, Heseltine was seen to shake his head in
disagreement.

On Wednesday 18 December, Mrs Thatcher summoned an informal
meeting at the flat in Downing Street with the Chief Whip John Wakeham,
Whitelaw, Brittan, Robert Armstrong and Bernard Ingham. In assembling
this small group, she was probably trying to learn from her mistake of the
ERM meeting the previous month. Although, in this case, she did not face
comparable isolation, she needed to have the wiliest minds in government
assisting her. Feeling that the standing of the entire government was
threatened, she wanted to find a way of stopping Heseltine in his tracks.
She believed that he was consciously and clearly breaking collective Cabinet responsibility.

At the start of the meeting, the politicians met alone, with the officials
kept on hand. Brittan, who, of those present, was suffering most from the
row, suggested that Mrs Thatcher should see Heseltine and order him to
stop his campaign. Although no one said it in so many words, this was
not going to happen, because the relationship between Mrs Thatcher and
Heseltine was simply too poor.[62] Another way of making the demarche to
Heseltine which Brittan wanted was for Mrs Thatcher to write him a letter. Wakeham felt this was a bad idea, because 'I wanted to steer the ship
into calmer waters,'[63] but did not think it was his place to say so. Instead
he suggested, 'Such a letter is bound to leak, so let's get the drafting exactly

right.'[64] Robert Armstrong was brought in. His draft, which survives, is short and blunt. 'You were on the front bench in the House yesterday when I made clear the Government's position concerning the future of Westlands,' he had Mrs Thatcher writing, 'namely that it is a matter for the company to decide.' This had been agreed, the draft went on, at E Committee on 9 December. An ultimatum followed: 'In this situation no Minister should use his position to promote one commercial option in preference to another – so long as he remains in government.'[65]

Once the draft was complete, Mrs Thatcher still could not decide whether the letter should be sent. Wakeham suggested that she send for Ingham for his opinion. On reading the draft, Ingham said: 'I think it's weak.' 'Weak!' exclaimed Mrs Thatcher. 'What's strong?' 'Sacking him,' said Ingham. 'Are you saying that I should sack him?' 'No, I'm just saying what's strong.'[66] The press secretary's view was that, if Heseltine received such a letter, or were summoned by Mrs Thatcher to be told the same thing orally, 'he would just resign.'[67] Mrs Thatcher later recalled Ingham saying, 'The public aren't ready for it, and wouldn't understand it.'[68] Brittan, still angry with Ingham over what he believed had been his role in demoting him in the reshuffle, protested that this political discussion should not be taking place in the presence of a non-political civil servant, which Ingham was.[69] He disliked Ingham's 'excessive and baleful influence'.[70]* But Mrs Thatcher agreed with Ingham: 'I didn't like sacking a Minister unless it was absolutely clear . . . that there were reasonable circumstances to do it.'[71] Ingham was not expelled from the meeting, and the letter was not sent.

So nothing happened. To Bernard Ingham, here was an example of how Willie Whitelaw, for all his prestige as a fixer, was 'a lightweight': 'He did nothing about Westland. He should have said to Heseltine, "We're not having this." '[72] Curiously enough, Heseltine also believed that Whitelaw 'might help broker an acceptable outcome',[73] but his messages to Whitelaw went unanswered because Whitelaw was away playing golf.[74]† Looking back on it all when she came to write her memoirs, Mrs Thatcher said that the most justified criticism of her was not for bullying or provoking Heseltine too much but for holding back from disciplining him. Her counter self-justification took its cue from Ingham's argument about public reaction: 'I knew the politics of it.'[75] Heseltine, in other words, was too

---

* Brittan also believed that Ingham simply did not understand the issues involved in the Westland case: 'Behind the façade of a blunt Yorkshireman was a blunt Yorkshireman' (Interview with Lord Brittan of Spennithorne).

† In Charles Powell's view, the level of detail in the Westland affair was simply too great for Whitelaw to cope with (Interview with Lord Powell of Bayswater).

popular with the party in the country. The ground for his departure had not been prepared.

The Cabinet met the following day, the last meeting before Christmas. 'I need a line on Westlands/Cabinet by 11a.m.,' wrote a rather exasperated Ingham to Nigel Wicks. 'I can continue to play resignation/sacking away (unless you advise caution),' he went on, and he wrote a question on his note leaving a blank for Wicks to fill in: 'Is Mr Heseltine isolated in Cabinet? Answer: ?'[76]

The short answer to Ingham's question was now 'Yes'. Leon Brittan stated the government line and the latest news about the company, which was that the shareholders would now decide its future on 13 January. According to Robert Armstrong's contemporaneous notes, Mrs Thatcher, supporting Brittan, said, 'No Minister . . . is authorised to lobby for one side or the other, because that goes against our decision.'[77] Then, as a challenge to Heseltine, she added, 'Is that clear? Is that accepted?' Heseltine said that, as minister, he would have to answer questions for both bids about what he called the government 'workload' on the company. 'It must not be done in any way wh: favours one bid rather than another,' Armstrong noted Mrs Thatcher saying, and she repeated similar words when Heseltine argued for the maximum margin of discretion. Nigel Lawson weighed in on her side, and so did Willie Whitelaw, who ended the discussion. The Prime Minister had to answer questions in the House that day, Whitelaw said. Turning to her, he went on, 'When you state the policy again, you must be speaking with united voice in Cabinet . . . Hope we can stick to that. Hope Cab. can agree you are speaking for whole Govt.' 'Is that confirmed?' Mrs Thatcher asked the assembled company. '<u>Cab</u>: Confirmed' is how Armstrong recorded the conclusion of the meeting. Whatever Heseltine's private thoughts, he acquiesced in the unanimity.

At Prime Minister's Questions that afternoon, Neil Kinnock sought to exploit the obvious differences between Heseltine and Mrs Thatcher. She was able to respond simply that the future of Westland was 'a matter for the company to decide . . . That is the position, and it was reaffirmed by the Cabinet this morning.'[78] The BBC that night reported this as a 'snub' for Heseltine. In private, Heseltine complained to friends of his 'humiliation' in Cabinet.[79]

Heseltine did not let up. If anything, he redoubled his campaign. He talked frequently to newspaper editors. Clive Whitmore, his Permanent Secretary, recalled him being 'always on the phone lobbying'.[80] Mrs Thatcher regarded him as a 'Svengali or Rasputin' attempting to threaten companies like BAe and GEC with the loss of MOD contracts if they did not back the European bid: it was 'real strong-arm stuff'.[81] She thought he saw himself as 'a knight in shining armour'.[82] She did not mean the phrase as a compliment.

Heseltine also sought to overthrow the Cabinet consensus on government neutrality over the bids for Westland. On 23 December, he wrote to Mrs Thatcher about what he said was a 'significant development'[83] – the latest version (20 December) of the European offer. He said he had not publicly expressed any 'personal preference' since the Cabinet meeting the previous week ('Said 6 Sea-kings [that is, the order for six Sea King helicopters] would only go to European offer on Sunday radio', scribbled Mrs Thatcher crossly). But now he believed that there were wider policy issues at stake which, 'in my view, would warrant further collective discussion'. The government would be criticized for 'having no preference' between what he called 'a British-led offer [his imaginative term for the European bid] and a US-led one'. His latest manoeuvre was to seize upon the Italian company Fiat, which was part of the Sikorsky bid, because Fiat was partially owned by Libya. Given the hostility of the Libyan leader, Colonel Gaddafi, there was a 'possible Libyan involvement' and the danger of 'grave embarrassment' to the government and to the national interest, he alleged.* He had asked the Joint Intelligence Committee (JIC) to look at this, he told her. The government should indicate, Heseltine concluded, that 'subject to the commercial interests of the parties being protected, it would prefer a British/European solution'.[84]

In an accompanying personal note to Mrs Thatcher which, he emphasized, he was not copying to colleagues, Heseltine reminded her that, in October, Leon Brittan had favoured a European solution. Referring to his last sentence about how the government should now back the European bid, he wrote, 'I know that [it] . . . will not be an easy one for you. I know also that you will understand the depth of my convictions in this matter.'[85] She did indeed understand, not least because Heseltine allies had leaked the points in his letter the previous weekend. They had also publicly promoted the suggestion that in no circumstances would the MOD buy Black Hawk helicopters. This was a way of saying that the Sikorsky bid would be a dead end for shareholders. On Christmas Eve, a letter was sent by the MOD to Lloyds, the merchant bank of the European consortium,

---

* The Libyan share of Fiat was 14 per cent, and the Fiat share of the Sikorsky Westland offer was 14.9 per cent. Fiat also provided lots of other defence products for Britain without any complaint from the government. So Heseltine was laying it on a bit thick.

stating that Westland would not be able to be part of any European heli-copter project if it went ahead with manufacturing Black Hawks, for which MOD had neither the need nor the money.

So strong, indeed, were the depths of Heseltine's convictions that he sought to sway John Cuckney directly. One of his greatest difficulties throughout had been that the chairman of the company whose future he was trying to decide did not like what he was doing. In defiance of the non-intervention agreed by the Cabinet on 19 December, Heseltine called Cuckney at home in Kent with talk of a 'programme' which would per-suade him to back the European bid.* Cuckney told him that he could not leave home because he was tending to his wife, who was seriously ill, so Heseltine said he would bring down a team to present the proposals. 'He angered me,' Cuckney recalled. 'It was not an attractive development. He was slightly insensitive.'[86] Reluctant to see Heseltine, he rang his lawyers, who advised against the meeting since Heseltine was 'trying to bounce you'.[87] The meeting did not take place. Cuckney told Heseltine on Christmas Eve that 'I have no power to do as you ask.'[88]

None of the participants in the Westland saga passed a very happy Christ-mas, with the likely exception of Gordon Reece, who knew that he was about to receive, at Mrs Thatcher's behest, the knighthood of which he had felt cheated in the previous Parliament (see Volume I, p. 410). He spent Christmas lunch at Chequers with her and Denis and the other guests.†

Michael Heseltine, with his usual flair for the dramatic, saw the chance to make a point. On Boxing Day, Chris Moncrieff,‡ the political editor of the Press Association, got a call from the Defence Secretary: 'Have you heard about my family holiday in Nepal? Well, I'm not going on it.' 'That's a story,' said Moncrieff. 'You've got to get it from my press office, not me,' said Heseltine. Farcically, when Moncrieff did as Heseltine had asked, the press secretary refused to check the story with Heseltine on the grounds that he should not disturb a Cabinet minister on Boxing Day. In the end, Heseltine had to arrange to be disturbed by his own press secretary, so that the story could get out.[89] He wanted it known as early as possible that he was staying at home to fight.

---

* This included a sweetener about German interest in the EH101 helicopter project in which Westland had been struggling with Italy and a threat that a Sikorsky-owned Westland would be shut out of Europe.

† Because of the importance of being seen to be neutral, Mrs Thatcher had no other direct contact with Reece throughout the Westland affair. Her informal conduit for messages from Reece was Woodrow Wyatt.

‡ Chris Moncrieff (1931–), political editor, the Press Association, 1980–94.

With the Westland shareholders' decision expected on 13 January, both sides spent the Christmas season preparing for a showdown. The struggle was now fought out through a series of letters. The first came from Cuckney, who was seeking to defuse a potentially powerful argument against the Sikorsky bid. Heseltine's camp claimed that, were a non-European entity to hold even a minority stake in the company, Westland would no longer be considered 'European' and would thus be shut out of the European market. Writing to Mrs Thatcher by prearrangement with Powell, Cuckney wanted an assurance that this would not be the case.[90] Mrs Thatcher, of course, obliged and the next day the draft reply to Cuckney, written by Charles Powell, reached Heseltine's office for comment. In short order, Downing Street then received a letter from the Attorney-General's office, giving the opinion of the Solicitor-General,* Sir Patrick Mayhew.† It warned Mrs Thatcher that the government was 'under a duty not to withhold any information it knows to be relevant'[91] and would be 'at serious risk' if it did not convey 'the fact that there are indications from European governments and companies that they take the view that a number of projects in which Westland are currently expecting to participate in co-operation with other European countries may be lost to Westland if the Sikorsky offer is accepted'. Mrs Thatcher put a loop and an exclamation mark linking the word 'fact' with the word 'indications'.

This letter, which infuriated Mrs Thatcher, had very obviously been inspired by Heseltine. Heseltine and Patrick Mayhew were old friends, going back to Oxford days. The Defence Secretary, seeking to trump Mrs Thatcher's proposed response to Cuckney, had rushed the Solicitor-General into it. Mayhew's letter was more a favour to a friend than a considered document that was strictly necessary from a legal point of view. The use of the Law Officers in government was (and is still) a sensitive issue because of the distinction between law and politics. Under the British system, this conflict is internalized: the Law Officers are politicians but, in their capacity of giving legal advice to government, they are not allowed to behave politically. By the same token, ministers are not supposed to abuse Law Officers' advice for political purposes or ever to disclose it – even its existence – without the agreement of the officers. Paradoxically, therefore,

---

* Mayhew's superior, the Attorney-General Sir Michael Havers, was absent because of illness.
† Sir Patrick Mayhew (1929–), educated Tonbridge and Balliol College, Oxford; Conservative MP for Royal Tunbridge Wells, February 1974–83; for Tunbridge Wells, 1983–97; Solicitor-General, 1983–7; Attorney-General, 1987–92; Secretary of State for Northern Ireland, 1992–7; knighted, 1983; created Lord Mayhew of Twysden, 1997; retired from the House of Lords, 2015.

the Law Officers' advice can be a potent political weapon because its apparent objectivity makes it difficult to challenge. Heseltine knew that Mrs Thatcher would have to go carefully in the face of such advice.

In her reply to Cuckney on New Year's Day, Mrs Thatcher followed Mayhew's legal advice. But she also confirmed that as long as Westland continued in the UK, the government would continue to regard it as a British – and therefore as a European – company: 'The Government would wish to see Westland play a full part in existing and future European collaborative projects.'[92] It would make sure that Westland was not discriminated against. Two days later, Heseltine fought back through yet another exchange of correspondence. Replying to a letter which he had himself inspired – indeed dictated to its sender by telephone – Heseltine wrote to David Horne of Lloyds Merchant Bank, which was acting for the European bid. In the guise of factual advice to Lloyds, he set out arguments which would sway the shareholders against the Sikorsky bid. He put in all the points which he had wanted Mrs Thatcher to include in her reply to Cuckney, but which she had not. 'The Government . . . has no intention of procuring the Black Hawk,' he wrote.[93] Mrs Thatcher was not shown the reply to Horne before Heseltine sent it. It was subsequently leaked from the MOD to *The Times*.

Although the government remained formally neutral about who should buy Westland, all the energies of both camps – Heseltine and 10 Downing Street – were now expended on fighting for one side or the other.

There is no evidence, as has sometimes been suggested, that Mrs Thatcher came under any US government pressure to support the Sikorsky bid. Nor did she have a strong personal opinion of the merits of the bids, although she certainly did dislike Heseltine's corporatist concoction. She was fired up for other reasons. As Powell put it, 'She did not want Sikorsky *per se*. She wanted a board solution [as opposed to a government-sponsored one] and one which would guarantee her triumph over Heseltine.'[94]

Powell was effectively in sole charge of the campaign to make sure she succeeded. His next move, however, came directly at the behest of Mrs Thatcher, who had become aware that Heseltine's recent letter to David Horne contained a factual mistake. As Powell recalled, 'I sat down with her at Chequers and she said, "We must make sure a Law Officer knows this." She then instructed me to contact Paddy Mayhew.'[95] Revenge was about to be executed. As Powell put it, 'Heseltine tried to deploy the Law Officers and got it right back between the eyes.'[96] Mrs Thatcher was now directly involved in a potentially dangerous game of retaliation. On 4 January 1986, Powell reported to Mrs Thatcher that he had got Brittan to speak to the Solicitor-General, who had not previously seen Heseltine's letter to David Horne. Having now read it, Patrick Mayhew had concluded that – in a phrase that was to become famous – 'it contained a material inaccuracy'.[97] Revealing irritation with what he saw as the Industry Secretary's feebleness, Powell went on,

> Since Mr Brittan does not appear to have done so, I am proposing to suggest to the Solicitor that he should write to Mr Heseltine to say that he has read a copy of his letter to Lloyds Bank International in the *Times* [where it had been published]; that he regrets that it was not cleared with him in advance; that it contains a material inaccuracy; that Mr Heseltine ought to issue a letter of correction.

Heseltine should also be made to give his letter to the press since he had done the same with his letter to Horne, Powell added. He then got in touch directly with Mayhew and 'told him', as he himself put it, 'what was expected of him'.[98] It cannot have been welcome to Mayhew, who did not rush to respond, but he made no objection.

The following day, a Sunday, Mrs Thatcher met Whitelaw and Wakeham at Chequers for a discussion of how to deal with Heseltine. She told them that the Solicitor-General was likely to object to what appeared in Heseltine's letter to Horne, though she did not say by what means. They agreed that Heseltine should be brought to order at the next Cabinet meeting on Thursday 9 January. She still did not want to sack him. 'I don't want to look petty,' she told Woodrow Wyatt on the telephone that evening.[99]* She and her colleagues were not even trying to engineer his resignation – though they realized it was a strong possibility that he would resign and therefore designated the Scottish Secretary, George Younger, as his replacement if one were needed. They were trying to devise a way of forcing Heseltine into line.

In the late morning of Monday 6 January, the Solicitor-General sent his letter to Michael Heseltine, very late in the day if it was to fulfil its declared

---

* Wyatt, who wrote columns for the *News of the World* and *The Times*, liked to act as an informal intermediary between Mrs Thatcher and Rupert Murdoch, who owned both papers. He was close to Mrs Thatcher and defended and interpreted her to his readers. He used to telephone her most Sundays and she usually took his calls. From 1985, he kept journals. When these were published, on his instructions, after his death in 1997, they were widely attacked and their reliability was questioned. Most of this anger, however, stemmed from the fact that Wyatt had broken confidences. Although one should allow for the inaccuracy and self-serving qualities endemic in the diary form, his diaries are a good source for the 'off duty' remarks and attitudes of many of the leading figures of the age, including Mrs Thatcher. They often reveal her private reactions to public events when she considered herself among friends.

purpose of informing the Westland board in time for their meeting that afternoon. The previous day, Mayhew had telephoned Heseltine to warn him of this approach: in his dealings throughout the affair, he was friendlier to Heseltine than to Mrs Thatcher, so much so that he did little more than go through the motions in rebuking the Defence Secretary. Although it was cautious and friendly in tone, however, his letter did make the point which Powell had wanted about 'material inaccuracies' in the letter to Horne. Heseltine had been mistaken in saying, said Mayhew, that *all* the companies in the European bid had stated that a Westland link with Sikorsky would rule out Westland participation in a European battlefield helicopter. Two had; one (the Italians) hadn't – hardly an earth-shattering point. Since the letter to Horne might be relied upon by the Westland board and shareholders in arriving at their decision, 'I therefore advise you that you should write again to Mr Horne correcting these inaccuracies.'[100] Passing this on to Mrs Thatcher, Charles Powell wrote on it: 'Very satisfactory'. No one pretended that this letter offered a finely tuned piece of legal advice. Like the first, this second Mayhew letter had been transparently inspired by ministers in their war with one another. This time the conflict intensified further. As Leon Brittan recalled, 'She and her entourage were extremely keen it be in the public domain.'[101] In a breach of accepted practice, the Law Officer's letter was leaked to the press. Colette Bowe, Brittan's press officer,* did this by reading part of its contents over the telephone just after 2 p.m. that day to Chris Moncrieff of the Press Association.

Writing as fast as he could that afternoon to Patrick Mayhew (to whom he had already spoken on the telephone), Heseltine complained about the leak, which he felt greatly exaggerated the criticism in Mayhew's letter. The fact of the leak made him feel free to make public his version of the full background. Even Cuckney, though pleased by the content of the Solicitor-General's letter, thought there was 'no business reason' which made the leak necessary – it was 'just anti-Heseltine'.[102]

Not only was the leak improper in itself: it was also partial – only the bit which was damaging to Heseltine, rather than the whole letter, had been read to Chris Moncrieff. 'It was', recalled Moncrieff, 'a major act of deception.'[103] It also – not surprisingly – enraged Mayhew. 'I was furious,' he remembered. 'I had no interest in the outcome of the row, but substantial interest in Law Officers not being perceived to be used for tendentious

* Colette Bowe (1946–), educated Notre Dame High School, Liverpool, Queen Mary College, University of London and LSE; director of information, DTI, 1984–7; chairman of Ofcom, 2009–14; created dame, 2014.

purposes.'[104] Since he had, in fact, allowed himself to be used twice in a week for tendentious purposes – first by Heseltine and then by Thatcher/Brittan – Mayhew must have been particularly irritated that his part in this had become visible. He immediately wrote sympathetically to Heseltine, to express his 'dismay' at the leak.* Mayhew directed his anger at those he presumed to be the culprits: 'I asked straightaway for an explanation from No. 10' since he knew that the DTI request for him to send the letter in the first place had come from Powell.[105] He threatened resignation. Mayhew was supported the next morning by the Attorney-General, Michael Havers, who was so annoyed by the leak that he came steaming back from sick leave and threatened privately to put the police into No. 10 to investigate it. Havers also wrote to Robert Armstrong demanding a formal leak inquiry.† This was a very dangerous development for Mrs Thatcher. The Law Officers were not normally front-rank figures, but if it could be proved that 10 Downing Street had been abusing their advice for political purposes, the Prime Minister's integrity would be at risk.

On Tuesday morning, the pro-Thatcher *Sun* ran the splash headline 'You Liar!' ('Tarzan gets rocket from top law man') in reference to Heseltine.[106]‡ Heseltine immediately sought – and was granted – leave from Michael Havers to sue the paper.§ He was moving inexorably to what he saw as higher moral ground.

Mrs Thatcher knew that she had to find a way to rein Heseltine in at the Cabinet meeting that Thursday. She studied her proposed speaking note on the subject of Westland, prepared by Brittan. In one of his characteristic glosses of material from ministers, Charles Powell described it in his covering note to her as 'a bit turgid and long-winded'.[107] Robert Armstrong worried about a 'needlessly provocative' passage telling Heseltine that he should not criticize John Cuckney: 'Heseltine is particularly enraged by Cuckney, and will rise to this sentence.'[108] But there was no

---

* Referring to additional material that Heseltine would have seen in drawing his conclusions, which he had not, Mayhew now gave Heseltine the freedom not to write the correction which he had demanded in his earlier letter. Heseltine seized upon this and promptly informed David Horne that no correction was required.

† Mayhew considered this 'very brave' of Havers, because he (Havers) wanted to be Lord Chancellor, and was risking this ambition by displeasing Mrs Thatcher. In fact, she gave Havers the job he wanted in June the following year. It probably would have looked too vindictive for her to have done otherwise. Charles Powell was less impressed: 'The biggest leaker was Havers – every lunch-time to his chums at the bar of the Garrick Club' (Interview with Lord Powell of Bayswater).

‡ It repeated the same headline on the other half of its front page referring to an explanation for a black eye given by the snooker player Alex 'Hurricane' Higgins.

§ The action was not pursued.

disagreement about the purpose of the Cabinet meeting. It was to make it clear to Heseltine that he must stop. Press cuttings were deployed: 'There's probably no paper which has been a more loyal supporter of this government than the *Sunday Telegraph* and it spoke last Sunday of a "National scandal . . . British Government . . . so pitifully divided". The affair "has brought ridicule on the government at home and abroad".' One simple sentence read: 'We cannot go on like this.'[109] This was no more than the truth. On one draft, Nigel Wicks wrote a list of which Cabinet ministers were to be lobbied by 'Willy' and which by 'Wakeham'. The preparation for the Cabinet meeting was intense. Bernard Ingham wrote to Mrs Thatcher: 'It will be important to move quickly on Westland. On the last occasion, the Lord President [Whitelaw] came out of Cabinet to brief me.'[110]

Even Ingham did not know just how quickly movement would be needed.

The Cabinet met as usual on Thursday 9 January, at 10 a.m. The Prime Minister set out the Westland situation and Brittan briefed colleagues on the coming Extraordinary General Meeting of the Westland shareholders. Robert Armstrong, as usual, scribbled, in his own version of shorthand, who said what in his Cabinet Secretary's notebook. Mrs Thatcher warned of 'great damage . . . just as things were getting better'.[111] 'We must restore standing of Govt,' she said, and asked everyone to observe collective responsibility and the conclusions of the previous Cabinet meeting before Christmas. At first, Heseltine was moderate in tone. He said that he had 'very little to add' and, in briefings on the Westland bids, would adopt 'an absolutely neutral stance'.

Disagreement did not seem inevitable. But Mrs Thatcher was keen to ensure no ambiguity about how questions on Westland should be now be handled by the government. She produced what Heseltine called 'a tatty piece of paper from her handbag'.[112] Given the sensitivity of the issue and the fact that it crossed departmental boundaries, she insisted that 'Answers to qu must be cleared through the Cabinet Office, so that they can be cleared with depts. concerned. That is what collective responsibility means.' Heseltine objected. He agreed he would not make any new statements, but he had to be able to answer questions himself about the European bid, since the answers depended on government defence policy. What, for example, if someone asked whether there was an MOD requirement for Black Hawk helicopters? If he were not allowed to answer, this would have the effect of favouring the Sikorsky bid. 'There are critical qus about procurement wh. have to be answered';[113] if answers had to be cleared, this could take twelve hours and would create uncertainty.

Norman Tebbit acted the role of candid friend to Heseltine. He had 'a great deal of personal sympathy' for the European bid, he said, but 'with reasonable good will' all ministers could stick to the same line. He warned Heseltine of 'pushing his luck too far . . . we have to be tolerant of each other.' Lawson, Geoffrey Howe and others also urged Heseltine to accept what Howe called the 'need for unity', but Heseltine would not let go. He persisted with variants on the theme of 'I don't intend to make further statements, but I must be able to reaffirm existing statements.'[114] Mrs Thatcher kept repeating her version of collective responsibility. At last she tried to end the debate, which was going nowhere: 'We reaffirm 19 Dec. Answers to be cleared through Cabinet Office.'* Heseltine said: 'There has been no coll. responsibility in the disc [discussion] of these matters. There has been a breakdown in the propriety of Cabinet discussions. I cannot accept the decision. I must therefore leave this Cabinet.'[115] With these words, at 11.05 a.m., he swept up his papers, rose from the table and walked out.

Watched by Charles Powell, who was sitting at the back of the Cabinet meeting, Heseltine turned sharp right out of the Cabinet Room and into the lavatory to 'comb his hair'.[116]† When he emerged, he walked out of the front door of No. 10 and was approached by a solitary waiting cameraman, who asked him what was happening. Heseltine said, 'I've resigned from the Cabinet, and I shall be making a full statement later on.'‡ Then he walked off, across the road to the Ministry of Defence. As he entered the office, his private secretary, Richard Mottram, who had naturally been expecting him much later in the morning, said: 'That's a bit quick.' 'I've resigned,' said Heseltine. Wondering, 'in my typical, civil servant way', whether this was really, formally, irretrievably so, Mottram said, 'Does anyone know?' 'Yes,' said Heseltine, 'I told the cameraman on the door.'[117] Mottram had worried that Heseltine was gearing up for resignation, and had warned Charles Powell, with whom he had good relations, but it had never occurred to him that this would happen in the middle of a Cabinet meeting. He did not believe that it had occurred to Heseltine either.

---

* It has been suggested, for example by John Campbell (Campbell, *Margaret Thatcher: The Iron Lady*, p. 488) that it was Nicholas Ridley, the Transport Secretary, who tipped Heseltine over the edge, having been 'primed' to push the point about the Cabinet Office clearance of all statements. The evidence of Armstrong's notebook – the only full record – does not support this, but Ridley, in his own memoirs (Nicholas Ridley, *My Style of Government: The Thatcher Years*, Hutchinson, 1991, p. 49), says he pressed Heseltine three times to agree to the clearance procedure.
† Heseltine denied this (Interview with Lord Heseltine).
‡ Clive Whitmore, Heseltine's Permanent Secretary, dined with him the night before, and formed no sense that he was about to resign. He wondered whether, if no cameraman had been outside in Downing Street, Heseltine would have resigned at all. (Interview with Sir Clive Whitmore.)

Heseltine privately agreed with this judgment. He resigned on the spur of the moment, he recalled, 'because of what the No. 10 machine would have done to me if I had accepted this humiliation'. Resignation was not in his best interests: 'It is very likely that I would have been Prime Minister if I hadn't resigned: but I'd never have faced myself.'[118] He also thought that Mrs Thatcher 'had not planned for or expected me to walk out of the Cabinet. Nor had I! I don't believe she wanted me to go.'[119]

Meanwhile, back in Downing Street, there was that mixture of consternation and suppressed merriment which politicians feel when something damaging and dramatic suddenly happens. Some thought that Heseltine had not resigned, but had merely staged an angry walk-out. Some even thought he might walk back in. Robert Armstrong was despatched to find out if he was still in the building, and returned to report privily to Mrs Thatcher that he had left and spoken to the media outside. Mrs Thatcher adjourned the Cabinet meeting for half an hour. By her own account, she was one of the few people not surprised by what had happened: 'I knew he was going to resign.'[120] She did not mean by this that she had known for a fact that he would resign at the meeting. She meant rather that resignation was the logical outcome of Heseltine's dramatically uncompromising stance. She had not expected it at that moment, but she had prepared for it, even hoped for it. The meeting had, as Charles Powell recalled, 'been intended to be decisive'.[121] She did not much mind that it had been so excitingly so. As soon as she understood what had happened, she had a private word with George Younger, and offered him the Defence portfolio, which he accepted,* and she replaced him at the Scottish Office with Malcolm Rifkind. She then returned to the Cabinet Room to introduce Younger in his new role. The remaining business of the Cabinet meeting then continued.

That afternoon, Heseltine made a resignation statement so long that some accused him of having prepared it before he walked out. He irritated MPs and former ministerial colleagues by speaking from the department from which he had just resigned rather than waiting, as is customary, to explain his departure to the House of Commons. At the same time, he used the MOD's own telegraphic network to tell European defence ministers that he would continue to work for the European consortium.

In his statement, Heseltine gave a narrative which was very damaging to Mrs Thatcher. He complained of 'ad hoc' meetings organized by the

---

* The private office also had to get immediate consent to the appointment from the Queen, who was at Sandringham (Correspondence with Lord Armstrong of Ilminster).

Prime Minister to get round colleagues and 'close off the European option'. He said that minutes of the Cabinet on 12 December had been circulated without containing any reference to the protest he said he had made about a lack of a chance to meet to discuss the European option. He protested at the leak of the Solicitor-General's letter, and about its content ('My answer needed no correction'). He complained that Leon Brittan, meeting Sir Raymond Lygo, the managing director of BAe, had tried to interfere with the bid process by warning Lygo to sever his company's link with the European consortium. Finally, he explained how, at that morning's Cabinet, he had not felt able to abandon assurances he had already given in relation to the European bid. He could not accept the constraint of the silence demanded of him. Hence his action: 'if the basis of trust between the Prime Minister and her Defence Secretary no longer exists, there is no place for me with honour in such a Cabinet.' Heseltine successfully wrung the occasion for every drop of drama it possessed and the airwaves contained nothing else.*

Mrs Thatcher was not displeased with the resignation itself. 'At last we shall get some decisions taken,' she said to Ingham.[122] But she was wilfully blind to the effects of what had happened. When Woodrow Wyatt rang her later in the day to discuss the debacle, she told him that Brittan, not she, would deal with its public presentation: 'I'm not going to speak about it on Monday in the House. Why should I? Just because a Minister resigns.'[123] This was an understandable expression of exasperation. She was probably right that most Conservative opinion thought Heseltine had gone too far over such a minor issue. He had badly overplayed his hand. What she failed to see, however, was that, in the process, he had damaged her, and she had damaged herself. In her memoirs, her treatment of the whole Westland affair is particularly unilluminating, since she barely engages with the issues raised about her actions or discloses much of what she did. Her assessment of Heseltine is accurate: she described Westland as 'a crisis created from a small issue by a giant ego',[124] but she never examined what she – also the possessor of a giant ego – had done or failed to do.

Stephen Sherbourne, the head of her political office, sent her an acute analysis of how the political landscape looked after Heseltine had walked

---

* The journalist Nicholas Coleridge happened to be ill at the time of the resignation, and so lay in bed watching the story continuously on television. He noted that Heseltine wore six different ties in the course of one day – blue and yellow designed by Gianfranco Ferré, a white tie 'embossed like a pie frill', a plain black tie, then 'green geometric Pucci of Florence, followed by the Guards tie for the *Six O'Clock News* and a restrained red polka dot on a black background for the late headlines'. (*Spectator*, 25 January 1986.)

out. 'I am not worried about the attack on your so-called "style of Government",' he wrote. 'People want Prime Ministers to be in charge and they expect that of you.'[125] The problem lay almost the other way: 'The most damaging effect of the Heseltine affair has been to show the Government in serious disarray and you looking, uncharacteristically, as though you are not in control.' So 'what matters is doing everything we can to show an image of unity and decisiveness.' This was true. Mrs Thatcher's characteristic combination of aggression with bursts of caution, often so effective, had, in this case, made the conduct of business very difficult. In relation to Heseltine, she had been willing to wound, but afraid to strike.

On the day of Heseltine's resignation, Bernard Ingham sent her a note explaining the media's objective in its wake. It was, he said, 'to set Conservative politician against politician; and to crawl over all allegations made against you and your style of government'.[126]* He called for a co-ordinated response, spreading the load with Douglas Hurd and Kenneth Baker as 'the most useful and soothing spokesmen'. Mrs Thatcher would have done better to enter into this spirit and lead the co-ordination. Instead, she laid the unpleasant parliamentary duty on to Brittan. His shoulders were not big enough to bear it.

Charles Powell relieved her feelings and perhaps his own by attacking the Cabinet Office draft of her reply to the letter of resignation Heseltine had sent her. The draft praised Heseltine's role in increasing 'the standing of the United Kingdom and its Armed Forces', planning to modernize the nuclear deterrent and stationing INF in Europe. 'None were his contributions,' Powell wrote to Nigel Wicks.[127] The letter finally sent thanked him only for less important achievements like improving procurement and reorganizing the ministry. Powell also prepared sixteen points of what he called 'Knocking copy' against Heseltine[128] for Bernard Ingham to use when briefing the Sunday lobby.

On the following Monday, 13 January, Brittan made a statement to the House about the whole affair, only to be ambushed by Heseltine. Brittan denied Heseltine's accusation that he had put any pressure on Ray Lygo to withdraw BAe from the European bid. At this, Michael Heseltine rose and asked an apparently artless question. He wanted to know 'whether the Government have received any letters from British Aerospace giving

---

* This memo is actually dated 8 January. If this dating were correct, it would sensationally prove that Mrs Thatcher had contrived Heseltine's resignation in advance. It is entitled 'Handling of Heseltine resignation'. Internal evidence, however, proves that it was written after the event, on 9 January.

its views of the [Brittan–Lygo] meeting'.[129] Heseltine asked because he knew that, shortly before Brittan came to the Commons, a letter had arrived at Downing Street from Sir Austin Pearce, the chairman of BAe, supporting Lygo's interpretation and complaining about Brittan's behaviour. Downing Street had informed Brittan's office of the letter and its contents but indicated that he should not refer to it in Parliament because it was labelled 'private and confidential'. Brittan's reply to Heseltine was 'I have not received any such letter.'[130] This was a lawyer's answer – literally true, since Downing Street, not he, had received it, but wholly misleading. Sitting beside Brittan on the front bench, Mrs Thatcher looked uncomfortable and offered Brittan no visible support. Rumours began to spread that a letter *had* been received, and that Brittan had therefore lied to the House. Late that night, he was forced to return to Parliament. He explained that he now had Pearce's agreement to mention the letter, and apologized for not having done so before. There were numerous calls for his resignation. John Smith,* the shadow DTI spokesman, pointed out that Mrs Thatcher could have lent over to correct him in the House that afternoon but had not chosen to do so.

The following day, Mrs Thatcher responded to growing pressure by announcing an inquiry into the leak of the Solicitor-General's letter, headed by Robert Armstrong, to be conducted in private. She had little choice, given the anger of the Law Officers, but her decision greatly increased the danger to her. The leak was rumoured to have come from Brittan's office (as indeed it had), which obviously made him vulnerable. It was widely understood that Brittan had worked closely with Mrs Thatcher against Heseltine in the Westland affair. Where might the inquiry lead? Setting up an inquiry meant that the leak was considered a grave transgression: any discovery that the Prime Minister had a hand in it could, in the febrile circumstances, prove fatal.

By this time, friends of Mrs Thatcher were getting seriously worried that her political position might be threatened. They knew that if, after all this, the European bid for Westland were to succeed, she would be badly wounded. Rupert Murdoch, the media mogul, who was also a director of United Technologies, the owner of Sikorsky, rang Woodrow Wyatt. He was thinking of trying to get Sikorsky to 'do a deal' over Westland.

---

* John Smith (1938–94), educated Dunoon Grammar School and Glasgow University; Labour MP for Lanarkshire North, 1970–83; for Monklands East, 1983–94; Secretary of State for Trade, 1978–9; Leader of the Labour Party and Leader of the Opposition from 1992 until his death from a heart attack in 1994.

Sikorsky would go in with BAe and GEC, exclude the Europeans and thus save Mrs Thatcher's bacon. He wanted Wyatt's help in persuading Lord Weinstock, GEC's managing director.[131] In fact, Weinstock, 'furious with Heseltine' for resigning and leaving him and other supporters of the European bid to face Mrs Thatcher's wrath,[132] had been trying to work out his own solution. His idea, following a conversation with Gianni Agnelli, the boss of Fiat, was that Sikorsky–Fiat be allowed to join the European consortium 'and all would be a great united family.'[133] Weinstock agreed that Wyatt should convey his idea to Mrs Thatcher. He did so that night. 'A glow of light', Mrs Thatcher exclaimed, and promised to tell no one, not even Leon Brittan.[134]

In the previous week, a mystery buyer had bought nearly 15 per cent of Westland shares. This was quickly revealed to be Lord Hanson. Part of his motive in doing so was to help Mrs Thatcher get the vote from Westland shareholders that she wanted. It seems that this was understood and supported in Downing Street before it became public.[135] This was probably part of a wider move. John Nott, the former Defence Secretary, having left Parliament at the 1983 election, was chairman and chief executive of the merchant bank Lazards at this time. Westland was Lazards' client. In his memoirs, Nott wrote, 'To this day [2002], Michael Heseltine, a good friend of mine, . . . clearly feels that the City conducted a series of manoeuvres to deny the victory to the European consortium. My recollections do not coincide with Michael's but nothing is to be gained from re-engaging in a contest which almost everyone but Michael has forgotten long ago.'[136] On the face of it, these bland words amount to very little. However, an inspection of the index for this page of Nott's book (p. 338) reveals three names – Agnelli, Hanson and Sir James Goldsmith – that do not appear in the text. The explanation is that Nott had given an account of these men's role in the Westland saga but then removed it, at the last minute, fearing that he had libelled them. No one, however, remembered to prune the index. Nott had indeed implied that the three men in question had planned to form a 'concert party'* or something like it.[137]† So Heseltine's suspicions were not without foundation.‡

In fact, neither the Agnelli–Weinstock nor the Murdoch scheme came to fruition, but there is no doubt that Mrs Thatcher's supporters in

---

* A 'concert party' is the term used when individuals, secretly acting in concert, buy up a company's shares to acquire control.

† When taxed with the suggestion of a concert party to back the Sikorsky bid, John Cuckney preferred a different phrase: it was a 'fan club', he said. (Quoted in Michael Heseltine, *Life in the Jungle*, Hodder & Stoughton, 2000, p. 323.)

‡ The author is grateful to Lord Heseltine for pointing this out to him.

business got involved in Westland primarily to help her rather than because they were interested in a small helicopter company.* Another buyer of Westland shares was Murdoch. Through his company TNT, he bought just under the 5 per cent limit which required disclosure of the buyer. Apart from his firm belief that Mrs Thatcher was good for his business and for Britain, Murdoch had a particular reason for not wanting to see her fall at this moment. He was about to make the dramatic move to produce all his papers on new technology at his plant in Wapping, taking on the might of print unions. He was counting on her support in the battles to come. Murdoch and Woodrow Wyatt were among the guests at a lunch party given by the Thatchers on Sunday 19 January at Chequers. After it, Murdoch took Wyatt on a guided tour of the Wapping plant.[138] Westland and Wapping were intertwined.

On Wednesday 15 January, Mrs Thatcher had to speak in the parliamentary debate which, after the Heseltine resignation, she had hoped to avoid. Although she made no catastrophic individual error, she was weak. John Whittingdale,† Brittan's special adviser, read the draft of her speech in the morning. 'Total cop out,' he confided to his diary. 'Did not attempt to demolish Heseltine or even suggest that he had behaved badly before his resignation.'[139] There were reasons for her chosen tack. The first, as she told Wyatt that morning, was that 'I can't attack Heseltine without making everything worse. I don't want to look as though I am attacking a colleague and giving him an excuse to do even more harm.'[140] The second reason was related to the first, and could not be said. Wyatt advised her to clear the air about the charge that Brittan had leaked the Solicitor-General's letter, but of course she could not. ' "There'll be the usual leaks procedure but there have been a lot of leaks all round in this affair," she said, sounding rather dismal.'[141] Because of her own role, she was feeling vulnerable, not wishing to say more or get into a fight, worried where it would all lead.

The effect of Mrs Thatcher's reticence was to direct unwelcome

---

* Alan Bristow, who came round to supporting the European bid, also bought shares. A secondary scandal broke out in February when he claimed that two Thatcher-backing peers – later named as Lords Forte and King – had tried to get him to switch sides with the offer of a knighthood. What precisely happened was unclear, but obviously neither man had the power to bestow honours.

† John Whittingdale (1959–), educated Winchester and University College London; Conservative MP for Colchester South and Maldon, 1992–7; for Maldon and East Chelmsford, 1997–2010; for Maldon, 2010–; special adviser to Secretary of State for Trade and Industry, 1984–7; political secretary to the Prime Minister, 1988–90; private secretary to Margaret Thatcher, 1990–92; Secretary of State for Culture, Media and Sport, 2015–.

attention on Brittan, and thus to weaken him. He made the wind-up speech for the government in that day's debate, but ran out of time* before he could launch his planned denunciation of Heseltine. Mrs Thatcher congratulated him warmly afterwards, but his reviews in the press the following morning were unenthusiastic. Two days later, Westland shareholders voted in favour of the Sikorsky bid, but not by the 75 per cent required to settle the matter at once. So the battle continued.

On Sunday, John Whittingdale had an alarming conversation with Colette Bowe, the DTI chief information officer, who had leaked the key words from the Solicitor-General's letter to the Press Association. So far, she had not been publicly identified. She was already worried that she would be named in the House as the leaker. She informed Whittingdale that she had told Armstrong about the true circumstances of the leak and 'would tell Select Cttee if asked'.[142] 'That was when', Whittingdale recalled, 'I realised we were going to have big trouble.'[143] Until this point, those involved had assumed that the facts could be covered up, but now it seemed that this might not be possible, particularly if officials could not be protected from having to appear before a select committee. Then they would have to be frank about what had happened. Bowe's account to Armstrong was bound to implicate at least some of her superiors and political masters. In his diary Whittingdale wrote, 'May finish us all.'[144] Three days later, news spread that Armstrong's leak inquiry had identified the DTI as the source of the leak. Tam Dalyell named Colette Bowe in the House.

Rumours began to circulate that Brittan would have to resign. In the afternoon, Brittan saw Armstrong, with Mrs Thatcher, to be told the inquiry's findings. It was agreed that Mrs Thatcher would make a statement about the report of the inquiry in the Commons the next day, 23 January, although the week before she had said she would not do this. There then ensued what Geoffrey Howe called a 'brief overnight tussle'.[145] Howe, who was a friend of Brittan, argued for a form of words which made his position more publicly defensible. The point was to convey the sense that Brittan had been acting with her authority. In Mrs Thatcher's memory, possibly exaggerated over time, this became an attempt by Howe and, through him, by Brittan to alter the wording of evidence already given to Robert Armstrong. 'I said [to Howe] you are a silk [that is, a QC], a former Solicitor-General, coming to ask me to alter the evidence being given to Robert Armstrong and you come at the instigation of another silk

---

* Parliamentary front-bench wind-up speeches always had to end precisely for each 10 p.m. vote, and so had to be curtailed if the earlier debate had run on too long. This meant they were sometimes severely abbreviated.

[Brittan].' It would also have seemed to her, though she did not say this, like a veiled threat to drag her down from someone who sought her job. Howe presented her with a piece of paper with his suggested changes on it, she recalled, and 'I tore it up . . . I tore it up.'[146] Whether any doctoring was really being suggested is doubtful (how could anyone, at that stage, have altered Armstrong's already completed report?), but she did, in fact, concede some of the points that Howe and Brittan wanted in her statement to the House. She felt close to being trapped.

Mrs Thatcher came to the House in the afternoon of 23 January. As she had indicated the previous week, she confirmed that Armstrong's report itself would not be published. This she defended in terms of precedent, but it obviously added to the outcry and charge of cover-up. The Prime Minister set out its main findings. She told the House that it had been 'a matter of duty' that Heseltine's 'material inaccuracies' be corrected and become public knowledge by 4 p.m. on 6 January before Cuckney's press conference that afternoon to announce the board's recommendation of the Sikorsky bid. Brittan, she said, had been told the contents of the Mayhew letter at 1.30 that day.* He wanted it leaked (she stuck with the word 'disclosure') and told his office that he would prefer this to be done by No. 10. 'Subject to the agreement of my office', however, she continued, Brittan was making it clear that 'he was giving authority for the disclosure to be made from the Department of Trade and Industry, if it was not made from 10 Downing Street.'[147] On how it should be disclosed, she said, Brittan 'expressed no view'.

Mrs Thatcher moved on to her own role, or lack of it. Her office, she said, had been duly approached and had given 'cover' (a key word that Brittan had demanded): 'They did not seek my agreement: they considered – and they were right – that I should agree with [Brittan]' that the material should be disclosed quickly. Her office 'accepted' that the DTI would disclose the letter by ringing the Press Association. 'Had I been consulted,' she went on, 'I should have said that a different way must be found of making the relevant facts known.' The Attorney-General, she added, having read Armstrong's report, saw no need for prosecutions under the Official Secrets Act. She named none of the officials involved. She was in the awkward position of half admitting that something bad had happened but not admitting that anyone (apart, of course, from Heseltine) had been at fault.

Alan Clark, who had been shown a copy of Mrs Thatcher's statement

---

* She did not say that he had to be fished out of lunch with his department's former Permanent Secretary at Morgan Grenfell bank, which was advising Sikorsky.

shortly before she made it, 'started a *faux-rire* . . . How *can* she say these things without faltering? But she did. Kept her nerve beautifully . . . It was almost as if the House, half horrified, half dumb with admiration, was cowed.'[148] Actually, the House was more sullen than cowed. The Conservative benches were uneasy, and one Tory, Alex Fletcher,* asked her pointedly if she was 'satisfied that the statement she has made this afternoon has enhanced the integrity of her Government'. On the other side, both Neil Kinnock and, more effectively, David Owen asked about what she herself had known and when. Owen wondered how she could 'continue to hold the high office that she does' when she had set up a leak inquiry 'in the full knowledge that her office, and by implication she herself, was fully involved in this whole sordid affair'.[149] As even her ardent admirer Woodrow Wyatt admitted, 'She is not free from her pursuers yet.'[150]

Given this failure to clear the air, the mood within the parliamentary Conservative Party became restive. Someone had to be blamed for the leak, many felt, although others felt that blaming Brittan, the only available ministerial victim apart from Mrs Thatcher, would make it more likely that she would be next. Her statement had opened up a gap between herself and Brittan, because it said that he definitely had ordered the leak and that she definitely had not. Her statement made Brittan vulnerable. Even before it, Clark reported bumping into the backbencher Marcus Kimball† in the Members' Lobby: he 'was standing about – always a sign that something is afoot. He told of dining with Willie the previous evening, and that there had been much talk of "too many jewboys in the Cabinet".'[151] At the 1922 Committee meeting that night, the current went strongly against Brittan and under it flowed some anti-Semitism. According to Gerry Malone,‡ Brittan's PPS, who was there, one backbencher§ 'disgracefully' complained that the Home Office – Brittan's earlier post – should only have been occupied by 'a proper Englishman'.[152] The feeling was that, if Brittan did not go, backbenchers would not support Mrs Thatcher in the next Westland debate which had now been called for Monday. The whips did not exert themselves to save Brittan. 'The mood

---

* Alexander Fletcher (1929–89), educated Greenock High School; Conservative MP for Edinburgh North, November 1973–83; for Edinburgh Central, 1983–7; Minister, DTI, 1983–5; knighted, 1987.

† Marcus Kimball (1928–2014), educated Eton and Trinity College, Cambridge; Conservative MP for Gainsborough, February 1956–83; created Lord Kimball, 1985.

‡ Gerald Malone (1950–), educated St Aloysius' College, Glasgow and Glasgow University; Conservative MP for Aberdeen South, 1983–7; for Winchester, 1992–7; PPS to Secretary of State, DTI, 1985–6; Deputy Chairman, Conservative Party, 1992–4; Minister of State, Department of Health, 1994–7.

§ This was Sir John Stokes, MP for Halesowen and Stourbridge.

was wholly supportive of her,' Clark recorded, 'and the Scapegoat was duly tarred.'[153]

This was unwelcome to Mrs Thatcher, partly because she felt Brittan deserved to be backed, but chiefly because she feared for her own political life. She ever afterwards maintained the position that she had wanted Brittan to stay while the 1922 Committee forced him to go. She greatly feared that Brittan, feeling ill treated, would try to lay the blame on her and bring her down. She knew he knew things which could do this. Brittan himself was conscious of this possibility and seems to have toyed with it. After the Solicitor-General's letter had been disclosed, he quickly told Gerry Malone that 'Mrs Thatcher personally authorised the leak.'[154] Speaking to the present author, he put it a bit differently – that the leak was '*in effect* authorized by her'.[155] Of this, 'there was no doubt at all,' Brittan continued; the letter was 'definitely intended and procured to be made public'.[156] Both he and Charles Powell, from their different perspectives, agreed that the first plan had been to get the Solicitor-General's letter sent straight to Mrs Thatcher. Then, when they realized that confidentiality rested, by law, with the recipient, they thought this unwise, and devised the ruse of getting the letter sent to Heseltine.[157] This indicates that leaking the document may have been an idea they shared. Brittan, by his later account, received a telephone call on the night of Sunday 5 January, the night before the leak, from 'those acting for her'.[158] Although he was naturally inhibited from turning against Mrs Thatcher by past loyalty, by hope of future advancement and by fear of being inextricably involved in the ensuing ruin, he was also angry. After the 1922 Committee meeting, Mrs Thatcher had to tread carefully.

The next morning, 24 January, Brittan gathered together the conflicting signals from media, civil servants and colleagues about whether he should resign. The advice of much of the press was unambiguous, with headlines such as 'Kick him out' (*Daily Star*), 'Brittan must go' (*Sun* and *Mirror*) and 'Maggie on the rack – Brittan must resign says majority of MPs' (*Express*).[159]

Brittan believed that Bernard Ingham was briefing against him. He saw John Wakeham, the Chief Whip, who indicated to him that he had lost the support of the party.[160]* In the afternoon, he saw Mrs Thatcher and told her he must go. She begged him to stay, with a strong show of sincerity. He was adamant, however, dreading a long-drawn-out process of refusing

---

* Brittan also spoke to Willie Whitelaw, who advised him to stay. Characteristically, the next day, after Brittan had resigned, Whitelaw told Woodrow Wyatt that 'Of course Brittan had to go' (Wyatt, *The Journals of Woodrow Wyatt*, vol. i, 25 January 1986, p. 71).

to resign and then having to do so later. In his letter of resignation, which he wrote at once, he said, 'Since your statement in the House yesterday it has become clear to me that I no longer command the full confidence of colleagues . . .' By linking her statement with his resignation, he was implying a criticism of what she had said, perhaps even a threat of revenge. Wishing to show her goodwill, Mrs Thatcher, in her letter of reply, began by saying, 'I am very sorry that despite all the arguments I could use I was unable to dissuade you this afternoon from resigning,' and she added, 'I hope that it will not be long before you return to high office to continue your Ministerial career.'[161] This was an unusual thing to say to a resigning minister. It had the force, in Brittan's mind, of 'an informal understanding'.[162]

There was a sense in which Brittan's resignation was worse for Mrs Thatcher than Heseltine's. It was clear to most that Heseltine had himself violated the collective Cabinet responsibility which he claimed to hold so dear, and had been absolutely determined to break with Mrs Thatcher on an issue of no great importance. She could be criticized severely for how she had handled his behaviour, but it was understood that things had got to a point where it was a case of 'him or her' – so naturally it had to be him. With Brittan, the case was different. He had tried to do what the Cabinet, and particularly Mrs Thatcher herself, had wanted. He had also conspired with her about how best to do Heseltine down. So his departure suggested both that her somewhat shady schemes had gone awry and that she had not stuck by a friend in trouble. Brittan's judgment nearly thirty years later was, 'If she'd *really* defended me, I think it would have blown over. I wouldn't criticize her, though – I was resigning as part of a balancing act.'[163] Contemporary judgments by many colleagues were less generous. The thought that she had been as weak in protecting an ally as she had in fighting an opponent was damaging. She now faced the Westland debate called by Labour in the Commons for the coming Monday without a praetorian guard of colleagues to protect her.

Mrs Thatcher's team made huge efforts to prepare her for the showdown. So many people became involved in the drafts of her speech that Stephen Sherbourne complained to Nigel Wicks that the work was becoming impossible. There were such crowds that they had to operate in the Cabinet Room, where Mrs Thatcher, preferring her study, did not like working. Sherbourne begged Wicks and Charles Powell to go through the whole thing with Mrs Thatcher 'very precisely . . . "Brian Walden style"* . . . Because the PM has got to be pinned down to be as precise as possible.'[164] 'I was

* A reference to the heavyweight television political interviewer.

worried', he recalled, 'that Kinnock would kill her with two or three questions.'[165] For example: what did her office tell her about the leak before
the publication of the inquiry report, and, indeed, before she set up the
inquiry? Did her office know that the DTI intended to disclose the letter
by partial leak to the Press Association? If so, why didn't they seek her
agreement, or counsel against? If neither, wasn't it 'tacit approval of something which the Prime Minister has since said was wrong?'[166] Had Brittan
told her of his role in the disclosure? If so, when?

Mrs Thatcher, exhausted and perplexed, allowed herself to be more or
less a passenger in this process. As she set off that Saturday evening for a
constituency function in Finchley, she was told that a local party dignitary
who had been expected to greet her would not be doing so because he was
having a nervous breakdown. 'HE's having a nervous breakdown!' she
exclaimed. 'What about me?'[167] When Wyatt rang her privately to ask how
she could explain the various things that had happened she wearily took
the line which was to be her public soundbite: ' "Truth is stranger than
fiction," she said several times.'[168] As a lawyer, and one with a keen sense
of the proprieties, she felt particularly awkward to be caught up in a scandal involving the Law Officers. She had a well-founded fear of being
subjected to legal-style interrogation. She must also have had an uneasy
conscience. For a brief time at least, she seems to have felt like a rabbit in
the headlights, incapable of action.

Mrs Thatcher was heartened, however, to get a call from the White
House before she set off for Finchley. With diplomatic correctness, the US
Embassy in London had kept out of sight during the Westland crisis, but
the Ambassador, Charlie Price, had sent Mrs Thatcher a personal letter
of support. Now President Reagan came on the telephone because 'he
thought she might like to hear a friendly voice.'[169] 'He was furious',
recorded Powell, 'that anyone had the gall to challenge her integrity. He
wanted her to know that "out here in the colonies" she had a friend. He
urged the Prime Minister to go out and do her darnedest.'* She was also
fortified by a bunch of flowers and a letter from a member of the public,
Andrew M. Fox, a young international bond dealer recently out of university. He dismissed suggestions that she had favoured the Sikorsky bid
to suck up to Reagan as 'totally overblown' and thanked her for the
changes in public attitudes she had brought about since 1979. 'Many

---

* In talking of friendship 'out here in the colonies' Reagan was echoing the jocular language
of his very first letter to Mrs Thatcher, in April 1975, when he had told her much the same
thing, albeit under very different circumstances (Reagan to Thatcher, 30 April 1975, Thatcher
MSS (http://www.margaretthatcher.org/document/110357)).

changes are irreversable [sic],' he wrote, 'but the struggle is to maintain the . . . commitment to the principles of liberty and free enterprise which offer young people such opportunities today.'[170] These friendly words inspired Mrs Thatcher to write on the letter a list of issues to which she wished to return: 'Rates Inner Cities Education – Teacher Pay Changes in Social Security . . . Public Order Privatisation', and she added, 'gather with renewed strength & determination to propound and implement these positive policies.'

The biggest fear (or, for some, hope) all weekend was that Leon Brittan would use his power to bring down the Prime Minister. Her vulnerability was emphasized by a television interview with Douglas Hurd on Sunday, in which he defended her but called for proper Cabinet government – a coded attack. He also said, 'The worst thing for the country now would be to lurch into discussion of the leadership,'[171] thereby making such discussion more likely. On this cue, John Patten,* claiming the support of two other young ministers on the left of the party, Chris Patten and William Waldegrave, suggested to Hurd that evening that he throw his hat into the ring for the leadership.[172] Hurd declined, but was probably not unhappy that the idea of a change of leadership was in circulation.

Hurd's television performance that Sunday was watched with interest at Chevening, Geoffrey Howe's official country residence. According to Howe's PPS, Richard Ryder, 'Geoffrey believed he would become leader' if Mrs Thatcher fell: 'He'd got all his ducks in a row.'[173] So friends of Howe watching the TV interview grumbled that Hurd was 'on manoeuvres'. Their man had decided to 'keep a low profile', but he told Ryder that if there were a contest he would stand. He sought Ryder's opinion of his chances. Hearing 'widespread rumours on the Commons Rialto', Ryder told him, 'I was 80 per cent sure he'd get it.'[174]

There were also stirrings on the back benches. Cranley Onslow, the chairman of the 1922 Committee (and a paid adviser to Westland), was, in Ryder's view, 'not always on her side'.[175] Even the ultra-loyal Ian Gow, who had telephoned Mrs Thatcher that day, had privately formed the view that it was all up with her.[176] Mrs Thatcher's advisers knew that nothing in her speech in Monday's debate should provoke Brittan. For several hours later on Sunday, Howe, Wakeham and other colleagues went through the draft with Armstrong, but deliberately without her tense and

* John Patten (1945–), educated Wimbledon College and Sidney Sussex College, Cambridge; Conservative MP for City of Oxford, 1979–83; for Oxford West and Abingdon, 1983–97; Minister of State, Home Office, 1987–92; Secretary of State for Education, 1992–4; created Lord Patten, 1997.

distracting presence, to 'satisfy themselves that the speech was as convincing as it could be, and left minimal risk of further intensifying the Government's political problems'.[177]

On the morning of the debate, Monday 27 January 1986, the fear of Brittan's reaction had not receded. The problem was not just Brittan himself, but the mutinous feelings of his officials, who resented being outmanoeuvred by Bernard Ingham and Charles Powell. That morning's *Financial Times* reported their anger with Ingham, because he had taken 'an active role in the decision on how the letter should be leaked' and had played a part in what happened earlier.[178] The same sources alleged that Mrs Thatcher had given an incomplete version of events to the Commons on Thursday. Ingham wrote to Nigel Wicks, complaining about 'all the gossiping by DTI'.[179] Sir Brian Hayes,* the Permanent Secretary at the DTI, told Wicks that morning, 'There is clearly a conflict of testimony and I think it right that this should be disclosed – I hope in a relatively innocuous way.'[180] Geoffrey Howe acted as Brittan's ambassador in discussion of the text of Mrs Thatcher's speech, and was part of a small group discussing it with her in Downing Street right up to the last minute. In front of this group, she said, 'I may not be Prime Minister by six o'clock tonight.'[181]† She thought this, according to Brittan, because she feared 'she would be shown to have plotted by underhand means against her own ministers. Because that is what she had done.'[182] Those present when she made this remark inwardly acknowledged that she might be right, and so did not protest. Howe found it piquant to be helping her in her hour of need because 'Even to my cautious eye it was not possible to discern any successor but myself.'[183]

The House was packed, with Members overflowing the benches and perching in all the gangways. Neil Kinnock opened the debate. Although he got in a few pertinent questions, he was quickly blown off course. He comically said 'Heseltine' when he meant Westland, got flustered, accused the Tories of being dishonest, and tangled with the Speaker. Then he fell back upon the rhetorical generalities for which he was well known. As Alan Clark put it, 'For a few seconds Kinnock had her cornered, and you could see fear in those blue eyes. But then he had an attack of wind, gave her time to recover.'[184] The mood of the House changed. Tony Blair, then

* Brian Hayes (1929–), educated Norwich School and Corpus Christi College, Cambridge; Permanent Secretary, DTI, 1985–9; knighted, 1980.
† Her anxiety can be seen in her repetition of this phrase (or variants of it) to David Norgrove in her study just before she went over to the House and to Robert Armstrong as she got into the car to leave Downing Street (Interviews with David Norgrove and Lord Armstrong of Ilminster).

a young Labour MP in his first Parliament, learnt from Kinnock's failure of leadership as he watched in the Chamber that day: 'As Neil went on, I could see the wave of relief pass over the Tories. She thought the guillotine was going to come. Instead, she got the reprieve.' Kinnock's approach was wrong: 'She was vulnerable to a forensic dissection. It needed a scalpel. All she got from Neil was a rather floppy baseball bat.'[185] Kinnock agreed with his critics: 'I added excessive points at the front of my speech. It was stupid. Entirely my own bloody fault.'[186] He had failed to expose what he called 'the effort of complicated deception'.[187] He missed his most important single moment so far as leader of the Opposition.

When Mrs Thatcher answered him, she got the worst bit out of the way quickly. She admitted how closely she had been involved in the decision to drum up an opinion from the Solicitor-General. She repeated her previously expressed regret that the letter had been leaked without reference to him, and she added, with more contrition than before: 'Indeed, with hindsight, it is clear that this was one, and doubtless there were others, of a number of matters that could have been handled better, and that, too, I regret.'[188] She explained that she had known something of the leak in the hours after it had happened. Attempting to account for the respective behaviour of her office and Brittan's in the DTI, she took refuge in Armstrong's self-parodically careful mandarin phrase: there had been 'a genuine difference of understanding' between the two offices. This was a better formulation than 'misunderstanding' would have been, because it implied fault on neither side. It dealt with Hayes's point about a 'conflict of testimony'. Her speech was successful, Sherbourne remembered, because 'She was *solid*,'[189] and that was enough. 'A brilliant performance, shameless and brave,' Alan Clark wrote. 'We are out of the wood.'[190]

With the forensic skill which Kinnock lacked, David Owen then made a series of strong specific points against Mrs Thatcher, dragging Powell and Ingham, by name, into the spotlight; but by then the House had decided that she had won. Heseltine intervened, saying he had previously intended not to. He declared that Mrs Thatcher's expression of regret had been 'a difficult and very brave thing for a Prime Minister to say in such circumstances', and that he had his own regrets about what he had done. She had, he said, now brought 'the politics of this matter to an end'. The Tory benches loudly cheered his apparent magnanimity. Brittan, speaking for the first time since his resignation, upheld the truthfulness of Mrs Thatcher's account, and took responsibility for his role in the leak. His officials, he said, were 'not to be blamed'. The great traditional Tory combination of loyalty and humbug had reasserted itself. Mrs Thatcher had survived.

46. **Her closest servants** (i): Charles Powell, foreign affairs private secretary, 1984–90, physically one step behind, but mentally right beside her. Here they confront the Italian 'ambush' at the Milan summit, 1985.

47. (ii): Robert Armstrong, Cabinet Secretary, 1979-87, entertaining Mrs Thatcher at home to mark his retirement. She respected him very much, but did not agree with him about Ireland.

48. (iii): Robin Butler, principal private secretary, 1982–5, between his boss and the US Secretary of State, George Shultz. Butler found that talking to her socially was 'like feeding a fierce animal'.

49. Mrs Thatcher and Garret FitzGerald, the Irish Prime Minister, present one another with the Anglo-Irish Agreement in Hillsborough Castle, November 1985. She was uneasy about what she was doing. Behind them, left to right, are Dermot Nally, the Irish Cabinet Secretary, Tom King, the Northern Ireland Secretary, Geoffrey Howe and a painting of Windsor Castle.

50. Mrs Thatcher puts her feet on the sofa – her only concession to informality – and studies her red boxes. It is just after nine o'clock at night – very early for her.

51. Michael Heseltine, ex–Defence Secretary, arrives with characteristic brio at the Westland heliport, Battersea, 12 January 1986. Three days earlier, he had resigned in Cabinet over the Westland crisis.

52. Leon Brittan, Trade and Industry Secretary, leaves a Cabinet meeting on 16 January 1986. On 24 January he too resigned.

53. Colette Bowe, Brittan's chief press secretary, on the day of his resignation. She was instructed to leak the Solicitor-General's letter. She could probably have brought the Thatcher government down, but refrained.

54. On the same day, Mrs Thatcher shows the strain. The following week, she finally routed those trying to get her out over Westland.

55. With Prince Bandar and the Downing Street Christmas tree, December 1984. He and she persuaded King Fahd of Saudi Arabia to agree to the Al-Yamamah deal – the biggest defence contract in British history.

56. With Sultan Qaboos of Oman, 1982. He was a good friend of Britain in the Gulf, but Mark Thatcher's business relations with his entourage brought her own judgement into question.

57. 'The plucky little King'. Hussein of Jordan, here on her visit to his country in September 1985, was Mrs Thatcher's favourite Middle Eastern monarch. She tried, but failed, to help him achieve a breakthrough in the Israel–Palestine dispute.

58. With the Israeli prime minister, Shimon Peres, in Jerusalem, May 1986.
She was a true, if cautious, friend of Israel.

59. Mrs Thatcher deploys her arts of flattery on King Fahd in London in 1987.
He found her extremely attractive.

60. 'Thy rod and thy staff comfort me'. On holiday with Denis in Imlau, Austria, August 1984. Back home, the miners' strike raged.

61. 'Red' Ken Livingstone, leader of the Greater London Council, marks its demise on the last day of March 1986 with a defiant party. Mrs Thatcher abolished it, setting Livingstone on his career as her cheekiest opponent.

62. In the middle of the road for once, the Prime Minister opens the M25 motorway round London in October 1986.

63. In 1985, the Thatchers bought 11 Hambledon Place, Dulwich, as their private house, almost on a whim. It was not a success: she found it too far from Parliament and Denis did not like the golf course.

64. On holiday in Cornwall, August 1986, with a borrowed dog. Margaret always wanted a pet, but Denis would not allow it. Her bandaged hand is the result of a recent operation for Dupuytren's contracture.

65. Mrs Thatcher and President Mitterrand agree to the Channel Tunnel project in the chapter house of Canterbury cathedral, February 1986. She was seduced by Mitterrand's idea for 'something exciting'.

66. Camp David again, November 1986. She felt she had succeeded in steering Reagan back to the need for a credible nuclear deterrent after the near-disaster of his Reykjavik summit with Gorbachev.

67. Watching the British Army of the Rhine on manoeuvres in West Germany, September 1986. Helmut Kohl is half-obscured by a British military arm.

68. Denis and Mrs Thatcher receive the Queen in Downing Street, October 1985, for a dinner to mark the 250th anniversary of No. 10 as the prime minister's residence. Always deferential to the monarch, Mrs Thatcher curtsies very low.

69. The Commonwealth review conference, Marlborough House, London, August 1986. Left to right, Brian Mulroney (Canada), Bob Hawke (Australia), MT, Sir Lynden Pindling (Bahamas), The Queen, Kenneth Kaunda (Zambia), Sir 'Sonny' Ramphal (Commonwealth Secretary-General), Rajiv Gandhi (India), Robert Mugabe (Zimbabwe). Mrs Thatcher was isolated over South African sanctions.

70. Nigel Lawson, Chancellor of the Exchequer from the start of the second term, and economic mastermind of the period. She admired him greatly, but considered him 'a gambler'.

71. David Young (Lord Young of Graffham). He tackled unemployment and held Mrs Thatcher's hand through the 1987 election campaign, to the irritation of Norman Tebbit.

72. **Clever young men** (i): Oliver Letwin, the Policy Unit's youngest brainbox.

73. (ii): John Redwood, successful head of the Policy Unit, 1983–5, and privatization expert.

74. (iii): William Waldegrave, mastermind of the poll tax.

75. Oleg Gordievsky, the most important double agent Britain ever had in the KGB. After he defected, Mrs Thatcher called him 'Mr Collins', for security reasons.

76. Laurens van der Post, South African writer, guru and flatterer of the mighty. He influenced her against sanctions.

77. Brian Walden, ex–Labour MP. He was the television interviewer who understood her best.

78. Rupert Murdoch (right), with Kelvin Mackenzie, editor of his paper, the *Sun*, on the day it was first printed at Wapping in January 1986. Without Mrs Thatcher, Murdoch believed, he could not have beaten the print unions.

79. Woodrow Wyatt, chairman of the Tote and columnist in the *News of the World* and *The Times* (both Murdoch-owned). She took his calls most Sundays.

80. David Hart, the most irregular of her 'Irregulars'. He fought the miners' strike from Claridge's and gave her inside information on the working miners.

81. **Moscow, March 1987**
(i): In beige suede boots and sable coat, Mrs Thatcher visits St Sergius monastery, Zagorsk.

82. (ii): Lighting a candle in the church at Zagorsk. Being a good Methodist, she did not know what to do with it.

83. (iii): Laying a wreath at the Tomb of the Unknown Warrior in Moscow.

84. (iv): Mrs Thatcher visits workers' housing in Moscow.
She got a hero's reception from the crowds.

85. (v): With Gorbachev in the Kremlin. Neither of them could stop talking.

86. An election press conference in Glasgow in 1987. A rate revaluation threatened to wipe the Tories out in Scotland. With her is Malcolm Rifkind, the Scottish Secretary.

87. Mrs Thatcher takes command in a Lancashire biscuit factory, for campaigning purposes, May 1987.

88. Striding out in her constituency, Finchley – but her steps in the campaign were often uncertain.

89. The winners: on election night, at the window of Conservative Central Office, Mrs Thatcher at last gives Norman Tebbit his due.

90. Victorious in Whitehall.

91. With Tim Bell (in later years). By secretly bringing him back to help her win in 1987, she caused bad feeling in her team.

92. Safely home: Denis and Mrs Thatcher begin their third stint in No. 10, 12 June 1987.

Her escape was reflected in the press the morning after. 'Tide stemmed by Thatcher' judged the *Telegraph*, 'Maggie Stops the Rot' proclaimed the *Daily Mail*, while the *Express* commented that she was 'Not, after all, the Wicked Witch'.[191] On 12 February, after a great deal of intervention by mystery buyers and other City jiggery-pokery, the Westland shareholders finally agreed to accept the Sikorsky bid, sparing Mrs Thatcher further embarrassment. But by then the political caravan had moved on, and few pretended any more that Westland itself mattered much. The details of this scandal, which lacked the usual preferred ingredients of sex, spies and money, faded into confusion and boredom.

Oddly, though, Heseltine had been too merciful to Mrs Thatcher in declaring the politics of the crisis at an end. The questions about what had really happened and what she had known still lurked, and these doubts were used against her officials and the way she governed. On the evening of her parliamentary triumph, Charles Powell wrote Mrs Thatcher a private letter of congratulation on her 'stirring performance',[192] and he thanked her 'for fighting so hard for Bernard & for me. Your loyalty and thoughtfulness towards your staff far exceeds anything which I have known in over 20 years in government service.' He stood ready to sacrifice himself: 'If you conclude that you would be better served by a less notorious Private Secretary, I would readily understand and offer to slip away – but would always be proud to have served you.'[193] Powell's letter was clearly couched as an offer which Mrs Thatcher could not accept, but in describing himself as 'notorious', he drew attention to an important aspect of the Westland affair. Until then, although he had already made a strong mark in Whitehall, Powell had been unknown to the public. The idea that a non-political official might be a known player was anathema, even more than it is today, to the Civil Service, and it was not what Powell, ambitious though he was, wanted. The brilliant 'regular', the top-class professional civil servant, had begun to look like one of her 'irregulars', using dark arts. Bernard Ingham, too, although much better known to the public than Powell, was also, unlike twenty-first-century press secretaries and media operatives, a career civil servant with no party affiliation. He never, for example, attended the Conservative Party conference nor, which is more surprising, sat regularly in on the Cabinet. The suggestion that Powell and Ingham were the two most powerful people below the Prime Minister, and in effect ran her government, was explosive, especially as it was not completely untrue. So was the idea, nowadays almost commonplace, that officials from different departments would be agents in media wars against one another's ministers.

In the case of Powell and Ingham, it did not help that the two often had uneasy relations with each other. Ingham thought that 'the real problem was Charles Powell because he made life so difficult for every other private secretary and for the Foreign Office and tried to run with the media too.'[194] Powell thought that Ingham was too jealous of his patch and had a tendency, when reporting from European and other summits, to have such a strong eye for the domestic press that he would stir up controversies which upset allies.[195]

Part of the difficulty arose from what was, in more normal circumstances, a huge advantage. Both men were outstandingly able, probably more so than anyone who had previously occupied their respective roles. No one else had Ingham's power for a crisp summation of a story, nor his instinct for Mrs Thatcher's attitudes and idiom. His daily press digest to Mrs Thatcher, complained about in many Cabinet ministers' memoirs for its suppression of bad news and distortion of her critics, was actually a very clear, amusing and useful summary of who said what and what mattered. It is rarely true, though it was often alleged, that Ingham hid news from Mrs Thatcher because she might not like it. Powell, for his part, was a man of astonishing industry and intelligence, and of speed and precision in writing. His memos to Mrs Thatcher, flowing almost constantly through day and night and often over weekends, form a uniquely full and eloquent documentation of the years he served her (1984–90). They expounded policy lucidly, and gave masterly, often witty explanations of diplomacy and dealing with other world leaders and with ministers. They also mirrored and prompted her thoughts, which enhanced their freedom to act and thus their power. 'Please don't misunderstand this, but in a strange sense it was quite hard to tell what was me and what was her,' Powell reflected.* 'I knew her way of doing things and what she wanted, so I could pretty much read her mind.'[196]† Mrs Thatcher was right to value Ingham and Powell extremely highly, and also to trust them. At the time of Westland, her private office was not working very well. Her principal private secretary, Nigel Wicks, though able and hard working, was too

---

* Powell's observation was shared by colleagues. As Percy Cradock later wrote, sometimes it was 'difficult to establish where Mrs Thatcher ended and Charles Powell began' (Percy Cradock, *In Pursuit of British Interests: Reflections on Foreign Policy under Margaret Thatcher and John Major*, John Murray, 1997, p. 14).

† In Powell's case, the master–servant relationship occasionally teetered on the edge of inverting itself. Returning from their gruelling trip to sign the Hong Kong Declaration (and see Reagan at Camp David) just before Christmas in 1984, Robin Butler arranged an informal drinks gathering for Mrs Thatcher. During the party, the phone on Charles Powell's desk rang. Mrs Thatcher picked it up without hesitation saying, 'I'm sorry, he's busy. Can I take a message?' (Correspondence with David Willetts.)

cautious, anxious and reactive to give the necessary lead. He and David Norgrove, her newish Treasury private secretary, had failed to foresee the embarrassment of being isolated at her meeting with Nigel Lawson and others over ERM entry in November 1985 (see Chapter 13). As the Westland trouble blew up, she needed a more adroit service. Powell saw the vacuum and filled it with panache. Indeed, it is completely impossible to imagine Mrs Thatcher being able to find her way through the Westland crisis without Powell's help. 'She was professionally extremely well served by Powell and Ingham,' Stephen Sherbourne recalled, 'and she relied on Charles even more than Bernard. But I do think it was a problem. They were too personal to her and too powerful.'[197]

Once Powell and Ingham were so widely reported, this became a problem in itself. As the several select committees geared up to investigate the Westland affair, one of the issues which arose was whether the officials involved, including Colette Bowe at the DTI and Powell and Ingham, should appear before them. Robert Armstrong had to deploy all his arguments about lack of precedent and 'double jeopardy' (he had already interviewed them for his own inquiry) to stop them being forced to appear. The highest official and political energies had to be put into the defence of people who, in theory, were not of the highest rank. This succeeded, though with considerable strain. Robert Armstrong appeared on behalf of the officials as, for the DTI, did Brian Hayes. As a result, both Ingham and Powell survived and grew in their importance to Mrs Thatcher, who had only to hear her good people attacked to defend them even more forthrightly. If they had fallen, that would have been disastrous for her, but the fact that they stayed on, their power undiminished, was damaging too. The pattern of Westland, the idea of a kitchen Cabinet more powerful than the real one, was established. It would recur in differing forms in the coming years.

After months of hearings and deliberations, the Defence Select Committee reported, in terms which, though scarcely pleasing to the government, did not cause Mrs Thatcher further personal damage. The heat had gone out of the issue. The day the report was published, Bernard Ingham wrote sardonically to Wicks about his press briefing on it:

> Remarkably little interest by a small lobby which lasted 10 minutes . . .
> I shook my head sadly, with much tut-tutting, about the splurge of leaks . . .
> This concern about leaks does not add up, I said . . . Would this be my last
> lobby? I doubted it; I hadn't packed my pictures. There had of course
> already been expressions of confidence in the officials mentioned.[198]

*

The select committee had not been able to establish precisely what did happen in the affair of the leaking of the Solicitor-General's letter. It raised the right questions about what the government was concealing, but could not fully answer them. The machine had managed – just – to exert enough discipline upon itself to stave off disaster. If the committee had known and published what had really happened, however, and had been allowed to question the officials involved, it is hard to see how Mrs Thatcher would have been able to remain in office.

The answers which Mrs Thatcher had given in the debate in which she finally prevailed over her enemies on 27 January had been the truth, but not the whole truth. She was lucky that the official at the centre of the leak row, Colette Bowe, was a highly professional civil servant and, in her private views, a strong supporter of the Thatcher 'revolution'. If she had not been, she could probably have brought the government down. Until speaking to the present author for this book, Bowe put all her personal records of the saga in a bank vault and said nothing to anyone, other than Armstrong's inquiry, about what had happened.*

Colette Bowe had served in the DTI since the late 1970s, most recently as press secretary to Norman Tebbit, remaining in post after Brittan took over. In her recollection, the department had 'felt a bit protective' towards its reluctant and bruised new minister. When, in November, Heseltine suddenly began to turn the Westland issue into 'a trial of strength with Mrs Thatcher', Bowe and her colleagues thought it was 'a bit unfair'.[199] Brittan was not totally into the brief of this seemingly quite minor matter. It seemed to his civil servants that Mrs Thatcher was giving him tacit support, but 'not explicit', and he had to pursue government policy alone.[200] Far from noticing Downing Street exerting too much authority, Bowe felt there was too little: 'I thought "Where's Nigel Wicks?" At that point, I had never even heard of Charles Powell.'[201] 'At the time,' she recalled, 'it all seemed puzzlingly chaotic. As I see it now, it looks as if there was some lack of control from the centre, and Heseltine was out of line: the Prime Minister was the only person who could really bring him back into line.'[202]

In the era before spin-doctors and mobile phones, let alone emails, holidays were considered sacred, and so when Colette Bowe took a fort-night's leave for Christmas, she was completely out of touch. The same

---

* This was despite numerous media provocations. One, from the *Sun*, was the headline 'DTI mole was nude model'. The paper felt able to write this because Colette Bowe, when a student, had taken part in a life-class for a friend at the Slade School of Art.

was true of Brittan's private secretary, John Mogg.* When both returned to work on Monday 6 January, 'it felt like a maelstrom,' and it still seemed that 'a central organising force was absent.'[203] She came into the office that morning 'not realising what was happening'.[204] As endless phone calls from the press came in, Bowe fended them off by saying that the Cabinet meeting on Thursday would settle matters.

At lunchtime that day, Bowe was asked by John Mogg to join him in the private office of Leon Brittan, who was out to lunch. He and Jon Michell, the other DTI civil servant chiefly involved, there showed her a copy of the Solicitor-General's letter to Heseltine, which had been expected and had recently arrived. The original had just been sent to Heseltine. Bowe read it: 'I sucked my teeth.'[205] Michell explained that the Westland board was holding its press conference at 4 p.m. and people needed to have heard the news of the letter by that time. Mogg then rang Brittan, fishing him out of his lunch. He told him that the letter had arrived and reminded him of the timing. 'It's her [that is, Mrs Thatcher's] letter,' Brittan told Mogg. 'If she wants it done, fine. Get it in the public domain, but clear it first with No. 10.'[206] Mogg recalled: 'I had to ring Charles [Powell] to confirm that action should take place.'[207] Powell told him that the letter must be got into the public domain. Both men spoke, in Mogg's view, as private secretary to private secretary, working on the implicit assumption that if the private secretary says something is wanted, he does so on behalf of his principal. Besides, 'Charles was extremely good at interpreting what his boss wanted: he was speaking with her authority.'[208] Mogg asked how best to get the letter out and Powell said, 'I've given a copy to Bernard.'[209] Powell also, however, 'somehow conveyed that No. 10 did not want to do the business itself'.[210] To Bowe, who previously had no inkling of No. 10's involvement, 'That did not seem an unreasonable position.'[211] Mogg then reported the call to Bowe and asked her to ring Ingham. 'Hang on,' said Bowe, worried at what was happening. 'This is a letter from a Law Officer. Let's ring Brian Hayes [the Permanent Secretary].'[212] They tried, but Hayes was out of town in a car (in the days before government cars were automatically supplied with car-phones)† and could not be reached. Given the pressure of time, she agreed to ring Ingham.

Bowe and Ingham were colleagues and had, she thought, 'a warm relationship'.[213] He was not her boss – in those days, unlike in the Blair

* John Mogg (1943–), educated Bishop Vesey's Grammar School, Sutton Coldfield and Birmingham University; PPS to Secretary of State for Trade and Industry, 1985–6; knighted, 2003; created Lord Mogg, 2008.
† The car-phone, attached to an apparatus fed by the car engine, was distinct from mobile phones which, at that time, were rare, and extremely bulky.

era, there was no media command system across Whitehall – but he was the most senior of her tribe. Because of the Mogg–Powell conversation, she did not believe that, in ringing Ingham, she was raising a question of whether or not the letter should be leaked. She thought she was having a conversation between professionals about 'ways and means' of leaking (she preferred the word 'disclosing'), about 'who does what'.[214] In his version of events, Ingham recalled that Bowe told him, 'I've got permission to leak this letter.'[215] 'My eyebrows [his most famous attribute: they were very bushy] hit the ceiling,' he said, and they did not resume their normal position when she went on, 'We want you to leak it.' He refused, but did not try to prevent her: 'I had no authority over her.'[216] For her part, Bowe remembered asking Ingham, 'What's supposed to be happening?' He replied, 'Charles has given a copy of the letter to me and says it must be got out.' He added, however, 'I've got to keep the PM above the fray.'[217]* 'I took a deep breath,' Bowe recalled, 'and thought "OK, I'll have to do it."' 'I'll give it to Chris [Moncrieff of the Press Association],' she told Ingham, who asked her if Moncrieff would protect the source. She said he would, so he agreed. She did not feel she was under orders from Ingham or that he had bullied her, but she did believe that if he had advised against she would not have leaked. 'There's an implicit contract here' was how she put it nearly thirty years later. 'I was either Rosencrantz,' Bowe said, 'or Guildenstern.'[218] She leaked, getting hold of Chris Moncrieff just after 2 p.m. All hell duly broke loose that afternoon.

The next morning, Colette Bowe was wrestling with the consequences of the leak when John Whittingdale, Brittan's special adviser, came to see her. He had just been to No. 10, he said, where it had been made clear to him that 'the PM is very relaxed about the Solicitor-General's letter.'[219] The idea was that this message should be conveyed to Brittan. In the minds of the DTI, therefore, they felt they had been given cover from No. 10 both before and after the fact. No one at No. 10 had criticized them for the leak. They were stunned when Mrs Thatcher announced the inquiry. 'We gasped. We said, "What on earth is this inquiry for?"'[220]

Charles Powell gave a different account of his conversation with John Mogg. He believed Mogg, 'a fairly devious fellow', had set him up, for use 'posthumously' when people started to ask questions.[221] Powell denied telling Mogg that the letter had to be made public. Instead, he recalled Mogg asking, 'Is this all going to reach the press?' to which Powell replied, 'I expect it will: everything else seems to.' Powell pointed to the

* Ingham's recollection, which supports Bowe's, was that he said, 'I have to keep the PM above that sort of thing' (Correspondence with Sir Bernard Ingham).

conversation between Ingham and Bowe 'which seems to have gone rather further than that'. That too was part of the 'set-up' by the DTI of No. 10, Powell believed. He did not give the DTI oblique permission to leak, he maintained: press relations were not his job. As soon as Brittan resigned, the former DTI Secretary wanted Powell out as well, as a punishment to Mrs Thatcher for letting her loyal minister go, inadequately defended.[222]

These 'who did what?' arguments – a customary form of recrimination after something goes wrong – might not have mattered much had it not been for Armstrong's inquiry. But once this began, the officials feared that it might turn into *sauve qui peut*. It was natural that Robert Armstrong, appalled by the damage done to the reputation of the Prime Minister, to his own Cabinet Office and to the Civil Service, would look for scapegoats, most likely Bowe, Mogg and Michell. Luckily for them, their Permanent Secretary, Sir Brian Hayes, insisted on accompanying Bowe to her meetings with Armstrong, and threatened to resign if his officials were punished.[223] Bowe was particularly incensed by the idea that her leak was a breach of the Official Secrets Act and was therefore being compared with the case of Clive Ponting. She had been acting under authority, she maintained, and her action had been inspired by the opposite motives to Ponting's – to save her minister and the government from embarrassment. She told Armstrong the full story, including about the message from No. 10, relayed by Whittingdale, to the DTI. She warned the Cabinet Office officials conducting the leak inquiry that if she were charged under the Official Secrets Act, 'I'll see you in court.'[224*]

Bowe's story explains why Armstrong's inquiry found as it did, and why the officials concerned could not be permitted to appear in front of the select committee. In his own evidence, Armstrong had to give an accurate account of what had happened which nevertheless involved a good deal of *suppressio veri*. If Bowe had told a parliamentary committee what had passed between her and Ingham (which in turn involved what Powell had said to Mogg), and had then revealed what she knew about Mrs Thatcher's support for the leak, the storm would have broken upon Mrs Thatcher's head. Hence the very careful words chosen by Mrs Thatcher in which she said that she had favoured the Solicitor-General's letter being in the public domain but had not known of the method of getting it there and would not have approved of it if she had. Hence the importance of stating that all the

* So angry was Colette Bowe at the threat of the Official Secrets Act that she even protested about being offered immunity under it, arguing that she had not committed any breach. She was eventually persuaded by Brian Hayes that she must accept this offer of protection.

officials involved were part of 'a genuine difference of understanding'. And hence, too, Mrs Thatcher's insistence that she had not asked what really happened before she heard the result of the Armstrong inquiry. Of course she had not asked what really happened: she was quite cunning enough to understand that the answer would be highly embarrassing to know. In the weeks in which the select committee was accumulating its material, Mrs Thatcher more than once wrote to her officials warning against what she called 'spurious accuracy'.[225] She meant, which is true, that people asked for formal evidence sometimes answer with a precision that their memory does not justify. But what she really feared in this case was accuracy itself. As Charles Powell himself put it, 'Her hands were not entirely clean.'[226]

At the end of January, Mrs Thatcher received two contradictory signals. Ingham warned her that, among the lobby, the government was seen as 'tossing on a sea of trouble . . . I get the feeling that there is a great deal of gossip going on in the party and that Cabinet Ministers are participants. They are described as extremely worried about the next election and in need of rallying.'[227] But her postbag told a different story. During the week of 31 January, the political office reported that Mrs Thatcher had received some 700 letters (five times the usual number). 'Virtually all these letters expressed their unqualified support for your leadership.'[228] By mid-February Mrs Thatcher was trying to move on from the affair. It had been 'a very, very difficult few weeks', she told the *Finchley Times*, but 'that's all behind us now.'[229] Armstrong wrote a letter to the DTI at the end of his inquiry saying that 'no official acted culpably or irresponsibly in this matter' and that all should continue in their work with their careers unaffected. But opinion was not so ready to give a clean bill of health to Mrs Thatcher. This was not because many agreed with Michael Heseltine. Although he was admired for his panache and supported by some in his interventionist industrial policies, few in the Tory Party shared his obsession with the Westland issue, and most of them thought it confected for his own advantage. His vanity was widely commented on ('What a conceited thing he is,' wrote the loyal backbencher Fergus Montgomery to Mrs Thatcher).[230] It was also acknowledged that it is not easy to run a government when one of its senior members decides to kick over the traces. In being slow to take Heseltine in hand, Mrs Thatcher had erred on the side of trusting colleagues rather than throwing her weight about. As she understandably protested, if she had acted earlier, critics would have said: 'there you are! Old Bossy Boots at it again.'[231] It really was not her fault that Heseltine sought a fight, and it is clear from the evidence that he, not she, was the first to throw a spanner in the works of collective responsibility.

It was the other things the Westland affair exposed which were so difficult for Mrs Thatcher. By the end of it all, her government resembled a man who has suddenly had a tooth knocked out, and has not been to the dentist for a long time. When he is examined, it turns out that his whole mouth is in bad shape. Not much worked well that December and January – not Cabinet government, nor the Cabinet Office; not the whips' management of party opinion, nor media presentation; not interdepartmental relations, nor her private office. Blame naturally attached to the woman supposed to be in charge of all of the above. This blame was not only *ex officio*: it also dwelt on her personal defects. If, in her own phrase, Westland was 'a drama of personalities, not realities',[232] one of the two main personalities was hers, and the story did not show her in a favourable light. Two of her strongest qualities – her leadership competence and her integrity – fell under question in a way that had not really happened before. 'The Tory Party isn't expected to behave like that,' she wrote to a supporter in the middle of the crisis.[233] The affair of the Solicitor-General's letter showed that she, too, had fallen short of expected behaviour.

As for her much discussed 'style of government', the crisis exposed how Mrs Thatcher, as Charles Powell put it, 'operated in two parallel universes'.[234] One was 'the Government', with its institutions, procedures, committees and so on. She saw this as somewhat alien and was quite capable of saying 'What on earth does the Government think it is up to?', as if she were not at its head. The other was 'her universe'[235] of 'inspiration, ideas, argument, great causes'. In her universe, 'she saw herself as a lonely campaigner' overcoming formalism and 'being an identifiable figure-head for change'. 'To use an Everest analogy,' Powell went on, 'she needed the Expedition/Government to get her up to a certain altitude. After that she just needed herself and a few Sherpas. The dangers of self-exaltation are obvious.' In the case of Westland, when the two universes collided, 'she showed an uncertain touch: seeing herself as leading a campaign for the right of the market to decide while lacking the political guile to dish Heseltine's squalid manoeuvres.'[236] Powell observed, in this case and at all times, 'a strange innocence or naivety about her which most people thought a fake, but was terrifyingly real!'[237]

Although Mrs Thatcher exhibited definite signs of unease at what she had done, she learnt the wrong lesson from the Westland debacle. Her most trusted associates, the objects of opprobrium in the crisis, noticed this more than anyone. According to Bernard Ingham, 'Her arteries certainly hardened.'[238] After Westland, 'She was always playing things very close to her chest and felt she had to in order to keep government going.' Charles Powell, who had 'thought I'd be made to walk the plank', was grateful for her loyalty, but noticed 'no regret or revision' in her mind about how to govern. Indeed, though temporarily reined in, she became more arbitrary in her attitudes. She was very angry, for example, that Clive Whitmore, her former principal private secretary, had not helped her deal with Heseltine. She ignored the fact that, as his Permanent Secretary, Whitmore owed his loyalty to him, not to her. 'It cost Clive Whitmore any possibility he might have had of being Cabinet Secretary,' she said when writing her memoirs, 'because I really felt at this time he should have warned us.'[239] Nor did she see the need to start cultivating backbenchers in the tea room again, as she had done in her early days. 'They've chosen someone to lead them, and that's what I do,' she told Powell: they could like it or lump it.[240] She was reinforced in her self-confidence by the view – surely correct in itself – that she had been right about the subject. It would have been ludicrous and inconsistent if the government she led had organized a European, monopolistic, state-backed rescue for Westland when a reasonable private sector buyer was available. She often was right when others were wrong, thanks to her courage and independence of mind; but, at this crucial juncture, she failed to pause and think self-critically about what had gone amiss.

The other big event in Britain at the beginning of 1986 was Rupert Murdoch's coup against the print unions. Under their noses, he had secretly prepared his Wapping plant to produce all his British newspapers – *The Times*, the *Sunday Times*, the *Sun* and the *News of the World*. For years, the print unions, perhaps the most unreformed and resistant to new technology of all British unions, had refused to agree to a move to Wapping from the papers' separate, existing 'hot-metal' sites at the back of their respective newspapers. Early in the spring of 1985, Murdoch decided to move against his long-standing tormentors. He had seen how the regional newspaper proprietor Eddie Shah had won his dispute with the unions over printing the *Warrington Messenger* in late 1983. Shah had invoked the Thatcher administration's new union laws to overcome the mass pickets which beset his plant after he had sacked six members of the print union, the National Graphical Association, and de-recognized the unions. 'We felt the atmosphere was changing. And we had this plant lying idle.'[241] Murdoch decided to go ahead without any agreement, in secret, and make Wapping ready with the new technology to prepare and print all his newspapers. He invented a cover story that he was using the site to launch a London '24-hour' paper, the *London Post*. With a strange lack of curiosity, neither the unions nor the media worked out what was really going on.

On 24 January 1986, the day, by coincidence, of Leon Brittan's resignation, 6,000 News International workers went on strike against the company's attempts to modernize technology and print an extra section of the *Sunday Times* in Wapping. This confrontation suited Murdoch's plan. On the same day, he activated it. Instead of the print unions, he had arranged with the right-wing Electricians' Union (the EETPU), which, under Frank Chapple and then Eric Hammond, had a long history of fighting Communist infiltration, to replace the printers with their members overnight, and get the papers out. He sacked all those who were on strike. To circumvent the attempted union boycott of newspaper distribution that followed, he used his own freight company, TNT, to transport the papers by road rather than rail. Large crowds of often violent pickets – several thousands on Saturday nights – assembled outside the Wapping plant to try to prevent workers going in. One of the tricks of the protesters was to throw darts into the rumps of police horses, causing them to rear up and making it look, for the benefit of cameras, as if they were trying to crush the pickets. Some journalists refused to take part in the move to Wapping. The Labour Party announced that it would not deal with representatives of the Murdoch papers.

Mrs Thatcher was not, naturally, part of this plan. According to Murdoch, he never rang her during the dispute: 'I avoided all contacts with her so that if anyone asked, she'd be in a stronger position.'[242] But in the summer of 1985, Charles Douglas-Home, the editor of *The Times* (who was to die of cancer later in the year), had been to see her to tell her 'This is a very serious thing, and we're going ahead.'[243] Murdoch believed that, as a result of this, Mrs Thatcher informed the then Home Secretary, Brittan, about the potential need for large numbers of police, as had been required so often in the miners' strike. As Murdoch himself put it, 'We would probably not have done it if she hadn't reformed the unions.'[244] News International's victory in the contest was extremely important to her. This was the first front-rank private sector fight with the unions since her reforms. If it turned out that the newspaper industry could be beaten, then her previous achievements in the field would be set back, and the issue which made so much of Fleet Street support her so strongly would have been lost.

Yet the astonishing fact is that, among the Prime Minister's papers in the government's possession, there is no file about the Wapping dispute, and virtually no mention of any kind. The same is almost equally true of Mrs Thatcher's private papers. This is not because her contacts over the dispute were considered too secret to be recorded, but because there were almost none. There is a perfectly good reason for this. She had brought about a reform of the law so successful that the battle needed no management by government. This reflects her success. But there is a further reason. Because of the Westland effect, Mrs Thatcher was so weakened that she did not dare engage in the argument which raged about Wapping. Her answers to Commons questions on the subject were fully supportive, but restrained and slightly distanced: 'I wish those newspapers well in their efforts to print on the latest equipment. Management and everyone else, including trade unions, are entitled to take full advantage of the law.'[245] Kenneth Clarke, her anti-Thatcherite employment minister, felt emboldened to criticize Murdoch for his bad 'public relations' in the dispute, and she did not feel strong enough to slap him down. Luckily for her, Murdoch prevailed: after about a year, the picketing collapsed. A new era for British newspapers had begun.

The weekend in which the Wapping dispute began coincided with Mrs Thatcher's preparation for her final showdown over Westland in the House of Commons on the coming Monday. Murdoch consulted Woodrow Wyatt: 'He says, "There's an unfortunate cartoon in the *News of the World* showing Mrs Thatcher choking on leek soup. Do you think she'll mind?" '[246] Wyatt thought not. At the end of that day's entry he recorded, 'When I spoke to Rupert I said I had two friends in difficulties, him and Margaret, and he said, "Yes, but I'm winning." '[247]

PART THREE

Recovery

15
TBW

'While she is with us, she is not with her own people'

The immediate effect of the Westland affair was to cut Mrs Thatcher down to size politically. 'Hurd warns Maggie' was the headline in the *Evening Standard* the day after the final Commons debate on Westland, after Hurd had told the BBC's *Today* programme that Mrs Thatcher 'must not run the Government as a one-woman band'.[1] All those Cabinet colleagues irritated by her approach and style now did their best to rein her in. John Biffen warned that 'Toryism is not a raucous political faction.' Peter Walker said that the Conservatives could still win the next general election if they could more successfully project their concern about unemployment, which had just risen, in the figures announced in January, to 3,407,729, the highest ever.[2] 'Collective responsibility', wrote Ferdinand Mount, 'is only a code phrase for "the quiet life with no radical or contentious stuff".'[3] It was also a phrase which always implied a criticism of Mrs Thatcher. She herself believed that many senior Tories were trying to get her out. 'I am not going,' she told Woodrow Wyatt. 'I will fight them all the way.'[4]

The spring of 1986 proved tough going for Mrs Thatcher. The immediate issue on which her Cabinet colleagues fastened was the future of British Leyland (BL). In her memoirs, she wrote that 'the most damaging effect of the Westland affair was the fuel which had been poured on the flames of anti-Americanism'.[5] The British motor industry was a good opportunity to stoke the fires higher.

Before the Westland crisis, questions about the future of BL had been becoming more urgent. During Westland, they became critical. For a long time, Mrs Thatcher had been impatient with BL's failure to fulfil its promises of improvement. 'Time after time, we had forecasts of improvements and they just didn't come,' she later recalled.[6] By 1986, BL had received some £2 billion from the British taxpayer over a ten-year period.[7] Mrs Thatcher believed the best future lay in separating the company into its constituent parts and, where possible, privatizing. This had happened

successfully with Jaguar, which demerged from BL and became a separate
publicly quoted company in July 1984. International interest grew. Honda,
from Japan, signed an agreement for joint model development with BL in
Swindon in April 1985. General Motors (GM) in the United States
expressed a desire for Leyland Truck and Bus and, separately, for Land
Rover. There was disagreement between Mrs Thatcher and Norman Tebbit, at that time the DTI Secretary. She wanted to open the market as
much as possible. Tebbit thought that Land Rover was 'a name strongly
identified with . . . British excellence in product design and engineering':[8]
'I do not believe it will be easy to gain public acceptance for . . . handing
such a particularly British undertaking to US control,' he told her. Mrs
Thatcher had little patience with such objections. 'There weren't any British solutions: that was the fact of the matter,' she later recalled. And she
harboured a greater fear: 'I didn't want it to go German.'[9] Tension rose
in the summer of 1985 when Tebbit suspected he was being leaked against
by her Policy Unit. Andrew Turnbull, her Treasury private secretary,
reported to Robin Butler, Tebbit's 'extreme sensitivity'. She might have to
'choose between pushing through her view on BL and keeping in with Mr
Tebbit'.[10] She reshuffled Tebbit in September 1985 before this choice
became unavoidable, and made him party chairman (see Chapter 13).

Replacing Tebbit, Leon Brittan pursued the GM discussions. But, as
Mrs Thatcher's Policy Unit warned her, 'GM are only at the starting line;
BL will provide plenty of chicanes before they reach the chequered flag.'[11]
So it proved. At the end of November, just when the Westland story was
becoming dramatic, Brittan told her that he would press ahead with the
sale to GM, but added that 'the real problem is political; the deal will
have enough natural opponents, some of them on our own backbenches,
to make it essential to avoid also bringing out against us the West Midlands lobbies associated with Austin Rover.'[12] This was the present danger
because, almost immediately after Brittan had sent his memo, Ford told
him of its own interest in Austin Rover, BL's volume car-maker. In one
way, this was great news for Mrs Thatcher's revolution in industry. At last
the once-moribund company was something whose bits the world wanted
to own. In another, it was terrible timing. As Peter Warry of the Policy
Unit put it to her, 'BL could be history by the middle of 1986. The downside is the political difficulty of selling the whole of BL to foreign
multinationals.'[13] The GM project was codenamed Salton, the Ford bid
Maverick.

In early December 1985, Mrs Thatcher, Brittan and Nigel Lawson met
and agreed to pursue the Ford discussions. Wisely, no one informed
Michael Heseltine of what was afoot. Mrs Thatcher was acutely aware of

the tricky politics. If the American bids could go forward without British or European companies being seen to have a chance to bid too, it would be Westland all over again, and on a far more important issue. On 27 January 1986, the day when she finally calmed Westland down in parliamentary terms, she was informed of Norman Tebbit's view that the combination of the two American bids was too controversial. He 'could not recommend' going ahead with the Ford deal at this time.[14] He said he preferred the idea of Austin Rover and Ford forming together a 'European holding company' which 'could be represented as an important step forward towards the creation of a European car industry'. Tebbit might no longer be the relevant departmental head on the subject but, since he was party Chairman and the administration's leading Thatcherite, his support was essential. If her greatest maverick did not like Maverick, how many others were likely to support it?

That weekend, news of the Ford interest and of the GM bid was leaked by – Mrs Thatcher believed – people in BL itself and reached the front pages of several Monday newspapers. What was good for General Motors, warned the *Daily Mail*, was not necessarily good for Britain.[15] On Monday 3 February, Paul Channon, who had taken over at the DTI after Brittan's resignation, had to come to the Commons to admit what was going on. The matter was debated in Parliament two days later, and Edward Heath, relishing his moment, led the charge against the government. 'Let us get away from this so-called anti-Americanism,' he said, stoking it;[16] 'because of Westland, and now because of this, the public are becoming anti-American. They do not want to see our country and our industries handed over more and more to the American firms.' His solution was almost spookily like that of Norman Tebbit, normally his bitter opponent: 'a European arrangement . . . which would be a joint operation'.[17] This was the mood of the House, reflected in the media. Mrs Thatcher considered it 'a kind of pseudo-patriotic hysteria'.[18]

The next day, at what she described as 'an extremely difficult meeting of the Cabinet',[19] Mrs Thatcher found herself supported only by Lawson in her desire to push on with Maverick. Colleagues were clamorous about the need not to repeat Westland. That afternoon, Channon told Parliament that the Ford bid would not be pursued. The press reported this decision as a 'climb-down' or a 'humiliation' for Mrs Thatcher. The *Express* claimed that it was the 'fastest U-turn on record'.[20]

It had been very much a decision of the Cabinet. 'We stopped it, you know,' Douglas Hurd told the present author a few days after the event, emphasizing the 'We'.[21] Mrs Thatcher was upset, and wrote to Donald E. Petersen, the chairman of the Ford Motor Company, to say how sorry she

was. She blamed the leak and the 'resulting speculation, uncertainty and
public apprehension'.[22] Ford did not doubt her own commitment, Petersen
said in reply, but had been amazed by the 'quite hostile responses' in
Britain to its 'honest initiative'[23] which it 'still felt hard to understand
completely'. Mrs Thatcher felt 'we were very vulnerable because Ford had
very big operations in England and it was dead easy for them to take them
to the Continent . . . We went to great lengths to reassure Ford and calm
them down.'[24]

Inevitably, the opposition to the Ford bid was unappeased by its victory
and moved its target to the GM one. Mrs Thatcher was furious. Officials
kept urging her to deal with the question collectively in government and
be seen to keep an open mind about other bids for Land Rover. To ensure
this, she set up a small ministerial group to work out the way forward
with GM. But the next day, 20 February, in Cabinet, colleagues warned
her that the GM takeover could not go ahead – 'My postbag enormous, &
universally hostile' (Tebbit), 'We are in danger of a major disaster'
(Whitelaw).[25] She moaned that she was 'Fed up with people of considerable
wealth [who] don't come forward with British bids, but want it all on
British taxpayer'. 'I fear consequences of what we did in rejecting Ford,'
she said.[26] Sure enough, the pressure of party and public opinion was too
great. A compromise attempt by the government to persuade GM to buy
just under half of Land Rover failed. On 25 March, Channon had to tell
the Commons that GM was not prepared to buy Leyland Trucks and its
freight business if it were not allowed control. The fact that Mrs Thatcher,
the most pro-American of modern British prime ministers, was compelled
to abort both these deals showed how politically weak she had become.

Just two weeks later, in early April, Mrs Thatcher found her pro-American
sympathies brought to the fore once again, in what was now a decidedly
hostile climate. For some time, terrorist attacks sponsored by Libya had
been a growing problem. There were several outrages in 1985. These
culminated in attacks at Rome and Vienna airports on 27 December, carried out by the Abu Nidal terrorist organization and supported by Libya,
which killed nineteen people. On 7 January 1986, Reagan had announced
sanctions against Libya in a televised press conference. He also threatened
'further steps' if sanctions proved inadequate. He wrote privately to European leaders, asking for their support.

Britain was in no doubt about the unpleasantness of Colonel Gaddafi's
Libyan regime. On 17 April 1984, WPC Yvonne Fletcher, policing an
anti-Gaddafi protest outside the Libyan Embassy in London, had been
killed by a shot fired from an Embassy window. Getting no co-operation

from Libya in finding the culprit, Britain broke off diplomatic relations, banned arms exports and put strict restrictions on credit and immigration.[27] It was 'very difficult to do much with Qadhafi* because he is mad', Mrs Thatcher told Vice-President George Bush in July 1985.[28] Nonetheless, she had a long-standing dislike of economic sanctions. She believed – most notably in the case of South Africa, where she stood out against almost all her fellow members of the Commonwealth (see Chapter 16) – that sanctions were ineffective and damaged the people who imposed them. 'Look!' she told American correspondents on 10 January, in response to Reagan's call for sanctions. 'Sanctions do not work if other people supply the goods. Other people do supply the goods.'[29] She believed that Reagan, who had supported her arguments in relation to South Africa, was now undermining the general case.

Worse was the possibility that the Americans might resort to military action. If so, she told Woodrow Wyatt in confidence, 'we can't support them.'[30] Presumably mindful of her unhappy experience over Grenada, at her press conference she tried to head the President off:

> I must warn you that I do not believe in retaliatory strikes which are against international law. We suffer from terrorism in this country and in Northern Ireland. What would you think if I said . . . that we would be entitled to go in hot pursuit or engage in retaliatory strikes? You would be absolutely against me, and so would I, because it would be contrary to international law . . . Now, I quite agree terrorism is against international law, but I believe that one has to fight it by legal means.[31]

She made this statement the day after Michael Heseltine had resigned as defence secretary in the midst of the Westland crisis. The last thing she needed at this point was entanglement in a controversial military adventure.

In her private reply to Reagan's letter, however, Mrs Thatcher concentrated on her case against sanctions, and said little about retaliation. Studying her response, Reagan's staff seized on this omission: 'The letter is perhaps more important for what it does <u>not</u> say. She makes no mention of her public remarks to the effect that international law prohibits punitive strikes against states that harbour terrorists. She does, however, subtly ask that "we remain in close touch as our thinking develops".'[32] The staffers were not wrong in noticing Mrs Thatcher's careful positioning for

---

* The name of the Libyan leader admits of many English spellings. This text uses 'Gaddafi' unless quoting directly from a written source.

what might lie ahead. She sensed that the Americans meant business on this issue, and she did not want to rule herself out of the discussion.

That week, the President sent his Deputy Secretary of State, John Whitehead, on a mission to European capitals to strengthen allied resolve against Libya. Whitehead conveyed the administration's anger. Mrs Thatcher's recent public remarks 'had been seen as a slap in the face to the President', he told Geoffrey Howe. Howe's office reported to Downing Street Whitehead's view that 'the time had come for offensive action to topple Qadhafi' – 'his private message was disquieting and his tone distinctly coercive.'[33]

By this stage, Mrs Thatcher's mind was churning about how she could help Reagan against Libya without sanctions and without entering the realms of illegality. On the following Monday, during a visit to Lille to announce the project for the Channel Tunnel (see Chapter 12), she discussed the problem with President Mitterrand. The United States was very 'cross' about the lack of British support over Libya, she told him, and she wondered whether military retaliation against terrorist training camps could be justified. She worried that it was little different from 'attacking the country'. Mitterrand told her that he would support 'precise attacks' (a phrase which Mrs Thatcher underlined in the record of their conversation). He also suggested that the allies should create 'internal difficulties' for Gaddafi, in secret.[34] A few days later, large quantities of Libyan rifles and ammunition – Gaddafi's supplies for the IRA – were found hidden in sites in Co. Sligo and Co. Roscommon in the Republic of Ireland. This discovery gave Mrs Thatcher, if she needed one, a reminder of how Gaddafi was actively threatening Britain. It may well have strengthened her desire to assist the United States. The British government looked into various ways of making life difficult for Gaddafi, while bearing in mind that the target should be 'the regime rather than the man'.[35] As Charles Powell scribbled on top of a Foreign Office note for her eyes, 'The (reluctant) conclusion is that there is not much we can do.'[36]

The Americans forced the issue, alone. In March, they began a series of naval manoeuvres in the Gulf of Sirte, international waters which Gaddafi claimed as his own. Coming under missile attack from the Libyan coast, the US attacked the launch site and sank two Libyan patrol boats. Gaddafi sent out a general message to all his European 'People's Bureaux' (as he preferred to call his country's embassies) ordering them to mount terrorist attacks on US military and civilian targets. This and other Libyan cable traffic carrying more specific messages were intercepted with assistance from GCHQ at Cheltenham. On 4 April, a message was picked up from the East Berlin People's Bureau to Tripoli saying, 'We have something planned that will make you happy . . . It will happen soon, the bomb will blow, American soldiers must be hit.'[37] The Libyans were as bad as their word. In the early hours of 5 April, a bomb went off in the La Belle discotheque in West Berlin, a haunt of US servicemen. Three people, one of them an American soldier, were killed. The Americans decided at once that they had now found the 'smoking gun' and could and should hit back. They despatched messages from the President to their allies.

The most important of these came to Mrs Thatcher. 'I have reluctantly taken the decision to use US military forces to exact a response to these Libyan attacks,' said the President.[38] He requested the use of British airfields where US F-111s were based, so that they could attack Libya.* His request arrived on 8 April, asking for an answer by noon (GMT) the following day. The Americans assumed, erroneously, that British agreement would be pretty much automatic. But Mrs Thatcher, meeting Howe and the new Defence Secretary George Younger after a formal dinner for the President of South Korea, played for time.† As Percy Cradock, her foreign policy adviser, later put it: 'We were not entirely surprised; but we were worried. The request was far from precise and we were not sure that the Administration had thought through the consequences . . . Above all, there were British hostages in the Lebanon [two employees of the American University in Beirut who were held by Libyan proxies, and were therefore at extreme risk].'[39] The fact that Reagan's request came when anti-American feeling was still running high following Westland and the abortive sale of British Leyland was also unhelpful. Mrs Thatcher's reply, sent early in the morning of the following day, ignored the US deadline for a decision and instead sought more information.‡ She reiterated her opposition to terrorism and her 'instinct' always to support the United States, but explained that 'your message causes me very considerable

* Militarily, the US could have launched the raids using navy assets alone. The decision to use the air force, and thus involve Mrs Thatcher so closely, was a consequence of internal politics (and rivalries) between the services. (Interviews with John Lehman and John Poindexter.)

† The Libya episode put further strain on Mrs Thatcher's relationship with her Foreign Secretary: 'It was the measure of Geoffrey Howe . . . It was George Younger who was very strong' (Thatcher Memoirs Materials, CAC: THCR 4/3).

‡ One problem that the British did not reveal to the Americans was that they were far from sure whether the 1952 agreement on US use of British bases required British *permission* for such flights. Officials thought that the worst outcome would be for Britain to refuse the request, 'but for the United States Government to go ahead all the same'. (Powell to Galsworthy, 9 April 1986, Prime Minister's Papers, Libya, Relations, Internal Political Situation, Part 4A (document consulted in the Cabinet Office).) To avoid such an outcome, was the implication, it would be better for Britain to agree.

anxiety ... I would like you to tell me more precisely what you have in mind.' What were the targets, she wondered? Would other countries be involved? She also raised wider concerns – the risk of 'getting us into a cycle of revenge and counter-revenge, in which many more innocent lives will be lost'. And she wanted to know the exact nature of the justification, once again raising the comparison with Northern Ireland: 'I have to live with the border between Northern Ireland and the Republic across which terrorists come daily. We have lost 2,500 of our people in the last ten years, but we have never crossed that border to exact revenge.' 'Indeed,' she added tartly, 'I wonder what the reaction would be in the United States if we did.'* Self-defence was a much better legal justification than punitive action. Besides, 'The effect in the Arab world, where we all have very major economic interests ... could be devastating.' 'I am deeply troubled by what you propose,' she concluded, but added that she wrote 'in the spirit of loyalty and friendship'.[40]

In her memoirs, Mrs Thatcher wrote that 'this initial response was probably too negative.'[41] Certainly, 'This was not the sort of cable we had expected to get back from Mrs Thatcher,' recalled Howard Teicher of the NSC staff,[42] but her questions did force the Americans to produce answers, and thus to think more clearly about what they were doing: 'I think it would be fair to say that she did have an influence on the President. He did take her seriously. He did say, "I need her help. I need to make sure I can look her in the eye and say I did everything I could to do what you asked us to do." '[43] As consultations and US military planning continued, the American deadline drifted.

But Reagan's reply to Mrs Thatcher, which she received soon after midnight on 10 April, was firm. He said that, although her concerns were 'understandable', the cycle of revenge which she feared had started a long time ago. The lack of a firm Western response, the President wrote, 'builds up Qadhafi and his prestige'. Contrary to the British view, other Arab governments were content that Libya be punished, and there was 'ample legal justification' for such an attack, although he did not mention the issue of self-defence which Mrs Thatcher considered so important. Reagan also answered her request to explain his targets. They would not be economic, and they would be focused on Gaddafi's 'primary headquarters and immediate security forces'.[44] Then the President made her feel the iron fist in his velvet glove: 'You should not underestimate the profound effect

* Mrs Thatcher later conceded her parallel was unsound. 'The difference is that Libya was directly state-sponsored terrorism. The Republic of Ireland is not, they are trying to stop the terrorists.' (Thatcher Memoirs Materials, CAC: THCR 4/3.)

on the American people if our actions to put a halt to these crimes continue to receive only lukewarm support or no support at all from our closest allies whom we have committed ourselves to defend . . . we are the only Western power in a position to act decisively. I do not feel I can shrink from this responsibility.'[45]

Mrs Thatcher underlined these words and made her decision in the small hours. Charles Powell remembered 'her coming down exceptionally early in the morning into the private office. She sat in the armchair beside my desk and said, "Charles, I've been thinking about this all night. We have to support the Americans on this. That's what allies are for." '[46] Powell went into action. 'The Prime Minister takes the view', he wrote to Geoffrey Howe's private office, 'that the reply [from Reagan] is well argued and leaves no doubt the President is determined to go ahead with military action against Libya. We are not going to deter him; and there is no point in being grudging in the further message which will now be required.'[47] In a meeting with Howe and Younger that morning Mrs Thatcher set out this position. Howe grumbled, saying that he 'remained sceptical whether the action proposed by the President would have the intended effects',[48] but both acquiesced. Without any formal meeting to seek ministerial approval, Mrs Thatcher replied to Reagan, editing out the more querulous tone of an earlier Cabinet Office draft. She said that she was 'much impressed' by his case: 'The main point of this message, therefore, is to assure you that you can count on our unqualified support for action directed against specific Libyan targets demonstrably involved in the conduct and support of terrorist activities.'[49] The President replied quickly and gratefully that her offer 'reaffirms the fundamental strength of the special relationship between our two countries'.[50]*

Once the thing was all over, Mrs Thatcher was inclined to lend colour to her own reasoning. When she saw the American arms reductions negotiator Paul Nitze almost two weeks later, she told him that her decision had been governed by her dislike of appeasement. The American view on Libya had ensured that 'for the first time she understood what Baldwin and Chamberlain had come up against and that she would fight it.'[51] It is true that, as Powell put it, 'Her resistance to terrorism was so powerful, so central to her being and existence, that there were no two ways about it';[52] but at the time, she weighed all the arguments very carefully: 'What worried her most was the fate of the British hostages in Lebanon. She

---

* Contrary to what has sometimes been written (e.g. Smith, *Reagan and Thatcher*, p. 193), Reagan and Mrs Thatcher did not discuss any of the Libyan question by telephone until after the US attacks had taken place.

agonized over it beforehand, because the advice was that they would be bumped off . . . It was a decision she took, knowing that she could be signing the death warrant of those guys.'[53] She also wanted to be quite sure that there was proper justification in international law for any attack. This led her, backed up by the opinion of the Attorney-General, to insist on self-defence under Article 51 of the UN Charter, rather than retaliation, as the legal justification. In the view of Percy Cradock, who was advising her on the subject, the 'principle of retaliation' was successfully 'twisted round' into that of self-defence.[54] Her readiness for strong, even violent action by allies was always heavily qualified by her belief in legality.

While Mrs Thatcher would not have agreed to Reagan's request unless she had been satisfied on these points, she was never actively enthusiastic for the attacks on Libya. What really swayed her was her judgment of American attitudes. Once she had worked out that the United States was determined to proceed, she had to decide whether Britain wanted to repeat the row over Grenada, this time without the rhetorical advantage of being able to complain afterwards that she had been kept in the dark. Reagan had consulted her, had reasoned with her and had invoked their overriding common interests. If she had refused to co-operate and he had gone ahead anyway, she would have let him down and exposed for all to see that, on this matter, she had been unable to sway him. She was unhappy, and strongly conscious that neither British public opinion nor her colleagues would be supportive, but she saw that opposition to the attacks was a dead end. She would get a couple of days' good headlines for 'standing up to America', but, in the longer term, gravely weaken the alliance and the relationship on which she had built so much. Officials observing her thought that she had moved weirdly fast from her grave doubts about the attacks to strong support in twenty-four hours. 'She had completely changed,' David Goodall recalled,[55] as if she had been leant on. She certainly had been leant on, but there is no evidence that she thought Reagan had applied pressure illegitimately. The change was typical of the way Mrs Thatcher usually made decisions. She was all hesitation, doubt and niggling until the moment of decision. Once she had decided, she was adamantine.

On 12 April, Reagan's envoy General Vernon Walters called on Mrs Thatcher to discuss US intentions in more detail. Walters remembered Mrs Thatcher as being 'magnificent': 'She said to me, "For forty years you have kept 350,000 of your young men in Europe to help us retain our freedom. How can anyone seriously expect me to say 'No' to your request to use the bases in the United Kingdom." '[56] She may have spoken thus, but the official record paints a markedly different picture. Without withdrawing the support she had promised the President, Mrs Thatcher pushed hard on every issue that worried her. She complained that the US had expanded the President's 'reasonably reassuring' definition of targets: 'The sort of targets identified by Secretary Shultz would make an attack look like a state of undeclared war. There was no knowing where this would lead. The longest journey started with the shortest step.'[57] She reiterated her insistence on self-defence as the justification for any attack; there must be no talk of 'retaliation, revenge, or reprisal'. So trenchant, indeed, were her remarks that the gist was leaked to *The Times* – most likely by sources hostile to the American raid – and presented two days later as a story that 'The Prime Minister is believed to have refused a request from the United States for the use of its F-111 bomber bases in Britain to mount an attack against Libya.'[58]

At noon that day, Monday 14 April, the issue was discussed and agreed at the OD Committee of the Cabinet, Mrs Thatcher having decided, on the advice of Robert Armstrong,[59] that this smaller and more secure body was more appropriate than the full Cabinet. Mrs Thatcher's speaking note for the meeting summed up all the problems, but concluded, 'We have got to stand by them as they stood by us over the Falklands.'[60] At 17.20, Downing Street heard that the F-111s would shortly take off from their British bases, and immediately so informed the Queen.

The planes' journey was elongated by the refusal of Spain and France (despite President Mitterrand's private talk of support for anti-Gaddafi operations) to allow over-flight. Powell noted Mrs Thatcher's contempt for the European allies' 'needlessly and deliberately endangering American lives'.[61] As the bombers were taking off, she was also facing a political crisis of an almost absurdly different kind – a classic example of the random concatenation of events which makes the office of prime minister so challenging.

In the Commons that night, the House was debating the controversial Shops Bill, which would have allowed more shops to open on Sundays. This reform had been brewing for several years. In deference to Christian principles, the law had always restricted Sunday trading, but social and technological change had eaten away at this. A mare's nest of laws now permitted some openings but prevented others. One anomaly, for example, was that it was legal to buy pornography on a Sunday, but not to buy a Bible. There was a move, naturally favoured by the larger retailers, to liberalize and straighten out the rules. Despite her Sabbatarian background as a Methodist girl from Grantham, Mrs Thatcher was in favour.

'I think this Bill is desirable,' she wrote about a prototype version four years earlier, 'and that it would provide more business and possibly more jobs.'[62] She persisted in this view even though well aware of what she called 'a strong alliance in the Commons against it of USDAW [the shopworkers' union], the Lord's [Day] Observance Society, and small shopkeepers'.[63] A government Bill to implement the changes was framed.

Among Mrs Thatcher's advisers, counsels were divided. The free-market beliefs of most of them favoured reform. Business interests, represented to her by the likes of Tim Bell and David Young, and often including contributors to Conservative Party funds, were powerful. On the other hand, Brian Griffiths, in charge of the Policy Unit, and her PPS, Michael Alison, were strong evangelicals, and opposed it. Writing 'as a churchwarden', Griffiths told her it would be 'yet another inducement to loosen family ties'.[64] Many of her supporters, he went on,

> welcome your moral stance on economic and social matters. They also feel that our traditional Sunday is part of our Christian heritage as a nation. They therefore find it puzzling, in view of your stand on other issues, that you are prepared to put the weight of the Government behind these proposed changes.

'As the Bill goes through Parliament,' he concluded, 'I would expect the opposition to it to grow considerably.'[65]

Griffiths knew whereof he spoke because he was close to the main campaigners against the Bill who came together as the 'Keep Sunday Special' campaign. It was formally launched, by ill chance, on the day of Michael Heseltine's resignation, and so attracted no public notice. This lulled the government into a false sense of security. The campaign's Operation Valentine, centred on St Valentine's Day, held close to 180 public meetings targeting the constituencies of backbench Conservative MPs, pushing the party's commitment to what its director, Michael Schluter, called 'the Judaeo-Christian ethos'.[66] Tory MPs began to be impressed by the strength of opposition. By early March, more than 32,000 letters against the Bill had arrived in Downing Street, and a month later petitions against had attracted more than a million signatures. 'The perceived inflexibility of the Government is now damaging your personal reputation,' hazarded Hartley Booth from the Policy Unit, adding that 'The Church in Scotland has come out strongly in favour of changing the law to <u>restrict</u> trading.'[67]* 'They would wouldn't they?' wrote Mrs Thatcher,

---

* A further anomaly exposed in the controversy was that Scotland, traditionally more Sabbatarian, did not have laws restricting Sunday trading. This was because Scots had not, until the late twentieth century, imagined that anyone would dare to trade on the Sabbath.

in imitation of Mandy Rice-Davies. In Brian Griffiths's view, 'She did not really want to know. She thought it was going to happen.'[68]

But there was a reputational danger for Mrs Thatcher, partly because the Shops Bill coincided with her wider post-Westland unpopularity and the resistance to selling BL to Americans. Her personal support for the Bill, which was not enthusiastically backed by her doubting Cabinet,* added to the feeling that she was uncaring, that her god was money and even that she was, somehow, unBritish. There was hypocrisy in all this, since the great majority of British people, including churchgoers, shopped on Sunday where and when they could; but then hypocrisy is a permanent British quality which politicians ignore at their peril.[69]

About a month before the vote, Michael Alison wrote his boss a long and typically courteous memo, describing himself as a 'conscientious objector' and asking to be allowed to abstain. He set out the true nature of opposition to the Bill, and advocated new legislation which would make Sunday 'special':

> So many traditional landmarks are slipping away, with ethnic and religious pluralism sweeping in, that a Government decision to legislate to make Sunday different would ... be a symbolic reaffirmation of the Christian values of our past ... This approach is analogous to keeping the Monarchy afloat, long after its real power has been ceded; indeed, the weaker the Monarchy in real terms, the greater the zeal and affection for it popularly! This accounts, I believe, for the paradoxical upsurge in zeal for Sunday among millions of good, church-going Conservatives who cheerfully shop on Sundays in a limited way.[70]

While consenting to Alison's plea to abstain, Mrs Thatcher's response to his broader points is not recorded. Her approach to similar criticisms was to listen politely, and on occasion authorize changes in tactics, but press on with the Bill regardless.

As the night of the vote approached, the revolt grew and the rebels began to feel safety in numbers. Because the contentious nine-hour debate stretched late into the night, Mrs Thatcher worried that the House would still be sitting when news of the Libyan bombing raid broke and feared that she would be called to explain then and there what was going on. She

---

* A list drawn up at the time of the Shops Bill suggests that the majority of the Cabinet were opposed to it, with 10 'For' and 12 'Against'. At more junior levels of government opposition was even stronger. The totals were: minister of state 4 For/18 Against, parliamentary under-secretary 9 For/38 Against, whips 6 For/7 Against, parliamentary private secretary 9 For /34 Against. (Handwritten note, CAC: THCR 1/3/21 (The list is undated but the context suggests it likely relates to the Shops Bill).)

and her staff waited in the Cabinet Room, anxiously checking the ticker tapes for the first reports of the attacks. In the event, the raids were delayed and only began to hit their targets at one in the morning (UK time). The government lost the Sunday Trading Bill by 14 votes. More than seventy Conservatives rebelled, and the absolutely loyal Michael Alison, as permitted by Mrs Thatcher, abstained. This was its first defeat of the Parliament and the only occasion in the whole of her time in office when a government Bill was lost on the second reading. The House then voted to adjourn. The news of the raid had not yet broken, so Mrs Thatcher was spared the need for a late-night statement.

It being much earlier in the evening in the United States, Reagan broadcast to the nation. The content of this speech had been the subject of considerable lobbying from London. Having convinced herself that military action was justifiable on grounds of self-defence, Mrs Thatcher was determined that Reagan, who often lapsed into talk of retaliation, should choose his words carefully. 'We were conscious of her insistence that we frame the attacks in terms of self-defence . . .' recalled Teicher, 'so definitely there would have been an impact on how things were framed as a result of her input.'[71] Reagan now provided the words Mrs Thatcher needed to hear: 'Self-defense is not only our right, it is our duty. It is the purpose behind the mission undertaken tonight, a mission fully consistent with Article 51 of the United Nations Charter.'[72]

At the Cabinet that day, and again on Thursday, ministers were extremely unenthusiastic. Willie Whitelaw said that 'The young regard Reagan as a dangerous old fool. They are frightened of him.'[73] Norman Tebbit, disgruntled by his exclusion from the inner counsels,[74] was particularly fierce. He took up Whitelaw's point, saying that Reagan's style was 'OK for Little Rock, Arkansas, but it grates on electors of Ryedale [the Yorkshire constituency, normally a safe Tory seat, where a by-election was imminent].'[75] Only Lord Hailsham, the Lord Chancellor, talking rather wildly about how his mother had been an American, positively supported the action.[76] But because she had already secured OD support, Mrs Thatcher was not in serious political danger from colleagues, and could not be accused of constitutional impropriety. It did little, however, for her already strained relations with Tebbit. 'This was the only time I can remember Norman getting into a complete rage, which lasted for about a fortnight,' recalled Andrew Lansley, his private secretary.[77] Tebbit's complaint was that, as party chairman, he needed advance notice of such things to enable him to defend them. At the time, Tebbit recalled, he was also worried that the permission for the raid would be politically damaging, but, in retrospect, formed the view that 'she was right: it was not.'[78] Certainly the immediate public reaction to British support for the raids was overwhelmingly negative. Stephen Sherbourne informed her that Conservative Central Office had received an 'unusually large number of calls expressing concern . . . the biggest reaction since the Falklands'.[79] 'Terrorism thrives on appeasement,' Mrs Thatcher wrote on the back of this note.

The Opposition in the House of Commons was in angry mood for Question Time and Mrs Thatcher's statement that afternoon. Against criticism from Tony Benn she stated her general theory: 'If one refuses to take any risks because of the consequences, the terrorist Governments will win and one can only cringe before them.'[80] During her statement, she was interrupted by insults (the Labour MP Andrew Faulds called Reagan 'her cretinous friend', an interjection which the Speaker forced him to withdraw). Mrs Thatcher kept returning in her remarks to the importance of self-defence. She defended her ground firmly, and faced no serious criticism from her own side. She 'could hardly have been more resolute as an ally and a friend', reported the US Ambassador, Charlie Price.[81] Afterwards, Reagan telephoned to thank her. She repeated to him what she had said to Benn, and he commented 'that Britain and America had learned over 40 years ago of the dangers of appeasement'.[82] He said that 'when, in the speech of the previous night, he had referred to the cooperation of European allies, he had only one country in mind: the United Kingdom. He was deeply grateful.'

No doubt these words produced a warm glow in Mrs Thatcher – and gave her the appeasement comparison which she was able to play back to Paul Nitze the following week – but in her conversation with Reagan she frankly expressed anxiety. She fretted – rightly, as it turned out – that the raids were not hugely effective or well targeted, and she told him that it was 'a difficult task to secure wide public understanding and support for this in the United Kingdom'.[83] She was effectively saying that he was in her debt.

What Mrs Thatcher called 'public understanding' did not improve much, from her point of view. BBC reporting of the bombing was clearly hostile, and so was much editorial comment in the British press. The action, judged the *Financial Times*, was 'futile, deplorable and almost certainly counter-productive . . . Mrs Thatcher was wrong to give in to US pressure.'[84] In a debate in the Commons the following day, Mrs Thatcher put in what Peter Riddell called 'one of her most effective performances',[85] sticking firmly to her line of principle: 'Terrorism has to be defeated; it cannot be tolerated or side-stepped. When other ways and other methods have failed – I am the first to wish that they had succeeded – it is right that the terrorist should know that firm steps will be taken to deter him.'[86] In order to press her point home in the debate, she had hoped to be able to refer to intelligence material which linked Libya with the terrorist attacks. But she was always ultra-conscious of the need to protect the secret services and approached the possibility of disclosing intelligence (famously used – or, according to critics, abused – by Tony Blair before the invasion of Iraq in 2003) with great care. In this case, she accepted the view of her officials that the sources involved were too sensitive to risk exposure. 'We refused intelligence about Gaddafi,' recalled Percy Cradock. 'She understood. She never compromised intelligence in any way.'[87] In the Commons, she tried to reassure doubters by saying – which Armstrong had agreed with the administration in advance – that no further US strikes would be launched from British bases without her express permission.

A MORI opinion poll the following day (admittedly based on research before her Commons speech) recorded 71 per cent disapproval of US use of the bases, and a dissatisfaction rating with Mrs Thatcher personally which had risen to 68 per cent from 61 per cent in March.[88] On 18 April, the bodies of Leigh Douglas and Philip Padfield, the two British hostages, held in the Lebanon, were found in Beirut (an American hostage was also murdered). Mrs Thatcher did not repent her decision to back the United States, and publicly reiterated that 'We cannot allow ourselves to be deflected in the struggle against terrorism by fear of reprisals.'[89] But she was naturally upset. 'She says she's been feeling very lonely,' her journalistic confidant Woodrow Wyatt recorded.[90] Price wrote directly to Reagan with a sympathetic assessment: 'While she has stood up to the political heat with her usual tenacity and style, it looks likely she will pay the price for her decision. As a result, I think it unlikely that Mrs Thatcher would support another similar strike absent an extremely compelling case.'[91]

Price was essentially right that Mrs Thatcher wanted no more of this, but it was typical of her attitude to difficult situations that she resisted internal attempts to back away. Charles Powell sent a tart note to the Foreign Office on her behalf. The Prime Minister was 'surprised', he said, at the minutes of the Ministerial Group on Libya saying that 'the Government had made clear to the United States that a further request by them to use bases in the United Kingdom would not be welcome and would not necessarily meet with a positive response . . . She is not aware of any decision made by Ministers in these terms.' The government of course gave 'no blank cheque' to the US, Powell went on, but nor did it rule out further action.[92] When Jacques Chirac, the French Prime Minister, visited her at Chequers that weekend, he told her that French opinion polls showed support both for the US attacks *and* for the French government's position. Mrs Thatcher exploded with rage:

> that reflected a cynical attitude: let the United States do the job and let France keep out of it. The crucial difference between France and the United Kingdom was that France did not have United States forces on its soil. France was in the fortunate position of being defended by the United States without undertaking a whole-hearted commitment to the Alliance . . . She would argue that this posed an added obligation to be helpful in an emergency.[93]

She summed up her approach: 'The Prime Minister said that the United Kingdom did not offer the United States blind devotion. Indeed, we frequently spoke very frankly to them. But there was a matter of loyalty.' She added acidly that 'France and the United Kingdom felt differently on this.'[94]

Two weeks after the raids, Mrs Thatcher's political difficulties rumbled on: 'while she is with us,' reported the US Embassy, 'she is not with her own people despite every effort on her part to turn around public opinion.'[95] In early May the government lost the Ryedale by-election as Tebbit had predicted. For all this, Mrs Thatcher did reap political benefits from her stance on Libya. One was that her conduct throughout, even though the policy was unpopular, helped restore the respect for her leadership which had been weakened by Westland. Whatever else might be said, her actions were not those of an indecisive or cowardly person. She had executed her decision clearly and defended it well. As time went on, she could also point to the fact that Libyan terrorism, despite the lack of physical success in the US raids, did go into retreat. With the glaring exception of the Lockerbie bombing in December 1988, Gaddafi was much subdued. According to Paul Bremer, then the State Department's Ambassador-at-Large for counter-terrorism, 'the Libyans had been planning 34 or 35 subsequent attacks on American targets in Europe. Those were stopped immediately.'[96]*

More important, the loyalty to allies of which she spoke so strongly to

---

* In discussions about the Thatchers' personal security in the wake of the Libyan bombing, 'the possibility of the detective carrying a protective mackintosh which could be placed around the Prime Minister's shoulders was raised' (Addison to Wicks, 23 April 1986, PM's Papers; Security: Arrangements for Mark Thatcher's Overseas Trips and Security (document consulted in the Cabinet Office)). Mrs Thatcher accepted this suggestion. This mackintosh was presumably an improvement on the one tried out on her before the Conservative Party conference in Blackpool the previous year. When Barry Strevens, her detective, helped her on with the bullet-proof garment provided, she collapsed under its weight (Interview with Barry Strevens).

Chirac was recognized in Washington and greatly increased her political capital. Reagan himself repeatedly expressed his gratitude, both in public and in private, in writing and in conversation. Howard Teicher recalled that 'in the immediate aftermath I suspect that the UK could have asked for and received almost anything it wanted.'[97]

Mrs Thatcher wanted US help over terrorist extradition. Despite the administration's general dislike of terrorism, American politics tended to make an exception of Northern Ireland. Irish Americans in Congress were, from a British point of view, unsound on the matter, and American politicians regularly had to bear the Irish vote in mind. The extradition treaty between the USA and Britain contained a loophole, barring extradition if the acts concerned were 'political' in nature. In December 1984, the New York federal court had denied the extradition of an IRA gunman, Joseph Doherty, on these grounds. The administration readily agreed to remove the loophole, but the resulting 'supplementary extradition treaty' was held up in the Senate. Leaders of the opposition to the change included John Kerry (who was to win the Democratic nomination for the presidential election of 2004 and later become President Obama's secretary of state) and Joe Biden (who, in 2009, would become vice-president of the United States). Explaining the situation to the President, John Poindexter, his National Security Advisor, set out how the 'political' exemption worked: 'For example, those who perpetrated the Brighton bombing – which nearly killed Mrs Thatcher – could not have been extradited back to the UK, assuming they had gotten to the US.'[98]

Mrs Thatcher herself did not use Libya 'explicitly as a "trade"', letting the British action 'speak for itself'.[99] But Price reported a conversation with Geoffrey Howe to Reagan: 'Geoffrey also reminded me with good humor of the urgent need to get the Extradition Treaty approved. I believe it would be a key demonstration of our appreciation for British support if we could capitalize on Thatcher's current popularity in Washington to press the treaty through.'[100]

Reagan took the promptings and swung into action. The following day he wrote to Richard Lugar, the chairman of the Senate Foreign Relations Committee: 'As Great Britain demonstrated once again last week, she is our staunchest Ally in the battle against international terrorism. Rejection of the Treaty would be viewed by the British – and the world at large – as a weakening of U.S. resolve. This must not happen.'[101] Reagan and Mrs Thatcher discussed the matter further when they met at the G7 summit in Tokyo in May. At the end of the month, the President appealed to the American people in his weekly radio broadcast. He rehearsed the arguments about closing the loophole in the treaty to 'prevent terrorists who have kidnapped, killed, or maimed people in Britain from finding refuge in our country'. Moreover, he went on: 'rejection of this treaty would be an affront to British Prime Minister Margaret Thatcher, one European leader who, at great political risk, stood shoulder to shoulder with us during our operations against Qadhafi's terrorism.'[102] On 17 July, the Senate ratified the treaty by 87 votes to 10, with even Senators Kerry, Biden and Ted Kennedy voting in favour.

Reagan rang Mrs Thatcher immediately with the news, apologizing for pulling her out of a dinner party with the government whips:

> Mrs Thatcher replied that she did not mind being disturbed at dinner, particularly to hear such good news. She graciously said that the President deserved all the credit for the positive outcome. He responded that it was a joint effort and that the Prime Minister and her government had played a large role in the Senate passage. The Prime Minister reemphasized that the outcome would not have been favourable without the President's many personal efforts.[103]

Mrs Thatcher's conclusion over the Libyan affair was that her loyalty to the American alliance had been vindicated, and that the unreliability of European allies had been proved: 'they are a feeble, weak lot . . .' she said later, 'we alone among Europe helped' the Americans.[104] At the end of May, just as Reagan's campaign for the extradition treaty was reaching its climax, she was asked to give written answers to questions for *The Rich Tide*, a forthcoming book about transatlantic relations by David Frost and Michael Shea. Charles Powell redrafted her proposed answers from what he called 'a late and poor draft from the Foreign Office'. Mrs Thatcher was delighted with his reworking. 'I think you have done wonders,' she scribbled. 'I have deleted just one sentence.'[105] The offending sentence was in answer to the question, 'Is there a special bond that exists between the United Kingdom and the United States that does not exist between the UK and any other country?' The Powell draft gave an affirmative answer, but added the qualification, 'We have very close relations with other countries too: with the democratic nations of the Commonwealth, and with Europe.' Mrs Thatcher struck this out, so that her answer ended with the unqualified words 'Special means unique, unique to Britain and the United States.'[106]

Just as the United States made ready to attack Libya, Mrs Thatcher was at Chequers, discussing, for the first time, how to approach the next general election. She was in an edgy mood, made edgier because she was not free to explain to colleagues why. Norman Tebbit had dined and slept at

Chequers the night before, but had learnt nothing about the Libyan plan from her. The political high command were present – Howe, Lawson, Tebbit, Young and Whitelaw (though he could only drop in, since he was entertaining royal guests at home). Tebbit was not pleased by the presence of Young, whom he suspected of muscling in on his responsibilities.[107] The grandees were assisted by Sherbourne, Brian Griffiths and Michael Dobbs, and also by John Sharkey,* the managing director of Saatchi and Saatchi, who had retained the Conservative account ever since Gordon Reece bestowed it on them, on Mrs Thatcher's behalf, in 1978. The specific purpose of the meeting, which was held on Sunday 13 April, was to consider the strategy for the run-up to the election, including the results of opinion research which Saatchis had carried out at Tebbit's request.

The research was presented by Dobbs. Though working full time for Tebbit, he remained deputy chairman of Saatchis, who had seconded him and were paying him. This created an uncomfortable feeling that Dobbs had an interest not only in Tory fortunes, but in supporting whatever Saatchis came up with. The opinion research, he reported, showed a public impression of confused leadership over the Westland crisis. As Sharkey recalled it, 'Perceptions of Mrs Thatcher had turned from largely positive to slightly negative.'[108] In the view of Saatchis and of Tebbit, it was a presentation 'about the sense of leadership, not about her personally'.[109] According to Stephen Sherbourne – although others remember this differently – the presentation involved clips of films in which various women were interviewed and spoke disparagingly of Mrs Thatcher herself.[110] At this time, the press were talking about what they called 'the TBW factor' as counting against the Conservatives with the public. TBW stood for 'That Bloody Woman'. Mrs Thatcher herself had known about it since the previous June, when David Frost had introduced her to the phrase on air.[111] Although the offensive acronym was naturally not used in the presentation, Mrs Thatcher sensed that this was what it was getting at.† She did not like what she was being told. There was no shouting match or scene, but when Dobbs was about to display the illustrative boards which summarized his talk, she seized them and 'threw them into a corner before they'd been shown'.[112]

It was not immediately obvious to all that things had gone badly wrong. Sharkey went away from the meeting thinking it had been 'reasonably

---

* John Sharkey (1947–), joint managing director, Saatchi & Saatchi UK, 1986–9; created Lord Sharkey, 2010.

† These findings were confirmed in ordinary opinion polls. In April 1986, Mrs Thatcher was viewed positively by only 28 per cent of those questioned. She had not had such low ratings since 1981. (See Campbell, *Margaret Thatcher: The Iron Lady*, p. 499.)

successful'.[113] Sherbourne, however, who knew Mrs Thatcher better, noticed her anger: 'Dobbs almost had to pick up his bags and go.'[114] It did not take long for rumours to filter back that all was not well. Dobbs soon found himself 'disinvited from every election planning meeting'.[115] Since he was Tebbit's right-hand man, this was, in effect, a rejection of Tebbit. The presentation at Chequers had upset her not only because it wounded her vanity but also because it confirmed her suspicions. Even when she had appointed Tebbit as chairman the previous September, she had not bestowed her full trust on him, and so had created a problem for him and for herself. He was too big and too popular a figure with party supporters for her to be easy with him in a role which might allow him to stand between her and her base. In the post-Westland atmosphere, there was a strong sense that her leadership was insecure. Robin Harris,* who, as head of the Conservative Research Department, saw a lot of both Mrs Thatcher and Tebbit at this time, recalled, 'I thought she'd be a goner over Westland. If she did go, Norman was a very likely successor. I wasn't plotting with him, but I did want him [to be leader if Mrs Thatcher fell]. It is absurd to suppose he was not even thinking about it.'[116] Young thought that 'Norman was just too popular: she suffered from ageing-lion syndrome in relation to him.'[117] She particularly feared his close relationship with Saatchis, hence her suspicion of Dobbs. A small symptom of her anxiety was apparent in an argument with Tebbit, just before appointing Dobbs early in the year, about what his job title should be. 'Deputy Chairman,' suggested Tebbit. 'No,' said Mrs Thatcher, 'PA.' The compromise was 'Chief of Staff'.[118]

Even before the Chequers meeting, some of those close to her had fed her anxieties. Tim Bell, the man who – with Gordon Reece – Mrs Thatcher liked the most of all those in the world of advertising and PR, had fallen out with Saatchis and left them. They had made a curious arrangement which paid him a retainer of £48,000 a year not to do any work for the Conservative Party without their agreement.[119]† This did not, however, prevent Mrs Thatcher privately seeing her old friend Bell, who naturally rejoiced that she wanted his advice. As Dobbs put it, 'Tim was sneaking in through the dustbins.'[120] Tebbit, however, was against Bell. He had learnt from Cecil Parkinson that Bell's drug-taking during the 1983 election

* Robin Harris (1952–), educated Canford School and Exeter College, Oxford; director, Conservative Research Department, 1985–9; member, No. 10 Policy Unit, 1989–90; adviser to Baroness Thatcher, 1990–2003; author of *Not for Turning: The Life of Margaret Thatcher*, Bantam, 2013.
† Tim Bell said that he never actually received any of the money promised (Interview with Lord Bell).

campaign had made him almost impossible to deal with.[121] He had firm, old-fashioned views on such matters. In 1985 Bell wrote to Mrs Thatcher to tell her about his problem with drugs, which he said he had now overcome. Her friendly response was 'If you've stopped, there's an end of it.'[122]* Bell was now undergoing rehabilitation, but Tebbit remained uneasy. Once he had decided that he did not want Bell on his Central Office team in any way, he had set himself on a collision course with Mrs Thatcher.[123]

Bell's ally in all this – and Tebbit's challenger for Mrs Thatcher's ear – was David Young. Although unelected, Young had exceptionally strong political ambitions, and had it in mind that he could be party chairman.[124] As a peer, he obviously presented no threat to Mrs Thatcher's leadership. As an adviser, he could influence her strongly, often against people who *were* elected. In the view of Stephen Sherbourne, Mrs Thatcher 'loved David and adored Tim'.[125] She had much more ambiguous feelings about Tebbit. In this area of political life, outside the stricter structures of policy and government, Mrs Thatcher was vulnerable to flattery and manipulation. There was too much of the atmosphere of a court. 'I began to understand Tudor history better,' recalled Tebbit.[126]

The presence of Bell and Young meant that there was, in effect, a parallel operation to prepare for the general election. Both men questioned the work of Saatchi and Saatchi, persuading Mrs Thatcher to look secretly at opinion research produced by a rival firm, Young and Rubicam.† According to that firm's chairman, John Banks, it was Mrs Thatcher 'at all times who wanted a restricted circulation [for Young and Rubicam's work] and for it to be kept clear of Tebbit'.[127] Bell and Young also disparaged Tebbit's efforts. 'Norman had never run anything,' recalled Young, 'and I could see that things hadn't got far at Central Office.'[128] What made matters particularly awkward was that there was some truth in their criticisms. Saatchis was going through an uncreative phase. Tebbit, though a brilliant public performer and political streetfighter, was not an organizer. As even Michael Dobbs admitted, 'Norman couldn't reach out to the people at Central Office. They didn't like not seeing enough of him. He'd be thinking about his wife at home.'[129] Central Office people considered that Tebbit and Dobbs were 'buddies who shut the door and laughed too much' instead of encouraging them all to work harmoniously: 'Norman

* Mrs Thatcher, though extremely innocent about drugs, did know that all had not been well with Bell during the 1983 campaign. 'How is Tim now?' she used to ask from time to time while he was out of action. (Interview with Lord Sherbourne of Didsbury.)
† The 'Young' of 'Young and Rubicam' was no relation of David Young.

was chaotic.'[130] 'They told me', Mrs Thatcher recalled, 'that he'd never been around Central Office.'[131] 'It was a bloody awful time,' Dobbs remembered.[132]

Naturally, all of this produced tremendous ill feeling. Mrs Thatcher was the last person to know how to sort it out because, although she was happy to have fierce arguments with colleagues about issues, she disliked personal conflicts. This was the dismal background to a series of by-election reverses. A week before the unhappy Chequers meeting, Labour had gained Fulham from the Tories. In early May, the Liberals grabbed the Conservative seat of Ryedale and came within a hundred votes of victory in West Derbyshire, where the seat was held for the Tories by Patrick McLoughlin,* an ex-miner.

Some of the mood may be charted from the diaries of John Biffen, the Leader of the House of Commons. Always independent-minded† and occasionally somewhat old-womanish, Biffen had never found Mrs Thatcher sympathetic, describing her, for example, as 'emotional and vindictive'.[133] In 1986, the complaints in his diary swell. After her survival in the Westland debate, he and Geoffrey Howe were 'much in agreement' about her 'bossy and intemperate manner . . . I cannot now see how she is secure, and I think she should go before the next election and probably won't.'[134]‡ In February, he quoted Willie Whitelaw worrying that she would 'take the Tory Party under'.[135] In May, invited on to the Brian Walden show just after the Ryedale and West Derbyshire results, Biffen opined: 'Nobody seriously supposes that the Prime Minister would be Prime Minister throughout the entire period of the next parliament. So therefore there is nothing extraordinary about the balanced ticket of the Prime Minister and some of the most powerful in the Conservative Party, one of whom would probably become Prime Minister in due course, being represented as a team.'[136]

---

* Patrick McLoughlin (1957–), educated Cardinal Griffin Catholic School, Cannock; mineworker, Littleton Colliery, 1979–85; Conservative MP for West Derbyshire, 1986–2010; for Derbyshire Dales, 2010–; Secretary of State for Transport, 2012–.

† Biffen was the most consistent Eurosceptic in the Cabinet. In the 1984 European election, he spoiled his ballot, writing 'Stuff Brussels' on the paper. (John Biffen, *Semi-Detached*, Biteback, 2013, p. 384.)

‡ Mrs Thatcher seems to have had her suspicions about the women involved as well. During a conversation at Chequers, Geoffrey Tucker, the veteran PR man from the Heath era, and Ronnie Millar, her speech-writer, went through the Cabinet 'showing how most of it was disloyal and how the wives of some Ministers, namely Biffen and Geoffrey Howe, were talking about the need for her to go. At one point she said "What about Norman?" and they nodded and she said, "I knew it." She was terribly upset by this. She could not understand how he had done it because she had had his wife out to Chequers and was devoted to them.' (David Butler Archive, Interview with Geoffrey Tucker, 27 July 1987.)

Since Biffen had publicly foreseen Mrs Thatcher's political end, his remarks were naturally picked up in the press. Bernard Ingham, speaking as usual through the anonymity of the lobby system, described Biffen as a 'semi-detached' member of the Cabinet. In Ingham's view, this was a pleasantly jokey (and accurate) way of defending Biffen's character against accusations of disloyalty,[137] but Biffen interpreted it as meaning he might be sacked. He admitted to being 'ham-fisted' in what he had said, but thought it was 'not a hanging offence'[138] and was oddly hurt by what was surely the inevitable reaction to such unguardedness: 'I sat by the PM for her questions [in Parliament]. There was not a single word. I will not be the first to speak.'[139] Besides, Biffen had meant what he had said: 'I do feel she got out of kimber in the second half of her time. She got to the point of "If I don't do it no one else will." '[140] This was well put. Mrs Thatcher did resemble the Little Red Hen in the folk tale of that name. In the story, the hen seeks help from a pig, a cat and so on, to plant a grain of wheat. All refuse. ' "Cluck, cluck, then I'll do it myself," said the Little Red Hen.' She does. Because of her efforts, the grain grows. Now the other animals want it, but she refuses them as a punishment for their laziness and eats it all alone.

Yet a 'balanced ticket', although certainly a coded criticism of Mrs Thatcher, was what those senior Tories who wished her to survive wanted too. They could appreciate the energy of the Little Blue Hen, though they found it very exhausting. They hoped to harness it. They sought, as politicians always do in tight situations, better presentation, and also a means of getting the government to work as one rather than she alone clucking round the political farmyard.

After the by-elections, and within days of Biffen's remarks to Walden, Mrs Thatcher reshuffled her Cabinet. The faithful Keith Joseph had indicated his wish to depart. The unspoken truth was that Joseph, so vital in her start on the road to radicalism and success, had been a disappointment to her as a minister, overborne by detail, by honest doubt and by his tendency to give in to officials. The net effect of his presence at Education was that the radical idea of vouchers had drained away. Not a great deal had happened. She replaced Joseph with Kenneth Baker, whose communicative skills she admired. She meant to move Education fast up her list of priorities. She was responding to research showing that the Conservatives were considered 'weak . . . on the so-called "caring issues" '.[141] This had already been the theme of her speech to the Scottish Conservative conference in Perth a few days earlier. Its refrain had been 'It is because we care about . . .',[142] and she had applied this to the old, the disabled, job creation and so on. With the same idea of 'caring', applied more personally, a programme of public engagements was drawn up which would show Mrs Thatcher herself in 'informal and human contexts'.[143]

Her new Secretary of State for Transport was John Moore, whose youthful good looks and Thatcherite success in advancing privatization made him stand well in her eyes. She also promoted Nicholas Ridley from Transport to Environment. She did not pretend that this was a presentational advantage: she did it because she wanted 'radical policies' for the manifesto and believed that his 'penetrating intellect' could deal with issues like housing and the coming community charge.[144] She kept Biffen in place, though from now on he felt 'on the skids'.[145]

Partly to improve the unity of the government and partly to prepare better for the election, Stephen Sherbourne proposed a sort of informal inner Cabinet. John Wakeham, the Chief Whip, took up the idea and wrote to Mrs Thatcher suggesting the setting up of a Strategy Group. This would mean that senior ministers would submit papers on areas of policy to co-ordinate an election-winning approach. 'You're so involved in running the government', he told Mrs Thatcher, 'that the party thinks you're not giving enough thought to running the next election.'[146] Typically, Wakeham regarded this not as a substantive exercise, but as one designed to show harmony and unity. 'Should the group's existence be secret or public?' Mrs Thatcher asked him when he put up the idea. 'I don't mind whether it even meets,' he replied. 'The point is that people should think it will, so it needs to be known about.'

In fact, the group did meet, and was immediately christened 'the A-Team' by the newspapers. It consisted of Mrs Thatcher, Whitelaw, Howe, Lawson, Tebbit, Hurd, Wakeham, but neither Biffen nor Young.* The clear majority of the A-Team thought of themselves as 'consolidators', but the policy groups the A-Team spawned – Lawson on the economy, Moore on young people, Ridley on planning and the environment – tended to be led by those described as 'go forwards', temperamentally and ideologically closer to Mrs Thatcher. The 'go forwards' believed that, as Brian Griffiths put it to her just before the Chequers meeting in April, 'Without radicalism, Thatcherism is dead.'[147] These different schools of thought represented permanent tendencies in the collective mind of conservatism. If the Conservatives were to succeed politically, they had to be held in balance.

The first A-Team meeting tried to accommodate both the opinion research produced by Tebbit and Saatchis and that from Young and

---

* Biffen considered that his exclusion proved he would not survive the next election. Young was to join at a later stage.

Rubicam.[148] It also agreed to discuss the theme for the coming party conference and the collection of themes for the election. Media relations and PR generally were to be co-ordinated.* The right pitch for the election was discussed. In the Strategy Group's second meeting, for example, Mrs Thatcher drew the attention of those present to a recent article by Ferdinand Mount called 'The Reclaiming of Yob England'. 'It was important to appeal to those who sought security – "the belongers" – and those – predominantly the young – who sought adventure.'[149] But Robin Harris, the secretary to the group, considered that the A-Team's actual products were 'not very useful'. The group's virtue was that 'It proved we wanted to win the election and we wanted to win under *her*.'[150]

It was Stephen Sherbourne who put to her more tactfully a message not dissimilar to that first presented by Dobbs and Tebbit. 'In the next election,' he wrote to Mrs Thatcher, 'the main issue will be you and your personality. Nobody, supporter or opponent, doubts the strength of your convictions.' Voters knew why they needed Mrs Thatcher in 1979 and 1983, but 'The subliminal question they will be asking at the next election is "What is there to be done in this third Parliament that only Mrs Thatcher can do?": in other words, "why do we need this strong woman?" '[151] Sherbourne was really approaching again the question which he had raised just before the April meeting at Chequers, only to have it swept away by Mrs Thatcher's anger at the Dobbs presentation. He had written then that there was famously 'no gratitude in politics', citing Churchill's defeat in 1945. 'For an incumbent government this problem becomes greater at each successive election – specifically, how does a government in office for 8 or 9 years present itself as fresh?'[152] Against this, Mrs Thatcher had written '1959' – the year in which the Tories, by that time led by Harold Macmillan, had won their third successive victory, the year which brought her into Parliament for the first time. By June, Mrs Thatcher felt readier to consider such questions than she had felt when she was under such immediate threat earlier in the year. What could not be said, but was obvious to all – none more so than Mrs Thatcher herself – was that although the Conservatives had previously won three general elections in a row (1951, 1955 and 1959), no party in the twentieth century had ever done this under one leader. A Thatcher-led third victory would be unprecedented.

Despite the improving sense of direction, all was still not well between

---

* Bernard Ingham felt strongly at this time that media handling was wrong. After the first A-Team meeting, he wrote to Mrs Thatcher about this. It was bad tactics for ministers to ring up the BBC and complain generally, rather than putting facts right: 'I am afraid Mr Tebbit has acquired a reputation with some broadcasters as simply a moaner.' (Ingham to Thatcher, 24 June 1986, CAC: THCR 2/7/5/8.)

party leader and party Chairman. In March, a front-page story had appeared in *The Times* saying that Norman Tebbit alone was going to write the manifesto.[153] Mrs Thatcher was displeased, both by the publicity, which seemed to have come from the Tebbit camp, and by the very idea. 'I did not like the previous [1983] manifesto,' she recalled when composing her memoirs, '. . . and I was determined to keep this one under my own grasp. Policy was my forte. Norman was a supreme politician,' but she added, 'We don't want to quarrel with Norman.'[154] What she was saying, in retirement, was that Tebbit had tried to usurp her prerogative. On the other hand, she did not want to suggest this publicly because by then – in adversity – he had become her friend once more. At the time, however, battle was almost openly joined. *The Times* story had convinced Robin Harris, for instance, that 'Norman had to be reined in.'[155] All through the summer, this conflict persisted, more or less underground. At the end of July and the beginning of August, a rash of articles appeared in the press which exposed the rift between party leader and party Chairman. These coincided with a Commonwealth crisis over South African sanctions, so it was a time of extreme tension for Mrs Thatcher. For his part, Tebbit, although on the A-Team, resented encroachment on what he saw as the work of Central Office, and was determined to fight off research (Young and Rubicam) which he had not himself commissioned and defend that which he had (Saatchis).

'The Chairman is coming to see you tomorrow. He has asked to see you alone, and therefore I will not be present,' Sherbourne warned Mrs Thatcher on 29 July. 'The press has been full of stories about your wish to drop Saatchis and replace them with Y & R.'[156] He went on: 'As far as I am aware, nobody from No 10 has said a word to the press about any of this. I do not know who started it, though it may be a fairly obvious Saatchi ploy. But now it is out in the open, it may be becoming a bit of a free-for-all.' She should consider whether to tell Tebbit that there were no plans to change the agency, while telling him that Young and Rubicam would also be used, or to tell him that the whole subject would be revisited in the autumn ('He won't like this . . . but equally you can say that the party cannot be bulldozed into taking decisions because of press speculation').

The next day, Tebbit arrived in Downing Street. He 'had his dark face on',[157] and bore a sheaf of press cuttings which he dumped in front of Mrs Thatcher, accusing her people of inspiring the stories. Mrs Thatcher denied all knowledge of such things – 'She was very good at not wanting to know.'[158] Tebbit said that if such stories did not stop he would resign. Mrs Thatcher asked him not to, but the meeting produced a new flood of press coverage. On 5 August, Mrs Thatcher went into the King Edward

VII Hospital for an operation on her right hand, which suffered from Dupuytren's contracture, a condition which causes the fingers to bend into the palm of the hand. Denis and her children were absent. Barry Strevens, her detective, who accompanied her, was troubled by 'how lonely she looked in the hospital, clutching a teddy bear that the Garden Room girls had given her' as she went to the operating theatre.[159]

She emerged after two days to a note from Sherbourne begging her to sort out the row, arrange weekly meetings with Tebbit to calm him down and make a decision between Young and Rubicam and Saatchis (he favoured sticking with Saatchis).[160] He told her that 'there are people who want to use your Y & R connection to cast doubt on your confidence in Central Office.' There was also a curt handwritten letter from Tebbit (a 'cri de coeur' warned Nigel Wicks),[161] addressing her as 'Prime Minister' – a bad sign in his case, since his informal notes normally called her 'Margaret'. He wished her a speedy recovery, but then stated, as through clenched teeth: 'the press speculation about my position as Party Chairman has continued and seems likely to do so until something is done to end it. While it continues it damages both Party and Government.'[162] He added that he was pressing ahead with party conference plans to involve ministers fully: 'I will need to secure your full backing for my approaches to colleagues by the end of this month.' With a circumlocutory expression of anxiety, Wicks advised, 'I wonder whether you might not wish to telephone NT and let it be known that you had telephoned so as to rest all the rumour-mongering once and for all.'[163]

On Wicks's note, Mrs Thatcher wrote: 'Have phoned Norman & asked Jim Coe [a No. 10 press officer] to kill the story.'[164] She did not banish Young and Rubicam, but she did express her confidence in Tebbit and permit him to continue with Saatchis. He felt their uncomfortable meeting had helped: 'Perhaps she had feared that I was the source of some of the adverse stories about her and my visit somehow reassured her that I was not.'[165] She set up the regular meetings Sherbourne had suggested. It was a truce, at least. Tebbit and his wife went off on holiday to France. Mrs Thatcher and Denis stayed with the Wolfsons in Cornwall, where they agreed to be photographed – she with her bandaged hand – holding a rather unruly borrowed dog on the beach.*

Yet another antagonist with whom Mrs Thatcher was wrestling was the BBC. Egged on by Denis, for whom the 'pinkoes' of the BBC were a

---

* Mrs Thatcher, who was fond of animals, always wanted a dog or cat as a pet, but Denis forbade it.

favourite topic of conversation, she had always considered the Corporation politically and personally hostile. This had become a matter of passionate concern to her during the Falklands War, when she felt that the BBC was making life difficult for the British Task Force and preaching defeatism (see Volume I, pp. 739–40). She had also long opposed the BBC for its 'extravagance', its broadcasting of material she considered indecent, its overmanned, unionized workforce, its journalistic methods* and its privilege of being funded by a compulsory, flat licence fee (a poll tax, in fact, but one which she was against) imposed on every owner or renter of a television in the land. She favoured the idea that the BBC should, in part at least, be funded by advertising – which, in the BBC's strict internal theology, was a sin against the Holy Ghost. There was almost nothing she liked about the BBC, with the important exceptions of its original high-minded 'Reithian standards' (so named after its original director-general, Sir John Reith), and its External Services, which broadcast in numerous languages. She believed these had a particular value when bringing accurate news to the Communist world, where all other broadcasting was propaganda.

From her earliest days as prime minister, Mrs Thatcher had criticized the BBC consistently and relentlessly, though more often in private than in public. In May 1980, for example, she had lunch at Broadcasting House with the main executives. She laid into the licence fee and suggested that Radio 1 (the pop music station) should carry advertising. Bernard Ingham, who was present, wrote it up afterwards:

> Mr Singer [Aubrey Singer, managing director of Radio] also objected to advertising on young people's programmes (eg Radio 1) because it would encourage 'covetousness' in them. There followed a lively exchange during which the Prime Minister demanded to know who around the table did not covet a higher standard of living and who had declined an increased salary . . . over the last 12 months.[166]

The lunch continued with her attacking the Corporation for its craven attitude to the IRA. There were a great many more of these 'lively exchanges' over the years, but her problem in bringing about change was that none of her successive Home Secretaries – the ministers responsible for the BBC – agreed with her. Of these, the most important was the first, Willie Whitelaw. Even after he had left the Home Office in 1983, and

---

* In 1982, for example, Mrs Thatcher was asked whether senior civil servants should take part in a BBC *Panorama* programme about information and propaganda during the Falklands War. 'Neither Ministers nor officials should appear on this programme,' she wrote. 'It is <u>not</u> being put on to reach the truth – but to try to justify the BBC.' (Armstrong to Thatcher, 6 August 1982, TNA: PREM 19/663 (http://www.margaretthatcher.org/document/134887).)

became deputy prime minister, he did everything he could to defend the BBC in its existing form, making it a personal sticking point. In 1986, he even told a ministerial meeting on the subject that he 'would not feel able to remain a member of the Government' if the BBC were to carry advertising.[167] Mrs Thatcher was clear in her own mind that Whitelaw's departure was not a price worth paying. As was quite often the case, her rhetoric was therefore more radical than her actions. Her views did not alter, however, and she rightly foresaw that technology – such as cable and direct broadcasting by satellite – would eventually undermine the duopoly power of the BBC and ITV, and hence the way the BBC was funded. She opposed the efforts of the BBC to capture each new technological area, wanting them all opened up to competition.

In her second term, Mrs Thatcher came to realize that the only way she could really affect the future of the BBC was by using the blunt instrument of the licence fee. The government had renewal of the fee in its power and the right to set its amount, and could therefore exercise leverage when these came up. In December 1984, she was secretly visited by Ian McIntyre,* the controller of Radio 3, the BBC's classical music station, a conservative-minded critic of his own organization. He had sent her a paper, full of criticisms of the BBC's 'poor leadership' which she had marked enthusiastically. 'One of the strengths of the BBC in the days of Reith', McIntyre concluded,

> was its ability to put a stamp on those who worked for it. Today it is the liberal consensus which has put its stamp on the BBC. Its prophets are the Galbraiths† and Dahrendorfs,‡ its holy writings the *Guardian* and the *Observer*, its political outlook (which it is not supposed to have) social democratic. Contemptuous of politicians and patronising towards its audience, it appears increasingly to see itself as a state within a state.[168]

Mrs Thatcher underlined the last phrase three times. She itched to overthrow the state within a state. McIntyre recommended that she seize her chance and increase the licence fee for only two years, setting conditions

---

* Ian McIntyre (1931–2014), educated Prescot Grammar School, St John's College, Cambridge and College of Europe, Bruges; controller, BBC Radio 4, 1976–8; controller, BBC Radio 3, 1978–87; associate editor, *The Times*, 1989–90.
† John Kenneth Galbraith (1908–2006), economist; Professor of Economics, Harvard University, 1949–75; US Ambassador to India, 1961–3; author of many books including *The Great Crash, 1929* (1954) and *The Affluent Society* (1958); lobbyist for liberal political causes.
‡ Ralf Dahrendorf (1929–2009), German sociologist, academic and political activist; EEC Commissioner, 1970–74; director, London School of Economics, 1974–84; author of many books including *Class and Class Conflict in Industrial Society* (1959); Warden, St Antony's College, Oxford, 1987–97; knighted, 1982; created Lord Dahrendorf, 1993.

which would force the BBC to 'do less better'. At the same time, she should set up a committee of inquiry into the 'objectives, organisation, management and scope of the BBC'.[169]*

Mrs Thatcher more or less followed McIntyre's advice, though she reluctantly accepted the Home Secretary Leon Brittan's recommendation not to go 'head on',[170] but to narrow the inquiry to future financing of the BBC, because of the political dangers of inquiring into journalistic standards. She told Brittan that the value of such an inquiry depended on who was chosen to run it: 'she suggested that Sir Woodrow Wyatt might be a good candidate.'[171] Brittan went away to think about this, and wrote back, arguing that Professor Alan Peacock,† a leading free-market economist, should chair the inquiry and that he and colleagues agreed it should confine itself to the question of introducing advertising and sponsorship to the BBC.[172] 'Not strong enough', wrote Mrs Thatcher beside Peacock's name, and she refused to agree to Brittan's proposal: 'No – the terms of reference are far too limited. Perhaps I might be consulted!?' She later told Brittan that Professor Peacock did not know enough 'to prevent the wool being pulled over his eyes',[173] but then gave in. She did succeed, however, in keeping the terms wide enough to include all aspects of the future financing of the BBC. In pushing for change in the financing, Mrs Thatcher was strongly backed by her own Policy Unit. Peter Warry wrote to her predicting that technology would 'undermine the justification for the licence by the 1990s': cable, DBS (direct broadcasting by satellite) and home computers would 'convert the television into a piece of household equipment, rather than an outlet solely for the BBC and ITV'.[174]‡

When Peacock reported in June 1986, he recommended, as the Home Office had hoped, that the BBC should not take advertising. This declaration, Douglas Hurd (then the Home Secretary) later wrote, came 'to my

---

* A private office covering note to Robin Butler warned him that Mrs Thatcher had squirrelled away McIntyre's paper: 'If you agree this should go to the Home Secy we shall need to recover it from the handbag' (Ingham to Butler, 14 December 1984, Prime Minister's Papers, Broadcasting, Television Licence Fees, Part 1 (document consulted in the Cabinet Office)).

† Alan Peacock (1922–2014), educated Grove Academy, Dundee High School and St Andrews University; Professor of Economic Science, University of Edinburgh, 1957–62; Professor of Economics, University of York, 1962–78; Professor of Economics, University College at Buckingham, 1978–80; Principal, 1980–83; Vice-Chancellor, University of Buckingham, 1983–4; knighted, 1987.

‡ It is a mark of the institutionalized power of the BBC which Mrs Thatcher failed to break that, although the Policy Unit's technological prophecy was proved correct within ten years, the Corporation still, at the time of writing (2015), collects the great bulk of its income from the licence fee.

great relief'.[175] Peacock also pointed out that technological change, with its multiplicity of channels, would eventually create a genuinely competitive broadcasting market. He was interested in the idea of 'pay-per-view'. The long-term consequences of Peacock were radical. The cosy system of the regional ITV franchises would be opened up to competitive tender. His recommendations provided the framework for reform of television as a whole, rather than just the BBC. Mrs Thatcher was to wrestle with all of this in her third term. But the short-term consequences were that her assault on the BBC was foiled, as she had suspected it would be when she had questioned Peacock's appointment in the first place. 'She thought it could have come out stronger,' recalled Brian Griffiths,[176] the head of her Policy Unit, who advised Mrs Thatcher on broadcasting as well as economic policy. The licence fee was secure, and was indexed to the Retail Price Index from 1 April 1988.*

Instead, attention switched to the personnel at the top of the organization, and one or two symbolic battles about programmes. At the end of August 1986, Stuart Young, the chairman of the BBC, died of cancer, aged only fifty-two. An accountant, and the brother of David Young, he had been Mrs Thatcher's appointment† to shake up the organization, but the BBC barons had proved too much for him. Mrs Thatcher now had the chance to put in a chairman who could make a difference. At the same time, two particular programmes were making the BBC vulnerable to her attack.

The case of a *Panorama* programme, 'Maggie's Militant Tendency', had been running since it was broadcast in January 1984. It had alleged that three Conservative MPs – Neil Hamilton, Harvey Proctor‡ and Gerald Howarth – had taken part in far-right activities. It evidence was thin, or worse. The programme did not prove the existence of any entryist organization in the Conservative Party like Militant in Labour. It also played tricks with film. For example, it showed a shot of Howarth wearing

---

* A minor recommendation of Peacock was that the BBC should auction off the late-night hours of broadcasting which it owned but did not use to much effect. At a ministerial meeting, Mrs Thatcher asked what was actually broadcast at these times. No one knew. Her private secretary was sent out to get a copy of the *Evening Standard* and Mrs Thatcher and colleagues then pored over its TV listings. 'Oh, look,' exclaimed Mrs Thatcher, lighting on the schedule for 3 a.m. 'There's one of Ronnie Reagan's films! I wonder if Denis knows.' (Interview with Lord Sterling of Plaistow.)
† The rule was that the government appointed the chairman of the BBC. The chairman and governors then appointed the director-general.
‡ Harvey Proctor (1947–), educated High School for Boys, Scarborough and University of York; Conservative MP for Basildon, 1979–83; for Billericay, 1983–7. Shortly after resigning as an MP, he was convicted on charges of gross indecency.

a steam-engine driver's uniform at a railway enthusiasts' rally and juxta-posed the picture with the claim that he had attended a fascist meeting in Italy, visually implying that the uniform was a fascist one. Hamilton and Howarth sued, and the BBC executives, led by the director-general, Alas-dair Milne,* assured the governors that the case was 'fire-proof'. Right up until it became clear that the case would come to court, late in 1986, they maintained this position, relying on the hope that the MPs, who had no private means, would not be able to afford it. Forced by the acting chairman, Lord Barnett,† to recognize that the programme would not stand up to legal scrutiny, they capitulated at the last moment. Their vic-tims eventually received roughly a million pounds in libel damages.‡

The other programme was the BBC's *Nine O'Clock News* on the night of the US raid on Libya. This had outraged Mrs Thatcher and Tebbit by what they saw as its readiness to accept Libyan government propaganda about the civilian casualties caused by the American bombs and its refusal to give airtime to the American and British positions. Live presentation from the reporter, Kate Adie, in Tripoli, had caused them particular dis-quiet. Unlike his predecessors as party chairman, who had preferred a more peaceful life, Tebbit had long since decided that it was a good idea to harry the BBC for bias and inaccuracy. In the case of 'Maggie's Militant Tendency', he had bombarded them with fifty-five complaints about the programme.[177] When it came to the Libyan coverage, he got Central Office to prepare a long, detailed dossier about mistakes and distortions in what had been broadcast and submitted the findings to an anonymous inde-pendent, 'academic' lawyer, who was actually the famous legal fixer and Labour-appointed peer Lord Goodman,[178] for a detached critique.

---

* Alasdair Milne (1930–2013), educated Winchester and New College, Oxford; controller, BBC Scotland, 1968–72; director of programmes, 1973–7; managing director, BBC TV, 1977–82; director-general, BBC, 1982–7.
† Joel Barnett (1923–2014), educated Derby Street Jewish School and Manchester Central High School; Labour MP for Heywood and Royton Division, Lancashire, 1964–83; Chief Secretary to the Treasury, 1974–9, during which time he devised the Barnett Formula which allocates public spending in Scotland, Wales and Northern Ireland; vice-chairman, Board of Governors, BBC, 1986–93; created Lord Barnett, 1983.
‡ For a fuller account of this case, see Jean Seaton's *'Pinkoes and Traitors': The BBC and the Nation 1974–1987*, Profile Books, 2015, pp. 309–13. In this official history, Seaton makes the strange claim that Mrs Thatcher was on the '[Jimmy] Savile shows' so often that the BBC tried to 'ration her appearances' (Seaton, *'Pinkoes and Traitors'*, p. 10). Savile, subsequently unmasked in the twenty-first century as a serial child-sex offender, presented many pro-grammes on the BBC, but he was not normally an interviewer and did not have shows suitable for frequent appearances by Mrs Thatcher. Seaton seems to be confusing Jimmy Savile with Jimmy Young, on whose Radio 2 show she liked to appear. She appeared on Savile's show *Jim'll Fix It* three times in her career, and on the *Jimmy Young Show* eighteen times.

Goodman found mainly in Tebbit's favour. On 30 October, Tebbit submitted his report to Barnett. 'You may conclude', he suggested, that the BBC coverage of the raid was 'a mixture of news, views, speculation, error and uncritical carriage of Libyan propaganda which does serious damage to the reputation of the BBC'.[179]

In trying to appoint Young's successor, Mrs Thatcher had almost no friends at the BBC to help her spy out the lie of the land. A rare exception, however, was Patricia Hodgson,* whom Mrs Thatcher had met in the 1970s when Hodgson ran the Bow Group. Mrs Thatcher took what Hodgson considered a motherly/sisterly interest in her career and used to invite her to tea or dinner every year.[180] Hodgson's own politics were Conservative, and she was upset by the way Milne and his executives had behaved over 'Maggie's Militant Tendency', which she regarded as indefensible. She thought the BBC had been over-politicized by the left. But her view of the organization was old-fashioned, public-service Reithian, rather than free-market. This was the side of the BBC tradition with which Mrs Thatcher had the most sympathy. When Patricia Hodgson was appointed secretary to the BBC in 1985, she told the panel that she knew Mrs Thatcher. Its members made her promise that her friendly meetings with the Prime Minister would cease. 'Don't be silly,' Hodgson replied, 'I can use this to the BBC's advantage,' but the selectors were adamant.[181] 'I'm going to Chequers shortly,' said Hodgson. 'I'll tell her that I can't come again.' From then on, Hodgson kept her word about not meeting Mrs Thatcher, but since part of her job was liaison with government, and since she attended the same north London church as Brian Griffiths she was able to discuss relevant matters with him, knowing that her comments would get back to Mrs Thatcher.

After Stuart Young died, Patricia Hodgson discovered from Griffiths that Mrs Thatcher's candidates for the chairmanship included Lord King of British Airways, Woodrow Wyatt (earlier proposed by her for what became the Peacock report) and the right-wing former leader of the electricians' union, Frank Chapple. Hodgson thought the list poor and was frightened that Mrs Thatcher would choose King, who would then have a confrontation with with the BBC journalists. She 'drew up a job spec for the chairmanship and gave it to Brian. I thought the chairman should understand the journalism.'[182] Griffiths thought King unsuitable for the

* Patricia Hodgson (1947–), educated Brentwood High School and Newnham College, Cambridge; deputy secretary, BBC, 1983–5; secretary, 1985–7; chair, Ofcom, 2014–; created dame, 2004.

same reason, and came up with the idea of Marmaduke 'Dukie' Hussey.*
Hussey had been the managing director of Times Newspapers during the
papers' shut-down, and had continued to work for the company after it
was bought by Rupert Murdoch. He was well connected, being married
to a lady-in-waiting to the Queen and brother-in-law to William Waldegrave, who also recommended him to Mrs Thatcher.[183]† He had the
necessary business toughness, establishment links and knowledge of journalism to fit the description that Patricia Hodgson had devised. Mrs
Thatcher appointed him. It was not considered important that he barely
watched television. According to John Birt,‡ whom Hussey was soon to
bring in, first as deputy director-general, to help transform the BBC, Hussey was 'a good intelligence gatherer, one for mood and flavour, not
precision. He had a great deal of courage. His own views and convictions
chimed with Mrs Thatcher's. But he was an old soldier and he had strong
views on public service.'[184] If the BBC under Hussey was to be Thatcher-
ized, it would be in Reithian form, not according to the principles of
market purity.

This combination of circumstances, at last favourable to Mrs Thatcher's hopes for the BBC, actually made Tebbit's attack on the Corporation
over Libya begin to seem dangerous. Brian Griffiths wrote to her warning
that a broadside from Tebbit might, at the last minute, unite the BBC
governors 'to rally round the flag of resisting outside political
interference'.[185]§ This would be terrible, because they were just gearing
up to sack Milne over 'Maggie's Militant Tendency', and should not be
deflected. Tebbit, recalled Griffiths, was 'so confrontational that he was
becoming counter-productive'.[186] There was also the possibility of an
internal government row, because Tebbit, angered by the BBC's brush-off
reply to his first letter, planned to send a second one. Douglas Hurd, as
Home Secretary, was responsible for BBC matters and did not feel easy
about another Cabinet minister, albeit acting in a party capacity, getting
into a serious fight with the Corporation. Labour hoped to exploit

---

* Marmaduke ('Dukie') Hussey (1923–2006), educated Rugby and Trinity College, Oxford;
served in Grenadier Guards in the Second World War; chairman, Board of Governors, BBC,
1986–96; created Lord Hussey of North Bradley, 1996.
† It is possible that it was Waldegrave who first suggested Hussey to Mrs Thatcher.
‡ John Birt (1944–), educated St Mary's College, Liverpool and St Catherine's College,
Oxford; deputy director-general, BBC, 1987–92; director-general, BBC, 1992–2000;
knighted, 1998; created Lord Birt, 2000.
§ On 4 November, Bernard Ingham reported to Mrs Thatcher the results of an NOP survey
for the *Independent*, which suggested that 'Mr Tebbit has misjudged the mood of the coun-
try: three quarters of those polled think the BBC is neutral' ('Press Digest', Ingham to
Thatcher, 4 November 1986, THCR 3/5/62).

differences here. Nigel Wicks wrote to Mrs Thatcher: 'I see a danger of some elements of this episode repeating the Westland troubles. A colleague with an obsession, doing things difficult to reconcile with collective responsibility. And all this at a time when things are going so well for the Government.'[187] Mrs Thatcher agreed. At her instruction, Stephen Sherbourne asked Dobbs to convey to Tebbit her wish to drop the second letter, or at least clear it with the A-Team.[188] In reality, Tebbit could hardly drop it at this late stage without a story breaking that he had been rebuked, so he did not. But after he had sent the second letter, he allowed the story to go away. As he put it, 'Eventually, the affair blew over.'[189] On balance, he was surely right to think that his fierceness against the BBC had helped force it to change its ways.

In January, Hussey, assisted by Patricia Hodgson, sacked Alasdair Milne and put in a sober accountant, Michael Checkland,* as the new director-general, with a brief to get the BBC's affairs in good order. Birt, who had made his name in the independent sector, was brought in as Checkland's deputy to sort out the programmes, especially those connected with news and current affairs. Mrs Thatcher felt well pleased. A few months after Hussey's appointment, Patricia Hodgson met Mrs Thatcher at a public function. 'Dukie is proving a great success,' said Hodgson. 'He's not frightened of BBC barons or journalists.' 'Of course he isn't,' said Mrs Thatcher, rather as if she alone had thought of the appointment. 'He lost his leg in the war.'[190]†

For all of Mrs Thatcher's earlier difficulties, Nigel Wicks had been right to speak in November of 'things . . . going so well for the Government'. The first seeds of this remarkable recovery in public esteem had been sown in Nigel Lawson's March Budget. The growth rate was up to 3.75 per cent, and the inflation rate was down to 3.4 per cent. After years of struggle, the PSBR was now modest, at 1.5 per cent of GDP. Lawson wished to hold it to 1.75 per cent in 1986–7 and was aware that oil revenues would fall, so he did not have great scope. He believed, however, not least for electoral reasons, that the government must cut taxes further. The politically extraordinary fact was that the 'tax-cutting' Tories had not cut the basic rate since Geoffrey Howe had brought it down to 30 per cent in his first Budget in 1979. Lawson's preferred, more targeted method of cutting

---

* Michael Checkland (1936–), educated King Edward's Grammar School, Five Ways, Birmingham and Wadham College, Oxford; director-general, BBC, 1987–92; knighted, 1992.
† Hussey was severely wounded in the spine at the battle of Anzio and was captured by the Germans and eventually lost a leg. He was reputed to remove his tin one occasionally and bang it on the table to alarm people.

income tax had been to raise the thresholds above inflation to take more
of the lowest earners out of tax.

Now, at the last minute, he changed his mind. He wanted tax cuts to
have a wider impact. He did not have much room for manoeuvre, however,
and he worried that a 1 per cent cut, the only amount he could really
afford, would be considered derisory. He feared that 29 per cent would
just look silly, set against the round figure of 30 per cent. Lawson credited his special adviser, Peter Cropper,* with seeing that this could be
turned to advantage: 'A reduction to 29 per cent', Cropper wrote to Lawson, 'would be seen as an unqualified commitment to cutting the burden
of taxation. It would be ludicrous to stop with a basic rate of 29 per cent
for more than a year or two: people will see that.'[191] Lawson, famous for
inventing the Medium-Term Financial Strategy, now invented what might
be described as a Medium-Term Tax Strategy. Announcing the one-penny
cut in his Budget, he reminded the Commons that this was the first cut
since 1979: 'So long as this Government remain in office, it will not be
the last.'[192] He revived the aim, first declared by Howe, of a basic rate of
25 per cent, making it clear that it would be necessary for voters to re-elect
a Conservative government to achieve this. In all of this, although she
warmly supported the one-penny cut, and needed some persuading by
Lawson about the promise of tax cuts to come,[193] Mrs Thatcher was little
more than an observer of the process, so weakened was she by Westland.
In her memoirs, she devotes only six lines – all of them favourable – to the
1986 Budget.[194]

As a result of the tax cut, Labour was in an awkward political spot.
The party decided to abstain in the Commons vote, but some on the left
rebelled and voted against. The Tories were starting once again to 'weap-
onize' tax issues politically, and Kinnock's Labour Party, trying rather
uncertainly to modernize, found it hard to respond in a united way. By
the autumn party conference season, the question of tax and the state of
the economy would take on electoral focus. Lawson's 1986 Budget set the
right political framework.

The work of the A-Team brought political benefit. It ensured that the programme of the government was now considered as a whole. For the
1986 party conference, Tebbit and Dobbs decided to obtain from every
departmental minister his legislative and policy plans for the next three

---

* Peter Cropper (1927–), educated Hitchin Grammar School and Gonville and Caius College,
Cambridge; special adviser to Chief Secretary to the Treasury, 1979–82; to Chancellor of
the Exchequer, 1984–8; director, Conservative Research Department, 1982–4.

years, and persuade them to include them in their platform speeches. They stitched these together under a slogan of 'THE NEXT MOVE FORWARD'. The phrase was designed both to emphasize the team work involved and to leave behind the tension and divisions of the early part of the year. In all probability, it would be the last conference before the general election; it was certainly planned and presented as if it were.

As usual, the Conservative conference was preceded first by that of the Liberals and then by Labour's. Both conferences voted in favour of unilateral nuclear disarmament. In the case of the Liberals, this split the party from its leadership (which had opposed the unilateralist motion) and from its more robust SDP partners in the Alliance. In the case of Labour, Neil Kinnock's strong unilateralism undid much of the modernizing work of the previous twelve months. In a television interview, he said a Britain without nuclear weapons would also refuse to be under the protection of the American nuclear umbrella, because this would be 'immoral'. The conference also voted to renationalize British Telecom and British Gas, which was about to be privatized, to remove the right for a secret ballot before a strike and to get rid of the right to buy a council house. Although the red rose, suggested by Kinnock's up-and-coming adviser Peter Mandelson,* replaced the red flag as the conference symbol, the party seemed politically rather redder than the previous year, when Kinnock had trounced Militant. It promised punitive taxes on the rich, and David Blunkett, the rising star of the left, proudly proclaimed that Labour's plans could not be paid for without increasing the standard rate of income tax as well.

When Mrs Thatcher came to Bournemouth for her party's conference on 6 October, she promptly tripped on a manhole cover and sprained her ankle quite badly. She was unwontedly cheerful, however, about the political opportunity now presenting itself after an extremely testing year. There was nothing she liked better than finding a clear dividing line between the Conservatives and the opposition parties. Now she had it. In her setpiece speech on the last day, she began by teasing Labour. 'The rose I am wearing is the rose of England.'[195] She trumpeted popular capitalism and the morality of choice. She boasted of having the lowest inflation rate for twenty years, the lowest basic rate of income tax for forty years and the lowest number of strikes for fifty years. She continued with the theme

---

* Peter Mandelson (1953–), educated Hendon County Grammar School and St Catherine's College, Oxford; director of campaigns and communications, Labour Party, 1985–90; Labour MP for Hartlepool, 1992–September 2004; Minister without Portfolio, Cabinet Office, 1997–8; Secretary of State for Trade and Industry, 1998; for Northern Ireland, 1999–2001; for Business, Enterprise and Regulatory Reform (later Business, Innovation and Skills), 2008–10; European Commissioner for Trade, 2004–8; created Lord Mandelson, 2008.

of caring, rushing her audience through hospitals she had visited all over the country, and announcing a new commitment to the quality of education. She put her strongest powder and shot into defence, emphasizing the 'utmost gravity' of the Labour decision the previous week: 'Exposed to the threat of nuclear blackmail, there would be no option but surrender.' A Labour Britain 'would be the greatest gain for the Soviet Union in forty years'. She reminded her audience of the leading Labour politicians in the past – Gaitskell, Bevan – who had opposed unilateral nuclear disarmament – in order to contrast them with Neil Kinnock. Labour's traditional patriotic voters could not be at home in his party. 'I believe the interests of Britain can now only be served by a third Conservative victory.' She even made a point of praising Norman Tebbit as chairman.

The shift of political circumstances allowed Mrs Thatcher to make exactly the sort of speech she loved best, yet without it containing any message of defiance of Wets or moderates in her own party. She later recalled that the conference was 'a total success. My recollection is at the end of that Bournemouth speech the message was you've really got to vote Conservative because Labour can't be trusted with defence. We really had something to bite on.'[196] The occasion was harmonious. The opinion polls responded, putting the Conservatives ahead of Labour for the first time since well before the Westland crisis.

A fortnight after the Conservative conference, Jeffrey Archer was accused in the *News of the World* of arranging a cash pay-off for a prostitute who said she had slept with him. After a short period of blustering, in which he tried to resist the bringer of bad news, Michael Dobbs, he resigned as deputy chairman of the party. This was embarrassing for Mrs Thatcher, since, in appointing Archer, she had overruled advice that his judgment was unreliable. Now hers was criticized. Norman Tebbit was relieved. He had not wanted Archer appointed in the first place, and the peripatetic novelist was not the man to help him with what he most needed – tightening the nuts and bolts of Conservative Central Office as a general election approached.

For this purpose, Tebbit had already, with Mrs Thatcher's agreement, appointed another deputy chairman, Peter Morrison. Morrison, liked by Mrs Thatcher as a supporter even before she became leader of the party, and respected by colleagues as a hard-working if unglittering junior minister, was suitable for the task. He was loyal, well connected in the party and no political threat to anyone.*

---

* He hated speaking at the despatch box of the House of Commons because it made him feel 'giddy' (Interview with Robin Harris).

There were two problems with Morrison, the first a fact, the second a rumour, the two conceivably connected. The first was that he drank too much. This had begun because of severe back-pain,[197] but had become habitual. Morrison was not a mercurial or loud-mouthed drunk, more a 'woozy' one, who 'would start on a vodka and tonic at 12 o'clock'[198] and could seem rather unfocused even as he toiled away. In the view of a doctor who observed him at the party conference at this time, he exhibited clear symptoms of alcoholism.[199] In a culture where being drunk was commonplace, his rather quiet drinking did not stand out, but it did cause anxiety.

The other problem was that rumours circulated about Morrison's sexual behaviour. There were no very precise allegations, but suggestions that Morrison might have attended gay parties and engaged in casual pick-ups. As early as before the 1983 general election, the press sometimes 'door-stepped' Morrison and even, on one occasion, pursued him to his family's estate on the island of Islay. Morrison was asked by whips about the accusations and always categorically denied them. The allegations put strain on him, and were thought to have contributed to his heavy drinking.[200] Tebbit recalled, 'I began to hear allegations, coming from his constituency [Chester], when he was with me at CCO, that he was excessively interested in schoolboys. I faced him. He swore absolutely that there was no truth in it. I wasn't absolutely convinced.'[201] Tebbit did not discuss the rumours with Mrs Thatcher, however, and she never raised them. The only effect of such stories was that an informal ceiling was put on Morrison's career. He was known to want to be chairman of the party after the 1987 election, but it was understood that this would be too risky.[202] Robin Butler recalled that, in his time as Mrs Thatcher's principal private secretary, which ended in 1985, no accusations came up about Morrison. When Butler became Cabinet secretary in 1987, however, allegations did surface. They were about homosexuality, and therefore the possibility of being compromised by Soviet agents, rather than about child abuse.[203]*

Unbeknown to Butler, the issue had arisen before. At the beginning of 1986, Robert Armstrong was made aware, through the Security Service, of rumours about Morrison. He asked his own office if there were any existing papers on the subject. An internal, undated, handwritten Cabinet Office note to him, signed 'MS', responded. 'We have none,' it

---

* The two were often confused in those days, partly because of general prejudice against homosexuals, but also because the age of consent for homosexual acts was twenty-one, whereas it was sixteen for heterosexual ones. Men had relationships with what people then called 'boys' who would now, in law, be considered adults. This was distinct from what is normally meant by paedophile acts.

said; 'it appears that previous contacts have been oral and not recorded.' It went on, 'the rumours persist and have become more widespread but do not necessarily indicate anything new since 1983.' The same note reported: 'Nigel Wicks says that the PM is aware of the issue. He does not want any further enquiries made – just to keep our ears open.'[204] On 13 January, Armstrong wrote to Sir Antony Duff, the head of MI5, telling him, 'I have made sure that the Prime Minister is aware that there is a potential problem.'[205]*

In June the following year, by which time Morrison was an energy minister as well as deputy chairman of the party, Armstrong wrote to Nigel Wicks, Mrs Thatcher's principal private secretary in succession to Butler. Armstrong had heard that Morrison was to make a ministerial visit to the Soviet Union. He warned that there had been:

> persistent rumours in Fleet Street over the last six years of homosexual activities on the part of Mr Morrison. He has made it clear that, if anything was published, he would sue for libel . . . There must, however, be a high probability, amounting to a racing certainty – that the rumours have come to the notice of Russian intelligence. Mr Morrison would be liable to Russian attempts to compromise him.[206]

Mrs Thatcher underlined this last sentence. Armstrong proposed that Morrison be accompanied at all times and 'be strongly advised not to drink alcohol when he is in Russia'. 'It would be a lot simpler for <u>Cecil Parkinson</u> to undertake this engagement at my request on seniority grounds,' Mrs Thatcher wrote.† Parkinson duly went instead of Morrison.

Similar questions about Morrison would later be raised, but the situation remained essentially the same. Mrs Thatcher was informed of nothing more than rumours, which Morrison had denied. No actual evidence was produced, nor did the police bring any charges, or even, so far as is known, issue a caution. Her attitude in such cases was to be careful (hence her suggestion of Parkinson replacing Morrison in Moscow), but

---

* Later that year, in November 1986, Duff told Armstrong about new rumours, coming from two separate sources, that Morrison 'has a penchant for small boys'. Morrison had been confronted about the rumours and had denied them. Duff concluded that 'the risks of political embarrassment to the government is [sic] rather greater than the security danger,' and the matter was not taken any further. (Duff to Armstrong, 4 November 1986, Cabinet Office Papers (document consulted in the Cabinet Office).) There is no evidence to suggest that Mrs Thatcher was made aware of these additional rumours. Duff's letter to Armstrong was contained in a Cabinet Office file which was revealed in 2015 following an Independent Review carried out by Peter Wanless and Richard Whittam QC (*The Times*, 23 July 2015).
† Parkinson returned to the Cabinet as energy secretary in June 1987.

not punitive. Anything else would, in her mind, have been unfair. It would also have been imprudent. Prime ministers are very frequently told unpleasant stories about their associates. They make terrible trouble for themselves if they follow all these whispers up. There was an added complication: what if Morrison, rather than breaking any law, had simply been trying to pick up homosexual partners? Mrs Thatcher did not herself approve of such behaviour, but neither did she think it was her business. As with the stories about Leon Brittan, Mrs Thatcher noted them, but did not act.

Stories about Peter Morrison also reached Mrs Thatcher by other means. Barry Strevens, her detective, recalled being asked by a senior officer in the Cheshire constabulary to convey to the Prime Minister, probably in the autumn of 1987, that journalists had been 'sniffing around' all-male parties in Peter Morrison's home in his Chester constituency, 'particularly in relation to a 15-year-old'.[207] She saw Strevens in her flat, in the presence of Archie Hamilton,* who had been appointed her parliamentary private secretary after the election. He told her about what he had been told, though not mentioning the fifteen-year-old. 'She just thanked me for telling her.'[208] But this story, too, did not constitute evidence. Indeed, according to Strevens, the police officer who told him himself 'said it was just rumours'. No one, it seems, thought the matter should be followed up. Hamilton confirmed Strevens's account of the meeting: 'It was alleged that he had held a party, exclusively for men. He may have said "including young men". The suggestion was that Peter was homosexual, not paedophile.'[209] Hamilton, who had been a whip from 1982 to 1986, remembered hearing, in relation to Morrison, 'vague rumours about public lavatories', this at a time when 'homosexuality itself was seen as dodgy.' The whips' attitude, however, was that if a crime had been suspected or committed, that was a matter for the police. They never heard any evidence or received any complaint. When Mrs Thatcher heard the story that Barry Strevens repeated, she said something like 'Oh dear, well, there we are.'[210] She did not feel that rumours of homosexuality (or of personal behaviour of which she privately disapproved) required any action on her part.

Whatever the truth about Morrison, he worked harmoniously with Tebbit in Central Office. The spirits of the Conservatives, and particularly of Mrs Thatcher herself, began to rise. Almost all the economic indicators

---

* Archibald ('Archie') Hamilton (1941–), educated Eton; Conservative MP for Epsom and Ewell, April 1978–2001; PPS to Prime Minister, 1987–8; Minister of State, MOD, 1988–93; knighted, 1994; created Lord Hamilton of Epsom, 2005.

were favourable. Even unemployment, which had hit its highest point ever in January 1986, was now starting to fall. In November, after the third monthly drop (and the sharpest since May 1983), it stood at 3,237,154.[211] At the end of October, Big Bang in the City began successfully. In early December, 4.5 million applications for British Gas were received when it was privatized. Mrs Thatcher was getting rid of the rates. Everything seemed to be coming together. Composing her memoirs in the early 1990s, Mrs Thatcher recalled:

> It was only about 1986 that I realised that it was all going to be all right, because until that time I had been worried to death that this country had taken so much socialism that I wondered if the spirit of enterprise had left us. We were not getting the rate of formation of small businesses. Then by 1986, we began to come back . . . So I knew it was all right and it was just a question of getting it across.[212]

It was about this time, Bernard Ingham recalled, that, one day sitting with Mrs Thatcher in Downing Street, 'She seemed to experience a moment of pure joy. She believed that, at last, her policies really were working.'[213]

16

Against Queen and Commonwealth

'Blacks and their families out of work. Moral? *Poof!'*

Over the summer of 1986, as Mrs Thatcher sought to recover her domestic political standing, she was also engaged in a struggle on the international stage over her approach to South Africa. Her opposition to economic sanctions designed to put pressure on the white minority government and her decision to maintain contact with the Prime Minister (later State President) P. W. Botha* were extremely controversial policies. Mrs Thatcher was accused at home and abroad of being a sympathizer with apartheid. The issue dominated two Commonwealth conferences – at Nassau in 1985 and London in 1986 – when friends and allies insisted that Mrs Thatcher was putting British business interests before the interests of the black people of South Africa. The rows over South Africa did lasting damage to Mrs Thatcher's relationship with her Foreign Secretary, Geoffrey Howe, and famously caused a rift between No. 10 and Buckingham Palace. In Mrs Thatcher's mind, however, there was a purpose behind all this conflict with the establishment, both at home and abroad. She wished to assert Britain's right to its own trade – Britain was one of South Africa's largest trading partners and the largest single investor – and its own foreign policy, and she saw domestic political advantage in doing this. She believed that British influence could do more for the multi-racial future of South Africa by engaging with its white government than by shunning it. While her policy earned her opprobrium in many quarters, it struck a chord with significant sections of British society.† By the end of 1986, she had survived the assaults of the Commonwealth and her

---

* Peter Willem (P. W.) Botha (1916–2006), Prime Minister of South Africa and Minister of National Intelligence Service, 1978–84; State President, 1984–9.

† In August 1986, Mrs Thatcher was informed that, of 7,000 recent letters to her on this subject, 5,000 supported her position. This represented a dramatic change since May, when there had been 'virtual unanimity against the Government'. (Flesher to Thatcher, 13 August 1986, CAC: THCR 1/3/21.)

own Foreign Secretary, and maintained her position to be developed in better days.

In her first term, Mrs Thatcher's approach to southern Africa had been governed by the problem of Rhodesia/Zimbabwe (see Volume I, Chapter 16). Once this had been settled, and with it the last British colonial responsibility in mainland Africa, she felt freer to concentrate on the most important country on the continent. Three factors predominated in her mind – the importance of British trade and kinship with South Africa, a desire to bring a peaceful end to apartheid and white minority rule, and a Cold War fear of Soviet adventurism in the region. She was more ambitious than her predecessors to influence change, but she saw it as her task to keep these three factors in balance. While it is true that Mrs Thatcher opposed the sanctions for which other nations were increasingly clamouring because she believed they would damage British business, she also believed that they would impoverish blacks in South Africa and make the white government retreat into the 'laager'. As early as 1980, she chided South Africa's Foreign Minister, R. F. 'Pik' Botha,* about his attitude to black Africans and told him not to assume that policy was 'only a question of economics and hunger: questions of dignity mattered.'[1] This simple sentiment filled out, later on, into a considered, if controversial policy.

In the mid-1980s, the Cold War factor was uppermost in Mrs Thatcher's mind. She was determined to get Cuban forces – proxies of the Soviet Union – out of the former Portuguese colony of Angola and to make sure that independence for Namibia,† which was illegally occupied by South African forces, should be linked with the withdrawal of the Cubans. She was suspicious of the largest black grouping in South Africa, the African National Congress (ANC), because of its links with the Communist Party and its intermittent use of violence. She feared its monopoly power: 'they don't represent all the Africans, all the interests must be protected'.[2]

There is no doubt, however, that Mrs Thatcher thought that apartheid was unjust – a form of oppressive 'racial socialism'[3] which forcibly moved people hither and thither, kept them poor and denied their human worth and their right to vote. All along, as the last State President of South

* Roelof Frederik ('Pik') Botha (1932–), MP (National Party), 1977–96; Minister of Foreign Affairs, South Africa, 1977–94; of Information, 1978–86; of Energy, 1994–6; Leader, Transvaal National Party, 1992–6.
† The South African government called Namibia South West Africa.

Africa, F. W. de Klerk,* recalled, the white leaders of South Africa knew that she 'never supported apartheid'.[4] Indeed, she regarded it with what she called 'total abhorrence and loathing'.[5] From 1984, she believed that Nelson Mandela,† the most prominent imprisoned black leader, and other ANC prisoners should be released from prison. Even in captivity, Mandela recognized Mrs Thatcher as a leader he would want to have on his side.‡ 'She *is* an enemy of apartheid,' he said not long after he was released from prison in 1990.[6]

Mrs Thatcher sought the replacement of white power, but not its violent overthrow. In this sense, her attitude to change in South Africa resembled her attitude to change in the Soviet Union in the Gorbachev era: she opposed the existing regime and wanted it replaced, but not in such a way that the country would collapse into revolution.

What was also true, however – unlike with the Soviet Union – was that Mrs Thatcher had personal sympathies with the tribe who dominated South Africa: the whites. Denis Thatcher had relations there, and often visited on business. It was to South Africa that he went in 1964, when he suffered a nervous breakdown and thought that his marriage to Margaret was on the rocks (see Volume I, pp. 173–4). He always called it 'God's own country',[7] resented attempts to break its participation in Test cricket and international rugby, and had a low opinion of the efficiency of black African governments. He was caustic, too, about the capacity of the Commonwealth either to understand or to improve the situation. This was what the Commonwealth Secretary-General, 'Sonny' Ramphal,§ called Mrs Thatcher's 'pillow-talk'[8] on the subject of South Africa. Denis's wife shared her husband's irritation with the Commonwealth, but was much less cynical about the possibility of majority rule in South Africa. She actively sought to meet dissidents and leaders of all races working for such change by peaceful means. She was more shocked than Denis by the

---

* Frederik Willem de Klerk (1936–), State President of South Africa, 1989–94; Deputy President, 1994–6; Leader of the Opposition, National Assembly of South Africa, 1996–7; winner, Nobel Peace Prize (with Nelson Mandela), 1993.

† Nelson Mandela (1918–2013), President, African National Congress, 1991–7; President of South Africa, 1994–9; anti-apartheid activist; sentenced to five years' imprisonment, 1962; tried for further charges, 1963–4, and sentenced to life imprisonment; released, 1990; winner, Nobel Peace Prize (with F. W. de Klerk), 1993.

‡ For an account of Mandela's interest in Mrs Thatcher's leadership qualities, see Anthony Sampson, *Mandela: The Authorised Biography*, Harper Press, 2011, pp. 333, 338.

§ Shridath ('Sonny') Ramphal (1928–), educated King's College London; lawyer; occupied several posts in the government of Guyana in the 1960s and 1970s, including foreign minister and attorney-general, 1972–3; Secretary-General of the Commonwealth, 1975–90; knighted, 1970.

indignities inflicted on the black population. Her views, in fact, rarely differed from those of Helen Suzman,* the veteran liberal white South African anti-apartheid politician, with whom she had friendly relations. She firmly believed, however, that British interests in South Africa and the interests of British passport holders in the country – of whom there were about 800,000† – must be looked after. So her strategy was peaceful transition, and her tactic was one of engagement with the people central to such a change – the white government itself.

Mrs Thatcher was correct that Britain, because of its history and its economic and human presence, had greater salience in South Africa than any other Western country. But she was also conscious that the same history made the issue a delicate one. The white government of South Africa was composed almost solely of Afrikaners, not those of British descent. The ruling National Party saw itself as the heir of the men who had fought the Boer War against British imperial domination at the turn of the twentieth century. Its victory in the South African elections of 1948 had been a repudiation of the British legacy. Full apartheid, which the new National Party government established after 1948, was seen by its supporters as a means of securing for Afrikaners the power and prosperity of which Britain had robbed them. So lectures from a British prime minister about how best the South African government should behave could easily backfire. In this sense – though both would have been enraged by the comparison – the South African Prime Minister (later President) P. W. Botha resembled the Zimbabwean Prime Minister (later State President) Robert Mugabe. Both saw themselves as part of a liberation struggle against Britain. Mrs Thatcher knew that if she were to persuade the National Party leaders of anything, she must not preach at them.

P. W. Botha was the almost perfect representative of the Afrikaner mentality. Born in 1916 into a 'bitter-ender' anti-British Boer family, he liked to boast in public that Afrikaners 'had nearly brought the British Empire to its knees'.[9] He had served as defence minister between 1966 and 1978, when he was known as 'Piet Skiet' (Piet the Shoot). He was extremely prickly at any criticism emanating from Britain. But his dour and

* Helen Suzman (1917–2009), prominent anti-apartheid campaigner; joined South African Parliament, 1953; founder member, Progressive Party (later renamed the Progressive Federal Party), 1959; remained an MP until retirement in 1989.

† The figure of 800,000, widely reported at the time, was based on Home Office estimates, though there was no accurate total (some reports put it at 1 million). In May 1986 figures showed that there were more people leaving South Africa than there were entering the country as immigrants, for the first time since the Soweto riots in 1976 (*Sunday Times*, 11 May 1986, and *The Times*, 16 June 1986).

charmless demeanour towards the outside world did him no harm in Afrikaner politics. He was sometimes called 'the Great Crocodile' because of his physical appearance and his political toughness. When he succeeded John Vorster as prime minister in 1978, however, he was not so stupid as to oppose all change. The following year, he made a famous speech, telling Afrikaners to 'adapt or die', eventually provoking a new Conservative Party to break away and oppose his reforms. It was with this unpromising, but not completely obdurate man that Mrs Thatcher decided to try to deal.

In November 1983, white voters endorsed in a referendum the new Constitution which Botha had offered them. It got rid of the all-white voting system, but gave votes only to Indians and so-called 'Cape Coloureds'* who helped make up a tri-cameral Parliament. Blacks, still voteless, were given more autonomy in the more or less bogus 'homelands' which the South African government had earlier established to balkanize black power. A state president was invented to take charge of a multi-racial but white-dominated President's Council. This role Botha designed for himself.

Although most international and internal black reaction to the changes was hostile, the British government gave them a cautious welcome. That month, at the Commonwealth Conference in New Delhi, signs appeared of disagreements which would soon become much more severe.† To the irritation of Commonwealth colleagues, Mrs Thatcher maintained her support for President Reagan's policy of 'linkage' between Cuban withdrawal from southern Africa and the independence of Namibia. But in March 1984, after South Africa and Mozambique had signed the Nkomati Accord, which agreed better security co-operation between the two nations, Mrs Thatcher supported Botha's consequent freezing out of REN-AMO, the anti-Communist guerrilla movement in Mozambique, even though this annoyed some of her friends in the Reagan administration.‡

* 'Cape Coloureds' was the term used to describe mixed-race South Africans, so called because they were the predominant ethnic group in the Western Cape.
† At this conference, Denis's irritation with the physical arrangements boiled over. During the leaders' 'retreat' in Goa, there were constant power cuts. He emerged on the balcony of the chalet allotted to the Thatchers and bellowed: 'This place is very high on the buggeration factor.' (Carol Thatcher, *Below the Parapet: The Biography of Denis Thatcher*, HarperCollins, 1996, p. 210.) At a more elevated political level, Mrs Thatcher agreed. She was annoyed by the Commonwealth's pretensions in issuing a 'declaration on international security', and wrote to Ronald Reagan: 'It is by no means an ideal document but you should have seen the earlier versions!' (Thatcher telegram 2018 to Reagan, 30 November 1983, Prime Minister's Papers, Commonwealth, The Commonwealth Heads of Government Meetings, Part 5 (document consulted in the Cabinet Office).)
‡ While bad news for the hardliners, Mrs Thatcher's opposition to RENAMO delighted

She felt strong enough to invite Botha on a 'working visit' to Britain to meet her.

Despite protests, most notably from Bishop Desmond Tutu,* who asked, extravagantly, 'Would you have collaborated with Hitler when he perpetrated the holocaust?',[10] the meeting went ahead.† P. W. Botha came to Chequers on 2 June.‡ He arrived in a helicopter, but Mrs Thatcher did not meet him as he landed because of the danger that the helicopter's blades would blow her hair all over the place.[11]§ In a plenary session, Mrs Thatcher set out her line to him: 'Many people in Britain had relatives in South Africa. So that was a natural reservoir of goodwill. But our political attitude was affected by one enormous problem: we felt strongly that people's rights should not be determined by the colour of their skin.'[12] According to the South African Foreign Minister, Pik Botha, who was present, Mrs Thatcher was the 'chairperson who ruled the roost'.[13]

Before this, Mrs Thatcher held a tête-à-tête meeting with P. W. Botha, entirely alone. Mrs Thatcher's speaking notes for the meeting are a clue to her priorities. Beside the 'General' heading, Mrs Thatcher scribbled the words 'Importance we attach to visit'. This was followed by:

Good to break isolation

Potential goodwill in West – but cannot be manifested because of internal situation

Our foreign policy dependent on internal liberalisation.[14]

Beside the last point Mrs Thatcher had written the words 'Adapt or Die', the phrase used by Botha himself in 1979. Botha, she reported to her

---

the centrists, who made hay. 'I never regarded RENAMO as a responsible organization,' recalled Frank Carlucci, later President Reagan's National Security Advisor. 'I used Margaret's name [with Reagan], saying, "Well, we can't get crossed wires with Margaret Thatcher," and that always did the trick. The last thing he wanted to do was to get crossed wires with Margaret.' (Interview with Frank Carlucci.)

* Desmond Tutu (1931–), Archbishop of Cape Town and Metropolitan of Southern Africa, 1986–96; general secretary, South African Council of Churches, 1978–85; leading spokesman for black South Africans; winner, Nobel Peace Prize, 1984.

† Given the controversy, many years later, about whether Mrs Thatcher should have called for Mandela's release more strongly, it is noteworthy that the anti-apartheid leaders writing to her about the Botha visit – Kaunda, Julius Nyerere of Tanzania, Bishop Trevor Huddleston, Tutu himself – did not raise the imprisonment of Mandela as one of their grievances.

‡ On his European tour, P. W. Botha also travelled to Bonn to meet Helmut Kohl. Kohl met him but refused to shake hands with him. (Theresa Papenfus, *Pik Botha and his Times*, Litera, Kindle edn (translated by Sandra Mills), 2010.)

§ Helicopters and hair were always a problem for Mrs Thatcher. Whenever she travelled in one, she had to wear the headphone link hanging beneath her chin rather than sitting on top of her head, in order not to disturb her coiffure.

private secretary, John Coles, immediately afterwards, had defended his constitutional changes and introduced a rag-bag of topics, including dropping hints (not taken up) that he wanted to buy new surveillance aircraft from Britain* and trying, unsuccessfully, to persuade Mrs Thatcher to close the ANC office in London.† For her part, Mrs Thatcher maintained the Gleneagles Agreement of 1977 which prevented sporting contacts. She opposed the forced removals of blacks, bringing Botha up sharply with a personal example. She recalled that when she had visited South Africa as education secretary, she 'had met a person in District 6 of Cape Town who had told her that he was obliged to move for the second time because land was being cleared for whites. Was Mr Botha saying that the object of removals was not to make way for whites?'[15] She also asked Botha what happened to people who refused to be moved. 'We have ways of persuading them,' he replied. She found this remark 'offensive to her concept of individual liberty'.[16]

Towards the end of the meeting, Mrs Thatcher 'took the opportunity to raise the case of Nelson Mandela. Mr Botha said that he noted the Prime Minister's remarks, but that he was not able to interfere in the judicial process.'‡ This passage of arms – the seeking of an imprisoned dissident's release by Mrs Thatcher and the attempted fob-off – mirrored almost exactly what happened whenever Mrs Thatcher pressed Soviet leaders for the release of leading prisoners of conscience such as Andrei Sakharov. In both cases, the tactic was to raise the issue, against the will of the interlocutor, without letting it prevent other negotiations or discussions. By using the phrase 'raise the case' rather than 'demand the release', Britain could avoid provoking a direct refusal. Nelson Mandela had been imprisoned since 1963, but Mrs Thatcher seems to have been the first British prime minister to request the South African government to release him.

---

* It was an irony of the sanctions debate that socialist France, though favouring sanctions, secretly provided the engines for combat aircraft sold to South Africa. Britain did not sell equivalent *matériel* or weapons.

† On her briefing cards Mrs Thatcher scribbled the words 'Terrorism – Have not called on U.S. Govt. to close down IRA/Noraid offices in U.S – and IRA have vote in UK' ('Mr Botha', speaking note c. 2 June 1984, CAC: THCR 1/10/154).

‡ The suggestion in Mrs Thatcher's speaking note was that she intended to raise Mandela's fate at the plenary session ('Sensitive issue – but a move to free Mandela and others would be widely welcomed'), but she did not do so. She may well have hoped that Botha would be more receptive one on one than with a broader audience. Finding little give, she jotted down Botha's excuses on the back of her speaking notes: ' "Nelson Mandela / ANC / Unpopular among electors / Under pressure from right / Never possible to satisfy internal opinion / Country of minorities." ' Her rough notes of the meeting formed the basis of Coles's record. (Thatcher's annotations 'Mr Botha', speaking note, c. 2 June 1984, CAC: THCR 1/10/154.)

The meeting was no breakthrough. Sensing Botha's instinctive anti-Britishness (as she did with some other leaders, such as Mugabe and the Israeli leader Menachem Begin), Mrs Thatcher 'did not particularly warm' to him.[17] In the opinion of Charles Powell, who took over the subject of South Africa as part of his brief when he replaced John Coles shortly after the Chequers summit, Mrs Thatcher 'mentally wrote Botha off after Chequers'.[18] This was not the case: the meeting did establish a basis of dialogue. Botha and Mrs Thatcher began to exchange occasional letters which, though quite often bursting into recrimination, did show mutual respect and an interest in each other's positions. At least in the early stages, Mrs Thatcher had some hopes of Botha personally. In any case, it was 'important to be seen to be trying':[19] she felt that reform would only come from within South Africa itself, and that, when it did, the South African government would see in her a trustworthy external interlocutor who could help it move forward. Her greatest fear was that the combination of white oppression and black violence would set the country aflame.

The following year, 1985, was probably the one in which her fear seemed most likely to be realized. International attention on South Africa had grown, symbolized by the award of the Nobel Peace Prize to Desmond Tutu in November 1984. In January 1985, announcing further reforms, Botha said publicly for the first time that he would release Mandela if he 'unconditionally rejected violence as a political instrument'. Mandela refused the offer, as he was bound to do since it did not extend to his ANC comrades, but the precedent of an offer being made at all was notable. Discussing it with Kenneth Kaunda of Zambia, Mrs Thatcher wrote that it was impossible to overlook 'the difficulty which his [Mandela's] refusal to renounce violence, however understandable in the South African context, presents President Botha'.[20] How could he retain his white constituency if he were to release someone actively committed to an armed struggle against its rule? In March, on the anniversary of the 1960 Sharpeville massacre, the black township of Langa played host to a funeral procession for fifteen black activists killed by police the previous week. In the ensuing disturbances, police shot and killed at least another nineteen people. Black activists retaliated with a new weapon – 'necklacing' – in which a petrol-filled tyre was put round the victim's neck and set alight. Mrs Thatcher, who sometimes fastened on a particularly extreme form of behaviour with strong personal horror, as with the IRA's 'dirty protest' (see Volume I, p. 597) in the Maze Prison, was deeply shocked.[21]*

---

* A year later, Nelson Mandela's controversial wife, Winnie, declared that 'With our boxes of matches and our necklaces, we shall liberate this country.' These words contributed greatly

But when, in June, South African forces raided suspected ANC bases in Botswana, Mrs Thatcher was furious. She wrote to Botha warning him that, if such a thing were to happen again, Britain would have to 'take specific steps to mark her repudiation of it'.[22] When Botha wrote back that she should understand his predicament, since she had always strongly condemned the IRA, her reply was sharp:

> You mention the IRA. There have, as you know, been a continuing series of terrorist incidents in Northern Ireland in which some 2000 soldiers, policemen, prison warders and ordinary citizens have lost their lives. What would the international community think if Britain retaliated by launching attacks across the border into the Irish Republic, where many of the terrorists are?[23]

Britain, she reminded him, 'stood almost alone in the international community . . . attempting to resist pressure for economic measures against South Africa'. She was always clear that the IRA comparison did not work: Irish republicans could vote in democratic elections, supporters of the ANC could not. A few days later, Botha imposed a state of emergency, the first since Sharpeville.

The world reacted. France imposed a unilateral freeze on new investment in South Africa, and called for a UN Security Council resolution demanding voluntary sanctions. In the United States, the moderate line of the Reagan administration was assailed, with the White House coming under increasing pressure from Congress. Most devastating was the decision of big American banks, led by Chase Manhattan, to stop rolling over loans to South African companies and freeze all unused lines of credit. There was a run on the rand and, in August alone, $400 million – about a tenth of the banks' loans – was withdrawn from South Africa. The situation was made more desperate by a big speech by P. W. Botha in the same month. It was hinted in advance that this might include a serious offer to Nelson Mandela and was billed by Pik Botha as a signal that the President would now lead white South Africa 'across the Rubicon' to negotiation. When it actually came, however, P. W. Botha backed off, probably because

---

to anxiety about the ANC. In 1985 Mrs Mandela had defied the banning order imposed by the South African government and returned to her home in Soweto. Commenting on a biography of Winnie Mandela which was published that year, Mrs Thatcher told the Rev. Canon Neville Chamberlain (who had sent her a copy), 'One or two of the passages which I have glanced at, particularly those dealing with the banning orders imposed on Mrs. Mandela, underline the unacceptable nature of apartheid and the abuses of human rights connected with it' (Thatcher to Chamberlain, 25 February 1986, CAC: THCR 3/2/184).

of warnings from the military. He told his supporters that he would not lead them 'on a road to abdication and suicide'.*

Those unfriendly to Mrs Thatcher laid blame at her door: 'Mr Botha wants to bludgeon the blacks into submission. He knows he will be supported by Mrs Thatcher and President Reagan and Chancellor Kohl.† They have made it quite clear that blacks in their view are expendable,' wrote Desmond Tutu.[24] Mrs Thatcher had had precious little benefit from her stand against sanctions so far, and plenty of obloquy. As she had implied when she complained to Botha about his attack on Botswana, she was isolated. Now the Commonwealth decided to make her feel it.

Mrs Thatcher was never instinctively enthusiastic about international institutions, although some, such as NATO, she regarded as essential. She resented their loquacity and what she saw as their hypocritical self-righteousness. She also regarded many of them as conspiracies against Western interests, keen to impose limits on her country's power. The Commonwealth was a particularly awkward case in point. It was, of course, the British Commonwealth in origin, though no longer in name. In principle, Mrs Thatcher liked the idea of a global family of 'the English-speaking peoples' – a phrase of Winston Churchill's which she loved to borrow. She was instinctively sympathetic to the Old Commonwealth of Canada, Australia and New Zealand, and to new Commonwealth countries which took democracy seriously, most notably India. In practice, however, she was annoyed that the Commonwealth refused to look at the tyrannical practices of some of its own members, and she felt that it liked to forge a too easy unity over South Africa, designed to put Britain in the dock. She was particularly incensed that Commonwealth countries which had little or no trade with South Africa tried to lay down the law on economic sanctions, and was scornful of those countries – such as Canada and the Frontline States‡ – which carried on trade while pretending not

* F. W. de Klerk, the man who eventually succeeded Botha as state president, recalled feeling dismayed at the Rubicon Speech. 'I was told that Mrs Thatcher was sitting in front of the television listening to the speech. I was one of the people who worked on what we thought we had agreed was going to be his speech. And then he threw it back at us.' (Interview with F. W. de Klerk.)
† Tutu's mention of Kohl as an important figure in the matter of South African sanctions was correct. West Germany had need of South African coal and was opposed to sanctions. Kohl and Mrs Thatcher, despite their other differences, were to work together quite closely on South Africa.
‡ The 'Frontline States' consisted of those countries bordering South Africa and Namibia – Angola, Botswana, Lesotho, Mozambique, Tanzania, Zambia and (from 1980) Zimbabwe – which had banded together to co-ordinate their opposition to apartheid.

to.* The Commonwealth Heads of Government Meetings (CHOGMs) were, she thought, inordinately long, pointless and ill organized. They often took place in hot holiday places, where pictures of leaders having fun at taxpayers' expense played badly at home. She felt that the leaders of poor countries spent far too much money on these jamborees. Mrs Thatcher was not blind to the cost to Britain. As Malcolm Rifkind, then the Foreign Office minister on the subject, recalled, there was a feeling that 'we provide a lot of funding for the Commonwealth, a bit like America and the United Nations, and all we are getting is a lot of stick in return. Occasionally she would have thought, why are we part of this organization?'[25]†

The CHOGM at Nassau, in the Bahamas, in October 1985, toxically combined all the things she disliked with the subject of South African sanctions. As was often the case before summits, Mrs Thatcher conducted trench warfare with her own officials to keep down the numbers of the British delegation, even trying (though failing) to exclude the Cabinet Secretary, Robert Armstrong ('The Prime Minister said she was tired of arguing about the subject').[26] She refused daily hair appointments as being too extravagant,[27] though Caroline Ryder, her diary secretary, slipped them back into the programme without permission because she thought they would be needed in the Bahamian heat. She also refused Lord King's offer of the use of Concorde to fly in the British delegation. She feared this would upstage the Queen who, as usual, was attending as head of the Commonwealth. 'Stick to VC10,' she scribbled.[28] As the conference approached, she became uneasily aware of the Sovereign's strong interest in getting Commonwealth agreement over South Africa. Charles Powell told her that the outcome on South Africa 'appears to be of great concern to the Palace',[29] and that the Queen would like to arrange an audience on 17 October, the day before the conference began, 'in the hope that she may be able to use what you tell her with other Commonwealth leaders'.[30]‡

* Privately, some of the leaders of the Frontline States were quite open about their reliance on trade with South Africa. In 1986, a note passed to Mrs Thatcher from the British High Commission in Zimbabwe reported the Deputy Prime Minister saying, 'We will never commit suicide by imposing sanctions on South Africa.' Another local politician explained: 'I am surprised that the British, who taught us hypocrisy, should find our attitude surprising.' (Melhuish to Reeve, 26 August 1986, CAC: THCR 1/3/21.)

† The racist saloon-bar joke of the time was that CHOGM stood for 'Coons Holidaying On Government Money'. This was attributed, falsely, to Denis Thatcher, but he liked the crack. (See Thatcher, *Below the Parapet*, p. 152.)

‡ Mrs Thatcher's office seems to have been informed of this in more detail by the Palace on 16 October. This missive – a note and a telegram – was considered so sensitive that Nigel

Mrs Thatcher was as restrictive in her attitude to the content of the conference as she was to the arrangements. In her speech at the opening session, she tried to move the focus away from South Africa. As Charles Powell put it, 'Our purpose is to try to get South Africa a bit into scale by "losing" it in the context of wider problems such as East/West, arms control etc.'[31] She also opposed the idea of a Commonwealth contact group for South Africa and, of course, resisted economic sanctions: 'she had heard it all before,' she told the Canadian Prime Minister Brian Mulroney on the first evening at Lyford Cay when he argued for new measures. Sanctions 'would only damage industry which was in the lead in breaking down apartheid'.[32] Mulroney, who wrote in his memoirs that 'the Queen personally asked me to work with other leaders to prevent a major split within the group' (that is, between Mrs Thatcher and all the rest),[33] tried to win Mrs Thatcher over by telling her how a British initiative over South Africa would make Commonwealth members 'all stand in line and salute'.[34] Mrs Thatcher was not tempted, believing, on the contrary, that the Commonwealth liked to treat Britain as a target, not a guiding star. The Labour Prime Minister of Australia, Bob Hawke,* tried a similar line to Mulroney's, saying that he did not want to embarrass the United Kingdom, and urging her to support the idea of a Commonwealth mission of eminent persons to South Africa. She disagreed, saying that the 'normal diplomatic channels' were better than special groups, as she had found when dealing with China over Hong Kong: 'The South African regime would never negotiate with a pistol to its head.'[35] She also thought it was 'unrealistic', in South Africa, to envisage 'one man, one vote in a unitary state': better to look to federal solutions to replace apartheid.[36]

In her separate discussions in the same two days with Kenneth Kaunda and with Robert Mugabe of Zimbabwe, she was equally disinclined to accept the proposition that there had to be a revolution to end apartheid. To Kaunda, who 'sobbed into his big white handkerchief'[37] about the possible break-up of the Commonwealth if there were no agreement at Nassau, she emphasized the need to give dignity to the black population and preserve a strong economy at the same time. She reminded Mugabe that his own Patriotic Front in Rhodesia had been made to give up violence. Some ANC leaders were heading the other way, she said – she

---

Wicks suggested to the Queen's private secretary that it be kept in the Palace archives and not in those of the Prime Minister, although today no copy survives in either repository. (See Wicks to Moore, 8 November 1985, Prime Minister's Papers, South Africa, Relations with South Africa, Part 8 (document consulted in the Cabinet Office).)

* Robert ('Bob') Hawke (1929–), educated University of Western Australia and University College, Oxford; Prime Minister of Australia, 1983–91.

wanted to support the moderates. 'History showed', Mugabe retorted, 'that the moderates were always doomed.'[38] She hotly replied that support for terrorism meant supporting the people who had murdered Mrs Gandhi the previous year. Mrs Thatcher insisted that she wanted to be 'a builder not a destroyer'. Accordingly, she emphasized to Mugabe, he must be in no doubt that she would not go along with economic sanctions. She said the same to the BBC. She recalled that in Rhodesia economic sanctions 'had not worked – they never do . . . I am not willing to start on that road.'[39] No one could accuse her of not being clear.

Commonwealth leaders did, however, accuse her of stirring things up. As the leaders gathered for their 'retreat' to settle key business in Lyford Cay that Friday, her statement against sanctions, Charles Powell reported, was 'clearly taken as a provocation by the Africans and others'.[40] The following day, an informal drafting committee of Mugabe, Mulroney, Kaunda, Hawke and Rajiv Gandhi* sketched out a proposed agreement, which they showed her. For two hours, Mrs Thatcher explained to them why it was unacceptable. In Powell's view, 'Their approach at this stage bordered on the naïve: an expectation that the Prime Minister would join the majority out of goodwill for the Commonwealth.'[41] Things went downhill after that, with a three-hour, wider meeting which was, 'at times, acrimonious, particularly exchanges between the Prime Minister and Mr Hawke'.† While this was going on, Brian Mulroney – always keen to exercise his considerable personal charm on Mrs Thatcher – passed her a handwritten note which said, 'I have concluded that this meeting is the <u>ultimate</u> test of the patience of any reasonable person of a conservative persuasion.'[42] If he was right, she failed his test pretty badly. Overnight, the British went off to prepare their own text. Sonny Ramphal was 'dejected . . . and spoke of a damaging and perhaps irreparable split in the Commonwealth'.[43]

The next day's plenary session was worse still: 'The Prime Minister was lectured on morality, on preferring British jobs to black African lives, on being concerned for pennies rather than principles,'[44] reported Powell. Characteristically, she 'reminded her critics of their own trade and other links with South Africa and some of the less satisfactory features of their societies, particularly when it came to human rights'. She pointed out that

---

* Rajiv Gandhi (1944–91), educated Shiv Niketan School, New Delhi, Imperial College of Science and Technology, University of London and Trinity College, Cambridge; Prime Minister of India, 1984–9 (took office after the assassination of his mother, Prime Minister Indira Gandhi); assassinated by a suicide bomber while campaigning in the 1991 elections.
† Hawke himself described their encounter, quite generously, as 'a vintage Thatcher performance, Margaret at her best and worst' (Bob Hawke, *The Hawke Memoirs*, Heinemann, 1994, p. 321).

they were perfectly willing to trade with the USSR, a more oppressive regime even than the South African one.

In these sessions, Mrs Thatcher exercised her unique mixture of conviction and guile. She was perfectly genuine in her principled opposition to sanctions, and in her anger with other member states, but she was also playing a game to minimize the demands made upon Britain. Contemptuous though she was of the moral pretensions of the Commonwealth, she did not, in fact, want a formal split. As the plenary session broke for lunch, she discussed with her officials the need 'to offer two very modest additional measures'[45] – a ban on the import of South African Krugerrands (gold coins) to Britain and the ending of official support for trade promotions to South Africa. These ideas had been prepared in advance of the conference by Mrs Thatcher and officials to keep up her sleeve. Britain would offer them if the Commonwealth would agree to call for 'a suspension of violence'.* The United Kingdom would take no further measures beyond these.

Mrs Thatcher now changed her act from anger to injury. At 3.30, she returned for 'a very chilly encounter'[46] with the drafting committee. She said she felt 'deep hurt' at some of the morning's remarks which were not 'in keeping with the Commonwealth spirit of fairness'. 'It was extraordinary', Mrs Thatcher recalled,

> how the pack instinct of politicians could change a group of normally courteous, in some cases even charming, people into a gang of bullies . . . So I began by saying that I had never been so insulted as I had by the people in that room and that it was an entirely unacceptable way of conducting international business.[47]

Feeling bad at this spectacle of a woman scorned, some of those present 'urged her not to take the remarks personally'. Mrs Thatcher exploited the moment to offer her two concessions, saying that it would be easier for her domestically if they were rejected, since her stand against sanctions was popular with her supporters at home. If her offer were not accepted, she would withdraw it and the United Kingdom would make a unilateral statement at the end of the conference. The leaders asked for a short break to reflect: 'Some ten minutes later a distinctly more cheerful Ramphal appeared to say that "We are in business."'[48]

At a meeting at 5 p.m., the text she sought was approved, unchanged. There were many speeches in praise of Mrs Thatcher, in what Powell

---

* The call for 'suspension' rather than an 'end' to violence was itself a concession by Mrs Thatcher. She reluctantly accepted the view of experts that the ANC would never forswear violence in principle, but might suspend it in practice.

described as 'a shame-faced reaction to the morning's session about which the Prime Minister had succeeded in making them all feel perfectly rotten. The meeting ended with a round of applause for the Prime Minister.'[49] 'I suddenly became a stateswoman for having accepted a "compromise",' Mrs Thatcher wrote mockingly in her memoirs.[50] The compromise was that the Commonwealth would indeed send an Eminent Persons Group (EPG) to investigate the situation in South Africa and report. If the eminences reported unfavourably on progress to ending apartheid, the issue of sanctions ('further measures' was the chosen, Thatcher-driven phrase to water down the concept) would be reopened.

In Powell's loyal but, in this case, correct view, Mrs Thatcher had overcome the difficulties she had faced with 'consummate skill'.[51] She had maximized her position of complete isolation on sanctions by making her opponents feel guilty. Calculating that they greatly preferred some sort of unanimous agreement to none, she had offered a couple of small inducements to include Britain in their final 'accord'. She had not persuaded any of them that she was right, but she had won the two things she most wanted – no sanctions, for now at least, and no serious compromise of Britain's right to take an independent view of the question.

As for the EPG, she thought no better of the idea than when it had first been floated, but because she had agreed to it, she could strongly influence its choice of members. She spoke privately about it to Geoffrey Howe at Lyford Cay. She was worried, she told him, that the South African government would refuse to see the group. This problem would be overcome if the Foreign Secretary himself would chair it. He 'would be the most effective spokesman and the person best able to keep some control of the Group's activities'.[52] She did not, apparently, see that the main minister of a British government with a policy of its own in the matter could not be accepted by the Commonwealth as its independent representative. According to Powell's official record, Howe was 'not averse' to her idea, though he was 'concerned about the compatibility of his obligations'. The actual mood of the meeting, however, was rather different. When Howe asked how his job could be done in his absence, Mrs Thatcher airily replied, 'Oh, that's all right. I'll be my own Foreign Secretary!' Howe, who shrank from conflict, made no direct protest, but this was, for him, 'the killer-blow'.[53] She was soon dissuaded from putting Howe's name forward, but she had clearly, almost artlessly, expressed her true wishes. For him, they were unforgettably humiliating.

As soon as the last-minute agreement was reached, Bernard Ingham wrote to Mrs Thatcher. What should he tell the press? Always and only concerned with the domestic audience, he framed the issue thus: 'Your main problem will be to kill the charge that you have had to give a lot in order to get an agreement – i.e. that you have done a U-turn – without immediately rubbishing as of no account the additional measures taken.'[54]

Achieving this balance was not something which Mrs Thatcher was instinctively good at. She was proud not of what she had agreed, but of what she hadn't. After all, she was not excited by the formal result – that the Commonwealth now had a policy on South Africa. When asked on television about the summit, she put her forefinger and thumb close to each other and said that she had moved only 'a tiny little bit', compared with 'what we were faced with'.[55] 'With four little words,' wrote Howe, who was sitting beside her when she uttered them, 'she had at one and the same time humiliated three dozen other heads of government, devalued the policy on which they had just agreed – and demeaned herself.'[56]* There is a vehemence in what he wrote which perhaps tries to make up for his failure to protest at the time. As he flew back to London with Mrs Thatcher, 'none of us said anything critical.'[57] He chewed the toad, as he had done before and would do again, but with increasing difficulty and distaste.†

The Commonwealth Eminent Persons Group took shape, with Lord Barber,‡ Edward Heath's former Chancellor of the Exchequer, as its British member.§ Mrs Thatcher was not enthusiastic about its work, and chafed at the caution of the Foreign Office in discouraging her from engaging with alternative sources of ideas, of all races, in South Africa. In November, when Enos Mabuza, the chief executive of KaNgwane, one of

---

* One fact that may have swayed Mrs Thatcher towards high-handedness was her irritation at the pretensions of Commonwealth leaders much less experienced than she. She regarded Rajiv Gandhi in particular as 'posturing and shallow' and believed that 'He and Mulroney were obviously keen to cut a figure at the meeting, but did not really have the experience for their self-appointed role.' (Powell to Acland, 21 October 1985, Prime Minister's Papers, Commonwealth, CHOGM, The Bahamas, Part 10 (document consulted in the Cabinet Office).)

† It had at first been planned that Denis should accompany Mrs Thatcher to the CHOGM in Nassau. In the end, he did not. The meticulous government records noted who in the prime ministerial party bought what at the duty-free shop before returning to Britain. Mrs Thatcher bought a multipack of Rothman's cigarettes for $6.50 and a bottle of gin for $4.97. Since she neither smoked nor drank gin, these must have been her present to her husband, who did both. (See 'Prime Minister, Duty Free', undated, Prime Minister's Papers, PM's Tours Abroad, CHOGM 1985, The Bahamas, Part 2 (document consulted in the Cabinet Office).)

‡ Anthony Barber (1920–2005), educated Retford Grammar School and Oriel College, Oxford; Conservative MP for Doncaster, 1951–64; for Altrincham and Sale, 1965–74; Chancellor of the Exchequer, 1970–74; chairman, Standard Chartered Bank Ltd, 1974–87; created Lord Barber, 1974.

§ Its co-chairmen were Malcolm Fraser, the former Prime Minister of Australia, and General Olusegun Obasanjo, twice Nigerian head of state.

the 'homelands', asked to see her, the Foreign Office advised her not to because he was not a political radical, but Charles Powell told her this was 'a bit stodgy. I gather Laurens van der Post would favour you seeing him.'[58] So she did.

Of the various 'irregulars' whose views, in most areas of life, she sought, van der Post was one of the most unusual. A brilliant, charming, beautiful old man of Afrikaner birth, he wrote powerfully about his native land, about history, literature and anthropology of the 'noble savage' variety. He was considered a spiritual counsellor by many, and was a guru to the Prince of Wales, who made him godfather to his elder son, Prince William. He was also, though this was unknown to Mrs Thatcher, something of a fantasist, claiming knowledge and experience that he did not always possess, and using it to establish connections with important people.* He was a genuine and long-standing opponent of apartheid, and also of the ANC, whose Communist elements he mistrusted. Part of his romantic obsession with the unWesternized glory of the black African was his admiration for the Zulus, whose language he falsely implied he could speak. This led him to favour the Inkatha movement led by the Zulu Chief Minister, Mangosuthu Buthelezi,† who opposed sanctions and was supported by large numbers of Zulus, particularly in the rural areas. It was van der Post who, in August 1985, first introduced Mrs Thatcher to Buthelezi and, in Charles Powell's view, 'fooled her'[59] that Buthelezi was more important and more influential than he was. Since, like van der Post, she was always looking for a plural black leadership rather than an ANC monopoly, Mrs Thatcher was readily persuaded. Buthelezi was the only non-ANC black leader with a large popular following. She would later go to considerable lengths to keep him in play as a counterbalance to ANC power.

Mrs Thatcher had known van der Post since being introduced to him in opposition by Airey Neave and Ian Gow, who was his solicitor. She fell for his mage-like wisdom and the flattering calls he made to her, particularly under the stress of the Falklands War. Charles Powell considered that he 'talked such transparent rubbish',[60] but he usually facilitated his

---

* Van der Post said, for example, that he had been brought up by a Bushman nanny, though this was not so. He also said he had been military-political adviser to Lord Mountbatten at the end of the Second World War, but this claim, which was not true, appeared in *Who's Who* only after Mountbatten was safely dead. This and other stories were controversially deconstructed by J. D. F. Jones in his authorized biography *Storyteller: The Many Lives of Laurens van der Post*, John Murray, 2001.

† Mangosuthu Buthelezi (1928–), Chief of the Buthelezi tribe, South Africa; founder of Inkatha Freedom Party, 1975; Leader, 1975–; Chief Minister, KwaZulu Legislative Assembly, 1976–94; Minister for Home Affairs, 1994–2004; Member, National Parliament, 1994–.

meetings with her and made sure she saw his letters on a range of subjects, of which South Africa was the most important.* Van der Post had real influence with Mrs Thatcher and gave her the feeling, which she always needed in all controversial policy areas, that there were genuine alternatives to the version which officials kept pushing on her.† Thanks to van der Post, No. 10 also had an informant at the top level of the South African government in the form of the minister Piet Koornhof,‡ who, from 1979, secretly provided information, via intermediaries, about the tensions in Botha's Cabinet and the opportunities for change. Koornhof led what van der Post called 'an enlightened movement in South African Internal policy'.[61] The sort of knowledge he furnished helped Mrs Thatcher to feel that her pressure might get somewhere.[62]

Her other source of alternative views on the subject was Fritz Leutwiler,§ the former president of the Swiss National Bank and chairman and president of the Bank for International Settlements. She had come to know and like Leutwiler while on holiday staying with Lady Glover in Switzerland, where he had warned her about the direction of her own monetary policy in 1980 (see Volume I, p. 530). In 1985, Leutwiler agreed to orchestrate the rescue of South Africa from the bank crisis provoked by Chase Manhattan. He was backed by the German and Swiss banks which were furious at their US equivalents for pulling the plug on their South African operations without consulting them. In this he was successful, and won Mrs Thatcher's admiration.[63] She agreed with his belief that the roll-over

---

* Van der Post's letters often began 'Margaret dear' and would tell her how beautiful she was, what a lovely dress she had been wearing, or how the Prince of Wales admired her: 'Prince Charles was with us here last night and I so wish you could have been there in your old chair to hear how he and we remembered, talked about you and are closer to you than ever.' (Van der Post to Thatcher, 30 October 1980, Prime Minister's Papers, Prime Minister's Meetings with Laurens Van der Post (document consulted in the Cabinet Office).)

† Other direct sources of advice to Mrs Thatcher which went against the standard Foreign Office line included George Guise, a member of her Policy Unit who specialized in science and business policy but had long experience of South Africa, Nicholas Elliott, the former MI6 man and friend of Airey Neave, Julian Amery MP, the old imperialist who had good connections with the white government and business elites, Harry Oppenheimer, the liberal South African head of Anglo American and De Beers, the gold and diamond mining giants, and her confidant Woodrow Wyatt. She also liked Ian Player, brother of the famous golfer, Gary. Player was a distinguished conservationist in southern Africa, instrumental in saving the white rhino. He helped push Mrs Thatcher in van der Post's pro-Zulu direction. He was also a friend of Charles Powell's wife, Carla.

‡ Pieter ('Piet') Koornhof (1925–2007), educated Stellenbosch and Oxford Universities; entered South African parliament in 1964; National Party Cabinet minister in various portfolios in 1970s and 1980s; South African Ambassador to the United States, 1987–91.

§ Fritz Leutwiler (1924–97), president of Swiss National Bank, 1974–84; chairman and president, Bank for International Settlements, 1982–4.

of debts which he negotiated would 'give time for political reforms to be introduced'[64] and with his warning that a white 'backlash' against Botha was likely if he went too far, too fast. Leutwiler shared her desire for an orderly end to apartheid and her anxieties about the ANC. At this time, he became her 'main contact' with P. W. Botha.[65]

Much as she preferred van der Post's gleaming-eyed accounts of warrior races, lost worlds and Zulu honour to being lectured at Commonwealth conferences, Mrs Thatcher retained a practical grasp of what was happening. Now that the EPG (the Eminent Persons Group agreed at Lyford Cay) existed, she realized that, rather than repudiate it, she had to try to steer it in the right direction. So when, on 12 November, P. W. Botha wrote to tell her that, despite her 'strong, principled stand [at Nassau] against economic sanctions', his government would not agree to her request to co-operate with the Commonwealth initiative,[66] she replied bluntly, 'I have to say that I am very disappointed by your message.'[67] In her own hand, after 'disappointed', she inserted 'and dismayed'. She went on:

> My ability to help preserve the conditions in which an internal dialogue of the sort you are seeking has a chance of success will be critically, perhaps fatally, undermined . . . If you value my continuing help, I most strongly urge you not to [refuse to co-operate]. I do not think I could be plainer.

Confronted with this, Botha quickly capitulated, and agreed to see the EPG.

At the same time, Mrs Thatcher was hearing from intelligence sources that the South African government had talked directly to Mandela about his possible release. Despite her refusal personally to talk to the ANC so long as it espoused violence, she was perfectly happy that MI6 should do so secretly outside South Africa itself – in Lusaka, for instance, and in London.[68] The ANC, the same sources said, would 'call a halt to all violence' if Mandela and all the imprisoned ANC leaders were released and the organization unbanned.[69] In a letter to Mrs Thatcher on 14 December, Botha told her that he wanted to continue with reforms and 'get moving with the negotiations . . . we are reconciled to the disappearance of white domination.'[70] Cheered up by all this, Howe told her that Botha 'obviously trusts you – you are perhaps the only Western leader in whom he feels he can confide.'[71] He suggested she set up an 'additional personal connection' so that Botha could talk to someone 'known to have your confidence', but then spoilt it by suggesting Gordon Richardson, the ex-Governor of the Bank of England, who was her particular *bête noire* (see Volume I, p. 462). 'She thinks that her card of entry to President Botha will decline in value', Powell replied on her behalf, 'if played too often; and she has other emissaries in mind whom she would prefer to use.'[72] The main one she was thinking of was Leutwiler, but she did not wish to share this with her Foreign Secretary. Another reason that Mrs Thatcher liked Leutwiler was that he was close to Helmut Kohl and advised him informally on South African matters. She was always keen to cement the alliance with Kohl against economic sanctions.*

Another contact, seeing Botha under his own steam at this time, was Julian Amery.† Did she want him to give Botha a message, he asked her early in 1986. Mrs Thatcher did, and scribbled out what it should be:

> The one L van der Post put to me – namely – he must get a majority against the extreme blacks by forming an alliance of
> Whites
> Indians
> Coloureds
> Zulus
> S. African Swazis
> Which together with some of the blacks they would carry with them, would give him a majority.[73]

This was a fair, if rough summation of how she wanted an internal settlement to come about.‡

In a major speech in January promising further reform, including a National Statutory Council for all races, Botha spoke publicly of the possibility of releasing Mandela. He put forward the suggestion that this could be a prisoner swap with a South African officer held in Angola and with the Soviet dissident Anatoly Shcharansky. This eccentric idea had come to him – via West Germans speaking to East Germans – from the Russians, as Mrs Thatcher was informed from reports.[74] Perhaps part of the

---

* Like Mrs Thatcher when dealing with Howe, Kohl concealed his own South African contacts from his Foreign Minister, Hans-Dietrich Genscher. In the German case, however, Genscher and Kohl led different political parties, so the lack of communication was less wounding in the German system than it was in the British.
† Julian Amery (1919–96), educated Eton and Balliol College, Oxford; Conservative MP for Preston North, 1950–66; for Brighton Pavilion, 1969–92; Minister for Housing and Construction, DOE, 1970–72; Minister of State, FCO, 1972–4; created Lord Amery, 1992.
‡ Mrs Thatcher, however, recognized that any settlement involving Buthelezi would not succeed if it fell short of meaningful reform. She told the Conservative MP Robert Jackson that this meant a 'firm commitment to the abolition of apartheid . . . I suspect he realises that without such a commitment no settlement which might be negotiated would be acceptable to the majority of the black population. The hope nurtured by some Afrikaners of a political deal which effectively maintains their power with the consent of the government does not seem to me a realistic one.' (Thatcher to Jackson, 27 February 1986, CAC: THCR 3/2/184.)

attraction of the scheme in Botha's mind was that the deal would confirm that the ANC was a tool of the Soviets. Whether it would really have been such a brilliant thing for the West if the Soviet Union had won the release of black Africa's greatest hero is something he seems not to have considered. Anyway, the ANC had little difficulty in refusing the offer.

Perhaps naively, Mrs Thatcher considered Botha's speech 'very courageous',[75] and was annoyed that the Foreign Office reaction was 'rather wan'.[76] She thought that Botha was moving away from old policies more decisively than was the case. Buthelezi announced that he would not join the new council, and P. W. Botha rebuked his own Foreign Minister, Pik, for saying that South Africa would one day have a black president. The international community remained unconvinced that real change was coming.

Some things were shifting, however. Lord Barber, for example, secretly relayed to the British government the news that Mandela, visited by an EPG colleague in prison, had said that he could work with Buthelezi if released, and had indicated that he wanted to give confidence to the white population.[77] In March, the whole seven-man EPG met Mandela. During this encounter, he turned to Barber and said: 'I am told Mrs Thatcher says President* Gorbachev is a man with whom she can do business. Will you please tell her that it would be far, far easier and very much safer to do business with Nelson Mandela.'[78] It is not clear that the message reached her in those precise terms, but Barber reported its essence to her and Howe. He told them that Mandela and Oliver Tambo† (whom he had also seen) would take part in negotiations with the South African government. The group's meetings with South African ministers had also been good. That with Botha, however, had been a 'disaster',[79] and Barber had concluded that the South African government did not envisage the full dismantling of apartheid. In that case, said Mrs Thatcher, it must change its position: 'There must be at least the prospect of change within a defined period.'

Please, Barber therefore asked her, would she introduce the EPG's 'negotiating concept' to Botha, who as yet knew nothing of it. The concept was that the South African government would end the state of emergency, withdraw troops from the townships, release Mandela and other ANC leaders and unban the ANC. In return, the ANC would agree to suspend violence and enter talks. Three days later, Mrs Thatcher wrote to Botha

---

* Gorbachev was not, in fact, president of the Soviet Union until 1990. At this stage, his title was general secretary of the Communist Party.
† Oliver Tambo (1917–93), deputy president-general, ANC, 1958; led ANC's mission in exile living in London, Tanzania and Zimbabwe, 1960–90; acting president-general, ANC, 1967–85; president, 1985–90; returned to South Africa from his exile base, 1990; national chairman, ANC, 1990–93.

and to President Reagan to explain this scheme.* To Botha, she said that the EPG concept 'offers a unique opportunity to make progress'.[80] Without some movement, she would have no chance of persuading Commonwealth colleagues to stay their hand on sanctions. To this, Botha responded positively, tacitly dropping his demand for the absolute forswearing of violence. He sought assurances, however, that the EPG would recognize that he would have to use punitive measures if violence continued after Mandela's release. He 'has some reason', Mrs Thatcher wrote to Powell on the face of his letter. 'He could not stand by if violence erupted again.'[81]

Powell did not want his boss to become Botha's intermediary with the EPG. He got her to write back saying that she could not 'try to insert myself as an honest broker'[82] between the two. She did add, however, that he could not ask for more than a 'suspension' of violence. She would support him if he took 'reasonable security measures', but the EPG could not give him a 'blank cheque'. She also defended the ANC to him: 'There is a readiness on their part to talk; but realistically they will need something they can show to their supporters to justify calling for a suspension of violence.' After Botha had received this, the South African government duly sent an encouraging message to the EPG. Mrs Thatcher also warned Botha that 'frustrated nationalism' was the breeding ground for Communism. This was interestingly echoed, a couple of weeks later, by a report from Helen Suzman on visiting Mandela in prison. He had 'stressed', said Suzman, 'that he was first and foremost a black African nationalist. He has said that he was not a Marxist.'[83] Ten days later, Mandela told Barber that 'he had no problem' with the EPG's negotiating concept and 'would be willing to cooperate'.[84] Irritated though she was by the pretensions of the Commonwealth, Mrs Thatcher was genuinely keen to push for the breakthrough their 'concept' sought.

It may help to understand the balance of hope and fear which surrounded the whole subject of South Africa at that time to note the report Mrs Thatcher received from the Cabinet's policy group on South Africa (MISC 118). It calibrated the different possibilities twenty years on. It put deterioration leading to a long-drawn-out civil war at 55 per cent, the breakdown of central government and 'black revolutionary takeover' at

---

* Reagan, who had domestic political problems about the South African issue, did not wish to make too much noise, but was on Mrs Thatcher's side. 'Through quiet support of efforts like Mrs Thatcher's,' wrote his National Security Advisor, John Poindexter, 'we can seek to maintain influence without signalling a direct US role or appearing to legitimize present ANC conduct.' (Poindexter to the President, 4 April 1986, Memo 19446, Exec Sec, NSC: System file, 8602655, Reagan Library.)

10 per cent, and 'peaceful transition to black majority rule' at 'perhaps 5 per cent'.[85] This sense of the precariousness of the situation weighed heavily with Mrs Thatcher.

On 19 May 1986, South African forces suddenly launched ground and air raids on ANC offices in Zambia, Zimbabwe and Botswana. One effect was to end the EPG's mission. For Mrs Thatcher, the raids must have seemed like Groundhog Day, as they so closely resembled the Botswana raids of the previous June. They evoked the same fury from her. She wrote to Botha wanting to know:

> what possible advantage to South Africa could outweigh the immense damage done to your international position and in particular to the Commonwealth initiative of which you make no mention [in a recent letter to her] but which I have supported so strongly, believing it to be in your interest. I frankly find this omission astonishing.[86]

He claimed that terrorists were not interested in negotiations, she went on, but the EPG had been in Lusaka, 'exploring this very point with the ANC', when the raids took place. People would say that these attacks were 'a deliberate attempt by your government to torpedo an initiative which was developing too well'. And she wished to register her sense of personal hurt: 'I myself find them hard to reconcile with the relationship of trust and confidence which I had thought we had established.' It was 'a watershed': 'I cannot emphasise enough the deep anxiety which we all feel about South Africa's future if what I believe may be the last chance for a negotiated settlement is rejected.' If she could get nothing out of this stubborn man, how could she hope to influence events in the direction she sought? It was probably from this time onward that Mrs Thatcher decided that real change within the white regime would not come from Botha and so began to look out for an Afrikaner Gorbachev.

Botha professed to be equally angry with Mrs Thatcher, complaining over eight pages. He spoke of her 'veiled threats'[87] and his 'deep disillusionment' with the contents and 'spirit' of her letter. If his government were forced to choose between 'accepting the domination of Marxist revolutionary forces and threats from certain Western countries and our determination to maintain civilised standards and our very existence – we will have no option', he concluded rather vaguely, 'but to follow the dictates of our own consciences.' On the same day, he sent her a separate, confidential document of the South African Communist Party, unearthed by his National Intelligence Service (NIS) and designed to shock her, about the revolutionary seizure of power. 'Not really a very illuminating document,' commented Powell drily. 'That's what Communist parties are like.'[88]

With this setback, Mrs Thatcher came under ever greater pressure from the Commonwealth and from her own Foreign Office. When Powell suggested that Howe should 'explore discreetly' Pik Botha's private suggestion that European heads of government might have a meeting with P. W. Botha, Mrs Thatcher scribbled, rather desperately, 'Yes – let's try every-thing we can. We must play for time.'[89] On 12 June, Botha reimposed the countrywide state of emergency he had earlier lifted. The EPG report was published on the same day. It said that South Africa was not making progress towards the abolition of apartheid. Although Charles Powell wrote disparagingly to Mrs Thatcher about the report, he drew favourable attention to what it had to say about Mandela personally: 'He clearly is a remarkable man.'[90]

When she met the co-chairmen of the EPG on the day of publication, Mrs Thatcher set out her overall case:

> in the end there had to be negotiations in South Africa between the Government and blacks ... She believed ... that Mandela held the key. But there must be a risk that his release would provoke further violence, even if this was not what he himself would wish. She also wondered to what extent Mandela would be able to control the ANC, let alone the young blacks in the townships. But in the absence of any other way forward, she thought that his release must be the focus of further efforts with the South African Government.

There was 'much to be said', she went on, 'for focussing attention on a single person and a single event'.[91] One of the two co-chairmen, the Nigerian General Olusegun Obasanjo, told Mrs Thatcher that she was 'the only person to whom President Botha would talk frankly about his fears and what he was prepared to do'.[92] This was 'interesting', Powell reported, but 'The Prime Minister deliberately did not respond to this. She thinks she has used up much of her credibility with Botha, for the time being at least.'[93] Talking to him might be a 'possible option' later. The very next day, Powell communicated Mrs Thatcher's emphasis on the importance of the release of Mandela to the South African Ambassador, Denis Worrall.* 'I am not passing this on to the Foreign Office,' he told Mrs Thatcher.[94]† As was the

---

* Denis Worrall (1935–), South African Ambassador to the UK, 1984–7; founder, Independent Party (South Africa), 1987.

† On 6 June Mrs Thatcher wrote to Lord Paget of Northampton, a Labour peer who supported her position on economic sanctions, outlining the case for Mandela's release: 'As you know, I loathe terrorism. But the status of Nelson Mandela as a black leader is accepted on

case in some other areas of diplomacy – aspects of the Cold War, relations with Saudi Arabia – South Africa became one of those subjects for which Mrs Thatcher and Powell worked out the direction of policy at the highest level in Downing Street and cut out Geoffrey Howe and his officials. Powell used the reformist Worrall, who had political ambitions of his own, almost as his spy within South African officialdom.

Ahead of the European Council in The Hague at the end of the month, Hawke and Mulroney lobbied Mrs Thatcher for the EEC to introduce sanctions. Still seeking delay, Mrs Thatcher revived her idea of Geoffrey Howe as an 'eminent person', but this time proposed that he should go to South Africa and the Frontline States as the European Council's special envoy. This was agreed, with notable support from Helmut Kohl. The Council announced a prospective ban on the import of gold coins, iron, steel and coal, and proposed a voluntary ban on new investment in South Africa, but not full-bodied sanctions. The Howe visit was allowed three months to work before any of the agreed action would be taken. This would make it more difficult, Mrs Thatcher hoped, for the Common-wealth London 'review conference', scheduled for the beginning of August, to throw its weight about. 'We must at all costs avoid bringing [his visit] to a premature conclusion,' Mrs Thatcher told Howe, perhaps uncon-sciously pleased at the thought that he would be away a lot. 'Anything less would be to let down the Germans, which the Prime Minister could not contemplate.'[95] She was not normally so tender about German feelings. Commonwealth leaders understood what she was up to, and were 'enraged' by it.[96]

Laurens van der Post rang to congratulate her on 'the best that could be done' at The Hague, and on avoiding sanctions once again: 'If we start on sanctions, it will be the end of South Africa.'[97] Botha thanked her too, for the same reason, but complained that the EEC had handed South Africa an ultimatum.[98] He told her haughtily that he would decide whether Howe, on his mission, could see Mandela, after he himself had seen Howe, if indeed he would see him at all. Reports warned that the ANC would not let Howe see Mandela anyway.[99]* Mrs Thatcher wrote back to Botha,

---

all sides and I am convinced that his release is a necessary step on the way to creating the right conditions for dialogue ... I realise that Nelson Mandela has not been prepared to renounce violence as a condition for his release (that of course is not the same as declaring that he would engage in terrorist activities).' (Thatcher to Paget, 6 June 1986, CAC: THCR 3/2/193.)
* Laurens van der Post talked up this point, telling Mrs Thatcher that 'Mandela was not just a prisoner of the South African Government, but also the ANC.' His Indian lawyer and Mrs Mandela, he said, were preventing him seeing Howe 'even though Mandela himself

maintaining her support for the EPG concept very clearly: 'a commitment to the early release of Nelson Mandela and the unbanning of the ANC, in exchange for a suspension of violence, would do more than any other step to create the climate of confidence in which a dialogue would become possible.'[100] It 'perturbs me considerably', she went on, that he would not see her Foreign Secretary: a meeting would be the best way of enabling her to 'defend what I perceive to be your interests as much as ours in the face of the rapidly mounting pressures for action against South Africa'. Faced with this plea, Botha, as was usually the case, backed down.* As for poor Howe, he resented the poisoned chalice which Mrs Thatcher had passed him, but could scarcely reject such an important role.

The ensuing month, leading up to and including the London review conference, was the most difficult in diplomatic terms that Mrs Thatcher had ever endured. She had to deal with the combined opposition of the Commonwealth leaders and the Commonwealth Secretariat (based in London), and the consequent anxieties of the Queen. Elizabeth II, as head of the Commonwealth, was worried about divisions between Britain and the other members. In addition, and related to the post-Westland anxieties about her style of government, Mrs Thatcher faced discontent among her own senior ministers over South Africa. Geoffrey Howe, in particular, found her attitude to the subject, her way of doing business and her treatment of him increasingly disagreeable. Against this, she had only the genuine but *sotto voce* support of Ronald Reagan and Helmut Kohl, and the strong backing of her supporters in the country, of several newspapers and of public opinion more widely. South African sanctions provided a classic example of Mrs Thatcher in action – reaching over policy elites and foreign leaders by reiterating what she saw as home truths, putting up with isolation in the belief that she would be proved right later.

There was a real danger, however, that the Commonwealth leaders, goaded beyond endurance by Mrs Thatcher and empowered by the sense of their own moral rectitude, would try to squash her once and for all. In planning this, they had several weapons – the London review conference, the fact that it coincided with the Commonwealth Games in Edinburgh, and the belief, encouraged by Sonny Ramphal at the Commonwealth Secretariat, that the Queen was on their side.

---

would wish to do so'. (Powell to Galsworthy, 8 July 1986, Prime Minister's Papers, Relations with South Africa, Part 11 (document consulted in the Cabinet Office).)

* All such letters to Botha, originally drafted, as was customary, by the Foreign Office, were heavily rewritten by Charles Powell, usually to make them less accusatory and more persuasive in tone.

Towards the end of June, the Queen received a letter from Desmond Tutu. The black people of South Africa had been loyal to her, he wrote, at a time when Hendrik Verwoerd (Prime Minister of South Africa from 1958 to 1966 and the arch-exponent of apartheid) had not been. Now he made an appeal: 'Madam, our country is on the brink of a monumental catastrophe.'[101] He was aged fifty-four, he said, a bishop and a Nobel Prize winner, but he could not vote. The EPG's work for peace had been scuppered by the cross-border raids. The South African government was being protected in its appalling behaviour by Britain, the United States and Germany. Why were there no sanctions against the 'most vicious system since Nazism'? 'Your Majesty, this is a *cri de coeur*. Please help us bring about a new South Africa.'

The letter immediately raised the ticklish problem of who should answer it. Since it came to Buckingham Palace from an Anglican bishop, by hand of the Archbishop of Canterbury's special representative, Terry Waite,* it might seem to be an appeal to the Queen in her role as supreme governor of the Church of England. On the other hand, since it dealt with foreign policy, should it not be a matter for the Queen's ministers? Yet again, though, since the Queen was head of the Commonwealth, and the London review conference was about to discuss the key matter of sanctions, was this really a matter for her British government at all? This was part of the awkwardness which could be produced by the Queen's different roles.

A fortnight after the letter was delivered, Charles Powell laid the problem before Mrs Thatcher: 'Bishop Tutu recently wrote to The Queen about South Africa in fairly objectionable terms. The fact of his letter is public.'[102] Geoffrey Howe, Powell reported, thought that the politics of the situation would be minimized if the Queen's own private secretary, Sir William Heseltine,† were to reply. Heseltine's draft, which Powell enclosed, said that the Queen was 'conscious of the historical connections to which you allude' and 'has followed developments in South Africa in recent months closely and with great concern'. She sought 'an end to the suffering and an early and peaceful solution to your country's problems' and emphasized the 'special responsibility of those in positions of influence to speak out against violence'. Powell questioned Howe's recommendation: 'The

---

* Terence ('Terry') Waite (1939–), educated Wilmslow and Stockton Heath, Cheshire and Church Army College, London; adviser to Archbishop of Canterbury on Anglican Communion Affairs, 1980–92. As an envoy for the Church of England he travelled to Lebanon to try to secure the release of four hostages. He was himself taken captive and held hostage from January 1987 to November 1991.

† William Heseltine (1930–), educated University of Western Australia; press secretary to the Queen, 1968–72; private secretary, 1986–90; knighted, 1982.

press would be bound to take it as somehow reinforcing the notion of a difference of opinion between The Queen and you.' He suggested that Howe should reply, in uncontroversial terms. Mrs Thatcher agreed: 'I think the proposed draft <u>does</u> involve The Queen in politics . . . I am very unhappy about the proposed advice. The Press is bound to claim that there is a rift between The Queen and Her Government.'[103] A variant on the Powell idea was that the British Ambassador in South Africa should reply to Tutu.

After a week's further cogitation, however, Sir William Heseltine wrote to Howe's office to say that the Queen had considered carefully the pros and cons of a letter to the Bishop from Buckingham Palace or from the Ambassador. Her Majesty had agreed it would be wrong to send a reply from the Foreign Secretary himself and, after much thought, decided that the balance of the argument rested with a letter from the private secretary.[104] Although the final draft differed little from the one that had worried him and Mrs Thatcher, Powell for some reason acquiesced happily. 'This is a simple and satisfactory solution,' he told Mrs Thatcher.[105]

There were no public explosions about the Queen's reply to Tutu, but the overall situation was not satisfactory for any of the parties. Mrs Thatcher was absolutely incensed, as she had been at Nassau, by the suggestion that her stand against sanctions was immoral. Indeed one of her favourite points, formulated by van der Post, was 'the immorality of sanctions' themselves. As usual, the disapproval of bishops, whose respect, in principle, she valued, did not help her temper. On 9 July, the day after Howe set off on his mission to South Africa and the Frontline States, Mrs Thatcher publicly denounced her critics. 'I find nothing *moral*', she told Hugo Young in the *Guardian*, 'about them sitting in comfortable circumstances, with good salaries, inflation-proof pensions, good jobs, saying that we, as a matter of *morality*, will put x hundred thousand black people out of work.'[106] The proposed fruit-and-vegetable boycott alone, she claimed, would put 95,000 people out of their jobs: 'blacks and their families out of work. *Moral?* Poof! *Moral?* No social security. *Moral?*'[107]

At the Commonwealth Secretariat, Sir Peter Marshall,* formerly a senior diplomat in the Foreign Office, was now Deputy Secretary-General. It was his job to make sure that Britain and the Commonwealth stayed close together, and he was dismayed. 'A dispiriting day,' he confided in his

* Peter Marshall (1924–), educated Tonbridge and Corpus Christi College, Cambridge; UK Representative on Economic and Social Council of UN, 1975–9; Ambassador and UK Permanent Representative to UN, 1979–83; Deputy Secretary-General of the Commonwealth, 1983–8; knighted, 1983.

diary, '. . . an impassioned interview with Hugo Young in the *Guardian* has added fuel to the flames.'[108] He noted the news that several nations were now pulling out of the Commonwealth Games: 'The gap is widening.'[109] As early as 20 June, he had asked himself, 'Is the Commonwealth able to cope with the magnitude of the issue or is it now a means of breaking us?'[110] As the review conference approached, that break seemed ever more likely.

True, the pressure was not all one way. Helmut Kohl strongly supported Howe's mission, and said that Botha's rudeness to Howe reminded him of his own mother's wisdom. She 'used to say to him, "Slam the door if you like, but remember you are going to have to open it again" '.[111] In Kohl's view, the ANC 'were a motley lot, and their leaders did not really want Mandela released: in prison he was a useful martyr, out of prison he would be a competitor for them.'[112] Reagan, under pressure of his own over sanctions in Washington, said it was 'unreasonable' to expect the whites 'to go immediately' to one man, one vote. He feared Communist penetration of the ANC, but 'did not exclude the possibility of dialogue with them'.[113] In a speech on 22 July the President went public with a call to resist 'this emotional clamor for punitive sanctions'.[114]

Nevertheless, those who disagreed with Mrs Thatcher on sanctions increasingly combined against her. She was inundated with messages from EPG members and other Commonwealth leaders trying to persuade her to change her mind. Brian Mulroney saw her when she visited Canada for Expo '86 and attempted to persuade her with his silken tongue. But he got the thick end of hers. 'Margaret, I am not a member of your government,' he stated as she became increasingly strident, 'I am the head of a sovereign nation!'[115] When he said British leadership of the Commonwealth would be 'imperilled' if she did not give ground at the review conference, she retorted that 'one had to draw a distinction between leadership and followership':[116] the way to get rid of apartheid was through negotiations, while sanctions would lead to violence. Mulroney told her they disagreed, and that this was 'not a happy situation'. 'You could tell how angry she was from her colour and her tight smile and her look at you – if she could have slit my throat and got away with it, she would probably have tried,' he remarked with a grin.[117] The ANC leader, Oliver Tambo, refused to see Geoffrey Howe in Lusaka because he (correctly) considered Howe's mission part of a policy of postponement: 'the statements made by the British Prime Minister have, to say the least, been wholly unhelpful.'[118]

What made things worse for Mrs Thatcher was the increasing restiveness of Geoffrey Howe himself. Although he had always agreed with her that South Africa 'should not be made the leper of the world',[119] Howe cared about the Commonwealth and agreed with its view that South Africa was part of its *cuisine interne*,[120] so he did not share Mrs Thatcher's indignation at Commonwealth involvement. He felt that she was needlessly putting Commonwealth unity at risk. On 24 June, he confided in Peter Marshall at a reception that 'the trouble is with the Prime Minister.'[121] The day before, Mrs Thatcher had been disagreeable to him in front of colleagues about his paper for the OD Committee in advance of the European Council. 'It gave the impression', she complained, 'that the mainspring of our policy should be to go along with the crowd.'[122] Trying, as with the British Leyland question after Westland, to rein in Mrs Thatcher through the power of ministers, Howe recruited senior colleagues on his side, causing Peter Walker to write to her: 'Willie [Whitelaw], Norman [Tebbit], Quintin [Hogg, Lord Hailsham], the Chief Whip [Wakeham] and I all have expressed our political judgment that we must be seen as positive in our desire to negotiate.'[123] The following day, in Cabinet, Howe won general support for further measures if his mission to South Africa should fail.[124]

The *Sunday Telegraph* built on this, reporting on 6 July that Howe was threatening to resign if Mrs Thatcher would not impose sanctions after his return from South Africa.[125]* His commitment to Commonwealth unity was symbolized by his presence at the Commonwealth–Foreign Office cricket match at Blenheim Palace, spreading goodwill. 'Elspeth [Howe] is batting,' recorded Peter Marshall, 'Sonny is fielding & takes 2 catches.'[126] Two days later, before setting off on the South African leg of his journey, Howe wrote to Mrs Thatcher to say that:

> The vigour and persistence with which we have continued to make the case against comprehensive sanctions has led [Commonwealth leaders] to conclude, contrary to the Hague understanding, that we have ruled out any move in that direction. This has prompted many of them to see us not just as the sole obstacle to that course, but often as the sole defender of apartheid.[127]

'This is what worries the Foreign Secretary most,' Powell glossed for her benefit. Howe urged her that Britain must concede something at the review conference.

Stories grew of royal anxieties about the future of the Commonwealth and dissatisfaction with Mrs Thatcher's handling of the issue. Some of

---

* Four days later, freed since January from the constraints of ministerial office, Leon Brittan became the first senior Conservative to break with Mrs Thatcher and call publicly for the imposition of sanctions (Associated Press, 10 July 1986).

this appeared in the press. Laurens van der Post rang Downing Street to say that he had just seen the Prince of Wales, who was 'very distressed that his mother was being pulled into the current controversy. Prince Charles told Laurens that they (the Royal Family) have never been more united behind you . . . Far from being critical they have total admiration for your stand.'[128] At lunch in Clarence House, Queen Elizabeth the Queen Mother told Woodrow Wyatt 'Without prompting . . . "How disgraceful it is that the press and people are trying to involve the Queen in the row about sanctions" '.[129] She denied any truth in the story that her daughter was at odds with Mrs Thatcher. 'I suspect', Wyatt added, 'she wants me to let Mrs T know the Queen is not against her.'

These two well-meant private remarks reflected the desire of the Queen to behave correctly and maintain good relations with her prime minister.* There is no known evidence that the two women ever exchanged hard words on the subject. But Buckingham Palace did indeed have different interests from Downing Street in this matter, and was working to promote them. The Queen had – and, in the twenty-first century, still has – a life-long commitment to maintaining the unity of the Commonwealth. She faithfully followed the view of her father, King George VI, settled with the independence of India in 1947, that ex-colonial republics, as well as ex-colonies which chose to retain the British Crown, could be members. As a result, the Commonwealth became a worldwide and multi-racial institution. It would be tragic for this legacy, Commonwealth supporters believed, if the institution were to break apart over the behaviour of its notorious ex-member, South Africa.

Accordingly, the Palace did what it could to keep things together – the more so, perhaps, because Sir William Heseltine, only recently promoted to the top job, was himself an Australian, the first non-Briton in the role – and therefore had Commonwealth fellow feeling. Heseltine stayed in close touch with Sonny Ramphal, consulting him about how best to outmanoeuvre Mrs Thatcher.[130] Ramphal himself, whom Mrs Thatcher 'couldn't stand',[131] took full advantage of the proximity of his offices in Marlborough House to see the Queen quite often. On 23 June, shortly before The Hague summit, he had met her, and afterwards reported to Peter Marshall that 'it went very well . . . She will do all she can to help.'[132] On 10 July, Powell informed Mrs Thatcher that although the Palace had previously

---

* It is hard to believe that van der Post's version was wholly accurate, however. One of the recent controversial press pieces had been a long anonymous profile of the Prince of Wales in the *Economist* which contained a good deal of criticism of Mrs Thatcher. It was based, though it did not say so, on an interview with the Prince by the paper's political editor Simon Jenkins. (*Economist*, 19 July 1986.)

shown 'not much enthusiasm ... for giving any sort of entertainment' during the review conference, the Queen was now 'actively considering giving a dinner on the Sunday evening' (the first day of the meeting).[133] According to William Heseltine, said Powell, the 'change of heart' had partly taken place because 'Sonny Ramphal has told the Palace that you were enthusiastic about the idea. I do not recall that.'[134] Nor did Mrs Thatcher. She put her disapproving wiggly line under the word 'enthusiastic'. What had actually happened was that the Queen, almost unprecedentedly breaking her summer stay at Balmoral, had decided to come up to London to save Commonwealth unity.[135] This move made life more difficult for Mrs Thatcher than for anyone else.

On 20 July, the campaign to get Mrs Thatcher to change her mind took a dramatic turn. Under the headline 'Queen dismayed by "uncaring" Thatcher', the *Sunday Times* reported that the rift between monarch and Prime Minister over South Africa and the Commonwealth was indeed real, and went wider. Relying on 'several briefings by the Queen's advisers, who were fully aware it would be published', the paper reported that 'the Queen considers the Prime Minister's approach often to be uncaring, confrontational and socially divisive.'[136] She felt the government should be more 'caring' towards the less privileged in society, it went on, feared

THE GOOD SAMARITAN

Garland illustrates tension between queen and prime minister over South African sanctions, *Daily Telegraph*, July 1986.

that as a result of the miners' strike 'long-term damage was being done to
the country's social fabric' and had 'misgivings' about the decision to allow
American bombers to use British bases to attack Libya. A big news feature
inside, entitled 'The African Queen', set out how Elizabeth II's Commonwealth role in that continent was at odds with Mrs Thatcher's approach.
In the view of Sonny Ramphal, who was in a position to know, 'The story
truly reflected the Palace view.'[137]

As the first copies came off the presses on the Saturday night, Buckingham Palace rushed out a statement, saying that 'As with all previous prime
ministers, The Queen enjoys a relationship of the closest confidentiality
with Mrs Thatcher, and reports purporting to be The Queen's opinion of
government policies are entirely without foundation.' Andrew Neil, the
editor of the *Sunday Times*,* was amazed, since the source for the story
(which, by journalistic convention, he could not reveal) was the Queen's
press secretary, Michael Shea. Neil was so angry at what he considered to
be double-dealing that he refused to print the Palace statement in his later
editions, a decision which, he afterwards admitted, had probably been a
mistake.[138]

In fact, the story, though it weakened itself by exaggeration, had foundation. The wording of the Palace statement was not, closely studied, a
denial, though it intended to give the impression that it was. Shea had
indeed told the *Sunday Times* most of what it published, and had even
had large sections of the full inside story (though not the front page) read
to him. What was even more extraordinary was that Shea had already,
pre-publication, boasted in private of what he had done. That Saturday,
19 July, was, by chance, the occasion for a meeting at Buckingham Palace
of the senior court officials of all the other European monarchies. Its subject
for discussion that morning was press handling and PR. 'Michael Shea',
as Sir William Heseltine recalled, 'came in to talk and . . . was so boastful
about this wonderful coup that he had with the *Sunday Times*.'[139] Shea felt
he had 'led them to publish a very sympathetic picture of the Queen: concerned about the coal miners and concerned for the Commonwealth'. Then,
in the middle of the afternoon, Shea 'came in with his tail between his legs,
looking thoroughly abashed, saying there's a sensational story appearing
in the *Sunday Times* which says there's a rift between the Prime Minister
and the Queen, and Bernard Ingham was in a state of frenzy'.[140]†

After frantic discussions, it was agreed between Heseltine and his

* Andrew Neil (1949–), educated Paisley Grammar School and University of Glasgow;
publisher, broadcaster and company chairman; editor, *Sunday Times*, 1983–94.
† Ingham had been informed because the *Sunday Times* had run the story past him.

counterpart at No. 10, Nigel Wicks, that it was pointless for Heseltine to ring Andrew Neil and ask him to kill the story since that would only provoke him to publish 'with additional relish'. Instead, Heseltine hurried to the Queen at Windsor, where she was about to give drinks to all the European royal court officials. He said to her, 'You know, this is going to be quite a screaming match and a sensation. I think it might be a good idea if you made personal contact with the Prime Minister.' This the Queen immediately did, by telephone to Chequers. She told Mrs Thatcher that (in Heseltine's paraphrase) she 'could not imagine how the story came to be circulated, and anyway it bears no relation to the truth as I understand it . . .' Queen and Prime Minister 'had a very amicable conversation'.[141]

Many people were naturally disposed to believe the Palace denial (or apparent denial), which was repeated by Heseltine in a letter to *The Times*. Much anger was hurled at the *Sunday Times*. But the fact that the story had come from the Queen's press secretary meant that the paper and its proprietor, Rupert Murdoch, were able to stand by it. It was clear to Mrs Thatcher, therefore, that there had been some truth in it. Murdoch informally authorized Woodrow Wyatt, who was, among other things, one of his columnists, to 'hint' to Mrs Thatcher who the source had been.[142] When he duly rang her, and indicated Shea's role, she said: 'Thank you for warning me. I shall know when and where to be careful.'[143] Wyatt suggested that, when asked about the story in Parliament, she should say, 'it's the silly season.' But Mrs Thatcher played by the rules, and replied: 'No . . . I will say that a denial has been issued from Buckingham Palace and I have nothing further to say.'[144]

She stuck to this, even in private. Mrs Thatcher was almost paralysingly correct about relations with the monarch and was never heard to gossip about, complain of or even quote in confidence anything the Queen had told her. After her weekly Tuesday audiences in Buckingham Palace – which, by tradition, never have any officials in attendance – she would emerge, 'panting for a whisky and soda',[145] to be debriefed by her own and the Queen's private secretaries. The audiences were rarely very productive, because Mrs Thatcher was nervous. She sat always on the edge of her chair and produced from her bag an agenda from which she launched forth. Far from being, as some docu-dramas and plays have depicted, little speeches in which Mrs Thatcher laid down the law to the Queen, what she said was usually an anodyne recitation of current business. Heseltine once asked the Queen if it was like Queen Victoria's experience of Gladstone – 'He speaks to me as if I were a public meeting.' No, said the Queen, 'It wasn't at all like that . . . but I wasn't given much encouragement to comment on what was said.'[146] Mrs Thatcher never had the confidence to make a friend of the Queen, as some of her predecessors had done, and so their relations were 'absolutely correct and perhaps not very cosy'. In Heseltine's view, 'There might have been fault on the Queen's side,' for not coming in when Mrs Thatcher drew breath and turning the talk into more of a discussion. Although the relationship between the two private offices was always good, the informal lines of communication between the principals were not.

So when it became clear that the Queen's own press secretary had put out a story so damaging to Mrs Thatcher, the Prime Minister did not have the sort of relaxed relationship with the Queen which could help smooth matters over. She knew what Shea had done, and she had even received sensitive reports about his boastful speech to the conference of royal private secretaries.[147] Although Shea – a Scottish social democrat in his views – was blamed for advancing his own political agenda, Mrs Thatcher had a sense that the story would never have reached a newspaper if he had not felt emboldened by those he worked for to put it out.* She felt, in the view of Robin Butler, 'desperately hurt. She would freeze, as she did over the row about her honorary degree at Oxford [see Chapter 19]. She never said how upset she was.'[148] Besides, Mrs Thatcher believed that the *Sunday Times* story would do her political harm. 'Those little old ladies will say Mrs Thatcher is upsetting the Queen. I'll lose votes,'† she told Charles Powell.[149] There was also risk the other way round. 'Does The Queen's known pro-Commonwealth stand raise problems within the UK?' Peter Marshall asked himself in his diary,[150] and answered his own question, 'Yes.' There was strong anti-sanctions feeling in Britain and 'The Commonwealth had better take note.'[151] Certainly the Palace saw the danger in what had happened and became even more politically cautious as a result.

Sensing Mrs Thatcher's political vulnerability, Geoffrey Howe saw his moment to press harder against his boss. Charles Powell was aware of this danger, which presented itself in an unusual form. On the previous Saturday, the day on which Shea had made his boast and the *Sunday Times*

---

* It was noted at the time that Willie Whitelaw, who had good royal connections, had been privately telling people that the Queen was worried about Mrs Thatcher's policies and was 'not unhappy that the story got out' (Interview with Andrew Neil).

† In the short term, at least, Mrs Thatcher's fears were probably justified. The monarchy, buoyed up by the popularity of Prince Andrew's marriage to Sarah Ferguson on 23 July, was a dangerous thing for an elected politician to fall foul of. An opinion poll in *The Times* on 1 August showed a sudden 9-point Labour lead; and the percentage thinking that the government was 'not tough enough on the South African government' had moved sharply up from 42 per cent to 56 per cent.

had written its story, Mrs Thatcher had been holed up all morning at Chequers with the journalist Graham Turner, who was interviewing her for the following week's *Sunday Telegraph*. Turner was a good friend of Mrs Thatcher, sympathetic to her politics, so she spoke very frankly to him, without officials present. By Thursday of the following week, two days before the *Sunday Telegraph* went to press, Powell alerted Mrs Thatcher. He had read the transcript of the Turner interview. It had alarmed him, and he had tried, via Bernard Ingham, to dissuade the *Sunday Telegraph* from using its more incendiary passages. But he had failed.* Mrs Thatcher had expressed trenchant views about the Commonwealth and South Africa. It was not the *British* Commonwealth, she reminded Turner, 'it is their club. It is their Commonwealth. If they wish to break it up, I think it is absurd.'[152] She also pointed out that lots of Commonwealth members were not democracies: 'Some of them have military governments, some of them have states of emergency, some of them have had censorship at various times, some of them have had terrible internal massacres, some of them have put people in opposition into jail without trial.'[153] To the suggestion that her position on sanctions was divisive, she cried, 'Poppycock!' She launched into the subject of necklacing: 'it is one of the things which, faster than anything else, turned my sympathies off any case which some of them might have been putting.' 'I am bound to say', Powell wrote to her, in the restrained language of the loyal adviser, 'that . . . the article runs the risk of exposing you to sharp criticism for dealing too vigorously with South African problems at a very sensitive moment' and also for speaking out when Geoffrey Howe, still in South Africa, is 'engaged in delicate negotiations'.[154]

Steamed up though she was about the issue of South Africa and the Commonwealth, Mrs Thatcher had no difficulty in seeing Powell's point. She blamed her unguardedness on the fact that the interview, when agreed, had not included the subject of South Africa. 'By all means try <u>very hard</u> to negotiate the deletions,' she told Powell, '. . . especially as things have <u>worsened</u> during the last week . . . Also – later events on Saturday and Sunday [the *Sunday Times* story] could put a complexion upon it that it was not intended to bear.'[155] As Powell reminded her the next day, events had indeed worsened. The review conference would meet in a week's time with 'no concrete progress to show on the release of Mandela'.[156] She

* Graham Turner remembered being 'threatened' by Ingham that, if he did not make the desired cuts, he would not be allowed to see Mrs Thatcher again. Ingham was as good as his word: Turner and Mrs Thatcher never met afterwards; but the tactic of 'bullying' annoyed Turner and made him dig his heels in. If he had been spoken to politely, he believed, he would have succumbed. (Interview with Graham Turner.)

would be outvoted 6:1 on further measures. All she could play for was to delay discussion of these until the Foreign Secretary's mission was finished at the end of September. 'This would be a messy outcome but we might just get by.'

Finding that he could not stop the *Sunday Telegraph*, Powell thought he should warn Howe, who was in South Africa. He was aware of the growing tension between his boss and her Foreign Secretary. 'I am not telegraphing the text,' he cabled, 'since there is nothing you can do about it . . . (I realise this may remind you of the Jewish telegram: "start worrying, letter follows"!).'[157] The *Sunday Telegraph* duly went to press with the interview on the evening of Saturday 26 July and was transmitted to Howe in Pretoria. The reply, from Howe's private secretary who was with him, was full of half-suppressed anguish: 'although [the interview] contains some positive things, it also contains some material that could not be less helpful.'[158] Howe, conscious that his own mission was failing, felt that 'the focus of the whole exercise . . . has already extended beyond its original aim of trying to influence the future of South Africa on to the defence of British interests which are increasingly threatened by our Commonwealth partners.' The *Sunday Telegraph* interview, he warned, 'will certainly not diminish that threat'. He had just seen P. W. Botha and found him 'truculent and totally oblivious of the pressures in the outside world'. He pleaded that Mrs Thatcher should stop attacking 'the immorality of sanctions' and instead make clear that Britain had taken measures – 'a number of recent episodes have jarred with the impression we need to give'; people would think the British government were 'defenders of apartheid'.

Strangely, the *Sunday Telegraph* interview did not produce further outcry. Perhaps it seemed a bit stale since it was declaredly conducted before the storm about the Queen and Mrs Thatcher had broken. But the Howe–Thatcher problem was now in some ways more serious than the hostility of the Commonwealth. Powell summed it up pretty frankly, replying to Howe's office: 'I have to say that some fundamental differences of assessment clearly remain.'[159] Mrs Thatcher's tactic, he explained, was to 'lay down a barrage' of firmness before the review meeting, and keep possible concessions up her sleeve. When a battered Howe returned home and saw Mrs Thatcher about his visit, he told her the United States would soon adopt additional measures and so should Britain.* She told Howe that he had 'conducted himself with great dignity and patience', and she

---

* That October, overriding President Reagan's veto, the US Congress passed the Comprehensive Anti-Apartheid Act imposing punitive sanctions on South Africa. According to

agreed that Britain should contemplate further measures if the whole of the EEC would participate, but 'She remained extremely reluctant to envisage the adoption, let alone recommendation, of further economic measures since she is absolutely convinced sanctions would not achieve internal change. Moreover the government's strong opposition to sanctions was receiving considerable support in the country'.[160] Howe presented her with his paper on the situation for the OD Committee of Cabinet. Powell advised her that it was not too bad, though it was 'designed to make your colleagues' flesh creep by describing the Dreadful Consequences should there be no agreement at the Commonwealth Meeting'.[161] He urged that the OD meeting be kept low key, because of political danger: 'I should keep off controversial themes which are bound to lead to argument with the Foreign Secretary, because a. they will provoke the Chancellor [Lawson] and the Home Secretary [Hurd] into supporting him, and b. it will be damaging to have stories of Cabinet/OD disunity.' She could bide her time: 'you will have the microphones at the Commonwealth Meeting and say what is necessary, so the most important thing is to avoid being tied down.' Bernard Ingham, seeking the line to give to the media, put it to Mrs Thatcher with his customary bluntness:

- Is the Lady for turning; and, if not
- will the Commonwealth crack up?[162]

It was Ingham, apparently, who caused Geoffrey Howe to snap. Howe's correct understanding of the OD meeting of 31 July, which passed off without incident, was that ministers had agreed to support further measures by the European Community. After the meeting concluded, however, it was reported to him that Ingham was briefing the lobby that the government was 'not in the business of further sanctions'.[163] Ingham told the lobby – so Howe believed – that Howe's promise of likely further measures in a statement to the House two weeks earlier was 'an albatross'. He predicted 'emotional outbursts from Kaunda, Mugabe and company' and would not mind if the review conference were to 'break up'. Unsourced rumours also circulated that Howe was about to resign. Urged on by Elspeth,[164] he sat down and wrote to Mrs Thatcher, producing drafts with the help of his PPS, Richard Ryder. It was a long and rather agonized letter, which he considered 'very important'.[165] He reprinted it in full in his memoirs.[166]

Howe set out how Ingham had behaved and how this might prejudice

---

Powell, rather than leading to a change of heart this only left Mrs Thatcher 'more embattled' (Interview with Lord Powell of Bayswater).

the review conference. But it was his last point which was, he said, 'more fundamental'. Although it was expressed as a criticism of Ingham, it was clearly directed at the principal as well as the messenger. 'We have worked together closely, and I like to think successfully, for more than 11 years.' He wanted to continue doing so and help win the next election. 'That means that we must continue to have confidence in each other: the partnership – for example, this weekend – is too close to survive without that.' It could not survive if the No. 10 press secretary set 'Minister against Minister', 'undermining our chances of securing a third term' and destroying 'what should still be the party's secret weapon' (loyalty). This must be tackled – though not during that fraught review-conference weekend – 'if we are to continue working together in confidence . . . I hope we may be able to find a chance to talk about it.' Mrs Thatcher chose to see this neither as a threat nor as a plea, but as a slightly cowardly attempt to get her loyal press secretary sacked. In the margins of pre-conference meetings, Howe raised it briefly with Mrs Thatcher, but she replied: 'Bernard isn't like that. But we can't talk about it now.'[167] In her own memoirs, she made no mention of Howe's demarche.* Howe had got close to Michael Heseltine's situation over Westland. There can be no doubt that, if he had chosen to resign, the damage done to Mrs Thatcher at this point would have been much greater. He was much more central than Heseltine to the whole Thatcher project, and was more widely respected as a calm and moderate person, with more allies in the party. Coming at a time when, for quite separate reasons, Mrs Thatcher was at loggerheads with Norman Tebbit (see Chapter 15), this row put her in some real danger. She was lucky that little of this became public, and lucky too that her Foreign Secretary was both too loyal and too infirm of purpose to press his point home.

On Saturday 2 August, the Thatchers visited the Commonwealth Games 'village' in Edinburgh, occupied by athletes of those countries (twenty-seven out of fifty-nine) which had not boycotted the games in protest at Britain's line on South African sanctions.† They were met with grumbles and a few catcalls. 'I did not disagree with Denis', she wrote in her memoirs, 'when

---

* Bernard Ingham, enclosing a copy of Geoffrey Howe's letter, wrote to the present author saying: 'I have not the slightest idea what he was on about. Nor have I any recollection that my offending briefing was raised with me. It would be remarkable if it had been because I briefed according to the line given to me after meetings I did not attend.' (Correspondence with Sir Bernard Ingham, 23 May 2012.)

† The games were boycotted by India and a number of the African and Caribbean nations whose governments were critical of Mrs Thatcher's position on sanctions. The nations

he remarked that this was "one of the most poisonous visits" we had ever made. It was a relief to dine that evening with my good friend Laurens van der Post who talks good sense about South Africa . . .'[168] She particularly resented the idea that Britain had to keep the games going and therefore to give concessions to save them. When Sonny Ramphal told her, 'Prime Minister, these are *your* games that are being spoilt,' Mrs Thatcher replied, 'No, Mr Secretary-General. They are not my games. These are *your* games.'[169] She was intensely irritated by the whole rigmarole of the Commonwealth – its combination of institutionalized anti-Britishness with riding on the coat-tails of British imperial prestige, its self-importance, and the complications caused by the involvement of the Queen. On the first night of the review conference, the seven leaders present, including Mrs Thatcher, plus Ramphal and Howe, dined at Buckingham Palace as planned. In Sonny Ramphal's view, the Queen 'made clear that the Commonwealth must not break up over this. Margaret did not like it. The Queen indicated her disagreement with Mrs Thatcher without ever having to say so.'[170]

The odd thing was that the conference itself did not, in fact, end in disaster. Mrs Thatcher operated from Peter Marshall's room in Marlborough House, where the conference was taking place ('We establish that Mrs T likes Haig whisky,' recorded Marshall).[171] Despite her tactical dispute with Howe about how best to play the British hand, she was looking for agreement. She accepted Powell's analysis on the eve of the meeting that Kaunda, Gandhi and so on 'for all the talk . . . would relish avoiding a bust-up'.[172] Since she was in such a difficult position, that was her attitude too. She even informed Helmut Kohl before the meeting began that she 'might have to concede a bit'.[173] She did not try to filibuster the Commonwealth's efforts to 'internationalize' further measures. She accepted Howe's warning not to repeat Nassau by belittling the deal afterwards. The review conference agreed that apartheid was not being dismantled and therefore that new measures were needed. Mrs Thatcher said that Britain would accept and implement the EEC measures agreed at The Hague (including the ban on the import of coal, iron, steel and Krugerrands) if the European partners would do the same.* No one publicly denounced anyone else.

---

attending the games included Australia, Canada and New Zealand as well as two of the Frontline States, Botswana and Lesotho.

* There was a piquant, *Yes, Minister*-style postscript to the review conference. In November 1986, Mrs Thatcher received a letter from Nigel Lawson in his role as master of the Mint. He said he wanted to strike a new 1-ounce gold coin called the Britannia, 'following the virtual demise of the Krugerrand'. (Lawson to Thatcher, 3 November 1986, Prime Minister's

Everything suddenly calmed down. Geoffrey and Elspeth Howe went off on holiday. Mrs Thatcher went into hospital to have a long-planned operation to correct Dupuytren's contracture on her fingers (see Chapter 15). Over a rather longer period of time, the government's low opinion of Michael Shea's behaviour was borne in upon Buckingham Palace,[174] and he was quietly edged out of his post ('not fast enough', in the view of Sir William Heseltine).[175]

What had this all been about? Was this a spectacular example of Mrs Thatcher's self-defeating obduracy and dogmatism? What was the point of upsetting the Queen and colleagues and numerous friendly powers? Certainly she had often caused unnecessary antagonism. Certainly, in the annals of normal diplomacy, this was no way to behave. It is also true that, at this stage, she had little positive to show for her attempts to move the white government. But then it was a strength as well as a fault in Mrs Thatcher that she did business in a unique way. She was quite sure that economic sanctions would not achieve the desired effect and she was not, unlike most politicians, cynical enough to agree to them anyway for the sake of a quiet life. She did not want to be boxed in, as Howe was encouraging her, by accepting principles which she really disagreed with. She did not want British companies to lose business or South African blacks to lose jobs. She believed that South Africa could change peacefully to a multi-racial government, negotiated after the release of Nelson Mandela, if the right interlocutors could be found. At this stage, she felt that South Africa would eventually end up with constitutional arrangements similar to the Swiss model of highly independent cantons. 'South Africa would never have a one-man, one-vote situation,' she told Reagan that November.[176] In this she was at odds with the ANC, but she certainly was not trying to prevent reform. As in her attitude to Gorbachev and the Soviet Union, she was optimistic about what could be done with the right partner at the head of the South African government. She had been disappointed by Botha over this, but she believed that such a partner would eventually

---

Papers, Economic Policy, The Coinage (document consulted in the Cabinet Office).) 'I assume we buy the gold from South Africa,' Mrs Thatcher inquired. Lawson replied that some of the gold probably would be South African. Geoffrey Howe wrote to Lawson to protest at this, given the Commonwealth ban. (Howe to Lawson, 17 December 1986. Ibid.) 'I trust that there will be no Russian [underlined three times] gold in it?' wrote Mrs Thatcher caustically. The Mint informed her that some of the gold probably would indeed be South African and some Russian. 'Go ahead,' instructed Mrs Thatcher, '– but I am at a loss for words! We can't import Krugerrands so we are going to strike a new coin which may . . . contain S. African & Russian gold. What a policy!!' (Norgrove to Thatcher, 3 November 1986. Ibid.)

emerge and hoped to help influence that process. In this way she would prove more far-sighted than those who wished only to parade their disapproval of apartheid rather than thinking how best to move beyond it.

Where she paid a higher price for her behaviour over South Africa and the Commonwealth was with Geoffrey Howe. Because she was, as Charles Powell put it, 'so at odds in methods, personality and views'[177] with Howe, she did not sufficiently respect him. Their disagreements over South Africa had been foreshadowed by Howe's frustration with Mrs Thatcher's handling of the Anglo-Irish negotiations in 1984–5. There was 'a fiery Celtic element to Geoffrey', recalled Richard Ryder, 'a Welsh hwyl. On the rare occasions when he gets angry, he gets very, very angry.'[178] In July 1986, he was angry about many things – about being made a fool of on his South African mission, about being disregarded by Mrs Thatcher, about her being, as he saw it, too kind to the white South African government and too rude to the Commonwealth.

He was also, perhaps, angry with himself for not challenging her more forcefully over Westland earlier in the year. He might already have missed the chance to succeed her, only to be blackguarded by Bernard Ingham.[179]* He was uneasily aware that when Mrs Thatcher failed to answer his letter about Ingham, he had done nothing further about it. He wrote in his memoirs that 'the questions I had raised were questions for her to consider'.[180] This was true, and he was right that she did not properly consider them; but neither did he resolve the point. So the issue festered.

On the day the London review conference came to a close, Peter Marshall had the chance of a long talk with Robert Armstrong: 'He says Mrs T doesn't trust Howe . . . She is filled with a sense of mission and there is no one to support her (Tebbit is out of favour).'[181] This was a fair summation.

---

* Howe's behaviour over South Africa actually formed part of Mrs Thatcher's charge-sheet against his leadership abilities. 'Howe has not got the calibre to be Prime Minister,' she told Woodrow Wyatt. 'At the Commonwealth Conference [in Nassau] it was she who had to fight the . . . other countries over the South African sanctions. He was feeble.' (Wyatt, *The Journals of Woodrow Wyatt*, vol. i, 9 February 1986, p. 87.)

17

Save the Bomb

'She was the exclamation point'

On 19 November 1985 Ronald Reagan and Mikhail Gorbachev held their long-awaited first summit in Geneva. This marked a milestone in efforts to engage with the Soviet Union, which Mrs Thatcher had been pressing on the President since before Gorbachev became general secretary. Reagan returned from Geneva with his confidence in her judgment confirmed. 'Maggie was right,' he began his White House debriefing meeting. 'We can do business with this man.'[1] The actual business transacted at Geneva had not been very great, but the symbolic value had been considerable. The occasion was recorded by 3,500 journalists, and the two men got on well with one another. As George Shultz wrote, 'Most of all, the precedent of serious and direct talk had been established.'[2] Following Mrs Thatcher's advice to Reagan the previous month, the leaders agreed at Geneva to hold two more summits, in Washington and Moscow.

As befitted a loyal and influential ally, Mrs Thatcher spent the next year doing what she could to move US–Soviet relations onwards. Indeed, during several months when the two superpower leaders circled one another, talking of meeting, but not actually setting a date, she encouraged them both to get on with it. When they finally did so, however, she experienced the most tremendous shock. Responding positively to an unexpected invitation from the Soviet leader to talk in advance of their long-planned Washington summit, President Reagan met Gorbachev alone in Reykjavik, the capital of Iceland, in October 1986. As news filtered out of what he seemed to be offering the Soviet leader, Mrs Thatcher was appalled. Even several months later, she still trembled when she remembered the event. She told two visiting Reagan administration officials Paul Nitze and Richard Perle that Reykjavik had 'come as an earthquake to the UK. It was the first time in her life that she had felt that there was no place on Earth on which she could put her feet and feel secure. It appeared that all Europe was to be sacrificed.'[3] It seemed to her that her most powerful friend and greatest ideological soulmate had come within a whisker of getting rid of what she believed kept the West safe and free – the nuclear deterrent.

The very strength of her relationship with Reagan caused Mrs Thatcher to be caught off-guard by what happened at Reykjavik. The level of trust between the two was such that disagreements could be frankly discussed. She saw it as her role both to win European support for American toughness and to ensure that the United States always remembered to consider European interests and feelings in its attitude to East–West relations. Before and immediately after the bombing of Libya in April 1986, for example, the administration's hawks, citing Soviet violations of the Strategic Arms Limitation Treaty (SALT II), wanted to renounce the limits imposed on the US by the treaty.* They were determined to send a clear message to Moscow that the US would not tolerate one-sided agreements. In the previous year, Mrs Thatcher had helped persuade the US to stick to the SALT rules, and now she tried again. 'As you know I regarded your decision last June to continue to adhere to SAL [sic] restraints as an important act of statesmanship,' she wrote to Reagan. 'I hope that you will feel able to maintain that position which earned the United States enormous respect.'[4] When Paul Nitze came to see her, on behalf of the President, just after the Libyan adventure, she sharpened her point. 'The Prime Minister said that if we announce that we are going to break the law, we will hand General Secretary Gorbachev an enormous victory . . .' noted the US record.

> Gorbachev will say 'this man . . . has just bombed Libya and is now announcing that he is going to break the law.' This Soviet propaganda will be very effective with public opinion. She said that she is very concerned about the alliance right now and about Europe and its fragility – 'they (the Europeans) are afraid and that is why they appease.'[5]

Having made her protest, however, Mrs Thatcher did not go public, and the expected row about the treaty did not materialize at the G7 summit in Tokyo that May. Reagan wrote to Mrs Thatcher later in the month, repeating that he could no longer adhere to the treaty 'unilaterally', but promising to exercise restraint so that the US would remain technically within its limits for several more months.[6] Realizing that this was not a battle which she should fight head-on, Mrs Thatcher decided to emphasize publicly that Reagan's decision was 'provisional'[7] and present it as an

---

* Although it had never been ratified, both sides had previously agreed voluntarily to adhere to the limits laid down in the treaty.

opportunity for the Soviets to bring themselves back into compliance. She was doing her best to be, though she always avoided the phrase, a bridge between America and Europe.

On the central issue of how to handle SDI and nuclear arms reduction, Mrs Thatcher and Reagan stayed in close touch. At Geneva, Gorbachev had well noted Reagan's obsession with ridding the world of nuclear weapons. He felt he could turn this to his advantage. In January 1986, he therefore wrote to Reagan offering the complete abolition of nuclear weapons by the year 2000, providing that the President gave up SDI. The Soviets made their proposal public immediately. This idea was entirely consistent with Moscow's long-standing efforts to present the West with a poisoned chalice by suggesting complete disarmament, especially when the Soviets feared the West was pulling ahead in the arms race. Many in the US administration accordingly doubted its value, but George Shultz saw the offer as marking a move towards Reagan's publicly stated position. Reagan agreed, wanting to go further. 'Why wait until the end of the century for a world without nuclear weapons?' he asked his advisers.[8] Naturally, Reagan had no intention of giving Gorbachev what he wanted about SDI, but he authorized a friendly reply. In a statement welcoming the Soviet proposal he reminded the world that he had called publicly for the total abolition of nuclear weapons as early as 1983: 'We, together with our allies, will give careful study to General Secretary Gorbachev's suggestions.'[9]

Mrs Thatcher's 'careful study' made her no less sceptical than before. She simply did not believe the underlying assumption that nuclear weapons could disappear from the face of the earth. She discussed the matter in private with Richard Perle: 'I recall her saying, "It is inconceivable that the Soviets would turn over their last nuclear weapon. They would cheat. I would cheat." '[10] And she was remarkably frank in public, ranging herself against both the world leaders. 'Both the President and Mr Gorbachev have said that they want to see a world without nuclear weapons,' she told Geoffrey Smith. 'I cannot see a world without nuclear weapons': it was 'pie in the sky'.[11] She was frightened that Reagan genuinely did not understand the truth which seemed so blindingly obvious to her: 'It was one of the few times, you know, when I think his aspirations left the reality of human nature.'[12] She therefore doubted its merit even as a tactic to wrong-foot the Soviets, because she knew that, on this subject, she and the President did not stand on the same ground.

On 11 February 1986, with the future of nuclear weapons much in mind, Mrs Thatcher wrote a six-page letter to Reagan, offering 'some thoughts on the handling of arms control issues at your next meeting with Mr Gorbachev'.[13] Choosing her words carefully, she gave the sort of warning about Gorbachev which, a year earlier, the Americans had been inclined to give her:

> He is clearly a more astute operator than his predecessors, far more aware of the scope for playing on public opinion in the West. But under the veneer he is the same brand of dedicated Soviet Communist that we have known in the past, relentless in pursuing Soviet interests and prepared to take time over this.

She explained his propaganda aims:

> When you launched the SDI, you set out the noble vision of a world without nuclear weapons. Gorbachev – and I think this is a good indication of his shrewdness – has latched on to this and produced his spurious timetable of simple steps for achieving the goal by the end of the century.

Her concern was that this would create unrealistic public expectations. A nuclear-free world, she reminded Reagan, 'would be a very risky place indeed unless there were concurrent steps to reduce the massive imbalance in the Soviet Union's favour in conventional forces. In particular, Western Europe would be very much more vulnerable.' She worried about proliferation, noting that 'while nuclear weapons themselves might in theory be abolished, the knowledge of how to make them never will be. But the risk lies above all in undermining public support for our agreed strategy of deterrence and flexible response.'[14]*

Mrs Thatcher reiterated her support for Reagan's view that SDI 'must be pursued', but expressed concern that the West could be outflanked in the propaganda war and that 'there remains the need to meet genuine Soviet anxieties'. She went on to suggest a series of ideas that would 'offer the Soviet Union a greater sense of reassurance about the likely shape, scope and timescale of possible development of the SDI'.[15]† Although she was careful to stress that her proposals would not restrict research, she was seeking limitations on the programme that went far beyond anything yet agreed by the administration. Away from SDI, her letter reiterated her

---

* Under 'flexible response' NATO, if attacked, could draw on a range of options, beginning with conventional forces, but escalating to tactical nuclear weapons, intermediate missiles and ultimately strategic nuclear forces. This preserved the credibility of NATO's nuclear deterrent by allowing the alliance to respond in kind to Soviet attacks of differing magnitudes.

† These included 'strengthening and refining the ABM Treaty, extending the period of notice required for unilateral withdrawal from it and a commitment not to enter particular phases of defensive programmes before certain specified dates' (Thatcher to Reagan, 11 February 1986, CAC: THCR 3/1/52).

anxiety about any attempt to draw Britain's nuclear deterrent into the arms control talks. She also cautioned against seeking the removal of Intermediate-range Nuclear Forces (INF) from Europe (the so-called 'zero option'), fearing for the credibility of NATO's nuclear deterrent.

Mrs Thatcher's broad concerns about Reagan's yearning for a nuclear-free world chimed with many of those within the President's own administration. 'I think Shultz probably supported the President,' recalled Admiral Poindexter, 'but the rest of us just didn't think it was realistic.'[16] The doubters argued with Reagan, but 'He would listen, understand all the arguments against and thank you warmly. And then ten minutes later he would start talking about what a great world it would be without nuclear weapons!'[17] Eventually, they decided that the best way to deal with the problem was to try to postpone the Reagan vision indefinitely. This was achieved by enumerating a series of conditions that would need to be in place before contemplating getting rid of nuclear weapons. As Ken Adelman, Director of the US Arms Control and Disarmament Agency, recalled, 'the conditions were basically everything – from no crime on the streets, no mugging and no tooth decay! We didn't really have much effect on Reagan's belief, but we did manage to get those conditions.'[18] Indeed, the conditions were set out in a formal National Security Decision Directive. They were wide-ranging – including not only complete conventional-force parity and 'the peaceful resolution of regional conflicts ... without interference', but also the very vague need for 'a demonstrated commitment by the Soviet leadership to peaceful competition'.[19]

The President replied to the Prime Minister before the end of February, including almost word for word all the conditions set out in his formal Directive. According to Charles Powell, this brought relief to Mrs Thatcher: 'I remember all the "buts" in the correspondence with Reagan. They were all our "buts" too. And they [the conditions] always seemed so unachievable that they were an absolute guarantee that you would never go to the phase of getting rid of nuclear weapons. So we could rest easy.'[20] Reagan's letter emboldened Mrs Thatcher to write at once to Gorbachev:

> I know that both you and President Reagan have embraced the goal of freeing the world of nuclear weapons. But this is a long-term aspiration, and simply to set down an arbitrary time-table for achieving it is not in my view a practical approach. We need to tackle the causes of the insecurity which make nuclear weapons necessary. As I said to you when you visited the United Kingdom – a visit which we remember with pleasure – nuclear weapons at present make an essential contribution to preserving peace and

stability. I am convinced that East and West will continue to rely on them in their deterrent role for the foreseeable future.[21]

Reagan also gave Mrs Thatcher some comfort about Britain's independent deterrent, which he pledged to keep out of any INF deal.[22] But he said virtually nothing about SDI. Mrs Thatcher duly wrote to thank Reagan for his INF ideas but sought more answers: 'I look forward in due course to hearing your reaction to the other points made in my letter of 11 February.'[23] On the subject of SDI, Reagan and his staff wished to remain as unencumbered as possible.* They were not rushing to discuss the matter, even with their closest ally.

While Mrs Thatcher was trying to nudge Reagan in her direction on SDI, Geoffrey Howe was trying to push her rather more firmly in his. In March, he sent Charles Powell an advance copy of a speech which referred to his RUSI address a year earlier in which he had attacked SDI (see p. 259). Powell proposed to Mrs Thatcher that this point be cut. She strongly agreed: 'The RUSI speech did <u>immense harm</u> and in my view was <u>intended</u> to undermine SDI. The arguments used are <u>Gorbachev's</u>.'[24] The following month, Howe wrote directly to Mrs Thatcher a fifteen-page letter of anxieties about the importance of not going beyond the research stage.[25] Branding it a 'cloudy missive', she commented, 'The Foreign Office gets more verbose by the day.' Four days later, she was surprised to receive a letter from Nigel Lawson, who never normally expressed an interest in such issues, supporting Howe's letter, and warning of 'a new spiral in the arms race'.[26] 'The Foreign Secretary is finding some allies,' Powell warned her. 'I can't think what the Treasury is doing writing a letter like this,' Mrs Thatcher scribbled.[27] It was indeed unusual, and could only have happened because senior ministers felt emboldened by her weakness after the Westland crisis. Lawson's letter was a small sign of danger, to which, perhaps, she did not pay enough attention. To adapt a phrase from the debate about SDI, one might say that a Howe–Lawson collaboration to keep Mrs Thatcher under control was now entering the research stage.

It was not until the summer that Mrs Thatcher received a substantive response from Reagan. His letter of 20 July proposed that the two

---

* An NSC analysis of Mrs Thatcher's suggestions cast doubt on whether a viable SDI research programme could really be sustained under the limitations she was proposing. Nonetheless, it grudgingly concluded that 'When all the smoke clears, we may ultimately have to make some move in the general direction suggested by the PM.' ('Critique of PM Thatcher's 11 Feb Letter', Mrs Thatcher on SDI/ABM, March 1986 (1), Box 92083, Robert Linhard Files, Reagan Library.)

superpowers should agree to keep all research, development and testing
of SDI technology within the bounds of the ABM Treaty for no fewer
than five years.* He went on, however, to offer a striking new proposal:
after the five years were passed, negotiations would begin over how to
share the benefits of strategic defence and to eliminate entirely the offensive ballistic weapons of both sides. If no agreement were reached after
two years, each side would be free to deploy SDI unilaterally after six
months' notice.[28]

The idea of abolishing all offensive ballistic missiles, the most potentially devastating nuclear weapons in existence, was at first glance an
astonishing thought. However, it naturally appealed to the American mind
because these missiles alone were capable of hitting any target in the
United States when launched from Soviet soil, and the Soviets had a large
numerical advantage in them. It also undermined the Soviet argument that
SDI would give the US an advantage in defending itself against ballistic
missiles: obviously this would no longer be true if ballistic missiles had
ceased to exist. SDI would therefore serve solely as a deterrent to reacquir-
ing the missiles later. The scheme looked much less dazzlingly brilliant to
America's NATO allies. It would undermine 'flexible response'. Worse, it
would put Britain's proposed new Trident in jeopardy, since Trident was
a ballistic missile supplied by the US. The plan stated that 'other nuclear
powers' would be expected to participate in the arms reduction talks. It
appeared that Britain's nuclear deterrent was to be negotiated away.

It is surprising – and it would be used against her in the arguments after
Reykjavik – that Mrs Thatcher made no great protest at this letter. At her
suggestion, Reagan did remove the reference to 'other nuclear powers'
from his proposals,[29] but the idea of eliminating all offensive ballistic
missiles – anathema to Mrs Thatcher – stayed. So Trident was threatened,
in fact if not by name, and eliminating ballistic weapons (while sharing
the benefits of SDI) took pride of place in a letter from Reagan to Gorbachev sent on 25 July. In her failure to react dramatically to these
proposals, Mrs Thatcher seems to have relied on Reagan's earlier assurances, including the conditions enshrined in his formal Directive and a
pledge in March that 'nuclear weapons will clearly remain the key element
for the foreseeable future.'[30] The British did not believe that such radical
proposals would overcome the paralysis of arms control negotiations in
the past. There was a certain complacency here. As Charles Powell put it,

---

* The exact nature of the research, development and testing permitted by the ABM Treaty
was a matter of great dispute between Washington and Moscow. Reagan's letter ignored this
controversy entirely.

'Whether we *should* have taken his comments on abolishing ballistic missiles seriously is something you can argue about, but we *didn't*. I think the attitude was "Oh, the old boy's got ideas of his own about nuclear weapons, but NATO strategy is NATO strategy and therefore it will all be fine." '[31]

It may also be that Mrs Thatcher was simply too interested by the prospect of her own role in a dialogue with the Russians to kick up a fuss at this point. Back in May, just before she had left London for the G7 in Tokyo, Leonid Zamyatin, the Soviet Ambassador to the UK, had informed Mrs Thatcher that Gorbachev was eager to arrange a summit with Reagan in Washington before the end of the year: 'The Ambassador made it clear that Gorbachev had personally asked him to convey his message about the Summit and to do it before she left for Tokyo.'[32] The implication was that Mrs Thatcher would now intercede with Reagan. In Tokyo, she duly passed on the message, tactfully noting that 'she did not really know what to make of it.'[33] Reagan assured her that he remained committed to a summit later that year. By early July, however, no progress had been made. Gorbachev then wrote to Mrs Thatcher to invite her to the Soviet Union, and asked again for her help in bringing about the hoped-for summit with the US and the 'change for the better in the international situation' which was not 'yet apparent'.[34] Charles Powell recommended to Mrs Thatcher that she hold her fire before replying to Gorbachev until the autumn, when the US–Soviet summit would be nearer and 'we may have important new points to make which would help bring the two sides closer.'[35] But Mrs Thatcher insisted on replying rather sooner.* She asked to come to Moscow in the first half of 1987. She reminded the Soviet leader of her relationship with his American interlocutor, saying that Reagan's response to the latest Soviet proposals at the Geneva talks 'was made after close consultation with me'. Since getting Gorbachev's letter, she said, 'I have . . . been in touch with President Reagan. He has confirmed that, like you, he is very keen to have a second summit . . . It is hard to imagine that any successor could be as well-placed as he is to persuade Congress to ratify the arms control agreements which I hope a Summit would reach.'[36]

Not until September, however, was a date for any meeting actually set. Moving boldly in the belief that progress with the US would help him push on with reform at home, Gorbachev suddenly proposed a private and

* The day before receiving Powell's recommendation, Mrs Thatcher had undergone the operation for Dupuytren's contracture on her right hand, which was therefore bandaged. Powell drew square boxes on his own memo, so that all she had to do, with her left hand, was to tick the option she preferred. This, incidentally, was the usual manner in which Reagan responded to recommendations from his staff.

informal meeting with Reagan in advance of the Washington summit. This would allow them to work out agreements which could then be signed in Washington. Gorbachev offered two possible venues, London or Reykjavik. These suggestions surprised and pleased the Americans, since both were NATO capitals. According to George Shultz, 'The President was tempted by London because he would have loved it if Margaret had sat in on the meeting, but he knew that was not proper.'[37]* But the Americans decided in favour of Reykjavik because of its much greater isolation. Before agreeing to the meeting at all, however, Reagan informed Mrs Thatcher (and other allies) of Gorbachev's invitation, and sought her advice.

Mrs Thatcher welcomed the idea of the meeting.† Encouraged by an earlier assurance from Gorbachev, she told Reagan that 'Soviet willingness to eliminate all reference to British and French forces is a great step forward and, of course, a condition for our accepting any agreement.' On the question of how many US and Soviet INF should remain in Europe, she wrote, 'I want you to know that we would accept an agreement based on any equal ceiling in Europe, always provided that the difference between this and the Asian ceiling [that is, INF stationed in Asia] is not excessive, and that other Allied conditions, above all on SR [Short Range] INF, are met.'[38] She reiterated the attitude to SDI which she had expressed in her February message: the 'key is to provide the Russians with reassurance that there will be no sudden break-out from research to deployment'.[39] Like the US administration, she saw the Reykjavik meeting as laying the ground for a major summit, and said as much in a letter to Gorbachev: 'I very much welcome the fact that you are coming together to prepare for a summit, which I hope will be held before the end of this year. I believe that it should be possible to reach agreements then on reductions in arms, as well as to register progress on regional disputes and human rights problems.'[40] She saw Reykjavik as a useful step in a process, nothing more. Indeed, she worried that the original draft of her letter to Reagan was much too long: 'we have to remember', she scribbled, 'that this is <u>NOT</u> the <u>Summit</u>.'[41]

---

* There is no evidence that Mrs Thatcher herself knew that London had been suggested as the possible host for the summit. If she had, she would surely have moved heaven and earth to get it. Charles Powell knew, but did not believe that the Americans were seriously contemplating it, and so did not tell her. (Interview with Lord Powell of Bayswater.) If she had succeeded in sitting in on the meeting, the proceedings would certainly have been different.

† Bernard Ingham was pleased with the timing: 'Reagan/Gorbachev well covered and eclipses Labour Party Conference,' he told Mrs Thatcher ('Press Digest', Ingham to Thatcher, 1 October 1986, CAC: THCR 3/5/61).

Reagan saw the forthcoming meeting in much the same way. He wrote to Mrs Thatcher on 8 October, just three days before the meeting began: 'My objective in Reykjavik is to increase the likelihood that the coming summit in the United States will be productive. I expect our meetings to be private and businesslike. I do not anticipate any formal agreements.'[42] He reassured Mrs Thatcher that he remained 'acutely aware of your special interest' in the area of any INF agreement. His 'highest priority' was 'significant and stabilising reductions in strategic offensive weapons'.[43] Reviewing the letter, Charles Powell wrote on it: 'Prime Minister. This crossed with your message. It is generally reassuring about the subjects to be discussed, but gives away little on substance.'[44] According to Roz Ridgway, head of the State Department's European Bureau and a senior negotiator at Reykjavik, Powell's assessment was correct: 'There was no new substance.'[45] The administration was concentrating on reduction, not abolition. Mrs Thatcher felt comfortable. Her last message to Reagan before the meeting did not concern the big issues, but thanked him for offering to raise the plight of Oleg Gordievsky's family with Gorbachev.

It was Gorbachev, the author of the Reykjavik proto-summit, who planned to spring the surprises. According to notes from the Politburo meeting beforehand, taken by Gorbachev's foreign policy adviser Anatoly Chernyaev, Gorbachev warned his colleagues that, if Reykjavik failed, 'we will be pulled into an arms race beyond our power, and we will lose this race' because 'we are presently at the limit of our capabilities.'[46] Gorbachev was under tremendous pressure not only from SDI but also from the growing effectiveness of Western conventional forces, which were now benefiting from new technologies. His goal was to undermine NATO by driving a wedge between Reagan and his allies. He explained to the Politburo that 'In order to move Reagan we have to give him something . . . We must emphasise that we are proposing the liquidation of nuclear weapons . . . If Reagan does not meet us halfway, we will tell the whole world about this.'[47] As Chernyaev understood it, Gorbachev meant to use Reykjavik to 'sweep Reagan off his feet'.[48] In Mrs Thatcher's eyes and much to her distress, he very nearly succeeded.

On the morning of Saturday 11 October 1986, Reagan and Gorbachev met in Höfði House, the official guesthouse of the Icelandic government, at first alone, except for interpreters and notetakers, and then joined by their foreign ministers, George Shultz and Eduard Shevardnadze.* Both

---

* Eduard Shevardnadze (1928–2014), First Secretary, Communist Party Central Committee, Georgia, 1972–85; member, Politburo, 1985–90; Minister of Foreign Affairs, USSR,

leaders expressed themselves in favour of the total elimination of nuclear weapons as an aspiration. To the surprise of the Americans, this quickly turned into specific offers of arms control by Gorbachev. What Gorbachev called a 'package' of Soviet proposals included a 50 per cent cut in strategic arms, the abolition of all INF in Europe and negotiations over those remaining in Asia (with French and British missiles ignored).[49] Gorbachev also proposed that both sides should agree to abide by the ABM Treaty for not less than ten years, followed by three to five years of negotiations about how to proceed; during this time, research on SDI would proceed but 'not outside of laboratories'. Reagan pronounced all this 'very encouraging',[50] rather alarming his staff. 'We had prepared responses to a variety of ideas already proposed by the Soviets,' recalled Roz Ridgway, 'but we didn't expect Gorbachev to come out with something new. And the President hadn't rehearsed this. Who knew where the President was going to take this stuff?'[51] Certainly Mrs Thatcher did not know. As things moved at a rapid pace, no information filtered out to the allies.

On the Sunday morning, Reagan and Gorbachev agreed to reduce their strategic forces by 50 per cent and to remove INF missiles from Europe entirely.* These were dramatic shifts in favour of long-standing US positions, the INF deal reflecting the 'zero option' Reagan had put forward in 1981. They were also far from what Mrs Thatcher had been expecting. As was clear from her letter to Reagan the previous month, she had been ready to accept a 'ceiling' on INF in Europe, but the word 'ceiling' did not, obviously, mean zero. Zero went beyond what Reagan had briefed allied leaders before Reykjavik.[52] Despite previous assurances to Mrs Thatcher that he was 'acutely aware' of her 'special interest', when Reagan negotiated the deal with Gorbachev on the Sunday morning, the news blackout remained absolute.

During a meeting Shultz held with the US team around midday, it began to dawn on the Americans that they should be doing more to keep the allies informed. They considered the proposed INF deal a great triumph and, as Adelman put it, were now eager to 'relay such glad tidings from Reykjavik' to their allies.[53] Ridgway promptly began telephoning European capitals. Charlie Price, the US Ambassador in London, remembered that everything moved so fast that Ridgway, hurrying to get the information out, rang him and others using open lines.[54] There was no suggestion

---

1985–90; founder, Movement for Democratic Reform, 1991; Chairman of Supreme Council and Head of State, Georgia, 1992–5; President of Georgia, 1995–2003; Hon. GCMG, 2000.
* At this stage it was suggested that the Soviets would keep 100 missiles in Asia and the US 100 in Alaska.

of consulting the allies, only of letting them know shortly before the whole world did.[55] It is not clear that even Ridgway's limited briefing reached Mrs Thatcher, who was becoming increasingly concerned by the information vacuum. Around lunchtime, Mrs Thatcher rang Charles Powell from Chequers. 'Have you heard what is going on at Reykjavik?' she asked Powell anxiously. 'We've got to do something, Charles.'[56] Powell leapt into a car and drove to Chequers immediately to help her take stock of the situation. Although concrete information as to what Reagan and Gorbachev were up to did not reach Mrs Thatcher until after 4 p.m., she was already getting nervous.

Back in Reykjavik, the stumbling block was SDI. Reagan was determined not to confine it to the laboratory for ten years, while Gorbachev was utterly unconvinced by the US offer to share it. During the Sunday-morning negotiations, planned as the final meeting of the summit, the two leaders went around in circles on this point, unable to reach agreement. Rather than end in deadlock they agreed to adjourn and give Shultz and Shevardnadze a chance to try to break the impasse.

The Americans now shifted to a radical and surprising course of action. While Shultz and Shevardnadze talked, Richard Perle and Robert Linhard, an NSC staffer, drafted a version of the zero ballistic missile proposal, first outlined in Reagan's letter to Gorbachev of 25 July. 'We hadn't planned to raise this at Reykjavik,' recalled Poindexter, who had discussed the possibility of introducing it, if necessary, with Reagan and Shultz the evening before.[57] Shultz now presented the draft to Shevardnadze (the specifics of which had not yet been cleared with Reagan). It proposed that neither side would withdraw from the ABM Treaty for ten years. During the first five years both sides would reduce their strategic nuclear forces by 50 per cent; during the second five years they would agree to abolish all remaining offensive ballistic missiles. Shevardnadze did not much like the idea, pointing out that it permitted SDI deployment after ten years, but the two foreign ministers agreed to brief their bosses so that they could discuss it in their final encounter.

After lunch, when Reagan and Gorbachev reconvened for a final session, discussions went to the brink. The Perle–Linhard proposal suggested the elimination of offensive ballistic missiles, where the Soviets had an advantage. But Gorbachev began the session by pressing for the elimination of all strategic arms, which would have left the US with no nuclear weapon capable of reaching the Soviet Union from within the homeland. Advised against accepting this, Reagan raised the game still further: 'At the end of a long discussion on the various categories of weapons being negotiated on, in which he seemed either not to have known or not to have cared about the difference between ballistic and strategic arms, Reagan declared that it would be fine with him "if we eliminated all nuclear weapons". Gorbachev replied, "We can do that. We can eliminate them." Shultz was not a silent spectator; he interjected to say, "Let's do it." [58] With understatement, Jack Matlock, Director of Soviet Affairs on the NSC staff, recalled that 'the President did get beyond what we had planned or thought he would do.'[59] Ridgway put it more colourfully: 'The dialogue between the President and Gorbachev was cosmic.'[60]

Nevertheless, the two leaders did not know what to do next. Gorbachev had insisted throughout on SDI being confined to the laboratory for ten years, and the Pentagon had equally insisted to the President that this would kill the programme. Reagan therefore refused Gorbachev's demand, and begged Gorbachev to ' "do this one thing", not to constrain SDI to the laboratory: "It is a question of one word. This should not be turned down over a word." Gorbachev responded that "it is not just a question of one word, it is a question of principle." '[61]

The meeting therefore broke up without agreement. And because Gorbachev's offer had been a 'package', no part of it now survived. All offers were off the table.

The lack of agreement, and the gloomy demeanour of George Shultz at the subsequent press conference, led the world to see the summit as a failure. But for Mrs Thatcher, at least at this stage, its failure was the only good thing about it.

She did not immediately know exactly how far Reagan had gone. Few people did, even within the administration. Most of those in the know, alarmed by what had transpired, worked hard to suppress the fact that Reagan and Gorbachev had come close to getting rid of all nuclear weapons, focusing instead on the elimination of ballistic missiles.* Nonetheless Mrs Thatcher picked up enough to be horrified. 'She was totally appalled,' recalled her principal private secretary, Nigel Wicks.[62] 'How could he do it? What is he doing?' she exclaimed.[63] According to Jacques Attali, then Mitterrand's special adviser, the aftermath of Reykjavik was 'the first time I heard Margaret Thatcher say the Americans were crazy'.[64] She was upset both by the content and by the manner of what had taken place. A nuclear-free world was, she had always maintained, an impossibility. If

---

* One exception was Don Regan, the President's Chief of Staff, who let the truth slip when he briefed the press immediately after the summit. 'We said to the Soviets, we will do away with all nuclear weapons . . .' he declared. 'Everything was on the table.' (*Washington Post*, 13 October 1986.)

the West sought it, therefore, it was pursuing a will o' the wisp, and would only make itself, particularly in Britain and Continental Europe, fatally vulnerable. Now the leader of the West *had* sought it, without agreeing his ideas with any of his allies. Since this had happened this way, against her wishes and without her knowledge, she felt a 'gnawing anxiety' that the disarmament proposals 'might well be put forward on some new occasion'.[65]

When Reagan telephoned Mrs Thatcher the following day, her sixty-first birthday, he confirmed what had been offered about ballistic missiles. Although initially he made no mention of abolishing all nuclear weapons, Mrs Thatcher seized upon this more accurate interpretation of what had almost transpired and sought to blame Moscow for the idea: 'the Soviet idea to eliminate all nuclear missiles in return for a 10-year agreement to restrict SDI research to the laboratory is extremely dangerous,' she insisted. Reagan seemed less convinced. When Mrs Thatcher reminded him of the conventional imbalance in Europe he disagreed, claiming that 'we do not believe the conventional situation is so imbalanced. Further-more, what the Soviets do not want is a war.'[66] She was careful to praise the President – he had 'performed marvellously',[67] she said, though she certainly did not believe this at the time – and she accused the Russians of trying to 'engineer a breakdown' at the meeting; but she clearly stated her anxieties. The proposal to eliminate nuclear weapons 'caused her considerable concern' and was 'unsettling to opinion in Europe'. Charles Powell, who noted the telephone conversation, considered it so sensitive that he made two versions, one for a very restricted circulation. In the latter, he noted anxiously that Reagan 'spoke dismissively' of the ABM Treaty, and recorded that when Mrs Thatcher 'repeatedly stressed the importance of nuclear deterrence in the face of the imbalance of conven-tional forces in Europe, the President's responses were rather vague.'[68] Reagan gave no ground to Mrs Thatcher: 'He showed no sign of backing down from his concept of eliminating nuclear weapons within ten years, indeed showed considerable pride in it.' He told her to read *Red Storm Rising*, the new novel by Tom Clancy and Larry Bond, set partly in Ice-land, which cast doubt on the idea of Soviet military success through conventional means.

In fact, the prospect of eliminating all nuclear weapons was very short lived. The small group of officials aware of Reagan's offer understood just how incendiary the idea was. It was understandable that they wished to erase a putative concession which, since it had not led to anything, they considered best forgotten. On 16 October, Admiral Poindexter wrote a long memo to the President, concluding thus:

I would strongly recommend that:

a) you step back from any discussion of eliminating all nuclear weapons in
10 years, and focus . . . on the elimination of all offensive ballistic missiles
in 10 years;

b) you make no further public comment endorsing the idea of the total
elimination of all nuclear weapons in 10 years as something discussed and
agreed with the General Secretary.[69]

Reagan reluctantly went along with this recommendation, but for Mrs
Thatcher it was only a small mercy. The President remained committed
to his plan to abolish all offensive ballistic missiles, which she considered
almost as bad as abolishing nuclear weapons altogether. As Poindexter
reminded Reagan, Mrs Thatcher questioned 'whether we can have effective deterrence without ballistic missiles. She does not believe it prudent
to make major reductions without redressing conventional and chemical
weapons imbalances. Mrs Thatcher also fears that elimination of ballistic
missiles will undercut her domestic political position.'[70]

This last point weighed very heavily on Mrs Thatcher's mind. Only the
day before Reykjavik, she had made defence the climax of her annual
party conference speech (see Chapter 15). In the previous week, the Labour
conference had voted for unilateral nuclear disarmament and the closing
of American nuclear bases in Britain. To her cheering audience in Bournemouth, Mrs Thatcher excoriated Neil Kinnock's leadership, and said that
'by repudiating NATO's nuclear strategy Labour would fatally weaken
the Atlantic Alliance and the United States' commitment to Europe's
defence'. That weekend, she went on, Reagan and Gorbachev would be
meeting in Reykjavik: 'Does anyone imagine that Mr Gorbachev would
be prepared to talk at all if the West had already disarmed?'[71] She saw
Labour's unilateralism as a key winner for her in the general election she
was free to call in 1987, just as it had been in 1983.

Two days after her oration, it began to look as if Reagan himself had
started dancing to Labour's tune. 'Giving up nuclear weapons is the sort
of thing that Neil Kinnock advocates,' Mrs Thatcher chided the President
over the phone. 'This would be tantamount to surrender, so we must be
very, very careful.'[72] Even the Labour Party, so wrapped up in itself at that
time that it barely noticed what was happening in the wider world, began
to spot a shift. Charles Clarke,* Kinnock's chief of staff, recalled that

---

* Charles Clarke (1950–), educated Highgate School and King's College, Cambridge; head,
office of Neil Kinnock, MP, 1981–92; Labour MP for Norwich South, 1997–2010; Minister

before Reykjavik Labour 'didn't appreciate enough Reagan's concerns about nuclear weapons. After Reykjavik, we did come to see them.'[73] It became possible to portray Kinnock's ideas as closer to Reagan's than Mrs Thatcher's. As Richard Perle, of all people the least likely to appeal to a Labour audience, put it, 'We were proposing to disarm the UK.'[74] But despite the pile of problems he had created for her, Mrs Thatcher remained careful to avoid any anger or rudeness in talking to the President. She ended her fraught telephone call on 13 October by thanking him 'for what she called a job well-done in Reykjavik. You lived up to the confidence we have in you.'[75] She was able to praise him, without total hypocrisy, because he had, in the end, held the line against Gorbachev and refused to give in over SDI. Even on the morning after the dreadful night before, she could begin to see how something could be made of the near-disaster at Reykjavik. SDI, towards which she had originally been lukewarm, would now become, by its power as a threat and by Reagan's unyielding adherence to it, the saviour of the West. Reykjavik, in retrospect, would become the moment when the Russians realized the game was up. 'Thank goodness. Thank goodness,' she reflected in retirement. '[The deal proposed at Reykjavik] would have given the Soviet Union all the superiority with conventional weapons. And everything we'd worked for would have been lost. Three cheers for the strength of purpose of Ronald Reagan, we go ahead with SDI. And so the whole thing failed.'[76]

Those observing Mrs Thatcher at close quarters often differed about her attitude to Ronald Reagan. The crisis of Reykjavik was the prime example of the problem. Some believed that, for all her proclaimed admiration, she had severe doubts. Poindexter said that 'At the time, she was always very friendly with the President, and tough. But my instinct was that she didn't really respect the President. I don't think she thought the President was very smart. She probably thought he was too simplistic.'[77] Robin Butler held a similar view, believing that she 'never had any illusions about getting below the surface with Reagan. Regularly after international meetings she would say, "But Robin, he didn't know anything about it!" '[78] Others thought that her regard was sincere. Colin Powell, who took over as Deputy National Security Advisor in the White House at the end of 1986, noted: 'A lot of foreign leaders might reflect the fact that they didn't think they were dealing with an intellectual equal. But Margaret never displayed that. She knew that she was dealing at the top level of abstraction and conceptualization with an intellectual equal.'[79] It sounds odd to

without Portfolio and Chairman of the Labour Party, 2001–2; Secretary of State for Education and Skills, 2002–4; Home Secretary, 2004–6.

speak of Ronald Reagan in terms like 'abstraction' and 'conceptualization', but Powell was right to think that Mrs Thatcher's respect for the
President came from her faith in the strength of his general beliefs, most
of which she shared. She did indeed believe that he was her intellectual
equal in that he grasped the political and ideological challenges of the age
in a way that other leaders in the West did not. This is why she clung to
him through thick and thin.

The other Powell – Charles – who probably knew her better than any
fellow official, noticed that she always tried to protect Reagan in her own
mind: 'She would always look for excuses for what she regarded as his
failure to measure up. Occasionally she would say, "Oh, they must be
concealing things from him if he thinks that." But there were some issues
on which she genuinely disagreed with him and was always a bit puzzled
that he didn't understand better why she disagreed.'[80] Of these, by far the
most important was the issue of nuclear weapons. So Reykjavik inevitably
put great strain on her trust in Reagan's wisdom, but it did not break that
trust. She tried to maintain a sort of platonic idea of what Reagan really
wanted. As she put it to Henry Kissinger a couple of months after the
Reykjavik 'earthquake', 'Her main concern remained to bring home to
the President that the effect of what he had done at Reykjavik ran flatly
contrary to his real objectives.'[81]

Her method of bringing this home to the President was to go and see
him. Mrs Thatcher over-dramatizes herself when, in her memoirs, she
claims that 'Somehow I had to get the Americans back onto the firm
ground of a credible policy of nuclear deterrence. I arranged to fly to the
United States to see President Reagan.'[82] In fact, her visit had been arranged
before Reykjavik. Circumventing the bureaucracy who were trying to
block her, she had got her request directly into Reagan's hand by means
of Charlie Price, and the President, quite exceptionally, had sent a handwritten note to aides granting her wish that it should be at Camp David
and detailing the arrangements: 'Margaret Thatcher would like to come
here for a one day meeting – just their ambas. + her sec. Charles Pow on
her side. She would arrive Nov. 14 & leave after lunch the 15th. She
expressed the wish this could be at Camp David. I'd like this if it could be
done. This is a weekend & is presently scheduled for Camp David.'[83] The
visit was only publicly announced after Reykjavik, however, so it looked
to the world like a response to the summit.

One irritated NSC memo complained: 'We think we have done everything to accommodate the British, indeed we cannot recall any previous
meeting in which the President played such a direct role in the arrangements. The British, nonetheless, continue to want more.'[84] But it was not

only over the logistics and 'face-time' that Mrs Thatcher was pressing. She was planning as carefully as she could to move Reagan's mind.

In calculating how best to do this, Mrs Thatcher and Charles Powell operated almost alone. 'You have a bilateral with the Foreign Secretary,' Powell reminded her nine days after Reykjavik, '– the plump chap with glasses who used to work across the road and whom we haven't seen for a long while! . . . He has been kept posted about your various discussions and the line you are taking.'[85] There was no suggestion that Geoffrey Howe should help craft the policy. Taking the model of the previous successful Camp David visit in 1984, Prime Minister and private secretary began by working out the press release they would like to see emerge. Mrs Thatcher deleted from Powell's draft the words 'We agree that very important progress was made at Reykjavik towards balanced and verifiable arms control agreements,' since she did not believe that either the balance or the verification was likely to be achieved.[86] The draft supported INF negotiations as the priority. It also supported SDI research. But it insisted that 'the security of the Western Alliance would continue for the foreseeable future to rest on nuclear deterrence.'[87]

A week later, Powell set out fully for Mrs Thatcher his advice on the best way to deal with Reagan post-Reykjavik. He commented unfavourably on a Foreign Office–MOD suggestion that Britain should 'try to get the Americans to negotiate agreed limits on SDI research with the Soviet Union'.[88] 'One has to ask how far this is realistic,' wrote Powell. 'It is precisely the point on which the President stood firm at Reykjavik and reaped great credit for doing so.' Mrs Thatcher underlined and ticked approvingly. Besides, Powell went on, such controls on SDI, as well as being unattainable, might not be 'actually desirable'. They might make it 'more likely that we shall be confronted with an agreement to eliminate nuclear weapons/ballistic missiles in a fixed time-span. We want the President to pay attention to our political needs – deterrence, Trident – so we must respect his political interests which are above all SDI.' Powell's view was that 'our present pickle' was caused by discussion focusing 'too exclusively on the symptoms (nuclear weapons) and not enough on the causes (ideological differences, Soviet subversion and so on)'.[89] Britain did not have the power to get the elimination of ballistic missiles off the table, but it might be able to get the Americans to see the proposal more tactically. He recommended a 'rather more basic approach to the President' and invented a little private speech that Mrs Thatcher could make to him at Camp David. She underlined it carefully.

'Ron, you did wonderfully at Reykjavik in reading Gorbachev's game-plan and refusing to let him bounce you into giving up the SDI. It just shows how careful you have to be in dealing with the Russians: you can simply never trust them, and every proposal they make needs to be crawled over in minute detail.' And so, the 'speech' went on, Reagan should hold out against 'unreasonable constraints' on SDI, pocket the real concessions that the Russians had already made on getting rid of their INF (while not including Britain and France in the INF negotiations), and going for really deep cuts in strategic nuclear weapons. He should make a step-by-step start with INF and 'break up the Reykjavik package into its constituent parts'. Then came the tough bit: 'The area where we have a real problem, Ron, is when you talk of the elimination of ballistic missiles within ten years. Now, I know why you do that . . . it's part of your vision of freeing the world of nuclear weapons . . . But you do need to take account of the impact in Europe, where the proposal is seen as equivalent to removing the US umbrella which has guaranteed the peace for 40 years and leaving Europe exposed to the massive Soviet preponderance . . . in conventional weapons.' The Europeans would not try to close the conventional gap; instead, they would turn towards neutralism, so when the President spoke of eliminating ballistic missiles, he must also speak of the conventional imbalance and of the need to 'tackle the political causes of the East/West conflict'.

The imagined oration ended with a personal plea from Mrs Thatcher to Reagan: 'You will also cause me very real political difficulties if you pursue your proposal for eliminating ballistic missiles too actively. In our people's minds it will raise two questions: isn't Labour right after all in wanting to get rid of nuclear weapons . . . ? And why on earth should we pay out all that money for Trident, if it's going to be abolished in 10 years?' The next British general election could 'turn' on these points, so 'you must help me deal with these arguments. The best way is to reaffirm strongly that the Alliance will continue to rely on nuclear deterrence for the foreseeable future.'[90]

Rarely does a civil servant's draft so clearly set out policy thinking and political tactics, and reveal such a close understanding of his principal's mind and character. Powell's high ability and confidence in doing so show why he had become indispensable to Mrs Thatcher, and therefore very irritating to the Foreign Office, whose officials felt – and were – excluded from the inner counsels. In response to the draft press statement, Geoffrey Howe argued for greater caution: a good agreement in Camp David might not be possible, and therefore it might be more prudent not to press for a joint statement at all.[91] But Powell was surely correct in his summary of the British problem, and in his bolder sense of how Mrs Thatcher could best argue her case personally with her closest ally. At the heart of this lay a crucial concession. To try to stave off the elimination of ballistic missiles, she needed to welcome the proposed zero for INF missiles in Europe. 'She didn't like the plans to get rid of INF,' recalled Powell. 'To be perfectly honest she never liked any disarmament at all. She had to be pushed and bullied into anything of that sort. I think that having gone all the way to secure the deployment of these missiles, she was reluctant to give them up. But she was sufficiently pragmatic to realize that there was no alternative to some sort of deal.'[92] Powell was also skilful in his methods. He had cultivated a close relationship with Price, the Ambassador, and he ensured that she privately passed Price her pre-Camp David thoughts so that they would go 'directly to the President, not put in telegrams which get [Mrs Thatcher underlined] splattered all round the State Department'.[93] In the end, she followed Powell's advice happily, and successfully.

Just as Mrs Thatcher was preparing for her visit to Washington, a story broke in a Beirut newspaper which threatened the stability of Reagan's presidency. The scandal, which eventually became known as 'Iran–Contra', began with revelations that the Reagan administration had been secretly engaged in efforts to sell weapons to Iran in return for the release of American hostages held by Iranian proxies in the Lebanon.* This ran contrary to US policy towards negotiating with terrorists, and was also, very likely, contrary to US law. There was talk of impeachment, if Reagan's knowledge of the operation could be proved. What had happened, it eventually emerged, was that the NSC staff, under Poindexter and his staffer, Colonel Oliver North, had been running the scheme without reference to Shultz and the State Department. As the story grew, Reagan denied it publicly, the day before Mrs Thatcher arrived in Washington. It was 'utterly false', he insisted.[94]

Although the White House probably did not realize it, Mrs Thatcher knew that Reagan was not telling the truth.[95] According to Charles Powell, 'We knew about it because of the extraordinarily close intermeshing of GCHQ, Cheltenham and NSA [the US National Security Agency] operations.'[96] Information provided to the Americans was gathered by GCHQ and passed through British channels. British analysts were thus able to work out that something was going on and make an accurate guess at what it was. Although Mrs Thatcher was unhappy with what was

---

* The word 'Contra' was added when it later came out that money from these sales was diverted to arming the Contra troops against the left-wing Sandinista government in Nicaragua.

happening, she calculated that there was nothing to be gained by pursuing the issue with the administration. 'We couldn't raise it because we weren't supposed to know about it,' Powell recalled. 'We didn't want to do anything frankly that would cut us off from the extraordinary flow of information which we got from the NSA.'[97] Because of this, and because the whole business had nothing to do with her, the best line open to Mrs Thatcher was 'Defend the man, not the policy.'[98] But the news added to the sense of crisis and drama surrounding her Washington visit.

In Washington, there was a good deal of support for Mrs Thatcher's views on the elimination of nuclear weapons, and sympathy with her difficult political position. Just as Charles Powell was drafting his 'speech' for his boss, the chairman of the Joint Chiefs of Staff, Admiral William Crowe, who considered the idea of zero ballistic missiles within ten years 'completely unacceptable',[99] told Reagan, at a meeting on 27 October, 'As your chief military adviser, I do not recommend that you submit the proposal, Mr President.'[100] Nevertheless, the policy of eliminating all ballistic missiles over ten years was not actually withdrawn, but was enshrined in a National Security Decision Directive, which the President signed on 3 November.[101] Shultz told Reagan that they wanted to secure Mrs Thatcher's agreement to this approach at Camp David. At the same time, though, he stressed that it was important that 'she returns to London stronger politically and reassured about the direction of our policies.'[102] On Trident, the Americans felt, they could give her reassurance, since the breakdown at Reykjavik meant that nuclear modernization could now go ahead, at least for the time being. The real task was 'to find a mutually acceptable formula that addresses Mrs Thatcher's insistence that drastic nuclear reductions such as the elimination of offensive ballistic missiles are inadvisable as long as conventional and chemical imbalances exist in Europe'.[103]

In line with Powell's advice, Mrs Thatcher had decided to welcome the zero INF deal, but the Americans did not yet know this. In the run-up to her visit, there was concern, if not irritation, at the idea that she might add this to her list of grievances. The Americans felt that the Europeans had been pushing them to negotiate reductions for years. Now that agreement had been reached to do away with the missiles, European leaders seemed to want to keep them after all. Reagan, advised Ty Cobb, an NSC staffer, should 'make this an issue with Thatcher, when she starts whining that "European interests were not taken into account." I know that RR doesn't like to talk tough, least of all with Thatcher, but I think its [sic] time to unload on them. They simply can't keep urging us to do this and that, then when we do they scurry for cover.'[104] Remembering what had happened at Camp David in 1984, the Americans were also jumpy about whether Mrs Thatcher would turn up with a draft joint statement at the ready. Powell told the London Embassy that 'the Prime Minister had no intention of doing so . . . The President and Prime Minister might agree that a joint statement would be desirable at the end of the talks, but that remained to be seen.'[105] In fact, American anxieties were well founded. Mrs Thatcher arrived in Washington on Friday 14 November with a text in her handbag.

The next morning Bernard Ingham sent her a note explaining how 'you should be able to turn this visit into a roaring success.'[106] He warned her that the press wanted rows on Reykjavik, the Iran scandal and US support for international criticisms of the fishing zone in the Falklands. The best outcome, he advised, would be to concentrate on what mattered to her: 'This visit is highly important in domestic political terms for you. You want to show back home that the old magic works with the Americans and that in your hands the West's defence is secure. The stronger your statement agreed at Camp David the more you should concentrate on this issue and play the rest away.' So she had every incentive to drive a hard, if friendly bargain with Reagan.

As was her preferred tactic, so that she could be calmer and politer when she met the President, Mrs Thatcher took out her frustration on others first. On the day she arrived, she had separate meetings with Caspar Weinberger and George Shultz. To Weinberger, she announced that her visit was 'possibly the most important she had ever made. The defence of the free world was at stake.'[107] To Shultz, Mrs Thatcher wisely proclaimed her support for the zero INF deal. Beyond this, as Shultz recalled, she gave him 'unshirted hell'.[108] She particularly emphasized the European perspective of sharing a continent with the much more heavily armed Soviets. Shultz tried to reassure her by saying that 'it was in practical terms impossible to conceive of them [the Reykjavik disarmament proposals] being brought to the point of agreement during President Reagan's remaining term in office.'[109] Mrs Thatcher was not much appeased – 'she could not emphasise too much the degree to which the United States proposal on ballistic missiles, and the failure to consult in advance about it, had undermined confidence in Europe.' The proposal would do nothing less than 'undermine the security of Western Europe', she told Shultz, before delivering her *coup de grâce*: if pursued, it would 'cause you to lose me and the British nation'.[110]

While Secretary of State and Prime Minister did not agree, given what was at stake they saw the necessity of finding the 'mutually acceptable formula' which Shultz had advocated to Reagan. Charles Powell and others worked late to redraft the statement that would be issued at the conclusion of the visit with what Mrs Thatcher praised as their 'golden pens'.[111] The next morning, as they flew to Camp David, the British passed their draft to Shultz, Poindexter and Ridgway, who accepted it. At one point, Mrs Thatcher was very persistent about a minor change. Poindexter was impressed: 'I remember thinking afterwards, that's why they refer to her as "the lady with the iron pants". Very tough.'[112] The hard work of negotiation was complete before Mrs Thatcher had even arrived at Camp David.

At Camp David, recalled Charles Powell, Mrs Thatcher was 'very nervous about her meeting with Reagan and needed intensive hand-holding'.[113] The stakes, of course, could hardly have been higher. In the end, it turned out that she had little to worry about other than the President's skills as a driver: 'There is a rather romantic photograph of her coming off the helicopter with Reagan holding his hands out. It's real "Gone with the Wind" stuff,' recalled Charles Powell, who watched as Mrs Thatcher climbed aboard the President's golf cart. 'She was petrified being driven around by Reagan. She was absolutely convinced he was going to tip her into the woods or something. She hated it. You could see the sort of fixed expression on her face.'[114] The two met for a tête-à-tête in Aspen Lodge, the President's cabin. Reagan explained the Iran business, misleadingly: 'He assured the Prime Minister that there had never been any question of bargaining for the release of the hostages.' Then he gave her a long account of his talks at Reykjavik. Mrs Thatcher repeated to the President, in more measured terms, the arguments she had put to George Shultz and 'underlined the inadequacy of airbreathing systems [that is, non-ballistic weapons that require the oxygen in the earth's atmosphere, such as cruise missiles and aircraft] alone to provide deterrence'.[115] For his part, Reagan 'left no doubt' about the US commitment to strategic nuclear modernization, the United Kingdom's independent deterrent and 'its modernisation with Trident'. At the end of all this, Mrs Thatcher laid a copy of the joint statement before him: 'The President accepted this without demur.'[116]

In came Shultz, Reagan's Chief of Staff Donald Regan, Poindexter and others for cocktails, lunch and a much more general conversation. It was all very genial, although Mrs Thatcher did indulge her habit of going on and on. Jim Kuhn, Reagan's executive assistant, managed to get Reagan aside during a break and told him, 'Mr. President . . . you haven't said anything. You have lots of points you need to make.' But 'The president just smiled. "Jim," he said, "you've got to understand that Maggie and I are old friends, and I just couldn't step in like that. She's much too dear of a friend." '[117] At last, however, Reagan got his chance, and gave a further description of his Reykjavik meetings. He praised Gorbachev for being 'the first Soviet leader not to reaffirm the goal of world Communist domination . . . He was also the first Soviet leader to propose the elimination of weapons which the Soviet Union already possessed.' On the other hand, 'he recalled Mr Gorbachev's refusal to have any serious discussion at Reykjavik of the causes of conflict between East and West.' Reagan remembered his own anger as the meeting broke down. 'Mr Gorbachev's parting words had been that it was still not too late, to which the President had replied: it is for me.'[118]

Before flying to Camp David that morning, Mrs Thatcher had breakfasted with Vice-President George Bush. He had spoken to her frankly about the crisis over the Iran arms-for-hostages affair. 'The climate was as ugly', he told her, 'as anything he had seen in a long time . . . People had not believed the President, for the first time in his Presidency. Congress was loaded for bear [that is, ready for a fight].'[119] With this gloomy view in her head though not on her lips, Mrs Thatcher raised the matter with Reagan and pointed out that she would be asked about it at the press conference. 'She would say that the President had reaffirmed to her that the United States did not pay ransom of any sort for hostages,' Powell recorded. 'That was of course our policy too.'[120]

Mrs Thatcher was so pleased with the agreed statement that she reprinted virtually its entire text in her memoirs.[121] She had good reason for her satisfaction. The statement announced that the priority in arms control would be 'an INF agreement with restraints on shorter-range systems; a 50 per cent cut over five years in United States and Soviet strategic offensive weapons; and a ban on chemical weapons'.[122] It stressed both leaders' support for 'the SDI research programme, which is permitted by the ABM Treaty'.* This was followed by a reassertion, crucial for Mrs Thatcher, of nuclear deterrence: 'We confirmed that NATO's strategy of forward defence and flexible response would continue to require effective nuclear deterrents based upon a mix of systems. At the same time, reductions in nuclear weapons would increase the importance of eliminating conventional disparities.' Finally, 'The President reaffirmed the United States

---

* Geoffrey Howe remained unhappy that Mrs Thatcher might be allowing Reagan too much leeway for developing SDI. A letter from his private office to Charles Powell argued that what she had said about SDI research had been 'merely stating a common sense fact' and should be expanded. (Budd to Powell, 20 November 1986, Prime Minister's Papers, Defence, Military Uses of Laser Technology in Space, Part 4 (document consulted in the Cabinet Office).) Mrs Thatcher scrawled on top: 'I do not accept that the common sense meaning of words should play no part in foreign policy.'

intention to proceed with its strategic nuclear modernisation programme, including Trident. He also confirmed his full support for arrangements made to modernise Britain's independent nuclear deterrent with Trident.'

Bernard Ingham gleefully reported to Mrs Thatcher that the press was full of 'glowing praise' for her performance at Camp David, mentioning in particular the *Telegraph*'s leading headline: 'Thatcher Trident Triumph'.[123] The only important omission from her prized statement was any language repudiating the idea of abolishing ballistic missiles. *The Times*'s diplomatic correspondent noticed: 'The chasm between Europe's cautious step-by-step view of nuclear disarmament and Washington's grand vision was not bridged during the talks.'[124] Each party could take refuge in the ambiguity of wording about nuclear deterrence being 'based on a mix of systems'. There was neither an agreement, nor an agreement to disagree: it was more an agreement to pretend to agree. What mattered, from Mrs Thatcher's point of view, was that the President had agreed to give priority to the proposals she favoured, inevitably pushing any discussion of the elimination of ballistic missiles into the indefinite future.

There were several factors, of course, in the weakening of Reagan's Reykjavik agenda for nuclear disarmament. There was institutional opposition, such as that of the Joint Chiefs. There was outside expert opposition, such as that offered by Henry Kissinger.* Above all, there was the effect of the Iran–Contra scandal. On 25 November, Oliver North was fired and John Poindexter resigned after revelations that profits from arms sales to Iran were being diverted to the Contras in Nicaragua.† Poindexter was replaced as National Security Advisor by Frank Carlucci, who, on appointment, told the President that he 'disagreed with Reykjavik'.[125] As he sought to return Reagan to the nuclear fold, Carlucci was happy to pray Mrs Thatcher in aid: 'I finally said, "Mr President, if you

---

* In the *Washington Post* of 18 November, Kissinger wrote that 'the Reykjavik edifice puts the entire postwar structure of deterrence into question because it makes it even more doubtful that the United States would use nuclear weapons in defense of its allies' (*Washington Post*, 18 November 1986).

† Mrs Thatcher strongly endeared herself to Reagan at this time by the moral support she gave him. In early December, she sent him, by private means, a handwritten letter of solidarity: 'The press and media are always so ready to criticise and get people down. I know what it's like. But your achievements in restoring America's pride and confidence and in giving the West the leadership it needs are far too substantial to suffer any lasting damage. The message I give to everyone is that anything which weakens you, weakens America; and anything that weakens America weakens the whole free world.' (Thatcher to Reagan, 4 December 1986, Presidential Handwriting File, Folder 169, Reagan Library.)

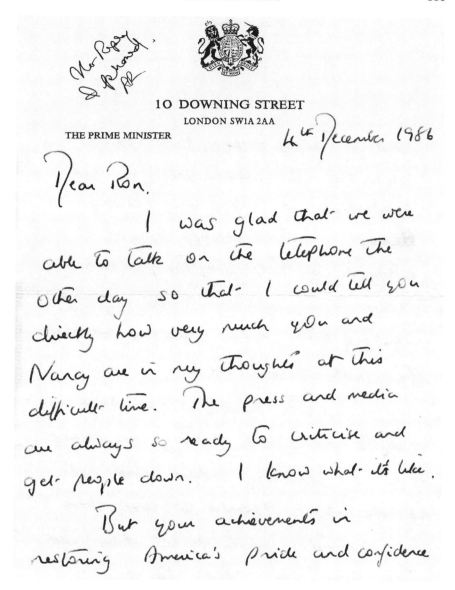

10 DOWNING STREET
LONDON SW1A 2AA

THE PRIME MINISTER

4ᵗʰ December 1986

Dear Ron,

I was glad that we were able to talk on the telephone the other day so that I could tell you directly how very much you and Nancy are in my thoughts at this difficult time. The press and media are always so ready to criticise and get people down. I know what it's like.

But your achievements in restoring America's pride and confidence

Mrs Thatcher's letter of comfort to Ronald Reagan at the height of the Iran–Contra affair, December 1986: 'anything which weakens you, weakens America; and anything that weakens America weakens the whole free world.'

move to get rid of nuclear weapons, Margaret will be on the phone in five minutes." "Oh, I don't want that," he said.'[126]

By the end of the year, Reagan had been forced to bend to the anxieties of Mrs Thatcher and those around him. The Soviets also made clear that they had no interest in pursuing the ballistic-missile proposal. The mood

and in giving the West the
leadership it needs are far too
substantial to suffer any lasting
damage. The message I give to
everyone is that anything which
weakens you, weakens America; and
anything that weakens America weakens
the whole free world.

Whatever happened over Iran
is in the past and nothing can change
it. I fervently believe that the
message now should be that there
is important work to be done and
that you are going to do it.

had changed: 'I don't remember Reykjavik being a burning issue when I
arrived as Deputy National Security Advisor on January 1, 1987,' said
Colin Powell.[127] The talk now was of nuclear-arms reduction, not of a
nuclear-free world. As George Shultz recalled, the proposal to abolish
ballistic missiles 'just sort of faded. She was the exclamation point, after
which there was nothing much.'[128]

In later years, Mrs Thatcher came to have a kinder view of what Reagan had achieved at Reykjavik. In her memoirs, she wrote that 'President Reagan's refusal to trade away SDI for the apparent near fulfilment of his dream of a nuclear-free world was crucial to the victory over communism. He called the Soviets' bluff.'[129] Many Reagan supporters took the view that Reagan had elicited concessions from Gorbachev which could never be taken back. By sticking to SDI, he had emerged stronger, Gorbachev weaker. In principle, Mrs Thatcher accepted this argument, but her most powerful memory of Reykjavik was of her fear of what might have happened. 'I don't think she ever came to see it as a success,' said Charles Powell.[130] 'I think the lesson of Reykjavik was that Reagan wasn't really reliable in international affairs,' said Bernard Ingham. 'He had to be kept on a strict rein. I suppose Reykjavik is the classic example where she found reason to worry about his understanding of life.'[131] But the aftermath of Reykjavik at Camp David also confirmed her sense of her own ability to influence events favourably, and to make good use of her real friendship with Ronald Reagan. Her staunch personal support over Iran–Contra – the reassuring sense she gave him that she would be with him in difficulty – helped keep that friendship strong. Once the Reykjavik difficulty had been overcome, the rest of Reagan's term would, by comparison, be plain-sailing for her.

18

To Moscow

'The light is coming from the West'

Fresh from her success at Camp David with President Reagan, Mrs Thatcher turned her attention again to Mikhail Gorbachev. Due to visit the Soviet Union in a matter of months, she was eager to keep in close touch with the Soviet leader. She felt she had persuaded Reagan to move away from the more radical approach espoused at Reykjavik and wanted to ensure that his interlocutor at the summit understood this. In correspondence, which was by now fairly frequent, Gorbachev had suggested that 'some European leaders seemed to be frightened by the prospect of a Soviet–American understanding.' Mrs Thatcher now dismissed this claim outright. 'The doubts we had were about the wisdom of trying to achieve an all-embracing arms control agreement in one leap, as the Soviet Union proposed at Reykjavik,' she explained. 'Events convince me that a progressive approach based on smaller, more attainable steps has a better chance. I hope very much that you will revert to that.'[1] She proposed concentrating on the areas she and Reagan had agreed at Camp David.

On 15 December 1986, Bryan Cartledge became the first British ambassador to be received alone by a Soviet general secretary since 1963. He came bearing Mrs Thatcher's letter, but before he read it out, he had to listen to what he reported as 'strong and at times angry criticism from Gorbachev of British positions post-Reykjavik'.[2] Gorbachev said he had a high regard for the Prime Minister as an 'interesting interlocutor', and he saw her forthcoming visit as timely – 'He wanted . . . to find out whether she looked to the future with a rifle in her hand or, as he believed, ready to reach out with a handshake.' The European reaction to Reykjavik, he complained, showed that 'As soon as a real possibility of eliminating nuclear weapons had appeared, there was a "panic" in London and Paris. British hostility to "socialism" was such that we could not accept Soviet ideas even when they were in our interest. The world was changing. The British Conservatives, however, were not.' Their attitude had 'the damp stagnant smell of the prehistoric cave'.

Cartledge then read out Mrs Thatcher's letter, and expounded it, emphasizing the importance of the step-by-step approach. This provoked displeasure: 'With considerable heat, Gorbachev attacked the UK for trying to dictate to the world, as she had done under Palmerston.'[3] He said that 'Mrs Thatcher had given him and President Reagan an "oral whipping" for getting carried away, "like small boys", in Reykjavik.' She boasted of her 'great achievement' at Camp David, but its effect was negative, producing impasse in Geneva: 'her great potential influence should be used to better effect than to read a sermon to the Soviet Union.' But despite what he called 'the occasionally harsh tone', Cartledge concluded that 'It was not a stilted meeting, and he [Gorbachev] was not unfriendly.' The dates for her visit to the Soviet Union (28 March–1 April 1987) were finally agreed. Gorbachev asked Cartledge to convey his 'warm personal greetings' to Mrs Thatcher.

Mrs Thatcher was pleased, as well she might be, by this flattering interpretation of her power, and by Gorbachev's correct, if critical, reading of her role. Charles Powell conveyed her congratulations to Cartledge for the way he had conducted the meeting. 'The Prime Minister', Powell wrote, 'has read [Cartledge's telegram] with great interest (and some merriment).'[4]

There was nothing in Gorbachev's combative style which irritated Mrs Thatcher, particularly as he was so declaredly eager to meet and talk. His attitude of stout argument combined with a keen interest in his opponent reflected hers. She felt a great hostility to the Soviet Union but also a growing curiosity about how it might change for the better. In the previous month, she had received the Russian dissident and leader of the Helsinki Monitoring Group in Moscow, Yuri Orlov. He counselled her against supporting the East–West 'human rights conference' which the Soviets wanted to hold in Moscow. She agreed and told him that people knew too little of the cruelty of the Soviet prison system and 'could easily be misled by the smooth, smart Gorbachevs' into thinking that 'the Soviet Union itself had changed'. She was always anxious that people should see the question in the round, rather than just as a matter of arms control: 'The genius of the Helsinki Accords was that they gave the West a locus for asking about human rights in the Soviet Union.'[5] Orlov encapsulated a point which was important to her thinking: the great Soviet 'fallacy' was that 'disarmament and peace were the same thing'.

Mrs Thatcher was interested both in highlighting Soviet oppression and in engagement which might improve matters. In December, Gorbachev at last relented and made a personal telephone call to Andrei Sakharov, the dissident and eminent scientist, allowing him to return to Moscow from his internal, KGB-supervised exile in Gorky. Mrs Thatcher, who had supported Sakharov publicly ever since his protests in the mid-1970s, sent him and his wife a Christmas card. Sakharov replied: 'We are deeply grateful for your many years of concern for our family. Happy New Year! With hope.'[6] She insisted on being allowed to see Sakharov as part of her Moscow trip in the spring.

In preparing for her Moscow visit, Mrs Thatcher was anxious to learn more about what was actually happening inside the Soviet Union, and to understand Gorbachev's two increasingly famous concepts of *glasnost* (openness) and *perestroika* (restructuring). 'I don't think I've ever prepared in so much detail and thought so carefully of what we wanted to do,' she said in an interview with her daughter Carol some time afterwards.[7] As she had done before when she wanted to think hard about the Soviet Union, she organized a seminar at Chequers ('No journalists,' she scribbled. 'They will use the fact of the seminar for their own purposes').[8] As usual, she did her utmost to keep the numbers down, excluding all but the most indispensable officials,* but including some outside experts. She even kept out the Cabinet Secretary, Robert Armstrong, and, despite Armstrong's protests, his deputy, the Soviet expert Christopher Mallaby.† Before the seminar was held on 27 February, Charles Powell wrote to her to focus on the purpose of the enterprise: 'You need to reach a judgment on how far Gorbachev really intends to change the Soviet Union and what the prospects of doing so successfully are. A great deal depends on that judgment, including how you handle your talks with him and how we present your visit.'[9] Powell also wanted her to consider whether Gorbachev would see her chiefly in her own right, or as 'guide and mentor' to Reagan. And it was not just a matter of Gorbachev alone – 'What message should you try to convey to the Soviet people, e.g. through television?'

As it turned out, the seminar – and all her wide accompanying reading – provided a lot of information, but did not make her judgment much easier to form. The experts, who included veterans of her 1983 seminar such as Ronald Amann, Archie Brown and Christopher Donnelly, were joined by Robert Conquest, Sir Michael Howard, Hugh Thomas and Seweryn Bialer, from Columbia University. Bialer answered Mrs Thatcher's demand that at least one American expert be present. Charles Powell summed up

---

* Those making the final cut were Charles Powell and Percy Cradock (Mrs Thatcher's office), Bryan Cartledge and David Ratford (Foreign Office) and Martin Nicholson (Cabinet Office).
† Christopher Mallaby (1936–), educated Eton and King's College, Cambridge; Head of Arms Control, Soviet and Eastern European Planning Departments, FCO, 1977–82; Deputy Secretary to the Cabinet, 1985–8; Ambassador to West Germany, 1988–92; to France, 1993–6; knighted, 1988.

their prolonged discussion in a way which, he conceded, 'may err slightly on the side of conveying too negative a view of what is happening in the Soviet Union'. He divided the experts into two camps – the 'enthusiasts', who tended to be more expert on the USSR, and the 'sceptics' who were 'principally non-specialists'.[10]

The enthusiasts said that Gorbachev was so 'shocked' by the poor performance of the Soviet economy that he had 'a strong sense of urgency'. A big change was in the air, and there were 'signs of greater pragmatism' about ideology and how to handle human rights cases. The sceptics, however, felt they 'had seen it all before', and compared it to the abortive reforms made, under Tsar Nicholas II, by Stolypin. The sceptics saw Gorbachev as 'a transient figure'. The conclusions drawn, noted Powell's record, were that 'fundamental change was not on his agenda' and 'The Soviet Union might at best evolve in 20 years' time into something resembling Yugoslavia today.'* As for the implications of what was happening for the West, the prospects seemed confusing. It was 'by no means self-evident' that it would be to the West's advantage if Gorbachev were to succeed in his economic reforms, but it would not be 'very practicable, and probably not desirable' to try to subject the Soviet economy to unbearable strain.[11] One person whose view was not sought was poor Geoffrey Howe. When he made as if to speak, Mrs Thatcher forestalled him: 'Don't worry, Geoffrey. We know exactly what you're going to say.'[12] Looking back on the whole session years later, Archie Brown concluded that many of the expectations aired proved erroneous: 'They won't get out of Afghanistan, there'll be no change in ideology, they won't allow any shred of independence to Eastern Europe. I would say that the judgments that came out of that seminar on the whole are less perspicacious than those that came out in 1983.'[13] As for Mrs Thatcher herself, she formed no clear conclusion from the seminar about Gorbachev's ultimate destination. By nature, she was in the sceptic camp, but she also hoped the enthusiasts might be right.† The questions she was asking could be answered only by her visit.

Mrs Thatcher also consulted Oleg Gordievsky. Their first meeting, at Chequers the previous May, had suffered from a certain absurdity. As

* Powell's record suggests that these conclusions 'seemed to command broad assent', but they clearly tilted towards the views of the sceptical majority. The divisions between the two camps remained too great to permit the emergence of a consensus.
† Archie Brown, whose comments on the next generation of Soviet leaders had attracted Mrs Thatcher's attention during the 1983 Chequers seminar, proved too much of an 'enthusiast' for her taste on this occasion. 'I'm not asking him again,' she told Robert Conquest afterwards. (Interview with Robert Conquest.)

Charles Powell had reported, 'The Prime Minister, who is very security-conscious, referred to Mr Gordievsky as Mr Collins throughout. If this confused anyone who was not supposed to be listening as much as it confused the guests, it was a very successful tactic.'[14] 'It was stupid,' recalled Gordievsky, 'because I was not Mr Collins and never had been!'[15] Mrs Thatcher had indulged her tendency to talk: 'The session lasted altogether some three and a half hours. The Prime Minister spent a considerable part of this in talking about life in general and Chequers in particular, in order to relax Mr Gordievsky/Collins ... The discussion of Soviet affairs is not easy to record since, rather than address questions to Mr Gordievsky, the Prime Minister tested out her views and assumptions about the Soviet Union on him.'[16] As Gordievsky recalled: 'I'm sorry to say it but she talked and talked and talked ... I could see it was her personal trait.'[17] He had been irritated by her loquacity, but also impressed by what she said: 'She knew of Communism only very basic things, but she had the same instinctive understanding of Communism as Reagan, but better than Reagan because more nuanced.' She had 'no historical understanding, but excellent moral understanding'. Mrs Thatcher had told Gordievsky that 'she did not expect to see any change in the nature of the Soviet Union in her time. But she was interested to know how that system could be influenced.'[18]

Now, the following March, with the deputy head of SIS, Colin McColl, to 'hold his hand',[19] Gordievsky had a more productive meeting with Mrs Thatcher, this time at No. 10. With everything focused on her meeting in Moscow at the end of the month, Mrs Thatcher was 'on the ball'.[20] Gordievsky recalled: 'She said, "I need material on what to say at the press conference and other interviews" ... I said, "Prime Minister, you couldn't have found a better man than me for it. I am a specialist in propaganda." '[21] He singled out points which would hit home with the Russian public, for example: ' "About 70 per cent of the British population live in independent dwellings. For the Russian population this is an absolutely sensational figure. Because they live in communal flats, like insects." It was a very good discussion.' He told her to be 'as clear and pungent as possible' whenever she appeared on television: she should 'spell out with statistics the reality of western prosperity'.[22]

Gordievsky also told Mrs Thatcher that Gorbachev was not popular with his own people – 'people resented the restrictions on alcohol, and thought he made far too many speeches.' Gorbachev's likely reforms would not lead to democracy. As for economic reforms, in 1922, the New Economic Policy (in which Lenin reversed his earlier dirigisme) had worked because the skills of a free economy still existed, but 'Now there was no one who would know how to take advantage of even a modest move towards a market economy.' The Soviet Union did want good relations with the West, because it was desperate for money, but Gorbachev's 'long-term aim was to denuclearise and neutralise Western Europe'. The Prime Minister 'should not mince her words' in pointing out that the West 'must rely on nuclear weapons in the absence of conventional dominance'. She should raise human rights issues and not be shy of discussing Soviet adventurism in the Third World.

Mrs Thatcher wanted to know what Gorbachev would be expecting from her visit. On the one hand, Gordievsky told her, he sought 'a chance to build up his prestige' and would 'want to be seen to be on good terms with the longest-serving Western leader'. On the other, 'he would fear that the Prime Minister's strong line on arms control might derail progress towards another US/Soviet Summit which he very much wanted.'[23] The combined effect, especially when set against the weakness of Reagan's position at home because of the Iran–Contra scandal, was to put Mrs Thatcher in a pivotal position.

The Prime Minister paid less respectful attention to the advice of her own Foreign Secretary. She ignored Geoffrey Howe's suggestions about trying to persuade the Russians and Americans to sink their differences over SDI, and she was much irritated by the draft of an article by Howe intended for the Soviet magazine *New Times*. As well as disliking the conciliatory, Foreign Office tone of the draft (she demanded '<u>Massive</u> deletions'), she objected to its *lèse-majesté*. 'Mrs Thatcher and I see this visit as an important opportunity,' Howe had written. Mrs Thatcher encircled the phrase 'Mrs Thatcher and I', and wrote '<u>No</u> no <u>no</u>'.[24] She was also unimpressed by the two silver-handled hairbrushes that the Foreign Office had selected as her official gift for Gorbachev. 'But he's completely bald,' she protested.[25]*

Knowing that a general election approached, the Labour Party was anxious to head off any potential success for Mrs Thatcher. On 19 March, the Shadow Foreign Secretary, Denis Healey, informed the Foreign Office that he was flying to Moscow immediately. The following day, however, Cartledge reported from Moscow that the Communist Party of the Soviet Union and the Ministry of Foreign Affairs were not interested in seeing Healey: 'We subsequently learned . . . that Mr Healey had found it "inconvenient" to travel to Moscow at this time. This was clearly a politically motivated self-invitation which misfired. The Russians were evidently not prepared to play ball.'[26] Beside this news, Mrs Thatcher happily wrote '!!'. Although the Soviets had more natural sympathy and closer contacts with

---

* The hairbrushes seem, nevertheless, to have been presented.

the Labour Party, they calculated that Mrs Thatcher was the more likely winner of the coming election, the one worth dealing with. Neil Kinnock made his own effort to take some of the shine off Mrs Thatcher's time in Moscow by planning a concurrent visit to Washington, DC. The White House, however, had no intention of doing anything to help Kinnock and the visit backfired spectacularly (see Chapter 20).

In Mrs Thatcher's calculations about her Moscow visit, of course, the imminence of the general election bulked large. In planning the visit, the Foreign Office had expressed concerns over the timing, fearing that the trip 'might get washed away by the election'.[27] Mrs Thatcher, however, took a very different view. The timing of the election 'dictated' the date for the visit, recalled Charles Powell. She was looking for a *coup de théâtre*.[28] Mrs Thatcher wanted to be successful not only in content, but in projecting the right visual impressions. Even more care than usual was taken about what she should wear. 'She was very excited about her Russian clothes,' recalled Amanda Ponsonby (formerly Colvin), who helped her pack them.[29] Crawfie, her personal assistant, who had noticed that Mrs Thatcher was much taken with Gorbachev's 'wonderful sparkly eyes', told her, 'If you're going to Moscow, I think we'd better buy you some new clothes. Mrs Gorbachev always wears Yves Saint Laurent so you'd better look nice.'[30] Crawfie saw a black coat in the window of Aquascutum, which she got on approval. She also found a camel-hair coat with a sable collar and borrowed a sable hat from a friend. Mrs Thatcher intended to make a splash. Everyone was conscious of how much the visit mattered. Denis, who did not accompany her, said 'Good luck, love' with untypical anxiety: 'We were all on edge.'[31]

In her final preparations, Mrs Thatcher was careful to communicate fully with her allies. On 23 March she saw, separately, both François Mitterrand and Helmut Kohl. The French President fell into the 'enthusiast' camp, though remaining staunch, from her point of view, that 'we must resist the attempt to denuclearise Europe'.[32] 'He believes Mr G prepared to go a very long way to changing the system,' Mrs Thatcher's own handwritten notes recorded, '– "when you change the form, you are on the way to changing the substance." '[33] The German Chancellor, on the other hand, qualified as a 'sceptic'. Kohl was worried by the effect of Soviet propaganda on his country, and he did not like what was happening in the Soviet Union – Gorbachev 'wants modern Communist system. Not a democratic system. More anti-religious than ever before.'[34]*

---

* While Mrs Thatcher was the first Western leader to forge a relationship with Gorbachev, Kohl was one of the last. In October 1986, the German leader had caused much offence in

Two days later, Mrs Thatcher wrote to Reagan, laying out in full her approach to her visit, which sometimes echoed Gordievsky's thoughts. 'I want first to make my own assessment of how serious Gorbachev is about internal political and economic restructuring: and what impact this will have on Soviet foreign policy . . . I am sceptical whether he is really able to take the necessary steps, or fully understands what is needed. People who have only lived under communism find it difficult to comprehend the workings of a free market.'[35] She would 'make clear that the West does not want to make change in the Soviet Union more difficult. Far from it: it is only when they start to treat their own people decently and implement the freedoms confirmed in the Helsinki Final Act that we shall be able to develop the trust and confidence which are necessary . . . we shall want to see actual results.'

As for arms control, on which, she predicted, they would spend the most time, she avoided the word 'Reykjavik'. 'My aim will be to get Gorbachev to accept in practice, if not formally, the priorities which you and I identified at Camp David last November.'[36] At the forefront of these proposals was a deal on INF. The prospects now looked better because, on 28 February, Gorbachev had announced, contrary to his Reykjavik all-or-nothing approach, that the Soviet Union would consider a stand-alone deal. So the 'zero option' was back on the table. She would accept the removal of intermediate missiles, so long as this was not a step, as Reagan was all too prone to see it, to denuclearizing Europe entirely: 'I shall remind him [Gorbachev] that although democratic countries are slow to do battle, he should not doubt our determination to retain strong defences based on nuclear deterrence. Nor should he be under any illusion that he can separate Europe from the United States.'[37] She also stood behind the Camp David position on SDI which they had agreed in 1984, but warned Reagan that she would raise with Gorbachev the possibility of giving him 'some assurance' about 'the shape, scope and timescale of programmes'. This was something she had raised with Reagan even before Reykjavik, but the President had shown little enthusiasm. In fact, Reagan had sought to discourage her from broaching the topic, but Mrs Thatcher brushed his concerns aside. She pledged not to imply that Reagan had endorsed her ideas, but she refused to take them off the table. She arrived in Moscow late on Saturday 28 March, and descended from the plane in her black coat and fur hat,

---

Moscow by drawing parallels between Gorbachev and the Nazi propagandist Joseph Goebbels. Kohl was not granted a meeting with the Soviet leader until the autumn of 1988 (see Archie Brown, *The Myth of the Strong Leader*, Bodley Head, 2014, pp. 136–7).

carrying a black crocodile skin handbag. Presented with a bunch of roses, as Crawfie recalled, 'she looked stunning.'[38]

A unique aspect of the Moscow visit was that Mrs Thatcher was permitted to go where she had asked, to meet Christians, dissidents and ordinary Soviet citizens, and to speak at length on Soviet television. Gorbachev encouraged this, to reinforce the impression that he believed in openness, and because he thought Mrs Thatcher's endorsement of his reforms would be valuable to him at home.* Public appearances alternated with talks, mainly with Gorbachev himself. But in Charles Powell's view, 'The most memorable aspect was the reaction of the Russian people. She was the first leader to go everywhere and insist on the right of the people to turn out to see her. There were huge crowds everywhere . . . She symbolized the opposition to communism.'[39] Amanda Ponsonby, who accompanied Mrs Thatcher as her personal secretary, was struck by how public excitement built up. As the party drove in from the airport, they saw no one on the streets, but the next day, when Mrs Thatcher visited the Orthodox monastery at Zagorsk, wearing smart beige boots and the camel coat with sable collar, people started to gather. At the service in the monastery church, Mrs Thatcher was asked to light a candle. Being a good Methodist, she had no experience of the liturgical role of candles and did not realize that lighting a candle is an occasion for placing it before the shrine and saying a prayer. She held it reverently but confusedly until told what to do. Mrs Thatcher noticed, in discussion afterwards, that at least some of her priestly interlocutors were supporters of the regime – the KGB had thoroughly penetrated what remained of the Orthodox hierarchy. 'Discarding my own prepared text, I answered [a speech by a patriarch against nuclear weapons] by stressing instead the need to release prisoners of conscience.'[40]

That afternoon, when Mrs Thatcher went to a supermarket and a show flat in Moscow, a woman standing outside another flat was desperate to meet her, and Ponsonby steered the Prime Minister through her door.† Friendly crowds gathered outside and 'She started to be mobbed.'[41] Mrs Thatcher recalled, 'I was determined to see some real live people as it were . . . The KGB would push them back and I would say "Stop it! Stop

---

* Scholars who were cynical about Gorbachev's reforms liked to point out that *glasnost* really meant not 'openness' but 'publicity'.

† Mrs Thatcher remembered that the supermarket was 'the most sparse for goods which I had ever seen in my life, there were one or two bits of bacon, very fat but not much, and there was some fish and some tinned fish and there was a little bit of chocolate. I had taken quite a lot of chocolate with me and I left some for the children.' (Thatcher Memoirs Materials, CAC: THCR 4/3.)

pushing them back!" '[42] By the last day of the visit, which ended in Tbilisi, Georgia, people stood 'seven-deep' on the pavements to see her pass. 'There was a feeling that she was a tremendous breath of fresh air. No one knew quite how to handle it, but everyone was very receptive,' Ponsonby remembered. 'She adores attention. She played to that.'

Mrs Thatcher met the Gorbachevs formally shortly after arriving in Moscow. On her second night, she went with them to watch *Swan Lake* at the Bolshoi Theatre. She wore a dress which Amanda Ponsonby's notes on her programme described as 'Eleanor black lace evening', Eleanor being the Christian name of Lady Glover, who had lent it to her.[43] At supper in the interval, over Georgian wine, Gorbachev told Mrs Thatcher that '*perestroika* though not easy of attainment was more feasible than the elimination of the Russians' love of (i.e. excessive) drink – indeed he deemed that impossible.'[44] The conversation so engrossed them that they were late returning, with the result that, as Mrs Thatcher's interpreter Richard Pollock reported, the 'audience had apparently been literally in the dark for five minutes'.[45]

On Monday Mrs Thatcher began her full talks with Gorbachev at the Kremlin, with Geoffrey Howe conspicuously absent. Mrs Thatcher, who by this stage preferred to travel without her Foreign Secretary whenever possible, had tried to prevent Howe from coming to Moscow at all. After strong protests from the Foreign Office she relented, but, as Tony Bishop, the Foreign Office veteran who had interpreted for Mrs Thatcher during her 1984 meeting with Gorbachev recalled, 'Mrs Thatcher characteristically had the final word by ensuring that whenever she was meeting Gorbachev during that trip, Howe would be meeting his opposite number Shevardnadze or others in a different building.'[46] As had been the case at Chequers, her conversations with Gorbachev were long, gruelling, sometimes rude, but successful. As Charles Powell, the only British official apart from the interpreter to be present for all seven hours, noted in the thirty-page report he drafted immediately afterwards: 'The talks were frank with no quarter asked or given. The Duke of Wellington would have recognised it as hard pounding. The mood varied considerably throughout, with some thunderstorms and occasional squalls but also some bright periods.'[47] They overran dramatically, with the consequence that Mrs Thatcher did not have time to return to the Embassy to change before the banquet that evening at the Kremlin. She thus decided to forsake her normal regard for formality and turn up 'in the short wool dress I had been wearing all day'.[48]*

---

* Amanda Ponsonby recalled hurrying round with a change of shoes and a hairbrush to get her ready (Interview with Amanda Ponsonby).

The discussions did not begin easily. 'Gorbachev at the start seemed keyed up,' noted Pollock, 'sitting back somewhat tensely, hands clasped across his midriff.'[49] Gorbachev's aide, Anatoly Chernyaev, also recorded the scene:

> She was, as always, extremely attractive,* earnest but determined, stubborn, sometimes didactic. He was ironic, sarcastic, at times even abrupt. Gorbachev's belief in the correctness of his cause translated into self-confidence in personal contacts . . . even with women. And Thatcher, for all her practical intelligence and astonishing competence, always showed a feminine side as well. She 'tenderly' looked over the men sitting in front of her as if also making sure about the impression she made as a woman.[50]

To Mrs Thatcher's surprise, Gorbachev began by raising the speech she had given to her party's Central Council in Torquay nine days earlier, in which she had promised 'realism and strength' against oppressive Soviet behaviour, as opposed to the 'illusion or surrender'[51] offered by Neil Kinnock, and attacked 'the slaughter in Afghanistan'. Gorbachev protested that he and his colleagues 'were feeling the breeze from the 1940s and 1950s'.[52] ' "Once again, communism and the Soviet Union were presented as 'evil forces'," he said. "It was the same old talk about strengthening the West's power position. We were very surprised by this. To tell you the truth, we even wondered if the prime minister would cancel her visit." "I can't believe this," she retorted. "You couldn't have thought that!" '[53]

Rather than backing off, though, Mrs Thatcher tried to explain why the West feared the Soviet Union. What she could have said in her Torquay speech, but didn't, she went on, was that there was 'no evidence' that the Soviets had 'given up the Brezhnev Doctrine'.[54]† They were subverting Southern Yemen, Ethiopia, Mozambique, Angola, Nicaragua, backing Vietnam to conquer Cambodia and occupying Afghanistan: 'We naturally drew the conclusion that the goal of the worldwide spread of Communism was still being pursued.'[55] She wanted to know whether his internal reforms would lead to changes in these external policies. Gorbachev's

---

* Chernyaev, who had a reputation as a ladies' man, encouraged Gorbachev to build a close relationship with Mrs Thatcher. He himself not only admired Mrs Thatcher but, according to his private diary, harboured sexual fantasies about her. (Diary of Anatoly Chernyaev, 16 September 1989, National Security Archive.)

† In explicitly referring to the Brezhnev Doctrine, she was taking up a suggestion of Robert Conquest ('A Note on Our Relations with Moscow: March 1987', CAC: THCR 1/10/113). This doctrine held that efforts to introduce capitalism into socialist countries were a problem for the entire socialist bloc, not merely for the country concerned. Such reforms would be resisted, if necessary through force.

immediate answer was that Communist world domination was 'only an extrapolation of Soviet theory . . . It was no more than a scientific concept,'[56] but her mention of the Brezhnev Doctrine stuck in his mind. For the moment, he hit back with an attack on Western meddling in the affairs of other countries: 'It might be more to the point to talk of Britain's support for the racist regime in South Africa.' 'Apartheid cannot last. It must go,' Mrs Thatcher responded, while insisting that sanctions against South Africa 'only aid mass starvation'.

The Soviets did not want to undermine the West's commercial needs, said Gorbachev, but they wanted the West 'to accept that socialism was a reality. It was no good seeing the October Revolution as an aberration and the Soviet Union as an error of history.' Each must respect the other's system. He would not be able to make a Communist out of Mrs Thatcher, he told her: she should not expect to make a capitalist out of him. 'The Prime Minister said that she was just trying to find out how much of a communist Mr Gorbachev really was.'[57] Mrs Thatcher did not let go her attack on Soviet adventurism. Once Communism was established in a country, she stated, 'all further choice ceased.' But look at bourgeois democracy, said Gorbachev: it 'had developed a mechanism which operated as exquisitely as ballet for fooling people about who really controlled the levers of power'. Mrs Thatcher and the Conservative Party, he complained, were 'too closely linked to the interests of the haves'. Mrs Thatcher countered that 'the capitalist system had shown that it could distribute far greater benefits to ordinary every day people than socialism could'.[58] She told Gorbachev, she recalled in her memoirs, that 'what I was trying to do was to create a society of "haves", not a class of them.'[59]

The argument was fierce, and, given the stubbornness of both the participants, circular. 'She is an audacious woman,' Gorbachev later reported to the Politburo; 'she acted as if she were in her own Parliament. You couldn't see this in any theater.'[60] Charles Powell recalled Gorbachev being 'very brutal' about the Conservative Party and against the British role in Northern Ireland. Sometimes the tension was so great that 'I thought we'd be thrown out at once.'[61] But then it was Mrs Thatcher who, according to Gorbachev, 'struck a more conciliatory note. Suddenly changing the course of the conversation, she said: "We follow your activity with great interest and we fully appreciate your attempts to improve the life of your people. I acknowledge your right to have your own system and security, just as we have the right to ours, and we suggest taking this as a basis for our debate." '[62] The contemporary record shows that she professed herself 'appalled' by some of the things Gorbachev had said, but that it had been

'helpful to clear the air'.[63] Yes, said Gorbachev, it had stirred up 'the stagnant pond'. And so the talk turned readily to arms control.

Once again, Gorbachev was fierce. Relaying the conversation to President Reagan two days later, Mrs Thatcher wrote, 'I endured a long lament
about how the West responded to Soviet initiatives by creating new link-
ages and conditions.'[64] She glossed over the fact that the lament was
directed more at her personally than at the West in general. The Soviet
leader was angry with her for her efforts, which had apparently succeeded
at Camp David, to move Reagan away from talk of eliminating nuclear
weapons. In effect, she was arguing against the desires of both the Soviet
and the American leaders. As ever, she insisted to Gorbachev that ridding
the world of nuclear weapons was unrealistic: what was true was that
there were far too many of them.

Gorbachev challenged her: 'You, Madam Thatcher, with your stance on
nuclear weapons, hamper the negotiations and hinder efforts to start a
process of genuine disarmament . . . When you solemnly declare that nuclear
weapons are beneficial, it's clear that you are an ardent supporter of them
who is prepared to accept the risk of war.'[65] This stung Mrs Thatcher. 'You
had to see what those words did to her,' wrote Chernyaev.

> She got very tense, blushed, and her expression hardened. She reached out
> and, touching Gorbachev's sleeve, began to talk without letting him get in
> a word. She poured forth the reasons why she considered it impossible to
> give up nuclear weapons: they had been ensuring peace in Europe for forty
> years . . . And how could he suspect her of such ghastly intentions?
>
> She became so excited that the conversation got completely out of hand.
> They started to interrupt each other, repeat themselves, assure each other
> of their best intentions. And compliments, compliments for Gorbachev and
> his new policies, which she hoped would be successful.[66]

Matters calmed down enough, however, for Mrs Thatcher to be able
to explain her more specific anxieties and put forward some of her specific
ideas. The Soviet leader must understand, she said, that Europe was
uniquely vulnerable to conventional war. She supported a 50 per cent
reduction in the strategic nuclear weapons of the two superpowers. She
also favoured an INF agreement. While Gorbachev spoke of the need to
stop the arms race and reduce the levels of nuclear weapons, she was looking for 'something deeper: a guarantee of the preservation of peace. She
would prefer peace based on a few nuclear weapons to the danger of war
with no nuclear weapons.'[67] As Powell recorded it, 'Mr Gorbachev said
sarcastically that surely he and the Prime Minister could agree to destroy
one nuclear weapon each.' Mrs Thatcher replied that 'Mr Gorbachev was

not taking the matter sufficiently seriously.' She urged him to hurry up and take advantage of the only one and a half years before President Reagan left office to get an agreement.

The meeting broke for lunch, which Mrs Thatcher (late again) had with Soviet dissidents led by Andrei Sakharov. They told her that they supported Gorbachev's reforms, and she 'told them firmly that it was not enough to support him now. They should continue to support him when the going got rough. The costs of reform would be evident long before the benefits came through.'[68] But she also listened, noting down Sakharov's remarks, one of which she relayed to Reagan in her conclusions about her visit: 'We have an interest in supporting his reform policies, even if their results are modest. As Sakharov has said, an open society is safer for its neighbours. We should push Gorbachev to recognise that.'[69]

After lunch, Mrs Thatcher returned to the Kremlin for her next session with Gorbachev, which took place in what Powell described as 'a jovial mood'[70] and began with his internal reforms. Even more loquacious than she, he inflicted a sixty-five-minute introduction on his visitor, explaining that *perestroika* had barely begun. He spoke with what Mrs Thatcher, writing to Reagan, called 'almost messianic fervour'[71] about his plans. Gorbachev said he wanted businesses to be free to earn foreign currency, and that he sought 'democratization'.[72] Individual enterprises would acquire their own rights, he said, taking power away from the Central State Planning Commission, and there would be much more scientific development. There was 'a boom in informations [sic] and computer technology. Soviet scientists had already constructed a computer capable of storing one billion bytes of information and by the end of the current five-year plan the figure would be 10 billion.* They had also solved the problem of personal computers and were now developing micro-processors for factories.'[73] He admitted to Mrs Thatcher that the Soviet Union 'lagged behind in the process of democracy', but urged that 'The conclusions which the Prime Minister should draw from the restructuring were that the West should forget any notion of putting the Soviet Union on the ash-heap of history and should abandon its evil-empire rhetoric.'[74]† Unlike in the earlier discussion, Mrs Thatcher did not pick an argument. She asked Gorbachev a polite question about the problems of applying science to industry ('Mr Gorbachev said that it had been a weak point'), but did little

---

* By the early twenty-first century, 1 billion bytes was roughly a fifth of the capacity of a typical DVD.

† President Reagan had first branded the Soviet Union an 'evil empire' in his speech to the National Association of Evangelicals in March 1983 (see Volume I, p. 565).

to interrupt his flow or question what he said. It was as if, accepting the importance of his direction of travel, she did not want to be too critical of the almost comical inadequacy of what had so far happened. She simply wanted to find out more about what was happening. Gorbachev, indeed, pre-empted potential criticism by admitting that 'the roots of the problem had scarcely been touched': she should 'come back in two or three years' time to look at progress'.[75]

They also discussed SDI. Despite Reagan's efforts to discourage her from supporting any sort of constraint, Mrs Thatcher told Gorbachev that 'she quite understood the Soviet Union's wish for predictability in this area.'[76] Proposed activities on both sides could be set out, and linked with an undertaking not to deploy SDI for a fixed period. This would allow the Soviet Union to 'decouple' the Strategic Arms Reduction Talks (the successor to the SALT talks) from questions of SDI constraints. Gorbachev commented carefully that this was 'an interesting, practical proposal'.[77]

The discussion was less combative than in the morning.* Mrs Thatcher (who once again raised the matter of Oleg Gordievsky's family, this time in the margins of the discussion with only the interpreter present) made a series of strong points about human rights, including better treatment of Jews and observing the Helsinki agreements. But she added, as she did so, that she was 'far more optimistic about the Soviet Union than she had ever been'.[78] Gorbachev, she reported to Reagan, 'objected strongly to my raising human rights, but nevertheless gave some quite useful assurances about the treatment of individual cases'.[79]

In her speech at the official banquet that evening, Mrs Thatcher did not pull her punches on human rights or the dangers of a nuclear-free world, but sought to strike a constructive tone. She ended with praise for Gorbachev's reform effort: 'you have certainly embarked upon a great endeavour and we most earnestly wish you and your people well.'[80]† This notwithstanding, the discussion over dinner became, in Pollock's view, 'more contentious' once again. Mrs Gorbachev who, Mrs Thatcher told Reagan, played a notably 'prominent role'[81] throughout her visit 'seemed keen . . . to resuscitate the "arms control" themes which had had a very

---

* The exception was a brief passage of arms in which Gorbachev criticized Mrs Thatcher over the Falklands and she replied that 'that was not a very wise remark' (Powell to Galsworthy, 30 March 1987, Prime Minister's Papers, Soviet Union, Prime Minister's Visit to the Soviet Union, Part 1 (document consulted in the Cabinet Office)).

† An earlier draft of the speech, addressing Mrs Thatcher's first meeting with Gorbachev in 1984, included the line: 'we were subsequently very pleased with ourselves for having spotted a winner.' While this accurately reflected Mrs Thatcher's feelings, the sentence was cut out of fear that it would appear 'patronising'. (Parker to Powell, 20 March 1987, CAC: THCR 5/1/5/549.)

thorough ventilation earlier in the day'.[82] Her husband concluded the evening by saying that 'he was beginning to think it would be easier to talk to the Americans than to the Prime Minister.' It was 'a somewhat sour tone on which to end the meal'. Pollock speculated that the Russians had 'a "negative" lobby which they have to keep happy at the moment – not least when talking "on the record"'. He may have been right, but Gorbachev's complaint reflected one side of the double-edged feelings he had about Mrs Thatcher – that she was his inveterate ideological opponent. The other side – which he felt, perhaps, even more strongly – was that she was an honest, intelligent and powerful leader with whom agreement could be reached. Three months later, Gorbachev discussed Mrs Thatcher with the Zimbabwean leader, Robert Mugabe, who was, of course, no friend to her. Gorbachev remarked on how fierce was her attachment to nuclear weapons and how she had 'an anti-Soviet mind-set . . . She is the vanguard of imperialist policies.'[83] 'She is a difficult woman,' Mugabe replied. But Gorbachev qualified his own thought: 'On the other hand . . . she is straightforward. She says what she thinks. She does not mince her words. She has a dislike for diplomatic fog.'[84]

The next morning, Mrs Thatcher had a rather *pro forma* meeting with the Prime Minister, Nikolai Ryzhkov. But the highlight of the day was her interview on Soviet television with three Soviet journalists. The Foreign Office had advised that her hosts were likely to adopt 'a pretty respectful posture' and that 'an interview with a visiting Prime Minister will probably not be regarded as the occasion for cut and thrust.'[85] While she carefully read and underlined the note, Mrs Thatcher, who always thrived on cut and thrust, did not take this to heart, readily challenging, interrupting and contradicting her stolid male interrogators. She explained to her audience how well the Soviet Union was stocked with nuclear weapons and put forward her argument in favour of the nuclear deterrent, and of the danger of conventional war. The Russians, she pointed out, had been invaded by Hitler and endured great suffering in the conventional age. She expounded her 'step-by-step' approach to nuclear disarmament, defended SDI and praised Gorbachev's reforms. The effect of the interview was sensational, not so much for any particular answer, but because the Soviet authorities allowed it to be broadcast that evening in its full, unedited form. Such a thing had never happened before. Tony Bishop monitored the broadcast and the reaction to it for the Foreign Office:

> From it the Soviet public learned for the first time so much about their own country, its armaments etc, that had hitherto remained concealed. Her

handling of the interviewers evoked widespread if sometimes rueful admiration . . . One Soviet trade unionist remarked, unattractively, to our Ambassador shortly afterwards: 'She squashed them like kittens' . . . And the Soviet public just loved it.[86]

'Yes, I took a risk,' Gorbachev said later, 'but it was my deliberate choice because I wanted her and everyone else to see that my policy of *Glasnost* was not a trick.'[87]

Percy Cradock passed on to Charles Powell one letter, in imperfect but expressive English, from 'a young Soviet intellectual', Alexei Yanshin, which he had written to a British fellow geologist. It captured the enormous personal impact of Mrs Thatcher on the Russian public. 'She acted extremely professional,' Yanshin wrote, 'very attractive and even sincerely . . . She was very rational and humanic. Now I often saw ladies dressed and hair-cutted a la Margaret Thatcher.' For two weeks afterwards, he said, crowds queued at the offices of the newspaper *Izvestia* to see the exhibition of photographs of Mrs Thatcher and Gorbachev: 'she change the whole attitude to UK – now . . . it's not considered that UK is a country with no face and only a political echo, mirror of USA. Now we suppose the UK is very interesting country, original.'[88] In Yanshin's view, Mrs Thatcher had outclassed her interviewers: 'When 3 huge, fat political commentators attacked her, they were . . . untactkful [sic], unprofessional, simply rude.' The interview had been the 'apopheosis [sic] of her visit'.

In the evening, Mrs Thatcher attended a small, informal dinner given by the Gorbachevs at the Soviet Foreign Ministry guesthouse, far more relaxed than that of the previous night. 'An effort had clearly been made', Charles Powell noted, 'to re-create the atmosphere at Chequers' large open fire.'[89] Only the Ryzhkovs, the two countries' ambassadors, Powell and the interpreters were present in addition. (Again, no Geoffrey Howe.) Mrs Gorbachev, Richard Pollock noted, was 'in very chirpy form',[90] arguing in a friendly way with her husband about what constituted the working class.[91] Ideas flowed freely as Gorbachev speculated on his plans for reform. 'Some of his ideas appear simplistic,' Mrs Thatcher later wrote to Reagan, but she was impressed by the way he was heading. At one point, Gorbachev raised the suggestion of 'paying people more and then charging them something for services like health and education',[92] a notion which even capitalist Britain tended to find heretical and dangerous. To hear such radical notions from the lips of a Soviet leader was indeed remarkable. The host, behaving in a manner for which colleagues at home often criticized Mrs Thatcher herself, was 'again dominating the conversation – surprising that he scarcely ever <u>invites</u> even his principal guest's views'.[93] Mrs Thatcher did not seem to object, however, and gave as good as she got. 'There can never have been a case where two heads of Government so radiated a kind of chemistry between them,' judged Cartledge. 'You could see sparks flying off.'[94] Charles Powell reported:

> As we sat down to dinner Mr Gorbachev pointed to a landscape on the wall depicting a farming scene with a clear sky in the background and observed that it reminded him of his talks with the Prime Minister, tempestuous but with great clarity. The Prime Minister pointed out that the light was coming from the West.[95]

Mrs Thatcher took leave of Gorbachev in the Kremlin the following morning. The occasion, wrote Pollock, was:

> very significant for Mrs Gorbachev's presence – and no one else's – with Gorbachev. Suggestive not only of their sincere personal commitment to the relationship . . . with the Prime Minister – but possibly too of Gorbachev's increasing confidence in his own position . . . There was no doubt whatever of the strength of friendship and respect those few words/minutes/facial expressions attested towards the Prime Minister and the United Kingdom.[96]

Nor was there any doubt in the minds of the participants on both sides that Mrs Thatcher's Moscow visit had been a great success. 'Remember how long we debated whether to invite her or not?' Gorbachev asked his Politburo colleagues. 'Now we can say we made the right choice.'[97] 'The visit', Cartledge wrote as it ended, 'has been the occasion for more candid and coherent exchanges on nearly all aspects of the East/West relationship than have, to my knowledge, ever taken place between a Soviet leader and the head of a Western government.'[98] In his report to Geoffrey Howe, Cartledge expanded on this idea:

> the visit was replete with paradox. On the major issues, no breakthroughs were expected or achieved: but the visit has nevertheless been accounted an outstanding succes [sic] by every objective observer. The areas of disagreement dwarfed those of agreement: but the warmth of the atmospherics, both personal and political, was striking. Despite – or perhaps, because of – these contradictions, I have no hesitation in describing the visit as historic. It established a new bench-mark for the quality of East–West dialogue.[99]

Mrs Thatcher also won plaudits from the press, across the political spectrum. In an April Fools' Day send-up, the *Daily Mirror*'s front page carried a mocked-up picture of Mrs Thatcher kissing Gorbachev marked

'Exclusive – Maggie Disarms Gorbachev'. The *Guardian*'s leader said that
Mrs Thatcher 'had acquitted the country pretty well in Moscow, not only
by what she said but by what she has listened to'. The *Sun* was more
direct: 'at home and abroad Margaret Thatcher is a lion.'[100]

It was of great significance that East–West dialogue now included discussion of Gorbachev's domestic reform agenda. Mrs Thatcher had arrived in
Moscow not quite sure what to make of *glasnost* and *perestroika*. During
her visit, she had not only heard about this reform effort from Gorbachev
first hand, but had also experienced some of the new openness for herself.
At this stage, she was less interested in the specifics of Gorbachev's reforms
than in getting a feel for what was under way. On this score she left Moscow
encouraged. She now believed that, while Gorbachev remained a committed
Communist, his effort at delivering reform was genuine and deserved support from the West. In her thank-you letter to him, she wrote: 'We both
enjoy frank speaking, and I am sure this is the best way to reach a better
understanding. I was pleased to be able to confirm to you personally our
welcome for your policies of open-ness, restructuring and democratisa-
tion.'[101] She had moved a fair way from the more cautious atmosphere of
the Chequers seminar, which had concluded that 'Public comments by
western governments on the reform process were unlikely to be of much
consequence one way or the other.' The importance of this was not lost on
Gorbachev. 'Her interest in what is happening in the Soviet Union is real,
and very strong . . .' he told the Politburo; 'probably unexpectedly to herself,
she said too many positive things about us. Something happened inside
her.' It was important, Gorbachev continued, 'that Thatcher practically
supported the policy of *perestroika*. The Americans are calling this her
biggest mistake.'[102] Mrs Thatcher's support for Gorbachev's reforms would
grow in the months and years that followed, even though, as Gorbachev
suggested, many in Washington questioned the wisdom of this course.

The visit was also, of course, very good for Mrs Thatcher politically.
'It showed her in a lead position, in a slightly glamorous position,' recalled
Charles Powell, '– the cold Russian winter with the fur collar and the fur
hat and tens of thousands of Russians turning out to cheer her in the street.
It really made it look as though her understanding of the changes in the
East/West relationship was a really significant factor in the world. She
was, as it were, leading the way.'[103] Here Gorbachev was complicit: 'it is
in our interest to raise the British role in international affairs,' he told his
colleagues, stressing that Mrs Thatcher's views could influence the Europeans and the Americans.[104] It was noted that Gorbachev had devoted an
unprecedented amount of time and trouble to looking after his visitor,
and that he had used her with the Russian people to advance his

reforms. Gorbachev believed that his insistence that her public comments be reported had 'disarmed her'.[105] However, his decision to allow her to be interviewed unedited also set a crucial precedent, making it possible for George Shultz, who visited two weeks later, to be given the same treatment. 'They played what I said on Afghanistan [on television],' Shultz recalled. 'That really showed things were changing.'[106]

Gorbachev had accepted more of what Mrs Thatcher said, particularly concerning the disconnect between his internal reforms and Moscow's unchanged, hardline foreign policy, than his combative style betrayed at the time. 'She emphasized trust,' he reported to the Politburo.

> She said the USSR had undermined trust in itself. 'We do not believe you. You take grave actions irresponsibly: Hungary, Czechoslovakia, Afghanistan. We could not imagine that you'd send troops to Czechoslovakia, but you did. The same again with Afghanistan. We are afraid of you. If you withdraw your medium-range missiles, and the Americans do the same, then we'll be defenceless before your armies.' This is how she thinks. She's sure that we have not given up the Brezhnev Doctrine. This is really something to ponder, comrades. We can't just brush it aside . . .[107]

The Russians lost no time in following up. On 8 April, Charles Powell reported a visit from a Mr Kossov of the Soviet Embassy in London. He explained to Powell that, before her visit, Moscow officials had been over-worried by Mrs Thatcher's Torquay speech, and this explained Gorbachev's aggression at the dinner on the second night. Kossov described Mrs Thatcher's ideas about predictability in SDI as having been 'very carefully noted',[108] and asked if they had been agreed by the Americans in advance. The US had been informed, but its agreement had not been sought, Powell replied. Kossov said that 'Mr Gorbachev wanted to maintain his "special relationship" with the Prime Minister.' The British official reaction registered pleasure as well as vigilance at this use of a phrase usually reserved for Britain and America. Derek Thomas, for the Foreign Office, replied to Powell that the idea was 'no doubt intended to be both flattering and wedge-driving. But we should not discount the possibility that it is also genuine . . . we should remain cautious about Soviet attempts to build up a special relationship, but not to the point of discouraging the Prime Minister from maintaining it.'[109]

Mrs Thatcher did not forget, however, where her real special relationship was. Her account to Reagan, written before she had even returned to Britain, was full, and more or less frank. She told Reagan that she thought she had been able to move Gorbachev towards 'the step-by-step approach [to disarmament] which we agreed at Camp David last year'.[110]

On INF, she said that Gorbachev would not accept the Western right to match Soviet levels of short-range systems '(which I said was a key point)'. 'His aim', she continued, 'is patently the denuclearisation of Europe. I left him in no doubt that I would never accept this.' But she thought, all the same, 'there is a pretty reasonable prospect of getting . . . an agreement which meets our requirements by the end of the year.' She wanted to be clear that she had not fallen for Gorbachev's blandishments: 'If ever I had any doubts whether Gorbachev is a true "believer" in the Communist system, my talks with him dispelled them.' But she argued strongly that her visit had been 'very well worthwhile'. 'Gorbachev needs to be told in plain, unvarnished terms what the Western viewpoint is. And he was . . . It was interesting that he did not allow my frankness to affect our personal relationship.' The West had an interest in supporting his reform policies. The response of the Russian people to her visit had been 'remarkable' – the West should use *glasnost* to promote its own messages.

Electorally, of course, there could be no better message than that the Iron Lady was also the person to bring peace. Mrs Thatcher was very conscious of this as she planned to go to the polls in June. But beyond political considerations at home, the Moscow visit was important. As Charles Powell put it, it was, 'in some ways, the beginning of the end of the Cold War'.[111]

Nicholas Garland, *Independent*, 1 April 1987.

19

What they saw in her

'Mrs Thatcher is the point at which all snobberies meet'

The success of the Moscow visit reinforced the perception of Mrs Thatcher as a bold and brave champion of the West. As she approached the end of her eighth year as prime minister, her battles at home and abroad were well known. Her longevity in office, and evident intention to continue, only served to confirm her dominance. Everyone recognized her; everyone had an opinion about her. She embodied the hopes of many and featured in the nightmares of some. The impact – psychological and cultural as well as directly political – of Mrs Thatcher at the height of her power was deep. She had become a mythological figure, the archetype of the 'strong woman' in all continents, the patron saint, some said, of taxi drivers and all those who strove to better themselves. Possibly for this very reason, she had become the object of unique scorn and vitriol among many British writers and intellectuals.

Ahead of the general election that would be held in June 1987, many of these critics spoke out. 'The chief function of this election', wrote the novelist Julian Barnes,* 'is to turn out Mrs Thatcher and her spayed Cabinet, whose main achievement in the last eight years has been the legitimation of self-interest.'[1] The television playwright Dennis Potter† thought Mrs Thatcher 'the most obviously repellent manifestation of the most obviously arrogant, dishonest, divisive and dangerous government since the war'.[2] David Hare‡ wrote of Mrs Thatcher, 'She is, as her teams

---

* Julian Barnes (1946–), educated City of London School and Magdalen College, Oxford; author of many novels, essays and short stories; winner of the 2011 Man Booker Prize for *The Sense of an Ending* (2011).
† Dennis Potter (1935–94), educated Bell's Grammar School, Coleford, St Clement Danes Grammar School, London and New College, Oxford; television dramatist, screenwriter and journalist; contested (Labour) East Herts, 1964; his works include a semi-autobiographical play, *Stand Up, Nigel Barton* (1965), and *The Singing Detective* (1986).
‡ David Hare (1947–), educated Lancing and Jesus College, Cambridge; playwright; his plays include *Plenty* (1978) and *Racing Demon* (1990); knighted, 1998.

of journalistic galley-slaves never tire of telling us, a crusader. Her crusade, however, is exclusively on behalf of herself, and those who share her peculiar temperament and ideas.'[3] He thought that voters would eventually recognize what he saw as her promotion of greed, and predicted, therefore, that her influence would disappear quickly after she left the political scene, 'leaving nothing but the memory of a funny accent and an obscure sense of shame'.[4] His reference to her accent gives a clue to the visceral way in which Mrs Thatcher's intellectual critics disliked her. She not only upheld ideas they found obnoxious: she almost physically embodied everything bad they conjured up in the use of the word 'suburban'. As the novelist and screenwriter Hanif Kureishi* later told the *Guardian*: 'England has become a squalid ... intolerant, racist, homophobic, narrow-minded, authoritarian rat-hole run by vicious, suburban-minded materialistic philistines.'[5]

Even without an election campaign, Mrs Thatcher as philistine-in-chief was a popular theme with Britain's leading thinkers and cultural figures, many of whom spoke to the journalist Graham Turner for an article which appeared in the *Sunday Telegraph*. The novelist and travel writer Jonathan Raban† saw her as a total philistine – 'she doesn't appreciate doubleness, contradictions, paradox, irony, ambiguity' and, to her, paintings, books and ideas were 'just so much Black Forest gateau'.[6] To David Hare she 'has no sense of personal morality'.[7] Alan Bennett also condemned Mrs Thatcher as a philistine and, in words which were not printed, depicted her as a type of bossy sexual ignorance: 'I see her as an assertive aunt ... a kind of maiden aunt who knows all about marriage.'[8] Mary Warnock,‡ the philosopher and Mistress of Girton College, Cambridge, said that Mrs Thatcher had 'a total lack of understanding of what universities were about' and that, even if her views changed, she would still not be acceptable because 'Watching her choose clothes at Marks and Spencer there

* Hanif Kureishi (1954–), educated King's College London; author of novels, short stories, screenplays and plays; his novel *The Buddha of Suburbia* won the Whitbread Prize for best first novel in 1990; his film scripts include *My Beautiful Laundrette* (1985).

† Jonathan Raban (1942–), educated University of Hull; essayist, travel writer and novelist; publications include *God, Man & Mrs Thatcher* (1989), a critical analysis of Margaret Thatcher's address to the General Assembly of the Church of Scotland.

‡ (Helen) Mary Warnock (1924–), educated St Swithun's, Winchester and Lady Margaret Hall, Oxford; headmistress, Oxford High School, 1966–72; Talbot Resident Fellow, Lady Margaret Hall, Oxford, 1972–6; Resident Fellow and Tutor in Philosophy, St Hugh's College, Oxford, 1976–84; Mistress of Girton College, Cambridge, 1985–91; member, Independent Broadcasting Authority, 1973–81; chairman, Committee of Inquiry into Special Education, 1974–8; chairman, Committee of Inquiry into Human Fertilization, 1982–4; created Lady Warnock, 1985.

was something really quite obscene about it.'⁹* Dr Jonathan Miller,† the theatre director and polymath, called her 'loathsome, repulsive in almost every way'¹⁰ and, in remarks which Turner decided not to print,¹¹ said that she had 'the diction of a perfumed fart'.

Any effort from Mrs Thatcher to show cultural interest met with derision from such critics. When the poet Philip Larkin had visited Mrs Thatcher in Downing Street in 1980, he had been much impressed by the fact that she had been able to quote from one of his poems. The poem is called 'Deceptions', and concerns a Victorian poor woman's account of having been drugged and raped. Mrs Thatcher had praised it to Larkin, and referred to the line 'Her mind was full of knives.' The original words are 'All the unhurried day, / Your mind lay open like a drawer of knives.' Alan Bennett wrote scornfully that 'Larkin liked to think that Madam knew the poem or she would not have been able to misquote it. Inadequate briefing seems a likelier explanation‡ and anyway, since the line is about an open mind it's not surprising that the superb creature got it wrong.'¹²§ Actually, it is striking that Mrs Thatcher fastened on that particular poem. Any other woman politician would have got some credit from the left for drawing attention to a poem about rape. But it was a special gift of Mrs Thatcher not only to inspire dislike in her opponents, but to goad them into an extravagance of condemnation. As the novelist Ian McEwan perceptively put it immediately after her death in 2013, 'It was never enough to dislike her. We *liked* disliking her.'¹³ This self-indulgence by her critics

---

* Mary Warnock and others complained afterwards about the selection of quotations used in the *Sunday Telegraph* interview: some of them, they said, had made more favourable remarks about Mrs Thatcher which were not included in the published text.

† Jonathan Miller (1934–), educated St Paul's and St John's College, Cambridge; writer, academic, broadcaster and director of numerous plays, operas, films and TV programmes; Fellow, University College London, 1981–; knighted, 2002.

‡ Despite Bennett's doubts, Mrs Thatcher had a genuine taste for poetry – especially Tennyson and Kipling – though not avant-garde poetry, and knew a good deal by heart. One reason that Denis Thatcher decided to propose to her was that, when he visited her once in her flat and quoted a line of verse, she capped the quotation and recited the whole poem. Unfortunately, he could not remember, in later years, which poem it was. (Interview with Sir Denis Thatcher.)

In general, Mrs Thatcher was never attracted by the avant-garde in the arts, and knew little about it. One day, at a meeting, she described something as being like 'Waiting for Godot', sounding the t in Godot. Lord Carrington whispered to her, 'It's pronounced Godo, Prime Minister.' 'How is it spelt?' she asked him sharply. He explained. 'Then it's Godot,' she insisted, sounding the t harder than ever. (Interview with Clare Pakenham.)

§ If Bennett really thought the line is about an open mind in the sense which he meant it, it was Mrs Thatcher who, to use other words from the poem, was the 'less deceived'. Larkin's image of the rape victim's mind lying open like a drawer of knives has nothing to do with free thought. It is an image of pure pain, echoing one of George Herbert's 'Affliction' poems: 'My thoughts are all a case of knives / Wounding my heart.'

tended to work to her advantage. Part of Mrs Thatcher's alleged 'philistin-
ism' was her failure to be automatically impressed by the status of highbrow
writers accustomed to praise from the upper reaches of society. 'Intellectuals in Britain had always dreamed of having influence with practical
politicians,' recalled David Hare, 'but the bitter irony was that when a
prime minister finally came along who did like intellectuals, it was the
blowhard right she wanted to listen to – Keith Joseph, Alfred Sherman,
Hugh Thomas – not, if you like, the usual suspects.'[14] 'She reads best-sellers'
was one of the attacks hurled at her by the novelist Anthony Burgess.[15]*
Few of the wider public regarded this as a crime.

Across British fiction, film, drama and music from and about the Thatcher
era, a similar extravagance of feeling tended to dominate. Freely acknowledging Mrs Thatcher's powerful influence, the singer/songwriter Billy
Bragg described her as 'my greatest inspiration . . . Like an angry line of
kettling coppers,† Thatcher's Tories pushed me around, forcing me to
question the assumptions I had made about the British state and my place
in it.'[16] In his song called 'Thatcherites' (1997), Bragg complained, 'You
privatize away and then you make us pay / We'll take it back some day,
mark my words, mark my words.'‡

Other songs about – and against – Mrs Thatcher included 'Ghost Town'
by the Specials, which was the number-one single during the riots of 1981,
'She'll Have To Go' by Simply Red (1989) and 'Margaret on the Guillotine'
by Morrissey (1988). In 'Tramp the Dirt Down' (1989), Elvis Costello sang,
'But when they finally put you in the ground / They'll stand there laughing
and tramp the dirt down.'§ The song 'Maggie', by the punk band the
Exploited (1985), had the refrain: 'Maggie, Maggie, you cunt / Maggie,
Maggie, Maggie, Maggie, you fucking cunt'. Also in 1985, the Angelic
Upstarts put a cartoon of Mrs Thatcher with her arms and legs blown off
on the cover of their single 'Brighton Bomb' and called on 'killers' to
'unite', presumably to do away with her. Oddly, the most successful
anti-Thatcher song was never released in Britain. By Renaud, 'the French

---

* Anthony Burgess (1917–93), educated Xaverian College, Manchester and Manchester
University; academic, author, critic and composer; novels include *A Clockwork Orange*
(1962), *Earthly Powers* (1980).
† 'Kettling' refers to a method of crowd control whereby the police confine protesters to a
small area.
‡ The sequence of Labour governments which came to power in that year and continued
until 2010 in fact did almost nothing to 'take back' any privatization.
§ This prediction was semi-fulfilled after Mrs Thatcher's death, when some anti-Thatcher
activists held parties and mock-funerals in celebration.

Bob Dylan', it was called 'Miss Maggie' and reached number one in France in 1984. It celebrated women for not being hooligans, assassins and committers of genocide, but proclaimed Mrs Thatcher as the sole exception. Its conclusion, translated from the French, was 'If I can't stay on earth, I will change into a dog so that I can use Madame Thatcher daily as a lamp-post.'

In Britain, much the best-known song about Mrs Thatcher remains the one sung in the stage version of the wildly successful musical *Billy Elliot*. The story, set against the backcloth of the miners' strike of 1984–5, concerns a young boy from a mining family who wishes to become a ballet dancer. Mrs Thatcher is the object of hatred. 'Merry Christmas Maggie Thatcher' is sung by the cast in chorus, including the words 'Merry Christmas, Maggie Thatcher / We all celebrate today / 'cos it's one day closer to your death.'*

Newspaper cartoonists, whose job is to depict politics through politicians, had a more directly professional challenge about how to deal with Mrs Thatcher. Although existing women politicians, such as Shirley Williams and Barbara Castle, were already widely caricatured, most cartoonists found that her sex, initially at least, made her a harder subject. Nicholas Garland,† who was the main political cartoonist, first at the *Daily Telegraph* and latterly at the *Independent*, throughout her time, recalled that he felt it 'freakish', at first, that a woman was in charge. He found Mrs Thatcher, 'very very difficult to draw', partly because of her sex: 'Women change more than men – hair, outfits, make-up. They are elusive.'[17] His first – unfavourable – impression of Mrs Thatcher was that she was simply 'tribal Tory woman'. When she was Education Secretary, he had dealt with her by concentrating on her 'puffball hats'[18] rather than her face. On the day she beat Heath for the leadership in 1975, he remembered thinking, 'I just can't do this.' Shortly afterwards, Mrs Thatcher attended a leader writers' conference at the *Daily Telegraph* and Garland was able to study her in the flesh. He was surprised to find that 'This woman turned out to be rather attractive, with considerable presence.'[19]

This personal encounter kept Garland out of the camp which reacted to Mrs Thatcher with disgust. Although of moderate left-wing views himself, and moving in Hampstead intellectual circles, he 'never hated her'. He recalled attending a dinner party of his great friend Jonathan Miller,

---

* When Margaret Thatcher actually did die in 2013, the show went on, with the words unaltered.

† Nicholas Garland (1935–), educated Slade School of Fine Art; political cartoonist, *Daily Telegraph*, 1966–86 and 1991–2011; *New Statesman*, 1971–8; *Independent*, 1986–91; he also drew regularly for the *Spectator*, 1979–95.

at which a fellow guest denounced Mrs Thatcher as a fascist. This was absolutely untrue, Garland protested: Mrs Thatcher was a democrat, chosen through democratic process. 'No one agreed with me.'[20] As a cartoonist, he began to study her more carefully, and noticed that 'She had slow eyes – the outside corners lower than the inside ones – strong, high cheekbones and a little, pursed mouth.'[21] He tried to draw in her face 'the power and the activism, which gave her a slightly bad-tempered look', and 'the underlying possibility of panic' expressed in her flashing eyes. 'Energy came off her. She was good at drama, which is a two-edged thing. She often had one finger raised, haranguing somebody.' Or she wielded the handbag as a weapon. Her handbag, of course, was an essential accoutrement for the cartoonist, like a crown for the Queen.

Garland's Thatcher followed several phases. She changed very much through the experience of the Falklands War, he noticed – 'I drew her more strong, frowning and vigorous.' Then there was a long period when she was a 'fixture' on the national scene, and he often showed her as Britannia or Queen Victoria. She also grew older, more hollow-cheeked and more chic in her dress and hair. Finally there was 'the tail-end period', roughly from 1988. In his cartoons, she became 'omnipotent; a bit mad'.[22]*

Other cartoonists treated her as mad – or bad – all along. Gerald Scarfe,† appearing mainly in the *Sunday Times*, emphasized her pointed nose and red lips. He turned her into a shark, a pterodactyl, a cannibal and a nuclear mushroom cloud. Steve Bell,‡ who was the principal cartoonist at the *Guardian* in the later Thatcher period, emphasized the fact that her left eye was rounder than her right. He made both eyes huge and threatening, and the left one crazed. He too turned Mrs Thatcher into a shark, as well as a vampire, a zombie and a sculpture worked out of South Atlantic penguin guano. Some of these – particularly the works of Bell – were powerful and inventive; but their relentless hostility and exaggeration meant that there was little room for jokes, or for degrees of satire. Since Mrs Thatcher was thoroughly evil in their eyes at all times, they missed the nuances of the time, so their cartoons were usually uninformative.

* During the defence cuts of the early 1980s, Garland drew Mrs Thatcher wearing a full suit of armour but with her knickers hanging round her ankles. His editor, Bill Deedes, spiked the drawing on grounds of bad taste. (Interview with Nicholas Garland.) Such qualms were rare in newspapers even then, however, and became rarer.
† Gerald Scarfe (1936–), educated Royal School of Art; political cartoonist, *Sunday Times*, 1967–; artist, *New Yorker*, 1993–; also works extensively in TV and film and has had many exhibitions of his art worldwide, including 'Milk Snatcher, Gerald Scarfe – The Thatcher Drawings', at the Bowes Museum, 2015.
‡ Steve Bell (1951–), educated Slough Grammar School; freelance cartoonist and illustrator since 1977; famous for his 'IF . . .' cartoon strip in the *Guardian*.

None of them 'nailed' her with one image. There was nothing like Vicky's encapsulation of Harold Macmillan as Supermac or Steve Bell's depiction of Mrs Thatcher's successor, John Major, wearing his underpants over his trousers. All shared, however, a strong preoccupation with Mrs Thatcher. A count of Garland cartoons through Mrs Thatcher's premierships,[23] for example, shows that on average 25 per cent of his daily cartoons featured her. This compares with only 6 per cent by David Low featuring Winston Churchill when prime minister. Mrs Thatcher outscored the combined appearances of her entire Cabinet.*

The subsidized theatre almost invariably treated Mrs Thatcher as a subject for attack. Indeed, *A Short, Sharp Shock* (1980) provoked an apology in the House of Commons by the Arts Minister, Norman St John-Stevas,† for the fact that public money had been spent on it. Written by Howard Brenton‡ and Tony Howard, the play showed, among many lurid scenes, Mrs Thatcher forcing her Employment Secretary Jim Prior to drink the sperm of the free-market economist Milton Friedman from a Coca-Cola bottle. In the same year, at the National Theatre, *The Romans in Britain*, also by Howard Brenton, drew a parallel between the Roman invasion of ancient Britain and the Thatcher government's treatment of Northern Ireland, using an explicit scene of male rape to make its point. Brenton also, with David Hare, wrote a much more observant play called *Pravda* (1985) which satirized, in pseudonymous form, the power of Rupert Murdoch in the Thatcher era.

Such plays did reflect feelings that were strong amid elements of the theatre-going classes. David Hare later recalled 'a tremendous blast of energy from the audience because they wanted an anti-Thatcher, anti-Murdoch blast'.[24] Brenton generalized the thought behind this energy when interviewed at the end of the Thatcher era:

---

* Mrs Thatcher, however, did not reciprocate the cartoonists' interest. Unlike many leading politicians, she did not buy the originals of cartoons about herself from the authors. A rare occasion on which she is known to have attempted this was after the death of Enoch Powell in 1998. Garland drew a cartoon of Mrs Thatcher looking at Powell's sculpted effigy in the manner of Rembrandt's *Aristotle Contemplating the Bust of Homer*. Mrs Thatcher tried to buy the original, but Powell's widow, Pam, also offered, and Garland decided in favour of Mrs Powell. (Interview with Nicholas Garland.)

† Norman St John-Stevas (1929–2012), educated Ratcliffe College, Fitzwilliam College, Cambridge and Christ Church, Oxford (he is thought to have been unique in holding office in both the Oxford and Cambridge Unions); barrister, author (editor of the complete works of Walter Bagehot); Conservative MP for Chelmsford, 1964–87; Leader of the House of Commons and Minister for the Arts, 1979–81; created Lord St John of Fawsley, 1987.

‡ Howard Brenton (1942–), educated Chichester High School for Boys and St Catharine's College, Cambridge; playwright; his numerous plays include *Christie in Love* (1969), *The Romans in Britain* (1980) and *In Extremis* (2006).

If there is one insight that comes from the most noted novels, television drama series and plays of the 1980s, it is that during the decade we were overtaken by something malevolent. It may seem exaggerated, but it was as if some kind of evil was abroad in our society, a palpable degradation of the spirit.[25]

Edward Bond,* who wrote plays such as *Derek* (1982), about the exploitation of a working-class man in the Falklands War, and *The War Plays*, which depicted nuclear war, was not untypical in such company in seeing Mrs Thatcher as a symbol of everything he hated. 'When I vote,' he told the *Guardian* just before the 1987 election, 'I shall keep faith with those who died to protect us from Fascism and militarism – and their sidekick Thatcherism.'[26] He did not identify those who had died in the struggle against Thatcherism.

Only one play of the era went strongly against the trend. This was *The Falklands Play* by Ian Curteis. Commissioned for television by the BBC, for whom Curteis had been a successful writer, the drama made Mrs Thatcher the unambiguous heroine of the Falklands story, depicting her as decisive when others had dithered and as a woman of compassion as well as courage. After initial enthusiasm for the play, the BBC went cold on the project. The head of plays, Peter Goodchild, told Curteis that he objected to scenes which showed Mrs Thatcher writing letters of sympathy to the widows of servicemen who had been killed, although she had indeed done this.[27] He wanted dialogue inserted showing Conservative politicians discussing the possible electoral advantages of war. Curteis refused. In July 1986, the BBC cancelled the drama, on the grounds that it might cause controversy in the run-up to the general election which was expected in 1987. This was widely interpreted as an excuse for canning the play altogether, and a huge row ensued in the press, with Curteis claiming he had been the victim of the BBC's politics. Michael Grade,† the controller of BBC1, added fuel to the flames by putting out the suggestion, which had not previously been made, that the play was simply not good enough. The BBC also stopped another Falklands drama, the much more anti-Thatcher *Tumbledown*, because of the coming election. But whereas *Tumbledown* was merely held over, and broadcast in 1988, *The Falklands*

---

* Edward Bond (1934–), playwright and director; author of numerous plays, among them *Saved* (1965), which included, famously, a scene featuring the stoning to death of a baby in its pram.
† Michael Grade (1943–), educated St Dunstan's College, London; controller, BBC1, 1984–6; director of programmes, BBC TV, 1986–7; chief executive, Channel 4, 1988–97; executive chairman and chief executive, ITV, 2007–9; created Lord Grade of Yarmouth, 2011.

Play was killed. It was not finally broadcast until the twenty-first century, treated as a historical curiosity. Altogether, the BBC ran seven Falklands dramas which were, to greater or lesser degrees, anti- the Falklands War, and none which was pro-.

In film, two pictures written by Hanif Kureishi sought to anatomize Thatcher's Britain unfavourably. *My Beautiful Laundrette* (1985), which was extremely successful, highlighted what Kureishi saw as Mrs Thatcher's bad effects on race relations. *Sammy and Rosie Get Laid* (1987), about the breakdown of communities, was ambitiously intended, according to its director, Stephen Frears,* 'to bring the government down'.[28] In this it failed, but the ardour of the intent reveals the mood of the moment. Other films, such as *Letter to Brezhnev* (1985), which compared the Liverpool ravaged by Mrs Thatcher unfavourably with the Soviet Union, and *Business as Usual* (1987), which was a thinly veiled anti-Thatcher polemic about predatory bosses and rights in the workplace, drew from similar wells of feeling. The latter starred John Thaw (later famous as Inspector Morse) and Glenda Jackson† who, in 1992, was to become a Labour MP.‡ *Top Girls* (1982), an explicitly anti-Thatcher play by Caryl Churchill,§ depicted Marlene, a woman so determined to succeed in business that she does not help other women and models her behaviour on that of unscrupulous men. The idea that Mrs Thatcher was not 'really' a woman was a common motif among her critics. This sorted oddly with the misogynistic instinct, also manifested by some of her critics, that her sex justified particularly extreme and obscene attack.

On television, *The Boys from the Blackstuff*, BBC2, a series written by Alan Bleasdale, the tale of five Liverpool tarmac layers, was later described by the British Film Institute as 'TV's most complete dramatic response to the Thatcher era',[29] although the original play on which the series was based had been written in 1978, when Jim Callaghan's Labour

---

* Stephen Frears (1941–), educated Gresham's School, Holt and Trinity College, Cambridge; film director. His films include *My Beautiful Laundrette* (1985), *Dangerous Liaisons* (1988), *High Fidelity* (2000).

† Glenda Jackson (1936–), educated West Kirby County Grammar School for Girls; RADA; actress, 1957–92; Labour MP for Hampstead and Highgate, 1992–2010; for Hampstead and Kilburn, 2010–15. She starred in many films including *Women in Love* (1971), *The Boyfriend* (1972), *Mary Queen of Scots* (1972).

‡ In the House of Commons adjournment debate after Mrs Thatcher's death in 2013, Glenda Jackson would attack Mrs Thatcher, saying that although she had been the first female prime minister, she did not embody her sex – 'A woman? Not on my terms' (Hansard, HC Deb 10 April 2013, 560/1650).

§ Caryl Churchill (1938–), educated Trafalgar School, Montreal and Lady Margaret Hall, Oxford; playwright; her plays include *Cloud Nine* (1979) and *Top Girls* (1982).

government was still in office. Sometimes such responses were well sat-irized by her critics themselves. A BBC comedy called *The Young Ones* (1982–4) featured four students sharing a squalid house while studying at Scumbag College. It contained lines like 'The bathroom is free. Unlike the country under a Thatcher junta!' Its stars and authors included Ben Elton, Rik Mayall and Alexei Sayle.

Even *Doctor Who*, the long-running children's programme, began a surreptitious effort to attack Mrs Thatcher. According to Sylvester McCoy, who acted the Doctor from 1987 to 1989, 'We were a group of politically motivated people and it seemed the right thing to do . . . Our feeling was that Margaret Thatcher was far more terrifying than any monster the Doctor had encountered.'[30] Andrew Cartmel recalled that he was asked by the show's producer in his interview for the post of script editor what he wanted to achieve in the role. 'My exact words were: "I'd like to over-throw the government." I was very angry about the social injustice in Britain under Thatcher and I'm delighted that came into the show.'[31] Under Cartmel, the villain of the drama for a three-part *Doctor Who* serial in 1988 called *The Happiness Patrol* became Helen A (played by the fiercely anti-Thatcher Sheila Hancock, wife of John Thaw), the tyrant of a human colony on the planet Terra Alpha. The Doctor persuaded the enslaved human beings to rise up against Helen A. The trouble for the BBC chil-dren's TV subversives, however, was that any explicit declaration of their political intent might have been fatal to their jobs, so they had to tread carefully. It seems that no one noticed what they were up to. The pro-gramme was going through a period of decline – its ratings fell from 16 million at their height to 3 million – which Helen A did nothing to redeem. A writer called Tony Attwood wrote a Doctor Who spin-off children's novel called *Turlough and the Earthlink Dilemma* at the time, with a villain called Rehctaht – Thatcher spelt backwards – but, again, few seemed to have noticed.

By far the most popular programme which dealt with Mrs Thatcher was *Spitting Image*, the ITV puppet show which ran from 1984 to 1996 and caricatured public figures of the period. It depicted Mrs Thatcher as the authority figure bossing her Cabinet,* frequently dressed as a

---

* *Spitting Image* embedded itself so deep in the public consciousness that the present author has often been approached by people who tell him a story about how Mrs Thatcher was asked by a waiter serving the Cabinet what meat she wanted. She answered, 'A raw steak, please.' Then the waiter asked, 'And the vegetables?' Mrs Thatcher replied, 'Oh, they'll have the same as me.' This is a *Spitting Image* skit, but people have turned it into a true story in their minds. (As part of the long-running joke about Mrs Thatcher being 'really' a man, the waiter in the sketch addresses her as 'Sir'.)

mannish dominatrix in a pinstripe suit and tie, sometimes with a Churchillian cigar.* On one occasion, it showed her standing up in a men's urinal. Although the treatment of her on the programme was harsh, its message constantly reinforced the impression of her power, so it probably did her more good than harm. It was her Cabinet colleagues, depicted, for the most part, as abject, who had more cause for complaint.

Oddly enough, the most successful and witty political television comedy of the era, *Yes, Minister* (BBC), by Antony Jay† and Jonathan Lynn,‡ did not really deal with the Thatcher phenomenon, even when it developed into *Yes, Prime Minister* from 1986 to 1988. In fact, much of the inspiration for the authors had come from the diaries of the Wilson–Callaghan period, since the show began in 1980 before any equivalents from the Thatcher era were available. The invariable plot structure was based on the joke that the civil servants (led by the Permanent Secretary, Sir Humphrey Appleby, played by Nigel Hawthorne) always get their way in the end by outwitting and then rescuing their minister. The minister, Jim Hacker (played by Paul Eddington), who eventually becomes prime minister, is an amiable if cowardly buffoon. The programme was a brilliant depiction of Whitehall ways, but it never tackled the clear and present danger of a prime minister who struck fear into civil servants. Perhaps because the satire was not near her knuckle, Mrs Thatcher felt free to say how much she enjoyed it. When Lynn congratulated her on her victory in 1983 she told him that she 'loved' his programmes. 'The dialogue & timing [are] <u>superb</u>. And the insight into the thought-processes of politicians & civil servants is supremely perceptive.'[32] She even agreed to take part in a rather stilted sketch with Eddington and Hawthorne at an awards ceremony in honour of the show in 1984.§ Another successful television serial, implicitly rather than directly anti-Thatcher, was *Paradise Postponed* (1986), the BBC's adaptation of John Mortimer's 1985 novel of the same

---

* *Spitting Image*'s creators, Peter Fluck and Roger Law, also commissioned a ceramic 'Mrs T-pot' in which the tea poured out of her nose. It did not sell well.

† Antony Jay (1930–), educated St Paul's and Magdalene College, Cambridge; freelance writer; BBC producer and editor, 1955–64; editor of the *Tonight* programme, 1962–3; writer (with Jonathan Lynn) of BBC television series *Yes, Minister* and *Yes, Prime Minister*, 1980–88; his publications include *Management and Machiavelli* (1967; 2nd edn 1987); knighted, 1988.

‡ Jonathan Lynn (1943–), educated Kingswood School, Bath and Pembroke College, Cambridge; director of numerous plays and films including (film): *Nuns on the Run* (1990) and *My Cousin Vinny* (1992); also actor and writer, including (with Antony Jay) of BBC television series *Yes, Minister* and *Yes, Prime Minister*, 1980–88.

§ Antony Jay had friendly relations with Mrs Thatcher and occasionally advised her on speeches and on the BBC.

name. Rather as Satan is the most exciting character in Milton's *Paradise Lost*, so is Leslie Titmuss (played by David Threlfall), the Norman Tebbit-ish Tory Cabinet minister and property developer, the most gripping though disgusting figure in *Paradise Postponed*. Mortimer intended Titmuss to represent all that he most disliked in Mrs Thatcher's overthrow of the 1945 settlement, but he portrayed Titmuss so convincingly that members of Kinnock's Shadow Cabinet were encouraged to read his book to understand the sort of arguments Labour would have to counter.[33]

Apart from Mortimer, fiction was slower than other creative media to try to get to grips with the Thatcher era, although in *The Satanic Verses* (1988), Salman Rushdie* did make a passing reference to 'Mrs Torture'. Most Thatcher-related novels appeared after her departure from office, and tended to use her as a straw woman to attack rather than a character to capture with the magic of fiction. *What a Carve Up!* (1994) by Jonathan Coe, for example, is a novel about a horrible Yorkshire family called the Winshaws, whose members embody perceived Thatcherite evils – the greedy banker, brutal farmer, unscrupulous art dealer, hypocritical tabloid journalist, arms dealer. *GB84* (2004) by David Peace is a ferociously anti-Thatcher thriller, set against the backcloth of the 1984–5 miners' strike and celebrating resistance to the 'massed power of the British state' at the Orgreave coking plant. Even novels with unpolitical subjects – Ian McEwan's *The Child in Time* (1987), for example – tended to create Thatcher-era settings that were dystopian, brutal, materialistic and decayed. In her novel *The Birds of the Air* (1980), Alice Thomas Ellis made fun of the English propensity for seeing human beings as animals:

> Even the leaders of the political parties had come to resemble little animals. On the left an old teddy [Michael Foot] . . . On the right a mouse – a shop mouse, her head stuck in a yellowed meringue, a mean little mouse bred on cheese rind and broken biscuit and the nutritionless, platitudinous parings of a grocer's mind.[34]

Sue Townsend's great comic creation, the disaffected teenager Adrian Mole, even wrote a poem in his fictional diary, entitled 'Mrs Thatcher':

> Do you weep, Mrs Thatcher, do you weep?
> Do you wake, Mrs Thatcher, in your sleep?
> Do you weep like a sad willow?

---

* (Ahmed) Salman Rushdie (1947–), educated Cathedral School, Bombay, Rugby and King's College, Cambridge; writer; works include *Midnight's Children* (1981) and *The Satanic Verses* (1988), which resulted in Ayatollah Khomeini's issuing a fatwa in 1989 calling for Rushdie's death; knighted, 2007.

On your Marks and Spencer's pillow?
Are your tears molten steel?
Do you weep?
Do you wake with '*Three Million*' on your brain?
Are you sorry that they'll never work again?
When you're dressing in your blue, do you see the waiting queue?
Do you weep, Mrs Thatcher, do you weep?[35]

Few authors tried to imagine sympathetically characters who were typical of the Thatcher era, such as 'upwardly mobile' members of the working class, people setting up their own business for the first time, or women who, because of Mrs Thatcher's example, felt empowered to pursue more ambitious careers. There is no reason, of course, why novelists should have felt under any pressure to be pro-Thatcher, but it is interesting that they seem to have felt strong pressure to be anti-, and disappointing artistically that they made so little effort to address what underlay the changes in both British life and the wider world in her time. As the novelist and critic D. J. Taylor put it, 'Scarcely a single contemporary novelist bothered him- or herself to try and comprehend the nature of Thatcher's appeal.'[36] Although seeing her from an extremely hostile point of view, David Hare, speaking for the theatre, agreed. The left had not seen Mrs Thatcher coming, he thought. They had predicted a left-wing revolution, and social breakdown, in the 1970s, but 'Suddenly, the person who wants change is coming from the right. There was a massive feeling of being wrong-footed. History took a different turn. I had nothing to say.'[37] It was only after about six years of Mrs Thatcher in office, Hare believed, that left-wing writers began to understand the full extent and (from her point of view) success of her project. He believed that she stood for selfishness, which he tried to capture in *Pravda*: 'Murdoch was at the heart of her venture, opening up the press to the nihilists.'[38]

One novelist actually interested in Mrs Thatcher's appeal was Philip Hensher,* who drew on his experiences as a clerk of the House of Commons at the end of Mrs Thatcher's period in office for his second novel *Kitchen Venom* (1996). It contains arresting vignettes of Mrs Thatcher's dominance of Parliament and the sense that, as a character called Jane says when surveying the Cabinet, 'It's only her that's at all remarkable.'[39] The book, which never names Mrs Thatcher, notes her parliamentary technique – how she used the hubbub of Prime Minister's Questions as 'the ritornello to an aria',[40] for example. There are passages in the novel

---

* Philip Hensher (1965–), educated Tapton School, Sheffield, Lady Margaret Hall, Oxford and Jesus College, Cambridge; clerk to the House of Commons, 1990–96; his novels include *The Northern Clemency* (2008) and *Scenes from Early Life* (2013).

in which Mrs Thatcher's inner thoughts are imagined, such as her rare experience of having 'half an hour to spare', and even some in which she is the narrator. Although Hensher was, by his own account, 'a weak-willed lefty'[41] at the time, he believed that the older generation of writers was much too obsessed with the question of Mrs Thatcher and social class and was inattentive to the way Britain had altered on such a large scale. So 'Paradoxically, she was fresh material':[42] as a novelist, 'You always want a clear voice. The Gloriana mode. It is a wonderful voice to carry a novel.'[43] A homosexual, Hensher was also conscious of Mrs Thatcher as a 'gay icon'. She had a 'magnificent, diva-like presence' and 'the quality of trans-formation'[44] about her appearance.

A paperback edition of *Kitchen Venom* shows a picture of the prime ministerial feet in high-heeled shoes treading on a cigarette. This is drawn from Hensher's description of how Mrs Thatcher walked: 'When she walked, she seemed to extinguish a cigarette beneath every pace; in her walk, it could be seen that she was in the right.'[45] He was not the only novelist to observe her gait. Alan Hollinghurst's novel *The Line of Beauty* (2004), perhaps the best-known fiction set in the Thatcher era so far pub-lished, tells the story of a young gay man, Nick Guest, experiencing a world that is grander and more glamorous than his own. The setting is the mid-Thatcher period of 1983 to 1987, the height of her power, and Nick, as lodger in the elegant house of a rising Tory politician called Gerald Fedden, witnesses some of it. The high point for Fedden is when he finally persuades Mrs Thatcher to come to a party held at his house, and she ends up (improbably) dancing – 'getting down rather sexily with Nick'. Describing Mrs Thatcher's entry to the party, Hollinghurst writes, 'She came in at her gracious scuttle, with its hint of a long-suppressed embarrassment, of clumsiness transmuted into power.'[46] This observant if superior way of describing Mrs Thatcher suggests how fruitful might have been fiction which imagined the circumstances and feelings of her and those like her as they fought to rise in the world.

Mrs Thatcher herself was not interested in how she was portrayed in fiction or on stage. This was not because she lacked egotism and pride, but because she had long learnt from hard knocks going back to the days of 'milksnatcher' not to waste emotional energy on thinking about how others saw her, particularly if those others were not important in winning votes. A rather sad result of this was that the drama she most disliked – *Anyone for Denis?* – was by no means the least friendly. This was simply because she saw it, and did not see the others. The play, which opened in May 1981 and closed, on grounds of taste, during the Falklands War, was the stage version of the *Private Eye* 'Dear Bill' letters. These, composed by John Wells* and Richard Ingrams,† purported to be written by Denis to an old chum, Bill, who was widely taken to be W. F. (Bill) Deedes,‡ at that time the editor of the *Daily Telegraph*, describing the slings and arrows of life under 'the Boss' or 'the old girl'. Mrs Thatcher was persuaded against her will by Tim Bell and others that it would look sporting for the couple to attend. They went to a special charity performance, in which press and audience watched intently for the Thatchers' reaction. The detectives, frightened of being photographed laughing at jokes against their principal, insisted on sitting inconspicuously behind her and made Bernard Ingham sit beside her.[47] Mrs Thatcher was, in Carol's words, 'acutely offended'[48] by the show, though she dutifully kept up the pretence of enjoyment, saying 'Marvellous farce' to the press through gritted teeth as she left. In her dislike of it, she took her cue from Denis, who was irritated to be portrayed as a drunken halfwit (though the adjective did not always lack foundation). The spoof letters themselves, however, did much to humanize the Thatcher marriage in people's minds. They also performed the useful service of convincing people that Denis was not the sort of person who could possibly have any political influence over his wife, although this was not the case. As Bill Deedes put it, '*Private Eye* made people think he could not be a serious figure: that put everyone off the scent.'[49]

Generally, however, Mrs Thatcher stuck to her line of paying little attention to her cultural depictions. This was almost certainly the psychologically correct thing to do. In her old age, the novelist Sebastian Faulks met her at a lunch party. Faulks told her she should read *The Line of Beauty*, since she appeared in it. She had not heard of the book, but listened attentively. As they parted, she said to Faulks, '*The Line of Duty*: I shall remember that.'[50] It was a characteristic mishearing, illustrating the gap between her way of thinking about the world and that of British metropolitan literary culture.

There were, of course, writers, intellectuals and people from the world of the arts who did admire Mrs Thatcher. In an interview for Graham

---

* John Wells (1936–98), educated Eastbourne College and St Edmund Hall, Oxford; writer, actor and director; played title role in *Anyone for Denis?* (as well as writing it, with Richard Ingrams) at Whitehall Theatre, 1981–2.

† Richard Ingrams (1937–), educated Shrewsbury and University College, Oxford; editor, *Private Eye*, 1963–86; *Oldie*, 1992–2014.

‡ W. F. ('Bill') Deedes (1913–2007), educated Harrow; journalist with *Morning Post*, 1931–7; Conservative MP for Ashford Division of Kent, 1950–September 1974; parliamentary secretary, Ministry of Housing and Local Government, 1954–5; Parliamentary Under-Secretary, Home Department, 1955–7; Minister without Portfolio, 1962–4; editor, *Daily Telegraph*, 1974–86; knighted, 1999; created Lord Deedes, 1986.

Turner's article, Kingsley Amis,* who, like many refugees from earlier leftism, was particularly attracted to Mrs Thatcher, praised her for one of the things which most enraged her cultural critics: 'the less the Government was involved with the arts, the better it was for the arts.'[51] He detected a certain jealousy of her on the left: 'Another thing – she's a woman and the Labour Party were supposed to have the first woman prime minister – the Tories have nipped in and stolen that.'[52] Barry Humphries,† writer, comedian and inventor of Dame Edna Everage, made a similar point when commenting after her death: 'Whenever feminists have complained in my presence about neglect of female high achievers . . . I always like to mention brilliant Margaret Thatcher. It always makes them furious.'[53] The novelist Peter Ackroyd‡ complained of the 'patronising snobbery' of those who despised Mrs Thatcher,[54] while Noël Annan,§ the leading academic and historian of British intellectual life, said that it 'was not true that there was no place for intellectuals in her scheme of things':[55] it was merely that she had changed who those intellectuals were. She also, said Annan, had 'a contempt for intellectuals as managers, and with justice'.[56]

Even the novelist John le Carré,¶ very far from Mrs Thatcher politically, found himself thinking well of her after the Falklands War: 'I never thought I would find her admirable, but I do somehow. Even though the immediate consequences, at least, are so wretched.'[57] She flatteringly encouraged le Carré to consider accepting an honour, which he turned down. Although himself instinctively on the left, he did not like the way left-wing writers 'cast her as the nanny, the tyrant'.[58] To him, she seemed 'a totally democratic person. Naturally adversarial. Entirely, in her own

---

* Kingsley Amis (1922–95), educated City of London School and St John's College, Oxford; his first novel, *Lucky Jim* (1955), won the Somerset Maugham Prize; *The Old Devils* (1986) received the Booker Prize; as well as twenty-four novels, Amis published collections of poetry, short stories and literary criticism; knighted, 1990.

† Barry Humphries (1934–), Australian comedian, actor, satirist and author; best known for writing and playing his on-stage and television alter egos Dame Edna Everage and Sir Les Patterson.

‡ Peter Ackroyd (1949–), educated St Benedict's School, Ealing, Clare College, Cambridge and Yale University; novelist, biographer and poet; novels include *The Last Testament of Oscar Wilde* (1983), *Hawksmoor* (1985); non-fiction includes *T. S. Eliot* (1984), *Thomas More* (1998) and *London: The Biography* (2000).

§ Noël Annan (1916–2000), educated Stowe and King's College, Cambridge; Provost of King's College, 1956–66; Vice-Chancellor, University of London, 1978–81; created Lord Annan, 1965.

¶ John le Carré (pseudonym of David Cornwell) (1931–), educated Sherborne, Berne University and Lincoln College, Oxford; author of spy novels, including *The Spy Who Came in from the Cold* (1963), *Tinker, Tailor, Soldier, Spy* (1974) and *Smiley's People* (1980).

way, fair.' He also found her very attractive, sensing that she 'gave a cry for protection which made me feel like one of her courtiers'.*

Intellectuals with direct experience of real tyranny thought of Mrs Thatcher very differently from her left-wing critics in Britain. She was greatly admired, for example, by Andrei Sakharov, the Soviet nuclear physicist and dissident (see Chapters 8 and 18), and by Vladimir Bukovsky,† the science student and writer who was released from a Soviet prison in 1977 and granted asylum in the West. 'She loved arguing,' Bukovsky recalled, 'Russians love arguing. People from Eton and Oxford were too polite to argue with a lady. Sometimes it would come to shouts and bangs on the table. I could see she enjoyed it.'[59] He felt he could trust her: 'She was an intensely loyal person, which always amazed me. We'd have a great quarrel [usually about her closeness to Gorbachev, of which Bukovsky vehemently disapproved], and then she'd go round introducing me in most flattering terms.' In Bukovsky's view, 'She was very cerebral. Zero intuition. One hundred per cent intellect. Reagan was the opposite.'[60] And yet she did not understand ideology, he thought: she simply had the correct perception that Communism was terrible. 'She was more man than all the others,' he judged, regarding this as a high compliment.

Mrs Thatcher was indeed well capable of using her powers of flattery upon intellectuals, which were made stronger by the fact that her admiration was usually genuine. She liked what she called 'wordsmiths', who could express things better than she believed she could, and also 'big minds'. When, for example, in 1986, the present author argued with her that she should not build the proposed new British Library but should revamp the old Reading Room of the British Museum, she replied that 'David Eccles‡ wants it. He is a big mind. When a big mind wants something, I do not stand in his way.'[61] This admiration for mental greatness was particularly apparent in her attitude to leading scientists, of whom

---

* There were a few occasions when even some of Mrs Thatcher's most dedicated foes did admire her. By chance, David Hare and Howard Brenton happened to be in Brighton, writing a play together, in the week of the 1984 bomb. When they watched her speech on the day that followed the bomb, Brenton said: 'I don't approve of her as prime minister, but by God she's a great tank commander.' (Interview with Sir David Hare.)

† Vladimir Bukovsky (1942–), Russian dissident, author and human rights activist; spent a total of twelve years in Soviet prisons, labour camps and so called 'psychiatric hospitals' in the 1960s and 1970s before his release and move to the UK.

‡ David Eccles (1904–99), educated Winchester and New College, Oxford; Conservative MP for Chippenham, 1943–62; held various ministerial posts in 1950s including Education, 1954–7 and 1959–62; returned to the government as paymaster-general and minister for the arts, 1970–73; trustee, British Museum, 1963–99; chairman, British Library Board, 1973–8; knighted, 1953; created Viscount Eccles, 1964.

she felt in awe. 'The only time I can remember seeing Mrs Thatcher in a flap, behaving just like a schoolgirl, meek and mild,' recalled Charles Powell, 'was when her former Oxford tutor, the Nobel-Prize-winning chemist Dorothy Hodgkin,* came to tea at No. 10.'[62] She was interested in leading intellectuals from all disciplines. When Allan Bloom's† book *The Closing of the American Mind* appeared, to great éclat, in 1987, George Walden,‡ then her universities minister, suggested that she should meet him. He was keen to get her to share Bloom's enthusiasm for non-utilitarian studies. Mrs Thatcher was receptive to Bloom's thesis that relativism in American education, far from opening new horizons for students, had disabled their ability to learn the canon of great thought. She invited Bloom to Chequers (with Walden) for lunch. When they arrived, Denis took Walden aside and asked him, ' "What the hell have you given Margaret to read that kept her up till 2.30?" At the lunch she asked detailed questions of Bloom, and listened carefully to the answers . . . I was impressed. Bloom was dazzled.'[63] Walden believed it was an example of Mrs Thatcher's genuine interest in such matters: 'She had had no reason to see this man – there was no press release – it was politically useless, but she was interested.'[64]

Philip Larkin admired Mrs Thatcher because 'Her great virtue is saying that two and two make four, which is as unpopular nowadays as it has always been.'[65] He liked the toughness of her politics, but he, too, enjoyed her admiration. He was very pleased when she offered him the poet-laureateship, although he turned it down. Writing to Robert Conquest in her praise for being so understanding about this, Larkin extolled her beauty, but added: 'The country will let her down, too idle and selfish.'[66] To the diarist James Lees-Milne, she was 'the greatest prime minister of the century'.[67]

Views differed strongly about Mrs Thatcher's attitude to the arts. The

---

* Professor Dorothy Hodgkin (1910–94), educated Sir John Leman School and Somerville College, Oxford; distinguished chemist, famous for her crystallographic analysis of the structure of molecules and later discovered important information about the structure of penicillin; winner, Nobel Prize for Chemistry, 1964; OM, 1965.
† Allan Bloom (1930–92), educated University of Chicago; American political philosopher, author and translator of works by Rousseau and Plato. His best-known book was *The Closing of the American Mind: How Higher Education Has Failed Democracy and Impoverished the Souls of Today's Students* (1987); he also wrote the collection of essays *Giants and Dwarfs* (1990), and *Love and Friendship* (published posthumously in 1993).
‡ George Walden (1939–), educated Latymer Upper School, Jesus College, Cambridge and Moscow University; diplomat, 1967–83; Conservative MP for Buckingham, 1983–97; Parliamentary Under-Secretary, Department for Education and Science, 1985–7.

artists Gilbert and George* expressed themselves succinctly: 'We admire Margaret Thatcher greatly. She did a lot for art. Socialism wants everyone to be equal. We want to be different.'[68] Some praised her enthusiasm, and even, in the area of music, her serious interest. Claus Moser,† the chairman of the Royal Opera House, recalled receiving her on one occasion in the royal box at Covent Garden for *Il trovatore*: 'She arrived looking marvellous – as though she didn't have a care in the world, unlike the rest of us who were all tired after a day's work. *Il trovatore*, as it happens, has one of the most complex plots in all opera. I certainly can't fathom it. Just before we took our seats, Mrs Thatcher said to me: "There's a little scene in the second act which I don't quite understand." Of course I couldn't explain it to her.'[69]

Mrs Thatcher was always anxious to acquire more cultural knowledge. In August 1984, while staying with Lady Glover in Switzerland, she went to the town of Anif in Austria to have lunch with the celebrated German conductor Herbert von Karajan‡ at his house there. Karajan, who disliked small talk, was delighted by the way she immediately started interrogating him: 'How, she asked, does a conductor create a sense of ensemble when the players are in different relationships with one another and at different distances? How do you best control an orchestra: is it by force of will or by persuasion? Is a conductor *necessary*?'[70] He so enjoyed this line of questioning that, having answered, he adopted a similar technique on her: 'Now it is my turn to ask you about your profession.'[71] He asked her comparable questions about the exercise of power and the nature of authority, making the lunch continue much longer than expected.

In Whitehall, Mrs Thatcher was notorious for noticing interesting works of art and furniture in the government collection and hijacking them for display at Downing Street. On one occasion, contrary to Whitehall rules that only specialist handlers could move a pair of valuable vases, she happily picked up one and ordered Robert Armstrong to carry the other.[72] She formed a friendly relationship with the director of the Government Art Collection, Wendy Baron, and asked her to provide works of art

---

* Gilbert Prousch (Italy, 1943–) and George Passmore (England, 1942–) met in 1967 at St Martin's School of Art in London and since then have worked in collaboration as artists.

† Claus Moser (1922–2015), born in Berlin to a Jewish family who escaped Nazi Germany to live in England in 1936; educated Frensham Heights School and LSE; statistician; held many senior posts in academia and the Civil Service, including professor of social statistics, LSE, 1961–70; director, Central Statistical Office and head of Government Statistical Service, 1967–78; chairman, Royal Opera House, 1974–87; knighted, 1973; created Lord Moser, 1981.

‡ Herbert von Karajan (1908–89), Austrian; principal conductor of the Berlin Philharmonic Orchestra, 1955–89.

which 'displayed the greatness of Britain'.[73] Dr Baron provided her with portraits of scientists, like Sir Humphry Davy, and Byron's daughter, Ada Lovelace, who invented the first algorithm intended to be carried out by machine, and a bust of Grantham's other most famous citizen, Sir Isaac Newton; also portraits of Wellington and Nelson, which she had demanded. Under the influence of Lord Gowrie, she was persuaded to display more modern work as well, including a sculpture by Henry Moore. She had idiosyncratic doctrines of her own about paintings, for example that they should have what she called 'focal points', by which she really meant little scenes of particular interest (hence an admiration for L. S. Lowry). Once, looking at a painting of the Camden School that Dr Baron had produced, she said, 'That's not a very good picture. I was taught at school one must never have more than two bright colours in one painting.'[74] The only picture that Mrs Thatcher specifically herself discovered and persuaded the government fund to buy for Downing Street was a (bad) painting of a sunset over water by Winston Churchill. She believed that Churchill had hung it in his study at Chartwell. She loved her surroundings. One August, thinking that Mrs Thatcher would be away, Dr Baron visited No. 10 to check up on the collection. She was surprised to come upon the Prime Minister busily dusting her cabinet full of porcelain on loan from the V&A. 'You know, Dr Baron,' she said, 'one of the things I shall most miss when I leave here is having all these beautiful pictures.'[75] She thought pictures were too expensive to buy herself, but she collected some things privately – Chinese scrolls, for instance, and Crown Derby – and was always eager to learn more, asking to be taken round museums by their directors *incognita* to be instructed about their collections.[76] John Pope-Hennessy, however, who, as director of the V&A when she was Education Secretary, had escorted Mrs Thatcher round the collection, recalled that she 'left me with the unambiguous impression that she was blind'.[77]

Rare was the intellectual who did not have strong feelings about Mrs Thatcher. Sir Isaiah Berlin* joked that it was a lack in himself that he could not muster passion against Mrs Thatcher or Ronald Reagan: 'I wish I could get up some kind of personal negative emotion against them in my breast, but I cannot. That is what some of my friends and allies have against me.'[78]

---

* Sir Isaiah Berlin (1909–97), educated St Paul's and Corpus Christi College, Oxford; Chichele Professor of Social and Political Theory, Oxford, 1957–67; president, British Academy, 1974–8; Fellow of All Souls College, Oxford; knighted, 1971.

The *locus classicus* for the conflict between Mrs Thatcher and intellectuals was the row over her honorary degree at Oxford in 1985. This had been foreshadowed in 1983, when the Royal Society, the country's most eminent scientific academy, decided to elect Mrs Thatcher, as the first scientist prime minister, to its fellowship. Forty-four Fellows of the Royal Society wrote to the magazine *Nature* to complain that it would be 'damaging to the good name' of the Society to grant her an honorary fellowship.[79] They did not prevail, although Mrs Thatcher's cause only narrowly won the two-thirds majority needed when the Society met to vote. Some of those who opposed her had cited her National Health Service policies and cuts in medical research funding. In 1981, the sums allocated by the government-funded University Grants Committee had been cut by 18 per cent over three years, to which Keith Joseph added a further 2 per cent cut in 1983. This led, by administrative complication rather than political intent, to a disproportionate cutting of the money for 'pure' (that is, non-applied) science. Academic feeling against these trends ran high. When Oxford's Hebdomadal Council proposed Mrs Thatcher for an honorary degree late in 1984, some of those who had tried, and failed, to stop her at the Royal Society tried again.

Mrs Thatcher herself was not well informed about the state of Oxford opinion. The proposal for her honorary degree would almost certainly have been uncontroversial if it had been made when she first became prime minister in 1979. The passage of time, however, had made it more controversial, because more resentment had accumulated against her. When she received the official invitation to allow her name to go forward for the degree, she also got a letter from the Conservative historian Robert Blake,* who was Provost of the Queen's College, Oxford. He said how delighted he was, and told her not to worry about the proviso that a vote on the matter might be taken in Congregation (that is, among all the university's academic staff): 'it is conceivable that some left-wing don might mount a challenge. I personally think it is very unlikely, but I might be wrong. I am confident, however, that if there were a vote, you would win it.'[80] Her principal private secretary, Robin Butler, was not so sure. He wrote a note accompanying Blake's letter warning her that 'left-wingers in the University will take the opportunity of running a campaign against you before

* Robert Blake (1916–2003), educated King Edward VI Grammar School, Norwich and Magdalen College, Oxford; Provost, the Queen's College, Oxford, 1968–87; a pro-vice-chancellor, Oxford University, 1971–87; historian, best known for his biography *Disraeli* (1966) and for *The Conservative Party from Peel to Churchill* (1970), revised and updated as *The Conservative Party from Peel to Thatcher* (1985); joint editor, *Dictionary of National Biography*, 1980–90; created Lord Blake, 1971.

the vote in Congregation.'[81] He advised her to reconsider the invitation at a later date. Mrs Thatcher appeared to acquiesce, but following a subsequent meeting with Lord Blake on 14 December she was persuaded to let her name go forward. She felt almost overawed by her old university. Answering Butler's anxiety, she said, 'Robin, if Oxford wants to confer an honorary degree on me, who am I to make terms about it?'[82] In her letter of acceptance, she said that the proposal gave her 'the greatest pride and pleasure',[83] which was true.

Her opponents were more diligent than her supporters. Drawing particularly on scientists and the faculty of Politics, Philosophy and Economics (PPE), they collected 275 protest signatures, including 11 Fellows of the Royal Society. Their statement said that Mrs Thatcher's government had done 'deep and systematic damage to the whole public education system in Britain'.

Their campaign took off. It drew strength from several factors – the usual anger that people feel when they receive less government money than in the past, a rejection of a vision of the universities which was considered too utilitarian, and a particular feeling against Mrs Thatcher heightened by the long-drawn-out struggle of the miners' strike, just then visibly moving towards defeat for Arthur Scargill. Following the constitution of the university, Oxford's Congregation met to debate the issue at the Sheldonian Theatre on 29 January 1985. Denis Noble,* a leading physiologist, argued against the degree. 'Virtually everyone', he said, 'who knows what is happening in the science laboratories of this country is extremely alarmed and deeply worried.'[84] He described the 'week to week' chaos about money in which the Research Councils found themselves as 'simply unbelievable'. But he also made a more general case: 'We are here to protect the intellectual heritage of hundreds of years': history would probably judge this as 'the watershed in determining whether we are *philistine* [his emphasis] enough to let this particular national heritage crumble'. That was more important, he argued, than the 'cosy tradition' of conferring honorary degrees on prime ministers.

That word 'philistine' tapped into the intellectuals' feeling against Mrs Thatcher which went much wider than Oxford. Peter Pulzer,† a political scientist, and another leader of the anti-Thatcher camp, reflected in after

---

* Denis Noble (1936–), educated Emanuel School, London and University College London; Burdon Sanderson Professor of Cardiovascular Physiology, Oxford University, 1984–2004; Tutorial Fellow, Balliol College, Oxford, 1963–84; Professorial Fellow, 1984–2004.
† Peter Pulzer (1929–), educated Surbiton County Grammar School, King's College, Cambridge and University of London; University Lecturer in Politics, Oxford, 1960–84; Official Student and Tutor in Politics, Christ Church, 1962–84; Gladstone Professor of Government

years that there had been a strong 'aesthetic' objection to Mrs Thatcher: 'It certainly weighed with me, and it weighed with a lot of other people . . . it was probably the biggest single common factor.'[85] He denied that this was because dons looked down on Mrs Thatcher socially. On the contrary, said Pulzer, who himself came from a modest grammar-school background, 'There was if anything this feeling that "She ought to be one of us, but isn't." '[86] Ill prepared for the level of controversy, the Council's leaders had not campaigned hard enough before the vote,* and did not really know how to fight back against the campaign. Congregation rejected an honorary degree for Mrs Thatcher by 738 votes to 319. No women spoke in the debate.

The reaction was excited, and polarized. Both sides in the argument saw themselves as bravely rebellious. Those who opposed the honorary degree thought they were standing up for the integrity of education against the powerful. The high Tory Peregrine Worsthorne,† though critical of Oxford for its vote, thought that Mrs Thatcher had partly brought it upon herself. 'Listening to Mrs Thatcher,' he wrote on the Sunday after the vote, 'one might be forgiven for supposing that the civilised governing class is part of the enemy which she, with the help of the people, is determined to eradicate – a real case of throwing out the Tory baby with the socialist bathwater.'[87]

Those who supported the honorary degree thought that the dons who voted it down were resentful of the loss of their privileged status in society as intellectuals automatically deferred to and subsidized by governments and saw Mrs Thatcher as a parvenue. The *Spectator* commented that the decision to snub a graduate of Somerville who had become the first woman prime minister 'will confirm many in their view that Oxford represents the "Establishment" and Mrs Thatcher is, as she prides herself, an outsider'.[88] Harold Macmillan had been elected chancellor of Oxford while prime minister and still held the position. What qualification did he have for that post that Mrs Thatcher lacked for a mere honorary degree? 'We can only think of one – a vanity equal to that of his *alma mater*.'[89]

---

and Public Administration, University of Oxford, 1985–96; Fellow of All Souls College, 1985–96.

* Geoffrey Warnock, the university's Vice-Chancellor, was privately reported, by John Patten, who was both an MP and a former Oxford don, to be making 'every effort' to get a good turnout for Mrs Thatcher. His wife, Mary Warnock, who later had such harsh things to say about Mrs Thatcher to the *Sunday Telegraph*, was 'doing a lot in the women's colleges' for Mrs Thatcher's cause, Patten relayed to Downing Street. (Patten to Alison, 28 January 1985, CAC: THCR 2/1/5/142.)

† Peregrine Worsthorne (1923–), educated Stowe, Peterhouse, Cambridge and Magdalen College, Oxford; columnist; associate editor, *Sunday Telegraph*, 1976–86; editor, 1986–9; knighted, 1991.

In a general assessment of Mrs Thatcher's place in history (written after her third general election victory), Professor John Vincent,* one of the few prominent academics to sympathize with Mrs Thatcher's subversive conservatism, and himself a victim of attack from the left in the 1980s, identified why she was such an object of hatred.

> It was because she offered 'earnest and practical dissent' to progressive orthodoxy. Mrs Thatcher is the point at which all snobberies meet: intellectual snobbery, social snobbery, the snobbery of Brooks's [the whiggish London club], the snobbery about scientists among those educated in the arts, the snobbery of the metropolis about the provincial, the snobbery of the South about the North, and the snobbery of men about career women.[90]

Both sides were able to adduce good arguments. But what seems most strange in retrospect is how little prominence was given to the point about Mrs Thatcher being Oxford's own, and the first of her sex. One needs to imagine Harvard refusing an honorary degree to America's first black president Barack Obama (who attended Harvard Law School) because of disagreement with his education policies, to see how extraordinary the Oxford decision looks today – and looked even at the time – to the wider world. Robin Butler's wife, Jill, an Oxford graduate, was clear: 'They would never have done this to a man.'[91] Her husband, who much later became the Master of University College, Oxford, and therefore experienced the consequences at first hand, recalled that Oxford's decision had 'a disastrous effect upon fund-raising for the university, especially in the United States'.[92]

Mrs Thatcher's own public reaction was laconic: 'If they do not wish to confer the honour, I am the last person who would wish to receive it.'[93] But Robin Butler felt that privately 'The degree of hurt was huge.'[94] Although she had not been exactly happy at Oxford, it had been the foundation of her public career, and she had a reverence for the place. To Anthony Quinton, the President of Trinity College, who had supported her, she wrote that, although she was 'naturally disappointed . . . I am not unaccustomed to rebuffs: and I am bound to say that my peace of mind is founded more upon my success in graduating successfully from the university than what is involved in gaining or failing to gain an honorary degree.'[95] To her friend Daphne Park, the Principal of her old college, Somerville, she wrote: 'I do assure you that the vote does not detract one jot from the affection I feel for the university which I knew, especially for

---

* Professor John Vincent (1937–), educated Bedales and Christ's College, Cambridge; Professor of Modern History, University of Bristol, 1970–84; Professor of History, 1984–2002. He was a columnist for the *Sun* and *The Times* in the 1980s.

Somerville. It was such a privilege to be there. Without that, I should never have been here [that is, in Downing Street].'[96]*

Mrs Thatcher later suggested that the story of her honorary degree showed the comfort family could bring. When the news came through, she said, Mark was in America, and saw it on television. He rang her at once and said, 'Don't worry, Mummy,' and 'within about two hours there were some flowers here.'[97] 'This kind of closeness', she said, '. . . is part of my life, every day.' That she cited this example indicates how much the degree refusal had upset her.

She certainly got full support from Denis, who was outraged. He wrote a real-life 'Dear Bill' letter to Bill Deedes. 'Why anybody takes this terrible job and lives in this awful atmosphere only our God knows. I literally wept. Bless you.'[98] 'I share your distress,' his friend and golfing partner replied, 'but let neither of you take this too much to heart. Oxford, alas, no longer implants a special culture of its own . . . On the contrary, she is prey to alien influences which infect less renowned seats of learning . . . Forgive the typewriter, but when I am cross my writing wobbles.'[99] Looking back on her years in office, Denis told the present author, he reckoned that the saga of the Oxford degree upset his wife more than anything else that happened to her in office, apart from her exit.[100]†

When told, in 1991, that Mrs Thatcher had been genuinely hurt by the vote, her leading Oxford opponent Peter Pulzer said: 'I have no sympathy with that. I think that a politician like her, who loses no time lecturing absolutely everybody on absolutely everything, must be prepared to accept snubs.'[101]

This snubbed woman, so suburban, harsh and philistine in many literary and academic minds, presented a very different persona to those who worked for her every day. On the whole, her staff – as opposed to her much bullied Cabinet colleagues – found it a much more pleasurable experience than, given her rather terrifying reputation, they had expected. This was true not only of those who performed the relatively humble tasks

---

* By way of commiseration, the friendly Oxford don Michael Gearin-Tosh sent Mrs Thatcher a gift of a rare edition of *Gulliver's Travels* by Jonathan Swift. She told him that 'The book has long been a favourite of mine – but it had not previously struck me that Swift was such a perceptive economist, as well as such a devastating satirist. I agree with everything you say in your letter about the economic and industrial facts of life – if only there were more realists among the clouds of Laputa!' (Thatcher to Gearin-Tosh, 14 February 1985, CAC: THCR 3/2/159.)

† Her revenge came later. In 1997, when the time came to place her papers in an archive, she gave them to Cambridge.

of driving, cooking, typing and so on; with these, Mrs Thatcher had always been friendly, direct and solicitous. It applied also to senior civil servants, a breed of whom, en masse, she was suspicious.

John Coles, Mrs Thatcher's foreign affairs private secretary from 1981 to 1984, wrote a short account of his experience working for her shortly after leaving her employment in June 1984.[102] In Coles's experience, the public perception of Mrs Thatcher often differed from the private reality. Physically, Coles found her 'Slightly dumpy, smaller than the popular imagination would have it.' She 'always took great trouble with her clothes, her hair and her make-up'. This care included consideration of the context of her clothes, both televisual and political. When she hosted a large banquet in the Great Hall of the People in Peking* in 1982 'she decided to appear in a brilliant scarlet dress, not of course as a sycophantic gesture to communist China but because she had been told that for the Chinese red signified happiness and that it would be an appropriate colour to wear for a celebratory occasion.' Coles considered that Mrs Thatcher's physical features were 'not particularly good, apart from her face which had great mobility; it was capable of an almost spitting fierceness, a beatific calm, flirtatiousness and the deepest concentration. You learned to watch the mood.'

Despite her fondness for expressing the great simplicities and discerning the 'fundamental principle' in any situation, Coles felt that 'everything about [her character] was complex':[103] 'The dominant characteristic was determination', but he nevertheless felt that the Iron Lady image was somewhat misleading. Although she did sometimes override all discussion, 'Much more often her approach to a new problem was hesitant and cautious. It is a mistake to assume that in her case determination meant dogmatism. It meant only that having reached a conclusion . . . and having rigorously examined the arguments, she then insisted on the application of the conclusion.'

Much of Mrs Thatcher's behaviour, Coles thought, derived from her unique situation as the only woman in power. This made her feel the need to maintain public toughness. She rarely expressed, for example, a general public compassion for the unemployed, though Coles noticed how often she took up 'individual cases of hardship' which came to her attention. She would reject the explanatory draft letters provided by Whitehall and 'insist that the case be re-examined and more humanity shown'. She feared that, as a woman among men, she would be considered unfit to lead if she

---

* It was customary for foreign diplomatic receptions to take place in the Great Hall, as well as those given by the Chinese.

made public displays of human emotion or 'could be shown to be given to unreasonable feminine behaviour'. The men in her Cabinet had resources deriving from male camaraderie in public schools, university, the armed services and clubs. 'They draw', wrote Coles, 'on a reserve of accepted thought and behaviour, of male humour, argument and sign-language from which a woman is excluded . . . She probably felt that the language of compromise itself had a male quality, the civilised talk of clubland.' She was outside all of that and had to prevent herself being suffocated by it.

It was well understood that this was so, thought Coles: 'Less commonly observed is the emotional cost to her of that process and the steps to which she had to resort to defy the conventions.'[104] Her situation led her to odd behaviour: 'To assert her will this very feminine woman had to – or at least chose to – adopt a strident tone with nearly all of her colleagues. At times her style was abusive, rude and unpleasant.' She was perfectly happy to take advantage of the sexist belief that women are irrational creatures: 'Not for her the logical chain of argument if she saw the chain leading in the wrong direction.' When a Cabinet minister threatened to resign, she did not understand – or preferred to ignore – the convention that such threats should elicit a plea to reconsider. On one such occasion, her response was 'That's up to you. But you would be extremely unwise to do so.' In such encounters, wrote Coles, 'She could display a quite unfeminine toughness and crudeness . . . But in general I insist on the femininity. She was a loving mother, with a mother's emotions. And she was devoted to her much older husband, even if their marriage, like most marriages at that age, lacked sparkle. She was easily moved by another's misfortunes.'

Her mind, too, worked more according to a female stereotype than her professional and educational qualifications implied:

> She did not proceed, as the scientist does, by . . . forming a conclusion only when the evidence clearly justifies it. Nor like the lawyer did she seek to build up a case by logical argument. I would be less than honest if I claimed fully to understand her intellectual processes. There were occasions when she moved with astonishing rapidity to a clear conclusion, apparently without needing any intervening steps. In these cases she had the fastest mind in the Cabinet by a long way. Whether she was guided by instinct or whether her agile mind simply concertinaed the chain of thought until it almost failed to exist, I never knew.[105]

Possibly this quality – and what Coles considered her 'inadequate literary grounding' – explained the fact that Mrs Thatcher was often 'rather incoherent' in communication. 'Time and again one saw baffled expressions on the faces of listeners as they attempted to make sense of a succession of sentences which tailed off into the air and seemed to bear little relation to each other.' Yet, despite this, her impromptu speeches were better than her setpiece ones which, perhaps by being over-prepared, did not have the style or feel for words of a Churchill. 'I do not think she ever made a great speech,' but nor did she ever make a bad one: 'She was always worth listening to. And audience after audience was fired by her conviction, clarity, enthusiasm, and the fact that she used language which, unlike much political jargon, could actually be understood.'

Although Mrs Thatcher was no intellectual, she was 'passionately attracted by ideas'. This was why she fought shy of the government machine, although she often admired and trusted individual members of it. She liked to see ideas 'in their original form, uncluttered by bureaucratic processing. She seized on what to her was a new idea with all the avidity and enthusiasm of a parched traveller, emerging thirsty from the desert to be presented with a goblet of ice-cold water.' For this reason, she was no respecter of persons and, though she could be most alarming in her dignity of office, 'she was probably the least pompous of all British Prime Ministers,' welcoming ideas whether they came from a Cabinet minister, an academic, an entrepreneur, 'or indeed the doorkeeper'.

Coles asked himself what motivated her. First, he concluded that it was her upbringing, especially what she had learnt from her father, and her consequent commitment to work, even when it entailed sacrifice of herself and others: 'She always had a stricken conscience that if she had spent more time with her children, their lives would have been easier.'[106] He added, rather tentatively, the idea that 'had the emotional side of her character been fully satisfied, she would never have developed the prodigious energy and determination that are two of her strongest qualities.' He was implying that never, in her marriage or in any other relationship, had she known the full force of sexual passion or unguarded love.

David Goodall, another senior civil servant who wrote a private account of Mrs Thatcher – in his case, after she had left office – had less natural rapport with her. As a strong sympathizer with Irish nationalism very concerned to solve the problem which he considered had been caused by the partition of Ireland, he disliked Mrs Thatcher's strong, if somewhat confused prejudices in the other direction. He worked closely with her in the Cabinet Office from 1982 to 1984 and quite closely from 1984 to 1987, when he was Deputy Under-Secretary in the Foreign Office and dealt with everything pertaining to the Anglo-Irish Agreement. 'Like so many of those who served under her, I liked, admired, and was repelled and exasperated by her in about equal measure. In retrospect, however, and on the whole, the admiration predominates.'[107]

He liked, for example, the fact that she could be teased. On one occasion, fed up with objections by officials to what she wanted to do, she exclaimed, ' "Don't keep saying 'No, no, Prime Minister.' " We substituted "But, Prime Minister". "But, but, but; too many buts," she complained. "If we can't say no and we can't say but, how are we to disagree with you?" I asked. She had the grace to laugh.'

Her interest in small matters or seemingly unimportant people was notable. When Goodall was appointed high commissioner in India in 1987, Mrs Thatcher saw him to wish him well. After a *tour d'horizon* of India, including her proclamation that its large middle class 'can pull all the rest up: that's what middle classes do', she turned to the subject of the servants' quarters in the Delhi High Commission. 'As the former colonial power, our servants shouldn't be less well looked after than the Germans' or the Americans'. And you have such a nice head bearer there – *such* a nice head bearer. So if you want my help bashing the Foreign Office over the head to improve the servants' quarters, don't hesitate.'[108] The head bearer, Kacheru, remained a preoccupation of hers. Some years after her resignation, she expressed outrage that he had not been given an adequately high honour; and she sent him a present.

There was something likeable and comic about her unpompous, immediate expression of what was on her mind to anyone who happened to be present. Early in her time as prime minister, Goodall was invited to brief her before a meeting with the Chancellor of Germany, Helmut Schmidt. He entered 10 Downing Street with Michael Palliser, the Permanent Secretary at the Foreign Office. Mrs Thatcher greeted them in the hall:

'What do you think of my new carpet? Much better than that dirty old coconut matting. By the way [to Palliser], have you got any lamps? I need some new lamps for the Pillared Room.' We stood reverentially on the edge of the carpet, contemplating it, when the front door opened and Lord Carrington [at that time Foreign Secretary] came in, looking rather cross and carrying a bundle of papers. 'Peter, you've just walked across a new and expensive carpet.' Carrington looked baffled. 'Carpet? What carpet?' 'And Peter, have you got any lamps?' 'Lamps? Lamps? Prime Minister, you're turning into an absolute magpie.'[109]

'What I liked', said Goodall,

was her downrightness, her clarity of mind, her ability to cut to the heart of a problem . . . and the courage and resolution with which she stuck to her guns. She was stimulating, capable of kindness and could be fun. What was less attractive was her narrowness of vision and above all what seemed to me a certain ungenerosity of spirit: she bridled at the word 'magnanimity' and the idea itself seemed alien to her.[110]

Robin Butler, one of her closest aides, was in many ways an admirer who came to believe that the only thing that history would remember about him and many of his colleagues was that they had worked for Mrs Thatcher. But he shared some uncomfortable feelings about her. 'My heart always fell when I had to sit next to her,' he recalled. She had no small talk, and he felt 'at risk'. Dealing with her face to face was 'like feeding a fierce animal'.[111]

Although almost no women had formal power during Mrs Thatcher's premiership, several were important in what might be called her court. They testified to aspects of her character which men tended to understand less well. In the opinion of Carla Powell, Charles's vivacious Italian wife, who frequently gave Mrs Thatcher informal assistance with clothes and home decoration, 'Everything about her was totally, totally feminine. She adored the details of clothes. I called her La Bionda [The Blonde] because she loved the boys [her private secretaries].'[112] Mrs Thatcher liked the way they prepared her for interviews and public appearances, and 'the boys' seemed to understand this. Robin Butler used an equestrian metaphor about getting her ready for Prime Minister's Questions in Parliament: 'It was important that there was the right amount of sweat on the flanks.'[113] With Mrs Thatcher, Carla Powell continued, 'everything was a woman thing'.[114] It was important not to upstage the Prime Minister. She recalled being lectured by Robin Butler: 'Remember that Mrs Thatcher is a woman, so don't overdress as you usually do.'[115] Because of her own attention to dress, Mrs Thatcher used to fret about her daughter Carol's more casual attitude: 'She wanted Carol to be better dressed. She looked as if she wanted to put her in a washing machine.'[116] This was connected in Mrs Thatcher's own mind, thought Carla, with her longing for her daughter to marry someone.* The subject of Carol, about whom Mrs Thatcher felt guilty, would bring tears to her eyes.† Her own marriage was undoubtedly

---

* At the time of writing, Carol has never married, but has a long-term partner, Marco Grass.
† If she felt her own children had been wronged, she was utterly unforgiving, although she tried also to appear to act professionally. In 1986, for example, Max Hastings, the new editor of the *Daily Telegraph*, decided to sack Carol from his features staff 'with the other dead wood' (Correspondence with Sir Max Hastings). 'Naively, I thought the PM would regard this as a normal piece of newspaper business, but she went potty, told CB [Conrad Black, the paper's proprietor] that I had behaved disgracefully etc . . . She never spoke to me again.' At the same time, however, Mrs Thatcher made sure to keep her relations with the Telegraph Group in good repair, courting Conrad Black and Andrew Knight, the then chief executive,

strong and even, according to Carla Powell's testimony, which differs in this from the consensus, flirtatious. She recalled a scrap of dialogue: 'Denis: "You know I don't like you dressed in black." Mrs Thatcher: "I have to. I'm the Prime Minister." Then Denis made a "Go on with you!" gesture.'[117] According to Cynthia Crawford, however, the marriage was 'not a huge love affair though they were great soulmates' and Mrs Thatcher always felt uneasy about Denis's first marriage, whose break-up had hurt him greatly. 'Crawfie,' she once said, 'I shall always be only the second Mrs Thatcher' (see Volume I, p. 110). For all her determination and success, she always suffered from insecurity.

Mrs Thatcher was ready to 'use her femininity'.[118] She could be 'totally, utterly ruthless', and part of this was to do with her idea of the role of her sex. Once she came across Carla Powell upset and crying over some argument. She tried to comfort her in her trouble and then said, 'Carla, if a woman takes on a battle, she has to win.' This was one of her strongest beliefs, and it may explain why she was not instinctively magnanimous. She believed men would close ranks against a woman: every inch had to be fought for. And yet this unyielding combativeness did not usually make her unpleasant to work for. She bestowed and received loyalty and 'She gave everyone love.'[119]

Even her demanding nature had its appeal. She had a surprising cosiness about her. On foreign trips in particular, she liked to have some of her secretaries – her 'girls' – about her.* Caroline Ryder, who went on several, recalled: 'She wanted us around early morning, late at night, late afternoon, to talk to. We were her daughters.'[120] Mrs Thatcher was always trying to find husbands for these younger women, often fastening on 'suitable' men who were, unbeknown to her, homosexual. She enjoyed gossip about such matters, especially about the absurdities of men in pursuit of women. Early in her leadership, for example, when Alison Ward told her how a young bachelor MP had made a 'massive lunge' at her in a taxi, scattering the contents of her handbag all over the floor, Mrs Thatcher 'cried with laughter'.[121] In such matters, her staff believed, she had learnt from early experiences of her own 'how to handle things'.[122] Although Mrs Thatcher had traditional views about marriage – she always disapproved of what were not then referred to as 'partners' – she was not personally censorious, preferring to see matters of love as part of the

---

who recalled her behaviour over the sacking of Carol as 'magnanimous' (Interview with Andrew Knight).

* Carol, her real daughter, was generous about this, and welcomed the fact that she was 'mightily fond of "her girls"' (Interview with Carol Thatcher).

comédie humaine. She never pushed anyone out because of a sexual relationship, unless, as in the case of Cecil Parkinson, the exterior pressure
became overwhelming.

Mrs Thatcher was often criticized by prominent women and by feminists for not doing enough for the cause of her sex. Certainly she was in
no hurry to seek out and surround herself with female talent in Parliament.
The testimony of individual women whom she knew, however, does suggest some solidarity with her sex. One example was Patricia Hodgson,
who first came across Mrs Thatcher in the early stages of her career.
In 1976, Patricia Hodgson became chairman of the Bow Group, the
influential party ginger group, and, in March 1976, presided over its
twenty-fifth-anniversary dinner, attended by the existing party leader and
her predecessors – Heath, Home and Macmillan – an august quad which
had never before been achieved. Careful preparations were made, and
Patricia Hodgson checked with Mrs Thatcher about what she would wear
in order to avoid any clash of clothes. It turned out to be the day of Harold
Wilson's resignation as prime minister, so this should have provided an
opportunity for Mrs Thatcher, but in fact she performed badly in the
Commons that day. She arrived at the dinner in a state of tension. To mark
the grand occasion, the young Patricia had gone out and bought herself a
cream oriental evening gown, forgetting her clothes agreement with the
leader's office. As she entered the room, Mrs Thatcher glared at her and
snapped: 'You said you'd wear blue.' Presumably because of the unexpected rush of the day, she seemed ill prepared for her speech and spent
the dinner saying and eating nothing, but scribbling her lines at the last
minute. The tension was worsened by the fact that Ted Heath talked across
the table to Macmillan within her hearing, shouting, 'We've got to get rid
of that dreadful woman.' Mrs Thatcher's speech was very poor, and she
seemed anguished about it, going literally down on her knees to Home
afterwards and beseeching, 'Was it all right?' It was not.[123]

The next day, Patricia Hodgson received a note of apology from Mrs
Thatcher for her discourtesy the previous night, and an invitation to come
and have tea. She accepted, and the tea – or sometimes dinner – became
a regular annual event until, in 1985, Hodgson was made the secretary of
the BBC. After the Corporation forbade further contact with the Prime
Minister (see p. 534) she and Hodgson had a 'farewell' lunch at Chequers
at which they drank cheap Liebfraumilch. 'It's terribly good, you know,'
Mrs Thatcher told her. 'It's a special offer from the *News of the World*.'[124]
In these meetings, Mrs Thatcher occasionally asked her to help with the
drafting of speeches, but otherwise appeared to have no 'agenda' in seeing
her. She wrote her a couple of letters of support when she was experiencing

a difficult pregnancy. Looking back at these various kindnesses, Patricia Hodgson said, 'I ask myself "Why?" and I conclude that she simply wanted to maintain links with other women.'

Mrs Thatcher kept in mind the pressures which women could experience in a man's world. On one occasion, her private office complained to her that too many ministers' wives were trying to get in on their husbands' official trips abroad 'often with a fairly flimsy justification'.[125] Would she intervene? 'I think not,' wrote Mrs Thatcher. 'Some wives have a rotten time because husbands are away so much and late at the House so often that the <u>odd</u> visit is a kind of compensation.' It should also be said, however, that most, though not all, ministers' wives considered themselves more or less ignored by Mrs Thatcher. She visibly preferred the conversation of the men. She also did not necessarily take the woman's side in questions of equality, and did not always realize that this might be held against her as indicating a lack of sisterly feeling. When the question of women priests came up, for example, she was instinctively against it, worrying that it would split the Church. One of her parliamentary private secretaries, Archie Hamilton, told her that, as a woman prime minister, she could not oppose the ordination of women. 'Anyway,' he said, 'I don't know what you are worried about: women are capable of greater spirituality than men and are less prone to sexual temptation.' 'Oh, I don't know about that,' Mrs Thatcher replied. Without conceding anything to Hamilton directly, she took his advice to heart and eventually came out in favour of women priests.[126]

A little later in Mrs Thatcher's career, one woman analysed her by unusual means. Professor Alice Coleman, a geographer whose experiments in how to reduce crime by improving housing environments were later to interest Mrs Thatcher, was also a graphologist. Before she had met Mrs Thatcher, she subjected her handwriting to an extensive graphological analysis. It reported that Mrs Thatcher's script showed her 'highly intelligent' and 'clear-minded', but without 'mental imagination': 'She lays great stress on facts and objectivity, and replaces imagination by empathy and intuitive insight.'[127] 'She has a talent for getting work finished. In fact, she has no fewer than 28 traits that can be described as intensifiers to job completion,' Professor Coleman thought. 'Without being pernickety, she pays good attention to details, seeing the trees as important components of the wood.' Professor Coleman even considered her to be 'capable of warm emotions', but added that 'One effect of [her] strong willpower and self-control is that her emotional expressiveness does not reflect her inner warmth and generous nature. It is predominantly objective or even cooler, to an extent that might cause some people to regard her as cold and hard.'[128] When she came to meet Mrs Thatcher, Coleman recalled that one thing particularly struck her, because it was rare in a politician: 'She wanted to round out her knowledge. She wanted to find things out properly.'[129]

As if to confirm the left-wing caricature of her habits and attitudes, Mrs Thatcher became, while prime minister, a suburban house-owner. At Easter 1985, after a tour of five countries in eleven days, in which she lost her voice while speaking to the Sri Lankan parliament, and everyone involved had returned to Britain utterly exhausted, the private secretaries begged her for a rest and asked if they – and therefore she – could have Whitsun off. She agreed, but as the Whitsun recess began to approach, she started to talk of holding an economic seminar at Chequers. 'If you let me go to Chequers,' she wailed, 'and don't let me do anything over Whitsun, I shall die.'[130] So the private office agreed to furnish one private secretary per day. Two of these days fell to Robin Butler. For the second, Mrs Thatcher had asked to visit the St Christopher Hospice in Sydenham, founded by Dame Cicely Saunders,* and the question arose as to what she should do afterwards. The hospice was near Butler's house in Dulwich, and when he asked Mrs Thatcher what she would like, she asked if she and Denis could simply have 'a quiet supper' with the Butlers there. Robin's wife Jill agreed, on condition that she would not have to entertain the Thatchers while getting supper ready, and so her husband took them for a walk in Dulwich Park, which was looking at its best with all its rhododendrons out. Because Mrs Thatcher was always interested in 'new build', Butler also arranged for her to see a development of executive houses which was going up beside the park. 'I thought this was entertainment,' he recalled. 'It never crossed my mind this would be a purchase.'[131]†

The Thatchers, however, were in house-moving mood, and ready to be seduced, as prospective buyers often are in early summer. They had decided not to try to renew the lease on their house in Flood Street, Chelsea, and had sold the remainder of it the previous year. They then looked at a house in Kent Terrace, Regent's Park, but felt stretched by the financial demands of its landlords, the Crown Estate. Mrs Thatcher believed she could not afford it. 'Of course, you can. Borrow!' advised Butler,[132] but Mrs Thatcher, always cautious with her own money, was not inclined to go down the path that so many British people were then following under the Chancellorship of Nigel Lawson. 'What happens if I die?' she riposted to Butler.

---

* Cicely Saunders (1918–2005), educated Roedean School and St Anne's College, Oxford; trained as a nurse, a medical social worker and a physician; pioneer of the modern hospice movement; founded St Christopher's Hospice, 1967; created dame, 1980; OM, 1989.
† Some other accounts of the Dulwich house story maintain that Robin Butler wanted Mrs Thatcher to buy the house, but there is no documentary evidence of this.

So when she saw the Barrett home under construction, and interrogated a plasterer on a ladder – who only realized halfway through the conversation that he was talking to the Prime Minister – about how best to do the cornices, Mrs Thatcher was smitten with the place. This was to be their bolthole and their retirement home. It was within 10 feet of the Dulwich and Sydenham golf course, and Mrs Thatcher immediately persuaded herself that this would be very nice for Denis, though in fact he had played on the course, which has heavy clay, and had 'absolutely loathed it'.[133] For his part, Denis decided that it would be very nice for Margaret because she could 'walk out and watch the Dulwich boys playing rugby'. 'I wondered', said Robin Butler, 'how two people married to each other for so long could know so little about each other's tastes.'[134]

Butler pointed out to Mrs Thatcher that she had arrived through Dulwich Park and had therefore not seen the much less pleasant route which she would have to take through Brixton (scene of the 1981 riots) to Westminster if she were to live there. His advice was ignored. The Thatchers bought the mock-Georgian five-bedroom house, 11 Hambledon Place, with the work still in progress, for about £350,000, shortly before her sixtieth birthday. She relayed to the media Denis's view that it was very important 'to get back into bricks and mortar' because prices were shooting up. 'For the first time in my life,' she enthused to *Woman's Own*, 'I've got the kitchen I've always wanted . . . It's going to be a country kitchen.'[135] She may have fantasized a little about cooking in it. Her daughter Carol recalled from her childhood that if her mother 'ever got any spare time from the flat-out pace of her life, she'd bake something'.[136] Mrs Thatcher probably spoke the truth when she said that 'planning the house and where everything will go will be the only relaxation I'll have.'[137] A decorator produced by the local Conservative MP Gerald Bowden* to help the Thatchers get the house ready for moving in in the autumn of 1985 was surprised, when he visited the house, to find the Prime Minister wearing a heavy workman's apron and thick rubber gloves. She got down on a kneeling pad and started to work away at paint spots on the bare floorboards in readiness for the laying of the carpets the following day.[138] Quite soon, the house was habitable, neatly and brightly furnished in the chintzy Peter Jones style which Mrs Thatcher favoured.

In fact, 11 Hambledon Place, was, as Denis much later put it, 'a great mistake'.[139] Its purpose, he told Bowden at the time, was 'not for me, you know. It's for the widow woman on her retirement. I shall be pushing up the daisies but she will be still on the go. She can toddle down to the

---

* Gerald Bowden (1935–), educated Battersea Grammar School and Magdalen College, Oxford; Conservative MP for Dulwich, 1983–92.

village shops with her basket. And if they need her for anything in the Lords, they can send a car.'[140]

But in fact, as Mrs Thatcher began to notice while still in office, it was too far from central London, and too ill protected from the security point of view, to work. The Thatchers spent only a handful of nights there in the whole remainder of their time in Downing Street, and the twins were not attracted to the place.* Carol remembered spending only one night there, and found, when she went there again after her mother left office, that she did not know the way.[141] As well as sheltering their money, however, the house performed a valuable psychological function which they naturally did not want to disclose at the time. Denis 'recalled the appalling situation when Ted Heath got flung out without any notice at all . . . He didn't have anywhere to go. I said to Margaret we've got to have somewhere to go when we go.'[142] If No. 10 failed, they now had No. 11.

Despite this insurance policy, Mrs Thatcher was always wary of acknowledging her political mortality. Once she had bought the house, Gerald Bowden encouraged her and Denis to register as voters in Dulwich, since it was a marginal seat and every vote counted. 'No, Gerry,' said Mrs Thatcher, 'we will not put our names on the register right now [1986]. If we did it would be seized on by some journalist to suggest we don't expect to be in Downing Street much longer. But after the next election, we shall most certainly register our residence at Hambledon Place.'[143] This she and Denis duly did after she won again in 1987.

Suburban housewife though, in some sense, she still was, the Margaret Thatcher of 1987 was a publicly much more majestic figure than when she had taken office eight years earlier. She was the senior statesman of the Western world, and she had learnt to dress accordingly. Those who advised her on clothes felt that she finally achieved her best style by 1987, both for her visit to see Gorbachev in Moscow in March and for the general election in June. 'Her look solidified at its purest,' according to the fashion historian Jane Mulvagh: it was the sartorial expression of the mental control which she exercised over government.[144] 'I introduced her to *Dynasty* padded shoulders,' claimed Carla Powell of the mid-1980s,[145] whereas Crawfie considered that it was she who persuaded her that her way of dressing looked old-fashioned. Crawfie enlisted the help of Margaret King at Aquascutum to put 'power suits' together for her which would give her the greatest

---

* Despite describing the golf course as 'lousy', Denis did play there, joining a group of like-minded retired members called the 'Wednesday Old Gentlemen', whose politically incorrect acronym amused them.

possible confidence. She also catalogued all the clothes, noting which was worn when and naming them according to the place at which each appeared ('Kiev', 'Versailles') or because of what they looked like ('Gloriana'). She was particularly pleased with the navy and white check suit which Mrs Thatcher wore in the election campaign, in which she 'looked a million dollars'.[146] Mrs Thatcher herself had a good memory for what she had worn when, and liked to wear old favourites, or, as she sometimes called them, 'recipes', revamped. They brought good luck, she believed.* She wore the same suit, for example, to sign the Hong Kong Agreement as she did for her Joint Address to both Houses of the US Congress.

Certainly Mrs Thatcher became a convert to the dictum of the famous *Vogue* editor Anna Wintour that 'everything comes from the shoulders', lessening the bust and narrowing the waist. She had moved from the provincial woman looking smart of the 1950s and 1960s, through the almost municipal styles of the 1970s – patterns, pussycat bows, waistcoats without sleeves, pie-crust frill blouses and designs which tended to make her shoulders look weak – to a clearer, stronger look which worked better on television. This clothed her in block colours – sapphire, cerise, jade green, canary yellow – which stood out against grey men, as well as the staple black, which suited her well. In some respects, she came to dress like the Queen, wearing, for example, thick-heeled patent-leather shoes, first from Rayne and later from Ferragamo, and carrying, of course, the famous patent-leather handbag. For someone who was so busy and needed to change fast, dresses were vulnerable and complicated: suits were better. In autumn and winter, she told Angela Huth for the BBC, showing her examples on air, 'I live a suit life.'[147] As Carol put it, 'She regarded her clothes as going with the job.'[148] It was important to use materials which would not be full of creases, Mrs Thatcher told Huth. She preferred tweeds, brocades and British wool, for example, to frail silks or linen, and was preoccupied with 'a very good line'.[149] Blouses provided the required element of softness. From her mother's expertise as a seamstress, she had learnt about attention to detail and quality, and various tips, such as not pressing a hem so hard that it became 'a knife's edge' and could not be let down later. She was well upholstered, well covered and always perfectly groomed and coiffed, although, when travelling, she never took a hairdresser but relied on local stylists.† 'She had very nice hair [although] a

---

* Crawfie noted, however, that Mrs Thatcher was not superstitious. She did not mind, for example, that her birthday was on the 13th of the month, and she chose to marry on the 13th (of December). (Interview with Cynthia Crawford.)
† Mrs Thatcher's personal assistants always travelled with Carmen rollers for her, just in

little bit on the fine side,' recalled Eivind Bjerke, her stylist of choice in the US. 'She liked it – in today's parlance – a little bit old fashioned. She liked her hair soft. She liked it teased. She liked it rolled. She liked it sprayed. It also had to be something that, when she was photographed from all angles, would look good.'[150] She was never informal, because she instinctively recognized that this would invite a familiarity which would weaken her, but she had learnt from her mother 'Do not sit around in good clothes.'[151] Could she ever afford to be 'flamboyant, daring, sexy', Angela Huth asked her: 'Never! Nor would I wish to be.'[152]* For the interview, the BBC had absolutely insisted that Angela Huth ask Mrs Thatcher where she bought her underwear, which she was loath to do. Huth only plucked up the courage to ask her at the very end of three hours of filming.[153] The reassuringly unsexy answer was Marks and Spencer.

Although Mrs Thatcher's style was, in a sense, conventional, she rejected the cliché of the female executive which sought to imitate men – the pinstripe, the dull navy suit. She made sure she stood out, and her female equivalent of armour made her feel powerful, but she knew that being powerful is like being a lady: if you have to tell people you are, you aren't. Her idea, though she probably did not put it to herself in this way, was that the story of her life was somehow told through her clothes.† She understood signifiers – and secretly regretted the fact that hats were too out of fashion for her to wear except on special occasions ('They complete the picture').[154] She also understood the importance of sentiment in jewellery, wearing a watch from Mark, and a South African bracelet of semi-precious stones in a gold setting and an eternity ring, both presents from Denis.

In a way, Mrs Thatcher's attitude to her clothes was like that of a medieval knight to his armour. What she wore had to be beautiful and well made but also to perform its combative function. Her clothes must attract all eyes and repulse all attacks. Thus armoured, she could feel ready for her third general election as leader of the Conservative Party.

---

case, as once happened in Thailand, the local service went badly wrong (Interview with Amanda Ponsonby).

* Once, at a dinner in Washington, the liberal film director Mike Nichols had sat next to Mrs Thatcher, and found her monologue about the evils of the Soviet Union punishing. After it, she came and sat with him again, sticking with the subject. Desperate, Nichols said, 'My friend John le Carré says you are a very sexy woman.' 'Well,' replied Mrs Thatcher, 'I'm not,' and resumed her diatribe. (Interview with Sir David Hare.)

† Those who knew Mrs Thatcher well disagreed about how good her own taste was. Carla Powell used to make a face and pull an imaginary lavatory chain when discussing it, but others thought she had a good eye for quality and an understanding of allure. Perhaps it does not matter what she would have done unaided: the point was that she acted on good advice.

The last victory

'There's a woman who will never fight another election'

'No one with a conscience votes Conservative,' said Norman Tebbit.[1] So *Guardian* readers were informed by their leading columnist, Hugo Young,* at the beginning of 1987, which was expected to be election year. The article, clearly benefiting from malicious but well-informed briefing, set out the differences between the party Chairman and Mrs Thatcher: 'He is, she now thinks, the worst appointment she has made in her 12 years as party leader.' In fact Tebbit had never uttered the words that Young attributed to him. He sued the *Guardian* for libel and eventually, more than a year later, won an apology, damages and costs.

Hugo Young's error was a striking example of a trap which, for the whole of Mrs Thatcher's time as prime minister, the left fell into again and again. Many of them – not only on the hard left, but also moderates who admired writers like Young – really hated her. They thought what she was doing was not merely mistaken, but evil, and they felt a visceral personal dislike for her. To such people, Norman Tebbit was the same, but even worse: the headline on Young's piece was 'A fate worse than Thatcherism'. These beliefs led them to make repeated, serious electoral mistakes. Since they thought Mrs Thatcher and her cronies were wicked, they tended to think that they had only to point this out loudly enough and voters would desert the Conservatives. Never, in any of the three general elections when they fought her, did they coldly analyse why she was winning, in order to ensure that she would lose. The Young piece was an example. Its essential subject – divisions between these two great figures of Thatcherism in the run-up to an election – was a politically important story, of potential use both to Labour and to the SDP–Liberal Alliance. But the false attribution to Tebbit of an unpleasant thought by

---

* Hugo Young (1938–2003), educated Ampleforth and Balliol College, Oxford; journalist, *Sunday Times*, 1965–84 (joint deputy editor, 1981–4); political columnist, *Guardian*, 1984–2003.

those who hated him distracted from this. The sense of being morally superior to Mrs Thatcher and the Conservatives fired up many in the Opposition parties, but it also made them ill disciplined and unelectable.

One person who understood this was Peter Mandelson, who had joined Labour Party HQ in 1985, and was working to 'rebrand' Labour and to change it. Although he disagreed with Mrs Thatcher and thought her 'a better destroyer than a creator',[2] he did not hate her, and he saw Tebbit as the man who 'embodied her appeal to the aspirant working class'. Tebbit was 'a huge danger to the Labour Party'. Mandelson thought Labour needed to understand that several of the things she was doing – controlling the deficit, reforming trade unions and nationalized industries, and maintaining the Bomb – were right. Before Mrs Thatcher came into office, 'there *was* a sense in which the trade unions had brought the country to its knees.'[3]

Mandelson's view was shared by the young Labour MP for Sedgefield, Tony Blair, who understood why she had 'broken through to some of our support'.[4] 'My dad was a huge supporter of hers: he had working-class Tory attitudes,' Blair recalled. In opposing her reforms which insisted on secret ballots before strikes, for example, 'We were on the wrong side.' Many of Blair's colleagues kept saying that Mrs Thatcher was a 'fascist', and they would 'sniff out' moderates like him who did not agree. They would not recognize that Mrs Thatcher had a 'philosophy which posed certain hard questions for us, a philosophy around aspiration'. They 'underestimated her intellectual capacity'. The task, Blair believed, was to sift out 'what was Tory in her and what was radical', opposing the first and harnessing the second.

In the run-up to the 1987 election, Labour was still not collectively ready for this task. At the Labour conference of 1986, Peter Mandelson had persuaded the party to adopt the red rose, rather than the red flag, as its emblem, and make itself what would now be called 'user-friendly'. It was he who, despite Labour's self-imposed ban – because of the Wapping dispute (see Chapter 14) – on any contact with Rupert Murdoch's newspapers, kept secretly in touch with them.[5] But although he knew that Neil Kinnock wanted to change the Labour Party and help it escape from its prison of left-wing dogmatism, in policy terms this had hardly begun. Kinnock had felt forced to devote most of his energies to fighting the hard left in his party rather than confronting the Prime Minister of the country. As Kinnock himself put it, 'She was partly winning because we were so brilliantly losing.'[6] From the time he had become leader in 1983, Kinnock had believed that it would take 'two innings' (that is, two elections) to defeat the Conservatives. First he had to control and heal his party, and fight off the threat from the SDP–Liberal Alliance, which, he feared, seemed to many like a better version: 'Labour with the Bomb and without the unions. It did really seem as if they could knock us into third place.'[7]

Besides, Kinnock was, in many ways, a soft-left sentimentalist. 'Peter, you're trying to strip me bare,' he protested when Mandelson urged him to move away from unilateral nuclear disarmament.[8] As Mandelson wrote: 'Our image and packaging were finally changing. Our product – as resolution after resolution at the party conference made clear – was not.'[9] This was what had made Mrs Thatcher so happy about the 1986 Labour conference. According to Charles Clarke, Kinnock's chief of staff, 'Margaret Thatcher's greatest strength was our uselessness.'[10] As the new year began, her confidence that the main opposition was still facing the wrong way grew. A few days after Hugo Young's article, a projection by the television programme *Weekend World* (based on a Harris poll), gave the Conservatives a majority of 100 in the next House of Commons. It was a statistical fact, of which Mrs Thatcher was informed, that in the previous seven general elections, the party in the lead four or five months before polling day had won.[11] So, despite Mrs Thatcher's habitual hesitation on this subject, early summer dates for the election were beginning to pencil themselves in to her diary.

At the end of February, the state of the electoral waters was tested with a by-election in the previously marginal Labour seat of Greenwich in south London. In the 1983 general election, the Alliance had come third and the Conservatives a close second. In the by-election, the Alliance candidate, Rosie Barnes, triumphed with more than half of the total vote, 6,611 votes ahead of Labour. The Conservatives slumped to a mere 11 per cent of the vote, but were not disheartened because the clear loser was Labour, who had needed to win. The Labour candidate was a supporter of the Ken Livingstone wing of the party. She was vilified by the press for her private life and unfavourably compared with the personable and family-minded Mrs Barnes. The fact that, despite all its alleged modernization, Labour could have chosen such a candidate at this moment was taken as a welcome sign by the Tories that it had not changed much.

Other events seemed to be good auguries for the Conservatives. In the same month, British Airways was at last privatized, with share applications eleven times oversubscribed. Days before this triumph of popular capitalism, the last big battle of militant trade unionism had been lost. After more than a year on strike, the print unions, beaten by the threat of fines and sequestration, by the 'scab' labour of the electricians' union and by a successful police operation to keep the plant open, surrendered in the Wapping dispute. Rupert Murdoch had succeeded in introducing the new technology to his newspapers, and had done so not by making a deal with the unions but by defeating them. The way was now open for all newspapers to follow suit, permitting them to make decent profits at last and escape from what they saw as the tyranny and disruption of militant trade unionism. Given how much favourable difference this change made to Fleet Street (which, as a geographical centre for newspapers, disappeared as a result), the support for Mrs Thatcher by most of the print media was sealed. So was their confidence in her future success. She was now virtually guaranteed a good press in any election campaign.

These events were all confirmations of Mrs Thatcher's power, and ability to bring change. So, on a global scale, was her visit to Moscow (described in Chapter 18). One of the few cards which the left had with public opinion on the nuclear issue was the claim that Mrs Thatcher was too confrontational with the Soviet Union, thus threatening world peace. This fitted in with criticisms of Mrs Thatcher for being too uncritically close to President Reagan. (The A-Team, or Strategy Group, conscious of the Westland–BL–Libya effects, had warned her of 'Ronald Reagan's crisis of credibility' and perceptions among the public of what it called British 'poodleism' towards the US government.)[12] That she was now going to talk to the Soviet leader – candidly, even fiercely, but in a friendly spirit – took this card away.

The prospect of Mrs Thatcher's Moscow visit made it all the more important for Neil Kinnock to seek respectability on the world stage and in the NATO alliance. 'I wanted to show', he recalled, 'that a Labour leader could go anywhere.'[13] This meant trying to get on terms with the US administration. Anxious to break with his predecessor, Michael Foot, who had been positively proud not to have visited America for twenty-five years, Kinnock had flown to Washington in February 1984, and there met President Reagan for the first time. He was, in many ways, an admirer of the American way of life, but on the subject of nuclear weapons, which he discussed with Edward Streator, Minister at the US Embassy in London, before his first visit, conversation 'came to a screeching halt'.[14] He said, Streator recalled, 'Glenys* would never let me stay married to her if

---

* Glenys Kinnock (1944–), educated Holyhead Comprehensive School and University College of Wales, Cardiff; Labour MEP for South Wales East, 1994–9; for Wales, 1999–2009; created Lady Kinnock of Holyhead, 2009.

I yield an inch on nukes. So I'm for nuclear disarmament.'[15] Reagan had been very reluctant to meet Kinnock. 'Why do I have to do it?' he asked. 'I've seen what the guy thinks. He thinks all the wrong things.'[16] Nonetheless, the 1984 meeting passed off 'reasonably amicably',[17] with the two men agreeing about the horror of nuclear weapons, though Reagan specifically stated his opposition to unilateral disarmament.

In the years that followed, the US Ambassador in London, Charlie Price, became increasingly worried by Kinnock's unilateralist position, and increasingly partisan in supporting Mrs Thatcher. According to Roz Ridgway, of the State Department, 'Price wouldn't talk to Kinnock. And we kept saying, "You're the Ambassador to the United Kingdom, not the Ambassador to Mrs Thatcher." '[18] Discussions with Labour were left to the career diplomat Raymond Seitz,* Streator's successor at the Embassy. As a good professional, Seitz was eager to keep channels open, but was in no doubt about the threat a Labour government was seen to pose to US interests, not only among Republicans, but in the bureaucracy:

> The State Department, the Pentagon and the CIA were all concerned about the possibility that the security arrangements with Britain would unravel . . . Our entire defence posture in Europe rested on the British Isles. If Kinnock had won . . . the result would have been catastrophic for the relationship not to mention for the Alliance.[19]

The Embassy even had a plan to influence the debate in the run-up to the election.[20] Informing Reagan that Kinnock would probably seek to meet him in the new year, Price told the President that he and colleagues 'were pulling out all the stops to assure that the full implications of Labor's defense policies are widely understood'. He recommended that Reagan see Kinnock 'in the hope that your persuasive powers can have some influence on him'.[21]

Against advice from colleagues, including the Shadow Foreign Secretary, Denis Healey, who thought there was nothing to be gained, Kinnock asked for a meeting with Reagan. His request was somewhat reluctantly granted by the White House, and the meeting was arranged for 27 March, the day before Mrs Thatcher was due to land in Moscow. Frank Carlucci, now National Security Advisor, explained to the President that the timing was designed by Kinnock 'to show that he, like Thatcher, is an important player in international affairs'.[22]

---

* Raymond Seitz (1940–), executive assistant to Secretary George Shultz, Washington, DC, 1982–4; Minister and Deputy Chief of Mission, US Embassy, London, 1984–9; Ambassador to the UK, 1991–4.

In preparation for the encounter, Kinnock shifted his defence policy a bit, declaring that a Labour government would accept cruise missiles on British soil, so long as progress continued to be made at the Geneva arms control talks (which aimed to remove these missiles altogether). At a lunch which Price finally decided to give him, Kinnock emphasized that 'Britain would remain a loyal ally under a Labor government . . . A call on the President, Kinnock said, is important symbolically to still the anti-American elements within his party.'[23] No one expected a meeting of minds. 'While Kinnock will want to accentuate the positive,' Carlucci told Reagan, 'our objectives are different: we want to make it clear that Labor's defense policies would adversely affect our common security interests and severely strain US–UK relations.'[24] Before the meeting, the President was warned by his advisers, 'Be careful what you say to Kinnock because he is going to use anything you say to show that you're supportive of his point.'[25] On the other hand, he should bear in mind that Kinnock might be the next prime minister. 'Well,' said Reagan simply, 'I want Margaret to win.'[26]

In the Oval Office, Kinnock was accompanied by Denis Healey, Charles Clarke and the British Ambassador, Sir Antony Acland; Reagan by George Shultz, Caspar Weinberger and a host of aides. The meeting seemed, in the minds of the Labour contingent, to pass off peacefully. Kinnock picked up on Reagan's unThatcherite dislike of nuclear weapons, and briefed the press accordingly: 'The President stated unequivocally that he wanted to see . . . the elimination of all nuclear weapons, which he described in his own words as "immoral and uncivilised" . . . Both I and Denis Healey stated that we shared this desire.'[27]*

The White House did not like this. In its view, Kinnock was misrepresenting the meeting, suggesting agreement where there was none. Marlin Fitzwater, the White House press secretary, decided that it could not stand. 'I agonised over it,' Fitzwater recalled. 'I knew it would be a big story and me slapping down Kinnock. But I could see no option.'[28] He duly called a press briefing of his own. The President had told Kinnock, Fitzwater insisted, that 'we disagree with Labor's defense policy'. It would have 'a strong effect on NATO, on East/West relations and would undercut our negotiating position at Geneva'.[29] Reagan had concluded by saying, 'We must be prepared, unlike before World War Two. We must not let that

---

* Kinnock thought that the President showed signs of mental decline at their meeting: 'I got the impression of an elderly man who, if I had been related to him, I would have been worried about. He read from postcards cut into shape in the palm of his hands.' (Interview with Lord Kinnock.)

happen again.' Fitzwater added that the meeting had gone on for 'slightly less than 20 minutes', not the twenty-eight minutes logged by the Kinnock party. The implication was that the President and Kinnock had not found enough to talk about to justify even the paltry twenty minutes originally allocated. A story (which was accurate) also began to seep out that Reagan had failed to recognize Healey and had greeted him with the words 'Nice to see you again, Mr Ambassador.'*

The press leapt at Fitzwater's briefing. 'Charade in the Oval Office' said the *Observer*.[30] 'Reagan takes his revenge on Kinnock' said the *Mail*.[31] Even the *Guardian* used the word 'debacle'.[32] The contrast with Mrs Thatcher's headlines coming out of Moscow was extreme. Her exciting encounters with Gorbachev, her reception by huge and enthusiastic crowds, her glamorous outfits, confirmed her already well-established role as a global superstar. The visit also helped position her as a figure of hope as well as strength, an attractive woman as well as the Iron Lady. Kinnock, by contrast, was left looking like a pipsqueak.

Although Kinnock himself did not want a public row about the Reagan meeting, Healey, once back in London, accused the White House of trying 'to help Mrs Thatcher in her election battles'.[33] In Kinnock's view, not expressed at the time, 'The thing was set up, not by Reagan, but by his staff.'[34]

Kinnock's suspicion was not ill founded. The official US record of the meeting does not support everything that Fitzwater said.† Provoked, perhaps, by Kinnock's original account, the White House seems to have decided to put out a version of events closer to the harsh briefing notes its staff had given to Reagan before the meeting than to what he actually said. In Acland's view, however, the White House was accurate in conveying Reagan's 'rather frosty' attitude: 'I think that the Americans wanted to short-change Kinnock to show disapproval . . . it was clear both before and at the meeting that there was no meeting of minds.'[35] Reagan's own diary confirmed this impression: 'It was a short meeting but I managed to get in a lick or two about how counter-productive "Labors" [sic] defense policy was in our dealings with the Soviets.'[36]

---

* According to Antony Acland, the new and actual Ambassador, this was not necessarily a preposterous or deliberate mistake by the President. He (Acland) was not yet well known to Reagan, and his predecessor, Oliver Wright, 'was not wholly unlike Healey in appearance. He was dark and had bushy eyebrows.' (Correspondence with Sir Antony Acland.)

† Reagan did not, for instance, tell Kinnock that his stance would 'undercut our negotiating position at Geneva'. The nearest the President came to condemnation of Labour's defence policies was when he said that they would 'have a deep effect on NATO and on East/West relations'. ('Summary of President's Meeting with UK Labor Party Leader Neil Kinnock', 27 March 1987, Chron 03/24/1987–03/29/1987, Box 92202, Sommer Files, Reagan Library.)

Kinnock and his office would have been even more outraged – and with justification – if they had known the full story of what had gone on. Charles Powell recalled: 'There was the famous meeting with Kinnock that I'm afraid we rather sabotaged.' The whole thing, Powell confessed, 'was a bit of a fix. We wanted to diminish the impact of the visit. Charlie Price read our signals and arranged that they would get only 20 minutes and that the whole thing would be really rather perfunctory. I'm ashamed to admit it now, but it is true.'[37]

Powell did not discuss this with Mrs Thatcher, who obviously was best kept out of it. Price supported Powell's case about collusion: 'There was, you could say, a certain amount of manoeuvring on the part of the British to see that the visit was brief.'[38] The fact was that the Reagan–Thatcher bond was unbreakable, and Kinnock had been foolish to imagine that he could make any impression on it. Kinnock's boyhood hero, the Welsh Labour politician Aneurin Bevan,* had famously warned that a unilateralist Labour Party would go 'naked into the conference chamber'. Kinnock had walked naked into the Oval Office.

By this time, Mrs Thatcher was increasingly prepared for a contest. On 17 March, Nigel Lawson had presented his fourth Budget. There was still no date for the election, but this was unmistakably an election Budget. The Chancellor gave himself a glowing report on a year of good revenues and healthy trends despite the collapse of the oil price, known as the 'Third Oil Shock'. The inflation rate was now only 3.5 per cent. There had been the largest six-monthly fall in unemployment since 1973 (though it was still well over 3 million). Manufacturing productivity, which had been the lowest in the G7 in the 1970s, was now the highest. Britain was enjoying the longest period of steady growth since the war and a PSBR which had reached, in advance of his own best expectations, what Lawson judged was its 'appropriate destination'[39] of only 1 per cent of GDP. What he called 'genuine popular capitalism' was spreading so successfully that 8.5 million people now owned shares – almost three times more than in 1979.

Lawson then translated all this good news more directly into measures which individual voters would notice. He announced that there would be no increase, not even indexing, to excise duties on alcohol and tobacco.

---

* Aneurin Bevan (1897–1960), educated Sirhowy Elementary School and Central Labour College; son of a miner and followed in same occupation after leaving school at thirteen; Labour MP for Ebbw Vale, 1929–60; Minister of Health, 1945–51; Treasurer, Labour Party, 1956–60. Originally a unilateralist, he changed his mind.

This was a way of making the Retail Price Index suggest a better picture for inflation than was actually the case, and was a good, comprehensible electoral bribe. As foreshadowed in his Budget the previous year, and in his party conference speech, he cut income tax by a further two pence, to twenty-seven pence. He also reaffirmed the aim of bringing it down to 25 per cent in the near future. The income tax reduction, he said, was 'a cut which the Labour Party is pledged to reverse, if it is given the chance, which it will not be'.[40]

According to Nigel Lawson himself, backbenchers considered this Budget to be 'a good election Budget but not blatantly so'.[41] He was also pleased with the *Financial Times* headline – 'Lawson Opts for Prudence in Last Budget Before Election' – 'Not bad for a package which took two pence off the basic rate'.[42] His Budget was not, in reality, very prudent at all. Commentators were already beginning to notice, in his managing down of the sterling exchange rate and his increasingly casual approach to monetary targets, the seeds of much inflationary trouble to come. In retrospect, Lawson considered that the content of his Budget had been right but admitted that 'I was insufficiently cautious in my language: I did get carried away.'[43] But this was not something which would damage the party's immediate electoral prospects: quite the reverse. Because Lawson was such a master of his subject, it was often assumed that he was an 'unpolitical Chancellor'. This was not the case: his background and interests were as much political as economic. No one worked harder to calculate how to win the election.

Naturally, Mrs Thatcher raised no objection to any of this. 'The *Sun* is marvellous,' she told Woodrow Wyatt. 'It was the best on the Budget with its headline, "Look What a Lot You Got".'[44] She continued to feel confidence in her Chancellor. He was, thought Charles Powell, 'in pretty good odour'.[45] She admired most of his stewardship of the economy and valued his policy suggestions for the election manifesto. When he went to see her at Chequers to discuss the Budget plans at the beginning of February, he asked her directly whether she wanted him to continue as Chancellor after the election. 'Yes; of course I do,' she replied.[46]

There was only one fly in the ointment. At the beginning of the year, the A-Team considered the report from the policy group which Lawson chaired, 'Managing the Economy'.[47]* Brian Griffiths sent her a note advising that all its recommendations were desirable, 'with the exception of joining the ERM'.[48] 'This report', he went on, 'advocates a major change

---

* There were eleven policy groups in total, each chaired by departmental ministers, who reported to the Strategy Group or 'A-Team'.

in tactics. It reaffirms that public expenditure needs to be controlled, but says nothing about the PSBR or the money supply. It does not even mention the MTFS. In its place it advocates a binding commitment to joining the ERM after the election.' This would be dangerous as an election policy, said Griffiths, leading to 'very damaging speculation' in the markets: 'Having won the election, there will be plenty of time to re-examine the case for ERM membership.' Mrs Thatcher accepted this counsel, and neither she nor Lawson pushed the argument further at this stage. But she had clocked what he and Geoffrey Howe – who was also involved in the scheme – were up to.

She had some reason to feel ganged up against. The policy group report on foreign affairs, Europe and defence, which had arrived on her desk at the same time as the economic one, also mentioned the ERM. In a section marked 'Liabilities' in its conclusions, it lamented 'our absence from the ERM of the EMS, which businessmen regret, and which is said to cloud our European credentials'.[49] One unnamed person who thought it had this clouding effect was Howe. The almost complete absence of Howe from any election plans was a mark of how far he and Mrs Thatcher had drifted apart.*

Despite the improvement in Tory fortunes in the last quarter of 1986, agreement had not really been reached about how the election campaign – whenever it came – should be run. Tebbit and Michael Dobbs at Conservative Central Office were not at one with Mrs Thatcher, nor with those who were close to her on these matters – David Young and (behind the curtain) Tim Bell. In the new year, the first of a series of 'war councils' was held at Alistair McAlpine's house, 17 Great College Street, three minutes' walk from Parliament. The mere fact of the meetings was secret, since if the press had known of them election speculation would have got out of hand. Mrs Thatcher was smuggled into Great College Street, with Sherbourne, to meet Tebbit, Michael Dobbs and others from Central Office.[50] Before the meeting, she had done her best to exclude Dobbs. 'She couldn't bear him,' Tim Bell recalled; 'she didn't think he was very good.'[51] But Sherbourne had pushed for his inclusion, insisting that Tebbit could not be expected to deal with all the Central Office questions alone.[52] Mrs Thatcher had reluctantly agreed, but henceforth ensured Dobbs was

* In a later meeting about the contents of the manifesto, Geoffrey Howe complained that there was not enough foreign policy included and demanded an encouraging reference to Conservative Members of the European Parliament. 'This is a British election, Geoffrey,' said Mrs Thatcher. 'I don't need to be reminded of that, Prime Minister,' replied Howe snappishly. (Correspondence with John O'Sullivan.)

not present at any of the 'war councils' she attended. There was no row at the meeting, and there was no real issue of ideological difference, or even of deep division about campaign strategy. It was less a matter of what Mrs Thatcher wanted than of whom she wanted. Particularly in relation to elections, which made her intensely anxious, she had to have people about her whom she had known for a long time and liked and trusted.

Since the Chequers meeting of April the previous year (see Chapter 15) – if not before – she had regarded Dobbs as the agent of Tebbit's supposed challenge to her leadership. She punished him, rather than directly confronting his principal. 'Saatchis had lent Michael to Norman, and I was none too happy about that,' she recalled,[53] as if Tebbit, Dobbs and Saatchis were all part of a plan to supplant or at least succeed her. In this she was not discouraged by Tim Bell, who regarded Dobbs as his opponent in his feud with Saatchis, or by Lord Young, who was seeking a bigger role.* For all his volatility, which made people like Cecil Parkinson uneasy about him and Tebbit turn against him, Bell did have a real gift for dealing with Mrs Thatcher. Parkinson himself recalled:

> Tim amused her. He was also one of the very few people who could hint at the truth to her. He could say something like: 'The public think you are very bossy,' and he would know how to balance it by adding, 'But they think you're a great leader.' As a result, she did listen to him.[54]

In Bell's view, the great problem with the 'That Bloody Woman' presentation at Chequers the previous year had been that it had 'made Margaret feel she was being told, "You're the least important person in the Conservative Party" '.[55] His own approach, learnt from Gordon Reece, was the opposite. He saw it as his job to make her happy, to 'deliver the things she liked'.[56] Mrs Thatcher herself never quite understood – or possibly she affected not to understand – the problem of Bell versus Saatchis. As Parkinson put it, 'she thought Tim *was* Saatchis.'[57] She recalled, when writing her memoirs, 'I remember, I had not much confidence in Saatchis. I said to them, "Look, I've never dealt with you before; I've always dealt with Tim Bell. Tim is a consultant to you and therefore I want to deal with him." They found that very difficult, so I didn't pursue it . . .'[58] It was true that she did not pursue it further with Saatchis, but neither did she give it

---

* Although not personally involved with any of the agencies, Young had found his much trusted special adviser, Howell James, through Tim Bell (Interview with Lord Young of Graffham). Young and James, though not umbilically linked in the manner of Tebbit and Dobbs, were effectively allies against them.

up. The 'parallel operation' which had begun early in 1986 never stopped. Mrs Thatcher approached the election campaign without ever deciding between her official and her unofficial advisers, or ever properly informing the former about the latter.

The other important figure influencing Mrs Thatcher was Alistair McAlpine, who was by now her longest and closest associate in the party set-up – 'the only person', according to Tim Bell, 'whom she always used to see alone' (because he told her confidential things about money).[59] His value to Mrs Thatcher was immense, as a generous host and a skilled treasurer who could bring in big businessmen and their large contributions to party funds, and also as a friend, who was not seeking anything from her in terms of extra office, power or access. Over the years, McAlpine had succeeded in seeing off the party chairmen – Thorneycroft and Gummer – who sidelined him, and had never lost his place in Mrs Thatcher's affections. Close to Tim Bell and Gordon Reece, he felt some resentment against Tebbit, who wished to exclude them, and him. As Richard Ryder put it, 'Cromwellian Tebbit didn't grasp the scale of Cavalier McAlpine's influence.'[60] In a wily, low-key way, McAlpine knew how to talk people up or down with Mrs Thatcher.* It was he who, once Tebbit became chairman, had spread stories about his ambitions. 'In so many words, he mentioned that Norman was doing his best but was rather losing the plot, campaign underpowered, never the same after Brighton.'[61] In Ryder's well-informed view, it was McAlpine who worked Bell back into Mrs Thatcher's company, and proposed David Young as the effective replacement for Tebbit. Young's diaries are full of glowing accounts of dinners and champagne with McAlpine. More than anyone, McAlpine opened Mrs Thatcher's door for him. More than anyone, McAlpine made Tebbit seem to Mrs Thatcher both threatening and churlish. As Mrs Thatcher's chief fund-raiser, he also had the power to pay for additional opinion research without the Chairman necessarily authorizing it.

On 15 March, David Young rang Mrs Thatcher at Chequers. By his own contemporary account,† he told her: 'Prime Minister, I'd just like you to know that I'm concerned about things at Central Office. I don't really think we are prepared . . . I would like to talk to you about ways in

---

* It was McAlpine, indeed, who first suggested to the present author that Tebbit had been organizing his leadership campaign from his hospital bed after the Brighton bomb (Interview with Lord McAlpine of West Green).

† Each night during the election campaign, Young dictated his Election Diary into a tape recorder. It was later transcribed, and used as the basis for part of his memoirs, *The Enterprise Years: A Businessman in the Cabinet*, Headline, 1990, but never published. It is a very useful, though obviously *parti pris* source for the period.

which I would help you and the campaign.'[62] He also told her that the latest news on unemployment (a drop, seasonally adjusted, of 44,000) represented 'the best unemployment figures since records were first kept'.[63]*

Two days later, en route to No. 10, Young decided to call on Tebbit to explain that he was seeing Mrs Thatcher to discuss the ways he might 'help in the election'.[64] Tebbit, Young recorded, 'seemed quite agreeable'. The two men had been friends when Tebbit was at the Department of Employment, and indeed it was Tebbit who had appointed Young head of the Manpower Services Commission, the job which was his springboard into politics. As Young reminded him, the combination of the two of them, plus Peter Morrison at Central Office, was a re-creation of 'the old team' at the Department of Employment. But by now the old team spirit had gone. The relationship had become wary, though there had been no open breach. In his memoirs, Tebbit writes: 'We had worked closely together in the past and had met regularly to discuss the coming campaign. What is more, Margaret Thatcher liked and trusted him. So I invited David into Central Office to help in the election campaign.'[65] While technically true, these words give almost no sense of what was actually happening, which was much more disagreeable for Tebbit.

Tebbit told Young that he planned a campaign which would expose the dangers of the Alliance by reminding people how the Lib–Lab Pact in the late 1970s had enabled the Winter of Discontent. This tactic arose from Tebbit's view that the party needed to have alternative strategies for fighting either the Alliance or Labour, depending on who was emerging as the main enemy. This was added to the Thatcher charge-sheet against him: 'It was too complicated for Margaret,' Tebbit recalled.[66] Her preferred tactic was always to concentrate fire on Labour and marginalize the Alliance, treating it mainly as the subject for comedy. 'Some Tory strategists – but not I', she later wrote, '– thought [the Alliance] were the principal threat to us.'[67]†

---

* By this Young meant that the figures showed the best drop ever: the total was still far, far higher than had ever been known before the Thatcher era.

† Mrs Thatcher did, however, hold a meeting about the Alliance threat at Downing Street at the end of April. One of those present was John Major, who afterwards wrote to Mrs Thatcher to set out the 'specific SDP/Liberal policies which would damage the self-interest of potential Tory defectors' (Major to Thatcher, 5 May 1987, CAC: THCR 2/7/5/41). Towards the end of the campaign, Major was present at the daily press conferences as the minister with responsibility for Social Security. According to John Whittingdale, 'that was when she first saw him . . . He did well in those briefings . . . I always thought it was during that campaign that she noticed him for the first time' (Thatcher Memoirs Materials, CAC: THCR 4/3).

After his conversation with Tebbit, Young obtained from Robert Armstrong's office the carefully guarded key which allowed passage from the Cabinet Office to 10 Downing Street, and went through to see Mrs Thatcher. He told her she should employ him to make everything ready for a general election from June if the local election results on 7 May were satisfactory. ' "Yes," she replied. "You must. You must first help with the presentation of the manifesto – the way it looks." '[68] Young advised her that the only really important thing was to get her on television all the time 'being met by adoring crowds'. Then the two descended from her study to the Cabinet Room where ministers were gathering to hear Lawson unveil the Budget that he would present to the Commons that afternoon. Lawson's good news 'received a marvellous reception'.[69] Mrs Thatcher asked Tebbit to stay behind at the end of the meeting, with Young. She told him that she had been thinking about the campaign: 'David's got some free time now, I'd like him to come and help.' According to Young, 'Norman looked only slightly surprised and said, "Well, of course that's no problem, I'd love that." '[70] He did not love it at all.

Before Young's new role was announced to the press, he had dinner with Peter Morrison. Morrison told Young that 'Norman was not the same Norman that we both worked for three years back, for since the bomb he was a different person. I began to get from Peter the same feeling that I was getting from people outside the Party about the state of Central Office.'[71] This refrain about Tebbit being 'not the same Norman' was frequently used against him – and also, more rarely, for him, by those who argued he had become a deeper, wiser man. For Young, as for Tim Bell, it was a means of legitimizing their ambition to marginalize him. A covert struggle was in progress to run the election campaign and thus to take credit for the expected victory. Tim Bell and Howell James had even found its chronicler, the journalist Rod Tyler, who was close to Mrs Thatcher and had previously, via Bell, been the 'ghost' for Ian MacGregor's autobiography. As he took up his work at Central Office, Young recorded, he had a drink with Tyler.[72] From then on, Tyler had access to the inner workings of Central Office and the Thatcher election entourage, and an informal prime ministerial blessing. His 'instant' book about it, *Campaign!* (1987), was well informed, but naturally took the part of those who got him in on it. Tebbit considered that Young was 'the prime briefer' against him to Mrs Thatcher, and was 'intensely ambitious'.[73]

All this was a recipe for conflict. On 5 April, Young was informed that 'Norman was spitting blood about my appointment,'[74] so he arranged to see the Chairman the following day. They met. By his account, Young began the conversation:

'I wanted to have a chat with you to see how we can work together.'

'Oh it's very difficult.'

'Norman, I'm only here to help you. If you want me to push off, just say the word and I'll go.' There followed the most difficult 45 minutes since I first tried to persuade a bank manager to give me my first overdraft.[75]

After expressing oblique resentment at Young's intrusion, Tebbit complained that Mrs Thatcher did not like the plan he had devised for her election tour. 'Norman . . . you know what she's like,' Young replied; '. . . if you produce the tour it's no good, if I produce the same tour it'll be fine.'[76] In Young's mind, this point was supposed to be 'a laugh' at Mrs Thatcher's expense. It is doubtful if Tebbit found it amusing. A non-working relationship was established before a shot had been fired in the general election. This mattered, because it was not merely a problem of ill feeling between Tebbit and Young. It related closely to Mrs Thatcher herself. 'Norman', recalled Michael Dobbs, 'would return from No. 10 and not know what to do next. He felt, rightly, that he wasn't part of her inner circle.'[77]

It gives perspective on the slight unreality of the situation to note that, in the midst of all this antagonism, the exterior political circumstances were extremely favourable. On 5 April, an opinion poll in the *Sunday Times*, taken in the wake of Mrs Thatcher's triumphant Moscow visit, showed the Conservatives 12 points ahead of the Alliance, with Labour now in third place.[78]

Despite the atmosphere of intrigue, the preparation of the manifesto had been relatively orderly. It depended on the idea of a hinge between what had happened since 1979 and what would happen next. Mrs Thatcher had commissioned a glossy pamphlet called *Our First Eight Years: The Conservative Party*, listing the achievements of two terms. This was conceived as a companion to the manifesto designed to win the third. The concept fitted neatly with the A-Team's attempt to make the government work as one and with the successful Tebbit framework for the previous year's party conference – 'The Next Move Forward'. Indeed, no one could think of a better title for the manifesto, except to make the ideas plural: it was called *The Next Moves Forward*.*

Mrs Thatcher felt the previous manifesto in 1983 had missed a chance

---

* After the title had been agreed, Stephen Sherbourne sensed that Mrs Thatcher was not completely happy with the choice and suggested a 'zippier and more buoyant' slogan of 'Britain on the Move Again'. Mrs Thatcher stuck to the original. (Sherbourne to Thatcher, 7 May 1987, CAC: THCR 2/7/5/11.)

to set out a full agenda. She wanted the next one to 'keep the forward momentum . . . on the lines of the fundamental principles'.[79] This would mean many more new ideas, more detail, and more specific promises than in 1983. The 'anchor man' for bringing the drafts together was John MacGregor, the Chief Secretary to the Treasury, whom Mrs Thatcher remembered as being 'nothing like as good as he was made out to be'[80] for this task. The chief draftsman was John O'Sullivan* of the Policy Unit, who had, she thought, 'a genius for presenting everything'[81] but also, according to some others, a genius for being late. He was assisted by Ronnie Millar, who contributed the more purple passages. O'Sullivan's draft was disparaged for its excessive length, but the unit's argument, which Mrs Thatcher accepted, was that 'We needed to prove *why* again,'[82] and to explain the reason that some things still remained to be done. The Conservative case had to be shown as a historical development which would reveal its logic: it was 'rolling Thatcherism'. The first term had been about rescuing the economy from disaster. The second had been about creating the right conditions for economic opportunity. The third would turn more to 'social Thatcherism' – the themes of responsibility and choice applied to the realm of public services. On health, however, where the Tories, always nervous on the subject, had no radical plans, the only tactic was to boast about how much had been spent. As Mrs Thatcher put it when preparing her memoirs, 'I had said "Well, we'll tackle education and housing this time, and we'll leave any detailed changes in the health service to come up after the election." '[83] This was not because she had a hidden agenda, but because she had very little agenda on health at all.†

It became more and more obvious to those involved that the election would be held in June. In practice, this did not include 4 June because this was a Jewish holiday, and Mrs Thatcher wanted to be sure that Jewish residents in her own constituency of Finchley would not be impeded from voting for her.[84] On Wednesday 15 April, Mrs Thatcher had a meeting at No. 10 with Maurice Saatchi. Tebbit was also present, on Sherbourne's recommendation, lest his exclusion 'cause a problem in the relationship between you and the Chairman which might spill over into the following day's meeting'.[85] At the Maundy Thursday meeting the next day, Young told her 'with a twinkle' that 'by coincidence' his department had booked lots of poster sites for May and June.[86] If an election were called,

* John O'Sullivan (1942–), educated St Mary's College, Crosby and University of London; special adviser to the Prime Minister (No. 10 Policy Unit), 1986–8. His journalistic positions have included parliamentary sketch-writer, *Daily Telegraph*; associate editor, *The Times*; editor, *National Review*; executive editor, Radio Free Europe and Radio Liberty.
† Mrs Thatcher's policies on health will be discussed in Volume III.

government advertising was forbidden and so the sites would fall vacant, and could be used for party advertising: 'It so happened that Saatchis would have an option on these sites.'

Mrs Thatcher then went off to Scotney Castle in Kent, where, because she now owned the Dulwich house, she was finally relinquishing her lease on the flat. She sorted out and packed up her possessions and then spent Easter Day at Chequers. The next morning she held an all-day meeting there, starting off 'at a tremendous rate of knots, saying that the manifesto wouldn't do and that it wasn't enough to talk about the past'.[87] As was her often infuriating wont, she went through everything, 'always saying "Why?"' By late afternoon, she 'started to get fidgety about the timing of the election', and also criticized Young for his choice of places for her to visit in the campaign. She kept saying, 'I must go to large factories, I must go to large factories.'

Meetings such as this, with Mrs Thatcher jumping all over the place, sometimes fastening on tiny things, sometimes reaching for the big picture, sometimes confident, sometimes unbearably anxious, were a constant feature of the prelude to the campaign. In all this time, no agreement was reached about several vital aspects. Tim Bell's role remained vague, and hidden from colleagues. There was talk of him being announced as a 'consultant' to Central Office, where he would 'be plugged into David Young, who would then channel Tim's ideas' to Mrs Thatcher.[88] But none of this was cleared with Tebbit, who kept complaining to Young that he did not know what was happening. Young, Sherbourne reported to Mrs Thatcher, felt that Tebbit was 'still a bit anxious' about his (Young's) involvement in the campaign and so suggested that she handle Tebbit carefully.[89] Young's role remained unclear. Although he now had the use of a room in Central Office, he had no job title and no defined task. Even as he made himself more and more central to the campaign, he kept asking Mrs Thatcher what she wanted him to do. She rarely gave a clear answer. Despite being one of her greatest admirers, Young felt that 'She just did not know how to deal with people.' Because she never resolved the Tebbit question, 'I was walking on eggshells.'[90] To the informed exterior eye, the situation was very strange and it was not obvious why the electoral 'virgin' Young was the man to take over the campaign. 'His was a ludicrous appointment,' Nigel Lawson considered.[91]

There were also conflicting views about who Mrs Thatcher should communicate with. Sherbourne warned her that 'if David Young is your contact man, then the danger is increased of messages between you and the Chairman going wrong; with misunderstandings arising.' He suggested that in an emergency Mrs Thatcher should speak either to Tebbit or to Peter Morrison.[92] This was the era when mobile phones were just coming into use. Young arranged for all Cabinet ministers and others most involved in the campaign to carry them as they travelled round the country, but they were not necessarily effective. Some ministers did not even know how to turn them on or off.[93] Young hoped Tebbit could be out on the road, where he was acknowledged as a good performer. This would have the added advantage of allowing Young to run Central Office. Mrs Thatcher sometimes favoured this idea but, fearing the misunderstandings of which Sherbourne wrote, sometimes got frightened that she might not be able to get hold of Tebbit at all times. She made clear that, despite Young's discouragement, she wanted him to stay put in Smith Square.*

The results of the local elections held on 7 May gave the Conservatives 40 per cent of the vote, Labour 30 per cent and the Alliance 27 per cent. There was therefore no remaining reason why the general election should not be held as quickly as possible.† Mrs Thatcher's closest ministers and advisers gathered at Chequers on Sunday 10 May to take a final view. The *Observer* called the ministers – Whitelaw, Howe, Lawson, Tebbit, Young, Hurd and Wakeham – the 'Seven Dwarfs'.‡ The night before, Mrs Thatcher arranged for Tim Bell to slip in, among family guests arriving for a dinner for Denis's seventy-second birthday, and see her there unannounced. Young and his wife were invited to stay that Saturday with Willie and Celia Whitelaw at Whitelaw's official residence, Dorneywood, before going over to Chequers the next day. The Hurds and Bakers were also present. Young was suddenly overcome with satisfaction at his new eminence among three of the other 'dwarfs'. 'We were talking in general about

---

* It was probably a blessing for everyone's nerves that Margaret Thatcher was of the last generation not to be a habitual mobile phone user. The thought that she could pursue ministers at all times telephonically would have been more than they could have borne. An additional danger was the threat to security and confidentiality caused by mobile phone calls which could easily be hacked. The *News of the World* paid an expert to hack into the lines on Mrs Thatcher's battlebus. It reported this. (*News of the World*, 24 May 1987.) What it did not report was that it had listened in to conversations between Stephen Sherbourne, who was on the bus, and Charles Powell in Downing Street. Since Powell, as a civil servant, was not supposed to be involved in the campaign, the contents of these chats might have been embarrassing. (Thatcher Memoirs Materials, CAC: THCR 4/3.)

† Rupert Murdoch had already decided to come to Britain for the duration of the election, without waiting to know the exact date. He wanted to be there to help Margaret Thatcher and, according to Woodrow Wyatt, 'we [Wyatt and Margaret Thatcher] can also perhaps tell him what we would like his newspapers to be saying . . . "He's marvellous," she replied.' (Wyatt, *The Journals of Woodrow Wyatt*, vol. i, 3 May 1987, p. 339.)

‡ This was a recycling of the joke Denis Healey had made about a similar ministerial meeting before the 1983 election (see p. 48 above).

political dispositions,' he wrote, 'and I suddenly realised for the first time that almost unknown to myself I'd become part of the charmed circle.'[94]*

Compared with Mrs Thatcher's almost absurd indecision about the date of the 1983 election (see Chapter 3), the Chequers meeting was fairly straightforward. Everyone recommended 11 June and she did not seriously demur. More controversial was the idea that Mrs Thatcher would take part in a video for the candidates' conference after the launch of the manifesto. At coffee after lunch, Young, who favoured her participation, sidled up to her.

> I saw my chance . . . and said 'Did you have a good meeting with Tim [who had also been pushing the idea of the video]?' She looked startled and said 'Ssshhh!' Evidently it was a very good meeting with Tim – she didn't want Norman to hear and I found out from her that she was now keen on the video.[95]†

Private opinion polls presented to her that afternoon, combined with an analysis of all the publicly available ones, encouraged her. An extrapolation from the local election results suggested a majority of 94. Tebbit gave her his cautious prediction – an overall majority of 19.[96] Mrs Thatcher said she would sleep on all this and decide the next day. At a special Cabinet meeting at 11 o'clock the following morning, she announced that the election date would be 11 June. She then went to the Palace to seek the formal agreement of the Queen. Parliament would be dissolved a week later, and then the election campaign proper would begin.

The intervening seven days did not go very well for Mrs Thatcher. Because of her long-standing belief that campaigns should be as short as possible, not much was organized for the first week. On the evening after firing the

---

* Having arrived in politics relatively late in life, without ever having to be elected to anything, Young had now conceived high ambitions. At various times in his Election Diary, he speculates on whether, after the election, he could continue as employment secretary, combine the job with being party chairman, become party chairman and Leader of the House of Lords, become secretary of state for trade and industry, or become Foreign Secretary. He eschews the departments of Health and of Energy, as being demotions. He even, although he reports this idea from the mouths of others, takes pleasure in the suggestion that a special Bill could be passed allowing him to renounce his peerage, be elected to the House of Commons, and become prime minister. In fact, it seems he did later entertain the idea seriously, using Alan Clark to sound out ministerial colleagues on the subject. (Interview with Lord Ryder of Wensum.)

† Margaret Thatcher initially had reservations about the video. 'I don't see enough use for what I think would be rather expensive and not as good as reading the original.' (Thatcher comment on Sherbourne note, 29 April 1987, CAC: THCR 2/7/5/24.)

"ONCE MORE UNTO THE BREACH, DEAR FRIENDS, ONCE MORE ..."

Nicholas Garland, *Independent*, 12 May 1987.

starting gun, however, she did agree to give an interview to the BBC that
provided the first gaffe of the campaign. She explained, on camera, that
the Conservatives had such a big agenda for the country that it would take
her quite some time to accomplish. 'Yes,' she continued, 'I hope to go on
[pause] and on.'[97] As soon as she had said this, she dropped her eyes from
the camera, as if she realized she had said more than she should. The idea
of her 'going on and on' fed into public anxieties about her domineering
personality, and was quickly used against her. Whereas the Conservatives
wished to emphasize the team and play down anything that would look
like a personality cult, the Opposition parties, especially Labour, wanted
to play on fear of her omnipotence. They could not deny her pre-eminence,
but they could criticize it. The message to voters that Mrs Thatcher might
be with them for ever if they let the Tories in again was calculated to put
off a good many of them. In the course of the week, the gap between the
Tories and the other parties shortened noticeably and Labour pulled well
ahead of the Alliance.

In her own memory of these events in retirement – though she was not
to be relied on about dates – Mrs Thatcher recalled Tebbit taking up this
hostile theme: 'During the election campaign . . . he was virtually telling
me that I was the problem. He'd say "People say 'TBW'." I'd say, "What
do you mean 'TBW'?" He'd say: "That Bloody Woman!" . . . He came to

the conclusion that I was stopping the party from winning, and I really wasn't going to admit that.'[98]

It was in the context of this personal criticism that the candidates' video (espoused by Young and Bell) became problematic. Introduced by Tebbit as if he were the conductor of the orchestra, the film showed six other ministers lauding the Tory achievements of the past eight years, including Geoffrey Howe making the rash claim that Britain was 'no longer quarrelling in Europe'. 'I feared it was bound to seem pretty insulting to Mrs Thatcher,' recalled John Wakeham, 'because to some it made Norman look like the quasi-Prime Minister.'[99] There was no interview with the actual Prime Minister. Instead, the film ended with rousing film clips of her with Reagan, Gorbachev, Kohl, Mitterrand, the Chinese and the Saudis. Those involved were proud of their work and Howell James arranged for Channel 4 to film them watching the video being put together. Young in particular, was pleased. 'The manifesto film made Norman the hero,' he told his diary. 'But I think Channel 4 . . . will be using some of today's filming and I think I will be seen to be the person behind it all.'[100]

The following Monday, Young arranged to show Mrs Thatcher the video in Downing Street. He noted what happened next:

> At the end she said: 'Marvellous! It's so fantastic – we should use it as a party election broadcast.' Then she added, 'Well, on the other hand it only shows me overseas. The manifesto is mine, but it all appears to be Norman. It is *my* manifesto!' She worked herself up in a rather embarrassing way . . . Really for the first time ever I thought she appeared very much a woman . . . This went on for more than a few minutes and it got quite difficult.[101]

Young left Downing Street promising to sort everything out for her: 'I got into the car and I really felt as if my whole world had come to an end . . . Not only did she not like it – she somehow felt I'd let her down.'[102] It was no longer so good to be seen as 'the person behind it all'.

In order not to cause a blow-up with Tebbit, and perhaps wanting to conceal from his rival that he had upset Mrs Thatcher so badly, Young concocted a story with John Wakeham in which they told Tebbit they had seen the video without showing it to Mrs Thatcher and were worried by the depiction of her, because it played to the current attack from the Alliance that she was 'happy to go to Moscow, but she never goes to Middlesbrough'. 'We need more of the home market,' said Wakeham. 'Put her in a white coat in a factory.'[103] While a factory visit was deemed impracticable in the time available, Wakeham and Young insisted that an interview with Mrs Thatcher needed shooting immediately to add to the end of the film.[104] Tebbit swallowed this line, and Mrs Thatcher, unaware of these shenanigans, went round to Great College Street that afternoon to have her new contribution recorded. As he often did for party political broadcasts, Tim Bell sat between the legs of the cameras looking straight at her and smiling, to reassure her. Always good when in a tight corner, Mrs Thatcher performed extremely professionally, giving a well-delivered encomium about the 'transformation' that Britain was undergoing.[105] When shown to candidates and the media, the video passed off without incident.

This farcical sequence of events was not an untypical example of the conduct of the whole campaign. It was the result of too many cooks spoiling the broth, and of the fact that, over the question of who should be head chef, Mrs Thatcher's indecision was final.

The following morning, the Conservative manifesto was unveiled at the first Conservative press conference of the campaign. The efforts to show 'the team' meant that too many ministers were crammed into the fairly small room at Central Office, sweating under television lights. The effect was to suggest tension rather than amity.

Although still quite long, the manifesto was a thoughtful and coherent document. 'I knew exactly what I wanted,' Mrs Thatcher claimed in later years.[106] Its argument was that 'A vast change separates the Britain of today from the Britain of the late 1970s.' 'Pride of ownership of homes, shares and pensions' had been established. Now it was time to offer 'greater choice and responsibility' in areas like housing and education. There would be a core national curriculum in state schools for the first time. These schools could opt out of management by their local education authority (LEA) and run themselves, collecting their money directly from central government.* 'The abuses of left-wing Labour councils have shocked the nation,' the manifesto said, and these would be ended by the replacement of the rates by 'the fairer Community Charge' which would 'strengthen local democracy and accountability'. Jobs would be assisted by a guaranteed place on the Youth Training Scheme for all sixteen- and seventeen-year-olds and all up to the age of twenty-five who had been out of work for six months or more. Inner cities would be revived by removing the Labour-imposed barriers against private investment: new Urban Development Corporations, like that which had been so successful in the

---

* Strenuous and repeated efforts had been made to include a pledge in the manifesto to close down asylums and hand the mentally ill over to 'care in the community', but Mrs Thatcher resisted on the grounds that such care would, in reality, be cruel (Interview with John O'Sullivan).

London Docklands, would be given powers to reclaim derelict land. As for the Bomb, the Conservatives alone promised to continue the replacement of Polaris with Trident nuclear missiles.[107]

The Labour manifesto, launched the same day, had no comparable depth. Its main policies – unilateral nuclear disarmament, increasing the basic rate of income tax by 2 per cent, repealing all the Tory trade union laws (including the restoration of secondary picketing, the weapon denied Arthur Scargill in the miners' strike) – were not appealing. Almost the only major concession to modernity was support, for the first time, for the right to buy council houses.* But journalists who came to Mrs Thatcher's cramped press conference from Kinnock's suave and spacious, red-rose-decorated one in the Queen Elizabeth II Centre near by, were struck by the contrast between the slick modernity projected by Labour and the stuffiness and confusion of the Conservatives. The idea that a contrast could be made between the fresh young personality of Kinnock and the strident one of Mrs Thatcher was beginning to catch fire – 'Mr Nice Guy vs TBW' was the shorthand. The same applied to the way the leaders' campaigns were organized. Kinnock's was a war of movement – travelling for days away from London and leaving most of the press conferences to his personable campaign chief, Bryan Gould.† Mrs Thatcher attended almost all the daily London press conferences, and went out on expeditions which, partly because of anxiety about IRA terrorism, kept her at too great a distance from the public. The fear in Central Office was that Mrs Thatcher's campaign would be 'overly "Prime Ministerial" and somewhat distant from the electorate, which might be contrasted unfavourably with Mr Kinnock's family, youth, man of the people image'.[108] 'It is a waste of your time pottering round supermarkets and schools and standing in empty fields shouting through a megaphone,' Woodrow Wyatt chided her, and she agreed.[109]

Two days after the manifesto launches, Labour produced its first party election broadcast of the campaign.‡ Filmed by Hugh Hudson, the director of the Oscar-winning film *Chariots of Fire*, it marked a revolution in

---

* It was pointed out to Mrs Thatcher, however, that Labour's policy would allow some local authorities discretion over the right to buy. This was 'no right at all'. ('Labour Manifesto 1987' Briefing prepared by the Conservative Research Department, 20 May 1987, CAC: THCR 2/7/5/33.)

† Bryan Gould (1939–), educated Auckland University and Balliol College, Oxford; Labour MP for Southampton Test, October 1974–9; for Dagenham, 1983–94; member of the Shadow Cabinet, 1986–92.

‡ Party election broadcasts were prescribed in their maximum length and the number permitted to each party, by law. When each party's broadcast went out, it was shown simultaneously on all television channels, so there was no escape for viewers, other than by

the genre. An RAF Tornado shot across the sky and seemed to transform itself into a seagull. Beneath the seagull were Neil and Glenys Kinnock, strolling hand in hand on the Great Orme headland by Llandudno. This film was interspersed with Kinnock explaining his compassionate attitudes and likeable working-class background, backed up by mainly Welsh friends and relations praising him. It also cut to his party-conference assault on Militant in 1985 and the election speech he had given in Llandudno the week before, in which, in an unscripted addition,[110] he had declared himself 'the first Kinnock in a thousand generations' to have attended university.* The message was about the freedom and opportunity for working people's natural talents if only a party would give them the 'platform' they needed. No policy was mentioned. The film kept using the word 'Kinnock' as if in an American presidential campaign, and never spoke the word 'Labour'. Mrs Thatcher was not mentioned or depicted, but it was she, by implication, who was denying ordinary people their platform.

The broadcast was a great success. It did not move the opinion polls much, although it did contribute to Labour's aim of reducing the Alliance threat: the double act of 'the two Davids', Steel and Owen, who were not on good terms, was not going well. But it galvanized interest in the campaign and convinced the media, bored with years of stories of Labour uselessness, that change was coming and that Kinnock was the man of the moment. It also suggested the political mortality of the Thatcher era. The film made much of Kinnock's youth (he was forty-five to Mrs Thatcher's sixty-one), and of course it was not easy to imagine Denis and Margaret holding hands on some Welsh cliffs.†

Mrs Thatcher had little time to watch television, did not enjoy the medium, and did not have a video-recorder, so she did not see the Kinnock broadcast.‡ She heard of its success, however, and was displeased. 'Labour

---

turning off the television altogether. As a result, the broadcasts were unpopular in principle, but widely watched.

* It was unkindly pointed out that, since there were only about a hundred generations back to Homer, there certainly had not been a thousand generations of Kinnocks (or of people at university).

† Age probably did play a small part, for the first time, in Mrs Thatcher's tetchiness during the campaign. Those close to her noticed that she tired more easily. 'She used to yawn a lot in meetings,' recalled David Young. 'She could have done with seven hours' sleep, but wouldn't admit it.' (Interview with Lord Young of Graffham.) Shortly after the election, Young said in a private interview that 'you had to recognise she was ageing' (Lord Young of Graffham interview, July 1987, David Butler Archive).

‡ Dismayed by Mrs Thatcher's lack of direct knowledge of what was appearing on television during the campaign, Lord Young arranged to send her videotapes of what had happened

had this thing with dear Neil and Glenys on the cliffs . . . The media were just determined that whatever Kinnock did was right . . .'[111] 'This is what we were up against, this remarkable guy who captured the imagination,' she added, in a sarcastic tone, when she remembered her rival's great moment. Labour considered the broadcast so successful that it made the unique decision to run it twice more in the campaign rather than show new ones.*

On the morning after the Kinnock broadcast, Mrs Thatcher made the second gaffe of her campaign. Answering a question at the press conference about schools policy, she seemed to say that schools opting out of local authority control might be able to charge fees on top of the standard costs paid by the government, and might also be able to have selective admission policies. This point had been left vague in the manifesto because Mrs Thatcher wanted such schools to be able to raise extra funds and Kenneth Baker did not.[112] Once the gaffe had been made, it could not be quickly corrected because no one could find the Education Secretary, Kenneth Baker, who had turned his mobile phone off. In Mrs Thatcher's mind, the problem had arisen because Baker was 'a big broadbrush man, very, very good at general speeches, but . . . I had to finish off the detail.'[113] In fact, she was forced more or less to back off, because of political damage. When David Willetts, who was handling policy questions for her at Central Office, advised that she should do this, she said, 'Even you, David, are racked by left-wing middle-class guilt,'[114] though she gave in. But the incident had been her fault, a carelessness which, in past campaigns, she had very rarely shown. It was 'a tragic fall at the first hurdle', Dobbs said privately shortly after the election: education 'was supposed to be the jewel in the crown'.[115]

At midnight, Mrs Thatcher telephoned Young to say that she had just been talking to her daughter Carol who 'had said we're about to lose the election the way things are going'.[116] A couple of days earlier, John Wakeham, who was almost completely inexperienced on television, had put in a very poor performance on *Election Call*, largely unable to answer the questions put to him. The Saturday-morning papers led with the education muddle, and spoke of a 'lost week' for the Tories.

---

each day. Stephen Sherbourne, knowing that she would have neither the time nor the inclination, simply put them in a drawer. (Interview with Lord Sherbourne of Didsbury.) Anyway, she would not have been able to watch any of them without descending to Bernard Ingham's office, where the only video-player in the building was to be found.

* This decision was partly determined by Labour's perception that its planned election broadcast about unemployment was wide of the mark, as the issue had subsided politically (see Rodney Tyler, *Campaign!: The Selling of the Prime Minister*, Grafton Books, 1987, p. 202).

That night, Mrs Thatcher had Tim Bell and Young in for drinks with Denis and Stephen Sherbourne in the flat at No. 10. Carol, whose role, according to Tim Bell, was 'like mine, to listen to her mother's rants',[117] was present. So was Denis, who 'was a bit aloof from the whole thing, but from time to time would say things like "The woman's getting grumpy: watch it!" '[118] Mrs Thatcher was in a mood of despair: 'It's hardly worth bothering, let's give up, it's the end.'[119] She raged against Wakeham's performance, saying that 'he can never even be a minister again.' Denis kept telling her to listen to Bell and Young. They expounded their idea that they should 'release Norman the assassin' to destroy Kinnock.

She calmed down a bit, but the next day she twice telephoned Young, full of anxieties. Her first call was to repeat the view of Woodrow Wyatt that she should be on more of her party's election broadcasts.* The second was to complain how appallingly scruffy her ministers, notably Lawson, Kenneth Clarke and Nicholas Ridley (whose crime was to wear a cardigan), looked on television: 'Nigel's got to get a haircut.' 'Absolutely right.' 'Will you tell him?' 'No, Prime Minister . . . you've got to tell him.' 'All right.'[120] In fact, she did not; his own wife did.[121] This combination of explosions of anger about various mistakes and shortcomings with a reluctance to speak directly to the people concerned also led her to strip Wakeham of his role co-ordinating television broadcasts for ministers without giving him the bad news herself. The task fell to Young, who executed her order, but was not pleased: 'She ensured I made an enemy for life.'[122] This atmosphere of unhappiness, anger, irresolution and intrigue dominated the whole campaign. Part of the trouble, caused by her long years at the top, was that she now had very few associates senior enough to stand up to her. Once, when she was firing so many angry questions at David Willetts that he could not get her to read the brief which answered them, David Wolfson intervened and said to Mrs Thatcher, 'Just shut up and read the bloody brief,'[123] but such courage was memorable by its rarity. All the difficulties came back to Mrs Thatcher's deep insecurity, and her lack of a team in which she could repose complete trust.

The wider political realities were much better for her. There was hardly any alteration in the opinion polls throughout May, except for a decline

---

* Wyatt's diaries confirm this conversation, and also indicate how he developed some of his ideas. When he called Margaret Thatcher, he was staying with Lord Weinstock in the country. Tim Bell came down for lunch. After seeing Bell, Wyatt told her: 'Tebbit is good in some ways but no good at organising. David Young is much better.' (Wyatt, *The Journals of Woodrow Wyatt*, vol. i, 24 May 1987, p. 351.) It seems reasonable to conjecture that it was Bell who had put this thought into his head at that moment.

of the Alliance which favoured Labour slightly more than the Conservatives. On policy, the Conservatives scored some palpable hits, and Labour did not. Indeed, when it came to the community charge, although press questioning revealed considerable Conservative incoherence about who would gain and who would lose, the Opposition largely stayed off the subject because of its fear of being saddled with blame for high rates and their association with the 'loony left'. As Young said in a private interview after the election, 'Labour missed a trick on the poll tax which certainly hadn't been properly thought out and on which the Conservatives were very vulnerable.'[124]

Running what he called 'my freelance election campaign' because he had been excluded from the nerve-centre by Young,[125] Nigel Lawson studied Labour's economic promises. His eye was caught by an oddly specific figure in the Labour manifesto. It promised a £7.36 per week increase in child benefit. He wondered why, and soon worked out that this was the amount that would be raised by abolishing the married man's tax allowance. Earlier drafts of the Labour manifesto had mentioned the abolition, in order to produce the £7.36 figure, but this had later been excised to prevent anger among married men. The tell-tale exact figure, however, had been carelessly left in,[126] exposing the deception. Lawson was also able to mount a wider attack on how Labour's spending promises must involve tax increases much larger than they were admitting. 'Nigel was very good at spotting the Labour weaknesses on taxation,' recalled Mrs Thatcher. 'Let us give credit where credit is due.'[127]

Even more helpful to the Conservatives was Labour's policy of unilateral disarmament. For this Saatchis produced an advertisement – their only one of the campaign which was universally described as a success. Its simple slogan was 'LABOUR'S POLICY ON ARMS', and it showed a British soldier with his hands held up in surrender.

On the same day that a despairing Mrs Thatcher was ringing up Young about Lawson's haircut, Kinnock was interviewed by David Frost on television. In an extremely convoluted answer about nuclear weapons, the Labour leader ended up saying that, since he did not believe that Britain could use nuclear weapons successfully, it would face 'the classical choice', when attacked, 'of either exterminating everything you stand for . . . or using the resources you've got to make any occupation totally untenable'.[128] By using the word 'occupation', Kinnock seemed to concede in advance the idea of defeat and surrender. The talk in the newspapers was that Kinnock was advocating that the British, if invaded, should 'take to the hills'. He was teased about wanting to create his own 'Dad's Army'. 'Norman the assassin' moved into action as agreed in principle the night before. 'Britain has no ambition to live under the red flag of socialism or the white flag of surrender,'[129] he declared.

Mrs Thatcher was offered a gift of a question about Kinnock's defence policy at her press conference on the Tuesday morning (the Monday was a bank holiday), but, to the exasperation of her staff she 'totally threw it away because she said that inner cities, not defence, was the subject of the day. She could be extraordinary sometimes.'[130] At a rally in Newport in Wales that night, however, she did launch into the sort of denunciation in which she specialized. She returned to the theme with which she had started the campaign – that Labour had an 'iceberg' manifesto, in which its dangers were concealed below the surface. She quoted Kinnock's words about occupation – 'A Soviet occupation, I presume. So now we know that Labour's non-nuclear defence policy is a policy for defeat, surrender, occupation and finally, prolonged guerrilla fighting . . . I do not understand how anyone who aspires to government can treat the defence of our country so lightly.'[131]*

On the last Sunday in May, the beginning of the last full week of the campaign, the opinion polls remained unaffected by the fierceness of the public battle being fought between the parties and, of course, by the hysterical atmosphere behind the scenes. The least favourable poll, a Gallup published in the *Sunday Telegraph*, gave the Tories an 8.5 per cent lead over Labour. Conservative candidates reported good levels of support. Travelling the country, Lawson recalled an even better atmosphere than in 1983, 'a huge, popular, positive response, a real feeling of a British economic miracle'.[132] He was talking his own book,† but there can be little doubt that voters were less worried than before about unemployment and widely convinced that good times had arrived and would stay.

Mrs Thatcher, however, and therefore most of those around her, remained extremely uneasy. They considered the polls alarming, though

---

* Two people who were not supposed to help her campaign, but did, were Ronald Reagan and Charles Powell. Both assisted on the nuclear issue. Reagan spoke publicly of Labour's 'grievous errors' on the subject (Reagan, Interview with Foreign Television Journalists Prior to the Venice Economic Summit, 27 May 1987, American Presidency Project (http://www. presidency.ucsb.edu/ws/index.php?pid=34337&st=&st1=)). Powell admitted that he took the Civil Service practice of scanning the manifesto for consistency with government policy to unusual lengths and suggested amendments to the defence aspect. He also proposed wording on foreign affairs and defence in Mrs Thatcher's speeches because policy was 'too important to leave in the hands of Central Office hacks'. (Correspondence with Lord Powell of Bayswater.)

† Literally his own book: his memoirs give a full account of that 'miracle' and his leading role in it.

they had barely shifted. The Sunday papers reported that Labour would move to more personal attacks on Mrs Thatcher, her arrogance and dictatorial ways. The young Tony Blair, by now a frontbench Treasury spokesman, spoke of 'her unchecked and unbalanced mind'.[133] In a note, Young told her how he thought the campaign should now go: 'You said when we left last night that it was not as clear as last week. Let me make clear: – 1. Between now and Wednesday/Thursday of this week we must stay on the ATTACK . . . The attack should be the fear issues . . . "They will destroy our industrial peace, they will destroy our safety on the streets and they will destroy the money in your pocket." '[134] Mrs Thatcher always liked attacking, and was pleased to concentrate on the simple case against Labour, the Alliance seemingly having been cleared out of the way. She spoke strongly in Edinburgh on the ensuing Tuesday (2 June), denouncing Labour's resort to 'personal abuse' and warned of what lay behind the 'mask of moderation'.[135] She also spoke directly to Scots: 'We pledged ourselves to abolish domestic rates and we have done so (Applause.) . . . And I am proud that we will first be introducing the Community Charge here in Scotland . . . It will be brought into operation. (Applause.)'

That night, a poll organized by Vincent Hanna of the BBC's *Newsnight* and using techniques which he claimed had been perfected in by-elections, gave the Conservatives a slightly less than 4 per cent lead over Labour, the worst figures of the campaign so far. Mrs Thatcher always became anxious if she was absent for too long from the centre of operations, and this was her first night not passed in London since the campaign had begun. Before she got back to Downing Street, the fighting mood in which she had started the week was debilitated by 'the onset of extremely painful toothache',[136] which was eventually diagnosed as an abscess. On Wednesday 3 June, she returned to find pain which, though not physical, was no less real.

Rumours in the City that afternoon had started share prices falling. A Gallup poll in the *Daily Telegraph* the following day confirmed them. It put the Tories on 40.5 per cent, Labour on 36.5 and the Alliance on 21.5. Her campaign was also rated 16 points behind that of Neil Kinnock. Stephen Sherbourne was with Mrs Thatcher in Downing Street when early news of the poll came through: 'Our response was quite unscientific. Panic gripped us all. "Is this a horrible turning point?" we asked ourselves.'[137]

Struggling back from making a speech in Southampton, Young reached Downing Street at about ten that night. He found a scene of distress. 'She started talking about the prospect of actually losing.'[138]

The next morning was worse. Mrs Thatcher had passed a sleepless night, racked by tooth pain, until given pills by Crawfie in the small hours, so she was groggy. After arriving at Central Office, she lashed out at

Tebbit and Young: 'You and David, you've been on too much and you're too old. We must have younger people on television.'[139] Although she was older than both of them, she wanted to be seen more herself: 'I thought that Norman was coming across too harsh, which is a strange thing for me to say. I said I have not been on television a great deal, I'm going on more now.'[140] She took the press conference. There she allowed herself to be trapped by a question about her private health treatment in the past. She said she had been so treated 'to enable me to go into hospital on the day I want, at the time I want and with the doctor I want'.[141] Her remarks contrasted unpleasingly with Kinnock's press conference across the road, which highlighted the case of a ten-year-old boy with a hole in the heart who had had to wait fifteen months for an operation. She did not seem to understand, when David Willetts discussed it with her afterwards, that the point at issue was not her right to have private treatment – which few potential Conservative voters doubted – but her implication that the National Health Service for which she was responsible did not offer the speed and quality which she valued to the average citizen who, unlike her, could not afford to go private.[142] She would be pursued for her remark until the end of the campaign.

Meeting the Chairman and others afterwards, Mrs Thatcher was 'almost hysterical, with her arms sweeping everywhere'.[143] 'Her eyes flashed: hatred shot out of them, like a dog about to bite you.'[144] She demanded to see Saatchis' proposed advertising. Despite the fact that the exiled Dobbs, because of his Saatchi role, had separated himself from advertising, the boards and other materials were kept in his office. John Wakeham came in and asked him to bring them to her. 'I'm not invited,' Dobbs replied. 'I'm not going in there without you,' said the now agitated Wakeham.[145] So Dobbs brought the advertisements in. 'She flayed me,' he recalled. 'She was screaming, foaming at the mouth. Norman was trying to talk sense into her. David Young was saying "Leave it to me, Margaret." Willie Whitelaw was rolling his oyster eyes.' The only coherent thing she said was that she wanted the material to dwell more on Conservative achievements.[146]

'I was getting more and more desperate,' Young told his diary,

> until eventually I said, 'Prime Minister, what do you want me to do?' And she just exploded. She said, 'I can't do all this myself, I can't tell you'. . . . Then she went on about the party election broadcast, and the meeting broke up without anything being resolved. I felt very depressed. I really thought . . . I was being left out in the cold and being blamed that things weren't going very well.[147]

He tottered off to arrange a meeting that afternoon with Tim Bell and others to try to put the advertising and the election broadcast right. Then – for the ordinary business of government still chugged on almost regardless – he had to attend a luncheon for the Chinese Minister for Aeronautical Industries.

Mrs Thatcher went to visit Alton Towers, the Staffordshire theme park, in heavy rain. The trip had been arranged in a desperate attempt to lighten the atmosphere of the campaign, but she now faced it, 'without quite being in the mood for jollity'.[148] After she had set off for Alton Towers, Whitelaw turned to Dobbs and said, 'There's a woman who will never fight another election.'[149]*

Rumours were sweeping Westminster and the markets of another unfavourable poll that evening, allegedly showing a 2 per cent Tory lead, so Young, Bell and co., scared by Mrs Thatcher's mood, believed they must be ready for her return early that evening. They saw a change in the campaign advertising as the only means of winning the election. They met in Downing Street. Bell, with his business partner Frank Lowe, had come up with a poster slogan 'BRITAIN'S A SUCCESS AGAIN – DON'T LET LABOUR RUIN IT', a slogan inspired by the Conservatives' victorious campaign for a third term in 1959: 'LIFE'S BETTER UNDER THE CONSERVATIVES. DON'T LET LABOUR RUIN IT'.[150] At the same time, Saatchis and Tebbit were frantically working on the same vague brief to replace their offering that had been rejected that morning.

Mrs Thatcher returned from her dismal outing by helicopter. Saatchis (Maurice Saatchi and John Sharkey) set out for Downing Street carrying their ideas carefully wrapped up and sealed against the torrential rain. Sherbourne and Willetts had to choreograph 'a scene from a Feydeau farce',[151] by which the representatives of the rival groups were kept in separate rooms, unaware of the presence of the other. Tebbit arrived separately. Young took him aside and showed him Bell's work, about which, until then, he had known nothing. ' "Who did this?" he asked . . . I said "Tim Bell." He said, "Well, that's it then, that's it." '[152] Young then 'got him by the shoulders and said, "Norman listen to me, we're about to lose this fucking election, you're going to go, I'm going to go, the whole thing is going to go. The whole election depends upon her being right for the next five days doing fine performances on television – she has to be happy, we have got to do this." ' Young was, as Tebbit put it, 'excessively excited'.[153] Rather cool-headedly, having inspected the offerings of the two sides,

---

* It was this highly charged occasion which inspired Dobbs to write his novel *House of Cards* (Interview with Lord Dobbs).

Tebbit decided that the one produced by his rivals was the better and more likely to please Mrs Thatcher.

After a further struggle, in which Young grabbed Maurice Saatchi, who was 'enraged',[154] by his lapels, and made a speech similar to the one he had made to Tebbit, Saatchis, encouraged by Tebbit, agreed to accept Bell's proposal so long as they were charged with executing and improving it. Their face-saving modification was 'BRITAIN'S GREAT AGAIN: DON'T LET LABOUR WRECK IT', which Bell considered 'unsubtle'[155] but, to the untutored eye, made very little difference. Once this was agreed, Tebbit said, 'Well, I want to go and tell her.'[156] Thus Mrs Thatcher was presented, at last, not with competing alternatives, but with a single, agreed suggestion. 'She looked very relieved,'[157] and accepted it. Early that evening, the news came through that the dreaded Marplan poll was fine – 44 per cent for the Conservatives and 34 for Labour. So all the heat went out of the rows, and the appalling twenty-four hours looked ridiculous.* 'What childish things we did,' recalled David Young.[158] That night, Mrs Thatcher, very uncharacteristically, failed to work on the draft of her next speech. This was because she was so tired she fell asleep at her desk.[159]

The next day (Friday 5 June), all rather uneasy with one another, but all working together, Tebbit, the Saatchis team and Young met in Central Office. Young argued for a huge blitz with the new advertising. Tebbit resisted, on the grounds that Central Office could not afford it, to which Young replied, 'Don't worry about the cost, because I've spoken to Alistair and there's plenty of money.'[160] It was the exact opposite tactic to the one employed in 1983, when the last few days of advertising were cancelled as an unnecessary extravagance (see Chapter 3), but in truth there was little need for this change. No poll at any point in the campaign ever remotely suggested that the Conservatives would lose. As Neil Kinnock himself recalled, 'We didn't seriously think we could win.'[161]

In the view of many seasoned campaigners, the whole business of Wobbly Thursday, as it came to be known, was absurd. Some blamed it on Lord Young. 'David panicked,' Nigel Lawson believed. 'It was infectious. There was no wobble. David Young didn't meet any voters.'[162] But although it was true that Young was electorally inexperienced, this was really beside the point. The ultimate problem lay with Mrs Thatcher herself. She was, in advertisers' jargon, the client (though technically the client was Central

---

* Mrs Thatcher resented the fact that she was not informed of the poll before going off for her next television encounter, with Jonathan Dimbleby (see Thatcher, *The Downing Street Years*, pp. 585–6).

BRITAIN NOW HAS THE FEWEST STRIKES FOR 50 YEARS.

The last Labour Government ended in The Winter of Discontent.

BRITAIN IS GREAT AGAIN. DON'T LET LABOUR WRECK IT. VOTE CONSERVATIVE ☒

A Saatchi poster in the 1987 campaign – following ferocious internal rows, the idea for the new slogan came from Tim Bell, backed by David Young.

Office); and in this election she was an impossible one – sure of nothing except that everything was going wrong. So Young and Bell were right to think that the key issue was to keep her happy and thus coax the best performances out of her. According to Charles Powell, the election campaign was 'one of her worst and scratchiest periods' and Wobbly Thursday 'made some of us feel that she had to be saved from herself'.[163]

One mysterious aspect of the affair is that Tebbit had told Mrs Thatcher as early as the middle of April that he had agreed with 'my Margaret' (his wife) not to accept office after the election. So it is odd that her suspicions of Tebbit persisted. Possibly she did not believe that he was unpersuadable on the subject: she always found it hard to imagine that people wanted to give up politics. Certainly she tried, including on election night itself, to get him to stay. Perhaps it was just that she never felt at ease with the rather stern Tebbit in the way that she did with louder, easier, more self-consciously charming men. For his part, Tebbit was more deeply hurt by what had happened than he – a proud man who had been treated very unfairly – liked to admit. At the party conference in 1987, meeting one colleague late at night, he 'embarked on a 10-minute fusillade of RAF expletives about his election treatment by the ghastly — —, an overrated PM'.[164] He was so incensed by what he had discovered about Mrs Thatcher using research behind his back during the election that he tried to telephone her at the Vancouver summit that autumn to insist she apologize to him publicly.[165] There was something tragic in this falling out, as there was about some of her other relationships with her most able senior colleagues. She admired Tebbit very much and yet, despite everything they had done together, their sense of common purpose had declined. In this sense, Wobbly Thursday may have been not so much a one-day wonder as a watershed.

In the final days, while her tooth still hurt, Mrs Thatcher recovered form. With plenty to do in the television studios, and a clear battle to fight under a clear slogan, she had a renewed sense of direction. Although still pursued on the subject of health, she fought back. On Sunday 7 June, when David Frost had a go at her, she asked him sweetly whether he too used private medicine, and he had to admit that he did. She remained tense, however. When she was interviewed by Robin Day for *Panorama* on the Monday night, she performed extremely well, but she was so upset by Day's attack on her as an 'uncaring' person that, once the filming was over, she was, recorded John Whittingdale, 'close to tears'.[166] 'In no other country would the Prime Minister be subjected to personal insults like that,' she said. Then she added, 'We must make a list of those in the media who are against us.'[167]

Mrs Thatcher immediately flew to Venice, for a truncated visit to the G7 summit. Her early departure caused disappointment in Washington where, as George Shultz told an NSC meeting, she was being relied upon to 'help secure our key objectives',[168] but the summit was a helpful reminder to the electorate of her global importance.* On her return to Gatwick,

---

* Margaret Thatcher also received from Reagan the startling news that he wanted to amend the US Constitution so that he could run for a third term as president. It was not completely clear whether he was joking. (Correspondence with Lord Powell of Bayswater.)

Stephen Sherbourne was waiting for her reaction to his draft of her speech to be delivered at Harrogate that night. Since she had actually torn up the draft he had given her for another speech the week before, he was extremely nervous, but Charles Powell, seeing Sherbourne across the tarmac, simply waved the speech in the air and put his thumb up.[169] She barely changed a word. This was a sign, unprecedented in the campaign, that she was content.

In an eve-of-poll interview, harassed by David Dimbleby about why she did not seem to care about the fate of the unemployed, Mrs Thatcher replied: 'If people just drool and drivel that they care, I turn round and say "Right, I also look to see what you actually do." '[170] Very untypically, she immediately retracted the phrase on air. 'I am sorry I used those words,' she said twice. If she had used them any earlier in the campaign, they would certainly have been brought up against her again, and probably have created as much trouble as her remarks on health. Yet the words were of the essence of Margaret Thatcher. First, they expressed fierce antagonism to the left's pretension to any moral high ground. Second, they encapsulated her tendency to judge by results and by action rather than by words. She did care about what happened to people without jobs, but she wished to be judged by how much she could improve their opportunities rather than by how nicely she spoke about them. She apologized, not because she thought she had said a wrong thing, but because she thought she had been politically imprudent. In all her social teaching, she kept asking the question, 'What is to be *done*?', and so she got angry when her critics cared, as she saw it, only about what should be said.

Although, as was almost traditional, Vincent Hanna's *Newsnight* poll two days before polling forecast a hung Parliament, and the BBC's exit poll did the same, the real result was never, once the votes started to be counted, in doubt.* On the day before polling day, Young told Mrs Thatcher he did not think she would get near a majority of 80. 'I must have an 80 majority, I must have it,' she replied. 'It won't look right if I don't.'[171] At 2.15 a.m. after Thursday's voting, the Conservatives achieved an overall majority. Once all the votes were counted, they had a majority of 102.

---

* Young's only duty on the day was to inform the Tigger-ish Jeffrey Archer that if he was coming to the election-night party in Central Office he must be sure not to be photographed with Mrs Thatcher (Lord Young of Graffham, unpublished Election Diary, 11 June 1987). Tim Bell, presumably by Tebbit's design, was not invited to the party at all. This enraged Mrs Thatcher. (Ibid., 12 June 1987.)

Mrs Thatcher's own result in Finchley, which saw her majority slightly reduced to 8,913, was:

Mrs M. Thatcher (Conservative)   21,603
J. R. M. Davies (Labour)   12,690
D. Howarth (Liberal)   5,580
Lord Buckethead (Independent)   131
M. J. St Vincent (Independent)   59

The total nationwide Conservative vote was 13,763,066 (42.2 per cent of the total) – a higher numerical, though not proportional, total than in 1979 or 1983. Labour added more than 1,500,000 votes to its terrible 1983 tally to get back just over 10,000,000, and achieved 30.8 per cent of the vote. The Alliance, with 22.5 per cent of the vote, was three percentage points down on 1983. The only serious blot on the Tory success was the sharp fall in the number of seats in Scotland, where voters had been the victims of rate revaluation – from twenty-one seats to ten.

On polling day, Bernard Ingham sent Mrs Thatcher a note of things she might want to say once her victory was certain:

> the main story tomorrow will be your historic winning of a third term . . . While savouring your triumph you _must_ give no impression of resting on your laurels . . . it would also be of longer term value to signal your concern to get on with the major 'caring' tasks which were interrupted by the General Election.[172]

Mrs Thatcher's own handwritten notes show her more or less following this advice. 'To be returned the third term is to make history,'[173] and she thanked Norman Tebbit for running 'the engine-room of victory'. Her notes referred to 'the duty that rests upon us to represent _all_ the people'. She wanted 'more choice in housing and education. Especially for those in inner cities'. What she actually said to the cameras, however, was 'We must do something about those inner cities.' Those were the words that were remembered.

But the facts spoke louder than anything Mrs Thatcher herself could say. No prime minister in the era of universal suffrage had ever won a third consecutive term before. Despite her own extreme anxiety, ill temper and misjudgments in the campaign, she had triumphantly done so. Thatcherism was now the dominant creed of the age.

The day after the Conservatives' victory was declared, Charles Powell wrote a letter of congratulation to his boss.[174] Although it was typed ('to save your eyes'), he reassured her that 'There are no copies.' 'If ever a party and a country were carried to success on the shoulders of one person,' he

told her, 'it has been over the last eight years.' But then he gave some brave
advice:

> All the same, I hope you will not put yourself through it again. The level
> of personal abuse thrown at you during the campaign was unbelievable and
> must take some toll, however stoic you are outwardly. There comes a point
> when your reputation and standing as a historic figure are more important
> to your party, to your cause and to the country than even you yourself can
> be . . . In two or three years time, you will have completed the most sweep-
> ing change this country has seen in decades and your place in history will
> be rivalled in this century only by Churchill. That's the time to contribute
> in some other area!

In her moment of greatest triumph, Mrs Thatcher was being reminded by
her closest associate that she was mortal.

Notes

ABBREVIATIONS

CAC Churchill Archives Centre, Churchill College, Cambridge
    THCR The Papers of Baroness Thatcher
    WTRS The Papers of Sir Alan Walters

FCO Foreign and Commonwealth Office

NAI The National Archives of Ireland, Dublin
    DFA   Department of Foreign Affairs
    TAOIS Department of the Taoiseach

TNA The National Archives, Kew
    CAB   Cabinet Office
    PREM Prime Minister's Office

References are also made to the Bush Library in College Station, TX; to the Reagan Library in Simi Valley, CA; and to The National Security Archive in Washington, DC.

CHAPTER I: LIBERAL IMPERIALIST

1. Speech to the UN General Assembly, 23 June 1982 (http://www.margaretthatcher. org/document/104974). 2. Ibid. 3. Speech to Conservative Party Conference, 8 October 1982 (http://www.margaretthatcher.org/document/105032). 4. Ibid. 5. Sir David Goodall, unpublished memoir, 2005. 6. Ibid. 7. Ibid. 8. Dame Margery Corbett-Ashby Memorial Lecture, 26 July 1982 (http://www.margaretthatcher. org/document/105007). 9. Speech to Conservative Party Conference, 8 October 1982 (http://www.margaretthatcher.org/document/105032). 10. Ibid. 11. TV interview for De Wolfe Productions, 30 December 1982, broadcast on ITV, 29 March 1983 (http://www.margaretthatcher.org/document/104849). 12. Ibid. 13. Ibid. 14. Speech at the Lord Mayor's Banquet, 15 November 1982 (http:// www.margaretthatcher.org/document/105054). 15. Ibid. 16. TV Interview for London Weekend Television, *Weekend World*, 16 January 1983 (http://www.marga retthatcher.org/document/105087). 17. Ibid. 18. Thatcher to Evans, 5 May 1983, CAC: THCR 3/2/116 (http://www.margaretthatcher.org/document/132330).

19. Speech to Conservative Central Council, 26 March 1983 (http://www.marga retthatcher.org/document/105285). **20.** Interview with Sir Percy Cradock. **21.** See Volume I, p. 365. **22.** Interview with Sir Stephen Wall. **23.** Carrington to Thatcher, 9 March 1982, TNA: PREM 19/789 (http://www.margaretthatcher.org/document/138420). **24.** See, for example, Christopher Patten, 'Pulling the dragon's teeth for Hong Kong', *Guardian*, 5 November 1979. **25.** Cradock to FCO, telegram 22, 12 January 1982, TNA: PREM 19/789 (http://www.margaretthatcher.org/document/138421). **26.** Acland to Armstrong, 7 July 1982, TNA: PREM 19/670 (http://www.margaretthatcher.org/document/138487). **27.** Armstrong to Coles, 28 July 1982. Ibid. **28.** Note of meeting between Thatcher and Pym, 28 July 1982, TNA: PREM 19/789 (http://www.margaretthatcher.org/document/138412). **29.** Ibid. **30.** Interview with Sir John Coles. **31.** Interview with Lord Butler of Brockwell. **32.** Interview with Sir Percy Cradock. **33.** Record of discussion at a working lunch at No. 10 Downing Street, 8 September 1982, TNA: PREM 19/790 (http://www.margaretthatcher.org/document/138485). **34.** Cradock to Donald, 16 September 1982, TNA: PREM 19/790 (http://www.margaretthatcher.org/document/138476). **35.** Interview with Lord Butler of Brockwell. **36.** *Independent*, 30 August 1992. **37.** Record of a conversation between Thatcher and Premier Zhao Ziyang, 23 September 1982, TNA: PREM 19/962 (http://www.margaretthatcher.org/document/128397). **38.** Interview with Sir Percy Cradock. **39.** Interview with Lord Butler of Brockwell. **40.** Record of meeting between Thatcher and Vice-chairman Deng Xiaoping, 24 September 1982, TNA: PREM 19/962 (http://www.margaretthatcher.org/document/128402). **41.** Ibid. **42.** Interview with Lord Butler of Brockwell. **43.** Ibid. **44.** Interview with Sir John Coles. **45.** Speech at Hong Kong business lunch, 27 September 1982 (http://www.margaretthatcher.org/document/105028). **46.** 'Prime Minister Thatcher in China: British Embassy Readout', 280954Z Sep 82, China-Foreign Relations-Hong Kong (9/27/82–10/20/82), Box 13, David Laux Files, Reagan Library. **47.** Cradock to Pym, 7 October 1982, TNA: PREM 19/962 (http://www.margaretthatcher.org/document/122698). **48.** Thatcher annotation on Coles to Thatcher, 6 October 1982, TNA: PREM 19/791 (http://www.margaretthatcher.org/document/138526). **49.** Interview with Henry Kissinger. **50.** Coles to Holmes, 15 November 1982, Prime Minister's Papers, USA, Henry Kissinger's visits to the UK (document consulted in the Cabinet Office). **51.** Kissinger to Thatcher, 20 December 1982. Ibid. **52.** Thatcher to Kissinger, 14 January 1983, CAC: THCR 3/2/109 (http://www.margaretthatcher.org/document/132262). **53.** Butler to Coles, 24 December 1982, TNA: PREM 19/1053 (http://www.margaretthatcher.org/document/138829). **54.** Note of a discussion on Hong Kong, 28 January 1983, TNA: PREM 19/1053 (http://www.margaretthatcher.org/document/138812). **55.** Pym to Thatcher, 16 February 1983, TNA: PREM 19/1053 (http://www.margaretthatcher.org/document/138799). **56.** Ibid. **57.** Thatcher's speaking note for Cabinet, 11 May 1983, TNA: PREM 19/1055 (http://www.margaretthatcher.org/document/139152). **58.** Cradock to FCO, telegram 417, 9 May 1983, TNA: PREM 19/1055 (http://www.margaretthatcher.org/document/139156). **59.** Cradock to FCO, telegram 416, 9 May 1983, TNA: PREM

19/1055 (http://www.margaretthatcher.org/document/139156). **60.** Interview with Lord Butler of Brockwell. **61.** Interview with John Gerson. **62.** Ibid.

CHAPTER 2: A RADICAL DISPOSITION

1. Taylor telegram 863, 12 October 1982, TNA: PREM 19/765. **2.** Ibid. **3.** Coles to Thatcher, 18 October 1982, TNA: PREM 19/765. **4.** Ibid. **5.** Taylor telegram 882, 18 October 1982, TNA: PREM 19/765. **6.** Taylor to Pym, 14 October 1982. Ibid. **7.** Pym to Thatcher, 14 October 1982, TNA: PREM 19/765 (http://www. margaretthatcher.org/document/137898). **8.** Note of meeting between Thatcher and Chancellor Kohl on 19 October, 20 October 1982, TNA: PREM 19/765 (http:// www.margaretthatcher.org/document/137895). **9.** Ibid. **10.** Ibid. **11.** Press conference with Chancellor Kohl, 19 October 1982 (http://www.margaretthatcher. org/document/105037). **12.** Joint press conference in Bonn, 29 October 1982 (http://www.margaretthatcher.org/document/105042). **13.** Interview with Sir John Coles. **14.** Remarks at the Berlin Wall, 29 October 1982 (Christopher Collins, ed., *Complete Public Statements of Margaret Thatcher 1945–90 on CD-ROM*, Oxford University Press, 1998/2000). **15.** Speech at the Golden Book ceremony, Berlin, 29 October 1982 (http://www.margaretthatcher.org/docu ment/105043). **16.** Interview with Sir John Coles. **17.** Interview with Lord Hannay of Chiswick. **18.** Conversation with Lady Thatcher. **19.** Thatcher annotation on Rhodes to Scholar, 26 October 1982, Prime Minister's Papers, Germany, PM's meetings with Chancellor Kohl of Germany, Part 4 (document consulted in the Cabinet Office). **20.** Helmut Kohl, *Erinnerungen 1982–1990*, Droemer Knaur, 2005, p. 60. **21.** Thatcher to Kohl, 23 December 1982, CAC: THCR 3/1/27 (http:// www.margaretthatcher.org/document/123598). **22.** Record of conversation between Thatcher and Chancellor Kohl, 4 February 1983, TNA: PREM 19/1307. **23.** Record of conversation between Thatcher and Chancellor Kohl and foreign secretaries, 4 February 1983, TNA: PREM 19/1307. **24.** Ibid. **25.** Joint press conference with West German Chancellor, 4 February 1983 (http://www.marga retthatcher.org/document/105249). **26.** 101209z Mar 83, 'Denis Healey, Labor Deputy Leader's Washington Visit, March 11', 10 March 1983, NSC: Country File, UK Vol. IV (1 of 5), Box 91330, Reagan Library. **27.** Interview with Richard Perle. **28.** Hansard, HC Deb 18 January 1983, 35/168 (http://hansard.millbanksystems. com/commons/1983/jan/18/engagements). **29.** Clark to Reagan, 'Meeting with UK Ambassador Sir Oliver Wright', 15 April 1983, UK (03/16/1983–04/14/1983), Box 20, Exec Sec, NSC: Country File, Reagan Library. **30.** Ibid. **31.** Interview with Ronald Lehman. **32.** Clark to Shultz/Weinberger, 'Reply to Mrs. Thatcher on Public Handling of Dual Key Issue', 29 April 1983, UK: PM Thatcher (8290407– 8390524), Exec Sec, NSC: Head of State, Reagan Library. **33.** Reagan to Thatcher, 1 May 1983, CAC: THCR 1/4/5 (part 2) (http://www.margaretthatcher.org/docu ment/130984); also Hansard, HC Deb 12 May 1983, 42/433W (http://hansard. millbanksystems.com/written_answers/1983/may/12/cruise-missiles). **34.** Correspondence with Lord Armstrong of Ilminster, 29 October 2011. **35.** Margaret

Thatcher, *The Downing Street Years*, HarperCollins, 1993, p. 268. **36.** *The Times*, 27 January 1982. Historical unemployment statistics for the 1980s are readily available from the Office of National Statistics. However, because this data has been revised (retroactively) on several occasions, it does not match the figures released at the time. The author has therefore relied upon the statistics reported contemporaneously in the press; these were the figures with which Mrs Thatcher had to contend. **37.** *Financial Times*, 5 July 1982. **38.** Sir Robert Armstrong, Cabinet Secretary's notebooks, 15 July 1982 (document consulted in the Cabinet Office). **39.** Ibid. **40.** Ibid. **41.** Interview with Sir John Sparrow. **42.** Interview with Lord Butler of Brockwell. **43.** Sir Robert Armstrong, Cabinet Secretary's notebooks, 9 September 1982 (document consulted in the Cabinet Office). **44.** Ibid. **45.** Private information. **46.** Thatcher, *The Downing Street Years*, p. 277. **47.** Interview with John Redwood. **48.** Interview with Sir John Sparrow. **49.** Armstrong to Thatcher, 9 August 1982, Prime Minister's Papers, Downing Street: Access to Papers by the Policy Unit (document consulted in the Cabinet Office). **50.** Interview with Ferdinand Mount. **51.** Ibid. **52.** Interview with Tim Flesher. **53.** Armstrong to Thatcher, 6 August 1982, Prime Minister's Papers, Government Machinery, Appointment of a Special Adviser to the PM (document consulted in the Cabinet Office). **54.** Armstrong to Thatcher, 8 October 1982. Ibid. **55.** Ibid. **56.** Butler to Thatcher, 8 October 1982. Ibid. **57.** Butler to Fall, 15 October 1982. Ibid. **58.** Note for the Record, 18 October 1982. Ibid . **59.** Ibid. **60.** Interview with Ferdinand Mount. **61.** Note for the record, 20 October 1982, Prime Minister's Papers, Government Machinery, Appointment of a Special Adviser to the PM (document consulted in the Cabinet Office). **62.** Sir Robert Armstrong, Cabinet Secretary's notebooks, 30 September 1982 (document consulted in the Cabinet Office). **63.** Ibid. **64.** Speech to Conservative Party Conference, 8 October 1982 (http://www.margaretthatcher.org/document/105032). **65.** Mount to Thatcher, 12 November 1982, TNA: PREM 19/1001. **66.** Ibid. **67.** Mount to Thatcher, 21 February 1983. Ibid. **68.** Flesher to Wilde, 8 March 1983. Ibid. **69.** Flesher to Wilde, 29 March 1983. Ibid. **70.** Interview with Oliver Letwin. **71.** Remarks at BT privatisation seminar, Centre for Contemporary British History and Churchill Archive Centre, 6 December 2006. **72.** Essay in Robert Blake and John Patten, eds., *The Conservative Opportunity*, Macmillan, 1976, p. 75. **73.** Hansard, HC Deb 12 June 1979, 968/249 (http://hansard.millbanksystems.com/commons/1979/jun/12/public-expenditure). **74.** See David Parker, *The Official History of Privatisation: The Formative Years 1970–1987*, vol. i, Routledge, 2009, p. 54. **75.** Remarks at BT privatisation seminar, 6 December 2006. **76.** See Nigel Lawson, *The View from No. 11*, Bantam Press, 1992, p. 211. **77.** Howe to Thatcher, 26 July 1982, TNA: PREM 19/988. **78.** Thatcher to Howe, 28 July 1982, CAC: THCR 3/3/4 (http://www.margaretthatcher.org/document/123653). **79.** Interview with Lord Lawson of Blaby. **80.** Interview with Oliver Letwin. **81.** Interview with Sir Peter Gregson. **82.** Interview with Lord Moore of Lower Marsh. **83.** Mount and Walters to Thatcher, 15 February 1983, TNA: PREM 19/989 (http://www.margaretthatcher.org/document/128138). **84.** Speech at Lord Mayor's Banquet, 10 November 1986 (http://www.margaretthatcher.org/document/106512).   **85.** Thatcher, *The Down-ing Street Years*, p. 676.   **86.** Interview with Sir Peter Gregson.   **87.** Interview with Lord Young of Graffham.   **88.** Ibid.   **89.** Interview with Sir Michael Scholar.   **90.** Remarks at BT privatisation seminar, 6 December 2006.   **91.** Kenneth Baker, *The Turbulent Years*, Faber & Faber, 1993, p. 78.   **92.** Remarks at BT privatisation seminar, 6 December 2006.   **93.** See Parker, *The Official History of Privatisation*, vol. i, p. 250.   **94.** Interview with Sir Michael Scholar.   **95.** Ibid.   **96.** Interview with Lord Jenkin of Roding.   **97.** Interview with Lord Young of Graffham.   **98.** Thatcher annotation on note from Mount to Thatcher, 17 December 1982, TNA: PREM 19/1100.   **99.** Speech to Conservative Party Conference, 8 October 1982 (http://www.margaretthatcher.org/document/105032).   **100.** Remarks at BT privatisation seminar, 6 December 2006.   **101.** Thatcher, *The Downing Street Years*, p. 644.   **102.** Heseltine memorandum, 'Alternatives to Domestic Rates', 8 June 1982, TNA: CAB 130/1210.   **103.** Ibid.   **104.** Heseltine memorandum to Thatcher, 9 June 1982, TNA: PREM 19/833.   **105.** Mount to Thatcher, 19 July 1982, TNA: PREM 19/835.   **106.** Heseltine memorandum to MISC 79, 15 December 1982, TNA: CAB 130/1211.   **107.** Cabinet Minutes, CC (83) 1st, 20 January 1983, TNA: CAB 128/76 (http://www.margaretthatcher.org/document/128241).   **108.** Sir Robert Armstrong, Cabinet Secretary's notebooks, 20 January 1983 (document consulted in the Cabinet Office).   **109.** Scholar to Mount, 7 February 1983, TNA: PREM 19/1079.   **110.** Transcript of interview for *The Times*, 3 May 1983 (http://www.margaretthatcher.org/document/105091).

CHAPTER 3: LANDSLIDE

1. Interview with Ferdinand Mount.   **2.** Interview with Lord Parkinson.   **3.** Interview with Lord Butler of Brockwell.   **4.** Ibid.   **5.** Ibid.   **6.** Chris Patten interview with David Butler, 13 November 1982, David Butler Archive, Nuffield College, Oxford.   **7.** Minutes of E Committee, 14 October 1982, Prime Minister's Papers, Industrial Policy, Industrial Relations Legislation, The Employment Bill, Part 9 (document consulted in the Cabinet Office).   **8.** Mount to Thatcher, 21 October 1982, TNA: PREM 19/1061 (http://www.margaretthatcher.org/document/128164).   **9.** Mount to Thatcher, 19 November 1982, TNA: PREM 19/1061 (http://www.margaretthatcher.org/document/128434).   **10.** Hansard, HC Deb 19 April 1983, 41/159 (http://hansard.millbanksystems.com/commons/1983/apr/19/engagements).   **11.** Thatcher Memoirs Materials, CAC: THCR 4/3.   **12.** Ingham to Thatcher, 6 May 1983, CAC: THCR 3/5/23.   **13.** Interview with Lord Jopling.   **14.** Interview with Lord Parkinson.   **15.** Britto to Gow, 10 May 1983, THCR 2/6/2/61 (http://www.margaretthatcher.org/document/131255). Interview with Keith Britto.   **16.** David Butler interview with Anthony Shrimsley, 14 June 1983, David Butler Archive.   **17.** Interview with Lord Parkinson.   **18.** Ibid.   **19.** Interview with Lord Jopling.   **20.** Ferdinand Mount, *Cold Cream: My Early Life and Other Mistakes*, Bloomsbury, 2008, p. 335.   **21.** Thatcher Memoirs Materials, CAC: THCR 4/3.   **22.** Ibid.   **23.** Interview with Peter Cropper.

24. Margaret Thatcher, *The Downing Street Years*, HarperCollins, 1993, p. 284. 25. Speech to Wembley Youth Rally, 5 June 1983 (http://www.marga retthatcher.org/document/105381). 26. Press conference to launch election manifesto (international press), 18 May 1983 (http://www.margaretthatcher.org/document/105320). 27. Press conference to launch election manifesto, 18 May 1983 (http://www.margaretthatcher.org/document/105319). 28. Election press conference, 20 May 1983 (http://www.margaretthatcher.org/document/105324). 29. Interview with Katharine Ramsay. 30. David Butler memo to self, 24 May 1983, David Butler Archive. 31. Interview with Lord Parkinson. 32. Ibid. 33. Interview with Lord Sherbourne of Didsbury. 34. *The Times*, 21 May 1983. 35. Ibid. 36. Thatcher Memoirs Materials, CAC: THCR 4/3. 37. Ibid. 38. David Butler interview with Keith Britto, 14 June 1983, David Butler Archive. 39. Radio Interview for BBC, 7 June 1983 (Christopher Collins, ed., *Complete Public Statements of Margaret Thatcher 1945–90 on CD-ROM*, Oxford University Press, 1998/2000). 40. Denis Kavanagh interview with Geoff Bish, 8 June 1983, David Butler Archive. 41. *The Times*, 26 May 1983. 42. Thatcher, *The Downing Street Years*, p. 424. 43. Speech in Cardiff, 23 May 1983, CAC: THCR 5/1/4/51 (http://www.margaretthatcher.org/document/105332). 44. Thatcher to Reagan, 9 May 1983, CAC: THCR 3/1/31 Part 1 (http://www.marga retthatcher.org/document/131540). 45. Reagan to Thatcher, 10 May 1983, CAC: THCR 3/1/31 Part 1 (http://www.margaretthatcher.org/document/131541). 46. Wright, telegram 1289, Washington, 10 May 1983, TNA: PREM 19/1008. 47. Armstrong to Thatcher, 14 March 1983, TNA: PREM 19/1007. 48. Walters to Thatcher, 25 April 1983, TNA: PREM 19/1008. 49. Howe to Thatcher, 4 May 1983, TNA: PREM 19/1008. 50. Record of conversation with Meese, 4 May 1983, TNA: PREM 19/1008. 51. Coles to Fall, 17 May 1983, TNA: PREM 19/1008. 52. Reagan to Thatcher, 24 May 1983, CAC: THCR 3/1/31 Part 2 (http://www.margaretthatcher.org/document/131885). 53. Thatcher, *The Downing Street Years*, p. 299. 54. Note of Meeting on 11:30 am at Williamsburg, 29 May 1983, 1 June 1983, TNA: PREM 19/1009. 55. Ibid. 56. See Thatcher, *The Downing Street Years*, p. 300. 57. General Election Press Conference, 31 May 1983 (http://www.margaretthatcher.org/document/105356). 58. Interview with Lord Parkinson. 59. Reagan to Thatcher, 15 June 1983, CAC: THCR 3/1/32 Part 1 (http://www.margaretthatcher.org/document/131545). 60. Interview with Lord Owen. 61. *Manchester Evening News*, 2 June 1983 (http://www.margaretthatcher.org/document/105361). 62. BBC TV Interview with John Cole, 3 June 1983 (http://www.margaretthatcher.org/document/105159). 63. Ibid. 64. Michael Spicer, *The Spicer Diaries*, Biteback, 2012, p. 66. 65. Thatcher, *The Downing Street Years*, p. 303. 66. John Campbell, *Margaret Thatcher*, vol. ii: *The Iron Lady*, Jonathan Cape, 2003, p. 193. 67. Conservative Party Election Broadcast, 7 June 1983 (http://www.margaretthatcher.org/document/105382). 68. David Butler memo attached to his interview with Cecil Parkinson, 27 May 1983, David Butler Archive. 69. Interview with Jeremy Sinclair. 70. Interview with Lord Parkinson. 71. Ibid. 72. Ibid. 73. Speech at Finchley Town Hall, 10 June 1983 (http://www.margaretthatcher.org/document/105393). 74. Interview with Peter Cropper.

CHAPTER 4: JOBS FOR HER BOYS

1. Flesher to Thatcher, 21 June 1983, CAC: THCR 1/11/13 (http://www.marga rethatcher.org/document/131086). **2.** Interview with Lord Butler of Brockwell. **3.** Ibid. **4.** Ingham to Thatcher, 7 June 1983, CAC: THCR 1/11/15. **5.** Interview with Lord Sherbourne of Didsbury. **6.** Interview with Lord Butler of Brockwell. **7.** Interview with Lady Ryder of Wensum. **8.** TV Interview for BBC, 10 June 1983 (http://www.margaretthatcher.org/document/105176). **9.** Thatcher Memoirs Materials, CAC: THCR 4/3. **10.** Ibid. **11.** Interview with William Rickett. **12.** Interview with Sir Michael Scholar. **13.** Ibid. **14.** Thatcher Memoirs Materials, CAC: THCR 4/3. **15.** Ibid. **16.** Interview with Lord Tebbit. **17.** Wolfson to Thatcher, 10 June 1983, CAC: THCR 1/11/15 (http://www.margaretthatcher.org/document/131085). **18.** Thatcher Memoirs Materials, CAC: THCR 4/3 **19.** Ibid. **20.** Interview with Lord Jopling. **21.** Thatcher Memoirs Materials, CAC: THCR 4/3. **22.** Interview with Jonathan Pym. **23.** Thatcher Memoirs Materials, CAC: THCR 4/3. **24.** Ibid. **25.** Margaret Thatcher, *The Downing Street Years*, HarperCollins, 1993, p. 307. **26.** Ibid. **27.** Interview with Lord Jopling. **28.** Thatcher Memoirs Materials, CAC: THCR 4/3. **29.** Interview with Lord Rees. **30.** Reported in *The Times*, 3 April 1986. **31.** Thatcher Memoirs Materials, CAC: THCR 4/3. **32.** Ibid. **33.** Alan Clark, *Diaries*, Weidenfeld & Nicolson, 1993, p. 8. **34.** Interview with Lord Wakeham. **35.** Clark, *Diaries*, p. 11. **36.** Interview with Lord Wakeham. **37.** Interview with Lord Deben. **38.** Interview with Lord Sherbourne of Didsbury. **39.** Interview with Tessa Gaisman. **40.** Interview with Lord Sherbourne of Didsbury. **41.** Interview with Rosie Alison. **42.** Matthew Parris, *Chance Witness: An Outsider's Life in Politics*, Viking, 2002, p. 350. **43.** Interview with Tessa Gaisman. **44.** Sparrow to Thatcher, 21 April 1983, TNA: PREM 19/1045. **45.** Interview with Sir John Sparrow. **46.** Sir Robert Armstrong, Cabinet Secretary's notebooks, 16 June 1983 (document consulted in the Cabinet Office). **47.** Interview with Ferdinand Mount. **48.** Interview with Lord Tebbit. **49.** Interview with Lord Lamont of Lerwick. **50.** Sir Robert Armstrong, Cabinet Secretary's notebooks, 16 June 1983 (document consulted in the Cabinet Office). **51.** Ibid. **52.** Stephen Wall, *A Stranger in Europe: Britain and the EU from Thatcher to Blair*, Oxford University Press, 2008, p. 22. **53.** Thatcher to Kohl, 1 July 1983, CAC: THCR 3/1/32 Part 2 (http://www.margaretthatcher.org/document/131930). **54.** Sir Robert Armstrong, Cabinet Secretary's notebooks, 23 June 1983 (document consulted in the Cabinet Office). **55.** Thatcher, *The Downing Street Years*, p. 314. **56.** Interview with Lord Weatherill. **57.** Ibid. **58.** Radio Interview for IRN, 28 July 1983 (http://www.margaretthatcher.org/document/105426). **59.** TV Interview for BBC, 28 July 1983 (http://www.margaretthatcher.org/document/105184). **60.** Interview with Thatcher, 5 July 1983, David Butler Archive. **61.** Ibid. **62.** Sir Robert Armstrong, Cabinet Secretary's notebooks, 7 July 1983 (document consulted in the Cabinet Office). **63.** Ibid. **64.** Walters to Thatcher, 14 July 1983, TNA: PREM 19/985 (http://www.margaretthatcher.org/

document/128136).   **65.** Ingham to Thatcher, 14 July 1983, TNA: PREM 19/985 (http://www.margaretthatcher.org/document/128135).   **66.** Sir Robert Armstrong, Cabinet Secretary's notebooks, 21 July 1983 (document consulted in the Cabinet Office).   **67.** Interview with Lord Fowler.   **68.** Nigel Lawson, *The View from No. 11*, Bantam Press, 1992, pp. 305–6.   **69.** Thatcher to Lord Bishop of Ely, 16 June 1983, CAC: THCR 3/2/119.   **70.** Private memoir by John Coles written on leaving Downing Street in 1984, 14 June 1984, CAC: THCR AS 3/24 (http://www.margaretthatcher.org/document/135761).   **71.** Ibid.   **72.** Interview with William Rickett.   **73.** Interview with Lord Butler of Brockwell.   **74.** Interview with Romilly, Lady McAlpine.   **75.** Thatcher personal minute to Cabinet Ministers, 5 August 1983, CAC: THCR 3/3/5 (http://www.margaretthatcher.org/document/131526).   **76.** Interview with William Rickett.   **77.** Mount to Thatcher, 5 August 1983, CAC: THCR 2/4/1/22 (http://www.margaretthatcher.org/document/131145).   **78.** Thatcher to Parkinson, 10 August 1983, CAC: THCR 2/4/1/22 (http://www.margaretthatcher.org/document/131150).   **79.** Clark, *Diaries*, 4 August 1983, pp. 35–6.   **80.** Ibid.   **81.** Interview with Lord Parkinson.   **82.** Thatcher Memoirs Materials, CAC: THCR 4/3.   **83.** Interview with Lord Deben.   **84.** Interview with Lord Sherbourne of Didsbury.   **85.** Ibid.   **86.** Thatcher Memoirs Materials, CAC: THCR 4/3.   **87.** Interview with Lord Deben.   **88.** Interview with Amanda Ponsonby.   **89.** Interview with Lord Parkinson.   **90.** *Private Eye*, 7 October 1983.   **91.** Interview with Lord Butler of Brockwell.   **92.** Ibid.   **93.** See Cecil Parkinson, *Right at the Centre*, Weidenfeld & Nicolson, 1992, pp. 249–50.   **94.** Ingham to Thatcher, 7 October 1983, CAC: THCR 1/12/16 Part 2 (http://www.margaretthatcher.org/document/131096).   **95.** Interview with Lord Parkinson.   **96.** Ferdinand Mount, *Cold Cream: My Early Life and Other Mistakes*, Bloomsbury, 2008, p. 343.   **97.** Interview with Lord Butler of Brockwell.   **98.** Interview with Lady Wakeham.   **99.** Interview with Amanda Ponsonby.   **100.** Interview with Lord Sherbourne of Didsbury.   **101.** Interview with Lady Ryder of Wensum.   **102.** Interview with Lord Parkinson.   **103.** Interviews with Lord McAlpine of West Green, Lord Sherbourne of Didsbury, Lord Young of Graffham.   **104.** Interview with Lord Deben.   **105.** Interview with Lord Tebbit.   **106.** Ibid.   **107.** Ingham, press digest, 17 October 1983, CAC: THCR 1/7/37 (http://www.margaretthatcher.org/document/130980).   **108.** Interview with Ferdinand Mount.   **109.** *Washington Post*, 28 September 1983.   **110.** Millar to Thatcher, 15 June 1983, CAC: THCR 1/3/10 (http://www.margaretthatcher.org/document/131026).   **111.** Interview with Ferdinand Mount.   **112.** David Young, 'The First Fifteen Months', with Mount to Thatcher, 8 June 1983, Papers of Sir Alan Walters, CAC: WTRS 1/81.   **113.** Karl Marx and Friedrich Engels, *The German Ideology*, Progress Publishers, 1976, p. 620.   **114.** Mount to Thatcher, 24 June 1983, CAC: THCR 1/15/9 Part 2 (http://www.margaretthatcher.org/document/131107).   **115.** Cockfield to Thatcher, 1 July 1983, Papers of Sir Alan Walters, CAC: WTRS 1/74.   **116.** Scholar to Walters, 5 July 1983, Papers of Sir Alan Walters, CAC: WTRS 1/74.   **117.** Ibid.   **118.** Ibid.   **119.** Ibid.   **120.** 'Unemployment Seminar' Note by Sir Alan Walters, Papers of Sir Alan Walters, CAC: WTRS 1/74.   **121.** Speech to Party Conference,

14 October 1983 (http://www.margaretthatcher.org/document/105454). **122.** Interview with Ferdinand Mount. **123.** Redwood to Thatcher, 23 December 1983, CAC: THCR 5/1/5/241 Part 4 (http://www.margaretthatcher.org/document/136300). **124.** Ibid. **125.** Interview with Ferdinand Mount. **126.** Redwood to Thatcher, 23 December 1983, CAC: THCR 5/1/5/241 Part 4 (http://www.margaretthatcher.org/document/136300). **127.** Coles, Record of a discussion, 15 June 1983, TNA: PREM 19/1055 (http://www.margaretthatcher.org/document/139124). **128.** Coles, Record of a Conversation, 24 June 1983. Ibid. **129.** Interviews with Charles Freeman, Burton Levin. **130.** Cradock telegram 580, Peking, 23 June 1983, TNA: PREM 19/1055 (http://www.margaretthatcher.org/document/139114). **131.** Interview with Lord Howe of Aberavon. **132.** Percy Cradock, *Experiences of China*, John Murray, 1994, pp. 202–3. **133.** Interview with Sir Percy Cradock. **134.** Interview with Lord Powell of Bayswater. **135.** Ibid. **136.** Private information. **137.** Howe draft statement for Luce for Hong Kong media, 23 September 1983, TNA: PREM 19/1057 (http://www.margaretthatcher.org/document/139249). **138.** Cradock, telegram 1325, 9 December 1983, TNA: PREM 19/1059 (http://www.margaretthatcher.org/document/139361). **139.** Coles, Record of a Discussion, 16 January 1984, TNA: PREM 19/1262 (http://www.margaretthatcher.org/document/139864). **140.** Howe to Thatcher, 29 March 1984, TNA: PREM 19/1263 (http://www.margaretthatcher.org/document/139894). **141.** Youde, telegram 859, Hong Kong, 29 March 1984, TNA: PREM 19/1263 (http://www.margaretthatcher.org/document/139893). **142.** Cradock telegram 1154, Peking, 7 November 1983, TNA: PREM 19/1059 (http://www.margaretthatcher.org/document/139275). **143.** Cradock to Howe, 12 December 1983, TNA: PREM 19/1059 (http://www.margaretthatcher.org/document/139414). **144.** Coles, Record of a Discussion, 6 April 1984, TNA: PREM 19/1264 (http://www.margaretthatcher.org/document/139742). **145.** Foreign policy in the 1980s: an event in honour of Sir John Boyd KCMG (outgoing Master of Churchill College), Churchill Archives Centre, 6 February 2006. **146.** Evans, telegram 739, Peking, 13 April 1984, TNA: PREM 19/1264 (http://www.margaretthatcher.org/document/139737). **147.** Coles, Record of a Discussion, 15 May 1984, TNA: PREM 19/1265 (http://www.margaretthatcher.org/document/139698). **148.** Draft letter from Thatcher to Zhao Ziyang, 10 July 1984, TNA: PREM 19/1266 (http://www.margaretthatcher.org/document/140351). **149.** Cradock, *Experiences of China*, p. 201. **150.** Ibid., p. 202. **151.** Youde, telegram 2176, Hong Kong, 31 July 1984, TNA: PREM 19/1266 (http://www.margaretthatcher.org/document/140307). **152.** Cradock to Thatcher, 3 August 1984, TNA: PREM 19/1267 (http://www.margaretthatcher.org/document/140010). **153.** Powell, Record of a Meeting, 19 September 1984, TNA: PREM 19/1267 (http://www.margaretthatcher.org/document/139963). **154.** Interview with Lord Powell of Bayswater. **155.** Ibid. **156.** Telegram 3047, Peking, 19 December 1984, TNA: PREM 19/1502. **157.** Interview with Lord Powell of Bayswater. **158.** Speech Signing the Joint Declaration, 19 December 1984 (http://www.margaretthatcher.org/document/105817). **159.** Interview with Lord Howe of Aberavon. **160.** Interview with Lord Powell of Bayswater. **161.** Interview with

Lady Dunn.   **162.** Telegram 2202, Hong Kong, 2 August 1984, TNA: PREM 19/1267 (http:/www.margaretthatcher.org/document/140011).

CHAPTER 5: REAGAN PLAYS HER FALSE

1. Record of Conversation, Thatcher and Bush, 24 June 1983, TNA: PREM 19/979 (http://www.margaretthatcher.org/document/128131).   **2.** Memorandum of Telephone Conversation, Reagan and Thatcher, 10 June 1983, United Kingdom – 1983 – 06/03/1983–06/15/1983, Box 90424, Peter Sommer Files, Reagan Library.   **3.** Coles to Fall, 10 June 1983, TNA: PREM 19/1404 (http://www.margaretthatcher.org/document/140750).   **4.** Cited in Jonathan Aitken, *Margaret Thatcher: Power and Personality*, Bloomsbury, 2013, p. 474.   **5.** Thatcher to Reagan, 12 November 1982, CAC: THCR 3/1/26 Part 2 (http://www.marga retthatcher.org/document/123549).   **6.** Interview with Sir Malcolm Rifkind.   **7.** Interview with Sir Nigel Broomfield.   **8.** Wright telegram 1989, 15 July 1983, TNA:PREM 19/1404 (http://www.margaretthatcher.org/document/140751).   **9.** Interview with Peter Robinson.   **10.** Address to the Nation on Defense and National Security, 23 March 1983, Public Papers of the Presidents, American Presidency Project (http://www.presidency.ucsb.edu/ws/index.php?pid=41093&st=&st1=).   **11.** Lord Heseltine, in 'The British Response to SDI', seminar, held 9 July 2003, Centre for Contemporary British History, p. 30 (http://www.kcl.ac.uk/sspp/departments/icbh/witness/PDFfiles/SDI.pdf).   **12.** Reagan to Thatcher, 23 March 1983, CAC: THCR 3/1/29 Part 2 (http://www.margaretthatcher.org/docu ment/131533).   **13.** Ibid.   **14.** Margaret Thatcher, *The Downing Street Years*, HarperCollins, 1993, p. 463.   **15.** Interview with Lord Armstrong of Ilminster.   **16.** Interview with Sir John Weston.   **17.** Hansard, HC Deb 29 March 1983, 40/178 (http://hansard.millbanksystems.com/commons/1983/mar/29/engage ments).   **18.** Interview with Lord Howe of Aberavon.   **19.** Cited in Thatcher, *The Downing Street Years*, p. 451.   **20.** Cited in Archie Brown, 'The Change to Engagement in Britain's Cold War Policy: The Origins of the Thatcher–Gorbachev Relationship', *Journal of Cold War Studies*, vol. 10, no. 3, Summer 2008, pp. 7–8.   **21.** Ibid.   **22.** Thatcher to Reagan, 15 September 1983, NSA Head of State file, UK PM Thatcher Cables (3), Box 35, Reagan Library.   **23.** Ibid.   **24.** Strategy Meetings on Foreign Affairs and Defence, Howe to Thatcher, 5 September 1983, Freedom of information request to FCO by the Machiavelli Center, University of Pavia, 2007 (http://www.margaretthatcher.org/document/111072).   **25.** Meeting at Chequers on 8 September 1983, Contemporary notes by Archie Brown, kindly made available to the author.   **26.** 8 September 1983, untitled handwritten note, CAC: THCR 1/10/53 (http://www.margaretthatcher.org/document/130942).   **27.** Meeting at Chequers on 8 September 1983, Contemporary notes by Archie Brown.   **28.** Cited in Brown, 'The Change to Engagement in Britain's Cold War Policy', p. 13.   **29.** Archie Brown, 'Leader of the Prologue', in Ferdinand Mount, ed., *Communism*, Harvill, 1992, p. 297.   **30.** Colquhoun to Neville-Jones, 12 September 1983, FCO papers, RSO13/1, cited in Brown, 'The Change to Engagement in Britain's Cold War Policy', p. 30. **31.** Interview with Sir Malcolm Rifkind. **32.** Ibid. **33.** Interview with Sir John Coles. **34.** Ibid. **35.** Ibid. **36.** Coles to Fall, 12 September 1983, FCO FOI request by the Machiavelli Center, University of Pavia (http://www.margaretthatcher.org/document/111075). **37.** Ibid. **38.** Ibid. **39.** Interview with Lord Powell of Bayswater. **40.** Interview with Michael Deaver. **41.** Ibid. **42.** Thatcher, *The Downing Street Years*, p. 321. **43.** Interview with Sir John Coles. **44.** Diary of Ronald Reagan, 29 September 1983, *The Reagan Diaries*, HarperCollins, 2007, p. 183. **45.** Memorandum of Conversation, The President and British Prime Minister Thatcher, 29 September 1983, Box 90424, Peter Sommer Files, Reagan Library. **46.** Speech at the Winston Churchill Foundation Award dinner, 29 September 1983 (http://www.marga retthatcher.org/document/105450). **47.** Ibid. **48.** Thatcher interview for *Daily Mail*, 4 November 1983, CAC: THCR 5/1/1E/46 Part 1 (http://www.marga retthatcher.org/document/105212). **49.** George Urban, *Diplomacy and Disillusion at the Court of Margaret Thatcher*, I. B. Tauris, 1996, p. 57. **50.** Interview with George Shultz. **51.** Speech to Conservative Party Conference, 14 October 1983 (http://www.margaretthatcher.org/document/105454). **52.** Interview with Oleg Gordievsky. **53.** Ibid. **54.** Ibid. **55.** Interview with Sir John Scarlett. **56.** Interview with Sir Colin McColl. **57.** Geoffrey Howe, *Conflict of Loyalty*, Macmillan, 1994, p. 350. **58.** Gordon Barrass, *The Great Cold War: A Journey through the Hall of Mirrors*, Stanford University Press, 2009, p. 299. **59.** Ibid., p. 301. **60.** Gordon Barrass offers perhaps the best account of this in ibid., pp. 298–305; see also Nate Jones, 'Countdown to Declassification: Finding Answers to a 1983 Nuclear War Scare', *Bulletin of the Atomic Scientists*, vol. 69, no. 6, 2013, pp. 47–57. **61.** 'Soviet Union: Concern about a Surprise NATO Attack', 8 May 1984, see Peter Burt, 'Thirty years ago: The Nuclear Crisis which Frightened Thatcher and Reagan into Ending the Cold War', *Nuclear Information Service*, 3 November 2013 (http://nuclearinfo.org/blog/peter-burt/2013/11/thirty-years-ago-nuclear-crisis-which-frightened-thatcher-and-reagan-ending). **62.** Interview with Sir Rodric Braithwaite. **63.** See Christopher Andrew, *The Defence of the Realm: The Authorized History of MI5*, Allen Lane, 2009, p. 709. **64.** 'Soviet Concern about a Surprise NATO Attack', 10 April 1984, see Burt, 'Thirty years ago: the nuclear crisis which frightened Thatcher and Reagan into ending the Cold War'. **65.** Interview with Sir John Scarlett. **66.** 241847z Oct 83, Reagan to Thatcher, NSC: Country File, UK Vol. V (3 of 3), Box 91331, Reagan Library. **67.** Thatcher, *The Downing Street Years*, pp. 330–31. **68.** Interview with Josephine Louis. **69.** Reagan to Thatcher, 2200 Zulu, 24 October 1983, CAC: THCR 3/1/33 Part 3 (http://www.margaretthatcher.org/document/131575). **70.** Howe, *Conflict of Loyalty*, p. 329. **71.** Interview with Lawrence Eagleburger. **72.** Interview with Bud McFarlane. **73.** Interview with Lord Howe of Aberavon. **74.** Interview with Bud McFarlane. **75.** 'G. P. Shultz – Turmoil Draft', Great Britain, Box 61, Papers of Charles Hill, Hoover Institution, Stanford, CA. **76.** Interview with Sir Derek Thomas. **77.** Interview with Lord Renwick of Clifton. **78.** Robin Renwick, *A Journey with Margaret Thatcher*, Biteback, 2013, p. 144. **79.** Report, 21 October 1983, Prime Minister's Papers, Grenada, Part 1 (document consulted in the Cabinet

Office).   80. Coles to Thatcher, 21 October 1983. Ibid.   81. Ibid.   82. Interview with John Poindexter.   83. See Duane Clarridge, *A Spy for All Seasons: My Life in the CIA*, Scribner, 2002, p. 252.   84. Hill to McFarlane, Grenada SSG, 22 October 1983, Exec Sec, NSC: Records of National Security Planning Group, 'NSPG0075 23 Oct 1983', Box 91306, Reagan Library.   85. Interview with Duane Clarridge.   86. Interview with Kenneth Adelman.   87. Interview with Jack Matlock.   88. Interview with Lord Howe of Aberavon.   89. Cited in H. W. Brands, *Reagan: The Life*, Doubleday, 2015, p. 401.   90. Wright telegram 3084, 22 October 1983, TNA: PREM 19/1048 (http://www.margaretthatcher.org/document/ 128213).   91. Interview and correspondence with Jonathan Howe.   92. Interview with Lord Luce.   93. Ibid.   94. Ibid.   95. Howe telegram 291, 22 October 1983, CAC: THCR 1/10/61 Part 1 (http://www.margaretthatcher.org/docu ment/131318).   96. Thatcher, *The Downing Street Years*, p. 330.   97. Renwick, *A Journey with Margaret Thatcher*, p. 144.   98. Interview with Lord Renwick of Clifton.   99. Howe, *Conflict of Loyalty*, p. 328.   100. Record of a conversation between Thatcher and Dam, 7 November 1983, TNA: PREM 19/1151 (http:// www.margaretthatcher.org/document/128198).   101. Hansard, HC Deb 24 October 1983, 47/30 (http://hansard.millbanksystems.com/commons/1983/oct/24/ grenada).   102. Thatcher annotation on House of Commons Statement by the Foreign Secretary, 24 October 1983, TNA: PREM 19/1048 (http://www.marga retthatcher.org/document/128146).   103. Bridgetown telegram 342, 23 October 1983, TNA: PREM 19/1048 (http://www.margaretthatcher.org/document/ 128217).   104. Washington telegram 3099, 24 October 1983, TNA: PREM 19/1048.   105. Interview with Sir John Coles.   106. Thatcher to Reagan, 25 October 1983, TNA: PREM 19/1048 (http://www.margaretthatcher.org/docu ment/128147).   107. Ibid.   108. Interview with Lord Butler of Brockwell.   109. Ibid.   110. Ibid.   111. Coles to Fall, 25 October 1983, TNA: PREM 19/1048 (http://www.margaretthatcher.org/document/128329).   112. Interview with Michael Deaver.   113. 250656z Oct 83, Reagan to Thatcher, 25 October 1983, Exec Sec, NSC: Country File, UK Vol. V (3 of 3), Box 91331, Reagan Library.   114. Ronald Reagan, *An American Life: The Autobiography*, Simon & Schuster, 1990, p. 454.   115. Coles to Ricketts, 26 October 1983, TNA: PREM 19/1048 (http://www.margaretthatcher.org/document/128224).   116. Ibid.   117. Kingston telegram 304, 26 October 1983, TNA: PREM 19/1048 (http://www. margaretthatcher.org/document/128225).   118. Interview with Lord Fellowes.   119. Interview with Sir John Ure.   120. Interview with James Baker.   121. Memorandum of telephone conversation, Prime Minister Margaret Thatcher, 26 October 1983, Exec Sec, NSC: Country File, UK Vol. V (3 of 3), Box 91331, Reagan Library. The Library has also released a tape of the call (RAC Box 53, White House Situation Room Records).   122. Ibid.   123. 'Memcon of conversation between President Reagan and Prime Minister Hawke re Grenada', 26 October 1983, Exec Sec, NSC: Country File, Australia (2/16/84–1/31/85), Box 6, Reagan Library.   124. 281444z Oct 83, 'President's call to Thatcher had a very favorable impact', State Department Archives, released under FOIA Case #200605058.   125. Sir Robert Armstrong, Cabinet Secretary's notebooks, 27 October 1983 (document consulted in the Cabinet Office).   **126.** Ibid.   **127.** Hansard, HC Deb 27 October 1983, 47/423 (http://hansard.millbanksystems.com/commons/1983/oct/27/engagements).   **128.** Radio interview for BBC World Service, 30 October 1983 (Christopher Collins, ed., *Complete Public Statements of Margaret Thatcher 1945–90 on CD-ROM*, Oxford University Press, 1998/2000).   **129.** Interview with John Lehman.   **130.** Interview with George Shultz.   **131.** 071453z Nov 83, McFarlane to Armstrong, 7 November 1983, Exec Sec, NSC: Country File, UK Vol. V (3 of 3), Box 91331, Reagan Library.   **132.** McFarlane to Armstrong, 2 November 1983, UK, Box 90762, Donald Fortier Files, Reagan Library.   **133.** Coles to Armstrong, 11 November 1983, TNA: PREM 19/1404 (http://www.margaretthatcher.org/document/140752).   **134.** *The Times*, 7 November 1983.   **135.** Renwick to Ure, 28 October 1983, TNA: PREM 19/1404.   **136.** Interview with Sir John Ure.   **137.** Diary of Kenneth Dam, 6–9 November 1983, State Department Archives, released under FOIA Case #200807054.   **138.** Correspondence with Kenneth Dam.   **139.** 081312z Nov 83, 'Deputy Secretary Dam's Meeting November 7 with Prime Minister Thatcher', State Department Archives, released under FOIA Case #200601766.   **140.** Record of a conversation between the Prime Minister and Mr. Dam of the US State Department, 7 November 1983, TNA: PREM 19/1151 (http://www.margaretthatcher.org/document/128198).   **141.** Interview with Kenneth Dam.   **142.** 101656z 'Thatcher and the US: Where we are, what to do', 10 November 1983, UK-1983-11/7/83–11/19/83, Box 90424, Sommer Files, Reagan Library.   **143.** Interview with Edward Streator.   **144.** Cobb to Poindexter, undated, UK-1983-12/4/83–12/10/83, Sommer Files, Reagan Library.   **145.** Bush to Thatcher, 9 December 1983, CO 167: 207639, WHORM File, Reagan Library.   **146.** Thomas to Thatcher, 15 December 1983, TNA: PREM 19/1404 (http://www.margaretthatcher.org/document/140753).   **147.** Ibid.

CHAPTER 6: THE ENEMY WITHIN

1. Hansard, HC Deb 27 February 1984, 55/28 (http://hansard.millbanksystems.com/commons/1984/feb/27/gchq-cheltenham).   **2.** Interview with Tony Comer.   **3.** Note for the Record, 10 March 1981, Prime Minister's Papers, Security, Changes in the Funding, Status and Staffing at GCHQ, Part 1 (document consulted in the Cabinet Office).   **4.** Interview with Lord Armstrong of Ilminster.   **5.** Thatcher Memoirs Materials, CAC: THCR 4/3.   **6.** Hansard, HC Deb 11 November 1982, 31/669–78 (http://hansard.millbanksystems.com/commons/1982/nov/11/security).   **7.** Interview with Lord Gowrie.   **8.** Ibid.   **9.** Armstrong to Thatcher, 21 September 1983, Prime Minister's Papers, Security, Changes in the Funding, Status and Staffing at GCHQ, Part 1 (document consulted in the Cabinet Office).   **10.** Hansard, HC Deb 25 January 1984, 52/917 (http://hansard.millbanksystems.com/commons/1984/jan/25/gchq-employment-protection-acts).   **11.** Armstrong to Thatcher, 25 January 1984, Prime Minister's Papers, Security, Changes in the Funding, Status and Staffing at GCHQ, Part 1 (document consulted in the Cabinet Office).   **12.** Hatfield to Butler, 26 January 1984 and 27 January 1984. Ibid.   **13.** Interview with Tony Comer.   **14.** Interview with Lord Butler of Brockwell.

15. Press Report, 16 February 1984, Security, Changes in the Funding, Status and Staffing at GCHQ, Part 1 (document consulted in the Cabinet Office).   **16.** Interview with Lord Armstrong of Ilminster.   **17.** Armstrong to Thatcher, 17 February 1984, Prime Minister's Papers, Security, Part 1 (document consulted in the Cabinet Office).   **18.** Butler to Thatcher, 22 February 1984. Ibid.   **19.** Record of a meeting with the Council of Civil Service Unions, 23 February 1984. Ibid.   **20.** Interview with Lord Armstrong of Ilminster.   **21.** Howe speech draft, 24 February 1984, Prime Minister's Papers, Security, Part 2 (document consulted in the Cabinet Office).   **22.** Geoffrey Howe, *Conflict of Loyalty*, Macmillan, 1994, pp. 347–8.   **23.** Interview with Lord Armstrong of Ilminster.   **24.** Thatcher Memoirs Materials, CAC: THCR 4/3.   **25.** Interview with Lord Gowrie.   **26.** Interview with Lord Butler of Brockwell.   **27.** Butler to Thatcher, 31 January 1984, Prime Minister's Papers, Security, Part 1 (document consulted in the Cabinet Office).   **28.** Interview with Lord Gowrie.   **29.** Interview with Tim Flesher.   **30.** Ingham to Thatcher, 19 February 1981, TNA: PREM 19/539 (http://www.margaretthatcher. org/document/126042).   **31.** Interview with Lord Butler of Brockwell.   **32.** Interview with Sir Peter Gregson.   **33.** Nigel Lawson, *The View from No. 11*, Bantam Press, 1992, p. 140.   **34.** Interview with Sir Peter Gregson.   **35.** Lawson, *The View from No. 11*, p. 150.   **36.** Interview with Sir Peter Gregson.   **37.** Armstrong to Thatcher, 21 July 1983, TNA: PREM 19/1329 (http://www.margaretthatcher.org/ document/133113).   **38.** Interview with Lord Sherbourne of Didsbury.   **39.** Lawson, *The View from No. 11*, p. 154.   **40.** Interview with Lord Walker of Worcester.   **41.** Interview with Tim Flesher.   **42.** Interview with Lord Walker of Worcester.   **43.** Gregson to Thatcher, 14 September 1983, TNA: PREM 19/1329 (http://www.mar garetthatcher.org/document/133119).   **44.** Record of a meeting in No. 10 Downing Street, 15 September 1983, TNA: PREM 19/1329 (http://www.margaretthatcher. org/document/133121).   **45.** Turnbull to Reidy, 2 November 1983, TNA: PREM 19/1329 (http://www.margaretthatcher.org/document/133128).   **46.** Ibid.   **47.** Pascall to Turnbull, 7 March 1984, TNA: PREM 19/1329 (http://www.margaretthatcher. org/document/133140).   **48.** Cabinet minutes, 13 March 1984, TNA: CAB 128/78 (http://www.margaretthatcher.org/document/133169).   **49.** See Ian MacGregor, *The Enemies Within: The Story of the Miners' Strike, 1984–5*, Collins, 1986, pp. 192–3.   **50.** Interview with Lord Turnbull.   **51.** Note for the Record, 14 March 1984, TNA: PREM 19/1329 (http://www.margaretthatcher.org/docu ment/133144).   **52.** Interview with Sir Brian Cubbon.   **53.** Note for the Record, 14 March 1984, TNA: PREM 19/1329 (http://www.margaretthatcher.org/docu ment/133145)   **54.** Interview with Lord Brittan of Spennithorne.   **55.** Interview with Sir Brian Cubbon.   **56.** Ibid.   **57.** Coles to Thatcher, telephone message from Turnbull, 19 March 1984, TNA: PREM 19/1329 (http://www.margaretthatcher.org/ document/140016).   **58.** Message from Energy Private Office, 16 March 1984, TNA: PREM 19/1329 (http://www.margaretthatcher.org/document/140015).   **59.** Turnbull to Thatcher, 24 May 1985, CAC: THCR 1/12/28 (http://www.margaretthatcher.org/ document/136462).   **60.** Interview with Lord Brittan of Spennithorne.   **61.** Interview with Lord Turnbull.   **62.** Interview with Lord Sherbourne of Didsbury.   **63.** *Panorama*, BBC 1, 9 April 1984 (http://www.margaretthatcher.org/document/

105538). **64.** Interview with Lord Butler of Brockwell. **65.** Turnbull to Thatcher, 30 May 1984, TNA: PREM 19/1330 (http://www.margaretthatcher.org/document/ 133357). **66.** Interview with Lord Sherbourne of Didsbury. **67.** Interview with Tim Flesher. **68.** David Hart, *Come to the Edge*, Hutchinson, 1988, p. 214. **69.** Interview with Lord Bell. **70.** Hart to Thatcher, 'Impressions from the coalfield', 26 April 1984, CAC: THCR 1/12/28 (http://www.margaretthatcher.org/document/ 136217). **71.** Interview with Tim Flesher. **72.** Redwood and Pascall to Thatcher, 18 April 1984, TNA: PREM 19/1330 (http://www.margaretthatcher.org/docu ment/133308). **73.** Cabinet Minutes, 3 May 1984, TNA: CAB 128/78 (http:// www.margaretthatcher.org/document/133176). **74.** Note of a meeting, 15 May 1984, TNA: PREM 19/1330 (http://www.margaretthatcher.org/document/ 133336). **75.** Ibid. **76.** Interview with Lord Turnbull. **77.** Ibid. **78.** Gregson to Thatcher, 18 May 1984, TNA: PREM 19/1330 (http://www.margaretthatcher. org/document/133343). **79.** Barclay to Neilson, 30 May 1984, TNA: PREM 19/1330 (http://www.margaretthatcher.org/document/133356). **80.** Speech at Banbury Cattle Market, 30 May 1984 (http://www.margaretthatcher.org/document/ 105691). **81.** Turnbull to Thatcher, 4 June 1984, TNA: PREM 19/1331 (http:// www.margaretthatcher.org/document/133365). **82.** Ibid. **83.** Interview with Lord Turnbull. **84.** Ibid. **85.** Ibid. **86.** Margaret Thatcher, *The Downing Street Years*, HarperCollins, 1993, p. 354. **87.** Turnbull to Thatcher, 8 June 1984, TNA: PREM 19/1331 (http://www.margaretthatcher.org/document/133369). **88.** Min utes of MISC 101 Meeting of 12 June, 13 June 1984, TNA: CAB 130/1268 (http:// www.margaretthatcher.org/document/133258). **89.** Turnbull to Thatcher, 13 June 1984, TNA: PREM 19/1331 (http://www.margaretthatcher.org/document/ 133374). **90.** Turnbull to Thatcher, 15 June 1984, TNA: PREM 19/1331 (http:// www.margaretthatcher.org/document/133377). **91.** Interview with Lord Turn bull. **92.** *Daily Telegraph*, 19 June 1984. **93.** Millar to Thatcher, 16 July 1984, CAC: THCR 1/12/24 (http://www.margaretthatcher.org/document/136443). **94.** Gregson to Thatcher, 2 July 1984, TNA: PREM 19/1331 (http://www.marga retthatcher.org/document/133402). **95.** Ibid. **96.** Ibid. **97.** Redwood to Thatcher, 13 July 1984, TNA: PREM 19/1331 (http://www.margaretthatcher.org/ document/133420). **98.** Thatcher's notes, Gregson to Turnbull, 16 July 1984, TNA: PREM 19/1331 (http://www.margaretthatcher.org/document/133422). **99.** Record of a Meeting at No. 10 Downing Street, 16 July 1984, TNA: PREM 19/1331 (http://www.margaretthatcher.org/document/133424). **100.** Gregson to Turnbull, 16 July 1984, TNA: PREM 19/1331 (http://www.margaretthatcher.org/ document/133422). **101.** Interview with Lord Butler of Brockwell. **102.** Reagan to Thatcher, 18 July 1984, TNA: PREM 19/1331 (http://www.margaretthatcher.org/ document/133430). **103.** Thatcher, *The Downing Street Years*, p. 358. **104.** Cabinet Minutes, 19 July 1984, TNA: CAB 128/79 (http://www.margaretthatcher.org/docu ment/133186). **105.** Thatcher to Reagan, 23 July 1984, TNA: PREM 19/1332 (http:// www.margaretthatcher.org/document/133437). **106.** Record of a meeting to discuss power station endurance, 25 July 1984, TNA: PREM 19/1332 (http://www. margaretthatcher.org/document/133441). **107.** Turnbull to Thatcher, 18 July 1984, TNA: PREM 19/1331 (http://www.margaretthatcher.org/document/133431).

108. Interview with Lord Sherbourne of Didsbury.   **109.** Quoted in Hugo Young, *One of Us*, Macmillan, 1989, p. 367.   **110.** Interview with Ken Livingstone. **111.** See Christopher Andrew, *The Defence of the Realm: The Authorized History of MI5*, Allen Lane, 2009, p. 677.   **112.** Speech to the 1922 Committee, speaking notes, 19 July 1984, CAC: THCR 1/1/19 (http://www.margaretthatcher.org/docu ment/136215).   **113.** *Spectator*, 4 May 1984.   **114.** Interview with Lord Kinnock   **115.** Ibid.   **116.** See, for example, Hansard, HC Deb 24 July 1984, 64/822 (http://hansard.millbanksystems.com/commons/1984/jul/24/coal-industry-dispute).   **117.** Hansard, HC Deb 31 July 1984, 65/241–52 (http://www.margaretthatcher.org/document/105732).   **118.** Interview with Sir Peter Gregson.   **119.** Ibid.   **120.** Ibid.   **121.** Daily Coal Report, 3 September 1984, TNA: PREM 19/1333 (http://www.margaretthatcher.org/document/133501). **122.** Turnbull to Thatcher, 3 September 1984, TNA: PREM 19/1333 (http://www. margaretthatcher.org/document/133505).   **123.** Record of a meeting on 4 September, 5 September 1984, TNA: PREM 19/1333 (http://www.margaretthatcher.org/ document/133507).   **124.** Interview with Lord Turnbull.   **125.** Interview with Lord Sherbourne of Didsbury.   **126.** Interview with Lord Turnbull.   **127.** Interview with Ken Livingstone.   **128.** Redwood to Thatcher, 13 September 1984, TNA: PREM 19/1333 (http://www.margaretthatcher.org/document/133539).   **129.** Hart to Thatcher, 18 September 1984, CAC: THCR 1/12/26 (http://www.marga retthatcher.org/document/136219).   **130.** Ibid.   **131.** Enthronement sermon of Bishop of Durham, 21 September 1984, TNA: PREM 19/1334 (http://www.mar garetthatcher.org/document/133575).   **132.** Butler to Thatcher, 26 September 1984, TNA: PREM 19/1334 (http://www.margaretthatcher.org/document/ 133581).   **133.** Sherbourne to Thatcher, 28 September 1984, CAC: THCR 5/1/4/80 (http://www.margaretthatcher.org/document/136256).   **134.** Draft Thatcher speech (on arrival at Brighton), 8 October 1984, CAC: THCR 5/1/4/82 (http://www.margaretthatcher.org/document/136222).   **135.** Ibid. **136.** Speech to Conservative Party Conference, 12 October 1984 (http://www. margaretthatcher.org/document/105763).   **137.** Note for the record, 15 October 1984, TNA: PREM 19/1334 (http://www.margaretthatcher.org/document/ 133622).   **138.** Ibid.   **139.** Ibid.   **140.** Ibid.   **141.** Memo of telephone conversation with Thatcher by Hart, 14 October 1984, Private Papers of the late David Hart.   **142.** Daily Coal Report, 24 October 1984, TNA: PREM 19/1335 (http:// www.margaretthatcher.org/document/133960).   **143.** Turnbull to Thatcher, 17 July 1984, CAC: THCR 1/12/24 (http://www.margaretthatcher.org/document/ 136445).   **144.** Ibid.   **145.** Undated MS in the Private Papers of the late David Hart.   **146.** See Andrew, *The Defence of the Realm*, pp. 679–80, 699.   **147.** Private information.   **148.** Armstrong to Butler, 5 November 1984, TNA: PREM 19/1335 (http://www.margaretthatcher.org/document/133996).   **149.** Francis Beckett and David Hencke, *Marching to the Fault Line: The 1984 Miners' Strike and the Battle for Industrial Britain*, Constable, 2009, p. 148.   **150.** Turnbull to Thatcher, 29 October 1984, TNA: PREM 19/1335 (http://www.margaretthatcher. org/document/133974).   **151.** Ibid.   **152.** Written on back of Turnbull to Thatcher, 17 September 1984, TNA: PREM 19/1333 (http://www.margaretthatcher.org/

document/133548). **153.** Ingham to Thatcher, 30 November 1984, TNA: PREM 19/1578 (http://www.margaretthatcher.org/document/140017). **154.** Ibid. **155.** Interview with Lord Kinnock **156.** 'My November 8 Call on the PM', 9 November 1984, State Department Archives, released under FOIA Case #200905115. **157.** Cabinet Minutes, 15 November 1984, TNA: CAB 128/79 (http://www.marga retthatcher.org/document/133196). **158.** Hansard, HL Deb 13 November 1984, 457/240 (http://hansard.millbanksystems.com/lords/1984/nov/13/address-in-reply-to-her-majestys-most). **159.** Warry to Turnbull, 13 November 1984, TNA: PREM 19/1335 (http://www.margaretthatcher.org/document/134024). **160.** Record of a meeting, 13 December 1984, TNA: PREM 19/1578 (http://www.margaretthatcher. org/document/138233). **161.** Neilson to Turnbull, 20 December 1984, TNA: PREM 19/1578 (http://www.margaretthatcher.org/document/138229). **162.** Thatcher to Mrs Linton, 4 February 1985, TNA: PREM 19/1579 (http://www.margaretthatcher. org/document/138171). **163.** Daily Coal Report, 8 February 1985, TNA: PREM 19/1579 (http://www.margaretthatcher.org/document/138107). **164.** 'The Final Push', Hart to Thatcher, 11 February 1985, TNA: PREM 19/1579 (http://www. margaretthatcher.org/document/138108). **165.** Ingham to Thatcher, 18 February 1985, TNA: PREM 19/1579 (http://www.margaretthatcher.org/docu ment/138183). **166.** Speaking note, 18 February 1985, TNA: PREM 19/1579 (http:// www.margaretthatcher.org/document/138183). **167.** Daily Coal Report, 27 February 1985, TNA: PREM 19/1579 (http://www.margaretthatcher.org/ document/138119). **168.** Daily Coal Report, 8 March 1985, TNA: PREM 19/1580 (http://www.margaretthatcher.org/document/138657). **169.** Remarks on the end of the miners' strike, 3 March 1985 (http://www.margaretthatcher.org/docu ment/105982). **170.** Lessons of the 1984/85 miners' strike, 20 May 1985, TNA: PREM 19/1580 (http://www.margaretthatcher.org/document/138716). **171.** Turnbull to Thatcher, 24 May 1985, CAC: THCR 1/12/28 (http://www.margaretthatcher. org/document/136462). **172.** Interview with Lord Butler of Brockwell. **173.** Addison to Turnbull and Flesher, 28 May 1985, TNA: PREM 19/1580 (http://www. margaretthatcher.org/document/138720). **174.** Interview with Lord Turnbull. **175.** Interview with John Redwood. **176.** Interview with Lord Sherbourne of Didsbury. **177.** Speech to Malaysian Institute of Public Administration, 6 April 1985 (http://www.margaretthatcher.org/document/106010). **178.** Ingham to Thatcher, 15 April 1985, TNA: PREM 19/1580 (http://www.margaretthatcher.org/ document/138710). **179.** Interview with Lord Sherbourne of Didsbury. **180.** Interview with Lord Bell. **181.** Interview with Tim Flesher. **182.** Interview with Lord Walker. **183.** Thatcher to Mrs Hackett, 4 April 1985, TNA: PREM 19/1580 (http://www.margaretthatcher.org/document/138713). **184.** Ibid.

CHAPTER 7: SALES OF THE CENTURY

1. Interview with Lord Lawson of Blaby. This was the view held by a number of his colleagues, although not by Lawson himself. See Nigel Lawson, *The View from No. 11*, Bantam Press, 1992, p. 246; also Margaret Thatcher, *The Downing Street*

Years, HarperCollins, 1993, p. 284.   **2.** Lawson, *The View from No. 11*, p. 271.
3. Ibid., p. 333.   **4.** Redwood to Thatcher, 27 January 1984, TNA: PREM
19/1197 (http://www.margaretthatcher.org/document/134125).   **5.** Interview with
Lord Tebbit.   **6.** Ibid.   **7.** Interview with Lord Sterling of Plaistow.   **8.** Lawson,
The View from No. 11, p. 336.   **9.** Lawson to Thatcher, 16 February 1984, TNA:
PREM 19/1197 (http://www.margaretthatcher.org/document/134134).   **10.** Lawson, *The View from No. 11*, p. 323.   **11.** Turnbull to Butler, 10 February 1984,
TNA: PREM 19/1197.   **12.** See Lawson, *The View from No. 11*, p. 323.
13. Interview with David Norgrove.   **14.** Turnbull to Thatcher, 23 January 1984,
TNA: PREM 19/1197.   **15.** Walters to Thatcher, 1 March 1984, TNA: PREM
19/1198 (http://www.margaretthatcher.org/document/134157).   **16.** Turnbull to
Thatcher, 24 February 1984, TNA: PREM 19/1197 (http://www.margaretthatcher.
org/document/134144).   **17.** Ingham to Thatcher, 2 March 1984, TNA: PREM
19/1198 (http://www.margaretthatcher.org/document/134160).   **18.** Lawson, *The
View from No. 11*, p. 357.   **19.** *Guardian*, 1 March 1984.   **20.** Hansard, HC Deb
13 March 1984, 56/286 (http://hansard.millbanksystems.com/commons/1984/
mar/13/introduction).   **21.** Walters to Thatcher, 1 March 1984, TNA: PREM
19/1198 (http://www.margaretthatcher.org/document/134157).   **22.** *Spectator*,
17 March 1984.   **23.** *Guardian*, 14 March 1984.   **24.** Redwood to Thatcher,
20 March 1984, CAC: THCR 2/6/3/131 Part 1 (http://www.margaretthatcher.org/
document/136305).   **25.** Interview with Oliver Letwin.   **26.** Interview with David
Pascall.   **27.** Interview with Bob Young.   **28.** Interview with David Pascall.
29. Ibid.   **30.** Interview for *The Times*, 3 May 1983 (http://www.margaretthatcher.
org/document/105091).   **31.** Thatcher note on Gregson to Thatcher, 25 October
1983, TNA: PREM 19/990.   **32.** Interview with Peter Warry.   **33.** Ibid.
34. Interview with Lord Tebbit.   **35.** Interview with Oliver Letwin.   **36.** Interview
with John Redwood.   **37.** Interview with Ferdinand Mount.   **38.** Correspondence
with David Willetts.   **39.** Ibid.   **40.** Interview with Lord Moore of Lower
Marsh.   **41.** Ibid.   **42.** Interview with David Pascall.   **43.** Interview with Bob
Young.   **44.** Interview with Lord Moore of Lower Marsh.   **45.** Interview with
John Redwood.   **46.** Ibid.   **47.** Interview with David Willetts.   **48.** Interview with
Lord Moore of Lower Marsh.   **49.** Lawson to Thatcher, 25 July 1983, TNA:
PREM 19/989 (http://www.margaretthatcher.org/document/128139).   **50.** Inter-
view with Lord Moore of Lower Marsh.   **51.** Lawson, Memo to E (A), Competition
and Privatisation, 19 October 1983, TNA: CAB 134/4685.   **52.** Mount to Thatcher,
21 October 1983, TNA: PREM 19/990.   **53.** Redwood to Mount, 20 October
1983, TNA: PREM 19/990.   **54.** Interview with Bob Young.   **55.** Walker to
Thatcher, 20 December 1983, TNA: PREM 19/990.   **56.** Redwood to Thatcher,
20 January 1984, TNA: PREM 19/990.   **57.** Interview with Lord Moore of Lower
Marsh.   **58.** Interview with Sir Gerry Grimstone.   **59.** Cockfield to Thatcher,
23 January 1984, TNA: PREM 19/1195.   **60.** Interview with Peter Warry.
61. Mount to Thatcher, 17 December 1982, TNA: PREM 19/1100.   **62.** Quoted
in Cecil Parkinson, *Right at the Centre*, Weidenfeld & Nicolson, 1992, p. 241.
63. Nicklaus Thomas-Symonds, *Nye: The Political Life of Aneurin Bevan*, I. B.
Tauris, 2015, p. 4.   **64.** Interview with Sir Peter Gregson.   **65.** *The Times*, 11

January 1985. **66.** *Financial Times*, 28 January 1984. **67.** Walker to Thatcher, 30 January 1984, TNA: PREM 19/1195. **68.** Turnbull to Thatcher, 30 January 1984, TNA: PREM 19/1195. **69.** Interview with Lord Lawson. **70.** Interview with John Redwood. **71.** Interview with Sir Martin Jacomb. **72.** Ibid. **73.** Interview with Oliver Letwin. **74.** Interview with David Willetts. **75.** Interview with Sir Martin Jacomb. **76.** Interview with Lord Moore of Lower Marsh. **77.** Ibid. **78.** Speech to Joint Houses of Congress, 20 February 1985 (http://www.margaretthatcher.org/document/105968). **79.** Interview with Lord Lawson. **80.** See Lawson, *The View from No. 11*, p. 224. **81.** Thatcher, *The Downing Street Years*, pp. 678–9. **82.** Scholar to Rees, 8 April 1982, TNA: PREM 19/1162. **83.** Gow to Thatcher, 24 May 1982, TNA: PREM 19/1162. **84.** Gregson to Thatcher, 23 July 1983, TNA: PREM 19/1162. **85.** Cockfield to Howe, 1 September 1982, TNA: PREM 19/1162. **86.** Cockfield to Brittan, 6 October 1982, TNA: PREM 19/1162. **87.** Wolfson to Thatcher, 15 November 1983, TNA: PREM 19/1162. **88.** Redwood and Young to Thatcher, 21 February 1984, TNA: PREM 19/1162. **89.** Turnbull to Nicholls, 12 September 1984, TNA: PREM 19/1163. **90.** Sherbourne to Turnbull, 26 September 1984, TNA: PREM 19/1163. **91.** For a full account of these efforts see Martyn Gregory, *Dirty Tricks: British Airways' Secret War against Virgin Atlantic*, Little, Brown, 1994, p. 35. **92.** Ibid. **93.** Interview with Sir Oliver Wright. **94.** Thatcher to Reagan, 29 March 1983, Exec Sec, NSA: Head of State, UK PM Thatcher, Box 35, Reagan Library. **95.** Interview with Sir Rodric Braithwaite. **96.** Reagan to Thatcher, 6 April 1983, Exec Sec, NSA: Head of State, UK PM Thatcher, Box 35, Reagan Library. **97.** Sommer to McFarlane, 24 June 1983, UK-1983-06/16/83–07/11/83, Box 90424, Peter Sommer Files, Reagan Library. **98.** 090908Z Nov 84, 'Laker Investigation: My Meeting with PM Thatcher', UK-1984-10/29/84–11/08/84, Box 90549, Peter Sommer Files, Reagan Library. **99.** 14 November 1983 [sic, actually 1984], Extraterritoriality – Laker (1), Box 28F, Fred Fielding Files, Reagan Library. **100.** Interview with Robert Kimmitt. **101.** Ronald Reagan, *The Reagan Diaries*, HarperCollins, 2007, 16 November 1984, p. 278. **102.** 170749z Nov 84, 'Talking Points for WAW, November 18 1984', State Department Archives, released under FOIA Case #200903260. **103.** 172342z Nov 84, 'Laker Case – Meeting with PM Thatcher', UK: Vol. IV(1), Exec Sec, NSC: Country File, Box 91333, Reagan Library. **104.** 181839z Nov 84, 'Laker Investigation: Meeting with PM Thatcher', State Department Archives, released under FOIA Case #200903260. **105.** Ibid. **106.** Thatcher to Reagan, 18 November 1984, CAC: THCR 3/1/42 (http://www.margaretthatcher.org/document/136658). **107.** Thatcher to Reagan, undated, Exec Sec, NSC: Head of State, UK PM Thatcher (8407695-8409063), Box 36, Reagan Library. **108.** 201317z Dec 84, 'Your meeting with PM Thatcher', Terrorism: US-British (11/20/1984–12/20/1984), Box 14, Oliver North Files, Reagan Library. **109.** Interview with Roger Maynard. **110.** Memcon, 'Mrs Thatcher at Camp David', 22 December 1984, Thatcher Visit – December 1984 (1), Exec Sec, European and Soviet Affairs Directorate, Box 90902, Reagan Library. **111.** Interview with George Shultz. **112.** Memcon, 22 December 1984, Thatcher Visit – December 1984 (1), Exec Sec, European and Soviet Affairs Directorate, Box

90902, Reagan Library. **113.** Interview with Lord Powell of Bayswater. **114.** Memcon, Private Meeting with PM Thatcher, 20 February 1985, Thatcher's Visit Feb 1985 (2), Exec Sec, European and Soviet Affairs Directorate, Box 90902, Reagan Library. **115.** Interview with Raymond Albright. **116.** Redwood to Thatcher, 19 July 1984, TNA: PREM 19/1196. **117.** Interview with Lord Lawson of Blaby. **118.** Lawson, *The View from No. 11*, p. 214. **119.** Interview with Sir Peter Gregson. **120.** Ibid. **121.** Lawson, *The View from No. 11*, p. 174. **122.** Ibid., p. 215. **123.** Peter Walker, *Staying Power*, Bloomsbury, 1991, p. 192. **124.** Interview with Lord Moore of Lower Marsh. **125.** Redwood to Thatcher, 19 July 1984, TNA: PREM 19/1196. **126.** Interview with Sir Peter Gregson. **127.** Interview with John Redwood. **128.** Interview with Sir Peter Gregson. **129.** Interview with Lord Young of Graffham. **130.** Interview with Sir Peter Gregson. **131.** Interview with Lord Turnbull. **132.** Thatcher, *The Downing Street Years*, p. 681. **133.** Interview with Sir Gerry Grimstone. **134.** Interview with David Norgrove. **135.** Interview with David Willetts. **136.** Interview with Sir Martin Jacomb. **137.** Interview with Sir Peter Gregson. **138.** Interview with Lord Turnbull. **139.** See David Parker, *The Official History of Privatisation*, vol. i, Routledge, 2009, p. 392. **140.** Interview with Sir David Walker. **141.** Thatcher to Wilson, 10 November 1980, TNA: PREM 19/1005 (http://www.marga retthatcher.org/document/137161). **142.** Interview with Sir Nicholas Goodison. **143.** Interview with Lord Parkinson. **144.** Interview with Sir David Walker. **145.** Interview with Lord Lawson of Blaby. **146.** Speech by Mr Jacob Rothschild to Financial Times conference, 24–25 October 1982, TNA: PREM 19/1005. **147.** Interview with David Willetts. **148.** Interview with Lord Lawson of Blaby. **149.** A full account of the OFT sequence of events appears in David Kynaston's history, *The City of London*, vol. iv: *A Club No More 1945–2000*, Chatto & Windus, 2001, pp. 616ff. **150.** Interview with Sir Nicholas Goodison. **151.** Interview with Lord Parkinson. **152.** Ibid. **153.** Interview with Sir David Walker. **154.** Interview with Sir Michael Scholar. **155.** Interview with Lord Parkinson. **156.** Interview with Sir Martin Jacomb. **157.** *Daily Telegraph*, 30 December 2014. **158.** Interview with Sir Michael Scholar. **159.** Ibid. **160.** Interview with Lord Parkinson. **161.** Interview with David Willetts. **162.** Interview with John Redwood. **163.** Draft statement by Secretary of State for Trade and Industry, 26 July 1983, TNA: PREM 19/1005. **164.** Redwood to Thatcher, 18 October 1983, TNA: PREM 19/1005 (http://www.margaretthatcher. org/document/137178). **165.** Redwood to Thatcher, 6 April 1984, TNA: PREM 19/1461 (http://www.margaretthatcher.org/document/137000). **166.** Turnbull to McCarthy, 10 April 1984, TNA: PREM 19/1461. **167.** Ibid. **168.** Redwood to Thatcher, 6 April 1984, TNA: PREM 19/1461 (http://www.margaretthatcher.org/ document/137000). **169.** Turnbull to McCarthy, 10 April 1984, TNA: PREM 19/1461. **170.** Interview with Lord Lawson of Blaby. **171.** Interview with David Norgrove. **172.** Griffiths and Willetts to Thatcher, 11 April 1986, TNA: PREM 19/1718. **173.** Redwood talk to Policy Unit, 11 June 1984, TNA: PREM 19/1199 (http://www.margaretthatcher.org/document/134173). **174.** Ibid. **175.** Ibid. **176.** Interview with Oliver Letwin. **177.** Ibid. **178.** Conservative

Central Council, 15 March 1986 (http://www.margaretthatcher.org/document/ 106348). **179.** *The Times*, 9 November 1985. **180.** Speech to Scottish Conservative Party Conference, 15 May 1987 (http://www.margaretthatcher.org/ document/106814). **181.** Interview with David Willetts. **182.** Interview with John Redwood. **183.** Interview with Lord Lawson of Blaby. **184.** Interview with Lord Moore of Lower Marsh. **185.** Interview with Lord Turnbull. **186.** Interview with Lord Lawson of Blaby.

CHAPTER 8: *GLASNOST* IN THE CHILTERNS

1. Thatcher to Alison, 31 December 1983, CAC: THCR 2/6/3/135 (http://www. margaretthatcher.org/document/131301). **2.** Coles to Fall, 21 December 1983, USA, Henry Kissinger's Visits to the UK. **3.** Ibid. **4.** Reagan, Address to the Nation and Other Countries on United States–Soviet Relations, 16 January 1984 (http://www.reagan.utexas.edu/archives/speeches/1984/11684a.htm). **5.** Thatcher to Reagan, 19 January 1984, CAC: THCR 3/1/36 (http://www.mar garetthatcher.org/document/136648). **6.** Interview with Sir John Coles. **7.** FCO steering brief, 24 January 1984, CAC: THCR 1/10/69 (http://www.marga retthatcher.org/document/133919). **8.** Ricketts to Coles, covering note to FCO steering brief, 19 January 1984, Prime Minister's Papers, PM's Tours Abroad: Visit to Hungary (document consulted in the Cabinet Office); see also 'Call on Mr Kadar', c.3 February 1984, THCR 1/10/69 (http://www.margaretthatcher.org/ document/133923). **9.** Thatcher to Reagan, 8 February 1984, CAC: THCR 3/1/36. **10.** Ibid. **11.** 'Handwritten notes re: Chequers 12 Feb 84', VP Trip to Europe & USSR, Donald Gregg Files, Bush Library. **12.** Interview with Lord Powell of Bayswater. **13.** Interview with Lord Butler of Brockwell. **14.** Written contribution from Tony Bishop, 9 September 2010. **15.** Margaret Thatcher, *The Downing Street Years*, HarperCollins, 1993, p. 458. **16.** Written contribution from Tony Bishop, 9 September 2010. **17.** Moscow telegram 217, 14 February 1984, Prime Minister's Papers, Soviet Union, Prime Minister's Attendance at Mr Andropov's funeral in Moscow (document consulted in the Cabinet Office). **18.** Written contribution from Tony Bishop. **19.** Archie Brown, 'The Change to Engagement in Britain's Cold War Policy: The Origins of the Thatcher–Gorbachev Relationship', *Journal of Cold War Studies*, vol. 10, no. 3, Summer 2008, p. 20. **20.** Interview with Sir Nigel Broomfield. **21.** Powell to Thatcher, 28 June 1984, TNA: PREM 19/1394 (http://www.margaretthatcher.org/document/134689). **22.** Reagan, Address to the 39th Session of the UN General Assembly in New York, 24 September 1984, Public Papers of the Presidents, American Presidency Project (http://www.presidency.ucsb.edu/ws/index.php?pid=40430&st=&st1=). **23.** Reagan to Thatcher, 26 September 1984, CAC: THCR 3/1/40. **24.** Thatcher to Reagan, 26 September 1984, CAC: THCR 3/1/40. **25.** Reagan to Thatcher, 3 October 1984, Exec Sec, NSC: Head of State, UK: PM Thatcher, Box 8491035, Reagan Library. **26.** Thatcher to Reagan, 9 October 1984, CAC: THCR 3/1/41. **27.** Powell note to Thatcher, undated, TNA: PREM 19/1394. **28.** Appleyard to Powell,

16 October 1984, TNA: PREM 19/1394 (http://www.margaretthatcher.org/document/134701).   **29.** Thatcher to Reagan, 8 November 1984, Exec Sec, NSC: Head of State, UK: PM Thatcher, Box 8491070, Reagan Library.   **30.** Ibid. **31.** McFarlane to President, 8 November 1984, UK 1984-10/29/84–11/09/84, Box 90549, Peter Sommer Files, Reagan Library.   **32.** Interview with Jack Matlock. **33.** Appleyard to Powell, 19 November 1984, TNA: PREM 19/1394 (http://www.margaretthatcher.org/document/134706).   **34.** Ibid.   **35.** Andrei Grachev, *Gorbachev's Gamble: Soviet Foreign Policy and the End of the Cold War*, Polity, 2008, pp. 50–51.   **36.** Sutherland, Moscow telegram 1382, 4 December 1984, TNA: PREM 19/1394 (http://www.margaretthatcher.org/document/134714).   **37.** Cradock to Powell, 11 December 1984, TNA: PREM 19/1394 (http://www. margaretthatcher.org/document/134724).   **38.** See Nicholas Elliott, *With my Little Eye: Observations along the Way*, Michael Russell, 1993 (especially p. 9). **39.** For a full account, see Christopher Andrew, *The Defence of the Realm: The Authorized History of MI5*, Allen Lane, 2009, pp. 671–3.   **40.** Ibid.   **41.** Interview with Sir Colin McColl.   **42.** Ibid.   **43.** Ibid.   **44.** Interview with Sir John Scarlett. **45.** Interview with Oleg Gordievsky.   **46.** Ibid.   **47.** Ibid.   **48.** See Andrew, *The Defence of the Realm*, p. 680.   **49.** Butler to Armstrong, 10 December 1984, TNA: PREM 19/1394 (http://www.margaretthatcher.org/document/134719).   **50.** Interview with Lord Jopling.   **51.** Mikhail Gorbachev, *Memoirs*, Doubleday, 1996, p. 160.   **52.** Written contribution from Tony Bishop.   **53.** Record of conversation between Thatcher and Gorbachev at Chequers, 16 December 1984, TNA: PREM 19/1647.   **54.** Record of conversation between Thatcher and Gorbachev at Chequers, 16 December 1984, TNA: PREM 19/1394 (http://www.margaretthatcher. org/document/134729).   **55.** Ibid.   **56.** Ibid.   **57.** Ibid.   **58.** Jonathan Aitken, *Margaret Thatcher: Power and Personality*, Bloomsbury, 2013, p. 481.   **59.** Record of conversation between Thatcher and Gorbachev at Chequers, 16 December 1984, TNA, PREM 19/1394 (http://www.margaretthatcher.org/document/134729). **60.** Written contribution from Tony Bishop.   **61.** Record of conversation between Thatcher and Gorbachev at Chequers, 16 December 1984, TNA: PREM 19/1394 (http://www.margaretthatcher.org/document/134729).   **62.** Thatcher, *The Downing Street Years*, p. 461.   **63.** Gorbachev, *Memoirs*, pp. 160–61.   **64.** Interview with Lord Powell of Bayswater.   **65.** Aitken, *Margaret Thatcher*, pp. 482–3.   **66.** Powell to Appleyard, 16 December 1984, TNA: PREM 19/1394 (http:// www.margaretthatcher.org/document/134730).   **67.** Ibid.   **68.** Ibid.   **69.** Ibid.   **70.** Written contribution from Tony Bishop.   **71.** Martin Nicholson, unpublished manuscript (kindly made available to the author by Martin Nicholson).   **72.** Cited in Deborah Hart Strober and Gerald Strober, *The Reagan Presidency: An Oral History of the Era*, Potomac, 2003, p. 327.   **73.** Written contribution from Tony Bishop.   **74.** Ibid.   **75.** Interview with Lord Powell of Bayswater.   **76.** Correspondence with Sir Bernard Ingham. See also Bernard Ingham, *Kill the Messenger*, Fontana, 1991, p. 270.   **77.** FCO telegram 2529 to Hong Kong, 20 December 1984, TNA: PREM 19/1394 (http://www.margaretthatcher.org/document/134737).   **78.** Andrei Grachev, 'Political and Personal: Gorbachev, Thatcher and the End of the Cold War', *Journal of European Integration History*, vol. 16, no. 1, 2010, p. 50.   **79.** Interview

with Oleg Gordievsky. **80.** Ibid. **81.** Interview with Sir John Scarlett. **82.** Ibid., **83.** Thatcher, *The Downing Street Years*, p. 463. **84.** Powell to Appleyard, 17 December 1984, TNA: PREM 19/1394 (http://www.margaretthatcher.org/document/134733). **85.** *Washington Post*, 21 December 1984. **86.** 201317z Dec 84, 'Your meeting with Prime Minister Thatcher', 20 December 1984, Terrorism: US–British (11/20/1984–12/20/1984), Box 14, Oliver North Files, Reagan Library. **87.** Thatcher's report to Reagan on meeting with Gorbachev, 22 December 1984, TNA: PREM 19/1394 (http://www.margaretthatcher.org/document/134740). **88.** Ibid. **89.** Interview with Lord Butler of Brockwell. **90.** Ibid. **91.** Washington telegram 21, 20 December 1984, TNA: PREM 19/1502. **92.** Annotation by Charles Powell, undated, Prime Minister's Papers, PM's Tours: Possible visit to Peking (document consulted in the Cabinet Office). **93.** Memcon, Margaret Thatcher at Camp David, 22 December 1984, Thatcher visit Dec. 84 (1), EASD, NSC, Box 90902, Reagan Library. **94.** Ibid. **95.** Ibid. **96.** Thatcher, *The Downing Street Years*, p. 466. **97.** Memcon, Margaret Thatcher at Camp David, 22 December 1984, Thatcher visit Dec. 84 (1), EASD, NSC, Box 90902, Reagan Library. **98.** Ibid. **99.** Record of a meeting between the Prime Minister and President Reagan, 22 December 1984, CAC: THCR 1/10/78 (http://www.margaretthatcher.org/document/136436). **100.** Memcon, Margaret Thatcher at Camp David, 22 December 1984, Thatcher visit Dec. 84 (1), EASD, NSC, Box 90902, Reagan Library. **101.** Interview with Lord Powell of Bayswater. **102.** Memcon, Margaret Thatcher at Camp David, 22 December 1984, Thatcher visit Dec. 84 (1), EASD, NSC, Box 90902, Reagan Library. **103.** Ibid. **104.** Interview with Bud McFarlane. **105.** Interview with Sir Bernard Ingham. **106.** Lord Powell of Bayswater, Interview for *The Downing Street Years* (BBC1), 1993. **107.** Interview with Lord Powell of Bayswater. **108.** Untitled draft, Thatcher Visit 12/22/84, OA 11623, Robert Sims Files (Press Secretary), Reagan Library. **109.** Interview with Lord Powell of Bayswater. **110.** Ibid. **111.** George Shultz, *Turmoil and Triumph*, Charles Scribner's Sons, 1993, p. 509. **112.** Interview with Richard Burt. **113.** William Safire, *New York Times*, 24 December 1984. **114.** Interview with Henry Kissinger. **115.** Interview with Richard Perle. **116.** Interview with Arthur Hartman. **117.** *Newsweek*, 3 December 1990. **118.** Interview with Roz Ridgway. **119.** Correspondence with George Shultz. **120.** Interview with Colin Powell. **121.** Powell to Ricketts, 9 January 1985, Prime Minister's Papers, USA, UK/US Relations, Part 3 (document consulted in the Cabinet Office). **122.** Quoted in Washington telegram 593, 20 February 1985, Prime Minister's Papers, USA, PM's visit to Washington, February 1985, Part 4 (document consulted in the Cabinet Office). **123.** Interview with Lord Powell of Bayswater. **124.** Thatcher, Speech to Joint Houses of Congress, 20 February 1985 (http://www.margaretthatcher.org/document/105968). **125.** Ibid. **126.** Interview with Lord Powell of Bayswater. **127.** Ronald Reagan, 'Foreword Written for a Report on the Strategic Defense Initiative', 28 December 1984, Public Papers of the Presidents (http://www.presidency.ucsb.edu/ws/index.php?pid=38499&st=&st1=). **128.** Thatcher's Handwritten Speaking Cards, 'Talks with President in Plenary', CAC: THCR 1/10/81. **129.** 'Record of a meeting on Arms Control between the Prime Minister and the President of the United States at the White House on Wednesday 20 February at 1330', CAC: THCR 1/10/81.   **130.** Ibid.   **131.** Thatcher, 'Remarks Departing the White House', 20 February 1985 (http://www.margaretthatcher.org/docu ment/105969).   **132.** Interview with Lord Powell of Bayswater.   **133.** Ken Adelman, Interview for *The Downing Street Years* (BBC1), 1993.   **134.** Ibid.   **135.** *Time*, 24 February 1985.   **136.** Interview with Bud McFarlane.

CHAPTER 9: ARMS AND THE WOMAN

1. 'Return to Moscow', Thatcher Memorandum, 16 March 1985, CAC: THCR 1/20/5 (http://www.margaretthatcher.org/document/139102).   **2.** Ibid.   **3.** Ibid.   **4.** Ibid.   **5.** Written contribution from Tony Bishop.   **6.** 'Return to Moscow', 16 March 1985.   **7.** Ibid.   **8.** Ibid.   **9.** Meeting with Gorbachev, speaking note (undated), Prime Minister's Papers, Soviet Union: Prime Minister's attendance at Mr Andropov's and Mr Chernenko's funeral (document consulted in the Cabinet Office).   **10.** Powell to Appleyard, 13 March 1985. Ibid.   **11.** Ibid.   **12.** Written contribution from Tony Bishop.   **13.** Diary of Anatoly Chernyaev, 14 March 1985, National Security Archive. Translation based on the kind suggestions of Martin Nicholson and Sir Rodric Braithwaite.   **14.** Powell to Appleyard, Meeting of Thatcher with Bush on 13 March, 14 March 1985, TNA: PREM 19/1646.   **15.** Ibid.   **16.** Interview with Lord Powell of Bayswater.   **17.** Sutherland telegram 685 to Thomas, 11 May 1985, CAC: THCR 1/10/91.   **18.** Interview with Lord Powell of Bayswater.   **19.** See Ivo Daalder, *The SDI Challenge to Europe*, Ballinger, 1987, pp. 13–16.   **20.** Interview with Lord Kerr of Kinlochard.   **21.** Interview with Richard Perle.   **22.** *The Times*, 20 March 1985.   **23.** Interview with Lord Powell of Bayswater.   **24.** *The Times*, 18 March 1985.   **25.** Thatcher to Reagan, 21 March 1985, CAC: THCR 3/1/45.   **26.** Wright to McFarlane, 23 March 1985, UK 1985-05/21/85–06/05/85, Box 90867, Peter Sommer Files, Reagan Library.   **27.** *The Times*, 23 March 1985.   **28.** 24 June 1985, Ronald Reagan, *The Reagan Diaries*, HarperCollins, 2007, p. 337.   **29.** Interview with Henry Kissinger.   **30.** Gorbachev to Thatcher, 7 May 1985, CAC: THCR 3/1/46.   **31.** Wright, Washington telegram 2220, 24 July 1985, Prime Minister's Papers, USA, Prime Minister's visit to the USA on 25/26 July 1985 (document consulted in the Cabinet Office).   **32.** Press conference, British Embassy in Washington, 26 July 1985 (http://www.margaretthatcher.org/document/106106).   **33.** Interview with General Jim Abrahamson.   **34.** Ibid.   **35.** Interview with Sir John Weston.   **36.** Interview with General Jim Abrahamson.   **37.** Thatcher meeting with Weinberger, 26 July 1985, Prime Minister's Papers, USA, Prime Minister's Visit to the USA on 25/26 July 1985 (document consulted in the Cabinet Office).   **38.** Ibid.   **39.** Ibid.   **40.** Correspondence with Lord Powell of Bayswater.   **41.** *New York Times*, 26 July 1985.   **42.** See Christopher Andrew, *The Defence of the Realm: The Authorized History of MI5*, Allen Lane, 2009, pp. 725–7.   **43.** Addison to Thatcher, 27 August 1985, Prime Minister's Papers, Soviet Union, UK/Soviet Relations, Part 4 (document consulted in the Cabinet Office).   **44.** Gorbachev to

Thatcher, 28 August 1985. Ibid.   **45.** Interview with Sir Bryan Cartledge.   **46.** Interview with Sir Christopher Curwen.   **47.** Interview with Sir Colin McColl.   **48.** See Oleg Gordievsky, *Next Stop Execution: The Autobiography of Oleg Gordievsky*, Macmillan, 1995, p. 368.   **49.** Interview with Oleg Gordievsky.   **50.** Interview with Lord Powell of Bayswater.   **51.** Armstrong to Thatcher, 11 September 1985, Prime Minister's Papers, Soviet Union, UK/Soviet Relations, Part 4 (document consulted in the Cabinet Office).   **52.** Powell to Appleyard, 15 September 1985. Ibid.   **53.** Powell to Budd, 30 September 1985. Ibid.   **54.** Cartledge, Third Impressions of the Soviet Union, 16 October 1985. Ibid.   **55.** Interview with Oleg Gordievsky.   **56.** Ibid.   **57.** Interview with Sir John Scarlett.   **58.** Gordievsky, *Next Stop Execution*, p. 354.   **59.** Ibid.   **60.** Thatcher to Reagan, 12 September 1985, CAC: THCR 3/1/49.   **61.** Ibid.   **62.** Ibid.   **63.** Ibid.   **64.** Interview with Jack Matlock.   **65.** Reagan to Thatcher, September 1985, Exec Sec, NSC: Head of State, UK: PM Thatcher (8590931–8591083), Reagan Library.   **66.** Ibid.   **67.** Cited in Martin Anderson and Annelise Anderson, *Reagan's Secret War: The Untold Story of his Fight to Save the World from Nuclear Disaster*, Crown Publishers, 2009, p. 224.   **68.** Ibid., p. 226.   **69.** Reagan to Thatcher, 20 September 1985, Prime Minister's Papers, Soviet Union, UK/Soviet Relations, Part 4 (document consulted in the Cabinet Office).   **70.** Gorbachev to Thatcher, 16 October 1985, CAC: THCR 3/1/50.   **71.** Speech to Conservative Party Conference, 11 October 1985 (http://www.margaretthatcher.org/document/106145).   **72.** Interview with Lord Powell of Bayswater.   **73.** Correspondence with Lord Carrington.   **74.** Wall to Cartledge, 14 June 1979, TNA: PREM 19/92.   **75.** Richards to Alexander, 30 January 1981, TNA: PREM 19/530.   **76.** Note of a Discussion with Mr Begin, 23 May 1979, TNA: PREM 19/92 (http://www.margaretthatcher.org/document/117934).   **77.** Note of a Conversation, 14 June 1979, TNA: PREM 19/92 (http://www.margaretthatcher.org/document/117939).   **78.** Interview with Sir Clive Whitmore.   **79.** Interview with Oliver Miles.   **80.** Interview with Lord Wolfson of Sunningdale.   **81.** Henderson to Carrington, 1 October 1981, TNA: PREM 19/532 (http://www.margaretthatcher.org/document/125895).   **82.** Conversation between Thatcher and Reagan, Blackpool, 12 October 1981, TNA: PREM 19/532 (http://www.margaretthatcher.org/document/125898).   **83.** 081312z Nov 83, 'Deputy Secretary Dam's meeting November 7 with Prime Minister Thatcher', 8 November 1983, State Department Archives, released under FOIA, on appeal, Case #200610766.   **84.** Thatcher to Reagan, 4 November 1983, CAC: THCR 3/1/34 (http://www.margaretthatcher.org/document/131580).   **85.** Thatcher to Reagan, 7 February 1984, CAC: THCR 3/1/36 (http://www.margaretthatcher.org/document/136654).   **86.** Thatcher to Reagan, 7 February 1984, CAC: THCR 3/1/36 (http://www.margaretthatcher.org/document/136665).   **87.** George Shultz, *Turmoil and Triumph*, Charles Scribner's Sons, 1993, p. 231.   **88.** Thatcher to Reagan, 30 September 1981, CAC: THCR 3/1/16 (http://www.margaretthatcher.org/document/121537).   **89.** Interview with Sir John Coles.   **90.** Richards to Ricketts, 18 November 1981, TNA: PREM 19/533.   **91.** Coles to Fall, 12 September 1983, TNA: PREM 19/1088.   **92.** Memorandum of Conversation, Margaret Thatcher at Camp David, 22 December 1984, Exec Sec, NSC: European and Soviet Affairs Directorate, Thatcher Visit – Dec. 1984 (1), Box 90902, Reagan Library. **93.** Thatcher to King Hussein, 27 February 1985, TNA: PREM 19/1570. **94.** King Hussein to Reagan, 24 March 1985. Ibid, part 12. **95.** Thatcher to Reagan, 15 April 1985. Ibid. **96.** Powell to Ricketts, 7 June 1985, TNA: PREM 19/1571. **97.** Thatcher to Reagan, 6 June 1985, CAC: THCR 3/1/47. **98.** Powell to Thatcher, 18 June 1985. Ibid. **99.** Powell to Thatcher, 25 June 1985. Ibid. **100.** Thatcher to King Hussein, 5 July 1985. Ibid. **101.** Reagan to King Hussein, oral message, 7 September 1985. Ibid. **102.** King Hussein to Reagan, 11 September 1985. Ibid. **103.** Record of a meeting, 19 September 1985. Ibid. **104.** Ibid. **105.** Interview with Sir John Coles. **106.** Thatcher to Reagan, 19 September 1985, TNA: PREM 19/1571. **107.** Interview with Lord Powell of Bayswater. **108.** Ibid. **109.** Thatcher to Coles, 23 September 1985, CAC: THCR 3/2/174. **110.** Interview with Sir John Coles. **111.** *Sun*, 23 September 1985. **112.** Fidler to Thatcher, 23 September 1985, CAC: THCR 5/2/183. **113.** Ingham to Thatcher, 23 September 1985, CAC: THCR 5/2/183. **114.** Interview with Richard Murphy. **115.** Wolfson to Powell, undated, probably 8 October 1985, Prime Minister's Papers, The Middle East, Situation in the Middle East, Part 14 (document consulted in the Cabinet Office). **116.** Powell to Thatcher, 13 October 1985. Ibid. **117.** Thatcher to Hussein, 14 October 1985. Ibid. **118.** Interview with Lord Powell of Bayswater. **119.** Speech at dinner given by the Israeli Prime Minister, 25 May 1986 (http://www.margaretthatcher.org/document/106402). **120.** Azriel Bermant, *Margaret Thatcher and the Middle East*, Cambridge University Press, forthcoming, 2016. **121.** Interview with Lord Powell of Bayswater. **122.** Telegram 244, Tel Aviv, Squire, 30 May 1986, CAC: THCR 1/10/104. **123.** Powell to Culshaw, 13 March 1987, Prime Minister's Papers, The Middle East, The Situation in the Middle East, Part 16 (document consulted in the Cabinet Office). **124.** Lever to Alexander, 19 December 1980, TNA: PREM 19/529. **125.** MOD report accompanying Pattie to Thatcher, 4 September 1980, TNA: PREM 19/413. **126.** Interview with Prince Bandar bin Sultan. **127.** Heseltine to Howe, 19 September 1983, TNA: PREM 19/1315. **128.** Michael Heseltine, *Life in the Jungle*, Hodder & Stoughton, 2000, p. 287. **129.** Interview with Wafic Saïd. **130.** Interview with Sir Clive Whitmore. **131.** Interview with Wafic Saïd. **132.** Ibid. **133.** Interview with Sir Richard Mottram. **134.** Ibid. **135.** Interview with Sir Clive Whitmore. **136.** Interview with Lord Blyth of Rowington. **137.** Interview with Wafic Saïd. **138.** Interview with Sir Richard Mottram. **139.** Interview with Prince Bandar bin Sultan. **140.** Ibid. **141.** See Jonathan Aitken, *Margaret Thatcher: Power and Personality*, Bloomsbury, 2013, p. 437. **142.** Interview with Prince Bandar bin Sultan. **143.** Interview with Lord Powell of Bayswater. **144.** Mottram to Powell, 25 September 1985, TNA: PREM 19/1571. **145.** Interview with Prince Bandar bin Sultan. **146.** Interview with Lord Blyth of Rowington. **147.** Interview with Lord Powell of Bayswater. **148.** Interview with Prince Bandar bin Sultan. **149.** Ibid. **150.** Ibid. **151.** Thatcher to King Fahd, 27 February 1985, CAC: THCR 3/1/44. **152.** Interview with Lord Butler of Brockwell. **153.** Aitken, *Margaret Thatcher*, p. 426. **154.** Interview with Lord

Blyth of Rowington.   **155.** Ibid.   **156.** Thatcher to King Fahd, 17 May 1986, CAC: THCR 3/1/54.   **157.** Interview with Prince Bandar bin Sultan.   **158.** Interview with Carol Thatcher.   **159.** *Observer*, 15 January 1984.   **160.** Interview with Sir Clive Whitmore.   **161.** See Paul Halloran and Mark Hollingsworth, *Thatcher's Gold: The Life and Times of Mark Thatcher*, Simon & Schuster, 1995, ch. 4.   **162.** Interview with Sir Tim Lankester.   **163.** Ibid.   **164.** *Sunday Times*, 4 March 1984. **165.** Ivor Lucas, *A Road to Damascus: Mainly Diplomatic Memoirs from the Middle East*, Radcliffe Press, 1997, p. 204.   **166.** BBC *Panorama*, 9 April 1984 (http://www.margaretthatcher.org/document/105538), quoted in Halloran and Hollingsworth, *Thatcher's Gold*, p. 91.   **167.** ITV *Weekend World*, 15 January 1984 (http://www.margaretthatcher.org/document/105503).   **168.** Interview with Sir Mark Thatcher.   **169.** Private information.   **170.** Interview with Sir Tim Lankester.   **171.** Interview with Sir Clive Whitmore.   **172.** Ibid.   **173.** Ibid. **174.** Interview with Sir Mark Thatcher.   **175.** Ibid.   **176.** Interview with Sir Clive Whitmore   **177.** Interview with Lord Butler of Brockwell.   **178.** Interview with Sir Mark Thatcher.   **179.** See Halloran and Hollingsworth, *Thatcher's Gold*, ch. 6. **180.** Interview with Wafic Saïd.   **181.** Interview with Prince Bandar bin Sultan. **182.** Interview with Wafic Saïd.   **183.** Interview with Sir Mark Thatcher.   **184.** Private information.   **185.** Interview with Wafic Saïd.   **187.** Ibid.   **188.** Thatcher note on codenamed intelligence telegram, 27 December 1984, Prime Minister's Papers, Security, Arrangements for Mark Thatcher's Overseas Trips and Security (document consulted in the Cabinet Office).   **189.** Interview with Lord Kerr of Kinlochard. **190.** Hollanby to Miss Gillett, 10 January 1985, Prime Minister's Papers, Security, Arrangements for Mark Thatcher's Overseas Trips and Security (document consulted in the Cabinet Office).   **191.** Interview with Lord Kerr of Kinlochard. **192.** Interview with Sir Mark Thatcher.   **193.** Wenick to Seitz, 4 February 1985, Prime Minister's Papers, Security, Arrangements for Mark Thatcher's Overseas Trips and Security (document consulted in the Cabinet Office).   **194.** Thatcher to Wicks, 18 April 1986. Ibid.   **195.** Wicks to Thatcher, 18 April 1986. Ibid.   **196.** Kerr to Wicks, 6 June 1986. Ibid.   **197.** Kerr to Wicks, 23 June 1986. Ibid.   **198.** Wicks to Denis Thatcher, 2 July 1986. Ibid.   **199.** See Wright telegram 1758, Washington, 2 July 1986. Ibid.   **200.** Wicks to Thatcher, 4 July 1986. Ibid.   **201.** See Wicks to Sheinwald, 8 July 1986. Ibid.   **202.** Wicks to Thatcher, 4 December 1986. Ibid. **203.** Tarling to Head of Chancery, 14 December 1986. Ibid.   **204.** Wicks to Thatcher, 6 January 1987. Ibid.   **205.** Halloran and Hollingsworth, *Thatcher's Gold*, p. 128. **206.** Interview with Lord Kerr of Kinlochard.

CHAPTER 10: IRISH AGREEMENT, BRIGHTON BOMB

1. 'Conversation between Mr Hume and Mrs Thatcher', 13 February 1984, NAI: DFA/2014/32/1940.   **2.** Thatcher Memoirs Materials, CAC: THCR 4/3.   **3.** Note by Kirwan, Assistant Secretary to the Government, 31 December 1982, NAI: TAOIS/2012/90/1007.   **4.** Ibid.   **5.** Interview with Lord Powell of Bayswater. **6.** Thatcher Memoirs Materials, CAC: THCR 4/3.   **7.** Ibid.   **8.** Ibid.   **9.** Interview with Conor Burns.   **10.** Interview with Dermot Nally.   **11.** Thatcher Memoirs

Materials, CAC: THCR 4/3.   **12.** Interview with Lord Armstrong of Ilminster.   **13.** Thatcher Memoirs Materials, CAC: THCR 4/3.   **14.** Ibid.   **15.** Interview with Sir David Goodall.   **16.** Interview with Lord Powell of Bayswater.   **17.** Armstrong to Thatcher, 8 July 1983, TNA: PREM 19/1070 (http://www.margaretthatcher.org/document/138073).   **18.** Ibid.   **19.** Interview with Michael Lillis.   **20.** Sir David Goodall, unpublished manuscript (kindly made available to the author by Sir David Goodall).   **21.** Ibid.   **22.** See Paul Bew, 'Irish Government and the Agreement', in Arthur Aughey and Cathy Gormley-Heenan, eds., *The Anglo-Irish Agreement: Re-Thinking its Legacy*, Manchester University Press, 2011, pp. 43-4.   **23.** Armstrong to Thatcher, 3 November 1983, TNA: PREM 19/1408.   **24.** Ibid.   **25.** Ibid.   **26.** Report, 2 November 1983, TNA: PREM 19/1408.   **27.** Goodall, unpublished manuscript.   **28.** Interview with Michael Lillis.   **29.** Geoffrey Howe, *Conflict of Loyalty*, Macmillan, 1994, p. 416.   **30.** Record of a Conversation, 7 November 1983, TNA: PREM 19/1408.   **31.** Goodall, unpublished manuscript.   **32.** *The Times*, 23 December 1983.   **33.** Remarks on Departing Belfast, 23 December 1983 (http://www.margaretthatcher.org/document/105500).   **34.** Goodall, unpublished manuscript.   **35.** Sir Robert Armstrong, Cabinet Secretary's notebooks, 16 February 1984 (document consulted in the Cabinet Office).   **36.** Ibid.   **37.** Ibid.   **38.** Ibid.   **39.** Thatcher Memoirs Materials, CAC: THCR 4/3.   **40.** BBC, *The World This Weekend*, 6 May 1984 (Christopher Collins, ed., *Complete Public Statements of Margaret Thatcher 1945-90 on CD-ROM*, Oxford University Press, 1998/2000).   **41.** Thatcher Memoirs Materials, CAC: THCR 4/3.   **42.** Goodall, unpublished manuscript.   **43.** Interview with Michael Lillis.   **44.** Ibid.   **45.** Interview with Judge William Clark.   **46.** Shultz to President, 14 May 1984, Exec Sec, NSC: Trip File, The President's Trip to Europe: Ireland, UK, and Normandy 06/01/1984-06/10/1984, Poindexter (1), RAC Box 8, Reagan Library.   **47.** Thatcher Memoirs Materials, CAC: THCR 4/3.   **48.** Interview with Lord Powell of Bayswater.   **49.** Thatcher Memoirs Materials, CAC: THCR 4/3.   **50.** Goodall to Powell, 29 August 1984, TNA: PREM 19/1408.   **51.** Ibid.   **52.** Powell to Appleyard, 3 September 1984, TNA: PREM 19/1408.   **53.** Ibid.   **54.** Goodall, unpublished manuscript.   **55.** Interview with Lord Butler of Brockwell.   **56.** Interview with Amanda Ponsonby.   **57.** Interview with Lord Sherbourne of Didsbury.   **58.** Interview with Lord Deben.   **59.** Interview with Tessa Gaisman.   **60.** Interview with Bob Kingston.   **61.** Ibid.   **62.** Interview with Lord Butler of Brockwell.   **63.** Thatcher Memoirs Materials, CAC: THCR 4/3.   **64.** Interview with Lord Deben.   **65.** Thatcher Memoirs Materials, CAC: THCR 4/3.   **66.** Ibid.   **67.** Ibid.   **68.** Interview with Lord Deben.   **69.** Margaret Thatcher, *The Downing Street Years*, HarperCollins, 1993, p. 380.   **70.** Interview with Lord Sherbourne of Didsbury.   **71.** Interview with Amanda Ponsonby.   **72.** TV interview for the BBC, 12 October 1984 (http://www.margaretthatcher.org/document/105574).   **73.** Interview with Lord Deben.   **74.** Interview with Lord Butler of Brockwell.   **75.** Thatcher Memoirs Materials, CAC: THCR 4/3.   **76.** Ibid.   **77.** Interview with Lord Butler of Brockwell.   **78.** Interview with Tessa Gaisman.   **79.** Interview with Amanda Ponsonby.   **80.** Interview with Lord

Sherbourne of Didsbury. **81.** Speech to Conservative Party Conference, 12 October 1984 (http://www.margaretthatcher.org/document/105763). **82.** Speech to Conservative Party Conference, 12 October 1984 (http://www.margaretthatcher. org/document/105763). **83.** Diary of Douglas Hurd, 12 October 1984 (kindly made available to the author by Lord Hurd of Westwell). **84.** Thatcher Memoirs Materials, CAC: THCR 4/3. **85.** Ibid. **86.** Interview with Harvey Thomas. **87.** Thatcher to Thorneycroft, 14 October 1984, CAC: THCR 3/2/149 (http://www. margaretthatcher.org/document/136237) **88.** Carol Thatcher, *Below the Parapet: The Biography of Denis Thatcher*, HarperCollins, 1996, p. 214. **89.** Thatcher Memoirs Materials, CAC: THCR 4/3. **90.** Private information. **91.** Interview with Lord Deben. **92.** Coles to Thatcher, 13 October 1984, CAC: THCR 1/1/23 (http://www.margaretthatcher.org/document/136330). **93.** Armstrong to Thatcher, 10 October 1984, TNA: PREM 19/1288 (http://www.margaretthatcher. org/document/134206). **94.** Powell to Thatcher, 18 October 1984, TNA: PREM 19/1288 (http://www.margaretthatcher.org/document/134216). **95.** Interview with Cynthia Crawford. **96.** Howe to Thatcher, 3 November 1984, TNA: PREM 19/1408 (http://www.margaretthatcher.org/document/134741). **97.** Interview with Lord Powell of Bayswater. **98.** Goodison, telegram 636, 12 November 1984, TNA: PREM 19/1408 (http://www.margaretthatcher.org/document/134751). **99.** Goodall, unpublished manuscript. **100.** Powell to Appleyard, 14 November 1984, TNA: PREM 19/1408 (http://www.margaretthatcher.org/document/134754). **101.** Ibid. **102.** 'Telephone discussion with Sir Robert Armstrong, Secretary to the Cabinet', 14 November 1984, NAI: DFA/2014/32/1944. **103.** Armstrong to Powell, 15 November 1984, TNA: PREM 19/1408 (http://www. margaretthatcher.org/document/134755). **104.** Interview with Lord Powell of Bayswater. **105.** Ibid. **106.** 'List of Points for the Taoiseach's tete-a-tete', 17 November 1984, NAI: TAOIS/2014/105/827, Part 1. **107.** Record of First Evening, 18 November 1984, TNA: PREM 19/1408 (http://www.margaretthatcher. org/document/134760). **108.** Goodall, unpublished manuscript. **109.** Record of Meeting, Chequers, 19 November 1984, TNA: PREM 19/1408 (http://www.mar garetthatcher.org/document/134762). **110.** Ibid. **111.** Ibid. **112.** Thatcher Memoirs Materials, CAC: THCR 4/3. **113.** Record of a Meeting, Chequers at noon, TNA: PREM 19/1408 (http://www.margaretthatcher.org/docu ment/134764). **114.** Interview with Garret FitzGerald; Draft Record of Plenary session, NAI: DFA/2014/32/2059. **115.** Press conference following the Anglo-Irish Summit, 19 November 1984 (http://www.margaretthatcher.org/document/105790). **116.** Interview with Lord Hurd of Westwell. **117.** Ryan to Assistant Secretary, 21 November 1984, NAI: TAOIS/2014/105/827. **118.** Cited in Anthony Kenny, *The Road to Hillsborough: The Shaping of the Anglo-Irish Agreement*, Pergamon, 1986, pp. 82–3. **119.** Interview with Michael Lillis. **120.** Interview with Dick Spring. **121.** Goodison telegram 682, 22 November 1984, TNA: PREM 19/1408 (http://www.margaretthatcher.org/document/134768). **122.** Interview with Lord Armstrong of Ilminster. **123.** 'Press Digest', Ingham to Thatcher, 22 November 1984, CAC: THCR 3/5/40. **124.** See Thatcher, *The Downing Street Years*, p. 400. **125.** FitzGerald to Thatcher, 22 November 1984, TNA: PREM

19/1408 (http://www.margaretthatcher.org/document/134769). **126.** Armstrong to Thatcher, 27 November 1984, TNA: PREM 19/1549. **127.** Interview with Lord Powell of Bayswater. **128.** Thatcher to FitzGerald, 29 November 1984, TNA: PREM 19/1549. **129.** Powell to Thatcher, 3 December 1984. Ibid. **130.** Ibid. **131.** Ibid. **132.** Interview with Dermot Nally. **133.** Interview with Lord Howe of Aberavon. **134.** Interview with Sir David Goodall. **135.** O'Neill to President, 13 December 1984, CO167:146000, WHORM File, Reagan Library. **136.** Memcon, Margaret Thatcher at Camp David, 22 December 1984, Thatcher visit Dec. 84 (1), EASD, NSC, Box 90902, Reagan Library. **137.** Interview with Sir Nigel Sheinwald. **138.** Powell, Note of a discussion over lunch, 20 February 1985, TNA: PREM 19/1658. **139.** Speech to Joint Houses of Congress, 20 February 1985 (http://www.margaretthatcher.org/document/105968). **140.** Howe to Thatcher, 28 March 1985, TNA: PREM 19/1549. **141.** Ibid. **142.** 'Anglo-Irish Relations', Howe and Hurd, 19 April 1985. Ibid. **143.** Ibid. **144.** Powell to Thatcher, 23 April 1985. Ibid. **145.** Note for the Record by Powell, 6 June 1985. Ibid. **146.** Interview with Garret FitzGerald. **147.** Interview with Lord Armstrong of Ilminster. **148.** Interview with Lord Powell of Bayswater. **149.** Ibid. **150.** Interview with Sir David Goodall. **151.** Powell to Thatcher, 19 June 1985, TNA: PREM 19/1549. **152.** Powell to Daniell, 29 June 1985. Ibid. **153.** Ibid. **154.** Ibid. **155.** Interview with Lord Hurd of Westwell. **156.** Armstrong to Thatcher, 26 July 1985, TNA: PREM 19/1550. **157.** Powell to Armstrong, 29 July 1985. Ibid. **158.** Powell to Thatcher, 2 August 1985. Ibid. **159.** Powell to Thatcher, 26 September 1985. Ibid. **160.** Interview with Lord King of Bridgwater. **161.** Ibid. **162.** Ibid. **163.** Powell to Thatcher, 27 September 1985, TNA: PREM 19/1550. **164.** King to Thatcher, 27 September 1985. Ibid. **165.** Ibid. **166.** Ibid. **167.** Howe to Thatcher, 28 September 1985. Ibid. **168.** Interview with Lord Powell of Bayswater. **169.** Ibid. **170.** Powell to Daniell, 2 October 1985, TNA: PREM 19/1551. **171.** Ibid. **172.** Thatcher to FitzGerald, 4 October 1985. Ibid. **173.** Powell to Thatcher, 27 October 1985. Ibid. **174.** Ibid. **175.** Powell to Armstrong, 1 November 1985, TNA: PREM 19/1552. **176.** Powell to Daniell, 9 November 1985. Ibid. **177.** Thatcher to FitzGerald, 11 November 1985. Ibid. **178.** Hansard, HC Deb 14 November 1985, 86/682 (http://hansard.millbank systems.com/commons/1985/nov/14/engagements). **179.** Interview with Richard Ryan. **180.** Ingham to Thatcher, 14 November 1985, TNA: PREM 19/1552. **181.** Goodall, unpublished manuscript. **182.** Ibid. **183.** Gow to Thatcher, 15 November 1985, CAC: THCR 2/1/6/41. **184.** Interview with Sir David Goodall. **185.** Interview with Lord Howe of Aberavon. **186.** Interview with Michael Lillis. **187.** Interview with Lord Armstrong of Ilminster. **188.** Goodall, unpublished manuscript. **189.** Interview with Lord King of Bridgwater. **190.** Joint press conference with the Irish Prime Minister, 15 November 1985 (http://www.margaretthatcher.org/document/106173). **191.** Interview with Lord King of Bridgwater. **192.** Kohl to Thatcher, 15 November 1985, CAC: THCR 3/1/51. **193.** Statement on the United Kingdom–Ireland Agreement Concerning Northern Ireland, 15 November 1985, American Presidency Project (http://www.presidency. ucsb.edu/ws/index.php?pid=38072&st=faithful+friends&st). **194.** Thatcher

Memoirs Materials, CAC: THCR 4/3. **195.** Garret FitzGerald, *All in a Life: Garret FitzGerald, an Autobiography*, Gill & Macmillan, 1991, p. 570. FitzGerald suggests, erroneously, that this meeting took place in Brussels rather than Luxembourg. **196.** Paul Bew and Gordon Gillespie, *Northern Ireland: A Chronology of the Troubles 1968–1999*, Gill & Macmillan, 1999, pp. 190–91. **197.** Interview with Lord King of Bridgwater. **198.** Thatcher to Griffiths, 25 March 1986, CAC: THCR 3/2/186. **199.** Thatcher Memoirs Materials, CAC: THCR 4/3. **200.** Interview with Michael Lillis. **201.** Charles Moore, contemporaneous private note, 26 November 1985. **202.** Thatcher Memoirs Materials, CAC: THCR 4/3. **203.** Thatcher, *The Downing Street Years*, p. 415. **204.** Interview with Lord Armstrong of Ilminster. **205.** Thatcher, *The Downing Street Years*, p. 410. **206.** Interview with Michael Lillis. **207.** Thatcher, *The Downing Street Years*, p. 415. **208.** Interview with Martin Mansergh. **209.** *Daily Telegraph*, 23 November 1998. **210.** Hansard, HC Deb 10 April 2013, 560/1621–3 (http://www.publications.parliament.uk/pa/cm201213/cmhansrd/cm130410/debtext/130410-0001.htm#1304104000296). **211.** Interview with Lord Powell of Bayswater. **212.** Interview with Dick Spring. **213.** Interview with Garret FitzGerald. **214.** Ibid. **215.** Interview with Garret FitzGerald. **216.** Howe, *Conflict of Loyalty*, p. 422. **217.** Ibid., p. 427. **218.** Interview with Lord Armstrong of Ilminster. **219.** Interview with Sir David Goodall. **220.** Interview with Lord Powell of Bayswater.

CHAPTER 11: POLL TAX

1. Margaret Thatcher, *The Downing Street Years*, HarperCollins, 1993, p. 644. **2.** Interview with Lord Turnbull. **3.** Sir Robert Armstrong, Cabinet Secretary's notebooks, 10 May 1983 (document consulted in the Cabinet Office). **4.** Interview with Lord Sherbourne of Didsbury. **5.** See Volume I, pp. 131–2. **6.** Article on local government in *Conservative Oxford*, 31 October 1949 (http://www.margaretthatcher.org/document/100843). **7.** Jenkin to Thatcher, 13 September 1983, TNA: PREM 19/1080 (http://margaretthatcher.org/document/140755). **8.** See Thatcher, *The Downing Street Years*, p. 284. **9.** Interview with Oliver Letwin. **10.** Scholar to Ballard, 13 July 1983, TNA: PREM 19/1080. (http://margaretthatcher.org/document/140754). **11.** Ingham to Jenkin, 16 December 1983, TNA: PREM 19/1303 (http://margaretthatcher.org/document/105968). **12.** Interview with Lord Jenkin of Roding. **13.** Turnbull, Note for the Record, 14 February 1984, TNA: PREM 19/1304 (http://www.margaretthatcher.org/document/141484). **14.** Interview with Lord Sherbourne of Didsbury. **15.** Interview with Sir Michael Scholar. **16.** Ingham press digest, 27 March 1984, CAC: THCR 3/5/3. **17.** Interview with Oliver Letwin. **18.** 'Press Digest', Ingham to Thatcher, 30 March 1984, CAC: THCR 3/5/32. **19.** Interview with Oliver Letwin. **20.** Ibid. **21.** Interview with David Norgrove. **22.** Letwin to Barclay, 30 May 1984, TNA: PREM 19/1305 (http://www.margaretthatcher.org/document/141490). **23.** Interview with Oliver Letwin. **24.** 'Press Digest', Ingham to Thatcher, 16 May 1984, CAC:

THCR 3/5/34. **25.** Ingham to Lord President, 28 June 1984, TNA: PREM 19/1306 (http://www.margaretthatcher.org/document/141497). **26.** Interview with Ken Livingstone. **27.** Ingham to Lord President, 28 June 1984, TNA: PREM 19/1306 (http://www.margaretthatcher.org/document/141497). **28.** Redwood to Thatcher, 29 August 1984, TNA: PREM 19/1307 (http://www.margaretthatcher.org/document/141493). **29.** Thatcher, *The Downing Street Years*, p. 646. **30.** Redwood to Thatcher, 25 September 1984, TNA: PREM 19/1307 (http://www.margaretthatcher.org/document/141492). **31.** Turnbull to Ballard, 27 September 1984, TNA: PREM 19/1307 (http://www.margaretthatcher.org/document/141491). **32.** Ibid. **33.** Rees to Thatcher, 3 October 1984, TNA: PREM 19/1308 (http://www.margaretthatcher.org/document/141496). **34.** Interview with Lord Lawson of Blaby. **35.** Draft Thatcher Speech, 8 October 1984, CAC: THCR 5/1/4/82 (http://www.margaretthatcher.org/document/136222). **36.** Interview with Lord Waldegrave of North Hill. **37.** Ibid. **38.** Ibid. **39.** Thatcher to Rothschild, 30 October 1984, TNA: PREM 19/1308 (http://www.margaretthatcher.org/document/141495). **40.** Interview with Jill Rutter. **41.** Interview with Lord Butler of Brockwell. **42.** Ibid. **43.** Interview with Oliver Letwin. **44.** Ibid. **45.** Letwin to Turnbull, 15 November 1984, CAC: THCR 2/6/3/131 Part 1 (http://www.margaretthatcher.org/document/137675). **46.** Letwin to Thatcher, 6 December 1984, CAC: THCR 2/6/3/131 Part 1 (http://www.margaretthatcher.org/document/136334). **47.** Letwin to Turnbull, 15 November 1984, CAC: THCR 2/6/3/131 Part 1 (http://www.margaretthatcher.org/document/137675). **48.** Gregson to Thatcher, 20 November 1984, TNA: PREM 19/1308 (http://www.margaretthatcher.org/document/141494). **49.** Telegram 1596, Immediate Peking, 18 December 1984, TNA: PREM 19/1309 (http://www.margaretthatcher.org/document/141498). **50.** Rothschild to Thatcher, 1 January 1985, TNA: PREM 19/1559. **51.** Ibid. **52.** Interview with Lord Sherbourne of Didsbury. **53.** Interview with Lord Baker of Dorking. **54.** Baker to Joseph, 31 January 1985, TNA: PREM 19/1559. **55.** Ibid. **56.** Alison, Note of a Meeting, 14 February 1985, TNA: PREM 19/1559. **57.** Ibid. **58.** Younger to Thatcher, 27 February 1985, PREM 19/1559. **59.** Interview with Oliver Letwin. **60.** Monro to Thatcher, 18 April 1985, CAC: THCR 2/1/4/90. **61.** Younger to Thatcher, 5 March 1985, TNA: PREM 19/1559. **62.** Butler to Thatcher, 15 March 1985, TNA: PREM 19/1559. **63.** Butler to Thatcher, 25 March 1985, TNA: PREM 19/1559. **64.** Interview with Lord Butler of Brockwell. **65.** Ibid. **66.** Interview with Lord Lawson of Blaby. **67.** Ibid. **68.** Interview with Lord Rees. **69.** Rothschild to Butler, 27 March 1985, TNA: PREM 19/1559. **70.** Redwood and Letwin to Thatcher, 29 March 1985, TNA: PREM 19/1559. **71.** Ibid. **72.** Butler to Ballard, 2 April 1985, TNA: PREM 19/1560. **73.** Interview with Lord Baker of Dorking. **74.** Interview with Lord Jenkin of Roding. **75.** Interview with Oliver Letwin. **76.** Interview with Sir Terry Heiser. **77.** Interview with Lord Butler of Brockwell. **78.** Interview with Lord Waldegrave of North Hill. **79.** Butler to Ballard, 2 April 1985, TNA: PREM 19/1560. **80.** Thatcher to Rothschild, 4 April 1985, CAC: THCR 3/2/163. **81.** Interview with Lord Turnbull. **82.** Interview with Ken Livingstone. **83.** Livingstone public letter to Scargill, 24 January 1985, quoted in the *Spectator*, 16 March 1985. **84.** Rothschild to Butler, 2 April 1985, TNA: PREM 19/1560. **85.** Redwood and Letwin to Thatcher, 17 May 1985, TNA: PREM 19/1560. **86.** Gregson to Thatcher, 17 May 1985, TNA: PREM 19/1560. **87.** Memo by Chancellor of the Exchequer, 16 May 1985, TNA: CAB 134/4878. **88.** Redwood and Letwin to Thatcher, 17 May 1985. Ibid. **89.** Interview with Lord Lawson of Blaby. **90.** Interview with Lord Waldegrave of North Hill. **91.** Interview with Lord Lawson of Blaby. **92.** Ibid. **93.** Interviews with Lord Waldegrave of North Hill and David Norgrove. **94.** Interview with Lord Waldegrave of North Hill. **95.** Interview with Oliver Letwin. **96.** Interview with Lord Lawson of Blaby. **97.** Interview with Oliver Letwin. **98.** Interview with Lord Lawson of Blaby. **99.** Sherbourne to Thatcher, 30 April 1985, CAC: THCR 2/1/4/90. **100.** See David Butler, Andrew Adonis and Tony Travers, *Failure in British Government: The Politics of the Poll Tax*, Oxford University Press, 1994, p. 80. **101.** *The Times*, 1 October 1985. **102.** *New York Times*, 2 October 1985, Kinnock speech, 1 October 1985 (http://www.britishpolitical-speech.org/speech-archive.htm?speech=191). **103.** Redwood and Letwin to Thatcher, 20 September 1985, TNA: PREM 19/1562. **104.** Interview with Jill Rutter. **105.** Butler covering note to Rothschild letter to Thatcher, 3 July 1985, TNA: PREM 19/1565 (http://www.margaretthatcher.org/document/141599). **106.** Unwin to Thatcher, 19 September 1985, TNA: PREM 19/1562. **107.** Turnbull to Ballard, 8 July 1985, TNA: PREM 19/1561. **108.** Letwin to Thatcher, 8 November 1985, TNA: PREM 19/1565 (http://www.margaretthatcher.org/document/141497). **109.** Interview with David Norgrove. **110.** Letwin to Thatcher, 8 November 1985, TNA: PREM 19/1565 (http://www.margaretthatcher.org/document/141497). **111.** Ibid. **112.** Letwin to Thatcher, 12 November 1985, TNA: PREM 19/1565 (http://www.margaretthatcher.org/document/141595). **113.** Interview with David Norgrove. **114.** Interview with Sir Brian Unwin. **115.** Unwin to Thatcher, 8 November 1985, TNA: PREM 19/1565 (http://www.margaretthatcher.org/document/141596). **116.** Interview with Oliver Letwin. **117.** Interview with Lord Waldegrave of North Hill. **118.** Ibid. **119.** Hurd to Baker, 30 September 1985, TNA: PREM 19/1565 (http://www.margaretthatcher.org/document/141598). **120.** Interview with Lord Waldegrave of North Hill. **121.** Ibid. **122.** Interview with David Norgrove. **123.** Interview with Lord Lawson of Blaby. **124.** Letwin to Thatcher, 13 December 1985, TNA: PREM 19/1565 (http://www.margaretthatcher.org/document/141594). **125.** Letwin to Thatcher, 30 December 1985. TNA: PREM 19/1565 (http://www.margaretthatcher.org/document/141593). **126.** Ibid. **127.** See Norgrove to Young, 31 December 1985, TNA: PREM 19/1565 (http://www.margaretthatcher.org/document/141601). **128.** Norgrove to Thatcher, 3 January 1986, Prime Minister's Papers, Local Government: The Future of the Rating System, Part 4 (document consulted in the Cabinet Office). **129.** Sir Robert Armstrong, Cabinet Secretary's notebooks, 9 January 1986 (document consulted in the Cabinet Office). **130.** Ibid. **131.** Kenneth Baker, *The Turbulent Years: My Life in Politics*, Faber & Faber, 1993, p. 126. **132.** Wicks to Young, 4 March 1986, Prime Minister's Papers, Local Government: The Future of the Rating System, Part 4 (document consulted in the Cabinet Office). **133.** Thatcher, *The Downing Street Years*, p. 649. **134.** Ibid. **135.** Ridley to Thatcher,

18 November 1986, Prime Minister's Papers, Local Government: The Future of the Rating System, Part 4 (document consulted in the Cabinet Office). **136.** Ridley to Thatcher, 10 April 1987. Ibid. **137.** Norgrove to Thatcher, 6 May 1987. Ibid. **138.** Fowler to Thatcher, 7 May 1987. Ibid. **139.** Interview with the Lord Lothian (Michael Ancram). **140.** Interview with Lord Sherbourne of Didsbury. **141.** Interview with Lord Lothian. **142.** Cabinet minutes, 13 November 1986, TNA: CAB 128/83 (http://www.margaretthatcher.org/document/136964). **143.** Rifkind to Whitelaw, 6 February 1987, Prime Minister's Papers, Local Government: The Future of the Rating System, Part 4 (document consulted in the Cabinet Office). **144.** Speech to Scottish Conservative Party Conference, 15 May 1987 (http://www. margaretthatcher.org/document/106814). **145.** Interview with Sir Terry Heiser. **146.** Interview with Lord Lothian. **147.** Interview with Lord Sherbourne of Didsbury. **148.** Ibid. **149.** Interview with David Norgrove. **150.** Interview with Sir Bernard Ingham.

CHAPTER 12: A SINGLE EUROPEAN

1. 'EU budget 2014–2020', House of Commons Library Briefing Paper, 22 May 2015, No. 06455. **2.** Interview with Pierre Morel. **3.** Helmut Kohl, *Erinnerungen 1982–1990*, Droemer Knaur, 2005, p. 283. **4.** Interview with Pierre Morel. **5.** Coles to Appleyard, Record of conversation between Thatcher and Kohl, 2 May 1984, Prime Minister's Papers, Germany, Chancellor Kohl's visit to UK, April 1983, and subsequent UK Visits, Part 8 (document consulted in the Cabinet Office). **6.** Interviews with Lord Hannay of Chiswick and Lord Renwick of Clifton. **7.** Interview with Lord Renwick of Clifton. **8.** Interview with Lord Williamson of Horton. **9.** Preface by Christopher Collins, 27 May 2015 (http:/www.margaret thatcher.org/document/139100). **10.** 'Fontainebleau', Thatcher Memorandum, undated, CAC: THCR 1/20/4 (http://www.margaretthatcher.org/document/ 139100). **11.** Interview with Lord Renwick of Clifton. This account also draws on his published account: Robin Renwick, *A Journey with Margaret Thatcher*, Biteback, 2013. **12.** 'Fontainebleau', undated. **13.** Ibid. **14.** Kohl, *Erinnerungen*, p. 283. **15.** Interview with Sir Michael Butler. **16.** Margaret Thatcher, *The Downing Street Years*, HarperCollins, 1993, p. 544. **17.** 'Fontainebleau', undated. **18.** Interview with Lord Renwick of Clifton. **19.** Interview with Hubert Védrine. **20.** Interview with Jacques Attali. **21.** David Hannay, *Britain's Quest for a Role: A Diplomatic Memoir from Europe to the UN*, I. B. Tauris, 2013, p. 106. **22.** Hansard, HC Deb 27 June 1984, 62/1008 (http://hansard.millbanksystems.com/ commons/1984/jun/27/european-council-fontainebleau). **23.** *Spectator*, 29 June 1984. **24.** Ingham to Thatcher, 'Your press conference', undated, Prime Minister's Papers, European Policy, European Council Meeting in Paris, Part 18 (document consulted in the Cabinet Office). **25.** 'Fontainebleau', undated. **26.** Study groups had looked into the matter in 1963, 1965, 1973 and 1975. For a full account, see Terry Gourvish, *The Official History of Britain and the Channel Tunnel*, Routledge, 2006. **27.** Brief for Thatcher's Meeting with MacGregor, 10 November 1981, Prime Minister's Papers, Transport, The Channel Tunnel, Part 1 (document consulted in the Cabinet Office). **28.** Ibid. **29.** Scholar to Mayer (Department of Transport), 17 November 1981. Ibid. **30.** MacGregor to Edwards, 31 March 1982, Prime Minister's Papers, Transport, The Channel Tunnel, Part 2 (document consulted in the Cabinet Office). **31.** Scholar note on Howell to Thatcher, 19 January 1982, Prime Minister's Papers, Transport, The Channel Tunnel, Part 1 (document consulted in the Cabinet Office). **32.** Biffen to Howell, 8 February 1982. Ibid. **33.** Pym to Thatcher, 12 May 1982, Prime Minister's Papers, Transport, The Channel Tunnel, Part 2 (document consulted in the Cabinet Office). **34.** Coles to Mayer, 18 May 1982. Ibid. **35.** Turnbull to Nichols, 14 March 1984. Ibid. **36.** Young to Thatcher, 11 May 1984. Ibid. **37.** See Gourvish, *The Official History of Britain and the Channel Tunnel*, pp. 250–51. **38.** Flesher to Thatcher, 31 October 1984, Prime Minister's Papers, Transport, The Channel Tunnel, Part 2 (document consulted in the Cabinet Office). **39.** Quoted in Gourvish, *The Official History of Britain and the Channel Tunnel*, p. 252. **40.** Ibid. **41.** Interview with Sir Bernard Ingham. **42.** Quoted in Gourvish, *The Official History of Britain and the Channel Tunnel*, p. 254. **43.** Ibid. **44.** Wybrew to Thatcher, 22 February 1985, Prime Minister's Papers, Transport, The Channel Tunnel, Part 2 (document consulted in the Cabinet Office). **45.** Henderson to Thatcher, 10 April 1985, Prime Minister's Papers, Transport, The Channel Tunnel, Part 3 (document consulted in the Cabinet Office). **46.** Ingham to Thatcher, 15 July 1985. Ibid. **47.** Powell to Thatcher, 10 December 1985. Ibid. **48.** Armstrong to Thatcher, 15 January 1986, Prime Minister's Papers, Transport, The Channel Tunnel, Part 4 (document consulted in the Cabinet Office). **49.** Wybrew to Thatcher, 20 December 1985. Ibid. **50.** Powell to C. R. (possibly Caroline Ryder), 20 January 1986. Ibid. **51.** Interview with Barry Strevens. **52.** Interview with Sir Michael Butler. **53.** Interview with Sir Bernard Ingham. **54.** Interview with Lord Renwick of Clifton. **55.** Ricketts to Coles, 24 February 1984, Prime Minister's Papers, Germany, Chancellor Kohl's visit to the UK, Part 8 (document consulted in the Cabinet Office). **56.** Interview with Lord Egremont. **57.** Carrington to Thatcher, 13 November 1981, Prime Minister's Papers, European Policy, Political Cooperation as discussed at meeting of Foreign Ministers at Venlo in May 1981 (document consulted in the Cabinet Office). **58.** Ibid. **59.** Coles to Thatcher, 16 February 1983. Ibid. **60.** Coles to Thatcher, 21 February 1983. Ibid. **61.** Pym to Thatcher, 28 February 1983. Ibid. **62.** Ibid. **63.** Interview with Sir Stephen Wall. **64.** Interview with *Die Welt*, 31 October 1984 (http://www.margaretthatcher.org/document/105580). **65.** Interview with Lady Thatcher. **66.** Powell note to Thatcher, undated, Prime Minister's Papers, European Policy, European Council meeting in Brussels, 29–30 March 1985, Part 20 (document consulted in the Cabinet Office). **67.** Howe to Thatcher, 14 March 1984, Prime Minister's Papers, European Policy, Appointment of the President of the European Commission, Part 2 (document consulted in the Cabinet Office). **68.** Howe to Thatcher, 10 July 1984. Ibid. **69.** Record of meeting between Thatcher and Dumas, 17 July 1984. Ibid. **70.** Interview with Jacques Delors. **71.** Interview with Lord Powell of Bayswater. **72.** Powell to Thatcher, 29 August 1984, TNA: PREM 19/1220. **73.** Powell to Budd, 15 October 1984. Ibid. **74.** Powell to Budd, 1 May 1985, Prime Minister's Papers, European Policy, Appointment of the President of the European Commission, Part 3 (document consulted in the Cabinet Office). **75.** Ibid. **76.** Interview with Jacques Delors. **77.** Powell to Budd, 16 October 1984, Prime Minister's Papers, European Policy, European Council Meeting in Milan, Part 21 (document consulted in the Cabinet Office). **78.** Budd to Powell, 1 February 1985, European Policy, Appointment of the President of the European Commission, Part 3 (document consulted in the Cabinet Office). **79.** Interview with Lord Renwick of Clifton. **80.** Quoted in Stephen Wall, *A Stranger in Europe: Britain and the EU from Thatcher to Blair*, Oxford University Press, 2008, pp. 41–2. **81.** Interview with Sir Malcolm Rifkind. **82.** Bullard to Powell, 25 September 1984, Prime Minister's Papers, Germany, Anglo-German Relations, Part 2 (document consulted in the Cabinet Office). **83.** Ibid. **84.** Powell to Thatcher, 27 September 1984. Ibid. **85.** Thatcher to Kohl, 28 September 1984. Ibid. **86.** See Powell to Thatcher, 11 October 1984, Prime Minister's Papers, Germany, Anglo-German Relations, Part 3 (document consulted in the Cabinet Office). **87.** Ibid. **88.** Powell to Thatcher, 7 February 1985. Ibid. **89.** Powell to Thatcher, 24 January 1985, Prime Minister's Papers, Germany, Chancellor Kohl's Visit to the UK, Part 9 (document consulted in the Cabinet Office). **90.** Bullard telegram 466, 8 May 1985. Ibid. **91.** Powell to Thatcher, 3 May 1985. Ibid. **92.** Ibid. **93.** Powell to Thatcher, 15 May 1985. Ibid. **94.** Powell to Appleyard, 19 May 1985. Ibid. **95.** Bullard telegram 508, 19 May 1985. Ibid. **96.** Kohl to Thatcher, 19 June 1985, Prime Minister's Papers, European Policy, European Council Meeting in Milan, 28–29 June 1985, Part 21 (document consulted in the Cabinet Office). **97.** Howe to Thatcher, 25 June 1985. Ibid. **98.** Powell to Budd, 27 June 1985. Ibid. **99.** Interview with Lord Powell of Bayswater. **100.** Notes manuscrites, 28 May 1985, Conseil Européen de Milan, 28 and 29 juin 1985, Archives Nationales de France, 5 AG4/EG41, Dossier 1. **101.** Jean Vidal note of meeting, 6 June 1985. Ibid. **102.** Ibid. **103.** Howe to Thatcher, 1 July 1985, Prime Minister's Papers, European Policy, European Council Meeting in Milan, 28–29 June 1985, Part 22 (document consulted in the Cabinet Office). **104.** Interview with Sir Stephen Wall. **105.** Interview with Lord Howe of Aberavon. **106.** Interview with Horst Teltschik. **107.** Cabinet minutes, 4 July 1985, TNA: CAB 128/81 (http://www.margaretthatcher.org/document/136791). **108.** Interview with Lord Renwick of Clifton. **109.** Ingham to Douglas-Home, 1 July 1985, Prime Minister's Papers, European Policy, European Council Meeting in Milan, 28–29 June 1985, Part 22 (document consulted in the Cabinet Office). **110.** Bullard telegram 687, 4 July 1985. Ibid. **111.** Interview with Lord Williamson of Horton. **112.** Powell to Thatcher, 22 November 1985, Prime Minister's Papers, Germany, Chancellor Kohl's Visit to the UK, Part 9 (document consulted in the Cabinet Office). **113.** Hannay telegram 4128, 27 November 1985, Prime Minister's Papers, European Policy, European Council Meeting in Luxembourg, 2–3 December 1985, Part 24 (document consulted in the Cabinet Office). **114.** Lawson to Thatcher, 28 November 1985. Ibid. **115.** Hannay, *Britain's Quest for a Role*, p. 131. **116.** Thatcher, *The Downing Street Years*, p. 555. **117.** Interview with Lord Williamson of Horton. **118.** Wall, *A Stranger in Europe*, p. 69. **119.** Quoted in Hugo Young, *This Blessed Plot: Britain and Europe from Churchill to Blair*, Papermac,

1999, p. 332. **120.** Hannay telegram 4235, 4 December 1985, Prime Minister's Papers, European Policy, European Council Meeting in Luxembourg, 2–3 December 1985, Part 24 (document consulted in the Cabinet Office). **121.** Thatcher, Opening Intervention, undated. Ibid. **122.** Lawson to Thatcher, 28 November 1985. Ibid. **123.** Ingham to Thatcher, 3 December 1985. Ibid. **124.** Ibid. **125.** Press conference after Luxembourg Summit, 4 December 1985 (http://www.mar garetthatcher.org/document/106187). **126.** Ibid. **127.** Interview with Lord Williamson of Horton. **128.** Interview with Sir Stephen Wall. **129.** Hansard, HC Deb 5 December 1985, 88/433 (http://hansard.millbanksystems.com/com mons/1985/dec/05/european-council-luxembourg). **130.** Interview with Lord Renwick of Clifton. **131.** Interview with Lord Young of Graffham. **132.** Ibid. **133.** Interview with Lord Williamson of Horton. **134.** Ibid. **135.** Interview with Lord Powell of Bayswater. **136.** Ibid. **137.** Thatcher, *The Downing Street Years*, pp. 556–7. **138.** Ibid. **139.** Interview with Lord Williamson of Horton.

CHAPTER 13: THE DEATH-KNELL OF MONETARISM

1. Interview with Lord Lawson of Blaby. **2.** *Financial Times*, 21 January 1984. **3.** Interview with Lord Griffiths of Fforestfach. **4.** Ibid. **5.** See, for example, Nigel Lawson, *The View from No. 11*, Bantam Press, 1992, p. 484. **6.** Ibid. **7.** Interview with Rachel Lomax. **8.** Thatcher to Reagan, 15 January 1985, CAC: THCR 3/1/43. **9.** Mulford to Regan, 'Briefing for your January 18 Breakfast with Chancellor Lawson', 17 January 1985, International Affairs (8), Box 51, Regan Papers, Library of Congress. **10.** Reagan to Thatcher, 16 January 1985, CAC: THCR 3/1/43. **11.** Lawson, *The View from No. 11*, p. 474. **12.** Turnbull to Lomax, 13 February 1985, Prime Minister's Papers, European Policy, European Monetary System, Part 2 (document consulted in the Cabinet Office). **13.** Ibid. **14.** Lawson, *The View from No. 11*, p. 489. **15.** Terry Burns, personal note, 13 February 1985 (kindly made available to the author by Lord Burns). **16.** Ibid. **17.** Ibid. **18.** Redwood to Thatcher, 1 February 1985 [Redwood's typist dated this memo 1 February 1984, but this is clearly a mistake], TNA: PREM 19/1455. **19.** Turnbull to Thatcher, 1 February 1985. Ibid. **20.** See Lawson, *The View from No. 11*, p. 365. **21.** Note for the Record, 4 February 1985, TNA: PREM 19/1455. **22.** Ingham to Turnbull, 19 November 1984. Ibid. **23.** See Lawson, *The View from No. 11*, p. 362. **24.** See Geoffrey Howe, *Conflict of Loyalty*, Macmillan, 1994, pp. 280–81. **25.** Turnbull to Thatcher, 8 February 1985, TNA: PREM 19/1455. **26.** Note for the Record, 13 February 1985. Ibid. **27.** Redwood to Thatcher, 13 February 1985. Ibid. **28.** 6th pre-Budget discussion at Cabinet, 14 February 1985, TNA: CAB 128/82 (http://www.marga retthatcher.org/document/136872). **29.** Turnbull to Thatcher, 27 February 1985, TNA: PREM 19/1455. **30.** Hansard, HC Deb 19 March 1985, 75/791 (http:// hansard.millbanksystems.com/commons/1985/mar/19/tax-reform). **31.** *Spectator*, 23 March 1985. **32.** Charles Moore, *Spectator*, 23 March 1985. **33.** Lawson, *The View from No. 11*, p. 330. **34.** Ibid., p. 331. **35.** Interview with James Baker.

36. Lawson, *The View from No. 11*, p. 493. **37.** Interview with Lord Lawson of Blaby. **38.** Lomax to Norgrove, 24 September 1985, Prime Minister's Papers, European Policy, European Monetary System, Part 2 (document consulted in the Cabinet Office). **39.** Redwood to Thatcher, 27 September 1985. Ibid. **40.** Norgrove to Thatcher, 27 September 1985. Ibid. **41.** Willetts to Thatcher, 27 September 1985. Ibid. **42.** Terry Burns, personal note, 30 September 1985 (kindly made available to the author by Lord Burns). **43.** Ibid. **44.** Ibid. **45.** Lomax to Norgrove, 1 October 1985, Prime Minister's Papers, European Policy, European Monetary System, Part 2 (document consulted in the Cabinet Office). **46.** Speech to Mansion House, 17 October 1985, HM Treasury. **47.** Lawson, *The View from No. 11*, p. 496. **48.** Norgrove to Wicks, Griffiths, Willetts, 4 November 1985, Prime Minister's Papers, European Policy, European Monetary System, Part 2 (document consulted in the Cabinet Office). **49.** Lomax to Norgrove, 6 November 1985. Ibid. **50.** Lomax to Norgrove, 11 November 1985. Ibid. **51.** Ibid. **52.** Norgrove to Thatcher, 12 November 1985. Ibid. **53.** Interview with Lord Wakeham. **54.** Interview with Sir Nigel Wicks. **55.** Correspondence with Lord Tebbit. **56.** Norgrove, Note for the Record, 14 November 1985, Prime Minister's Papers, European Policy, European Monetary System, Part 2 (document consulted in the Cabinet Office). **57.** Terry Burns, personal note, 13 November 1985 (kindly made available to the author by Lord Burns). **58.** Interview with Lord Wakeham. **59.** Terry Burns, personal note, 13 November 1985. **60.** Interview with Lord Kingsdown. **61.** Interview with David Norgrove. **62.** Norgrove, Note for the Record, 14 November 1985, Prime Minister's Papers, European Policy, European Monetary System, Part 2 (document consulted in the Cabinet Office). **63.** Interview with Lord Burns. **64.** Interview with Lord Wakeham. **65.** Interview with Sir Nigel Wicks. **66.** Interview with Lord Burns. **67.** Interview with Sir Peter Middleton. **68.** Lawson, *The View from No. 11*, p. 501. **69.** Interview with Lord Lawson of Blaby. **70.** Interview with David Norgrove. **71.** Interview with Lord Wakeham. **72.** Ibid. **73.** Interview with David Norgrove. **74.** Margaret Thatcher, *The Downing Street Years*, HarperCollins, 1993, p. 698. **75.** Interview with Lord Burns. **76.** *The Times*, 3 May 1985. **77.** Thatcher Memoirs Materials, CAC: THCR 4/3. **78.** Ibid. **79.** Interview with Sir Gerald Howarth. **80.** Manuscript minutes by Gerald Howarth (kindly made available to the author by Sir Gerald Howarth). **81.** Ibid., 18 June 1985. **82.** Interview with Sir Gerald Howarth. **83.** Ibid. **84.** Sherbourne to Thatcher, 20 May 1985, CAC: THCR 2/7/5/5. **85.** Butler to Thatcher, 22 May 1985, CAC: THCR 1/14/14. **86.** Thatcher Memoirs Materials, CAC: THCR 4/3. **87.** Turnbull to Hatfield, 20 June 1985, TNA: PREM 19/1463. **88.** Turnbull to Macnaughton, 10 July 1985. Ibid. **89.** *Sun*, 19 July 1985. **90.** Owen to Thatcher, 22 July 1985. Ibid. **91.** Ibid. **92.** Flesher to Thatcher, 8 August 1985. Ibid. **93.** Thatcher, *The Downing Street Years*, p. 417. **94.** Lawson to Thatcher, 28 October 1985, TNA: PREM 19/1463. **95.** See Thatcher, *The Downing Street Years*, p. 417. **96.** Norgrove to Thatcher, 29 November 1985, TNA: PREM 19/1463. **97.** Interview with Lord Sherbourne of Didsbury. **98.** Thatcher, *The Downing Street Years*, p. 417. **99.** Thatcher to Bramall, 31 July 1985, CAC: THCR 3/2/170. **100.** Ingham to Thatcher, 2 August

1985, CAC: THCR 1/14/14. **101.** Redwood to Thatcher, 2 August 1985, CAC: THCR 2/7/5/5. **102.** Ibid. **103.** Thatcher Memoirs Materials, CAC: THCR 4/3. **104.** Interview with Lord Gowrie. **105.** Ibid. **106.** Ibid. **107.** Ibid. **108.** Thatcher Memoirs Materials, CAC: THCR 4/3. **109.** Ibid. **110.** Wakeham to Thatcher, 22 August 1985, CAC: THCR 1/14/14. **111.** Sherbourne to Thatcher, 22 August 1985. Ibid. **112.** Wolfson to Thatcher, undated. Ibid. **113.** Interview with Andrew Lansley. **114.** Ibid. **115.** Ibid. **116.** Interview with Lord Tebbit. **117.** Interview with Lord McAlpine of West Green. **118.** Interview with Lord Dobbs. **119.** Thatcher, *The Downing Street Years*, p. 422. **120.** Thatcher Memoirs Materials, CAC: THCR 4/3. **121.** Interview with Lord Tebbit. **122.** Interview with Andrew Lansley. **123.** Interview with Lord Dobbs. **124.** Tebbit to Thatcher, 27 August 1985, CAC: THCR 1/14/14. **125.** Thatcher Memoirs Materials, CAC: THCR 4/3. **126.** Ibid. **127.** Ibid. **128.** Interview with Sir Bernard Ingham. **129.** Interview with Lord Jopling. **130.** Interviews with Lord Wakeham and Sir Bernard Ingham. **131.** Interview with Sir Bernard Ingham. **132.** Armstrong, Note for the Record, 27 June 1984, Cabinet Office Papers (document consulted in the Cabinet Office). **133.** See, for example, Chris Moncrieff in the *Daily Mail*, 22 January 2015. **134.** Armstrong, Note for the Record, 27 June 1984, Cabinet Office Papers (document consulted in the Cabinet Office). **135.** *Private Eye*, 29 June 1984. **136.** *Guardian*, 27 June 1984. **137.** Cohen to Thatcher, 29 June 1984, Cabinet Office Papers (document consulted in the Cabinet Office) **138.** Thatcher to Cohen, 9 July 1984. Ibid. **139.** Interview with Lord Sherbourne of Didsbury. **140.** Interview with Lord Brittan of Spenithorne. **141.** Interview with Lord Wakeham. **142.** Ibid. **143.** Thatcher Memoirs Materials, CAC: THCR 4/3. **144.** Interview with Lord Tebbit. **145.** Interview with Lord Dobbs. **146.** Thatcher Memoirs Materials, CAC: THCR 4/3. **147.** Ibid. **148.** Ibid. **149.** Interview with Lord Young of Graffham. **150.** Hugo Young, *One of Us*, Macmillan, 1989, p. 516. **151.** Alan Clark, *Diaries*, Weidenfeld & Nicholson, 1993, 24 April 1985, p. 109. **152.** Interview with Lord Young of Graffham. **153.** Ibid. **154.** Thatcher Memoirs Materials, CAC: THCR 4/3. **155.** Interview with Lord Tebbit. **156.** Speech to Conservative Party Conference, 11 October 1985 (http://www.margaretthatcher.org/document/106145). **157.** *Evening Standard*, 18 April 2000. **158.** *Spectator*, 11 October 1985. **159.** Ibid. **160.** Speech to Conservative Party Conference, 11 October 1985 (http://www.margaretthatcher.org/document/106145). **161.** Thatcher to Blakelock, 14 October 1985, CAC: THCR 3/2/175. **162.** Wicks to Taylor (Home Office), 7 October 1985, Prime Minister's Papers, Home Affairs, Civil Disorder, Part 3 (document consulted in the Cabinet Office). **163.** Booth to Thatcher, 8 November 1985. Ibid. **164.** Ibid. **165.** Interview with Lord Sherbourne of Didsbury. **166.** Thatcher Memoirs Materials, CAC: THCR 4/3. **167.** Baker to Thatcher, 3 October 1985, Prime Minister's Papers, Regional Policy, Inner City Policing and Problems, Part 7 (document consulted in the Cabinet Office). **168.** Booth and Letwin to Thatcher, 12 November 1985. Ibid. **169.** Ibid. **170.** Archbishop Runcie to Thatcher, 27 November 1985. Ibid. **171.** Interview with the Reverend John Witheridge. **172.** *Faith in the City: A Call for Action by Church and Nation,*

Church House Publishing, 1985, p. 208.   **173.** Griffiths to Thatcher, 29 November 1985, Prime Minister's Papers, Regional Policy: Inner City Policy and Problems, Part 7 (document consulted in the Cabinet Office); see also *Faith in the City*, p. 360.   **174.** Interview with Bishop Richard Chartres.   **175.** Booth to Thatcher, 2 December 1985, Prime Minister's Papers, Regional Policy, Inner City Policing and Problems, Part 7 (document consulted in the Cabinet Office).   **176.** Griffiths to Thatcher, 29 November 1985. Ibid.   **177.** Ingham to Lord President, 28 November 1985. Ibid.   **178.** *Sunday Times*, 1 December 1985.   **179.** Interview with Lord Deben.   **180.** Interview with John Witheridge.   **181.** Ibid.   **182.** Interview with Lord Deben.   **183.** *Faith in the City*, pp. 135–6.   **184.** Interview with Lord Deben. The fullest discussion of Mrs Thatcher's religious background and opinions is Eliza Filby's *God & Mrs Thatcher: The Battle for Britain's Soul*, Biteback, 2015. **185.** See Speech at the retirement of Lord Jakobovits, 21 February 1991 (http://www.margaretthatcher.org/document/108261).   **186.** Griffiths and Booth to Thatcher, 29 January 1986, Prime Minister's Papers, Regional Policy, Inner City Policing and Problems, Part 7 (document consulted in the Cabinet Office). **187.** Armstrong to Thatcher, undated but late January 1986. Ibid.

CHAPTER 14: HELICOPTER CRASH

1. Thatcher Memoirs Materials, CAC: THCR 4/3.   **2.** Interview with Lord Hannay of Chiswick.   **3.** Heseltine to Thatcher, 30 April 1985, TNA: PREM 19/1415 (http://www.margaretthatcher.org/document/136734).   **4.** Kaunda to Thatcher, 8 June 1985, TNA: PREM 19/1415 (http://www.margaretthatcher.org/document/136736).   **5.** Howe to Thatcher, 17 July 1985, Prime Minister's Papers, Aerospace: Westland Helicopters, Part 1 (document consulted in the Cabinet Office).   **6.** Tebbit to Heseltine, 1 July 1985, TNA: PREM 19/1415 (http://www.margaretthatcher.org/document/136742).   **7.** Owen to Thatcher, 5 July 1985, TNA: PREM 19/1415 (http://www.margaretthatcher.org/document/136743).   **8.** Turnbull to Mogg, 8 July 1985, TNA: PREM 19/1415 (http://www.margaretthatcher.org/document/136846).   **9.** Interview with Lord Cuckney.   **10.** Interview with Lord Sherbourne of Didsbury.   **11.** Interview with Lord Lamont of Lerwick.   **12.** Interview with Lord Heseltine.   **13.** Interview with Lord Brittan of Spennithorne.   **14.** Interview with Lord Powell of Bayswater.   **15.** Interview with Lord Heseltine.   **16.** See Nigel Lawson, *The View from No. 11*, Bantam Press, 1992, p. 674.   **17.** Interview with Lord Tebbit.   **18.** Brittan to Thatcher, 4 October 1985, TNA: PREM 19/1415 (http://www.margaretthatcher.org/document/136745).   **19.** Powell to Thatcher, 4 October 1985, TNA: PREM 19/1415 (http://www.margaretthatcher.org/document/136847).   **20.** Interview with Lord Brittan of Spennithorne.   **21.** Hosker to Mottram, 18 October 1985, TNA: PREM 19/1415.   **22.** Interview with Lord Cuckney.   **23.** Interview with Lord Heseltine.   **24.** Interview with Lord Powell of Bayswater.   **25.** Interview with Lord Cuckney.   **26.** Powell to Thatcher, 29 November 1985, TNA: PREM 19/1415.   **27.** Interview with Lord Cuckney.   **28.** MacGregor to Heseltine, 3 December 1985,

TNA: PREM 19/1415 (http://www.margaretthatcher.org/document/136750). **29.** Warry to Powell, 4 December 1985, TNA: PREM 19/1415 (http://www.mar garetthatcher.org/document/136851). **30.** Powell to Thatcher, 5 December 1985, TNA: PREM 19/1415 (http://www.margaretthatcher.org/document/ 136752). **31.** Powell to Mogg, 6 December 1985, TNA: PREM 19/1415 (http:// www.margaretthatcher.org/document/136753). **32.** Ibid. **33.** Interview with Lord Heseltine. **34.** Powell to Thatcher, 8 December 1985, TNA: PREM 19/1415 (http://www.margaretthatcher.org/document/136754). **35.** Ibid. **36.** Ibid. **37.** Interview with Sir Richard Mottram. **38.** Interview with Lord Powell of Bayswater. **39.** Interview with David Norgrove. **40.** Interview with Lord Powell of Bayswater. **41.** Interview with Lord Heseltine. **42.** Interview with Lord Powell of Bayswater. **43.** Lawson, *The View from No. 11*, p. 677. **44.** Interview with Lord Cuckney. **45.** Ibid. **46.** Interview with Lord Heseltine. **47.** Correspondence with Lord Armstrong of Ilminster. **48.** Sir Robert Armstrong, Cabinet Secretary's notebooks, 12 December 1985 (document consulted in the Cabinet Office). **49.** Interview with Lord Brittan of Spennithorne. **50.** Heseltine telegram, 11 December 1985, TNA: PREM 19/1416 (http://www. margaretthatcher.org/document/136758). **51.** Interview with Lord Heseltine. **52.** Interview with Lord Brittan of Spennithorne. **53.** Wiggins to Unwin, 12 December 1985, TNA: PREM 19/1416 (http://www.margaretthatcher.org/ document/136759). **54.** Ibid. **55.** Ibid. **56.** Powell to Thatcher, 13 December 1985, TNA: PREM 19/1416 (http://www.margaretthatcher.org/docu ment/136866). **57.** Ibid. **58.** Cuckney to Thatcher, 13 December 1985, TNA: PREM 19/1416. **59.** See Armstrong to Wicks, 16 December 1985, TNA: PREM 19/1416 (http://www.margaretthatcher.org/document/136767). **60.** Interview with Lord Heseltine. **61.** *The Times*, 17 December 1985. **62.** Interview with Tim Flesher. **63.** Interview with Lord Wakeham. **64.** Ibid. **65.** Draft letter to Heseltine, 18 December 1985, CAC: THCR 1/4/11. **66.** Interview with Lord Wakeham. **67.** Interview with Lord Brittan of Spennithorne. **68.** Thatcher Memoirs Materials, CAC: THCR 4/3. **69.** Ibid. **70.** Interview with Lord Brittan of Spennithorne. **71.** Thatcher Memoirs Materials, CAC: THCR 4/3. **72.** Interview with Sir Bernard Ingham. **73.** Interview with Sir Richard Mottram. **74.** Interview with Lord Heseltine. **75.** Thatcher Memoirs Materials, CAC: THCR 4/3. **76.** Ingham to Wicks, 19 December 1985, TNA: PREM 19/1416. **77.** Sir Robert Armstrong, Cabinet Secretary's notebooks, 19 December 1985 (document consulted in the Cabinet Office). **78.** Hansard, HC Deb 19 December 1985, 89/564 (http://hansard.millbanksystems.com/commons/1985/dec/19/engage ments). **79.** Wicks to Thatcher, 23 December 1985, TNA: PREM 19/1416 (http:// www.margaretthatcher.org/document/136773). **80.** Interview with Sir Clive Whitmore. **81.** Thatcher Memoirs Materials, CAC: THCR 4/3. **82.** Ibid. **83.** Heseltine to Thatcher, 23 December 1985, TNA: PREM 19/1416 (http://www. margaretthatcher.org/document/136774). **84.** Ibid. **85.** Ibid. **86.** Interview with Lord Cuckney. **87.** Ibid. **88.** See Magnus Linklater and David Leigh, *Not with Honour: The Inside Story of the Westland Scandal*, Sphere Books, 1986, p. 119. **89.** Interview with Chris Moncrieff. **90.** Cuckney to Thatcher, 30

December 1985, TNA: PREM 19/1667.   **91.** Saunders to Powell, 31 December 1985. Ibid.   **92.** Thatcher to Cuckney, 1 January 1986, TNA: PREM 19/1667.   **93.** Heseltine to Horne, 3 January 1986. Ibid.   **94.** Interview with Lord Powell of Bayswater.   **95.** Ibid.   **96.** Ibid.   **97.** Powell to Thatcher, 4 January 1986, TNA: PREM 19/1667.   **98.** Interview with Lord Powell of Bayswater.   **99.** Woodrow Wyatt, *The Journals of Woodrow Wyatt*, vol. i, Macmillan, 1998, 5 January 1986, p. 46.   **100.** Mayhew to Heseltine, 6 January 1986, TNA: PREM 19/1667.   **101.** Interview with Lord Brittan of Spennithorne.   **102.** Interview with Lord Cuckney.   **103.** Interview with Chris Moncrieff.   **104.** Interview with Lord Mayhew of Twysden.   **105.** Ibid.   **106.** 'Press Digest', Ingham to Thatcher, 7 January 1986, CAC: THCR 3/5/52.   **107.** Draft speaking note, 7 January 1986, TNA: PREM 19/1667.   **108.** Armstrong, annotation advice on draft, 8 January 1986. Ibid.   **109.** Draft speaking note, 8 January 1986. Ibid.   **110.** Ingham to Thatcher, 8 January 1986. Ibid.   **111.** Sir Robert Armstrong, Cabinet Secretary's notebooks, 9 January 1986 (document consulted in the Cabinet Office).   **112.** Interview with Lord Heseltine.   **113.** Armstrong, Cabinet Secretary's notebooks, 9 January 1986.   **114.** Ibid.   **115.** Ibid.   **116.** Interview with Lord Powell of Bayswater.   **117.** Interview with Sir Richard Mottram.   **118.** Interview with Lord Heseltine.   **119.** Ibid.   **120.** Thatcher Memoirs Materials, CAC: THCR 4/3.   **121.** Interview with Lord Powell of Bayswater.   **122.** Interview with Sir Bernard Ingham.   **123.** Wyatt, *The Journals of Woodrow Wyatt*, vol. i, 9 January 1986, p. 49.   **124.** Margaret Thatcher, *The Downing Street Years*, HarperCollins, 1993, p. 433.   **125.** Sherbourne to Thatcher, 10 January 1986, CAC: THCR 2/1/5/57.   **126.** Ingham to Thatcher, 8 [actually 9] January 1986, TNA: PREM 19/1667.   **127.** Draft Thatcher letter re Heseltine resignation, 9 January 1986. Ibid.   **128.** Powell to Thatcher, 10 January 1986. Ibid.   **129.** Hansard, HC Deb 13 January 1986, 89/780 (http://hansard.millbanksystems.com/commons/1986/jan/13/westland-plc-1).   **130.** Ibid.   **131.** Wyatt, *The Journals of Woodrow Wyatt*, vol. i, 14 January 1986, p. 55.   **132.** Ibid., 18 January 1986, p. 60.   **133.** Ibid., 12 January 1986, p. 51.   **134.** Ibid., p. 52.   **135.** Private information.   **136.** John Nott, *Here Today, Gone Tomorrow: Recollections of an Errant Politician*, Politico's, 2002, p. 338.   **137.** Interview with Sir John Nott.   **138.** See Wyatt, *The Journals of Woodrow Wyatt*, vol. i, 19 January 1986, p. 63.   **139.** John Whittingdale, unpublished diary, 15 January 1987 (kindly made available to the author by John Whittingdale).   **140.** Wyatt, *The Journals of Woodrow Wyatt*, vol. i, 15 January 1986, p. 56.   **141.** Ibid.   **142.** Whittingdale, unpublished diary, 19 January 1986.   **143.** Thatcher Memoirs Materials, CAC: THCR 4/3.   **144.** Whittingdale, unpublished diary, 19 January 1986.   **145.** Geoffrey Howe, *Conflict of Loyalty*, Macmillan, 1994, p. 470.   **146.** Thatcher Memoirs Materials. CAC: THCR 4/3.   **147.** Hansard, HC Deb 23 January 1986, 90/449–51 (http://hansard.millbanksystems.com/commons/1986/jan/23/westland-plc).   **148.** Alan Clark, *Diaries*, Weidenfeld & Nicholson, 1993, p. 134.   **149.** Hansard, HC Deb 23 January 1986, 90/453–4 (http://hansard.millbanksystems.com/commons/1986/jan/23/westland-plc).   **150.** Wyatt, *The Journals of Woodrow Wyatt*, vol. i, 24 January 1986, p. 70.   **151.** Clark, *Diaries*, p. 133.   **152.** Interview with Gerald

Malone. **153.** Clark, *Diaries*, p. 134. **154.** Interview with Gerald Malone. **155.** Interview with Lord Brittan of Spennithorne. **156.** Ibid. **157.** Ibid. **158.** Ibid. **159.** 'Press Digest', Ingham to Thatcher, 24 January 1986, CAC: THCR 3/5/52. **160.** Interview with Lord Brittan of Spennithorne. **161.** *The Times*, 25 January 1986. **162.** Interview with Lord Brittan of Spennithorne. **163.** Ibid. **164.** Sherbourne to Wicks, 25 January 1986, TNA: PREM 19/1669. **165.** Interview with Lord Sherbourne of Didsbury. **166.** Sherbourne to Wicks, 24 January 1986, TNA: PREM 19/1669. **167.** Interview with Lord Sherbourne of Didsbury. **168.** Wyatt, *The Journals of Woodrow Wyatt*, vol. i, 25 January 1986, p. 71. **169.** Charles Powell, Note for the record, 25 January 1986, TNA: PREM 19/1669. **170.** Fox to Thatcher, 25 January 1986. Ibid. **171.** *Weekend World*, 26 January 1986. **172.** Douglas Hurd, *Memoirs*, Abacus, 2003, p. 399. **173.** Interview with Lord Ryder of Wensum. **174.** Ibid. **175.** Ibid. **176.** Private information. **177.** Correspondence with Lord Armstrong of Ilminster. **178.** *Financial Times*, 27 January 1986. **179.** Ingham to Wicks, 27 January 1986, TNA: PREM 19/1669. **180.** Hayes to Wicks, 27 January 1986. Ibid. **181.** Howe, *Conflict of Loyalty*, p. 471. **182.** Interview with Lord Brittan of Spennithorne. **183.** Howe, *Conflict of Loyalty*, p. 471. **184.** Clark, *Diaries*, p. 135. **185.** Interview with Tony Blair. **186.** Interview with Lord Kinnock. **187.** Ibid. **188.** Hansard, HC Deb 27 January 1986, 90/653–71 (http://hansard. millbanksystems.com/commons/1986/jan/27/westland-plc). **189.** Interview with Lord Sherbourne of Didsbury. **190.** Clark, *Diaries*, p. 135. **191.** Ingham to Thatcher, 28 January 1986, CAC: THCR 3/5/52. **192.** Powell to Thatcher, 27 January 1986, TNA: PREM 19/1669. **193.** Ibid. **194.** Interview with Sir Bernard Ingham. **195.** Interview with Lord Powell of Bayswater. **196.** Ibid. **197.** Interview with Lord Sherbourne of Didsbury. **198.** Ingham to Wicks, 24 July 1986, TNA: PREM 19/1670. **199.** Interview with Dame Colette Bowe. **200.** Ibid. **201.** Ibid. **202.** Ibid. **203.** Ibid. **204.** Ibid. **205.** Ibid. **206.** Interview with Lord Brittan of Spennithorne. **207.** Interview with Lord Mogg. **208.** Ibid. **209.** Interview with Lord Mogg. **210.** Ibid. **211.** Interview with Dame Colette Bowe. **212.** Ibid. **213.** Ibid. **214.** Ibid. **215.** Interview with Sir Bernard Ingham. **216.** Ibid. **217.** Interview with Dame Colette Bowe. **218.** Ibid. **219.** Ibid. **220.** Ibid. **221.** Interview with Lord Powell of Bayswater. **222.** Ibid. **223.** Private information. **224.** Interview with Dame Colette Bowe. **225.** For example, 3 March 1986, Armstrong, draft memorandum to the Select Committee on Defence, TNA: PREM 19/1670. **226.** Interview with Lord Powell of Bayswater. **227.** Press Digest, Ingham to Thatcher, 31 January 1986, CAC: THCR 3/5/52. **228.** Hawkins to Thatcher, 31 January 1986, CAC: THCR 2/6/3/134, underlined by Mrs Thatcher. **229.** *Finchley Times*, 20 February 1986. **230.** Montgomery to Thatcher, 27 January 1986, CAC: THCR 1/4/11. **231.** *Face the Press*, Channel 4, 26 January 1986 (Christopher Collins, ed., *Complete Public Statements of Margaret Thatcher 1945–90 on CD-ROM*, Oxford University Press, 1998/2000). **232.** Thatcher Memoirs Materials, CAC: THCR 4/3. **233.** Thatcher to Lady Tilney, 17 January 1986, CAC: THCR 1/4/11. **234.** Correspondence with Lord Powell of Bayswater. **235.** Ibid. **236.** Ibid. **237.** Ibid. **238.** Interview with

Sir Bernard Ingham. **239.** Thatcher Memoirs Materials, CAC: THCR 4/3.
240. Interview with Lord Powell of Bayswater. **241.** Interview with Rupert Murdoch. **242.** Ibid. **243.** Ibid. **244.** Ibid. **245.** Hansard, HC Deb 30 January 1986, 90/1089 (http://hansard.millbanksystems.com/commons/1986/jan/30/engagements). **246.** Wyatt, *The Journals of Woodrow Wyatt*, vol. i, 25 January 1986, p. 72.
247. Ibid., p. 73.

CHAPTER 15: TBW

1. *Evening Standard*, 28 January 1986. **2.** *The Times*, 31 January 1986.
3. *Spectator*, 15 February 1986. **4.** Woodrow Wyatt, *The Journals of Woodrow Wyatt*, vol. i, Macmillan, 1998, 9 February 1986, p. 87. **5.** Margaret Thatcher, *The Downing Street Years*, HarperCollins, 1993, p. 436. **6.** Thatcher Memoirs Materials, CAC: THCR 4/3. **7.** *The Times*, 25 March 1986. **8.** Tebbit to Thatcher, 25 January 1985, Prime Minister's Papers, Industrial Policy, The Future of British Leyland, Part 8 (document consulted in the Cabinet Office). **9.** Thatcher Memoirs Materials, CAC: THCR 4/3. **10.** Turnbull to Butler, 7 June 1985, Prime Minister's Papers, Industrial Policy, The Future of British Leyland, Part 10 (document consulted in the Cabinet Office). **11.** Warry to Thatcher, 29 November 1985. Ibid. **12.** Brittan to Thatcher, 25 November 1985. Ibid. **13.** Warry to Thatcher, 29 November 1985. Ibid. **14.** Lansley to Norgrove, 27 January 1986. Ibid.
15. 'Press Digest', Ingham to Thatcher, 4 February 1986, CAC: THCR 3/5/53.
16. Hansard, HC Deb 5 February 1986, 91/326–8 (http://hansard.millbanksystems.com/commons/1986/feb/05/british-leyland). **17.** Ibid. **18.** Thatcher, *The Downing Street Years*, p. 440. **19.** Ibid. **20.** 'Press Digest', Ingham to Thatcher, 7 February 1986, CAC: THCR 3/5/53. **21.** Charles Moore, private note of conversation, February 1986. **22.** Thatcher to Petersen, 14 February 1986, Prime Minister's Papers, Industrial Policy, The Future of British Leyland, Part 10 (document consulted in the Cabinet Office). **23.** Petersen to Thatcher, 5 March 1986. Ibid. **24.** Thatcher Memoirs Materials, CAC: THCR 4/3. **25.** Sir Robert Armstrong, Cabinet Secretary's notebooks, 20 February 1986 (document consulted in the Cabinet Office). **26.** Ibid. **27.** For Gaddafi's support for the IRA and the NUM see Chapter 6. **28.** 'Vice President's Meeting with British PM Margaret Thatcher, Friday, July 26 1985', Meetings with Foreigners, Donald Gregg Files, Bush Library. **29.** Press conference for American correspondents, 10 January 1986 (http://www.margaretthatcher.org/document/106300). **30.** Woodrow Wyatt, unpublished diaries, 5 January 1986 (kindly made available to the author by Diana Rawstron on behalf of the estate of the late Lord Wyatt of Weeford).
31. Press conference for American correspondents, 10 January 1986 (http://www.margaretthatcher.org/document/106300). **32.** Sommer to Poindexter, 'Presidential Reply to Mrs Thatcher: Libyan sanctions', 16 January 1986, Exec Sec, NSC: System File, 8600439, Reagan Library. **33.** Appleyard to Powell, 17 January 1986, Prime Minister's Papers, Libya, Relations, Internal Political Situation, Part 4B (document consulted in the Cabinet Office). **34.** Record of conversation between

Thatcher and Mitterrand, 20 January 1986. Ibid. **35.** Appleyard to Powell, 10 February 1986. Ibid. **36.** Ibid. **37.** Brian Davis, *Qaddafi, Terrorism and the Origins of the US Attack on Libya*, Praeger, 1990, p. 115. **38.** Reagan to Thatcher, 8 April 1986, Libya–El Dorado Canyon (1), Box 91747, James Stark Files, Reagan Library. **39.** Percy Cradock, *In Pursuit of British Interests: Reflections on Foreign Policy under Margaret Thatcher and John Major*, John Murray, 1997, p. 74. **40.** Thatcher interim reply to Reagan, 9 April 1986, Prime Minister's Papers, Libya, Relations, Internal Political Situation, Part 4A (document consulted in the Cabinet Office). **41.** Thatcher, *The Downing Street Years*, p. 443. **42.** Interview with Howard Teicher. **43.** Ibid. **44.** Reagan to Thatcher, 9 April 1986, Libya (Fortier File) (6), Box 91673, Donald Fortier Files, Reagan Library. **45.** Ibid. **46.** Interview with Lord Powell of Bayswater. **47.** Powell to Galsworthy, 10 April 1986, Prime Minister's Papers, Libya, Relations, Internal Political Situation, Part 4A (document consulted in the Cabinet Office). **48.** Powell to Galsworthy re 'further meeting' of ministers and officials, 10 April 1986. Ibid. **49.** Thatcher to Reagan, 10 April 1986. Ibid. **50.** Reagan to Thatcher, 11 April 1986, Libya (Fortier File) (5), Box 91673, Donald Fortier Files, Reagan Library. **51.** 'RSVP: Nitze meeting with PM Thatcher', 23 April 1986, State Department Archives, released under FOIA Case #200801161. **52.** Interview with Lord Powell of Bayswater. **53.** Ibid. **54.** Interview with Sir Percy Cradock. **55.** Interview with Sir David Goodall. **56.** Vernon Walters, *The Mighty and the Meek: Dispatches from the Front Line of Diplomacy*, St Ermin's Press, 2001, p. 147. **57.** Powell to Galsworthy, 12 April 1986, Prime Minister's Papers, Libya, Relations, Internal Political Situation, Part 5 (document consulted in the Cabinet Office). **58.** *The Times*, 14 April 1986. **59.** Interview with Lord Armstrong of Ilminster. **60.** Speaking note for OD: Libya, 13 April 1986, Prime Minister's Papers, Libya, Relations, Internal Political Situation, Part 5 (document consulted in the Cabinet Office). **61.** Interview with Lord Powell of Bayswater. **62.** Pattison to Thatcher, 12 February 1982, Prime Minister's Papers, Home Affairs, Review of the Restrictions on Shopping Hours and Sunday Trading, Part 1 (document consulted in the Cabinet Office). **63.** Turnbull to Taylor, 8 March 1985. Ibid. **64.** Griffiths to Thatcher, 5 November 1985. Ibid. **65.** Ibid. **66.** Interview with Dr Michael Schluter. **67.** Booth to Thatcher, 4 March 1986, Prime Minister's Papers, Home Affairs, Review of the Restrictions on Shopping Hours and Sunday Trading, Part 2 (document consulted in the Cabinet Office). **68.** Interview with Lord Griffiths of Fforestfach. **69.** For more on the religious and political feelings involved in the Sunday trading debate see Eliza Filby, *God & Mrs Thatcher: The Battle for Britain's Soul*, Biteback, 2015, pp. 229–32. **70.** Alison to Thatcher, 4 March 1986, CAC: THCR 1/3/20. **71.** Interview with Howard Teicher. **72.** Reagan, Address to the Nation on the United States Air Strike against Libya, 14 April 1986, American Presidency Project (http://www.presidency.ucsb.edu/ws/index.php?pid=37131&st=&st1=). **73.** Sir Robert Armstrong, Cabinet Secretary's notebooks, 15 April 1986 (document consulted in the Cabinet Office). **74.** Ingham to Powell, 24 April 1986, Prime Minister's Papers, Libya, Relations, Internal Political Situation, Part 6 (document consulted in the Cabinet Office). **75.** Ibid.

76. Interview with Lord Powell of Bayswater.   **77.** Interview with Andrew Lansley.   **78.** Interview with Lord Tebbit.   **79.** Sherbourne to Thatcher, 15 April 1986, CAC: THCR 1/10/99.   **80.** Hansard, HC Deb 15 April 1986, 95/724 (http://hansard.millbanksystems.com/commons/1986/apr/15/engagements).   **81.** 'Libya – Support from PM Thatcher', 16 April 1986, State Department Archives, released under FOIA Case #200903792.   **82.** Powell to Galsworthy, 15 April 1986, Prime Minister's Papers, Libya, Relations, Internal Political Situation, Part 5 (document consulted in the Cabinet Office).   **83.** Ibid.   **84.** *Financial Times*, 16 April 1986.   **85.** *Financial Times*, 17 April 1986.   **86.** Hansard, HC Deb 16 April 1986, 95/875 (http://hansard.millbanksystems.com/commons/1986/apr/16/libya).   **87.** Interview with Sir Percy Cradock.   **88.** *The Times*, 17 April 1986.   **89.** *Newsweek*, 28 April 1986.   **90.** Wyatt, *The Journals of Woodrow Wyatt*, vol. i, 20 April 1986, p. 124.   **91.** Price to President, 21 April 1986, United Kingdom–1986–04/21/1986–04/24/1986, Box 90901, Peter Sommer Files, Reagan Library.   **92.** Powell to Galsworthy, 24 April 1986, Prime Minister's Papers, Libya, Relations, Internal Political Situation, Part 6 (document consulted in the Cabinet Office).   **93.** Powell to Galsworthy, 26 April 1986. Ibid.   **94.** Ibid.   **95.** 'Libya Raid: UK Perception 2 weeks on', 29 April 1986, State Department Archive, released under FOIA Case #200907365.   **96.** Interview, Paul Bremer, Frontline, PBS, September 2001 (http://www.pbs.org/wgbh/pages/frontline/shows/target/interviews/bremer.html).   **97.** Interview with Howard Teicher.   **98.** Poindexter to President, Letters to Senators Lugar and Dole, United Kingdom – 1986 – 04/21/1986–04/24/1986, Box 90901, Peter Sommer Files, Reagan Library.   **99.** Interview with Lord Powell of Bayswater.   **100.** 221653z Apr 86, 21 April 1986 (US Action in Libya, 1986) (4/4), Box 91747, James Stark Files, Reagan Library.   **101.** Reagan to Lugar, 22 April 1986, The American Presidency Project (http://www.presidency.ucsb.edu/ws/index.php?pid=37172).   **102.** Reagan, Radio Address to the Nation on Terrorism, 31 May 1986, American Presidency Project (http://www.presidency.ucsb.edu/ws/index.php?pid=37376).   **103.** President's Telephone Conversation with Prime Minister Thatcher, 17 July 1986, Terrorism; United States–British, Box 14, North Files, Reagan Library.   **104.** Thatcher Memoirs Materials, CAC: THCR 4/3.   **105.** Powell to Thatcher, 30 May 1986, Prime Minister's Papers, USA, UK/USA Relations, Part 4 (document consulted in the Cabinet Office).   **106.** Ibid.   **107.** Interview with Lord Sharkey.   **108.** Ibid.   **109.** Interview with Lord Dobbs.   **110.** Interview with Lord Sherbourne of Didsbury.   **111.** Interview for *TV-am*, 7 June 1985 (http://www.margaretthatcher.org/document/105826).   **112.** Interview with Lord Dobbs.   **113.** Interview with Lord Sharkey.   **114.** Interview with Lord Sherbourne of Didsbury.   **115.** Interview with Lord Dobbs.   **116.** Interview with Robin Harris.   **117.** Interview with Lord Young of Graffham.   **118.** Interview with Lord Sherbourne of Didsbury.   **119.** David Butler Archive, Interview with John Sharkey, 16 June 1987.   **120.** Interview with Lord Dobbs.   **121.** Ibid.   **122.** Interview with Lord Bell.   **123.** Interview with Lord Dobbs.   **124.** Interview with Lord Wakeham.   **125.** Interview with Lord Sherbourne of Didsbury.   **126.** Interview with Lord Tebbit.   **127.** David Butler Archive, Interview with John Banks, 21 July 1987.   **128.** Interview with Lord Young of

Graffham. **129.** Interview with Lord Dobbs. **130.** Interview with Robin Harris. **131.** Thatcher Memoirs Materials, CAC: THCR 4/3. **132.** Interview with Lord Dobbs. **133.** John Biffen, *Semi-Detached*, Biteback, 2013, p. 374. **134.** Ibid., pp. 390–91. **135.** Ibid., p. 394. **136.** Ibid., pp. 399–400. **137.** Interview with Sir Bernard Ingham. **138.** Interview with Lord Biffen. **139.** Biffen, *Semi-Detached*, p. 403. **140.** Interview with Lord Biffen. **141.** Thatcher, *The Downing Street Years*, p. 562. **142.** Speech to Scottish Conservative Party Conference, 16 May 1986 (http://www.margaretthatcher.org/document/106394). **143.** Addison to Wicks, 20 June 1986, CAC: THCR 2/6/3/129. **144.** Thatcher, *The Downing Street Years*, p. 563. **145.** Interview with Lord Biffen. **146.** Interview with Lord Wakeham. **147.** Griffiths to Thatcher, 11 April 1986, CAC: THCR 1/15/14. **148.** See Minutes of the Strategy Group, 23 June 1986, CAC: THCR 2/7/5/6. **149.** Minutes of the Strategy Group, 30 June 1986. Ibid. **150.** Interview with Robin Harris. **151.** Sherbourne to Thatcher, 26 June 1986, CAC: THCR 2/7/5/6. **152.** Sherbourne to Thatcher, 10 April 1986, CAC: THCR 2/7/5/1. **153.** *The Times*, 10 March 1986. **154.** Thatcher Memoirs Materials, CAC: THCR 4/3. **155.** Interview with Robin Harris. **156.** Sherbourne to Thatcher, 29 July 1986, CAC: THCR 2/6/3/57. **157.** Interview with Lord Sherbourne of Didsbury. **158.** Interview with Lord Dobbs. **159.** Interview with Barry Strevens. **160.** Sherbourne to Thatcher, 6 August 1986, CAC: THCR 2/6/3/57. **161.** Wicks to Thatcher, 8 August 1986. Ibid. **162.** Tebbit to Thatcher, 8 August 1986. Ibid. **163.** Wicks to Thatcher, 8 August 1986. Ibid. **164.** Ibid. **165.** Interview with Lord Tebbit. **166.** Ingham to Whitmore, 7 May 1980, Prime Minister's Papers, Broadcasting, Legislation on Broadcasting, Part 1 (document consulted in the Cabinet Office). **167.** Norgrove to Thatcher, 14 October 1986, Prime Minister's Papers, Broadcasting, Television Licence Fees, Part 3 (document consulted in the Cabinet Office). **168.** McIntyre paper, undated, Prime Minister's Papers, Broadcasting, Television Licence Fees, Part 1 (document consulted in the Cabinet Office). **169.** Ingham to Butler, 14 December 1984. Ibid. **170.** Barclay to Taylor, 9 January 1985. Ibid. **171.** Ibid. **172.** Brittan to Thatcher, 28 February 1985. Ibid. **173.** Butler to Taylor, 6 March 1985. Ibid. **174.** Warry to Thatcher, 20 December 1984. Ibid. **175.** Douglas Hurd, *Memoirs*, Abacus, 2003, p. 369. **176.** Interview with Lord Griffiths of Fforestfach. **177.** See Jean Seaton, '*Pinkoes and Traitors': The BBC and the Nation 1974–87*, Profile Books, 2015, p. 313. **178.** Interview with Lord Tebbit. **179.** Tebbit to Barnett, 30 October 1986, Prime Minister's Papers, Broadcasting, Television Licence Fees, Part 3 (document consulted in the Cabinet Office). **180.** Interview with Dame Patricia Hodgson. **181.** Ibid. **182.** Ibid. **183.** Interview with Lord Waldegrave of North Hill. **184.** Interview with Lord Birt. **185.** Griffiths to Thatcher, 24 October 1986, CAC: THCR 2/7/5/6. **186.** Interview with Lord Griffiths of Fforestfach. **187.** Wicks to Thatcher, 13 November 1986, CAC: THCR 2/6/3/61. **188.** Sherbourne to Thatcher, 13 November 1986, CAC: THCR 2/6/3/61. **189.** Norman Tebbit, *Upwardly Mobile*, Weidenfeld & Nicolson, 1988, p. 257. **190.** Interview with Dame Patricia Hodgson. **191.** Quoted in Nigel Lawson, *The View from No. 11*, Bantam Press, 1992, p. 374. **192.** Hansard, HC Deb 18 March 1986, 94/183 (http://

hansard.millbanksystems.com/commons/1986/mar/18/income-tax). **193.** See Lawson, *The View from No. 11*, p. 375. **194.** Thatcher, *The Downing Street Years*, p. 673. **195.** Speech to Conservative Party Conference, 10 October 1986 (http://www.margaretthatcher.org/document/106498). **196.** Thatcher Memoirs Materials, CAC: THCR 4/3. **197.** Interview with Francis Maude. **198.** Interview with Robin Harris. **199.** Private information. **200.** Interview with Lord Hamilton of Epsom. **201.** Interview with Lord Tebbit. **202.** Interview with Lord Brooke of Sutton Mandeville. **203.** Interview with Lord Butler of Brockwell. **204.** 'Ms' to Sir Robert Armstrong, Cabinet Office Papers, undated (document consulted in the Cabinet Office). **205.** Armstrong to Duff, 13 January 1986, Cabinet Office Papers (document consulted in the Cabinet Office). **206.** Armstrong to Wicks, 22 June 1987. Ibid. **207.** Interview with Barry Strevens. **208.** Ibid. **209.** Interview with Lord Hamilton of Epsom. **210.** Ibid. **211.** *The Times*, 14 November 1986. **212.** Thatcher Memoirs Materials, CAC: THCR 4/3. **213.** Interview with Sir Bernard Ingham.

CHAPTER 16: AGAINST QUEEN AND COMMONWEALTH

1. Record of a conversation, 12 November 1980, Prime Minister's Papers, Visit by the South African Foreign Minister Mr Pik Botha (document consulted in the Cabinet Office). **2.** Wyatt, unpublished diaries, 23 June 1986 (kindly made available to the author by Diana Rawstron on behalf of the estate of the late Lord Wyatt of Weeford). **3.** Guise to Thatcher, 22 April 1988, CAC: THCR 1/10/119. **4.** Interview with F. W. de Klerk. **5.** Speaking note on South Africa, undated, October 1985, CAC: THCR 5/1/5/352. **6.** *The Times*, 5 July 1990. **7.** Interview with Sir Denis Thatcher. **8.** Interview with Sir Sonny Ramphal. **9.** See Anthony Sampson, *Black and Gold: Tycoons, Revolutionaries and Apartheid*, Coronet, 1987, p. 59. **10.** Tutu to Thatcher, 25 May 1984, TNA: PREM 19/1392. **11.** Interview with Sir Malcolm Rifkind. **12.** Record of a Conversation, 2 June 1984, TNA: PREM 19/1392. **13.** Theresa Papenfus, *Pik Botha and his Times*, Litera, Kindle edn (translated by Sandra Mills), 2010. **14.** 'Mr Botha speaking notes', 2 June 1984, CAC: THCR 1/10/154. **15.** Coles to Bone, 2 June 1984, TNA: PREM 19/1392. **16.** Correspondence with Sir John Coles. **17.** Margaret Thatcher, *The Downing Street Years*, HarperCollins, 1993, p. 515. **18.** Interview with Lord Powell of Bayswater. **19.** Ibid. **20.** Thatcher to Kaunda, 18 April 1985, CAC: THCR 3/1/46. **21.** Interview with Lord Renwick of Clifton. **22.** Thatcher to Botha, 4 July 1985, CAC: THCR 3/1/48. **23.** Thatcher telegram to Botha, 11 July 1985. Ibid. **24.** *Financial Times*, 17 August 1985. **25.** Interview with Sir Malcolm Rifkind. **26.** Powell to Appleyard, 12 July 1985, Prime Minister's Papers, PM's Tours Abroad, CHOGM 1985, The Bahamas, Part 1 (document consulted in the Cabinet Office). **27.** Ryder to Thatcher, 26 September 1985. Ibid. **28.** Powell to Allan (Department of Transport), 6 June 1985. Ibid. **29.** Powell to Thatcher, 11 October 1985, Prime Minister's Papers, PM's Tours Abroad, CHOGM 1985, The Bahamas, Part 2 (document consulted in the Cabinet

Office). **30.** Powell to Thatcher, 12 October 1985. Ibid. **31.** Powell to Thatcher, 10 October 1985, THCR 5/1/5/352. **32.** Powell to Ricketts, 16 October 1985, Prime Minister's Papers, Commonwealth, CHOGM, The Bahamas, Part 10 (document consulted in the Cabinet Office). **33.** Brian Mulroney, *Memoirs: 1939–1993*, McClelland & Stewart, 2007, p. 402. **34.** Ibid. **35.** Powell to Ricketts, 17 October 1985, Prime Minister's Papers, Commonwealth, CHOGM, The Bahamas, Part 10 (document consulted in the Cabinet Office). **36.** Ibid. **37.** Interview with Lord Powell of Bayswater. **38.** Powell to Ricketts, 18 October 1985, Prime Minister's Papers, Commonwealth, CHOGM, The Bahamas, Part 10 (document consulted in the Cabinet Office). **39.** BBC *Newsnight*, 18 October 1985 (http://www. margaretthatcher.org/document/105921). (Christopher Collins, ed., *Complete Public Statements of Margaret Thatcher 1945–90 on CD-ROM*, Oxford University Press, 1998/2000.) **40.** Powell to Acland, 21 October 1985, Prime Minister's Papers, Commonwealth, CHOGM, The Bahamas, Part 10 (document consulted in the Cabinet Office). **41.** Ibid. **42.** Handwritten note to Thatcher from Mulroney, undated. Ibid. **43.** Powell to Acland, 21 October 1985, Prime Minister's Papers, Commonwealth, CHOGM, The Bahamas, Part 10 (document consulted in the Cabinet Office). **44.** Ibid. **45.** Ibid. **46.** Ibid. **47.** Thatcher, *The Downing Street Years*, p. 518. **48.** Powell to Acland, 21 October 1985, Prime Minister's Papers, Commonwealth, CHOGM, The Bahamas, Part 10 (document consulted in the Cabinet Office). **49.** Ibid. **50.** Thatcher, *The Downing Street Years*, p. 518. **51.** Powell to Acland, 21 October 1985, Prime Minister's Papers, Commonwealth, CHOGM, The Bahamas, Part 10 (document consulted in the Cabinet Office). **52.** Powell to Thatcher, 22 October 1985. Ibid. **53.** Interview with Lord Powell of Bayswater. **54.** Ingham to Thatcher, 20 October 1985, Prime Minister's Papers, Commonwealth, CHOGM, The Bahamas, Part 10 (document consulted in the Cabinet Office). **55.** Press Conference at Nassau Commonwealth Summit, 20 October 1985 (http://margaretthatcher.org/document/106151). **56.** Geoffrey Howe, *Conflict of Loyalty*, Macmillan, 1994, p. 483. **57.** Ibid. **58.** Appleyard to Powell, 7 November 1985, Prime Minister's Papers, Relations with South Africa, Part 8 (document consulted in the Cabinet Office). **59.** Interview with Lord Powell of Bayswater. **60.** Ibid. **61.** Van der Post to Alexander, 27 October 1980, Prime Minister's Papers, Prime Minister's Meetings with Laurens van der Post (document consulted in the Cabinet Office). **62.** Interview with Lord Powell of Bayswater. **63.** Interviews with Lord Powell of Bayswater and Sir Claude Hankes. **64.** Powell to Budd, 6 February 1986, Prime Minister's Papers, Relations with South Africa, Part 8 (document consulted in the Cabinet Office). **65.** Interview with Lord Powell of Bayswater. **66.** Botha to Thatcher, 12 November 1985, Prime Minister's Papers, Relations with South Africa, Part 8 (document consulted in the Cabinet Office). **67.** Thatcher to Botha, 17 November 1985. Ibid. **68.** See, for example, *Guardian*, 23 March 2000. **69.** Report, 3 December 1985. Ibid.; Report, 4 December 1985. Ibid. **70.** Botha to Thatcher, 14 December 1985. Ibid. **71.** Howe to Thatcher, 20 December 1985. Ibid. **72.** Powell to Appleyard, 20 December 1985, Prime Minister's Papers, Relations with South Africa, Part 8 (document consulted in the Cabinet Office). **73.** Powell to Thatcher, 6 January

1986. Ibid.   **74.** Cradock to Powell, 7 February 1986. Ibid.   **75.** Powell to Thatcher, 30 January 1986. Ibid.   **76.** Powell to Budd, 3 February 1986. Ibid.   **77.** Solesby telegram 009, Pretoria, 24 February 1986. Ibid.   **78.** Malcolm Fraser and Margaret Simons, *Malcolm Fraser: The Political Memoirs*, Miegunyah Press, 2010, p. 650.   **79.** Powell to Budd, 17 March 1986, Prime Minister's Papers, Relations with South Africa, Part 9 (document consulted in the Cabinet Office).   **80.** Thatcher to Botha, 20 March 1986. Ibid.   **81.** Botha to Thatcher, 10 April 1986. Ibid. **82.** Thatcher to Botha, 18 April 1986. Ibid.   **83.** Moberly, Cape Town, telegram 252, 6 May 1986. Ibid.   **84.** Moberly, Cape Town, telegram 267, 16 May 1986. Ibid.   **85.** MISC 118 report, 2 May 1986. Ibid.   **86.** Thatcher to Botha, 21 May 1986. Ibid.   **87.** Botha to Thatcher, 26 May 1986. Ibid.   **88.** Ibid.   **89.** Howe to Thatcher, 28 May 1986. Ibid.   **90.** Powell to Thatcher, 11 June 1986, Prime Minister's Papers, Relations with South Africa, Part 10 (document consulted in the Cabinet Office).   **91.** Powell to Budd, 12 June 1986. Ibid.   **92.** Ibid.   **93.** Ibid. **94.** Powell to Thatcher, 13 June 1986. Ibid.   **95.** Powell to Galsworthy, 3 July 1986, Prime Minister's Papers, Relations with South Africa, Part 11 (document consulted in the Cabinet Office).   **96.** Interview with Sir Sonny Ramphal. **97.** Ryder to Powell, 1 July 1986, Prime Minister's Papers, Relations with South Africa, Part 11 (document consulted in the Cabinet Office).   **98.** Botha to Thatcher, 1 July 1986.   Ibid.   **99.** Cradock to Powell, 3 July 1986.   Ibid. **100.** Thatcher to Botha, 4 July 1986. Ibid.   **101.** Waite to Heseltine (William), 23 June 1986. Ibid.   **102.** Powell to Thatcher, 8 July 1986. Ibid.   **103.** Ibid. **104.** W. Heseltine to Galsworthy, 15 July 1986. Ibid.   **105.** Ibid.   **106.** *Guardian*, 9 July 1986.   **107.** Ibid.   **108.** Sir Peter Marshall, unpublished diaries, 9 July 1986 (kindly made available to the author by Sir Peter Marshall).   **109.** Ibid. **110.** Ibid., 20 June 1986.   **111.** Bullard, Bonn, telegram 624, 18 July 1986, Prime Minister's Papers, Relations with South Africa, Part 11 (document consulted in the Cabinet Office).   **112.** Ibid.   **113.** Wright, Washington, telegram 1902, date illegible, but from context 18 July 1986. Ibid.   **114.** Reagan, Remarks to Members of the World Affairs Council and the Foreign Policy Association, 22 July 1986, American Presidency Project (http://www.presidency.ucsb.edu/ws/?pid=37643). **115.** Interview with Brian Mulroney.   **116.** Powell to Budd, 14 July 1986, Prime Minister's Papers, Relations with South Africa, Part 11 (document consulted in the Cabinet Office).   **117.** Interview with Brian Mulroney.   **118.** Tambo to Howe, 22 July 1986, Prime Minister's Papers, Relations with South Africa, Part 11 (document consulted in the Cabinet Office).   **119.** Interview with Sir Percy Cradock. **120.** Interview with Sir Colin Budd.   **121.** Marshall, unpublished diaries, 24 June 1986.   **122.** Powell to Budd, 23 June 1986, Prime Minister's Papers, Relations with South Africa, Part 10 (document consulted in the Cabinet Office).   **123.** Walker to Thatcher, 24 June 1986. Ibid.   **124.** Howe, *Conflict of Loyalty*, p. 486. **125.** *Sunday Telegraph*, 6 July 1986.   **126.** Marshall, unpublished diaries, 13 July 1986.   **127.** Howe to Thatcher, 15 July 1986, Prime Minister's Papers, Relations with South Africa, Part 11 (document consulted in the Cabinet Office).   **128.** Ryder to Thatcher, 16 July 1986, Prime Minister's Papers, Relations with South Africa, Part 12 (document consulted in the Cabinet Office).   **129.** Woodrow Wyatt, *The*

Journals of Woodrow Wyatt, vol. i, Macmillan, 1998, 17 July 1986, p. 167.
130. Interview with Sir Sonny Ramphal   **131.** Interview with Lord Powell of Bayswater.   **132.** Marshall, unpublished diaries, 24 June 1986.   **133.** Powell to Thatcher, 10 July 1986, Prime Minister's Papers, Commonwealth, CHOGM on South Africa in London (document consulted in the Cabinet Office). **134.** Ibid.   **135.** Interview with Sir Sonny Ramphal.   **136.** *Sunday Times*, 20 July 1986.   **137.** Interview with Sir Sonny Ramphal.   **138.** For a full account of this incident, see Andrew Neil, *Full Disclosure*, Macmillan, 1996, pp. 195ff. **139.** Interview with Sir William Heseltine.   **140.** Ibid.   **141.** Ibid.   **142.** Wyatt, *The Journals of Woodrow Wyatt*, vol. i, 21 July 1986, p. 174.   **143.** Wyatt, unpublished diaries, 21 July 1986.   **144.** Wyatt, *The Journals of Woodrow Wyatt*, vol. i, 21 July 1986, p. 174   **145.** Interview with Sir William Heseltine.   **146.** Ibid. **147.** Interview with Lord Powell of Bayswater.   **148.** Interview with Lord Butler of Brockwell.   **149.** Interview with Lord Powell of Bayswater.   **150.** Marshall, unpublished diaries, 26 July 1986.   **151.** Ibid.   **152.** Interview for *Sunday Telegraph*, 19 July 1986 (http://www.margaretthatcher.org/document/106269). **153.** Ibid.   **154.** Powell to Thatcher, 24 July 1986, Prime Minister's Papers, Relations with South Africa, Part 12 (document consulted in the Cabinet Office). **155.** Ibid.   **156.** Powell to Thatcher, 25 July 1986, Prime Minister's Papers, Commonwealth, CHOGM on South Africa in London (document consulted in the Cabinet Office).   **157.** Powell to Howe private office, 25 July 1986, Prime Minister's Papers, Relations with South Africa, Part 12 (document consulted in the Cabinet Office).   **158.** FCO telegram 161, *Sunday Telegraph* article, Prime Minister's Papers, Commonwealth, CHOGM on South Africa in London (document consulted in the Cabinet Office).   **159.** Powell telegram 183 to Howe private office, 28 July 1986, Prime Minister's Papers, Relations with South Africa, Part 12 (document consulted in the Cabinet Office).   **160.** Powell to Galsworthy, 30 July 1986. Ibid.   **161.** Powell to Thatcher, 30 July 1986. Ibid.   **162.** Ingham to Thatcher, 29 July 1986, Prime Minister's Papers, Commonwealth, CHOGM on South Africa in London (document consulted in the Cabinet Office).   **163.** Howe, *Conflict of Loyalty*, pp. 492–3.   **164.** Interview with Lord Ryder of Wensum.   **165.** Interview with Lord Howe of Aberavon.   **166.** Howe, *Conflict of Loyalty*, pp. 493–6. **167.** Ibid., p. 496.   **168.** Thatcher, *The Downing Street Years*, p. 521.   **169.** Interview with Sir Sonny Ramphal.   **170.** Ibid.   **171.** Marshall, unpublished diaries, 3 August 1986.   **172.** Powell to Thatcher, 30 July 1986, Prime Minister's Papers, Commonwealth, CHOGM on South Africa in London (document consulted in the Cabinet Office).   **173.** Powell to Galsworthy, 1 August 1986. Ibid.   **174.** Interview with Lord Ryder of Wensum.   **175.** Interview with Sir William Heseltine. **176.** 'Summary of President's Meeting with Prime Minister Thatcher', 15 November 1986, State Department Archives, released under FOIA Case #200802013. **177.** Interview with Lord Powell of Bayswater.   **178.** Interview with Lord Ryder of Wensum.   **179.** Private information.   **180.** Howe, *Conflict of Loyalty*, p. 498.   **181.** Marshall, unpublished diaries, 4 August 1986.

CHAPTER 17: SAVE THE BOMB

1. Max Kampelman in *New York Times*, 24 April 2006.   **2.** George Shultz, *Turmoil and Triumph*, Charles Scribner's Sons, 1993, p. 607.   **3.** 'Nitze/Perle meeting with Prime Minister Thatcher on SDI and ABM Treaty', 26 February 1987, State Department Archives, Released under FOIA Case #200801161.   **4.** Thatcher to Reagan, 11 February 1986, CAC: THCR 3/1/52.   **5.** 'RSVP: Nitze Meeting with PM Thatcher', 23 April 1986, State Department Archives, released under FOIA Case #200801161.   **6.** Reagan to Thatcher, 23 May 1986, Exec Sec, NSC: Head of State, UK: PM Thatcher (8690401–8690687), Box 37, Reagan Library.   **7.** *The Times*, 28 May 1986.   **8.** Shultz, *Turmoil and Triumph*, p. 700.   **9.** *New York Times*, 16 January 1986.   **10.** Interview with Richard Perle.   **11.** Geoffrey Smith, *The Times*, 28 March 1986.   **12.** As she told Geoffrey Smith in a private interview in January 1990. See Geoffrey Smith, *Reagan and Thatcher*, Bodley Head, 1990, p. 58.   **13.** Thatcher to Reagan, 11 February 1986, Exec Sec, NSC: Head of State, UK: PM Thatcher (8591145–8690149), Box 37, Reagan Library.   **14.** Ibid.   **15.** Ibid.   **16.** Interview with John Poindexter.   **17.** Interview with Ken Adelman.   **18.** Ibid.   **19.** NSDD #210, 4 February 1986, RAC Box 9, Exec Sec, NSC: NSDDs, Reagan Library.   **20.** Interview with Lord Powell of Bayswater.   **21.** Thatcher to Gorbachev, 27 February 1986, CAC: THCR 3/1/52.   **22.** Reagan to Thatcher, 22 February 1986. Ibid.   **23.** Thatcher to Reagan, 24 February 1986. Ibid.   **24.** Powell to Thatcher, 14 March 1986, Prime Minister's Papers, Defence, Military Uses of Laser Technology in Space, Part 4 (document consulted in the Cabinet Office).   **25.** Howe to Thatcher, 28 April 1986. Ibid.   **26.** Lawson to Thatcher, 2 May 1986. Ibid.   **27.** Ibid.   **28.** Reagan to Thatcher, 20 July 1986, CAC: THCR 3/1/56.   **29.** Reagan to Thatcher, 26 July 1986. Ibid.   **30.** Reagan to Thatcher, 14 March 1986, CAC: THCR 3/1/53.   **31.** Interview with Lord Powell of Bayswater.   **32.** Draft Record of Conversation, 4 May 1986, Exec Sec, NSC: System File, #8603794, Reagan Library.   **33.** Ibid.   **34.** Gorbachev to Thatcher, 10 July 1986, Prime Minister's Papers, Soviet Union, UK/Soviet Relations, Part 6 (document consulted in the Cabinet Office).   **35.** Powell to Thatcher, 6 August 1986. Ibid.   **36.** Thatcher to Gorbachev, 20 August 1986. Ibid.   **37.** Interview with George Shultz.   **38.** Thatcher to Reagan, 6 October 1986, Prime Minister's Papers, Foreign policy, East/West Relations, Part 6 (document consulted in the Cabinet Office).   **39.** Ibid.   **40.** Thatcher to Gorbachev, 3 October 1986, CAC: THCR 3/1/58.   **41.** Draft reply to Reagan, 3 October 1986. Ibid.   **42.** Reagan to Thatcher, 8 October 1986, CAC: THCR 3/1/58.   **43.** Ibid.   **44.** Ibid.   **45.** Interview with Roz Ridgway.   **46.** Chernyaev's notes of 4 October 1986, 'The Reykjavik File', National Security Archive. Cited in Ken Adelman, *Reagan at Reykjavik: Forty-Eight Hours that Ended the Cold War*, HarperCollins, 2014, p. 75.   **47.** Chernyaev's notes of 4 October 1986, *The Reykjavik File*, National Security Archive. Cited in Steven Hayward, *The Age of Reagan: The Conservative Counterrevolution 1980–89*, Crown Forum, 2009, p. 493.   **48.** Anatoly Chernyaev, *My Six Years with Gorbachev*, Pennsylvania State

University Press, 2000, p. 81.   **49.** See Paul Lettow, *Ronald Reagan and his Quest to Abolish Nuclear Weapons*, Random House, 2005, p. 219.   **50.** Reykjavik Summit First Session, Reagan/Gorbachev Memcon, 11 October 1986, Box 92140, Jack Matlock Files, Reagan Library. (See also: http://www.margaretthatcher.org/docu ment/109177.)   **51.** Interview with Roz Ridgway.   **52.** See Jack Matlock, *Reagan and Gorbachev: How the Cold War Ended*, Random House, 2004, pp. 228–9.   **53.** Adelman, *Reagan at Reykjavik*, p. 141.   **54.** Interview with Charles Price.   **55.** Interview with Roz Ridgway.   **56.** Interview with Lord Powell of Bayswater.   **57.** Interview with John Poindexter.   **58.** Lettow, *Ronald Reagan and his Quest to Abolish Nuclear Weapons*, p. 225.   **59.** Interview with Jack Matlock.   **60.** Interview with Roz Ridgway.   **61.** Lettow, *Ronald Reagan and his Quest to Abolish Nuclear Weapons*, p. 225.   **62.** Interview with Sir Nigel Wicks.   **63.** Ibid.   **64.** Interview with Jacques Attali.   **65.** Margaret Thatcher, *The Downing Street Years*, HarperCollins, 1993, pp. 471–2.   **66.** Telephone conversation, Reagan/Thatcher 10/13/1986, Thatcher visit – 11/15/1986–11/16/1986, Box 92116, Robert Linhard Files, Reagan Library.   **67.** Powell to Budd, 13 October 1986, Prime Minister's Papers, Foreign Policy, East/West Relations, Part 6 (document consulted in the Cabinet Office).   **68.** Powell to Budd, 14 October 1986. Ibid.   **69.** Poindexter to President, 'Why We Can't Commit To Eliminating All Nuclear Weapons Within 10 Years', 16 October 1986, Reykjavik Briefing: Memo re Eliminating Nuclear, Box 91636, Alton Keel Files, Reagan Library.   **70.** Poindexter to President, Meeting with Prime Minister Margaret Thatcher, 15 November 1986, CO 167 (440030), WHORM File, Reagan Library.   **71.** Speech to Conservative Party Conference, Bournemouth, 10 October 1986 (http://www.margaretthatcher.org/document/106498).   **72.** Telephone conversation, Reagan/Thatcher 10 October 1986, Thatcher visit – 11/15/1986–11/16/1986, Box 92116, Robert Linhard Files, Reagan Library.   **73.** Interview with Charles Clarke.   **74.** Interview with Richard Perle.   **75.** Telephone conversation Reagan/Thatcher, 10 October 1986, Thatcher visit – 11/15/1986–11/16/1986, Box 92116, Robert Linhard Files, Reagan Library.   **76.** Lady Thatcher, Interview for *The Downing Street Years* (BBC1), 1993.   **77.** Interview with John Poindexter.   **78.** Interview with Lord Butler of Brockwell.   **79.** Interview with Colin Powell.   **80.** Interview with Lord Powell of Bayswater.   **81.** Powell to Galsworthy, 3 December 1986, Prime Minister's Papers, USA, Henry Kissinger's Visits to the UK (document consulted in the Cabinet Office).   **82.** Thatcher, *The Downing Street Years*, p. 472.   **83.** Untitled, undated handwritten note by President Reagan, CO 167 (440030), WHORM File, Reagan Library.   **84.** Lavin and Sommer to Poindexter, 10 November 1986, Thatcher Visit November 15 1986 (4), Exec Sec, NSC: European and Soviet Affairs Directorate, Box 90902, Reagan Library.   **85.** Powell to Thatcher, 21 October 1986, Prime Minister's Papers, PM's Bilaterals with the Foreign Secretary (document consulted in the Cabinet Office).   **86.** Powell to Thatcher, 23 October 1986, Prime Minister's Papers, USA, PM's Visit to Washington (Camp David), 14–15 November 1986, Part 6 (document consulted in the Cabinet Office).   **87.** Ibid.   **88.** Powell to Thatcher, 30 October 1986. Ibid.   **89.** Ibid.   **90.** Ibid.   **91.** Budd to Powell, undated. Ibid.   **92.** Interview with Lord

Powell of Bayswater.   **93.** Powell to Thatcher, 11 November 1986, Prime Minister's Papers, USA, PM's Visit to Washington (Camp David), 14–15 November 1986, Part 6 (document consulted in the Cabinet Office).   **94.** Richard Reeves, *President Reagan: The Triumph of Imagination*, Simon & Schuster, 2006, p. 264.   **95.** For the first public account of this knowledge, see Geoffrey Smith's book, *Reagan and Thatcher*, pp. 204–7.   **96.** Interview with Lord Powell of Bayswater.   **97.** Ibid.   **98.** Smith, *Reagan and Thatcher*, p. 211.   **99.** William Crowe, *The Line of Fire: From Washington to the Gulf, the Politics and Battles of the New Military*, Simon & Schuster, 1993, p. 267.   **100.** Ibid., p. 268.   **101.** See NSDD #250, 3 November 1986, RAC Box 10, Exec Sec, NSC: NSDDs, Reagan Library.   **102.** Shultz to President, 'Visit of UK Prime Minister Thatcher November 15 1986', 12 November 1986, CO167 43000–44099, WHORM File, Reagan Library.   **103.** Ibid.   **104.** 'Thatcher Memo', Note from Tyrus Cobb, 12 November 1986, November 86 – Breakfast Meeting with UK Prime Minister Thatcher, Meetings with Foreigners, Donald Gregg Files, Bush Library.   **105.** 052220z Nov 86, 'Mrs Thatcher's visit to Washington', 5 November 1986, Archives of the State Department, released under FOIA Case #200601516.   **106.** Ingham to Thatcher, 15 November 1986, Prime Minister's Papers, USA, PM's Visit to Washington (Camp David), 14–15 November 1986, Part 6 (document consulted in the Cabinet Office).   **107.** Powell to Galsworthy, 'Meeting with Secretary Weinberger', 16 November 1986. Ibid.   **108.** Interview with George Shultz.   **109.** Powell to Galsworthy, 'Meeting with Secretary Shultz', 14 November 1986, Prime Minister's Papers, USA, PM's Visit to Washington (Camp David), 14–15 November 1986, Part 6 (document consulted in the Cabinet Office).   **110.** Evening Reading Item, 'My meeting with Prime Minister Thatcher', 14 November 1986, State Department Archives, released under FOIA Case #F–200601579.   **111.** Smith, *Reagan and Thatcher*, p. 222.   **112.** Interview with John Poindexter.   **113.** Correspondence with Lord Powell of Bayswater.   **114.** Interview with Lord Powell of Bayswater.   **115.** Powell to Galsworthy, 'Meeting with President Reagan', 16 November 1986, Prime Minister's Papers, PM's Visit to Washington (Camp David), 14–15 November 1986, Part 6 (document consulted in the Cabinet Office).   **116.** Ibid.   **117.** Jim Kuhn, *Ronald Reagan in Private: A Memoir of my Years in the White House*, Sentinel, 2004, p. 142.   **118.** Powell to Galsworthy, 'Meeting with President Reagan', 16 November 1986, Prime Minister's Papers, PM's Visit to Washington (Camp David), 14–15 November 1986, Part 6 (document consulted in the Cabinet Office).   **119.** Powell to Galsworthy, 16 November 1986, Meeting with Vice-President Bush, Prime Minister's Papers, USA, PM's Visit to Washington (Camp David), 14–15 November 1986, Part 6 (document consulted in the Cabinet Office).   **120.** Powell to Galsworthy, 'Meeting with President Reagan', 16 November 1986, Prime Minister's Papers, PM's Visit to Washington (Camp David), 14–15 November 1986, Part 6 (document consulted in the Cabinet Office).   **121.** Thatcher, *The Downing Street Years*, p. 473.   **122.** Press Conference, British Embassy Rotunda, Washington, DC, 15 November 1986 (http://www.margaretthatcher.org/document/106514).   **123.** 'Press Digest', Ingham to Thatcher, 17 November 1986, CAC: THCR 3/5/62.   **124.** *The Times*, 17 November 1986.   **125.** Interview with

Frank Carlucci. **126.** Ibid. **127.** Interview with Colin Powell. **128.** Interview with George Shultz. **129.** Thatcher, *The Downing Street Years*, p. 471. **130.** Interview with Lord Powell of Bayswater. **131.** Interview with Sir Bernard Ingham.

CHAPTER 18: TO MOSCOW

1. Thatcher to Gorbachev, undated, CAC: THCR 3/1/59. **2.** Cartledge telegram 1504, 15 December 1986, Prime Minister's Papers, Soviet Union, UK/Soviet Relations, Part 6 (document consulted in the Cabinet Office). **3.** Ibid. **4.** Powell to Galsworthy, 16 December 1986. Ibid. **5.** Powell to Budd, 28 November 1986, Prime Minister's Papers, Soviet Union, Human Rights and the Position of Dissidents in the Soviet Union, Part 2 (document consulted in the Cabinet Office). **6.** Letter from Sakharov to Thatcher, received 6 January 1987, Prime Minister's Papers, Soviet Union, The Arrest and Subsequent Sending into Exile of Andrei Sakharov (document consulted in the Cabinet Office). **7.** *Life*, October 1987. **8.** Powell to Thatcher, 'Memorandum on seminar on the Soviet system under Gorbachev', 18 December 1986, Prime Minister's Papers, Soviet Union, UK/Soviet Relations, Part 6 (document consulted in the Cabinet Office). **9.** Powell to Thatcher, 'List of Questions', 20 February 1987. Ibid. **10.** Powell to Galsworthy, 'Note on Seminar on the Soviet Union', 1 March 1987. Ibid. **11.** Ibid. **12.** Interview with Sir Michael Howard. **13.** Interview with Archie Brown. **14.** Powell to Galsworthy, 28 May 1986, Prime Minister's Papers, Soviet Union, UK/Soviet Relations, Part 6 (document consulted in the Cabinet Office). **15.** Interview with Oleg Gordievsky. **16.** Powell to Galsworthy, 28 May 1986, Prime Minister's Papers, Soviet Union, UK/Soviet Relations, Part 6 (document consulted in the Cabinet Office). **17.** Interview with Oleg Gordievsky. **18.** Powell to Galsworthy, 28 May 1986, Prime Minister's Papers, Soviet Union, UK/Soviet Relations, Part 6 (document consulted in the Cabinet Office). **19.** Interview with Sir Colin McColl. **20.** Ibid. **21.** Interview with Oleg Gordievsky. **22.** Powell to Galsworthy, 'PM's meeting with Mr Gorbachev', 19 March 1987, Prime Minister's Papers, Soviet Union, UK/Soviet Relations, Part 6 (document consulted in the Cabinet Office). **23.** Ibid. **24.** Galsworthy to Powell, 16 March 1987, Prime Minister's Papers, Soviet Union, Prime Minister's Visit to the Soviet Union 28 March–1 April 1987, Part 1 (document consulted in the Cabinet Office). **25.** Robin Renwick, *A Journey with Margaret Thatcher*, Biteback, 2013, p. 167. **26.** Cartledge telegram 423, 20 March 1987, Prime Minister's Papers, Soviet Union, Prime Minister's Visit to the Soviet Union 28 March–1 April 1987, Part 1 (document consulted in the Cabinet Office). **27.** Interview with Michael Llewellyn Smith. **28.** Interview with Lord Powell of Bayswater. **29.** Interview with Amanda Ponsonby. **30.** Interview with Cynthia Crawford. **31.** Interview with Amanda Ponsonby. **32.** Margaret Thatcher, *The Downing Street Years*, HarperCollins, 1993, p. 477. **33.** 'President Mitterrand Mon 23 March', 23 March 1987, CAC: THCR 1/10/113. **34.** 'Chancellor Kohl's comments', undated, CAC: THCR 1/10/113. **35.** Thatcher to Reagan, 25 March 1987, CAC: THCR 3/1/61. **36.** Ibid. **37.** Ibid. **38.** Interview with Cynthia Crawford. **39.** Interview with Lord Powell of Bayswater. **40.** Thatcher, *The Downing Street Years*, p. 479. **41.** Interview with Amanda Ponsonby. **42.** Thatcher Memoirs Materials, CAC: THCR 4/3. **43.** Interview with Amanda Ponsonby. **44.** Pollock to Powell, 6 April 1987, CAC: THCR 1/10/117. **45.** Ibid. **46.** Written contribution from Tony Bishop. **47.** Powell to Galsworthy, 30 March 1987, Prime Minister's Papers, Soviet Union, Prime Minister's Visit to the Soviet Union, Part 1 (document consulted in the Cabinet Office). **48.** Thatcher, *The Downing Street Years*, p. 483. **49.** Pollock to Powell, 6 April 1987, CAC: THCR 1/10/117. **50.** Anatoly Chernyaev, *My Six Years with Gorbachev*, Pennsylvania State University Press, 2000, p. 99. **51.** Speech to Conservative Central Council, 21 March 1987 (http://www.margaretthatcher.org/document/106769). **52.** Powell to Galsworthy, 30 March 1987, Prime Minister's Papers, Soviet Union, Prime Minister's Visit to the Soviet Union, Part 1 (document consulted in the Cabinet Office). **53.** Chernyaev, *My Six Years with Gorbachev*, p. 99. **54.** Powell to Galsworthy, 30 March 1987, Prime Minister's Papers, Soviet Union, Prime Minister's Visit to the Soviet Union, Part 1 (document consulted in the Cabinet Office). **55.** Ibid. **56.** Ibid. **57.** Ibid. **58.** Ibid. **59.** Thatcher, *The Downing Street Years*, p. 482. **60.** Session of CC CPSU Politburo, 16 April 1987, Notes by Anatoly Chernyaev, the Gorbachev Foundation. Kindly provided by Svetlana Savranskaya of the National Security Archive. **61.** Interview with Lord Powell of Bayswater. **62.** Mikhail Gorbachev, *Memoirs*, Doubleday, 1996, p. 434. **63.** Powell to Galsworthy, 30 March 1987, Prime Minister's Papers, Soviet Union, Prime Minister's Visit to the Soviet Union, Part 1 (document consulted in the Cabinet Office). **64.** Thatcher to Reagan, 1 April 1987, Prime Minister's Papers, Soviet Union, Prime Minister's Visit to the Soviet Union, Part 2 (document consulted in the Cabinet Office). **65.** Chernyaev, *My Six Years with Gorbachev*, p. 103. **66.** Ibid. **67.** Powell to Galsworthy, 30 March 1987, Prime Minister's Papers, Soviet Union, Prime Minister's Visit to the Soviet Union, Part 1 (document consulted in the Cabinet Office). **68.** Rodric Braithwaite, 'Gorbachev and Thatcher', *Journal of European Integration History*, vol. 16, no. 1, 2010, p. 36. **69.** Thatcher to Reagan, 1 April 1987, Prime Minister's Papers, Soviet Union, Prime Minister's Visit to the Soviet Union, Part 2 (document consulted in the Cabinet Office). **70.** Powell to Galsworthy, 30 March 1987, Prime Minister's Papers, Soviet Union, Prime Minister's Visit to the Soviet Union, Part 1 (document consulted in the Cabinet Office). **71.** Thatcher to Reagan, 1 April 1987, Prime Minister's Papers, Soviet Union, Prime Minister's Visit to the Soviet Union, Part 2 (document consulted in the Cabinet Office). **72.** Powell to Galsworthy, 30 March 1987, Prime Minister's Papers, Soviet Union, Prime Minister's Visit to the Soviet Union, Part 1 (document consulted in the Cabinet Office). **73.** Ibid. **74.** Ibid. **75.** Ibid. **76.** Ibid. **77.** Cartledge, telegram 537, 1 April 1987, Prime Minister's Papers, Soviet Union, Prime Minister's Visit to the Soviet Union, Part 2 (document consulted in the Cabinet Office). **78.** Powell to Galsworthy, 30 March 1987, Prime Minister's Papers, Soviet Union, Prime Minister's Visit to the Soviet Union, Part 1 (document consulted in the Cabinet Office). **79.** Thatcher to Reagan, 1 April 1987, Prime Minister's Papers, Soviet Union, Prime Minister's Visit to the Soviet Union, Part

2 (document consulted in the Cabinet Office).   80. Speech at Soviet Official Banquet, 30 March 1987 (http://www.margaretthatcher.org/document/106776).   81. Thatcher to Reagan, 1 April 1987, Prime Minister's Papers, Soviet Union, Prime Minister's Visit to the Soviet Union, Part 2 (document consulted in the Cabinet Office).   82. Pollock to Powell, 6 April 1987, CAC: THCR 1/10/117.   83. Igor Korchilov, *Translating History: Thirty Years on the Front Lines of Diplomacy with a Top Russian Interpreter*, Scribner, 1997, p. 36.   84. Ibid., p. 37.   85. Parker to Powell, 20 March 1987, CAC: THCR 5/1/5/461.   86. Written contribution from Tony Bishop.   87. Jonathan Aitken, *Margaret Thatcher: Power and Personality*, Bloomsbury, 2013, p. 496.   88. Cradock to Powell, 24 June 1987, Prime Minister's Papers, Soviet Union, Prime Minister's Visit to Soviet Union, Part 2 (document consulted in the Cabinet Office).   89. Powell to Galsworthy, 31 March 1987, Prime Minister's Papers, Soviet Union, Prime Minister's Visit to the Soviet Union, Part 1 (document consulted in the Cabinet Office).   90. Pollock to Powell, 6 April 1987, CAC: THCR 1/10/117.   91. Powell to Galsworthy, 31 March 1987, Prime Minister's Papers, Soviet Union, Prime Minister's Visit to the Soviet Union, Part 1 (document consulted in the Cabinet Office).   92. Thatcher to Reagan, 1 April 1987, Prime Minister's Papers, Soviet Union, Prime Minister's Visit to the Soviet Union, Part 2 (document consulted in the Cabinet Office).   93. Pollock to Powell, 6 April 1987, CAC: THCR 1/10/117.   94. Sir Bryan Cartledge, British Diplomatic Oral History Programme, Churchill College, Cambridge (https://www.chu.cam.ac.uk/media/uploads/files/Cartledge.pdf).   95. Powell to Galsworthy, 31 March 1987, Prime Minister's Papers, Soviet Union, Prime Minister's Visit to the Soviet Union, Part 1 (document consulted in the Cabinet Office).   96. Pollock to Powell, 6 April 1987, CAC: THCR 1/10/117.   97. Session of CC CPSU Politburo, 16 April 1987, Gorbachev Foundation.   98. Cartledge, telegram 537, 1 April 1987, Prime Minister's Papers, Soviet Union, Prime Minister's Visit to the Soviet Union, Part 2 (document consulted in the Cabinet Office).   99. Cartledge telegram 538, 1 April 1987. Ibid.   100. 'Press Digest', Perks to Thatcher, 1 April 1987, CAC: THCR 3/5/67; *Guardian*, 1 April 1987.   101. Thatcher to Gorbachev, 2 April 1987, CAC: THCR 3/1/62.   102. Session of CC CPSU Politburo, 16 April 1987, Gorbachev Foundation.   103. Interview with Lord Powell of Bayswater.   104. Session of CC CPSU Politburo, 16 April 1987, Gorbachev Foundation.   105. Cited in Chernyaev, *My Six Years with Gorbachev*, p. 104.   106. Interview with George Shultz.   107. Cited in Chernyaev, *My Six Years with Gorbachev*, p. 104.   108. Powell to Galsworthy, 8 April 1987, Prime Minister's Papers, Soviet Union, Prime Minister's Visit to the Soviet Union, Part 2 (document consulted in the Cabinet Office).   109. Thomas to Powell, 10 April 1987. Ibid.   110. Thatcher to Reagan, 1 April 1987, Prime Minister's Papers, Soviet Union, Prime Minister's Visit to the Soviet Union, Part 2 (document consulted in the Cabinet Office).   111. Interview with Lord Powell of Bayswater.

CHAPTER 19: WHAT THEY SAW IN HER

1. *Observer*, 7 June 1987.   **2.** *Daily Telegraph*, 13 June 1987.   **3.** *Spectator*, 22 May 1987.   **4.** Ibid.   **5.** *Guardian*, 30 May 1988.   **6.** 'Why Britain's Eggheads Look Down on Mrs Thatcher', *Sunday Telegraph*, 10 January 1988.   **7.** Graham Turner, interview transcripts (by kind permission of Graham Turner).   **8.** Ibid. **9.** Ibid.   **10.** Ibid.   **11.** Ibid.   **12.** Alan Bennett, *Writing Home*, Picador, 1994, p. 558.   **13.** *Guardian*, 9 April 2013.   **14.** Interview with Sir David Hare. **15.** Anthony Burgess, 'Thoughts on the Thatcher Decade' (1989), reprinted in *One Man's Chorus*, Carroll & Graf, 1998, p. 148.   **16.** *Guardian*, 11 April 2009. **17.** Interview with Nicholas Garland.   **18.** Ibid.   **19.** Ibid.   **20.** Ibid. **21.** Ibid.   **22.** Ibid.   **23.** Colin Seymour-Ure, *Prime Ministers and the Media: Issues of Power and Control*, Blackwell, 2003, p. 237.   **24.** Graham Turner, interview transcripts.   **25.** *Guardian*, 29 November 1990.   **26.** *Guardian*, 8 June 1987.   **27.** Interview with Ian Curteis.   **28.** Lester Friedman, *Fires Were Started: British Cinema and Thatcherism*, University of Minnesota Press, 1993, p. 235. **29.** *Guardian*, 29 March 2014.   **30.** *Sunday Times*, 14 February 2010. **31.** Ibid.   **32.** Thatcher to Lynn, 15 June 1983, CAC: THCR 2/4/1/19 (http://www. margaretthatcher.org/document/131132).   **33.** See Mortimer's obituary, *Daily Telegraph*, 17 January 2009.   **34.** Alice Thomas Ellis, *The Birds of the Air*, Duckworth, 1980, p. 57.   **35.** Sue Townsend, *The Growing Pains of Adrian Mole*, Puffin Books, 1984, entry for Saturday, 6 November.   **36.** *New Statesman*, 20 September 1999.   **37.** Interview with Sir David Hare.   **38.** Ibid.   **39.** Philip Hensher, *Kitchen Venom*, Hamish Hamilton, 1996, p. 90.   **40.** Ibid., pp. 149–50.   **41.** Interview with Philip Hensher.   **42.** Ibid.   **43.** Ibid.   **44.** Ibid.   **45.** Hensher, *Kitchen Venom*, p. 90.   **46.** Alan Hollinghurst, *The Line of Beauty*, Picador, 2004, pp. 385, 376.   **47.** Carol Thatcher, *Below the Parapet: The Biography of Denis Thatcher*, HarperCollins, 1996, p. 146.   **48.** Ibid., p. 147.   **49.** Interview with Lord Deedes of Aldington.   **50.** Interview with Sebastian Faulks.   **51.** *Sunday Telegraph*, 10 January 1988.   **52.** Turner transcripts.   **53.** *Spectator*, 13 April 2013.   **54.** *Sunday Telegraph*, 10 January 1988.   **55.** Ibid.   **56.** Turner transcripts.   **57.** Letter from John le Carré to Hugh Thomas, October 1982. **58.** Interview with David Cornwell (John le Carré).   **59.** Interview with Vladimir Bukovsky.   **60.** Ibid.   **61.** Charles Moore, contemporary record.   **62.** Interview with Lord Powell of Bayswater.   **63.** Interview with George Walden. **64.** Ibid.   **65.** Interview with Philip Larkin by Graham Lord, *Sunday Express*, 8 August 1979.   **66.** Letter to Robert Conquest, 22 December 1984.   **67.** James Lees-Milne, *Diaries 1984–97*, John Murray, 2008, 25 November 1990; James Lees-Milne, *Ceaseless Turmoil: Diaries 1988–92*, John Murray, 2004.   **68.** *Daily Telegraph*, 5 July 2009.   **69.** Interview with Lord Moser.   **70.** Richard Osborne, *Herbert von Karajan: A Life in Music*, Pimlico, 1999, p. 695.   **71.** Ibid.   **72.** Interview with Lord Armstrong of Ilminster.   **73.** Interview with Dr Wendy Baron. **74.** Ibid.   **75.** Ibid.   **76.** Interview with Lord Luce.   **77.** *Guardian*, 14 April 1989.   **78.** Isaiah Berlin unpublished letter to Arthur Fried, 29 November 1988,

Isaiah Berlin Literary Trust Archive, Wolfson College, Oxford, © The Trustees of the Isaiah Berlin Literary Trust 2015. **79.** *Nature*, 29 September 1983. **80.** Blake to Thatcher, 2 November 1984, CAC: THCR 6/2/115. **81.** Butler to Thatcher, 29 November 1984. Ibid. **82.** Interview with Lord Butler of Brockwell. **83.** Thatcher to Dorey, 17 December 1984, CAC: THCR 6/2/115. **84.** Text of Professor Noble's speech in the possession of Professor Sir Brian Harrison (kindly made available to the author by Sir Brian Harrison). **85.** Interview with Professor Peter Pulzer by Brian Harrison, 1991. **86.** Ibid. **87.** *Sunday Telegraph*, 3 February 1985. **88.** *Spectator*, 2 February 1985. **89.** Ibid. **90.** John Vincent, 'Margaret Thatcher: Her Place in History', in John Campbell, Martin Holmes and G. W. Jones (eds.), 'The Thatcher Years', *Contemporary Record*, vol. 1, issue 3, 1987, pp. 23–4. **91.** Interview with Lady Butler of Brockwell. **92.** Interview with Lord Butler of Brockwell. **93.** *Mail on Sunday*, 3 February 1985. **94.** Interview with Lord Butler of Brockwell. **95.** Thatcher to Quinton, 26 February 1985, CAC: THCR 2/1/5/121. **96.** Thatcher to Park, 1 February 1985, CAC: THCR 3/2/159. **97.** Interview with Press Association, 3 May 1989 (http://www.marga retthatcher.org/document/107427). **98.** See Stephen Robinson, *The Remarkable Lives of Bill Deedes*, Little, Brown, 2008, p. 320. **99.** Deedes to Denis Thatcher, 30 January 1985, CAC: THCR 3/1/15. **100.** Interview with Sir Denis Thatcher. **101.** Brian Harrison interview with Professor Peter Pulzer, 7 August 1991. **102.** Private memoir by John Coles written on leaving Downing Street in 1984, 14 June 1984, CAC: THCR 3/24 (http://www.margaretthatcher.org/docu ment/135761). **103.** Ibid. **104.** Ibid. **105.** Ibid. **106.** Ibid. **107.** Goodall, unpublished manuscript (kindly made available to the author by Sir David Goodall). **108.** Ibid. **109.** Ibid. **110.** Ibid. **111.** Interview with Lord Butler of Brockwell. **112.** Interview with Lady Powell of Bayswater. **113.** Interview with Lord Butler of Brockwell. **114.** Interview with Lady Powell of Bayswater. **115.** Ibid. **116.** Ibid. **117.** Ibid. **118.** Ibid. **119.** Ibid. **120.** Interview with Lady Ryder of Wensum. **121.** Interview with Lady Wakeham. **122.** Interview with Amanda Ponsonby. **123.** Interview with Dame Patricia Hodgson. **124.** Ibid. **125.** Flesher to Thatcher, 26 March 1986, Prime Minister's Papers, Ministers, Rules Governing Travel by Ministers, Part 2 (document consulted in the Cabinet Office). **126.** Interview with Lord Hamilton of Epsom. **127.** Unpublished handwriting analysis of Margaret Thatcher by Alice Coleman (kindly made available to the author by Alice Coleman). **128.** Ibid. **129.** Interview with Professor Alice Coleman. **130.** Interview with Lord Butler of Brockwell. **131.** Ibid. **132.** Ibid. **133.** Ibid. **134.** Ibid. **135.** Interview with *Woman's Own*, 12 October 1985. **136.** Interview with Carol Thatcher. **137.** Interview with *Woman's Own*, 12 October 1985. **138.** Gerald Bowden, 'The Thatchers' Dulwich Days', private article (kindly made available to the author by Gerald Bowden). **139.** Interview with Sir Denis Thatcher. **140.** Bowden, private article. **141.** Interview with Carol Thatcher. **142.** Interview with Sir Denis Thatcher. **143.** Bowden, private article. **144.** Interview with Jane Mulvagh. **145.** Interview with Lady Powell of Bayswater. **146.** Interview with Cynthia Crawford. **147.** *An Englishwoman's Wardrobe*, BBC2, 18 July

1986 (Christopher Collins, ed., *Complete Public Statements of Margaret Thatcher 1945–90 on CD-ROM*, Oxford University Press, 1998/2000).   **148.** Interview with Carol Thatcher.   **149.** *An Englishwoman's Wardrobe*, 18 July 1986. **150.** Interview with Eivind Bjerke.   **151.** *An Englishwoman's Wardrobe*, 18 July 1986.   **152.** Ibid.   **153.** Interview with Angela Huth.   **154.** Interview with Lady Thatcher.

CHAPTER 20: THE LAST VICTORY

1. *Guardian*, 9 January 1987.   **2.** Interview with Lord Mandelson.   **3.** Ibid. **4.** Interview with Tony Blair.   **5.** See Peter Mandelson, *The Third Man: Life at the Heart of New Labour*, Harper Press, 2010, p. 90.   **6.** Interview with Lord Kinnock.   **7.** Ibid.   **8.** Interview with Lord Mandelson.   **9.** Mandelson, *The Third Man*, p. 93.   **10.** Interview with Charles Clarke.   **11.** See Thatcher's handwritten comment on p. 12 of 'CCO Election Campaign Plans', December 1986, CAC: THCR 2/7/5/3; Peter Riddell, *Financial Times*, 31 December 1986.   **12.** 'Report of strategy group on foreign affairs, Europe and defence', 18 December 1986, CAC: THCR 2/7/5/10.   **13.** Interview with Lord Kinnock.   **14.** Interview with Edward Streator.   **15.** Ibid.   **16.** Interview with Robert McFarlane.   **17.** Interview with Lord Kinnock.   **18.** Interview with Roz Ridgway.   **19.** Interview with Raymond Seitz.   **20.** See 221627z Sep 86, 'Preparing for the Next British Elections', 22 September 1986, UK-1986-09/01/1986–09/24/1986, Box 90901, Sommer Files, Reagan Library.   **21.** Price to Reagan, 15 October 1986, CO167 4265485, WHORM File, Reagan Library.   **22.** Carlucci to President, 'Meeting with Neil Kinnock', 26 March 1987, CO167 464657, WHORM File, Reagan Library.   **23.** 201733z Mar 87, 'Ambassador's lunch with Neil Kinnock: Cruise could stay, loony Left must go', 20 March 1987, UK-1987-Cables (2), Box 92082, Ledsky Files, Reagan Library. **24.** Carlucci to President, 'Meeting with Neil Kinnock', 26 March 1987, CO167 464657, WHORM File, Reagan Library.   **25.** Interview with Marlin Fitzwater. **26.** Ibid.   **27.** 302200z Mar 87, 'Visit of Neil Kinnock to Washington: National Press Club News Conference March 27, 1987', 30 March 1987, State Department, released under FOIA Case #200905655.   **28.** Interview with Marlin Fitzwater.   **29.** Press briefing by Marlin Fitzwater, 27 March 1987, Press Briefing Files, Reagan Library.   **30.** *Observer*, 29 March 1987.   **31.** *Daily Mail*, 28 March 1987.   **32.** *Guardian*, 30 March 1987.   **33.** *Financial Times*, 30 March 1987. **34.** Interview with Lord Kinnock.   **35.** Correspondence with Sir Antony Acland. **36.** Ronald Reagan, *The Reagan Diaries*, HarperCollins, 2007, 27 March 1987, p. 486.   **37.** Interview with Lord Powell of Bayswater.   **38.** Correspondence with Charles Price.   **39.** Hansard, HC Deb 17 March 1987, 112/818–48 (http://hansard. millbanksystems.com/commons/1987/mar/17/public-sector-borrowing).   **40.** Ibid. **41.** Nigel Lawson, *The View from No. 11*, Bantam Press, 1992, p. 689. **42.** Ibid.   **43.** Interview with Lord Lawson of Blaby.   **44.** Woodrow Wyatt, *The Journals of Woodrow Wyatt*, vol. i, Macmillan, 1998, 2 March 1987, p. 316. **45.** Correspondence with Lord Powell of Bayswater.   **46.** Lawson, *The View from*

No. 11, p. 692.   **47.** 'Managing the Economy: Report of a Policy Group – Autumn 1986', 19 December 1986, CAC: THCR 2/7/5/49. See also, 'Minutes of the Strategy Group: Eleventh Meeting: Monday 19th January 1987', 21 January 1987, CAC: THCR 2/7/5/7.   **48.** Griffiths to Thatcher, 16 January 1987, CAC: THCR 2/7/5/7.   **49.** 'Report of policy group on foreign affairs, Europe and defence', 18 December 1986, CAC: THCR 2/7/5/10.   **50.** Sherbourne to Thatcher, 25 November 1986, CAC: THCR 2/7/5/5.   **51.** Interview with Lord Bell.   **52.** Interview with Lord Sherbourne of Didsbury.   **53.** Thatcher Memoirs Materials, CAC: THCR 4/3.   **54.** Interview with Lord Parkinson.   **55.** Interview with Lord Bell.   **56.** Ibid.   **57.** Correspondence with Lord Parkinson.   **58.** Thatcher Memoirs Materials, CAC: THCR 4/3.   **59.** Interview with Lord Bell.   **60.** Interview with Lord Ryder of Wensum.   **61.** Ibid.   **62.** Lord Young of Graffham, introduction to unpublished Election Diary (kindly made available to the author by Lord Young of Graffham).   **63.** Ibid.   **64.** Ibid.   **65.** Norman Tebbit, *Upwardly Mobile*, Weidenfeld & Nicolson, 1988, p. 262.   **66.** Interview with Lord Tebbit.   **67.** Margaret Thatcher, *The Downing Street Years*, HarperCollins, 1993, p. 578.   **68.** Young, introduction to unpublished Election Diary.   **69.** Ibid.   **70.** Ibid.   **71.** Ibid.   **72.** Ibid.   **73.** Interview with Lord Tebbit.   **74.** Young, introduction to unpublished Election Diary.   **75.** Young, unpublished Election Diary, 6 April 1987.   **76.** Ibid.   **77.** Interview with Lord Dobbs.   **78.** *Sunday Times*, 5 April 1987.   **79.** Thatcher Memoirs Materials, CAC: THCR 4/3.   **80.** Ibid.   **81.** Ibid.   **82.** Interview with John O'Sullivan.   **83.** Thatcher Memoirs Materials, CAC: THCR 4/3.   **84.** Wicks to Thatcher, 20 March 1987, CAC: THCR 2/7/5/42.   **85.** Sherbourne to Thatcher, 8 April 1987. Ibid.   **86.** Young, unpublished Election Diary, 16 April 1987.   **87.** Ibid., 20 April 1987.   **88.** Sherbourne to Thatcher, 14 April 1987, CAC: THCR 2/7/5/24.   **89.** Ibid.   **90.** Interview with Lord Young of Graffham.   **91.** Interview with Lord Lawson of Blaby.   **92.** Sherbourne to Thatcher, 15 April 1987, CAC: THCR 2/7/5/45.   **93.** Interview with Lord Young of Graffham.   **94.** Young, unpublished Election Diary, 9 May 1987.   **95.** Ibid., 10 May 1987.   **96.** Ibid.   **97.** TV Interview for BBC, 12 May 1987 (http://www.margaretthatcher.org/document/106615).   **98.** Thatcher Memoirs Materials, CAC: THCR 4/3.   **99.** Interview with Lord Wakeham.   **100.** Young, unpublished Election Diary, 15 May 1987.   **101.** Ibid., 18 May 1987.   **102.** Ibid.   **103.** Interview with Lord Wakeham.   **104.** Young, unpublished Election Diary, 18 May 1987.   **105.** Conservative Election Video, *The Next Moves Forward*, Adrian Rowbotham Films.   **106.** Thatcher Memoirs Materials, CAC: THCR 4/3.   **107.** *The Next Moves Forward*, Conservative Party Manifesto 1987, CAC: THCR 2/7/5/14.   **108.** 'CCO Election Campaign Plans', December 1986, CAC: THCR 2/7/5/3.   **109.** Wyatt, *The Journals of Woodrow Wyatt*, vol. i, 4 June 1987, p. 359.   **110.** Interview with Lord Kinnock.   **111.** Thatcher Memoirs Materials, CAC: THCR 4/3.   **112.** Interview with David Willetts.   **113.** Thatcher Memoir Materials, CAC: THCR 4/3.   **114.** Interview with David Willetts.   **115.** Michael Dobbs interview, 23 June 1987, David Butler Archive.   **116.** Young, unpublished Election Diary, 22 May 1987.   **117.** Interview with Lord Bell.   **118.** Ibid.   **119.** Young, unpublished Election Diary, 23 May 1987.   **120.** Ibid., 24 May

1987. **121.** Interview with Lord Lawson of Blaby. **122.** Interview with Lord Young of Graffham. **123.** Interview with David Willetts. **124.** Lord Young of Graffham interview, July 1987, David Butler Archive. **125.** Interview with Lord Lawson of Blaby. **126.** See Lawson, *The View from No. 11*, p. 703. **127.** Thatcher Memoirs Materials, CAC: THCR 4/3. **128.** See David Butler and Dennis Kavanagh, *The British General Election of 1987*, Macmillan, 1992, p. 103. **129.** See Rodney Tyler, *Campaign!: The Selling of the Prime Minister*, Grafton Books, 1987, p. 186. **130.** Thatcher Memoirs Materials, CAC: THCR 4/3. **131.** Speech to Conservative rally in Newport, 26 May 1987 (http://www.margaretthatcher.org/document/106843). **132.** Interview with Lord Lawson of Blaby. **133.** Tyler, *Campaign!*, p. 204. **134.** Young to Thatcher, 30 May 1987, CAC: THCR 2/7/5/64. **135.** Speech to Conservative Rally in Edinburgh, 2 June 1987 (http://www.margaretthatcher.org/document/106861). **136.** Thatcher, *The Downing Street Years*, p. 584. **137.** Interview with Lord Sherbourne of Didsbury. **138.** Young, unpublished Election Diary, 3 June 1987. **139.** Ibid., 4 June 1987. **140.** Thatcher Memoirs Materials, CAC: THCR 4/3. **141.** 'General Election Press Conference (Health and Social Security)', 4 June 1987 (http://www.margaretthatcher.org/document/106866). **142.** Interview with David Willetts. **143.** Interview with Lord Sherbourne of Didsbury. **144.** Interview with Robin Harris. **145.** Interview with Lord Dobbs. **146.** See Tyler, *Campaign!*, pp. 216–17. **147.** Young, unpublished Election Diary, 4 June 1987. **148.** Thatcher, *The Downing Street Years*, p. 585. **149.** Interview with Lord Dobbs. **150.** Interview with Lord Bell. **151.** Interview with David Willetts. **152.** Young, unpublished Election Diary, 4 June 1987. **153.** Interview with Lord Tebbit. **154.** Interview with Lord Sharkey. **155.** Interview with Lord Bell. **156.** Young, unpublished Election Diary, 4 June 1987. **157.** Ibid. **158.** Interview with Lord Young of Graffham. **159.** Thatcher Memoirs Materials, CAC: THCR 4/3. **160.** Young, unpublished Election Diary, 5 June 1987. **161.** Interview with Lord Kinnock. **162.** Interview with Lord Lawson of Blaby. **163.** Interview with Lord Powell of Bayswater. **164.** Private information. **165.** Interview with Lord Sherbourne of Didsbury. **166.** Thatcher Memoirs Materials, CAC: THCR 4/3. **167.** Ibid. **168.** NSC 147 21 May 1987, Exec Sec, NSC: Meeting File, Box 9, Reagan Library. **169.** Interview with Lord Sherbourne of Didsbury. **170.** TV interview for BBC, 10 June 1987 (http://www.margaretthatcher.org/document/106649). **171.** Lord Young of Graffham interview, July 1987, David Butler Archive. **172.** Ingham to Thatcher, 11 June 1987, CAC: THCR 2/7/5/63. **173.** Thatcher Speaking Notes, 11 June 1987, CAC: THCR 2/7/5/64. **174.** Powell to Thatcher, 13 June 1987, CAC: THCR 1/3/23.

Bibliography

PRIMARY SOURCES

Manuscript collections (UK)

Churchill Archives Centre, Cambridge
    The papers of Baroness Thatcher (THCR)
    The papers of Sir Alan Walters (WTRS)
The National Archives, Kew
    Cabinet Office Papers (CAB)
    Prime Minister's Papers (PREM)

Manuscript collections (abroad)

Archives Nationales de France, Paris
The Archives of the United Nations, New York, NY
The George H. W. Bush Presidential Library, College Station, TX
The Hoover Institution, Stanford, CA
The Library of Congress, Washington, DC
The National Archives and Records Administration, College Park, MD
The National Archives of Ireland, Dublin
    Papers of the Department of Foreign Affairs (DFA)
    Papers of the Department of the Taoiseach (TAOIS)
The National Security Archive, George Washington University, Washington, DC
The Ronald Reagan Presidential Library, Simi Valley, CA

Selected online resources

The American Presidency Project (http://www.presidency.ucsb.edu/ws/)
CAIN Web Service, University of Ulster (http://cain.ulst.ac.uk/)
Hansard (http://hansard.millbanksystems.com/)
Oxford Dictionary of National Biography (http://www.oxforddnb.com)
The Margaret Thatcher Foundation (www.margaretthatcher.org)
Who's Who Online (http://www.ukwhoswho.com)

Witness seminars

'Britain and South Africa, 1985–91', Witness Seminars, 23 January 2009, IDEAS, London School of Economics (ed. M. D. Kandiah) (http://issuu.com/fcohistorians/docs/witness_seminars_pretoria)

'The British Response to SDI', seminar held on 9 July 2003, Centre for Contemporary British History, Senate House, University of London (http://www.kcl.ac.uk/sspp/departments/icbh/witness/PDFfiles/SDI.pdf)

'The Privatisation of British Telecom, 1984', held in association with the BT Archives and the Cabinet Office's Official Histories programme, 5 December 2006, Telecom Tower, London (available at Churchill Archives Centre)

Other unpublished works and private collections made available to the author

Bowden, Gerald, 'The Thatchers' Dulwich Days', private article

Brown, Archie, contemporary notes

Burns, Terry, personal notes

Butler, David, private archive

Coleman, Alice, handwriting analysis of Margaret Thatcher

Coles, John, private memoir

Deedes, W. F., private papers

Goodall, David, private memoir

Harrison, Brian, private papers

Hart, David, private papers

Howarth, Gerald, personal notes

Marshall, Peter, private diaries

Turner, Graham, unpublished interviews

Whittingdale, John, private diaries

Wyatt, Woodrow, unedited diaries

Young, David, private Election Diary

SECONDARY SOURCES
Books

Adelman, Ken, *Reagan at Reykjavik: Forty-Eight Hours that Ended the Cold War*, HarperCollins, 2014

Aitken, Jonathan, *Margaret Thatcher: Power and Personality*, Bloomsbury, 2013

Aldous, Richard, *Reagan and Thatcher: The Difficult Relationship*, W. W. Norton, 2012

Alexander, Michael, *Managing the Cold War: A View from the Front Line*, RUSI, 2005

Alison, Michael and Edwards, David L., eds., *Christianity and Conservatism*, Hodder & Stoughton, 1990

Anderson, Martin and Anderson, Annelise, *Reagan's Secret War: The Untold Story of his Fight to Save the World from Nuclear Disaster*, Crown Publishers, 2009

Andrew, Christopher, *The Defence of the Realm: The Authorized History of MI5*, Allen Lane, 2009

Attali, Jacques, *Verbatim*, Fayard, 1993

Aughey, Arthur, *Under Siege: Ulster Unionism and the Anglo-Irish Agreement*, Palgrave Macmillan, 1989.

Aughey, Arthur and Gormley-Heenan, Cathy, eds., *The Anglo-Irish Agreement: Re-Thinking its Legacy*, Manchester University Press, 2011

Baker, Kenneth, *The Turbulent Years: My Life in Politics*, Faber & Faber, 1993

Barrass, Gordon, *The Great Cold War: A Journey through the Hall of Mirrors*, Stanford University Press, 2009

Beckett, Francis and Hencke, David, *Marching to the Fault Line: The 1984 Miners' Strike and the Battle for Industrial Britain*, Constable, 2009

Beinart, William, *Twentieth Century South Africa*, Oxford University Press, 2001

Bell, Tim, *Right or Wrong: The Memoirs of Lord Bell*, Bloomsbury, 2014

Bennett, Alan, *Writing Home*, Picador, 1994

Berlinski, Claire, *There Is No Alternative: Why Margaret Thatcher Matters*, Basic Civitas, 2011

Bermant, Azriel, *Margaret Thatcher and the Middle East*, Cambridge University Press, forthcoming, 2016

Bew, Paul and Gillespie, Gordon, *Northern Ireland: A Chronology of the Troubles 1968–1999*, Gill & Macmillan, 1999

Bew, Paul and Patterson, Henry, *The British State and the Ulster Crisis: From Wilson to Thatcher*, Verso Books, 1985

Biffen, John, *Semi-Detached*, Biteback, 2013

Blake, Robert and Patten, Chris, eds., *The Conservative Opportunity*, Macmillan, 1976

Bloomfield, Kenneth, *A Tragedy of Errors: The Government and Misgovernment of Northern Ireland*, Liverpool University Press, 2007

Booker, Christopher and North, Richard, *The Great Deception: A Secret History of the European Union*, Continuum, 2003

Braithwaite, Rodric, *Across the Moscow River: The World Turned Upside Down*, Yale University Press, 2002

Brands, H. W., *Reagan: The Life*, Doubleday, 2015

Brittan, Samuel, *Against the Flow*, Atlantic Books, 2005

Brown, Archie, *The Myth of the Strong Leader: Political Leadership in the Modern Age*, Basic Books, 2014

Burgess, Anthony, *One Man's Chorus: The Uncollected Writings*, Carroll & Graf, 1998

Butler, David, Adonis, Andrew and Travers, Tony, *Failure in British Government: The Politics of the Poll Tax*, Oxford University Press, 1994

Butler, David and Butler, Gareth, *British Political Facts since 1979*, Palgrave Macmillan, 2006

Butler, David and Kavanagh, Dennis, *The British General Election of 1983*, Macmillan, 1984

Butler, David and Kavanagh, Dennis, *The British General Election of 1987*, Macmillan, 1992

Butler, Michael, *Europe: More than a Continent*, Heinemann, 1986

Campbell, John, *Margaret Thatcher*, vol. i: *The Grocer's Daughter*, Jonathan Cape, 2001

Campbell, John, *Margaret Thatcher*, vol ii: *The Iron Lady*, Jonathan Cape, 2003

Campbell, John, *Roy Jenkins: A Well-Rounded Life*, Jonathan Cape, 2014

Cannon, Lou, *President Reagan: The Role of a Lifetime*, Simon & Schuster, 1991

Carrington, Peter, *Reflect on Things Past: The Memoirs of Lord Carrington*, HarperCollins, 1988

Carvel, John, *Citizen Ken: Biography of Ken Livingstone*, Chatto & Windus, 1984

Chernyaev, Anatoly, *My Six Years with Gorbachev*, Pennsylvania State University Press, 2000

Clark, Alan, *Diaries*, Weidenfeld & Nicolson, 1993

Clark, Alan, *Diaries: Into Politics*, Weidenfeld & Nicolson, 2000

Clark, Nancy L. and Worger, William H., *South Africa: The Rise and Fall of Apartheid*, Routledge, 2013

Clarridge, Duane, *A Spy for All Seasons: My Life in the CIA*, Scribner, 2002

Cochrane, Feargal, *Unionist Politics and the Politics of Unionism since the Anglo-Irish Agreement*, Cork University Press, 2002

Cockett, Richard, *Thinking the Unthinkable*, HarperCollins, 1994

Coles, John, *Making Foreign Policy: A Certain Idea of Britain*, John Murray, 2000

Collins, Christopher, ed., *Complete Public Statements of Margaret Thatcher 1945–90 on CD-ROM*, Oxford University Press, 1998/2000

Congdon, Tim, *Keynes, the Keynesians and Monetarism*, Edward Elgar, 2007

Congdon, Tim, *Money in a Free Society*, Encounter Books, 2011

Congdon, Tim, *Reflections on Monetarism*, Edward Elgar, 1992

Cooke, Alistair, ed., *Tory Policy-Making: The Conservative Research Department 1929–2009*, CRD, 2009

Cradock, Percy, *Experiences of China*, John Murray, 1994

Cradock, Percy, *In Pursuit of British Interests: Reflections on Foreign Policy under Margaret Thatcher and John Major*, John Murray, 1997

Crick, Michael, *Scargill and the Miners*, Penguin, 1985

Crocker, Chester A., *High Noon in Southern Africa: Making Peace in a Rough Neighborhood*, W. W. Norton, 1992

Croft, Stuart, ed., *British Security Policy: The Thatcher Years and the End of the Cold War*, HarperCollins Academic, 1991

Crowe, William, *The Line of Fire: From Washington to the Gulf, the Politics and Battles of the New Military*, Simon & Schuster, 1993

Crozier, Brian, *Free Agent: The Unseen War 1941–1991*, HarperCollins, 1993

Curteis, Ian, *The Falklands Play: A Television Play*, Hutchinson, 1988

Daalder, Ivo, *The SDI Challenge to Europe*, Ballinger, 1987

Dale, Iain, *Margaret Thatcher: In her own Words*, Biteback, 2010

Davis, Brian, *Qaddafi, Terrorism and the Origins of the US Attack on Libya*, Praeger, 1990

Deaver, Michael, *A Different Drummer: My Thirty Years with Ronald Reagan*, HarperCollins, 2001

Delaney, Sam, *Mad Men and Bad Men: What Happened When British Politics Met Advertising*, Faber & Faber, 2015

Delors, Jacques, *Mémoires*, Plon, 2004

Denham, Andrew and Garnett, Mark, *Keith Joseph*, Routledge, 2001

Dobrynin, Anatoly, *In Confidence: Moscow's Ambassador to America's Six Cold War Presidents*, Random House, 1995

Dorman, Andrew, *Defence under Thatcher*, Palgrave, 2002

Dumbrell, John, *A Special Relationship: Anglo-American Relations in the Cold War and After*, St Martin's Press, 2001

Dunlop, Frank, *Yes Taoiseach*, Penguin, 2004

Edwardes, Michael, *Back from the Brink*, William Collins, 1983

Ellis, Alice Thomas, *The Birds of the Air*, Duckworth, 1980

Faith in the City: A Call for Action by Church and Nation, Church House Publishing, 1985

Filby, Eliza, *God & Mrs Thatcher: The Battle for Britain's Soul*, Biteback, 2015

FitzGerald, Garret, *All in a Life: Garret FitzGerald an Autobiography*, Gill & Macmillan, 1991

FitzGerald, Garret, *Ireland in the World: Further Reflections*, Liberties Press, 2005

FitzGerald, Garret, *Reflections on the Irish State*, Irish Academic Press, 2002

Fowler, Norman, *Ministers Decide: A Personal Memoir of the Thatcher Years*, Chapmans Publishers, 1991

Fraser, Malcolm and Simmons, Margaret, *Malcolm Fraser: The Political Memoirs*, Miegunyah Press, 2010

Friedman, Lester, *Fires Were Started: British Cinema and Thatcherism*, University of Minnesota Press, 1993

Gaffikin, Frank and Morrissey, Mike, *Northern Ireland: The Thatcher Years*, Zed Books, 1989

Garnett, Mark and Aitken, Ian, *Splendid! Splendid!: The Authorized Biography of Willie Whitelaw*, Jonathan Cape, 2002

Gates, Robert, *From the Shadows: The Ultimate Insider's Story of Five Presidents and How They Won the Cold War*, Simon & Schuster, 1996

Gergen, David, *Eyewitness to Power*, Simon & Schuster, 2000

Gilmour, Ian, *Dancing with Dogma: Britain under Thatcherism*, Simon & Schuster, 1992

Gorbachev, Mikhail, *Memoirs*, Doubleday, 1996

Gordievsky, Oleg, *Next Stop Execution: The Autobiography of Oleg Gordievsky*, Macmillan, 1995

Gourvish, Terry, *The Official History of Britain and the Channel Tunnel*, Routledge, 2006

Grachev, Andrei, *Gorbachev's Gamble: Soviet Foreign Policy and the End of the Cold War*, Polity, 2008

Green, E. H. H., *Thatcher*, Bloomsbury Academic, 2006

Greenwood, Sean, *Britain and the Cold War*, St Martin's Press, 2000

Gregory, Martyn, *Dirty Tricks: British Airway's Secret War against Virgin Atlantic*, Little, Brown, 1994

Guise, George, *Inside the Tank*, Bretwalda Books, 2015

Haig, Alexander, *Caveat: Realism, Reagan and Foreign Policy*, Macmillan, 1984

Halloran, Paul and Hollingsworth, Mark, *Thatcher's Gold: The Life and Times of Mark Thatcher*, Simon & Schuster, 1995

Hannaford, Peter, *The Reagans: A Political Portrait*, Coward-McCann, 1983

Hannay, David, *Britain's Quest for a Role: A Diplomatic Memoir from Europe to the UN*, I. B. Tauris, 2013

Harris, Robert, *Good and Faithful Servant: The Unauthorized Biography of Bernard Ingham*, Faber & Faber, 1990

Harris, Robin, *Not for Turning: The Life of Margaret Thatcher*, Thomas Dunne Books, 2013

Harrison, Brian, *Finding a Role? The United Kingdom 1970–1990*, Oxford University Press, 2011

Harrison, Nancy, *Winnie Mandela: Mother of a Nation*, Grafton, 1985

Hart, David, *Come to the Edge*, Hutchinson, 1988

Hawke, Bob, *The Hawke Memoirs*, Heinemann, 1994

Hayward, Steven, *The Age of Reagan: The Conservative Counterrevolution: 1980–89*, Crown Forum, 2009

Heath, Edward, *The Course of my Life*, Hodder & Stoughton, 1998

Heffer, Simon, *Like the Roman: The Life of Enoch Powell*, Weidenfeld & Nicolson, 1998

Henderson, Nicholas, *Mandarin: The Diaries of an Ambassador, 1969–1982*, Weidenfeld & Nicolson, 1994

Hennessy, Peter, *The Prime Minister*, Allen Lane, 2000

Hennessy, Peter, *Whitehall*, Secker & Warburg, 1989

Hennessy, Thomas, *Hunger Strike: Margaret Thatcher's Battle with the IRA: 1980–81*, Irish Academic Press, 2014

Hensher, Philip, *Kitchen Venom*, Hamish Hamilton, 1996

Heseltine, Michael, *Life in the Jungle: My Autobiography*, Hodder & Stoughton, 2000

Horne, Alistair, *Harold Macmillan*, vol. ii: *1957–1986*, Macmillan, 1989

Hoskyns, John, *Just in Time: Inside the Thatcher Revolution*, Aurum Press, 2000

Howe, Geoffrey, *Conflict of Loyalty*, Macmillan, 1994

Hurd, Douglas, *An End to Promises: Sketch of a Government, 1970–74*, HarperCollins, 1979

Hurd, Douglas, *Memoirs*, Abacus, 2003

Hyam, Ronald and Henshaw, Peter, *The Lion and the Springbok: Britain and South Africa since the Boer War*, Cambridge University Press, 2007

Ingham, Bernard, *Kill the Messenger*, Fontana, 1991

Jackson, Ben and Saunders, Robert, *Making Thatcher's Britain*, Cambridge University Press, 2012

Jenkins, Peter, *Mrs Thatcher's Revolution: Ending of the Socialist Era*, Jonathan Cape, 1989

Jenkins, Roy, *A Life at the Centre*, Macmillan, 1993

Jenkins, Simon, *Thatcher and Sons: A Revolution in Three Acts*, Penguin, 2007

Jones, J. D. F., *Storyteller: The Many Lives of Laurens van der Post*, John Murray, 2001

Keays, Sara, *A Question of Judgement*, Quintessential Press, 1985

Keegan, William, *Mr Lawson's Gamble*, Hodder & Stoughton, 1989

Kengor, Paul and Clark Doerner, Patricia, *The Judge: William P. Clark, Reagan's Top Hand*, Ignatius Press, 2007

Kenny, Anthony, *The Road to Hillsborough: The Shaping of the Anglo-Irish Agreement*, Pergamon, 1986

Kissinger, Henry, *Years of Renewal*, Simon & Schuster, 1999

Kohl, Helmut, *Erinnerungen 1982–1990*, Droemer Knaur, 2005

Korchilov, Igor, *Translating History: Thirty Years on the Front Lines of Diplomacy with a Top Russian Interpreter*, Scribner, 1997

Kuhn, Jim, *Ronald Reagan in Private: A Memoir of my Years in the White House*, Sentinel, 2004

Kynaston, David, *The City of London*, vol iv: *A Club No More 1945–2000*, Chatto & Windus, 2001

Lawson, Nigel, *The View from No. 11*, Bantam Press, 1992

Lees-Milne, James, *Diaries 1984–97*, John Murray, 2008

Lettow, Paul, *Ronald Reagan and his Quest to Abolish Nuclear Weapons*, Random House, 2005

Letwin, Oliver, *Privatising the World*, Cassell, 1988

Linklater, Magnus and Leigh, David, *Not with Honour: The Inside Story of the Westland Scandal*, Sphere Books, 1986

Lucas, Ivor, *A Road to Damascus: Mainly Diplomatic Memoirs from the Middle East*, Radcliffe Press, 1997

Luce, Richard, *Ringing the Changes: A Memoir*, Michael Russell Publishing, 2007

McAlpine, Alistair, *Once a Jolly Bagman: Memoirs*, Weidenfeld & Nicolson, 1997

MacGregor, Ian, *The Enemies Within: The Story of the Miners' Strike 1984–5*, HarperCollins, 1986

McSmith, Andy, *No Such Thing as Society*, Constable, 2010

Major, John, *The Autobiography*, HarperCollins, 2010

Mandelson, Peter, *The Third Man: Life at the Heart of New Labour*, Harper Press, 2010

Mann, James, *About Face: A History of America's Curious Relationship with China, from Nixon to Clinton*, Vintage, 2000

Mann, James, *The Rebellion of Ronald Reagan: A History of the End of the Cold War*, Penguin, 2009

Mantel, Hilary, *The Assassination of Margaret Thatcher: Stories*, Fourth Estate, 2014

Marx, Karl and Engels, Friedrich, *The German Ideology*, Progress Publishers, 1976

Matlock, Jack, *Reagan and Gorbachev: How the Cold War Ended*, Random House, 2004

Mawhinney, Brian, *Just a Simple Belfast Boy*, Biteback, 2013

Meese, Edwin, *With Reagan: The Inside Story*, Regnery Publishing, 1992

Millar, Ronald, *A View from the Wings*, Weidenfeld & Nicolson, 1989

Milne, Seumas, *The Enemy Within: The Secret War against the Miners* (30th Anniversary Edition), Verso, 2014

Morris, Edmund, *Dutch: A Memoir of Ronald Reagan*, Random House, 1999

Mount, Ferdinand, *Cold Cream: My Early Life and Other Mistakes*, Bloomsbury, 2008

Mount, Ferdinand, *Communism*, Harvill, 1992

Mulroney, Brian, *Memoirs: 1939–1993*, McClelland & Stewart, 2007

Nau, Henry, *The Myth of America's Decline: Leading the World Economy into the 1990s*, Oxford University Press, 1990

Neil, Andrew, *Full Disclosure*, Macmillan, 1996

Nott, John, *Here Today, Gone Tomorrow: Recollections of an Errant Politician*, Politico's, 2002

O'Malley, Padraig, *Biting at the Grave: The Irish Hunger Strike and the Politics of Despair*, Beacon Press, 1990

O'Sullivan, John, *The President, the Pope, and the Prime Minister: Three Who Changed the World*, Regnery Publishing, 2006

Orman, Stanley, *Faith in G. O.D.S: Stability in the Nuclear Age*, Elsevier, 1991

Osborne, Richard, *Herbert von Karajan: A Life in Music*, Pimlico, 1999

Palmer, Dean, *The Queen and Mrs Thatcher: An Inconvenient Relationship*, History Press, 2015

Papenfus, Theresa, *Pik Botha and his Times*, Kindle edn, Litera (trans. Sandra Mills), 2010

Parker, David, *The Official History of Privatisation*, vol. i: *The Formative Years 1970–1987*, Routledge, 2009

Parkinson, Cecil, *Right at the Centre: An Autobiography*, Weidenfeld & Nicolson, 1992

Parris, Matthew, *Chance Witness: An Outsider's Life in Politics*, Penguin Viking, 2002

Patterson, Henry, *Ireland's Violent Frontier: The Border and Anglo-Irish Relations during the Troubles*, Palgrave Macmillan, 2013

Pipes, Richard, *Vixi: Memoirs of a Non-Belonger*, Yale University Press, 2003

Powell, Jonathan, *Great Hatred, Little Room: Making Peace in Northern Ireland*, Bodley Head, 2008

Pravda, Alex and Duncan, Peter, eds., *Soviet–British Relations since the 1970s*, Cambridge University Press, 1990

Prior, James, *A Balance of Power*, Hamish Hamilton, 1986

Purdy, Ann, *Molyneaux: The Long View*, Greystone Books, 1989

Pym, Francis, *The Politics of Consent*, Hamish Hamilton, 1984

Ramphal, Shirdath, *Glimpses of a Global Life*, Hansib, 2014

Reagan, Nancy, *My Turn: The Memoirs of Nancy Reagan*, Random House, 1989

Reagan, Ronald, *An American Life: The Autobiography*, Simon & Schuster, 1990

Reagan, Ronald, *The Reagan Diaries*, HarperCollins, 2007

Reagan, Ronald, *The Reagan Diaries Unabridged*, 2 vols, HarperCollins, 2009

Reed, Thomas, *At the Abyss: An Insider's History of the Cold War*, Random House, 2004

Reeves, Richard, *President Reagan: The Triumph of Imagination*, Simon & Schuster, 2006

Renwick, Robin, *Economic Sanctions*, Harvard Center for International Affairs, 1981

Renwick, Robin, *The End of Apartheid: Diary of a Revolution*, Biteback, 2015

Renwick, Robin, *A Journey with Margaret Thatcher: Foreign Policy under the Iron Lady*, Biteback, 2013

Renwick, Robin, *Unconventional Diplomacy in Southern Africa*, Macmillan, 1997

Ridley, Nicholas, *My Style of Government: The Thatcher Years*, Hutchinson, 1991

Robinson, Stephen, *The Remarkable Lives of Bill Deedes*, Little, Brown, 2008

Roy, Subroto and Clarke, John, *Margaret Thatcher's Revolution*, Continuum, 2006

Saltoun-Ebin, Jason, ed., *The Reagan Files: The Untold Story of Reagan's Top-Secret Efforts to Win the Cold War*, CreateSpace, 2010

Sampson, Anthony, *Black and Gold: Tycoons, Revolutionaries and Apartheid*, Coronet, 1987

Sampson, Anthony, *Mandela: The Authorised Biography*, Harper Press, 2011

Sawatsky, John, *Mulroney: The Politics of Ambition*, Macfarlane Walter & Ross, 1991

Schluter, Michael with Lee, David J., *Keeping Sunday Special*, Marshall Pickering, 1988

Schweizer, Peter, *Reagan's War: The Epic Story of his Forty-Year Struggle and Final Triumph over Communism*, Doubleday, 2002

Seaton, Jean, *Pinkoes and Traitors: The BBC and the Nation*, Profile Books, 2015

Seldon, Anthony, *Major: A Political Life*, Weidenfeld & Nicolson, 1997

Seldon, Anthony and Collings, Daniel, *Britain under Thatcher*, Pearson Education, 2000

Seymour-Ure, Colin, *Prime Ministers and the Media: Issues of Power and Control*, Blackwell, 2003

Shepherd, Gillian, *The Real Iron Lady: Working with Margaret Thatcher*, Biteback, 2013

Sherman, Alfred, *Paradoxes of Power*, Imprint Academic, 2005

Shultz, George, *Turmoil and Triumph: My Years as Secretary of State*, Charles Scribner's Sons, 1993

Skinner, Kiron K., Anderson, Annelise and Anderson, Martin, eds., *Reagan: A Life in Letters*, Free Press, 2003

Skinner, Kiron K., Anderson, Annelise and Anderson, Martin, eds., *Reagan, in his own Hand*, Free Press, 2001

Smith, Geoffrey, *Reagan and Thatcher*, Bodley Head, 1990

Spicer, Michael, *The Spicer Diaries*, Biteback, 2012

Stein, Herbert, *Presidential Economics: The Making of Economic Policy from Roosevelt to Clinton*, AEI Press, 1994

Stephens, Philip, *Politics and the Pound*, Macmillan, 1996

Stewart, Graham, *Bang! A History of Britain in the 1980s*, Atlantic Books, 2014

Strober, Deborah and Strober, Gerald, *The Reagan Presidency: An Oral History of the Era*, Potomac, 2003

Stuart, Mark, *Douglas Hurd: The Public Servant – An Authorised Biography*, Mainstream Publishing, 1998

Talbott, Strobe, *Deadly Gambits: The Reagan Administration and the Stalemate in Nuclear Arms Control*, Alfred A. Knopf, 1984

Tatchell, Peter, *The Battle for Bermondsey*, Heretic, 1983

Tebbit, Norman, *Upwardly Mobile*, Weidenfeld & Nicolson, 1988

Thatcher, Carol, *Below the Parapet: The Biography of Denis Thatcher*, HarperCollins, 1996

Thatcher, Margaret, *The Downing Street Years*, HarperCollins, 1993

Thatcher, Margaret, *The Path to Power*, HarperCollins, 1995

Thorpe, D. R., *Supermac*, Chatto & Windus, 2010

Torrance, David, *We in Scotland: Thatcherism in a Cold Climate*, Birlinn, 2009

Turner, Alwyn, *Rejoice! Rejoice! Britain in the 1980s*, Aurum Press, 2013

Tyler, Rodney, *Campaign!: The Selling of the Prime Minister*, Grafton Books, 1987

Urban, George, *Diplomacy and Disillusion at the Court of Margaret Thatcher: An Insider's View*, I. B. Tauris, 1996

Urquhart, Brian, *A Life in Peace and War*, Harper & Row, 1987

Vinen, Richard, *Thatcher's Britain: The Politics and Social Upheaval of the 1980s*, Pocket Books, 2010

Waldegrave, William, *A Different Kind of Weather: A Memoir*, Constable, 2015

Walden, George, *Lucky George: Memoirs of an Anti-Politician*, Penguin, 2000

Walker, Peter, *Staying Power: An Autobiography*, Bloomsbury, 1991

Wall, Stephen, *A Stranger in Europe: Britain and the EU from Thatcher to Blair*, Oxford University Press, 2008

Walters, Dennis, *Not Always with the Pack*, Constable, 1989

Walters, Vernon, *The Mighty and the Meek: Dispatches from the Front Line of Diplomacy*, St Ermin's Press, 2001

Wapshott, Nicholas, *Ronald Reagan and Margaret Thatcher: A Political Marriage*, Penguin, 2007

Wapshott, Nicholas and Brock, George, *Thatcher*, Macdonald, 1983

Warner, Gerald, *The Scottish Tory Party: A History*, Weidenfeld & Nicolson, 1988

Weinberger, Caspar, *Fighting for Peace: Seven Critical Years in the Pentagon*, Warner Books, 1990

Weinberger, Caspar W., *In the Arena: A Memoir of the 20th Century*, Regnery Publishing, 2003

Westlake, Martin, *Kinnock: The Authorized Biography*, Little, Brown, 2001

Whisler, Timothy R., *The British Motor Industry, 1945–1994: A Case Study in Industrial Decline*, Oxford University Press, 1999

White, Brian, *Britain, Détente and Changing East–West Relations*, Routledge, 1992

Whitelaw, William, *The Whitelaw Memoirs*, Aurum Press, 1989

Wilsher, Peter, MacIntyre, Donald and Jones, Michael, with the Sunday Times Insight Team, *Strike: Thatcher, Scargill and the Miners*, Coronet, 1985

Wilson, James, *The Triumph of Improvisation: Gorbachev's Adaptability, Reagan's Engagement, and the End of the Cold War*, Cornell University Press, 2015

Wirthlin, Dick, *The Greatest Communicator: What Ronald Reagan Taught Me about Politics, Leadership, and Life*, John Wiley & Sons, 2004

Wyatt, Woodrow, *The Journals of Woodrow Wyatt*, vol. i, Macmillan, 1998

Young, David, *The Enterprise Years: A Businessman in the Cabinet*, Headline, 1990

Young, Hugo, *One of Us*, Macmillan, 1989

Young, Hugo, *This Blessed Plot: Britain and Europe from Churchill to Blair*, Papermac, 1999

Young, Hugo, *The Hugo Young Papers: Thirty Years of British Politics – Off the Record*, Allen Lane, 2008

Ziegler, Philip, *Edward Heath: The Authorised Biography*, Harper Press, 2010

Articles

Agar, Jon, 'Thatcher, Scientist', *Notes and Records of the Royal Society of London*, vol. 65, no. 3, 20 September 2011

Bale, Tim, 'In Life as in Death? Margaret Thatcher (Mis)Remembered', *British Politics*, vol. 10, issue 1, April 2015

Blundell, John, 'Margaret Thatcher's Revolution: How it Happened and What it Meant', *Economic Affairs*, vol. 26, no. 1, 2006

Braithwaite, Rodric, 'Gorbachev and Thatcher', *Journal of European Integration History*, vol. 16, no. 1, 2010

Brown, Archie, 'The Change to Engagement in Britain's Cold War Policy: The Origins of the Thatcher–Gorbachev Relationship', *Journal of Cold War Studies*, vol. 10, no. 3, Summer 2008

Burt, Peter, 'Thirty Years Ago: The Nuclear Crisis which Frightened Thatcher and Reagan into Ending the Cold War', *Nuclear Information Service*, 3 November 2013

Campbell, Beatrix, 'Margaret Thatcher: To Be or Not to Be a Woman', *British Politics*, vol. 10, issue 1, April 2015

Evans, Stephen, 'The Not So Odd Couple: Margaret Thatcher and One Nation Conservatism', *Contemporary British History*, vol. 23, no. 1, 2009

Grachev, Andrei, 'Political and Personal: Gorbachev, Thatcher and the End of the Cold War', *Journal of European Integration History*, vol. 16, no. 1, 2010

Harrison, Brian, 'Mrs Thatcher and the Intellectuals', *Twentieth Century British History*, vol. 5, no. 2, 1994

Jones, Nate, 'Countdown to Declassification: Finding Answers to a 1983 Nuclear War Scare', *Bulletin of the Atomic Scientists*, vol. 69, no. 6, 2013

Jones, Nicholas, 'Thatcher's 1984 Cover-Up: The Secret Hit-list', Campaign for Press and Broadcasting Freedom (http://www.cpbf.org.uk/body.php?id=3007)

King, Anthony, 'The Outsider as Political Leader: The Case of Margaret Thatcher', *British Journal of Political Science*, vol. 32, no. 3, 2002

Lillis, Michael and Goodall, David, 'Edging towards Peace', *Dublin Review of Books*, issue 16, Winter 2010

Onslow, Sue, 'Thatcher, the Commonwealth and Apartheid South Africa' (http://blogs.lse.ac.uk/africaatlse/2013/04/09/thatcher-the-commonwealth-and-apartheid-south-africa/), 9 April 2013 (accessed 03/03/2015)

Index

MT = Margaret Thatcher. Main biographical notes are indicated by * (e.g. 632*); references to other footnotes are indicated by n (e.g. 210n).